MATHEMATICAL ECONOMICS

AKIRA TAKAYAMA

Purdue University

THE DRYDEN PRESS

Hinsdale, Illinois

To my parents

Preface

This book is intended to provide a systematic treatment of mathematical economics, a field that has progressed enormously in recent decades. It discusses existing theories in the field and attempts to extend them. The coverage herein is much broader than in any other book currently used in the field.

The literature on mathematical economics is enormous. The traditional method of education in economics—that of assigning many books and articles to be read by the student—is clearly inappropriate for the study of mathematical economics. This is both because of the size and complexity of the field and because the traditional method fails to make the student aware of the importance of the analytical character of economic theory. Here an attempt is made to provide all of the material usually obtained from a multitude of different sources but within a single framework, using consistent terminology, and requiring a minimum of outside reading.

More than a mere survey of the literature, this book strongly emphasizes both the unifying structure of economic theory and the mathematical methods involved in modern economic theory with the intention of providing the reader both the technical tools and the methodological approach necessary for doing original research in the field.

Furthermore, the book is not an exposition of elementary calculus and matrix theory with applications to economic problems; rather it is a book on economic problems using mathematical tools to aid in the analysis. Nor is it an introduction to a higher level text. It begins at a rather elementary level and brings the reader right to the frontiers of current research. Care is also taken so that each chapter can be read more or less independently (that is, each chapter can be read without careful reading of other chapters).

Needless to say, economics is concerned with real world problems, and its development has been crucially dependent on a strong demand and stimulus from such problems. However, the large number of viewpoints based on diversified vested interests in a particular policy often obscures transparent theoretical understanding. Hence it is very important for economists to find the basic logical structure of each problem and to be fully equipped with the major analytical tools, although many important economic theories obviously can be neither mathematical nor analytical.

This book deals with the analytical and the mathematical aspects of economic theory. It thus emphasizes a systematic exposition and extensions of various mathematical tools of analysis which can be useful in many diversified branches of economics, *and* of two topics in economic theory— competitive equilibrium and economic growth—both which, with their rigor and theoretical thoroughness, will provide basic prototypes of analysis and frames of reference for many other economic theories. Clearly, the topics of interest in economics change rapidly from time to time, reflecting the changing current concern with problems in the real world, and no book can possibly cover all of these topics. However, I think that the material presented in this book is useful and basic in analyzing many economic problems, old and new.

In spite of the fact that the book is conspicuously analytical and mathematical and that it is designed to bring the reader to the frontiers of mathematical economics, the mathematical prerequisites have been kept to a minimum. In virtually all sections of the book, the requirements include only that level of knowledge of elementary calculus and elementary matrix theory (say, the knowledge of matrix multiplication) which is now a standard requirement for entering economics students in graduate schools in major U.S. universities.

With regard to prerequisites in economic theory, the author can think of several excellent introductory texts available on many of the topics discussed herein. More generally, a rigorous second or third year undergraduate course should provide the reader with sufficient economic background to take up this study. Readers who are acquainted with books such as Dorfman, Samuelson, and Solow, *Linear Programming and Economic Analysis*, New York, McGraw-Hill, 1958, and Hicks, *Value and Capital*, 2nd ed., Oxford, Clarendon Press, 1946, may benefit more from reading this book than those unfamiliar with these works; however, familiarity with such texts is by no means necessary.

The book is suitable for use as a textbook in graduate courses in economic theory and mathematical economics and is also intended to serve as a reference work for professional economists who wish to become familiar with some of the topics and techniques of mathematical economics.

In addition, this book represents a record of my lectures on mathematical economics and economic theory given to first- and second-year graduate students at the University of Minnesota, the University of Rochester, the University of Hawaii, and Purdue University during the past eight years. In spite of considerable revisions and attempts to update the book during those years, it is natural and inevitable that the book carries some flavor of the period 1965–1966 when the entity of the book was first tried out at Minnesota.

In the course of writing the manuscript, I found that I owe a great debt to an excellent graduate education in economics received at the University of Rochester. I am also grateful for the atmosphere favorable to this modern approach to economic theory existing at the University of Minnesota and Purdue University, as well as at the University of Rochester. This atmosphere, sponsored and nurtured by such distinguished scholars as Professors Leonid Hurwicz, John S. Chipman, Marcel K. Richter, Stanley Reiter, and Robert L. Basmann, as well as Lionel W. McKenzie, Ronald W. Jones, and Edward Zabel of Rochester, has provided a great deal of stimulation.

My greatest debt is to the students at Minnesota, Rochester, Hawaii, and Purdue who took my courses on the topic and have constantly given me stimulation, encouragement, and criticism. A number of people, in addition to students in my classes, have read a portion or the whole of the manuscript. Among them, I would like to express my gratitude to Michihiro Ohyama, James C. Moore, William A. Brock, Mohamed A. El-Hodiri, Takashi Negishi, Jinkichi Tsukui, Hiroshi Atsumi, Sheng Cheng Hu, John Z. Drabicki, Yuji Kubo, Raj K. Jain, Kenneth Avio, and Fred Nordhauser. In addition, I am grateful to Professor Richard E. Quandt of Princeton, who read the entire manuscript and provided me with numerous comments as well as encouragement. My special thanks also go to John Drabicki, for without his help and encouragement, the completion of this book may have been further delayed and hampered. I also appreciate the capable research assistance provided by Erik Haites, Gene Warren, Robert Parks, Frank Maris, and James Winder, as well as the excellent stenographic services of Mrs. Gladys Cox, Mrs. Helen Antonienko, and others whose assistance was made available to me, for the most part, through Purdue University.

I am also grateful to Professor Leonid Hurwicz for his readiness in giving me permission to quote the results of one of his unpublished works ("LH-Oct. 1966" as revised, July 2, 1970). I would also like to record my gratitude to those professors who have granted their kind permission to quote many very interesting and illuminating passages from their writings. The precise source and the author of each quotation is given in the respective place of each quotation. Thanks are also due to the editors of *Metroeconomica* and the *Quarterly Journal of Economics* for permission to include in this book some articles by the author which were originally published by them.

I am also grateful to Deans Emanuel T. Weiler, John S. Day, Rene

P. Manes, and Jay W. Wiley of the Krannert School of Industrial Administration of Purdue University, who have provided me with generous encouragement as well as unusually favorable research conditions. Finally, my wife, Machiko, greatly helped me in preparing the indexes of the book, as well as providing me with encouragement.

A. T.

December, 1973
West Lafayette, Indiana

Contents

Some Frequently Used Notations

1. Sets

$x \in X$ x belongs to X (x is a member of X)

$x \notin X$ x does not belong to X (x is not a member of X)

$\{x:$ properties of $x\}$ set notation

ϕ the empty set

R the set of real numbers

R^n the n-dimensional real space

Ω^n the non-negative orthant of R^n (or simply Ω when the dimension n is clear in the context)

X^c the complement of X

X^o the open kernel (the interior of X)
(for example, $\Omega^o =$ the positive orthant)

$X \subset Y$ X is contained in Y (X is a subset of Y)

$X = Y$ X is equal to Y (that is, $X \subset Y$ and $Y \subset X$)

$X \cap Y$ the intersection of X and Y

(similarly, $\bigcap_{i=1}^{n} X_i$ or $\bigcap_{t \in T} X_t$)

$X \cup Y$ the union of X and Y

(similarly, $\bigcup_{i=1}^{n} X_i$ or $\bigcup_{t \in T} X_t$)

$X + Y$ the vector sum of X and Y (that is, $\{x + y: x \in X, y \in Y\}$

(similarly, $\sum_{i=1}^{n} X_i$, $\alpha X + \beta Y$, and so on)

$X - Y$ the vector difference between X and Y
(that is, $\{x - y: x \in X, y \in Y\}$

$X \backslash Y$ $\{x: x \in X, x \notin Y\}$

$\bigotimes_{i=1}^{n} X_i$ the Cartesian product of the X_i's

(similarly, $X \otimes Y$, and so on)

2.   Vectors

$\| x \|$ the norm of x
$d(x, y)$ the distance between x and y
$x \cdot y$ the inner product of x and y
Given two vectors x and y in R^n
        a. $x \geq y$ means $x_i \geq y_i$ for all i
        b. $x \geqq y$ means $x_i \geqq y_i$ for all i *and* with strict inequality for at least one i
        c. $x > y$ means $x_i > y_i$ for all i

3.   Matrix and Vector Multiplication

Let A be an $m \times n$ matrix
        $A \cdot x$ implies x is an n-dimensional column vector
        $x \cdot A$ implies x is an m-dimensional row vector
        $x \cdot A \cdot y$ implies x is an m-dimensional row vector and y is an n-dimensional
        column vector
In other words, we do not use any transpose notation for vectors, unless so specified.

4.   Preference Ordering

$x \circledgeqq y$ x is not worse than y
              (that is, y is not preferred to x)
$x \circledeq y$ x is indifferent to y
$x \circledgt y$ x is preferred to y

5.   Others

$\Rightarrow$ means "implies"
$\because$ means "because"
$\equiv$ means "is by definition equal to" (or "is identically equal to")
det A: determinant of matrix A
$\text{Re}(\omega)$:   real part of a complex number ω
Abbreviation resp. stands for respectively

INTRODUCTION

Section A
SCOPE OF THE BOOK

The essential feature of modern economic theory is that it is analytical and mathematical. Mathematics is a language that facilitates the honest presentation of a theory by making the assumptions explicit and by making each step of the logical deduction clear. Thus it provides a basis for further developments and extensions. Moreover, it provides the possibility for more accurate empirical testing.[1] Not only are some assumptions hidden and obscured in the theories of the verbal and the "curve-bending" economic schools,[2] but their approaches provide no scope for accurate empirical testing, simply because such testing requires explicit and mathematical representations of the premises of the theories to be tested.

Hence it is often argued that the "institutionalists" (as representing a methodological approach to economic problems) have been largely driven out of the temple and, furthermore, the relative weights of the curve-bending and the mathematical methodologies have been moving in the direction of the latter in many departments of economics in U.S. universities. But yet, economics is a complex subject and involves many things that cannot be expressed readily in terms of mathematics. Commenting on Max Planck's decision not to study economics, J. M. Keynes remarked that economics involves the "amalgam of logic and intuition and wide knowledge of facts, most of which are not precise."[3] In other words, economics is a combination of poetry and hard-boiled analysis accompanied by institutional facts. This does not imply, contrary to what many poets and institutionalists feel, that hard-boiled analysis is useless. Rather, it is the best way to express oneself honestly without being buried by the millions of institutional facts. Abstract economic theorizing with analytical and mathematical methodology does provide an excellent way to investigate real-world problems and institutions. An analogy here would be that of Tycho Brahe vs. Kepler, Galilei and Newton.[4] Clearly both are important, but this book chooses to discuss the analytical and mathematical approach.

Mathematical economics is a field that is concerned with complete and hard-boiled analysis. The essence here is the *method* of analysis and not the resulting collection of theorems, for actual economies are too complex to allow ready application of these theorems. J. M. Keynes once remarked that "the theory of economics does not furnish a body of settled conclusions immediately applicable to policy. It is a method rather than a doctrine, an apparatus of the mind, a technique of thinking, which helps its possessor to draw conclusions."[5]

An immediate corollary of this is that the theorems are useless without explicit recognition of the assumptions and complete understanding of the logic involved. It is important to get an intuitive understanding of the theorems (by means of diagrams and so on, if necessary), but this understanding is useless without a thorough knowledge of the assumptions and the proofs. Hence, in this book, all the major theorems are stated in full and proved rigorously. An introductory account of each topic is given to help provide an intuitive understanding of the theory involved. Care is taken to make the proofs as simple (or at least conceptually as elementary) as possible and no steps are omitted (so that they can be followed by readers of a nonmathematical inclination). Furthermore, a special effort is made to make the economic meaning of the theorems and the concepts involved in the theorems explicit and clear.

Modern economic theory may be discussed either in terms of the analytical techniques employed, or in terms of the topics discussed. Economists have lavished particular attention on two topics—the theory of competitive markets and the theory of growth, especially their general equilibrium aspects—with the results that both have achieved the status of rigorous, elegant theories, a state of theoretical development unmatched by any other branch of economics. The perfection of these theories has been very closely tied to the exploration, advancement, and elaboration of various mathematical techniques. This book will be restricted to these two theories—the theory of competitive markets and the theory of growth—and to those mathematical techniques that will assist in explaining and clarifying them. The book adopts a unified viewpoint—that of general equilibrium analysis.

The great danger in a book of this kind is that it may tend to become a patchwork of theories that are collected from different sources and artificially pasted together. The reader of such a book may be embarrassed by the knowledge he gains because he will be unaware of the relationships among the theories. Particular emphasis is placed herein on the relationships among the theories by bringing out the principles common to them. Also, insofar as is possible, a consistent body of terminology and notation is employed.

There exists a great deal of work in the profession indicating the utility of this approach as well as the utility of mathematical analysis in economic theory, for example, Samuelson's *Foundations of Economics Analysis* (1947). This book follows this pattern, paying particular attention to the advancements of economic science over the past 25 years.

It is tempting, in a study of this type, to treat the mathematical techniques and the economic theories separately. However, the fact that the mathematical techniques are closely related to economic theories seems to make it difficult to treat them effectively by themselves. In addition, treating the mathematical techniques first might discourage the student before he gets to the economic theories, whereas treating the economic theories first would not enable him to take advantage of the mathematical techniques. The author takes the view that this is not a difficulty but rather an advantage, in the sense that developments in economic theory can be used to provide the unifying structure for the book. The mathematical techniques can then be explained in connection with the theoretical developments to which they are related. Mathematical theorems will thus become more interesting and exciting to economists.

The author fully realizes some of the limitations of the book. For example, in spite of quite a comprehensive coverage of the topics (which is broader than in any other book currently in the field), it misses at least three important topics, namely, the theory of uncertainty, the theory of social systems and organizations,[6] and the theory of conflicts and interactions.[7] There is no question that these topics are important and that significant contributions will be made in the next few decades. They were excluded only because their inclusion would make the book massive and because, in view of the current research carried out in these fields, the materials covered would probably become obsolete by the time of publication of this work.[8]

Furthermore, even the topics covered in this book have important deficiencies, in spite of the elegance and importance of all the literature related to them. For example, in the case of the theory of competitive equilibrium one may ask the following questions: (1) What is the rationale justifying assumptions such as a fixed number of commodities, a fixed number of consumers, and a fixed technology set? (2) Granting all the premises of the theory, how can we reach an equilibrium? Walras offered the *tâtonnement* process, which provides a way to reach an equilibrium without knowing individuals' preferences, technology sets, and so forth.[9] But the process excludes the possibility of intermediate trading. When intermediate trading is permitted, the equilibrium depends on the trading paths. (3) Even if the *tâtonnement* process is accepted, convergence to an equilibrium is still an open question. So far, the proof of stability depends on heroic assumptions such as "gross substitutability."[10]

Although the monopoly of the nonanalytical methodology seems to be over, mathematical economics, as it may be represented by this book, is no doubt transitory. Future economists, completely free from prejudices against mathematics and well trained in mathematics, econometric methods, and the theory of measurement, and skilled in methods of electronic computation and simulation, may be able to deal successfully with the institutional and political-economy aspects of economics.[11] However, the basic methodology and the framework of thinking developed in mathematical economics will no doubt remain. Future economists may be less concerned with such "large" problems as the competitive equilibrium of the entire economy, and instead be more concerned with smaller aspects of the economy. But they will still realize the importance of the analytical method and the mode of developing analysis utilizing formally and honestly constructed models. Furthermore, with the proper training, future economists will not be in danger of overlooking the general equilibrium aspects of such models.

In ending, it must be stressed that we should not overlook the importance of the mathematical techniques developed in the course of the emergence of mathematical economics. Although I would be the last person to argue whether or not so-and-so's work is "good economics," I will be the first to defend the importance of making the mathematical tools available to economists. These are tools for every economist. Hence I have no hesitation to place heavy emphasis on mathematical techniques, almost on a par with my emphasis on economics.

Section B
OUTLINE OF THE BOOK

This book is essentially divided into three parts. The first part (Chapter 0) provides the background materials in mathematics and economics necessary for reading the rest of the book and also for further research in mathematical economics. The second and the third parts constitute the main body of the book. Roughly speaking, the second part (Chapters 1 through 4) is primarily concerned with the theory of competitive markets, and the third part (Chapters 5 through 8) is primarily concerned with the theory of growth. The above division between the second and the third parts is a rough one, since the mathematical techniques are closely interwoven with the economic topics, and it is not possible to classify these techniques according to economic topics. For example, the theory of non-linear programming (Chapter 1) is a mathematical technique which lies at the heart of the theory of competitive markets, yet it is an important technique also for growth theory and for other fields of economics.

The first part, consisting of only one chapter (Chapter 0), is divided into three sections. Section A collects the basic mathematics that will be useful for reading the rest of the book and also for the reader's further study in economic theory. Unlike the remainder of the book, most theorems here are stated without proof so that the reader can grasp the basic mathematical concepts and ideas without being led astray by the details of the proofs. Care is taken, however, not to misguide the reader into thinking that our world is always Euclidian, and thus this section becomes more than a mere exposition of the mathematics necessary for later sections of the book.

Section B of Chapter 0 is an exposition of separation theorems, one of the most important of all mathematical theories which contribute to the foundations of modern economic theory. One of the important features of modern economic theory is that it is set-theoretic, and Section C offers an exposition of activity analysis, which represents one of the most basic materials for the set-theoretic feature of modern economic theory. Separation theorems are the important mathematical technique used here.

The main content of the book starts with the exposition of nonlinear programming theory (Chapter 1), which is probably the most important mathematical technique in modern economic theory. There are many approaches one can take in this theory. Our approach utilizes the separation theorems of convex sets because this approach seems more natural (than, say, the implicit function theorem approach) in providing results that do not require differeniability. Section B of this chapter summarizes such results. Differentiation is introduced in Section C, and Section D summarizes the major results on the characterization of the solution of the constrained maximum problem in terms of derivatives. Section E provides an exposition of some additional (yet important) topics such as quasi-concave programming, vector maximization, the characterization of concave or quasi-concave functions in terms of Hessian matrices, and the second-order (necessary or sufficient) conditions for an optimum. The last section (F) of Chapter 1 provides examples of various economic applications. Obviously, the applications of nonlinear programming are not exhausted in Section F. Only some of the well-known examples are given. No doubt these applications have stimulated the interest of economists in the theory of nonlinear programming. It is probably natural to assume that the readers of this book have already confronted the standard use of the classical optimization theory (for example, Hicks's *Value and Capital*, Mathematical Appendix), so that they are motivated to read the treatment of the modern theory in Chapter 1 without too much economic introduction. Applications are thus placed at the end of the chapter. In the Appendix to Section F, we summarize the classical theory of optimization and its standard applications to comparative statics analysis, in order to make this book sufficiently self-contained.

Chapter 2 deals with the theory of competitive markets, especially its welfare aspects and the existence problem. Section B introduces the discussion of consumers and consumer preferences. Section C proves the two classical propositions of welfare economics: (1) a competitive equilibrium always realizes a Pareto optimum, and (2) for any Pareto optimum, there exists a reallocation of initial resources such that it can be supported by a competitive equilibrium. In the Appendix to Section C, we attempt an introductory exposition of the theory of the core, a topic which has recently attracted great interest. It is hoped that interest is aroused among readers to study the theory of n-person games, which has great potential with regard to its applications to economics. Section D deals with demand theory. Two main results, the continuity property of demand functions and the Hicks-Slutsky equation, are the central themes here. In the

Appendix to Section D, related mathematical concepts and theorems are discussed. In particular, we discuss the relation among the various concepts of semicontinuity and a useful mathematical theorem known as the "maximum theorem." Section E deals with the existence of a competitive equilibrium. Mathematical techniques known as "fixed point theorems" play a central role here. Various approaches to the existence problem are discussed, for each approach has an interesting feature and contains potential applications to other problems. The Appendix to Section D contains a brief discussion of the uniqueness of equilibrium. The last section (F) attempts to make it clear that the mechanism of competitive markets can be viewed as a mechanism that generates a solution to a nonlinear programming problem. Thus the topics of the two chapters on nonlinear programming and competitive markets are now related. In particular, we prove the two classical propositions of welfare economics and the existence of a competitive equilibrium from the point of view of nonlinear programming.

Chapter 3 deals with the stability of competitive markets. The *tâtonnement* process provides an institutional scheme under which one can find a competitive equilibrium without actually knowing each consumer's preferences and each producer's technology set. After a discussion of the historical background of the topic in Section C, the Arrow-Block-Hurwicz proof of global stability under the gross substitutes case is duscussed in Section E. Section F provides certain remarks on this main result, the most important of which is Scarf's example of instability. Section G questions the institutional plausibility of the *tâtonnement* mechanism and discusses non-*tâtonnement* processes. Owing to the strictness of the gross substitutability assumptions coupled with Scarf's counter-example, and with the doubt about the institutional plausibility of the *tâtonnement* process, there are certain economists who are left cold by the entire stability analysis. However, this analysis has made economists aware of the importance of disequilibrium analysis and adjustment processes toward an equilibrium. Moreover, it has also made economists realize the importance of the differential equations technique in economics. The exposition of this technique is attempted in Section B and the Liapunov second method, a powerful tool for stability analysis, is explained in Section H. An important diagrammatical technique, the phase diagram, is also made available to economists through stability analysis. This technique, discussed in Section D, has many applications in dynamic economic theories.

Chapter 4 deals with the mathematical techniques developed in connection with Frobenius' theorems and dominant diagonal matrices. These are developed in connection with the Leontief input-output analysis and stability analysis. In Section A, we motivate our discussion of this chapter by using the Leontief input-output model, which in turn is a model of a general equilibrium competitive economy. Section B deals with Frobenius' theorems, and Section C deals with dominant diagonal matrices in cases where off-diagonal elements are either all nonnegative or all nonpositive. After the rather tedious mathematical discussions of Sections B and C, economic applications are taken up in Section D.

Section D begins with a summary of the results of B and C, and the reader, if he so wishes, can skip most of the reading of B and C. The rich and wide applications shown in Section D will illustrate the power of this technique in economic theory.

Chapter 5 has the dual purpose of introducing modern growth theory in the form of an aggregate optimal growth model and of making the reader familiar with an important mathematical tool, the calculus of variations. The calculus of variations has had an unfortunate history among economists in that it was immediately forgotten after the initial economic works of Roos, Evans, and Ramsey, in the 1920s and 1930s. However, the power of this technique in physics is well known, and economists are becoming more aware of its use in economics. The optimal growth model gives an interesting example of its economic applications. In Section A, we make an expository account of this technique for the simplest case. In Section B, we enter into a study of the second-order characterizations, which may be useful for the reader's further reading and research. It is also shown there that, just as in nonlinear programming, concavity is sufficient to guarantee that the first-order characterization ("Euler's condition") is necessary and sufficient for an optimum. Section C digresses from the optimization problem and attempts a compact summary of the one-sector growth model. Section D then deals with the one-sector optimal growth model. An enormous amount of literature in this field is treated in a unified and simple manner. Chapter 5 ends with the Appendix to Section D, in which we deal with the discrete-time analogue of our discussion of Section D. This Appendix is intended to illustrate the relation between the "continuous-time" model and the "discrete-time" model, and to give an expository account of the existence problem and of the important "sensitivity" results.

Chapter 6 discusses two important multisector growth models, the von Neumann model and the dynamic Leontief model. In spite of many limitations, the von Neumann model turns out to be fundamental in modern growth theory. Section A deals with this model. Section B is concerned with the dynamic Leontief model, which is particularly important among empirical economists. This model, however, seems to have several important theoretical limitations. We point out these difficulties. The Appendix to Section B uses a one-sector model and points out these difficulties more sharply.

Chapter 7 deals with optimal growth in a multisector context. Section A discusses some of the old results in this topic, namely, the "turnpike theorems." In this material the role of consumption is completely subsumed and society is concerned only with the terminal stock of goods. Our emphasis here is on an elegant turnpike theorem due to Radner. Although the turnpike theorems of Section A mark a great advance in theory compared with the von Neumann theory, the above weakness is quite strong. This prompted the "neo-turnpike theorems," notably that of David Gale. However, we deal with consumption more explicitly than did Gale. Incidentally, we carry out our discussions of Chapters 6 and 7 in terms of the discrete-time model, which the reader may, if he so wishes, translate to the continuous-time model. In Chapter 7, where we discuss the optimization problem, we see that the nonlinear programming technique (Chapter 1) is again found to have important economic applications.

Chapter 8 is the last chapter of the book and deals with one important and powerful technique, optimal control theory. In Section A we summarize the important results obtained by Pontryagin and others with some illustrations of the applications of these results. In Section B we discuss, in full, two applications of these results: the problem of regional allocation of investment and the optimal growth problem with a linear objective. The latter is particularly useful as an illustration of the "bang-bang" solution. In Section C we return to the basic theory again and discuss some important generalizations of the results summarized in Section A. In addition to the usual Pontryagin-type differential equation constraint, constraints of other forms (such as $g[x, u, t] \geq 0$, integral constraints, and so on) are introduced. The major theorem here is due to Hestenes. We again point out the importance of concavity and present a result which is slightly more general than Mangasarian's sufficiency theorem. Section D deals with some applications of the results of Section C. Optimal growth is again taken up because of the reader's familiarity with this topic. Another application in Section D is concerned with the peak-load problem. In Section E, we study the neoclassical theory of investment as an application of the optimal control technique, and present various theories in a unified and generalized fashion. In spite of our rather complete treatment of investment theory in Section E, our emphasis in Chapter 8 is still to expose the reader to this powerful technique rather than to discuss in detail all possible economic applications. It is hoped that the reader will find other important economic applications of the technique. Although economic applications in the literature have been concerned almost exclusively with growth theory, there should be no such restriction. Obviously the interpretation of t does not have to be confined to "time." The variable t can refer to Mr. t in the continuum of traders model or to income "t" in the taxation model, and so forth.

FOOTNOTES

1. By empirical testing, I do not mean the "curve-fitting school," which relies heavily on regression analysis. Although this school is fashionable among certain empirical economists, it seems to represent institutionalism in one of its worst forms. Not only does it suffer from a poor theoretical basis, but also it often ignores the elementary theory of measurement.
2. However, there is no question that "diagrams" are often very useful tools for understanding important theories and that "common sense" verbal arguments are often essential in leading to economically fruitful theories.
3. Keynes, J. M., "Alfred Marshall, 1842–1924," *Economic Journal*, XXXIV, September 1924, p. 333.
4. The analogy is imperfect, for we do not know of any economic theory which is

as successful in its application as is Newtonian mechanics in physics. Thus Planck decided not to study economics.

5. Keynes, J. M., "Introduction" (to the series), *Cambridge Economic Handbooks* (the first book in the series, *Supply and Demand* by H. D. Henderson, appeared in 1922, published by Harcourt Brace and Co.).

6. A classical study in this field is L. Hurwicz, "Optimality and Informational Efficiency in Resource Allocation Processes," in *Mathematical Methods in the Social Sciences, 1959*, ed. by K. J. Arrow, S. Karlin, and P. Suppes, Stanford, Calif., Stanford University Press, 1960. In the study of the problems of social choice, the classical work is K. J. Arrow, *Social Choice and Individual Values*, 2nd ed., New York, Wiley, 1963 (1st ed., 1951).

7. These three topics are obviously interrelated. An important example of this interrelationship is found in the body of mathematical knowledge known as the "theory of games." The list of good textbooks on the theory of games has been expanding, consequently discouraging me from including the subject in this book.

8. There seems to be no question that the topics covered in this book will provide a basis for further research in the above three fields. For example, the theory of competitive equilibrium is a theory of a social system—competitive markets— given *a priori*, operating under conditions of certainty. The theory of growth provides an understanding of the complications that arise when the possibility of intertemporal choice is explicitly introduced. In view of the prior importance of the theory of competitive equilibrium and the theory of growth, the omission might not be as serious as it may seem.

9. H. Scarf recently offered a method of computing the competitive equilibrium when we know the aggregate technology set and certain information on the preferences of individual consumers. See his article "On the Computation of Equilibrium Prices," in *Economic Studies in the Tradition of Irving Fisher*, New York, Wiley, 1967, and "An Example of an Algorithm for Calculating General Equilibrium Prices," *American Economic Review*, LIX, September 1969.

10. Some of these points are discussed in the book. See our discussion on the non-*tâtonnement* processes (Chap. 3, Section G), for example. Incidentally, disequilibrium analysis is another important topic whose rapid progress is expected in the next few decades.

11. Needless to say, they should still have ample knowledge of data and institutions as well as deep insight into the workings of the real world. Lacking these, there is some doubt as to whether they are qualified to be called "economists."

0

PRELIMINARIES

Section A

MATHEMATICAL PRELIMINARIES[1]

a.   SOME BASIC CONCEPTS AND NOTATIONS[2]

A **set** is a collection of objects (of any kind). For example, the collection of all the positive integers is a set, the collection of all human beings on earth is a set, and the collection of all the transistor radios made in Japan during the year 1973 is a set. Words such as "family," "collection," and "class" are often used synonymously with the word "set." If x is a member of a set S, we denote that by $x \in S$. If x is not a member of S, we denote that by $x \notin S$. A set is often denoted by braces, $\{\ \}$. Inside the brace, a colon often separates two descriptions: the first denotes a typical element of the set and the second denotes the properties that a typical element must have to belong to the set. For example, if I is the set of all the positive integers, we may denote it by $I \equiv \{n : n \text{ is a positive integer}\}$. The set of points on the unit circle in the two-dimensional plane can be denoted by $\{(x, y) : x \in R, y \in R, x^2 + y^2 = 1\}$, where R is the set of all real numbers. That any S can be written in the form $\{x : P(x)\}$, where $P(x)$ are the properties for x to be a member of S, is sometimes called the **axiom of specification** (see Halmos [6], p. 6). In this book, unless otherwise stated, R will always refer to the set of all real numbers.[3] A set with a finite number of elements can (in principle) be denoted by enumerating its elements; for example, $\{x, y, z\}$, $\{0\}$, and so on. An element of a set is often called a "point" in the set.

Given two sets A and B, if every element of A is an element of B, we say that A is a **subset** of B or B **includes** A; we write $A \subset B$ or $B \supset A$. Note that $A \subset A$. We say that two sets A and B are **equal** if they have the same elements, and we write $A = B$ or $B = A$. (This is often called the **axiom of extension**; see Halmos [6], pp. 2–3.) It is easy to see that $A = B$ if and only if both $A \subset B$ and $B \subset A$.

The collection of all the elements which belong to both set A and B is denoted by $A \cap B$ and is called the **intersection** of A and B; that is, $A \cap B \equiv$

1

$\{x: x \in A$ and $x \in B\}$. The collection of all the elements which belong to set A or set B is denoted by $A \cup B$ and is called the **union** of A and B; that is, $A \cup B \equiv \{x: x \in A$ or $x \in B\}$. The **difference** between two sets A and B (denoted by $A\backslash B$) is defined by $A\backslash B \equiv \{x: x \in A$ and $x \notin B\}$. The set that has no elements is also considered a set. It is called the **empty set** and is denoted by $\emptyset$. If two sets A and B have no elements in common, A and B are said to be **disjoint** or **nonintersecting**. In other words, $A \cap B = \emptyset$.

The union (or intersection) can be taken over a finite or infinite collection of sets. For example, if $S_1, S_2, \ldots, S_n, \ldots$ are sets, we can consider

$$\bigcup_{i=1}^{n} S_i \quad \text{or} \quad \bigcup_{i=1}^{\infty} S_i$$

In fact, the index i does not have to be an integer. For example, letting T be the set of all real numbers between 0 and 1, we may consider the union $\cup_{t \in T} S_t$. If S_t is the set of all the human beings on earth at time t, $\cup_{t \in T} S_t$ is the set of all human beings on earth during the period T. The reader should easily understand the notations

$$\bigcap_{i=1}^{M} S_i, \quad \bigcap_{i=1}^{\infty} S_i, \quad \bigcap_{t \in T} S_t$$

If I is the set of all positive integers, we may write

$$\bigcup_{i=1}^{\infty} S_i = \bigcup_{i \in I} S_i$$

When S is a subset of set X, the set of elements which belongs to X but not to S is said to be the **complement of** S relative to X. When it is obviously "relative to X," we often omit this phrase and denote it by S^c where $S^c \equiv \{x: x \in X, x \notin S\}$. Clearly $X^c = \emptyset$ and $(S^c)^c = S$.

Given two sets X and Y, consider an ordered pair (x, y) where $x \in X$ and $y \in Y$. The collection of all those ordered pairs is called the **Cartesian product** of X and Y and is denoted by $X \otimes Y$. The ordinary two-dimensional plane can be written as $R \otimes R$, also R^2 where R is the set of real numbers. Given sets X_1, $X_2, \ldots$, we may consider the Cartesian product such as

$$\bigotimes_{i=1}^{n} X_i, \quad \bigotimes_{i=1}^{\infty} X_i$$

When T is some index set (not necessarily the positive integers), we may consider the Cartesian product such as $\bigotimes_{t \in T} X_t$. If T is the set of all the positive integers, clearly

$$\bigotimes_{t \in T} X_t = \bigotimes_{i=1}^{\infty} X_i$$

If we write $x = (x_1, x_2, \ldots, x_n) \in \bigotimes_{i=1}^{n} X_i$, x_i is called the *i*th **coordinate** of a point. Similarly in $\otimes_{t \in T} X_t$, $x_t \in X_t$ is the *t*th **coordinate** of the respective point. The set X_t is called the *t*th **coordinate set**.

Given two sets X and Y, if we can associate each member of X with an element of Y in a certain manner, which we denote by $f(x)$, then we say f is a **function** from X into Y, denoted by $f: X \to Y$. The set X is said to be the **domain** of f and the set $\{f(x): x \in X\}$ [often denoted by $f(X)$] is said to be the **range** of f; $f(x)$ is the **value** or the **image** of x under f.[4] The terms **map, transformation, operator,** and **function** are synonymous. If we can associate more than one point in Y for each point x in X, we call it a **set-valued function**, a **multivalued function**, or a **correspondence**. When only one point in Y is associated with each point of X, we call it a **single-valued function** or simply a **function**.[5] Even if a function is single-valued, it is still possible that more than one point in X is associated with the same value in Y under this function. An example is $f: R \to R$ with $f(x) = a$ for all x (called a **constant function**). Let A be a subset of $f(X)$. The set defined as $\{x: x \in X, f(x) \in A\}$ is called the **inverse image** of A under f and is denoted by $f^{-1}(A)$. If A consists of only one element, say, $A = \{y\}$, then $f^{-1}(A)$ is the inverse image of y under f. For example, if $f(x) = 3$, $x \in R$, then $f^{-1}(3) = R$. One can define a mapping f^{-1} of Y into X by $x = f^{-1}(y)$ if and only if $y = f(x)$. The function f^{-1} can be either single-valued or multivalued. When both f and f^{-1} are single-valued, then f is said to be **one to one** or an **injection**. If, in addition, $f(X) = Y$, then f is called **one to one and onto** or a **bijection**. If f is a function from X into Y and if g is a function from $f(X)$ into Z, then we can define a function h from X into Z by first applying f, then g. That is, $h = g[f(x)]$, $x \in X$. We call h the **composite function** of f and g and denote it by $h = g \circ f$. Let f be a function from X into Y. Then the set defined by $\{(x, y): (x, y) \in X \otimes f(X), y = f(x)\}$ is called the "graph" of f. The graphs on R^2 shown in Figure 0.1 may be useful illustrations.

Let S be a set of real numbers, that is, $S \subset R$. Then S is said to be **bounded from above** if there exists an $a \in R$ (a is not necessarily in S) such that $x \leq a$ for all $x \in S$,

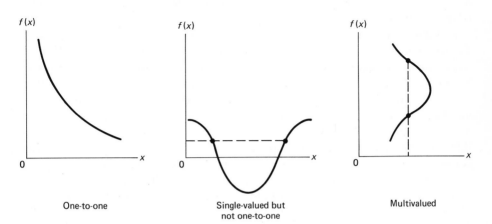

One-to-one   Single-valued but   Multivalued
not one-to-one

Figure 0.1. Functions.

and a is called an **upper bound** of S. Similarly, S is said to be **bounded from below** if there exists a $b \in R$ (b is not necessarily in S) such that $x \geq b$ for all $x \in S$; b is called the **lower bound** of S. Clearly there can be many upper bounds and lower bounds for a given set of real numbers. We do not discuss the axioms of the real number system here (the interested reader can refer to any relevant book in pure mathematics). But from these axioms, one can easily derive the following proposition:

   (i) *If S is bounded from above, there is a smallest element in the set of upper bounds of S.*

From *(i)*, we can then derive *(ii)*:

   (ii) *If S is bounded from below, there is a largest element in the set of lower bounds of S.*

In other words, if S is bounded from above, the set U of its upper bounds, $U \equiv \{a: a \in R, a \geq x \text{ for all } x \in S\}$, is not empty. Proposition (i) asserts that there exists an $\tilde{a} \in U$ such that $x < \tilde{a}$ implies $x \notin U$; $\tilde{a}$ is called the **supremum** or the **least upper bound** of S. It is denoted as sup $S \equiv \tilde{a}$ or $\sup_{x \in S} x \equiv \tilde{a}$. If S is bounded from below, the set L of its lower bounds, $L \equiv \{b: b \in R, b \leq x \text{ for all } x \in S\}$, is not empty. Proposition (ii) asserts that there exists a $\check{b} \in L$ such that $x > \check{b}$ implies $x \notin L$. $\check{b}$ is called the **infimum** or the **greatest lower bound** of S. It is denoted as inf $S \equiv \check{b}$ or $\inf_{x \in S} x \equiv \check{b}$. Given a set S, a subset of R, S may not contain its least upper bound even if it is bounded from above. Similarly, S may not contain its greatest lower bound even if it is bounded from below. For example, the set S defined by $S \equiv \{1/q: q = 1, 2, \ldots\}$ is clearly a subset of R, and sup $S = 1$ and inf $S = 0$. Note that $1 \in S$ and $0 \notin S$. That is, inf $S \notin S$. In general, given an arbitrary subset S of R, if $\tilde{a} \equiv$ sup S is in S, $\tilde{a}$ is called the **maximum** element of S. Similarly, if $\check{b} \equiv$ inf S is in S, $\check{b}$ is called the **minimum** element of S. The above is an example of the case in which a set does not contain its infimum.

   Finally, we may note that the notation "$\Rightarrow$" is often used to mean "imply." For example $A \Rightarrow B$ is read as "statement A implies statement B." If $A \Rightarrow B$ holds, we say that B is a **necessary condition** for A and that A is a **sufficient condition** for B. When $A \Rightarrow B$ holds, it is not necessarily the case that $B \Rightarrow A$ holds (that is, "the converse is not necessarily true"). For example, let Q be the set of all rational numbers and J be the set of all integers; then $x \in J \Rightarrow x \in Q$ but $x \in Q$ does not necessarily imply $x \in J$. When $A \Rightarrow B$ and $B \Rightarrow A$ both hold, then we may say that A is a **necessary and sufficient condition** for B or B is a necessary and sufficient condition for A. In this case A and B are also said to be **logically equivalent**. When $A \Rightarrow B$ holds, then "B does not hold $\Rightarrow A$ does not hold" is true. On the other hand, if we can show "B does not hold $\Rightarrow A$ does not hold," then $A \Rightarrow B$. This is often used to prove the statement "$A \Rightarrow B$."

b. R^n AND LINEAR SPACE[6]

Let R be the set of all real numbers. Consider an n-tuple of real numbers, $x = (x_1, x_2, \ldots, x_n)$. Write R^n for the set of all n-tuples of real numbers, that is, $R^n \equiv \{x = (x_1, x_2, \ldots, x_n): x_i \in R, i = 1, 2, \ldots, n\}$. Then R^n is the n-fold Cartesian product of R. The ith element x_i of $x \in R^n$ is the ith coordinate of x. Define the addition of any two arbitrary members x and y of R^n by coordinate-wise addition, that is, $x + y = z$ means $z_i = x_i + y_i$, $i = 1, 2, \ldots, n$. Clearly $z \in R^n$ if x, $y \in R^n$. In other words, R^n is **closed** under addition. Given an arbitrary scalar $\alpha \in R$, define the multiplication of an arbitrary member x of R^n by α (called **scalar multiplication**) by coordinate-wise multiplication, that is, $z = \alpha x = x\alpha$ means $z_i = \alpha x_i$, $i = 1, 2, \ldots, n$. Clearly $x \in R^n$, $\alpha \in R$ implies $\alpha x \in R^n$. In other words, R^n is "closed" under scalar multiplication.

When $n = 2$, we can illustrate the above concepts of coordinates, addition, and scalar multiplication in Figure 0.2. This diagram should be well known.

Given the above rule of addition and scalar multiplication in R^n, we can readily check that the following eight properties hold for arbitrary elements x, y, and z of R^n and scalars $\alpha, \beta \in R$.

(L-1)   (**Associative Law**) $x + (y + z) = (x + y) + z$.
(L-2)   There exists an element called 0 such that $x + 0 = 0 + x = x$.
(L-3)   There exists an element $(-x)$ for every x such that $x + (-x) = 0$.
(L-4)   (**Commutative Law**) $x + y = y + x$.
(L-5)   (**Associative Law**) $\alpha(\beta x) = (\alpha \beta)x$.
(L-6) $1x = x$.
(L-7)   (**Distributive Law**) $\alpha(x + y) = \alpha x + \alpha y$.
(L-8)   (**Distributive Law**) $(\alpha + \beta)x = \alpha x + \beta x$.

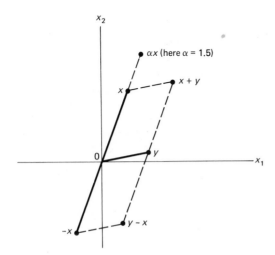

Figure 0.2.   An Illustration of R^2.

A little notational caution is needed here about the symbol 0, which can mean either the scalar zero or the n-tuple of 0's. The latter is sometimes called the **origin** for the obvious geometric reason (see Figure 0.2).

Given an arbitrary set X (not necessarily R^n), if "addition" and "scalar multiplication" are defined, if X is closed under these two operations, and if the above properties (L-1) to (L-8) are satisfied, then we call X a (real) **linear space** or (real) **vector space**, and an element of X is called a **vector**. Of course R^n with the above rule of addition and scalar multiplication is only one *example* of a linear space. From now on we shall regard R^n as a particular one in which such addition and multiplication are defined. We henceforth call R^n "(n-dimensional) real space." For illustrative purposes we give the following as examples of linear spaces other than R^n.

> **EXAMPLE 1:** The set F of real-valued functions defined on the interval $[a, b]$. Given $f, g \in F$, "addition" $(f + g)$ is defined by $f(x) + g(x)$ for each $x \in [a, b]$ and scalar multiplication (αf) is defined by $\alpha f(x)$ for each $x \in [a, b]$.
>
> **EXAMPLE 2:** $x = (x_1, x_2, \ldots, x_n, \ldots)$, where $\sum_{k=1}^{\infty} x_k < \infty$, with a similar definition of addition and scalar multiplication as in R^n.
>
> **EXAMPLE 3:** The set of all two-by-two matrices with real number entries.
>
> **EXAMPLE 4:** The set of all continuous functions defined on the closed interval $[0, 1]$ into R (denoted by $C_{[0,1]}$), with the same rules of addition and scalar multiplication as in example 1.
>
> *REMARK*: Given an arbitrary set X, if "addition" is defined on X and x, $y \in X$ implies $x + y \in X$ with the properties (L-1) to (L-4), we say X is an **Abelian (additive) group**.

A subset S of a linear space X is called a **linear subspace** or **vector subspace** if $x, y \in S \Rightarrow x + y \in S$ and $x \in S$, $\alpha \in R \Rightarrow \alpha x \in S$. It should be clear that a linear subspace is also a linear space [that is, the above axioms (L-1) to (L-8) are satisfied in S]. If S_i, $i = 1, 2, \ldots, n$ are linear subspaces in linear space X, then the intersection $\cap_{i=1}^{n} S_i$ is also a linear subspace.

> *REMARK*: Given a linear space X, an arbitrary subset of X is not necessarily a linear space. In fact, in most cases it is not. However, the cases in which a subset itself is a linear space are important, for we can then utilize the above eight properties (L-1) to (L-8). The set R^3 is a linear space and its subsets $S_1 \equiv \{(x_1, 0, 0) \in R^3 : x_1 \in R\}$ and $S_2 \equiv \{(x_1, x_2, 0) \in R^3 : x_1, x_2 \in R\}$, respectively, are linear subspaces of R^3. However, $S_1 \cup \{(1, 1, 1)\}$ is not a linear space.
>
> *REMARK*: In the above definition of linear space, scalar multiplication is confined to multiplication by real numbers. In general we do not have to

restrict the "scalars" to real numbers. If a linear space is defined over complex numbers, we call it a **complex linear space** or a **linear space with complex field**. In fact, we can use anything as a scalar in the defining properties of a linear space, if it satisfies the properties of the algebraic concept "field." However, in this book, we confine ourselves to a "real linear space," or a "linear space with real field" (that is, the case in which the scalars are the real numbers). Hence, when we subsequently refer to a linear space, we mean it to be a real linear space as was defined above.

Let S_1 and S_2 be two subsets in a linear space X. Since addition and scalar multiplication are defined in a linear space, we can define the following set S, for fixed scalars α and β

$$S \equiv \{\alpha x + \beta y : x \in S_1, y \in S_2, \text{ and } \alpha, \beta \in R\}$$

We denote S by $\alpha S_1 + \beta S_2$ and call it a **linear sum** of S_1 and S_2. Clearly S is in X. Given m sets, $S_1, S_2, \ldots, S_m$ in a linear space X, we can analogously define $S \equiv \sum_{i=1}^{m} \alpha_i S_i$, $\alpha_i \in R$, $i = 1, 2, \ldots, m$. The linear sum of sets must be distinguished from the union of sets (such as $\cup_{i=1}^{m} S_i$).

Given any two arbitrary members $x = (x_1, x_2, \ldots, x_n)$ and $y = (y_1, y_2, \ldots, y_n)$ of R^n, we may define a rule for multiplication of x and y as follows:

$$x \cdot y \equiv \sum_{i=1}^{n} x_i y_i$$

Note that $x \cdot y$ is a real number; $x \cdot y$ computed by the above rule is called the inner product in R^n.

In general, given an arbitrary linear space X (over a real field), an **inner product** is defined as a real-valued function defined on the Cartesian product $X \otimes X$ (denoted by $x \cdot y$ or $< x, y >$ where $x \in X$ and $y \in X$), which satisfies the following properties. For arbitrary elements x, y and $z \in X$ and $\alpha, \beta \in R$,

(I-1) $x \cdot y = y \cdot x$.
(I-2) $(\alpha x + \beta y) \cdot z = \alpha (x \cdot z) + \beta (y \cdot z)$.
(I-3) $x \cdot x \geq 0$ and $x \cdot x = 0$ if and only if $x = 0$.

A linear space with an inner product defined is called an **inner product space**. Clearly the inner product defined above for R^n satisfies the above axioms (I-1) to (I-3). We call it the usual (Euclidian) inner product.

Given a point $x = (x_1, x_2, \ldots, x_n)$ in R^n, the distance between x and the origin can be computed by

$$d(x, 0) \equiv \sqrt{\sum_{i=1}^{n} x_i^2} = \sqrt{x \cdot x}$$

Similarly, given any two arbitrary points $x = (x_1, x_2, \ldots, x_n)$ and $y = (y_1, y_2, \ldots,$

y_n) in R^n, the distance between x and y can be computed by

$$d(x,y) \equiv \sqrt{\sum_{i=1}^{n}(x_i - y_i)^2} = \sqrt{(x-y)\cdot(x-y)}$$

The "distance" defined in the above formula is called the **Euclidian distance**. The Euclidian distance is illustrated in Figure 0.3.

We can easily show that the Euclidian distance defined above satisfies the following properties.

(M-1) $d(x, y) = 0$ if and only if $x = y$.
(M-2) **(Triangular inequality)** $d(x, y) + d(y, z) \geq d(z, x)$.
(M-3) $d(x, y) \geq 0$ for all x and y.
(M-4) **(Symmetry)** $d(x, y) = d(y, x)$.

Properties (M-3) and (M-4) can be obtained from (M-1) and (M-2). Given an arbitrary set X, if a function d from $X \otimes X$ into R is defined and if d satisfies the above properties (M-1) and (M-2) [hence also (M-3) and (M-4)], then X is called a **metric space**, d is called a **metric**, and $d(x, y)$ is called the **distance** between two points x and y in $X \otimes X$. The metric space is denoted by (X, d). The metric (or distance) is a function from $X \otimes X$ into R.

> REMARK: The first example of a metric space is obviously R^n with the Euclidian distance defined, from which the concept is formulated. However, it is possible to think of many different kinds of metric spaces. In the following example the reader can easily check that the axioms (M-1) and (M-2) of metric spaces are satisfied.

Let X be an arbitrary nonempty set and define

$$d(x, y) \equiv \begin{cases} 0 \text{ if } x = y \\ 1 \text{ if } x \neq y \end{cases}$$

This example shows that every nonempty set can be regarded as a metric space.

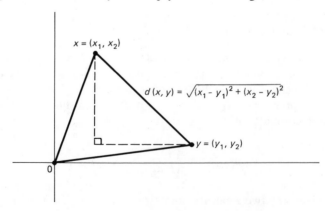

Figure 0.3.   An Illustration of Euclidian Distance.

This example is often used to show that certain statements which hold true in R^n (with the Euclidian distance) do not necessarily hold true in an arbitrary metric space.

Given a point x in R^n, the Euclidian distance between x and the origin, $d(x, 0)$, is also called the **Euclidian norm** of x. We denote it by $\| x \|$. Then $d(x, y)$ can be denoted by $\| x - y \|$. Given arbitrary points x and y in R^n and a scalar $\alpha \in R$, we can easily verify that the following three properties hold for the Euclidian norm.

(N-1) $\| x \| \geq 0$ and $\| x \| = 0$ if and only if $x = 0$.

(N-2)   **(Triangular inequality)** $\| x + y \| \leq \| x \| + \| y \|$.

(N-3) $\| \alpha x \| = |\alpha| \, \| x \|$.

Given an arbitrary vector space X (not necessarily R^n), if we define the real-valued function, called a **norm**, which satisfies the above three properties, we call X a **normed vector space**, or a **normed linear space**. Clearly every normed linear space is a metric space with respect to the induced metric defined by $d(x, y) = \| x - y \|$. It should be noted that the choice of a norm is not necessarily unique. For example, R^n is a normed linear space with the Euclidian norm, but it can also be a normed linear space with the following norms:

$$\| x \| \equiv \max |x_i|, \quad 1 \leq i \leq n$$

or

$$\| x \| \equiv \sum_{i=1}^{n} |x_i|$$

The reader can check that either of the above two satisfies all three properties (N-1) to (N-3).

We should note that an arbitrary metric space cannot necessarily be a normed linear space, for it may not be a linear space in the beginning.

Given a linear space X, we can also induce the concept of a norm from the concept of an inner product. That is, let X be an inner product space and define

$$\| x \| \equiv (x \cdot x)^{\frac{1}{2}}, \quad \text{or} \quad \| x \|^2 = (x \cdot x)$$

We can easily verify all the properties of a norm, (N-1) to (N-3); hence X becomes a normed linear space as well as an inner product space. Note that in R^n this relation holds when $\| x \|$ is the Euclidian norm and $(x \cdot x) \equiv \sum_{i=1}^{n} x_i^2$.

Thus given an arbitrary linear space X, if we first define an inner product and if we induce the norm and then the metric in the way described above, then X becomes a normed, metric, and inner product linear space. Thus all the properties (N-1) to (N-3), (M-1) to (M-4), (I-1) to (I-3), and (L-1) to (L-8) are available. In particular, R^n can be such a space with its usual Euclidian norm, metric, and inner product. Unless otherwise stated, we consider R^n as such a space. That is, given x and y in R^n, we have

$$x \cdot y \equiv \sum_{i=1}^{n} x_i y_i, \quad \| x \| \equiv (x \cdot x)^{\frac{1}{2}}$$

and

$$d(x, y) \equiv \| x - y \| = [(x - y) \cdot (x - y)]^{\frac{1}{2}}$$

with (N-1) to (N-3), (M-1) to (M-4), (I-1) to (I-3), (L-1) to (L-8), and all the properties derived from them.

   We remark that to have a norm it is not necessary to have an inner product at all. We also remark that there are normed linear spaces over which one cannot define an inner product that will "generate" or "induce" the norm on the space. In other words, there may not exist any inner product such that $x \cdot x = \| x \|^2$, where $\| x \|$ is the norm on the space. However, if further conditions are imposed on the norm, then one can guarantee the existence of an inner product that will induce the norm.

c.   BASIS AND LINEAR FUNCTIONS[7]
   We begin this subsection by defining some important concepts of a linear space.

Definition: Let X be a linear space. Given m vectors in X, $x^1, x^2, \ldots, x^m$, the vector x defined by

$$x \equiv \sum_{i=1}^{m} \alpha_i x^i, \quad \alpha_i \in R, i = 1, 2, \ldots, m$$

is called a **linear combination** of these m vectors.

   REMARK: In order that the above definition of x be meaningful, X cannot be an arbitrary set. That is, scalar multiplication and addition must be defined on the set.[8] Note also that x is in X since X is a linear space. Note also that m must be a finite number, since a linear combination is defined only with respect to a finite sum.

Definition: A finite set of vectors $\{x^1, x^2, \ldots, x^m\}$ in a linear space is called **linearly independent** if

$$\sum_{i=1}^{m} \alpha_i x^i = 0 \text{ implies that } \alpha_i = 0 \text{ for every } i$$

An arbitrary (finite or infinite) collection of vectors, S, is said to be **linearly independent** if every finite subset is linearly independent. The collection of vectors S is said to be **linearly dependent** if it is not linearly independent; S is linearly dependent if and only if there exists a linear combination of (a finite number of) vectors in S, say $x^1, x^2, \ldots, x^m$, such that

$$\sum_{i=1}^{m} \alpha_i x^i = 0 \text{ for some } \alpha_i \in R, \alpha_i \neq 0, i = 1, 2, \ldots, m$$

REMARK: If S is finite, say, $\{x^1, x^2, \ldots, x^m\}$, S is linearly dependent if and only if there exist scalars, $\alpha_1, \alpha_2, \ldots, \alpha_m$, all in R and not vanishing simultaneously such that $\sum_{i=1}^{m} \alpha_i x^i = 0$.

The following proposition is an immediate but very important corollary of the above definitions.

Corollary: *The set of nonzero vectors, $\{x^1, x^2, \ldots, x^m\}$, is linearly dependent if and only if one of the vectors in the set—say, x^i—can be expressed as a linear combination of other vectors in the set.* (For the proof, see Halmos [5], pp. 9–10, for example.)

Definition: Let X be a linear space. A linearly independent set S in X, with the property that every vector x in X can be expressed as a linear combination of the vectors in S, is called a **basis** (or a **Hamel basis**) for X.

REMARK: A basis S may consist of a finite or infinite number of members. If it is finite, X is said to be **finite dimensional** (and otherwise **infinite dimensional**).

REMARK: The usual Cartesian coordinate system of R^n, that is, n vectors, $(1, 0, \ldots, 0)$, $(0, 1, \ldots, 0)$, $\ldots$ $(0, \ldots, 0, 1)$, each consisting of n members, forms a basis for R^n. Obviously there can be many bases for a given linear system X.

The following theorem is basic.

Theorem 0.A.1:

(i) *Every linear space has a basis.*

(ii) *Any two bases of a linear space are in one-to-one correspondence.*

PROOF: See Wilansky [12], pp. 16–17, for example.

REMARK: The proof of (i) requires Zorn's lemma; an understanding of this lemma is not required in this book. The interested reader can refer to any standard textbook on set theory or topology (for example, Halmos [6], sec. 16, and Kelley [7], p. 33).

A corollary of (ii) in the above theorem is that the number of elements in any basis of a finite dimensional linear space is the same as in any other basis. Hence we can define the number of elements of a basis of a finite dimensional linear space as the dimension of the space. Moreover, if X is an n-dimensional linear space, then every set of $(n + 1)$ vectors in X is linearly dependent.

We now define an important class of functions, "linear functions." For the remainder of this section, all functions are taken to be *single-valued.*

Definition: A function f from a linear space X into a linear space Y is said to be a **linear function** if

(i) $f(x + x') = f(x) + f(x')$ for every $x, x' \in X$;

(ii) $f(\alpha x) = \alpha f(x)$ for every $\alpha \in R$ and $x \in X$.

REMARK: In particular, if $Y \subset R$ (that is, if f is real-valued), then f is often called a **linear form** or a **linear functional**. A real-valued function which may not be linear is simply called a **functional**.

REMARK: In the above definition addition, such as $x + x'$ and $f(x) + f(x')$, and scalar multiplication, such as αx and $\alpha f(x)$, are meaningful because both X and Y are linear spaces. Note also that if f is a linear function, then $-f$ is also a linear function.

EXAMPLES OF LINEAR FUNCTIONALS:

1. Define $f: R^n \rightarrow R$ by $f(x) = a \cdot x$ where $x \in R^n$ and a is any (fixed) vector in R^n.
2. Let $C_{[a,b]}$ be the set of all continuous functions defined on the closed interval $[a, b]$. Define $f: C_{[a,b]} \rightarrow R$ by $f(x) = \int_a^b x(t)dt$, where $x(t) \in C_{[a,b]}$. Incidentally, $C_{[a,b]}$ is a linear space but not finite dimensional.

Consider now the collection of all linear functions of a linear space X into a linear space Y. We denote this collection by $L[X, Y]$. First, note that a function which maps $x \in X$ into $0 \in Y$ is in $L[X, Y]$, and we shall reserve the notation 0 to denote this, that is, $0 \in L[X, Y]$ and $0(x) = 0$. Now define the addition of any two elements, say, f and g, of $L[X, Y]$ by $[f + g](x) = f(x) + g(x)$, for each $x \in X$. Define $[-f]$ by $[-f](x) = -f(x)$ for each $x \in X$ and $f \in L[X, Y]$. We can easily see that $f + [-f] = 0$. Furthermore, $[-f]$ is the only g in $L[X, Y]$ such that $f + g = 0$. Using the defining properties (i) and (ii) of linear functions, the argument can be continued to establish $L[X, Y]$ as a linear space. In particular, the set of linear functions of a linear space X into itself (that is, $L[X, X]$) is a linear space, and the set of linear functionals $L[X, R]$ is a linear space.

Consider now $L[X, X]$. Denote as L the set of those $f \in L[X, X]$ for which $f(X) = X$ (that is, "onto"). The identity function which maps each element of X into itself is in L. We reserve the notation 1 for this function; thus we can write $1 \in L$ and $1(x) = x$.

Let $f, g \in L$. Define the **multiplication** of linear functions f and g (denoted by $f \circ g^0$ or simply $f \cdot g$) by $[f \circ g](x) \equiv f[g(x)]$. It should be noted that the order of transformation of $f \circ g$ is to transform first by g and then by f. In general, $f \circ g$ is not the same as $g \circ f$.

Definition: The function $f \in L$ is said to be **invertible** if the following hold:

(i) $x, x' \in X$ with $x \neq x'$ implies $f(x) \neq f(x')$.

(ii) For every $y \in X$, there exists at least one $x \in X$ such that $f(x) = y$.

Definition: Let $f \in L$ be invertible. Define the **inverse** of f (again denoted by f^{-1}) as follows. If y_0 is any vector in X, we may by (ii) find an x_0 in X such that $f(x_0) = y_0$. Moreover, by (i) this x_0 is unique. Define $f^{-1}(y_0)$ to be this x_0.

REMARK: From the definition it is easy to see that 0 is not invertible and that "f is invertible" implies "$f \circ f^{-1} = f^{-1} \circ f = 1$."

For finite dimensional spaces, we have the following remarkable result.

Theorem 0.A.2:   *Let X be a finite dimensional linear space and define L as above; $f \in L$ is invertible if and only if $f(x) = 0$ implies $x = 0$.*

PROOF: See Halmos [5], p. 63, for example.

REMARK: In finite dimensional spaces "f is not invertible" therefore implies that "there exists an $x \in X, x \neq 0$ such that $f(x) = 0$." Such an f is often called **singular** and an invertible f is often called **nonsingular**.

Let X be an n-dimensional linear space where n is a finite positive integer. Let $S = \{x^1, x^2, \ldots, x^n\}$ be a basis of X. Let $f \in L$; thus $f(x) \in X$. Hence in particular $f(x^j) \in X, j = 1, 2, \ldots, m$. From the definition of basis, $f(x^j)$ can be written as

$$f(x^j) = \sum_{i=1}^{n} a_{ij} x^i, \quad j = 1, 2, \ldots, n$$

where $a_{ij} \in R, i, j = 1, 2, \ldots, n$. Consider the following array of the a_{ij}'s.

$$A \equiv \begin{bmatrix} a_{11} & a_{12} & \cdots & a_{1n} \\ a_{21} & a_{22} & \cdots & a_{2n} \\ \cdots & \cdots & \cdots & \cdots \\ \cdots & \cdots & \cdots & \cdots \\ a_{n1} & a_{n2} & \cdots & a_{nn} \end{bmatrix}$$

or simply $A = [a_{ij}]$. Such an array is called a **matrix**.

It should be noted that the matrix A is determined with respect to a particular set of basis vectors. That is, a matrix A is a representation of a linear function f when a particular basis is chosen. When a different basis is chosen, we obtain a different array of scalars. To emphasize this we used different notations, f for a linear function and A for its matrix representation under a particular basis, which is contrary to the usual convention.

Note also that in the matrix representation of a linear function, the order of the basis chosen is important. When the basis is defined as a set of vectors, the order of the vectors is clearly not particularly important. However, in order to fix the matrix representation of linear functions, we also have to fix the order of the basis vectors.

In the above, a matrix is defined in connection with f applied on a basis $\{x^1, \ldots, x^n\}$. Consider now an arbitrary vector x in X. Let $x = \sum_{j=1}^{n} \xi_j x^j$ in terms of these basis vectors. Then noting $f(x) = \sum_{j=1}^{n} \xi_j f(x^j)$ since f is linear, we again obtain an array of scalars $[\alpha_{ij}]$, where $\alpha_{ij} \equiv a_{ij}\xi_j$. Note that if $y = f(x) = \sum_{i=1}^{n} \eta_i x^i$, then $\eta_i = \sum_{j=1}^{n} a_{ij}\xi_j$. Considering x and y as (column) vectors whose ith element is ξ_i and η_i respectively, $y = f(x)$ is represented by the usual textbook matrix notation $\eta_i = \sum_{j=1}^{n} a_{ij}\xi_j$, or $y = Ax$.

Using a fixed basis (often called a **coordinate system**), we obtain the matrix representation $A = [a_{ij}]$ of a linear function f. It can be shown that this representation is one to one, that is, matrices of two different functions in L are different. Moreover, we can also assert that every array $[a_{ij}]$ of n^2 scalars is the matrix of some linear function in L. For the proofs of these statements, see Halmos [5], pp. 67–68, for example. Moreover, we can assert that this association between L and the set of matrices preserves addition, multiplication, and the 0 and identity element.

For this purpose, consider the set of all matrices $[a_{ij}]$, $[b_{ij}]$, and so on, $i, j = 1, 2, \ldots, n$, and define addition, scalar multiplication, product, the 0 element (0), and the identity element (I) in this set by

$$[a_{ij}] + [b_{ij}] = [a_{ij} + b_{ij}]$$

$$\alpha[a_{ij}] = [\alpha a_{ij}]$$

$$[a_{ij}][b_{ij}] = \left[\sum_{k=1}^{n} a_{ik}b_{kj} \right]$$

$$0 \equiv [0_{ij}] \quad \text{where} \quad 0_{ij} = 0 \in R \text{ for all } i \text{ and } j$$
$$I \equiv [e_{ij}] \quad \text{where} \quad e_{ij} = 0 \in R \text{ if } i \neq j$$
$$= 1 \in R \text{ if } i = j$$

Then we can assert

Theorem 0.A.3:   *Given L and the set T of all matrices $[a_{ij}]$ defined by $f(x^j) \equiv \sum_{i=1}^{n} a_{ij}x^i$ with a fixed basis of X, $(x^1, x^2, \ldots, x^n)$, there exists an* **isomorphic** *correspondence, that is, a one-to-one correspondence between L and T that preserves addition, scalar multiplication, product, and the 0 and identity elements, when these operations on the matrices are defined as above.*

PROOF: See Halmos [5], pp. 67–68, for example.

REMARK: To arrive at the above theorem, we restricted L to be the set of linear functions of an n-dimensional linear space X onto itself. However, we may extend our consideration in an analogous fashion to the case where L is the set of linear functions defined on an n-dimensional linear space X onto an m-dimensional linear space Y. In this case we do not get square matrices, but obtain ($n \times m$) rectangular matrices as the representation of such linear functions.

We have come a rather long way. Starting from the definitions of basis, linear functions, and so on, we finally reached "matrices," which, after all, must be familiar to the readers who have finished an elementary course in matrix algebra. We should note, however, that we have discovered that these "matrices" have much more profound meaning than a mere array of numbers. Namely, the set of these matrices is an "isomorphic" representation of the set of linear functions on a finite dimensional linear space.

Some remarks on notations are in order now. In this book the dot (·) between a matrix and a vector (or a matrix) indicates the multiplication of the matrix with the vector (or the matrix). We will not make a distinction between "row" or "column" vectors. We assume that the readers of this book know the rules of the multiplication of two matrices—say, A and B, of a matrix A and vector x, and of two vectors x and y—so that there should be clear understanding of the meaning of $A \cdot B$, $A \cdot x$, and $x \cdot y$ (and $y \cdot x$) and no misunderstanding about the distinction between $A \cdot x$ and $x \cdot A$. After all, it is much more plausible to consider a vector as an element of a linear space rather than as an array of numbers and a matrix as a representation of a linear function rather than as an array of numbers.[10]

We close this subsection by mentioning the definition of "linear affine" functions, since they are often confused with linear functions.

Definition: Let f be a function on a linear space X into R (that is, a linear functional). The function f is said to be **linear affine** or **affine** if $f(x) - f(0)$ is linear.

REMARK: Obviously a linear function is a special case of a linear affine function. Let $X \subset R^n$ and $Y = R$, and define $f(x) \equiv \alpha \cdot x + k = \sum_{i=1}^{n} \alpha_i x_i + k$, where $\alpha, x \in R^n$, $k \in R$, and α and k are constants. In elementary mathematics and in most literature in economics, such a function f is known as a "linear function." However, as long as $k \neq 0$, f does not satisfy the definition of linear functions; it is a linear affine function. Similarly, let $F(x)$ be defined by $F: R^n \rightarrow R^m$, $F(x) = A \cdot x + k$, where $x \in R^n$, $k \in R^m$ and A is an ($m \times n$) matrix. Then F is also a linear affine function as long as $k \neq 0$.

REMARK WITH REGRET: In the course of this book, as long as the context is clear we do not stick closely to this distinction between linear functions and linear affine functions. In other words, we sometimes call a linear affine function a "linear function" as long as this does not cause any confusion. Although obviously imprecise, this is rather inevitable in view of the common usage in economics. For example, linear programming typically contains the "linear constraint" of the type $f(x) \equiv \alpha \cdot x + k \leq 0$ ($k \neq 0$). As remarked above, f is linear affine and not linear. Similarly, F in the constraint $F(x) \equiv A \cdot x + k \leq 0$ ($k \neq 0$) is also linear affine. But it is too pedantic to rename linear programming "linear affine programming" and linear constraints "linear affine constraints." There are too many such examples in economics to rename the relevant functions as "linear affine."

d. CONVEX SETS[11]

Here we consider an arbitrary linear space X. This X does not necessarily have to be R^n. However, the reader can certainly confine his attention to R^n (instead of X) if he so wishes.

Definition: Given x and y in a linear space X, z defined by $z \equiv \theta x + (1 - \theta)y$, $0 \leq \theta \leq 1$, $\theta \in R$, is called a **convex combination** of x and y.

REMARK: The concept of a convex combination can be illustrated in R^2 by Figure 0.4.

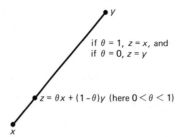

if $\theta = 1$, $z = x$, and
if $\theta = 0$, $z = y$

$z = \theta x + (1 - \theta)y$ (here $0 < \theta < 1$)

Figure 0.4. An Illustration of a Convex Combination.

Definition: Let $S \subset X$, where X is a linear space. If an arbitrary convex combination of any two points of S is in S, then S is called a **convex set**. That is, S is convex if $x, y \in S$ implies $\theta x + (1 - \theta)y \in S$ for $0 \leq \theta \leq 1$.

REMARK: A circle is *not* a convex set, but a disk that includes all the interior points of a circle is a convex set. The area covered by the Chinese character 凸 (translation "convex") is *not* convex (see Figure 0.5).

Definition: Given m points, $x^1, x^2, \ldots, x^m$ in a linear space X, x defined by

$$x = \sum_{i=1}^{m} \theta_i x^i \quad \text{where} \quad 0 \leq \theta_i \leq 1, \theta_i \in R, \ i = 1, \ldots, m \quad \text{and} \quad \sum_{i=1}^{m} \theta_i = 1$$

is called a **convex combination** of these m points.

The proof of the following theorem is easy to do and so is left for the reader.

Theorem 0.A.4:

(i) *A set S in a linear space X is convex if and only if every convex combination of (two or more) points in S belongs to S.*

(ii) *Any intersection (finite or infinite) of convex sets is also convex.*

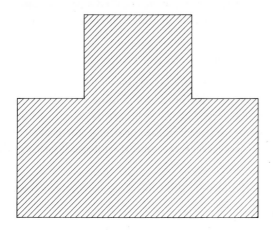

Figure 0.5. Chinese Character "Convex"—Not a Convex Set.

REMARK: The empty set $\emptyset$ and sets consisting of only one point are considered convex sets.

Definition: Let $S \subset X$, where X is a linear space. Given m points in $S, x^1, x^2, \ldots,$ x^m, x defined by $x \equiv \sum_{i=1}^{m} \alpha_i x^i$ where $\alpha_i \in R$ and $\alpha_i \geq 0, i = 1, 2, \ldots, m$ is called a **nonnegative linear combination** of these m points.

REMARK: As we defined earlier, if we do not restrict α_i to be nonnegative, x is simply called a **linear combination** of those points. Given any arbitrary m points in S, a subset of a linear space X, neither a convex combination nor a (nonnegative) linear combination of these m points has to be in S, although both of them are in X.

The following theorem is very useful.

Theorem 0.A.5: *Let S_i, $i = 1, 2, \ldots, m$ be convex sets in a linear space X. Then the following are true.*[12]

(i) *Their linear sum $\sum_{i=1}^{m} \alpha_i S_i$ is also convex;*
(ii) *Their Cartesian product $\bigotimes_{i=1}^{m} S_i$ is also convex (the Cartesian product of the S_i's is the set of all m-tuples $(x^1, x^2, \ldots, x^i, \ldots, x^m), x^i \in S_i, i = 1, 2, \ldots, m$).*

Definition: Let $K \subset X$, where X is a linear space; K is called a **cone** with vertex at the origin if $\alpha \geq 0$, $\alpha \in R$, and $x \in K$ imply $\alpha x \in K$.

Definition: Let $K \subset X$, where X is a linear space; K is called a **convex cone** with vertex at the origin if it is a cone with vertex at the origin, with the following property:

$$x, y \in K \quad \text{implies} \quad x + y \in K$$

REMARK: It is possible to define a (convex) cone with vertex at a point other than the origin. However, in this book we confine our discussion of convex cones to those with the vertex at the origin (this does not hamper the generality of the discussion, for the choice of the origin can be arbitrary). Hence when we refer to (convex) cones, we omit the phrase "vertex at the origin."

REMARK: From the above definitions the following properties should be obvious.

   (i) *Every convex cone is a convex set.*
   (ii) *Every cone contains the origin.*

REMARK: The set consisting of two different half lines starting from the origin is a cone, but not a convex cone. If we include the area inside two half lines with an acute angle, then it is a convex cone.

Theorem 0.A.6:

   (i) $\sum_{i=1}^{m} K_i$ *is a convex cone if K_i is a convex cone for all i.*
   (ii) *Any (finite or infinite) intersection of convex cones is also a convex cone.*

REMARK: The empty set $\emptyset$ is considered a convex cone. Note that $K_1 \cup K_2$ is not necessarily a convex cone even if both K_1 and K_2 are convex cones.

Definition: Given a set S in a linear space X, the intersection of all the convex cones containing S is called a **convex cone spanned by** S or a **convex cone generated by** S, and we denote it by $K(S)$.

REMARK: We can show that $K(S)$ is the "smallest" convex cone containing S. That is, K is a convex cone containing S implies that $K(S) \subset K$. We can also show that $K(S)$ can be written as

$$K(S) = \left\{ \sum_{i=1}^{m} \alpha_i x^i \colon x^i \in S, \alpha_i \in R, \alpha_i \geq 0, i = 1, 2, \ldots, m \right\}$$

where m and the choice of x^i and α_i are arbitrary.[13]

REMARK: When S is a set consisting of a finite number of points, $K(S)$ is called a **convex polyhedral cone**.[14] In R^2, for example, the set of two points

(0, 1) and (1, 0) will generate a convex polyhedral cone $K(S)$ which is the nonnegative orthant of R^2.

In the previous subsection, we defined such concepts as the dimension of a linear space and linear functions. With the aid of these concepts we can obtain the following important characterization of convex sets and so forth.

Theorem 0.A.7:   *Let f be a linear function of a linear space X into a linear space Y. If S is a convex subset (resp. cone, linear subspace) of X, then its image f(S) is a convex subset (resp. cone, linear subspace) of Y.*

PROOF: See Berge [1], p. 143, for example.

EXAMPLES: Let $X = R^n$ and $S \subset X$. Consider the following examples:

1. $f: S \rightarrow X$ by $f(x) = \alpha x$, where $\alpha \in R$. Then αS is a convex subset of X if S is convex.
2. $f: S \rightarrow R^m$ by $f(x) = A \cdot x$, where A is an $(m \times n)$ matrix with real entries. Then the set defined by $\{y: y = A \cdot x, x \in S\}$ is a convex subset in R^m if S is convex.

e.   A LITTLE TOPOLOGY[15]

Consider a point x_0 in a metric space (X, d), say, R^n, and define a set $B_r(x_0)$ by

$$B_r(x_0) \equiv \{x: x \in X, d(x, x_0) < r\}$$

where r is some positive real number and $d(x, x_0)$ refers to the (Euclidian) distance between x and (the fixed point) x_0. The set $B_r(x_0)$ is called the **open ball about** x_0 **with radius** r. The point x_0 is called the **center** of $B_r(x_0)$. An open ball is always nonempty, for it contains its center. Figure 0.6 illustrates some examples of an open ball.

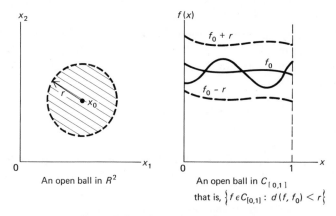

An open ball in R^2

An open ball in $C_{[0,1]}$
that is, $\{f \in C_{[0,1]} : d(f, f_0) < r\}$

Figure 0.6.   Illustration of Open Balls.

There is one very important characteristic in the concept of an open ball. Given an open ball—say, $B_r(x_0)$ in R^n—pick any point—say, x—in $B_r(x_0)$. Then we can always find another open ball about this point x which is contained in $B_r(x_0)$. This is illustrated in Figure 0.7. Given an arbitrary set S in (X, d), if S has this characteristic, S is called an **open set**. In other words, we have the following definition.

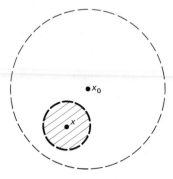

Figure 0.7.   A Property of an Open Ball.

Definition: Let S be a subset in a metric space (X, d). This set S is called an **open set**, if, for any x in S, there exists a positive real number r such that $B_r(x) \subset S$.

REMARK: It is easy to check that every open ball is an open set.

Now consider the collection of all the open sets in X. Note that X itself is an open set. The empty set $\emptyset$ can be considered as a trivial example of an open set. We denote the collection of all the open sets in X by τ. We can easily check that τ satisfies the following properties:

(T-1) $X \in \tau, \emptyset \in \tau$.
(T-2) $V_i \in \tau, i = 1, 2, \ldots, m$ implies $\cap_{i=1}^m V_i \in \tau$.
(T-3) $V_\alpha \in \tau$ for all $\alpha \in A$ implies $\cup_{\alpha \in A} V_\alpha \in \tau$.

Given an arbitrary set X (it does not have to be a metric space or a linear space), if we define a collection of subsets τ of X which satisfies the properties (T-1), (T-2), and (T-3), we can call it a **topological space** with **topology** τ. We denote a topological space by (X, τ). A member of τ is called an **open set**. In fact, as the reader can easily check, any set X can be a topological space for either one of the following topologies:

1. $\tau \equiv \{X, \emptyset\}$ (called the **indiscrete topology**).
2. $\tau \equiv$ all the subsets of X (called the **discrete topology**).

In fact, many kinds of topologies other than the above two can be defined on an arbitrary set. That is, there are many ways to transform a given arbitrary set to a topological space. The symbol τ in the notation (X, τ) refers to the topology specified for this topological space X.

In a metric space we are often concerned with the collection of open sets defined in terms of open balls as a topology. We call this the **usual topology** in the metric space or **the topology induced by the metric**. Although there are many ways to make a metric space into a topological space, we henceforth refer to this usual topology as the topology in metric space, unless otherwise specified.

Note that an arbitrary topological space does not have to be a metric space, although every metric space can be a topological space by the topology induced by the metric. Note also that an arbitrary topological space may not be a linear space, although every normed linear space is a topological space by the topology induced by the norm.

Real space, R^n, is a metric space with the Euclidian metric; hence it is also a topological space with the usual topology. Moreover, R^n is also a linear space, a normed linear space, and an inner product space. In other words, it has all the features of these spaces. Conversely, we may say that the properties of each of these spaces are abstracted from R^n. This means that one can always get an intuitive understanding of these concepts by a graphical representation in R^2. However, the reader should note that this is also very dangerous, for these concepts are far more general and broader than R^2 (or R^n).

We now define closed sets.

Definition: Let (X, τ) be a topological space. Then a subset S of X is called a **closed set** if its complement is an open set, that is, $S^c \in \tau$ (where S^c denotes X/S).

REMARK: Note that the empty set $\emptyset$ and X are also closed sets (as well as open sets). Open intervals in R, such as $(a, b), (-\infty, a), (b, \infty)$, are all open sets in R, and closed intervals in R, such as $[a, b]$, are closed sets. The sets $[b, \infty)$ and $(-\infty, a]$ are also closed sets. However, $(a, b]$ and $[a, b)$ (where a and b are finite) are neither open sets nor closed sets.

REMARK: It is an elementary exercise in set theory to show the following propositions:

    (i)   *Any (finite or infinite) intersections of closed sets is closed.*
    (ii)   *Any finite union of closed sets is closed.*

Definition: Given a topological space (X, τ) and a subset S of X, a point x_0 of X is called a **limit point** or an **accumulation point** of S if every open set containing x_0 contains a point of S other than x_0.[16] A point x_0 of S is called an **isolated point** of S if it is contained in an open subset of X which has no other points in S. The set of all the limit points of S is called the **derived set** of S. The union of S and its derived set is called the **closure** of S, which we denote by $\overline{S}$.[17]

REMARK: If S is a set which consists of only one point, that is, $S \equiv \{x_0\}$, then x_0 cannot be a limit point of S, for S has no point other than x_0.

REMARK: A limit point of S can be a point of S, but it is not necessary that it be a point of S. For example, let S be an interval $[0, 1]$ of the real line with the usual metric in R [that is, $d(a, b) \equiv |b - a|$]; then every point in S is a limit point of S. But point 0, which does not belong to S, is also a limit point of S.

Definition: Given a metric space (X, d), a point x_0 in X, and a subset S of X, a sequence[18] $\{x^q\}$ in S is said to **converge to** x_0 (denoted by $x^q \to x_0$ or $\lim x_q = x_0$) if for any real number $\varepsilon > 0$, there exists a positive integer $\overline{q}$ such that $q \geq \overline{q}$ implies $d(x_0, x^q) < \varepsilon$. The point x_0 is called the **limit** of $\{x^q\}$, and such a sequence $\{x^q\}$ is called a **convergent sequence** in S if $x_0 \in S$.

REMARK: Intuitively speaking, this means that if the terms of a sequence approach a limit, they get close together. Note again that x_0 does not have to be in S. For example, let S be an interval $(0, 1]$ with the usual metric. The sequence $\{1/q\}$, where the q's are positive integers, is a sequence whose values are in S. The point 0 is the limit of this sequence, but it is not in S.

REMARK: The concept of convergence can be generalized for a topological space which is not necessarily a metric space. Given a topological space (X, τ), a sequence $\{x^q\}$ in X is called **convergent in** X if there exists a point $x_0 \in X$ such that for every open set V containing x_0, there exists a positive integer $\overline{q}$ such that $q \geq \overline{q}$ implies $x^q \in V$. The point x_0 is called a **limit** of $\{x^q\}$, and we say x^q **converges to** x_0. However, such a limit may not be unique in an arbitrary topological space.

REMARK: Given an arbitrary sequence in a metric space, say, $\{x^q\}$, it may have a limit or it may not have a limit (nonconvergent sequence). But if the limit exists, it can be shown easily from the definition of a limit that the limit is always unique in *metric spaces*. Moreover, if a sequence has a limit, *every* subsequence[19] of the sequence has the same limit. If a sequence has no limit, a subsequence of the sequence may have a limit or may have no limit. For example, $\{0, 1, 0, 1, \ldots\}$ has no limit but has two convergent subsequences $\{0, 0, \ldots, 0\}$ and $\{1, 1, \ldots 1\}$ with limits 0 and 1 respectively.

REMARK: A common confusion is in the distinction between "limit" and "limit point." These two terms are different. A sequence is not a set of points; rather, it is a *function* defined on the positive integers ($q = 1, 2, \ldots$) with values in the sets (that is, $x^q \in S$). Moreover, (the value of) the limit of a sequence may not be a limit point of the set. That is, that $x^q \to x_0$, where $\{x^q\} \in S$, does not necessarily imply that x_0 is a limit point of S. For example, let S be a set which consists of a single point 1; then a sequence $\{1, 1, 1, \ldots\}$ is a convergent sequence whose values are in S, with limit 1. But the point 1 is *not* a limit point of S, for S, consisting of a single point, cannot have any limit points, as we remarked after the definition of the limit point.

The following theorem is easy to prove and is useful to relate the two concepts of "limit" and "limit point."

Theorem 0.A.8: *Let $S \subset R^n$. Then a point x_0 in R^n is a limit point of S if and only if there exists a sequence $\{x^q\}$ in $S \backslash \{x_0\}$ such that*

$$\lim_{q \to \infty} x^q = x_0$$

PROOF: The sufficiency part of the theorem is obvious. For the proof of the necessity part, see Rudin [10], p. 42, and Kelley [7], p. 73, for example.

REMARK: Restriction of S to be in the real space R^n is necessary to prove the necessity part only. In fact, this can be relaxed by requiring that $S \subset X$, where X is a topological space satisfying the "first axiom of countability." The reader is not required to understand the concept of the first axiom of countability. However, he can always find its definition from any textbook on general topology; see, for example, Kelley [7], p. 50, and footnote 28 of the present section.

REMARK: Let $\{x^q\}$ be a sequence in X. The convergence of this sequence depends on the metric or topology defined on X. For example, $\{x^q\}$ may be convergent under one metric but may not be convergent under another metric. Moreover, even if $\{x^q\}$ is convergent under two different metrics, the limit may be different depending on the metric chosen. In the real space R^n, the following three metrics are well known and important.

$$d_1(x, y) \equiv \sqrt{\sum_{i=1}^{n} (x_i - y_i)^2}$$
$$d_2(x, y) \equiv \max_i |x_i - y_i|$$

$$d_3(x, y) \equiv \sum_{i=1}^{n} |x_i - y_i|$$

It can be shown that if a sequence $\{x^q\}$ is convergent under any of d_1, d_2, and d_3, it is also convergent under the other two metrics, and the limits under these three metrics are all the same. (For the proof, see Nikaido [9], sec. 11, for example.)

The following theorems are rather easy to prove but important.

Theorem 0.A.9:   *Let S be a subset in a topological space (X, τ). Then the following hold:*

(i) *S is closed if and only if S contains all its limit points (that is, if it contains its derived set).*

(ii) *S is closed if and only if $S = \overline{S}$.*

PROOF: See, for example, Kelley [7], pp. 41–43; Simmons [11], sec. 17.

REMARK: If the derived set of S is empty (that is, if S has no limit point), then S is always closed. Hence, for example, a set of only one element is a closed set. A set consisting of a finite number of points is closed as is a finite union of closed sets.

Definition: Let S be a subset of a topological space (X, τ). A point x_0 in S is called an **interior point** of S if S contains an open set containing x_0. The set of all the interior points of S is called the **interior** (or the **open kernel**) of S (denoted by S^o or "interior S"). If a point is in $\overline{S}$ (the closure of S) but not in S^o, then it is called a **boundary point** of S. The collection of all the boundary points of S is called the **boundary** of S and is denoted by "boundary S."

REMARK: It is not difficult to prove (see Kelley [7], p. 44, for example) the following propositions:

(i) *S^o is an open set and it is the largest open subset of S.*

(ii) *S is open if and only if $S = S^o$,*

(iii) *$\overline{S} = S \cup boundary\ S$ and boundary $S = \overline{S} \cap \overline{S^c}$.*

All these properties are obvious when X is a metric space with the usual topology in the metric space.

EXAMPLE: An open ball $B_r(x_0) \equiv \{x : x \in X, d(x, x_0) < r\}$ in a metric space (X, d) is not a closed set. However, $\{x : x \in X, d(x, x_0) \leq r\}$, called a **closed ball**, is a closed set and, in fact, is a closure of $B_r(x_0)$. The open ball $B_r(x_0)$ is the open kernel of this set $\overline{B_r(x_0)}$. The set $\{x : x \in X, d(x, x_0) = r\}$ is the boundary of $B_r(x_0)$ and $\overline{B_r(x_0)}$. Any point in this boundary is a limit point of the open ball $B_r(x_0)$ but is clearly not in $B_r(x_0)$.

REMARK: We started the discussion of topology with open sets. Open sets satisfy the axioms of a topological space (that is, a finite intersection of open sets is open and any union of open sets is open). A closed set is then defined to be the complement of an open set. Then we showed that any closed set contains all its limit points. A point x in a set X is a limit point of S, a subset of X, if there exists a sequence of points other than x in S which converges to x. Hence, in a closed set, every converging sequence of points in the set converges to a point in the set. In other words, a closed set is a set which is closed under the limit operation.

We can reverse the construction of a topology or topological spaces by confining ourselves to a metric space, thus defining convergence in terms of a metric; that is, we start with the definition of a closed set as a set that is closed under the limit operation and then define an open set as the complement of a closed set. We can then show that a finite union of closed sets is closed and any intersection of closed sets is closed. From the definition of open set, we can then trivially conclude the properties of topological spaces.

Now we define the very important concept of a "continuous function." As remarked before, function here always refers to a *single-valued* function.

Definition: Let f be a function from a metric space (X, d_1) into a metric space (Y, d_2). The function f is called **continuous at a point** x_0 **in** X if for any real number $\epsilon > 0$, there exists a real number δ such that $d_1(x, x_0) < \delta$ and $x \in X$ imply $d_2(f(x), f(x_0)) < \epsilon$. The function f is called **continuous** in X if it is continuous at every point of X.

It is easy to show that this definition is equivalent to either of the following two statements (see Simmons [11], p. 76, for example).

(i) For each open ball $B_\epsilon(f(x_0))$ with center $f(x_0)$, there exists an open ball $B_\delta(x_0)$ with center x_0 such that $f(B_\delta(x_0)) \subset B_\epsilon(f(x_0))$.

(ii) $x^q \to x_0$ implies $f(x^q) \to f(x_0)$.

Note that the above definition of continuity is strictly analogous to the one in R^n. We have the following important theorem:

Theorem 0.A.10:   *Let f be a function from a metric space (X, d_1) into a metric space (Y, d_2). The function f is continuous in X if and only if $f^{-1}(V)$ is open in X whenever V is open in Y.*

PROOF: See Simmons [11], pp. 76–77, for example.

This theorem induces the definition of continuity in an arbitrary *topological space* (not necessarily a metric space). That is, we say that a function from a topological space (X, τ_1) to (Y, τ_2) is **continuous** if $f^{-1}(V) \in \tau_1$ whenever $V \in \tau_2$. Therefore the concept of the continuous function is quite a general one for it is not confined to metric spaces.[20]

Corollary: *The function f is continuous in X if and only if $f^{-1}(V)$ is closed whenever V is closed in Y.*

REMARK: The statement "f is continuous in X and V is an open set (resp. a closed set)" does *not* necessarily imply "$f(V)$ is an open set (resp. a closed set)." For a counterexample, see Kolmogorov and Fomin [8], sec. 12.

EXAMPLE 1:   A constant function is a continuous function.

EXAMPLE 2:   The Euclidian norm on R^n is a continuous function into R. In fact, *any* norm $\|x\|$ on an arbitrary linear space X is a continuous function into R with respect to the metric induced by the norm [that is, $d(x, y) \equiv \|x - y\|$], because $x, y \in X$ and $d(x, y) < \delta$ imply that $|\|x\| - \|y\|| < \delta$ $(\because |\|x\| - \|y\|| \leq \|x - y\|$ owing to the triangular inequality).

EXAMPLE 3:   The distance (or metric) function $d(x, x_0)$ on $X \otimes X$ (that is, $x_0, x \in X$) is a function on X into R when we fix x_0, and it is continuous because $x, y \in X$, and $d(x, y) < \delta$ imply $|d(x, x_0) - d(y, x_0)| < \delta$.

EXAMPLE 4:   The function $r(x, y)$ of $R^n \otimes R^n$ into R^n defined by $r(x, y) \equiv x + y$ is continuous.

EXAMPLE 5:   The function $k(\alpha, x)$ of $R \otimes R^n$ into R^n defined by $k(\alpha, x) \equiv \alpha x$ is continuous. (The proofs of Examples 4 and 5 are easy, or see Berge and Ghouila-Houri [2], p. 38).

REMARK: In the expression $\lim_{x \to a} f(x) = b$ or $(f(x^q) \to b$ as $x^q \to a)$, it is neither required that f be defined at a nor that $f(a) = b$ when f is defined at a. The function f is "continuous" at a if f is defined at a and $f(x^q) \to f(a)$ as $x^q \to a$.

REMARK: Let X be a subspace of R^n and let $x \cdot y \equiv \sum_{i=1}^n x_i y_i$. Let α be a fixed point in R^n and $\{x^q\}$ be a sequence in X such that $x^q \to x_0$, $x_0 \in X$, as $q \to \infty$. Suppose $x^q \cdot \alpha > a$ for all q, where a is a fixed real number. We can conclude that $x_0 \cdot \alpha \geq a$. To prove this, note that $x_0 \cdot \alpha$ is a continuous function on X, and obtain a contradiction[21] if $x \cdot \alpha < a$. Similarly, if $\{x^q\}, \{y^q\}$ are two sequences in X such that $x^q \to x_0$ and $y^q \to y_0$ with $x^q \cdot \alpha > x^q \cdot y^q$ for all q, then we can show $x_0 \cdot \alpha \geq x_0 \cdot y_0$. (Note that $x \cdot y$ is continuous on $X \otimes X$.)[22]

The following theorem is important.

Theorem 0.A.11:

   (i)   *A continuous function of a continuous function is also continuous.*

   (ii) *The Cartesian product of continuous functions is also continuous (that is, let f_i, $i = 1, \ldots, m$ be continuous functions from S into T_i; then a function from S into $\otimes_{i=1}^m T_i$ defined by $f(x) \equiv [f_1(x), \ldots, f_m(x)]$ is also continuous).*

  (iii) *The converse of statement (ii) is also true.*

PROOF: Statement (i) follows directly from the definition of continuity. For (ii) and (iii), see Kelley [7], p. 91, for example.

REMARK: For the usual Euclidian topology, the proofs of (ii) and (iii) are straightforward (see Rudin [10], pp. 75–76, for example). However, the construction of a topology on the product space $\bigotimes_{i=1}^{m} T_i$ as the one naturally induced from the component spaces is extremely important and is not easy. See Kelley [7], pp. 88–90, and Simmons [11], pp. 115–118. The topology thus constructed is known as the **product topology**, and the usual topology of the product space is this product topology.[23] We take up this topic once again in connection with the Tychonoff theorem on compact sets.

REMARK: Given $f = [f_1, \ldots, f_m]$, f_i is called the *i*th **projection** of *f*. Statement (iii) says that every projection of a continuous function is also continuous. The identity transformation $f(x) = x$ on R^n is continuous; hence $f_i(x) = x_i$, $i = 1, 2, \ldots, n$ are also continuous functions of *x*.

Theorem 0.A.11 holds for any continuous function from a metric (or topological) space into a metric (or topological) space. Suppose now that the range of the function is in a linear space. We can then talk meaningfully about such things as $f + g$, αf, and so on. In particular, we consider the properties of a continuous function whose range is in R^n (or R). Then we can show the following.[24]

Theorem 0.A.12:

(i)   *Let f_i: $X \to R^n$ and α_i: $X \to R$, $i = 1, 2, \ldots, m$, where X is a metric space, be continuous functions, then $f \equiv \sum_{i=1}^{m} \alpha_i(x) f_i(x)$ is also continuous in X.*

(ii) *Let f_i be real-valued continuous functions on a metric space X ($i = 1, 2, \ldots, m$). Then $\Pi_{i=1}^{m} f_i$ is also continuous.[25] If f: $X \to R$ is continuous in X, $1/f$ is also continuous for all $x \in X$ with $f(x) \neq 0$.*

(iii) *Let f_i be continuous functions on a metric space X ($i = 1, 2, \ldots, m$). Then $\max_i \{ f_i(x) \}$ and $\min_i \{ f_i(x) \}$ are also continuous on X.*

REMARK: Two corollaries of the above theorem are (1) *every polynomial is a continuous function,* and (2) *the Cobb-Douglas function,* $\prod_{i=1}^{n} x_i^{\alpha_i}$ ($\equiv x_1^{\alpha_1} x_2^{\alpha_2} \ldots x_n^{\alpha_n}$), $0 < \alpha_i < 1$ *for all i and* $\sum_{i=1}^{n} \alpha_i = 1$, *is a continuous function.*

We may note the following important theorem, the proof of which can be done by using the concept of a continuous function.

Theorem 0.A.13: *Every convex polyhedral cone is a closed set.*

PROOF: See, for example, Nikaido [9], theorem 5, sec. 27, for such a proof. For a similar but an alternative proof, see Hestenes, M. R., *Calculus of Variations and Optimal Control Theory*, New York, Wiley, 1966, pp. 15–16 (lemma 5.5).

REMARK: Note that an arbitrary convex set may not be closed, but every convex polyhedral cone is closed by the above theorem.

Next we discuss another very important topological concept, "compactness." In the real space R^n, a set is called "compact" if it is a closed set *and* if it is bounded (that is, if there exists an open ball with a finite radius that contains the set). Then it can be shown that a set is compact if and only if every open "cover" of the set contains a finite subcover (the Heine-Borel theorem). It is now argued that this theorem probes very deeply into the nature of "compactness," and the conclusion of the Heine-Borel theorem is converted into a definition of compactness.

Definition: Let (X, τ) be a topological space. Then a class of open sets $\{V_\alpha\}$, $\alpha \in A$, in (X, τ) (where A is an index set), is called an **open cover** of S, a subset of X, if each point of S belongs to at least one V_α. A subclass of an open cover which is itself an open cover is called a **subcover**.

Definition: A subset S of X in a topological space (X, τ) is called **compact** if every open cover of S has a finite subcover.

REMARK: Note that the set must be in a topological space if compactness is to be defined at all.

In a metric space (not necessarily R^n) compactness with the usual topology has the following important consequence.

Theorem 0.A.14: *Let (X, d) be a metric space with the usual topology defined. Then we have the following*:

(i) *The set S is a compact subset of X if and only if every infinite subset of S has a limit point (this is known as the* **Bolzano-Weierstrass property**).

(ii) *The set S is compact if and only if every sequence in S has a convergent subsequence and its limit is in S (this is known as* **sequential compactness**).

REMARK: Let S be a set of two points 0, 1 in R, that is, $S \equiv \{0, 1\}$. Clearly S is closed and bounded in R, and it is compact (see Theorem 0.A.16). Consider an infinite sequence in S, $\{0, 1, 0, 1, \ldots\}$. This sequence is clearly not convergent, but it has convergent subsequences such as $\{0, 0, \ldots\}$ or $\{1, 1, \ldots\}$. The property of sequential compactness is useful for obtaining many important results. Nikaido [9], for example, exploited this property throughout his book.

Given a collection of topological spaces (X_α, τ_α) where $\alpha \in A$ and A is an index set, form the Cartesian product $\bigotimes_{\alpha \in A} X_\alpha$ and denote it by X. There will be many ways to generate a topology τ in X from τ_α. The question is whether we can generate τ in such a way that the product of compact sets in X_α in terms of τ_α, $\alpha \in A$, is also a compact set in terms of τ. The answer is yes; that is, there is a way to generate τ such that this is possible. Thus generated, τ is the product topology mentioned before. We do not discuss how to generate the product topology, but we will state the result of its construction, known as the Tychonoff theorem, which is probably the most important theorem in general topology.

Theorem 0.A.15 (Tychonoff): *The product of any nonempty class of compact sets is compact with the product topology.*

The proof of this theorem is not easy, and, in fact, many of the past proofs are known to be wrong. The proof requires use of Zorn's lemma. A consequence of this theorem is the classical **Heine-Borel theorem.**

Theorem 0.A.16 (Heine-Borel): *Every subset of R^n is compact if and only if it is closed and bounded.*[26]

> PROOF: See Kelley [7], pp. 144–145, and Simmons [11], pp. 119–120, for example.

This theorem immediately shows the following examples of compact sets in R^n: (1) a closed ball, (2) the boundary of a closed ball, and (3) the set defined by

$$\{x: x \in R^n, x_i \geq 0, i = 1, 2, \ldots, n, \sum_{i=1}^{n} x_i \leq 1\}$$

The following theorem is useful and easy to prove.

Theorem 0.A.17: *Let (X, τ) be a topological space. Then*

    (i)   *Any closed subset of a compact set in (X, τ) is compact.*

    (ii) *Any continuous image of a compact set in (X, τ) is compact.*

    (iii) *Let X be a linear space and X_i, $i = 1, 2, \ldots, m$, be subsets in X. Then their linear sum set $\sum_{i=1}^{m} \alpha_i X_i$, $(\alpha_i \in R, i = 1, 2, \ldots, m)$ is compact if all the X_i's, $i = 1, 2, \ldots, m$, are compact.*

    (iv) *The union of a finite number of compact sets in (X, τ) is compact.*

> PROOF: For (i) and (ii), see Simmons [11], p. 111, for example. Statement (iii) follows immediately from (ii), and (iv) follows immediately from the definition of compactness.

Statement (ii) of the above theorem has an important corollary, known as the **Weierstrass theorem.**

Theorem 0.A.18 (Weierstrass): *Let (X, τ) be a topological space and f be a real-valued continuous function on X. Let S be a compact subset of X. Then f achieves a maximum and a minimum in S.*

PROOF: Since f is continuous and S is compact, $f(S)$ is compact. Also, since $f(S) \subset R$, it is closed and bounded in R by the Heine-Borel theorem. Hence f has a maximum $f(a)$ and a minimum $f(b)$, where both a and b are in S.

(Q.E.D.)

REMARK: For example, $f(x) = x$ defined on the unit open interval $(0, 1)$ of the real line is a continuous function, but it does not achieve a maximum (or minimum) at any point in $(0, 1)$. If $f(x) = x$ is defined on $[0, 1]$ instead, then it achieves the maximum (resp. minimum) at $x = 1$ (resp. at $x = 0$). Note that $[0, 1]$ is closed and bounded in R, hence compact.

REMARK: Note that Theorem 0.A.18 holds even if X is not Euclidian.

Important concepts which are closely related to concepts such as limit, continuity, and compactness are the **separation properties** of topological spaces. We introduce some of them in the following definitions.

Definition: Let (X, τ) be a topological space. Then

(i)   The space X is said to be a T_1-**space** if $x, x' \in X$, and $x \neq x'$ imply that there exist $V, V' \in \tau$ with $x \in V$ and $x' \in V'$, such that $x \notin V'$ and $x' \notin V$.

(ii)   The space X is said to be a T_2-**space**, or **Hausdorff space**, if $x, x' \in X$, and $x \neq x'$ imply that there exist $V, V' \in \tau$, with $x \in V$ and $x' \in V'$ such that $V \cap V' = \emptyset$.

(iii)   The space X is said to be a **normal space** if whenever U and U' are two disjoint closed sets in X, then there exist V and V' in τ with $U \subset V$, $U' \subset V'$ such that $V \cap V' = \emptyset$. The space X is said to be a T_4-**space** if it is normal and T_1.

REMARK: In addition to T_1-, T_2-, and T_4-spaces, T_0-, T_3-, T_π-, and T_5-spaces, and so forth, are defined and discussed in general topology. Clearly every T_4-space is a T_2-space and every T_2-space is a T_1-space. Converses of these statements do not necessarily hold. Note also that any set can be a normal space under the discrete topology.

The following theorem is an easy consequence of the above definition.

Theorem 0.A.19:

(i)   *A topological space X is a T_1-space if and only if each point in X, considered as a set, is a closed set in X.*

(ii)   *Every compact subset of a Hausdorff space is closed.*

(iii)   *Every compact Hausdorff space is a T_4-space.*

(iv)   *Every metric space is a T_4-space (hence a Hausdorff space).*

(v)   *Let $\{x^q\}$ be a sequence in a Hausdorff space. If $\{x^q\}$ is convergent, then it has a unique limit.*[27]

(vi) *The Cartesian product of any nonempty class of Hausdorff spaces is also a Hausdorff space.*

PROOF: See, for example, Simmons [11], pp. 130–134; also Berge [1], IV.5 and IV.6; Wilansky [12], 9.1; Kelley [7], pp. 56–57, pp. 112–113.

REMARK: Statement (v) implies that the proofs of theorems which involve the limit of a sequence would usually require that the relevant set be a Hausdorff space. Statement (iv) says that in a metric space we do not have to worry about this.[28]

A set X is a topological space if it is equipped with a topology (say, τ). What about a subset S of X? We may construct a topology in S (in a natural way) so that S is a topological space also.

Definition: Let (X, τ) be a topological space and S be a subset of X. Then $t \equiv \{U: U = V \cap S, V \in \tau\}$, that is, the collection of all intersections of members of τ with S, is called the **relative topology** of S.

REMARK: It is easy to see that t is indeed a topology so that (S, t) is a topological space. The space (S, t) is called a **subspace** of (X, τ); $U \in t$ is said to be **open in** S and $S \backslash U$ is said to be **closed in** S whenever $U \in t$.

REMARK: Let S be a subset of a topological space (X, τ). Let A be a subset of S. Since A is also a subset of X, we can determine whether A is open or not by the topology τ. However, we can also determine whether A is open or not in the topological space (S, t) by the relative topology t. One may conjecture that A is open (closed) in (S, t) if and only if A is open (closed) in (X, τ). However, this conjecture is not true, as one can see by considering the following example.

EXAMPLE: Consider R (the set of all real numbers) with its usual topology. Let S be the set of all rational numbers. The set S itself is a closed set in the space S. However, S is *not* a closed set in R since $\overline{S}$ (the closure of S) $= R$ so that $\overline{S} \neq S$.

REMARK: In this book the statement "A is open (closed)" will mean that A is open (closed) in X with topology τ.[29] If A is open (closed) *with respect to the relative topology* t, we shall explicitly specify the relative topology (unless it is clear from the context).

The following theorem is important but follows immediately from the definition of relative topology.

Theorem 0.A.20:   *Let (X, τ) be a topological space and let (S, t) be a subspace of (X, τ). Let $A \subset S$. Then the following hold:*

(i) *The set A is closed in (S, t) if and only if $A = B \cap S$ for some closed set B in (X, τ).*

(ii) *A point x_0 in X is a limit point of A with respect to t if and only if it is a limit point of A with respect to τ.*

FOOTNOTES

1. The basic mathematics, which will be useful for the later sections and chapters and for the reader's further study in economic theory, are sketched here. No prerequisite knowledge is necessary to read this section. The reader, if he so wishes, may restrict his attention to the usual "Euclidian space," or R^n. However, it should also be noted that special care is taken not to misguide readers into thinking that our world is always Euclidian. Consequently, this section becomes more than a mere exposition of the mathematics necessary for later sections of this book. This approach to mathematical preliminaries will be useful for readers who are serious about further study and research in modern economic theory. Unlike the remainder of the book, most theorems here are stated without proofs in order that the reader can grasp the basic mathematical concepts and ideas without being led astray by complicated proofs. For those readers who wish to see the proofs, references are given from time to time.

2. For a more detailed exposition, see, for example, Kolmogorov and Fomin [8], chap. 1, Rudin [10], chap. 1 (also pp. 21–27); Nikaido [9], secs. 6–8; Berge [1], II.1; and Simmons [11], chap. 1. For a more complete exposition of set theory, see Halmos [6], for example.

3. When the number of elements of a set is finite, it is often called a **finite set**. It is called an **infinite set** if it is not finite. For example, R is an infinite set. A set is called **countably infinite** if there is a one-to-one mapping between the set and the set of all positive integers. (The phrase "one-to-one mapping" will be explained shortly.) A set which is either finite or countably infinite is called **countable**; and a set which is not countable is called **uncountable**. Then R is uncountable.

4. Let $S \subset X$; then $f(S)$ is called the **image** of S under f. When $Y = f(X)$, f is said to be **onto**.

5. It should be noted, however, that in many treatments in the literature, "function" usually refers to a single-valued function.

6. For a more detailed exposition, see, for example, Kolmogorov and Fomin [8], secs. 8 and 21; Berge [1], IV.1, VII.2; Halmos [5], secs. 1–4; Simmons [11], secs. 9,14, and 15. In this subsection, concepts such as "linear space," "inner product" (space), "metric space," "norm," and "normed linear space" will be discussed. The reader will realize that these concepts, although they are abstracted from R^n, have much broader scope than R^n.

7. See Halmos [5], secs. 5–8 and 32–38; Nikaido [9], secs. 9 and 10; Wilansky [12], 2.1–2.4.

8. This is certainly the case, if X is a linear space as is assumed in the above definition.

9. The notation is justified, for, after all, the multiplication of f and g is defined as the composite function of f and g.

10. Strictly speaking, $A \cdot B$ may have to be denoted as $A \circ B$. However, this is too pedantic. In fact, following the usual convention, we often denote it simply as AB, unless it is confusing.

11. For a more detailed exposition see, for example, Fenchel [3], I.1, I.2, II.1, and II.2; Berge [1], VII.4; Berge and Ghouila-Houri [2], 1.4 and 1.5; Nikaido [9], sec. 27; or Fleming [4], 1.4. The proofs of the theorems are fairly easy. The reader can enhance his understandings of the content of this subsection by trying to prove these theorems by himself.

12. The proof of statement (i) is easy if we utilize a later theorem, Theorem 0.A.7.

13. The corresponding concept to $K(S)$ is **convex hull**, which is defined as the smallest convex set containing a given set S. Denoting this by $C(S)$, we can easily prove that $C(S)$ can be written as $C(S) = \{\sum_{i=1}^{m} \alpha_i x^i : x^i \in S, \; \alpha_i \in R, \; \alpha_i \geq 0, \; i = 1, 2, \ldots, m, \; \sum_{i=1}^{m} \alpha_i = 1\}$, where m and the choice of x^i and α_i are arbitrary. Note the difference between $C(S)$ and $K(S)$.

14. Corresponding to this concept, the convex hull of a finite number of points in X is called a **convex polyhedron**, or a **convex polytope**.

15. The material here is standard in general topology, and many textbooks are available for those who wish to see the proofs of the theorems in this subsection and to study this topic further. See, for example, Simmons [11]; Kelley [7]; and Berge [1]. Kelley [7] is a standard textbook on this topic; however, Simmons [11] is easier to read than Kelley [7]. Again, most of the proofs are omitted so that the reader can grasp the basic ideas without being led astray in the "jungles" of the proofs.

16. It is important to notice that the concept of limit point becomes concrete only when the topology of the space is specified. In other words, whether a particular point is a limit point or not depends on the topology. Let X be the set of real numbers. With its usual topology the open interval $(0, 1)$ is an open set and every point of the closed interval $[0, 1]$ is a limit point of $(0, 1)$. However, if the discrete topology is chosen for X, then *no* subset of X has the limit point.

17. For example, the closed interval $[a, b]$ in R is the closure of (a, b), $(a, b]$, and $[a, b)$ in R with its usual topology.

18. The reader of this book must have encountered the term "sequence" some time earlier in his study of mathematics. A rigorous definition is as follows. A **sequence** in X is a function defined on the set of all positive integers and whose range is included in X. If the range of this function is a set of real numbers, then it is called a **sequence of real numbers**. In general, however, the range can be any set. A sequence is usually denoted by $\{x^1, x^2, \ldots\}$ or, in short, $\{x^q\}$, where $x^1, x^2, \ldots, x^q, \ldots$ are the images of the function (and are called the **values** of the sequence, or the **terms** of the sequence). If $x^q \in S$ for all q, then $\{x^q\}$ is said to be a **sequence in (set)** S.

19. Given a sequence $\{x^q\}$, consider a sequence $\{q_s\}$, where $q_1 < q_2 < \ldots < q_s < \ldots$. Then the sequence $\{x^{q_s}\}$ is called a **subsequence** of x^q.

20. This remark with respect to Theorem 0.A.10 also means that the continuity of a particular function depends on the topology specified in the space.

21. If $x_0 \cdot \alpha < a$, then for a sufficiently large q, we have $x^q \cdot \alpha < a$, for $x \cdot \alpha$ is a continuous function. This contradicts the assumption.

22. Similarly, we can also prove that (1) if $x^q \to x_0$ and $x^q \cdot \alpha < a$ for all q, then $x_0 \cdot \alpha \leq a$, and (2) if $x^q \to x_0$, $y^q \to y_0$ with $x^q \cdot \alpha < x^q \cdot y^q$ for all q, then $x_0 \cdot \alpha \leq x_0 \cdot y_0$. The propositions in the present remark with this footnote are often utilized in economic theory (for example, consider α as a price vector).

23. Again the basic motivation here is found in R^n. The set I of all the open intervals (a, b) in R, under the usual topology of R, is called the **open base** of R in the sense that *every* open set of R can be expressed as a union of open intervals. In other words, every open set of R can be generated from I. Then define **open cube** in R^n by $\{(x_1, x_2, \ldots, x_n): a_i < x_i < b_i, a_i, b_i, x_i \in R, i = 1, 2, \ldots, n\}$. We can prove that the set of open cubes is an open base for R^n, that is, it will generate every open

set of R^n. In other words, we produced a topology for R^n starting from that of R. This idea of generating a product topology for R^n is used for the general case.

24. For the proof, see any standard textbook on elementary analysis, or try to prove it by yourself.

25. $\Pi_{i=1}^{m} f_i$ denotes $f_1 f_2 \cdots f_m$.

26. A set S in R^n (or any metric space) is said to be **bounded** if there exists an open ball with a finite radius which contains S.

27. As we remarked earlier, we can define a **limit** of a sequence in an arbitrary topological space (X, τ); that is, x_0 is a **limit** of sequence $\{x^q\}$ if for each open set V containing x_0 there exists a $\bar{q}$ such that $q \geqq \bar{q}$ implies $x^q \in V$. However, as we cautioned earlier, such a limit may not be unique: for example, consider $\tau \equiv \{X, \emptyset\}$ (indiscrete topology); then any sequence converges to every point of X. A remarkable feature of the Hausdorff space is that if a limit exists it is always unique.

28. In this section, we induced the concept of a topology from a metric and thus observed that a topology is closely related to the concept of the "limit of a sequence." We may reverse the problem; that is, given a topological space (X, τ), what is the situation in which the topology can be described in terms of sequences alone? This question then leads us to the Moore-Smith convergence theory in terms of "directed sets" and "nets." We do not go into this discussion (see Kelley [7], chap. 2). In any case, it turns out that the most satisfactory situation in which a topology can be described by sequences alone is the case of the "first axiom of countability." A topological space (X, τ) is said to satisfy the **first axiom of countability**, if, for each point x in X, there exists a *countable* class of open sets such that every open set containing x is a union of sets in this class. In short, (X, τ) satisfies the "first axiom of countability" if it has a countable open base at each of its points. An **open base** is a class of open sets such that every open set is a union of sets in this class (see Kelley [7], p. 50; Simmons [11], pp. 99–100). The first axiom of countability makes the following statement meaningful for general topological spaces. "A point x_0 is a limit point of a set S if and only if there exists a sequence in $S \backslash \{x_0\}$ which converges to x_0" (see Kelley [7], theorem 8, p. 72, and problem B, p. 76). It is known that every metric space satisfies the first axiom of countability (for example, see Kelley [7], theorem 11, p. 120). Hence, when we induced the concept of topology from a metric, the first axiom of countability had already crept into our discussion. In other words, the metric space with its induced topology is a "nice" topological space in terms of sequences, for it satisfies the first axiom of countability as well as being Hausdorff.

29. In the remainder of this book, we usually assume that X is R^n. Hence the statement "A is open" will mean, unless otherwise specified, that A is open in R^n with its usual topology.

REFERENCES

1. Berge, C., *Topological Spaces*, New York, Macmillan, 1963 (French original, 1959).

2. Berge, C., and Ghouila-Houri, A., *Programming, Games and Trasportation Networks*, New York, Wiley, 1965 (French original, 1962).

3. Fenchel, W., *Convex Cones, Sets, and Functions* (hectographed), Princeton, N.J., Princeton University Press, 1953.

4. Fleming, W. H., *Functions of Several Variables*, Reading, Mass., Addison-Wesley, 1965.

5. Halmos, P. R., *Finite Dimensional Vector Spaces*, 2nd ed., Princeton, N.J., Van Nostrand, 1958.

6. ———, *Naive Set Theory*, Princeton, N.J., Van Nostrand, 1960.

7. Kelley, J. L., *General Topology*, New York, Van Nostrand, 1955.

8. Kolmogorov, A. N., and Fomin, C. V., *Functional Analysis*, Vol. I, Rochester, N. Y., Grayrock, 1957 (Russian original, 1954).

9. Nikaido, H., *Introduction to Sets and Mappings in Modern Economics*, tr. K. Sato, Amsterdam, North-Holland, 1970 (Japanese original, Tokyo, 1960).

10. Rudin, W., *Principles of Mathematical Analysis*, 2nd ed., New York, McGraw-Hill, 1964.

11. Simmons, G. F., *Introduction to Topology and Modern Analysis*, New York, McGraw-Hill, 1963.

12. Wilansky, A., *Functional Analysis*, New York, Blaisdell, 1964.

Section B

SEPARATION THEOREMS

Optimization problems deeply underlie many branches of economic theory. The theorem (known as the **separation theorem**) which asserts the existence of a hyperplane that separates two disjoint convex sets is probably the most fundamental theorem in the mathematical theory of optimization. In this section, we study the essence of this theorem by confining ourselves to a simple but very important case—that is, the whole space is the real space, R^n—and considering it both as a vector space and a topological space (with the usual metric topology of R^n).

Definition: Let $p \in R^n$ with $p \neq 0$, $\| p \| < \infty$,[1] and $\alpha \in R$. The set H defined by $H \equiv \{x : p \cdot x = \alpha, x \in R^n\}$ is called a **hyperplane** in R^n with normal p.

REMARK: If $n = 3$, H is a plane; and if $n = 2$, H is a straight line.

REMARK: Suppose that there are two points, x^* and y^*, in H. Then by definition $p \cdot x^* = \alpha$ and $p \cdot y^* = \alpha$. Hence $p \cdot (x^* - y^*) = 0$. In other words, vector p is orthogonal to the line segment $(x^* - y^*)$, or to H. [See footnote 5.] For the two-dimensional case ($n = 2$), we may illustrate this as in Figure 0.8.

Definition: Given two nonempty sets X and Y in R^n and a hyperplane $H \equiv \{x : p \cdot x = \alpha, x \in R^n\}$, we say X **and** Y **are separated by** H (or H **separates** X **and** Y) if

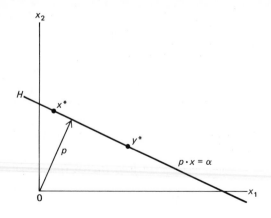

Figure 0.8. An Illustration of a Hyperplane.

$$p \cdot x \leq \alpha \qquad \text{for all } x \in X$$

and

$$p \cdot x \geq \alpha \qquad \text{for all } x \in Y$$

If we have strict inequalities in the above two inequalities, that is, $p \cdot x > \alpha$ for all $x \in X$ and $p \cdot x < \alpha$ for all $x \in Y$, then we say X and Y are **strictly separated by** H.

> *REMARK:* The above definition obviously holds even if X and/or Y is a set consisting of only one point.

> *REMARK:* A hyperplane H in R^n divides R^n into two "half spaces." In particular, $H \equiv \{x: p \cdot x = \alpha, x \in R^n\}$ determines the following two **closed half spaces**.

$$\{x: p \cdot x \geq \alpha, x \in R^n\} \quad \text{and} \quad \{x: p \cdot x \leq \alpha, x \in R^n\}$$

It can be seen readily that a closed half space is convex as well as closed. A hyperplane itself is clearly closed and convex.

Definition: Given a nonempty set X in R^n, a hyperplane H is called **bounding for** X if X is contained in one of the two closed half spaces determined by H. If H is bounding for X *and* H has a point in common with the boundary of X (that is, $\inf_{x \in X} p \cdot x = \alpha$), then H is called a **supporting hyperplane** to X.

Definition: An intersection of hyperplanes is called a **linear manifold**.

We first prove a separation theorem in its simplest version.

Theorem 0.B.1: *Let $\bar{X}$ be a nonempty closed convex set in R^n. Let $x_0 \notin \bar{X}$. Then the following are true.*

(i) *There exists a point $a \in \overline{X}$ such that $d(x_0, a) \leq d(x_0, x)$ for all $x \in \overline{X}$, and $d(x_0, a) > 0$.*

(ii) *There exists a $p \in R^n$, $p \neq 0$, $\| p \| < \infty$, and an $\alpha \in R$ such that*
$$p \cdot x \geq \alpha \qquad for\ all\ x \in \overline{X}$$

and

$$p \cdot x_0 < \alpha$$

In other words, $\overline{X}$ and x_0 are separated by a hyperplane $H = \{x: p \cdot x = \alpha, x \in R^n\}$.

PROOF:

(i) Let $\overline{B}(x_0)$ be a closed ball with center at x_0 and meeting $\overline{X}$ [that is, $\overline{B}(x_0) \cap \overline{X} \neq \emptyset$]. Write $A \equiv \overline{B}(x_0) \cap \overline{X}$. The set A is nonempty, closed and bounded (hence compact). Since A is compact and the distance function is continuous, $d(x_0, x)$ achieves its minimum in A as a result of Weierstrass's theorem. That is, there exists an $a \in A$ such that $d(x_0, a) \leq d(x_0, x)$ for all $x \in A$. Hence *a fortiori* $d(x_0, a) \leq d(x_0, x)$ for all $x \in \overline{X}$. Since $x_0 \notin \overline{X}$ and $a \in \overline{X}$, $d(x_0, a) > 0$.

(ii) Let $p \equiv a - x_0$ and $\alpha \equiv p \cdot a$. Note first that $p \cdot x_0 = (a - x_0) \cdot x_0 = (a - x_0) \cdot (x_0 - a) + (a - x_0) \cdot a = -(a - x_0) \cdot (a - x_0) + (a - x_0) \cdot a = -\| p \|^2 + \alpha < \alpha$, where $0 < \| p \| < \infty$. Let $x \in \overline{X}$ (arbitrary point). Since $\overline{X}$ is convex and $a \in \overline{X}$, $x(t) \in \overline{X}$, where $x(t) \equiv (1 - t)a + tx$, $0 < t \leq 1$. Then $d(x_0, a) \leq d(x_0, x(t))$ by (i). In other words: $\| a - x_0 \|^2 \leq \| x(t) - x_0 \|^2 = \| (1 - t)a + tx - x_0 \|^2 = \| (1 - t)(a - x_0) + t(x - x_0) \|^2 = (1 - t)^2 \| a - x_0 \|^2 + 2t(1 - t)(a - x_0) \cdot (x - x_0) + t^2 \| x - x_0 \|^2$. Hence we obtain $0 \leq t(t - 2) \| a - x_0 \|^2 + 2t(1 - t)(a - x_0) \cdot (x - x_0) + t^2 \| x - x_0 \|^2$. Divide both sides by $t (t > 0)$, and we obtain $0 \leq (t - 2) \| a - x_0 \|^2 + 2(1 - t)(a - x_0) \cdot (x - x_0) + t \| x - x_0 \|^2$. Take a limit as $t \rightarrow 0$. Then we obtain

$$0 \leq -2 \| a - x_0 \|^2 + 2(a - x_0) \cdot (x - x_0)$$

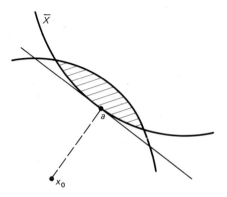

Figure 0.9.   An Illustration of the Proof of Theorem 0.B.1.

or

$$0 \geq (a - x_0) \cdot (a - x_0) - (a - x_0) \cdot (x - x_0) = (a - x_0) \cdot a - (a - x_0) \cdot x$$

Since $p \equiv (a - x_0)$, we have $p \cdot x \geq p \cdot a = \alpha$ for all $x \in \overline{X}$.

(Q.E.D.)

REMARK: Note that the convexity of $\overline{X}$ is used only in (ii) of the above proof.

REMARK: Since $0 < \| p \| < \infty$, we may choose p such that $\| p \| = 1$.[2]

REMARK: The above proof is essentially due to von Neumann and Morgenstern [11]. Debreu [4] offers the following alternative argument for the second part (ii) of the above proof, which avoids the use of the limit process (that is, $t \to 0$). His argument is rather intuitive (see Figure 0.10). A rigorous proof along this line can be seen in Berge [1], p. 162, or Berge and Ghouila-Houri [2], pp. 53–54. The proof is done by contradiction. That is, suppose that there is a point x of $\overline{X}$ which is strictly on the same side of H as x_0. Consider the point $x(t)$ on the line segment $\overline{ax}$ such that $\overline{x_0 x(t)}$ is orthogonal to $\overline{ax}$. Since $d(x_0, x) \geq d(x_0, a)$, the point $x(t)$ is between a and x. Thus $x(t) \in \overline{X}$ and $d(x_0, x(t)) < d(x_0, a)$, which contradicts the choice of a.

REMARK: Note that the hyperplane $H \equiv \{x: p \cdot x = \alpha, x \in R^n\}$ is a supporting hyperplane to $\overline{X}$. This hyperplane separates set $\overline{X}$ from the given point x_0(which itself is a convex set). Hence the existence of such a supporting hyperplane to $\overline{X}$ is the crux of the theorem. Given a nonempty closed convex set (say, $\overline{X}$) and a point (say, a) in the boundary of $\overline{X}$, we can assert that there exists at least one supporting hyperplane to $\overline{X}$ passing through the point a. In Theorem 1, we saw that such a hyperplane played an important role in the theorem. In fact, such a supporting hyperplane also plays a more crucial role in other versions of the separation theorem, which we prove in this section (Theorems 0.B.2 and 0.B.3). If the (hyper-) curve which defines the boundary of $\overline{X}$ is smooth ("differentiable") at the given

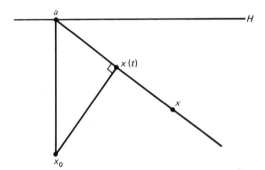

Figure 0.10   Debreu's Argument.

boundary point a, then the tangent (hyper-) plane at the point gives such a supporting hyperplane. In this case there is only one supporting hyperplane passing through the given point a. However, if the (hyper-) curve is not smooth, then there can be many supporting hyperplanes passing through the given point. These two cases are illustrated in Figure 0.11. It is important to note that the above tangent hyperplane conceptually links the separation theorems to calculus. The power of the separation theorem is that the boundary (hyper-) curve does not have to be smooth (differentiable) at a, and that it is more direct and set-theoretic.

Theorem 1 is sometimes stated in the following form.

Corollary: *Let $\overline{X}$ be a nonempty closed convex set in R^n not containing the origin. Then there exists a $p \in R^n$, $p \neq 0$, $\| p \| < \infty$, and an $\alpha \in R$, $\alpha > 0$ such that*

$$p \cdot x \geqq \alpha \qquad \text{for all } x \in \overline{X}$$

and this inequality can be made strict.

PROOF: In Theorem 1, let x_0 be the origin. Then, as a result of the theorem, there exist $p \neq 0$ and α such that $p \cdot x \geqq \alpha$ for all $x \in \overline{X}$, where p and α are defined as $p \equiv a - x_0 = a$ and $\alpha \equiv p \cdot a$. By this definition, $\alpha > 0$.

(Q.E.D.)

REMARK: Obviously, this corollary is really equivalent to Theorem 1, for the choice of the origin can be arbitrary. The inequality in the statement of the corollary can be made strict by choosing a point strictly in between a and the origin (instead of a).

In the above theorem, $\overline{X}$ is assumed to be a closed set. In fact, we can relax this assumption and we can obtain the following theorem.

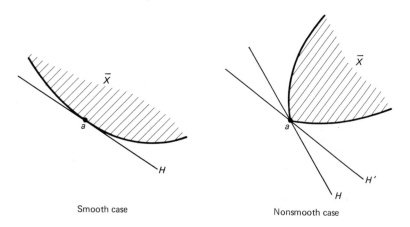

Smooth case   Nonsmooth case

Figure 0.11.   Supporting Hyperplanes.

Theorem 0.B.2:   *Let X be a nonempty convex set in R^n (not necessarily closed). Let x_0 be a point in R^n which is not in X. Then there exists $p \in R^n$, $p \neq C$, $\| p \| < \infty$ such that*[3]

$$p \cdot x \geqq p \cdot x_0 \qquad \text{for all } x \in X$$

PROOF:

(i) Suppose $x_0 \notin \overline{X}$, where $\overline{X}$ is the closure of X. Then, by Theorem 1, there exist $p \in R^n$, $p \neq 0$, and $\alpha \in R$ such that $p \cdot x \geqq \alpha$ for all $x \in \overline{X}$ and $p \cdot x_0 < \alpha$. Thus $p \cdot x > p \cdot x_0$ for all $x \in \overline{X}$. Hence, *a fortiori*, $p \cdot x > p \cdot x_0$ for all $x \in X$.

(ii) Suppose $x_0 \in \overline{X}$. Since $x_0 \notin X$ (that is, $x_0 \in X^c$) by assumption, x_0 is a boundary point of $\overline{X}$. Then, for any open ball containing x_0, there exists a point which is not in $\overline{X}$. That is, there exists a sequence $\{x^q\}$ such that $x^q \notin \overline{X}$ and $x^q \to x_0$. Since $x^q \notin \overline{X}$ and $\overline{X}$ is nonempty, closed, and convex, there exist, by Theorem 0.B.1, $p^q \in R^n$, $p^q \neq 0$ such that $p^q \cdot x > p^q \cdot x^q$ for all $x \in \overline{X}$. This is illustrated in Figure 0.12. Now without a loss of generality, we can choose p^q such that $\| p^q \| = 1$. Then the sequence $\{p^q\}$ moves in the unit sphere of R^n. Since the unit sphere is compact, there exists a convergent subsequence in the sphere; that is, there exists a subsequence such that $p^{q_s} \to p$ with $\| p \| = 1$, where $\{p^{q_s}\}$ corresponds to $\{x^{q_s}\}$. Take the limit of $p^{q_s} \cdot x > p^{q_s} \cdot x^{q_s}$ as $q_s \to \infty$. Since an inner product is a continuous function, we have $p \cdot x \geqq p \cdot x_0$ for all $x \in \overline{X}$. Hence, *a fortiori*, $p \cdot x \geqq p \cdot x_0$ for all $x \in X$.   (Q.E.D.)

Theorem 0.B.3 (Minkowski):   *Let X and Y be nonempty convex sets in R^n (not necessarily closed) such that $X \cap Y = \emptyset$. Then there exist $p \in R^n$, $p \neq 0$, $\| p \| < \infty$, and $\alpha \in R$ such that $p \cdot x \geqq \alpha$ for all $x \in X$ and $p \cdot y \leqq \alpha$ for all $y \in Y$.*[4]

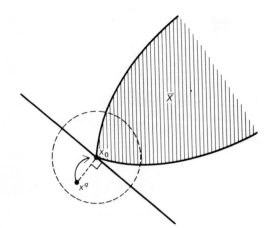

Figure 0.12.   An Illustration of the proof of Theorem 0.B.2.

PROOF: Consider $S \equiv X + (-Y)$ (the set obtained by vector addition). Since X and Y are convex, S is also convex. Also $0 \notin S$. (If $0 \in S$, then there exist $x^* \in X$ and $y^* \in Y$ such that $x^* + (-y^*) = 0$, or $x^* = y^*$. This contradicts $X \cap Y = \emptyset$.) Hence, owing to Theorem 0.B.2, there exists a $p \neq 0$ such that $p \cdot z \geq p \cdot 0 = 0$ for all $z \in S$. Write $z = x - y$, $x \in X$, $y \in Y$. Thus we have $p \cdot x \geq p \cdot y$ for all $x \in X$ and $y \in Y$. In other words, $\inf_{x \in X} p \cdot x \geq \sup_{y \in Y} p \cdot y$. Hence we can pick α in such a way that the conclusion of the theorem holds.   (Q.E.D.)

REMARK: If, in addition, X is closed and Y is compact, then we can strengthen the conclusion of Theorem 0.B.3 as $p \cdot x > \alpha$ for all $x \in X$ and $p \cdot y < \alpha$ for all $y \in Y$. For the proof of this theorem, see Berge [1], pp. 163–164; and Berge and Ghouila-Houri [2], p. 55.

REMARK: Theorem 0.B.2 is clearly a special case of Theorem 0.B.3, in which one of the two sets is a set consisting of only one point (which is obviously convex). The previous remark states the theorem which generalizes Theorem 0.B.1, since a set consisting of only one point is compact.

REMARK: In the above theorems we used expressions such as

$$p \cdot x \geq \alpha \qquad \text{for all } x \in X \quad (\text{or } p \cdot x > \alpha \qquad \text{for all } x \in X)$$

and

$$p \cdot y \leq \alpha \qquad \text{for all } y \in Y \quad (\text{or } p \cdot y < \alpha \qquad \text{for all } y \in Y)$$

The directions of these inequalities are immaterial to the essence of the theorems, for we can easily reverse the direction of the inequalities by defining $\tilde{p} \equiv -p$ and $\tilde{\alpha} \equiv -\alpha$. Then $\tilde{p} \cdot x \leq \tilde{\alpha}$ for all $x \in X$ (or $\tilde{p} \cdot x < \tilde{\alpha}$ for all $x \in X$), and $\tilde{p} \cdot y \geq \tilde{\alpha}$ for all $y \in Y$ (or $\tilde{p} \cdot y > \tilde{\alpha}$ for all $y \in Y$). Notice also that in the statement of the above theorems we did not specify the signs of α and of each component of p.

We finish our discussion of the separation theorems by showing one of their important applications. We will prove the Minkowski-Farkas lemma by using Theorem 0.B.1. In order to do this we need the following lemma.

Lemma: *Let K be a cone, with the vertex at the origin, in R^n, and let p be a given point in R^n. If $p \cdot x$ is bounded from below for all $x \in K$, then $p \cdot x \geq 0$ for all $x \in K$.*

PROOF: By assumption, there exists an $\alpha \in R$ such that $p \cdot x \geq \alpha$ for all $x \in K$. Since K is a cone with the vertex at the origin, $x \in K$ implies $\theta x \in K$ for all $\theta \geq 0$. Hence $p \cdot (\theta x) \geq \alpha$ or $p \cdot x \geq \alpha/\theta$ for all $x \in K$ and $\theta > 0$. Taking the limit as $\theta \to \infty$ yields $p \cdot x \geq 0$.   (Q.E.D.)

We can now prove the following theorem.

Theorem 0.B.4 (Minkowski-Farkas lemma):   *Let* $a^1, a^2, \ldots, a^m$ *and* $b \neq 0$ *be points in* R^n. *Suppose that* $b \cdot x \geq 0$ *for all* x *such that* $a^i \cdot x \geq 0$, $i = 1, 2, \ldots, m$. *Then there exist coefficients* $\lambda_1, \lambda_2, \ldots, \lambda_m$, *all* ≥ 0 *and not vanishing simultaneously, such that* $b = \sum_{i=1}^{m} \lambda_i a^i$.

PROOF: Let K be a convex polyhedral cone generated by $a^1, a^2, \ldots, a^m$. Then K is a closed set. We want to show that $b \in K$. Suppose $b \notin K$. Then K is a nonempty, closed, convex set which is disjoint from b. Hence from Theorem 0.B.1, there exist $p \in R^n$, $p \neq 0$, and $\alpha \in R$ such that

$$p \cdot x \geq \alpha \qquad \text{for all } x \in K \text{ and } p \cdot b < \alpha$$

Thus $p \cdot x$ is bounded from below for all $x \in K$. Because of the previous lemma, we have $p \cdot x \geq 0$ for all $x \in K$. Also note that $0 \in K$ means $p \cdot 0 \geq \alpha$, or $\alpha \leq 0$. Thus we have $p \cdot b < 0$. Since $a^i \in K$ for all i, $p \cdot a^i \geq 0$ for all i. Thus for this p, we have $b \cdot p < 0$ with $a^i \cdot p \geq 0$, $i = 1, 2, \ldots, m$. This contradicts the hypothesis of the theorem. Hence $b \in K$. In other words, there exist $\lambda_1, \lambda_2, \ldots, \lambda_m$, all ≥ 0, such that $b = \sum_{i=1}^{m} \lambda_i a^i$. Since $b \neq 0$, the λ_i's cannot vanish simultaneously.   (Q.E.D.)

REMARK: If $b = 0$, then it is possible that $\lambda_i = 0$ for all $i = 1, 2, \ldots, m$.

REMARK: The converse of the above theorem is also true. *If* $a^1, a^2, \ldots, a^m$ *and* $b \neq 0$ *are points in* R^n, *and if there exist coefficients* $\lambda_1, \lambda_2, \ldots, \lambda_m$, *all* ≥ 0 *(not vanishing simultaneously), such that* $b = \sum_{i=1}^{m} \lambda_i a^i$, *then* $b \cdot x \geq 0$ *for* x *such that* $a^i \cdot x \geq 0$, $i = 1, 2, \ldots, m$.

PROOF: Suppose $\lambda_1, \lambda_2, \ldots, \lambda_m$, all ≥ 0, are such coefficients that $b = \sum_{i=1}^{m} \lambda_i a^i$; then $b \cdot x = (\sum_{i=1}^{m} \lambda_i a^i) \cdot x = \sum_{i=1}^{m} \lambda_i (a^i \cdot x) \geq 0$.   (Q.E.D.)

Owing to the above remark, the Minkowski-Farkas lemma can also be stated in the following form.

Theorem 0.B.5:   *Given points* a^i, $i = 1, 2, \ldots, m$ *and* $b \neq 0$ *in* R^n, *exactly one of the following two alternatives holds.*

(i)   *There exist* λ_i, $i = 1, 2, \ldots, m$, *all* ≥ 0 *(not vanishing simultaneously), such that*

$$b = \sum_{i=1}^{m} \lambda_i a^i \qquad or$$

(ii)   *There exists an* $x \in R^n$ *such that*

$$b \cdot x < 0 \quad and \quad a^i \cdot x \geq 0, i = 1, 2, \ldots, m$$

REMARK: Theorem 0.B.5 is stated as follows: "if (ii) does not hold, then (i) holds."

Defining an $m \times n$ matrix $A \equiv \begin{bmatrix} a^1 \\ a^2 \\ \vdots \\ a^m \end{bmatrix}$, a column vector $x \equiv \begin{bmatrix} x_1 \\ x_2 \\ \vdots \\ x_n \end{bmatrix}$

and a row vector $\lambda \equiv (\lambda_1, \lambda_2, \ldots, \lambda_m)$, we can state the above alternatives (i) and (ii) in the following forms:

(i) The equation $b = \lambda \cdot A$ has a nonnegative solution $\lambda \geq 0$, $\lambda \neq 0$.
(ii) The inequalities $b \cdot x < 0$ and $A \cdot x \geq 0$ have a solution x.

Theorem 0.B.4 can be restated as "$b \cdot x \geq 0$ for all x such that $A \cdot x \geq 0$ implies that there exists a $\lambda \geq 0$ with $\lambda \neq 0$ such that $b = \lambda \cdot A$."

REMARK: A geometric interpretation of Theorem O.B.4 is as follows:[5]

(i)   The inequality $a^i \cdot x \geq 0$ for all i means that x is in the cone *POQ* (the shaded area).
(ii) The inequality $b \cdot x \geq 0$ means that x is in the half space, determined by the hyperplane $H \equiv \{x : b \cdot x = 0, x \in R^n\}$, which contains the point b.
(iii) The conclusion of the theorem is "$b \in K$," where $K \equiv \{y : y = \lambda \cdot A, \lambda \geq 0\}$.
(iv) If $b \in K$ (Case *a*), then we have $b \cdot x \geq 0$ for all x such that $a^i \cdot x \geq 0$,

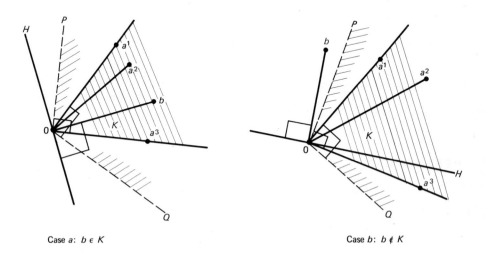

Case *a*: $b \in K$ 　　　　　　　　　　　　　　Case *b*: $b \notin K$

Figure 0.13. A Geometric Interpretation of the Minkowski-Farkas Lemma.

$i = 1, 2, \ldots, m$ (that is, the cone *AOB* is contained in the half space, determined by *H*, which contains *b*).

(v) If $b \notin K$ (Case *b*), then we *cannot* have $b \cdot x \geq 0$ for all x such that $a^i \cdot x \geq 0$, $i = 1, 2, \ldots, m$. In other words, there exists a point—say, $\tilde{x}$—in the cone *AOB*, but not in the half space which contains *b* (Figure 0.13, Case *b*).

REMARK: The Minkowski-Farkas lemma plays an important role in the theory of linear programming (for example, the duality theorem), game theory (for example, the zero-sum two-person game), and the theory of nonlinear programming (for example, the Kuhn-Tucker theorem), and so on. There are many ways to prove this theorem. The above proof (the proof of Theorem 0.B.4) is a minor modification of the proof by Berge [1], p. 164. Alternative proofs can be found, for example, in Gale [6], pp. 44–46; Goldman, A. J., and Tucker, A. W., "Polyhedral Convex Cones" in [7]; Nikaido [8], sec. 29, [9] I.3; and Hestenes, M. R., *Calculus of Variations and Optimal Control Theory*, New York, Wiley, 1966, pp. 13–15.

FOOTNOTES

1. By $\| p \| < \infty$, we mean $\| p \|$ is finite. Note also that $p \neq 0$ means $\| p \| > 0$.

2. In the statement of the theorem, $p \cdot x \geq \alpha$ for all $x \in \overline{X}$ and $p \cdot x_0 < \alpha$, redefine p and α by $p/\| p \|$ and $\alpha/\| p \|$ respectively. Needless to say, $\| p/\| p \| \| = 1$.

3. Again, p can be chosen such that $\| p \| = 1$, if one wishes to do so.

4. Again, p can be chosen such that $\| p \| = 1$, if one wishes to do so.

5. Given two vectors x and y in R^n, we can prove that $x \cdot y = \| x \| \ \| y \| \cos \theta$, where $\| x \|^2 = \sum_{i=1}^{n} x^2 = x \cdot x$ and θ is the angle between the two vectors x and y ($0 \leq \theta \leq \pi$). (To prove this, use the cosine law of trigonometry, $\| x - y \|^2 = \| x \|^2 + \| y \|^2 - 2 \| x \| \ \| y \| \cos \theta$.) If $x = 0$ or $y = 0$, $x \cdot y = 0$. Assuming that $x \neq 0$ and $y \neq 0$, we have $x \cdot y > 0$ if $0 \leq \theta < \pi/2$, $x \cdot y = 0$ if $\theta = \pi/2$, and $x \cdot y < 0$ if $\pi/2 < \theta \leq \pi$. Incidentally, from the above relation $x \cdot y = \| x \| \ \| y \| \cos \theta$, we can also obtain $(x \cdot y)^2 \leq \| x \|^2 \| y \|^2$, which is called the **Cauchy-Schwartz inequality** (in fact, this relation holds for any inner product space).

REFERENCES

1. Berge, C., *Topological Spaces*, New York, Macmillan, 1963 (French original, 1959), esp. chap. VIII.

2. Berge, C., and Ghouila-Houri, A., *Programming, Games and Transportation Networks*, New York, Wiley, 1965 (French original, 1962).

3. Debreu, G., *Theory of Value*, New York, Wiley, 1959.

4. Debreu, G., "Separation Theorem for Convex Sets," in "Selected Topics in Eco-

nomics Involving Mathematical Reasoning" by Koopmans, T. C., and Bausch, A. F., *SIAM Review*, 1, July 1959.

5. Fenchel, W., *Convex Cones, Sets, and Functions*, Princeton, N.J., Princeton University, 1950 (hectographed).
6. Gale, D., *The Theory of Linear Economic Models*, New York, McGraw-Hill, 1960.
7. Kuhn, H. W., and Tucker, A. W., eds., *Linear Inequalities and Related Systems*, Princeton, N.J., Princeton University Press, 1956.
8. Nikaido, H., *Introduction to Sets and Mappings in Modern Economics*, tr. K. Sato, Amsterdam, North-Holland, 1970 (Japanese original, Tokyo, 1960).
9. ———, *Convex Structures and Economic Theory*, New York, Academic Press, 1969.
10. Valentine, F. A., *Convex Sets*, New York, McGraw-Hill, 1964.
11. von Neumann, J., and Morgenstern, O., *Theory of Games and Economic Behavior*, 2nd ed., Princeton, N.J., Princeton University Press, 1947 (1st ed., 1944).

Section C

ACTIVITY ANALYSIS AND THE GENERAL PRODUCTION SET

The central concept of the traditional (or "neoclassical") analysis of production is that of a *production function*. A production function is a function which describes the technological relation between various outputs and various inputs. If we denote the output vector by $x = (x_1, x_2, \ldots, x_k)$ and the input vector by $v = (v_1, v_2, \ldots, v_r)$, then a "production function" can be written as $F(x, v) = 0$. This relation is usually supposed to define a unique surface on the x-plane for a given value of v. In order to understand the meaning of the traditional production function analysis more fully, let us first consider the case where there is no joint production so that $x = x_1$. In this case a production function is usually written in the form $x = f(v)$. It is generally supposed that this relation assigns a *unique* value of x for each value of the vector v. In other words, f is assumed to be a single-valued function. Then the traditional analysis usually proceeds with a further assumption, the differentiability of function f, and the analysis then becomes one which may best be described as "marginal analysis."

It has long been realized that this concept of a production function is unnecessarily restrictive. It, in a sense, presupposes the existence of an "efficient manager." Given available quantities of factors, the efficient manager maximizes the amount of output produced. In the joint production case, this manager supposedly maximizes the production of one arbitrary output with all the other outputs held constant. Thus the efficient manager in this case defines the unique surface with a given amount of inputs.

"Activity analysis" revolutionizes traditional production analysis by discarding the above concepts of a production function and an "efficient manager." Instead, it postulates the *set* of production processes available in a given economy. (Here the word "economy" can mean a firm, a collection of firms, the entire national economy, or the whole world.) This set is called a **production set**. An element of this set is an *n*-tuple which describes the technological relation of the input-output combination of one process of production. An element of the production set is called a **process** or an **activity**. We may also call it a **blueprint** to stress its technological character. There is no presupposition about the existence of an "efficient manager," so that nothing in the beginning is specified about what processes or blueprints in the production set should be adopted or discarded. If one likes, one can include the managerial ability of Mr. A in the list of commodities. We assume that there are *n* "commodities" in the economy and each commodity is qualitatively homogeneous. In general, a **commodity** is defined here by a specification of all its physical characteristics, of its availability location, and of its availability date. Hence, for example, flows of technically the same commodity in two different locations represent two different commodities.[1] Note that we may always regard different commodities as one commodity, if this facilitates a sharper and deeper analysis of a particular problem.

The production process is described by an ordered *n*-tuple of these commodities. (The dimension *n* is usually assumed to be a *finite*, positive integer, but can be infinity.) The production set is the collection of these *n*-tuples. The following example is from Koopmans and Bausch [9], pp. 99–100. Here we consider an economy with four commodities and two processes.

		Process 1 (Tanning)	Process 2 (Shoemaking)
Commodity 1	(shoes)	0	1
Commodity 2	(leather)	1	$-\frac{1}{4}$
Commodity 3	(hides)	-1	0
Commodity 4	(labor)	$-\frac{1}{10}$	$-\frac{1}{2}$

In each process inputs are represented by negative numbers and outputs are represented by positive numbers. Note also that there can be any number of processes for tanning or shoemaking. Moreover, each process can have more than one positive entry. This is the case of joint production. For example, in a process which produces cow hides, beef may also be produced.

The scope of activity analysis is not limited to statics. The convention of **dating commodities** (which is due to Hicks [5]) extends the scope of activity analysis to dynamics and capital theory, in which time is involved in an essential manner. For example, consider the Åkerman-Wicksell model of the durability of capital. Assume that one unit of the capital good (an axe) whose durability is j days is produced by l_j units of labor. Assume that l_j men are used as input the first day, leaving one unit of the axe for the second day. Assume that the axe of durability j lasts for j days after it is built with the same efficiency and suddenly "dies" at the end of the $(j + 1)$th day with zero scrap value. Then the jth production process which produces the axe of durability j can be expressed by the following vector:

$$(-l_j, 1, 1, \ldots, 1, 0, \ldots, 0)$$

where there are (j) 1's in this vector. Assuming that the maximum durability in use one can obtain (with any amount of the initial labor input) is m days, there are $(m - j)$ 0's in the above vector. There are m processes for the production of the axe, and the choice of the durability of the axe amounts to choosing a proper process from these m processes. Clearly this convention of "dating commodities" can also be applied to the Böhm-Bawerk-Wicksell theory of the period of production. If the inputs (say grape juice) are "sunk" for certain periods of time, as in the Wicksellian model of vintage wine, then there are zeros in the production process vector corresponding to such periods. The choice of the period of production amounts to choosing a proper process among the set of processes which are distinguished by the number of these zeros. For a completely general treatment on capital theory from the activity analysis viewpoint, we simply refer to Malinvaud [10]. Clearly, it is also possible to build a model of growth or capital without following the convention of dating commodities. Simpler treatments are often possible.

The *modus operandi* of activity analysis is through the use of set theory and other branches of modern mathematics. Activity analysis is axiomatic, more fundamental, and more rigorous than the traditional production function analysis. Separation theorems will play an important role in activity analysis just as derivatives played an important role in production function analysis. If we like, however, we can characterize the production set by some functional relations and pursue an analysis using these relations. The analysis then looks similar to the traditional analysis except that it is more general. Now we will study the elements of this modern production analysis. This will provide a good bridge to the modern economic theory which we propose to study in subsequent chapters.

Let Y be the set of all the technically possible production processes in a given "economy." We assume $Y \subset R^n$, and $y \in Y$ denotes a production process in the economy. We use the convention that the ith component, y_i, of y, represents an "output" if $y_i > 0$ and represents an "input" if $y_i < 0$.[2] The quantity $|y_i|$ indicates the amount of the ith "commodity" involved in this process y. We first impose the following two postulates.

(A-1) (**Additivity**) $y \in Y$ *and* $y' \in Y$ *imply* $y + y' \in Y$.
(A-2) (**Proportionality**) $y \in Y$ *implies* $\alpha y \in Y$ *for all* $\alpha \geqq 0$, $\alpha \in R$.

Thus Y is a convex cone. Due to the proportionality, if $a^j \in Y$, then

$$\lambda_j a^j \in Y \text{ for all } \lambda_j \geq 0, \lambda_j \in R, \text{ where } a^j \equiv \begin{bmatrix} a_{1j} \\ \vdots \\ a_{nj} \end{bmatrix}$$

The vector a^j may be referred to as the *j*th activity (or process) of Y in its unit level of operation. Here a_{ij} denotes the amount of the *i*th good involved in one unit operation of the *j*th activity; λ_j signifies the **activity level** of the *j*th activity.
    Now we impose the third postulate:

(A-3) **(Finite number of basic activities)** *There exist a finite number of a^j's such that Y is a convex polyhedral cone generated by these a^j's. These a^j's are called* **basic activities**.

In other words, a typical element y in Y can be expressed as a nonnegative linear combination of $a^1, a^2, \ldots a^m$, where m is a finite positive integer. Owing to the above postulates, the production set Y in activity analysis can be written as $Y = \{y: y = A \cdot \lambda, \lambda \geq 0\}$, where A is an $n \times m$ matrix (with real-number entries) formed by $[a^1, \ldots, a^m]$ and λ is an *m*-vector whose *j*th element is λ_j.

    It should be clear that the proportionality postulate means *complete divisibility of all the commodities and constant returns to scale* and that the additivity postulate means the independent action of each activity (no interactions among activities): in Scitovsky's terminology, there are *no* ("*technological*") *external economies* or *diseconomies*.

    That Y is a convex polyhedral cone implicitly entails several other features. Some important ones are the following:

(i) $0 \in Y$ **(possibility of inaction)**. That is, it is possible for the producer to do nothing.

(ii) Y is a closed set. (This is mathematically both a very important and a nice feature. Economically it means that any production process that can be approximated by processes in Y is itself in Y.)

Koopmans [7] imposed the following three additional important postulates (whose economic meanings should be self-evident).

(A-4) **(Productiveness)** *There exists at least one positive element for some y in Y.*
(A-5) **(No land of Cockaigne)** $y \geq 0$ *implies $y \notin Y$. Or $Y \cap \Omega = \{0\}$.*[3]
(A-6) **(Irreversibility)** $y \in Y$ *and $y \neq 0$ imply $-y \notin Y$. Or $Y \cap (-Y) = \{0\}$.*

The two diagrams of Figure 0.14 illustrate the meaning of some of the above postulates. In case a, (A-4) and (A-5) hold but not (A-6). In case b, (A-4), (A-5), and (A-6) all hold. We may note one important consequence of (A-5), which illustrates the meaning of the above postulates. For a detailed investigation of the implications of these postulates, see Koopmans [7], chap. III.

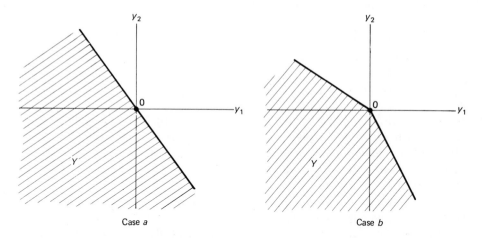

Figure 0.14   Illustrations of Two Cases

Theorem 0.C.1:   *Let $Y \equiv \{y: y = A \cdot \lambda, \lambda \geqq 0\}$. Y satisfies postulate* (A-5) *if and only if there exists a $p > 0$, $p \in R^n$, $\| p \| < \infty$, such that $p \cdot y \leqq 0$ for all $y \in Y$.*

PROOF:

    (i) (Sufficiency) $y \geqq 0$ implies $p \cdot y > 0$ for any $p > 0$. Hence by assumption $y \notin Y$.

    (ii) (Necessity) Omitted (an interesting exercise for the use of the separation theorems).[4]

REMARK: If we interpret p as a **price** vector, then $p \cdot y$ represents the *profit* from y. Hence, for example, $p \cdot y \leqq 0$ for all $y \in Y$ means that the maximum profit is at most 0.

We stated postulates (A-4), (A-5), and (A-6) in connection with the production set Y which is a convex polyhedral cone. In general these postulates can be stated even if Y is *not* a convex polyhedral cone. When Y represents the collection of input-output combinations that are technically feasible in a given economy, and when we do not require Y to be a convex polyhedral cone, we call Y a **general production set**. We can list some of the important postulates that we may wish to impose on the general production set Y. (Most of the results in activity analysis follow in an arbitrary *normed linear space*, as well as in R^n.)

    (i)   The set Y is closed.

    (ii)   Possibility of inaction ($0 \in Y$).

    (iii) Productiveness $\left[\text{that is, (A-4)}\right]$.

(iv)   No land of Cockaigne ($Y \cap \Omega \subset \{0\}$).[5]

(v)   Irreversibility ($Y \cap (-Y) \subset \{0\}$).

(vi)   **Free disposability** $\left[y \in -\Omega \text{ implies } y \in Y, \text{ or } Y \supset (-\Omega) \right]$.

(vii-a) The set Y is a convex polyhedral cone.

(vii-b) The set Y is a convex cone.

(vii-c) The set Y is convex.

Note that (vii-a) implies (i) and (ii) and that (vii-b) implies (ii). Statements (vii-c) and (ii) together imply that if $y \in Y$, then $\alpha y \in Y$ for all $0 \leqq \alpha \leqq 1$; in other words, *nonincreasing returns to scale* prevail (or increasing returns to scale are ruled out). Note also that the convexity of Y presupposes the *divisibility* of all the goods involved.

The production set Y as described above indicates the technological possibilities in a given economy; hence it is free from resource limitations. In other words, $y \in Y$ indicates how much output can be produced after specifying the amounts of the inputs, and we do not ask whether these inputs are, in fact, available in the economy. (Thus we called $y \in Y$ a "blueprint.") In this sense it corresponds to the concept of the classical production function. However, we can also take resource limitations into account. For example, Y can indicate a "truncated" convex polyhedral cone, such as $Y \equiv \{y: y = A \cdot \lambda, \lambda \geq 0, \lambda \in R^m,$ and $y + \bar{z} \geq 0\}$, where $\bar{z} \geq 0$ denotes the resource limitation of the economy. With the no land of Cockaigne postulate, such a set is no longer a convex polyhedral cone, although it is still convex. Note that the set is compact now. This truncation can easily be illustrated by Figure 0.15.

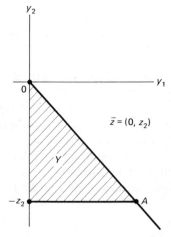

Figure 0.15 A Truncated Production Cone.

REMARK: Strictly speaking, the use of the words "activity analysis" may have to be confined to a study of production processes when the number of basic activities is finite. In other words, Y must be confined to a convex polyhedral cone or a "truncated" convex polyhedral cone. We will *not* adopt this narrow definition. The revolutionary character of activity analysis is not in a particular shape of Y. It is in the set-theoretic approach which is more fundamental and powerful than the traditional smooth (differentiable) production function approach. We now introduce the most important concept in activity analysis.

Definition: Let $Y \subset R^n$ be a general production set. A point $\hat{y}$ in Y is called an **efficient point** of Y if there does not exist a $y \in Y$ such that $y \geq \hat{y}$.

REMARK: An efficient point represents a boundary point, and it corresponds to a point on the classical production function. It is an input-output combination such that no output can be increased without decreasing other outputs or increasing inputs. In terms of the previous diagram, $0A$ is the set of efficient points in the truncated production cone. If the production set is the entire cone, the half line from 0 passing through A is the set of the efficient points.

REMARK: An efficient point is often defined with an explicit recognition of the resource constraint. As we discussed in the previous remark, a general production set Y can also be regarded as the one which takes the resource constraint into account. Thus our concept of an efficient point can include such a case. However, we also note that our interpretation of Y is rather flexible in the sense that it also allows the case in which no resource constraints are taken into account. Hence our concept of an efficient point is also flexible accordingly. If no resource constraints are taken into account in Y, then some efficient points may not be attainable in the given economy because they may be outside the range of the resource constraints.

REMARK: In activity analysis a distinction among primary, intermediate, and desired commodities is often made. The *primary commodities* are the ones which flow into production from outside the production system; the *intermediate commodities* are the ones which are produced only for use as inputs for further production; and the *desired goods* are the ones which are produced for consumption or other uses outside the production system. However, these distinctions can be arbitrary. For example, the same commodity can often be used either for final consumption or as an input for further production. Hence we do *not* emphasize these distinctions.

We now state and prove two fundamental theorems in activity analysis.

Theorem 0.C.2: *Let Y be a general production set in R^n. A point $\hat{y}$ in Y is an efficient point of Y if there exists a $p > 0$, $p \in R^n$, and $\| p \| < \infty$ such that $p \cdot \hat{y} \geq p \cdot y$ for all $y \in Y$.*

PROOF: Suppose not. Then there exists $y \in Y$ such that $y \geq \hat{y}$. Thus $p \cdot y > p \cdot \hat{y}$, since $p > 0$, which is a contradiction.   (Q.E.D.)

REMARK: The above theorem specifies nothing with respect to the postulates on Y.

In order to prove Theorem 0.C.3, we need the following lemma.

Lemma: *Let Y be a general production set in R^n. If $\hat{y}$ is an efficient point of Y, then $(Y - \hat{y}) \cap \Omega^o = \emptyset^6$, where Ω^o is the positive orthant of R^n (that is, the interior of the nonnegative orthant of R^n, Ω).*

PROOF: Suppose not. Then there exists a $z > 0$ (that is, $z \in \Omega^o$) such that $z \in (Y - \hat{y})$. Hence $z + \hat{y} \in Y$. Thus $\hat{y}$ is not an efficient point of Y, which is a contradiction.   (Q.E.D.)

Theorem 0.C.3: *Let Y be a convex production set in R^n. If $\hat{y}$ is an efficient point of Y, then there exists $p \geq 0$, $p \in R^n$, $\| p \| < \infty$ such that $p \cdot \hat{y} \geq p \cdot y$ for all $y \in Y$.*

PROOF: Let $X \equiv Y - \hat{y}$. Then X is convex as it is a linear sum of two convex sets. (See Theorem 0.A.5.) Since $\hat{y}$ is an efficient point of Y, we have $X \cap \Omega^o = \emptyset$ by the previous lemma. Thus we have two disjoint nonempty convex sets. Hence, from the Minkowski separation theorem (Theorem 0.B.3), there exists a $p \in R^n$, $p \neq 0$, $\| p \| < \infty$, and $\alpha \in R$ such that

$$p \cdot z \geq \alpha \qquad \text{for all } z \in \Omega^o$$

and

$$p \cdot x \leq \alpha \qquad \text{for all } x \in X$$

Note that $0 \in X$ for $\hat{y} \in Y$. Hence $\alpha \geq 0$. Then we have $p \geq 0$. For if not, there exists an element of p (say, p_i) which is negative, since $p \neq 0$. By choosing the corresponding element of z (say, z_i) large enough in Ω^o, we can have $p \cdot z < 0$, which is a contradiction. Also $\alpha \leq 0$, for if not, then $p \cdot z \geq \alpha > 0$ for all $z \in \Omega^o$. This is impossible, for by choosing $\| z \|$ small enough we can have $p \cdot z < \alpha$. Since $\alpha \geq 0$ and $\alpha \geq 0$, we have $\alpha = 0$. Therefore $p \cdot x \leq 0$ for all $x \in X$ with $p \geq 0$, or $p \cdot (y - \hat{y}) \leq 0$; that is, $p \cdot \hat{y} \geq p \cdot y$ for all $y \in Y$ with $p \geq 0$.   (Q.E.D.)

REMARK: Because of the homogeneity of relation $p \cdot \hat{y} \geq p \cdot y$, we may choose p so that $\sum_{i=1}^{n} p_i = 1$.

REMARK: If Y is a convex polyhedral cone in the above theorem, then it can be shown that we can choose $p > 0$.[7]

REMARK: By Theorem 0.C.3, the concept of "efficient point" is now characterized by **profit maximization**; that is, maximization of $p \cdot y$ with respect to y over Y. The existence of a solution for this maximization problem is guaranteed if, *for example*, Y is a compact set (the Weierstrass theorem), since the inner product is a continuous function.

REMARK: Suppose that Y can be characterized by linear inequalities such as:

$$\sum_{j=1}^{m} a_{ij}\lambda_j \leq r_i, \; i = 1, \ldots, n, \qquad \lambda_j \geq 0, j = 1, 2, \ldots, m$$

Then the problem of finding $\lambda \equiv (\lambda_1, \ldots, \lambda_m)$ which maximizes $p \cdot y$ *where* $y \equiv \sum_{j=1}^{m} a_{ij}\lambda_j$, subject to the above constraints is a typical linear programming problem, of which the computational method is well known and widely used in practice (the "simplex method"). Hence activity analysis also has practical and computational significance.

REMARK: It is important to realize the basic features of the neoclassical "smooth" production function approach in terms of activity analysis terminology. These are essentially the following. (1) It deals with a production set which cannot be generated from a finite number of activities (that is, it is *not* a convex polyhedral cone); rather a continuum of vectors is required to characterize the set. (2) The "efficient manager" is presupposed, so that production always takes place at an efficient point, that is, on the set of efficient points (called "production frontier"), which is nothing but the set defined by the production function. (3) This set of efficient points constitutes a differentiable function.

FOOTNOTES

1. "Services" and "factors of production" as well as ordinary "goods" are commodities.
2. Clearly y_i may be 0 for some i; $y_i = 0$ means that the ith commodity is used neither as an input nor as an output for the process y—that is, it is not involved in the production process y.
3. Given two vectors $x, y \in R^n$, the notation $x \geqq y$ means that every element of x is greater than or equal to the corresponding element of y; that is, $x_i \geqq y_i$ for all $i = 1, 2, \ldots, n$, *and* $x_i > y_i$ for at least one i. This should be distinguished from the notation $x \geq y$ which requires only the first of the above conditions, that is, $x_i \geqq y_i$ for all i. The notation $x > y$ is used to mean $x_i > y_i$ for all $i = 1, 2, \ldots, n$. The symbol Ω denotes the nonnegative orthant of R^n.
4. The sketch of the proof is as follows. By hypothesis, Y does not contain any $y \geqq 0$. Let $Y^* = \{p: p \cdot y \leqq 0 \text{ for all } y \in Y\}$ (called the **negative polar cone** of Y). We can then show that there exists $p \in Y^*$ such that $p > 0$, which completes the proof. [Suppose not. Then Y^* does not contain any interior points of Ω, the positive orthant of R^n (that is, Ω^o). Let $M \equiv \Omega^o - Y^*$; then we can show that M does not contain the origin. Moreover, M is convex because both Ω and Y^* are convex. Thus

we can have a hyperplane passing through the origin and bounding for M, as a result of the separation theorem (recall Theorems 0.B.1 and 0.B.2). Thus there exists an $\alpha \in R^n$, $\alpha \geq 0$, such that $\alpha \cdot p \leq 0$ for all $p \in Y^*$. From this we can show $\alpha \in Y$ with $\alpha \geq 0$, contradicting the hypothesis.]

5. The notation $Y \cap \Omega \subset \{0\}$ means that the intersection of Y with Ω contains *at most* 0, the origin. That is, $Y \cap \Omega$ can be an empty set, as in the case in which $0 \notin Y$. If Y is a convex polyhedral cone, then $0 \in Y$; hence (iv) is replaced by $Y \cap \Omega = \{0\}$ as in (A-4).

6. The notation $Y - \hat{y}$ denotes $Y - \{\hat{y}\} \equiv \{z : z = y - \hat{y}, y \in Y\}$.

7. The proof is not too difficult.

REFERENCES

1. Afriat, S., "Economic Transformation," *Krannert Institute Paper*, Purdue University, no. 152, November 1966.

2. Baumol, W. J., "Activity Analysis in One Lesson," *American Economic Review*, LXVIII, December 1958.

3. Debreu, G., *Theory of Value*, New York, Wiley, 1959, esp. chap. 2 and 3.

4. Dorfman, R., Samuelson, P. A., and Solow, R. M., *Linear Programming and Economic Analysis*, New York, McGraw-Hill, 1958.

5. Hicks, J. R., *Value and Capital*, 2nd ed., London, Oxford University Press, 1946.

6. Hicks, J. R., "Linear Theory," *Economic Journal*, LXV, December 1960.

7. Koopmans, T. C., ed., *Activity Analysis of Production and Allocation*, New York, Wiley, 1951, esp. chap. III (by Koopmans).

8. Koopmans, T. C., *Three Essays on the State of Economic Science*, New York, McGraw-Hill, 1957, esp. pp. 66–104.

9. Koopmans, T. C., and Bausch, A. F., "Selected Topics in Economics Involving Mathematical Reasoning," *SIAM Review*, 1, July 1959, esp. Topic 3.

10. Malinvaud, E., "Capital Accumulation and Efficient Allocation of Resources," *Econometrica*, 21, April 1953; also "Corrigendum," *Econometrica*, 30, July 1962.

11. von Neumann, J., "A Model of General Economic Equilibrium," *Review of Economic Studies*, XIII, no. 1., 1945–1946. Translation from German original published in *Ergebnisse eines mathematischen Kolloquiums*, no. 8, 1937.

12. Wicksell, K., *Lectures on Political Economy*, London, Routledge & Kegan Paul, 1936 (Swedish original, 3rd ed., 1928).

1

DEVELOPMENTS OF NONLINEAR PROGRAMMING

In many economic problems, as well as problems in science and engineering, it is often necessary to maximize or minimize a certain real-valued function, say $f(x)$, where $x \in X$, a subset of R^n, subject to certain constraints, say,

$$g_1(x) \geqq 0, g_2(x) \geqq 0, \ldots, g_m(x) \geqq 0$$

where each g_j is a real-valued function.[1] For example, in the theory of consumer choice $f(x)$ is a utility function for an individual and x is his n-commodities consumption vector. If his income is given by M, when price p prevails, a "competitive" consumer, being unable to affect the level of p, maximizes his satisfaction $f(x)$ subject to the constraints $M - p \cdot x \geqq 0$, $x \geqq 0$.

When the functions $f, g_1, g_2, \ldots, g_m$ are all linear functions, except for constant differences, the problem is known as the **linear programming** problem. For example, a country may wish to maximize the value of her national output (n-vector x), which can be measured by $p \cdot x$ (linear function) if price vector p prevails. Let a_{ij} be the amount of the jth resource necessary to produce one unit of the ith commodity and let r_j be the amount of the jth resource available in this country. Then the constraints of the problem are the linear functions,

$$r_j - a^j \cdot x \geqq 0, \quad j = 1, 2, \ldots, m \quad \text{and} \quad x \geqq 0$$

where a^j represents the vector whose ith component is a_{ij}. In this formulation we implicitly assumed that only one production process is available for each commodity, but if one wishes one can easily introduce as many processes as one likes for each industry. The problem remains a linear programming problem.

Linear programming, first formulated by the Russian mathematician Kantorovich but developed chiefly in the United States by G. Dantzig and others, is applicable to many different problems.[2] The activity analysis of production, as sketched in the preceding chapter, was no doubt influenced by linear programming. There is perhaps little doubt that interest in linear programming was prompted, at least in its earlier stage, by the invention of the computational algorithm known as the "simplex method."

The development of linear programming also prompted the study of the optimization problem when the f and g_j's are not necessarily linear. We now see that the theoretical apparatus[3] which was developed in connection with linear programming can be used in or extended to the problem of nonlinear programming.[4] The simplex method also encouraged study of algorithms for certain nonlinear (notably quadratic) programming problems. In this study we are not concerned with algorithms as such; rather we are concerned with the theoretical structure of the nonlinear programming problem and with its connection to modern economic theory. The crucial paper in the development of nonlinear programming is Kuhn and Tucker [3].[5]

We may now explain the problem we are going to deal with in this chapter. A functional relation $g_j(x) = 0$, whether it is linear or nonlinear, may define a surface (or curve) on x-space (or plane). Suppose that it divides the space R^n into two regions, the region where $g_j(x) \geq 0$ and the region where $g_j(x) \leq 0$. The surface of $g_j(x) = 0$ serves as the common boundary of these two regions. In Figure 1.1, $g_j(x) \equiv 1 - x_1 - x_2 = 0$ defines a straight line on the x-plane and divides R^2 into two regions. In the region which contains the origin (the shaded region), we can easily show that $1 - x_1 - x_2 \geq 0$, and in the other region we have $1 - x_1 - x_2 \leq 0$.

In Figure 1.2, the shaded region satisfies the four functional relations, $g_1(x) \geq 0, g_2(x) \geq 0, g_3(x) \geq 0$, and $x \geq 0$ on R^2. It may happen that a set of functional relations is **inconsistent** in the sense that it does not allow any x which satisfies all the relations. Mathematically, we may express this by saying that the set $C \equiv \{x : x \in X, g_j(x) \geq 0, j = 1, 2, \ldots, m\}$ is empty. For example, $g_1(x) \equiv 1 - x_1 - x_2 \geq 0$ and $g_2(x) \equiv x_1 + x_2 - 2 \geq 0$ do not allow any (x_1, x_2) which *satisfies* these two relations simultaneously, even if $X = R^2$, the entire space.

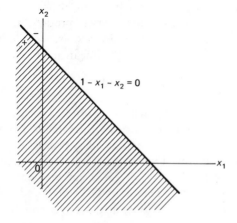

Figure 1.1. The Division of the Space.

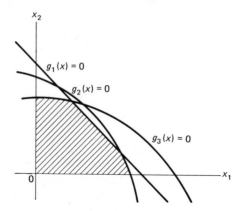

Figure 1.2. The Constraint Set.

Hence the nonlinear programming problem of maximizing $f(x)$ subject to $g_j(x) \geq 0$, $j = 1, 2, \ldots, m$, can be considered as one of choosing the x which maximizes $f(x)$ over the nonempty set C. The set C is called the **constraint set** or the **feasible set**.[6] The following two diagrams (Case a and Case b of Figure 1.3) illustrate the problem. Case a is concerned with the case in which $f(x)$ and the $g_j(x)$'s are all linear or linear affine (the problem of linear programming), and Case b is concerned with the case in which these functions are nonlinear. The optimum point[7] is denoted by $\hat{x}$, where in both cases $X = R^2$.

Note that in both Cases in Figure 1.3 the optimum point $\hat{x}$ is strictly inside the region of the constraints, $g_3(x) \geq 0$ and $g_4(x) \geq 0$. We say that these constraints

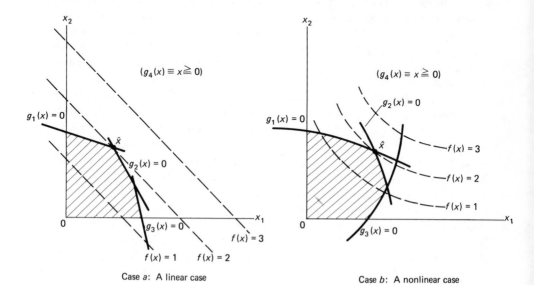

Case a: A linear case

Case b: A nonlinear case

Figure 1.3. The Optimal Point.

are **inactive** (or **ineffective**) at $\hat{x}$. The constraints $g_1(x) \geq 0$ and $g_2(x) \geq 0$ are **active** (or **effective**) at $\hat{x}$ in both Case a and Case b of Figure 1.3 in the sense that $g_1(\hat{x}) = 0$ and $g_2(\hat{x}) = 0$. Note also that the boundary surfaces of the constraint sets (the shaded areas of Case a and Case b of Figure 1.3) do not allow derivatives at $\hat{x}$ (that is, the boundary curve is not "differentiable" at $\hat{x}$). In economics, one of the constraints is often the **nonnegativity constraint**, such as $x \geq 0$, since economic variables such as price and output are usually nonnegative. And, if $\hat{x}$ is a solution of the problem, we typically have a situation such that $\hat{x} > 0$; that is, the constraint $x \geq 0$ is ineffective at $\hat{x}$.

In the classical maximization problem due to Lagrange and Euler, we are concerned with the case in which all the constraints are always effective [that is, the problem is the one of maximizing $f(x)$ subject to $g_j(x) = 0, j = 1, 2, \ldots, m$]. Although this form of constraint is often very inconvenient in dealing with economic problems, it is also true that there are situations in which we know that the constraints are always effective. For example, one of the constraints may be a definitional equation, which is not an inequality. Can we then handle the problem with equality constraints within the above formulation of the nonlinear programming problem? The answer is simply yes, for we can rewrite an equality constraint[8]

$$g_j(x) = 0$$

as

$$g_j(x) \geq 0 \quad \textit{and} \quad -g_j(x) \geq 0$$

The solution $\hat{x}$ as defined above maximizes $f(x)$ subject to $g_j(x) \geq 0, j = 1, 2, \ldots, m$, over the *entire* domain of f, that is, X. In this sense, it is often said that $\hat{x}$ achieves a **global maximum**. In the traditional Lagrange-Euler formulation, we are also concerned with a local maximum. The point $\hat{x}$ is said to achieve a **local maximum** of $f(x)$ subject to $g_j(x) \geq 0, j = 1, 2, \ldots, m$, and $x \in X$, if there exists an open ball B about $\hat{x}$ (which may be very small) intersecting with the constraint set C (that is, $B \cap C \neq \emptyset$) such that $f(\hat{x}) \geq f(x)$ subject to $g_j(x) \geq 0, j = 1, 2, \ldots, m$, and $x \in X \cap B$ (that is, $f(\hat{x}) \geq f(x)$ for all x in $B \cap C$). We will introduce these concepts in a proper context. We may note that the concept of *local* maximum or minimum, being concerned with a (small) neighborhood, is closely associated with calculus. When we treat the problem by means other than calculus, it is not necessarily the case that we restrict ourselves to the local concept of optimization. Moreover, the calculus approach obviously presupposes the differentiability of certain functions. This is often considered too restrictive.

Given the problem of maximizing (or minimizing) a certain real-valued function $f(x)$, where x is an n-vector, subject to the constraints of m real-valued functions $g_1(x) \geq 0, g_2(x) \geq 0, \ldots, g_m(x) \geq 0$, and $x \in X$, there is no guarantee that a solution $\hat{x}$ exists for this problem. First, as remarked above, the set $C \equiv \{x: x \in X, g_j(x) \geq 0, j = 1, 2, \ldots, m\}$ may be empty, in which case it is clear that the solution for this problem does not exist. Even if the constraint set is nonempty, we may still have a situation in which the solution does not exist.

For example, consider the problem of maximizing $f(x) = x$, $x \in R$, over the constraint set $C = (0, 1)$, the unit open interval on R. Again the solution does not exist. What, then, are the conditions which guarantee the existence of a solution of the above problem? One powerful condition is obtained by utilizing the Weierstrass theorem which asserts the existence of a maximum (and minimum) of a continuous function over a compact set (Theorem 0.A.18). In regard to our present problem, this means that if the maximand function is continuous and the constraint set C is compact, then, from the Weierstrass theorem, we can assert that there exists a solution for the present nonlinear programming problem.

In the above formulation of the nonlinear programming problem we confined ourselves to the real space R^n or some subset X. However, we can extend the analysis to the case in which X is a subset of some linear space—say, L—with a certain topological structure defined so that we can talk about such things as continuous functions. In particular, we may be concerned with the problem of choosing a certain function $x(t)$ from a certain set of functions X. The set of functions often constitutes a linear space so that we may be able to regard X as a subset of a certain linear space. For example, consider a consumer who wants to maximize the sum of the utility stream $u[x(t)]$ attained by the consumption stream $x(t)$ over his lifetime. Suppose that he knows his income at time t, $y(t)$, and the commodity-price vector at time t, $p(t)$, for all t in the span of his lifetime. Let ρ and r respectively denote his subjective discount rate and the market rate of interest, both of which are assumed to be positive constants. Assume that this consumer is "small" enough so that his choice of $x(t)$ does not affect the $p(t)$ and r that prevail in the market. Then the problem may be formulated as follows:

Maximize: $I[x(t)] \equiv \int_0^T u[x(t)] e^{-\rho t} dt$

Subject to: $g[x(t)] \equiv \int_0^T p(t) \cdot x(t) e^{-rt} dt \leqq M$

and $x(t) \geqq 0$, $t \in [0, T]$, where $M \equiv \int_0^T y(t) e^{-rt} dt$

This integral constraint contains the assumption that the consumer can borrow or lend any amount at the fixed rate of interest r. In any case, this is a problem of choosing a function $x(t)$ from a set of (say, continuous) functions, X, defined over the interval $[0, T]$ such as to maximize a real-valued function $I[x(t)]$ subject to the constraints $g[x(t)] \leqq M$ and $x(t) \geqq 0$. This is clearly similar, at least formally, to the problem discussed above. In fact, there has been a considerable effort recently to consider this kind of problem as a natural extension of nonlinear programming theory to problems in linear spaces (not necessarily R^n).[9] However, in this chapter we restrict ourselves to R^n or its subset X, as formulated above. In this way we can treat the theory in a much simpler manner. We discuss the question of programming in a linear space later in the book when we discuss such topics as the calculus of variations and optimal control theory.[10]

Now let us come back to the usual nonlinear programming problem, that is, the one of maximizing $f(x)$ subject to $g_j(x) \geq 0, j = 1, 2, \ldots, m$, and $x \in X$, where X is a subset of R^n, or in other words, maximizing $f(x)$ subject to $x \in C \equiv \{x: x \in X, g_j(x) \geq 0, j = 1, 2, \ldots, m\}$. The following questions are the natural questions involved in any nonlinear programming problem.

QUESTION 1: Is the set C nonempty; that is, does there exist a **feasible point**?

QUESTION 2: Does there exist a *solution* $\hat{x}$, a point which maximizes $f(x)$ subject to $x \in C$?

QUESTION 3: What are the characteristics of this optimum $\hat{x}$?

QUESTION 4: Is the solution $\hat{x}$ unique, or is there any other solution besides $\hat{x}$?

QUESTION 5: What is the algorithm to find all the solutions?

Because this is a book dealing primarily with economic theory, we are not interested in Question 5. Much work is being done on the problem of finding algorithms, but no definite methods have yet been found, except in some special cases.[11] Readers are referred to articles in professional journals.

Owing to our interest in theory, we pay greatest attention here to Question 3,[12] discussing, in particular, the "saddle-point characterization" and the "quasi-saddle-point characterization." Question 3 should also be of central concern to those interested in algorithms.

In Section B, we discuss the problem posed when the functions f and g_j belong to a certain class of functions, called "concave" (or "convex") functions. We do not assume differentiability of these functions, and global results are obtained. The central characterization of optimality is that of a "saddle point." In Section C we remind the reader of certain basic facts, such as the definition of differentiability and the unconstrained maximum problem. This section will prepare the way for Section D, in which we study problems where we can assume the differentiability of f and the g_j's. The basic characterization for optimality under such an assumption is well known and is called the first-order condition (or "quasi-saddle-point condition"). The central theorems are Kuhn and Tucker's main theorem and the Arrow-Hurwicz-Uzawa theorem. In the Appendix to Section D, we sketch the proof of the Arrow-Hurwicz-Uzawa theorem. In Section E, we extend the nonlinear programming theory established thus far. In particular, we discuss (1) quasi-concave programming, (2) the vector maximum problem, and (3) the characterization of concave (or quasi-concave) functions and the second-order conditions. In Section F we illustrate economic applications of the theory established in this chapter.[13] In the Appendix to Section F, we summarize the classical theory of optimization and its standard applications to comparative statics analysis. The reader may find this appendix a useful review.

FOOTNOTES

1. The maximization problem is equivalent to the minimization problem, for one can easily convert one to the other. For example, if this problem is taken to be one of minimizing $f(x)$, subject to a certain set of constraints, it can be converted to one of maximizing $[-f(x)]$, subject to the same set of constraints.

2. To name just a few, we have the transportation problem, the production scheduling problem, the diet problem, the gasoline mixing problem, and the allocation problem.

3. For the theoretical apparatus developed in linear programming and its applications to economic theory, see, for example, H. W. Kuhn and A. W. Tucker, eds., *Linear Inequalities and Related Systems*, Princeton University Press, 1956.

4. The term *non*linear programming is a little confusing. It customarily includes linear programming as a special case.

5. Linear programming aroused interest in constraints in the form of inequalities and in the theory of linear inequalities and convex sets. The Kuhn-Tucker study [3] appeared in the middle of this interest with a full recognition of such developments. However, the theory of nonlinear programming when the constraints are all in the form of equalities has been well known for a long time—in fact, since Euler and Lagrange. The inequality constraints were treated in a fairly satisfactory manner already in 1939 by Karush [2]. Karush's work is apparently under the influence of a similar work in the calculus of variations by Valentine. Unfortunately, Karush's work has been largely ignored more or less.

6. The function $f(x)$ is called the **maximand function** or the **objective function**.

7. The point $\hat{x}$ is also called **a maximum point, a solution, an optimal solution,** and **an optimal program**.

8. See Section D of this chapter, for example.

9. For a pioneering work in this direction, see Hurwicz [1]. Programming in linear spaces would presumably include such topics as the calculus of variations and optimal control theory. The reverse approach—that is, treating the usual nonlinear programming as a special case of optimal control theory—is also possible. This has been recently investigated, especially after the interest aroused in the variational approach by Pontryagin *et al.*, Hestenes, and so on. See, for example, M. Canon, C. Cullum, and E. Polak, "Constrained Maximization Problem in Finite-Dimensional Spaces," *Journal of SIAM Control*, vol. 4, no. 3, August 1966.

10. The dynamic optimum consumption problem as stated above has recently been treated in a more sophisticated manner by M. El-Hodiri, M. Yaari, A. Douglas, K. Avio, and so on, by using the calculus of variations and optimal control theory. See, for example, K. Avio, "Age-dependent Utility in the Lifetime Allocation Problem," *Krannert Institute Paper*, Purdue University, no. 260, November 1969, for this problem and the references. See also Chapter 8, Section C. Note also that the dynamic consumption problem can also be treated by using the usual nonlinear programming technique.

11. This does not imply, of course, that the scope of available algorithms is very limited. On the contrary, thanks to electronic computers we are able to handle a sufficiently large number of practical problems.

12. Moreover, we will not treat such topics as integer programming, stochastic programming, and the like, as such.

13. Although this chapter was written prior to and independently of Mangasarian [4], the reader may benefit from reading this excellent treatise on nonlinear programming along with this chapter.

REFERENCES

1. Hurwicz, L., "Programming in Linear Spaces," in *Studies in Linear and Nonlinear Programming*, ed. by K. J. Arrow, L. Hurwicz, and H. Uzawa, Stanford, Calif., Stanford University Press, 1958.
2. Karush, W., *Minima of Functions of Several Variables with Inequalities as Side Conditions*, Master's Thesis, University of Chicago, 1939.
3. Kuhn, H. W., and Tucker, A. W., "Nonlinear Programming," *Proceedings of Second Berkeley Symposium on Mathematical Statistics and Probability*, ed. by J. Neymann, Berkeley, Calif., University of California Press, 1951, pp. 481–492.
4. Mangasarian, O. L., *Nonlinear Programming*, New York, McGraw-Hill, 1969.

Section B

CONCAVE PROGRAMMING— SADDLE-POINT CHARACTERIZATION

In this section we discuss one important characterization of the solution of the nonlinear programming problem: the **saddle-point characterization**. A major feature in this characterization is that we need no assumptions with regard to the differentiability of any functions involved, and hence we do not have to talk about differentiation here.

Definition: Let $\Phi(x, y)$ be a real-valued function defined on $X \otimes Y$ where $x \in X$ and $y \in Y$. A point $(\hat{x}, \hat{y})$ in $X \otimes Y$ is called a **saddle point** of $\Phi(x, y)$ if

$$\Phi(x, \hat{y}) \leq \Phi(\hat{x}, \hat{y}) \leq \Phi(\hat{x}, y) \text{ for all } x \in X \text{ and } y \in Y$$

REMARK: Clearly a saddle point may never exist, and even if it exists, it is not necessarily unique. Note that, for a fixed value $\hat{y}$, $\hat{x}$ achieves the maximum of $\Phi(x, \hat{y})$ and that, for a fixed value $\hat{x}$, $\hat{y}$ achieves the minimum of $\Phi(\hat{x}, y)$. In other words, $\Phi(\hat{x}, \hat{y}) = \max_{x \in X} \Phi(x, \hat{y})$ and $\Phi(\hat{x}, \hat{y}) = \min_{y \in Y} \Phi(\hat{x}, y)$. Intuitively, this could produce a picture like a horse saddle, as illustrated in Figure 1.4. We should note, however, that there is a common misconception that a saddle point always looks similar to such a saddle. Nikaido [11], pp. 142–143, gave the following example of a saddle point, which does not look like a saddle.

EXAMPLE: $\Phi(x, y) \equiv 1 - x + y, 0 \leq x \leq 1, 0 \leq y \leq 1$.
Point $(0, 0)$ is a saddle point of $\Phi(x, y)$. As can be seen from Figure 1.5, Φ does not look like a saddle.

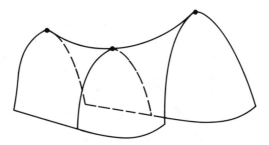

Figure 1.4.   An Illustration of a Saddle Point.

Definition: Let f be a real-valued function defined on a convex set X in R^n. The function f is called a **concave function** if, for all $x, y \in X$, and $0 \leqq \theta \leqq 1$,

$$f[\theta x + (1 - \theta)y] \geqq \theta f(x) + (1 - \theta)f(y)$$

If the inequalities in the above definition are strict for all $x, y \in X$ with $x \neq y$, and $0 < \theta < 1$, that is, if $f[\theta x + (1 - \theta)y] > \theta f(x) + (1 - \theta)f(y)$, for all $\theta, 0 < \theta < 1$, and for all $x, y \in X$ with $x \neq y$, then f is called a **strictly concave function**. On the other hand, f is called a **convex** (resp. **strictly convex**) function if $(-f)$ is concave (resp. strictly concave).

> *REMARK*:   A (strictly) concave function is illustrated in Figure. 1.6 (where $X = R$). Needless to say, every strictly concave function is concave (and every strictly convex function is convex).

> *REMARK*:   Intuitively, f is a concave function if the chord joining any two points on the function lies on or below the function. The set X must be convex; otherwise $\theta x + (1 - \theta)y$ may not be in X, so that the LHS of the in-

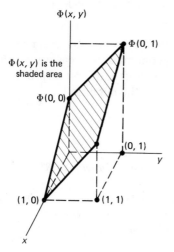

Figure 1.5.   Nonsaddle-like Saddle Point.

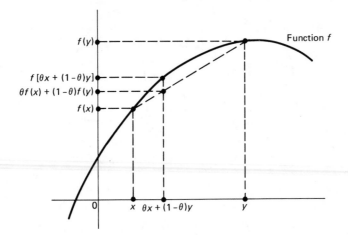

Figure 1.6. An Illustration of a Concave Function.

equality may be meaningless. Henceforth X is automatically taken to be a convex set if it is a domain of a concave function.

REMARK: If, in particular, f can be written as $f(x) = a \cdot x + a_0$ where a is a constant vector in R^n and a_0 is a constant real number,[1] then f is *both* concave and convex, but neither strictly concave nor strictly convex. Clearly there are many real-valued functions that are neither concave nor convex (hence certainly neither strictly concave nor strictly convex).

REMARK: Note that the concept of concave (or convex) functions is a global concept in the sense that the defining property is concerned with all the points of the domain. Note also that the above definition still holds even if we replace R^n by any linear space.[2]

The class of concave functions (and convex functions) probably forms the most important class of functions in economics, for reasons which will become clear in reading this book. We now list some of the important properties of concave functions, which follow immediately from the definition.

Theorem 1.B.1

(i) *Let f be a concave function on a convex subset X of R^n. Then $S \equiv \{x: x \in X, f(x) \geq 0\}$ is a convex set.*

(ii) *A nonnegative linear combination of concave functions is also concave. In other words, if $f_i(x)$, $i = 1, 2, \ldots m$, are concave functions on a convex subset X of R^n, then $f(x) \equiv \sum_{i=1}^{m} \alpha_i f_i(x)$, where $\alpha_i \in R$, $\alpha_i \geq 0$, $i = 1, 2, \ldots, m$, is also a concave function on X.*

(iii) *Every concave function is continuous in the interior of the domain of the function.*[3]

PROOF:

    (i)   Let $x, y \in S \subset X$. Then $f(x) \geq 0$ and $f(y) \geq 0$. Also $\theta x + (1 - \theta) y \in X$, for $0 \leq \theta \leq 1$, since X is convex. Using the concavity of f, we have

$$f[\theta x + (1 - \theta)y] \geq \theta f(x) + (1 - \theta)f(y) \geq 0 \quad \text{for} \quad 0 \leq \theta \leq 1$$

Hence $[\theta x + (1 - \theta)y]$ must also be in S.

    (ii) Let $x, y \in X$. Then $\theta x + (1 - \theta)y \in X$, for $0 \leq \theta \leq 1$, due to the convexity of X. Using the concavity of the f_i's, we obtain

$$f[\theta x + (1 - \theta)y] = \sum_{i=1}^{m} \alpha_i f_i [\theta x + (1 - \theta)y]$$

$$\geq \sum_{i=1}^{m} \alpha_i [\theta f_i(x) + (1 - \theta)f_i(y)] = \theta \sum_{i=1}^{m} \alpha_i f_i(x) + (1 - \theta) \sum_{i=1}^{m} \alpha_i f_i(y)$$

$$= \theta f(x) + (1 - \theta)f(y) \quad \text{for} \quad 0 \leq \theta \leq 1$$

Hence f is also a concave function.

   (iii) Proof is omitted. It is an easy exercise which follows in a straightforward way from the definitions of continuity and concavity. For this proof, the reader may refer to Fenchel [3], pp. 75–76; Berge [1], pp. 193–194; or Fleming [4], pp. 26–27.   (Q.E.D.)

REMARK: Let $f(x)$ be a real-valued function on a convex subset X of R^n; then the following can be shown:

    (i)   *If f is concave, then the set $\{x:x \in X, f(x) \geq \alpha\}$ (for each $\alpha \in R$) is convex in R^n.* [For the proof, simply observe (i) and (ii) of Theorem 1.B.1.]

    (ii) *The function f is concave if and only if the set $\{(x, \alpha):x \in X, \alpha \in R, f(x) \geq \alpha\}$ is convex in R^{n+1}.* [The proof follows directly from the definitions.]

   (iii) *The function f is concave if and only if, for each integer $m \geq 1$,*

$$f(\theta_1 x^1 + \theta_2 x^2 + \cdots + \theta_m x^m) \geq \theta_1 f(x^1) + \theta_2 f(x^2) + \cdots + \theta_m f(x^m)$$

for all $x^j \in X$, $\theta_j \in R$, $\theta_j \geq 0$, $j = 1, 2, \ldots, m$, with $\sum_{j=1}^{m} \theta_j = 1$. [For the proof use (ii) above.]

   (iv) *If $f_i(x)$, $i = 1, 2, \ldots, k$, are concave functions on X which are bounded from below, then $f(x) \equiv \inf_i f_i(x)$ is also concave.* [For the proof, use (ii) above.]

    The converse of (i) of the above remark is *not* necessarily true. A weaker property than the concavity of f will suffice to guarantee the convexity of the set (later we discuss it as the quasi-concavity of a function). The set $\{x: x \in X, f(x) \geq \alpha\}$ is often called the **upper contour set** (see Figure 1.7). [In the theory of consumer demand, f is a utility function and the set $\{x: x \in X, f(x) = \alpha\}$ is often called an **indifference curve.**]

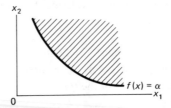

x_2

$f(x) = \alpha$

x_1

0

Figure 1.7.   Upper Contour Set.

REMARK: Let $g_j, j = 1, 2, \ldots, m$, be concave functions on X in R^n. Let $C \equiv \{x: x \in X, g_j(x) \geq 0, j = 1, 2, \ldots, m\}$ (the constraint set). Then C is a convex set since it is an intersection of the convex sets $C_j \equiv \{x: x \in X, g_j(x) \geq 0\}$ (that is, $C = \cap_{j=1}^{m} C_j$).

We now prove the fundamental theorem of concave functions from which many of the important implications of concave functions can be proved.

Theorem 1.B.2 (Fundamental Theorem):   *Let X be a convex set in R^n and let $f_1, f_2, \ldots, f_m$ be real-valued concave functions defined on X. If the system*

$$f_i(x) > 0, \; i = 1, 2, \ldots, m$$

admits no solution x in X, then there exist coefficients $p_1, p_2, \ldots, p_m$, all $p_i \geq 0$ (not vanishing simultaneously) and $p_i \in R, \; i = 1, 2, \ldots, m$, such that

$$\sum_{i=1}^{m} p_i f_i(x) \leq 0 \qquad \text{for all } x \in X$$

If we wish, we may choose p_i such that $\sum_{i=1}^{m} p_i = 1$.

PROOF: Given a point x in X, define a set Z_x by

$$Z_x \equiv \{(z_1, z_2, \ldots, z_i, \ldots, z_m) \in R^m: z_i < f_i(x), \; i = 1, 2, \ldots, m\}$$

Then consider a set Z defined by

$$Z \equiv \bigcup_{x \in X} Z_x$$

Set Z is illustrated by Figure 1.8. By assumption, Z does not contain the origin [∵ if it does, $0 \in Z_x$ for some Z_x, or $0 < f_i(x)$ for all i and for some x, which is a contradiction]. Also Z is convex, since if $z \in Z_x$ and $z' \in Z_{x'}$ and $\theta \in R$ such that $0 \leq \theta \leq 1$, then

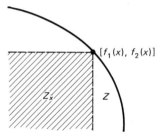

Figure 1.8.   Illustration of Set Z.

$$\theta z_i + (1 - \theta)z'_i < \theta f_i(x) + (1 - \theta)f_i(x') \leq f_i\left[\theta x + (1 - \theta)x'\right]$$
$$\text{for } i = 1, 2, \ldots, m,$$

and so $\theta z + (1 - \theta)z' \in Z_{[\theta x + (1 - \theta)x']} \subset Z\left[\because \theta x + (1 - \theta)x' \in X \text{ since } X\right.$ is convex]. Thus we have a convex set which is disjoint from a point, that is, the origin. Hence, owing to Theorem 0.B.2 (or Theorem 0.B.3), there exists a $\tilde{p} \neq 0$ such that

$$\tilde{p} \cdot z \geq \tilde{p} \cdot 0 = 0 \qquad \text{for all } z \in Z$$

Since z_i can take any absolutely large negative value, $\tilde{p} \leq 0$. Write $p \equiv -\tilde{p}$. Then

$$p \cdot z \leq 0 \qquad \text{for all } z \in Z$$

where $p \geq 0$. An arbitrary point $z \in Z$ can be expressed by $z_i = f_i(x) - \epsilon_i$ for some x and some $\epsilon_i > 0$. By varying x in X and $\epsilon_i > 0$, we can obtain all points $z \in Z$. Hence we obtain $\sum_{i=1}^{m} p_i[f_i(x) - \epsilon_i] \leq 0$ for all $x \in X$ and all $\epsilon_i > 0$ $(i = 1, 2, \ldots, m)$. In other words, $\sum_{i=1}^{m} p_i f_i(x) \leq \epsilon$ for all $x \in X$ and all $\epsilon > 0$, where $\epsilon \equiv \sum_{i=1}^{m} p_i \epsilon_i$. Since this relation holds for all $\epsilon > 0$, we have $\sum_{i=1}^{m} p_i f_i(x) \leq 0$ for all $x \in X$, as required. We can suppose that $\sum_{i=1}^{m} p_i = 1$ by dividing each p_i by the number $p_1 + p_2 + \cdots + p_m > 0$.   (Q.E.D.)

REMARK: Theorem 1.B.2 is essentially due to K. Fan, I. Glicksberg, and A. J. Hoffman, "Systems of Inequalities Involving Convex Functions," *American Mathematical Society Proceedings*, 8, 1957. See also Berge [1], pp. 201–202, and Berge and Ghouila-Houri [2], pp. 62–64.

REMARK: In the case where $m > n + 1$, we can take all but $(n + 1)$ of the numbers $p_1, p_2, \ldots, p_m$ to be zero. For the proof of this statement (which requires "Helly's theorem"), see Berge and Ghouila-Houri [2], p. 64. For the exposition of Helly's theorem, see, for example, [1], pp. 165–166; and [2], p. 62. The following corollary follows immediately.

Corollary: *Let X be a convex set in R^n and let $f_1, f_2, \ldots, f_m$ be real-valued convex functions. Then either the system $f_i(x) < 0, i = 1, 2, \ldots, m$, admits a solution $x \in X$,* *or there exist p_1, p_2, ..., p_m, all ≥ 0 and not vanishing simultaneously, such that $\sum_{i=1}^{m} p_i f_i(x) \geq 0$ for all $x \in X$.[4] If we wish, we may choose the p_i's such that $\sum_{i=1}^{m} p_i = 1$.*

REMARK: There are several important applications of this fundamental theorem. Berge and Ghouila-Houri ([2], pp. 64–68) proved, for example, the theorem due to Bohnenblust, Karlin, and Shapley, the von Neumann minimax theorem, and a generalized Minkowski-Farkas lemma as applications of this theorem.

We now prove the major theorem of this section, which is again a corollary of Theorem 1.B.2.

Theorem 1.B.3 (Kuhn-Tucker, Uzawa):   *Let f, g_1, g_2, ..., g_m be real-valued concave functions defined on a convex set X in R^n. Suppose that $\hat{x}$ achieves a maximum of $f(x)$ on X subject to $g_j(x) \geq 0, j = 1, 2, \ldots m, x \in X$. Then there exist coefficients $\hat{p}_0, \hat{p}_1, \hat{p}_2, \ldots, \hat{p}_m$, all ≥ 0, not all equal to zero, such that*

$$\hat{p}_0 f(x) + \hat{p} \cdot g(x) \leq \hat{p}_0 f(\hat{x}) \quad \text{for all } x \in X$$

where $\hat{p} = (\hat{p}_1, \hat{p}_2, \ldots, \hat{p}_m)$ and $g(x)$ is the m-vector whose jth component is $g_j(x)$.

Also, $\hat{p} \cdot g(\hat{x}) = 0$. If one wishes, $\hat{p}_j$ may be chosen such that $\sum_{j=0}^{m} \hat{p}_j = 1$.

PROOF: By hypothesis, the system

$$g_j(x) \geq 0, j = 1, 2, \ldots, m$$
$$f(x) - f(\hat{x}) > 0$$

has no solution in X. Hence, *a fortiori*, the system

$$g_j(x) > 0, j = 1, 2, \cdots, m$$
$$f(x) - f(\hat{x}) > 0$$

has no solution in X. Thus, by the fundamental theorem, there exist coefficients $\hat{p}_0, \hat{p}_1, \hat{p}_2, \ldots, \hat{p}_m$, all ≥ 0, not all equal to zero, which can be chosen with $\sum_{j=0}^{m} \hat{p}_j = 1$ such that

$$\hat{p}_0 [f(x) - f(\hat{x})] + \sum_{j=1}^{m} \hat{p}_j g_j(x) \leq 0, \quad \text{for all } x \in X$$

or

$$\hat{p}_0 f(x) + \hat{p} \cdot g(x) \leq \hat{p}_0 f(\hat{x}), \quad \text{for all } x \in X, \quad \text{where} \quad \hat{p} = (\hat{p}_1, \hat{p}_2, \ldots, \hat{p}_m)$$

To show $\hat{p} \cdot g(\hat{x}) = 0$, set $x = \hat{x}$ in the above inequality. Then we obtain $\hat{p} \cdot g(\hat{x}) \leq 0$. But $\hat{p} \geq 0$ and $g(\hat{x}) \geq 0$ so that $\hat{p} \cdot g(\hat{x}) \geq 0$. Therefore we have $\hat{p} \cdot g(\hat{x}) = 0$.   (Q.E.D.)

We now state and prove the immediate corollary of the above theorem. The above theorem is better known in the form of the following corollary.

Corollary:[5]   *Suppose that the following additional condition is satisfied for Theorem 1.B.3.*[6]

(S)   *There exists an $\bar{x}$ in X such that $g_j(\bar{x}) > 0, j = 1, 2, \ldots, m$.*

Then we have $\hat{p}_0 > 0$. Hence under the assumptions of the theorem together with condition (S), there exist coefficients, $\hat{\lambda}_1, \hat{\lambda}_2, \ldots, \hat{\lambda}_m$, all ≥ 0, such that

(SP) $\Phi(x, \hat{\lambda}) \leq \Phi(\hat{x}, \hat{\lambda}) \leq \Phi(\hat{x}, \lambda)$, *for all $x \in X$ and all $\lambda \geq 0$, where $\Phi(x, \lambda) \equiv f(x) + \lambda \cdot g(x)$, and $\lambda \equiv (\lambda_1, \lambda_2, \ldots, \lambda_m)$.*

In other words, $(\hat{x}, \hat{\lambda})$ is a saddle point of $\Phi(x, \lambda)$ on $X \otimes \Omega^m$ where Ω^m is the nonnegative orthant of R^m.

PROOF: Suppose $\hat{p}_0 \ngtr 0$. Then $\hat{p}_0 = 0$ and $\hat{p} \geq 0$. Hence by the above theorem we have

$$\hat{p} \cdot g(x) \leq 0 \text{ for all } x \in X$$

In particular, $\hat{p} \cdot g(\bar{x}) \leq 0$. Since $\hat{p} \geq 0$, this contradicts the above condition (S). Therefore, we must have $\hat{p}_0 > 0$. Write $\lambda_j \equiv \hat{p}_j/\hat{p}_0, j = 1, 2, \ldots, m$. Then the first part of the above relation (SP) follows immediately from the statement of the theorem. The second part of (SP) also follows immediately from $\hat{\lambda} \cdot g(\hat{x}) = 0, g(\hat{x}) \geq 0$ and $\lambda \geq 0$.   (Q.E.D.)

REMARK: The above condition (S) is known as **Slater's condition**[7] (see Slater [12]). Slater's condition (S) can be replaced by the following condition (K).

(K)   For any $p \geq 0$, there exists an $\bar{x}$ in X such that $p \cdot g(\bar{x}) > 0$.

This condition is known as **Karlin's condition**, for it is due to Karlin ([7], p. 201). It can easily be shown that condition (S) and condition (K) are, in fact, equivalent.[8] In any case, condition (S) or condition (K) guarantees a strictly positive $\hat{p}_0$ in the statement of Theorem 1.B.3. Such a condition is often called the **normality condition**.

REMARK: In the original paper by Kuhn and Tucker [8], the need for a normality condition such as Slater's condition is not explicitly stated. It was hidden in a condition called the **Kuhn-Tucker constraint qualification**, which we take up in Section D. The first really elegant proof of the above theorem using Slater's condition (and without relying on the Kuhn-Tucker constraint qualification and the differentiability of the g_j's) is provided by Uzawa [13]. Uzawa's proof does not utilize the fundamental theorem (that is, Theorem 1.B.1); rather, it directly utilizes the separation theorem. The present proof is a slight modification of the proof by Berge [1], which is essentially similar to the one by Uzawa. We may note that our theorem is slightly more general than Uzawa's, for we do not assume the set X to be the nonnegative orthant, Ω^n. Also note that Uzawa's proof essentially amounts to re-proving the above fundamental theorem which is originally due to Fan, Glicksberg, and Hoffman.

REMARK: If Slater's condition (S) is not satisfied, then the conclusion of the above corollary does not necessarily follow. Consider the problem of maximizing $f(x) = x$ on $x \in R$, subject to $g(x) = -x^2 \geq 0$. Clearly, $\hat{x} = 0$ is the solution of this constrained maximization problem. However, it can be shown easily that the point $(0, \hat{\lambda})$ cannot be a saddle point of $\Phi(x, \lambda) \equiv f(x) + \lambda g(x)$ for any nonnegative $\hat{\lambda}$. (Notice that $\partial \Phi / \partial x$ evaluated at $\hat{x} = 0$ is positive for any value of $\hat{\lambda}$.)[9]

REMARK: The function $\Phi(x, \lambda) \equiv f(x) + \lambda \cdot g(x)$ [or, but much less often, $p_0 \cdot f(x) + p \cdot g(x)$] defined on $X \otimes \Omega^m$ is called the **Lagrangian function** or simply the **Lagrangian** of the above nonlinear programming problem. The above characterization (SP) of the solution of the problem in terms of the saddle point of the Lagrangian function Φ is called the **saddle-point characterization**. Any nonlinear programming problem with both concave objective and constraint functions (that is, the f and the g_j's) is called a **concave programming problem**.

We now prove the converse of the above corollary.

Theorem 1.B.4: *Let $f, g_1, g_2, \ldots, g_m$ be real-valued functions defined over X in R^n. If there exists a point $(\hat{x}, \hat{\lambda})$ in $X \otimes \Omega^m$ such that*

$$\Phi(x, \hat{\lambda}) \leq \Phi(\hat{x}, \hat{\lambda}) \leq \Phi(\hat{x}, \lambda) \quad \textit{for all } x \in X \textit{ and all } \lambda \in \Omega^m$$

where $\Phi(x, \lambda) \equiv f(x) + \lambda \cdot g(x)$, then

(i) *The point $\hat{x}$ maximizes $f(x)$ subject to $g_j(x) \geq 0, j = 1, 2, \ldots, m$, and $x \in X$.*

(ii) *$\hat{\lambda} \cdot g(\hat{x}) = 0$.*

PROOF: The inequality $\Phi(\hat{x}, \hat{\lambda}) \leq \Phi(\hat{x}, \lambda)$ for all $\lambda \in \Omega^m$ implies that $\hat{\lambda} \cdot g(\hat{x}) \leq \lambda \cdot g(\hat{x})$ for all $\lambda \in \Omega^m$. Thus $\lambda \cdot g(\hat{x})$ is bounded from below for all $\lambda \in \Omega^m$, and Ω^m is a convex cone. Therefore, we have $\lambda \cdot g(\hat{x}) \geq 0$ for all $\lambda \geq 0$. (Recall the lemma immediately preceeding Theorem 0.B.4.) Thus $g_j(\hat{x}) \geq 0, j = 1, 2, \ldots, m$. (Thus $\hat{x}$ satisfies the constraints.) Putting $\lambda = 0$ in the above inequality $\hat{\lambda} \cdot g(\hat{x}) \leq \lambda \cdot g(\hat{x})$, we obtain $\hat{\lambda} \cdot g(\hat{x}) \leq 0$, which proves (ii) since $\hat{\lambda} \cdot g(\hat{x}) \geq 0$. Now note that by assumption, $\Phi(x, \hat{\lambda}) \leq \Phi(\hat{x}, \hat{\lambda})$ for all $x \in X$. This means $f(x) + \hat{\lambda} \cdot g(x) \leq f(\hat{x})$, since $\hat{\lambda} \cdot g(\hat{x}) = 0$; or $f(\hat{x}) - f(x) \geq \hat{\lambda} \cdot g(x)$. [That is, $f(\hat{x}) - f(x) \geq 0$ for all $x \in X$ such that $\hat{\lambda} \cdot g(x) \geq 0$.] In particular, $f(\hat{x}) - f(x) \geq 0$ for all $x \in X$ such that $g_j(x) \geq 0$, $j = 1, 2, \ldots, m$.   (Q.E.D.)

REMARK: In the above theorem we do not assume the concavity of the f and the g_j's, nor do we assume the convexity of X.

Combining Theorem 1.B.3 and its corollary, we immediately obtain the following useful theorem.

Theorem 1.B.5: *Let $f, g_1, g_2, \ldots, g_m$ be concave functions defined over a convex set X in R^n. Suppose that Slater's condition (S) is satisfied. Then $\hat{x}$ achieves a maximum of $f(x)$ subject to $g_j(x) \geq 0, j = 1, 2, \ldots, m$, if and only if there exists a $\hat{\lambda} \geq 0$ such that $(\hat{x}, \hat{\lambda})$ achieves the saddle point of the Lagrangian $\Phi(x, \lambda)$, that is, $\Phi(x, \hat{\lambda}) \leq \Phi(\hat{x}, \hat{\lambda}) \leq \Phi(\hat{x}, \lambda)$ for all $x \in X$ and $\lambda \geq 0$.*

REMARK: The above statement of the theorem presupposes the existence of $\hat{x}$. We may also restate the theorem in the following way:

There exists a solution, $\hat{x}$, for the problem of maximizing $f(x)$ subject to $g_j(x) \geq 0, j = 1, 2, \ldots, m$, if and only if there exists a saddle point for $\Phi(x, \lambda)$ such that $\Phi(x, \hat{\lambda}) \leq \Phi(\hat{x}, \hat{\lambda}) \leq \Phi(\hat{x}, \lambda)$ for all $x \in X, \lambda \geq 0$.

REMARK: In the above characterization of the solution of a nonlinear programming problem, the solution $\hat{x}$ is a global solution; that is, it does not refer to any small neighborhood about $\hat{x}$. The solution $\hat{x}$ is defined for the entire domain X.

REMARK: In certain cases, Slater's condition (S) can be dispensed with. For example, linear programming is a special case of concave programming and it is known (by the "Goldman-Tucker theorem") that the above theorem holds without (S) for the linear programming problem. We discuss this later in Sections D and F of this chapter.

POSTSCRIPTS (FOR FURTHER READING): Here we are concerned with the problem of finding $x \in X \subset R^n$ to maximize a real-valued function $f(x)$ on X subject to m real-valued function constraints $g_j(x) \geq 0, j = 1, \ldots, m$. Let Ω^m be the m-dimensional nonnegative orthant of R^m. Then, writing $g(x) \equiv [g_1(x), \ldots, g_m(x)]$, we may rephrase this problem as one of maximizing $f(x)$ subject to $g(x) \in \Omega^m$. Now notice that Ω^m is a convex cone. Thus we can generalize the above problem to finding $x \in X \subset R^n$ so as to

$$\text{Maximize: } f(x)$$
$$\text{Subject to: } g(x) \in K$$

where K is a convex cone in R^m. Note that this allows equality constraints as well as inequality constraints. For example, this reformulation allows the following constraints:

$$g_j(x) \geq 0, j = 1, 2, \ldots, m'$$

and

$$g_j(x) = 0, j = m' + 1, \ldots, m$$

Besides, $g(x) \in K$ allows the extension to a general linear space in which the meaning of the ordering $\geq$ has to be defined properly.[10]

Confining himself to real spaces, R^n, R^m, and so on, Moore [9] recently examined concave programming. In order to cope with the extension of Ω^m to a general convex cone K, he, following Hurwicz [6], redefined the concavity of the g_j's in terms of "K-concavity."

Definition: Let g be a function of X into R^m, where X is a convex subset of R^n. The function g is said to be K-**concave** if

$$g[\theta x + (1 - \theta)x'] - [\theta g(x) + (1 - \theta)g(x')] \in K \qquad \text{for all } x, x' \in X$$

and $0 \leqq \theta \leqq 1$, $\theta \in R$, where K is a convex cone in R^m.

We may define K-**convexity** analogously. If K is the nonnegative orthant of $R(m = 1)$, this definition of K-concavity (or K-convexity) coincides with the usual definition of concavity (or convexity).[11] Moore restricted his attention to the case in which g is K-concave.[12]

Although Moore's paper is quite general, his analysis is still confined to Euclidian spaces. The analysis of a more general case, that is, the case of real linear topological spaces, is thoroughly discussed by Hurwicz [6]. We may note that as a result of this restriction to Euclidian spaces, Moore was able to simplify some of the proofs considerably. Hence reading his paper may serve as a guide to the difficult paper of Hurwicz, at least for the concave programming case.

Strictly speaking, Moore's results are not all special cases of Hurwicz [6]. We record one of his main results as a theorem for those readers who are interested in [9] (his theorem 3).

Moore's Theorem: *Let f be a real-valued concave function of X, a convex subset of R^n, and let $g(x) \equiv [g^1(x), g^2(x)]$ be a function of X into R^m. Suppose that $\hat{x} \in X$ achieves a maximum of $f(x)$ subject to $g^1(x) \in K_1$ and $g^2(x) \in K_2$, where K_1 is a convex cone in R^{m_1}, K_2 is a convex cone in R^{m_2}, and $m_1 + m_2 = m$. Assume the following:*

    (i)   *The function g^1 is linear affine*[13] *and g^2 is K_2-concave.*
    (ii)   *Interior $X \neq \emptyset$ and Interior $K_2 \neq \emptyset$ (in R^{m_2}).*
    (iii) *There exists an $\tilde{x} \in$ Interior X such that $g^1(\tilde{x}) \in K_1$.*
    (iv) *There exists an $\overline{x} \in X$ such that $g^1(\overline{x}) \in K_1$ and $g^2(\overline{x}) \in$ Interior K_2.*

Then there exists a $\hat{\lambda} \in K^*$, where K^* denotes the nonnegative polar cone[14] *of $K \equiv K_1 \otimes K_2$, such that $(\hat{x}, \hat{\lambda})$ is a saddle point of $f(x) + \lambda \cdot g(x)$.*

    REMARK: The corollary of Theorem 1.B.3 is not really a special case of the above theorem in view of the requirement that Interior $X \neq \emptyset$ in the above theorem. This theorem was apparently conceived as a generalization of Uzawa's theorem 3 ([13], pp. 35–37). As Moore pointed out, Uzawa's theorem 3 is not correct in a strict sense.[15]

FOOTNOTES

  1. In other words, f is linear affine.
  2. In an arbitrary linear space the meaning of the ordering $\geqq$ is not obvious. Usually it is defined as follows: Let X be a linear space and x and x' be points in X; $x \geqq x'$ if

$x - x' \in K$, where K is a given fixed convex cone in X. If $X = R^n$ and Y is Ω^n, then this definition coincides with the usual definition. In any case, in terms of this definition of $\geq$ in a linear space, the concavity or convexity of functions on a linear space can be defined analogously to the case of a real space. See Hurwicz [6], for example.

3   It is important to note that a concave function may not be continuous at its boundary points. For example, define f on $[0, \infty)$ by $f(x) = 0$ if $x = 0$ and $f(x) = 1$ if $x > 0$. This function is clearly concave but not continuous at $x = 0$. It is continuous on $(0, \infty)$.

4.   Write $f = (f_1, f_2, \ldots, f_n)$ and $p = (p_1, p_2, \ldots, p_n)$. If there exists an $\bar{x} \in X$ with $f(\bar{x}) < 0$, then clearly $p \cdot f(\bar{x}) < 0$ for any $p \geq 0$; that is, "$p \cdot f(x) \geq 0$ for all $p \geq 0$, $x \in X$" does not hold. On the other hand, if $f(x) < 0$ admits no solution for $x \in X$, then $-f(x) > 0$ admits no solution for $x \in X$. Hence, as a result of Theorem 1.B.2, there exists a $p \geq 0$ such that $p \cdot [-f(x)] \leq 0$ or $p \cdot f(x) \geq 0$ for all $x \in X$. This proves the corollary.

5.   A generalization of this corollary and Theorem 1.B.3 to the case of linear topological spaces is accomplished by Hurwicz [6], theorem V.3.1., pp. 91–93.

6.   In many economic problems, we are often concerned with the problem of choosing $x \in R^n$ which maximizes $f(x)$ subject to $g_j(x) \geq 0, j = 1, 2, \ldots, m,$ and $x \geq 0$. For such a problem it can easily be shown that Slater's condition is slightly weakened so that there exists an $\bar{x} \geq 0$ such that $g_j(\bar{x}) > 0, j = 1, 2, \ldots, m$. For a more general result with linear (affine) constraints such that $A \cdot x + b \geq 0$, instead of $x \geq 0$, see Moore's theorem later in this section.

7.   The need for some requirement for constraints when all the constraints are in the form of inequalities was first investigated in 1939 by Karush in his Master's thesis at the University of Chicago (*Minima of Functions of Several Variables with Inequalities as Side Conditions*).

8.   If (S) holds, then $g(\bar{x}) > 0$ so that $p \cdot g(\bar{x}) > 0$ for $p \geq 0$; that is, (K) holds. Conversely, if (K) holds, then there exists no $p \geq 0$ such that $p \cdot g(x) \leq 0$ for all $x \in X$. Then, owing to the corollary of Theorem 1.B.2, the system $g(x) > 0$ admits a solution, say, $\bar{x}$ in X; that is, (S) holds. The equivalence of these two conditions for a more general space is provided by L. Hurwicz and H. Uzawa, "A Note on the Lagrangian Saddle-Points," in *Studies in Linear and Non-Linear Programming*, Stanford, Calif., Stanford University Press, 1958.

9.   Slater's own counterexample is the following: $f(x) = x - 1$ and $g(x) = -(x - 1)^2$, $x \in R$. The above example, due to Uzawa [13], p. 34, is obviously a slight modification of Slater's example. In spite of this well-known counterexample, there seems to be a confusion among economists on this point. See, for example, K. Lancaster, *Mathematical Economics*, New York, Macmillan, 1968, p. 75 (the second proposition of his "existence theorem"). See also p. 64.

10.   For such a definition, recall our earlier remark in footnote 2.

11.   The above definition of the K-concavity (or the K-convexity) is clearly motivated by the definition of $\geq$ in a linear space. The reader should not confuse this concept with that of the S-concavity (or S-convexity), which is discussed in Berge [1], and so on.

12.   In Moore's analysis [9], f is not restricted to a real-valued function but can be vector-valued; that is, $f = [f_1, \ldots, f_n]$, where $f_i, i = 1, \ldots, n$, are real-valued. Such a problem is called the "vector maximum problem" and we discuss it later in Section E.

13.   Thus $g^1(x)$ can be written as $g^1(x) = A \cdot x + b$, where A is an $m_1 \times n$ matrix with entries of real numbers and $b \in R^{m_1}$.

14.   Let K be a convex cone in R^m; then the **nonnegative polar cone** can be defined as

$K^* \equiv \{z: z \in R^m, y \cdot z \geqq 0, \text{for all } y \in K\}$. It is easy to see that K^* is also a convex cone. Also, if $K = \Omega^m$, then $K^* = \Omega^m$:

15. There is a counterexample to Uzawa's theorem 3, as it is stated. This is pointed out by Moore [9], p. 61.

REFERENCES

1. Berge, C., *Topological Spaces*, New York, Macmillan, 1963 (French original, 1959).
2. Berge, C., and Ghouila-Houri, A., *Programming, Games and Transportation Networks*, New York, Wiley, 1965 (French original, 1962).
3. Fenchel, W., *Convex Cones, Sets and Functions*, Princeton, N.J., Princeton University, 1953 (hectographed).
4. Fleming, W. H., *Functions of Several Variables*, Reading, Mass., Addison-Wesley, 1965.
5. Hadley, G., *Nonlinear and Dynamic Programming*, Reading, Mass., Addison-Wesley, 1964, chap. 3.
6. Hurwicz, L., "Programming in Linear Spaces," in *Studies in Linear and Non-linear Programming*, ed. by K. J. Arrow, L. Hurwicz, and H. Uzawa, Stanford, Calif., Stanford University Press, 1958.
7. Karlin, S., *Mathematical Methods and Theory in Games, Programming, and Economics*, Vol. 1, Reading, Mass., Addison-Wesley, 1959, esp. sec. 7.1, 7.2, and appendix B.
8. Kuhn, H. W., and Tucker, A. W., "Non-linear Programming," in *Proceedings of the Second Berkeley Symposium on Mathematical Statistics and Probability*, ed. by J. Neyman, Berkeley, Calif., University of California Press, 1951.
9. Moore, J. C., "Some Extensions of the Kuhn-Tucker Results in Concave Programming," in *Papers in Quantitative Economics*, ed. by J. P. Quirk and A. Zarley, Lawrence, Kansas, University of Kansas Press, 1968.
10. Nikaido, H., *Introduction to Sets and Mappings in Modern Economics*, tr. by K. Sato, Amsterdam, North-Holland, 1970 (Japanese original, Tokyo, 1960).
11. ———, *Linear Mathematics for Economics*, Tokyo, Baifukan, 1961, (in Japanese), esp. chap. III, sec. 4.
12. Slater, M., "Lagrange Multipliers Revisited: A Contribution to Non-linear Programming," *Cowles Commission Discussion Paper*, Math. 403, November 1950; also RM-676, August 1951.
13. Uzawa, H., "The Kuhn-Tucker Theorem in Concave Programming," in *Studies in Linear and Non-linear Programming*, ed. by K. J. Arrow, L. Hurwicz, and H. Uzawa, Stanford, Calif., Stanford University Press, 1958.

Section C

DIFFERENTIATION AND THE UNCONSTRAINED MAXIMUM PROBLEM

In this section we summarize some important results, a few of which are probably known to readers who have finished an advanced calculus course. However, this review is necessary as a bridge to the next important section. We begin by reminding the reader of the definition of differentiation on a real line R.

a. DIFFERENTIATION

Definition: A real-valued function f defined on a subset X of R is said to be **differentiable at** x^0, where x^0 is an interior point of X, if there exists a real number a which depends on x^0 such that

$$\lim_{\substack{h \to 0 \\ h \neq 0}} \frac{f(x^0 + h) - f(x^0)}{h} = a$$

or

$$\lim_{\substack{h \to 0 \\ h \neq 0}} \frac{f(x^0 + h) - f(x^0) - ah}{h} = 0$$

We call a **the derivative of** f **at** x^0 and denote it by $f'(x^0)$. We can easily see that $f'(x^0)$, if it exists, is unique.

> *REMARK:* Since x^0 is an interior point of X, it is assumed that X contains an open interval (α, β) such that $x^0 \in (\alpha, \beta)$. This guarantees that $x^0 + h \in (\alpha, \beta)$ when h is small enough. Hence such an h, if it is small enough, can be either negative or positive. If, on the other hand, f is defined on the closed interval $[\alpha, \beta]$, then this is no longer the case. For example, if $x^0 = \alpha$, h, however small it may be, cannot be negative. To deal with such a situation the concepts of the "left-hand derivative" and "the right-hand derivative" are formulated. In other words,
>
> $$\lim_{\substack{h \to 0 \\ h > 0}} \frac{f(x^0 + h) - f(x^0)}{h} = a^+$$
>
> and
>
> $$\lim_{\substack{h \to 0 \\ h < 0}} \frac{f(x^0 + h) - f(x^0)}{h} = a^-$$

The numbers a^+ and a^- are respectively called the **right-hand derivative** and the **left-hand derivative** of f at x^0, and are denoted by $f'^+(x^0)$ and $f'^-(x^0)$ respectively. At $x = \alpha$ in $[\alpha, \beta]$, only $f'^+(\alpha)$ can be defined, and at $x = \beta$, only $f'^-(\beta)$ can be defined; $f'(x^0)$ exists only if $f'^+(x^0)$ and $f'^-(x^0)$ both exist and are equal.

Now suppose that f is defined on R^n. The above definition of differentiability needs to be modified, for h must now be a vector as x^0 is a vector in R^n. Letting $\| x \|$ be the usual Euclidian norm of x, the following modified definition is a natural generalization of the definition given above.

Definition: A real-valued function defined on a subset X of R^n is said to be **differentiable** at $x^0 \in X$ where x^0 is an interior point of X, if there exists an n-vector a which depends on x^0 such that

$$\lim_{\substack{h \to 0 \\ h \neq 0}} \frac{f(x^0 + h) - f(x^0) - a \cdot h}{\| h \|} = 0$$

where h is, of course, an n-vector also. The above a is denoted by $f'(x^0)$ and is called the **derivative of f at x^0**.

REMARK: In the above definition, $a \cdot h$ is called the **differential** of f at x^0. It clearly depends on x^0 and h. If f is differentiable at every point in a subset S of X, f is called **differentiable in S**. If X is open and if f is differentiable in X, then f is called a **differentiable function**.[1]

REMARK: Also, we can show that $f'(x^0)$, if it exists, is unique.

REMARK: Note that X in the above definition does not have to be an open set. However, x^0 is restricted to be an interior point. Hence it is assumed that there is an open ball about x^0 which is contained in X.

REMARK: When X is a **(closed) rectangular region**, that is,

$$X = \{x : x \in R^n, a_i \leq x_i \leq b_i, i = 1, 2, \ldots, n\}$$

we can define the concept of the left-hand and right-hand derivatives by analogy. For example, an n-vector a^+ is the **right-hand derivative** of f at x^0, if

$$\lim_{\substack{h \to 0 \\ h \geq 0}} \frac{f(x^0 + h) - f(x^0) - a^+ \cdot h}{\| h \|} = 0$$

Clearly the above concept can be defined even if X is not bounded (for example, Ω^n). It should be clear, however, that the above concept is rather limited because the closed rectangular region is a very special kind of domain.

REMARK: The definition of differentiation is often restated in the following manner: "f is *differentiable at* $x^0 \in X$, where x^0 is an interior point of $X \subset R^n$, if there exists an $a \in R^n$ such that

$$f(x^0 + h) - f(x^0) = a \cdot h + o(\| h \|)$$

where $o(\| h \|)$ is an infinitesimal of higher order than h." [More rigorously, $o(\| h \|)$ denotes that for any $\epsilon > 0$, there exists a $\delta > 0$ such that $\| h \| < \delta$ implies $o(\| h \|) < \epsilon \| h \|$]. In other words,

$$\lim_{\substack{h \to 0 \\ h \neq 0}} \frac{o(\| h \|)}{\| h \|} = 0$$

This $o(\cdot)$ is often called **Landau's o-symbol**. The notation $r(h) = o(\| h \|)$ means that $\| r(h) \| / \| h \| \to 0$ as $h \to 0$ with $h \neq 0$. In general, r is a vector-valued function.

REMARK: In fact, in the above definition of differentiability, it is *not* necessary that x^0 be restricted to an interior point of R. In other words, $f(x)$ can be defined to be **differentiable at** $x^0 \in X$, if there exists a linear function $a \cdot (x - x^0)$ such that

$$f(x) - f(x^0) = a \cdot (x - x^0) + o(\| x - x^0 \|)$$

That is, only the *existence* of the differential is crucial in the definition of differentiability.

REMARK: In the above definition, although we let $\| x \|$ be the usual Euclidian norm, there is no necessity for this. As long as we consistently use one norm, the choice of a norm is really immaterial. In fact, in R^n we can show that if f is differentiable at x^0 under a certain norm, then f is differentiable at x^0 under any other norm.[2]

REMARK: We may also note that it is not necessary that our space be R^n. The above definition can be extended word for word to the case in which X is an arbitrary normed linear space (not necessarily R^n), except that $a \cdot h$ is replaced by a linear functional $a(h)$. Then $a(h)$ is called the **differential of f at** x^0. Note that $a(h)$ depends on x^0, as was the case above [so it is often also denoted as $a(x^0, h)$]. This linear functional $a(h)$, defined on a normed linear space, is also called the **Fréchet differential** and the $o(\| h \|)$ is called the **remainder** of the differential. (See Vainberg [7], p. 40, for example.)[3]

Definition: Let e^i be an n-vector with the ith coordinate equal to 1 and all other coordinates equal to 0. A real-valued function f on a subset X of R^n is said to have a **partial derivative with respect to** x_i at x^0, where x^0 is an interior point of X, if there exists a scalar a_i such that

$$\lim_{\substack{h \to 0 \\ h \neq 0}} \frac{f(x^0 + he^i) - f(x^0) - a_i h}{h} = 0$$

where h is a *scalar*. The scalar a_i is called the **partial derivative of f at** x^0 and is often denoted by $\partial f / \partial x_i|_{x=x^0}$.

We now state the basic theorems about derivatives, the proofs of which can be found in any book on elementary analysis or advanced calculus.

Theorem 1.C.1.

(i) *If a real-valued function $f(x)$ on $X \subset R^n$ is differentiable at x^0, then it is continuous at x^0 and has partial derivatives with respect to each of its coordinate variables such that*

$$a = (a_1, a_2, \ldots, a_n)$$

that is,

$$f'(x^0) = \left[\frac{\partial f}{\partial x_1}, \cdots, \frac{\partial f}{\partial x_n} \right]_{x=x^0}$$

(ii) *The function f is differentiable at x^0 and its differential is continuous at x^0 if and only if f has continuous partial derivatives at x^0 with respect to each of its coordinate variables.*

REMARK: The function f is said to be **continuously differentiable at** x^0 if it is differentiable at x^0 *and* if $f'(x^0)$ is continuous at x^0.

REMARK: The vector $f'(x^0)$ is sometimes called the **gradient vector** of f at $x = x^0$. When notational simplicity is required, we will denote it by f_x^0.

REMARK: Although the differentiability of f implies the continuity of f,[4] the converse is not necessarily true. (For example, $f(x) = |x|$, $x \in R$, is continuous but not differentiable at $x = 0$.) Weierstrass constructed an example of a continuous function on R which is nowhere differentiable.[5]

REMARK: The partial derivatives $\partial f / \partial x_1$, $\ldots$, $\partial f / \partial x_n$ are often called the **first-order partial derivatives**. The $\partial f / \partial x_i$'s are also functions on X as x^0 varies over X. Thus the **second-order partial derivatives** are defined analogously [for example, $f(x, y) = x^2 y$, $x, y \in R$, $\partial f / \partial x = 2xy$, $\partial^2 f / \partial x^2 = 2y$, $\partial^2 f / \partial y \partial x = 2x$, $\partial f / \partial y = x^2$, $\partial^2 f / \partial y^2 = 0$, $\partial^2 f / \partial x \partial y = 2x$]. The partial derivatives of f of order $q = 3, 4, \ldots$, are also defined analogously. If the qth order ($q = 1, 2, \ldots$) partial derivatives of f exist and are continuous in the domain, then f is said to be a **function of class** $C^{(q)}$. If f is simply continuous, f is a function of **class** $C^{(0)}$; $C^{(0)}$ and $C^{(1)}$ are often denoted respectively by C and C'. In Theorem 1.C.1, (ii) says that if and only if $f \in C^{(1)}$, f is (continuously) differentiable; and (i) says that $f \in C^{(1)}$ implies $f \in C^{(0)}$. As remarked above, $f \in C^{(0)}$ does not necessarily imply $f \in C^{(1)}$.

It can be shown that $f \in C^{(2)}$ implies $\partial^2 f / \partial x_i \partial x_j = \partial^2 f / \partial x_j \partial x_i$ for all i and j and for all points in the domain.[6] When $f \in C^{(2)}$, f is said to be **twice continuously differentiable**.

In the definition of differentiation and in the above theorem, we assume that f is a real-valued function. We can extend the concept of differentiation to the case in which f is a vector-valued function.

Definition: Let f be a function from a subset X of R^n into R^m. Then f is said to be **differentiable at** x^0, where x^0 is an interior point of X, if there exists an $m \times n$ matrix A with real number entries such that

$$f(x^0 + h) - f(x^0) = A \cdot h + o(\| h \|)$$

We can show that A, if it exists, is unique.

REMARK: Writing $f(x) = [f_1(x), \ldots, f_m(x)]$, we can easily show that $f(x)$ is differentiable at x^0 if and only if $f_i(x)$ is differentiable at x^0 for all $i = 1, \ldots, m$. The above A can be written in the form

$$A = \begin{bmatrix} \dfrac{\partial f_1}{\partial x_1} & \cdots & \dfrac{\partial f_1}{\partial x_n} \\ \vdots & & \vdots \\ \dfrac{\partial f_m}{\partial x_1} & \cdots & \dfrac{\partial f_m}{\partial x_n} \end{bmatrix} \Big|_{x = x^0}.$$

This matrix is sometimes called the **Jacobian matrix** of f at x^0.

REMARK: If X and Y are normed linear spaces (not necessarily R^n), we replace $A \cdot h$ by a linear function $A(h)$ from X into Y. The function $A(h)$ is called the **differential of f at** x^0, or the **Fréchet differential** of f at x^0, and $o(\| h \|)$ is the **remainder** of the differential.

REMARK: A theorem analogous to Theorem 1.C.1 also holds for vector-valued functions. For example, let $f(x) = [f_1(x), \ldots, f_m(x)]$. Then f has a continuous differential at x^0 if and only if the partial derivatives of $f_i (i = 1, 2, \ldots, n)$ exist and are continuous at x^0.

We now state the extension of an important theorem (called the **chain rule**) in elementary calculus.

Theorem 1.C.2 (Composite Function Theorem):   *Let f be a function from $X \subset R^n$ into R^m, and let g be a function from $Y \subset R^m$ into R^k where $f(X) \subset Y$. Suppose that*

f is differentiable at $x^0 \in X$ and g is differentiable at $f(x^0) \in Y$; then the function $h \equiv g \circ f: X \to R^k$ is differentiable at x^0, and $h'(x^0) = g'[f(x^0)] \circ f'(x^0)$.

REMARK: Note that $g'[f(x^0)]$ is the $(k \times m)$ Jacobian matrix of g and $f'(x^0)$ is the $(m \times n)$ Jacobian matrix of f, so that $h'(x^0)$ can simply be expressed as the product of these two matrices. This is the formula for the generalized chain rule.

EXAMPLE: $(n=1, k=1)$: Let $f(x) = [f_1(x), \ldots, f_m(x)]$ and $h(x) = g[f(x)]$, where $x \in R$ and $h(x) \in R$. Writing $y_i = f_i(x)$, we have

$$h'(x) = \sum_{i=1}^{m} \frac{\partial g}{\partial y_i} \frac{\partial f_i}{\partial x}$$

In particular, we may consider

$$h(t) = g[f(t)]$$

where $f(t) = a + bt$ with $a, b \in R^m$, $t \in R$ (a, b are constant vectors). Then we have

$$h'(t) = g_y \cdot b$$

We conclude this part by noting a very important characterization of a concave or convex function in terms of the gradient vector of the function.

Theorem 1.C.3: *Let f be a differentiable real-valued function defined on an open convex set X in R^n. Then f is concave if and only if, for any x and x^0 in X,*

$$f_x^0 \cdot (x - x^0) \geq f(x) - f(x^0)$$

where f_x^0 is the gradient vector of f at x_0.

PROOF: (Necessity) Suppose f is concave; then we have

$$f[(1-t)x^0 + tx] \geq (1-t)f(x^0) + tf(x) \qquad \text{for all } t, 0 \leq t \leq 1$$

or

$$f[x^0 + t(x - x^0)] - f(x^0) \geq t[f(x) - f(x^0)], \qquad \text{for all } t, 0 \leq t \leq 1$$

Let $h \equiv x - x^0$. Subtract $tf_x^0 \cdot h$ from both sides of the above relation and divide by $t > 0$. Then we obtain

$$\frac{f[x^0 + th] - f(x^0) - tf_x^0 \cdot h}{t} \geq f(x) - f(x^0) - f_x^0 \cdot h$$

Now take the limit of $t \to 0$ ($t > 0$). Then the LHS of the above relation goes to 0 by definition of $f_x{}^0$. Therefore we obtain

$$f_x{}^0 \cdot (x - x^0) \geq f(x) - f(x^0)$$

(Sufficiency)   We suppose the above inequality holds and show that f is concave. Let x^1 and x^2 be arbitrary points in X such that $x^1 \neq x^2$. Let $x^0 \equiv (1 - t)x^1 + tx^2, 0 < t < 1, t \in R$ and $h \equiv x^1 - x^0$. Then $x^2 = x^0 - \left[(1 - t)/t\right] h$. As a result of the above presupposed inequality, we have

$$f(x^1) - f(x^0) \leq f_x{}^0 \cdot h$$

$$f(x^2) - f(x^0) \leq f_x{}^0 \cdot \left(-\frac{1 - t}{t} h\right)$$

Hence we obtain

$$\left(\frac{1 - t}{t} f(x^1) + f(x^2)\right) - \left(\frac{1 - t}{t} + 1\right) f(x^0) \leq 0$$

or

$$(1 - t) f(x^1) + t f(x^2) \leq f(x^0), \ 0 < t < 1$$

When $t = 1$ or 0, this inequality obviously holds.   (Q.E.D.)

REMARK: The above theorem can be illustrated by Figure 1.9.

REMARK: If f is strictly concave, then we have, for any two points x and x_0, $x \neq x^0$, in X,

$$f_x{}^0 \cdot (x - x^0) > f(x) - f(x^0)$$

The converse of this statement is also true. The proof of this remark is analogous to the proof of the above theorem.

REMARK: The function f is convex if and only if the inequality of the above theorem is reversed, that is,

$$f_x{}^0 \cdot (x - x^0) \leq f(x) - f(x^0)$$

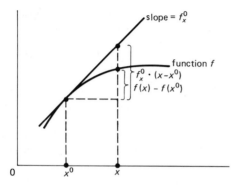

Figure 1.9.   Illustration of Theorem 1.C.3.

The function f is strictly convex if and only if the above holds with strict inequality for any $x \neq x^0$ in X.

b.   UNCONSTRAINED MAXIMUM

We now consider the maximization problem and its relation to derivatives. The minimization problem is essentially the same as the maximization problem, for the maximization of $f(x)$ is equivalent to the minimization of $-f(x)$, and vice versa. In this section we take up the unconstrained maximum problem.

Definition: A real-valued function f defined on X in R^n is said to achieve its **local** (or **relative**) **maximum at** $\hat{x} \in X$ if there exists an open ball $B_\epsilon(\hat{x})$ with center $\hat{x}$ and radius $\epsilon > 0$ such that $f(\hat{x}) \geq f(x)$ for all $x \in A$ where $A \equiv B_\epsilon(\hat{x}) \cap X$. If $f(\hat{x}) > f(x)$ for all $x \in A$, we say that f achieves its **strong** (or **unique**) local maximum at $\hat{x}$.

> *REMARK*:   Note that in the above definition X is not necessarily open. Also note that ϵ can be very small.

Definition: A real-valued function f defined on X in R^n is said to achieve its **global** (or **absolute**) **maximum at** $\hat{x} \in X$ if $f(\hat{x}) \geq f(x)$ for all $x \in X$. If $f(\hat{x}) > f(x)$ for all $x \in X$, then we say that f achieves its **strong** (or **unique**) global maximum at $\hat{x}$.

> *REMARK*:   **Local minimum, strong local minimum, global minimum,** and **strong global minimum** are defined analogously. We say **extremum** for either maximum or minimum.

> *REMARK*:   In the above definitions of maximum and minimum, the domain of f does not necessarily have to be R^n. For the concept of global extremum, X can be anything. For the concept of local extremum it has to be a set in a metric space in order for the concept "open ball" to be meaningful. If we replace "open ball" by "open set," X does not even have to be in a metric space, although it has to be in a topological space.

> *REMARK*:   Theorem 1.B.3 of the previous section may be reworded as follows:
>
> *If f, g_1, g_2, $\ldots$, g_m are concave functions on a convex set X in R^n, and if f achieves its maximum at $\hat{x}$, subject to $g(x) \geq 0$, then there exist $\hat{p}_0$, $\hat{p}_1$, $\ldots$, $\hat{p}_m$, all ≥ 0, not all equal to zero, such that*
>
> $$L(\hat{x}) \geq L(x) \text{ for all } x \in X, \text{ where } L(x) \equiv \hat{p}_0 f(x) + \hat{p} \cdot g(x)$$
>
> Note that this theorem thus says that the *global* maximum of f *over* the constraint set $C \equiv \{x: x \in X \text{ and } g(x) \geq 0\}$ implies the *global* maximum of L over X.

Obviously any global maximum (resp. minimum) point is also a local maximum (resp. minimum) point. The converse is not necessarily true. However, when f is a concave (resp. convex) function, the converse is also true. In particular, we prove the following:

Theorem 1.C.4: *Let $f(x)$ be a concave function over a convex set X in R^n. Then any local maximum of $f(x)$ in X is also a global maximum of $f(x)$ over X.*

PROOF: Suppose f achieves its local maximum at $\hat{x}$ with respect to an open ball $B_\epsilon(\hat{x})$. Suppose that $\hat{x}$ is *not* a global maximum point. In other words, there exists an $x^* \in X$ such that

$$f(x^*) > f(\hat{x})$$

Clearly, $x^* \notin B_\epsilon(\hat{x})$. Since $f(x)$ is concave, we have

$$f[tx^* + (1 - t)\hat{x}] \geq tf(x^*) + (1 - t)f(\hat{x}) \qquad \text{for all } t, 0 \leq t \leq 1$$

Since $f(x^*) > f(\hat{x})$, the RHS of the above inequality exceeds $f(\hat{x})$, if $t \neq 0$, so that

$$f[tx^* + (1 - t)\hat{x}] > f(\hat{x}) \qquad \text{for all } t, 0 < t \leq 1$$

Let $x \equiv tx^* + (1 - t)\hat{x}$ for $t < \bar{t}$ with $\bar{t}$ chosen such that $\bar{t} < 1$ and $0 < \bar{t} \leq \epsilon/\|\hat{x} - x^*\|$, so that x is inside $B_\epsilon(\hat{x})$ (note that $x \in X$ for X is a convex set). Then $f(x) > f(\hat{x})$ for all t, $0 < t < \bar{t}$, which contradicts the fact that $f(x)$ takes a local maximum at $\hat{x}$ with respect to the ball $B_\epsilon(\hat{x})$.   (Q.E.D.)

Theorem 1.C.5: *Let f be a concave function defined on a convex set X in R^n. Let S be the set of points in X at which f takes on its global maximum. Then S is a convex set.*

PROOF: If the global maximum is taken on at just a single point, then the result is obvious. Suppose then that the global maximum is taken on at two different points $\hat{x}$ and x^*. Let $\tilde{x} \equiv tx^* + (1 - t)\hat{x}, 0 \leq t \leq 1$. Since f is concave and since $f(\hat{x}) = f(x^*)$, we have

$$f(\tilde{x}) \equiv f[tx^* + (1 - t)\hat{x}] \geq tf(x^*) + (1 - t)f(\hat{x}) = f(\hat{x}), 0 \leq t \leq 1$$

Since $f(\tilde{x})$ cannot be greater than $f(\hat{x})$, $f(\tilde{x}) = f(\hat{x})$. Therefore $\tilde{x} \in S$, or $tx^* + (1 - t)\hat{x} \in S$ for all t, $0 \leq t \leq 1$.   (Q.E.D.)

REMARK: It should be clear that Theorems 1.C.4 and 1.C.5 remain correct if we replace "f is concave" by "f is convex" and "maximum" by "minimum."

REMARK: Hence, if the global maximum is taken at two different points, it is also taken at all the points in between those two points. It should also be clear that if $f(x)$ is a *strictly* concave function, then the global maximum is taken at a *unique* point. To prove this, suppose that the global maximum is taken on at two distinct points, $\hat{x}$ and x^*. Then we have $f(\tilde{x}) > tf(x^*) + (1 - t)f(\hat{x}) = f(\hat{x})$, where $\tilde{x} \equiv tx^* + (1 - t)\hat{x}$, $0 < t < 1$. That is, we have $f(\tilde{x}) > f(\hat{x})$, which contradicts the fact that $f(\hat{x})$ is the global maximum.

We now prove the following basic theorem.

Theorem 1.C.6: *Let f be a real-valued function on an open set X in R^n. If f has a local extremum at $\hat{x}$ and f is differentiable at $\hat{x}$, then $f'(\hat{x}) = 0$.*

PROOF: Let v be a vector in R^n such that $\| v \| = 1$, where $\| v \|$ is the Euclidian norm of v. Consider $\alpha(t) \equiv f(\hat{x} + tv)$, where $t \in R$ and $x + tv \in X$. By assumption $\alpha(t)$ has a local extremum at $t = 0$; hence by elementary calculus $\alpha'(0) = 0$. But $\alpha'(0) = f'(\hat{x}) \cdot v$ by the chain rule (Theorem 1.C.2). Since the choice of v is arbitrary, this implies $f'(\hat{x}) = 0$.

REMARK: Hence $f'(\hat{x}) = 0$ is a necessary condition that $\hat{x}$ furnish a local extremum of f, and it is called the **first-order condition**. It is not a sufficient condition. In other words, the converse of the above theorem is not necessarily true. For example, consider $f(x) = x^3$, $x \in R$. We know that $f'(x) = 3x^2$ is 0 at $x = 0$ [that is, $f'(0) = 0$], but 0 is not an extremum point. However, when f is a concave (or a convex) function [note $f(x) = x^3$ is neither concave nor convex in R], the converse of the above theorem is also true.

Thus we have Theorem 1.C.7.

Theorem 1.C.7: *Let $f(x)$ be a differentiable and concave function over an open convex set X in R^n. The function $f(x)$ achieves its global maximum at $x = \hat{x}$ if and only if $\hat{f}_x = 0$, where $\hat{f}_x \equiv f'(\hat{x})$ (the gradient vector of f at $\hat{x}$). Moreover, $\hat{x}$ furnishes a unique maximum of f if f is strictly concave.*

PROOF: If the global maximum is taken on at $x = \hat{x}$, clearly we have $\hat{f}_x = 0$. Conversely, if $\hat{f}_x = 0$, then, as a result of Theorem 1.C.3, $0 \geq f(x) - f(\hat{x})$ for all $x \in X$, or $f(\hat{x}) \geq f(x)$ for all $x \in X$.   (Q.E.D.)

REMARK: Analogously, $f(x)$ achieves its global minimum at $\hat{x}$ if and only if $f'(\hat{x}) = 0$, when f is a convex function. Likewise, $\hat{x}$ furnishes a unique minimum of f if f is strictly convex.

REMARK: In the literature there are usually discussions on the "second-order sufficiency conditions" assuming $f \in C^{(2)}$. When f is specified as concave (or convex), we can see from the above theorem that such considerations can be dispensed with. The second-order conditions are, however, related to the concavity or the convexity of a function in a neighborhood of the relevant point (see Section E, subsection c). Moreover, note that Theorem 1.C.7 says that $\hat{f}_x = 0$ is a necessary and sufficient characterization of a *global* maximum and not simply that of a local maximum. But this can easily be understood in view of Theorem 1.C.4, which asserts that under concavity every local maximum is a global maximum. In other words, the concavity of f also plays a crucial role in establishing the global characterization of a maximum.

REMARK: Consider the constrained maximum problem of maximizing $f(x)$ subject to $g_j(x) \geqq 0$, $j = 1, \ldots, m$, $x \in X \subset R^n$. Let $C \equiv \{x \in X : g_j(x) \geqq 0$, $j = 1, 2, \ldots, m\}$ (the constraint set). If $\hat{x}$ is a solution of this problem, then $\hat{x}$ maximizes $f(x)$ over C. Hence identifying set X in Theorems 1.C.4 and 1.C.5 with set C and assuming that C is convex, we can assert under the concavity of f that every local maximum of f over C is a global maximum of f over C, and that $S \equiv \{\hat{x} : f(\hat{x}) \geqq f(\hat{x}), x \in C\}$ is convex. Furthermore, if f is strictly concave (and C is convex), $\hat{x}$ is unique.

REMARK: Again consider the constrained maximum problem of maximizing $f(x)$ over C. Suppose that the solution $\hat{x}$ is in the *interior* of C, so that there exists an open ball about $\hat{x}$ [say, $B_\epsilon(\hat{x})$] which is in C. Then Theorems 1.C.6 and 1.C.7 can be applied directly to such a constrained maximum problem by identifying X in these theorems with $B_\epsilon(\hat{x})$. In other words, the constrained maximum problem is reduced to an unconstrained maximum problem. But there is nothing surprising in this, for that the solution $\hat{x}$ is in the interior of C means that *none* of the constraints $g_j(x) \geqq 0, j = 1, \ldots,$ m, are effective at $\hat{x}$.

FOOTNOTES

1. When $X = R$, there are now two different definitions of differentiability. That is, f is differentiable at x° (i) if both the right-hand and the left-hand derivatives exist and they are equal, *or* (ii) if the differential exists at x° in the above sense. It can be shown that these two definitions are equivalent. See, for example, Brown and Page [1], pp. 266–267, especially theorem 7.1.9.

2. In other words, if f is differentiable at x° in one norm in R^n, then f is differentiable at x° in another norm in R^n and the two derivatives coincide. See, for example, Brown and Page [1], p. 273.

3. In infinite dimensional (normal linear) spaces, the differentiability and the value of differentials, in general, depend on the choice of the norm.

4. For the proof of this statement, see, for example, Fleming [2] and Rudin [6]. Here it is crucial that X is in a finite dimensional space such as R^n. If X is in an infinite dimensional space, the function may be differentiable at x° but may fail to be continuous at x°. See, for example, Brown and Page [1], p. 274 (exercise 3).

5. Weierstrass showed that the function $f(x) \equiv \sum_{n=0}^{\infty} a^n \cos(b^n x)$ is continuous but nowhere differentiable when b is an odd integer, $0 < a < 1$ and $ab > 1 + (3/2)\pi$. This was first published by du Bois Reymond in 1875. Since then simpler examples have been constructed. One of the simplest was given by B. L. van der Waerden

in 1930. A systematic discussion of nowhere differentiable functions is given in E. W. Hobson, *The Theory of Functions of a Real Variable*, Vol. 2, 2nd ed., Cambridge University Press, 1926, pp. 401–412.

6. If $f \notin C^{(2)}$ or if the second partial derivatives of f are not continuous. then we do not necessarily have $\partial^2 f / \partial x_i \, \partial x_j = \partial^2 f / \partial x_j \, \partial x_i$. A usual counterexample in text-books is the function f defined by $f(x, y) = xy(x^2 - y^2)/(x^2 + y^2)$ if $(x, y) \neq (0, 0)$, and $f(0, 0) = 0$. It can be shown easily that $\partial^2 f / \partial y \, \partial x = -1$ at $(0, 0)$ and $\partial^2 f / \partial x \, \partial y = 1$ at $(0, 0)$. See also Section E of this chapter.

REFERENCES

1. Brown, A. L., and Page, A., *Elements of Functional Analysis*, London, England, Van Nostrand Reinhold, 1970.

2. Fleming, W. H., *Functions of Several Variables*, Reading, Mass., Addison-Wesley, 1965, esp. chapters 1, 2, 3, and 4.

3. Goffman, C., *Calculus of Several Variables*, New York, Harper & Row, 1965, esp. chapters 2 and 3.

4. Hadley, G., *Nonlinear and Dynamic Programming*, Reading, Mass., Addison-Wesley, 1964, esp. chapters 1 and 3.

5. Loomis, L. H., and Sternberg, S., *Advanced Calculus*, Reading, Mass., Addison-Wesley, 1968, esp. chapter 3.

6. Rudin, W., *Principles of Mathematical Analysis*, 2nd ed., New York, McGraw-Hill, 1964, esp. chapter 9.

7. Vainberg, M. M., *Variational Methods for the Study of Nonlinear Operators*, (translated by Feinstein from the Russian original published in 1956), San Francisco, Holden-Day, 1964, esp. chapter 1.

Section D

THE QUASI-SADDLE-POINT CHARACTERIZATION

Supposing that we are given real-valued functions $f(x)$, $g_1(x)$, $g_2(x)$, $\ldots$, $g_m(x)$, on X in R^n, in Section B we discussed the following two conditions:

(M) (**Maximality condition**) There exists an $\hat{x}$ in X which maximizes $f(x)$ subject to $g_j(x) \geq 0$, $j = 1, 2, \ldots, m$, and $x \in X$.

(SP) (**Saddle-point condition**) There exists an $(\hat{x}, \hat{\lambda})$, in $X \otimes \Omega^m$ such that $(\hat{x}, \hat{\lambda})$ is a saddle point of $\Phi(x, \lambda)$; that is, $\Phi(x, \hat{\lambda}) \leq \Phi(\hat{x}, \hat{\lambda}) \leq \Phi(\hat{x}, \lambda)$, for all $x \in X$ and $\lambda \in \Omega^m$, where $\Phi(x, \lambda) \equiv f(x) + \lambda \cdot g(x)$.

In Section B, we showed that condition (M) implies condition (SP) if f and the g_j's are all concave functions (where X is a convex set) and if a normality condition such as Slater's condition is satisfied. We also showed that condition (SP) implies condition (M) (with no conditions such as the concavity of f and the g_j's or Slater's condition). In this section, unlike section B, we assume that f and the g_j's are *differentiable* on X. First we introduce the following condition, which is *also* known as the **first-order condition** or the **Kuhn-Tucker-Lagrange condition**.

(QSP) (**Quasi-saddle-point condition**) There exists an $(\hat{x}, \hat{\lambda})$ in $X \otimes \Omega^m$ such that $\hat{f}_x + \hat{\lambda} \cdot \hat{g}_x = 0$, $g(\hat{x}) \geq 0$ and $\hat{\lambda} \cdot g(\hat{x}) = 0$, where $\hat{f}_x = f'(\hat{x})$ and $\hat{g}_x = g'(\hat{x})$. (Here X is an open set to make differentiation meaningful.)[1]

> REMARK: In the above we supposed $X \subset R^n$. The space R^n can be replaced by a normed linear space.

> REMARK: Note that condition $\hat{f}_x + \hat{\lambda} \cdot \hat{g}_x = 0$ can be spelled out as the following:

$$\frac{\partial f}{\partial x_i} + \sum_{j=1}^{m} \hat{\lambda}_j \frac{\partial g_j}{\partial x_i} = 0, \ i = 1, 2, \ldots, n$$

(where the partial derivatives are evaluated at $x = \hat{x}$). If we write $L(x)$ $[\equiv \Phi(x, \hat{\lambda})] = f(x) + \hat{\lambda} \cdot g(x)$, then this condition can also be written as

$$\left. \frac{\partial L(x)}{\partial x_i} \right|_{x=\hat{x}} = 0, i = 1, 2, \ldots, n$$

Now we can immediately observe the following theorem.

Theorem 1.D.1: *Let $f, g_1, g_2, \ldots, g_m$ be real-valued differentiable functions on an open set X in R^n.*

(i) *Condition (SP) implies condition (QSP).*

(ii) *If, in addition, f and $g_1, \ldots, g_m$ are all concave functions, then (QSP) implies (SP) (where X is now taken to be convex).*

PROOF:

(i) By assumption, $\Phi(x, \hat{\lambda}) \leq \Phi(\hat{x}, \hat{\lambda})$ for all $x \in X$. [That is, $\hat{x}$ achieves a global (hence local) maximum of $\Phi(x, \hat{\lambda})$ on X.] Therefore, by Theorem 1.C.7, $\Phi_x(\hat{x}, \hat{\lambda}) = 0$ or $\hat{f}_x + \hat{\lambda} \cdot \hat{g}_x = 0$. Also, by Theorem 1.B.4, (SP) implies $\hat{\lambda} \cdot g(\hat{x}) = 0$. Hence $\Phi(\hat{x}, \hat{\lambda}) \leq \Phi(\hat{x}, \lambda)$ for all $\lambda \geq 0$ implies that $\lambda \cdot g(\hat{x}) \geq 0$ for $\lambda \geq 0$. Hence, in particular, $g(\hat{x}) \geq 0$.

(ii) Since $\Phi(x, \hat{\lambda}) = f(x) + \hat{\lambda} \cdot g(x)$ is a nonnegative linear combination of f and g_j's, and since f and the g_j's are concave functions, $\Phi(x, \hat{\lambda})$ is also a concave function. Then, by Theorem 1.C.7, we have $\Phi(x, \hat{\lambda}) \leq \Phi(\hat{x}, \hat{\lambda})$, and $\Phi(\hat{x}, \hat{\lambda}) \leq \Phi(\hat{x}, \lambda)$ follows trivially from the fact that $\hat{\lambda} \cdot g(\hat{x}) = 0$, $g(\hat{x}) \geq 0$ and $\lambda \geq 0$. (Q.E.D.)

Combining the above theorem with the corollary of Theorem 1.B.3, Theorem 1.D.2 follows at once.

Theorem 1.D.2: *Let* f, g_1, g_2, ..., g_m *be concave and differentiable on an open convex set* X *in* R^n. *Assume that Slater's condition holds, that is,*

(S)   *There exists an* $\bar{x} \in X$ *such that* $g_j(\bar{x}) > 0$ *for all* $j = 1, 2, \ldots, m$.

Then condition (M) holds if and only if (QSP) holds.

> *REMARK*: We illustrate schematically some important results obtained so far in this chapter in Figure 1.10. The arrow here reads "implies" under the conditions stated with the arrow.

> *REMARK*: In economics it is often necessary to take into account explicitly a nonnegativity condition such as $x \geq 0$. So here let us consider the problem of maximizing $f(x)$ subject to $g_j(x) \geq 0$, $j = 1, 2, \ldots, m$, *and* $x \geq 0$, where $x \in R^n$. Note that the set X in the above theorem is now taken to be the whole space R^n, which is obviously open and convex. We can write the (QSP) condition for the present case as follows:
> There exist $\hat{x}$, $\hat{\lambda}$, $\hat{\mu}$ such that

$$\hat{f}_x + \hat{\lambda} \cdot \hat{g}_x + \hat{\mu} = 0$$
$$\hat{\lambda} \cdot g(\hat{x}) + \hat{\mu} \cdot \hat{x} = 0$$

and

$$g(\hat{x}) \geq 0, \quad \hat{x} \geq 0$$
$$\hat{\lambda} \geq 0, \quad \hat{\mu} \geq 0$$

This condition can easily be converted to the following *equivalent* and better known condition, which we call **condition (QSP′)**.[2]

(QSP′)   There exist $\hat{x} \geq 0$ and $\hat{\lambda} \geq 0$ such that

$$\hat{f}_x + \hat{\lambda} \cdot \hat{g}_x \leq 0, \quad (\hat{f}_x + \hat{\lambda} \cdot \hat{g}_x) \cdot \hat{x} = 0$$
$$\hat{\lambda} \cdot g(\hat{x}) = 0 \quad \text{and} \quad g(\hat{x}) \geq 0$$

We illustrate the above condition in Figure 1.11. Here $X = R$ and we have only one constraint, $x \geq 0$. From the diagram, $\hat{x} = 0$ achieves the maximum of $f(x)$ subject to $x \geq 0$, and $f'(x) < 0, f'(\hat{x}) \cdot \hat{x} = 0$. In this problem, if we take $X = \Omega$ (that is, $\{x : x \in R, x \geq 0\}$), then the explicit constraint will disappear; $f'(\hat{x})$ should be replaced by the right-hand derivative $f'^+(\hat{x})$.

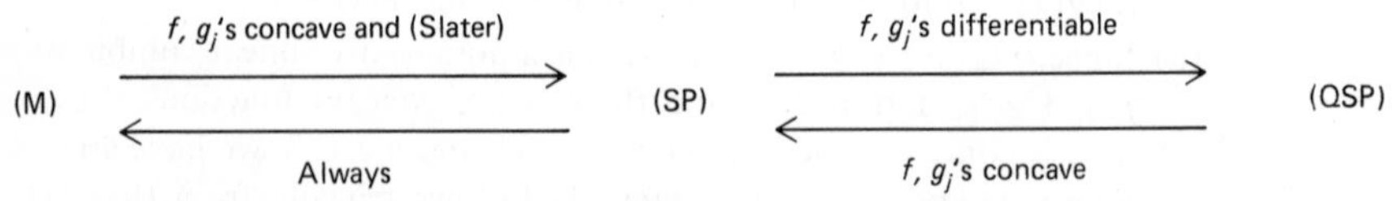

Figure 1.10.   Relationships between (M), (SP), and (QSP) under Concavity.

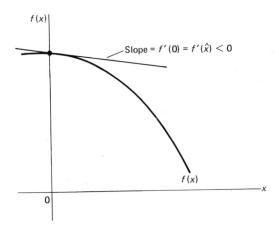

Figure 1.11. An Illustration of Corner Solution.

In Theorem 1.D.2 we considered the relation between (M) and (QSP) by going through (SP). We are now concerned with the problem of finding the relation between (M) and (QSP) without going through (SP). This is, in fact, the approach adopted by Kuhn and Tucker in their famous paper [10]. To do this, we first discuss the following condition, (KTCQ), which was introduced by Kuhn and Tucker and is now called the **Kuhn-Tucker constraint qualification**. Here X is assumed to be an open subset of R^n, and the g_j's are assumed to be differentiable in X.

(KTCQ)   Let C be the constraint set defined by $C \equiv \{x : x \in X, g_j(x) \geq 0, j = 1, 2, \ldots, m\}$. Let $\hat{x}$ be a point in C with $g_j(\hat{x}) = 0$ for $j \in E$ where $E \subset \{1, 2, \ldots, m\}$ and $E \neq \emptyset$. Let $\bar{x}$ be any point in X such that $g_j'(\hat{x}) \cdot (\bar{x} - \hat{x}) \geq 0$ for all $j \in E$. It is supposed that there exists a function $h(t)$ on $[0, 1]$ into X, which is differentiable at 0 with the following properties.

(i) $h(0) = \hat{x}$, and $h(t) \in C, 0 \leq t \leq 1$,
(ii) $h'(0) = \alpha(\bar{x} - \hat{x})$ for some positive number α.

Because of $h(t)$, this condition (KTCQ) may be referred to as the **parameterizability condition**.

REMARK: Intuitively speaking, (KTCQ) says the following: For every "line" originating from $\hat{x}$ and lying in the set defined by

$$Y \equiv \{\bar{x} : \bar{x} \in X, g_j'(\hat{x}) \cdot (\bar{x} - \hat{x}) \geq 0, j \in E\}$$

there exists a differentiable curve $h(t)$ which lies in the constraint set C such that at $\hat{x}$, $h(t)$ is tangent to the line.

This (KTCQ) is illustrated in Figure 1.12. In either of the two cases, (KTCQ) is satisfied.

The case in which (KTCQ) is not satisfied is illustrated in Figure 1.13. This is the case where there is some irregularity (such as a "cusp") on the boundaries. It should be clear that for a point such as $\bar{x} \in Y$ in Figure 1.13, there is no function $h(t)$ satisfying (i) and (ii) of (KTCQ).

Before we state Kuhn-Tucker's main theorem, we also should modify condition (M) [note that (M) implies (LM)].

(LM) **(Local maximality condition)** There exists an $\hat{x}$ in X such that $f(x)$ has a local maximum at $\hat{x}$ subject to $g_j(x) \geqq 0, j = 1, 2, \ldots, m$, and $x \in X$.

In other words, there exists an open ball $B(\hat{x})$ about $\hat{x}$ such that $A \equiv B(\hat{x}) \cap C \neq \emptyset$ and $f(\hat{x}) \geqq f(x)$ for all $x \in A$, where C is the constraint set.

We now state and prove the theorem.

Theorem 1.D.3 (Kuhn-Tucker's main theorem): *Let $f, g_1, g_2, \ldots, g_m$ be real-valued, differentiable functions on an open set X in R^n. Assume that the functions $g_j, j = 1, 2, \ldots, m$, satisfy* (KTCQ). *Then condition* (LM) *implies condition* (QSP).

PROOF: Let $\hat{x}$ be a local maximum. If $g_j(\hat{x}) > 0$ for all $j = 1, 2, \ldots m$, then it follows easily that $f'(\hat{x}) = 0$ (Theorem 1.C.6, unconstrained local maxi-

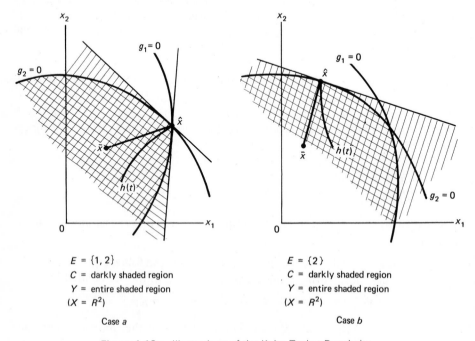

E = {1, 2}
C = darkly shaded region
Y = entire shaded region
(X = R²)

Case *a*

E = {2}
C = darkly shaded region
Y = entire shaded region
(X = R²)

Case *b*

Figure 1.12. Illustrations of the Kuhn-Tucker Regularity.

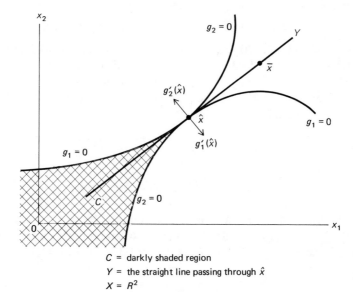

C = darkly shaded region
Y = the straight line passing through $\hat{x}$
X = R^2

Figure 1.13.   An Illustration of the Kuhn-Tucker Irregularity.

mum). Then if we choose $\hat{\lambda}_1 = \hat{\lambda}_2 = \ldots = \hat{\lambda}_m = 0$, the (QSP) condition is satisfied. Now suppose

$$g_j(\hat{x}) = 0 \qquad j \in E$$
$$g_j(\hat{x}) > 0 \qquad j \notin E$$

where $E \subset J \equiv \{1, 2, \ldots, m\}$ and $E \neq \emptyset$. Let $\bar{x}$ be an arbitrary point in X such that

$$g_j'(\hat{x}) \cdot (\bar{x} - \hat{x}) \geqq 0 \qquad \text{for } j \in E$$

We consider $h(t)$ in (KTCQ), with $h(0) = \hat{x}$. Write $x \equiv h(t)$. By the definition of differentiation, we have

$$f(x) - f(\hat{x}) = f'(\hat{x}) \cdot (x - \hat{x}) + o(\| x - \hat{x} \|)$$

Also

$$x - \hat{x} = h(t) - h(0) = h'(0)t + o(\| t \|) \quad \text{and} \quad o(\| x - \hat{x} \|) = o(\| t \|)$$

Hence

$$f(x) - f(\hat{x}) = f'(\hat{x}) \cdot [h'(0)t + o(\| t \|)] + o(\| t \|)$$

Therefore

$$f(x) - f(\hat{x}) = f'(\hat{x}) \cdot h'(0)t + o(\| t \|)$$

or

$$f(x) - f(\hat{x}) = \alpha f'(\hat{x}) \cdot (\bar{x} - \hat{x})t + o(\| t \|)$$

Since $x \equiv h(t) \in C$ for $0 \leqq t \leqq 1, f(x) - f(\hat{x}) \leqq 0$ for sufficiently small t from the local maximality of $f(\hat{x})$ in C. Hence for sufficiently small $t, f'(\hat{x}) \cdot (\bar{x} - \hat{x}) \leqq 0$. Write $\xi \equiv (\bar{x} - \hat{x})$. Then $-f'(\hat{x}) \cdot \xi \geqq 0$ for all ξ with $g'_j(\hat{x}) \cdot \xi \geqq 0$, $j \in E$. Therefore, by the Minkowski-Farkas lemma (Theorem 0.B.4), there exist $\hat{\lambda}_j \geqq 0$, for all $j \in E$, such that

$$-f'(\hat{x}) = \sum_{j \in E} \hat{\lambda}_j g'_j(\hat{x})$$

or

$$f'(\hat{x}) + \sum_{j \in E} \hat{\lambda}_j g'_j(\hat{x}) = 0$$

Choose $\hat{\lambda}_j = 0$ if $j \notin E$. We have now obtained $(\hat{x}, \hat{\lambda}_1, \ldots, \hat{\lambda}_m)$ such that $f'(\hat{x}) + \sum_{j=1}^m \hat{\lambda}_j g'_j(\hat{x}) = 0$. That $g_j(\hat{x}) \geqq 0$ for all j follows immediately from (LM). Since $g_j(\hat{x}) = 0$ for $j \in E$, and $\lambda_j = 0$ for $j \notin E$, we have

$$\sum_{j=1}^m \hat{\lambda}_j g_j(\hat{x}) = 0$$

(Q.E.D.)

REMARK: It should be clear from the above proof that the theorem follows almost immediately from (KTCQ). Note also that the above theorem and proof follow almost word for word when f and the g_j's are real-valued functions defined over X, where X is a "Banach space" (that is, a complete normed linear space).[3] See Ritter [13]. The Minkowski-Farkas lemma holds almost as it is when X, the domain of the f and g_j's, is an arbitrary linear space (which can be infinite dimensional and does not even have to be normed). See Fan [4], especially theorem 4, p. 104.

REMARK: In the (QSP) condition, we required, among others, the following relation:

$$\hat{f}_x + \hat{\lambda} \cdot \hat{g}_x = 0$$

If we do not have (KTCQ), (LM) does *not* necessarily imply (QSP) (in particular, the above relation). In other words, a statement such as "the first-order conditions are the necessary conditions for a local maximum" is *not* necessarily true. A special regularity condition such as (KTCQ) is required to make this statement valid.

However, if we modify the above expression to

$$\hat{\lambda}_0 \hat{f}_x + \hat{\lambda} \cdot \hat{g}_x = 0 \text{ where } \hat{\lambda}_0 \geqq 0$$

allowing the coefficient $\hat{\lambda}_0$ for $\hat{f}_x$ (with the possibility of $\hat{\lambda}_0 = 0$), then (LM) always implies (QSP) with *this modification*. In other words, the role of (KTCQ) is to guarantee that $\hat{\lambda}_0 > 0$ (which in turn enables us to set $\hat{\lambda}_0 = 1$). Hence the regularity condition such as (KTCQ) is really *the normality con-*

dition, which we discussed in Section B of this chapter. The theorem which states that (LM) implies the above *modified* (QSP) was proved by Fritz John in 1948 [8].

To make clear this point about $\hat{\lambda}_0$, let us consider the following example (**Slater's example**) again.

$$\text{Maximize: } f(x) \equiv x \qquad \text{on } x \in R$$
$$\text{Subject to: } g(x) \equiv -x^2 \geq 0$$

Clearly $\hat{x} = 0$ is a solution of this problem. Since the Lagrangian is written as $\Phi(x, \lambda) \equiv f(x) + \lambda g(x) = x - \lambda x^2$, we have $f_x + \lambda g_x = 1 - 2\lambda x$. Therefore $\hat{f}_x + \lambda \hat{g}_x = 1 - 2\lambda \hat{x} = 1$. In other words, $(\hat{f}_x + \lambda \hat{g}_x) \neq 0$ at $\hat{x} = 0$. Hence the usual first-order condition is *not* a necessary condition for maximality in this case. However, the condition

$$\hat{\lambda}_0 \hat{f}_x + \hat{\lambda} \hat{g}_x = 0$$

is certainly satisfied at $\hat{x} = 0$ with $\hat{\lambda}_0 = 0$.

When the condition (KTCQ) is satisfied, such a nonlinear programming problem is called **Kuhn-Tucker regular**, and in this case we have $[(LM) \Rightarrow (QSP)]$ (with $\hat{\lambda}_0 = 1$ as (QSP) is usually defined). However, (KTCQ) is not the only condition that guarantees $[(LM) \Rightarrow (QSP)]$. In fact, in Theorem 1.D.2 we already observed that Slater's condition (S) together with the concavity of the function f and the g_j's are also sufficient to guarantee $[(LM) \Rightarrow (QSP)]$; hence they are also the conditions for normality. We can check easily (as in fact we already remarked in Section B) that Slater's example given above does violate Slater's condition (S).

We are now interested in finding some other conditions that would guarantee $[(LM) \Rightarrow (QSP)]$. To begin, we may observe that (KTCQ) is not a particularly easy condition to check, so that we may be interested in finding conditions that are easier to apply. Second, we may also relate the present theory to the linear programming theory and to the classical maximization theory in which all the constraints are expressed as equalities. In this connection we may recall that in linear programming no normality condition such as (KTCQ) is required and that in the classical theory the normality condition called the "rank condition" is required.

With this background, we are now ready to state beautiful results by Arrow, Hurwicz, and Uzawa which provide us with important conditions that replace the (KTCQ) condition.

Theorem 1.D.4 (Arrow-Hurwicz-Uzawa):   *If any one of the following five conditions holds, then (KTCQ) in Theorem 1.D.3 can be dispensed with [that is, (LM) implies (QSP)], where X is an open convex subset of R^n.*

(i)   *The functions $g_j(x), j = 1, 2, \ldots, m$, are convex functions.*

(ii)   *The functions $g_j(x)$, $j = 1, 2, \ldots, m$, are linear or linear affine functions.*

(iii)   *The functions $g_j(x)$, $j = 1, 2, \ldots, m$, are concave functions and there exists an $\overline{x}$ in X such that $g_j(\overline{x}) \geq 0$ for $j \in E'$ and $g_j(\overline{x}) > 0$ for $j \in E''$, where E' is the set of indices for the effective constraints (at $\hat{x}$) which are linear (affine), and E'' is the set of indices for the effective constraints (at $\hat{x}$) which are not linear (affine).*

(iv)   *The constraint set, $C = \{x : g(x) \geq 0, j = 1, 2, \ldots, m, x \in R^n\}$, is convex and possesses an interior point, and $g_j'(\hat{x}) \neq 0$ for all $j \in E$, where E is the set of indices of all the effective constraints at $\hat{x}$.*

(v)   **(Rank condition)** *The rank of $\left[g_j'(\hat{x})\right]_{j \in E}$ equals the number of effective constraints at $\hat{x}$,[4] where the rank of the $k \times n$ matrix is defined as the (maximum) number of its linearly independent rows (which is equal to the maximum number of its linearly independent columns).[5]*

PROOF: Omitted. See Arrow, Hurwicz, and Uzawa [1], especially their theorem 3. See also the appendix to this section.

REMARK: We may call the above five conditions the **Arrow-Hurwicz-Uzawa** (or the **A-H-U**) **conditions**. Condition (ii) is obviously a special case of condition (i). Condition (ii) is important in connection with linear programming. Note that Slater's condition is a special case of condition (iii). Conditions (iv) and (v) presuppose no concavity or convexity of the g_j's. Condition (v) is famous from classical Lagrangian multiplier theory which deals with the case in which *all* the constraints are effective (that is, all the constraints are "equality constraints"). It is important to note that all the above five conditions are concerned with the constraints only.

REMARK: We illustrate Theorems 1.D.3 and 1.D.4 schematically in Figure 1.14.

If f and the g_j's are concave, then (QSP) implies (LM), hence (M). This was already discussed in Theorem 1.D.2.

We now show one immediate corollary of the above theorem.

Theorem 1.D.5:   *Let $f(x)$ be a real-valued concave differentiable function on R^n. Let a^j, $j = 1, 2, \ldots, m$, be points in R^n. Let $g_j(x) \equiv r_j - a^j \cdot x$, $j = 1, 2, \ldots, m$, where $r_j \in R$. Then $\hat{x}$ achieves a maximum of $f(x)$ subject to $g_j(x) \geq 0, j = 1, 2, \ldots, m$, if and only if*

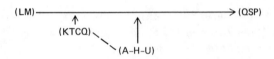

Figure 1.14.   An Illustration of Theorems 1.D.3 and 1.D.4.

(i) *There exists a $\hat{\lambda} \geq 0$ such that $(\hat{x}, \hat{\lambda})$ is a saddle point of $\Phi(x, \lambda) = f(x) + \lambda \cdot g(x)$ over $R^n \otimes \Omega^m$; that is, $\Phi(x, \hat{\lambda}) \leq \Phi(\hat{x}, \hat{\lambda}) \leq \Phi(\hat{x}, \lambda)$ for all $x \in R^n$ and all $\lambda \geq 0$.*

Or

(ii) *There exists a $\hat{\lambda} \geq 0$ such that $(\hat{x}, \hat{\lambda})$ satisfies (QSP).*

PROOF: Since $g_j(x)$ is linear affine for all j, condition (ii) of the Arrow-Hurwicz-Uzawa theorem is satisfied. Hence (M) implies (QSP). Moreover, f is concave and the g_j's are linear affine, hence concave; therefore (QSP) is sufficient for the maximality (M). Thus statement (ii) in the above theorem is proved. Owing to the differentiability of f and the g_j's, (SP) implies (QSP). Owing to the concavity of f and the g_j's, (QSP) implies (SP). Since (QSP) is necessary and sufficient for (M), (SP) is now also necessary and sufficient for (M), which proves statement (i) of the theorem.   (Q.E.D.)

REMARK   To prove the above theorem, we really do not need the machinery of the Arrow-Hurwicz-Uzawa theorem. But the extreme simplicity of the above proof will indicate the power of the theorem, as well as enhance the reader's understanding of the theorem.

REMARK: It may be worthwhile to recall the warning that we gave earlier. That is, in order that an expression such as $\hat{f}_x + \hat{\lambda} \cdot \hat{g}_x = 0$ in (QSP) be meaningful, $\hat{x}$ must be an interior point in X. If this condition is not satisfied, the theorems which involve (QSP) become meaningless and those theorems whose proofs require (QSP) may not hold. Consider the following example from Moore [12].

$$\text{Maximize: } f(x) \equiv \sqrt{1 - x^2}$$
$$\underset{x \in R}{}$$

$$\text{Subject to: } g(x) \equiv x - 1 \geq 0$$

Note that the domain of $f(x)$ is restricted to a closed interval $[-1, 1]$ in R, in order that $f(x)$ be a real-valued function. Hence, in view of the constraint $x - 1 \geq 0$, the constraint set consists of only one point $x = 1$. The solution of the above problem is obviously $\hat{x} = 1$. However, we cannot state the (QSP) condition since f' is not defined at $\hat{x} = 1$. Note that the Lagrangian $\Phi \equiv \sqrt{1 - x^2} + \lambda(x - 1)$ does not have a saddle point at $\hat{x} = 1$. Note also that the constraint function $g(x)$ is linear affine in this case, so that condition (ii) of the A-H-U theorem is satisfied.

It may be worthwhile now to summarize some of the results obtained with respect to the characterization of a solution. For the sake of simplicity, we assume $X = R^n$, which, in particular, implies that X is open and convex. Moreover, whenever (QSP) appears, the differentiability of f and the g_j's is assumed. First we remind ourselves of the problem and various conditions.

PROBLEM: Maximize: $f(x)$
$\quad\quad\quad\quad\quad$ x
$\quad\quad\quad\quad$ Subject to: $g_j(x) \geq 0, j = 1, 2, \ldots, m$
$\quad\quad\quad\quad\quad\quad\quad\quad$ $x \in X = R^n$

or

$\quad\quad\quad\quad$ Maximize: $f(x)$
$\quad\quad\quad\quad\quad$ x
$\quad\quad\quad\quad$ Subject to: $x \in C$, where $C \equiv \{x \in X: g_j(x) \geq 0, j = 1, \ldots, m\}$

Condition (M) $\hat{x}$ is a solution of the above problem.
Condition (LM)   There exists an open ball (or neighborhood) $B(\hat{x})$ such that $\hat{x}$ maximizes $f(x)$ subject to $x \in B(\hat{x}) \cap C$.
Condition (SP)   The point $(\hat{x}, \hat{\lambda})$ is a saddle-point of $\Phi(x, \lambda) \equiv f(x) + \lambda \cdot g(x)$.
Condition (QSP)   (Or the **first-order conditions**) The point $(\hat{x}, \hat{\lambda})$ is a quasi-saddle-point of $\Phi(x, \lambda)$; that is,

(i) $\hat{f}_x + \hat{\lambda} \cdot \hat{g}_x = 0$
(ii) $\hat{\lambda} \cdot g(\hat{x}) = 0, \quad g(\hat{x}) \geq 0$

and

(iii) $\hat{\lambda} \geq 0, \hat{\lambda} \in R^m, \hat{x} \in X$

Condition (KTCQ)   The constraint functions g_j's satisfy the Kuhn-Tucker constraint qualification.
Condition (A-H-U)   The constraint functions g_j's satisfy any one of the five conditions of the Arrow-Hurwicz-Uzawa theorem. For example,

(i)   The g_j's are all convex or linear (affine).
(ii)   The g_j's are all concave and satisfy the Slater condition (S):
$\quad\quad$ (S) $\exists \bar{x} \in X$ such that $g_j(\bar{x}) > 0$ for all j.
(iii)   The rank condition is satisfied.

Condition (Conc.)   The functions $f, g_j, j = 1, 2, \ldots, m$, are all concave.

We are now ready to obtain the diagram which shows the logical connections of the above conditions (Figure 1.15).

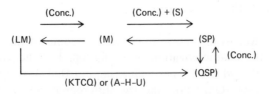

Figure 1.15.   Characterization of $\hat{x}$.

In Figure 1.15, the arrow again reads "implies" under the conditions stated with the arrow. If no conditions are stated, then no conditions are necessary to obtain the given implication. In practical applications of nonlinear programming theory to economics, the following conditions are often satisfied.

(i)   The function f is concave and the g_j's are all concave and satisfy (S), or

(ii) The function f is concave and the g_j's are all linear (affine).

In such a "nice" situation, we can easily see that Figure 1.15 is considerably simplified to Figure 1.16; that is, (LM), (M), (SP), and (QSP) are all equivalent.

The classical Lagrangian problem is concerned with the problem of "equality constraints," that is, finding $\hat{x} \in X$, an open subset of R^n, which maximizes $f(x)$ subject to $g_j(x) = 0$, $j = 1, 2, \ldots, m$, where f and the g_j's are real-valued continuously differentiable functions on X in R^n. As we remarked earlier, these constraints can be converted into $g_j(x) \geqq 0$ and $-g_j(x) \geqq 0$, $j = 1, 2, \ldots, m$. Clearly if the constraints are all linear, then the constraint qualification is satisfied as a result of condition (ii) of the A-H-U theorem. However, suppose that the g_j's are not linear. Condition (i) cannot be applied, for if g_j is convex, then $-g_j$ is concave. Condition (iii) cannot be applied either, for if $g_j(\bar{x}) > 0$ for some $\bar{x}$, we cannot have $-g_j(\bar{x}) > 0$. The rank constraint (v) may not seem applicable, for the rank of the $(2m \times n)$ matrix.

$$\begin{bmatrix} \dfrac{\partial g_j}{\partial x_i} \\[2mm] -\dfrac{\partial g_j}{\partial x_i} \end{bmatrix}$$

is certainly not equal to $2m$, for any $x \in X$, where $2m$ is apparently the number of effective constraints. However, this is not correct reasoning. We have to note that the constraints $g_j(x) \geqq 0$ and $-g_j(x) \geqq 0$ are not distinct constraints when the values of x are such that $g_j(x) = 0$. Hence, although there are $2m$ constraints in appearance, the number of distinct constraints for x with $g_j(x) = 0$ is m, and the rank condition for the problem should be stated that the rank of the $(m \times n)$ matrix $[\partial g_j / \partial x_i]$ should be equal to m. Hence we obtain the following classical theorem, which was originally conceived by Lagrange and later developed by Carathéodory [2] and Bliss.[6]

Theorem 1.D.6. (Lagrange):   *Suppose that $\hat{x}$ satisfies (LM).[7] Suppose also that*

Figure 1.16.   Characterization of $\hat{x}$ for a "Nice" Case.

the rank of the $(m \times n)$ matrix $\left[\partial g_j / \partial x_i\right]$ evaluated at $\hat{x}$ is equal to m, where it is assumed that $m < n$. Then (QSP) holds for this $\hat{x}$.

REMARK: The Lagrangian for this problem is written as

$$\Phi \equiv f(x) + \sum_{j=1}^{m}(\mu_j - v_j)g_j(x) = f(x) + \sum_{j=1}^{m}\lambda_j g_j(x)$$

where $\lambda_j \equiv \mu_j - v_j, j = 1, 2, \ldots, m$. Although in (QSP) we may require $\hat{\mu}_j \geq 0$ and $\hat{v}_j \geq 0$, we cannot require $\hat{\lambda}_j \geq 0$ $(j = 1, 2, \ldots, m)$; that is, $\hat{\lambda}_j$ can be either positive or negative.

EXAMPLE: Consider the problem of choosing $(x_1, x_2) \in R^2$ to
Maximize: $x_1 x_2$
Subject to: $g(x) \equiv x_1^2 + x_2^2 - 1 = 0$

Using a diagrammatical representation of the problem, we can easily obtain the solution of the problem as $\hat{x}_1, \hat{x}_2 = \pm 1/\sqrt{2}$. We now obtain this as an application of the above theorem. Define the Lagrangian by $\Phi \equiv x_1 x_2 + \lambda(x_1^2 + x_2^2 - 1)$. The (QSP) conditions can be written as

$$\frac{\partial \hat{\Phi}}{\partial x_1} = \hat{x}_2 + 2\hat{\lambda}\hat{x}_1 = 0, \frac{\partial \hat{\Phi}}{\partial x_2} = \hat{x}_1 + 2\hat{\lambda}\hat{x}_2 = 0, \text{ and } \hat{x}_1^2 + \hat{x}_2^2 - 1 = 0$$

From these three equations we can easily obtain $\hat{x}_1, \hat{x}_2 = \pm 1/\sqrt{2}$ and $\hat{\lambda} = \frac{1}{2}$. The rank condition which validates the above computation is that the rank of $(\partial g / \partial x_1, \partial g / \partial x_2) = (2x_1, 2x_2)$ must be equal to one at $(\hat{x}_1, \hat{x}_2)$. It is obvious that this condition holds.

The above consideration of the case with the equality constraints enables us to extend our analysis to the case in which both equality and inequality constraints are present (the case of **mixed constraints**). In other words, consider the problem of finding x so as to

Maximize: $f(x)$
$x \in X$

Subject to: $g_j(x) \geq 0, j = 1, 2, \ldots, m$
$h_k(x) = 0, k = 1, 2, \ldots, l$

It is assumed that f, and the g_j's and h_k's are continuously differentiable. Let $\hat{x}$ be a solution of this problem and let E be the set of indices such that $g_j(\hat{x}) = 0$ (that is, the effective constraints). Let m_e be the number of elements in E. Then we can obtain the following theorem, assuming $m_e + l < n$.

Theorem 1.D.7:   *Suppose that $\hat{x}$ satisfies (LM).[8] Suppose also that the rank of the $(m_e + l) \times n$ matrix*

$$\begin{bmatrix} \dfrac{\partial g_j}{\partial x_i} \\[2mm] \dfrac{\partial h_k}{\partial x_i} \end{bmatrix} \qquad \textit{where } j \in E \textit{ and } k = 1, 2, \ldots, l$$

evaluated at $\hat{x}$, is equal to $(m_e + 1)$. Then (QSP) holds for this $\hat{x}$ where the Lagrangian for the above theorem is defined as

$$\Phi \equiv f(x) + \lambda \cdot g(x) + \mu \cdot h(x)$$

Here (QSP) requires $\hat{\lambda} \geq 0$, while $\hat{\mu}$ can be either positive or negative.

REMARK: For a further and a more vigorous consideration of mixed constraints, see Mangasarian [11], chapter 11.

EXAMPLE: Consider the problem of choosing $(x_1, x_2) \in R^2$ to

> Maximize: $x_1 x_2$
> Subject to: $g(x) \equiv x_1 + 8x_2 - 4 \geq 0$
> $h(x) \equiv x_1^2 + x_2^2 - 1 = 0$

Using the diagrammatical representation of the problem, the solution of this problem can be obtained easily as $\hat{x}_1 = \hat{x}_2 = 1/\sqrt{2}$. The Lagrangian of this problem is defined as $\Phi \equiv x_1 x_2 + \lambda_1(x_1 + 8x_2 - 4) + \lambda_2(x_1^2 + x_2^2 - 1)$, and the (QSP) conditions are written out as

$$\frac{\partial \hat{\Phi}}{\partial x_1} = \hat{x}_2 + \hat{\lambda}_1 + 2\hat{\lambda}_2\hat{x}_1 = 0$$

$$\frac{\partial \hat{\Phi}}{\partial x_2} = \hat{x}_1 + 8\hat{\lambda}_1 + 2\hat{\lambda}_2\hat{x}_2 = 0$$

$$\hat{x}_1^2 + \hat{x}_2^2 - 1 = 0$$
$$\hat{\lambda}_1(\hat{x}_1 + 8\hat{x}_2 - 4) = 0$$
$$\hat{\lambda}_1 \geq 0$$

Solving this, we can also obtain $\hat{x}_1 = \hat{x}_2 = 1/\sqrt{2}$ as well as $\hat{\lambda}_1 = 0$ and $\hat{\lambda}_2 = -\frac{1}{2}$. Note that the Lagrangian multiplier $\hat{\lambda}_2$ which corresponds to the equality constraint is negative here. It can easily be seen that the constraint $g(x) \geq 0$ is ineffective at $(\hat{x}_1, \hat{x}_2)$, that is, $1/\sqrt{2} + 8/\sqrt{2} - 4 > 0$. Hence the rank condition for this problem is that the rank of $(\partial h/\partial x_1, \partial h/\partial x_2) = (2x_1, 2x_2)$ be equal to 1 at $\hat{x}_1 = \hat{x}_2 = 1/\sqrt{2}$, which is trivially satisfied.

POSTSCRIPT: This section and Section B constitute the main characterizations of optimal solutions. Our approach here is via the theory of convex sets utilizing the separation theorems and the Minkowski-Farkas lemma. This approach was motivated by the development of linear programming. Historically there is another route, that is, via calculus. The classical Lagrangian theorem is concerned with the case in which all the constraints are equalities. Karush [9], much prior to Kuhn and Tucker [10], considered the inequality constraints, reducing them to the equality constraints by adding to, or subtracting from each inequality the square of a real number.[9] For example, the constraints $g_j(x) \geq 0, j = 1, 2, \ldots, m$, can be converted into the following equality constraints:

$$g_j(x) - \delta_j^2 = 0, \text{ where } \delta_j^2 \geq 0, j = 1, 2, \ldots, m$$

Unfortunately, this work has been unduly ignored. El-Hodiri [3] rediscovered Karush [9] and put it in a better perspective. The essential tool in the calculus approach is the implicit function theorem. Although several approaches are possible in this calculus route, three expositions seem to be most useful, that is, Hestenes [6], Mangasarian [11], and El-Hodiri, M. A. (*Constrained Extrema: Introduction to the Differentiable Case with Economic Applications*, Berlin, Springer-Verlag, 1971).

Next to Karush [9], but still prior to Kuhn and Tucker [10], Fritz John ([8], 1948) considered the nonlinear programming problem with inequality constraints. He assumed no qualification except that all functions are continuously differentiable. Here the Lagrangian expression looks like $(\lambda_0 f + \lambda \cdot g)$ instead of $(f + \lambda \cdot g)$, and λ_0 can be 0 in the first-order conditions. The Kuhn-Tucker constraint qualification ([10], 1951) amounts to providing a condition which guarantees $\lambda_0 > 0$ (that is, a normality condition). Arrow-Hurwicz-Uzawa ([1], 1961) then provided a weaker normality condition than the Kuhn-Tucker constraint qualification, and also provided us with some very useful constraint qualifications that imply their normality condition. Their normality condition was shown to be the weakest possible if the constraint set is convex. Since then there have been some efforts to weaken the normality condition. In 1967, Abadie introduced a new normality condition which neither implies nor is implied by the Arrow-Hurwicz-Uzawa condition. Evans (1969) then provided us with a normality condition that was weaker than any of those mentioned above. The normality condition for the case in which both inequality and equality constraints are present was considered by Mangasarian and Fromovitz in 1967 and by Mangasarian ([11], chap. 11). They presented a normality condition for the case of mixed constraints. A further investigation for the case of mixed constraints was done by Gould and Tolle (1971).[10]

FOOTNOTES

1. In order that the expression $\hat{f}_x + \hat{\lambda} \cdot \hat{g}_x = 0$ be meaningful, $\hat{x}$ must be an interior point in X. That is, there exists an open ball about $\hat{x}$ which is contained in X. Intuitively, $\hat{x}$ is surrounded by points in X. If X is an open set, this condition is satisfied. In many nonlinear programming problems, it is simply assumed that $X = R^n$.
2. This is often known as the **nonnegative quasi-saddle-point condition**.

3. A **Banach space** is a normed space that is "complete" as a metric space induced by the norm. A metric space is called **complete** if every sequence $\{x^q\}$ in X which has the following property is convergent. For each $\epsilon > 0$, there exists a positive integer $\bar{q}$ such that $d(x^q, x^{q'}) < \epsilon$ for all $q, q' \geq \bar{q}$. (Any sequence satisfying this property is called a **Cauchy sequence**.) The set of all the continuous functions defined on a closed interval in R is an example of a Banach space, when the norm is properly defined.

4. These constraints $g_j(x) \geq 0, j = 1, 2, \ldots, m$, must be **distinct**. For example, the two constraints $x_1 + x_2 < 1$ and $2x_1 + 2x_2 < 2$ are not distinct. More formally, the functions $g_j, j = 1, 2, \ldots, m$, must be linearly independent. It is easy to see that this rank condition will not hold under any circumstances if we allow non-distinct constraints.

5. The maximum number of linearly independent rows of any (possibly rectangular) matrix is equal to the maximum number of its linearly independent columns. This is often known as the **rank theorem**. See D. Gale, *The Theory of Linear Economic Models*, New York, McGraw-Hill, 1960, pp. 36–37. Here it is assumed that the number of effective constraints is less than n.

6. Carathéodory [2] stated and proved the theorem in which the normality condition is not involved (thus the coefficient for f, λ_0, appears in the Lagrangian). See his theorem 2, p. 177. The proof is a simple application of the implicit function theorem. See also G. A. Bliss, *Lectures on the Calculus of Variations*, Chicago, Ill., University of Chicago Press, 1946.

7. The definition of (LM) must be modified to cope with the equality constraint. Such a modification must be obvious, that is, $g_j(x) \geq 0$ in the definition of (LM) is replaced by $g_j(x) = 0$.

8. Again, $g_j(x) \geq 0, j = 1, 2, \ldots, m$, in the definition of (LM) should be replaced by $g_j(x) \geq 0, j = 1, 2, \ldots, m$, and $h_k(x) = 0, k = 1, 2, \ldots, l$.

9. This is obviously motivated by the similar procedure in the calculus of variations by Valentine. See F. A. Valentine, "The Problem of Lagrange in the Calculus of Variations with Inequalities as Added Side Conditions," in *Contributions to the Calculus of Variations (1933–1937)*, Chicago, Ill., University of Chicago Press, 1937.

10. The works cited in this paragraph are as follows: J. Abadie, "On the Kuhn-Tucker Theorem," in *Nonlinear Programming*, ed. by J. Abadie, New York, Wiley, 1967; J. Evans, "A Note on Constraint Qualifications," *Report 6917*, Center for Mathematical Studies in Business and Economics, University of Chicago, June 1969; O. L. Mangasarian, and S. Fromovitz, "The Fritz John Necessary Optimality Conditions in the Presence of Equality and Inequality Constraints," *Journal of Mathematical Analysis and Applications*, 17, January 1967; F. J. Gould, and J. W. Tolle, "A Necessary and Sufficient Qualification for Constraint Optimization," *SIAM Journal on Applied Mathematics*, 20, March 1971.

REFERENCES

1. Arrow, K. J., Hurwicz, L., and Uzawa, H., "Constraint Qualifications in Maximization Problems," *Naval Research Logistics Quarterly*, vol. 8, no. 2, June 1961.

2. Carathéodory, C., *Calculus of Variations and Partial Differential Equations of the First Order, Part II, Calculus of Variations*, San Francisco, Holden Day, 1967 (translated from the German original published in 1935).

3. El-Hodiri, M., "The Karush Characterization of Constrained Extrema of Functions of a Finite Number of Variables," Ministry of Treasury UAR, *Research Memoranda*, series A, no. 3, July 1967.

4. Fan, Ky, "On Systems of Linear Inequalities," in *Linear Inequalities and Related Systems*, ed. by Kuhn and Tucker, Princeton, N.J., Princeton University Press, 1956.

5. Hadley, G., *Nonlinear and Dynamic Programming*, Reading, Mass., Addison-Wesley, 1964, esp. chap. 6.

6. Hestenes, M. R., *Calculus of Variations and Optimal Control Theory*, New York, Wiley, 1966, esp. chap. 1.

7. Hurwicz, L., "Programming in Linear Spaces," in *Studies in Linear and Non-linear Programming*, ed. by Arrow, Hurwicz, and Uzawa, Stanford, Calif., Stanford University Press, 1958.

8. John, F., "Extremum Problems with Inequalities as Subsidiary Conditions," *Studies and Essays*, Courant Anniversary Volume, New York, Interscience, 1948.

9. Karush, W., *Minima of Functions of Several Variables with Inequalities as Side Conditions*, Master's Thesis, University of Chicago, 1939.

10. Kuhn, H. W., and Tucker, A. W., "Non-linear Programming," *Proceedings of the Second Berkeley Symposium on Mathematical Statistics and Probability*, ed. by Neyman, Berkeley, Calif., University of California Press, 1951, pp. 481–492.

11. Mangasarian, O. L., *Nonlinear Programming*, New York, McGraw-Hill, 1969.

12. Moore, J. C., "Some Extensions of the Kuhn-Tucker Results in Concave Programming," in *Papers in Quantitative Economics*, ed. by J. P. Quirk and A. Zarley, Lawrence, Kansas, University of Kansas Press, 1969.

13. Ritter, K., "Duality for Nonlinear Programming in a Banach Space," *SIAM Journal on Applied Mathematics*, vol. 15, no. 2, March 1967.

14. Samuelson, P. A., *Foundations of Economic Analysis*, Cambridge, Mass., Harvard University Press, 1947, esp. appendix A.

Appendix to Section D: A Further Note on the Arrow-Hurwicz-Uzawa Theorem[1]

In Section D, we introduced a very useful result due to Arrow, Hurwicz, and Uzawa (Theorem 1.D.4) that provided five conditions, any one of which replaces the (KTCQ). In other words, if any of these five conditions holds, the (LM) condition implies the (QSP) condition. The beauty of these conditions is that it is much easier to apply them than the (KTCQ). In proving this theorem, Arrow, Hurwicz, and Uzawa [2] first proposed the "condition W," as they called it, which replaces (KTCQ) but which is "slightly weaker" than (KTCQ). Then they prove that any one of the above five conditions implies this condition W.

Later in a lecture at Minnesota [5], Hurwicz simplified the proof of the Arrow-Hurwicz-Uzawa theorem considerably.[2] The purpose of this Appendix is to provide an expository account of this new proof of the Arrow-Hurwicz-Uzawa theorem.

We consider the following nonlinear programming problem.

$$\text{Maximize: } f(x)$$
$$\text{Subject to: } g_j(x) \geqq 0, j = 1, 2, \ldots, m$$
$$x \in X$$

We assume that X is a nonempty convex open set in R^n. Let $\hat{x}$ be a point in X which achieves a local maximum of $f(x)$, subject to the constraints [that is, the condition (LM) is realized by $\hat{x}$]. Let E be the set of indices for the effective constraints at $\hat{x}$; that is, $g_j(\hat{x}) = 0$, if $j \in E$, $E \subset \{1, 2, \ldots, m\}$. Let J be the set of indices for the convex effective constraints and let J' be the set of indices for the nonconvex effective constraints. In other words, $j \in J$ means $j \in E$ and $g_j(x)$ is convex on X, and $j \in J'$ means $j \in E$ and $g_j(x)$ is not convex on X. Clearly $E = J \cup J'$. We now define the following condition due to Arrow, Hurwicz, and Uzawa [2] (p. 183, theorem 3), which we call **condition (AHU)** or the **Arrow-Hurwicz-Uzawa constraint qualification.**

(AHU)   There exists an $h^* \in R^n$ such that

$$g_j'(\hat{x}) \cdot h^* \geqq 0 \quad \text{for all } j \in J$$

and

$$g_j'(\hat{x}) \cdot h^* > 0 \quad \text{for all } j \in J'$$

This condition plays an important role in Arrow-Hurwicz-Uzawa [2] and will play a crucial role in the following proof. We are now ready to state the main theorem of this appendix.

Theorem 1.D.8:   *Let $f, g_1, g_2, \ldots, g_m$ be real-valued differentiable functions defined on a nonempty open convex set X in R^n. Suppose that condition (AHU) is satisfied. Then (LM) implies (QSP). In other words, if $\hat{x}$ achieves a local maximum of the problem, there exists a $\hat{\lambda}$ such that the quasi-saddle-point condition (QSP) is satisfied.*[3]

PROOF (HURWICZ):

   (i)   Suppose $g_j(\hat{x}) > 0$ for all $j = 1, 2, \ldots, m$ (that is, $E = \emptyset$). It follows that $f'(\hat{x}) = 0$, for we have in this case the unconstrained maximization problem. By choosing $\hat{\lambda}_1 = \hat{\lambda}_2 = \ldots = \hat{\lambda}_m = 0$, the (QSP) condition is satisfied. Now we concentrate on the case in which $E \neq \emptyset$.

   (ii)   Suppose $g_j(x)$ is convex (that is, $j \in J$). Then $g_j(\hat{x} + th^*) - g_j(\hat{x}) \geqq g_j'(\hat{x}) \cdot (th^*)$ for all $t \in R, t \geqq 0$, and any $h^* \in R^n$ such that $(\hat{x} + th^*) \in X$. But by condition (AHU), we can choose h^* such that $g_j'(\hat{x}) \cdot h^* \geqq 0$. Hence $g_j(\hat{x} + th^*) - g_j(\hat{x}) \geqq 0$ for all $t \geqq 0, t \in R$, such that $\hat{x} + th^* \in X$.

   (iii)   Suppose $g_j(x)$ is not convex (that is, $j \in J'$). By the definition of differentiation, we have

$$g_j(x) - g_j(\hat{x}) = g_j'(\hat{x}) \cdot (x - \hat{x}) + o(\|x - \hat{x}\|) \quad \text{for all } x \in X$$

Let $x(t) \equiv \hat{x} + th^*$ such that $x(t) \in X$ and $t > 0, t \in R$. Then $g_j[x(t)] - g_j(\hat{x}) = g_j'(\hat{x}) \cdot (th^*) + o(\| t \|)$. But by condition (AHU), we c.n choose h^* such that $g_j'(\hat{x}) \cdot h^* > 0$. Hence $g_j[x(t)] - g_j(\hat{x}) > 0$ for sufficiently small t.[4] Hence choosing t sufficiently small, say $0 < t < \bar{t}$, we can have $g_j[x(t)] - g_j(\hat{x}) > 0$ for all $j \in J'$.

(iv) Let $x(t) \equiv \hat{x} + th^*$, where $0 \leq t < \bar{t}$ with $x(t) \in X$. Then combining (ii) and (iii) we have $g_j[x(t)] - g_j(\hat{x}) \geq 0$ for all $j \in E$, or $g_j[x(t)] \geq 0$ for all $j \in E$. Moreover, $g_j[x(t)] \geq 0$ for all $j \notin E$, for sufficiently small t, say $\bar{\bar{t}}$, owing to the fact that $g_j(\hat{x}) > 0$ for all $j \notin E$ and the continuity of the g_j's. Thus $x(t) \in C$, where C is the constraint set $\{x \in X : g_j(x) \geq 0, j = 1, 2, \ldots, m\}$, if t is sufficiently small (that is, $t < \min \{\bar{t}, \bar{\bar{t}}\}$).

(v) Now define $\Psi(t) \equiv f[x(t)] - f(\hat{x})$ for $0 \leq t < \tilde{t}$ where $\tilde{t} = \min \{\bar{t}, \bar{\bar{t}}\}$. Note that $\Psi(0) = 0$. Also $\Psi(t) \leq 0$ for sufficiently small t, say, $0 \leq t \leq t_0 < \tilde{t}$ where $t_0 > 0$, because, by assumption, $x(t) \in C$ and $\hat{x}$ achieves a local maximum of $f(x)$ subject to $x \in C$. Let $\Psi'_+(0)$ be the right-hand derivative of Ψ at $t = 0$.[5] Then by the chain rule, we have $\Psi'_+(0) = f'(\hat{x}) \cdot h^*$. Note that $\Psi(t) \leq 0 = \Psi(0), 0 \leq t \leq t_0$, which implies that $\Psi(t)$ is non-increasing at $t = 0$, or $\Psi'_+(0) \leq 0$. Hence $f'(\hat{x}) \cdot h^* \leq 0$. Since the choice of h^* can be arbitrary as long as condition (AHU) is satisfied, we have thus established $f'(\hat{x}) \cdot h^* \leq 0$ for any h^* in which condition (AHU) is satisfied. Note that condition (AHU) is *a fortiori* satisfied if there exists an $\bar{h} \in R^n$ such that $g_j'(\hat{x}) \cdot \bar{h} > 0$ for all $j \in E$. Hence for any $\bar{h} \in R^n$ for which $g_j'(\hat{x}) \cdot \bar{h} > 0$ for all $j \in E$, we have $f'(\hat{x}) \cdot \bar{h} \leq 0$.

(vi) Now consider any h satisfying $g_j'(\hat{x}) \cdot h \geq 0$ for all $j \in E$. Then we have $g_j'(\hat{x}) \cdot (h + th^*) > 0$ for all $j \in E$ and for any $t > 0, t \in R$, if condition (AHU) is satisfied for h^*. Then as a result of the conclusion obtained in (v), we have

$$f'(\hat{x}) \cdot (h + th^*) \leq 0$$

Take the limit as $t \to 0$. Then, owing to the continuity of the inner product, we obtain

$$f'(\hat{x}) \cdot h \leq 0$$

Thus we have established that $f'(\hat{x}) \cdot h \leq 0$ for all h such that

$$g_j'(\hat{x}) \cdot h \geq 0, \qquad j \in E$$

(vii) Hence, from the Minkowski-Farkas lemma (Theorem 0.B.4), there exist $\hat{\lambda}_j$'s, all ≥ 0, such that

$$-f'(\hat{x}) = \sum_{j \in E} \hat{\lambda}_j g_j'(\hat{x})$$

or

$$f'(\hat{x}) + \sum_{j \in E} \hat{\lambda}_j g_j'(\hat{x}) = 0$$

Choose $\hat{\lambda}_j = 0$ if $j \notin E$. Then

$$f'(\hat{x}) + \sum_{j=1}^{m} \hat{\lambda}_j g_j'(\hat{x}) = 0$$

That $g_j(\hat{x}) \geq 0$ for all j follows immediately from condition (LM). Since $g_j(\hat{x}) = 0$ for all $j \in E$ and $\hat{\lambda}_j = 0$ for $j \notin E$, we obtain

$$\sum_{j=1}^{m} \hat{\lambda}_j \, g_j(\hat{x}) = 0$$

(Q.E.D.)

REMARK: Just as (KTCQ), the above condition (AHU) is again the normality condition. Notice also that it is a qualification for the constraints (that is, nothing is mentioned about the maximand function f).

We are now ready to derive the conclusion of the Arrow-Hurwicz-Uzawa theorem. In particular, we want to show that any one of the five conditions in the A-H-U theorem implies condition (AHU). This part of the A-H-U theorem is really a corollary of the above theorem and has already been established in the original paper by Arrow, Hurwicz, and Uzawa (see the corollaries of their theorem 3 in [2]).

First, note that if $g_j(x)$ is convex for all $j \in E$, then condition (AHU) is trivially satisfied. This can be seen easily by choosing $h^* = 0$ in the statement of condition (AHU). Clearly if *either* of the following two conditions is satisfied, then $g_j(x)$ is convex for all $j \in E$.

(i)   The function $g_j(x)$ is convex for all $j = 1, 2, \ldots, m$.
(ii) The function $g_j(x)$ is linear for all $j = 1, 2, \ldots, m$.

Since every linear function is convex, (ii) is really a special case of (i); however, it has a powerful implication, for, as remarked before, it implies that, in linear programming, condition (AHU) is automatically satisfied.

Next we will see that the following modification of the Slater condition implies condition (AHU):

(iii) The function $g_j(x)$ is concave for $j = 1, 2, \ldots, m$ and there exists an $\bar{x} \in X$ such that $g_j(\bar{x}) > 0$ for all $j = 1, 2, \ldots, m$.

To see this, first recall the following basic inequality for concave functions.

$$g_j'(\hat{x}) \cdot (x - \hat{x}) \geq g_j(x) - g_j(\hat{x}) \quad \text{for any } x, \hat{x} \in X$$

In particular, set $x = \bar{x}$ and let $h \equiv \bar{x} - \hat{x}$. Then we have

$$g_j'(\hat{x}) \cdot \bar{h} \geq g_j(\bar{x}) > 0 \qquad \text{for all } j \in E$$

That $g_j(\bar{x}) > 0$ (for all j) follows from the above condition (iii). Thus condition (AHU) is satisfied if condition (iii) is satisfied. It should be clear that, in view of (ii), condition (iii) can be slightly weakened as in (iii′).

(iii′) The functions $g_j(x)$, $j = 1, 2, \ldots, m$, are all concave and there exists an $\bar{x}$ in X such that $g_j(\bar{x}) \geq 0$ for $j \in E'$ and $g_j(\bar{x}) > 0$, $j \in E''$, where E' is the set of indices for the effective constraints (at $\hat{x}$) for which the g_j's are linear, and E'' is the set of indices for the effective contraints (at $\hat{x}$) for which the g_j's are not linear (but concave).

Next we show that the following rank condition implies condition (AHU):

(iv) The rank of the $m \times n$ matrix $g'(\hat{x})$ (that is, the Jacobian matrix) is equal to the number of effective constraints at $\hat{x}$.

Let $g'_E(\hat{x})$ be the submatrix of $g'(\hat{x})$ obtained from $g'(\hat{x})$ by deleting the rows which correspond to the constraints that are not effective at $\hat{x}$ [that is, "$g'_j(\hat{x})$ is a row of $g'_E(\hat{x})$" means $j \in E$]. Let k be the number of effective constraints at $\hat{x}$. Then, owing to condition (iv), the number of linearly independent rows of the matrix $g'(\hat{x})$ is equal to k. Note that owing to an elementary property of matrices, the rank of matrices cannot exceed the number of columns or rows.[6] Hence $k \leq n$ as well as $k \leq m$. Since all the rows of $g'_E(\hat{x})$ are linearly independent, there are k linearly independent columns in $g'_E(\hat{x})$. Without loss of generality we may suppose that the first k columns of $g'_E(\hat{x})$ are linearly independent. Let A be the $k \times k$ square matrix obtained from $g'_E(\hat{x})$ by deleting the $(k + 1)$th to the nth column (if $k < n$). Let u be the k-vector whose elements are all equal to 1. Since A is a nonsingular square matrix, there exists a k-vector $\tilde{h}$ such that $A \cdot \tilde{h} = u$. Let an n-vector h^* be defined such that $h^*_i = \tilde{h}_i$ for $i = 1, 2, \ldots, k$, and $h^*_i = 0$ for $i = k + 1, \ldots, n$. Then clearly we have $g'_E(\hat{x}) \cdot h^* = u > 0$, or $g'_j(\hat{x}) \cdot h^* > 0$ for $j \in E$. This establishes condition (AHU). Hence the rank condition (iv) implies condition (AHU).

There is another condition in the Arrow-Hurwicz-Uzawa theorem which implies condition (AHU): The constraint set C is convex and has an interior and $g'_j(\hat{x}) \neq 0$ for every $j \in E$. The proof that this condition implies condition (AHU) is a little complicated, and hence is omitted. Interested readers are referred to Arrow, Hurwicz, and Uzawa [2], p. 184.

Fritz John's famous theorem, originally obtained in 1948 ([4], theorem I, pp. 188–189),[7] is an easy consequence of Theorem 1.D.8.

Theorem 1.D.9 (John): *Let $f, g_1, \ldots, g_m$ be real-valued differentiable functions defined on a nonempty open set X in R^n. Suppose that (LM) is satisfied; that is, $\hat{x}$ achieves a local maximum of f subject to $g_j(x) \geq 0, j = 1, 2, \ldots, m$, and $x \in X$. Then there exist $\hat{\lambda}_j \geq 0, j = 0, 1, 2, \ldots, m$, not vanishing simultaneously, such that*

$$\hat{\lambda}_0 f'(\hat{x}) + \sum_{j=1}^{m} \hat{\lambda}_j g'_j(\hat{x}) = 0$$

PROOF (HURWICZ):

(i) Suppose that, for some $h^* \in R^n$, $g'_j(\hat{x}) \cdot h^* > 0, j \in E$. Then condition (AHU) is satisfied. Hence from the previous theorem, we are guaranteed the existence of $\hat{\lambda}_j \geq 0, j = 0, 1, 2, \ldots, m$, with $\hat{\lambda}_0 = 1$.

(ii) Suppose now that there exists *no* $h^* \in R^n$ for which

$$g'_j(\hat{x}) \cdot h^* > 0, j \in E$$

Define the set Z by[8]

$$Z \equiv \{z \in R^k: z = g'_E(\hat{x}) \cdot h, \, h \in R^n\}$$

Then Z does not contain any strictly positive element $z > 0$. Let R^k_+ be the positive orthant of R^k, that is, $\{z \in R^k: z > 0\}$. Then R^k_+ and Z are two disjoint convex sets. Hence, owing to the Minkowski separation theorem (Theorem 0.B.3), there exists an $\alpha \in R^k$, $\alpha \neq 0$, such that[9]

$$\alpha \cdot z \geq 0 \qquad \text{for all } z \in R^k_+$$

and

$$\alpha \cdot z \leq 0 \qquad \text{for all } z \in Z$$

From the first relation, it is clear that $\alpha \geq 0$. In the second relation, if $\alpha \cdot z < 0$ for some $z \in Z$, then $\alpha \cdot (-z) > 0$, since $z \in Z$ implies $-z \in Z$. This is a contradiction. Hence

$$\alpha \cdot z = 0 \qquad \text{for all } z \in Z$$

Thus $\alpha \cdot \left[g'_E(x) \cdot h \right] = 0$ for all h. Therefore

$$\alpha \cdot g'_E(\hat{x}) = 0$$

Let $\hat{\lambda}_0 = 0$, $\hat{\lambda}_j = \alpha_j$ if $j \in E$ and $\hat{\lambda}_j = 0$ if $j \notin E$. Then we obtain the desired $\hat{\lambda}_j$'s.

(Q.E.D.)

FOOTNOTES

1. I am grateful to Leonid Hurwicz for giving me permission to quote the results and the derivation from his unpublished paper [5], from which much of the material in this appendix is borrowed. Needless to say, any possible misunderstanding of [5], and hence mistakes, are mine.

2. The essence of Hurwicz [5] is to provide a proof without by-passing the use of (KTCQ).

3. Condition (QSP) says that there exist $\hat{x} \in X$ and $\hat{\lambda} \in R^m$, $\hat{\lambda} \geq 0$, such that $f'(\hat{x}) + \hat{\lambda} \cdot g'(\hat{x}) = 0$, $g(\hat{x}) \geq 0$, and $\hat{\lambda} \cdot g(\hat{x}) = 0$, where $g = (g_1, \ldots, g_m)$. If the nonnegativity constraint $x \geq 0$ is made explicit in addition to $g(x) \geq 0$, then (QSP) is modified to (QSP'): There exist $\hat{x} \in X$, $\hat{x} \geq 0$, $\hat{\lambda} \in R^m$, $\hat{\lambda} \geq 0$ such that $f'(\hat{x}) + \hat{\lambda} \cdot g'(\hat{x}) \leq 0$, $\hat{x} \cdot [f'(\hat{x}) + \hat{\lambda} \cdot g'(\hat{x})] = 0$, $g(\hat{x}) \geq 0$, and $\hat{\lambda} \cdot g(\hat{x}) = 0$. Recall our discussion on this point in Section D of this chapter.

4. It should be clear why $g'_j(\hat{x}) \cdot h^* > 0$ (instead of ≥ 0) is required for $j \in J'$. If $g'_j(\hat{x}) \cdot h^* = 0$ is allowed for $j \in J'$, then we cannot guarantee that $g_j[x(t)] - g_j(\hat{x}) \geq 0, j \in J'$ for sufficiently small t.

5. Note that $\Psi'_+(0)$ exists because f is differentiable in X.

6. The "rank" of a (rectangular) matrix is defined as the number of linearly independent rows. As remarked before it can be shown that it is equal to the number of linearly independent columns (the rank theorem).

7. When all the constraints are in the equality forms, that is, $g_j(x) = 0, j = 1, 2, \ldots, m$, then the theorem corresponding to Fritz John's theorem is known in the name of

Lagrange and Euler. As remarked before, the proof of such a theorem is provided by Carathéodory ([3], pp. 176–177, theorem 2). See also theorem 76.1 of G.A. Bliss, *Lectures on the Calculus of Variations*, Chicago, Ill., University of Chicago Press, 1946.

8. Recall that k is the number of effective constraints and that $g'_E(\hat{x})$ denotes the $k \times n$ matrix which is obtained from $g'(\hat{x})$ by deleting the rows which correspond to the ineffective constraints (ineffective at $\hat{x}$).

9. It should be clear that the separating hyperplane passes through the origin of R^k.

REFERENCES

1. Abadie, J., "On the Kuhn-Tucker Theorem," in *Nonlinear Programming*, ed. by J.Abadie, New York, Interscience, 1967.

2. Arrow, K. J., Hurwicz, L., and Uzawa, H., "Constraint Qualifications in Maximization Problems", *Naval Research Logistics Quarterly*, vol. 8, no. 2, June 1961.

3. Carathéodory, C., *Calculus of Variations and Partial Differential Equations of the First Order, Part II, Calculus of Variations*. San Francisco, Holden Day, 1967 (tr. by Robert Dean from German original, 1935).

4. John, F., "Extremum Problems with Inequalities as Subsidiary Conditions," *Studies and Essays*, Courant Anniversary Volume, New York, Interscience, 1948.

5. Hurwicz, L., "LH–Oct. 1966," *Lecture Note* at the University of Minnesota, October 1966, revised July 2, 1970.

Section E

SOME EXTENSIONS

In this section we extend the nonlinear programming theory established so far. This extension, set out under three principal topics, will provide us with useful applications in economic theory.

The first topic is concerned with constraint maximization problems where the maximand function $f(x)$ and the constraint functions are not necessarily concave but "quasi-concave." As we will see later, the quasi-concavity of the consumer's utility function corresponds to the ordinary utility function whose indifference curves are convex to the origin, and the quasi-concavity of the production function allows increasing returns to scale. These observations alone should be sufficient to motivate a study of "quasi-concave programming."

The second topic is the constrained vector maximum problem. So far we have assumed that the maximand function $f(x)$ is a real-valued function. We want to extend this to problems where $f(x)$ is a vector-valued function. The constrained vector maximum problem will be related to the concept of "efficient point" in activity analysis and the concept of "Pareto optimum" in welfare economics.

The third topic is the characterization of differentiable concave or quasi-concave functions in terms of the Hessian matrix. This will clarify the relation between the theory of nonlinear programming and the ordinary second-order conditions, and it will give a useful method of determining whether or not a particular function is concave or quasi-concave. At the end, we will discuss the so-called "second-order (necessary or sufficient) conditions" for an optimum.

a. QUASI-CONCAVE PROGRAMMING

Definition: A real-valued function $f(x)$ defined over a convex set X in R^n is called **quasi-concave** if

$$f(x) \geq f(x') \text{ implies } f[tx + (1 - t)x'] \geq f(x') \qquad \text{for all } x, x' \in X \text{ and } 0 \leq t \leq 1$$

REMARK: Therefore, $f(x)$, over a convex set X, is a quasi-concave function if and only if $\{x: x \in X, f(x) \geq \alpha\}$ is a convex set for all $\alpha \in R$.

Definition: A real-valued function $f(x)$ defined over a convex set X in R^n is called **quasi-convex** if $-f(x)$ is quasi-concave. The function $f(x)$ is called **strictly quasi-concave** if

$$f(x) \geq f(x') \text{ implies } f[tx + (1 - t)x'] > f(x') \text{ for all } x \neq x' \in X \text{ and } 0 < t < 1$$

The function $f(x)$ is called **strictly quasi-convex** if $-f(x)$ is strictly quasi-concave.

REMARK: Clearly a strictly quasi-concave (-convex) function is always quasi-concave (-convex), but not vice versa.

We can easily show the following theorem.

Theorem 1.E.1:

(i)   *Any concave function is also quasi-concave, but the converse does not necessarily hold. Similarly, any strictly concave function is also strictly quasi-concave, but the converse does not necessarily hold.*

(ii)   *Any monotone increasing (or decreasing) function is quasi-concave if $X \subset R$.*

(iii)   *Any monotone nondecreasing function of a quasi-concave function is also quasi-concave.*

REMARK: An ordinary utility function whose corresponding indifference curve is drawn convex to the origin is an example of a quasi-concave function. If the indifference curve does not contain a linear segment, then the utility function is strictly quasi-concave. Although a quasi-concave function is not necessarily concave, a quasi-concave function can be transformed into a concave function, under a certain regularity condition, by a strict positive transformation. See Fenchel [6], pp. 115–137. This observation is interesting, since utility is usually supposed to be an index so that the utility function must be invariant under a monotone transformation.

Some examples of a quasi-concave function which is *not* concave are the following:

(1) $f(x) = x^2$, where $x \in R$, $x \geq 0$

(2) $Y = L^\alpha K^\beta$ where $\alpha + \beta > 1$, $\alpha > 0$, $\beta > 0$, $(L \geq 0, K \geq 0)$

It can also be shown that any homogenous function with degree less than or equal to one is a concave function, if it is a quasi-concave function.

We are now concerned with the problem of maximizing a quasi-concave function $f(x)$ over the n-dimensional nonnegative orthant Ω^n subject to the constraints $g_j(x) \geq 0$, $j = 1, 2, \ldots, m$, where the g_j's are all quasi-concave functions defined on Ω^n. More specifically, we are interested in characterizing the maximality condition of the problem in terms of the (QSP') condition. The (QSP') condition for the present problem can be written (as discussed in the remark following Theorem 1.D.2.) as

(**QSP'**)   There exists an $(\hat{x}, \hat{\lambda})$ such that

$$\hat{f}_x + \hat{\lambda} \cdot \hat{g}_x \leq 0, \qquad \hat{x} \cdot (\hat{f}_x + \hat{\lambda} \cdot \hat{g}_x) = 0$$
$$\hat{\lambda} \cdot g(\hat{x}) = 0, \qquad g(\hat{x}) \geq 0$$
$$\hat{x} \geq 0 \qquad \text{and} \qquad \hat{\lambda} \geq 0$$

The maximality condition (M') would be the same as before, that is,
(**M'**)   There exists an $\hat{x} \in \Omega^n$ which maximizes $f(x)$ subject to $g_j(x) \geq 0$, $j = 1$, $2, \ldots, m$, and $x \geq 0$ with $x \in R^n$.

We now introduce a new concept and state a sufficiency theorem for the maximum.

Definition: Given the constraint set $C \equiv \{x : x \in \Omega^n, g_j(x) \geq 0, j = 1, 2, \ldots, m\}$, we call the ith coordinate variable x_i a **relevant variable** if there exists an $\bar{x}$ in C such that $\bar{x}_i > 0$.

> *REMARK*:   As Arrow and Enthoven ([1], p. 783) explained, it is a variable "which can take on a positive value without necessarily violating the constraints."

Theorem 1.E.2 (Arrow-Enthoven):   *Let $f, g_1, g_2, \ldots, g_m$ be differentiable, quasi-concave, real-valued functions of the n-dimensional vector x on R^n with $x \geq 0$. Then (QSP') implies (M'), provided that one of the following conditions is satisfied.*

(i) *$\hat{f}_{x_i} < 0$ for at least one variable x_i, where $\hat{f}_{x_i}$ is the partial derivative of $f(x)$ with respect to x_i, evaluated at $x = \hat{x}$.*

(ii) *$\hat{f}_{x_i} > 0$ for some relevant variable x_i.*

(iii) $\hat{f}_x \neq 0$ *and* $f(x)$ *is twice differentiable in the neighborhood of* $\hat{x}$.
(iv) *The function* $f(x)$ *is concave.*

PROOF: Omitted. See Arrow and Enthoven [1].

REMARK: In concave programming, we assume that *both* f and $g_j(j = 1, 2, \ldots, m)$ are concave. Condition (iv) in Theorem 1.E.2 is a slight weakening of this. Note also that if all g_j's are quasi-concave, then the constraint set $C \equiv \{x: x \in \Omega^n, g_j(x) \geq 0, j = 1, 2, \ldots, m\}$ is a convex set.

REMARK: The requirement that the constraint functions $g_1(x), \ldots, g_m(x)$ be quasi-concave can be replaced by the weaker condition that the constraint set $C \equiv \{x: x \in \Omega^n, g_j(x) \geq 0, j = 1, 2, \ldots, m\}$ be a convex set. Obviously C is convex if g_j is quasi-concave for all j, but it can also be convex if some g_j's are not quasi-concave. See Arrow and Enthoven [1], p. 788. Note that if f and $g_j, j = 1, 2, \ldots, m$, are all concave, then all the requirements of the theorem are satisfied. Thus (QSP') implies (M'). This is nothing but the result obtained as part of Theorem 1.D.2.

REMARK: If all the variables are relevant (the usual case in economic theory), then (i) and (ii) of Theorem 1.E.2 simply reduce to $\hat{f}_x \neq 0$.

Referring again to Arrow and Enthoven [1], we state the following theorem, which really corresponds to the Arrow-Hurwicz-Uzawa theorem [Theorem 1.D.4, conditions (iii) and (iv)]. The theorem is concerned with a necessary condition for the maximum.

Theorem 1.E.3: *Let* $g_j(x), j = 1, 2, \ldots, m$, *be differentiable quasi-concave real-valued functions. Suppose that there exists an* $\bar{x} \geq 0$ *such that* $g_j(\bar{x}) > 0$ *for all* j. *Then* (M') *implies* (QSP'), *provided that either of the following conditions is satisfied*:

(i) *The functions* $g_j(x)$ *are concave for all* j.
(ii) *The functions* $g_j'(x) \neq 0$ *for all* j *and for all* $x \in C$.

REMARK: We must note a very unpleasant fact about quasi-concave functions. As we mentioned before, any nonnegative linear combination of concave functions is also concave. But a nonnegative linear combination of quasi-concave functions is *not* necessarily quasi-concave. As we will see later, this will restrict the applicability of quasi-concave programming. (We call the constrained maximization problem **quasi-concave programming** if the maximand function and the constraint functions are all quasi-concave).

Finally, we should mention the concept of "explicit" quasi-concavity (or quasi-convexity).[1]

Definition: A real-valued function $f(x)$ defined over a convex set X in R^n is called **explicitly quasi-concave** if it is quasi-concave *and* if

$$f(x) > f(x') \text{ implies } f[tx + (1 - t)x'] > f(x')$$

for all $x, x' \in X$ (with $x \neq x'$) and for all t with $0 < t \leq 1$.

REMARK: The two properties required in the above definition are independent. For example, consider $f(x)$, $x \in R$, defined by

$$f(x) = -1 \text{ if } x = 0, \text{ and } f(x) = 0 \text{ if } x \neq 0$$

Then f is not quasi-concave, but it satisfies the second property required in the above definition. However, if f is continuous, the second property implies the quasi-concavity of f, so that quasi-concavity is superfluous in the above definition. The proof is easy and is left to the interested reader.

REMARK: Note that every strictly quasi-concave function is explicitly quasi-concave, and that every explicitly quasi-concave function is quasi-concave.

Definition: A real-valued function $f(x)$ defined over a convex set X in R^n is called **explicitly quasi-convex** if $-f(x)$ is explicitly quasi-concave.

REMARK: The following very useful propositions can easily be proved:

(i) *If $f(x)$ is a concave (resp. convex) function defined on the convex set X in R^n, then f is explicitly quasi-concave (resp. explicitly quasi-convex) in X.*[2]

(ii) *Let $f(x)$ be an explicitly quasi-concave (resp. explicitly quasi-convex) function on a convex set X in R^n. Then every local maximum (resp. local minimum) of f in the constraint set C, which is convex, is also a global maximum.*[3]

(iii) *Let $f(x)$ be strictly quasi-concave on a convex set X in R^n. Then if $\hat{x}$ achieves a local maximum of f in the constraint set C and if C is a convex set, then it achieves a unique global maximum over C.*[4]

b. THE VECTOR MAXIMUM PROBLEM

So far we have been concerned with the problem of maximizing a certain real-valued function $f(x)$ subject to certain constraints. Here we are concerned with the problem of maximization when $f(x)$ is a vector-valued function.

Definition: Let $f_1(x), f_2(x), \ldots, f_k(x)$ and $g_1(x), g_2(x), \ldots, g_m(x)$ be real-valued functions defined on X in R^n. We say that $\hat{x}$ in X gives a **vector (global) maximum** of $f(x) \equiv [f_1(x), f_2(x), \ldots, f_k(x)]$ *subject to* $g_j(x) \geq 0, j = 1, 2, \ldots, m$, if the following conditions exist:

(i) $g_j(\hat{x}) \geq 0, j = 1, 2, \ldots, m$, and $\hat{x} \in X$.
(ii) There exists no $\tilde{x}$ satisfying

$$f_i(\tilde{x}) \geq f_i(\hat{x}) \qquad \text{for all } i = 1, 2, \ldots, k$$
$$f_i(\tilde{x}) > f_i(\hat{x}) \qquad \text{for some } i$$
$$g_j(\tilde{x}) \geq 0, j = 1, 2, \ldots, m, \qquad \text{and } \tilde{x} \in X$$

REMARK: The reader may realize that the concept of "efficient point" in activity analysis is a special case of the vector maximum where $f(x) = x$. One may also note that the vector maximum problem has immediate relevance to the concept of Pareto optimum, which is important in economic theory.

REMARK: The definition of vector *local* maximum is analogous to the above definition of vector global maximum. For the distinction between a local maximum and a global maximum, see Section C of this chapter. The concept of a local maximum is concerned with maximization with respect to *some* open ball (which can be very small).

REMARK: It follows from the above definition that if $f(\hat{x})$ is a constrained vector maximum, *then*

$\hat{x}$ maximizes $f_{i_0}(x)$ [that is, $f_{i_0}(\hat{x}) \geq f_{i_0}(x)$]
Subject to:
$$f_i(x) \geq f_i(\hat{x}) \qquad \text{for all } i \neq i_0$$
$$g_j(x) \geq 0 \qquad j = 1, 2, \ldots m$$

where the choice of i_0 is arbitrary. For if not, there exists an $\tilde{x}$ and an $\tilde{i}$ such that

$$f_{\tilde{i}}(\tilde{x}) > f_{\tilde{i}}(\hat{x})$$

and

$$f_i(\tilde{x}) \geq f_i(\hat{x}) \qquad \text{for all } i \neq \tilde{i}$$
$$g_j(\tilde{x}) \geq 0 \qquad j = 1, 2, \ldots, m$$

This is a contradiction of the assumption that $\hat{x}$ is a vector maximum.

Utilizing this remark, we now prove the following theorem. The method of proof using the above remark is due to El-Hodiri [4], who, in turn, attributes the idea to Leonid Hurwicz.

Theorem 1.E.4:   *Let* $f_1, f_2, \ldots, f_k, g_1, g_2, \ldots, g_m$ *be real-valued concave functions defined on a convex set X in* R^n. *Assume that Slater's condition (S) holds; that is, there exists an* $\bar{x}$ *in X such that*

$$g_j(\bar{x}) > 0 \qquad \text{for all } j$$

Then if $\hat{x}$ *achieves a vector maximum of* $f(x) \equiv [f_1(x), \ldots, f_k(x)]$ *subject to* $g_j(x) \geq 0$, $j = 1, 2, \ldots, m$, *there exist* $\alpha \in R^k$, $\hat{\lambda} \in R^m$ *with* $\alpha \geq 0$, $\hat{\lambda} \geq 0$, *and* $\alpha \neq 0$ *such that* $(\hat{x}, \hat{\lambda})$ *is a saddle point of* $\Phi(x, \lambda) \equiv \alpha \cdot f(x) + \lambda \cdot g(x)$; *that is,*

$$\Phi(x, \hat{\lambda}) \leq \Phi(\hat{x}, \hat{\lambda}) \leq \Phi(\hat{x}, \lambda) \qquad \text{for all } x \in X \text{ and } \lambda \geq 0$$

PROOF: As a result of the above remark and Theorem 1.B.4, fixing i_0, there exist α_{ii_0}, $i = 1, 2, \ldots, k$, $\hat{\Lambda}_{ji_0}$, $j = 1, 2, \ldots, m$, with $\alpha_{ii_0} \geqq 0$, $\hat{\Lambda}_{ji_0} \geqq 0$ for all i and j but not all equal to 0, such that

$$\alpha_{i_0 i_0} f_{i_0}(x) + \sum_{i \neq i_0} \alpha_{ii_0}[f_i(x) - f_i(\hat{x})] + \sum_{j=1}^{m} \hat{\Lambda}_{ji_0} g_j(x)$$

$$\leqq \alpha_{i_0 i_0} f_{i_0}(\hat{x}) + \sum_{i \neq i_0} \alpha_{ii_0}[f_i(\hat{x}) - f_i(\hat{x})] + \sum_{j=1}^{m} \hat{\Lambda}_{ji_0} g_j(\hat{x}) \qquad \text{for all } x \in X$$

and

$$\sum_{j=1}^{m} \hat{\Lambda}_{ji_0} g_j(\hat{x}) = 0$$

These can easily be simplified to the following:

$$\alpha_{i_0 i_0} f_{i_0}(x) + \sum_{i \neq i_0} \alpha_{ii_0}[f_i(x) - f_i(\hat{x})] + \sum_{j=1}^{m} \hat{\Lambda}_{ji_0} g_j(x) \leqq \alpha_{i_0 i_0} f_{i_0}(\hat{x}) \qquad \text{for all } x \in X$$

or,

$$\sum_{i=1}^{k} \alpha_{ii_0} f_i(x) + \sum_{j=1}^{m} \hat{\Lambda}_{ji_0} g_j(x) \leqq \sum_{i=1}^{k} \alpha_{ii_0} f_i(\hat{x}) + \sum_{j=1}^{m} \hat{\Lambda}_{ji_0} g_j(\hat{x}) \qquad \text{for all } x \in X$$

and

$$\sum_{j=1}^{m} \hat{\Lambda}_{ji_0} g_j(\hat{x}) = 0 \qquad ,$$

Summing this inequality and equation over i_0 from 1 to k, and defining

$$\alpha_i \equiv \sum_{i_0=1}^{k} \alpha_{ii_0}, \quad \hat{\Lambda}_j \equiv \sum_{i_0=1}^{k} \hat{\Lambda}_{ji_0}$$

we obtain

$$\sum_{i=1}^{k} \alpha_i f_i(x) + \sum_{j=1}^{m} \hat{\Lambda}_j g_j(x) \leqq \sum_{i=1}^{k} \alpha_i f_i(\hat{x}) + \sum_{j=1}^{m} \hat{\Lambda}_j g_j(\hat{x}) \qquad \text{for all } x \in X$$

and

$$\sum_{j=1}^{m} \hat{\Lambda}_j g_j(\hat{x}) = 0$$

Or in vector notation,

$$\alpha \cdot f(x) + \hat{\Lambda} \cdot g(x) \leqq \alpha \cdot f(\hat{x}) + \hat{\Lambda} \cdot g(\hat{x}) \qquad \text{for all } x \in X$$

and

$$\hat{\lambda} \cdot g(\hat{x}) = 0$$

Now we want to show that $\alpha \neq 0$. Suppose that $\alpha = 0$; then $\hat{\lambda} \neq 0$. Also, owing to the above relation we have $\hat{\lambda} \cdot g(x) \leq 0$, for all $x \in X$. Let $x = \bar{x}$ for condition (S); then we obtain a contradiction, since $\hat{\lambda} \neq 0$ and $\hat{\lambda} \geq 0$. Now we show $\Phi(\hat{x}, \hat{\lambda}) \leq \Phi(\hat{x}, \lambda)$ for all $\lambda \geq 0$; that is, $\alpha \cdot f(\hat{x}) + \hat{\lambda} \cdot g(\hat{x}) \leq \alpha \cdot f(\hat{x}) + \lambda \cdot g(\hat{x})$ for all $\lambda \geq 0$. Or we want to show

$$0 \leq \lambda \cdot g(\hat{x}) \qquad \text{for all } \lambda \geq 0$$

But this is obvious since $\hat{x}$ is a solution of this vector maximum problem, so that $g_j(\hat{x}) \geq 0$ for all j.

(Q.E.D.)

REMARK: We should note that Slater's condition (S) in the above theorem is used to guarantee $\alpha \neq 0$. Without this condition, α can be zero.

REMARK: It is possible to prove the above theorem directly from the separation theorem or the fundamental theorem of concave functions (Theorem 1.B.2), as we did for Theorem 1.B.3. But the above proof seems to be conceptually the simplest. See also Karlin [11], pp. 216–218, and Kuhn and Tucker [12].[5]

We now prove a sufficiency theorem.

Theorem 1.E.5: *Let f_i, $i = 1, 2, \ldots, k$, and g_j, $j = 1, 2, \ldots, m$, be real-valued functions over X in R^n. Suppose that there exist $\hat{x} \in X$, $\alpha > 0$ and $\hat{\lambda} \geq 0$, such that*

$$\alpha \cdot f(x) + \hat{\lambda} \cdot g(x) \leq \alpha \cdot f(\hat{x}) + \hat{\lambda} \cdot g(\hat{x}) \qquad \text{for all } x \in X$$

and

$$\hat{\lambda} \cdot g(\hat{x}) = 0, \quad g(\hat{x}) \geq 0$$

Then $\hat{x}$ achieves a vector maximum subject to $g(x) \geq 0$, $x \in X$.

PROOF: The proof is almost trivial. By the hypothesis of the theorem, we have $\alpha \cdot f(\hat{x}) - \alpha \cdot f(x) \geq \hat{\lambda} \cdot g(x)$ for all $x \in X$. Hence $\hat{x}$ maximizes a real-valued function $\alpha \cdot f(x)$ subject to the constraints $g(x) \geq 0$ and $x \in X$. Now suppose $\hat{x}$ is *not* a vector maximum point. Then there exists an $\tilde{x} \in X$ such that $f_i(\tilde{x}) \geq f_i(\hat{x})$ for all $i = 1, 2, \ldots, k$ with strict inequality for at least one i and $g_j(\tilde{x}) \geq 0$, $j = 1, 2, \ldots, m$. Hence we have $\alpha \cdot f(\tilde{x}) > \alpha \cdot f(\hat{x})$ with $g(\tilde{x}) \geq 0$, $\tilde{x} \in X$. This contradicts the above observation that $\hat{x}$ maximizes $\alpha \cdot f(x)$ subject to $g(x) \geq 0$ and $x \in X$.

(Q.E.D.)

REMARK: Note that we do not need the concavity of the f_i and g_j nor the convexity of X in Theorem 1.E.5. From the above proof we can immediately see the following useful theorem.[6]

Theorem 1.E.6: *Let f_i, $i = 1, \ldots, k$, and g_j, $j = 1, 2, \ldots, m$, be real-valued functions over X in R^n. Suppose that there exists an $\hat{x} \in X$ and coefficients $\alpha_1, \alpha_2, \ldots, \alpha_k$ in R with $\alpha_i > 0$ for all i, such that $\hat{x}$ maximizes $\alpha \cdot f(x)$ subject to $g(x) \geq 0$ and $x \in X$. Then $\hat{x}$ gives a vector maximum of $f(x)$ subject to $g(x) \geq 0$, $x \in X$. Here $f(x) \equiv [f_1(x), \ldots, f_k(x)]$ and $g(x) \equiv [g_1(x), \ldots, g_m(x)]$.*

We can obtain the following theorem, whose proof is analogous to that of Theorem 1.B.4.

Theorem 1.E.7: *Let f_i, $i = 1, 2, \ldots, k$, and g_j, $j = 1, 2, \ldots, m$, be real-valued functions over X in R^n. Suppose that there exist coefficients $\alpha_1, \alpha_2, \ldots, \alpha_k$ in R with $\alpha_i > 0$ for all i and a saddle point $(\hat{x}, \hat{\lambda})$ in $X \otimes \Omega^m$ such that*

$$\Phi(x, \hat{\lambda}) \leq \Phi(\hat{x}, \hat{\lambda}) \leq \Phi(\hat{x}, \lambda) \qquad \text{for all } x \in X \text{ and all } \lambda \in \Omega^m$$

where

$$\Phi(x, \lambda) \equiv \alpha \cdot f(x) + \lambda \cdot g(x)$$

Then

    (i) *$\hat{x}$ achieves a vector maximum of $f(x)$ subject to $g(x) \geq 0$ and $x \in X$.*
    (ii) *$\hat{\lambda} \cdot g(\hat{x}) = 0$.*

PROOF: Since $\Phi(\hat{x}, \hat{\lambda}) \leq \Phi(\hat{x}, \lambda)$, we have $\hat{\lambda} \cdot g(\hat{x}) \leq \lambda \cdot g(\hat{x})$ for all $\lambda \geq 0$. Hence $\lambda \cdot g(\hat{x})$ is bounded from below for all λ in Ω^m. Therefore $\lambda \cdot g(\hat{x}) \geq 0$ for all $\lambda \geq 0$, so that we obtain $g(\hat{x}) \geq 0$. (Recall the lemma immediately preceeding Theorem 0.B.4.) Putting $\lambda = 0$ in the above inequality, we obtain $\hat{\lambda} \cdot g(\hat{x}) \leq 0$. But $\hat{\lambda} \cdot g(\hat{x}) \geq 0$, since $\hat{\lambda} \geq 0$. Hence $\hat{\lambda} \cdot g(\hat{x}) = 0$.

    Now note that $\Phi(x, \hat{\lambda}) \leq \Phi(\hat{x}, \hat{\lambda})$ for all $x \in X$; that is, $\alpha \cdot f(x) + \hat{\lambda} \cdot g(x) \leq \alpha \cdot f(\hat{x})$ ($\because \hat{\lambda} \cdot g(\hat{x}) = 0$). This means that $\hat{x}$ maximizes $\alpha \cdot f(x)$ subject to $g(x) \geq 0$ and $x \in X$ with $\alpha > 0$. Owing to the above theorem, $\hat{x}$ achieves a vector maximum subject to $g(x) \geq 0$ and $x \in X$.   (Q.E.D.)

Now let us assume that the f_i's and g_j's are all differentiable in an open set X in R^n. Then we can extend the above analysis of the constrained vector maximum problem in a manner similar to the analysis in Section D. Since the proof will be analogous to the proofs given above and in Section D, we need only list the main results. First we must define certain concepts.

    Given differentiable vector-valued functions $f(x) = [f_1(x), f_2(x), \ldots, f_k(x)]$ and $g(x) = [g_1(x), \ldots, g_m(x)]$ defined over an open set X in R^n, we define the following conditions.

(VM)   There exists an $\hat{x} \in X$ which achieves a vector maximum of $f(x)$ subject to $g(x) \geq 0$, $x \in X$.

(LVM)   There exists an open ball $B_\epsilon(\hat{x})$ with radius ϵ in X about $\hat{x}$ such that $\hat{x}$ achieves a vector maximum of $f(x)$ subject to $g(x) \geq 0$ and $x \in B_\epsilon(\hat{x})$.

(VQSP)   There exist $\alpha \in R^k$ with $\alpha \geq 0$ (that is, $\alpha \neq 0$) and $(\hat{x}, \hat{\lambda})$ in $X \otimes \Omega^m$

such that $\alpha \cdot \hat{f}_x + \hat{\lambda} \cdot \hat{g}_x = 0$ and $\hat{\lambda} \cdot g(\hat{x}) = 0$ with $g(\hat{x}) \geq 0$ where $\hat{f}_x \equiv f'(\hat{x})$ and $\hat{g}_x \equiv g'(\hat{x})$.

Now we are ready to list the theorems, whose proofs are obvious.

Theorem 1.E.8:   *Suppose that the f_i's and g_j's are all concave differentiable functions defined over an open convex set X in R^n. Suppose also that Slater's condition is satisfied; that is,*

(S)   *There exists an $\bar{x} \in X$ such that $g(\bar{x}) > 0$.*

Then (VM) implies (VQSP).

Theorem 1.E.9:   *Suppose that the g_j's satisfy (KTCQ) or (A-H-U) as defined in Section D. Then (LVM) implies (VQSP).*

Theorem 1.E.10:   *Suppose that the f_i's and g_j's are all concave differentiable functions defined over an open convex set in R^n. Then (VQSP) implies (VM), where α in (VQSP) is assumed to be strictly positive.*

PROOF OF THEOREM 1.E.10:   Since $\alpha \cdot f(x) + \hat{\lambda} \cdot g(x)$ is a nonnegative linear combination of concave functions, it is concave. Hence by Theorem 1.C.7, we obtain from (VQSP)

$$\alpha \cdot f(x) + \hat{\lambda} \cdot g(x) \leq \alpha \cdot f(\hat{x})$$

Since $\alpha > 0$, this proves that $\hat{x}$ achieves a vector maximum of $f(x)$ subject to $g(x) \geq 0$ and $x \in X$.   (Q.E.D.)

c.   QUADRATIC FORMS, HESSIANS, AND SECOND-ORDER CONDITIONS

In this section we are interested in characterizing concave or quasi-concave functions in terms of their "Hessian matrices" and in general order (necessary or sufficient) conditions for an optimum. To do this we first have to introduce the useful properties of symmetric matrices, their negative or positive (semi) definiteness. We also define the second-order derivatives to which the Hessian matrix corresponds. Since these concepts are important in mathematical economics, we will discuss them in detail before we come to the characterization of the concave or quasi-concave functions. We will also discuss the relation between this characterization and the so-called "second-order condition" for the maximization problem.

We begin this discussion with some elementary concepts in linear algebra.

Definition: Given an $n \times n$ *symmetric* matrix $A = [a_{ij}]$, whose entries are real numbers, and an *n*-vector, $x = (x_1, x_2, \ldots, x_n) \in R^n$,

$$f(x, x) \equiv \sum_{i=1}^{n} \sum_{j=1}^{n} a_{ij} x_i x_j \equiv x \cdot A \cdot x$$

is called the **quadratic form** associated with A over the real field.

REMARK: Clearly $f(x, x)$ is a real-valued function defined over $R^n \otimes R^n$, and it is **bilinear** in the sense that

$$\begin{bmatrix} f(x + y, x) = f(x, x) + f(y, x) & \text{for all } x, y \in R^n \\ f(\alpha x, x) = \alpha f(x, x) & \text{for all } \alpha \in R, x \in R^n \end{bmatrix}$$

and

$$\begin{bmatrix} f(x, x + y) = f(x, x) + f(x, y) & \text{for all } x, y \in R^n \\ f(x, \alpha x) = \alpha f(x, x) & \text{for all } \alpha \in R \text{ and } x \in R^n \end{bmatrix}$$

In general, a real-valued function $f(x, x)$ defined over $X \otimes X$ where X is a linear space (not necessarily finite dimensional) is called a **quadratic functional** if the above bilinearity holds (where R^n in the above definition is replaced by X). Every quadratic functional can be expressed as a quadratic form (that is, in the form of $x \cdot A \cdot x$) if X is finite dimensional.

Definition: Let $Q(x) = f(x, x)$ be a quadratic functional (or quadratic form) on a linear space X. Then $Q(x)$ is said to be **negative (positive) definite** if $Q(x) < 0 (> 0)$ for all nonzero x in X, and $Q(x)$ is said to be **negative (positive) semidefinite** if $Q(x) \leq 0 (\geq 0)$ for all $x \in X$.

If $Q(x) = x \cdot A \cdot x$, where A is a symmetric matrix, the matrix A is said to be **negative (positive) definite** if $Q(x)$ is negative (positive) definite. The matrix A is said to be **negative (positive) semidefinite** if $Q(x)$ is negative (positive) semidefinite.

EXAMPLES:

1. If $x = (x_1, x_2)$ and $A = \begin{bmatrix} 1 & 0 \\ 0 & 1 \end{bmatrix}$

   then $Q(x) = x \cdot A \cdot x = x_1^2 + x_2^2$. Hence $Q(x) > 0$ for all nonzero $x \in R^2$.

2. If $x = (x_1, x_2)$ and $A = \begin{bmatrix} 0 & 1 \\ 1 & 0 \end{bmatrix}$

   then $Q(x) = x \cdot A \cdot x = 2x_1 x_2$. Here $Q(x)$ can be negative, positive, or zero, depending on the value of x_1 and x_2.

3. $X_1 = C_{[0,1]}$ (the set of all continuous functions on $[0, 1]$); $Q(f) = \int_0^1 [f(t)]^2 dt$ where $f(t) \in X$ is a quadratic functional that is positive definite.

We call a quadratic form $Q(x) = x \cdot A \cdot x$ a **real quadratic form** if $x \in R^n$ and $A = [a_{ij}]$ with $a_{ij} \in R$. We are concerned with real quadratic forms. Given an $n \times n$ matrix $A = [a_{ij}]$, we may define the following determinants.

$$D_k \equiv \begin{vmatrix} a_{11} & a_{12} & \dots & a_{1k} \\ a_{21} & a_{22} & \dots & a_{2k} \\ \dots & \dots & \dots & \dots \\ a_{k1} & a_{k2} & \dots & a_{kk} \end{vmatrix}, \quad k = 1, 2, \dots, n$$

The determinants $D_1, D_2, \dots, D_n$ are called the **successive principal minors** of A. Given A, we may also define the following $k \times k$ determinant

$$\tilde{D}_k \equiv \begin{vmatrix} a_{ii} & a_{ij} & \dots & a_{ik} \\ a_{ji} & a_{jj} & \dots & a_{jk} \\ \dots & \dots & \dots & \dots \\ a_{ki} & a_{kj} & \dots & a_{kk} \end{vmatrix}$$

where $(i, j, \dots, k)$ is any permutation of k integers from the set of integers $\{1, 2, \dots, n\}$. The determinant $\tilde{D}_k$ is called **principal minor** of A with order k. Note that every $\tilde{D}_n$ has the same sign as the determinant of A, since both rows and columns are interchanged in the process of permutation.

EXAMPLES:

$$A = \begin{bmatrix} a_{11} & a_{12} \\ a_{21} & a_{22} \end{bmatrix}; \quad D_1 = a_{11}, \quad D_2 = \begin{vmatrix} a_{11} & a_{12} \\ a_{21} & a_{22} \end{vmatrix}$$

$$\tilde{D}_1 = a_{11} \text{ and } a_{22}, \tilde{D}_2 = \begin{vmatrix} a_{11} & a_{12} \\ a_{21} & a_{22} \end{vmatrix} \text{ and } \begin{vmatrix} a_{22} & a_{21} \\ a_{12} & a_{11} \end{vmatrix}$$

The following theorem is concerned with the characterization of a real quadratic form.

Theorem 1.E.11: *Let $Q(x) = x \cdot A \cdot x$, $x \in R^n$ be a real quadratic form.[7] Then*

(i) *$Q(x)$ is positive definite if and only if $D_1 > 0, D_2 > 0, \dots, D_n > 0$ (that is, all the successive principal minors are positive).*

(ii) *$Q(x)$ is negative definite if and only if $D_1 < 0, D_2 > 0, \dots, (-1)^n D_n > 0$ (that is, the successive principal minors alternate in signs).*

(iii) *$Q(x)$ is positive semidefinite if and only if all $\tilde{D}_1 \geq 0, \tilde{D}_2 \geq 0, \dots, \tilde{D}_n \geq 0$.*

(iv) *$Q(x)$ is negative semidefinite if and only if all $\tilde{D}_1 \leq 0, \tilde{D}_2 \geq 0, \dots, (-1)^n \tilde{D}_n \geq 0$.*

(v) *A positive (negative) semidefinite $Q(x)$ is positive (negative) definite if and only if A is a nonsingular matrix.*

PROOF: See Gantmacher [7], pp. 306–308, and Hestenes [9], pp. 20–21, for example.

REMARK: The determinants $\tilde{D}_k$ have all the same signs if $\{i, j, \ldots, k\}$ is the same index set, since both rows and columns are interchanged in the process of permutation. For example,

$$A = \begin{bmatrix} a_{11} & a_{12} & a_{13} \\ a_{21} & a_{22} & a_{23} \\ a_{31} & a_{32} & a_{33} \end{bmatrix}$$

has three kinds of $\tilde{D}_2$, each kind having its own sign and value,

$$\tilde{D}_2{}^1 = \begin{vmatrix} a_{11} & a_{12} \\ a_{21} & a_{22} \end{vmatrix} \text{ and } \begin{vmatrix} a_{22} & a_{21} \\ a_{12} & a_{11} \end{vmatrix}$$

$$\tilde{D}_2{}^2 = \begin{vmatrix} a_{11} & a_{13} \\ a_{31} & a_{33} \end{vmatrix} \text{ and } \begin{vmatrix} a_{33} & a_{31} \\ a_{13} & a_{11} \end{vmatrix}$$

$$\tilde{D}_2{}^3 = \begin{vmatrix} a_{22} & a_{23} \\ a_{32} & a_{33} \end{vmatrix} \text{ and } \begin{vmatrix} a_{33} & a_{32} \\ a_{23} & a_{22} \end{vmatrix}$$

REMARK: Statements (i) and (ii) of the above theorem can be restated as the following: $Q(x)$ is positive definite if and only if $D_k > 0, k = 1, 2, \ldots, n$, and $Q(x)$ is negative definite if and only if $(-1)^k D_k > 0, k = 1, 2, \ldots, n$.

REMARK: The determinants $\tilde{D}_k$ in statements (iii) and (iv) of the above theorem cannot be replaced by D_k. For example, let

$$A = \begin{bmatrix} 0 & 0 \\ 0 & 1 \end{bmatrix}$$

Then $D_1 = 0, D_2 = 0$ (but $\tilde{D}_1 = 0$ *and* 1). Hence this satisfies the condition of (iv) if $\tilde{D}_k$ is replaced by D_k, but $Q(x) = x \cdot A \cdot x = x_2{}^2$ is *not* negative semi-definite (while it is positive semidefinite but not positive definite).

Now we define the second derivative.

Definition: Let f be a real-valued differentiable function on an open subset X in R^n; f is said to be **twice differentiable at** x^0 where $x^0 \in X$, if there exists an n-vector a and an $n \times n$ matrix A such that

$$f(x^0 + h) - f(x^0) = a \cdot h + \tfrac{1}{2} h \cdot A \cdot h + o(\| h \|^2)$$

The n-vector a is called the **first derivative of** f **at** x^0 and A is called the **second derivative of** f **at** x^0. The **first differential of** f **at** x^0 is the name given to $a \cdot h$, and $h \cdot A \cdot h$ is called the **second differential of** f **at** x^0. The first and the second differentials are denoted by δf(or df) and $\delta^2 f$(or $d^2 f$), respectively. Note that $d^2 f = d(df)$.

REMARK: If X is a (normed) linear space which is not necessarily finite dimensional, then $a \cdot h$ is replaced by the linear functional $a(h)$ and $h \cdot A \cdot h$ is replaced by the quadratic functional $A(h)$. The above definition and this remark are natural extensions of the concept of a derivative and differential as discussed in Section C. It can be shown that a and A in the above definition are unique if they exist.

REMARK: If f is twice differentiable at $x^0 \in X$, an open subset of R^n, then the second partial derivatives $\partial^2 f(x)/\partial x_i \partial x_j$ $(i, j = 1, 2, \ldots, n)$ exist at x^0 and the second derivative A (at x^0), also denoted by $f''(x^0)$, has the following expression:

$$
A = \begin{bmatrix}
\dfrac{\partial^2 f}{\partial x_1^2} & \dfrac{\partial^2 f}{\partial x_1 \partial x_2} & \cdots & \dfrac{\partial^2 f}{\partial x_1 \partial x_n} \\[2ex]
\dfrac{\partial^2 f}{\partial x_2 \partial x_1} & \cdots & \cdots & \dfrac{\partial^2 f}{\partial x_2 \partial x_n} \\[2ex]
\cdots & \cdots & \cdots & \cdots \\[2ex]
\dfrac{\partial^2 f}{\partial x_n \partial x_1} & \dfrac{\partial^2 f}{\partial x_n \partial x_2} & \cdots & \dfrac{\partial^2 f}{\partial x_n^2}
\end{bmatrix}
$$

where $\dfrac{\partial^2 f}{\partial x_i \partial x_j} \equiv \dfrac{\partial}{\partial x_i} \left(\dfrac{\partial f}{\partial x_j} \right)$ (evaluated at x^0), $i, j = 1, 2, \ldots, n$. If the second partial derivatives are continuous at x^0, then f'' is continuous at x^0 and $\dfrac{\partial^2 f}{\partial x_i \partial x_j} = \dfrac{\partial^2 f}{\partial x_j \partial x_i}$, $i, j = 1, 2, \ldots, n$ (evaluated at x^0). In other words, the above matrix A is symmetric. The matrix A is called the **Hessian matrix** of f at x^0.[8]

REMARK: According to the usual convention in mathematics, the notation $[f''(x^0) \leq 0]$ means that the Hessian matrix $f''(x^0)$ is negative semidefinite, and *not* that each element of the matrix $f''(x^0)$ is nonpositive. Similarly, $[f''(x^0) < 0]$ means that the Hessian matrix $f''(x^0)$ is negative definite, and not that each element of $f''(x^0)$ is negative. When x^0 is a scalar, this convention does not create any confusion. But when the dimension of x^0 is greater than or equal to 2, this convention might cause confusion to some readers.[9] In this book, following the usual convention in economics, we reserve the notation $A \leq 0$ to mean that each element of the matrix A is nonpositive. Similarly, $A < 0$ means that each element of A is negative.

The following theorem offers a characterization of concave functions in terms of the Hessian matrix.

Theorem 1.E.12: *Let $f(x)$ be twice continuously differentiable real-valued function on an open convex set X in R^n, and let $f''(x)$ be a Hessian matrix. Then*

(i) *The function f is concave on X if and only if $f''(x)$ is negative semidefinite for all $x \in X$.*

(ii) *The function f is strictly concave on X if $f''(x)$ is negative definite for all $x \in X$.*
(iii) *The function f is convex on X if and only if $f''(x)$ is positive semidefinite for all $x \in X$.*
(iv) *The function f is strictly convex on X if $f''(x)$ is positive definite for all $x \in X$.*

PROOF: See Fenchel [6], pp. 87–88.

REMARK: Note that concavity or convexity is a *global* concept. Hence in each statement of Theorem 1.E.12, the phrase "for all $x \in X$" is needed. If $f(x)$ is concave (or convex) in a convex subset S of its domain X, then X in all four statements should be replaced by S.

REMARK: The converse of (ii) and the converse of (iv) do not necessarily hold. For example, $f(x) = -(x-1)^4, x \in R$, is strictly concave, but $f''(1) = 0$.[10]

Combining Theorem 1.E.12 with Theorem 1.E.11, we obtain Theorem 1.E.13.

Theorem 1.E.13: *Let $f(x)$ be a twice continuously differentiable real-valued function on an open convex set X in R^n. Let $f''(x) = [a_{ij}]$ be the Hessian matrix of f for $x \in X$. Let D_k and $\tilde{D}_k (k = 1, 2, \ldots, n)$, respectively, be the successive principal minors and principal minors of $f''(x)$. Then the following are true.*

(i) *The function f is concave if and only if $\tilde{D}_1 \le 0, \tilde{D}_2 \ge 0, \ldots, (-1)^n\tilde{D}_n \ge 0$ for all $x \in X$.*
(ii) *The function f is strictly concave if $D_1 < 0, D_2 > 0, \ldots, (-1)^nD_n > 0$ for all $x \in X$.*
(iii) *The function f is convex if and only if $\tilde{D}_1 \ge 0, \tilde{D}_2 \ge 0, \ldots, \tilde{D}_n \ge 0$.*
(iv) *The function f is strictly convex if $D_1 > 0, D_2 > 0, \ldots, D_n > 0$.*

REMARK: The converse of (ii) and the converse of (iv) are not necessarily true, since the converse of (ii) and the converse of (iv) in Theorem 1.E.12 are not necessarily true.

EXAMPLES:

1. $Y = F(L, K)$ $(L, K, Y \in R$, and all $> 0)$ is a concave function if $F_{LL} < 0$, $F_{KK} < 0$, and F is linear homogeneous, where $F_{LL} \equiv \partial^2 F/\partial L^2$, $F_{KK} \equiv \partial^2 F/\partial K^2$.
2. In particular, $F(L, K) = L^\alpha K^\beta > 0$ is a strictly concave function if $\alpha + \beta < 1$.[11]

REMARK: Recall that the second-order conditions are never mentioned in the theorems developed in the previous sections when f and the g_j's are concave. If the g_j's are concave (or even quasi-concave), the constraint set $C \equiv \{x \in X: g_j(x) \ge 0, j = 1, 2, \ldots, m\}$ is convex. Under the convexity of C, the concavity of f implies that every local maximum is a global maximum; f is concave if and only if the Hessian of f is negative semidefinite for all

$x \in X$. That is, $(-1)^k \tilde{D}_k \geqq 0$, $k = 1, 2, \ldots, n$ for *all* $x \in X$. In other words, a global maximum of f corresponds to the Hessian of f being *globally* negative semidefinite.

We now turn to the characterization of quasi-concave functions.

Definition: Let $f(x)$ be a real-valued function on an open subset X of R^n, which is twice differentiable at x^o in X. Then the following matrix B is called the **bordered Hessian matrix** of f evaluated at x^o.

$$B \equiv \begin{bmatrix} 0 & f_1 & f_2 & \cdots & f_n \\ f_1 & f_{11} & f_{12} & \cdots & f_{1n} \\ \cdots & \cdots & \cdots & \cdots & \cdots \\ f_n & f_{n1} & f_{n2} & \cdots & f_{nn} \end{bmatrix}$$

where $f_i \equiv \partial f / \partial x_i$, and $f_{ij} \equiv \partial^2 f / \partial x_i \partial x_j$, $i, j = 1, 2, \ldots, n$, all evaluated at x^o.

Denote the $(k + 1)$th successive principal minor of B by B_k, which we call the kth (successive) **bordered Hessian determinant** evaluated at x^o. In other words,

$$B_k \equiv \begin{bmatrix} 0 & f_1 & f_2 & \cdots & f_k \\ f_1 & f_{11} & f_{12} & \cdots & f_{1k} \\ \cdots & \cdots & \cdots & \cdots & \cdots \\ f_k & f_{k1} & f_{k2} & \cdots & f_{kk} \end{bmatrix}, \quad k = 1, 2, \ldots, n$$

When x^o moves in X, the values of the B_k's also change in general.

Theorem 1.E.14: *Let $f(x)$ be a twice continuously differentiable real-valued function on R^n. Then the following holds for $x \geqq 0$.*

(i) *If $f(x)$ is quasi-concave, then $B_2 \geqq 0$, $B_3 \leqq 0$, $\ldots$, $(-1)^n B_n \geqq 0$ for all $x \in R^n$ ($B_1 \leqq 0$ holds always).*

(ii) *Conversely, if $B_1 < 0$, $B_2 > 0$, $B_3 < 0$, $\ldots$, $(-1)^n B_n > 0$ for all $x \in \Omega^n$, then $f(x)$ is quasi-concave on Ω^n, where Ω^n is the nonnegative orthant of R^n.*

PROOF: See Arrow and Enthoven [1], especially their theorem 5.

We now turn to the discussion of the second-order conditions. The following characterization of the unconstrained maximum problem is a classical result.

Theorem 1.E.15: *Let $f(x)$ be a twice continuously differentiable real-valued function on an open set X in R^n and $f''(\hat{x})$ be the Hessian matrix of f at $\hat{x}$. Then*

(i) *If f has a local maximum at $\hat{x} \in X$, then $f'(\hat{x}) = 0$ and $f''(\hat{x})$ is negative semidefinite.*

(ii) *Conversely, if $f'(\hat{x}) = 0$ and $f''(\hat{x})$ is negative definite, then there exists an open ball $B_\epsilon(\hat{x})$ about $\hat{x}$ with radius $\epsilon > 0$ and a positive number θ such that*

$$f(\hat{x}) \geq f(x) + \theta \parallel x - \hat{x} \parallel^2 \qquad \text{for all } x \text{ in } B_\epsilon(\hat{x})$$

PROOF: The proof is easy and therefore is omitted. (See, for example, Hestenes [9], pp. 18–20).

REMARK: That $f''(\hat{x})$ be negative *semi*definite in the above theorem is called the **second-order necessary condition**. That $f''(\hat{x})$ be negative definite is called the **second-order sufficient condition**.[12]

Next we consider the second-order conditions for the constrained maximum problem. We consider, for the sake of generality, constraints which are a mixture of inequalities and equalities. In other words, we consider the problem of finding $x \in X$, an open subset of R^n, such as to

Maximize: $f(x)$
Subject to: $g_j(x) \geq 0, j = 1, 2, \ldots, m$
$\qquad\qquad h_k(x) = 0, k = 1, 2, \ldots, l$

where f, g_j, $j = 1, 2, \ldots, m$, and h_k, $k = 1, 2, \ldots, l$, are all real-valued twice continuously differentiable functions on X.

In view of the presence of the equality constraints, we cannot use conditions such as Slater's condition. We will assume the following **rank condition** (R).

(R) Let E be the set of indices j for which $g_j(\hat{x}) = 0$. Let m_e be the number of such j's (that is, the number of effective g-constraints at $\hat{x}$). Then it is required that the rank of the $(m_e + l) \times n$ matrix

$$G = \left[\frac{\partial g_j}{\partial x_i} \quad \frac{\partial h_k}{\partial x_i} \right] , j \in E; k = 1, 2, \ldots, l; i = 1, 2, \ldots, n$$

where each partial derivative is evaluated at $\hat{x}$, be equal to $(m_e + l)$.[13]

We define the Lagrangian for the present problem by

$$L(x) \equiv f(x) + \hat{\lambda} \cdot g(x) + \hat{\mu} \cdot h(x)$$

where $\hat{\lambda} = (\hat{\lambda}_1, \hat{\lambda}_2, \ldots, \hat{\lambda}_m) \in \Omega^m$ and $\hat{\mu} = (\hat{\mu}_1, \hat{\mu}_2, \ldots, \hat{\mu}_l) \in R^l$. The **quasi-saddle-point conditions** or the **first-order conditions** for this problem are written as follows:

(FOC) There exists an $(\hat{x}, \hat{\lambda}, \hat{\mu})$ in $X \otimes \Omega^m \otimes R^l$ such that $\hat{f}_x + \hat{\lambda} \cdot \hat{g}_x + \hat{\mu} \cdot \hat{h}_x = 0$, $\hat{\lambda} \cdot g(\hat{x}) = 0$, $g(\hat{x}) \geq 0$, $\hat{\lambda} \geq 0$, and $h(\hat{x}) = 0$, where $\hat{f}_x \equiv f'(\hat{x})$, $\hat{g}_x \equiv g'(\hat{x})$ and $\hat{h}_x \equiv h'(\hat{x})$.

The **(local) maximality condition** is written out as:

(LM) There exists an $\hat{x}$ in X such that $f(x)$ has a local maximum at $\hat{x}$ subject to $g_j(x) \geq 0, j = 1, 2, \ldots, m$, and $h_k(x) = 0, k = 1, 2, \ldots, l$.

We are now ready to state an important theorem which characterizes (LM). The first statement is concerned with the **second-order necessary conditions** for

(LM) and the second statement is concerned with the **second-order sufficient conditions** for (LM).

Theorem 1.E.16:[14]

(i) *Suppose that conditions (LM) and (R) are satisfied; then we have (FOC) and*

$$\xi \cdot H \cdot \xi \leqq 0 \quad where \quad \xi \equiv x - \hat{x}$$

satisfying

$$g_j'(\hat{x}) \cdot \xi = 0, j \in E, \ and \ h_k'(\hat{x}) \cdot \xi = 0, k = 1, 2, \ldots, l$$

where H is the Hessian matrix of L evaluated at $\hat{x}$, that is, $H \equiv L''(\hat{x})$.

(ii) *Suppose that conditions (FOC) and (R) are satisfied. Furthermore, suppose that*

$$\xi \cdot H \cdot \xi < 0 \quad where \quad \xi \equiv x - \hat{x} \neq 0$$

satisfying

$$g_j'(\hat{x}) \cdot \xi = 0, j \in E, \quad and \quad h_k'(\hat{x}) \cdot \xi = 0, k = 1, 2, \ldots, l$$

Then there exists an open ball $B_\epsilon(\hat{x}) \subset X$ about $\hat{x}$ with radius $\epsilon > 0$ and a positive number $\theta > 0$ such that

$$f(\hat{x}) \geqq f(x) + \theta \| x - \hat{x} \|^2 \quad for \ all \ x \in B_\epsilon(\hat{x})$$

PROOF: See Hestenes [9], chapter 1, sections 9 and 10, and El-Hodiri [4].

REMARK: Note that if *f*, the g_j's, and the h_k's are all concave *and* if all the multipliers $\hat{\lambda}_j$'s and $\hat{\mu}_k$'s are nonnegative, then the Lagrangian function *L*, as a nonnegative linear combination of concave functions, is concave. Hence the Hessian matrix of *L* is negative semidefinite for *all* $x \in X$. In particular, *H* is negative semidefinite. In other words, $\xi \cdot H \cdot \xi \leqq 0$ for *all* ξ. It should also be noted that Theorem 1.E.16 is concerned with only the local characterization. The (quasi-) concavity of *f* together with the convexity of the constraint set guarantees a global characterization.

As is well known, it is possible to characterize the second-order conditions in terms of the bordered Hessians. Let $A = [a_{ij}]$ be any $n \times n$ matrix with real entries and $B = [b_{ij}]$ be any $m \times n$ matrix with real entries. Here *A* and *B* are *not* necessarily Hessian or Jacobian matrices. Now define the following submatrices of *A* and *B*.

$$A_r \equiv \begin{bmatrix} a_{11} & a_{12} & \cdots & a_{1r} \\ a_{21} & a_{22} & \cdots & a_{2r} \\ \cdots & \cdots & \cdots & \cdots \\ a_{r1} & a_{r2} & \cdots & a_{rr} \end{bmatrix}, \qquad B_{mr} \equiv \begin{bmatrix} b_{11} & b_{12} & \cdots & b_{1r} \\ b_{21} & b_{22} & \cdots & b_{2r} \\ \cdots & \cdots & \cdots & \cdots \\ b_{m1} & b_{m2} & \cdots & b_{mr} \end{bmatrix}$$

where $m < n$ is assumed. Furthermore, define the following determinants $|C_r|$.

$$|C_r| \equiv \det \begin{bmatrix} 0 & B_{mr} \\ B'_{mr} & A_r \end{bmatrix}, \quad r = m + 1, m + 2, \ldots, n$$

where B'_{mr} is the transpose of B_{mr} and 0 is the $m \times m$ matrix whose entries are all zero. Then we have the following theorem to characterize the second-order sufficient conditions.

Theorem 1.E.17:   *Let A be symmetric and B_{mm} be nonsingular. Then*

(i) $\xi \cdot A \cdot \xi < 0$ *for all $\xi \neq 0$ such that $B \cdot \xi = 0$, if and only if*

$$(-1)^r |C_r| > 0, r = m + 1, m + 2, \ldots, n$$

(ii) $\xi \cdot A \cdot \xi > 0$ *for all $\xi \neq 0$ such that $B \cdot \xi = 0$, if and only if*

$$(-1)^m |C_r| > 0, r = m + 1, m + 2, \ldots, n$$

REMARK: In (i), the sign of $|C_r|$ depends on r; thus (i) says that the last $(n - m)$ successive principal minors of the bordered matrix C_n alternate in signs. In (ii), the sign of $|C_r|$ depends on m; thus (ii) says that the last $(n - m)$ successive principal minors of C_n all have the identical sign $(-1)^m$.

REMARK: Theorem 1.E.17 became well known to economists through Hicks's *Value and Capital* (Mathematical Appendix) and Samuelson's *Foundations of Economic Analysis* (especially pp. 376–378). A complete and sound proof of this theorem is given by Debreu [3]. It is well known that this theorem, together with Theorem 1.E.16, plays an important role in the comparative statics analysis.[15]

REMARK: Let

$$|\check{C}_r| \equiv \det \begin{bmatrix} A_r & B'_{mr} \\ B_{mr} & 0 \end{bmatrix}, \quad r = m + 1, \ldots, n$$

Then the bordered principal minors conditions of Theorem 1.E.17 can also be written in terms of $|\check{C}_r|$; that is,

$$(-1)^r |C_r| > 0 \text{ if and only if } (-1)^r |\check{C}_r| > 0 \ (r = m + 1, \ldots, n)$$

and

$$(-1)^m |C_r| > 0 \text{ if and only if } (-1)^m |\check{C}_r| > 0 \ (r = m + 1, \ldots, n)$$

As an example of the applications of Theorems 1.E.16 and 1.E.17, consider the problem of choosing $x \in R^n$ so as to

Maximize: $f(x)$
Subject to: $g(x) \equiv M - p \cdot x = 0$

where $p \geq 0$ is a constant vector in R^n and M is a positive constant. Define the Lagrangian by $L(x) \equiv f(x) + \hat{\lambda}(M - p \cdot x)$ and let A be the Hessian matrix of $L(x)$ evaluated at $\hat{x}$; that is, $A = L''(\hat{x})$ so that $a_{ij} = \partial^2 L(\hat{x})/\partial x_i \partial x_j$. Let B be the gradient vector $(\partial g/\partial x_1, \ldots, \partial g/\partial x_n) = (-p_1, -p_2, \ldots, -p_n)$. Then combining (ii) of Theorem 1.E.16 and (i) of Theorem 1.E.17, we can assert that a sufficient condition for $\hat{x}$ to achieve a local maximum of $f(x)$ subject to the constraint is $L'(\hat{x}) = 0$ *and*

$$\begin{vmatrix} 0 & -p_1 & -p_2 \\ -p_1 & a_{11} & a_{12} \\ -p_2 & a_{21} & a_{22} \end{vmatrix} > 0, \quad \begin{vmatrix} 0 & -p_1 & -p_2 & -p_3 \\ -p_1 & a_{11} & a_{12} & a_{13} \\ -p_2 & a_{21} & a_{22} & a_{23} \\ -p_3 & a_{31} & a_{32} & a_{33} \end{vmatrix} < 0, \ldots .$$

or equivalently,

$$\begin{vmatrix} a_{11} & a_{12} & -p_1 \\ a_{21} & a_{22} & -p_2 \\ -p_1 & -p_2 & 0 \end{vmatrix} > 0, \quad \begin{vmatrix} a_{11} & a_{12} & a_{13} & -p_1 \\ a_{21} & a_{22} & a_{23} & -p_2 \\ a_{31} & a_{32} & a_{33} & -p_3 \\ -p_1 & -p_2 & -p_3 & 0 \end{vmatrix} < 0, \ldots .$$

Note that the rank condition (R) is satisfied because $p \neq 0$ by assumption.

FOOTNOTES

1. Note the difference between "strictly quasi-concave" and "explicitly quasi-concave." Clearly if f is strictly quasi-concave (resp. strictly quasi-convex), then it is explicitly quasi-concave (resp. explicitly quasi-convex). The converse does not necessarily hold. Mathematicians often use the term "strictly quasi-concave" for the second property of "explicitly quasi-concave." See Ponstein [15], for example. The terms such as "explicitly quasi-concave" and "explicitly quasi-convex" are used in Martos [14], one of the papers which introduced the concept for the first time in the literature.

2. This statement can be proved by applying the **arithmetic mean theorem**; that is, $\min \{a, b\} \leq ta + (1 - t)b \leq \max \{a, b\}$, where $a, b, t \in R$, and $0 < t < 1$. Let $a = f(x)$ and $b = f(x')$, and apply the left inequality. Note the converse of the statement does not necessarily hold.

3. Prove by contradiction. Suppose $\hat{x}$ is a local maximum point in C which is not global. Then there exists $\bar{x} \in C$ such that $f(\bar{x}) > f(\hat{x})$. Due to the explicit quasi-concavity of f, this means $f[t\bar{x} + (1 - t)\hat{x}] > f(\hat{x})$ for all t, $0 < t \leq 1$. Choosing t close enough to zero, we get a contradiction of the local maximality of $\hat{x}$. Note that only the *second property* of explicit quasi-concavity is used in the proof. See Ponstein [15], for example.

4. That $\hat{x}$ achieves a global maximum follows from the previous statement since every strictly quasi-concave function is explicitly quasi-concave. To show the uniqueness, suppose the contrary. That is, $f(\hat{x}) = f(x^*)$ with $\hat{x} \neq x^*$ and $\hat{x}, x^* \in C$, where $\hat{x}$ and x^* both achieve global maximum. Let $\tilde{x} \equiv \frac{1}{2}\hat{x} + \frac{1}{2}x^*$. Then $\tilde{x} \in C$ and $f(\tilde{x}) > f(x^*)$, which is a contradiction.

5. However, it should also be noted that the consideration of the case in which the maximand function f is real-valued is not really a prerequisite for considering the case in which f is *vector*-valued. Without too much difficulty, the reader should be able to rephrase our discussions on Sections B and D such that they hold for the case in which f is vector-valued. See also Hurwicz [10], for example.

6. For example, consider the problem of (vector-) maximizing $x \in R^n$ subject to $g(x) \geq 0$, $x \geq 0$. Interpret $g(x)$ as the usual production transformation locus and x as the output vector. Theorems 1.E.5 and 1.E.6 signify that the solutions of the problems of maximizing $\alpha \cdot x$ with $g(x) \geq 0$ and $x \geq 0$ ($\alpha \in R^n$, $\alpha > 0$), when α varies, trace the points on the transformation locus. (The points on the transformation locus are the solutions of the above vector maximum problem.) The vector α may be interpreted as a "price vector."

7. The quadratic form $Q(x)$ in each of the following statements may be replaced by the symmetric matrix A.

8. If the second partial derivatives of f exist and are continuous for all x in the domain, then f is called **twice continuously differentiable** (as remarked in Section C). In this case, the Hessian matrix $f''(x)$ is symmetric for all x in the domain.

9. Needless to say, a matrix can be negative definite without each element of A being negative. Conversely, A may not be negative definite, even if each element of A is negative.

10. There seems to be a confusion among economists on this point. For example, K. Lancaster writes, "If $f(x)$ is strictly convex (concave), its Hessian is positive (negative) definite." (See his *Mathematical Economics*, New York, Macmillan, 1968, p. 333.) This statement is wrong in view of the above counterexample.

11. If $\alpha + \beta = 1$, F is no longer strictly concave, although it is strictly quasi-concave. In general, if $f(x)$ on $x \in X$, a convex subset of R^n, is linear homogeneous, it *cannot* be strictly concave. The strict concavity of f requires $f[(x + y)/2] > f(x)/2 + f(y)/2$ for all $x \neq y$ in X. But this is impossible under the linear homogeneity of f, if y is a scalar multiple of x (say $y = \alpha x$, for some $\alpha \in R$). To see this, observe $f[(x + y)/2] = (1 + \alpha)f(x)/2 = f(x)/2 + \alpha f(x)/2 = f(x)/2 + f(y)/2$.

12. There seems to be a confusion among economists between the second-order necessary condition and the second-order sufficient condition. For example, Hicks writes, "In order that u should be a true maximum, it is necessary to have not only $du = 0 \ldots$ but also $d^2u < 0$," (*Value and Capital*, 2nd ed., p. 306). Consider the problem of maximizing $f(x) \equiv -(x - 1)^4$, $x \in R$. Clearly f reaches its maximum at $x = 1$. Note that $f''(1) = 0$. In other words, $f''(1) < 0$ is by no means *necessary* for a maximum.

13. Assume $m_e + l < n$.

14. Recall that Theorem 1.D.7 has already established that (LM) and (R) imply (FOC). This is the first statement of (i) of the present theorem.

15. See, for example, chapters 2, 3, 4, and 5 of Samuelson [16]. See also Appendix to Section F of this chapter for a complete summary of the local maximization theory and its applications to the comparative statics problem.

REFERENCES

1. Arrow, K. J., and Enthoven, A. C., "Quasi-Concave Programming," *Econometrica*, 29, October 1961.

2. Arrow, K. J., Hurwicz, L., and Uzawa, H., "Constraint Qualifications in Maximization Problems," *Naval Research Logistics Quarterly*, vol. 8, no. 2, June 1961.

3. Debreu, G., "Definite and Semidefinite Quadratic Forms," *Econometrica*, 20, April 1952.

4. El-Hodiri, M. A., *Constrained Extrema: Introduction to the Differentiable Case with Economic Applications*, Berlin, Springer-Verlag, 1971 (originally "Constrained

Extrema of Functions of a Finite Number of Variables: Review and Generalizations," *Krannert Institute Paper*, No. 141, Purdue University, 1966).

5. ———, "The Karush Characterization of Constrained Extrema of Functions of a Finite Number of Variables," UAR Ministry of Treasury, *Research Memoranda*, series A. no. 3, July 1967.

6. Fenchel, W., *Convex Cones, Sets, and Functions*, Princeton, N.J., Princeton University, 1953 (hectographed).

7. Gantmacher, F. R., *The Theory of Matrices*, Vol. 1, New York, Chelsea Publishing Co., 1959, esp. chap. X (tr. from Russian).

8. Hadley, G., *Linear Algebra*, Reading, Mass., Addison-Wesley, 1961, esp. chap 7.

9. Hestenes, M. R., *Calculus of Variations and Optimal Control Theory*, New York, Wiley, 1966.

10. Hurwicz, L., "Programming in Linear Spaces," in *Studies in Linear and Non-linear Programming*, ed. by Arrow, Hurwicz, and Uzawa, Stanford, Calif., Stanford University Press, 1958.

11. Karlin, S., *Mathematical Methods and Theory in Games, Programming, and Economics*, Vol. 1, Reading, Mass., Addison-Wesley, 1959, esp. pp. 216–218 and appendices A and B.

12. Kuhn, H. W., and Tucker, A. W., "Non-linear Programming," in *Proceedings of the Second Berkeley Symposium on Mathematical Statistics and Probability*, ed. by J. Neyman, Berkeley, Calif., University of California Press, 1951.

13. Marcus, M., and Minc, H., *A Survey of Matrix Theory and Matrix Inequalities*, Boston, Allyn and Bacon, 1964, esp. part II.

14. Martos, B., "The Direct Power of Adjacent Vertex Programming Methods," *Management Science*, Series A, 12, November 1965.

15. Ponstein, J., "Seven Kinds of Convexity," *SIAM Review*, vol. 9, January 1967.

16. Samuelson, P. A., *Foundations of Economic Analysis*, Cambridge, Mass., Harvard University Press, 1947, esp. appendix A.

Section F

SOME APPLICATIONS

In this section we give applications of some of the theorems established in the previous sections of this chapter. This will indicate the practical importance of these theorems and at the same time enhance our understanding of them. First we derive two important theorems in linear programming as simple corollaries of the theorems established thus far. Then we illustrate the applications to consumer's choice, theory of production, activity analysis, and the Ricardo-Mill problem in the theory of international trade.

a.   LINEAR PROGRAMMING

Probably the most fundamental relation in the theory of linear programming is the dual relation. The dual relation is concerned with the following two types of problems, each one of which is called the "dual problem" of the other.

$$(M_{LP}) \quad \text{Maximize: } p \cdot x$$
$$x \in R^n$$

$$\text{Subject to: } A \cdot x \leq r \text{ and } x \geq 0$$

where p is a given vector in R^n, r is a given vector in R^m, and A is an $m \times n$ matrix

$$(m_{LP}) \quad \text{Minimize: } w \cdot r$$
$$x \in R^n$$

$$\text{Subject to: } A' \cdot w \geq p \text{ and } w \geq 0$$

where A' is the transpose of A.

We may recall here the convention of multiplying a vector by a matrix or by another vector. We do not make a distinction in our notation between a "row" or a "column" vector, assuming that the reader will be able to tell the difference by use. The dot ($\cdot$) between a matrix (or a vector) and a vector indicates multiplication of the matrix (or the vector) with the vector. The reader should ensure that he knows the result of this product. In the above two problems, one should note the following:

(i)   The **evaluating vector** p in (M_{LP}) appears in the constraint of (m_{LP}), and the evaluating vector r in (m_{LP}) appears in the constraint of (M_{LP}).

(ii) The constraint matrices are each other's transpose.

(iii) Except for the nonnegativity condition, the inequality in the constraint is reversed.

We now prove two important theorems in connection with dual problems: the duality theorem and the Goldman-Tucker theorem. These theorems were originally proved without using the theory of nonlinear programming, and, in fact, played an important role in the development of the theory of nonlinear programming. Here we prove them using the theorems established in the previous sections.

Theorem 1.F.1 (LP duality theorem):

(i)   *There exists an optimal solution $\hat{x}$ for (M_{LP}) if and only if there exists an optimal solution $\hat{w}$ for (m_{LP}).*

(ii) *The inequalities $\hat{x} \geq 0$ and $\hat{w} \geq 0$ satisfy $A \cdot \hat{x} \leq r$, $A' \cdot \hat{w} \geq p$, and $\hat{w} \cdot (r - A \cdot \hat{x}) = \hat{x} \cdot (A' \cdot \hat{w} - p) = 0$ if and only if $\hat{x}$ is optimal for (M_{LP}) and $\hat{w}$ is optimal for (m_{LP}) (moreover, in this case, $p \cdot \hat{x} = r \cdot \hat{w}$).*

PROOF: (i) Suppose $\hat{x}$ is optimal for (M_{LP}). Then by Theorem 1.D.5, there exists $\hat{w} \geq 0$ such that $(\hat{x}, \hat{w})$ is a saddle point of $\Phi(x, w) \equiv p \cdot x + w \cdot (r - A \cdot x)$, that is,

$$(1) \qquad \Phi(x, \hat{w}) \leq \Phi(\hat{x}, \hat{w}) \leq \Phi(\hat{x}, w) \qquad \text{for all } x \geq 0, w \geq 0$$

Define

$$\Psi(w, x) \equiv -\Phi(x, w) = -p \cdot x - w \cdot (r - A \cdot x)$$
$$= -w \cdot r + x \cdot (A' \cdot w - p)$$

Then from (1) we have

$$\Psi(w, \hat{x}) \leq \Psi(\hat{w}, \hat{x}) \leq \Psi(\hat{w}, x) \qquad \text{for all } x \geq 0, w \geq 0$$

Hence from the corollary of the Arrow-Hurwicz-Uzawa theorem, $\hat{w}$ maximizes $-w \cdot r$ subject to $w \geq 0$, $A' \cdot w \geq p$; that is, $\hat{w}$ is optimal for (m_{LP}).

Conversely, if $\hat{w}$ is optimal for (m_{LP}), then, proceeding as before, there exists an $\hat{x} \geq 0$ such that $\Psi(w, x)$ has a saddle point at $(\hat{w}, \hat{x})$. This in turn implies $\Phi(x, w)$ has a saddle point at $(\hat{x}, \hat{w})$, which implies $\hat{x}$ is optimal for (M_{LP}).

(ii) If $\hat{x}$ and $\hat{w}$ are optimal solutions of (M_{LP}) and (m_{LP}), respectively, then by the reasoning of part (i), $(\hat{x}, \hat{w})$ is a saddle point of $\Phi(x, w)$, and $(\hat{w}, \hat{x})$ is a saddle point of $\Psi(w, x)$. But then by Theorem 1.B.4 (ii),

$$\hat{w} \cdot (r - A \cdot \hat{x}) = \hat{x} \cdot (A' \cdot \hat{w} - p) = 0$$

Moreover, since $\Phi(\hat{x}, \hat{w}) = -\Psi(\hat{w}, \hat{x})$, we then have $p \cdot \hat{x} = \hat{w} \cdot r$, which verifies the parenthetical remark in (ii).

Conversely, suppose that there exist $\hat{x} \geq 0$ and $\hat{w} \geq 0$ such that

$$(2) \qquad \hat{w} \cdot (r - A \cdot \hat{x}) = \hat{x} \cdot (A' \cdot \hat{w} - p) = 0$$

and

$$(3) \qquad A \cdot \hat{x} \leq r, \qquad A' \cdot \hat{w} \geq p$$

Then if $\hat{x} \geq 0$ and $\hat{w} \geq 0$ we have, using (3), (2), and (3) in turn,

$$\Phi(x, \hat{w}) = p \cdot x + \hat{w} \cdot (r - A \cdot x) = \hat{w} \cdot r + (p - \hat{w} \cdot A) \cdot x$$
$$\leq \hat{w} \cdot r = \hat{w} \cdot r - \hat{x} \cdot (A' \cdot \hat{w} - p) = p \cdot \hat{x} + \hat{w} \cdot (r - A \cdot \hat{x})$$
$$= \Phi(\hat{x}, \hat{w}) = p \cdot \hat{x} \leq p \cdot \hat{x} + w \cdot (r - A \cdot \hat{x}) = \Phi(\hat{x}, w)$$

Hence, again by Theorem 1.D.5, it follows that $\hat{x}$ is optimal for (M_{LP}). The fact that $\hat{w}$ is optimal for (m_{LP}) then follows from (i).   (Q.E.D.)

REMARK: There are a variety of proofs of the *LP* duality theorem which do not rely on the theory of nonlinear programming. For these, see any standard textbook on linear programming. Two proofs that are among the simplest and most interesting are one by Nikaido [12], which proves the *LP* duality theorem as an application of the Minkowski-Farkas lemma, and the other by Dantzig ([4], pp. 129–134), which proves the theorem as an application of the *LP* simplex method. Our proof will enhance the reader's understanding of the nonlinear programming theory developed in this chapter.

In the course of the proof of the duality theorem, we also proved the following theorem.

Theorem 1.F.2 (Goldman-Tucker): *There exist optimal solutions for* (M_{LP}) *and* (m_{LP})*, denoted by* $\hat{x}$ *and* $\hat{w}$ *respectively, if and only if there exists* $(\hat{x}, \hat{w})$*, which is a saddle point of* $\Phi(x, w) \equiv p \cdot x + w \cdot (r - A \cdot x)$*; that is,*

$$\Phi(x, \hat{w}) \leq \Phi(\hat{x}, \hat{w}) \leq \Phi(\hat{x}, w) \qquad \text{for all } x \geq 0, \text{ and all } w \geq 0$$

REMARK: For the original proof, which obviously does not rely on nonlinear programming theory, see Goldman and Tucker [8], especially theorem 6, pp. 77–78. They obtained this theorem from the *LP* duality theorem.

REMARK: In Figure 1.17 we illustrate schematically the logical structure of some of the important theorems established so far.

REMARK: We proved the fundamental theorem of activity analysis (Theorem 0.C.3) by using the separation theorem. As we will see later, this theorem can also be proved by an extension of the concave programming theorem. The proof of the Minkowski-Farkas lemma by utilizing the *LP* duality theorem and the proof of the *LP* duality theorem by utilizing the Minkowski-Farkas lemma are not too difficult and will be interesting exercises for the reader.

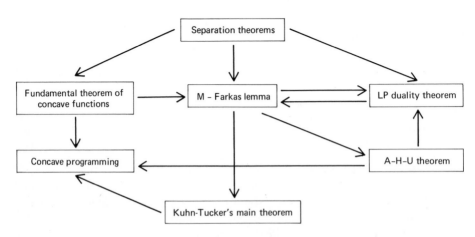

Figure 1.17. Logical Structure of Some Important Theorems.

b. CONSUMPTION THEORY

In the classical theory of consumer's choice as explained in Hicks [10], for example, a consumer is supposed to maximize his satisfaction over the budget set. Let $x \in R^n$ be his n-commodity consumption bundle and $u(x)$, a real-valued function defined over R^n, be his utility function. Suppose that this consumer is a "competitive consumer" so that he cannot influence the prices of the commodities in the market. Then if a price vector p prevails, his budget constraint can be expressed as $p \cdot x \leq M$ (with $x \geq 0$) where M is his income. Although the non-negativity condition $x \geq 0$ is not mentioned in Hicks, it is implied in the context. Hicks wrote the budget constraint in the form of the equality $p \cdot x = M$. This means that the consumer must spend all his income. We will use the inequality constraint $p \cdot x \leq M$ instead, allowing the consumer the possibility of not spending all his income. Later we will find a condition under which this constraint becomes effective (that is, he spends all his income).

We can now write the problem for each consumer as follows:

$$\text{Maximize: } u(x)$$
$$\scriptstyle x \in R^n$$
$$\text{Subject to: } p \cdot x \leq M \quad \text{and } x \geq 0$$

Following the classical analysis, we assume that $u(x)$ is differentiable[1] everywhere. Hence we can use the theory developed in Sections D and E. Since the constraints are linear, owing to the (A-H-U) theorem (Theorem 1.D.4), the (QSP') condition is a necessary condition for global maximality. In other words, if $\hat{x}$ is a solution of the above problem, then there exists a $\hat{\lambda} \in R$ such that

(4) $\qquad \hat{u}_{x_i} - \hat{\lambda} p_i \leq 0, \qquad i = 1, 2, \ldots, n$

(5) $\qquad \hat{x} \cdot (\hat{u}_x - \hat{\lambda} p) = 0$

(6) $\qquad \hat{\lambda}(M - p \cdot \hat{x}) = 0, \quad \hat{\lambda} \geq 0$ $\qquad$ **(QSP')**

(7) $\qquad M - p \cdot \hat{x} \geq 0, \quad \hat{x} \geq 0$

Here $\hat{u}_x \equiv u'(\hat{x})$, $\hat{u}_{x_i} \equiv \partial u / \partial x_i$ (evaluated at $x = \hat{x}$), and $\hat{u}_x \equiv (\hat{u}_{x_1}, \ldots, \hat{u}_{x_n})$. Conversely, assuming $u(x)$ is a concave function, if there exist $\hat{x}$ and $\hat{\lambda}$, both nonnegative, such that the above (QSP') condition holds, then, owing to Theorem 1.D.2, $\hat{x}$ is a solution of the above constrained maximum problem for the consumer. In other words, under the concavity of $u(x)$, the above (QSP') becomes a *necessary and sufficient* condition for $\hat{x}$ to furnish a global maximum of the above constrained maximum problem (see Theorem 1.D.5). Hence our attention will be shifted to finding the values of $\hat{x}$ and $\hat{\lambda}$ which satisfy the above (QSP'). If $u(x)$ is not concave but rather quasi-concave, then we need an additional assumption. In particular, we assume

(A-c) $\hat{u}_{x_i} > 0$ for some *relevant* variable x_i (that is, positive "marginal utility" for some relevant variable).[2]

Then, applying the Arrow-Enthoven theorem (Theorem 1.E.2), we can again conclude that (QSP') provides a *necessary* as well as *sufficient* condition for the above constrained maximum problem.

With these remarks, we now shift our attention to (QSP'). First observe that conditions (6) and (7) of (QSP') mean

$$(8) \qquad\qquad \hat{\lambda} > 0 \text{ implies } M - p \cdot \hat{x} = 0$$

Since $\hat{u}_{x_i} \leq \hat{\lambda} p_i$ for all i from condition (4) above, $\hat{u}_{x_i} > 0$ (positive marginal utility) for *some* commodity i is consistent only with $\hat{\lambda} > 0$ and a positive price of that commodity ($p_i > 0$). We may recall that $\hat{u}_{x_i} > 0$ for some relevant x_i is assumed [(A-c)] when we adopt quasi-concave programming. In other words, if we assume that there exists at least one commodity in which the consumer is never satiated, then $\hat{\lambda} > 0$ so that $M = p \cdot \hat{x}$ [resulting from relations (6) and (7)]. This could mean that the nonsatiation assumption will be a crucial assumption in the sense that it guarantees that all the income is spent. Thus we have revealed one crucial assumption which underlies the Hicksian equality constraint $M = p \cdot x$.

Next note that conditions (4) and (5) of the above (QSP') mean

$$(9) \qquad\qquad \hat{x}_i(\hat{u}_{x_i} - \hat{\lambda} p_i) = 0, \qquad i = 1, 2, \ldots, n$$

Hence if we assume an interior solution for all i (that is, $\hat{x}_i > 0$ for all i), then we obtain

$$(10) \qquad\qquad \hat{u}_{x_i} = \hat{\lambda} p_i, \qquad i = 1, 2, \ldots, n$$

Note that this interior solution assumption is usually made implicit in the classical analysis, as it is explained in Hicks, for example. In general, this assumption does not necessarily hold. It is quite possible that $\hat{x}_i = 0$ for some i. A typical situation is illustrated in Figure 1.18.

Following the classical analysis, we now proceed with the interior solution assumption (that is, $\hat{x}_i > 0$ for all i). By relation (10), if $p_i \neq 0$ for some i, then $\hat{\lambda} > 0$. In other words, under the assumption that the consumer consumes a positive amount of every commodity, $p_i \neq 0$ for some i guarantees $\hat{\lambda} > 0$. Then we have $M = p \cdot \hat{x}$ [from (8)]. This and equation (10) provide $n + 1$ equations which are

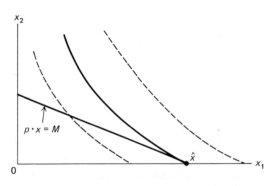

Figure 1.18. An Illustration of Corner Solution.

available to determine $(n + 1)$ variables, that is, $\hat{x}_1, \hat{x}_2, \ldots, \hat{x}_n$, and $\hat{\lambda}$. This is the classical procedure as explained in Hicks [10] (especially the mathematical appendix). Assuming that there exist "equilibrium" values of these variables, we can then go to comparative statics and obtain the "fundamental equation of value theory" (or the "Hicks-Slutsky equation").[3] We may note that these equilibrium values of the $\hat{x}_i$'s will furnish a *global* maximum for the above constrained maximum problem, which clearly has important implications in comparative statics.

We may note here that (10) implies that $\hat{u}_{x_i} > 0$ if and only if $p_i > 0$ (with $\hat{\lambda} > 0$). This means of course that if the consumer decides to consume a positive amount of some commodity (which enters into his original choice problem), then the positive price of a particular commodity implies a positive marginal utility for that commodity. Note that this allows the possibility of a negative price for a certain commodity. If the price of a certain commodity is negative, the marginal utility of this commodity must be negative. Conversely, if a certain commodity has a negative marginal utility (thus is "undesired") for every consumer, then it must have a negative price. To pursue this converse problem more precisely, we would have to construct a model of the economy into which *all* the relevant consumers and producers are included. We will not pursue this problem here.

Next we note the bordered Hessian condition as discussed in Hicks. Hicks pointed out the following second-order condition as a sufficient condition for (local) maximality of the constrained maximum problem: $(-1)^k B_k > 0, k = 1, 2, 3, \ldots, n$, *at a solution* $\hat{x}$ *of the problem, where*

$$B_k \equiv \begin{vmatrix} 0 & u_1 & u_2 & \cdots & u_k \\ u_1 & u_{11} & u_{12} & \cdots & u_{1k} \\ u_2 & u_{21} & u_{22} & \cdots & u_{2k} \\ \cdots & \cdots & \cdots & \cdots & \cdots \\ u_k & u_{k1} & u_{k2} & \cdots & u_{kk} \end{vmatrix}$$

where $u_i \equiv \partial u / \partial x_i$ and $u_{ij} \equiv \partial^2 u / \partial x_i \partial x_j$ (all the partial derivatives are evaluated at $x = \hat{x}$).

By Theorem 1.E.14, if the above condition holds for all x, then $u(x)$ is quasi-concave. In other words, quasi-concave programming enables us to dispense with the above bordered Hessian condition and provides us with a *global* maximum (instead of a local maximum). Note that if u is *strictly* quasi-concave, we would have a *unique* global maximum. Needless to say, the quasi-concavity of the utility function (that is, the convex-to-the-origin indifference curves) is more intuitively appealing than to say that the utility function satisfies the bordered Hessian condition.[4]

If $u(x)$ is concave, then the above bordered Hessian condition is replaced by the stronger Hessian condition, as discussed in Section E. *Strict* concavity will give a *unique* solution.

This finishes our critical review of the classical theory of consumer's choice in terms of (quasi-) concave programming. The following points were made explicit:

(i) The formulation of the problem as a modern theory of (quasi-) concave programming problem.
(ii) The assumption which guarantees the equality $M = p \cdot \hat{x}$ (that is, the non-satiation assumption).
(iii) The possibility of a corner solution.
(iv) The possibility of negative prices.
(v) The relation between the second-order condition and quasi-concave programming theory.

Finally, we should stress that the theory of concave (or quasi-concave) programming provides a global characterization of the problem. The classical treatment in terms of the Euler-Lagrange necessary conditions and the Hessian (or bordered Hessian) condition (as utilized by Hicks and so on) only provides a local characterization; that is, it is concerned with the properties in some (possibly very small) neighborhood of a solution point, and there may be many solution points, each giving a different value for maximal utility.

c. PRODUCTION THEORY

The production activity of an economy is concerned with transforming one set of commodities, called "inputs," denoted by a vector $v = (v_1, v_2, \ldots, v_m)$ into another set of commodities called "outputs," denoted by a vector $x = (x_1, x_2, \ldots, x_n)$. In activity analysis, inputs were denoted by negative numbers, outputs were denoted by positive numbers, and we called a vector $y = (-v, x)$ an "activity vector" (after normalization with respect to a certain commodity, to define the "activity level"). Then we considered the set of these y's, Y, and called it the "production set." We now wish to describe this set by a functional relation in order to obtain an application of the theory established in this chapter. By the explicit introduction of such a functional relation, our analysis will also serve as a critical review of an important part of the classical production theory (as explained in Hicks [10] and Carlson [2]). In the following analysis, we denote inputs—say, v_j—by positive numbers (instead of negative numbers).

The functional relation that describes a production set can be written as

$$F(v, x) \geq 0$$

We assume $v \in R^m$ and $x \in R^n$ with $v \geq 0$ and $x \geq 0$. In the case where v and x are real numbers, we may illustrate the above relation as in Figure 1.19. Here the shaded area illustrates the values of (v, x) which satisfy the above functional relation.

We note that if $F(v, x) \equiv f(v) - x$, the relation $x = f(v)$ can be obtained by solving $F(v, x) = 0$. This relation $x = f(v)$ or $F(v, x) = 0$ (where $v \in R^m, x \in R^n$ with $v \geq 0, x \geq 0$) is the familiar **production function** in the traditional analysis. We may call such a surface a **production frontier**. In the functional relation $F(v, x) \geq 0$, we allowed the possibility of points which are not on the surface $F(v, x) = 0$. This is illustrated in Figure 1.19. Points such as A are on the curve defined by

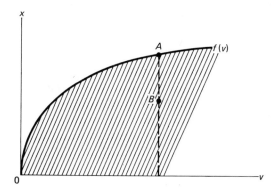

Figure 1.19.   An Illustration of Production Set.

$F(v, x) = 0$ [or $x = f(v)$]. However, we also allow the possibility of points such as B. Such points are allowed for either (or both) of the following two reasons.

(i) We allow the possibility of production processes that are technically inferior to some other processes. In other words, we do not assume the existence of an "efficient" manager.

(ii) We assume free disposability of commodities so that some inputs and outputs can be thrown away in the process. This can happen, for example, if some commodities (either inputs or outputs) become "free" due to an excess supply of those commodities in the economy.

Now let $p = (p_1, p_2, \ldots, p_n)$ be the price vector for outputs and $w = (w_1, w_2, \ldots, w_m)$ be the price vector for inputs. Then the profit which can be obtained by transforming v into x may be written as

$$\pi \equiv p \cdot x - w \cdot v$$

Suppose that the "producer" is "competitive" so that he cannot affect the level of prices, p and w, that prevails in the market. Suppose further that his behavioral rule is profit maximization (for otherwise he will sooner or later be ruled out of a typically "competitive" market). Then his problem is the following nonlinear programming problem.

$$\text{Maximize: } \pi \equiv p \cdot x - w \cdot v$$
$$_{(x,v)}$$
$$\text{Subject to: } F(v, x) \geq 0 \text{ and } v \geq 0, x \geq 0$$

First, let us suppose that $F(v, x)$ is a differentiable concave function with respect to v and x, and that the following Slater's condition holds.

(S)   There exist $\bar{v} \geq 0$, $\bar{x} \geq 0$ such that $F(\bar{v}, \bar{x}) > 0$.

This condition (S) can be accepted without much difficulty. Essentially it allows an interior point in the production set which is possible as a result of either (i) or (ii) above. Under these assumptions, we can apply Theorem 1.D.2. In other words, $\hat{x} \geq 0$ is a solution of the above problem if and only if there exists a scalar $\hat{\lambda} \geq 0$ such that

$$(11) \qquad p_i + \hat{\lambda}\hat{F}_{x_i} \leq 0, \qquad i = 1, 2, \ldots, n$$

$$(12) \qquad -w_j + \hat{\lambda}\hat{F}_{v_j} \leq 0, \qquad j = 1, 2, \ldots, m$$

$$(13) \qquad \hat{x} \cdot (p + \hat{\lambda}\hat{F}_x) + \hat{v} \cdot (-w + \hat{\lambda}\hat{F}_v) = 0$$

$$(14) \qquad F(\hat{v}, \hat{x}) \geq 0, \quad \hat{\lambda}F(\hat{v}, \hat{x}) = 0$$

$$(QSP')$$

where $\hat{F}_{x_i} \equiv \partial F/\partial x_i$, $\hat{F}_{v_j} \equiv \partial F/\partial v_j$, $i = 1, 2, \ldots, n$, $j = 1, 2, \ldots, m$ [each evaluated at $(v, x) = (\hat{v}, \hat{x})$], and $\hat{F}_x \equiv (\hat{F}_{x_1}, \hat{F}_{x_2}, \ldots, \hat{F}_{x_n})$, $F_v \equiv (\hat{F}_{v_1}, \hat{F}_{v_2}, \ldots, \hat{F}_{v_m})$.

By conditions (11) and (12), condition (13) of the above (QSP') is equivalent to

$$(15) \qquad \hat{x}_i(p_i + \hat{\lambda}\hat{F}_{x_i}) = 0, \qquad i = 1, 2, \ldots, n$$

$$(16) \qquad \hat{v}_j(-w_j + \hat{\lambda}\hat{F}_{v_j}) = 0, \qquad j = 1, 2, \ldots, m$$

We assume that at least one output (say, i_0) is produced (that is, $\hat{x}_{i_0} > 0$) or at least one input (say, j_0) is used in production (that is, $\hat{v}_{j_0} > 0$). Then from (15) or (16)

$$(17) \qquad\qquad\qquad \hat{\lambda} > 0$$

as long as $p_{i_0} > 0$ or $w_{j_0} > 0$.

Then from (14), we have $F(\hat{v}, \hat{x}) = 0$. In other words, under the above assumption of $\hat{x}_{i_0} > 0$ or $\hat{v}_{j_0} > 0$ (for some i_0 or j_0), production will take place on the production frontier *if and only if* the producer maximizes his profit. This corresponds to the fundamental theorems of activity analysis (Theorems O.C.2 and O.C.3).

If we assume an interior solution for every output and input (that is, $\hat{x}_i > 0$, $\hat{v}_j > 0$ for all i and j), as in Hicks [10], conditions (11) and (12) can be rewritten as follows:

$$(11') \qquad\qquad -p_i = \hat{\lambda}\hat{F}_{x_i}, \qquad i = 1, 2, \ldots, n$$

$$(12') \qquad\qquad w_j = \hat{\lambda}\hat{F}_{v_j}, \qquad j = 1, 2, \ldots, m$$

Under the assumption of an interior solution, we have $\hat{\lambda} > 0$, as noted above, which in turn implies $F(\hat{x}, \hat{v}) = 0$. Combining this equation with conditions (11') and (12'), we obtain $(n + m + 1)$ equations, which, in turn, would presumably determine $(n + m + 1)$ variables, that is, $\hat{\lambda}$, the $\hat{x}_i$'s, and the $\hat{v}_j$'s as functions of the p_i's and w_j's. By changing the values of the p_i's and w's, we get a comparative statics analysis which will lead to Hick's fundamental equation. In the above analysis, the fact that (QSP') is *necessary and sufficient* for a (global) maximum depends on our assumption that $F(v, x)$ is a concave function. The function $F(v, x)$ is concave if and only if the following Hessian condition holds (assuming that F is twice differentiable). (See Theorem 1.E.13.)

$$\tilde{D}_1 \leq 0, \tilde{D}_2 \geq 0, \ldots, (-1)^{m+n}\tilde{D}_{m+n} \geq 0$$

where $\tilde{D}_k$ is defined as in Section E.

If F is quasi-concave instead of concave, we can still say that the above (QSP′) is sufficient for the optimality of $(\hat{v}, \hat{x})$ since the maximand function is linear and hence concave [condition (iv) of the Arrow-Enthoven theorem, Theorem 1.E.2]. Moreover, (QSP′) is also necessary for the optimality if a certain constraint qualification is satisfied. The constraint qualifications which require neither the concavity nor the convexity of the constraint functions are provided, for example, in (KTCQ) and the Arrow-Hurwicz-Uzawa theorem [conditions (iv) and (v) of Theorem 1.D.4 or condition (ii) of Theorem 1.E.3]. For example, assuming that there exist $\bar{v} \geq 0$, $\bar{x} \geq 0$, with $F(\bar{v}, \bar{x}) > 0$, (QSP′) is necessary for $(\hat{v}, \hat{x})$ to furnish a maximum, if[5]

(18) $$\hat{F}_x \neq 0 \text{ or } \hat{F}_v \neq 0$$

If we have an interior solution for some i or some j, then (11′) and (12′) imply (18). Hence, assuming an interior solution, (QSP′) becomes necessary and sufficient for an optimum under the quasi-concavity of the function F. The quasi-concavity of F can be characterized in terms of the bordered Hessian conditions, which corresponds to Hicks's discussion of the topic ([10], p. 320). A condition that is alternative to (18) can be obtained by utilizing the rank condition (Theorem 1.D.4). The rank condition for the present problem is stronger than (18). Even with $\hat{x} > 0$, $\hat{v} > 0$, we may, for example, require[6]

(18′) $$\hat{F}_x \neq 0 \text{ and } \hat{F}_v \neq 0$$

Again under the quasi-concavity of F, (QSP′) provides a set of necessary and sufficient conditions for an optimum.[7]

The quasi-concavity of $F(v, x)$ implies that the following bordered Hessian condition holds (assuming that F is twice differentiable).

(19) $$B_1 \leq 0, B_2 \geq 0, \ldots, (-1)^{m+n} B_{m+n} \geq 0$$

where B_k is defined as in Section E (Theorem 1.E.14). We again emphasize that the concept of concavity or quasi-concavity is more intuitively appealing than the Hessian or the bordered Hessian conditions.

In order to understand further the meaning of the above (QSP′) condition, we now assume that there is only one output in this production, so that x and p are now scalars. We also assume that $F(x, v) \geq 0$ can be written as $f(v) \geq x$. Then our (QSP′) condition can be rewritten as follows:

(20) $$p - \hat{\lambda} \leq 0$$

(21) $$-w_j + \hat{\lambda}\hat{f}_{v_j} \leq 0, j = 1, 2, \ldots, m$$

(22) $$(p - \hat{\lambda})\hat{x} + \hat{v} \cdot (-w + \hat{\lambda}\hat{f}_v) = 0$$

(23) $$\hat{\lambda}[f(\hat{v}) - \hat{x}] = 0, f(\hat{v}) - \hat{x} \geq 0, \hat{x} \geq 0, \hat{v} \geq 0$$

Conditions (20), (21), and (22) imply that

$$(24) \qquad\qquad (p - \hat{\lambda})\hat{x} = 0$$

and

$$(25) \qquad\qquad \hat{v}_j(-w_j + \hat{\lambda}\hat{f}_{v_j}) = 0, \qquad j = 1, 2, \ldots, m$$

Assume $p > 0$; then $\hat{\lambda} > 0$ as a result of (20). Then, in view of (23), $\hat{x} = f(\hat{v})$, which means that the production takes place on the production frontier at an optimum. Note that this does not preclude the possibility of $\hat{x} = 0$. In other words, it is possible that zero output is optimum. Assume that $\hat{x} > 0$, for otherwise it would not be of interest to discuss the problem. Then from (24), $p = \hat{\lambda}$. In other words, the Lagrangian multiplier $\hat{\lambda}$ for the problem is equal to the price of the output p which is given to the producer. Thus the set of conditions (20), (21), (22), and (23) are rewritten as follows:

$$(26) \qquad\qquad p\hat{f}_{v_j} \leqq w_j, \qquad j = 1, 2, \ldots, m$$

$$(27) \qquad\qquad \hat{v}_j(w_j - p\hat{f}_{v_j}) = 0, \qquad j = 1, 2, \ldots, m$$

$$(28) \qquad\qquad f(\hat{v}) = \hat{x}$$

Conditions (26), (27), and (28) provide the *necessary and sufficient* conditions for $(\hat{x}, \hat{v})$ to be optimal under the quasi-concavity of $[f(v) - x]$ or the concavity of $f(v)$, given the proper additional conditions discussed above.

Condition (26) says that the value of the jth factor's marginal product cannot exceed the price of the jth factor. Condition (27) says that if the price of the jth factor exceeds the value of its marginal product, then this jth factor will not be used in the profit maximizing activity. Condition (28) says that only profit maximization is compatible with "efficient" production (production on the frontier). We may also note that the nonnegativity conditions $(x \geq 0, v \geq 0)$ are now explicitly considered.

d.   ACTIVITY ANALYSIS

Let a_{ij} be the amount of the ith commodity involved in a unit operation of the jth activity and let a^j be the vector for the jth activity whose ith element is a_{ij}. Assume that there are n commodities and m activities. Let x_j be the activity level of the jth activity and let x be the activity vector whose jth element is x_j. Then, as we discussed in Chapter 0, Section C, the production set Y is given by

$$(29) \qquad\qquad Y \equiv \{y: y = A \cdot x, x \geq 0\}, \text{ where } A = [a_{ij}]$$

or

$$Y \equiv \{y: y = \sum_{j=1}^{m} a^j x_j, \ x \geq 0\}$$

An *efficient point* $\hat{y}$ of Y is a point such that there does not exist a $y \in Y$ such that $y \geq \hat{y}$. In other words, this $\hat{y}$ can be obtained as a solution of the following vector maximum problem.

(Vector) Maximize: y
Subject to: $y \in Y$

Then from Theorem 1.E.4, if $\hat{y}$ is a solution of this problem, there exists $p \geq 0$ such that

(30) $\qquad\qquad p \cdot \hat{y} \geq p \cdot y \qquad$ for all $y \in Y$

Obviously this holds even if Y is not restricted to the form (29). Only the convexity of Y is required. Relation (30) corresponds to Theorem 0.C.3. Although the converse of the theorem is easy to obtain, as discussed in Theorem 0.C.2, we can also obtain this converse by using Theorem 1.E.6. In other words, if there exists a $p > 0$ such that $p \cdot \hat{y} \geq p \cdot y$ for all $y \in Y$, then $\hat{y}$ is an efficient point of Y (or a solution of the above vector maximum problem).

We now consider a resource constraint which we write as follows:

(31) $\qquad\qquad y + z \geq 0, \quad y \in Y$

where z_i, the ith component of z, denotes the amount of this ith commodity ("resource") available in the economy. The feasible set Y_F of this economy is then

$$Y_F = \{y: y \in Y, y + z \geq 0\}$$

Now we are interested in the problem of finding an efficient point of this feasible set Y_F. The point $\hat{y}_F$ is an efficient point of Y_F if there does not exist $y \in Y_F$ such that $y \geq \hat{y}_F$. Hence an efficient point of Y_F can be obtained as a solution of the following vector maximum problem.

Maximize: y
Subject to: $y + z \geq 0$ and $y \in Y$

Assume Slater's condition so that there exists a $\bar{y} \in Y$ such that $\bar{y} + z > 0$. Then using Theorem 1.E.4, if $\hat{y}$ is a solution of this problem, there exists a $p \geq 0 \, (p \neq 0)$ and $\hat{\lambda} \geq 0$ such that

(SP) $\Phi(y, \hat{\lambda}) \leq \Phi(\hat{y}, \hat{\lambda}) \leq \Phi(\hat{y}, \lambda)$, for all $y \in Y$ and $\lambda \geq 0$, and $\hat{\lambda} \cdot (\hat{y} + z) = 0$, where $\Phi(y, \lambda) \equiv p \cdot y + \lambda \cdot (y + z)$.

The first inequality of the above (SP) can be written as follows:

(32) $\qquad p \cdot y + \hat{\lambda} \cdot (y + z) \leq p \cdot \hat{y} + \hat{\lambda} \cdot (\hat{y} + z) \qquad$ for all $y \in Y$

or

(32') $\qquad\qquad q \cdot y \leq q \cdot \hat{y} \qquad$ for all $y \in Y$, where $q \equiv p + \hat{\lambda}$

which means "profit maximization" with respect to q. Also note that, under Slater's condition and the convexity of Y, (32) and $\hat{\lambda} \cdot (\hat{y} + z) = 0$ are equivalent to (cf. Theorem 1.B.5):

(33) $$p \cdot \hat{y} \geq p \cdot y \qquad \text{for all } y \in Y \text{ such that } y + z \geq 0$$

which means profit maximization with respect to p subject to the resource constraint.

Conversely, if there exist $p > 0$, $\hat{\lambda} \geq 0$, and $\hat{y} \in Y$ such that the above (SP) condition holds, then $\hat{y}$ is a solution of the above constrained vector maximum problem (Theorem 1.E.5). This corresponds to Theorem 0.C.2. Certainly, this is a difficult way to reach such a theorem, but it does illustrate one use of the vector maximum problem.

Now consider the following linear programming problem.

$$\text{Maximize: } \alpha \cdot y$$
$$y$$
$$\text{Subject to: } y + z \geq 0 \text{ and } y \in Y, \text{ where } \alpha \in R^{n}, \alpha \geq 0$$

or

$$\text{Maximize: } \alpha \cdot A \cdot x$$
$$x$$
$$\text{Subject to: } A \cdot x + z \geq 0 \text{ and } x \geq 0, x \in R^{n}$$

Clearly those two problems are equivalent. Hence if $\hat{x}$ is a solution of the latter problem, $\hat{y} \equiv A \cdot \hat{x}$ is a solution of the former problem. Now $\hat{y}$ is a solution of the former problem if and only if there exists a $\hat{\lambda} \geq 0$ such that

(SP) $\quad \Phi(y, \hat{\lambda}) \leq \Phi(\hat{y}, \hat{\lambda}) \leq \Phi(\hat{y}, \lambda)$, for all $y \in Y$, and $\lambda \geq 0$, where $\Phi(y, \lambda) \equiv \alpha \cdot y + \lambda \cdot (y + z)$.

We can prove this by slightly modifying our proof of the Goldman-Tucker theorem. In any case, this saddle-point condition means that if $\hat{y}$ is a solution of the above constrained vector maximum problem, then it is a solution of the first linear programming problem. Conversely, if we can find a solution $\hat{x}$ of the latter linear programming problem with $\alpha > 0$, then $\hat{y} \equiv A \cdot \hat{x}$ is a solution of the above constrained vector maximum problem, thus providing an efficient point of Y_F. By varying α, we can obtain the set of efficient points.

e. RICARDO'S THEORY OF COMPARATIVE ADVANTAGE AND MILL'S PROBLEM

Consider a two-country world, where each country (1 and 2) is able to produce two commodities, X and Y, using one factor, "labor." Let l_{xi} and l_{yi} be the amount of labor necessary to produce one unit of X and Y respectively in country $i (i = 1, 2)$, which are assumed to be positive constants. Let L_i be the total supply of labor in country i. We suppose that labor is immobile between the countries, and that the transport costs of X and Y are negligible. The production activities are described in the following table.

	Country 1		Country 2	
Commodity X	1	0	1	0
Commodity Y	0	1	0	1
Labor of country 1	$-l_{x1}$	$-l_{y1}$	0	0
Labor of country 2	0	0	$-l_{x2}$	$-l_{y2}$

Note that we are assuming that each country has only one production process for the production of each commodity. Letting x_i and y_i be the output of X and Y respectively for country i, the resource constraints for the two countries can be written as follows:

(34)
$$l_{x1}x_1 + l_{y1}y_1 \leqq L_1$$

(35)
$$l_{x2}x_2 + l_{y2}y_2 \leqq L_2$$

Or we can write

(36)
$$\frac{x_1}{L_1/l_{x1}} + \frac{y_1}{L_1/l_{y1}} \leqq 1$$

(37)
$$\frac{x_2}{L_2/l_{x2}} + \frac{y_2}{L_2/l_{y2}} \leqq 1$$

We may also write

(38)
$$\frac{x_1}{a_1} + \frac{y_1}{b_1} \leqq 1$$

(39)
$$\frac{x_2}{a_2} + \frac{y_2}{b_2} \leqq 1$$

where

$$a_i \equiv \frac{L_i}{l_{xi}}, \quad b_i \equiv \frac{L_i}{l_{yi}} \quad (i = 1, 2)$$

The production possibility sets for the two countries are illustrated in Figure 1.20.

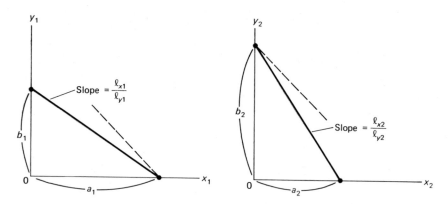

Figure 1.20.   Each Country's Production Possibility Set.

In the above diagrams we assumed that

(40)
$$\frac{l_{x1}}{l_{y1}} < \frac{l_{x2}}{l_{y2}} \quad \text{or} \quad \frac{b_1}{a_1} < \frac{b_2}{a_2}$$

This condition is called **Ricardo's condition of comparative advantage**. Essentially, this says that country 1 is comparatively more "efficient" in producing commodity X and less "efficient" in producing commodity Y than country 2. Letting x and y be the total world output for the two commodities (that is, $x \equiv x_1 + x_2, y \equiv y_1 + y_2$), and using Figure 1.20, we obtain Figure 1.21 where the block 0SRQ describes the world production set.

Mathematically, the world production set can be described as the set of points (x, y) which satisfy the following constraints with $x \geq 0, y \geq 0$:

$$\frac{x}{a_1} + \frac{y}{b_1} \leq \frac{b}{b_1}, \quad \frac{x}{a_2} + \frac{y}{b_2} \leq \frac{a}{a_2},$$

where $x \equiv x_1 + x_2, y \equiv y_1 + y_2, a \equiv a_1 + a_2$, and $b \equiv b_1 + b_2$. We can also check algebraically that these constraints are equivalent to the constraints for the individual countries given above (see Chipman [3], p. 485).

Now consider the vector maximum problem of maximizing (x, y) subject to the above constraints and $x \geq 0, y \geq 0$. The set of solutions of this problem is the kinked line QRS. Since Slater's condition is trivially satisfied (or since the constraints are all linear) in this problem, we can immediately apply Theorem 1.E.4. Hence, if $(\hat{x}, \hat{y})$ is a solution of this problem, there exist $p \equiv (p_x, p_y)$, $\hat{\Lambda} \equiv (\hat{\Lambda}_1, \hat{\Lambda}_2)$, $p \geq 0$, $\hat{\Lambda} \geq 0$, such that

(41) $\Phi(x, y; \hat{\Lambda}) \leq \Phi(\hat{x}, \hat{y}; \hat{\Lambda}) \leq \Phi(\hat{x}, \hat{y}; \Lambda)$ for all $x, y, \lambda \geq 0$

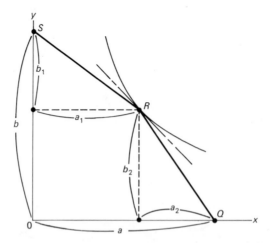

Figure 1.21.   The World Production Possibility Set.

where

$$\Phi(x, y; \lambda) \equiv p_x x + p_y y + \lambda_1 \left[\frac{b}{b_1} - \frac{x}{a_1} - \frac{y}{b_1} \right] + \lambda_2 \left[\frac{a}{a_2} - \frac{x}{a_2} - \frac{y}{b_2} \right]$$

and

(42)
$$\hat{\lambda}_1 \left[\frac{b}{b_1} - \frac{\hat{x}}{a_1} - \frac{\hat{y}}{b_1} \right] = 0$$

(43)
$$\hat{\lambda}_2 \left[\frac{a}{a_2} - \frac{\hat{x}}{a_2} - \frac{\hat{y}}{b_2} \right] = 0$$

Conversely, from Theorem 1.E.7, if there exist $p > 0$ and $\hat{\lambda} \geq 0$ such that the above saddle-point condition (41) holds, then $(\hat{x}, \hat{y})$ is a solution for the vector maximum problem. It is easy to see that the values of p_x and p_y determine the location of the solution on the line QRS.

Now consider the following linear programming problem [where $p \equiv (p_x, p_y) \geq 0$].

Maximize: $p_x x + p_y y$
(x,y)

Subject to: $\dfrac{x}{a_1} + \dfrac{y}{b_1} \leq \dfrac{b}{b_1}$

$\dfrac{x}{a_2} + \dfrac{y}{b_2} \leq \dfrac{a}{a_2}$

$x \geq 0, y \geq 0$

Then from the Goldman-Tucker theorem (Theorem 1.F.2), $(\hat{x}, \hat{y})$ is a solution of this problem if and only if there exist $(\hat{x}, \hat{y}) \geq 0$ and $\hat{\lambda} \geq 0$ such that

(44) $\Phi(x, y; \hat{\lambda}) \leq \Phi(\hat{x}, \hat{y}; \hat{\lambda}) \leq \Phi(\hat{x}, \hat{y}; \lambda)$ for all $x, y, \lambda \geq 0$

Hence the solutions for the above vector maximum problem are characterized by this linear programming problem. In other words, if $(\hat{x}, \hat{y})$ is a solution of the above vector maximum problem, it is a solution of the above linear programming problem. And conversely, if $(\hat{x}, \hat{y})$ is a solution of the above linear programming problem with $p_x > 0$, $p_y > 0$, then it is also a solution of the above vector maximum problem.

If in the linear programming problem we choose p_x and p_y such that $p_x > 0$, $p_y > 0$, and

(R)
$$\frac{l_{x1}}{l_{y1}} < \frac{p_x}{p_y} < \frac{l_{x2}}{l_{y2}}$$

then we obtain point R of Figure 1.21 (as can be seen at once from the diagram). This point R is called **Ricardo's point** by DOSSO ([6], p. 35),[8] for this is exactly the problem that David Ricardo was concerned with in his celebrated theory of comparative advantage. Note that point R is obtained if country 1 specializes in the production of commodity X and country 2 specializes in the production of commodity Y. In short, Ricardo was concerned with the problem of finding the frontier of the world production set (the line QRS) and he specified point R by specifying the slope of the "price line," p_x/p_y. Point R is the point of **complete specialization** for each country. Borrowing the terminology of activity analysis, we may call the line QRS the **world efficient frontier**.

Note that when price vector p prevails with condition (R), then, as a solution of the above linear programming problem, $(\hat{x}, \hat{y})$ at point R maximizes the value of total world output. Note also that if price vector p prevails with condition (R) after free trade (with no transport cost), then each country's national product is maximized. This can easily be seen from Figure 1.20 which describes the production possibility sets for the two countries (the price line is indicated by the dotted lines). In other words, point R is the "optimum" point from the point of view of both the world as a whole and each country individually.[9] Also note that if price vector p prevails with condition (R), then point R (which signifies complete specialization for both countries) is obtained under the competitive rule, assuming that the price ratio of the two commodities in each country will be equal to the slope of its production possibility line before trade. This can be seen as follows: Suppose that international trade is initiated between the two countries with price vector p such that condition (R) holds. Then each country's merchants will come to the world market and trade the commodities at the world price vector p, thus maximizing their profit. This, in turn, will bring each country to the point of complete specialization (country 1 in commodity X and country 2 in commodity Y). The above logic can be easily seen from the dotted price lines in Figure 1.20.

The above analysis has one serious drawback: It does not involve a consideration of the utility of each country's consumers (that is, the so-called "demand conditions"). Let us now take up this problem.

Assume for the sake of simplicity that we can write the world welfare obtained by consuming the bundle (x, y) by $u(x, y)$, where u is a quasi-concave continuously differentiable function on the nonnegative orthant of R^2. Now consider the following nonlinear programming problem.

$$
\begin{aligned}
\text{Maximize:} \quad & u(x, y) \\
{\scriptstyle (x, y)} \\
\text{Subject to:} \quad & \frac{x}{a_1} + \frac{y}{b_1} \leq \frac{b}{b_1} \\
& \frac{x}{a_2} + \frac{y}{b_2} \leq \frac{a}{a_2} \\
& x \geq 0, y \geq 0
\end{aligned}
$$

This is essentially the problem that John Stuart Mill was trying to solve in [11]. For the utility function u, he assumed:

As the simplest and most convenient, let us suppose that in both countries any given increase of cheapness produces an exactly proportional increase of consumption: or, in other words, that the value expended in the commodity, the cost incurred for the sake of obtaining it, is always the same, whether the cost affords a greater or a smaller quantity of the commodity. ([11], p. 155)

Chipman noted ([3], pp. 484–485) that such a demand function is yielded by a utility function of the form $u = x^\alpha y^\beta$, and Mill chose a special case in which $\alpha = \beta = 1$. We generalized his utility function by assuming it to be quasi-concave.

Now let us return to the above nonlinear programming problem. Noting that the constraints are all linear, we apply the Arrow-Hurwicz-Uzawa theorem (Theorem 1.D.4). As a result of this theorem, the following (QSP′) condition is a necessary condition for the optimum:

(**QSP**$'_m$) There exist $(\hat{x}, \hat{y})$ and $\hat{\lambda} = (\hat{\lambda}_1, \hat{\lambda}_2)$ such that

(45)
$$\hat{u}_x - \frac{\hat{\lambda}_1}{a_1} - \frac{\hat{\lambda}_2}{a_2} \leqq 0, \qquad \hat{u}_y - \frac{\hat{\lambda}_1}{b_1} - \frac{\hat{\lambda}_2}{b_2} \leqq 0$$

(46)
$$\left[\hat{u}_x - \frac{\hat{\lambda}_1}{a_1} - \frac{\hat{\lambda}_2}{a_2}\right] \hat{x} + \left[\hat{u}_y - \frac{\hat{\lambda}_1}{b_1} - \frac{\hat{\lambda}_2}{b_2}\right] \hat{y} = 0$$

(47)
$$\frac{b}{b_1} - \frac{\hat{x}}{a_1} - \frac{\hat{y}}{b_1} \geqq 0, \qquad \frac{a}{a_2} - \frac{\hat{x}}{a_2} - \frac{\hat{y}}{b_2} \geqq 0$$

(48)
$$\hat{\lambda}_1 \left[\frac{b}{b_1} - \frac{\hat{x}}{a_1} - \frac{\hat{y}}{b_1}\right] + \hat{\lambda}_2 \left[\frac{a}{a_2} - \frac{\hat{x}}{a_2} - \frac{\hat{y}}{b_2}\right] = 0$$

$$\hat{x} \geqq 0, \hat{y} \geqq 0, \hat{\lambda}_1 \geqq 0, \hat{\lambda}_2 \geqq 0$$
[where $\hat{u}_x \equiv \partial u/\partial x$, $\hat{u}_y \equiv \partial u/\partial y$, both evaluated at $(\hat{x}, \hat{y})$]

To establish the converse of the above statement, we apply Arrow and Enthoven's theorem of quasi-concave programming (Theorem 1.E.2). In this problem we can assume $\hat{u}_x > 0$, or $\hat{u}_y > 0$, which is the case for the utility function $u(x, y) = x^\alpha y^\beta$. Then, from the Arrow-Enthoven theorem, the above (QSP$'_m$) condition is sufficient for the optimum. Hence we can assert that $(\hat{x}, \hat{y})$ is a solution of the above nonlinear programming problem *if and only if* the above (QSP$'_m$) holds.

Now assume

(49)
$$\frac{b_1}{a_1} < \frac{b_2}{a_2} \left(\text{that is, } \frac{l_{x1}}{l_{y1}} < \frac{l_{x2}}{l_{y2}}\right)$$

as above and find the condition under which country 1 specializes in the production of X and country 2 specializes in the production of Y (the Ricardian pattern of complete specialization). This is the question raised by J. S. Mill. Mathematically speaking, we are now seeking the condition under which the Ricardian pattern of specialization ($\hat{x} = \hat{x}_1 = a_1$, $\hat{y} = \hat{y}_2 = b_2$, $\hat{y}_1 = 0$, and $\hat{x}_2 = 0$) is the solution of the above nonlinear problem [hence satisfies the above (QSP$'_m$)].

The solution of Mill's problem is rather easy to see from Figure 1.21 and it does not need the above machinery of nonlinear programming such as (QSP'_m). Assuming that the utility function is nicely shaped, such as $u(x, y) = x^\alpha y^{1-\alpha}$, $0 < \alpha < 1$, we can easily see from Figure 1.21 that the necessary and sufficient condition for (a_1, b_2) to be the solution of the above nonlinear programming problem is simply that the slope of the indifference curve at (a_1, b_2) be between the slopes of the lines QR and RS. Letting $(\hat{x}, \hat{y}) = (a_1, b_2)$, we can write this condition as follows:

(50) $$\frac{b_1}{a_1} \le \frac{\hat{u}_x}{\hat{u}_y} \le \frac{b_2}{a_2} \quad \text{(with at least one strict inequality)}$$

where $\hat{u}_x$ and $\hat{u}_y$ are now defined respectively as u_x and u_y both *evaluated at* (a_1, b_2). This condition is often called **Mill's condition**.

We now obtain this *necessary and sufficient* condition mathematically. This procedure is more tedious than the one in terms of the above diagram, but it is useful in order to become familiar with our nonlinear programming theory as well as to obtain the precise understanding of the solution. Moreover, it will facilitate a further generalization (see Takayama [17]). First introduce the following assumption on the utility function, which will guarantee that $\hat{x} > 0, \hat{y} > 0$. Notice that if we cannot guarantee $\hat{x} > 0, \hat{y} > 0$, then (a_1, b_2) cannot be a solution.

(A-m) $$u(x, 0) = 0 \text{ and } u(0, y) = 0$$

$$u_x \equiv \frac{\partial u}{\partial x} > 0 \text{ and } u_y \equiv \frac{\partial u}{\partial y} > 0 \quad \text{for all } x > 0, y > 0$$

An example of a utility function that satisfies the above assumption is one of the Cobb-Douglas type, $u = x^\alpha y^{(1-\alpha)}$, $0 < \alpha < 1$. The feasible set for our nonlinear programming problem is $M \equiv \{(x, y): (x, y) \ge 0, x/a_1 + y/b_1 \le b/b_1, x/a_2 + y/b_2 \le a/a_2\}$. The set M is nonempty and contains a point $(\bar{x}, \bar{y})$ with $\bar{x} > 0$ and $\bar{y} > 0$. (Note that this also implies that Slater's condition holds for the present problem.) Hence from the above assumption, $u(\bar{x}, \bar{y}) > u(x, 0)$ for all $x \ge 0$ and $u(\bar{x}, \bar{y}) > u(0, y)$ for all $y \ge 0$. Therefore, an optimal point $(\hat{x}, \hat{y})$ must be such that $\hat{x} > 0$ and $\hat{y} > 0$. Then the first two conditions (45) and (46) of the above (QSP'_m) can be converted to the following equivalent condition:

(51) $$\hat{u}_x - \frac{\hat{\lambda}_1}{a_1} - \frac{\hat{\lambda}_2}{a_2} = 0, \qquad \hat{u}_y - \frac{\hat{\lambda}_1}{b_1} - \frac{\hat{\lambda}_2}{b_2} = 0$$

Mill's problem is that of finding the condition under which Ricardo's point (a_1, b_2) is optimal. Since at (a_1, b_2) the two relations in condition (47) of the above (QSP'_m) hold with equality, (48) is automatically satisfied; thus at (a_1, b_2) both (47) and (48) of (QSP'_m) are satisfied. Hence the *necessary and sufficient* condition for Ricardo's point (a_1, b_2) to be optimal is reduced to the following condition:

(52) There exists $\hat{\lambda}_1 \ge 0$, $\hat{\lambda}_2 \ge 0$ (with at least one strict inequality)[10] such that condition (51) holds *at* (a_1, b_2).

From (51) we obtain

(53-a)
$$\hat{\lambda}_1 - \frac{a_2}{a_1}\frac{b_1}{b_2}\hat{\lambda}_1 = (\hat{u}_y - \frac{a_2}{b_2}\hat{u}_x)b_1$$

(53-b)
$$\hat{\lambda}_2 - \frac{a_1}{a_2}\frac{b_2}{b_1}\hat{\lambda}_2 = (\hat{u}_y - \frac{a_1}{b_1}\hat{u}_x)b_2$$

where $\hat{u}_x \equiv u_x(a_1, b_2)$ and $\hat{u}_y \equiv u_y(a_1, b_2)$. Since $b_1/a_1 < b_2/a_2$ by hypothesis, we have

(54)
$$\frac{a_2}{a_1}\frac{b_1}{b_2} < 1$$

Therefore, recalling $\hat{\lambda}_1 \geq 0$ and $\hat{\lambda}_2 \geq 0$, we obtain from (53-a) and (53-b)

(55-a)
$$\hat{u}_y > \left(\frac{a_2}{b_2}\right)\hat{u}_x \qquad \text{if } \hat{\lambda}_1 > 0$$

and

$$\hat{u}_y = \left(\frac{a_2}{b_2}\right)\hat{u}_x \qquad \text{if } \hat{\lambda}_1 = 0$$

(55-b)
$$\hat{u}_y < \left(\frac{a_1}{b_1}\right)\hat{u}_x \qquad \text{if } \hat{\lambda}_2 > 0$$

and

$$\hat{u}_y = \left(\frac{a_1}{b_1}\right)\hat{u}_x \qquad \text{if } \hat{\lambda}_2 = 0$$

Hence, recalling that $\hat{\lambda}_1$ and $\hat{\lambda}_2$ cannot vanish simultaneously, we obtain from (55-a) and (55-b)

(56)
$$\frac{b_1}{a_1} \leqq \frac{\hat{u}_x}{\hat{u}_y} \leqq \frac{b_2}{a_2} \quad \text{(with at least one strict inequality)}$$

which is the Mill's condition. Therefore, if condition (52) is satisfied, then Mill's condition (56) is satisfied. Conversely, if (56) is satisfied, then we can obtain condition (52). If (56) holds with strict inequalities, then obtain $\hat{\lambda}_1$ and $\hat{\lambda}_2$ from (53-a) and (53-b). If (56) holds with one equality, say, $b_1/a_1 = \hat{u}_x/\hat{u}_y$, then define $\hat{\lambda}_2$ as $\hat{\lambda}_2 = 0$ and obtain $\hat{\lambda}_1$ from (53-a) as $\hat{\lambda}_1 = b_1\hat{u}_y$. Thus obtained, $\hat{\lambda}_1$ and $\hat{\lambda}_2$ will satisfy condition (52). This finishes the mathematical proof that Mill's condition is a necessary and sufficient condition for Ricardo's point to be optimal.

It should be noted that Mill's condition and the above observation are crucially dependent on the specification of the utility function. If we adopt a different form of u, then we will obtain a different condition. As Chipman noted ([3], p. 489), Mill realized this point and attempted to analyze more general cases [more general, that is, than the case in which $u(x, y) = xy$]. (See [11], Book

III, chap. 18. esp. secs. 8 and 9.) However his mathematical equipment precluded the derivation of any exact condition.

FOOTNOTES

1. The utility function u may not be defined outside Ω^n, the nonnegative orthant of R^n. However, it would be more convenient to conceive that u is defined over the entire space R^n, in order to avoid the possibility of "corner" derivatives when we talk about the (QSP') condition. Clearly, the consumer cannot place any utility outside his consumption set Ω^n; hence the definition of u outside of Ω^n can be more or less arbitrary, as long as differentiability is preserved. This convention of extending the domain of the function is often useful in many economic problems in which many functions are, strictly speaking, defined only on the nonnegative orthant, and in which we are concerned with (QSP').

2. For the meaning of the "relevant variable," see Section E of this chapter or Arrow and Enthoven [1], p. 783. This concept does not create any problem in the present problem of consumer's choice.

3. Most readers are probably familiar with the procedure of obtaining the Hicks-Slutsky equation. Clearly the author is not discounting any of the glory of the classical demand theory à la Slutsky, Hicks, and so on. In the Appendix to this section, we attempt the exposition of the classical demand theory, as an example of the time-honored technique in economics, comparative statics. Later we will take up a modern approach to the Hicks-Slutsky equation (Chapter 2, Section D).

4. The (strict) quasi-concavity of the utility function means that the consumer desires to consume a *variety* of commodities rather than to consume any one commodity.

5. Here we are using condition (iv) of Theorem 1.D.4 (the A-H-U theorem), which is the same as condition (ii) of Theorem 1.E.3 under the quasi-concavity of F. The condition requires (a) condition (18) in addition to (b) the quasi-concavity of F (or the convexity of the constraint set), and (c) the existence of $(\overline{v}, \overline{x}) \geq 0$ with $F(\overline{v}, \overline{x}) > 0$ (or the existence of an interior point in the constraint set).

6. As remarked above, assuming that at least one output is produced at the optimum, we have $\hat{\lambda} > 0$ so that $F(\hat{v}, \hat{x}) = 0$. In other words, the constraint $F(v, x) \geq 0$ is effective at the optimum. If we do not have the constraint $(\hat{v}, \hat{x}) \geq 0$, the rank condition is satisfied if condition (18) holds (which ensures $[\hat{F}_v, \hat{F}_x] \neq 0$). A stronger condition such as (18') is required for the present problem in view of the non-negativity constraints, $\hat{x} \geq 0$ and $\hat{v} \geq 0$. Note that, to ensure the rank condition, neither the quasi-concavity of F nor the existence of $(\overline{v}, \overline{x}) \geq 0$ with $F(\overline{v}, \overline{x}) > 0$ is required.

7. Under the rank condition, (QSP') is necessary for an optimum. Under the quasi-concavity of F, (QSP') is sufficient for an optimum.

8. DOSSO is the standard nickname of Dorfman, Samuelson, and Solow [6].

9. The optimality here is defined as the maximization of the value of output under a *fixed* price vector p. Notice that the maximization of $p_x x + p_y y$(resp. $p_x x_i + p_y y_i, i = 1, 2$) is equivalent to the maximization of "real income" $(p_x/p_y)x + y$ or $x + (p_y/p_x)y$ [resp. $(p_x/p_y)x_i + y_i$ or $x_i + (p_y/p_x)y_i, i = 1, 2$], as long as (p_x, p_y) is a fixed vector. Notice also that a country can increase its welfare from the above "optimum" position if it is allowed to alter p or the terms of trade p_x/p_y. This will, in general, imply a loss to the other country. The optimum tariff argument is concerned with the choice of p_x/p_y by means of tariffs so as to maximize one country's welfare.

10. If $\hat{\lambda}_1 = \hat{\lambda}_2 = 0$, then from (51) we obtain $\hat{u}_x = \hat{u}_y = 0$ which, in view of $\hat{x} > 0$ and $\hat{y} > 0$, contradicts (A-m) (in particular, $u_x > 0$, $u_y > 0$ for all $x > 0$ and $y > 0$).

REFERENCES

1. Arrow, K., and Enthoven, A. C., "Quasi-Concave Programming," *Econometrica*, vol. 29, October 1961.

2. Carlson, S., *A Study on the Pure Theory of Production*, Oxford, Basil Blackwell, 1956.

3. Chipman, J. S., "A Survey of the Theory of International Trade, Part 1, The Classical Theory," *Econometrica*, vol. 33, July 1965.

4. Dantzig, G. B., *Linear Programming and Extensions*, Princeton, N.J., Princeton University Press, 1963.

5. Dantzig, G. B., and Orden, A., "Notes on Linear Programming: Part II, Duality Theorem," Rand Corporation, *Research Memorandum*, RM 1265, October 30, 1953.

6. Dorfman, R., Samuelson, P. A., and Solow, R. M., *Linear Programming and Economic Analysis*, New York, McGraw-Hill, 1958.

7. Eisenberg, E., "Duality in Homogeneous Programming," *Proceedings of the American Mathematical Society*, 12, October 1961.

8. Goldman, A. J., and Tucker, A. W., "Theory of Linear Programming," in Linear *Inequalities and Related Systems*, ed. by H. W. Kuhn and A. W. Tucker, Princeton, N.J., Princeton University Press, 1956.

9. Hadley, G., *Linear Programming*, Reading, Mass., Addison-Wesley, 1962.

10. Hicks, J. R., *Value and Capital*, 2nd ed., Oxford, Clarendon Press, 1946.

11. Mill, J. S., *Principles of Political Economy*, 3rd ed., London, Parker & Co., 1852 (1st ed. 1848 by Parker, 9th ed. 1885 by Longmans, Green & Co.).

12. Nikaido, H., *Introduction to Sets and Mappings in Modern Economics*, tr. by K. Sato, Amsterdam, North-Holland, 1970 (the Japanese original, Tokyo, 1960).

13. Ricardo, D., *On the Principles of Political Economy and Taxation*, London, John Murray, 1817, in *The Works and Correspondence of David Ricardo*, Vol. I, ed. by P. Sraffa, Cambridge, Cambridge University Press, 1951.

14. Samuelson, P. A., *Foundations of Economic Analysis*, Cambridge, Mass., Harvard University Press, 1947.

15. Shephard, R. W., *Cost and Production Functions*, Princeton, N.J., Princeton University Press, 1953.

16. Takayama, A., *International Economics*, Tokyo, Toyo-Keizai Shimpo-sha, 1963 (in Japanese).

17. ——, *International Trade—An Approach to the Theory*, New York, Holt, Rinehart and Winston, 1972, chaps. 4, 5, 6, and 7.

Appendix to Section F: Optimization and Comparative Statics—A Local Theory[1]

a. THE CLASSICAL THEORY OF OPTIMIZATION

The classical theory of optimization and comparative statics has become very well known to economists through Hicks [8], Samuelson [12], and many textbooks on price theory. The purpose of this Appendix is to review this topic concisely so that the reader may be able to refresh his understanding of the theory in a proper perspective.

Let $f(x, \alpha)$ and $g_j(x, \alpha), j = 1, 2, \ldots, m$, be real-valued functions defined on $X \otimes A$ where X and A are, respectively, open subsets of R^n and R^l. We assume

(A-1) All the second partial derivatives of f and $g_j, j = 1, 2, \ldots, m$, exist *and are continuous* for all (x, α) in $X \otimes A$.

Consider the following maximization problem:

Maximize: $f(x, \hat{\alpha})$
$\quad x$

Subject to: $g_j(x, \hat{\alpha}) = 0, j = 1, 2, \ldots, m$, and $x \in X$

where $\hat{\alpha}$ is a given vector in A. The $\hat{\alpha}_k$'s are called the **shift parameters**. The *local maximum condition (LM)* is written as:

(LM) $\exists \, \hat{x} \in X$ such that it achieves a local maximum of f subject to the constraints.

The *first-order condition (FOC)* of this problem can be stated as follows:

(FOC) $\exists \, \hat{x} \in X$ and $\lambda \in R^m$ such that

(1) $$\Phi_x(\hat{x}, \hat{\lambda}, \hat{\alpha}) = 0, \qquad g(\hat{x}, \hat{\alpha}) = 0$$

where

(2) $$\Phi(x, \lambda, \hat{\alpha}) \equiv f(x, \hat{\alpha}) + \lambda \cdot g(x, \hat{\alpha})$$

and $g(x, \hat{\alpha}) \equiv [g_1(x, \hat{\alpha}), \ldots, g_m(x, \hat{\alpha})]$. Here Φ_x denotes the gradient vector of Φ with respect to x.[2]

Next, we write the *second-order necessary condition (SONC)* and the *second-order sufficient condition (SOSC)*, respectively, as

(SONC) $\xi \cdot A \cdot \xi \leq 0$ for all ξ such that $B \cdot \xi = 0$.
(SOSC) $\xi \cdot A \cdot \xi < 0$ for all $\xi \neq 0$ such that $B \cdot \xi = 0$.

where $A = [a_{ij}]$ and $B = [b_{ij}]$ are, respectively, $(n \times n)$ and $(m \times n)$ matrices defined by[3]

(3-a) $$A \equiv \Phi_{xx}(\hat{x}, \hat{\lambda}, \hat{\alpha}); \text{ that is, } a_{ij} \equiv \frac{\partial^2 \Phi(\hat{x}, \hat{\lambda}, \hat{\alpha})}{\partial x_i \partial x_j}$$

(3-b) $$B \equiv g_x(\hat{x}, \hat{\lambda}, \hat{\alpha}); \text{ that is, } b_{ij} \equiv \frac{\partial g_i(\hat{x}, \hat{\lambda}, \hat{\alpha})}{\partial x_j}$$

The **rank condition (R)** is[4], assuming $m < n$,

(R) Rank $B = m$.

The fundamental theorem of the classical optimization theory is now stated.[5]

Theorem 1.F.3   *Assume that condition (R) holds. Then*
  (i)   *(LM) implies (FOC) and (SONC).*
 (ii)   *(FOC) and (SOSC) imply (LM).*

In the classical optimization theory, all the constraints are assumed to be effective for all $x \in X$. Now suppose we consider the following problem with inequality constraints.

$$\text{Maximize: } f(x, \hat{\alpha})$$
$$\phantom{\text{Maximize: }}_{x}$$

Subject to: $g_j(x, \hat{\alpha}) \geqq 0, j = 1, 2, \ldots, m, x \geqq 0$ and $x \in R^n$

The first-order conditions of this problem may be stated as[6]

(QSP′) $\exists \; \hat{x} \geqq 0$ and $\hat{\lambda} \geqq 0$ where $\hat{x} \in X$ and $\hat{\lambda} \in R^m$ such that

$$\Phi_x(\hat{x}, \hat{\lambda}, \hat{\alpha}) \leqq 0, \; \Phi_x(\hat{x}, \hat{\lambda}, \hat{\alpha}) \cdot \hat{x} = 0, \; g(\hat{x}, \hat{\alpha}) \geqq 0, \; \hat{\lambda} \cdot g(\hat{x}, \hat{\alpha}) = 0$$

If we can assume $\hat{x} > 0$ and $\hat{\lambda} > 0$, then this condition is reduced to

$$\Phi_x(\hat{x}, \hat{\lambda}, \hat{\alpha}) = 0 \quad \text{and} \quad g(\hat{x}, \hat{\alpha}) = 0$$

which then looks precisely the same as (FOC). Therefore, we may regard the above (FOC) as (QSP′) with $\hat{x} > 0$ and $\hat{\lambda} > 0$, and we can carry out a similar comparative statics analysis using (QSP′). However, in (FOC) of the classical theory, there are no provisions to guarantee $\hat{x} \geqq 0$ and $\hat{\lambda} \geqq 0$. Note also that if f and the g_j's are all concave and if $\hat{\lambda} \geqq 0$, then Φ is concave in x so that the Hessian matrix Φ_{xx} is negative semidefinite *for all x in X.* Thus (SONC) is automatically satisfied.

In any case, we proceed here with the classical theory.[7] As remarked earlier (Theorem 1.E.17), (SOSC) is equivalent to the following **bordered Hessian condition** (BHC), assuming that rank $B_{mm} = m$ and $m < n$.

$$(BHC) \quad (-1)^r \begin{vmatrix} 0 & B_{mr} \\ B'_{mr} & A_r \end{vmatrix} > 0, \quad r = m + 1, \ldots, n$$

or equivalently,

$$(BHC') \quad (-1)^r \begin{vmatrix} A_r & B'_{mr} \\ B_{mr} & 0 \end{vmatrix} > 0, \quad r = m + 1, \ldots, n$$

where A_r and B_{mr} are defined by

$$A_r \equiv \begin{bmatrix} a_{11} & a_{12} & \cdots & a_{1r} \\ a_{21} & a_{22} & \cdots & a_{2r} \\ \cdots & \cdots & \cdots & \cdots \\ \cdots & \cdots & \cdots & \cdots \\ a_{r1} & a_{r2} & \cdots & a_{rr} \end{bmatrix}, \; B_{mr} \equiv \begin{bmatrix} b_{11} & b_{12} & \cdots & b_{1r} \\ b_{21} & b_{22} & \cdots & b_{2r} \\ \cdots & \cdots & \cdots & \cdots \\ \cdots & \cdots & \cdots & \cdots \\ b_{m1} & b_{m2} & \cdots & b_{mr} \end{bmatrix}$$

Here B'_{mr} is the transpose of B_{mr}.

b.   COMPARATIVE STATICS

Hereafter, we assume (LM) and (R), so that (FOC) and (SONC) hold. Condition (FOC) provides $(n + m)$ equations, which are then available to determine the $(n + m)$ variables, $\hat{x}_1, \hat{x}_2, \ldots, \hat{x}_n, \hat{\lambda}_1, \ldots, \hat{\lambda}_m$. Assume

$$\text{(A-2)} \quad \det \begin{vmatrix} 0 & B \\ B' & A \end{vmatrix} \neq 0$$

Then under assumptions (A-1) and (A-2), we can directly apply the implicit function theorem.[8] Thus we can conclude that there exist continuously differentiable functions x and λ such that $\hat{x} = x(\hat{\alpha})$ and $\hat{\lambda} = \lambda(\hat{\alpha})$ and

$$\text{(4-a)} \qquad \Phi_x[x(\alpha), \lambda(\alpha), \alpha] = 0$$

$$\text{(4-b)} \qquad g[x(\alpha), \alpha] = 0 \, [9]$$

for all α in some neighborhood of $\hat{\alpha}$, say, $N(\hat{\alpha})$.

The comparative statics analysis in the context of optimization is to establish the effect of changes in the α_k's on the values of $x(\alpha)$ and $\lambda(\alpha)$, using (4-a) and (4-b). Differentiating (4-a) and (4-b) with respect to α_k, we obtain (for each k)

$$\text{(5)} \qquad \begin{bmatrix} \Phi_{xx} & \Phi_{x\lambda} \\ & \\ \Phi_{\lambda x} & 0 \end{bmatrix} \begin{bmatrix} \dfrac{\partial x(\alpha)}{\partial \alpha_k} \\ \\ \dfrac{\partial \lambda(\alpha)}{\partial \alpha_k} \end{bmatrix} + \begin{bmatrix} \Phi_{x\alpha_k} \\ \\ \Phi_{\lambda\alpha_k} \end{bmatrix} = 0$$

for all $\alpha \in N(\hat{\alpha})$, or equivalently,

$$\text{(5')} \qquad \begin{bmatrix} 0 & \Phi_{\lambda x} \\ & \\ \Phi_{x\lambda} & \Phi_{xx} \end{bmatrix} \begin{bmatrix} \dfrac{\partial \lambda(\alpha)}{\partial \alpha_k} \\ \\ \dfrac{\partial \lambda(\alpha)}{\partial \alpha_k} \end{bmatrix} + \begin{bmatrix} \Phi_{\lambda\alpha_k} \\ \\ \Phi_{x\alpha_k} \end{bmatrix} = 0$$

for all $\alpha \in N(\hat{\alpha})$, where all the second partials of Φ are evaluated at α; that is, $\Phi_{xx} \equiv \Phi_{xx}[x(\alpha), \lambda(\alpha), \alpha]$, and so on. Needless to say, $\Phi_{x\lambda} = \Phi_{\lambda x} = g_x[x(\alpha), \alpha]$.[10]

Define the $(m + n) \times (m + n)$ matrices H and $\hat{H}$ by[11]

$$\text{(6)} \qquad H \equiv \begin{bmatrix} 0 & \Phi_{\lambda x} \\ \Phi_{x\lambda} & \Phi_{xx} \end{bmatrix} \text{ and } \hat{H} \equiv \begin{bmatrix} 0 & B \\ B' & A \end{bmatrix}$$

By (A-1) and the continuity of the functions $x(\alpha)$ and $\lambda(\alpha)$, every element of H is continuous in α. But by (A-2), $\hat{H}$ is nonsingular. Hence H is also nonsingular for all α in some neighborhood of $\hat{\alpha}$, say, $\bar{N}(\hat{\alpha})$, where $\bar{N}(\hat{\alpha}) \subset N(\hat{\alpha})$. Therefore, from (5) we obtain[12]

(7)
$$
\begin{bmatrix} \dfrac{\partial \lambda(\alpha)}{\partial \alpha_k} \\[2ex] \dfrac{\partial x(\alpha)}{\partial \alpha_k} \end{bmatrix} = - \begin{bmatrix} 0 & \Phi_{\lambda x} \\[1ex] \Phi_{x\lambda} & \Phi_{xx} \end{bmatrix}^{-1} \begin{bmatrix} \Phi_{\lambda \alpha_k} \\[1ex] \Phi_{x\alpha_k} \end{bmatrix}
$$

for all α in $\bar{N}(\hat{\alpha})$. This equation is the **fundamental equation of comparative statics** obtained from (FOC).

c. THE SECOND-ORDER CONDITIONS AND COMPARATIVE STATICS

It is clear from (7) that the key to establishing the comparative statics results is in the matrix H^{-1}. The concavity of the functions f and the g_j's would provide very useful global information on H^{-1}, as we shall see later (for example, see Chapter 4, Section D). Here we investigate the local information which can be deduced from the second-order conditions.

In Theorem 1.F.3, we stated that (LM) together with (R) imply (SONC) as well as (FOC). It can be shown that (SONC) and (A-2) together imply

$$
\xi \cdot A \cdot \xi < 0 \qquad \text{for all } h \neq 0 \text{ such that } B \cdot h = 0
$$

that is, (SOSC), hence (BHC). In other words, under (LM) and (R), (A-2) implies that the last $(n - m)$ principal minors of $\hat{H}$ alternate signs, as in (BHC). Since every element of H is continuous in α, the last $(n - m)$ principal minors of H alternate in signs for each fixed α in $\bar{N}(\hat{\alpha})$. In other words,[13]

(8) $\qquad (-1)^i H_i > 0, \, i = 2m + 1, \ldots, m + n$, for all $\alpha \in \bar{N}(\hat{\alpha})$

where H_i is the ith successive principal minor of H.

Write H^{-1} as

(9)
$$
H^{-1} = \frac{1}{\det H} \begin{bmatrix} h_{11} & h_{21} & \cdots & h_{m+n,1} \\ h_{12} & h_{22} & \cdots & h_{m+n,2} \\ \cdots & \cdots & \cdots & \cdots \\ \cdots & \cdots & \cdots & \cdots \\ h_{1,m+n} & \cdots & \cdots & h_{m+n,m+n} \end{bmatrix}
$$

where h_{ji} is the cofactor of the i-j element of H and $\det H$ is the determinant of H. Then in view of (8), we can conclude that, for each $\alpha \in \bar{N}(\hat{\alpha})$

(10) $\qquad\qquad \text{sgn}(\det H) = (-1)^{m+n}$

and

(11) $$\mathrm{sgn}\ h_{ii} = (-1)^{m+n-1}, i = 1, 2, \ldots, m + n^{14}$$

Therefore, for each $\alpha \in \bar{N}(\hat{\alpha})$,

(12) $$\mathrm{sgn}\ \frac{h_{ii}}{\det H} = -1, i = 1, 2, \ldots, m + n$$

Next decompose the matrix H^{-1} as

(13) $$H^{-1} = \begin{bmatrix} K_1 & K_2 \\ K_3 & K_4 \end{bmatrix}$$

where K_1, K_2, K_3, and K_4 are, respectively, $m \times m$, $m \times n$, $n \times m$, and $n \times n$ matrices.[15] Since H is symmetric, so is H^{-1}, K_1 and K_4 are also symmetric. Moreover, by condition (R) and (8), we can conclude that, for all $\alpha \in \bar{N}(\hat{\alpha})$,

(14) $$\xi \cdot K_4 \cdot \xi \leq 0 \text{ for all } \xi$$

that is, K_4 is negative semidefinite.[16]

In summary, K_4 [that is, the $(n \times n)$ southeast submatrix of H^{-1}] is symmetric, negative semidefinite, and its diagonal elements are all negative. Also H^{-1} is symmetric and its diagonal elements are all negative.

We now illustrate this discussion in terms of the Hicks-Slutsky equation. The purpose here is only for illustration, and a more general (and elegant) discussion is postponed to Chapter 2, Section D.

d.   AN EXAMPLE: HICKS-SLUTSKY EQUATION

Consider the problem of choosing $x \in R^n$ so as to

$$\begin{aligned} \text{Maximize:} \quad & u(x) \\ \text{Subject to:} \quad & g(x) \equiv \hat{M} - \hat{p} \cdot x = 0 \end{aligned}$$

where $\hat{p} > 0$ and $\hat{M} > 0$ are the parameters of the problem. We assume that (A-1) holds with respect to the functions u and g. That $p \neq 0$ ensures the rank condition (R), since

$$\left(\frac{\partial g}{\partial x_1}, \ldots, \frac{\partial g}{\partial x_n} \right) = (-\hat{p}_1, -\hat{p}_2, \ldots, -\hat{p}_n) \neq 0$$

for all x. Thus $B = -\hat{p}$. Define the Lagrangian by

(15) $$\Phi(x, \lambda, \hat{p}, \hat{M}) \equiv u(x) + \lambda(\hat{M} - \hat{p} \cdot x)$$

Assume that there exists an $\hat{x} > 0$ which satisfies the (LM) condition. Then the first-order condition (FOC) for this problem is now written as follows:

(16-a) $$\hat{M} - \hat{p} \cdot \hat{x} = 0$$

(16-b) $$u_i(\hat{x}) - \hat{\lambda}\hat{p}_i = 0, i = 1, 2, \ldots, n$$

where $u_i(\hat{x}) = \partial u(\hat{x})/\partial x_i$. Define the bordered Hessian matrix H by

$$(17) \quad H \equiv \begin{bmatrix} 0 & -p_1 & -p_2 & \cdots & -p_n \\ -p_1 & u_{11} & u_{12} & \cdots & u_{1n} \\ -p_2 & u_{21} & u_{22} & \cdots & u_{2n} \\ \cdots & \cdots & \cdots & \cdots & \cdots \\ \cdots & \cdots & \cdots & \cdots & \cdots \\ -p_n & u_{n1} & u_{n2} & \cdots & u_{nn} \end{bmatrix} = \begin{bmatrix} 0 & -p \\ -p' & (u_{ij}) \end{bmatrix}$$

where $u_{ij} \equiv \partial^2 u/\partial x_i \partial x_j$. Evaluate these u_{ij}'s at $\hat{x}$ and set $p = \hat{p}$ in the above H. Denote it by H, and assume

$$(18) \quad \det \hat{H} \neq 0$$

which corresponds to (A-2). We can then apply the implicit function theorem to (16-a) and (16-b) and obtain the continuously differentiable functions $\lambda(p, M)$ and $x(p, M)$ with $\hat{\lambda} = \lambda(\hat{p}, \hat{M})$, $\hat{x} = x(\hat{p}, \hat{M})$, and

$$(19\text{-a}) \quad M - p \cdot x(p, M) = 0$$

$$(19\text{-b}) \quad u_i[x(p, M)] - \lambda(p, M)p_i = 0, \, i = 1, 2, \ldots, n$$

for all (p, M) in some neighborhood of $(\hat{p}, \hat{M})$

Partially differentiating (19) with respect to p_j, we obtain

$$(20) \quad \begin{bmatrix} 0 & -p \\ -p' & (u_{ij}) \end{bmatrix} \begin{bmatrix} \dfrac{\partial \lambda}{\partial p_j} \\ \dfrac{\partial x}{\partial p_j} \end{bmatrix} = \left.\begin{bmatrix} x_j \\ 0 \\ \vdots \\ 0 \\ \lambda \\ 0 \\ \vdots \\ 0 \end{bmatrix}\right) (j + 1)$$

for all (p, M) in the neighborhood of $(\hat{p}, \hat{M})$, where $\lambda = \lambda(p, M)$ and $x = x(p, M)$. Let e_j be the $(n + 1)$-vector whose jth element is one and all other elements are zero. The RHS of (20) can be rewritten as

$$x_j e_1 + \lambda e_{j+1}$$

Since H is nonsingular in some neighborhood of $(\hat{p}, \hat{M})$—say, $\bar{N}(\hat{p}, \hat{M})$—from (18), we obtain

$$(21) \quad \begin{bmatrix} \dfrac{\partial \lambda}{\partial p_j} \\ \dfrac{\partial x}{\partial p_j} \end{bmatrix} = x_j(p, M) H^{-1} e_1 + \lambda(p, M) H^{-1} e_{j+1}$$

for all (p, M) in $\bar{N}(\hat{p}, \hat{M})$, where $\lambda = \lambda(p, M)$ and $x = x(p, M)$.

Next, partially differentiating (19) with respect to M and taking account of (18), we obtain

(22)
$$\begin{bmatrix} \dfrac{\partial \lambda}{\partial M} \\[2ex] \dfrac{\partial x}{\partial M} \end{bmatrix} = -H^{-1}e_1$$

for all (p, M) in $\bar{N}(\hat{p}, \hat{M})$, where $\lambda = \lambda(p, M)$ and $x = x(p, M)$. Therefore, combining (21) with (22), we obtain the following fundamental equation.

(23)
$$\begin{bmatrix} \dfrac{\partial \lambda}{\partial p_j} \\[2ex] \dfrac{\partial x}{\partial p_j} \end{bmatrix} = \lambda H^{-1} e_{j+1} - x_j \begin{bmatrix} \dfrac{\partial \lambda}{\partial M} \\[2ex] \dfrac{\partial x}{\partial M} \end{bmatrix}$$

for all (p, M) in $\bar{N}(\hat{p}, \hat{M})$, where $\lambda = \lambda(p, M)$ and $x = x(p, M)$. In particular,

(24)
$$\frac{\partial x_i(p, M)}{\partial p_j} = S_{ij}(p, M) - x_j(p, M)\frac{\partial x_i(p, M)}{\partial M}, \quad i, j = 1, 2, \ldots, n$$

where

(25)
$$S_{ij} = \lambda(p, M)\frac{h_{j+1, i+1}}{\det H}, \quad i, j = 1, 2, \ldots, n$$

and

(26)
$$H^{-1} = \frac{1}{\det H}[h_{ij}]$$

as defined in (9). Equation (24) is called the **Hicks-Slutsky equation**. By (19-b), $\lambda(p, M) > 0$ if $u_i[x(p, M)] > 0$ for all i (nonsatiation).

We now obtain the basic properties of S_{ij}.

Define S by

(27)
$$S \equiv \begin{bmatrix} S_{11} & S_{12} & \cdots & S_{1n} \\ S_{21} & S_{22} & \cdots & S_{2n} \\ \cdots & \cdots & \cdots & \cdots \\ \cdots & \cdots & \cdots & \cdots \\ S_{n1} & S_{n2} & \cdots & S_{nn} \end{bmatrix}$$

Then S corresponds to K_4 in (13). Therefore, from our discussion on K_4, we can immediately conclude that, for all (p, M) in $\bar{N}(\hat{p}, \hat{M})$,

(28)
$$S_{ij} = S_{ji}, \quad i, j = 1, 2, \ldots, n$$

(29)
$$S_{ii} < 0, \quad i = 1, 2, \ldots, n[17]$$

(30)
$$S \text{ is negative semidefinite}$$

Next observe that $x_i(p, M)$ is homogeneous of degree zero in p and M.[18] Hence by the Euler equation, we obtain

$$(31) \qquad \sum_{j=1}^{n} \frac{\partial x_i(p, M)}{\partial p_j} p_j + \frac{\partial x_i(p, M)}{\partial M} M = 0, \qquad i = 1, 2, \ldots, n$$

for all (p, M) in $\bar{N}(\hat{p}, \hat{M})$. Combining this with (24), we obtain

$$(32) \qquad \sum_{j=1}^{n} S_{ij} p_j = 0, \qquad \text{for all } (p, M) \text{ in } \bar{N}(\hat{p}, \hat{M})$$

Next, partially differentiating the budget equation (19-a) with respect to p_j and M, respectively, we obtain

$$(33\text{-a}) \qquad \sum_{i=1}^{n} p_i \frac{\partial x_i(p, M)}{\partial p_j} + x_j = 0, \qquad j = 1, 2, \ldots, n$$

$$(33\text{-b}) \qquad \sum_{i=1}^{n} p_i \frac{\partial x_i(p, M)}{\partial M} = 1$$

Combining (33) with (24), or also directly from (28) and (32), we obtain

$$(34) \qquad \sum_{i=1}^{n} p_i S_{ij} = 0 \qquad \text{for all } (p, M) \text{ in } \bar{N}(\hat{p}, \hat{M})$$

Equations (28), (29), (30), (32), and (34) exhaust all the important properties of S.[19]

We may note that the following relations can be obtained directly from the budget equation (19-a) by utilizing (33) but without using (24):

$$(35\text{-a}) \qquad \sum_{i=1}^{n} \theta_i \eta_{ij} = -\theta_j \quad \textbf{(the Cournot aggregation property)}$$

$$(35\text{-b}) \qquad \sum_{i=1}^{n} \theta_i \pi_i = 1 \quad \textbf{(the Engel aggregation property)}$$

where

$$(36\text{-a}) \qquad \eta_{ij} \equiv \frac{\partial x_i(p, M)}{\partial p_j} \frac{p_j}{x_i} \quad (\textit{price elasticity})$$

$$(36\text{-b}) \qquad \pi_i \equiv \frac{\partial x_i(p, M)}{\partial M} \frac{M}{x_i} \quad (\textit{income elasticity})$$

$$(36\text{-c}) \qquad \theta_i \equiv \frac{p_i x_i}{M} \quad \text{(budget proportion of commodity)}$$

Also from homogeneity, or (31), we obtain

(37) $$\sum_{j=1}^{n} \eta_{ij} + \pi_i = 0, i = 1, 2, \ldots, n$$

Finally, utilizing (19-b) and assuming that $\lambda(p, M) \neq 0,$[20] rewrite the bordered Hessian in this problem as defined in (17) as follows:

(38) $$H = \begin{bmatrix} 0 & u_1 & u_2 & \cdots & u_n \\ u_1 & u_{11} & u_{12} & \cdots & u_{1n} \\ u_2 & u_{21} & u_{22} & \cdots & u_{2n} \\ \cdots & \cdots & \cdots & \cdots & \cdots \\ \cdots & \cdots & \cdots & \cdots & \cdots \\ u_n & u_{n1} & u_{n2} & \cdots & u_{nn} \end{bmatrix}$$

Then it should be clear that there is a close relation between the present formulation and quasi-concave programming (that is, Theorems 1.E.2, 1.E.3, and 1.E.14). The only important difference between the two approaches is that the quasi-concavity of u together with the linearity (hence the concavity) of the constraint function ensure the *global* result by specifying the signs of the principal minors of H *for all* x.

e.   THE ENVELOPE THEOREM[21]

As before, consider the problem of choosing x so as to

Maximize: $f(x, \alpha)$

Subject to: $g_j(x, \alpha) = 0, j = 1, 2, \ldots, m$, and $x \in X$ (an open subset of R^n)

Let $x(\alpha)$ and $\lambda(\alpha)$ be the functions corresponding to (4-a) and (4-b). It is assumed that (LM) holds as well as (R) so that (FOC) and (SONC) hold. Define the functions $F(\alpha)$ and $\Psi(\alpha)$ by[22]

(39) $$F(\alpha) \equiv f[x(\alpha), \alpha]$$
(40) $$\Psi(\alpha) \equiv f[x(\alpha), \alpha] + \lambda(\alpha) \cdot g[x(\alpha), \alpha]$$

Then we have the following theorem.

Theorem 1.F.4:[23]   *Assume that F and Ψ are continuously differentiable in α. Then*

(41) $$\frac{\partial F(\alpha)}{\partial \alpha_k} = \frac{\partial \Psi(\alpha)}{\partial \alpha_k} = \frac{\partial \Phi(x, \lambda, \alpha)}{\partial \alpha_k}, \quad k = 1, 2, \ldots, l$$

where

(42) $$\frac{\partial \Phi(x, \lambda, \alpha)}{\partial \alpha_k} = \frac{\partial f(x, \alpha)}{\partial \alpha_k} + \lambda \cdot \frac{\partial g(x, \alpha)}{\partial \alpha_k}, k = 1, 2, \ldots, l$$

REMARK: In the vector notation, (41) and (42) are respectively written as[24]

(43) $$F_\alpha = \Psi_\alpha = \Phi_\alpha$$
(44) $$\Phi_\alpha = f_\alpha + \lambda \cdot g_\alpha$$

REMARK: It is possible that F and Ψ are *not* continuously differentiable in α. See Uzawa [15], for example.

PROOF:[25]   Simply observe that

$$\Psi_\alpha = \Phi_x \cdot x_\alpha + \Phi_\lambda \cdot \lambda_\alpha + \Phi_\alpha = \Phi_x \cdot x_\alpha + g \cdot \lambda_\alpha + \Phi_\alpha$$
$$= \Phi_\alpha \; [\text{by using (4-a) and (4-b)}]$$
$$F_\alpha = f_x \cdot x_\alpha + f_\alpha$$
$$= -\lambda \cdot g_x \cdot x_\alpha + f_\alpha \; [\text{since } f_x = -\lambda \cdot g_x \text{ from (4-a)}]$$
$$= \lambda \cdot g_\alpha + f_\alpha \; [\text{since } g_x \cdot x_\alpha + g_\alpha = 0 \text{ by (4-b)}]$$
$$= \Phi_\alpha \qquad\qquad (\text{Q.E.D})$$

REMARK: Notice that $\partial\Psi/\partial\alpha_k$ measures the *total* effect of a change in α_k on the Langrangian, while $\partial\Phi/\partial\alpha_k$ measures the *partial* effect of a change in α_k on the Langrangian with x and λ being held constant. Note that every partial derivative in (41) is evaluated at $[x(\alpha), \lambda(\alpha), \alpha]$.

From Theorem 1.F 4,

$$\frac{\partial F(\alpha)}{\partial\alpha_k} = \frac{\partial f}{\partial\alpha_k} + \lambda \cdot \frac{\partial g}{\partial\alpha_k}$$

Now change the original maximization problem in such a way that the kth parameter α_k is considered as one of the choice variables (such as the x_i's). Then from the first-order conditions of this new problem, we have

$$\frac{\partial f}{\partial\alpha_k} + \lambda \cdot \frac{\partial g}{\partial\alpha_k} = 0$$

Thus

$$\frac{\partial F(\alpha)}{\partial\alpha_k} = 0$$

Write $(\alpha_1, \ldots, \alpha_{k-1}, \alpha_{k+1}, \ldots, \alpha_l) \equiv \beta$. Then we have the following two equations:

(45) $$\phi(F, \beta, \alpha_k) \equiv F - F(\alpha) = 0$$
(46) $$\psi(\beta, \alpha_k) \equiv \frac{\partial F(\alpha)}{\partial\alpha_k} = 0$$

Keeping α_k constant, $\phi(F, \beta, \alpha_k) = 0$ defines a surface in the $(F\text{-}\beta)$-space. By changing α_k, we then obtain a family of such surfaces. By solving this equation (45) together with equation (46), we obtain the envelope of such a family of surfaces.[26] For example, if β is a scalar, then (45) defines a curve in the $(F\text{-}\beta)$-plane for a given value of α_k. By changing α_k, we obtain a family of curves. The envelope of this family of curves in the $(F\text{-}\beta)$-plane may be obtained by eliminating α_k from (45) and (46) as

(47) $$F = \varepsilon(\beta) \quad \text{or} \quad \tilde{\varepsilon}(F, \beta) = 0$$

The famous Wong-Viner envelope theorem that the long-run cost curve is the envelope of the family of short-run cost curves is an example of the above consideration, as we will see later (Example 4).

We now show some examples of the applications of Theorem 1.F.4. We hope that these examples will illustrate the use of this theorem.

EXAMPLE 1 (marginal utility of income):
Consider the following problem again:

$$\text{Maximize: } u(x)$$
$$\phantom{\text{Maximize: }} x$$
$$\text{Subject to: } M - p \cdot x = 0, \ x \in R^n$$

Let $x(p, M)$ and $\lambda(p, M)$, respectively, correspond to $x(\alpha)$ and $\lambda(\alpha)$ in (4). Define

(48) $$U[p, M] \equiv u[x(p, M)] \text{ (indirect utility function)}$$

and $$\Phi[x, \lambda, p, M] \equiv u(x) + \lambda(M - p \cdot x)$$

Then by Theorem 1.F.4, we obtain

(49) $$\frac{\partial U}{\partial M} = \lambda(p, M)$$

which is the well-known result that the Lagrangian multiplier of the problem signifies the marginal utility of income. We also obtain

(50) $$\frac{\partial U}{\partial p_j} = -\lambda x_j, \quad j = 1, 2, \ldots, n$$

Hence if $\lambda(p, M) > 0$, then an increase in any price will decrease the consumer's satisfaction. Also, from (49) and (50), we have $(\partial U/\partial p_j)/(\partial U/\partial M) = -x_j(p, M)$.

EXAMPLE 2 (the meaning of the multipliers): In general, consider the problem of choosing $x \in R^n$ so as to

$$\text{Maximize: } f(x)$$
$$\text{Subject to: } g_j(x) = b_j, j = 1, 2, \ldots, m$$

Let $x(b)$ and $\lambda(b)$ correspond to $x(\alpha)$ and $\lambda(\alpha)$ in (4), where $b \equiv (b_1, b_2, \ldots, b_m)$. Define

(51-a) $$F(b) \equiv f[x(b)]$$

and

(51-b) $$\Phi(x, \lambda, b) \equiv f(x) + \lambda \cdot [b - g(x)]$$

Then by Theorem 1.F.4, we obtain

(52) $$\frac{\partial F(b)}{\partial b_j} = \lambda_j(b), \quad j = 1, 2, \cdots, m$$

Thus the jth Lagrangian multiplier signifies the marginal rate of change of the optimal value of the objective function with respect to a change in the jth constraint. Example 1 is clearly a special case of this. Interpreting b_j as the amount of the jth resource supply, λ_j signifies the **shadow price** of the jth resource.

EXAMPLE 3 (cost minimization):
Consider the following problem:

Maximize: $-w \cdot x$ ($=$ Minimize: $w \cdot x$)
$\quad x$

Subject to: $M - p \cdot x = 0, x \in R^n$

where $w > 0$, $y > 0$, and $g(x)$, respectively, signify the input price vector, the output (scalar), and the production function. Let $x(w, y)$ and $\lambda(w, y)$, respectively, correspond to $x(\alpha)$ and $\lambda(\alpha)$ of (4).
Define[27]

(53-a) $$C(w, y) \equiv w \cdot x(w, y)$$

and

(53-b) $$\Phi(x, \lambda, w, y) \equiv -w \cdot x + \lambda[g(x) - y]$$

Then by Theorem 1.F.4,[28]

(54) $$\frac{\partial C}{\partial y} = \lambda(w, y)$$

so that the multiplier signifies the long-run marginal cost. Also we obtain

(55) $$\frac{\partial C}{\partial w_i} = x_i(w, y), \quad i = 1, 2, \ldots, n$$

so that an increase in any factor price increases the minimum total cost C. From (55), we obtain

$$\sum_{i=1}^{n} \frac{\partial C(w, y)}{\partial w_i} w_i = \sum_{i=1}^{n} w_i x_i(w, y) = C(w, y)$$

for all (w, y). Hence by Euler's theorem, the minimal cost function $C(w, y)$ is homogeneous of degree one in w. Also noting that $\partial^2 C/\partial w_i \partial y =$

$\partial^2 C/\partial y\partial w_i$, we obtain from (54) and (55)

(56)
$$\frac{\partial x_i(w, y)}{\partial y} = \frac{\partial \lambda(w, y)}{\partial w_i}$$

Then, using (54), (53), and (56) successively, we can observe

$$\lambda(w, y) = \frac{\partial C}{\partial y} = \sum_{i=1}^{n} w_i \frac{\partial x_i(w, y)}{\partial y} = \sum_{i=1}^{n} w_i \frac{\partial \lambda}{\partial w_i} \qquad \text{for all } (w, y)$$

Thus $\lambda(w, y)$ is also homogeneous of degree one in w. Recall that by the first-order condition, we have

$$w_i = \lambda(w, y) g_i(x), \qquad i = 1, 2, \ldots, n$$

where $g_i(x) = \partial g(x)/\partial x_i$. Therefore if, *in particular*, the production function is homogeneous of degree one in x so that $\sum_{i=1}^{n} g_i(x) x_i = g(x)$ for all x, then we obtain

$$C(w, y) = \sum_{i=1}^{n} w_i x_i = \lambda \sum_{i=1}^{n} g_i(x) x_i = \lambda(w, y) y$$

From this we can conclude that,[29] for all (w, y),

(57)
$$\frac{C}{y} = \frac{\partial C}{\partial y} (= \lambda)$$

(58)
$$\frac{\partial \lambda(w, y)}{\partial y} = 0$$

EXAMPLE 4 (the envelope of the short-run cost curves):   In the problem of the previous example, reinterpret x as the vector of *variable* factor inputs and consider the following problem.

$$\text{Maximize:} - [w\cdot x + f(k)] \quad [= \text{Minimize: } w\cdot x + f(k)]$$
$$x$$
$$\text{Subject to: } g(x, k) = y \text{ and } x \in R^n$$

where k and $f(k)$, respectively, signify the "size of the plant" and the "fixed cost." For the sake of simplicity, k is assumed to be a scalar rather than a vector signifying the spectrum of capital goods. Let $x(w, y, k)$ and $\lambda(w, y, k)$, respectively, correspond to $x(\alpha)$ and $\lambda(\alpha)$ of (4). Define[30]

(59-a)
$$C(w, y, k) \equiv w\cdot x(w, y, k) + f(k)$$

and

(59-b)
$$\Phi(x, \lambda, w, y, k) \equiv -[w\cdot x + f(k)] + \lambda[g(x, k) - y]$$

Then from Theorem 1.F.4,

(60)
$$\frac{\partial C(w, y, k)}{\partial y} = \lambda(w, y, k)$$

so that the multiplier λ in this problem signifies the short-run marginal cost. Assume that w is fixed and define the function ϕ by

(61)
$$\phi(C, y, k) \equiv C - C(w, y, k) = 0$$

For a fixed value of k, the graph of ϕ in the $(C$-$y)$-plane denotes a short-run (total) cost curve. In the long-run case in which k is allowed to adjust, we have

(62)
$$\frac{\partial \Phi}{\partial k} = -f'(k) + \lambda \frac{\partial g}{\partial k} = 0$$

from the first-order conditions. Since $\partial C(w, y, k)/\partial k = -\Phi_k$ by Theorem 1.F.4, we obtain from (61) and (62)

(63)
$$\frac{\partial \phi(C, y, k)}{\partial k} = 0$$

Suppose that we can obtain the unique relation between C and y by eliminating k from (61) and (63) as

(64)
$$C = \varepsilon(y)$$

Then the graph of ε in the $(C$-$y)$-plane signifies the long-run cost curve as the envelope of the short-run cost curves.

FOOTNOTES

1. This section is indebted to Otani [11] as well as Hicks [8] and Samuelson [12].
2. Therefore, $\Phi_x = f_x + \lambda \cdot g_x$, where g_x denotes the Jacobian matrix of g with respect to x, and f_x denotes the gradient vector of f with respect to x.
3. In other words, Φ_{xx} denotes the Jacobian matrix of Φ_x with respect of x, so that it is the Hessian matrix of Φ in x.
4. The rank of a rectangular matrix is equal to the number of linearly independent rows, which is equal to the number of linearly independent columns. Rank B denotes "the rank of the matrix B."
5. Recall Theorem 1.E.16.
6. Recall, for example, Chapter 1, Section D.
7. To save space, we will not attempt to make detailed comments in the subsequent discussions from the viewpoint of modern theory. The reader is urged to do this job by himself.
8. The **implicit function theorem** states the following: Let $f_i(y, \alpha)$, $i = 1, 2, \ldots, s$, be continuously differentiable real-valued function on $Y \otimes A$ where Y and A, respectively, are open subsets of R^s and R^l. Let $f_i(\hat{y}, \hat{\alpha}) = 0$, $i = 1, 2, \ldots, s$, for some $(\hat{y}, \hat{\alpha}) \in Y \otimes A$, and assume that the determinant of the Jacobian matrix $[\partial f_i(\hat{y}, \hat{\alpha})/\partial y_j]$ is nonvanishing. Then there exists a continuously differentiable function h such that $\hat{y} = h(\hat{\alpha})$ and $f_i[h(\alpha), \alpha] = 0$, $i = 1, 2, \ldots, s$, for all α in some neighborhood of $\hat{\alpha}$. For the proof of this theorem, see any textbook of advanced

calculus. It is important to realize that this is a "local" theorem in the sense that the above neighborhood may be very small.

9. Let Φ_λ be the gradient vector of Φ with respect to λ. Then by definition of Φ, we can rewrite (4-b) as $\Phi_\lambda[x(\alpha), \alpha] = 0$.

10. Here $\Phi_{x\alpha_k}$ is the n-dimensional column vector whose ith element is $\partial^2\Phi[x(\alpha), \lambda(\alpha), \alpha]/\partial x_i \partial \alpha_k$, and similarly for $\Phi_{\lambda\alpha_k}$. Clearly the jth element of $\Phi_{\lambda\alpha_k}$ is equal to $\partial g_j[x(\alpha), \alpha]/\partial \alpha_k$.

11. Clearly, $\hat{H}$ is obtained from H by evaluating every element of H at $\hat{\alpha}$.

12. One should note that, in many applications in economics, (A-2) fails to hold; thus H^{-1} fails to exist. The homogeneity and the concavity of the relevant functions are often the source of such singularity.

13. This also means that (SOSC) holds for all α in $\bar{N}(\hat{\alpha})$. Therefore, under (FOC) and (R), we can conclude that, for each fixed α in $\bar{N}(\hat{\alpha})$, $x(\alpha)$ achieves a local maximum of $f(x, \alpha)$ subject to $g(x, \alpha) = 0$, $x \in X$.

14. Note that $h_{m+n,m+n}$ is the $(m + n)$-$(m + n)$ confactor of H; hence it has the sign opposite of det H as a result of (8). Thus sgn $h_{m+n,m+n} = (-1)^{m+n-1}$. From this, we can deduce (11) by using the property of a determinant that a simultaneous permutation of rows and columns does not alter the sign and the value of the determinant.

15. They respectively correspond to 0, $\Phi_{\lambda x}$, $\Phi_{x\lambda}$, and Φ_{xx} in H.

16. In general, we have the following theorem. Let H be any $(m + n) \times (m + n)$ symmetric matrix with real entries. Assume that H is decomposed in the form of (6) as $\hat{H}$. Assume also that rank $B = m$ and that A is negative definite subject to $B \cdot h = 0$. Then H^{-1} exists and K_4 of H^{-1} [where H^{-1} is decomposed as (14)] is negative semidefinite. See Carathéodory ([4], pp. 195–196). Samuelson ([12], pp. 378–379) contains the statement of such a theorem.

17. Since $S_{ii} < 0$, we have $\partial x_i(p, M)/\partial p_i < -x_i \partial x_i(p, M)/\partial M$, $i = 1, 2, \ldots, n$, from (24). Commodity i is defined as **Giffen** if $\partial x_i(p, M)/\partial p_i > 0$, and **inferior** if $\partial x_i(p, M)/\partial M < 0$. Hence it is clear that every Giffen commodity is inferior, but not necessarily vice versa.

18. The homogeneity of $x(p, M)$ is due to the fact that, in the original maximization problem, $\hat{M} - \hat{p} \cdot x = 0$ if and only if $c\hat{M} - (c\hat{p}) \cdot x = 0$ for all scalars $c > 0$, so that $\hat{x} = x(\hat{p}, \hat{M}) = x(c\hat{p}, c\hat{M})$ for all $c > 0$.

19. The term S_{ij} is called the **net (or pure) substitution term**. To understand the meaning of this term, consider the problem of choosing $x \in R^n$ so as to minimize $p \cdot x$ (expenditures) subject to $u(x) = u$, where u is fixed. Denote the solution to this dual problem by $x = h(p, u)$. If $u = u[x(p, M)]$, then the solution of the utility maximization problem becomes the solution of this outlay minimization problem, and it can be shown that $S_{ij} = \partial h_i(p, u)/\partial p_j$, that is, a change in the demand for i when p_j is changed with a **compensated change in income** so as to keep the level of utility u fixed. Two commodities $i \neq j$ are said to be **substitutes** if $S_{ij} > 0$ and **complements** if $S_{ij} < 0$. From (34), it is clear that at least one pair must be substitutes (that is, it is not possible that all commodities are complements).

20. This is satisfied if $u_i[x(p, M)] > 0$ for all i (nonsatiation), as remarked earlier.

21. The discussion here can easily be carried out in the global context under proper assumptions.

22. By definition of Φ, we may also write (40) as $\Psi(\alpha) = \Phi[x(\alpha), \lambda(\alpha), \alpha]$.

23. The relation $\partial F/\partial \alpha_k = \partial \Phi/\partial \alpha_k$ is due to Afriat ([1], pp. 355–357). The proposition in the form of this theorem is found in Otani [11]. See also D. G. Luenberger, *Optimization by Vector Space Methods*, New York, Wiley, 1969, pp. 221–223.

24. The notations F_α, Ψ_α and Φ_α, respectively, denote the gradient vectors of F, Ψ, and Φ with respect to α.

25. Here, x_α is the $(n \times l)$ (Jacobian) matrix whose $(i\text{–}k)$ element is $\partial x_i / \partial \alpha_k$. Similarly, λ_α is the $(m \times l)$ matrix whose $(j\text{–}k)$ element is $\partial \lambda_j / \partial \alpha_k$. The proof is a simple application of the chain rule (Theorem 1.C.2) with the first-order conditions [in the form of (4-a) and (4-b)].

26. Consider, for example, the family of curves $y = (x - \alpha)^2$ in the $(x\text{-}y)$-plane where α is a parameter. This is the family of parabolas obtained by translating $y = x^2$ in the direction of the x-axis. Clearly the x-axis (that is, $y = 0$) is the envelope. This is obtained by eliminating α from $f(x, y, \alpha) \equiv y - (x - \alpha)^2 = 0$ and $\partial f / \partial \alpha = 2(x - \alpha) = 0$. In general, consider $f(x, y, \alpha) = 0$ where $(x, y) \in R^2$ and $\alpha \in R$. Regarding α as a parameter, we obtain a family of curves in the $(x\text{-}y)$-plane. **An envelope** of a family of curves is a curve with the following two properties: (1) At every one of its points it is tangent to at least one curve of the family; (2) it is tangent to every curve of the family at at least one point. An envelope may not be unique [for example, consider the family of circles, $(x - \alpha)^2 + y^2 = 1$]. **The envelope** of a family of curves is the union of its envelopes. The envelope is obtained by eliminating α from the two equations $f(x, y, \alpha) = 0$ and $\partial f(x, y, \alpha)/\partial \alpha = 0$. In general, the envelope of multiparameter surfaces, $f(z_1, z_2, \ldots, z_n; \alpha_1, \alpha_2, \ldots, \alpha_s) = 0$, is obtained by eliminating α from this equation together with $\partial f(z, \alpha)/\partial \alpha_k = 0$, $k = 1, 2, \ldots, s$. It is, of course, possible that a family of curves or surfaces may never generate an envelope. The above procedure only gives a necessary (but not necessarily a sufficient) condition to obtain an envelope. The exposition of the envelope is found in most textbooks of advanced calculus (for example, E. B. Wilson, 1911; W. F. Osgood, 1925; H. B. Fine, 1937; D. V. Widder, 1947; J. M. H. Olmsted, 1961, and so on) and classical treatments of differential geometry.

27. Here $C(w, y)$ is the long-run minimum (total) cost for given (w, y). Fixing w, the graph of C as a function of y is the total cost curve that appears in many textbooks on price theory.

28. Note that $\partial C/\partial y = -\partial \Phi/\partial y$ by Theorem 1.F.4.

29. Equation (57) says that the average cost is equal to the marginal cost if constant returns to scale prevail. To obtain (58), note that $\partial(C/y)/\partial y = [(\partial C/\partial y) - (C/y)]/y$, which is equal to zero by (57). Equation (58) says that the function λ is independent of y. Hence we may write $\lambda(w, y) = \mu(w)$. Relations (57) and (58) are important in the results known as the **Shephard-Samuelson theorem**. See Shephard [13] and Takayama ([14], pp. 549–551).

30. The function $C(w, y, k)$ signifies the short-run minimum total cost, for given (w, y, k).

REFERENCES

1. Afriat, S. N., "Theory of Maxima and the Method of Lagrange," *SIAM Journal on Applied Mathematics*, 20, May 1971.

2. Bliss, G. M., *Lectures on the Calculus of Variations*, Chicago, University of Chicago Press, 1946.

3. Burger, E., "On Extrema with Side Conditions," *Econometrica*, 23, October 1955.

4. Carathéodory, C., *Calculus of Variations and Partial Differential Equations of the First Order*, Part II, San Francisco, Holden Day, 1967, esp. chap. 11 (German original, 1935).

5. Debreu, G., "Definite and Semidefinite Quadratic Forms," *Econometrica*, 20, April 1952.

6. El-Hodiri, M. A., *Constrained Extrema: Introduction to the Differentiable Case with Economic Applications*, New York, Springer-Verlag, 1971.

7. Hestenes, M. R., *Calculus of Variations and Optimal Control Theory*, New York, Wiley, 1966, chap. 1.

8. Hicks, J. R., *Value and Capital*, 2nd ed., Oxford, Clarendon Press, 1946 (1st ed. 1939).

9. Mangasarian, O. L., *Nonlinear Programming*, New York, McGraw-Hill, 1969.

10. Mann, H. B., "Quadratic Forms with Linear Constraints," *American Mathematical Monthly*, 1943: reprinted in *Readings in Mathematical Economics*, ed. by P. Newman, Baltimore, Md., Johns Hopkins Press, Vol. I, 1968.

11. Otani, Y., *Microeconomic Theory*, lecture notes at Purdue University, Fall 1971.

12. Samuelson, P. A., *Foundations of Economic Analysis*, Cambridge, Mass., Harvard University Press, 1947.

13. Shephard, R. W., *Cost and Production Functions*, Princeton, N.J., Princeton University Press, 1953.

14. Takayama, A., *International Trade—An Approach to the Theory*, New York, Holt, Rinehart and Winston, 1972.

15. Uzawa, H., "A Note on the Menger-Wieser Theory of Imputation," *Zeitschrift für Nationalökonomie*, XVIII, August 1958.

2

THE THEORY OF COMPETITIVE MARKETS

In this chapter, we study the theory of competitive markets. We consider an economy which consists of two types of "economic agents," one called a "producer" and the other a "consumer." There are m consumers and k producers in the economy. These economic agents are concerned with "commodities." A commodity bundle is considered to be an element of R^n; that is, it is an n-dimensional vector whose components are real numbers. Usually a "commodity" is defined by the specification of all its physical characteristics, its availability location, and its availability date. Services are also considered to be commodities. We call attention to the fact that each commodity is dated. Hence today's apple is a different commodity from tomorrow's apple. Thus the time element is introduced into the model. There is a "price" for each commodity and the price vector is an element in R^n. It is assumed in the theory of "competitive" markets that each economic agent is so "small" relative to the size of the economy that he cannot affect the price level that prevails in the economy (or, more precisely, the impact of his action, as a producer or a consumer, on market prices is negligible). This assumption obviously implies that there are many producers and consumers in the economy. A behavioral rule is assumed for each economic agent. It is assumed that each consumer maximizes his satisfaction over the set of commodity bundles that he can afford to buy with his income, and that each producer maximizes his profit using the process or processes available in his production set. Activity analysis is most typically concerned with a characterization of such a competitive producer when his production set is a convex polyhedral cone. For example, we showed that every efficient point of a production set is a profit maximization point under a certain fixed price vector and that every profit maximization point (under a certain fixed price vector) is an efficient point (Theorems 0.C.2 and 0.C.3). In Section D of this chapter we are concerned with the theory of a competitive consumer. In describing the theory of consumer's choice, we assume that only the commodity bundles that a consumer wishes to consume enter into his decision making and that the prices of the commodities do not affect his preferences. In real life, one may wish to consume a certain commodity mainly because it is expensive. Such a "snob effect" is assumed away in this chapter. In this connection, we must note that there is an important complication in the theory of consumer's choice. Unlike the theory of production, we do not have a measurable behavioral criterion such as profit. However, it turns out that important results in the theory of consumer's choice and the subsequent results in the theory of competitive markets can be obtained without any reference to the measurability of individual's satisfaction. We will observe this throughout the chapter.

In addition to the study of the behavior of each type of economic agent, the theory of competitive markets is also concerned with the interaction of many agents in the economy. This is the question of a competitive *equilibrium.* Essentially, a competitive equilibrium is a state of affairs in which each consumer maximizes his satisfaction given his budget set defined by the prevailing price vector, each producer maximizes his profit given the same price vector, and the total supply of commodities is equal to the total demand for commodities.[1] In this chapter we study the following two aspects of a competitive equilibrium.

    (i) The welfare implication of a competitive equilibrium (Section C).
    (ii) The existence of a competitive equilibrium (Section E).

The existence of a competitive equilibrium depends on whether or not there exists a price vector such that a competitive equilibrium as described above can be sustained. In other words, it is essentially concerned with the "consistency" of the concept of a competitive equilibrium and the model of a competitive economy in the sense of whether the actions of numerous "competitive" producers and "competitive" consumers can be consistent with each other.

In developing such a theory of competitive markets, one fundamental assumption is often made and usually plays a crucial role in establishing the major results. This is the assumption of the absence of "externalities." In other words, it is usually assumed that the interdependence among the economic agents (consumer vs. consumer, consumer vs. producer, producer vs. producer) is negligible. One type of interdependence among consumers is known as the "demonstration effect." In essence, the "independence" among consumers says that each consumer cares only about the consumption bundle that he consumes and does not care about the consumption bundles of others. If this is the case, the consumer is said to be **selfish** or **individualistic**.[2] One type of interdependence among producers is known as the (technological) **external economies and diseconomies**. A famous example of the interdependence between producer and consumer is the dissatisfaction incurred by the public as a result of smoke from a factory's chimney. The theory of such externalities is making rapid progress in economics. Here we only point out that fresh views are given for the entire theory by Hurwicz [2] and by the "core" theorists.[3]

Some preliminary remarks on notations are now in order. The production process y_j for the jth producer is an n-vector whose negative elements denote "inputs" and whose positive elements denote "outputs." The set of possible consumption bundles for the ith individual is denoted by X_i, and is called his **consumption set**. Given a price vector p and income M_i, his **budget set** is $\{x_i : x_i \in X_i$ and $p \cdot x_i \leqq M_i\}$. Each individual receives his income either by selling (or offering) his "resources" in the market or by receiving a gift from someone else. His resources may be physical goods such as apples or labor services performed by him. Whether there is money in the economy or not is immaterial here since we do not consider its specific features as such in this chapter. Money, if it exists in this economy, serves mainly as a unit of measurement of prices and the generally accepted means of payment. In a "money" economy he receives his "money income" by selling his resources to the market, while in a barter economy he obtains a bundle of goods and services for his consumption in exchange for his resources. The convenience due to the existence of money when compared with the barter economy may enter the utility function of each consumer. But since money, then, is like a public good and the amount of satisfaction to each individual cannot be well described, we might as well assume that money does not enter the individual's utility function. Or we may just consider that money is simply inherent to the institutional scheme of the monetary economy, so that one does not obtain any particular utility from it. If the reader so desires, for the sake of simplicity of discussion, he can assume that our entire discussion is confined to a barter economy.

The relationships between a consumer's budget set and his consumption bundle require additional clarification. First, the word "income" may be misleading, as from the above argument it can be considered to be the total value of his "resources." For example, one can sell the land that he owns if he so wishes, instead of selling the *services* from the land. In other words, the stocks of those commodities which are marketable can enter the definition of the consumer's budget constraint. Thus by the word "income" we mean the total value of all the flows and stocks of the commodities that he can sell to the markets. Hence the word "income" may more properly be replaced by "wealth." However, once the above point is recognized, it is rather immaterial whether we call it "income" or "wealth," and thus we stick to the more conventional word "income." Note also that as long as the commodities are dated, income may also be dated, so that the possibility of borrowing and lending will affect the consumer's budget set.[4]

One implication of dating commodities is that it is assumed that each consumer knows all of the bundles of commodities that he will want to consume in the future and all of the price vectors that will prevail; that is, we assume that each consumer has perfect foresight. This assumption can easily be justified in a stationary state (or even on a "balanced growth" path),[5] though under any other conditions justification for the assumption is difficult. The extension of the theory of competitive markets to the world of uncertainty has recently been explored.

In any case, let us now return to Mr. i's consumption vector x_i. Traditionally,

x_i is taken to be a vector whose components are all nonnegative. If Mr. i has resources $\bar{x}_i$ and if he gets all his income by selling this $\bar{x}_i$, his income will be $p \cdot \bar{x}_i$, when price vector p prevails in the market. His **budget constraint** is thus

$$p \cdot x_i \leqq p \cdot \bar{x}_i$$

We may note that Mr. i, if he wishes, can retain a part of his resources for his own consumption. One way to handle this is to (fictitiously) suppose that he sells all his resources in the market and buys some of them back (with zero transaction cost).

Some simple examples may clarify the above budget relation. Suppose Mr. i has holdings of only one commodity, A. Suppose further that his initial holding of A is the amount $\bar{X}_a$ and that he sells a part of A, say, $\tilde{X}_a$. His consumption of A will then be $(\bar{X}_a - \tilde{X}_a)$. Now let us assume that he also consumes commodity B of which he has no initial holding. Letting p_a and p_b denote the price of A and B, respectively, his budget constraint can be written as

$$p_a(\bar{X}_a - \tilde{X}_a) + p_b X_b \leqq p_a \bar{X}_a$$

We may suppose that this budget constraint means that he sells all his initial holdings of A, $\bar{X}_a$, and that he buys back the amount $(\bar{X}_a - \tilde{X}_a)$. The commodities A and B could be such goods as apples and bananas, or one of them could be labor services (or leisure). In other words, we may interpret $\bar{X}_a = 24$ hours a day, $\tilde{X}_a =$ the amount of labor he sells to the market per day, and $(\bar{X}_a - \tilde{X}_a) =$ the amount of leisure he consumes per day.

The above budget relation could also be written as

$$p_b X_b \leqq p_a \tilde{X}_a$$

If we write the equation this way, we have to infer from $\tilde{X}_a$ the amount of commodity A which enters into his consumption and his preference ordering. This can be done by specifying the value of $\bar{X}_a$ and computing the value of $(\bar{X}_a - \tilde{X}_a)$.

As long as the total amounts of resources held by him are fixed, it does not make any fundamental difference how we write the budget relation. In fact, we may rewrite the above relation as

$$p_a(-\tilde{X}_a) + p_b X_b \leqq 0$$

We then consider his consumption bundle as $(-\tilde{X}_a, X_b)$ and his total budget (income) as zero. We may suppose that his preference ordering (or utility function) is defined on all possible values of $(-\tilde{X}_a, X_b)$ instead of all possible values of $(\bar{X}_a - \tilde{X}_a, X_b)$. One caution to note is that under this supposition, his consumption vector is no longer nonnegative.

In general, we can rewrite $p \cdot x_i \leqq p \cdot \bar{x}_i$ as $p \cdot z_i \leqq 0$, where $z_i \equiv x_i - \bar{x}_i$, and consider z_i as his consumption bundle and 0 as his total budget. Negative elements in z_i represent quantities of commodities supplied and positive elements in z_i represent quantities received. In this convention, the consumption set X_i is the set of all possible consumptions and trades (of the ith consumer). Usually, it is assumed that X_i is a subset of R^n.

Further complications arise when we consider the producers. First, producers may hold certain resources. The question is: Who claims the income from these resources? There is one simple answer (not the only answer). We may assume that all the resources are initially held by the consumers (and none by producers) and some of them are sold to the producers (for example, labor service). Thus consumers get the income. Second, producers may get positive (negative or zero) profit. Who has the claim to the profit? This can be solved simply by assuming that all the firms are owned by the consumers, and that ownership is represented by stocks issued by the producers. Clearly some consumers may never own stocks and hence receive no income from the profits that producers make. Let $y_j \in R^n$ be the production point (input-output combination) chosen by the jth producer when price vector p prevails. The negative elements of y_j denote inputs and the positive elements of y_j denote outputs. His profit is represented by $p \cdot y_j$.[6] Let θ_{ji} be the fraction of the stock of the jth producer that the ith consumer owns. Thus

$$\sum_{i=1}^{m} \theta_{ji} = 1 \text{ for all } j \quad \text{and } \theta_{ji} \geq 0 \qquad \text{for all } j \text{ and } i$$

Then Mr. i gets the dividend from the jth producer in the amount of $\theta_{ji}(p \cdot y_j)$.

Letting $\bar{x}_i$ be the total amount of resources initially made available to Mr. i, his total wealth (or income), prior to any consumption, can now be represented by

$$p \cdot \bar{x}_i + \sum_{j=1}^{k} \theta_{ji}(p \cdot y_j)$$

(he owns the stock issued by producer $j = 1, \ldots, k$).[7] Note that this formulation does not preclude the possibility that the same individual is a consumer and a producer at the same time. In this case he, as a consumer, owns 100 percent of the stock of himself as a producer.

Needless to say, the set of all possible input-output combinations for the jth producer is the *production set* of j (which we denote by Y_j). Clearly $y_j \in Y_j$. In this chapter we assume that Y_j is a subset of R^n. If there are no external economies and diseconomies, the *aggregate production set* of the economy, denoted by Y, can be defined by

$$Y \equiv \sum_{j=1}^{k} Y_j$$

Finally, we may remark that the definition of a competitive equilibrium *can*, in fact, be independent of the question of who owns the resources, because one can describe a consumer's behavior not by specifying how much his total income is, but by specifying the point chosen by him. We may simply define each consumer's behavior as being described by the choice of which consumption bundle is preferred or equivalent to all other alternatives in his consumption set that are of equal or less value. Note that in this definition of consumer's behavior, nothing is said about how he obtains his income.

With these remarks, we now enter the theory of competitive markets. This is probably the most rigorously and elegantly developed field in economics. It certainly deals with a very simple type of economy, a "competitive economy." Because it is simple, we can more fully appreciate many of the difficult problems which arise at this stage. The study of this theory is very important in order to better understand a more complicated or more "realistic" model (which may not yet be well covered in the literature).[8] We may also remind the reader that there was at least one period of time in history (if not now) in which the model of competitive equilibrium is thought to have approximated the real world fairly well. After all, Walras did not draw his theory from a hat. Great economists such as Walras and Marshall, who were concerned with the competitive economy, were all interested in the real world. The theory of competitive markets has probably the longest history of any subject in economics, and the literature is voluminous. But we should also note that most of the modern development that took place in the 1950s is due to economists such as Arrow, Debreu, Hurwicz, McKenzie, Gale, Nikaido, and Uzawa after the classical contributions of Walras, Hicks, Samuelson, and so on.

FOOTNOTES

1. It is possible to suppose that the total demand for commodities does not exceed the total supply of commodities. Note that this convention, allowing excess supply of commodities, presupposes the free disposability of commodities.

2. Since this assumption does not involve any ethical connotation, the word "individual-istic" seems to be better than "selfish."

3. The theory of the core will be explained later (in the appendix to Section C of this chapter). For the theory of externalities, see also T. Negishi, *General Equilibrium Theory and International Trade*, Amsterdam, North-Holland, 1972, esp. chapter 4.

4. Note that if we date commodities, then prices are also "dated" in the sense that interest rates between various dates are incorporated into the model.

5. However, even in a stationary state, it is difficult for the consumer to know the time of his death with perfect certainty.

6. The definition of "profits" depends upon what is included in the list of commodities. For example, if "entrepreneurial skills" are not included in the list, the returns to them constitute a part of the profits. On the other hand, if such items are included in the list of commodities, the production set may become a convex cone, so that the maximum profit becomes zero.

7. Such a convention is seen, for example, in Debreu [1]. One possible difficulty here is that the explanation of the distribution of the θ_{ji}'s is not clear. This is especially true if entrepreneurial skills are not included in the list of commodities.

8. The basic methods involved in the studies of competitive equilibrium (existence,

welfare, stability, and comparative statistics) are also useful and important when we study even much simpler models in other branches of economics. Still another important reason for the study of competitive markets is its welfare significance. See our discussions in Section C and its appendix in this chapter and Section G of Chapter 3.

REFERENCES

1. Debreu, G., *Theory of Value*, New York, Wiley, 1959.
2. Hurwicz, L., "Optimality and Informational Efficiency in Resource Allocation Processes," in *Mathematical Methods in Social Sciences, 1959*, ed. by K. J. Arrow, S. Karlin, and P. Suppes, Stanford, Calif., Stanford University Press, 1960.
3. Koopmans, T. C., *Three Essays on the State of Economic Science*, New York, McGraw-Hill, 1957.
4. Walras, L., *Elements of Pure Economics*, tr. by W. Jaffé, Homewood, Ill., Richard D. Irwin, 1954.

Section B

CONSUMPTION SET
AND PREFERENCE ORDERING

a.   CONSUMPTION SET

The basic concept in the theory of consumer's choice is the "consumption set," which is the set of all possible consumption bundles for a particular consumer. This concept is clearly analogous to the concept of the production set, which was discussed in Chapter 0, Section C. The consumption set, which we will denote by X, is traditionally taken to be the entire nonnegative orthant of R^n. We should realize that this convention implicitly or explicitly contains the following assumptions:

(A-1)   The set X is a convex set.
(A-2)   An individual can consume any amount of goods (however large it may be).
(A-3)   An individual can survive as long as he has a positive quantity of some commodity. Thus, for example, the origin is a minimum subsistence consumption.
(A-4)   The set X is a subset of a finite dimensional vector space.

The third assumption implies that every individual has the same starvation point regardless of his physiological capability if everybody in the market has the nonnegative orthant as his consumption set.[1] The second assumption may not be considered a strong one, for one may get satisfaction just from owning commodities. However, we may then argue that we should distinguish the consumption activity of actually consuming a commodity from that of simply owning it. After all, eating cakes may provide a different kind of satisfaction to an individual from owning cakes. The first assumption is very convenient but quite a strong one, for it implies, among other things, the perfect divisibility of every commodity, including commodities such as automobiles. We may note, however, that every commodity can be made perfectly divisible if we consider consumption per unit of time of the commodity, since time is a continuum. For example, the consumption of an electric bulb can be measured by the amount of time we use the bulb. If the bulb lasts 1000 hours and if one consumed 10π hours of lighting by the bulb, we may say that he consumed $10\pi/1000$ of the bulb (which is an irrational number). In this context, we may even question the need to assume that X is a subset of a linear space. For a linear space, by definition, must allow multiplication by any scalar. It may be worthwhile to investigate the extent of the theory in which the consumption set is not embedded in either the linear space structure or the topological structure. By assuming that X is in R^n, these structures may unnecessarily creep into the theory. Note also that even if we assume that every commodity is perfectly divisible, X may cease to be a subset of a *finite* dimensional vector space. This is true, for example, if we date each commodity by continuum time. In this case, a consumption vector is a function of time, $x(t)$, so that $x(t) \in X$ (which typically presupposes X to be a subset of an infinite dimensional linear space).[2] In Figure 2.1 we illustrate the consumption set in R^2 where one of the two commodities is indivisible. The consumption set is the set of points on the horizontal lines.

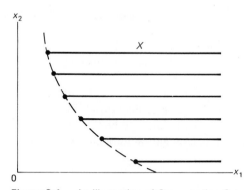

Figure 2.1.   An illustration of Consumption Set.

b.   QUASI-ORDERING AND PREFERENCE ORDERING

Let X be the consumption set for a certain individual, say, Mr. A. Given two elements (consumption bundles) x, y in X, we suppose that Mr. A can say (from the point of view of the satisfaction he obtains from consuming these bundles of goods) such things as: (1) "I prefer x to y"; (2) "x is no worse than y"; (3) "x and y are equivalent to me." This means that he is defining a certain "relation" (called a "preference relation") on two elements of his consumption set X. If we wish, we may consider such a relation to be a collection of ordered pairs (x, y) where $x \in X$ and $y \in X$. For example, we may interpret this ordered pair as "x is preferred to y." If we wish, we may use symbols such as $x \bigcirc y$ or $x \, P \, y$. If we want to stress that this is Mr. A's ordering, we may write it as $x \bigcirc_A y$ or $x \, P_A \, y$.

In general, a (**binary**) **relation** is a mathematical concept which is a set of ordered pairs (x, y). If R is a relation, we can write $(x, y) \in R$. This is also written as "$x \, R \, y$," and we say that x **is R-related to** y. More intuitively, "relation" is defined on a certain set—say, X—such that the statement $x \, R \, y$, where R is a verbal phrase such as "is not worse than," is meaningful in the sense that it can be classified definitely as "true" or "false." For example, if X is the set of all positive integers, we can define a relation by interpreting R as "is less than"; that is, $x \, R \, y$ means $x < y$ where x and y are positive integers.

Definition: A relation R on X is called a (**partial**) **quasi-ordering**, or (**partial**) **pre-ordering**, if it satisfies

(i) $x \, R \, x$ for every $x \in X$ (**reflexivity**).
(ii) $x \, R \, y$ and $y \, R \, z$ imply $x \, R \, z$ where $x, y, z \in X$ (**transitivity**).

If, in addition, $x \, R \, y$ and $y \, R \, x$ imply "$x = y$," then the relation is called a **partial ordering** or simply an **ordering**. Furthermore, if in a quasi-ordering R on X, we necessarily have either $x \, R \, y$ or $y \, R \, x$ for arbitrary elements $x, y \, (x \neq y)$ of X, we call R a **total quasi-ordering** or a **complete quasi-ordering**. Similarly, we can define **total ordering**.

Definition: A relation R on X is called an **equivalence relation** if it satisfies (i) and (ii) above (that is, reflexivity and transitivity) *and*

(iii) $x \, R \, y$ implies $y \, R \, x$ (**symmetry**).

In other words, an equivalence relation is a quasi-ordering which is symmetric. An equivalence relation is denoted by $x \sim y$.

EXAMPLE: The relation "is not less than" (that is $\geqq$) defined on the set of positive integers is a total ordering. The relation "is equal to" is an equivalence relation. If X is the set of all fractions a/b where a and b are integers with $b \neq 0$, then we can define the equivalence relation by saying that $a/b \sim c/d \, (d \neq 0)$ whenever $ad = bc$ holds, where ad and bc are integers in the usual sense (for instance, $\frac{1}{2} \sim \frac{2}{4}$). The preference relation "is not worse than" (denoted by $\bigcirc$) can be a quasi-ordering which is not necessarily an ordering. The relation $\bigcirc$ is often assumed to be total, but this is not necessarily the case. In fact, $\bigcirc$ can even fail to be a (partial) quasi-ordering by missing the transitivity axiom.[3] The preference relation "is indifferent to" can be an example of an equivalence relation.[4] If $X = R^n$ and if we define $x \geq y$ for x, $y \in R^n$ by $x_i \geq y_i$, $i = 1, 2, \ldots, n$, this relation $\geq$ is a partial ordering which is not total.

NOTATION: We use the following notations for the "preference ordering."[5]

(a) **x is preferred to y**: $x \bigcirc\!\!\!> y$ or $y \bigcirc\!\!\!< x$.
(b) **x is not preferred to y**: $x \bigcirc\!\!\!\leq y$ or $y \bigcirc\!\!\!\geq x$.
(c) **x is indifferent to y**: $x \ominus y$ or $y \ominus x$.

If we wish to indicate the individual (say, i) for whom the preference ordering holds, we write

$$ x \bigcirc\!\!\!>_i y, \quad x \bigcirc\!\!\!\geq_i y, \quad x \ominus_i y $$

REMARK: In the "usual" theory of consumer's choice, the preference ordering of a consumer is assumed to be defined on a consumption set whose elements consist of his own consumption bundles alone. That is, his preference ordering is independent of the consumption bundles of other people and of the pattern of production, and so on. This is clearly a strong restriction imposed on the preference ordering, although it is known to be powerful enough to produce important results. The preference ordering with this restriction is called **selfish** or **individualistic**, as mentioned in Section A.

REMARK: Figure 2.2 may be useful for the understanding of the above concepts.

Definition: Let X be the consumption set of a given individual and let $\hat{x} \in X$. Then

(i) The set $\{x : x \in X, x \bigcirc\!\!\!\geq \hat{x}\}$ is called the **no-worse-than-$\hat{x}$ set** or the **upper contour set of $\hat{x}$**.
(ii) The set $\{x : x \in X, x \bigcirc\!\!\!\leq \hat{x}\}$ is called the **not-better-than-$\hat{x}$ set** or the **lower contour set of $\hat{x}$**.

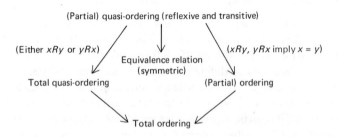

Figure 2.2. Relations among Various Orderings.

(iii) The set $\{x: x \in X, x \bigcirc \hat{x}\}$ is called the **preferred-to-$\hat{x}$ set**, or the **better-than-$\hat{x}$ set**.

(iv) The set $\{x: x \in X, x \bigcirc \hat{x}\}$ is called the **worse-than-$\hat{x}$ set**.

(v) The set $\{x: x \in X, x \bigcirc \hat{x}\}$ is called the **indifferent-to-$\hat{x}$ set** or the **indifference set** of $\hat{x}$.

c. UTILITY FUNCTION

Let X be the consumption set of a particular individual (say, Mr. A), and let us suppose that Mr. A's satisfaction from consumption can be expressed by an index which is a real number. This is called his **utility index**. The utility index is a function from X into R where R is the set of real numbers. This function, denoted by $u(x)$, is called the **utility function** (of Mr. A). Since the set of real numbers has the natural ordering $\geq$ or $>$, this amounts to assuming that Mr. A's preference is **representable** by the natural order of real numbers.[6] In other words,

(i) $x \bigcirc y$ if and only if $u(x) \geq u(y)$,
(ii) $x \bigcirc y$ if and only if $u(x) > u(y)$, and
(iii) $x \bigcirc y$ if and only if $u(x) = u(y)$.

The fundamental characteristic of such a utility function is that it can be replaced by any of its monotone increasing function without altering anything substantial (that is, ordering). In other words, if Φ is a real-valued function such that

$$\Phi(u^1) \gtreqless \Phi(u^2) \text{ according to whether } u^1 \gtreqless u^2$$

then

(i) $x \bigcirc y$ if and only if $\Phi[u(x)] \geq \Phi[u(y)]$.
(ii) $x \bigcirc y$ if and only if $\Phi[u(x)] > \Phi[u(y)]$.
(iii) $x \bigcirc y$ if and only if $\Phi[u(x)] = \Phi[u(y)]$.

Classical consumer's theory assumes that the consumption set is the non-negative orthant of R^n and a utility (index) function $u(x)$ is defined on this.[7] In the diagrammatical analysis, which is so common in the traditional analysis, the concept of an "indifference curve" is used. The indifference curve is the locus of $x = (x_1, x_2)$ on R^2 such that $u(x) = $ constant. Traditionally, indifference curves are drawn convex to the origin, indicating a diminishing marginal rate of substitution between the two commodities.[8] It is generally supposed that $u(x)$ increases as each element of x increases. However, this does not have to be true. It may so happen that a consumer is satiated with some commodity—say, i_0—at an amount—say, $x_{i_0}^*$—so that $u(x) \leq u(x^*)$ where $x_i = x_i^*$ for all $i \neq i_0$ and for all x_{i_0} with $x_{i_0} > x_{i_0}^*$. Note that it is possible to have $u(x) < u(x^*)$, that is, the utility may actually decrease beyond a certain level of consumption (for example, the amount of light in a room). Moreover, we may also question whether $u(x, y) = $ constant can define a unique curve, say, $x = v(y)$. It is possible that we can have "thick" indifference

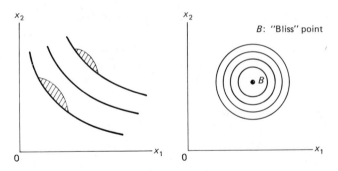

Figure 2.3. Illustration of Indifference "Curves."

loci. In Figure 2.3 we illustrate such indifference "curves." On the left, the indifference curves take the customary shape except that some of them contain "thick" portions. On the right, we illustrate indifference curves for which $u(x)$ is *not* monotone increasing with respect to a coordinate-wise increase in x.

The question will arise as to whether we can represent the preference ordering $\gtreqless$ (say, for Mr. A) by a utility function (that is, by real numbers).

This question was first solved by Debreu [3], [4] and later generalized by Rader [9]. To state Debreu's theorem, we need the following two concepts.

Definition: Let X be a topological space. Then X is called a **connected set** if it cannot be represented as the union of two disjoint, nonempty, open sets.

> *REMARK:* From the definition it follows that X is connected if and only if the only subsets of X which are both open and closed are X itself and the empty set $\emptyset$. A subset S of X becomes a topological space with the relative topology of S. The set S is called **connected** (subset of X) if it is connected as a topological space with the relative topology. Hence it follows that S is connected if and only if it cannot be partitioned into two disjoint nonempty subsets of X which are open in S with respect to the relative topology. Intuitively speaking, a set is connected if it is of "one piece" (but possibly with holes).

Definition: A preference ordering $\gtreqless$ on X is called **continuous** or **closed** if for every $\hat{x} \in X$, the two sets $\{x: x \in X, x \gtreqless \hat{x}\}$ and $\{x: x \in X, x \lesseqgtr \hat{x}\}$ are both closed sets. In other words, if $\{x^q\}$ is a sequence in X with $x^q \gtreqless \hat{x}$ for all q (resp. $x^q \lesseqgtr \hat{x}$ for all q), then $x^q \to x^0$ implies $x^0 \gtreqless \hat{x}$ (resp. $x^0 \lesseqgtr \hat{x}$).[9]

We are now ready to state Debreu's theorem.

Theorem 2.B.1 (Debreu): *Let X be a connected subset of R^n and let $\gtreqless$ be a continuous total quasi-ordering defined on X. Then there exists a continuous utility function on X for $\gtreqless$.*[10]

REMARK: A well-known example of a preference ordering which is *not* representable by a real-valued function is the **lexicographic ordering.**[11] The lexicographic ordering can be illustrated in R^2 by

$x \bigcirc\!\!\!> y$ if $x_1 > y_1$ *or* if $x_2 > y_2$ with $x_1 = y_1$

$x \bigcirc\!\!\!- y$ if and only if $x = y$, where $x = (x_1, x_2)$ and $y = (y_1, y_2)$

In other words, in the lexicographic ordering, preference ordering is arranged according to the dictionary rule. The British Treasury may have a lexicographic ordering for its employees in the sense that it always prefers the Oxbridge graduates to others and the American Defense Department may have a lexicographic ordering for its employees in the sense that it always prefers noncommunists to communists. The upper contour set (of $\hat{x}$) with the above lexicographic ordering is illustrated by the shaded area in Figure 2.4. Clearly it is not a closed set, for it does not contain the dotted line. Obviously we can consider a more general lexicographic ordering of which the upper contour set (of $\hat{x}$) can be illustrated by the shaded area in Figure 2.5. For discussions on lexicographic orderings, see Georgescue-Roegen [5], and Chipman [2].

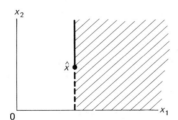

Figure 2.4.   A Lexicographic Ordering.

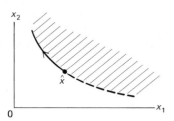

Figure 2.5.   A More General Lexicographic Ordering.

d.   THE CONVEXITY OF PREFERENCE ORDERING

Given a preference ordering $\bigcirc\!\!\!\geqq$ (hence $\bigcirc\!\!\!>$ and $\bigcirc\!\!\!-$ are also given) on X, we may define the following relations *on the assumption that X is a convex set.*[12] For any two points x and y in X we may have

(i) $x \bigcirc\!\!\!\geqq y$ implies $tx + (1 - t)y \bigcirc\!\!\!\geqq y, 0 < t < 1$, where $x \neq y$.

(ii) $x \bigcirc\!\!\!> y$ implies $tx + (1 - t)y \bigcirc\!\!\!> y, 0 < t < 1$, where $x \neq y$.

(iii) $x \ominus y$ implies $tx + (1 - t)y \oslash y, 0 < t < 1$, where $x \neq y$.

(iv) $x \ominus y$ implies $tx + (1 - t)y \oslash y, 0 < t < 1$.

A preference ordering is called **weakly convex** if (i) holds; it is called **convex** if (ii) and (iv) hold; and it is called **strictly convex** if (ii) and (iii) hold.[13] These preference orderings are illustrated by the indifference curves in Figure 2.6. Note that a weakly convex preference ordering allows a "thick" indifference curve (band) and a convex preference ordering allows a "flat" indifference curve. For a discussion of the relationship among these convexities, see Debreu [4] section 4.7. We may note that if the preference ordering is representable by a real-valued function (utility function), then the strict quasi-concavity of the utility function corresponds to the strict convexity of the preference ordering and the quasi-concavity of the utility function corresponds to the weak convexity of the preference ordering. The explicit quasi-concavity of the utility function corresponds to the convexity of the preference ordering.

REMARK:[14]

1. Condition (i) implies that all the upper contour sets of X must be convex.
2. If the preference ordering is continuous, then (ii) implies (i).
3. If the preference ordering is continuous, then (iii) implies (ii).

REMARK: In showing that the behavior of consumers without transitive preferences is compatible with most results in the theory of competitive equilibria, Sonnenschein [12] had to rely on a rather strong assumption that all the upper contour sets of X are convex. However, it is also true that in proving major theorems of the competitive equilibrium theory, such an assumption is required. The reason why only the convexity is required in place of the transitivity can be seen (intuitively) from the following example in [12] (p. 216). Suppose that X contains three points x, y, and z with $x \oslash y \oslash z \oslash x$. Then any budget set which contains these three points may

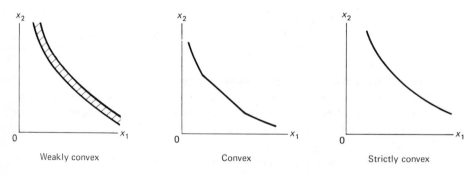

Figure 2.6.   Illustrations of the Convexity of Preference Ordering.

not contain any optimal consumption plan. However, the convexity of preferences ensures the existence of points in the budget set which are preferred to all three.

FOOTNOTES

1. As long as we consider a single consumer, the assumption that the origin denotes a minimum (subsistence) level of consumption is not as strong as it appears. If $\{x \in R^n : x \geq \bar{x} > 0\}$ is his consumption set, then by moving the origin properly, we can obtain the origin as a minimum level of subsistence. His consumption set may be denoted by $\{y \in R^n : y \geq 0\}$ where $y \equiv x - \bar{x}$. However, if we consider more than one consumer, then it involves the assumption that the minimum subsistence levels of consumption are identical for all consumers.

2. In the analysis of consumer's behavior, it is well known that the different characteristics of the commodities play an important role. For example, a consumer may consider a blue Valiant to be a different commodity from a red Valiant even if all other specifications are the same. Kelvin Lancaster, therefore, has recently proposed a "new approach to consumer theory" by emphasizing the "different characteristics" aspect of the commodities. See his "New Approach to Consumer Theory," *Journal of Political Economy*, LXXIV, April 1966. However, he apparently assumes that these characteristics are measurable quantities; see, for example, his phrase "the amount of the ith characteristic" (p. 135). When the consumption set is considered to be a subset of R^n, we have to be careful that anything measured on each coordinate is representable by real numbers. The characteristics cannot be represented by real numbers regardless of whether such a representation is ordinal or cardinal. A statement such as "the quantities of the characteristics are directly proportional to the quantities of the goods" is thus meaningless.

3. That $\geq$ is total means that the consumer can give his preference ordering $\geq$ for any two elements of his consumption set. Its plausibility is sometimes questioned, for some of the decisions in the consumption set might involve highly hypothetical situations which our consumer never faces in real life. In such cases, he cannot make any decisions. It is known that many theorems can be proved without this axiom. A still more questionable axiom involved in regarding the preference ordering as a total quasi-ordering may be the transitivity axiom. For example, we can show that the relation $\geq$ on $X = \{x \in R : x \geq 0\}$ defined by $x' \geq x$ if and only if $x' \geq x - 1$ is intransitive. The existence of thick regions of indifference would often cause intransitivity of $\geq$. The intransitivity can be quite normal. See K.O. May, "Transitivity, Utility, and Aggregation in Preference Patterns," *Econometrica*, 22, 1954, for example. In a remarkable paper [12], Sonnenschein showed that the transitivity axiom can be dispensed with in proving many important results of the theory of competitive equilibrium.

4. However, the relation "is different to" can be intransitive. In that case, it cannot be an equivalence relation.

5. Given the consumption set X of a particular individual, we do not have to define $\otimes$, $\geq$, $\ominus$, $\oslash$, $\odot$ all independently. We may first define $\geq$ as a total quasi-ordering on X; then define $\ominus$ by $x \geq y$ and $y \geq x$; $\otimes$ is defined by $x \geq y$ but not $y \geq x$; $x \odot y$ is defined by $y \geq x$; and $x \oslash y$ is defined by $y \otimes x$.

6. The preference ordering represented by real numbers is obviously transitive, for the natural order of the real numbers is transitive.

7. Note that this assumes that the preference ordering of the consumer is individualistic.

In general, we should write individual i's utility function, u_i, as $u_i(x^1, x^2, \ldots, x^i, \ldots, x^m)$, $x^i \in X_i$, $i = 1, 2, \ldots, m$, where X_i is individual i's consumption set.

8. Note that if the utility function is replaceable by its monotone increasing transformation, then the classical concept of "marginal utility" becomes rather meaningless, although the concept of marginal rate of substitution can still be meaningful. Consider a differentiable utility function $u(x)$ and a differentiable monotone transformation Φ (where $\Phi' > 0$). Then clearly we have $(\partial u/\partial x_i)/(\partial u/\partial x_j) = (\partial \Phi[u]/\partial x_i)/(\partial \Phi[u]/\partial x_j)$.

9. It can be shown that we can restate this (in an equivalent form) as follows: Let $\{x^q\}$ and $\{\bar{x}^q\}$ be two sequences in X such that $x^q \to x$ and $\bar{x}^q \to \bar{x}$. Suppose $\bar{x}^q \gtrapprox x^q$ for all q; then $\bar{x} \gtrapprox x$.

10. Rader [9] relaxed the transitivity assumption involved in Debreu's theorem.

11. For the proof, see Debreu [4], pp. 72–73.

12. As remarked before, this requires, among other things, that all commodities are perfectly divisible.

13. The following quotation from J. S. Chipman might be of some use in understanding the significance of the convexity of preference.

> Two pillars form the foundations of economic activity. One is the law of convexity of preferences, which states that people desire to consume a variety— or average—of products rather than limit their consumption to any one commodity alone. . . .

See his "The Nature and Meaning of Equilibrium in Economic Theory," in *Functionalism in the Social Sciences*, Philadelphia, Pa., American Academy of Political and Social Science, February 1965, p. 35.

14. For the proofs, see Debreu [4], pp. 60–61.

REFERENCES

1. Birkoff, G., *Lattice Theory*, rev. ed., Providence, R. I., American Mathematical Society, 1961.

2. Chipman, J. S., "Foundations of Utility," *Econometrica*, 28, April 1960.

3. Debreu, G., "Representation of Preference Ordering by a Numerical Function," in *Decision Processes*, ed. by Thrall, Coombs, and Davis, New York, Wiley, 1954, pp. 159–165.

4. ———, *Theory of Value*, New York, Wiley, 1959.

5. Georgescu-Roegen, N., "Choice Expectations, and Measurability," *Quarterly Journal of Economics*, 58, November 1954.

6. Hicks, J. R., *Value and Capital*, 2nd ed., Oxford, Clarendon Press, 1946.

7. Koopmans, T. C., *Three Essays on the State of Economic Science*, New York, McGraw-Hill, 1957.

8. Kuratowski, K., *Introduction to Set Theory and Topology*, Oxford, Pergamon Press, 1961 (tr. from Polish original).

9. Rader, T., "Existence of a Utility Function to Represent Preferences," *Review of Economic Studies*, 30, October 1963.

10. Richter, M. K., "Revealed Preference Theory," *Econometrica*, 34, July 1966.

11. Sonnenschein, H. F., "The Relationship between Transitive Preference and the Structure of the Choice Space," *Econometrica*, 33, July 1965.

12. ———, "Demand Theory without Transitive Preferences, with Applications to the Theory of Competitive Equilibrium," in *Preferences, Utility, and Demand: A Minnesota Symposium*, ed. by J. S. Chipman, L. Hurwicz, M. K. Richter, and H. F. Sonnenschein, New York, Harcourt Brace Jovanovich, 1971.

Section C

THE TWO CLASSICAL PROPOSITIONS OF WELFARE ECONOMICS

When we discussed activity analysis in Chapter 0, we proved that a point in the production set which maximizes profit under a certain "price" vector is an efficient point and that we can associate a price vector with every efficient point such that it becomes a profit maximization point. (For the latter, we needed the convexity of the production set.) In a competitive market, every producer is a price taker—that is, he cannot affect the prices which prevail in the market—and he must maximize his profit under the given price vector. The above results from activity analysis indicate a strong relationship between competitive pricing and the efficient point. Before we explore this further, we must recall the behavior of the other important economic unit in this economy, the consumer. In a competitive market, every consumer is a price taker—that is, he cannot affect the prices that prevail in the market—so he maximizes his satisfaction over the bundles of commodities which can be purchased under a given price vector. Assuming that an economy consists of these two basic types of economic units, and assuming that the total supply of commodities is equal to the total demand for commodities, a natural question is whether such an economy achieves a certain optimum of social welfare. The concept of "efficient production point" is concerned with such an optimality concept in production. But this is valid from the society's point of view only if we disregard consumers. What happens if we introduce consumers? When we introduce consumers into our consideration, we immediately recall that an individual's utility cannot be measured[1] so that we cannot add individual utilities to get a measure of social welfare. The search for a concept of social welfare, as is well known, led to the concept of the Pareto optimum, the state in which nobody can be better off without making others worse off, given that the total supply of commodities is equal to total demand for commodities.[2] Since a consumer presumably gets his satisfaction from his consumption activity, the phrases "better off" or "worse off" refer to the welfare of each individual consumer with respect to his preference ordering.

Now the natural question becomes: What is the relationship between "competitive equilibrium" and "Pareto optimum"? In particular, we may be interested in asking whether every competitive equilibrium realizes a Pareto optimum and whether a Pareto optimal state can be achieved and supported by a competitive equilibrium. These are the two main questions in classical welfare economics. If each question can be answered in the affirmative, then we want to know the precise conditions which support each conclusion. This is the task of this section.

Before we start our analysis, we may note that the above questions are not really new in economics. A principal theme of Adam Smith was that "free competition" realizes a "social optimum." Obviously, Smith did not have precise concepts of "free competition" and "social optimum."

There have been many attempts in the history of economics to formalize the above theme. The Ricardian theory of comparative advantage is probably the first such attempt to be successful in connection with productive efficiency. Wicksell [23] gave a formulation of how perfect competition maximizes production, which corresponds to the results from activity analysis mentioned above. The concept of the Pareto optimum is due to Pareto but was apparently introduced at the insistence of his friends, Pantaleoni and Barone. Pareto perceived the Pareto optimum significance of a competitive equilibrium (for this point, see Samuelson [22], pp. 212–214). Apparently it is Barone [3] who first stated exactly and proved that a competitive equilibrium, under quite general conditions, realizes a Pareto optimum.[3]

A somewhat converse proposition, that is, that a Pareto optimum state is supported by a competitive equilibrium, also came from Pareto and from Barone [3], Lange [14], Lerner [16], and others. Combined with the previous proposition, these two propositions constitute the so-called "fundamental theorems of welfare economics."

The studies of these propositions in the 1930s and 1940s by Lerner [15], [16], Lange [14], Hicks [8], Samuelson [22], and others are characterized by their recognition of the relationship between the marginal equivalences and a competitive equilibrium.

The first rigorous formulation and proof of these propositions using a modern set-theoretic approach was carried out by Arrow [1] and Debreu [4] and has been further generalized by Debreu [5], Moore [17], and so forth. The revolutionary character of this development is analogous to the advance from the traditional production function approach in production theory to the activity analysis approach (see Chapter 0, Section C). Our discussion in this section is based on the modern version. The author has greatly benefited from excellent expositions by Koopmans [12], and Koopmans and Bausch [13].

Before we turn to this modern approach, we may illustrate the problem by a simple diagram. Figure 2.7 illustrates the choice of a competitive consumer, whose consumption set is the nonnegative orthant of R^2. If he is faced with a price vector

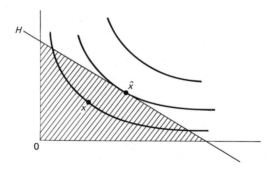

Figure 2.7.   Rational Consumer and Price Line.

indicated by the line H (in which the price of each commodity is positive), and if he has chosen the point $\hat{x}$, then, assuming that he is a "rational" consumer, we can immediately conclude that he must be maximizing his satisfaction over the points such as x, in the nonnegative orthant, which are on or below the line H (the shaded region).[4] *No* point in the shaded region costs more than $\hat{x}$ under this price line H.

Now consider an economy which consists of two consumers but no producers. The consumers exchange commodities with each other. Assuming that there are only two commodities in the economy and assuming also that each consumer's consumption set is the nonnegative orthant of R^2, the well-known Edgeworth-Bowley box diagram can be drawn. Any allocation of commodities between the two consumers is possible as long as the point which represents such an allocation stays inside or on the boundary of the box ("feasibility condition").[5] In Figure 2.8, point R, for example, is not a Pareto optimal point, because it is possible to improve one person's welfare without decreasing the other person's welfare simply by moving within the "lens" formed by the indifference curves of the two in-

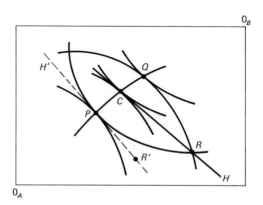

Figure 2.8.   An Illustration of the Two Classical Propositions.

dividuals which pass through R. However, any point on the curve PQ is a Pareto optimal point. Clearly, point C is a competitive equilibrium if the price indicated by H prevails, for each person maximizes his satisfaction in the sense described above. Note that at point C the price line is tangent to each person's indifference curve. In fact, this tangency condition is sufficient to guarantee that each person maximizes his satisfaction in the sense described above.

As it can easily be seen from Figure 2.8 and as is well known, any Pareto optimal point in the ordinary box diagram is a point at which the indifference curves of the two individuals are tangent. (The collection of such points is called the **contract curve**.) As was seen above, any competitive equilibrium point must be on a line which is tangent to the indifference curve of the individual and it must be at the point of tangency.[6] Hence it follows immediately that any competitive equilibrium point realizes a Pareto optimum.

Note also that at any Pareto optimal point (that is, any point on the contract curve), it is possible to draw a line which is tangent to an indifference curve for *each* consumer. At point C, H is such a line, and at point P, H' is such a line. Representing the price vector by the slope of such a line, we can at once conclude that every Pareto optimal point can be achieved and supported by competitive pricing.[7]

Note that the above statement does not say that any Pareto optimal point can be achieved by competitive pricing after starting from any arbitrary initial point. For example, if point R represents the initial resource point, point C can be achieved by pure exchange, with each individual acting as a competitive consumer —that is, a price taker—under a price line H. But point P *cannot* be achieved directly from R. It requires some reshuffling of goods so that point R is translated to a point such as R' on the H' line.

The above "proofs" of the two classical propositions of welfare economics look very simple, but they rely on many implicit assumptions. In fact, this is a prime example of traditional economic theory, whose reasoning is so crucially dependent on the diagram. We may ask the following questions, for example.

(i)   How crucial is the assumption that the consumption set is the entire non-negative orthant?

(ii)   Is it necessary to assume the convexity of each consumer's consumption set; and how essential is the divisibility assumption of each commodity?

(iii)   Does the consumption set of every consumer have to include the *same* list of n commodities?

(iv)   Does an individual's indifference curve have to be (strictly) convex to the origin?

(v)   Does it have to be smooth? [Or is it necessary that we can define a *unique* tangent line (such as H) for the individual's indifference curve?]

(vi)   Do we have to assume the continuity of the individual's utility function (if its differentiability can be dispensed with)?

(vii)   What is the role of consumer's satiation in the above analysis?

(viii)   What happens if the price line which should support a Pareto optimum coincides with one of the edges of the box? Can we still have a competitive equilibrium?

(ix) What happens if we introduce production? What assumptions are necessary when production is introduced into the model?

(x) Will the conclusions be altered if there are more than two consumers and two commodities and if there is an arbitrary number of producers?

(xi) What is the minimum possible set of assumptions which will guarantee all the conclusions of the classical propositions?

Although we may get considerable insight into the above questions from Figure 2.8,[8] nothing precise and definite can be said on the basis of it alone. Here we may quote the following remark from Koopmans ([12], p. 174):

> Nothing in the process of reading a diagram forces the full statement of assumptions and the stepwise advance, through successive implications to conclusions that are characteristic of logical reasoning. Assumptions may be concealed in the manner in which the curves are "usually" drawn and conclusions may be accepted unconditionally although they actually depend on such unstated assumptions.

We now turn to the modern formulation and the proof of the above classical propositions of welfare economics. The author hopes that the reader will fully appreciate the above remark by Koopmans in the process of reading the following exposition of the modern approach to welfare economics. In the following, we use the minimal possible assumptions which are known at present.[9] Any relaxation of assumptions will be interesting and important. Some important counter-examples will be offered when some of the assumptions are violated. Diagrams will be useful to show such counterexamples.

Let x_i be an n-vector of consumption by consumer $i(i = 1, 2, \ldots, m)$, and let y_j be an n-vector of production by producer $j(j = 1, 2, \ldots, k)$. The negative elements of y_j denote inputs and the positive elements of y_j denote outputs. Let $x \equiv \sum_{i=1}^{m} x_i$ and $y \equiv \sum_{j=1}^{k} y_j$. Denote by X_i the consumption set of i and by Y_j the production set of j. We assume that both X_i and Y_j are subsets of R^n. We denote by X the aggregate consumption set and by Y the aggregate production set.[10] We assume that the preference ordering $\succcurlyeq_i$ is defined for each consumption set X_i.[11] Given price p, the profit of producer j can be written as $p \cdot y_j$. There is an initial bundle of commodities available in the economy. We denote it by $\bar{x}$. This bundle of commodities can be held by consumers so that if we denote the initial resource held by the ith consumer by $\bar{x}_i$, then $\sum_{i=1}^{m} \bar{x}_i = \bar{x}$.

We now define (in the usual manner) feasibility, Pareto optimum, and competitive equilibrium.

Definition (feasibility): An array of consumption vectors $\{x_i\}$ is said to be **feasible** if there exists an array of production vectors $\{y_j\}$ such that $x = y + \bar{x}$.

Definition (Pareto optimality):   A *feasible* $\{\hat{x}_i\}$ is said to be **Pareto optimal (P.O.)** if there does not exist a feasible $\{x_i'\}$ such that x_i' $\textcircled{\geq}_i$ $\hat{x}_i$ for all $i = 1, 2, \ldots, m$ with $\textcircled{>}_i$ for at least one i.

Definition (competitive equilibrium):   An array of vectors $[\hat{p}, \{\hat{x}_i\}, \{\hat{y}_j\}]$ is called a **competitive equilibrium (C.E.)**, if $\hat{x}_i \in X_i, i = 1, 2, \ldots, m, \hat{y}_j \in Y_j, j = 1, 2, \ldots, k$, *and*

(i) $\hat{x}_i$ $\textcircled{\geq}_i$ x_i for all $x_i \in X_i$ such that $\hat{p} \cdot x_i \leq \hat{p} \cdot \hat{x}_i$,
        $i = 1, 2, \ldots, m$ (consumer's equilibrium)
(ii) $\hat{p} \cdot \hat{y}_j \geq \hat{p} \cdot y_j$ for all $y_j \in Y_j$,
        $j = 1, 2, \ldots, k$ (profit maximization)
(iii) $\hat{x} = \hat{y} + \bar{x}$ (feasibility)

REMARK: In the definition of feasibility above, we required the equality $\hat{x} = \hat{y} + \bar{x}$. In the literature, this is often replaced by $\hat{x} \leq \hat{y} + \bar{x}$, allowing an excess supply of commodities. This implicitly or explicitly assumes "free disposability" of commodities.[12] If free disposability is assumed, it is necessary that the price vector $\hat{p}$ in the definition of competitive equilibrium be nonnegative. We do not assume free disposability; hence the "undesired commodity" cannot be freely disposed of and its price will be negative. Under the free disposability assumption, not only do we require $\hat{x} \leq \hat{y} + \bar{x}$ for feasibility, but we also change condition (iii) of the definition of competitive equilibrium as follows:

(iii') $\hat{x} \leq \hat{y} + \bar{x}, \hat{p} \cdot (\hat{y} + \bar{x} - \hat{x}) = 0$, and $\hat{p} \geq 0$

The second relation in (iii') states that if there is an excess supply of some commodity, its price must be zero. As we will see shortly, the case $\hat{p} = 0$ will be precluded, under the assumption that $\hat{x}_i$ is a "local nonsatiation chosen point."

Definition (chosen point):   When price $\hat{p}$ prevails, a point $\hat{x}_i \in X_i$ is called a **chosen point** of the *i*th consumer, if

$$\hat{x}_i \textcircled{\geq}_i x_i \text{ for all } x_i \in X_i \text{ with } \hat{p} \cdot x_i \leq \hat{p} \cdot \hat{x}_i$$

Definition (local nonsatiation point):   A point $x_i \in X_i$ is called a **local nonsatiation point**, if there exists a $\delta > 0$ with $B_\delta(x_i) \cap (X_i \setminus x_i) \neq \emptyset$ such that for any $\epsilon, 0 < \epsilon < \delta$, with $B_\epsilon(x_i) \cap (X_i \setminus x_i) \neq \emptyset$, we have $x_i' \textcircled{>}_i x_i$ for some $x_i' \in B_\epsilon(x_i) \cap X_i$, where $B_\delta(x_i)$ and $B_\epsilon(x_i)$ are open balls with center x_i and radii δ and ϵ, respectively.

REMARK: The above definition of "local nonsatiation point" *assumes* that there exists at least one commodity which is divisible (since ϵ, the radius of the ball, can be *any* real number with $0 < \epsilon < \delta$)[13] and that the consumer is

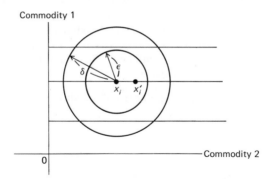

Figure 2.9.   An Illustration of the Local Nonsatiation Point.

"not satiated" with respect to this divisible commodity at point x_i (that is, there exists a point such as $x_i' \ominus_i x_i$ for each ϵ). Figure 2.9 illustrates the case in which one commodity is perfectly divisible and the other commodity is indivisible.[14] The consumption set here is assumed to be the collection of the horizontal lines in the nonnegative orthant.

REMARK: Suppose $\hat{x}_i$ is a chosen point under $\hat{p}$ so that $\hat{x}_i \ominus_i x_i$ for all $x_i \in X_i$ with $\hat{p} \cdot x_i \leq \hat{p} \cdot \hat{x}_i$. Then $\hat{p}$ can*not* be a zero vector if $\hat{x}_i$ is a local nonsatiation point. (For if $\hat{p} = 0$, then $\hat{p} \cdot x_i \leq \hat{p} \cdot \hat{x}_i$ holds for any $x_i \in X_i$.)

Definition (locally nonsaturating $\geqq_i$):   The preference ordering $\geqq_i$ is called **locally nonsaturating** if, given any local nonsatiation point x_i, $x_i' \ominus_i x_i$ implies that x_i' is also a local nonsatiation point.

We now introduce the following assumption.

(A-1) The preference ordering $\geqq_i$ is locally nonsaturating for every consumer.

REMARK: This assumption presupposes that there exists at least one perfectly divisible commodity.

Lemma: *Let $\hat{x}_i$ be a locally nonsatiating chosen point for the ith consumer when price $\hat{p}$ prevails. Then under (A-1),*

(i)   *$x_i \oslash_i \hat{x}_i$ implies $\hat{p} \cdot x_i > \hat{p} \cdot \hat{x}_i$.*
(ii) *$x_i \ominus_i \hat{x}_i$ implies $\hat{p} \cdot x_i \geqq \hat{p} \cdot \hat{x}_i$.*

PROOF:
(i)   Suppose not; that is, $\hat{p} \cdot x_i \leqq \hat{p} \cdot \hat{x}_i$. Since $\hat{x}_i$ is a chosen point, $\hat{x}_i \ominus_i x_i$, which is a contradiction.
(ii) Let $x_i \ominus_i \hat{x}_i$ and suppose that $\hat{p} \cdot x_i < \hat{p} \cdot \hat{x}_i$. Since $\hat{x}_i$ is not a point of

local satiation, neither is x_i [by (A-1)]. Hence for all ϵ, $0 < \epsilon < \delta$, there exists $x_i' \in X_i$ and $x_i' \in B_\epsilon(x_i)$ such that $x_i' \bigcirc_i x_i$, which in turn implies $x_i \bigcirc_i \hat{x}_i$ by the transitivity of the preference ordering.[15] We may choose x_i' close enough to x_i so that $\hat{p} \cdot x_i' < \hat{p} \cdot \hat{x}_i$ (which is possible because the value function $\hat{p} \cdot x_i$ is continuous). This contradicts the assumption that $\hat{x}_i$ is a chosen point under $\hat{p}$.   (Q.E.D.)

REMARK: The proof of statement (ii) of the above lemma can be illustrated by Figure 2.10.

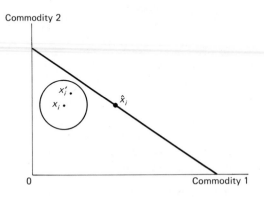

Commodity 2

0   Commodity 1

Figure 2.10.   An Illustration of the Lemma $(X = \Omega^2)$.

REMARK: The reader should realize that the choice of x_i' *close* enough to $\hat{x}_i$ so that $\hat{p} \cdot x_i' < \hat{p} \cdot \hat{x}_i$ needs the assumption that there exists at least one commodity which is divisible.

Theorem 2.C.1:   *Let* $[\hat{p}, \{\hat{x}_i\}, \{\hat{y}_j\}]$ *be a competitive equilibrium such that* $\hat{x}_i$ *is a local nonsatiation point for all* $i = 1, 2, \ldots, m$. *Suppose assumption (A-1) holds for all* i. *Then* $[\{\hat{x}_i\}, \{\hat{y}_j\}]$ *is a Pareto optimum.*

PROOF: Suppose $[\{\hat{x}_i\}, \{\hat{y}_j\}]$ is *not* a Pareto optimum. Then there exist $[\{x_i\}, \{y_j\}]$ such that $x_i \in X_i$, $i = 1, 2, \ldots, m$, $y_j \in Y_j$, $j = 1, 2, \ldots, k$, *and*

(i) $x = y + \bar{x}$ (feasibility)
(ii) $x_i \bigcirc_i \hat{x}_i$ for all $i = 1, 2, \ldots, m$
(iii) $x_i \bigcirc_i \hat{x}_i$ for some i

Hence from the previous lemma we have

$$\sum_{i=1}^{m} \hat{p} \cdot x_i > \sum_{i=1}^{m} \hat{p} \cdot \hat{x}_i \quad \text{or} \quad \hat{p} \cdot x > \hat{p} \cdot \hat{x}$$

But condition (iii) of C.E. requires $\hat{p} \cdot \hat{x} = \hat{p} \cdot \hat{y} + \hat{p} \cdot \bar{x}$. Hence we have

$\hat{p} \cdot x > \hat{p} \cdot \hat{y} + \hat{p} \cdot \bar{x}$. Condition (ii) of C.E. requires $\hat{p} \cdot \hat{y}_j \geqq \hat{p} \cdot z_j$ for all $z_j \in Y_j$, $j = 1, 2, \ldots, k$. Hence, in particular, $\hat{p} \cdot \hat{y}_j \geqq \hat{p} \cdot y_j$, $j = 1, 2, \ldots, k$. Or, summing over j, $\hat{p} \cdot \hat{y} \geqq \hat{p} \cdot y$. Therefore we now have

$$\hat{p} \cdot x > \hat{p} \cdot y + \hat{p} \cdot \bar{x}$$

or $\hat{p} \cdot (x - y - \bar{x}) > 0$. This contradicts the feasibility of $\{x_i\}$.   (Q.E.D.)

REMARK: Since $\hat{x}_i$ is a local nonsatiating chosen point, we have $\hat{p} \neq 0$.

REMARK: In the proofs of the above theorem and the preceding lemma, no convexity of the preference ordering is assumed.

REMARK: Although Theorem 2.C.1 states that every competitive equilibrium realizes a Pareto optimum under the extremely weak assumption (A-1), it does not say that a competitive equilibrium can *exist* under the same assumption.[16] At present the proof of the existence of competitive equilibrium requires a more stringent set of assumptions. This will be discussed in Section E of this chapter.

REMARK: We may easily construct an example in which a competitive equilibrium does *not* realize a Pareto optimum if $(A\text{-}1)$ is not satisfied. We illustrate this by the Edgeworth-Bowley diagram (Figure 2.11) which deals with a two-person pure exchange economy. In the diagram, 0_A represents the origin for individual A and 0_B represent the origin for individual B. The initial resource point is illustrated by R. The indifference curves are drawn in the ordinary convex fashion. Note that individual A is satiated over and above his indifference curve, and each point in the satiation region (the shaded region) gives him the same level of satisfaction.

Point C is a competitive equilibrium under the price represented by line H. But this point C is *not* a Pareto optimal point, for by moving from point C to point P, individual B certainly can increase his satisfaction without affecting A's satisfaction. (Note that P is a Pareto optimal point.) We may also note that in this example, point C can be achieved from point R

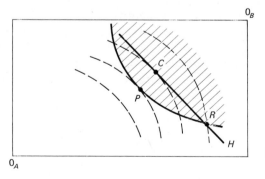

Figure 2.11.   (C.E. $\not\Rightarrow$ P.O.)

by competitive pricing under price line H. We may, however, recall that the above definition of C.E. does not require that point C should be achieved from an arbitrary initial resource point (say, R). The reader should be able to construct an example in which a competitive equilibrium does not realize a Pareto optimum when *none* of the commodities are divisible.[17]

In the above definition of competitive equilibrium, we have not specified how each consumer obtains the income which enables him to purchase commodities with a value of $\hat{p} \cdot \hat{x}_i$. One typical case is that the ith consumer receives the values of his *resources* $\bar{x}_i$ (where $\bar{x}_i \in R^n$ and $\sum_{i=1}^{m} \bar{x}_i = \bar{x}$) and shares θ_{1i}, $\theta_{2i}, \ldots, \theta_{ji}, \ldots, \theta_{ki}$ of the profit of the 1st, $\ldots$, jth, $\ldots$, kth producer (where $\theta_{ji} \in R$ with $\theta_{ji} \geq 0$ and $\sum_{i=1}^{m} \theta_{ji} = 1$). The $\bar{x}_i$'s are the given quantities of the commodities that he owns *a priori*, and θ_{ji} can be interpreted as the fraction of the stock of the jth producer that he owns.

The case thus described can be called the **private ownership economy**. We now wish to relate the definition of a competitive equilibrium as defined above to the competitive equilibrium of the private ownership economy.

Definition (competitive equilibrium of the private ownership economy): An array of vectors $[\hat{p}, \{\hat{x}_i\}, \{\hat{y}_j\}, \{\theta_{ji}\}]$ is a **competitive equilibrium of the private ownership economy (C.E.P.O.E.)** if $\hat{x}_i \in X_i$, $i = 1, 2, \ldots, m$, $\hat{y}_j \in Y_j$, $j = 1, 2, \ldots, k$, *and*

(i) $\hat{x}_i \ominus_i x_i$ for all $x_i \in X_i$ such that $\hat{p} \cdot x_i \leq M_i$, where $M_i = \hat{p} \cdot \bar{x}_i + \sum_{j=1}^{k} \theta_{ji} \hat{p} \cdot \hat{y}_j$, $i = 1, 2, \ldots, m$.

(ii) $\hat{p} \cdot \hat{y}_j \geq \hat{p} \cdot y_j$ for $y_j \in Y_j$, $j = 1, 2, \ldots, k$.

(iii) $\hat{x} = \hat{y} + \bar{x}$.

Clearly if $[\hat{p}, \{\hat{x}_i\}, \{\hat{y}_j\}, \{\theta_{ji}\}]$ is a C.E.P.O.E., then it is a C.E. It is easy to check that every C.E. can be derived from some C.E.P.O.E. This can be done by giving the ith consumer the resources $\bar{x}_i \equiv \hat{x}_i - (1/m)\hat{y}$ and the shares $\theta_{ji} \equiv 1/m$ (observe that $\sum_{i=1}^{m} \theta_{ji} = 1$, $\bar{x} + \hat{y} = \hat{x}$, and so on), where $[\hat{p}, \{\hat{x}_i\}, \{\hat{y}_j\}]$ is a C.E.[18]

We now turn to a deeper or at least a more difficult theorem, that is, a proposition somewhat converse to Theorem 2.C.1. Given the fact that an economy is in a Pareto optimal state, we want to know whether or not there exists a price vector such that it can be supported as a competitive equilibrium with this price vector (allowing a redistribution of ownership of the resources, if necessary). The answer is affirmative under a stronger set of assumptions than that required in Theorem 2.C.1. It will be shown that the crucial tool in establishing such a theorem is the separation theorem and that the slope of the separating hyperplane will give such a price vector. We start our discussion by recalling some definitions introduced in the previous section.

Definition (convex preference ordering): We call a preference $\ominus_i$ on X_i convex if

(i)   The set X_i is convex.

(ii) $x \succ_i x'$ implies $tx + (1 - t) x' \succ_i x'$, for $0 < t < 1$.

(iii) $x \succeq_i x'$ implies $tx + (1 - t) x' \succeq_i x'$, for $0 < t < 1$.

Here i refers to the ith consumer.

REMARK: The convexity of X_i is necessary to make statements (ii) and (iii) of the above definition meaningful. The convexity of X_i presupposes the the *divisibility* of *all* the commodities.

Definition: Let

$$C_i(\hat{x}_i) \equiv \{x_i: x_i \in X_i, x_i \succeq_i \hat{x}_i\}$$
$$\overline{C}_i(\hat{x}_i) \equiv \{x_i: x_i \in X_i, x_i \succ_i \hat{x}_i\}$$

The set $C_i(\hat{x}_i)$ is the **no-worse-than-$\hat{x}_i$ set** for i, and $\overline{C}_i(\hat{x}_i)$ is the **preferred-to-$\hat{x}_i$ set** for i.

REMARK: The convexity of the preference ordering (for i) implies the convexity of $C_i(\hat{x}_i)$ and $\overline{C}_i(\hat{x}_i)$ for all $\hat{x}_i \in X_i$.

We now introduce the following assumptions:

(A-2)   The preference ordering $\succeq_i$ is convex for each $i = 1, 2, \ldots, m$.

(A-3)   The set Y is convex.

(A-4)   **(cheaper-point)**[19] *Given a point $\hat{x}_i$ and a prevailing price vector $\hat{p}$, there exists $x_i' \in X_i$ such that $\hat{p} \cdot x_i' < \hat{p} \cdot \hat{x}_i$.*

(A-5)   **(continuity of $\succeq_i$)** *For each $i = 1, 2, \ldots, m$, the set $\{x_i: x_i \in X_i, x_i \succeq_i x_i'\}$ is closed for all $x_i' \in X_i$ (that is, if $\{x_i^q\}$ is a sequence in X_i such that $x_i^q \succeq_i x_i'$ and $x_i^q \to x_i^0$, then we have $x_i^0 \succeq_i x_i'$).*

REMARK: Assumption (A-3) does *not* require that the production set for each producer (Y_j) be convex. Assumption (A-4) is also called the **minimum wealth assumption.**

Definition (nonsatiation):   The ith consumer is said to be **nonsatiated at $\hat{x}_i$** if there exists an $x_i \in X_i$ such that $x_i \succ_i \hat{x}_i$.

Theorem 2.C.2:   *Suppose that $[\{\hat{x}_i\}, \{\hat{y}_j\}]$ is a Pareto optimum such that at least one consumer is not satiated. Then under assumptions (A-2) and (A-3), there exists a (price) vector $\hat{p} \neq 0$ such that*

(i) $\hat{p} \cdot \hat{x}_i \leq \hat{p} \cdot x_i$ *for all* $x_i \in X_i$ *with* $x_i \succeq_i \hat{x}_i$, $i = 1, 2, \ldots, m$.

(ii) $\hat{p} \cdot \hat{y}_j \geq \hat{p} \cdot y_j$ *for all* $y_j \in Y_j$, $j = 1, 2, \ldots, k$.

(iii) $\hat{x} = \hat{y} + \overline{x}$.

REMARK: This theorem does not require (A-4) and (A-5) but does not quite say that to every Pareto optimum we can adjoin a price vector such that it is supported by C.E. Condition (i) states that each consumer minimizes his expenditure over his no-worse-than-$\hat{x}_i$ set, but it does not necessarily imply the maximization of satisfaction over the budget set. To prove the latter, we use (A-4) and (A-5). We first prove the above theorem.

PROOF: Without loss of generality, we can suppose that the first consumer is nonsatiated (at $\hat{x}_1$). Let $\overline{C}(\hat{x}_1, \hat{x}_2, \ldots, \hat{x}_m) \equiv \overline{C}_1(\hat{x}_1) + \sum_{i=2}^{m} C_i(\hat{x}_i)$. For notational simplicity, we abbreviate $\overline{C}(\hat{x}_1, \hat{x}_2, \ldots, \hat{x}_m)$ by $\overline{C}$. By (A-2), $\overline{C}$ is convex. Let $W = \{w : w = y + \bar{x}, y \in Y\}$. Since Y is convex by (A-3), W is also convex. By the definition of P.O., $z \in \overline{C}$ implies $z \notin W$. Hence $\overline{C}$ and W are two nonempty disjoint convex sets. Hence by the Minkowski separation theorem (Theorem 0.B.3), there exists a $\hat{p} \neq 0$ and a real number α such that

$$\text{(a)}\quad \hat{p} \cdot w \leq \alpha \qquad \text{for all } w \in W$$

and

$$\text{(b)}\quad \hat{p} \cdot z \geq \alpha \qquad \text{for all } z \in \overline{C}$$

We now show that $\hat{p} \cdot \hat{x} = \alpha$.

Since $\hat{x} = \hat{y} + \bar{x}$ and $\hat{y} \in Y$, we have $\hat{x} \in W$, so that $\hat{p} \cdot \hat{x} \leq \alpha$. Suppose $x' \in \overline{C}$; then we can find $x_1' \in \overline{C}_1(\hat{x}_1)$ and $x_i' \in C_i(\hat{x}_i)$, $i = 2, 3, \ldots, m$, such that $x' = \sum_{i=1}^{m} x_i'$. Now let $x_i(t) \equiv t x_i' + (1 - t) \hat{x}_i$, $0 < t < 1$, $i = 1, 2, \ldots, m$, and $x(t) \equiv \sum_{i=1}^{m} x_i(t)$. By (A-2), $x_1(t) \in \overline{C}_1(\hat{x}_1)$ and $x_i(t) \in C_i(\hat{x}_i)$, $i = 2, 3, \ldots, m$. Hence $x(t) \in \overline{C}$. Now suppose that $\hat{p} \cdot \hat{x} < \alpha$. Then from (b) above, we obtain $\hat{p} \cdot z > \hat{p} \cdot \hat{x}$ for all $z \in \overline{C}$. In particular, $\hat{p} \cdot x(t) > \hat{p} \cdot \hat{x}$ for $0 < t < 1$. Since, by choosing t small enough, $x(t)$ can be arbitrarily close to $\hat{x}$, this is a contradiction. Thus we have $\hat{p} \cdot \hat{x} \not< \alpha$. This together with $\hat{p} \cdot \hat{x} \leq \alpha$ gives $\hat{p} \cdot \hat{x} = \alpha$ (that is, the hyperplane separating the two sets W and $\overline{C}$ goes through $\hat{x}$).[20] Hence (a) and (b) may be rewritten as follows:

$$\text{(a')}\quad \hat{p} \cdot w \leq \hat{p} \cdot \hat{x} \qquad \text{for all } w \in W$$

and

$$\text{(b')}\quad \hat{p} \cdot z \geq \hat{p} \cdot \hat{x} \qquad \text{for all } z \in \overline{C}$$

That $w \in W$ means w can be written as $w = \sum_{j=1}^{k} y_j + \bar{x}$ where $y_j \in Y_j, j = 1, 2, \ldots, k$. Therefore, from (a') we obtain

$$\hat{p} \cdot \left[\sum_{j=1}^{k} y_j + \bar{x} \right] \leq \hat{p} \cdot \hat{x}, \qquad \text{for all } y_j \in Y_j, j = 1, 2, \ldots, k$$

But $\hat{x} = \hat{y} + \bar{x}$ (feasibility of P.O.). Hence

$$\hat{p} \cdot \left[\sum_{j=1}^{k} y_j + \bar{x} \right] \leq \hat{p} \cdot \left[\sum_{j=1}^{k} \hat{y}_j + \bar{x} \right], \qquad \text{for all } y_j \in Y_j, j = 1, 2, \ldots, k$$

Or

$$\sum_{j=1}^{k} \hat{p} \cdot \hat{y}_j \geq \sum_{j=1}^{k} \hat{p} \cdot y_j, \qquad \text{for all } y_j \in Y_j, j = 1, 2, \ldots, k$$

Fix $j = j_0$ and let $y_j = \hat{y}_j$ for all $j \neq j_0$. Then $\hat{p} \cdot \hat{y}_{j_0} \geq \hat{p} \cdot y_{j_0}$ for all $y_{j_0} \in Y_{j_0}$. Since the choice of j_0 is arbitrary, this proves condition (ii) of Theorem 2.C.2. Condition (iii) of Theorem 2.C.2 is automatically satisfied by the feasibility condition of P.O.

Similarly, from (b') we obtain

(c) $\hat{p} \cdot x_1 \geq \hat{p} \cdot \hat{x}_1$ for all $x_1 \in \overline{C}_1(\hat{x}_1)$

and

(d) $\hat{p} \cdot x_i \geq \hat{p} \cdot \hat{x}_i$ for all $x_i \in C_i(\hat{x}), i = 2, 3, \ldots, m$

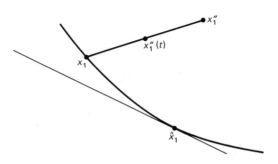

Figure 2.12. An Illustration of $x_1''(t)$ and x_1''.

We wish to assert that $\hat{p} \cdot x_1 \geq \hat{p} \cdot \hat{x}_1$ for all $x_1 \in C_1(\hat{x}_1)$. To do this we have to show that $x_1 \ominus_1 \hat{x}_1$ implies $\hat{p} \cdot x_1 \geq \hat{p} \cdot \hat{x}_1$. Since $\hat{x}_1$ is not a satiation point, we can find a point $x_1'' \oslash_1 \hat{x}_1 \ominus_1 x_1$. Let $x_1''(t) \equiv t x_1'' + (1 - t)x_1, 0 < t < 1$. Then by the convexity of $\oslash_1$ [(A-2)], $x_1''(t) \oslash_1 x_1, 0 < t < 1$, so that $x_1''(t) \oslash_1 \hat{x}_1, 0 < t < 1$. Then, from (c) above, $\hat{p} \cdot x_1''(t) \geq \hat{p} \cdot \hat{x}_1$. Hence by the continuity of the function $\hat{p} \cdot x_1$, it follows that $\hat{p} \cdot x_1 \geq \hat{p} \cdot \hat{x}_1$. Thus we obtain

(e) $\hat{p} \cdot x_i \geq \hat{p} \cdot \hat{x}_i$ for all $x_i \in C_i(\hat{x}_i), i = 1, 2, \ldots, m$

This proves condition (i) of the theorem.   (Q.E.D.)

Corollary: *If in addition (A-4) holds with respect to $\hat{x}_i$ and $\hat{p}$ in the above theorem, and if (A-5) holds, then for every Pareto optimum $[\{\hat{x}_i\}, \{\hat{y}_j\}]$, there exists $\hat{p} \neq 0$ such that $[\hat{p}, \{\hat{x}_i\}, \{\hat{y}_j\}]$ is a competitive equilibrium.*[21]

PROOF: It suffices to show that condition (i) of C.E. holds. In the above theorem we obtained

(e) $\hat{p} \cdot x_i \geq \hat{p} \cdot \hat{x}_i$ for all $x_i \in C_i(\hat{x}_i), i = 1, 2, \ldots, m$

This does not preclude the existence of an $x_i \in X_i$ such that $\hat{p} \cdot x_i = \hat{p} \cdot \hat{x}_i$ and $x_i \bigotimes_i \hat{x}_i$. We will show that this cannot happen under (A-4) and (A-5). Suppose the contrary. In other words, suppose that there exists an $x_i \in X_i$ such that

$$\hat{p} \cdot x_i = \hat{p} \cdot \hat{x}_i \text{ and } x_i \bigotimes_i \hat{x}_i$$

From (A-4), there exists an $x_i' \in X_i$ such that $\hat{p} \cdot x_i' < \hat{p} \cdot \hat{x}_i$. Relation (e) implies $x_i' \bigotimes_i \hat{x}_i$. Now consider $z_i \equiv t x_i' + (1 - t) x_i, 0 < t < 1$. Obviously, $\hat{p} \cdot z_i < \hat{p} \cdot x_i = \hat{p} \cdot \hat{x}_i$. By choosing t small enough, we can make z_i arbitrarily close to x_i. Then, from (A-5), we obtain[22]

$$z_i \bigotimes_i \hat{x}_i, \text{ but } \hat{p} \cdot z_i < \hat{p} \cdot \hat{x}_i$$

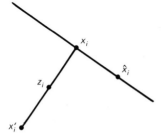

Figure 2.13.   An Illustration of the Proof of the Corollary.

This contradicts relation (e) above. Hence there cannot exist an $x_i \in X_i$ such that $\hat{p} \cdot x_i = \hat{p} \cdot \hat{x}_i$ and $x_i \bigotimes_i \hat{x}_i$. This means that $\hat{p} \cdot x_i = \hat{p} \cdot \hat{x}_i, x_i \in X_i$, implies $x_i \bigoplus_i \hat{x}_i$. Note that relation (e) means (taking its contraposition) that $\hat{p} \cdot x_i < \hat{p} \cdot \hat{x}_i, x_i \in X_i$, implies $x_i \bigotimes_i \hat{x}_i$. Hence we have obtained that

$$\hat{p} \cdot x_i \leq \hat{p} \cdot \hat{x}_i, x_i \in X_i, \text{ implies } x_i \bigoplus_i \hat{x}_i$$

In other words, $\hat{x}_i \bigoplus_i x_i$ for all $x_i \in X_i$ with $\hat{p} \cdot x_i \leq \hat{p} \cdot \hat{x}_i$. This proves condition (i) of C.E.   (Q.E.D.)[23]

REMARK: Note that the competitive equilibrium in the above corollary can be achieved by allocating from the aggregate income of the society, $p \cdot (y + \bar{x})$, the amount $p \cdot \hat{x}_i, i = 1, 2, \ldots, m$, to each consumer [note that condition (iii) in the definition of C.E. guarantees that all the income of the society is completely absorbed by all the consumers in the society]. In other words, without such a reallocation of ownership, a Pareto optimum can*not*, in general, be supported by competitive pricing.

As we remarked above, Theorem 2.C.2 does not quite establish that a Pareto optimum can be realized through a competitive equilibrium. To establish this (the above corollary), we needed the additional assumptions (A-4) and (A-5). An example showing that the conclusion of the corollary does not follow when the cheaper point assumption (A-4) is missing was first offered by Arrow [1], and we illustrate this with the Edgeworth-Bowley box diagram shown in Figure 2.14. The consumption set for each consumer is assumed to be the nonnegative orthant, so that one consumer's (consumer *A*) consumption set is the northeast orthant from

Figure 2.14. Arrow's Anomalous Case.

0_A and the other consumer's (consumer B) consumption set is the southwest orthant from 0_B. There is no production in the economy.

In the diagram, point P is a Pareto optimal point. The line tangent to the two consumers' indifference curves is the line going through $0_A P Q$ (the upper contour set for each consumer at P is represented by the shaded area). But this cannot represent the price line which supports a competitive equilibrium at point P. For under this price line, the price of commodity X is zero and consumer A is certainly *not* maximizing his satisfaction subject to his budget at point P. He can increase his satisfaction by moving in the direction of Q (this is possible since he can get commodity X free with the given price line). Note that at point P, the value of his commodity bundle is zero and he has no point in his consumption set below this line ($0_A P Q$). In other words, the cheaper point assumption (A-4) is not satisfied. Note also that all the other assumptions for the corollary can be satisfied in the above example.

This example does not allow production in the economy. An example that does allow production is offered by Koopmans ([12], pp. 34–35; [13], pp. 92–93). His example is concerned with an economy which involves only one consumer and one producer (if one likes, one can visualize a situation in which one person—say, Mr. Robinson Crusoe—performs two roles: one as a consumer and the other as a producer). Since there is only one consumer, a Pareto optimal point will be the point at which this consumer achieves his maximum satisfaction given the "feasibility condition," that is, given the entire supply of goods in the economy. (Recall that we denoted the aggregate supply set of the economy by W in the proof of Theorem 2.C.2.) We now illustrate Koopman's example in Figure 2.15.

In this economy there are only two commodities, food and labor service. The consumption set X of the consumer in this economy is the region above the curve $QRPS$. The consumer's indifference curves are represented by the dotted lines. Assume that the indifference curve passing through point P is tangent to the line PR (but stops at P and does not go farther along PR). Note also that any point on the line RP (except point P) is better than P for this consumer. Now in the diagram, point P is the only Pareto optimal point in this economy, simply because it is the

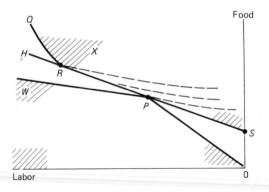

Figure 2.15.   Koopmans's Example.

only feasible point (set X and set W have no intersection except at point P). The line H (that is, the one which goes through PR) is the only line that separates the sets X and W. (Recall that in the proof of Theorem 2.C.2 and its corollary the slope of the separating hyperplane of X and W gave the price vector which supports a competitive equilibrium.) But this line contains a point (say, R) in X. In other words, point R is a better point than point P but has the same value as point P; hence, if the price represented by line H prevails, Robinson the consumer will certainly increase his satisfaction by trading the commodity bundle represented by P for the bundle represented by R with Robinson the producer. That is, the separation of decision-making functions by the price H has given rise to incompatible decisions by the two Robinsons. Hence the Pareto optimal point P cannot be supported by competitive pricing. Note that in this example there is no point of X below the line H. In other words, the cheaper point assumption (A-4) is again violated. (The reader should check that all the other assumptions can be satisfied by this example.)

If there is a point in X below the separating line, then a Pareto optimal point can be supported by decentralized pricing. This is illustrated by Figure 2.16, which

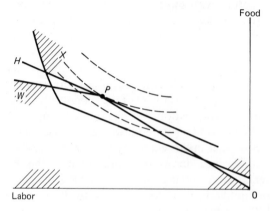

Figure 2.16.   (P.O. $\Rightarrow$ C.E.)

is again indebted to Koopmans ([12], p. 36). Note that under the price represented by line *H*, Robinson the consumer maximizes his satisfaction, Robinson the producer maximizes profit, and the feasibility condition is satisfied. Hence the separation of decision-making functions has given rise to compatible decisions by the two Robinsons.[24]

FOOTNOTES

1. The measurability of individuals' utility is a long debated question. At present we do not know any way of measuring it; we customarily treat it as nonmeasurable. However, the important empirical and theoretical consequences known in the literature do not depend on the measurability; hence it suffices to assume only the ordinality of utility. That is, the general practice of using ordinal utility (rather than cardinal utility) is a use of Occam's razor.

2. We may replace the last phrase of this sentence by "given that the total demand for commodities does not exceed the total supply of commodities." In fact, this may be a more common phraseology. However, we should note that if we allow excess supply of commodities, as above, then we are implicitly assuming free disposability of those commodities that are in excess supply.

3. The term "Pareto optimum" was apparently coined by I. M. D. Little in *A Critique of Welfare Economics*, Oxford, Clarendon Press, 1950, p. 89.

4. Note that we do not ask here how this point $\hat{x}$ is achieved. In other words, we do not ask here how the consumer obtains his "income" that brings him to point $\hat{x}$. This observation will later become relevant when we discuss the price implication of a Pareto optimum (Theorem 2.C.2).

5. It goes without saying that the same point in the box should be chosen by the two consumers. This is required for the demand for *each* commodity to be equal to (or not to exceed) its supply.

6. In other words, at any competitive equilibrium point, the "price line" is tangent to each individual's indifference curve. In view of the fact that the demand for each commodity should be equal to its supply in a competitive equilibrium (so that a common point in the box must be chosen by the two consumers), this implies that any competitive equilibrium point is a point in which the indifference curves for the two consumers are tangent to each other.

7. The calculus proof and a quite rigorous statement of the above two classical propositions of welfare economics are seen in Lange [14]. Although his treatment is compact and elegant, mathematical limitations restrict the generality of his exposition. This leads the way to a further generalization by Arrow [1] and Debreu [4].

8. Although diagrammatical analysis is not often accepted by serious economic theorists as the proof (or even the formulation) of a particular theorem that the analysis is concerned with, any serious theorist will not question the usefulness of diagrams in yielding an insight into the problem. It is often very advisable to think the problem through in terms of diagrams before one mathematizes it.

9. A complete scrutiny of the literature on the topic covered in this section is done by Moore [17], especially part I, with further extensions and interesting counter-examples.

10. Here we define: $X \equiv \sum_{i=1}^{m} X_i$ and $Y \equiv \sum_{j=1}^{k} Y_j$. Both are subsets of R^n. That Y is the

aggregate production set means that there are no (technological) *external economies and diseconomies*.

11. Note that $X_i \subset R^n$. Here it is assumed that individual i's preference ordering depends only on his own consumption bundle and not on the consumption bundles of other consumers (nor on the pattern of production). This assumption of the lack of "externality" is one of the most crucial assumptions in the theorems of this section. In the literature, this assumption is referred to as **individualistic** or **selfish** preference ordering, as we remarked earlier.

12. Notice, however, that this does not preclude the possibility of the existence of production processes which dispose of various types of waste.

13. Intuitively, a point is a local nonsatiation point if there are *arbitrarily close* points which are preferred to it. The concept of a local nonsatiation point was first introduced by Koopmans [12] and used again in [13]. Moore ([17], part I) reaffirmed the importance of the concept in the literature.

14. An alternative way to state the above definition is as follows: $x_i \in X_i$ is called a **local nonsatiation point** (for the ith consumer) if there exists $x_i'' \in X_i$ such that $x_i' \bigcirc_i x_i$ and $x_i' \in X_i$ where $x_i' \equiv tx_i + (1 - t)x_i''$, for *all* t, $0 < t < 1$.

15. If $\bigcirc_i$ is such that $x_i \bigcirc_i z_i'$ implies $tz_i + (1 - t)z_i' \bigcirc_i z_i'$, $0 < t < 1$, for $z_i \neq z_i'$ (which is true if $\bigcirc_i$ is strictly convex) with convex X_i, then the transitivity assumption can be dispensed with. To see this, suppose $x_i \bigcirc_i \hat{x}_i$ with $p \cdot x_i < p \cdot \hat{x}_i$ as above and let $x_i(t) = tx_i + (1 - t)\hat{x}_i$, $0 < t < 1$. Then $x_i(t) \bigcirc_i \hat{x}_i$, but $p \cdot x_i(t) < p \cdot \hat{x}_i$, which contradicts (i) above.

16. It simply says that "*if a competitive equilibrium exists, then* it realizes a Pareto optimum with (A-1)."

17. Such an example can be found in Quirk and Saposnik [20], p. 134. (Caution: Indifference curves should take on values only on the lattice points.)

18. See Debreu [6], pp. 93–94.

19. A slightly stronger version of this assumption, which is also used in the literature, is the following: For a given point $\hat{x}_i$, there exists $x_i' \in X_i$ such that $p \cdot x_i' < p \cdot \hat{x}_i$ for *all* price vectors p.

20. The separating hyperplane can be written as $H = \{x : x \in X, \hat{p} \cdot x = \hat{p} \cdot \hat{x}\}$, where $X = \sum_{i=1}^{m} X_i$.

21. Assumption (A-4) is rather awkward. It is certainly desirable to obtain the present corollary replacing (A-4) by a more plausible assumption, that is, one that is based directly on some properties of the preference orderings and/or the consumption and production sets. For an investigation of such a point, see Moore [17], part I.

22. Suppose not. That is, suppose $z_i \bigcirc_i \hat{x}_i$ for any small $t > 0$. Let $t \to 0$ so that $z_i \to x_i$. Then by (A-5), $x_i \bigcirc_i \hat{x}_i$, which contradicts $x_i \bigcirc_i \hat{x}_i$.

23. In establishing Theorem 2.C.2, which leads to the above corollary, we saw that the separation theorem played a crucial role. In Chapter 1, we obtained theorems of nonlinear programming (notably that of concave programming) using the separation theorem. We can conjecture that the above theorem and the corollary can be proved using a theorem in concave programming. We attempt to do so in Section F of this chapter.

24. The compatibility of decentralized decision making in terms of prices is the essence of the concept of competitive equilibrium. The essence of Theorem 2.C.2 is that if a separating hyperplane exists, it defines a price system that makes such a decentralization possible.

REFERENCES

1. Arrow, K. J., "An Extension of the Basic Theorems of Classical Welfare Economics," *Proceedings of the Second Berkeley Symposium on Mathematical Statistics and Probability*, ed. by J. Neyman, Berkeley, Calif., University of California Press, 1951.

2. Arrow, K. J., and Debreu, G., "Existence of an Equilibrium for a Competitive Economy," *Econometrica*, 22, July 1954.

3. Barone, E., "The Ministry of Production in the Collectivist State," in *Collectivist Economic Planning*, ed. by F. A. von Hayek, London, Routledge, 1935 (Italian original, 1908).

4. Debreu, G., "The Coefficient of Resource Utilization," *Econometrica*, 19, July 1951.

5. ———, "Valuation Equilibrium and Pareto Optimum," *Proceedings of the National Academy of Sciences of the U.S.A.*, 40, 1954.

6. ———, *Theory of Value*, New York, Wiley, 1959, esp. chap. 6.

7. Dorfman, R., Samuelson, P. A., and Solow, R. M., *Linear Programming and Economic Analysis*, New York, McGraw-Hill, 1958.

8. Hicks, J. R., "The Foundations of Welfare Economics," *Economic Journal*, XLIX, December 1939.

9. Hurwicz, L., "Optimality and Informational Efficiency in Resource Allocation Processes," in *Mathematical Methods in the Social Sciences, 1959*, ed. by K. J. Arrow, S. Karlin, and P. Suppes, Stanford, Calif., Stanford University Press, 1960.

10. Karlin, S., *Mathematical Methods and Theory in Games, Programming, and Economics*, Vol. I., 1st ed., Reading, Mass., Addison-Wesley, 1959.

11. Koopmans, T. C., "Efficient Allocation of Resources," *Econometrica*, 19, October 1951.

12. ———, *Three Essays on the State of Economic Science*, New York, McGraw-Hill, 1957, esp. secs. 1 and 2 of the first essay.

13. Koopmans, T. C., and Bausch, A., "Selected Topics Involving Mathematical Reasoning," *SIAM Review*, 1, July 1959, esp. pp. 83–95.

14. Lange, O., "Foundations of Welfare Economics," *Econometrica*, 10, January–October 1942.

15. Lerner, A. P., "The Concept of Monopoly and Measurement of Monopoly Power," *Review of Economic Studies*, 1, June 1934.

16. ———, *Economics of Control*, New York, Macmillan, 1944.

17. Moore, J. C., "On Pareto Optima and Competitive Equilibria (Part I: Relationships Among Equilibria and Optima; Part II: The Existence of Equilibria and Optima)," *Krannert Institute Paper*, nos. 268 and 269, April 1970, Purdue University.

18. Pareto, V., *Manuel d'Économie Politique*, 2nd ed., Paris, Giard, 1927 (1st ed., 1909), esp. chap. VI.

19. Pigou, A. C., *The Economics of Welfare*, 4th ed., London, Macmillan, 1932, esp. chaps. IX, X, XI.

20. Quirk, J., and Saposnik, R., *Introduction to General Equilibrium Theory and Welfare Economics*, New York, McGraw-Hill, 1968, esp. chap. 4, sec. 5.

21.   Rader, J. T., "Pairwise Optimality and Noncompetitive Behavior," in *Papers in Quantitative Economics*, Vol. I, ed. by J. Quirk and A. M. Zarley, Lawrence, Kansas, University of Kansas Press, 1968.

22.   Samuelson, P. A., *Foundations of Economic Analysis*, Cambridge, Mass., Harvard University Press, 1947.

23.   Wicksell, K., *Lectures on Political Economy*, Vol. I, London, Routledge & Kegan Paul, Ltd., 1935 (Swedish original, 1901).

Appendix to Section C: Introduction to the Theory of the Core

a.   INTRODUCTION

Consider a simple two-person, two-commodity pure exchange economy, which may be illustrated by the familiar Edgeworth-Bowley box diagram. Let $\bar{x}_i$ and $\bar{y}_i$, respectively, be the amounts of commodities X and Y which are initially held by consumer i, where $i = 1, 2$. We suppose that the two people, starting from such an initial position, wish to improve their satisfaction by engaging in the trade of these two commodities. The situation is illustrated in Figure 2.17.

In Figure 2.17, the indifference curves of the two people are denoted by the usual strictly convex shapes $(\alpha_1, \alpha_2, \ldots,$ and $\beta_1, \beta_2, \ldots)$. The initial endowment point is denoted by point R. The curve passing through points P, E, and Q is the contract curve, which is the locus of points at which two individuals' indifference curves are tangent to each other. Any point on the contract curve is a Pareto optimum point.

If the two consumers, starting from the initial point R, trade with each other, the result is a reallocation of the total amounts of the two commodities between them, which may be denoted by a point in the Edgeworth-Bowley box

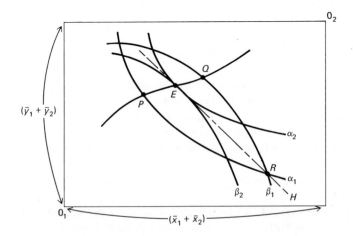

Figure 2.17.   Two-Person, Two-Commodity Pure Exchange Economy.

shown in the Figure 2.17. If the competitive price mechanism[1] is introduced into the trading, then we obtain a competitive equilibrium reallocation E, where the H-line signifies the equilibrium price ratio.

That the competitive equilibrium allocation is on the contract curve (and hence is Pareto optimal) is an important welfare result of the competitive price mechanism. But any other allocation on the contract curve is also a Pareto optimum.

Suppose that the competitive price mechanism is dropped from the trading scheme. Clearly the resulting allocation depends on the trading rule. However, it is also clear that, under any trading rule, the resulting allocation of the two people will not fall outside the lens-shaped region defined by the two indifference curves α_1 and β_1. For if it does, at least one person will be worse off compared to the initial position R, and he can always refuse to trade. It is clear that the final resulting allocation of the two people should lie on the PQ segment of the contract curve.

Hence we may say that, given the initial endowment point R, the allocations on the PQ segment of the contract curve should occupy a more privileged place compared to allocations outside the PQ segment. More strongly, any point on the curve outside the PQ segment is irrelevant to our consideration when the initial endowment point is given as R. We term the PQ segment the **core** of the above economy.[2] Note that the competitive allocation E is on the PQ segment.

In order to single out the importance of the competitive solution, Edgeworth [11] in 1881 considered an expanded economy of $2n$ consumers, in which there are two "types" of consumers. Every consumer of the same type has identical tastes and identical initial endowments. In other words, the above box diagram economy is replicated n times. Edgeworth then argued that as n tends to infinity, the above PQ segment shrinks to one point: the competitive allocation E (or the set of competitive equilibria if it is not unique)![3] In 1963, Debreu and Scarf [10] elegantly and rigorously proved Edgeworth's result.

The general principle given by Edgeworth was that of "recontracting." Consider any subgroup of consumers. Suppose that it is possible for its members to distribute their initial resources among themselves in such a way that no member of the subgroup is made worse off, while one or more members of the subgroup are made better off. Whenever this happens, "recontracting" takes place without others' consent. "Final settlement"[4] comes when a contract cannot be amended by the recontract of any such subsets. For the two-person economy, the above PQ segment, the "core," constitutes the set of final settlements, that is, the set of allocations which result in no further recontracting. What Edgeworth has shown is that, in the economy of $2n$ consumers of two "types," such a set of allocations decreases as n increases and converges to the set of competitive equilibria as $n \to \infty$.

It was Shubik [28] who related the Edgeworth notion of "final settlement" in "recontracting" to Gillies' [12] concept of the "core" in the theory of n-

person games. This, in turn, stimulated various works on the problem including Scarf and Debreu [10], mentioned above. The *n*-person game theory is concerned with situations in which individuals ("players") with conflicting interests compete, and hence it probes deeply into the question of the theory of competitive equilibrium. Therefore it is quite natural that economists should attempt to master the intricacies of game theory and the theory of the core.

As indicated above, the "core" of the economy is the set of allocations which cannot be "blocked" by any subgroup ("coalition") of members of the economy. Note that the concept of the core is free from prices. In other words, the core solution provides an alternative approach to the price-guided competitive solution, as well as offering an important characterization of competitive equilibrium through the results of Debreu-Scarf [10], and others. Moreover, the concept of "blocking coalition" in the theory of games and the core offers a fresh interpretation of the concept of Pareto optimum. A Pareto optimum allocation is one that will not be blocked by the coalition involving *all* participants of the economy. This then means that the core gives a stronger characterization of competitive equilibrium than does Pareto Optimum. In fact, the precision of this characterization is quite strong, as the above Edgeworth-Debreu-Scarf result indicates. An important merit of the core-theoretic approach here is that it permits freedom of choice for each individual of the economy and deduces that if the number of these individuals increases, each person might behave as if he were a price taker. In the theory of competitive markets, on the other hand, each individual is assumed (or destined) to be a price taker.[5]

With the increasing interest in the concept of the core, economists are now more concerned with the theory of *n*-person games (for example, the publication of a series of joint articles by Shapley and Shubik [22], [23], [24], [25], [26], and so on, in economic journals). This is quite natural, as we have already remarked. In the classical treatments of game theory such as the theory of von Neumann and Morgenstern [32], it is assumed that payoffs are made in "utils," which are cardinal and, like money, fully transferable among the players. It is further assumed that these utils are linear in money. Such an assumption is quite convenient, since the classical theory of games is almost exclusively concerned with cooperative games with side payments.[6] However, the appropriateness of this assumption of money-like transferable utils is naturally very questionable to economists and others, and it has been extensively debated. This, no doubt, prompted the development of the theory of cooperative games without side payments (for example, Aumann and Peleg [5]). There are a few necessary steps to be able to reach ordinality of preferences. The classical N-M theory assumed cardinal utils which are linear in money, but Shapely and Shubik [21] pointed out that linearity and perfect transferability are not essential to the theory. What remains is an ordinal theory.[7] Scarf's approach [17] with strictly ordinal utility is good in terms of the Occam's Razor principle. There seems little question that this advance in game theory has made the theory much more attractive to economists.

It is *not* the intention of the author to give an expository account of the theory of cooperative games.[8] The author wishes only to point out the relevance and the importance of the theory of games to economics. The purpose of this appendix is to attempt an introductory exposition of the theory of the core, to the extent that it requires no exposition of game theory. Moreover, it is not the intention of the author to make a comprehensive survey of the entire literature. The literature in the field has been expanding quite rapidly. The aim of this Appendix is thus a much more modest one; it is simply to familiarize the reader with some basic concepts in the theory of the core and the important result of Debreu and Scarf, which hopefully will facilitate further study on the theory of the core. The author then hopes that this will further increase the inquisitiveness of the reader about the general topic of game theory. In order to simplify our exposition, we will confine our attention to the pure exchange economy. The extension to an economy in which production is involved is more or less straightforward in certain cases.[9]

b.   SOME BASIC CONCEPTS

Let x_i be an n-vector of consumption by consumer i and $\bar{x}_i$ be an n-vector of initial resources held by the ith consumer. There are m consumers and let M be the set of all consumers, that is, $M \equiv \{1, 2, \ldots, m\}$. Denote by X_i the consumption set of i, where $X_i \subset R^n$ and by X we denote $\bigotimes_{i=1}^{m} X_i$. It is assumed that each consumer's preference ordering is represented by a continuous real-valued function $u_i(x_i)$ defined on X_i, $i = 1, 2, \ldots, m$. Clearly such a representation is, in general, not unique.[10] We arbitrarily select one of them for each consumer, and the analysis remains purely ordinal. That is, the representation here is only for convenience and is not essential in the subsequent discussion.[11] An array of consumption vectors $x = (x_1, x_2, \ldots, x_m)$, where $x \in X$ (that is, $x_i \in X_i$, $i = 1, 2, \ldots, m$), is called an **allocation**. An allocation x is said to be **feasible** if

$$(1) \qquad \sum_{i=1}^{m} x_i = \sum_{i=1}^{m} \bar{x}_i$$

Let A be the set of all feasible allocations, that is,

$$(2) \qquad A \equiv \{x: x \in X, \sum_{i=1}^{m} x_i = \sum_{i=1}^{m} \bar{x}_i\}$$

The central concept in the theory of the core is that of blocking.

Definition: By a **coalition** we mean a nonempty subset S of the set M of all consumers. A feasible allocation $x \in A$ is said to be **blocked** by a coalition S if there exists another feasible allocation x' such that

(3)
$$\begin{cases} u_i(x_i') \geq u_i(x_i) & \text{for all } i \in S \\[2mm] u_i(x_i') > u_i(x_i) & \text{for some } i \in S \end{cases}$$

and

(4)
$$\sum_{i \in S} x_i' = \sum_{i \in S} \bar{x}_i$$

We then say that x' is **S-block superior** to x, or x' **dominates** x **by coalition** S, and denote this by $x' B_S x$, where B_S is a binary relation defined on A.

> REMARK: Intuitively, an allocation x is "blocked" by a coalition S if there is another allocation which is feasible among the members of S and makes no consumers in S worse off while betters at least one consumer in S. The consumers outside the coalition are "discriminated" against by the coalition in the sense that some or all of them can be worse off in x' compared to the initial allocation x.[12]

> REMARK: Note that the coalition S may consist of all consumers in the economy, that is, $S = M$. A Pareto optimal allocation is one that is not blocked by the coalition involving *all* consumers.

Define the binary relation B on A by $[x' B x]$ if and only if $x' B_S x$ for *some* coalition S of M. Given a feasible allocation x in A, define set-valued functions $B_S(x)$ and $B(x)$ by

(5)
$$B_S(x) \equiv \{z \colon z B_S x, \, z \in A\}$$

(6)
$$B(x) \equiv \{z \colon z B x, \, z \in A\}$$

In other words, $B_S(x)$ is the set of all feasible allocations that block x by a *particular* coalition S in M, and $B(x)$ is the set of all feasible allocations that block x by *some* coalition in M.

Definition: The **core** is the set of all feasible allocations that are not blocked by any coalition. In other words, it is equal to

$$\{x \in A \colon B(x) = \emptyset\}$$

> REMARK: That x is Pareto optimal means that $B_M(x) = \emptyset$. Hence if x is in the core, then x is Pareto optimal, whereas a Pareto optimal allocation need not belong to the core.

Let $x_S = [x_i]_{i \in S}$ be a subvector of a feasible allocation x, in which $x_i \in x_S$ implies $i \in S$. Denote by A_S the allocations attainable among the members of the coalition S. That is,

(7)
$$A_S \equiv \{x_S \in X_S \colon \sum_{i \in S} x_i = \sum_{i \in S} \bar{x}_i\}$$

where $X_S \equiv \bigotimes_{i \in S} X_i$ and $x \in A$. Assuming that X_i, $i = 1, 2, \ldots, m$, are all closed and bounded from below, A_S is compact in $R^{n \times s}$ for any coalition S, where s is the number of members of coalition S. It is easy to show that A_S is convex for any S if the X_i, $i = 1, 2, \ldots, m$, are all convex. Let the function u_S: $A_S \rightarrow R^S$ be defined by $u_S(x_S) \equiv [u_i(x_i)]_{i \in S}$. That an allocation $\hat{x}$ is not blocked by a coalition S [that is, $B_S(\hat{x}) = \emptyset$] means that $\hat{x}_S$ is a solution of the vector maximum problem of maximizing $u_S(x_S)$ subject to $x_S \in A_S$.

Definition: The set $U(S)$ defined by

(8) $$U(S) \equiv \{u_S(x_S): x_S \in A_S\}$$

is called the **utility possibility set** of coalition S.

> REMARK: Clearly
>
> (8′) $$U(S) = \{u_S: \exists\, x_S \in A_S \text{ such that } u_S = u_S(x_S)\}$$
>
> Note that $U(S)$ is compact if A_S is compact (∵ the u_i's are all continuous).

> REMARK: The concept of the utility possibility set corresponds to that of a "characteristic function" in game theory. In economics, such a concept (when $S = M$) is well known through Samuelson [27] and others.[13]

In the theories of the core and games, a weaker concept than that of $U(S)$ is often used.[14] In other words, define the set $V(S)$ by

(9) $$V(S) \equiv \{u_S: \exists\, x_S \in A_S \text{ such that } u_S \leq u_S(x_S)\}$$

Clearly $U(S) \subset V(S)$, but the converse does not necessarily hold. As an example of $V(S) \not\subset U(S)$, it suffices to consider the case in which the consumption set of each consumer has a "hole." Obviously the relevant concept in the theory of the core should be $U(S)$. However, it is often convenient and useful (for obtaining sharper results) to carry out an analysis by simply assuming (or starting out with the assumptions which imply) $U(S) = V(S)$.

For the sake of illustration, suppose that the number of consumers in the economy is 3 ($m = 3$). Assume also that the consumption set for each consumer is Ω, the nonnegative orthant of R^n. In such an economy, there are obviously seven possible coalitions, that is, $\{1, 2, 3\}$, $\{1, 2\}$, $\{2, 3\}$, $\{1, 3\}$, $\{1\}$, $\{2\}$, and $\{3\}$. Denote the sets $V(\{1, 2, 3\})$, $V(\{1, 2\})$, $V(\{1\})$, and so on, by $V_{(123)}$, $V_{(12)}$, $V_{(1)}$, and so on. Thus, for example,

(10) $$V_{(123)} \equiv \{(u^1, u^2, u^3): u^i \leq u_i(x_i) \text{ for some } x_i \in \Omega, i = 1, 2, 3,$$
$$\text{with } x_1 + x_2 + x_3 = \bar{x}_1 + \bar{x}_2 + \bar{x}_3\}$$

(11) $$V_{(12)} \equiv \{(u^1, u^2): u^i \leq u_i(x_i) \text{ for some } x_i \in \Omega, i = 1, 2,$$
$$\text{with } x_1 + x_2 = \bar{x}_1 + \bar{x}_2\}$$

(12) $V_{(1)} \equiv \{u^1 : u^1 \leq u_1(x_1) \text{ for some } x_1 \in \Omega \text{ with } x_1 = \bar{x}_1\}$

The concepts of $V_{(12)}$, $V_{(1)}$, and $V_{(2)}$ are illustrated in Figure 2.18.[15] It should be clear that if $u^1 \in V_{(1)}$ and $(u^2, u^3) \in V_{(23)}$, then $(u^1, u^2, u^3) \in V_{(123)}$. Moreover, as Scarf [17] has shown,

$$\left.\begin{array}{l} (u^1, u^2) \in V_{(12)} \\[1mm] (u^2, u^3) \in V_{(23)} \\[1mm] (u^1, u^3) \in V_{(13)} \end{array}\right\} \quad \text{imply } (u^1, u^2, u^3) \in V_{(123)}$$

provided that the u_i's are quasi-concave. To show this, first observe that the assumptions imply

$$u^1 \leq u_1(x_1), u^2 \leq u_2(x_2) \text{ with } x_1 + x_2 = \bar{x}_1 + \bar{x}_2$$

$$u^2 \leq u_2(y_2), u^3 \leq u_3(y_3) \text{ with } y_2 + y_3 = \bar{x}_2 + \bar{x}_3$$

$$u^1 \leq u_1(z_1), \ u^3 \leq u_3(z_3) \text{ with } z_1 + z_3 = \bar{x}_1 + \bar{x}_3$$

But the allocation $[(x_1 + z_1)/2, (x_2 + y_2)/2, (y_3 + z_3)/2]$ is feasible for the coalition consisting of all three consumers, for we have

(13) $$\frac{x_1 + z_1}{2} + \frac{x_2 + y_2}{2} + \frac{y_3 + z_3}{2} = \bar{x}_1 + \bar{x}_2 + \bar{x}_3$$

Moreover, in view of the quasi-concavity of u_1, $u_1[(x_1 + z_1)/2] \geq \min \{u_1(x_1), u_1(z_1)\} \geq u_1$. Similarly, we also have $u_2[(x_2 + y_2)/2] \geq u_2$ and $u_3[(y_3 + z_3)/2] \geq u_3$. Therefore, $(u^1, u^2, u^3) \in V_{(123)}$.

It is important to note that the quasi-concavity assumption plays a crucial role in connecting the three "two-consumer" coalitions to the coalition of all three consumers. Using this as a guide, Scarf [17] proved a remarkable theorem which

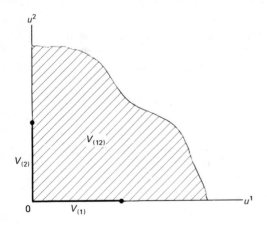

Figure 2.18.   An Illustration of $V(S)$.

states that the core of any "balanced m-person game" is always nonempty,[16] and then he remarked that an exchange economy with convex preferences always gives rise to a balanced m-person game; hence its core is nonempty. For the concept of a "balanced m-person game" and the proof of the above theorem, we simply refer to Scarf's elegant paper. For a recent generalization of Scarf's result, we refer to Billera [6].[17]

That the core is nonempty is obviously important, for the core can indeed be empty, and if the core is empty any discussion on the properties of the core becomes meaningless. Moreover, in view of the close relation between the core and the set of competitive equilibria, the study of the conditions for a nonempty core can be utilized in the study of competitive equilibrium, such as the existence of competitive equilibria. As we will show in the next subsection, every competitive equilibrium is in the core. Hence if the core is empty, there exists no competitive equilibrium.[18]

An example of an economy with an empty core (which is due to Scarf, Shapley, and Shubik) is mentioned by Debreu and Scarf [10] and by Shapley and Shubik [23]. The example is concerned with a pure exchange economy with two commodities and three consumers, each of whom has nonconvex preferences, as described by the indifference curves of Figure 2.19.

Mathematically, the utility function for Figure 2.19 may, for example, be written as

$$(14) \qquad u(x, y) \equiv \begin{cases} x & \text{if } x \leq \dfrac{y}{2} \\[2mm] \dfrac{y}{2} & \text{if } \dfrac{y}{2} < x < y \\[2mm] \dfrac{x}{2} & \text{if } x = y \\[2mm] \dfrac{x}{2} & \text{if } y < x < 2y \\[2mm] y & \text{if } x \geq 2y \end{cases}$$

Assuming that each consumer has *one* unit of each commodity initially, the proof that the core of this economy is empty may be sketched roughly as follows:

(i) Suppose that an allocation $c = (c_1, c_2, c_3)$ is in the core where c_i represents the consumption bundle of Mr. $i(i = 1, 2, 3)$. Since c cannot be blocked by a coalition consisting of one person, we must have $u(c_i) \geq u(1, 1) = \frac{1}{2}$, $i = 1, 2, 3$.

(ii) Moreover, c cannot be blocked by the coalition consisting of any two persons. But the coalition of any two persons can give each member $u(\frac{2}{3}, \frac{4}{3}) = u(\frac{4}{3}, \frac{2}{3}) = \frac{2}{3}$ by redistributing the resources between the two as

$$\begin{bmatrix} \frac{4}{3} \\[1mm] \frac{2}{3} \end{bmatrix} + \begin{bmatrix} \frac{2}{3} \\[1mm] \frac{4}{3} \end{bmatrix} = \begin{bmatrix} 2 \\[1mm] 2 \end{bmatrix}$$

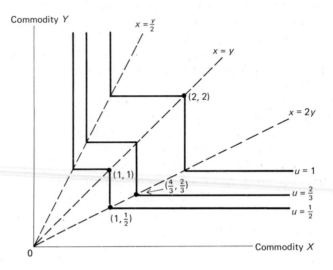

Figure 2.19. Preferences for the Empty Core.

(iii) Therefore, at least two consumers (say, Mr. 1 and Mr. 2) have $u_i \geq \frac{2}{3}$ for each $i (i = 1, 2)$.

(iv) Hence assume that $u_1 \geq \frac{2}{3}$, $u_2 \geq \frac{2}{3}$. Among all the possible allocations that give Mr. 1 and Mr. 2 at least satisfaction $\frac{2}{3}$, choose the one that gives Mr. 3 at least satisfaction $\frac{1}{2}$.

(v) It turns out from (14) that the only c_3 possible is the one such that $u(c_3) = \frac{1}{2}$. This implies that in view of (14), Mr. 3 must have either of the two commodities in the amount of one unit. Note that owing to the lack of convexity of preferences, $u(1, \frac{1}{2}) = u(1, 1) = u(\frac{1}{2}, 1) = \frac{1}{2}$.

(vi) Suppose that Mr. 3 gets a unit amount of X. Then we can show that the coalition of 1 and 3 can block such an allocation.

(vii) With a similar analysis for the case where Mr. 3 receives one unit of Y, we show that an allocation c can always be blocked by some coalition. Hence c cannot be in the core. Thus the core is empty.

In view of the above example, we can see that the convexity of preferences plays a crucial role in asserting the nonemptiness of the core. In a recent study by Shapley and Shubik [23], it is suggested, however, that the convexity of preferences is not as crucial as it appears in the above example, if the number of participants is large. They showed that the core can be empty but that there is a set of allocations which can be blocked only with very small preference on the part of the blocking coalition. In other words, assuming that a coalition "blocks" an allocation only when the increase in preferences (money-like utils) of the blocking coalition is at least as great as some positive number ϵ, a quasi-core (called the **ϵ-core**) defined in terms of such a "blocking" is always nonempty when the number of participants is large enough. Thus the core is "approximately" nonempty if the number of participants is large enough, and the ϵ-core shows such an approximation. Although the convexity of preferences is not required in establishing this result, it is obtained under a prohibitively strong assumption, that is, that of "transferable utility." Later on we will point out another result in the literature: if there is a continuum of participants, then the core in the strict sense is nonempty even with nonconvex preferences and nontransferable utility.

c. THEOREMS OF DEBREU AND SCARF

It is important to note that the concept of the core is free from any considerations of the particular price system. The redistribution of commodities in the concept of blocking coalitions can take place even when trading is not constrained by prices. Suppose now that trading is restricted by the competitive price mechanism; that is, each trader takes the prices as given, the prices are the same for all traders, and each trader maximizes his satisfaction subject to his budget determined by prices. Our next concern is then to relate the concept of the core to such an economy, that is, one that is guided by competitive prices.

Definition: An array of vectors $[\hat{x}, \hat{p}]$ is said to be a **competitive equilibrium** (or **C. E.**) if $\hat{x} \in A$ and $\hat{p} \in R^n$, $\hat{p} \geq 0$, such that

(i) $u_i(\hat{x}_i) \geq u_i(x_i)$ for all $x_i \in X_i$ with $\hat{p} \cdot x_i \leq \hat{p} \cdot \bar{x}_i$, $i = 1, 2, \ldots, m$

(ii) $\sum\limits_{i=1}^{m} \hat{x}_i = \sum\limits_{i=1}^{m} \bar{x}_i$

REMARK: Let $[\hat{x}, \hat{p}]$ be a C. E. In view of (ii), $\sum_{i=1}^{m} \hat{p} \cdot (\hat{x}_i - \bar{x}_i) = 0$. But $\hat{p} \cdot (\hat{x}_i - \bar{x}_i) \leq 0$ for all i by (i). Hence we have $\hat{p} \cdot \hat{x}_i = \hat{p} \cdot \bar{x}_i$ for all i.

In Section C, we proved that if $u_i(\hat{x}_i) \geq u_i(x_i)$ for all x_i with $\hat{p} \cdot x_i \leq \hat{p} \cdot \hat{x}_i$ and if the preference ordering is locally nonsaturating at $\hat{x}_i$, then

(15-a) $u_i(x_i) > u_i(\hat{x}_i)$ implies $\hat{p} \cdot x_i > \hat{p} \cdot \hat{x}_i$

and

(15-b) $u_i(x_i) = u_i(\hat{x}_i)$ implies $\hat{p} \cdot x_i \geq \hat{p} \cdot \hat{x}_i$

Suppose that these relations hold for each i; then we can prove the following theorem.

Theorem 2.C.3: *Every competitive equilibrium is in the core.*

PROOF: Let $[\hat{x}, \hat{p}]$ be a competitive equilibrium, and suppose that it is not in the core. Then there exists a coalition S such that $x' B_S x$, for some feasible allocation x' with $\sum_{i \in S} x'_i = \sum_{i \in S} \bar{x}_i$. Hence $u_i(x'_i) \geq u_i(\hat{x}_i)$ for all $i \in S$ with strict equality for at least one i. Hence by (15-a) and (15-b), we have

$\hat{p} \cdot x_i' \geqq \hat{p} \cdot \hat{x}_i$ for all $i \in S$ with strict inequality for at least one i, so that $\sum_{i \in S} \hat{p} \cdot x_i' > \sum_{i \in S} \hat{p} \cdot \hat{x}_i$, which contradicts $\sum_{i \in S} x_i' = \sum_{i \in S} \bar{x}_i$.   (Q.E.D)[19]

REMARK: As remarked before, every allocation in the core is a Pareto optimal allocation, while the converse does not necessarily hold. Hence the above theorem is an extension of the result which says that every competitive equilibrium realizes a Pareto optimum. Moreover, the above theorem also asserts that if a competitive equilibrium exists, then the core is nonempty, and that if the core is empty, there exists no competitive equilibrium.

Definition: Two consumers—say, i and j—are said to be **of the same type** if they have identical utility functions (that is, $u_i = u_j$) with identical consumption sets (that is, $X_i = X_j$) and if they have the same initial endowment (that is, $\bar{x}_i = \bar{x}_j$).

Suppose that there are r consumers in each of k categories ("types") of consumers in the economy (so that $kr = m$). Write the consumption bundle for each consumer as

$$x_{ij}, \quad i = 1, 2, \ldots, k; \, j = 1, 2, \ldots, r$$

That is, x_{ij} is the consumption vector of the jth consumer of the ith type. An allocation vector then is written as $(x_{11}, \ldots, x_{1r}, \ldots, x_{k1}, \ldots, x_{kr})$. The utility function and the consumption set of any consumer of the ith type is denoted by u_i and X_i, respectively. His initial endowment vector is denoted by $\bar{x}_i$, so that the aggregate endowment vector of the economy is equal to $\sum_{i=1}^{k}(r\bar{x}_i)$.
We now impose the following assumption.

(A-1) The consumption sets X_i are convex for all i and the utility functions u_i are strictly quasi-concave for all i.[20]

Theorem.2.C.4: *Suppose that (A-1) holds. If $(x_{11}, \ldots, x_{1r}, \ldots, x_{k1}, \ldots, x_{kr})$ is an allocation in the core, then $x_{i1} = x_{i2} = \cdots = x_{ir}$ for each $i = 1, 2, \ldots, k$; that is, an allocation in the core assigns the same consumption to all consumers of the same type.*[21]

PROOF: Suppose not, so that the consumption vectors $x_{i_0 1}, \ldots, x_{i_0 r}$ are not identical for some i_0. For such an i_0, let $x_{i_0 j_0}$ be the least desired consumption vector (that is, Mr. j_0 of the i_0th type is the "underdog" of the i_0th type). Then owing to the strict quasi-concavity of u_i, we have, for such a j_0,

(16) $$u_{i_0}(\frac{1}{r}x_{i_0 1} + \cdots + \frac{1}{r}x_{i_0 r}) > u_{i_0}(x_{i_0 j_0})$$

while for any other i we have

(17) $$u_i(\frac{1}{r}x_{i1} + \cdots + \frac{1}{r}x_{ir}) \geqq u_i(x_{ij}), \text{ for some } j$$

On the other hand, we have

(18)
$$\sum_{i=1}^{k} [(\frac{1}{r}x_{i1} + \cdots + \frac{1}{r}x_{ir}) - \bar{x}_i] = 0$$

since

$$\sum_{i=1}^{k} (x_{i1} + \cdots + x_{ir}) = \sum_{i=1}^{k} (r\bar{x}_i)$$

Therefore the coalition consisting of one consumer of each type, each of whom receives a least preferred consumption (that is, the "underdogs"), would block.[22]   (Q.E.D.)

REMARK: Suppose that the above theorem holds so that for each i, $x_{i1} = x_{i2} = \cdots = x_{ir}$, which we write as x_i to simplify the condition. Then under this theorem, an allocation in the core may be described by $(x_1, x_2, \ldots, x_k)$, where $\sum_{i=1}^{k} x_i = \sum_{i=1}^{k} \bar{x}_i$.

We now proceed with our analysis by assuming that (A-1) holds. Consider the set of all allocations in the core. Clearly it depends on r, the number of consumers in each category. We then denote the core by $C(r)$. It is easy to see that if an allocation $(x_1, \ldots, x_k)$ with r members of each type is blocked by a coalition S, then $(x_1, \ldots, x_k)$ with $(r + 1)$ members of each type is blocked by S. Hence $C(r + 1) \subset C(r)$. In other words, the core "shrinks," or at least is nonincreasing, as r increases. The main theorem obtained by Debreu and Scarf [10] says that if $(x_1, \ldots, x_k)$ is in the core for all r, then it is a competitive allocation. Intuitively, this means that the core shrinks to the set of competitive equilibria as $r \to \infty$. The result is known as a **limit theorem**, which, as remarked earlier, was originally discussed by Edgeworth [11] when $k = 2$.

In order to simplify our exposition, we impose the following assumption in place of (A-1).

(A-1')   For each i, the consumption set X_i is Ω, the nonnegative orthant of R^n. The utility functions u_i are strictly quasi-concave for all i.

Also assume **nonsatiation**, that is

(A-2)   For all $x_i \in \Omega$, there exists an $x_i' \in \Omega$ such that $u_i(x_i') > u_i(x_i), i = 1, 2, \ldots, k$.

Furthermore, we impose the **interior-point assumption**, that is

(A-3) $\bar{x}_i > 0$ for all i.

Assumption (A-3) implies that if a "price" vector $p \geq 0$ prevails, then there exists an $x_i' > 0$ such that $p \cdot x_i' < p \cdot \bar{x}_i$. In other words, (A-3) amounts to the **cheaper-point assumption**.

We now prove the following theorem.

Theorem 2.C.5   *Suppose that (A-1'), (A-2), and (A-3) hold. Then if $(\hat{x}_1, \ldots, \hat{x}_k)$ is in the core for all r, it is a competitive equilibrium.*

    PROOF: The proof is carried out in four steps.

    (i)   Define set Γ_i by

        (19) $\Gamma_i \equiv \{z_i \in \Omega : u_i(z_i + \bar{x}_i) > u_i(\hat{x}_i)\}, i = 1, 2, \ldots, k$

Since the nonsatiation assumption (A-2) holds and u_i is strictly quasi-concave, Γ_i is nonempty and convex. Define set Γ by[23]

    (20) $\Gamma \equiv \{z : z = \sum_{i=1}^{k} \alpha_i z_i, \ \sum_{i=1}^{k} \alpha_i = 1, \alpha_i \geqq 0, z_i \in \Gamma_i, i = 1, 2, \ldots, k\}$

Clearly Γ is nonempty and convex. This set Γ is illustrated in Figure 2.20. Next we show that the origin 0 does not belong to Γ (allowing us to utilize the separation theorem between 0 and Γ).

    (ii)   Suppose that $0 \in \Gamma$. Then there exists $\alpha_i^* \geqq 0, z_i^* \in \Gamma_i, i = 1, 2, \ldots, k$, with $\sum_{i=1}^{k} \alpha_i^* = 1$ such that

    (21) $\sum_{i=1}^{k} \alpha_i^* z_i^* = 0$

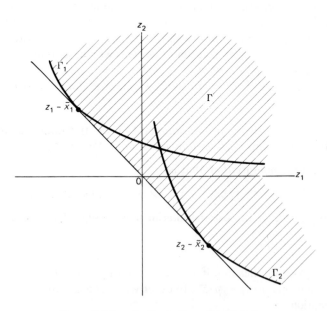

Figure 2.20.   An Illustration of the Set Γ.

Choose s from any positive integer with $s \leq r$. Let a_i^s be the smallest integer greater than or equal to $s\alpha_i^*$ and let I be the set of i for which $\alpha_i^* > 0$. For each i in I, define z_i^s by

$$(22) \qquad z_i^s \equiv \frac{s\alpha_i^*}{a_i^s} z_i^*$$

Observe that z_i^s approaches z_i^* as s tends to infinity. Therefore, z_i^s belongs to Γ_i for a sufficiently large s, since Γ_i is an open set (for each i) and any point sufficiently close to a point in Γ_i (such as z_i^*) is in Γ_i. Observe also

$$(23) \qquad \sum_{i \in I} a_i^s z_i^s = s \sum_{i \in I} \alpha_i^* z_i^* = 0$$

Now consider the coalition consisting of a_i^s members of each type $i \in I$, to each one of which we assign $(z_i^s + \overline{x}_i)$. Such a coalition is possible owing to (23). Also $u_i(z_i^s + \overline{x}_i) > u_i(\hat{x}_i)$ for all $i \in I$, if s is large enough (so that $z_i^s \in \Gamma_i$). Therefore this coalition blocks $(\hat{x}_1, \hat{x}_2, \ldots, \hat{x}_k)$ for a sufficiently large s, which contradicts the assumption that $(\hat{x}_1, \hat{x}_2, \ldots, \hat{x}_k)$ is in the core for all r. Therefore $0 \notin \Gamma$.

(iii) Hence, from the Minkowski separation theorem (Theorems 0.B.2 or 0.B.3), there exists a $\hat{p} \in R^n$, $\hat{p} \geq 0$, such that[24]

$$(24) \qquad \hat{p} \cdot z \geq 0 \qquad \text{for all } z \in \Gamma$$

Now consider $x_i' \in \Omega$ such that $u_i(x_i') > u_i(\hat{x}_i)$. Then $(x_i' - \overline{x}_i)$ is in Γ_i, so also in Γ. Hence from (24), $\hat{p} \cdot x_i' \geq \hat{p} \cdot \overline{x}_i$. In other words,

$$(25) \qquad u_i(x_i') > u_i(\hat{x}_i) \text{ implies } \hat{p} \cdot x_i' \geq \hat{p} \cdot \overline{x}_i, \, i = 1, 2, \ldots, k$$

From (A-2) and the strict quasi-concavity of u_i, there exists an $x_i'' \in \Omega$ in every neighborhood of $\hat{x}_i$ such that $u_i(x_i'') > u_i(\hat{x}_i)$. Then we obtain $\hat{p} \cdot \hat{x}_i \geq \hat{p} \cdot \overline{x}_i$ [for if $\hat{p} \cdot \hat{x}_i < \hat{p} \cdot \overline{x}_i$, then we can choose a point $\tilde{x}_i \in \Omega$ close enough to $\hat{x}_i$ so that $\hat{p} \cdot \tilde{x}_i < \hat{p} \cdot \overline{x}_i$, and yet $u_i(\tilde{x}_i) > u_i(\hat{x}_i)$, which contradicts (25)]. On the other hand, we also have $\sum_{i=1}^{k} (\hat{x}_i - \overline{x}_i) = 0$. Combining this with $\hat{p} \cdot \hat{x}_i \geq \hat{p} \cdot \overline{x}_i$, we obtain

$$(26) \qquad \hat{p} \cdot \hat{x}_i = \hat{p} \cdot \overline{x}_i, \, i = 1, 2, \ldots, k$$

(iv) We now show that $\hat{x}_i$ satisfies condition (i) of competitive equilibrium. For this purpose, it remains to be shown that $u_i(x_i') > u_i(\hat{x}_i)$ implies $\hat{p} \cdot x_i' > \hat{p} \cdot \hat{x}_i$ [$\because$ (25) and (26)]. To prove this, suppose that there exists $x_i' \in \Omega$ such that $u_i(x_i') > u_i(\hat{x}_i)$ and $\hat{p} \cdot x_i' = \hat{p} \cdot \hat{x}_i$. Then by the cheaper-point assumption (A-3),[25] there exists $x_i^* \in \Omega$ such that $\hat{p} \cdot x_i^* < \hat{p} \cdot \hat{x}_i$. Hence we can choose a point $x_i^0 \in \Omega$ which is close enough to x_i' so that $u_i(x_i^0) > u_i(\hat{x}_i)$, and yet $\hat{p} \cdot x_i^0 < \hat{p} \cdot \hat{x}_i (= \hat{p} \cdot \overline{x}_i)$. This contradicts (25).

$$\text{(Q.E.D.)}$$

REMARK: In view of Theorem 2.C.3, this theorem implies that the core is equal to the set of competitive equilibria in the limit ($r \to \infty$).

d.   SOME ILLUSTRATIONS

The purpose of this subsection is to illustrate some of the concepts and theorems discussed thus far. To simplify the exposition, we assume that the utility functions of all consumers are identical and are denoted by $u(x_i)$, $i = 1, 2, \ldots, m$. Assume that the consumption set for each consumer is Ω, the nonnegative orthant of R^n, and that u takes nonnegative values with $u(0) = 0$. Furthermore, impose the following restrictive assumption on the function u.

(A-4)   The function $u(z)$ is linear homogeneous, concave, and

$$u[tz^1 + (1 - t)z^2] > tu(z^1) + (1 - t)u(z^2)$$

for all $0 < t < 1$ and $z^1, z^2 \in \Omega$ with $z^1 \neq \beta z^2$ for any $\beta \in R, \beta \geq 0$, and $z_1 \neq 0$, $z_2 \neq 0$.

> *REMARK:*   The last part of (A-4) says that $u(z)$ is *strictly* concave for all *nonproportional* z^1 and z^2. Note that u cannot be linear homogeneous and strictly concave for proportional z^1 and z^2.[26] An example of $u(z)$ which satisfies (A-4) is[27]
>
> $$u: \Omega \to R, \; u(z) = \zeta_1^{\alpha_1}\zeta_2^{\alpha_2} \cdots \zeta_n^{\alpha_n}$$
>
> where $z = (\zeta_1, \zeta_2, \ldots, \zeta_n)$, $\sum_{i=1}^{n}\alpha_i = 1$, $\alpha_i > 0$, $i = 1, 2, \ldots, n$.

> *REMARK:*   It may be worthwhile to observe some consequences of the homogeneity and concavity requirements imposed in (A-4). Let $f(z)$ be a linear homogeneous and concave function defined on a convex subset Z of R^n. Let $z_1, z_2, \ldots, z_m$ be m points of Z. Note that the concavity of f alone implies

(27) $$f\left[\sum_{i=1}^{m} t_i z_i\right] \geq \sum_{i=1}^{m} t_i f(z_i)$$

for all $t_i \geq 0$, $i = 1, \ldots, m$, with $\sum_{i=1}^{m} t_i = 1$. Since f is linear homogeneous as well as concave, then for any $\alpha_i \geq 0$, $i = 1, 2, \ldots, m$, $\sum_{i=1}^{m}\alpha_i > 0$,

$$f\left[\sum_{i=1}^{m}\alpha_i z_i\right] = \alpha f\left[\sum_{i=1}^{m}\frac{\alpha_i}{\alpha}z_i\right] \geq \alpha \sum_{i=1}^{m}\frac{\alpha_i}{\alpha}f(z_i)$$

$$= \sum_{i=1}^{m}\alpha_i f(z_i), \quad \text{where } \alpha \equiv \sum_{i=1}^{m}\alpha_i$$

That is,

(28) $$f\left[\sum_{i=1}^{m}\alpha_i z_i\right] \geq \sum_{i=1}^{m}\alpha_i f(z_i)$$

for any $\alpha_i \geq 0$, $i = 1, 2, \ldots, m$, with $\sum_{i=1}^{m} \alpha_i > 0$. Note that $\sum_{i=1}^{m} \alpha_i$ does not have to be equal to one. For example, we have

$$f(z_1 + z_2 + \cdots + z_m) \geq f(z_1) + \cdots + f(z_m)$$

for such a function f. If f is linear homogeneous and strictly concave for non-proportional vectors, then the above inequality (28) is replaced by (28').

(28')
$$f\left[\sum_{i=1}^{m} \alpha_i z_i\right] > \sum_{i=1}^{m} \alpha_i f(z_i)$$

for all $\alpha_i > 0$, $i = 1, 2, \ldots, m$, provided that at least one z_{i_0} is not proportional to the others, that is, $z_{i_0} \neq \beta z_i$ for any $\beta \geq 0$ and any $i \neq i_0$, and that the z_i's do not vanish.

We now prove the following lemma, which justifies the power of (A-4) for the purpose of simplifying the illustration.

Lemma: *Let u be the identical utility function of all m consumers and assume that u satisfies (A-4). Let V be defined by*

(29)
$$V \equiv \{(u^1, \ldots, u^m): \sum_{i=1}^{m} u^i = u(\omega)\}, \text{ where } \omega \equiv \sum_{i=1}^{m} \bar{x}_i$$

If $(u^1, \ldots, u^m)$ is in V, then there exists a feasible allocation $x = (x_1, \ldots, x_m)$ such that $u(x_i) = u^i$, $i = 1, 2, \ldots, m$, and that x is Pareto optimal. Conversely, if x is a Pareto optimal allocation, then $(u^1, \ldots, u^m) \equiv [u(x_1), \ldots, u(x_m)]$ is in V.[28]

PROOF: The first two steps (i) and (ii) of the proof are concerned with the first statement of the lemma, and the last step (iii) is concerned with the second statement of the lemma.

(i)   First we show that there exists a feasible allocation $(x_1, \ldots, x_m)$ which satisfies $\sum_{i=1}^{m} u^i = u(\omega)$, where $u^i = u(x_i)$, $i = 1, \ldots, m$. Let

(30)
$$x_i \equiv \frac{u^i}{u(\omega)} \omega, \, i = 1, 2, \ldots, m$$

To show $u^i = u(x_i)$, $i = 1, 2, \ldots, m$, simply observe

$$u(x_i) = u\left[\frac{u^i}{u(\omega)} \omega\right] = \frac{u^i}{u(\omega)} u(\omega) = u^i, \, i = 1, 2, \ldots, m$$

where we employ the linear homogeneity of u. Now observe that

(31)
$$\sum_{i=1}^{m} x_i = \sum_{i=1}^{m} \frac{u^i}{u(\omega)} \omega = \omega$$

since $\sum_{i=1}^{m} u^i = u(\omega)$. In other words, the allocation $(x_1, \ldots, x_m)$ defined by (30) is feasible.

(ii) Next we show that if $\left[u(x_1), \ldots, u(x_m) \right] = (u^1, \ldots, u^m)$ is in V, then $(x_1, \ldots, x_m)$ is Pareto optimal. Suppose the contrary and assume that there exists $y_i \geqq 0$, $i = 1, 2, \ldots, m$, such that $\sum_{i=1}^{m} y_i = \omega$ and $u(y_i) \geqq u^i$ for all i with strict inequality for at least one i. Then using the concavity of u, we can observe

$$u(\omega) = u\left[\sum_{i=1}^{m} y_i \right] \geqq \sum_{i=1}^{m} u(y_i) > \sum_{i=1}^{m} u^i = u(\omega)$$

which is a contradiction.

(iii) To show that $\left[u(x_1), \ldots, u(x_m) \right]$ is in V for every Pareto optimal allocation $(x_1, \ldots, x_m)$, it suffices to show that $(x_1, \ldots, x_m)$ is **proportional** in the sense that

(32) $x_i = \alpha_i \omega$, for some $\alpha_i > 0$, $i = 1, 2, \ldots, m$, with $\sum_{i=1}^{m} \alpha_i = 1$

where $\omega \equiv \sum_{i=1}^{m} \bar{x}_i$, the aggregate endowment vector. For then we have

$$\sum_{i=1}^{m} u(x_i) = \sum_{i=1}^{m} u(\alpha_i \omega) = \sum_{i=1}^{m} \alpha_i u(\omega)$$

To show that every Pareto optimal allocation $(x_1, \ldots, x_m)$ is proportional, suppose the contrary. Then in view of (A-4), we have $u\left(\sum_{i=1}^{m} x_i \right) > \sum_{i=1}^{m} u(x_i)$ from (28'). But, since $\sum_{i=1}^{m} x_i = \omega$, this implies that $u(\omega) > \sum_{i=1}^{m} u(x_i)$. Define $y_i \equiv u(x_i) \omega / \sum_{i=1}^{m} u(x_i)$, $i = 1, 2, \ldots, m$, and observe that $(y_1, \ldots, y_m)$ is a feasible allocation and that

$$u(y_i) = \frac{u(x_i) u(\omega)}{\sum_{i=1}^{m} u(x_i)} > u(x_i), \quad i = 1, 2, \ldots, m$$

This contradicts the assumption that $(x_1, \ldots, x_m)$ is Pareto optimal.
(Q.E.D.)

REMARK: Observe that, in (iii) of the above proof, we showed that every Pareto optimal allocation is proportional in the sense of (32).[29]

Next we turn to an illustration of the Edgeworth-Debreu-Scarf limit theorem.[30] Assume now that there are two types of consumers and that there are r consumers of each type. There are two commodities X and Y in the economy. Assume for the sake of illustration that the consumers of both types have identical utility functions of the "Cobb-Douglas" form

(33) $u(x, y) = x^\alpha y^{1-\alpha}$, $0 < \alpha < 1$, where $x \geqq 0$ and $y \geqq 0$

As remarked before this utility function satisfies (A-4) [as well as (A-1')]. The consumers in the two different types are distinguished by their initial endowments.

Denote by $(\bar{x}_i, \bar{y}_i)$ the initial endowments of any consumer of the ith type $(i = 1, 2)$. Denote the aggregate endowments of X and Y by a and b, respectively, that is,

$$(34) \qquad a \equiv r\bar{x}_1 + r\bar{x}_2 \text{ and } b \equiv r\bar{y}_1 + r\bar{y}_2$$

We are interested in characterizing the core of such a replicated economy. Since any allocation in the core assigns identical consumption bundles to every consumer of the same type (the parity theorem of Subsection c), we may represent an allocation in the core by $[(x_1, y_1), (x_2, y_2)]$ where (x_i, y_i) denotes the consumption bundle of any consumer of the ith type. Moreover, we know, by definition of the core, that any allocation in the core is Pareto optimal. Furthermore, as we observed in this subsection, any Pareto optimal allocation is proportional; that is, it satisfies (32). Hence any allocation in the core is proportional. In other words, any allocation in the core assigns the two commodities in the ratio of a/b, that is,

$$(35) \qquad \frac{x_i}{y_i} = \frac{a}{b} \qquad \text{for all } i = 1, 2$$

Therefore, we may write

$$(36\text{-a}) \qquad x_1 = \theta \frac{a}{r} \text{ and } y_1 = \theta \frac{b}{r}$$

$$(36\text{-b}) \qquad x_2 = (1 - \theta)\frac{a}{r} \text{ and } y_2 = (1 - \theta)\frac{b}{r}$$

where $0 \leq \theta \leq 1$. Recalling that $a \equiv r(\bar{x}_1 + \bar{x}_2)$ and $b \equiv r(\bar{y}_1 + \bar{y}_2)$, we may rewrite this as

$$(37) \qquad x_1 = \theta\bar{x}, \, y_1 = \theta\bar{y}, \, x_2 = (1 - \theta)\bar{x} \text{ and } y_2 = (1 - \theta)\bar{y}$$

where $\bar{x}$ and $\bar{y}$ are defined by

$$(38) \qquad \bar{x} \equiv \bar{x}_1 + \bar{x}_2 \text{ and } \bar{y} \equiv \bar{y}_1 + \bar{y}_2$$

Therefore, each consumer of type 1 obtains the satisfaction represented by $\theta\bar{x}^\alpha\bar{y}^{1-\alpha}$. Similarly, each person of type 2 obtains the satisfaction represented by $(1 - \theta)\bar{x}^\alpha\bar{y}^{1-\alpha}$.

Consider the coalition consisting of s arbitrary consumers of type 1 and t arbitrary consumers of type 2. If $[(x_1, y_1), (x_2, y_2)]$ is an allocation in the core, then it cannot be blocked by any such coalition. In other words, using the lemma of this subsection, we obtain

$$(39) \qquad s\theta\bar{x}^\alpha\bar{y}^{1-\alpha} + t(1 - \theta)\bar{x}^\alpha\bar{y}^{1-\alpha} \geq (s\bar{x}_1 + t\bar{x}_2)^\alpha(s\bar{y}_1 + t\bar{y}_2)^{1-\alpha}$$

for any integers s and t with $0 \leq s, t \leq r$. Dividing both sides of (39) by $s\bar{x}^\alpha\bar{y}^{1-\alpha}$ and writing $t/s \equiv \sigma$ (where $s \geq 1$), we obtain

(40)
$$\theta + (1 - \theta)\sigma \geq \left(\frac{\bar{x}_1}{\bar{x}} + \frac{\bar{x}_2}{\bar{x}}\sigma\right)^\alpha \left(\frac{\bar{y}_1}{\bar{y}} + \frac{\bar{y}_2}{\bar{y}}\sigma\right)^{1-\alpha}$$

for any σ. Denote the RHS of this relation by $\phi(\sigma)$. Then we immediately obtain

(41)
$$\theta \geq \frac{[\phi(\sigma) - \sigma]}{(1 - \sigma)}, \quad \text{if } \sigma < 1$$

We may rewrite this as

(42)
$$\theta \geq 1 - \frac{\phi(1) - \phi(\sigma)}{1 - \sigma}, \quad \text{if } \sigma < 1$$

where we note that $\phi(1) = 1$. Similarly, we have

(43)
$$\theta \leq 1 - \frac{\phi(1) - \phi(\sigma)}{1 - \sigma}, \quad \text{if } \sigma > 1$$

Write

(44)
$$\psi(\sigma) \equiv \frac{\phi(1) - \phi(\sigma)}{1 - \sigma}$$

Then

(45)
$$\psi'(\sigma) = \frac{-1}{(1 - \sigma)^2}\left[\phi'(\sigma)(1 - \sigma) - \{\phi(1) - \phi(\sigma)\}\right]$$

On the other hand, we can compute

(46)
$$\phi'(\sigma) = \phi(\sigma)\left[\frac{\alpha\bar{x}_2}{\bar{x}_1 + \bar{x}_2\sigma} + \frac{(1 - \alpha)\bar{y}_2}{\bar{y}_1 + \bar{y}_2\sigma}\right]$$

so that $\phi'(\sigma) > 0$ for all σ. It is easy to check that $\phi(\sigma)$ is a strictly concave function[31] and therefore

(47)
$$\phi'(\sigma)(1 - \sigma) > \phi(1) - \phi(\sigma) \quad \text{for all } \sigma \neq 1$$

Hence from (45) we conclude

(48)
$$\psi'(\sigma) < 0 \quad \text{for all } \sigma \neq 1$$

Now for $\sigma < 1$, $\psi(\sigma)$ reaches a minimum when $\sigma(\equiv t/s)$ is as close as possible to 1, that is, $t = r - 1$ and $s = r$. For $\sigma > 1$, $\psi(\sigma)$ reaches a maximum when $\sigma(\equiv t/s)$ is as close as possible to 1, that is, $t = r$ and $s = r - 1$. Therefore from (42) and (43), we should have

(49)
$$1 - \phi\left(\frac{r - 1}{r}\right) \leq \theta \leq 1 - \phi\left(\frac{r}{r - 1}\right)$$

Now consider the limit as $r \to \infty$. Clearly when $r \to \infty$, $r/(r - 1) \to 1$ and $(r - 1)/r \to 1$. Therefore, we have, in view of (49),

(50)
$$1 - \lim_{\substack{\sigma \to 1 \\ \sigma < 1}} \frac{\Delta\phi}{\Delta\sigma} \leq \theta \leq 1 - \lim_{\substack{\sigma \to 1 \\ \sigma > 1}} \frac{\Delta\phi}{\Delta\sigma}$$

But by the differentiability of $\phi(\sigma)$, we have

(51)
$$\lim_{\substack{\sigma \to 1 \\ \sigma < 1}} \frac{\Delta\phi}{\Delta\sigma} = \lim_{\substack{\sigma \to 1 \\ \sigma > 1}} \frac{\Delta\phi}{\Delta\sigma} = \phi'(1)$$

where $\phi'(1)$ is easily computed from (46) as

(52)
$$\phi'(1) = \frac{\alpha\bar{x}_2}{\bar{x}} + \frac{(1-\alpha)\bar{y}_2}{\bar{y}}$$

From (50) and (51) we obtain

(53)
$$\theta = 1 - \phi'(1) = 1 - \left(\frac{\alpha\bar{x}_2}{\bar{x}} + \frac{(1-\alpha)\bar{y}_2}{\bar{y}}\right)$$

in the limit as $\sigma \to 1$. It is easy to see that $0 < \theta < 1$. In particular, if the type 1 consumers do not have Y initially and the type 2 consumers do not have X initially (that is, $\bar{y}_1 = 0$ and $\bar{x}_2 = 0$), then we have

(54)
$$\theta = \alpha$$

In any case, an allocation in the core when $r \to \infty$ is uniquely determined and easily computed as

(55)
$$x_i = \alpha\bar{x}_i + (1-\alpha)\bar{y}_i\frac{\bar{x}}{\bar{y}}, \, i = 1, 2$$

and

(56)
$$y_i = \alpha\bar{x}_i\frac{\bar{y}}{\bar{x}} + (1-\alpha)\bar{y}_i, \, i = 1, 2$$

When $\bar{x} = \bar{x}_1$ and $\bar{y} = \bar{y}_2$ so that $\theta = \alpha$, the computation is even simpler, and we obtain

(57)
$$x_1 = \alpha\bar{x}, x_2 = (1-\alpha)\bar{x}, y_1 = \alpha\bar{y}, \text{ and } y_2 = (1-\alpha)\bar{y}$$

Finally we relate the above discussions to the theory of competitive equilibrium. For this purpose we have to introduce prices. Denote by $p \equiv p_x/p_y$ the relative price of X vis-à-vis Y. It is assumed that each consumer chooses his consumption bundle so as to maximize his satisfaction subject to his budget constraint. In other words, his consumption bundle (x_i, y_i) is a solution of the following nonlinear programming problem. For each $i = 1, 2$,

Maximize: $\quad x_i^\alpha y_i^{1-\alpha}$
(x_i, y_i)

Subject to: $\quad px_i + y_i \leqq p\bar{x}_i + \bar{y}_i, x_i \geqq 0, y_i \geqq 0$

The solution of this problem can be computed easily and (as is well known) takes the following form:[32]

(58-a) $$x_i = \frac{\alpha}{p}(p\bar{x}_i + \bar{y}_i), \; i = 1, 2$$

(58-b) $$y_i = (1 - \alpha)(p\bar{x}_i + \bar{y}_i), \; i = 1, 2$$

where the notation (such as $\wedge$) which denotes the optimal value is omitted to simplify the notation. The condition for a competitive equilibrium is described by

(59) $$x_1 + x_2 = \bar{x}_1 + \bar{x}_2$$

Therefore, combining this with (58-a), we can compute the unique equilibrium price ratio $\hat{p}$ as

(60) $$\hat{p} = \frac{\alpha}{1 - \alpha}\frac{\bar{y}}{\bar{x}}$$

Therefore, the unique competitive allocation is computed by (58-a) and (58-b) using this $\hat{p}$. The resulting expressions for x_i and y_i, $i = 1, 2$, are identical to the ones in (55) and (56). In other words, when $r \to \infty$, the core allocation is unique and coincides with the competitive allocation. It may be emphasized here that both the core allocation (when $r \to \infty$) and the competitive allocation are unique as a result of (A-4), especially the assumption that u is strictly concave with respect to nonproportional vectors. If this assumption is relaxed, then the uniqueness does not necessarily follow.

e.   SOME REMARKS

The limit theorem obtained by Debreu and Scarf [10] has aroused great interest among mathematicians and economists working on the theory of the core and has produced various attempts to extend the Debreu-Scarf analysis. One focal point is the particular way of increasing the number of persons in the economy. It is assumed that there are k types of participants in the economy with r members of each type. Debreu and Scarf then obtained their result by letting r increase. The crucial step in obtaining the limit theorem is the equal treatment theorem which says that an allocation in the core assigns the same consumption to all consumers of the same type. In this way they avoid the difficulty of the feasibility condition

$$\sum_{i=1}^{m} x_i = \sum_{i=1}^{m} \bar{x}_i$$

becoming meaningless when m is directly increased rather than r. However, the assumption that there is an equal number of individuals ($= r$) of every type is a strong assumption indeed. Moreover, the Debreu-Scarf limit theorem is concerned with the case in which r is far larger than k, the number of types of individuals. In general, an economy would contain a different number of individuals in each of various types, and the number of types may exceed the number of individuals in any one type. If this is the case, then the equal treatment theorem breaks down and simple counterexamples can be found easily in which a core allocation does not assign the same consumption to two individuals of the same type.[33] Since the equal treatment theorem is crucial in the proof of the Debreu-Scarf limit theorem, it is then natural to explore whether or not a result similar to their limit theorem holds when we directly increase m. One such attempt is that of Vind [31]. Define the set Γ_i by (19), following Debreu and Scarf [10], and let $\Gamma_i(\epsilon) \equiv \{z_i \in \Omega: N_\epsilon(z_i) \subset \Gamma_i\}$, where $N_\epsilon(z_i)$ is an ϵ neighborhood of z. Let $\rho(p, \epsilon)$ be the number of persons such that $H \cap \Gamma_i(\epsilon) \neq \emptyset$, where $H \equiv \{z_i: p \cdot z_i \leq 0\}$. Let $\Gamma(\epsilon)$ be the convex hull of $\cup_{i=1}^m \Gamma_i(\epsilon)$. If we can prove that $0 \notin \Gamma(\epsilon)$, then using the separation theorem we can prove that there exists $\hat{p} \geq 0$ such that $\rho(\hat{p}, \epsilon) = 0$. Hence if we can prove $0 \notin \Gamma(\epsilon)$ for any $\epsilon > 0$ when $m \to \infty$, then we have a generalization of the Debreu-Scarf limit theorem. However, such a proof is impossible. What Vind [31] has shown is that we can find an upper bound for $\rho(p, \epsilon)$, which is independent of m, for every core allocation. In other words, if $(\hat{x}_1, \ldots, \hat{x}_m)$ is a core allocation, then there exists a $\hat{p} \geq 0$ such that $\rho(\hat{p}, \epsilon) \leq \bar{\rho}$ for any $\epsilon > 0$, where $\bar{\rho}$ is defined as[34]

$$\bar{\rho} \equiv \left[\frac{c(\epsilon)}{\epsilon}\right]^2 \text{ and } c(\epsilon) \equiv \sup d(0, H \cap \Gamma(\epsilon))$$

Clearly this result is useful only when $\bar{\rho}$ is finite for any m. However, ρ becomes infinite when, for example, a particular individual has a complete monopoly over a certain scarce resource in the production economy. The assumption that $\bar{\rho}$ is finite then seems to play a role similar to the Debreu-Scarf equal treatment theorem.

Another approach to the theory of the core and the limit theorem starts with Aumann's assumption of an "atomless" set or a continuum of traders [2]. In other words, the concept of a competitive equilibrium requires that the influence of each participant be zero, which is possible only when the number of participants in the economy is infinity. Then Aumann assumed that the economy contains a continuum of traders of as many real numbers as in the unit interval $I \equiv [0, 1]$. Define the initial endowment and the feasible allocation, respectively, as the functions $\bar{x}$ and x defined over I to Ω, such that

and

$$\int_I \bar{x} \equiv \int_I \bar{x}_i di > 0$$

$$\int_I x \equiv \int_I x_i di = \int_I \bar{x}_i di$$

where the integral is defined componentwise. Note that the integral gives the area under the curve defined by the integrand, and therefore the area under a single point—say, x_i—is zero. This is the basis of the "atomless" set of participants. In the actual treatment of core theory with an atomless space of participants, a branch of mathematics called "measure theory" is extensively used. Thus the above integrals are taken in the sense of Lebesgue,[35] and $\bar{x}_i$ and x_i are Lebesgue integrable functions in i. Let $\mu(S)$ denote the Lebesgue measure where S is a Lebesgue measurable subset of I. The core C_I and the set of competitive allocations E_I are respectively defined by

$$C_I \equiv \{x: u_i(x_i') > u_i(x_i), i \in S, \mu(S) > 0 \text{ imply } \int_S x_i' di \nleq \int_S \bar{x}_i di\}$$

$$E_I \equiv \{x: \exists \, \hat{p} \geq 0 \text{ such that } x_i' \in D_{\hat{p}}(i) \text{ implies } u(x_i) > u_i(x_i') \text{ for a.e. } i \in I\}$$

where $D_{\hat{p}}(i) \equiv \{z \in \Omega: \hat{p} \cdot z \leq \hat{p} \cdot x_i\}$. The existence of a competitive equilibrium then amounts to asserting that $E_I \neq \emptyset$, which is proved by Aumann.[36] The proof of the statement $E_I \subset C_I$ is almost trivial.[37] This in turn implies that $C_I \neq \emptyset$ as long as $E_I \neq \emptyset$. Using the Minkowski separation theorem, Aumann [2] showed that $C_I \subset E_I$, which together with $E_I \subset C_I$ implies $C_I = E_I$.

A remarkable feature in Aumann's proof of the nonemptiness of E_I and hence C_I is that no assumption is necessary with regard to the quasi-concavity of an individual's utility function (or the convexity of an individual's preference ordering). However, as we remarked before, in the economy consisting of a finite number of consumers, the core can be empty when preference orderings lack convexity (recall Figure 2.19). Another remarkable feature is that in his proof of $C_I = E_I$, which corresponds to Debreu-Scarf's limit theorem, there is no need to suppose various "types" of consumers with the same number of members in each type. These two features are clearly very powerful, and there has been active research in the field of an atomless space of economic agents.[38] The cost of obtaining these features is the assumption of a continuum of economic agents. Although this assumption may appear to be the natural consequence of the assumption that the influence of each agent is nil, this is indeed a striking assumption for economists. Clearly the number of economic agents is finite. It seems too far-fetched to leave Debreu and Scarf's world of countably many agents and to jump into a world with a continuum of agents. Furthermore, the fundamental notion of a competitive equilibrium is that each agent is a price taker rather than that the influence of each agent is nil. The latter implies the former, but not vice versa. It is true that each agent would be silly to act as a price taker if he can influence prices; but the amount of his influence may be so small and the cost of obtaining information with regard to his influence and of forming coalitions may be so large that each agent may end up acting as a price taker. In other words, one can argue that the influence of each agent in a competitive market is nil, not because he is atomless, but because the high cost of a coalition forces him to be a price taker.

That there is a cost involved in any coalition can possibly constitute a serious weakness in the theory of the core, for it usually ignores such a cost. Consider the case in which the number of participants m is finite. The cost to each participant of finding a coalition which blocks a given allocation can be very large indeed if m is large, and if every participant is not somewhat like the others. Hence to find a core allocation, that is, an allocation that cannot be blocked by *any* coalition, may become practically impossible because of the information cost involved in finding the effects of all coalitions.

On the other hand, the price mechanism involved in the competitive economy is quite remarkable in this respect. Each participant is required to know only the prices given to him, and even though no more information is required for his actions, yet the economy, by this mechanism, reaches an allocation that cannot be blocked by any possible coalition of the economy, that is, a core allocation. One crucial difference here is that the competitive price mechanism does not involve excessive information cost. The Debreu-Scarf limit theorem then says that, under certain assumptions, every core allocation can be obtained as a competitive equilibrium!

The question then boils down to the problem of finding an equilibrium price vector. The *tâtonnement* process, which we discuss in Chapter 3, provides one method of finding an equilibrium price vector, as long as the process converges to an equilibrium. The beauty of this process is that the "market manager" of this process does not have to know the preferences of each consumer and the production set of each producer. A major weakness of the process is that the convergence of this process to an equilibrium is established only under a restrictive situation in which all commodities are "gross substitutes." Recently Scarf [18 and 19], as mentioned before, offered a constructive method of finding an equilibrium price vector. Electronic computers will "quickly" calculate the equilibrium price vector,[39] if we know the technology available in the economy, the initial endowment of each consumer, and have certain information with regard to each consumer's demand function.[40] If one can successfully compute the equilibrium price vector, then the existence of competitive equilibrium of a given economy can also be ascertained.

That the core can be characterized "almost" completely by competitive equilibrium has one important corollary. That is, if we can find circumstances in which the core is empty, then the competitive mechanism will "fail," and conversely, if the competitive mechanism "fails," then there is a good possibility that the core may be empty (assuming that the number of participants is large).[41] In the literature, the cases in which the competitive mechanism fails are known as the cases of **market failures**.[42] This suggests the close connection between the theory of the core and the theory of market failures (and the theory of monopoly).

A famous case for market failures is the case of external economies and diseconomies in production or consumption that effect the welfare of outsiders regardless of their desires. A classical example of external economies is that of an apple grower and a beekeeper in the adjacent field. External diseconomies have attracted a greater attention recently due to smoke, noise, and many forms of air and water pollution. Recently a fresh look at this problem has been taken by Shapley and Shubik [25], who considered the problem of externality from the viewpoint of the theory of the core. They argue, for example, that in certain cases of diseconomies, the core may be empty. Needless to say, if the core is empty, the competitive equilibrium, in general, does not exist. Here we may quote Shapley and Shubik ([25], p. 681) for such an example.

> *The Garbage Game.* Each player has a bag of garbage which he must dump in someone's yard. The utility of having b bags dumped in one's yard is $-b$.

It can be shown easily that if there are more than two players in this "game," there is no core.[13]

Another example of market failures may be the commodity called "information." It is true that certain kinds of information can be traded in the market just as can any other commodity. For example, information with regard to technical know-how is traded for certain prices, called "royalties." Similarly, insurance premiums can be considered as the price for the information with regard to certain uncertainties. However, there are some types of information that are not traded in the market. The most important example would be "basic research," which in practice is often carried out in universities through funds given by the government, foundations, and so on, according to somewhat arbitrary principles. Clearly such information plays a role very similar to that of the externalities discussed above.[44]

Even if information can be treated as any other commodity, it is still possible that we do not have a competitive economy in practice. Inequalities in the distribution of information can cause fundamental inequalities among the members of the society and thus generate a possibility of blocking coalitions. For example, some forms of technical know-how that may be crucial for the production of certain commodities[45] cannot easily be imitated by others.[46] Then the possessor of this know-how can form a blocking coalition, thus giving rise to a monopoly. Similarly, some specialized skills that are scarce relative to the size of the economy can give rise to monopolies. Examples would be associations such as the American Medical Association or an electricians' union.

In this connection, we may recall our previous discussion with regard to the cost of coalitions. For example, a particular commodity such as "unskilled labor" may be indispensable for the production of any commodity, but the cost of the coalition of "working men of all countries" may be prohibitively high. The U.S. textile workers may refuse to have a coalition with the Japanese textile workers. On the other hand, in the above examples of specialized skills that are scarce relative to the size of the economy, the cost of coalition would be relatively small.

In fact, the relative differences in the costs of coalitions among the possible coalitions in the economy may be more important in explaining monopoly than the scarcities of skills, technical know-how, and so on. Monopoly can arise solely as the result of the ease of coalition and without any regard to the scarcities of skills, know-how, and the like. Incidentally, the cost of coalition may not be confined to the pecuniary cost alone; such things as differences in social class (such as caste in India), and matriculation from a university (say, Oxbridge) can explain various coalitions in a given society.

Some monopolies (or oligopolies) can be explained in terms of indivisibilities of certain commodities which give rise to increasing returns to scale. The production of electricity, automobiles, and so on, is often cited as an example. Here again the way in which a coalition is formed to obtain the initial capacity may be crucial in explaining the birth of these monopolies and oligopolies. Such coalitions are not formed by considering all the possible coalitions in the society under the assumption that the cost of forming each coalition is zero.

These considerations suggest an urgent need for introducing the cost of coalitions in the existing theory of the core. The author has a serious doubt with regard to the existing theory of the core, which considers all possible coalitions of the economy but ignores completely the cost of coalitions. The explicit introduction of the cost of coalitions will provide another important area for applications of the theory of the *n*-person cooperative game. Instead of exploring allocations which cannot be blocked by *any* coalition, one may be more inclined to study the coalitions which block certain allocations. Such a study may give rise to a fresh approach to the study of monopolies and oligopolies and to the study of various other forms of social establishment.

FOOTNOTES

1. Note the following features of the competitive price mechanism: (1) Each economic agent (here the consumer) is a price taker, and (2) there exists a price system which is the same for all economic agents. The price system can exist, of course, without each agent being a price taker. In the box diagram model, one or both can be empowered to name the price. For a game-theoretic exposition, see Shapley and Shubik [22].
2. Note that the core is a subset of the set of Pareto optimal points, in the sense that the entire contract curve is now restricted to its *PQ* segment. In this sense, the core is stronger than a Pareto optimum. The meaning of the core will be discussed more fully below.
3. See Edgeworth [11], pp. 35–39, in particular.
4. Edgeworth's definitions of terms such as "recontracting," "final settlement," and so on, appear in [11], pp. 18–19.
5. There is a slight oversell of the core theory here. The Debreu-Scarf result assumes that there are an equal number of individuals of each "type." The power of this assumption lies in its consequence that the individuals of the same type are treated identically (that is, each has the same consumption bundle). If there are different numbers of individuals of each type, then this parity (or equal treatment) result does not follow (that is, there is a core allocation which treats individuals of the same type differently). On the other hand, the basic premise of competitive equilibrium is obviously that of equal treatment. Thus both the theory of competitive equilibrium and the Debreu-Scarf result have one basic feature in common, that is, equal treatment.
6. The game is said to be **cooperative** if the players are allowed to communicate before each play and to make binding agreements about the strategies they will use. **Side payments** are allowed when there is a medium of exchange—say, "money"—which is freely transferable between the players and each player's utils are linear in (or proportional to) money. It is known that cooperative games without side payments include cooperative games with side payments as a special case. Noncooperative games include cooperative games as a special case.
7. See, for example, Aumann [4] and Aumann and Peleg [5].
8. For an excellent survey of the theory of *n*-person games without side payments, see Aumann [3].
9. Debreu and Scarf [10] suggested a way to generalize the results so as to incorporate production into the model. Nikaido [15], and Arrow and Hahn [1] have rigorous formulations and the proofs of such a generalization.
10. Any order-preserving (that is, monotone increasing) function of a particular utility function can also be a utility function. For the discussion of the representability of preferences by a continuous real-valued function ("utility function"), see Debreu [9]. Also recall our discussion in Section B.

11. The reader should find no difficulty (in most cases) in carrying out an analysis similar to the one which follows, replacing the function u_i by the usual preference ordering.

12. Note, however, that a person will not be worse off compared to his initial endowment position, since he can always refuse trading. In other words, the existence of a coalition does not mean that it would necessarily "take effect."

13. One of the most important applications of this concept in economics is the "compensation principle" problem in welfare economics. For an exposition of the compensation principle, see Takayama [29], chapter 17. Clearly this problem offers an interesting application of the theory of n-person (cooperative) games in economics.

14. A **game** (without side payments) can be defined by specifying $V(S)$ for all coalitions S and $U(M)$. In the theory of games, some or all of the following assumptions are imposed: (i) $V(S)$ is convex, closed, and nonempty for each S; (ii) $v \in V(S)$ and $v' \leq v$ where $v' \in R^s$ imply that $v' \in V(S)$; and (iii) $V(S) \otimes V(S') \subset V(S \cup S')$ if S and S' are two disjoint coalitions. Sometimes these assumptions are used as the axioms of the theory.

15. In Figure 2.18, it is implicitly assumed that the normalization of units is made with regard to the representation by the u_i's such that $u_i(0) = 0$ for all i.

16. Let e_S be a vector in R^s whose ith element e_{Si} is defined as $e_{Si} = 1$ if $i \in S$, and $= 0$ if $i \notin S$. A collection T of coalitions, $\{S\}$, is called **balanced** if it is possible to assign to each S in T a nonnegative number δ_S such that $\sum_{S \in T} \delta_S e_S = e_M$. If $M = \{1, 2, 3\}$, then $T = \{\{1, 2\}, \{2, 3\}, \{1, 3\}\}$ is balanced where the δ_S are given by $\delta_{\{1,2\}} = \delta_{\{2,3\}} = \delta_{\{1,3\}} = 1/2$. An m-person game is said to be **balanced** if for every balanced collection T, $u_S \in V(S)$ for all $S \in T$ implies $u \in V(M)$.

17. Not only did he generalize Scarf's result, but he also obtained necessary and sufficient conditions for a nonempty core for games whose payoff sets are assumed to be convex.

18. On the other hand, the method of proving that the core is nonempty can be utilized in the proof of the existence of competitive equilibrium. Apparently from this viewpoint, Scarf [18; 19] showed a constructive proof of the existence of competitive equilibrium. Compare these articles with [17].

19. It is easy to see that, in establishing this theorem, no stronger assumptions than those needed in proving Theorem 2.C.1 ("every competitive equilibrium realizes a Pareto optimum") are required.

20. A real-valued function f defined on a convex subset Z of R^n is called **strictly quasi-concave** if $f(z) \geq f(z')$ implies $f[tz + (1 - t)z'] > f(z')$ for all $z, z' \in Z$ with $z \neq z'$, and for all $t, 0 < t < 1$ (see Chapter 1, Section E). Using this definition, we can prove the following: Let f be strictly quasi-concave on Z, and let $z_1, z_2, \ldots, z_m$ be m points in Z. Suppose that one of these m vectors—say, z_{j_0}—is distinct from any other points with $f(z_j) \geq f(z_{j_0})$ for all $j = 1, 2, \ldots, m$. Then we have $f(\theta_1 z_2 + \cdots + \theta_m z_m) > f(z_{j_0})$ for all $\theta_j > 0, \sum_{j=1}^{m} \theta_j = 1$, such that $z_{j_0} \neq \sum_{j=1}^{m} \theta_j z_j$.

21. In this sense, Theorem 2.C.4 may be termed the **parity theorem** or the **equal treatment theorem**.

22. In other words, the coalition of the underdogs can block the original allocation by redistributing their own initial holdings among themselves, where the "underdog" of the ith group now receives $(x_{i1}/r + \cdots + x_{ir}/r)$. Such a coalition is feasible as a result of (18) and (17).

23. Such a set is the **convex hull** generated by the sets Γ_i.

24. That $\hat{p} \neq 0$ follows directly from the separation theorem. That $\hat{p} \geq 0$ is then obvious from (24).

25. This use of the cheaper-point assumption is standard practice. See the proof of the corollary to Theorem 2.C.2.

26. To see this, let $z^2 = \beta z^1$ for some β and observe that $u[(z^1 + z^2)/2] = u(z^1)/2 + u(z^2)/2$ using linear homogeneity. But this contradicts strict concavity. Note also that if $z^2 = 0$ and if $u(0) = 0$, then we again have $u[(z^1 + z^2)/2] = u(z^1)/2 + u(z^2)/2$, contradicting strict concavity.

27. To prove that $u(z)$ is strictly concave for all nonproportional vectors, show that $u'(z^1) \cdot (z^2 - z^1) > u(z^2) - u(z^1)$ for all nonproportional $z^1 \neq 0$ and $z^2 \neq 0$. To show this, utilize the following well-known inequality: $\theta_1^{\alpha_1}\theta_2^{\alpha_2}\cdots\theta_n^{\alpha_n} \leqq \alpha_1\theta_1 + \alpha_2\theta_2 + \cdots + \alpha_n\theta_n$ (the equality holds if and only if $\theta_1 = \theta_2 = \cdots = \theta_n$), where $\sum_{i=1}^{n}\alpha_i = 1$, $\alpha_i > 0$, and $\theta_i \geqq 0$ for all i.

28. A similar result is obtained in E. Eisenberg, "Aggregation of Utility Functions," *Management Science*, 7, July 1961.

29. In terms of the box diagram, this means that the contract curve coincides with the diagonal line of the box.

30. I learned recently that a similar example was discussed by Herbert Scarf in his lecture at Yale.

31. Compute $\phi''(\sigma)$ and examine $\phi''(\sigma) < 0$ for all σ. Alternatively, write $\phi(\sigma) = \Phi[f(\sigma), g(\sigma)]$, where $f(\sigma) \equiv (\bar{x}_1/\bar{x} + \bar{x}_2\sigma/\bar{x})^\alpha$ and $g(\sigma) \equiv (\bar{y}_1/\bar{y} + \bar{y}_2\sigma/\bar{y})^{1-\alpha}$. Observe that both $f(\sigma)$ and $g(\sigma)$ are strictly concave. Also note that Φ is strictly concave and monotone (that is, $\partial\Phi/\partial f > 0$ and $\partial\Phi/\partial g > 0$). These establish the strict concavity of ϕ.

32. First note that the Cobb-Douglas form of the utility function guarantees an interior solution. The condition requiring the tangency between an indifference curve and the budget line is stated as $p = [\alpha/(1-\alpha)](y_i/x_i)$. This together with $px_i + y_i = p\bar{x}_i + \bar{y}_i$ constitutes a necessary and sufficient quasi-saddle-point characterization of the solution and yields (58-a) and (58-b).

33. Green [13] contains such an example, which he acknowledges to Alan Kirman. Green [13] then argues that there are bounds on the inequality of treatments. See also Vind [31].

34. Let $X \subset R^n$ and $a \in R^n$. Then $d(a, X)$ denotes the "distance" between a and X, meaning $d(a, X) \equiv \inf_{x \in X} \| x - a \|$.

35. Since the reader is not expected to know measure theory, the subsequent paragraph may be omitted.

36. See R. J. Aumann, "Existence of Competitive Equilibrium in Markets with a Continuum of Traders," *Econometrica*, 34, January 1966. A crucial assumption is that of "monotonicity" in the sense that $x_i' \geq x_i$ implies $u_i(x_i') > u_i(x_i)$, and not the (quasi-) concavity of the u_i's.

37. Suppose that there exists $x \in E_I$ but $x \notin C_I$. Since $x \notin C_I$, there exists x' and $S \subset I$ with $\mu(S) > 0$, such that $u_i(x_i') > u_i(x_i)$, $i \in S$ and $\int_S x' = \int_S \bar{x}$. But, since $x \in E_I$, there exists $\hat{p} \geq 0$ such that $\hat{p} \cdot x_i' > \hat{p} \cdot \bar{x}_i$, $i \in S$, which implies $\hat{p} \cdot [\int_S x_i' di] > \hat{p} \cdot [\int_S \bar{x}_i di]$. This contradicts the feasibility condition of the coalition S, $\int_S \int_S x_i' di = \int_S \bar{x}_i di$.

38. For example, Vind [30] showed a different derivation of Aumann's result $E_I = C_I$ in [2]. Hildenbrand [14] introduced production, while Aumann and Vind assumed a pure exchange economy. Moreover, Hildenbrand showed that the monotonicity assumption can be relaxed and that the consumption set does not have to be restricted to the nonnegative orthant of R^n.

39. Scarf writes ([19], p. 669)

    A considerable body of computational experience with larger models has already been gathered. Over one hundred examples have been tested, ranging from three to twenty sectors. The computational time, which is dependent on the number of sectors, has never exceeded five minutes on an IBM 7094, and in most cases is substantially smaller.

40. It is assumed that each consumer has a set of demand functions which can be expressed as $x_{ij}(p) = a_{ij}f_i(p)/p_j^{b_i}$, where x_{ij} denotes consumer i's demand function of the jth commodity, a_{ij} measures the intensity of i's demand for j, and b_i is the elasticity of substitution for i. For computation, it is required that the a_{ij}'s and the b_i's be known.

41. It is to be pointed out that competitive equilibrium may fail to exist for various reasons, such as the nonconvexity of preferences and of the aggregate production set. But the core can still be nonempty or at least "approximately" nonempty as in the Shapley-Shubik theory of the ϵ-core [23]. This is a great merit of the theory of the core. But it is also to be noted that the core can be very large, and its practical significance may be greatly hampered.

42. The purpose of our discussion here is not to make a comprehensive survey of the theory of market failures. For an early exposition of this topic, see F. M. Bator, "The Anatomy of Market Failure," *Quarterly Journal of Economics*, LXXII, August 1958. See also K. Imai, H. Uzawa, R. Komiya, T. Negishi, and Y. Murakami, *Price Theory II*, (in Japanese), Tokyo, Iwanami, 1971, Chapter 7.

43. Shapley and Shubik [25], on the other hand, indicated that the core will exist in the case of external economies if they are internalized by being listed as explicit commodities. This apparent asymmetry between external economies and diseconomies makes their result highly suspect, or at least urges us to consider this problem further. See discussions on Shapley and Shubik [25] by K. J. Arrow and T. Rader, in *American Economic Review*, LX, May 1970, pp. 462–464. Arrow, for example, suspects that the lack of the core in the above garbage game may really be due to a possible lack of convexity in the production set, instead of the presence of an external diseconomy (p. 463).

44. Actually there are some important cases of market failures that we have not discussed here. For example, "the market fails" as a result of certain "public goods" in which the beneficiaries of these goods cannot be distinguished from the nonbeneficiaries (the lack of "exclusion") as a result of the lack of "future markets" for certain commodities, or simply as a result of future generations being unable to participate in the market.

45. The information may be indispensable for the production of a certain new commodity, or the information may provide a significant cost saving method of production of an existing commodity.

46. The information may be protected by patent rights and the possessor of the right may refuse to sell the information; or the possessor of the information may simply hide it, for publication of the information through patent rights may cause his techniques to be imitated.

REFERENCES

1. Arrow, K. J., and Hahn, F. H., *General Competitive Analysis*, San Francisco, Holden Day, 1971.

2. Aumann, R. J., "Markets with Continuum of Traders," *Econometrica*, 32, January–April 1964.

3. ———, "A Survey of Cooperative Games without Side Payments," *Essays in Mathematical Economics in Honor of Oscar Morgenstern*, ed. by M. Shubik, Princeton, N.J., Princeton University Press, 1967.

4. ———, "The Core of a Cooperative Game without Side Payments," *Bulletin of the American Mathematical Society*, XCVIII, March 1961.

5. Aumann, R. J., and Peleg, B., "von Neumann-Morgenstern Solutions to Cooperative

Games without Side Payments," *Transactions of the American Mathematical Society*, LXVI, May 1960.

6. Billera, L., "Some Problems on the Core of an N-Person Game without Side-Payments," *SIAM Journal on Applied Mathematics*, 18, May 1970.

7. Chipman, J. S., "The Nature and Meaning of Equilibrium Economic Theory," in *Functionalism in Social Sciences*, American Academy of Political and Social Science, Philadelphia, February 1965.

8. Debreu, G., "On a Theorem of Scarf," *Review of Economic Studies*, XXX, October 1963.

9. ———, *Theory of Value*, New York, Wiley, 1959.

10. Debreu, G., and Scarf, H., "A Limit Theorem on the Core of an Economy," *International Economic Review*, 4, September 1963.

11. Edgeworth, F. T., *Mathematical Psychics*, London, Kegan Paul, 1881.

12. Gillies, D. B., *Some Theorems on N-Person Games*, Ph.D. Thesis, Princeton University, 1953.

13. Green, J., "A Note on the Cores of Trading Economies," unpublished manuscript, University of Rochester, May 1969.

14. Hildenbrand, W., "On the Core of an Economy with a Measure Space of Economic Agents," *Review of Economic Studies*, XXXV, October 1968.

15. Nikaido, H., *Convex Structures and Economic Theory*, New York, Academic Press, 1968, esp. sec. 17.2.

16. Scarf, H. E., "An Analysis of Markets with a Large Number of Participants," in *Recent Advances in Game Theory*, ed. by M. Maschler, Princeton, N.J., Princeton University Press, 1962.

17. ———, "The Core of an *N*-Person Game," *Econometrica*, 35, January 1967.

18. ———, "On the Computation of Equilibrium Prices," in *Ten Economic Studies in the Tradition of Irving Fisher,* New York, Wiley, 1967.

19. ———, "An Example of an Alogarithm for Calculating General Equilibrium Prices," *American Economic Review*, LIX, September 1969.

20. Shapley, L. S., "On Balanced Sets and Cores," *Naval Research Logistics Quarterly*, 14, December 1967.

21. Shapley, L. S., and Shubik, M., "Solution of *N*-Person Games with Ordinal Utilities" (abstract), *Econometrica*, 21, April 1953.

22. ———, and ———, "Concepts and Theories of Pure Competition," *Essays in Mathematical Economics in Honor of Oscar Morgenstern*, ed. by M. Shubik, Princeton, N.J., Princeton University Press, 1963.

23. ———, and ———, "Quasi-cores in a Monetary Economy with Nonconvex Preferences," *Econometrica*, 34, October 1966.

24. ———, and ———, "On Market Games," *Journal of Economic Theory*, 1, June 1969.

25. ———, and ———, "On the Core of an Economic System with Externalities," *American Economic Review*, LIX, September 1969.

26. ———, and ———, "Pure Competition, Coalitional Power, and Fair Division," *International Economic Review*, 10, October 1969.

27. Samuelson, P. A., "Evaluation of Real National Income," *Oxford Economic Papers*, 2, January 1950.

28. Shubik, M., "Edgeworth Market Games," in *Contributions to the Theory of Games*, IV, ed. by A. W. Tucker, and R. D. Luce, Princeton, N.J., Princeton University Press, 1959.

29. Takayama, A., *International Trade—An Approach to the Theory*, New York, Holt, Rinehart and Winston, 1972.

30. Vind, K., "Edgeworth-Allocations in an Exchange Economy with Many Traders," *International Economic Review*, 5, May 1964.

31. ———, "A Theorem on the Core of an Economy," *Review of Economic Studies*, XXXII, January 1965.

32. von Neumann, J., and Morgenstern, O., *Theory of Games and Economic Behavior*, 3rd ed., Princeton, N.J., Princeton University Press, 1953.

Section D

DEMAND THEORY

The purpose of this section is to study the theory of demand for a "competitive" consumer. Traditionally (as explained in Hicks [5]), this theory is developed by postulating for each consumer a preference ordering representable by a real-valued "utility" function. Each consumer is supposed to maximize his utility subject to his budget constraint. The maximality condition (the first-order condition) provides the demand function that relates the individual's demand for a commodity to the prices of all commodities and his income. A comparative statics analysis with regard to the maximality condition will yield the Hicks-Slutsky equation and the properties of the substitution terms. The other approach, which is due to Samuelson [13], is called the **revealed preference theory**. This theory neither presupposes the utility function nor the preference ordering. It goes directly to the demand for commodities. If a certain bundle of commodities is actually purchased by a certain consumer at a certain price vector, it is supposed to "reveal" that he prefers this bundle of commodities to the bundles of goods which cost less than, or the same amount as, the bundle purchased. Using the consistency condition which is essentially due to this observation (later called the **weak axiom of revealed preference**), Samuelson proved most of the properties of the demand function, especially the properties of the "substitution terms." However, he failed to prove the symmetry of the substitution matrix, which was later proved by Houthakker [6] by imposing another condition (called the "strong axiom of revealed preference"). The natural question which arises is, What is the relation between the traditional approach and the revealed preference approach?

(i) Given a demand function, can we tell whether it could be induced by a *utility function*? This question is called the **integrability problem** and has recently been studied by Samuelson [14], Houthakker [6], Uzawa [15], and so forth. The converse of this problem is the traditional analysis explained in Hicks [5]. An excellent survey article on the ("local") integrability problem is now available in Hurwicz [7].

(ii) Given a demand function, can we tell whether it could be induced by a *preference relation*? Aspects of this problem have been studied by Uzawa [15] and Arrow [1]. The converse of this problem was studied by McKenzie [8]. As discussed in Section B of this chapter, we can deduce the utility function from a preference relation under certain assumptions. Then the converse problem will be the same as the converse of problem (i).

One highlight of these discussions is seen in a recent elegant paper by Richter [12]. One of his conclusions (his theorem 1, p. 639) is that a consumer acts "rationally" according to his preference ordering, which is a total quasi-ordering, if and only if he is "congruous" in the sense that this action satisfies the Samuelson-Houthakker revealed preference axiom in a more general sense (which essentially takes account of satiation and the nonuniqueness of demand function). His theorem on the integrability problem, concerning whether the strong axiom of revealed preference is sufficient to suppose that a consumer acts as though he has a real-valued "utility" function ("representable" consumer preferences), needs further assumptions. The purpose of this section is not to give an exposition of this article, although we strongly encourage the reader to read this elegant masterpiece. Here we want to stick to a more or less traditional approach, starting from a preference relation (if not a utility function). By imposing a preference relation which is total, over an individual's consumption set, we want to obtain the Hicks-Slutsky equation—in particular, the properties of the substitution terms. This is the approach adopted by McKenzie [8] and Yokoyama [16]. The author believes that this will be very helpful in understanding the basic structure of modern demand theory, for the McKenzie approach, although it is essentially based on the traditional approach, is greatly influenced by the revealed preference theory and appears to have influenced recent discussions of the integrability problem (for example, a paper by Hurwicz and Richter in [3]). On the other hand, the reader who is interested in the integrability problem (local or global) is referred to some articles in [3] as well as [12].

Another important aspect of demand theory is the continuity property of the demand function. First, the demand function is not necessarily single-valued. Hence a new concept of continuity is needed for multivalued functions. In particular, we will prove that under certain conditions, the demand function is "upper semicontinuous." This property is obtained by presupposing the preference relation on the consumption set. As we see in the next section, this will play a very important role in the proof of the existence of competitive equilibria. In Debreu [4], this property is proved by using a theorem which Berge [2] called the **maximum theorem**. We do not use this theorem in our proof. We derive it directly from our consideration of a preference relation. In the Appendix, we attempt an expository account of the "maximum theorem." In addition to the upper semicontinuity of the demand function, we establish some other important facts in demand theory. This section has two parts. In the first part we want to prove the upper semicontinuity of the demand function, and in the second part, we obtain the Hicks-Slutsky equation and related results.[1]

Let X be the consumption set of a certain individual. We assume that it is a compact[2] subset of R^n and totally quasi-ordered by $\geqslant$.[3] At the outset, we do not assume that X is convex. Let $p \in R^n, p \neq 0$, be the price vector which prevails in the market. We suppose that this individual is a "competitive" consumer in the sense that he cannot affect the prices that prevail in the market. We also suppose that his behavioral rule as a consumer is to maximize his satisfaction from the consumption bundles that he can afford with his income. Let M, a positive number, denote his (money) income. We are tempted to define the "budget set" $H(p, M)$ by $\{x: x \in X, p \cdot x \leq M\}$. But this definition is not quite right, for we have not specified the domain of price vector p and income M so that $H(p, M)$ can be empty. The set $H(p, M)$ would be empty if the prices became so high compared to his income that he could not afford to buy anything in his consumption set X. He may starve to death. To remedy this difficulty, we first define the set S of price-income pairs (p, M) by $S \equiv \{(p, M) \in R^{n+1}: \phi(p, M) \neq \emptyset\}$, where $\phi(p, M) \equiv \{x: x \in X, p \cdot x \leq M\}$. We then *assume* that this set hence S is nonempty, and we have the following definition.

Definition: Let H be a multivalued function from S into X such that $H(p, M) = \{x: x \in X, p \cdot x \leq M\}$. The function H is called the **budget function** and $H(p, M)$ is called the **budget set** when the consumer's income is M and price p prevails. In many cases, it is more convenient to explicitly write $M \equiv p \cdot \bar{x}$, where $\bar{x}$ is the endowment vector of the consumer. Then we define his budget set $H(p)$ by $H(p) \equiv \{x: x \in X, p \cdot x \leq p \cdot \bar{x}\}$, where p is taken in the subset of R^n in which $H(p)$ is nonempty.

Definition (demand function):[4] The **demand function** is a multivalued function, F, from $S \subset R^{n+1}$ into X such that $x \in F(p, M)$ means $p \cdot x \leq M$ and $x \geqslant z$ for all z such that $p \cdot z \leq M$. We assume that $F(p, M)$ is nonempty.

REMARK: If $x \in F(p, M)$, it means that $x \in H(p, M)$ and $x \geqslant z$ for all $z \in H(p, M)$. Figure 2.21 illustrates the points of $F(p, M)$. The left-hand diagram illustrates the case when $F(p, M)$ is single-valued and the right-hand diagram illustrates the case when $F(p, M)$ is multivalued. The curves, which are drawn convex to the origin in the diagram, indicate the utility indifference curves. Although it is not shown in Figure 2.21, it is possible to have $x \in$ *interior* $H(p, M)$ for some $x \in F(p, M)$; that is, x can be a satiation point.

REMARK: When $M \equiv p \cdot \bar{x}$, we may write $F(p, M)$ as $F(p)$. To obtain the Hicks-Slutsky equation and the traditional results in the demand theory, it would be more convenient to use $F(p, M)$. However, to discuss the upper semicontinuity of the demand function (and the lower semicontinuity of the

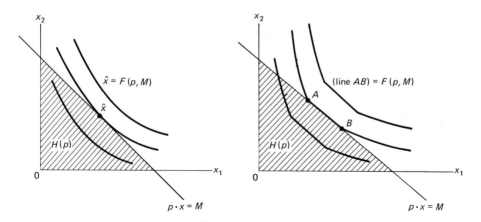

Figure 2.21.   Demand Functions $(X = \Omega^2)$.

budget set), it would be more useful, especially in connection with Section E, to consider $F(p)$ instead of $F(p, M)$ (and $H(p)$ instead of $H(p,M)$).

The following theorem is an immediate consequence of the definition of the demand function.

Theorem 2.D.1:   *Let $F(p, M)$ be a single-valued demand function. Then $F(p, M)$ is positively homogeneous of degree zero in (p, M); that is, $x = F(p, M)$ means $x = F(tp, tM)$ for any positive number t.*

PROOF: Since F is single-valued, we may write $x = F(p, M)$. From the definition of F, $x = F(p, M)$ if and only if $x \geqslant z$ for z with $p \cdot z \leq M$. But $p \cdot z \leq M$ if and only if $tp \cdot z \leq tM$ where t is any positive number. Hence $x = F(tp, tM)$. (Q.E.D.)

REMARK: From the above proof it is also clear that if $x \in F(p, M)$ (that is, F is multi-valued), then $x \in F(tp, tM)$ for any $t > 0$. Also if $x \in H(p,M)$, then $x \in H(tp, tM)$.

We introduce the following two basic assumptions, **(A-1)** and **(A-2)**, of demand theory.

(A-1)   (continuity of $\geqslant$)   *Let $\{x^q\}$ and $\{\bar{x}^q\}$ be two arbitrary sequences in X such that $x^q \to x$ and $\bar{x}^q \to \bar{x}$. Then $x^q \geqslant \bar{x}^q$ implies $x \geqslant \bar{x}$.*

REMARK: The set X is compact, hence closed. Thus $x^q \to x$ and $\bar{x}^q \to \bar{x}$ imply $x \in X$ and $\bar{x} \in X$. We may rewrite (A-1) as follows:

(A-1'):   Let $\{x^q\}$ be a sequence in X such that $x^q \to x$. If $x^q \geqslant \bar{x}$ for all q, then $x \geqslant \bar{x}$. And if $x^q \leqslant \bar{x}$ for all q, then $x \leqslant \bar{x}$.

(A-2) **(local nonsatiation)** Let $x \in F(p, M)$. Then there exists a positive number δ such that for *any* ϵ, $0 < \epsilon < \delta$, there exists a point $x' \in B_\epsilon(x)$ and $x' \in X$ with $x' \bigcirc x$, where $B_\epsilon(x)$ is an open ball about x with radius ϵ, and $B_\delta(x) \cap (X \setminus x) \neq \emptyset$.

> *REMARK:* This is the same assumption which was adopted in the previous section. The following concept was also used in the previous section.

Definition: $C_x \equiv \{z : z \in X, z \bigcirc x\}$ is called the **no-worse-than-x set**.

Lemma 2.D.1: *The set C_x is closed, if (A-1) holds.*

> PROOF: Let $x^q \to \bar{x}$ where $x^q \in C_x$. Then $\bar{x} \in X$ since X is a closed set. Also $x^q \bigcirc x$ implies $\bar{x} \bigcirc x$ from (A-1). Hence C_x is a closed set. (Q.E.D.)

> *REMARK:* Since X is bounded, C_x is bounded, hence compact.

Definition: $M_x(p) \equiv \min p \cdot z \qquad$ for $z \in C_x$.

> *REMARK:* Since C_x is compact, there exists a $\hat{z}$ in C_x which minimizes $p \cdot z$. The function $M_x(p)$ is called the **minimum expenditure function** (which achieves a level of satisfaction that is at least as great as the satisfaction obtained from x at price p).[5] This function $M_x(p)$ is illustrated in Figure 2.22.

Lemma 2.D.2: *Given $p \in R^n$, select an $x \in X$ such that $p \cdot x < \alpha$ where $\alpha \in R$. Then (A-2) implies that there exists an $x' \in X$ such that $x' \bigcirc x$ and $p \cdot x' < \alpha$.*

> PROOF: By (A-2), there exists a $\delta > 0$ such that for all ϵ, $0 < \epsilon < \delta$, there exists an $x' \in B_\epsilon(x)$, $x' \in X$, with $x' \bigcirc x$. Because of the continuity of the value function $p \cdot z$, we may choose x' close enough to x so that $p \cdot x' < \alpha$. (Q.E.D.)

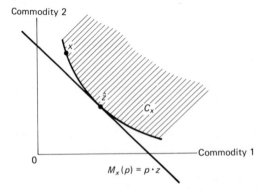

Figure 2.22. An Illustration of $M_x(p)$.

REMARK: The idea of this lemma was used in the proof of Theorem 2.C.1, especially in the proof of the lemma preceding the theorem.

Theorem 2.D.2:   Let $x \in F(p, M)$. If (A-2) holds for x, then $p \cdot x = M$. If (A-2) holds for all $z \in F(p, M)$, then $p \cdot x = M_x(p)$.

PROOF:

(i)   By definition of $F(p, M)$, $p \cdot x \leq M$. Suppose $p \cdot x < M$. Then, using Lemma 2.D.2, (A-2) implies that there exists an $x' \in X$, such that $x' \bigotimes x$ with $p \cdot x' < M$. This contradicts the definition of $F(p, M)$. Hence $p \cdot x = M$.

(ii) By the definition of $M_x(p)$, $M_x(p) \leq p \cdot x = M$. Suppose $M_x(p) < M$. Then $p \cdot x'' < M$ for some $x'' \bigotimes x$. Then $x'' \in F(p, M)$. Hence by (A-2), there exists $x' \in X$, such that $x' \bigotimes x''$ with $p \cdot x' < M$. This contradicts the definition of $F(p, M)$. Therefore we have $M_x(p) = M$.   (Q.E.D.)

REMARK: Theorem 2.D.2 means, among other things, that the local non-satiation at a chosen point implies that all the income is spent.

To study the continuity property of $H(p)$, we introduce the following assumptions.

(A-3) (interior point) The set X contains an interior point $\bar{x}$.
(A-4) The set X is convex.

REMARK: As remarked before, assumption (A-3) amounts to *the cheaper-point assumption* (that is, there exists an $\tilde{x}$ in X such that $p \cdot \tilde{x} < p \cdot \bar{x}$). Assumption (A-4) implies perfect divisibility of every commodity. This is a restrictive although a very useful assumption.

We now explain important mathematical concepts, upper and lower semi-continuity.

Definition: Let ϕ be a multivalued function from $X \subset R^m$ into $Y \subset R^n$ where Y is assumed to be *compact*. Let x^0 be a point in X.

(i)   Let $\{x^q\}$ be a sequence in X such that $x^q \rightarrow x^0$, and let $\{y^q\}$ be a sequence in Y such that $y^q \in \phi(x^q)$. If $y^q \rightarrow y^0$ implies $y^0 \in \phi(x^0)$, then ϕ is called **upper semicontinuous at x^0**.

(ii) Let $\{x^q\}$ be a sequence in X such that $x^q \rightarrow x^0$. If $y^0 \in \phi(x^0)$ implies "there exists a sequence $\{y^q\}$ in Y such that $y^q \rightarrow y^0$ and $y^q \in \phi(x^q)$," then ϕ is called **lower semicontinuous at x^0**.

(iii) The function ϕ is called **continuous at x^0** if it is both upper semicontinuous *and* lower semicontinuous at x^0.

REMARK: The above concepts are illustrated in Figure 2.23. The graph of ϕ is the shaded region, boundary included; $\phi(x^0)$ is the interval $[a, b]$.

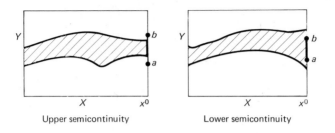

Upper semicontinuity   Lower semicontinuity

Figure 2.23.   An Illustration of Semicontinuity.

REMARK: Semicontinuity and continuity *on X* can be defined as semicontinuity and continuity at every point of X.

Assuming that the range set Y is *compact*, the following statements follow easily from the above definition (see Berge [2], chapter VI, for example).

(i)   The function ϕ is upper semicontinuous on X if and only if its graph, $\{(x, y):$ $x \in X$ and $y \in \phi(x)\}$, is closed.

(ii)   An upper (resp. lower) semicontinuous function of a continuous function is upper (resp. lower) semicontinuous.

(iii) The Cartesian product of upper (resp. lower) semicontinuous functions ϕ_i, that is, $(\phi_1, \phi_2, \ldots, \phi_m)$, is also upper (resp. lower) semicontinuous.

Theorem 2.D.3:   *The function $H(p)$ is lower semicontinuous for $p \geq 0$, under (A-3) and (A-4).*[6]

PROOF: By (A-3) there exists an $\tilde{x} \in X$, and $p \cdot \tilde{x} < p \cdot \bar{x}$. Consider a sequence $\{p^q\}$ with $p^q \to p$. Then $p^q \cdot \tilde{x} < p \cdot \bar{x}$ for q large enough. Let z be an arbitrary point of $H(p)$; we want to find a sequence $\{z^q\}$, $z^q \in H(p^q)$, such that $z^q \to z \in H(p)$, as $p^q \to p$. For large enough q, we define $z^q \equiv t^q z + (1 - t^q) \tilde{x}$ where t^q is maximal for $t^q \in [0, 1]$ such that $z^q \in H(p^q)$. We claim such a $\{z^q\}$ is the sequence we want to find. That is, we want to show $z^q \to z$ as $p^q \to p$. Note that $z^q \to z$ if and only if $t^q \to 1$. (Hence if we show $t^q \to 1$ as $p^q \to p$, we are done.) If $t^q = 1$ (that is, if $p^q \cdot z \leq p^q \cdot x$) for large enough q, we are done. Hence it suffices to consider the case in which $t^q < 1$ for large enough q. Note that $t^q < 1$ implies $p^q \cdot z^q = p^q \cdot \bar{x}$, for q large enough, or else t^q is not a maximum. Suppose $t^q \nrightarrow 1$. Since the interval $[0, 1]$ is a compact set, there exists a subsequence of $\{t^q\}$—say, $\{t^s\}$—such that $t^s \to t$, where $0 \leq t < 1$. Since $t < 1$, $p^s \cdot z^s = p^s \cdot \bar{x}$ for sufficiently large s. Write $z^s \equiv t^s z + (1 - t^s) \tilde{x}$. Since $t^s \to t$, $z^s \to z^\infty$, where $z^\infty \equiv tz + (1 - t)\tilde{x}$. Since $p^s \cdot z^s = p^s \cdot \bar{x}$ for large s, we have

(*) $$tp \cdot z + (1 - t) p \cdot \tilde{x} = p \cdot z^\infty = p \cdot \bar{x}$$

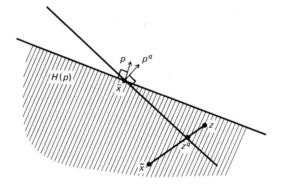

Figure 2.24. An Illustration of the Proof of Theorem 2.D.3.

as $s \to \infty$. But since $p \cdot \tilde{x} < p \cdot \bar{x}$, (*) yields $p \cdot z > p \cdot \bar{x}$, contradicting $z \in H(p)$. Hence we must have $t^q \to 1$.   (Q.E.D.)

REMARK: The graph of $H(p)$ is obviously closed. Hence $H(p)$ is upper semicontinuous.[7] Thus from the above theorem, $H(p)$ is in fact continuous.

REMARK: Note that the cheaper-point assumption (or the interior-point assumption) plays a crucial role in the above theorem. If the consumer starves to death when the price moves beyond a certain point (hence no "cheaper point" in his consumption set), his budget function $H(p)$ would become discontinuous.

Write $F(p)$ for $F(p,M)$ where $M \equiv p \cdot \bar{x}$. Then we can prove the following theorem.

Theorem 2.D.4: *The demand function $F(p)$ is upper semicontinuous with respect to p, if $H(p)$ is lower semicontinuous in p, and (A-1) holds.*

PROOF: Consider a sequence $\{p^q\}$ such that $p^q \to p$, as $q \to \infty$. Let z be an arbitrary point of $H(p)$. Then as a result of the lower semicontinuity of $H(p)$, there exists a sequence $\{z^q\}$ such that $z^q \in H(p^q)$ and $z^q \to z$. Let $x^q \in F(p^q)$. Then by the definition of F, $x^q \gtrsim z^q$. When a different element z is chosen from $H(p)$, we have a different sequence $\{z^q\}$. But whatever the sequence, $x^q \gtrsim z^q$ always holds by the definition of F and $z^q \in H(p^q)$. Owing to the compactness of X, there is a subsequence of $\{x^q\}$—say, $\{x^s\}$— such that $x^s \to x'$ where $x' \in X$; $p^s \cdot x^s \leq p^s \cdot \bar{x}$ implies $p \cdot x' \leq p \cdot \bar{x}$ (take the limit of $s \to \infty$). Thus $x' \in H(p)$. From (A-1) (the continuity of $\gtrsim$), $x^s \gtrsim z^s$ implies $x' \gtrsim z$. Since this holds, whatever the choice of z, $x' \in F(p)$. This, together with the compactness of the range space X, proves the theorem.
                                (Q.E.D.)

REMARK: As a result of this theorem, $F(p)$ is upper semicontinuous in p if (A-1), (A-3), and (A-4) hold.

REMARK: Note the importance of the cheaper-point assumption in establishing the above theorem. As we remarked in connection with Theorem 2.D.3, if the consumer starves to death when the price goes beyond a certain point, his demand function becomes discontinuous.

We now introduce a fifth assumption.

(A-5) (strict convexity of $\gtreqqless$) Let x, $x' \in X$ with $x \neq x'$ where X is assumed to be convex; $x \gtreqqless x'$ implies $x'' \gtrless x'$ where $x'' = tx + (1 - t)x', 0 < t < 1$.

REMARK: Note that (A-5) presupposes (A-4).

Theorem 2.D.5: *The demand function $F(p, M)$ is single-valued under (A-5)*

PROOF: Let x and $x' \in F(p, M)$. Then by definition,

$$x \gtreqqless z \qquad \text{for all } z \in X \text{ such that } p \cdot z \leq M$$

$$x' \gtreqqless z \qquad \text{for all } z \in X \text{ such that } p \cdot z \leq M$$

Suppose $x \neq x'$. Then from (A-5), $x'' \gtrless x$ where $x'' = \frac{1}{2}x + \frac{1}{2}x'$. But $p \cdot x'' \leq M$. This contradicts the condition that $x \in F(p, M)$. Hence $x = x'$.

(Q.E.D.)

REMARK: This theorem gives a *sufficient* condition for the single-valuedness of the demand function. It does *not* provide a *necessary* condition.

REMARK: From the above proof, it should be clear that $F(p)$ is also single-valued under (A-5). Therefore, under (A-1), (A-3), and (A-5), $F(p)$ is single-valued and continuous.

We now come back to the minimum expenditure function $M_x(p)$. Using this concept, we would eventually like to obtain the Hicks-Slutsky equation, especially the properties of the "substitution term." Obviously, the Hicks-Slutsky equation can be obtained by performing a comparative static analysis on the maximality condition obtained from maximizing a consumer's utility, $u(x)$, subject to his budget constraint. The essence of the comparative statics procedure is fully explained and discussed in Hicks [5] and in our Appendix to Section F, Chapter 1. Here we will arrive at the Hicks-Slutsky equation without having to resort to the concept of a utility function. The essential idea in this procedure is to use $M_x(p)$, which, as is mentioned above, is due to McKenzie [8]. The fact that the utility function is dispensed with in the analysis is an exercise of Occam's Razor, as McKenzie points out ([8], p. 185). The importance of the following analysis lies in its simplicity, its directness, and the clarification of the structure of demand theory. It is direct in the sense that it does not presuppose any knowledge or development of nonlinear programming. It does not even require the separation theorem.

We first modify the interior-point assumption (A-3) as follows.

(A-3′) (cheaper point)   Let $x \in F(p, M)$. Then there exists a positive number δ such that for *any* ϵ, $0 < \epsilon < \delta$, there exists a point $\tilde{x} \in X$ and $\tilde{x} \in B_\epsilon(x)$ with $p \cdot \tilde{x} < p \cdot x$, where $B_\epsilon(x)$ is an open ball about x with radius ϵ and $B_\delta(x) \cap (X \setminus x) \neq \emptyset$.

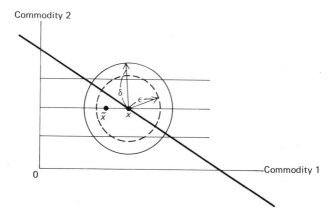

Figure 2.25.   An Illustration of (A-3′).

REMARK: If X is convex (hence all commodities are divisible), then the above assumption is simplified as follows: [Let $x \in F(p, M)$. Then there exists an $\tilde{x} \in X$ such that $p \cdot \tilde{x} < p \cdot x$.] Note that the convexity of X implies $x' \equiv [t\tilde{x} + (1 - t)x] \in X$ for all $0 \le t \le 1$, and obviously $p \cdot x' < p \cdot x$ for all $0 < t \le 1$.

In order to sharpen the argument, we henceforth assume that the demand function $F(p, M)$ is *single-valued*. First we prove the following lemma.

Lemma 2.D.3:   *Let $x = F(p, M)$ and $x' = F[p', M_x(p')]$ with $x' \neq x$. Suppose that (A-3′) holds at x'. Suppose also that (A-1) holds. Then if (p', x') lies sufficiently close to (p, x), $x \ominus x'$.*

PROOF:

(i) $(x' \ominus x)$:   By definition of F, $p' \cdot x' \le M_x(p')$. As we remarked in the definition of the minimum expenditure function, there exists $z \in C_x$ such that $p' \cdot z = M_x(p')$, since C_x is compact. [In other words, z can be purchased with income $M_x(p')$.] From the definition of x', $x' \ominus z$. Hence $x' \in C_x$ or $x' \ominus x$.

(ii) $(x \ominus x')$:   Since (p', x') is sufficiently close to (p, x), by (A-3′), there exists an $\tilde{x} \in X$ such that $x^q \equiv [t^q \tilde{x} + (1 - t^q)x'] \in X$ with $p' \cdot x^q < p' \cdot x'$, for all $0 < t^q < 1$. [Note that $p' \cdot \tilde{x} < p' \cdot x'$ implies $p' \cdot x^q < p' \cdot x'$ for all $0 < t^q < 1$, since $p' \cdot x^q = t^q p' \cdot \tilde{x} + (1 - t^q)p' \cdot x'$.] But $p' \cdot x' \le$

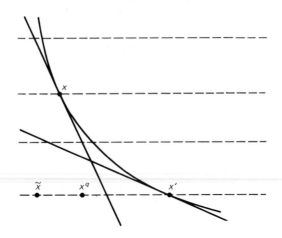

Figure 2.26.   An Illustration of the Proof of Lemma 2.D.3.

$M_x(p')$ by definition of F, so that we have $p' \cdot x^q < M_x(p')$. Hence from the definition of $M_x(p')$, $x^q \notin C_x$. Or $x \bigcirc x^q$. Letting $t^q \to 0$, by (A-1), $x \bigcirc x'$. Combining this with $(x' \bigcirc x)$, we obtain $x \bigcirc x'$.   (Q.E.D.)

REMARK: Lemma 2.D.3 amounts to asserting that there is an indifference curve in the neighborhood of (p, x).

Definition: Let $f_x(p) \equiv f[p, M_x(p)]$, which is defined in the neighborhood of (p, x), in which (A-3′) holds. The function $f_x(p)$ is called the **compensated demand function**.

REMARK: When it is convenient and not confusing, we abbreviate $f_x(p)$ by $f(p)$. Now $f(p)$, like $F(p, M)$, is a vector-valued function, the ith component of which can be written as $f_i(p)$. Thus $f_i(p)$ is the compensated demand function for the ith commodity. The concept of the compensated demand function is important in classical demand theory. The compensated demand function $f_x(p)$ indicates the point chosen at price p, when a consumer's income is guaranteed (compensated) such that it is just sufficient for him to obtain a level of satisfaction as great as at point x. This concept is illustrated in Figure 2.27. Note that $x = F(p, M)$ obviously means $x = f_x(p)$. Lemma 2.D.3 says that if $x = f_x(p)$ and (p', x') is close enough to (p, x) such that $x' = f_x(p')$, then $x \bigcirc x'$.

Theorem 2.D.6:   *If $f_x(p)$ is differentiable and if (A-1), (A-2), and (A-3′) hold, then*

$$p \cdot \frac{\partial f_x(p)}{\partial p_j} = 0, \qquad j = 1, 2, \ldots, n$$

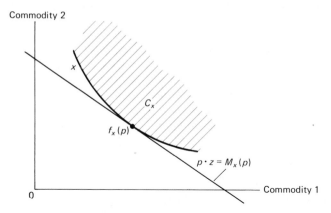

Figure 2.27.   An Illustration of $f_x(p)$.

PROOF: Let $z = f_x(p)$, and let $z' = f_x(p')$ where (p', z') is sufficiently close to (p, z). Then by Lemma 2.D.3, $z' \ominus z$, so that $z' \in C_x$. But by the definition of $M_x(p)$, $M_x(p) \leq p \cdot z'$ for all $z' \in C_x$. Since (A-2) holds, $M_x(p) = p \cdot z$ by Theorem 2.D.2. Therefore $p \cdot z \leq p \cdot z'$ for all $z' \in C_x$, or $p \cdot f_x(p) \leq p \cdot f_x(p')$ for all p', where (p', z') is sufficiently close to (p, z). In other words, for a fixed p, $p \cdot f_x(p')$ is minimized with respect to p' at p. Hence using the first-order characterization of a minimum, we obtain:

$$p \cdot \frac{\partial f_x(p')}{\partial p_j'} = 0 \text{ at } p' = p, \quad j = 1, 2, \ldots, n \qquad \text{(Q.E.D.)}$$

REMARK: It may so happen that $f_x(p)$ [hence $M_x(p)$ also] is *not* differentiable. This happens, for example, when there is a "kink" in the indifference curve. In Figure 2.28 (compare Hurwicz [7], p. 196), there is a kink at the point $\bar{x}$ in the sense that there are two tangent lines to the difference curve α at the point $\bar{x}$.

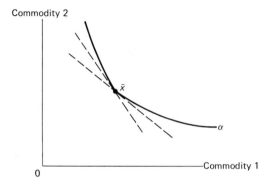

Figure 2.28.   Nondifferentiable $f_x(p)$.

Theorem 2.D.7:   If $(A-1)$, $(A-2)$, and $(A-3')$ hold at $x = f(p)$, where $f(p) \equiv f_x(p)$, and $f(p)$ is differentiable at p, then,

$$\frac{\partial M_x(p)}{\partial p_i} = f_i(p) \quad \text{and} \quad \frac{\partial f_i(p)}{\partial p_j} = \frac{\partial^2 M_x(p)}{\partial p_i \partial p_j} \quad (i, j = 1, 2, \ldots, n)$$

If $M_x(p)$ is twice continuously differentiable at p, then

$$\frac{\partial f_i(p_i)}{\partial p_j} = \frac{\partial f_j(p)}{\partial p_i}$$

PROOF: (i) By Theorem 2.D.2, $M_x(p) = p \cdot x = p \cdot F(p, M) = p \cdot f(p)$. Hence $\partial M_x(p)/\partial p_i = \partial[p \cdot f(p)]/\partial p_i = f_i(p) + p \cdot \partial f/\partial p_i = f_i(p)$, by the previous theorem. That $\partial f_i(p)/\partial p_j = \partial^2 M_x(p)/\partial p_i \partial p_j$ follows immediately from this. If $M_x(p)$ is twice continuously differentiable at p, then clearly $\partial f_i(p)/\partial p_j = \partial f_j(p)/\partial p_i$.   (Q.E.D.)

REMARK: The partial derivative $\partial f_i/\partial p_j$ signifies the rate at which the consumer varies the consumption of the ith good per unit change of the jth price when income changes are made at the same time and by a proper magnitude to keep the consumer on the same indifference locus; $\partial f_i/\partial p_j$ is called the **substitution term** by Hicks ([5], p. 103).

Lemma 2.D.4:   The function $M_x(p)$ is concave[8] for all $p \geq 0$.

PROOF: Let $p \equiv tp'' + (1 - t)p'$, $0 \leq t \leq 1$. By definition of $M_x(p)$, $M_x(p) \leq p \cdot z$ for all $z \in C_x$. Then there exists a point $\bar{z} \in C_x$ such that $M_x(p) \geq p \cdot \bar{z} - \epsilon$ for all $\epsilon > 0$.[9] Hence $M_x(p) \geq tp'' \cdot \bar{z} + (1 - t)p' \cdot \bar{z} - \epsilon$ for all $\epsilon > 0$ and $0 \leq t \leq 1$. Since $\bar{z} \in C_x$, $p'' \cdot z \geq M_x(p'')$ and $p' \cdot \bar{z} \geq M_x(p')$. Therefore we have $M_x(p) \geq tM_x(p'') + (1 - t)M_x(p') - \epsilon$ for all $\epsilon > 0$ and $0 \leq t \leq 1$. Therefore $M_x(p) \geq tM_x(p'') + (1 - t) M_x(p')$, $0 \leq t \leq 1$.   (Q.E.D.)

Theorem 2.D.8: $\sum_i \sum_j (\partial f_i/\partial p_j) \, dp_i dp_j \leq 0$, almost everywhere.

PROOF: $\partial f_i/\partial p_j = \partial^2 M_x(p)/\partial p_i \partial p_j$. Since $M_x(p)$ is a concave function by Lemma 2.D.4, and since the Hessian matrix of a concave function is negative semidefinite (Chapter 1, Section F,c), the statement of the theorem follows trivially.[10]   (Q.E.D.)

Lemma 2.D.5:   The function $M_x(p)$ is positively homogeneous of degree one.

PROOF: By definition, $M_x(p) = $ inf. $p \cdot z$ for $z \in C_x$. But this is true if and only if $tM_x(p) = $ inf. $tp \cdot z$, for all $z \in C_x$, $t > 0$.   (Q.E.D.)

Theorem 2.D.9:   The function $f_x(p)$ is positively homogeneous of degree zero.

PROOF: By definition, $f_x(p) = F[p, M_x(p)]$

$$= F[tp, tM_x(p)] \quad \text{(by Theorem 2.D.1)}$$
$$= F[tp, M_x(tp)] \quad \text{(by Lemma 2.D.5)}$$
$$= f_x(tp) \quad \text{(by definition)} \quad \text{(Q.E.D.)}$$

REMARK: Using the Euler equation for the homogeneous function of degree zero, we may write,

$$\sum_{j=1}^{n} \frac{\partial f_i}{\partial p_j} p_j = 0$$

where f_i is the ith component of $f_x(p)$.

REMARK: Writing $S_{ij} = \partial f_i / \partial p_j$ and $S = [S_{ij}]$ ($n \times n$ matrix), we may summarize the results obtained in Theorems 2.D.6 through 2.D.9 as follows:[11]

(i) $p \cdot S = 0$ (or $\sum_{i=1}^{n} p_i S_{ij} = 0$)   (Theorem 2.D.6)

(ii) S is symmetric (or $S_{ij} = S_{ji}$)   (Theorem 2.D.7)

(iii) S is negative semidefinite (or $\sum_{i,j}^{n} S_{ij} p_i p_j \leq 0$)   (Theorem 2.D.8)

(iv) $S \cdot p = 0$ (or $\sum_{j=1}^{n} S_{ij} p_j = 0$)   (Theorem 2.D.9)

(v) $S_{ii} \leq 0$ [from (iii) above]

Finally we obtain the Hicks-Slutsky equation.

Theorem 2.D.10:   *Suppose that (A-2) and Theorem 2.D.7 hold at $x = F(p, M)$ and that F is differentiable in p and M. Then*

$$\frac{\partial F_i(p, M)}{\partial p_j} = \frac{\partial f_i(p)}{\partial p_j} - f_j(p) \frac{\partial F_i(p, M)}{\partial M}$$

where $f(p) \equiv f_x(p)$.

PROOF: Since (A-2) holds, Theorem 2.D.2 holds, so that $p \cdot x = M = M_x(p)$. Therefore

$$\frac{\partial f_i(p)}{\partial p_j} = \frac{\partial F_i[p, M_x(p)]}{\partial p_j} = \frac{\partial F_i(p, M)}{\partial p_j} + \frac{\partial F_i(p, M)}{\partial M} \frac{\partial M_x(p)}{\partial p_j}$$

$$= \frac{\partial F_i(p, M)}{\partial p_j} + f_j(p) \frac{\partial F_i(p, M)}{\partial M} \quad \text{(by Theorem 2.D.7)}$$

(Q.E.D.)

FOOTNOTES

1. For the subject matter of this section, we have relied heavily on McKenzie [8] and his lectures at the University of Rochester. An exposition of McKenzie's approach is also seen in S. Karlin, *Mathematical Methods and Theory in Games, Programming, and Economics*, Vol. I, Reading, Mass., Addison-Wesley, 1959, pp. 271–273. For a more complete exposition of (static) demand theory, see D. W. Katzner, *Static Demand Theory*, New York, Macmillan, 1970.

2. The compactness of X is assumed just for the simplicity of exposition. It can be weakened. For example, it suffices to assume that X is closed and bounded from below. This is due to the fact that X can be restricted to a set which is bounded from above as a result of the budget constraint (that is, a finite income).

3. That is, we assume that the relation $\geqq$ is reflexive, transitive, and total. However, we may note that the transitivity axiom is not essential in obtaining many results in this section. In other words, in many results, it suffices to regard $\geqq$ only as a binary relation on X, which is total. Needless to say, the transitivity axiom is needed in obtaining some results here (such as Lemma 2.D.3 and Theorem 2.D.6).

4. The crucial underlying fact here is the assumption that some point—say, x—is "chosen" [that is, $F(p, M)$ is nonempty]. The power of this axiom of selection in demand theory is well illustrated in the theory of revealed preference. Starting from preference orderings, it is possible that such a choice is impossible. Here we may recall Sonnenschein's example (quoted in Section B of this chapter): Assume that the budget set consists of only three points x, y, and z, and suppose that our consumer's preference is $x \oslash y \oslash z$ but $z \oslash x$ (the case of intransitivity). Here no choice is possible. Needless to say, if $\oslash$ is intransitive, then $\geqq$ is also intransitive.

5. The minimum expenditure function $M_x(p)$ plays a crucial role in McKenzie's approach to demand theory. As will be shown later, $M_x(p)$ turns out to be a concave function, hence its Hessian matrix is negative semidefinite. It will also be pointed out later that the elements of this Hessian matrix correspond to the effect of a compensated price change on demand, that is, the substitution terms in the Hicks-Slutsky theory. In other words, the discovery of the crucial role played by the minimum expenditure function in demand theory is one of the important contributions of McKenzie [8].

6. Similarly, we can prove the lower semicontinuity of $H(p, M)$. Such a proof is given by Debreu [4], pp. 63–65. Our proof is due to Lionel McKenzie.

7. The function $H(p)$ is upper semicontinuous if its graph is closed *and* if its range space X is compact. Similarly, we can establish the lower semicontinuity and hence continuity of $H(p, M)$.

8. Since every concave function is continuous in the interior of the domain (compare Theorem 1.B.1), $M_x(p)$ is continuous for all $p > 0$.

9. To see this, suppose the contrary. That is, suppose that for some $\bar\epsilon > 0, M_x(p) < p \cdot z - \bar\epsilon$ for all $z \in C_x$. Let $\hat z$ be a point in C_x such that $p \cdot \hat z = M_x(p)$. Then we have $p \cdot \hat z < p \cdot \hat z - \bar\epsilon$, which is a contradiction.

10. It is known that every concave function is differentiable almost everywhere (that is, except for sets of measure zero). See, for example, W. Fenchel, *Convex Cones, Sets, and Functions*, Princeton University, September 1953 (hectographed).

11. Note that (iv) can also be obtained from (i) and (ii). Similarly, (i) can also be obtained from (ii) and (iv).

REFERENCES

1. Arrow, K. J., "Rational Choice Functions and Orderings," *Economica*, N.S., 26, May 1959.
2. Berge, C., *Topological Spaces*, New York, Macmillan, 1963 (French, 1959).
3. Chipman, J. S., Hurwicz, L., Richter, M. K., and Sonnenschein, H. F., eds., *Preferences, Utility, and Demand: A Minnesota Symposium*, New York, Harcourt Brace Jovanovich, 1971.
4. Debreu, G., *Theory of Value*, New York, Wiley, 1959.
5. Hicks, J. R., *Value and Capital*, 2nd ed., Oxford, Clarendon Press, 1946.
6. Houthakker, H. S., "Revealed Preference and the Utility Function," *Economica*, N.S., 17, May 1950.
7. Hurwicz, L., "On the Problem of Integrability of Demand Functions," in *Preferences, Utility, and Demand*, New York, Harcourt Brace Jovanovich, 1971, chap. 9.
8. McKenzie, L. W., "Demand Theory without a Utility Index," *Review of Economic Studies*, XXIV, June 1957.
9. ———, "Further Comments," *Review of Economic Studies*, XXV, June 1958.
10. Newman, P. K., and Read, R. C., "Demand Theory without a Utility Index; Comment," *Review of Economic Studies*, XXV, June 1958.
11. Newman, P. K., *The Theory of Exchange*, Englewood Cliffs, N.J., Prentice-Hall, 1965.
12. Richter, M. K., "Revealed Preference Theory," *Econometrica*, 34, July 1966.
13. Samuelson, P. A., *Foundations of Economic Analysis*, Cambridge, Mass., Harvard University Press, 1947.
14. ———, "The Problem of Integrability in Utility Theory," *Economica*, N.S., XVII, November 1950.
15. Uzawa, H., "Preferences and Rational Choice in the Theory of Consumption," in *Mathematical Methods in the Social Sciences*, ed. by Arrow, Karlin, and Suppes, Stanford, Calif., Stanford University Press, 1960. A revised version of this paper is included in [3], chapter 1.
16. Yokoyama, T., "A Logical Foundation of the Theory of Consumer's Demand," *Osaka Economic Papers*, 2, 1953.

Appendix to Section D: Various Concepts of Semicontinuity and the Maximum Theorem[1]

a. VARIOUS CONCEPTS OF SEMICONTINUITY

In the literature various definitons of semicontinuity of a multivalued function are used, and the definitions given by different authors do not always coincide. Hence one should be careful in applying the theorems obtained in the (mathematics) literature to economic problems whenever such problems involve the concept of semicontinuity. Here we take up a few of these definitions of semicontinuity and point out the relations among them.

We start our discussion by introducing the following concepts.

Definition: Let ϕ be a function, multivalued or single-valued, from a set X into a set Y. The **lower inverse** of ϕ, denoted by ϕ^-, is the mapping from $\phi(X) \subset Y$ into X defined as

$$\phi^-(y) \equiv \{x: x \in X, y \in \phi(x)\}$$

Let B be a nonempty subset of Y, then we define $\phi^-(B)$ as

$$\phi^-(B) \equiv \{x: x \in X, \phi(x) \cap B \neq \emptyset\}$$

Let $B \subset Y$; then the **upper inverse** of ϕ, denoted by ϕ^+, is defined as

$$\phi^+(B) \equiv \{x: x \in X, \phi(x) \subset B\}$$

REMARK: If $B = \emptyset$, then we define $\phi^-(B) \equiv \emptyset$. Note that, by definition of ϕ^+, we have $\phi^+(\emptyset) = \{x: x \in X, \phi(x) = \emptyset\}$. Note also that for all $B \subset Y$, $B \neq \emptyset$, we have $\phi^+(B) \subset \phi^-(B)$. If, in particular, ϕ is single-valued, then we have $\phi^+(B) = \phi^-(B) = \phi^{-1}(B)$.

The following example, given by Berge [1] (p. 25), may be useful in understanding the above concepts, as well as being somewhat amusing to the reader.

EXAMPLE: Let X be the set of possible positions in the game of chess: A position consists of the coordinates of the different pieces on the chess board and player whose move is next. Let X_1 be the set of positions in which White can move. Clearly $X_1 \subset X$. Let $x \in X_1$ and define $\phi(x)$ as the set of positions which White can reach immediately after position x.[2] The image $\phi^-(x)$ is the set of possible positions which could have occurred before position x. If A is a nonempty subset of X_1, $\phi^+(A)$ is the set of positions that can give only a position belonging to A in the following move. If K denotes the set of positions in which Black is checkmated, then the set of positions White can mate "in two moves" is $\phi^- \circ \phi^+ \circ \phi^-(K)$.

As a second example, let $X = Y = [0, 1]$, the unit interval on the real line, and let ϕ be a function of X into Y. The two diagrams of Figure 2.29 illustrate the concepts of lower inverse and upper inverse, where the shaded region of each diagram denotes the graph of ϕ.

Now we restrict our sets X and Y to be topological spaces: ϕ is now a (multivalued) function of a topological space X into a topological space Y.[3] We then define the following concepts.

Definition:

(i)   The function ϕ is called **upper semicontinuous** (abbreviated u.s.c.) **at** x^0 if for each open set V containing $\phi(x^0)$ there exists a neighborhood $N(x^0)$ (or an open set containing x^0) such that

$$x \in N(x^0) \text{ implies } \phi(x) \subset V$$

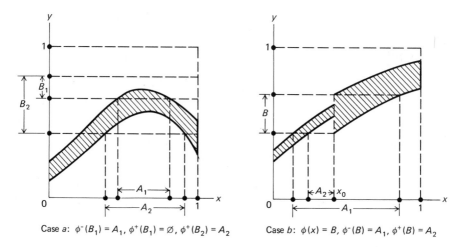

Case a: $\phi^-(B_1) = A_1$, $\phi^+(B_1) = \varnothing$, $\phi^+(B_2) = A_2$ Case b: $\phi(x) = B$, $\phi^-(B) = A_1$, $\phi^+(B) = A_2$

Figure 2.29.   Illustrations of Lower Inverse and Upper Inverse.

(ii) The function ϕ is called **lower semicontinuous** (abbreviated l.s.c.) **at** x^0 if for each open set V containing $\phi(x^0)$ there exists a neighborhood $N(x^0)$ (or an open set containing x^0) such that

$$x \in N(x^0) \text{ implies } \phi(x) \cap V \neq \varnothing$$

(iii) The function ϕ is called **continuous at** x^0 if it is both u.s.c. and l.s.c. at x^0.

REMARK: When ϕ is single-valued, we know that ϕ is continuous at x^0 if and only if for each open set V containing $\phi(x^0)$, there exists a neighborhood $N(x^0)$ (or an open set containing x^0) such that

$$x \in N(x^0) \text{ implies } \phi(x) \in V$$

In other words, ϕ is both u.s.c. and l.s.c. at x^0.

We are now ready to state various definitions of semicontinuity in X.

Definition:

(i)   We say that ϕ is **closed in** X if, for each $x^0 \in X$, "$x^q \rightarrow x^0$, $y^q \rightarrow y^0$, where $x^q \in X$, $y^q \in \phi(x^q)$" implies "$y^0 \in \phi(x^0)$."

(ii) We say that ϕ is **G-closed in** X if the graph of ϕ, $\{(x, y): x \in X, y \in \phi(x)\}$, is closed in $X \otimes Y$.

(iii) We say that ϕ is **quasi upper semicontinuous** (abbreviated q.u.s.c.) **in** X^4 if ϕ is u.s.c. at each x in X.

(iv) We say that ϕ is **upper semicontinuous** (u.s.c.) **in** X if ϕ is q.u.s.c. in X and $\phi(x)$ is compact for each x in X.

(v) We say that ϕ is **lower semicontinuous** (l.s.c.) **in** X if ϕ is l.s.c. at each x in X.

(vi) We say that ϕ is **continuous in** X if it is both u.s.c. and l.s.c. in X.

REMARK: Definitions (i) and (ii) are equivalent.[5] If ϕ is single-valued, then (i), (ii), (iii), (iv), (v), and (vi) are all equivalent.

REMARK: Definition (ii) is equivalent to saying that for each $x^0 \in X$, "$y^0 \in Y$, $y^0 \notin \phi(x^0)$" implies that "there exist open sets U in X and V in Y with $x^0 \in U$ and $y^0 \in V$ such that $\phi(x) \cap V = \emptyset$ for all $x \in U$."

We now state theorems which would clarify the meaning of the various definitions of semicontinuity and link these definitions.

Theorem 2.D.11 (Berge):[6]

(i)   *The function ϕ is l.s.c. in X if and only if for each open set V in Y the set $\phi^-(V)$ is open in X.*

(ii) *The function ϕ is u.s.c. in X if and only if for each open set V in Y the set $\phi^+(V)$ is open in X and $\phi(x)$ is compact for each $x \in X$.*

PROOF: See Berge [1], pp. 109–110.

Theorem 2.D.12:   *The function ϕ is u.s.c. in X if and only if ϕ is closed in X and Y is compact.*

PROOF: See Berge [1], p. 112 (corollary of theorem 7), and Moore [4], lemma 1-d and lemma 2.

REMARK: It is important to note that the compactness of Y is crucial here.[7] It is not accidental that in Debreu's definition of upper semicontinuity ([2], p. 17) and our definition in Chapter 2, Section D, Y is assumed to be compact.

REMARK: Theorem 2.D.12 implies that every u.s.c. function is closed.

REMARK: Berge also proved that if ϕ is u.s.c. in X, then $\phi(A)$ is compact in Y whenever A is compact in X ([1], p. 110).

REMARK: For the lower semicontinuity, we may conjecture that ϕ is l.s.c. in X if and only if for each $x^0 \in X$, "$y^0 \in \phi(x^0)$" implies that there exists a sequence $\{y^q\}$ in T such that $y^q \to y^0$.[8]

Theorem 2.D.13 (*Berge*):

(i)   *The function $\phi \circ \psi$ is l.s.c. (resp. u.s.c.) if both ϕ and ψ are l.s.c. (resp. u.s.c.).*

(ii) *The union (resp. intersection) of a family (finite or infinite) of l.s.c. (resp. u.s.c.) functions is also l.s.c. (resp. u.s.c.).*

(iii) *The union of a finite number of u.s.c. functions is also u.s.c. (no corresponding property holds for l.s.c. functions).*

(iv) *The Cartesian product of a finite number of u.s.c. (resp. l.s.c.) functions is also u.s.c. (resp. l.s.c.).*

PROOF: See [1], pp. 113–115.

REMARK: Moore ([4], pp. 135–137) also proved the following.
   (i) The function $\phi \circ \psi$ is q.u.s.c. if both ϕ and ψ are q.u.s.c.
   (ii) The function $\phi \circ \psi$ is closed if ϕ is closed and ψ is u.s.c.

b.   THE MAXIMUM THEOREM

Consider a typical competitive consumer with a utility function $u(x)$ defined on his consumption set X. The function $u(x)$ is real-valued from X into R. He chooses x (his "action") such as to maximize $u(x)$. His choice is restricted to a subset of X, called the "budget set." Suppose that his income is M and he is faced with a market price vector p. Let S be the set of all possible values of (p, M). Then his budget set can be defined by a set-valued function, H, from S into X. In the theory of consumer choice, H is defined in terms of $p \cdot x \leqq M$. However, given an arbitrary value of (p, M), $H(p, M)$ may not have an image in X, that is, $H(p, M)$ can be empty. We assume that there is at least one value of (p, M) in S such that $H(p, M)$ has an image in X, that is, $H(p, M)$ is nonempty for some $(p, M) \in S$. We then restrict the set S to its subset Z such that $H(p, M)$ is nonempty. In other words, $H(p, M)$ is nonempty for all (p, M) in Z. Now his action x (consumption vector) is such as to maximize $u(x)$ over the budget set $H(p, M)$.

In general, let us consider an economic agent who has a set of actions, which is *a priori* available to him, denoted by X. Let Z be the set of his possible environments. Given an element $z \in Z$, we suppose that his action is restricted to a subset of X by a set-valued function from Z into X. In other words, his action is restricted to $\phi(z) \subset X$. We assume that $\phi(z)$ is nonempty for all z in Z. Let us consider the outcome of action x when his environment is z. His action x is restricted to $\phi(z) \subset X$. In particular, we define a real-valued function u on $Z \otimes X$, called the **gain function**; $u(z, x)$ represents the gain when his environment is z and his action is x. Here the value of u may depend only on the action x which is taken. Hence $u(z, x)$ may simply be written $u(x)$. In demand theory, u is the utility function of the consumer, z is a price-income pair (p, M), X is the set of possible consumptions, and $\phi(z)$ is the budget set. In the theory of production, the economic agent is a producer, X is his production set (given the resource constraints), Z is the set of price-resource pairs, and u is the profit function.

Hence the above formulation of the function u defined on $Z \otimes X$ with $x \in \phi(x)$ has a wider application to economic problems. Let us suppose that the agent maximizes $u(z, x)$ for all $x \in \phi(z)$ with a given $z \in Z$. Let V be the value of this action, that is, $V(z) \equiv \sup \{u(z, x): x \in \phi(z)\}$. In other words, $V(z)$ is a real-valued function (and obviously single-valued) defined on Z. Let T be the set of such "optimal" actions. In other words, $T(z) = \{x: x \in \phi(z), u(z, x) = V(z)\}$. In general, $T(z)$ is a multivalued function from Z into X. We assume that X and Z are Hausdorff spaces. Berge ([1], pp. 115–116) stated and proved the following theorem which has many important applications.

Theorem 2.D.14 (maximum theorem):   *Let $u(z,x)$ be a real-valued (and single-valued) continuous function in $Z \otimes X$, and $\phi(z)$ be a multivalued function from Z into X such that $\phi(z) \neq \emptyset$ for all $z \in Z$ and $\phi(z)$ is continuous in Z. Then $V(z)$ is continuous and $T(z)$ is u.s.c. in Z.*

> *REMARK:*   In the above theorem, the requirement that $u(z,x)$ is continuous in $Z \otimes X$ can be replaced by the requirement that $u(x)$ is continuous in X. This is owing to the continuity of $\phi(z)$. This observation would be useful for the application of the theorem to demand theory, for example.

> *REMARK:*   In demand theory, $u(x)$ is the individual's utility function, $\phi(z)$ is his budget function, $V(z)$ is his indirect utility function, and $T(z)$ is his demand function (multivalued). The lower semicontinuity of $\phi(z)$ corresponds to the lower semicontinuity of $H(p, M)$. The upper semicontinuity of $T(z)$ corresponds to the upper semicontinuity of the demand function $F(p, M)$.

> *REMARK:*   Let $Y \subset R^n$ be the production set for a certain "competitive" producer. When price p prevails, his profit is $p \cdot y$, for action $y \in Y$. Let Z be the subset of R^n such that $p \cdot y$ attains a maximum over Y. We assume that Z is nonempty. Define $u(p, y)$ on $Z \otimes Y$ such that $u(p, y) \equiv p \cdot y$. There is no restriction by ϕ on Y; $V(p) \equiv \sup p \cdot y, y \in Y$. The supply function of this producer (multivalued function in general) is $T(p)$. Then from the above theorem (since $p \cdot y$ is obviously continuous), we can immediately conclude that his supply function $T(p)$ is upper semicontinuous and his profit function $V(p)$ is continuous.

> *REMARK:*   Theorem 2.D.14 was used by Debreu [2] to establish upper semicontinuity of the demand function and the supply function, but no explicit mention of the literature for the above theorems (such as Berge [1]) was made by him.

FOOTNOTES

1.   In the material of this Appendix, we have relied heavily on Berge [1] and Moore [4].
2.   Let X_2 be the set of positions in which Black can move and X_0 be the set of positions of checkmate or stalemate. Clearly X is the union of X_1, X_2, and X_0; ϕ is the mapping of $X \setminus X_0$ into X.
3.   It is assumed that X and Y satisfy the "first axiom of countability." A few definitions may be recalled here from Chapter 0, Section A. A topological space is said to satisfy the **first axiom of countability** if it has a countable open base at each of its points. An **open base** is a class of open sets such that every open set is a union of sets in this class.

The first axiom of countability practically enables a topology to be defined in terms of sequences alone. Clearly the usual Euclidian space satisfies the first axiom of countability. We further restrict Y to be a Hausdorff space. A topological space Y is called a **Hausdorff space** if for any two different points y^1 and y^2 in Y, there exist disjoint open sets V_1 and V_2 in Y such that $y^1 \in V_2$ (recall Chapter 0, Section A). This restriction of Y is required to obtain the subsequent results. It is known that every metric space is a Hausdorff space and also satisfies the first axiom of countability.

4. A function may be q.u.s.c. in X but may fail to be G-closed. A counterexample is the following: $X = R$, $Y = [0, 1]$ and define ϕ by $\phi(x) \equiv (0, 1)$ for all $x \in E$ (see Moore [4], pp. 131–132). As Moore points out ([4], p. 138, footnotes 7 and 8), there seems to be a slight confusion about this point in Karlin ([3], P. 409).

5. See Berge [1], p. 111, and Moore [4], p. 130.

6. Recall that when ϕ is single-valued, ϕ is continuous if and only if for each open set V in Y, the set $\phi^{-1}(V)$ is open in X. The definitions of lower inverse and upper inverse are thus linked in a natural way to the concepts of (semi-) continuity.

7. When Y fails to be compact, Theorem 2.D.12 fails to be valid. For an example of a G-closed function which fails to be q.u.s.c. (hence also fails to be u.s.c.), see Moore [4], p. 132.

8. The latter is the usual definition of l.s.c. appearing in the literature. See Debreu [2], p. 17.

REFERENCES

1. Berge, C., *Topological Spaces*, tr. by Patterson, New York, Macmillan, 1963 (French original, 1959).

2. Debreu, G., *Theory of Value*, New York, Wiley, 1959.

3. Karlin, S., *Mathematical Methods and Theory in Games, Programming, and Economics*, Vol. I, Reading, Mass., Addison-Wesley, 1959.

4. Moore, J. C., "A Note on Point-Set Mappings," in *Papers in Quantitative Economics*, Vol. I, ed. by J. P. Quirk, and A. M. Zarley, Lawrence, Kansas, University of Kansas Press, 1968.

Section E

THE EXISTENCE OF COMPETITIVE EQUILIBRIUM

a. HISTORICAL BACKGROUND

An economic model is constructed by specifying the economic agents involved, their behavioral rules, and the various equilibrium relations. The model is called a **general equilibrium model** if all the equilibrium relations in the model are specified. It is called a **partial equilibrium model** if only a part of the equilibrium relations is specified. The unspecified portion then is covered by the assumption that "other things are equal." A partial equilibrium analysis is convenient for a deeper analysis of some particular segment of the economy. However, it should be realized that any partial equilibrium analysis presupposes a general equilibrium analysis. For without knowing precisely under what conditions "other things are equal," the partial equilibrium analysis is rather meaningless.

Full recognition of the importance of general equilibrium analysis and the construction of the first general equilibrium model of a national economy is attributable to Léon Walras [42]. Moreover, Walras stated his general equilibrium system in mathematical forms whose impact on modern economic theory is immense. The model of a competitive equilibrium that we have considered so far in this chapter is an outgrowth of the Walrasian general equilibrium model. The important properties of such a general equilibrium—the optimality, the existence, and the stability of the equilibrium—have already been considered by Walras. Although his consideration was not too satisfactory from the present point of view, he was very much ahead of his time. The Walrasian construction of general equilibrium models goes from a simple model to more complicated models.[1]

We illustrate his model and his consideration of the existence of an equilibrium by using his model with production[2] ([42], part IV). (We use our own notation.) Let a_{ij} be the amount of the ith productive resource necessary to produce one unit of the jth commodity (good or service). Let $x_j, j = 1, 2, \ldots, n$, be the output of the jth commodity in the economy. Let $v_i, i = 1, 2, \ldots, m$, be the amount of the ith factor made available in the economy. Let p be an n-vector which gives the prices of the commodities that prevail in the economy, and let w be an m-vector that gives the prices of the factors. The jth component of p is denoted by p_j and the ith component of w is denoted by w_i. The demand for the jth commodity is a function of p and w. Similarly, the supply of the ith factor is a function of p and w. Thus the Walrasian general equilibrium system of competitive markets with production can be summarized by the following system of simultaneous equations.

(1)
$$\sum_{j=1}^{n} a_{ij} x_j = v_i \qquad i = 1, 2, \ldots, m$$

(2)
$$\sum_{i=1}^{m} w_i a_{ij} = p_j \qquad j = 1, 2, \ldots, n$$

(3)
$$v_i = v_i(p, w) \qquad i = 1, 2, \ldots, m$$

(4)
$$x_j = x_j(p, w) \qquad j = 1, 2, \ldots, n$$

Equation (1) determines the total demand for each factor, of which the supply is given by (3). The demand for each commodity is given by (4). Note that the same notation is used to denote the demand for and the supply of each factor and each commodity (that is, v_i and x_j). This implicitly assumes the equilibrium relation (the demand for each factor is equal to its supply and the demand for each commodity is equal to its supply). Equation (2) denotes the familiar profit condition which states that under perfect competition, profit is eliminated. Although it is not made explicit in the above model, Walras derived the above relations from the behavioral rules of the economic agents (competitive consumers and competitive producers). The market demand for commodity j was obtained by adding up the individual demands for commodity j over all consumers. Each consumer's demand for j was obtained by assuming that he maximizes his utility subject to his budget condition. The a_{ij}'s are the coefficients of production (or "coefficients of fabrication"). Walras initially assumed that they were constant but later (in the third edition; see lesson 36 of the fourth edition) showed that they were determined by the cost minimization behavior of each producer.[3] Alternatively the a_{ij}'s can be determined by the profit maximization behavior of each producer. Hence in the above system of equations we may consider $a_{ij} = a_{ij}(p, w)$.

Altogether there are $(2m + 2n)$ equations in the above system, and there are $(2m + 2n)$ variables to be determined in the system (that is, p_j, x_j, $j = 1, 2, \ldots, n$; w_i, v_i, $i = 1, 2, \ldots, m$). The price of one of the commodities for factors can be used as a numéraire to measure the relative prices of the other commodities and factors.[4] Letting $p_1 = 1$, we thus reduce the number of variables by one. Then Walras showed that there can be only $(2m + 2n - 1)$ *independent* equations in the above system, for one of the variables can be obtained from the identity, which is later called **Walras' Law**.[5]

$$\sum_{j=1}^{n} p_j x_j = \sum_{i=1}^{m} w_i v_i$$

For example, x_1 can be obtained as

$$x_1 = -\sum_{j=2}^{n} p_j x_j + \sum_{i=1}^{m} w_i v_i$$

Now there are $(2m + 2n - 1)$ variables and $(2m + 2n - 1)$ independent equations. Walras' fundamental method with regard to the existence of an equilibrium was that there exists an "equilibrium" (that is, the solution for the equilibrium values of the p_j's, x_j's, w_i's, and v_i's) because the number of equations and the number of variables are the same.

Although his recognition of the importance of the question of whether or not there exists an equilibrium is very ingenious and quite beyond his time, the logic used to obtain the conclusion, as described above, is clearly wrong. For example, the following two simultaneous equations in the variables $x, y \in R$, will not yield any solution, for these two equations are inconsistent (they are clearly independent).

$$\begin{cases} x + y = 1 \\ x + y = -1 \end{cases}$$

Moreover, even if there is a solution, there is a question as to whether the solution is economically meaningful. For example, the following system with one equation yields a solution, but the solution is usually economically meaningless:

$$x^2 = -1$$

Even a simpler example would be $x = -1$, where x denotes "output."[6] Hence Walras' method of counting the number of equations and the number of variables is quite unsatisfactory.[7] Although this method often gives a necessary condition for the existence of an equilibrium solution,[8] it is not a sufficient condition.

Although the above Walrasian procedure of showing the existence of an equilibrium solution is unsatisfactory, it was accepted for a long time without question.[9] The first satisfactory treatment came in the 1930s from Karl Menger's seminar in Vienna. One of the most important contributions made here was the reformulation of the Walras-Cassel system allowing inequalities.[10] Based upon such reformulations, in particular the ones due to Schlesinger [34] and Zeuthen [43], Abraham Wald [39][11] gave the first satisfactory and rigorous proof of the existence of an equilibrium solution. Alternative proofs of the existence of an equilibrium solution for Schlesinger's reformulation of the Walras-Cassel model have recently been given independently by Kuhn [19] and DOSSO [13]. The proofs by Kuhn and DOSSO are essentially similar in the sense that they are based on the idea of utilizing the duality theorem of linear programming.

Schlesinger's reformulation of the Walras-Cassal system can be described as follows (in terms of the above notation):

(5)
$$\sum_{j=1}^{n} a_{ij}x_j \leqq v_i, \qquad i = 1, 2, \ldots, m$$

(6)
$$\sum_{j=1}^{n} a_{ij}x_j < v_i \text{ implies } w_i = 0$$

(7)
$$\sum_{i=1}^{m} w_i a_{ij} = p_j, \qquad i = 1, 2, \ldots, n$$

(8) $p_j = f_j(x_1, x_2, \cdots, x_n), j = 1, 2, \cdots, n$ [or, in short, $p = f(x)$]

(9) $v_i = \bar{v}_i$ (constant) $i = 1, 2, \ldots, m$

(10) $p_j \geq 0, x_j \geq 0, \qquad j = 1, 2, \ldots, n$
        $w_i \geq 0, \qquad i = 1, 2, \ldots, m$

The model is almost self-explanatory, given the above explanation of Walras' system. Relation (6) says that if there is an excess supply of the ith factor, its price will be zero. Equation (8) is the "inverse" demand function, expressing the price of each commodity as a function of the quantity demanded. This convention facilitated the proof by Wald.[12] Wald proved the existence of a unique solution (p, x, v)

in the above system under the following assumptions:

(i) $a_{ij} \geq 0$ for all i and j.
(ii) $\bar{v} > 0$, $a_{ij} =$ constant for all i, j (fixed coefficients).
(iii) For each j there exists at least one i such that $a_{ij} > 0$.
(iv) The demand function f_j is single-valued, continuous, and defined for all $x > 0$.
(v)   If $\{x^q\}$ is a sequence of commodity vectors such that $x^q \to \bar{x}$ with $\bar{x}_j = 0$, then $f_j(x^q) \to \infty$.
(vi) Given $x, x' > 0$, and letting $p = f(x)$ and $p' = f(x')$, we have either (a) $p \cdot x < p \cdot x'$ or (b) $p' \cdot x' < p' \cdot x$.

Assumption (iii) precludes the Land of Cockaigne. Assumption (v) says that if the demand for the jth commodity goes to zero, its price goes to infinity. This means that the demand for each commodity will never be zero for any (finite) price, however large. This assumption is clearly unrealistic. It is introduced primarily to facilitate the proof. Assumption (vi) is needed in the proof of the *uniqueness* of the equilibrium solution.

Since Wald's original proof is rather tedious, we will sketch the proof by Kuhn [19] and DOSSO [13],[13] which should be of interest in itself because of its relation to the theory of linear programming.

Let $X \equiv \{x\colon x \geq 0,\ A \cdot x \leq \bar{v}\}$, where $A = [a_{ij}]$, (the feasible set). We can easily show that X is nonempty, compact, and convex. Then consider the following linear programming problem:

$$\text{Maximize: } p \cdot x$$
$$x$$
$$\text{Subject to: } A \cdot x \leq \bar{v}, \text{ and } x \geq 0$$

Define $p \equiv f(x)$ for all $x > 0$ such that $x \in X$. For a fixed value of x, we first obtain the value of p and then solve the above linear programming problem with this value of p. We obtain a solution x^* (which is obviously not necessarily unique). We now have a mapping $x \to p \to x^*$ which we denote by $F(x)$. It is a function from the interior of X into X. Extend this mapping to the whole X and denote it by $\Phi(x)$; that is, $\Phi(x) = F(x)$ for all $x > 0$. The extension can be achieved by taking the closure of the graph of F in $X \otimes X$ (see Kuhn [19], pp. 269–270). Using the continuity of $f(x)$, we can show that $\Phi(x)$ is upper semicontinuous and $\Phi(x)$ is nonempty and convex, for all $x \in X$. Now use the following theorem, known as the **Kakutani fixed point theorem**.

Theorem 2.E.1 (Kakutani):   *Let S be a nonempty, compact, convex subset of R^n. Let F be an upper semicontinuous function from S into itself such that, for all $p \in S$, the set $F(p)$ is nonempty and convex.[14] Then there exists a $\hat{p}$ in S such that $\hat{p} \in F(\hat{p})$.*

This theorem is a generalization of the following theorem, which is called **Brouwer's fixed point theorem**.

Theorem 2.E.2 (Brouwer):   *Let S be a nonempty, compact, convex subset of R^n, and let F be a single-valued continuous function from S into itself. Then there exists a $\hat{p}$ in S such that $\hat{p} = F(\hat{p})$.*

Both Brouwer's and Kakutani's theorems probe deeply into combinatorial topology. For rather simple proofs, see Nikaido [30],[31], for example.[15] Brouwer's theorem is illustrated in Figure 2.30. Here S is the unit interval $[0, 1]$. A continuous function from S to S must cross the diagonal line; thus $F(\hat{p}) = \hat{p}$.

> *REMARK*:   The method of actually computing a fixed point in connection with the theory of competitive equilibrium has been recently provided by Scarf [33]; his paper can also be considered to give a constructive proof of the existence of competitive equilibrium. See also Arrow and Hahn [4], Appendix C.

Reading the statement of Kakutani's fixed point theorem, we at once realize that this theorem is applicable to the present problem. In other words, there exists an $\hat{x} \in X$ such that $\hat{x} \in \Phi(\hat{x})$. Then, using assumption (v), we can show that $\hat{x} > 0$. Thus we can find $\hat{x} > 0$ and $\hat{p} = f(\hat{x})$ such that $\hat{x}$ solves the above linear programming problem. Then from the duality theorem of linear programming, there exists a solution $\hat{w}$ for the following dual problem.

$$\text{Minimize: } w \cdot \overline{v}$$
$$\text{Subject to: } A' \cdot w = \hat{p}, \ w \geq 0$$

Then $(\hat{p}, \hat{x}, \hat{w})$ constitutes a solution for Schlesinger's version of the Walras-Cassel model.[16] Using (vi), the uniqueness can be proved.[17] Note that Wald requires the equality $A' \cdot w = p$. This implies that the price of every commodity has to be strictly positive [under (iii)]. Assumption (v) is required to guarantee $\hat{x} > 0$ so that $A' \cdot \hat{w} = \hat{p}$. This assumption says roughly that every commodity is indispensable to the consumer. Note also that if we allow an inequality here—that is, $A' \cdot \hat{w} \geq \hat{p}$—then (from the duality theorem) we admit zero production for some goods and the difficulty of introducing assumption (v) disappears (See Kuhn [19]). (However, some sort of

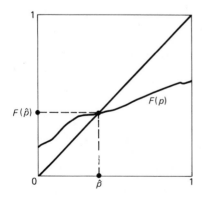

Figure 2.30.   An Illustration of Brouwer's Fixed Point Theorem.

indispensability assumption seems still to be needed to guarantee that the output of at least one commodity will be positive.)

Wald's original proof is quite tedious because he obviously could not utilize the duality theorem. Although we now have a simple proof by Kuhn and DOSSO, there are some unsatisfactory points in the above formulation. For example, it is not clear what will guarantee the existence of the inverse demand function and its continuity.[18] No behavioral rule for the consumers or for the producer is stated. The production set implied from the model is for the entire economy and is not for each producer. Only a special type of production set is considered. Thus we are forced to return to a model such as the one discussed in the previous sections of this chapter. In other words, we first specify the consumption set for each consumer, the production set for each producer, the behavioral rule for each economic agent, and a competitive equilibrium. Then, using the assumptions on the consumption set and the production set, and so forth, we want to prove the existence of an equilibrium. The problem then is no longer one of finding a solution for the simultaneous equations or inequalities. The stress now lies in the *compatibility* of each economic agent's behavior. The following excerpts from Koopmans ([17], p. 60) point this out precisely.

> The problem is no longer conceived as that of proving that a certain set of equations has a solution. It has been reformulated as one of proving that a number of maximization of individual goals under independent restraints can be simultaneously carried out.

This is the essence of the modern formulation of the existence question. The first successful formulation and proof of this problem is due to Arrow and Debreu [3].[19]

The essential idea of their paper is to consider the model of competitive markets as the model of an *n*-person noncooperative game and to utilize a theory developed in game theory. Independently, Gale [14] and Nikaido [28],[29] presented other proofs of existence at almost the same time. Their proofs and the proof given in Debreu [11] are quite similar. The development of their proofs can be obtained easily from our discussion in the previous sections of this chapter, especially Section D.

Starting with each consumer's consumption set and preference ordering, we can show that his demand function, $x_i(p)$, is an upper semicontinuous function of the price vector p, where p includes the price of all commodities including primary factors. The aggregate demand function is obtained as the sum of individual demand functions, that is, $x(p) = \sum x_i(p)$, assuming the absence of interactions among consumers' preferences. Since a linear combination of upper semicontinuous functions is also upper semicontinuous (which can be shown easily), the aggregate demand function $x(p)$ is also upper semicontinuous.[20] Similarly, we can show that the supply function of an individual producer (who is a profit maximizer) is upper semicontinuous (see Appendix to Section D of this chapter). Then, assuming no "(technological) externalities" among the producers, the aggregate supply function, $y(p)$, is the sum of the individual supply functions, that is, $y(p) = \sum y_j(p)$, and $y(p)$ is upper semicontinuous. Here a negative element of $y_j(p)$ is an input for j. Assuming no externalities among the producers and the consumers, we write the (aggregate) excess supply function as $z(p) \equiv y(p) + \bar{x} - x(p)$, where $\bar{x}$ is the total supply of resources available in the economy. Then $z(p)$ is also upper semicontinuous. Assuming free disposability, we write the feasibility condition as $z(p) \cap \Omega \neq \emptyset$; or, equivalently, there exists a $z \in z(p)$ such that $z \geq 0$. We say that $[\hat{p}, \{\hat{x}_i\}, \{\hat{y}_j\}]$ is a **competitive equilibrium** if

(i) $\hat{x}_i \in x_i(\hat{p}), \hat{y}_j \in y_j(\hat{p})$ for all i and j,

and

(ii)   *there exists a* $\hat{z} \in z(\hat{p})$ *such that* $\hat{z} \geq 0$, *where* $\hat{z} = \sum \hat{y}_j + \bar{x} - \sum \hat{x}_i$.

We normalize the price vector p by setting $\sum_{i=1}^{n} p_i = 1$. This corresponds to and replaces the Walrasian convention of setting $p_1 = 1$. The underlying assumption which makes the normalization possible is the "homogeneity postulate"; that is, each element of vectors $x_i(p)$'s and $y_j(p)$'s [hence $z(p)$ also] is homogeneous of degree zero [thus $z(\alpha p) = z(p)$, for all p, for any $\alpha > 0, \alpha \in R$, for example], so that an equilibrium is unaltered if all prices are multiplied by the same positive constant. Hence, without loss of generality, we can assume that $\sum_{i=1}^{n} p_i = 1$ or $p_1 = 1$ (see footnote 4). Note also that if we wish to choose a particular commodity (say commodity 1) to be *numéraire*, then its price should not be zero, at least in equilibrium (so that we can set $p_1 = 1$). If there exists a commodity for which the excess demand is positive whenever its price is zero, regardless of the prices of all other commodities, then such a commodity is a good candidate for *numéraire*.

Let $P \equiv \{p: \sum_{i=1}^{n} p_i = 1, p_i \geq 0, i = 1, 2, \ldots, n\}$. From a consideration of the individual's demand function, we prove that each $x_i(p)$ and each $y_j(p)$ is a convex set. [The convexity of the set $x_i(p)$ follows from the assumption of the weak convexity and the continuity of the preference ordering, and the convexity $y_j(p)$ follows from the convexity of the production set Y_j.] Here we simply assume this.

Let θ_{ji} be the share of the profits of the jth producer going to the ith consumer. If all the resources are held by consumers (so that $\bar{x} = \sum \bar{x}_i$), then each consumer's budget constraint can be written as

$$p \cdot x_i \leq p \cdot \bar{x}_i + \sum_{j=1}^{n} \theta_{ji} \, p \cdot y_j$$

where x_i is the consumption vector of i and y_j is the production vector of j. Summing over i and recalling that $\sum_{i=1} \theta_{ji} = 1$, we obtain

$$p \cdot x \leq p \cdot \bar{x} + p \cdot y, \text{ where } x \equiv \sum x_i \text{ and } y \equiv \sum y_j$$

or

$$p \cdot z \geq 0$$

This corresponds to Walras' Law.[21] We will now use the following lemma, which is proved independently in the literature by Gale [14] and Nikaido [28].[22] The lemma, which practically is the proof of the existence of competitive equilibrium, can easily be proved if we use Kakutani's fixed point theorem. (For such a proof, see Debreu [11], pp. 82–83, and Nikaido [31], pp. 266–267).[23]

Lemma 2.E.1 (Gale, Nikaido):   *Let P be the $(n-1)$-unit simplex in R^n, that is, $P \equiv \{p: p \in R^n, \sum_{i=1}^n p_i = 1, p \geq 0\}$, and let S be a nonempty compact subset of R^n. Let F be an upper semicontinuous function from P to S, such that $F(p)$ is nonempty and convex for all $p \in P$ and $p \cdot F(p) \geq 0$ [that is, $p \cdot z \geq 0$ for all $z \in F(p)$]. Then there exists a $\hat{p} \in P$ such that $F(\hat{p}) \cap \Omega \neq \emptyset$.*

This lemma is illustrated in Figure 2.31. By the assumption that $p \cdot F(p) \geq 0$, $F(p)$ must be above the line passing through the origin and orthogonal to p. As p moves in P, $F(p)$ must intersect with Ω.

Now let P be the $(n-1)$-unit simplex of price vectors as defined above. Then for each element p of P, we obtain $x_i(p)$ and $y_j(p)$. Define $z(p)$ as $z(p) \equiv \sum y_j(p) + \bar{x} - \sum x_i(p)$. We see immediately that this $z(p)$ satisfies the assumptions of the lemma. Hence there exists a $\hat{p} \in P$ such that $z(\hat{p}) \cap \Omega \neq \emptyset$. Let $\hat{z} \in z(\hat{p})$ with $\hat{z} \geq 0$. Then there exist $\hat{x}_i \in x_i(\hat{p})$ and $\hat{y}_j \in y_j(\hat{p})$ such that $\hat{z} \in z(\hat{p})$, where $\hat{z} \equiv \sum \hat{y}_j + \bar{x} - \sum \hat{x}_i$. This completes the proof of the existence of a competitive equilibrium in the manner of Gale [14], Nikaido [28], and Debreu [11].

In the above sketch of the proof of the existence of a competitive equilibrium by Gale, Nikaido, and Debreu, we relied heavily on results obtained in the previous sections. Hence it was not made explicit what the crucial assumptions are or how they are used. The reader can check this by going back to the previous sections of this chapter.[24] Now we present a complete proof of the existence of a competitive equilibrium. Our proof and the formulation are based essentially on McKenzie [22] and [21]. We do not use the most general version of McKenzie's model; for our purpose, the proof of a simpler formulation will suffice. Moreover, this will serve as a guide to McKenzie's rather difficult article [22]. For this purpose the author is also indebted to McKenzie for his lectures at the University of Rochester.

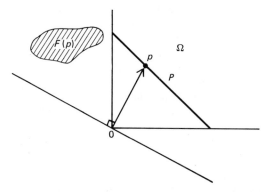

Figure 2.31.   An Illustration of the Gale-Nikaido Lemma.

Before we go on to McKenzie's proof, let us sketch an outline of some of the important and difficult problems in the proof of existence, which are not clearly or explicitly stated in the above expositions and proofs. The first thorough recognition of these problems (and hence the meaning of the assumptions) is due to Arrow and Debreu [3], whose work remains the standard reference for the problem.

(i)   The **survival problem**. This is the question of assuring that every consumer can survive, given the equilibrium conditions. If an equilibrium exists, the equilibrium prices of the resources held by some consumer may be so low that he may not be able to subsist on the income he obtains from his resources. The first requirement for this problem, of course, is that the aggregate supply set contain a point which is the sum of the minimal subsistence consumption requirements for each consumer (otherwise some consumer is bound to die). In terms of the notation of Section C, this means that there exist $x_i \in X_i$, for all i and $y \in Y$ such that $x = y + \bar{x}$, where $x \equiv \sum x_i$. The second requirement is that each consumer be able to subsist with the resources (including labor) he holds without engaging in exchange. This can be guaranteed if each consumer's consumption set, with his resources added, has an intersection with the aggregate production set of the economy. In fact, we need a little more. For example, we may require that not only must such an intersection be nonempty, it must also have an interior point.[25] This corresponds to the cheaper-point assumption discussed in the previous section. Essentially, it guarantees the (upper semi-) continuity of each consumer's demand function.

(ii)   **Satiation**. When an equilibrium price prevails, some consumer, because the prices of his resources are very high, may be able to purchase a consumption bundle such that he is satiated. As we said in the previous section, the nonsatiation assumption is needed to establish the lower semicontinuity of the budget function (hence the upper semicontinuity of the demand function). Arrow and Debreu simply assumed that every consumer is nonsatiated in his (somewhat modified) consumption set. This is a strong assumption. The relaxation of this assumption is possible and is attempted in the literature (for example, McKenzie [21], [22]).

(iii)   **Utility function and the production set**. Arrow and Debreu assume the existence of a continuous utility function for each consumer. McKenzie's formulation is in terms of a preference relation, although his assumptions imply the existence of a continuous utility function. The crucial assumption in this connection, which is common in all the existence proofs, is the convexity of individual preferences. Arrow and Debreu [3] assume the existence of a fixed number of firms, each of which has a convex production set.[26] McKenzie [22] assumes that the aggregate production set is a convex cone so that constant returns to scale prevails in the aggregate. McKenzie does not assume the irreversibility of the production processes, nor does he assume free disposability of commodities.

(iv)   **The number of producers**.[27] In Arrow and Debreu [3] and subsequent works such as Debreu [11], it is assumed that the total number of firms (producers) is fixed (at, say, k). It is well known and can easily be checked that diminishing returns to scale for an individual producer implies a positive profit, which in turn should imply that firms enter the market. Constant returns to scale for the aggregate production set can be justified on the basis of an adjustment in the number of firms, which are small in size compared to the industry. Diminishing returns to scale for an individual firm typically occur when there are certain limitational fixed factors, such as managerial ability or entrepreneurship, which are *not* explicitly introduced in the model (and are not marketed). Therefore, diminishing returns to scale (for each firm) plus a finite fixed set of firms imply the scarcity of certain commodities (factors) *and* freezing the assignment to various production processes of these commodities. (Such a model will not be useful for exploring possible effects of a redistribution of these resources.) Under diminishing returns to scale, firms may make profits, which are attributable to payments for the use of such resources as entrepreneurial skills or special talents of some kind. In McKenzie's model [22], such resources are explicitly included in the list of commodities (and marketed) and the number of firms need not be fixed, so that we can safely assume constant returns to scale for the aggregate production set. McKenzie also shows the concordance of his model with the usual Hicksian model of a fixed number of firms, each of which has a closed and convex production set (pp. 66–67).

b.   MCKENZIE'S PROOF

Essentially, we follow the proof due to McKenzie [22]. In order to understand the principal problems and difficulties involved in the proof, we consider his simpler case.[28]

Let x_i be an n-commodity consumption vector for consumer i ($i = 1$, $2, \ldots, m$) and let X_i be his consumption set, which is assumed to be a subset of R^n. We adopt the convention that the positive components of x_i represent the commodities demanded and the negative components represent commodities supplied by the ith consumer (recall the discussion in Section A for this convention). We do not take into explicit account a resource vector such as v_i; it is imbedded in our convention of x_i. Let Y be the aggregate production set. We now state and explain the assumptions which will be used in the present proof of the existence of a competitive equilibrium.

(i) Assumptions on consumption sets.

(A-1)   The set X_i is convex, closed, and bounded.
(A-2)   The set X_i is totally quasi-ordered by a strictly convex and continuous preference ordering $\gtrsim_i$.

> *REMARK*:   For discussions of the compactness of X_i, see Debreu [11], Arrow and Debreu [3], and Nikaido [30]. They show how we can restrict our attention to a compact consumption set. The crucial part of this assumption is that X_i is bounded from below.

> *REMARK*:   We recall the following definitions:
> **(strict convexity of $\gtrsim_i$)** Preference ordering $\gtrsim_i$ is called **strictly convex**

if X_i is convex and $x_i' \circleq_i x_i$ and $x_i' \neq x_i$ imply $[tx_i' + (1-t)x_i] \circgt_i x_i, 0 < t < 1$.
(**continuity of** $\circleq_i$) Preference ordering $\circleq_i$ is said to be **continuous** if for any sequences $\{x_i{}^q\}$, $\{\bar{x}_i{}^q\}$ in X_i with $x_i{}^q \to x_i$ and $\bar{x}_i{}^q \to \bar{x}_i$, $x_i{}^q \circleq_i \bar{x}_i{}^q$ for all q implies $x_i \circleq_i \bar{x}_i$.

(ii) **Assumptions on the aggregate production set** Y.

(A-3)   The set Y is a closed convex cone.
(A-4) $Y \cap \Omega = \{0\}$ (the impossibility of the Land of Cockaigne).

REMARK: Assumption (A-3) does not necessarily imply that each Y_j is convex. It means constant returns to scale for the *aggregate* production set.[29] As mentioned earlier, diminishing returns to scale for a particular producer (firm) can be subdued in the aggregate by increasing the number of firms in which the entrepreneurial factor is not private to the firm. The absence of technological external economies and diseconomies (interactions among production processes) is assumed here. The absence of Marshallian external economies and diseconomies is also assumed. The Marshallian externalities are due to a change in the size of an industry; hence they are external to each firm, but internal to the industry or the economy. Such externalities should be distinguished from the purely technological externalities. Note also that (A-3) and (A-4) do not assume the free disposability nor the irreversibility of production.

REMARK: From (A-3) and (A-4), the total profit in the economy is zero (recall our discussion of activity analysis, Chapter 0, Section C). We can suppose that each consumer receives zero shares of profit income. Or we can suppose that the profit share from a particular producer to a particular consumer is simply the return to the resources offered by the consumer to the producer. In any case, we suppose that each consumer's income is restricted to the value of the resources that he offers to the market. Hence his budget constraint can be expressed by $p \cdot x_i \leq 0$, $x_i \in X$, if price $p \in R^n$ prevails.

Definition: The **budget set** for the ith consumer, denoted by $H_i(p)$, is defined by

$$H_i(p) \equiv \{x_i: p \cdot x_i \leq 0, x_i \in X_i\}$$

We assume $H_i(p)$ is nonempty for all possible p. Recall our discussion on this assumption in Section D and its appendix.

Definition: Define the sets $C_i(p)$ and $C(p)$ by

$$C_i(p) \equiv \{x_i': x_i' \circleq_i x_i \text{ for all } x_i \in H_i(p)\}$$

$$C(p) \equiv \sum_{i=1}^{m} C_i(p)$$

The set $C_i(p)$ is the ith **upper contour set** under price p and $C(p)$ is the **economy's upper contour set** under price p.

The concept of the upper contour set, $C_i(p)$, is illustrated in Figure 2.32. The dotted lines indicate the indifference curves of the ith consumer.

Definition: We say that the ith consumer is **satiated at** x_i if $x_i \gtrsim_i x_i'$ for all $x_i' \in X_i$ and that the ith consumer is **satiated at price p** if $x_i \gtrsim_i x_i'$ for all $x_i' \in C_i(p)$.

(iii) Assumptions relating consumption and production sets.

(A-5)   The set $X_i \cap Y$ has an interior point for all i.
(A-6)   *Either* (1) no consumer is satiated at p, *or* (2) if some consumer is satiated at p, then $C(p) \cap Y = \emptyset$.

> REMARK: Assumption (A-5) guarantees that every consumer can supply a positive amount of every (unproduced) commodity to the producers.[30] Thus every consumer always has some income, given nonzero prices, so that his budget set contains a point in his consumption set, and he can trade with others. Assumption (A-5) guarantees the subsistence of every consumer and it also corresponds to the cheaper-point (minimum-wealth) assumption used in Sections C and D. This assumption, (A-5), is illustrated in Figure 2.33.

> REMARK: Assumption (A-6) says that if some consumer is satiated while trading at price p, then the total demand at p will exceed the possible production. This concept is illustrated in Figure 2.34, in which we assume that there is only one consumer in the economy. In this diagram, point x represents a point of satiation. In other words, if the price of a certain commodity becomes low enough (relative to other commodities), a consumer may be able to purchase a large quantity of that good (in exchange for other commodi-

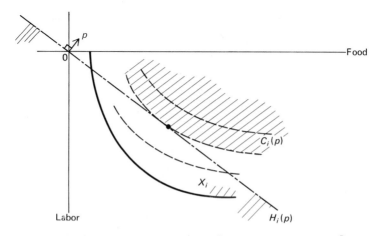

Figure 2.32.   An Illustration of $C_i(p)$. $\left[C_i(p) = \text{the shaded area}\right]$.

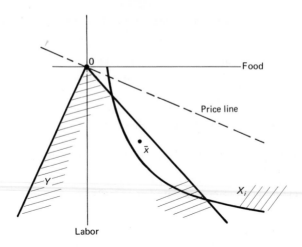

Figure 2.33.   An Illustration of (A-5).

ties), and thus he may be satiated with that good. Assumption (A-6) says that
if this occurs, the demand for that good is beyond the society's productive
capacity. Therefore (A-6), in effect, precludes such a possibility. Analytic-
ally, (A-6) corresponds to the nonsatiation assumption of demand theory.

We are now ready to start the proof of the existence of a competitive equilibrium. First we define competitive equilibrium (in the usual manner).

Definition (competitive equilibrium):   An array of vectors $\left[\{\hat{x}_1, \hat{x}_2, \ldots, \hat{x}_m\}, \hat{y}, \hat{p}\right]$

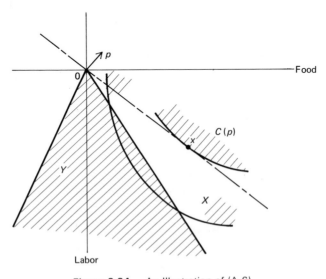

Figure 2.34.   An Illustration of (A-6).

is called a **competitive equilibrium** if the following hold:

(i) $\hat{x}_i \in C_i(\hat{p}) \cap H_i(\hat{p})$, $i = 1, 2, \ldots, m$.
(ii) $\hat{y} \in Y$ and $\hat{p} \cdot \hat{y} = 0$, $\hat{p} \cdot y \leq 0$ *for all* $y \in Y$.

(iii) $\sum\limits_{i=1}^{m} \hat{x}_i = \hat{y}$.

REMARK: Condition (i) is the familiar one of a consumer maximizing his satisfaction over his budget set ("demand condition"). Condition (iii) is the requirement that total demand be equal to total supply. This is stated as an *equality*; hence no free disposability is assumed, and negative prices are allowed. Condition (ii) is the familiar zero profit condition of a competitive economy. If there exists a $y' \in Y$ such that $\hat{p} \cdot y' > 0$, then consumers, as owners of resources, could receive higher returns for their resources by offering some of their resources at a production point $\alpha y'$ for some $\alpha > 0$ (α can be less than one, of course). Hence some consumers can be made better off by engaging in such trades. Thus the situation would not be stable. On the other hand, if $\hat{p} \cdot y < 0$, some returns would be reduced.

REMARK: Note that $\hat{p} \cdot \hat{y} = 0$ and $\hat{p} \cdot y \leq 0$ for all $y \in Y$. If we suppose that the number of the producers in the economy is fixed ($j = 1, 2, \ldots, k$), and that there are no externalities among the producers, then we can write $\hat{y} = \sum_{j=1}^{k} \hat{y}_j$ and $y = \sum_{j=1}^{k} y_j$, where $\hat{y}_j, y_j \in Y_j, j = 1, 2, \ldots, k$. Then $\hat{p} \cdot \hat{y} = 0$, and $\hat{p} \cdot y \leq 0$ for all $y \in Y$ means

$$\sum_{j=1}^{k} \hat{p} \cdot y_j \leq \sum_{j=1}^{k} \hat{p} \cdot \hat{y}_j = 0 \qquad \text{for all } y_j \in Y_j, j = 1, 2, \ldots, k$$

Fix $j = j_0$ and put $y_j = \hat{y}_j$ for all j except $j = j_0$. Then $\hat{p} \cdot y_{j_0} \leq \hat{p} \cdot \hat{y}_{j_0}$ for all $y_{j_0} \in Y_{j_0}$. Since the choice of j_0 is arbitrary, this shows the profit maximization of *each* producer.

In order to prove the existence of a competitive equilibrium, it is sufficient to confine our attention to a price vector p which satisfies condition (ii) of a competitive equilibrium.

Definition: The **polar cone of** Y, denoted by Y^*, is defined by

$$Y^* \equiv \{p: p \cdot y \leq 0, y \in Y\}$$

Let $\bar{x}_i \in$ interior $(X_i \cap Y)$, $i = 1, 2, \ldots, m$. This exists for all i from (A-5). Write $\sum_{i=1}^{m} \bar{x}_i \equiv \bar{x}$; then $\bar{x} \in$ interior Y.

Definition: We define P, called the **normalized polar cone of** Y, by[31]

$$P \equiv \{p: p \in Y^*, \text{ and } p \cdot \bar{x} = -1\}$$

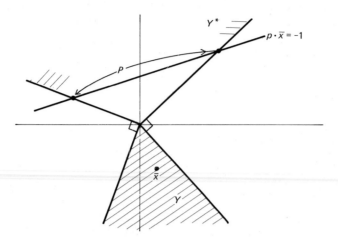

Figure 2.35.   An Illustration of Y^* and P.

REMARK: The normalization of the price vector is done for convenience. Since some prices can be negative, we cannot use a more customary normalization such as $\sum_{i=1}^{n} p_i = 1$. It turns out that the above normalization is convenient for the present analysis.

Lemma 2.E.2:   *The set P is convex and compact.*

PROOF: We prove this in three steps.

(i) (Convexity) Let p, $p' \in P$, and let $p'' \equiv tp + (1 - t)p'(0 \leq t \leq 1)$. But $p \cdot y \leq 0$ and $p' \cdot y \leq 0$ imply $p'' \cdot y \leq 0$. Hence $p'' \in Y^*$, $p \cdot \bar{x} = -1$, and $p' \cdot \bar{x} = -1$ imply $p'' \cdot \bar{x} = -1$. Hence $p'' \in P$. Therefore P is convex.

(ii) (Closed) Let $p^q \to p$, $p^q \in P$; $p^q \cdot y \leq 0$ implies $p \cdot y \leq 0$ for $y \in Y$ (as a result of the continuity of inner product). Hence $p \in Y^*$. $p^q \cdot \bar{x} = -1$ implies $p \cdot \bar{x} = -1$. Hence $p \in P$. Therefore P is closed.

(iii) (Bounded) Suppose there exists a sequence $\{p^q\}$ such that $\| p^q \| \to \infty$, $p^q \in P$. Consider $p^q / \| p^q \| \equiv \bar{p}^q$. Then $\bar{p}^q \in Y^*$, since Y^* is a convex cone and $p^q \in Y^*$. Moreover, $\bar{p}^q$ is an element of the intersection of Y^* and the $(n - 1)$-dimensional unit sphere. That is, $\bar{p}^q$ is an element of a compact set. Hence there exists a subsequence of $\{\bar{p}^q\}$—say, $\{\bar{p}^s\}$—such that $\bar{p}^s \to \bar{p}$, where $\| \bar{p}^s \| = \| \bar{p} \| = 1$. Moreover, $\bar{p} \in Y^*$, for Y^* is closed. Consider $\bar{p}^s \cdot \bar{x}$. Since $p^s \cdot \bar{x} = -1$ ($\because p^s \in P$), $\bar{p}^s \cdot \bar{x} = -1 / \| p^s \|$. Then $\| p^s \| \to \infty$ implies that $\bar{p}^s \cdot \bar{x} \to 0$ as $s \to \infty$, that is, $\bar{p} \cdot \bar{x} = 0$. But this is a contradiction, for $\bar{p} \in Y^*$ and $\bar{x} \in$ interior Y means $\bar{p} \cdot \bar{x} < 0$. Therefore no such sequence $\{p^q\}$ can exist. Thus P is bounded, so that it is compact.   (Q.E.D.)

Definition: The *i*th **demand function**, denoted by $f_i(p)$, is defined by

$$f_i(p) \equiv C_i(p) \cap H_i(p), \qquad p \in P$$

The following lemma was proved in Section D.

Lemma 2.E.3:   *Under (A-1), (A-2), and (A-5),*

(i)   *The function $f_i(p)$ is single-valued and continuous on P.*

(ii)   *If the i-th consumer is not satiated at $x_i = f_i(p)$, $p \cdot f_i(p) = 0$.*

(iii)   *The function $f_i(p)$ is positively homogeneous of degree zero.*

Let z be a point which is *not* an interior point of Y, and consider a chord join-ing $\bar{x}$ and z: $t\bar{x} + (1 - t)z$, $0 \leq t \leq 1$. Now consider the minimum of t subject to $t\bar{x} + (1 - t)z \in Y$. Since t varies over the (closed) unit interval $[0, 1]$, there exists a t in $[0, 1]$ for which t achieves its minimum. Denote this minimum by t_z. In other words, we define $t_z \equiv \min t$ such that $t\bar{x} + (1 - t)z \in Y, 0 \leq t_z \leq 1$. Now consider a function $h(z)$ from such $z \notin$ interior Y into Y by

$$h(z) = t_z \, \bar{x} + (1 - t_z)z$$

This function $h(z)$ is illustrated in Figure 2.36.

Lemma 2.E.4:   *The function $h(z)$ is continuous for $z \notin$ interior Y.*

PROOF: Consider a sequence $\{z^q\} \notin Y$ such that $z^q \to z$. Let $y^q \equiv h(z^q)$. Suppose $h(z)$ is *not* continuous. That is, suppose $y^q \to y \equiv h(z)$ does not hold. Then by the compactness of the unit interval ($\because t_z$ varies in $[0, 1]$), there is a

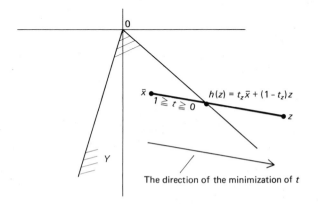

Figure 2.36.   An Illustration of $h(z)$.

subsequence $\{y^s\}$ such that $y^s \to y'$, where $y' \neq y \equiv h(z)$, and $y' = t'\bar{x} + (1 - t')z$ for some t', $0 \leq t' \leq 1$. Since $\bar{x} \in$ interior Y, and t^q and t_z are all less than 1, $y^q \neq \bar{x}$, $y' \neq \bar{x}$, and $y \neq \bar{x}$.

By the definition of t_z, we cannot have $t' < t_z$. Hence $t' \geq t_z$. But $t' = t_z$ implies $y = y'$, so that we have $t' > t_z$. This implies $y' = \theta\bar{x} + (1 - \theta)y$ for some θ, where $0 < \theta \leq 1$. Since $\bar{x} \in$ interior Y, there exists an open ball $B_\epsilon(\bar{x})$ about $\bar{x}$ with radius $\epsilon > 0$, such that $B_\epsilon(\bar{x}) \subset Y$. Let $w \in B_\epsilon(\bar{x})$ and define $w' \equiv \theta w + (1 - \theta)y$. Then $w' \in Y$, since both w and y are in Y. Hence we have an open ball $B_{\theta\epsilon}(y')$ about y' with radius $\theta\epsilon > 0$, such that $B_{\theta\epsilon}(y') \subset Y$. Hence y' is an interior point of Y. Therefore $y^q \in$ interior Y for large q. This contradicts the definition $y^q \equiv h(z^q)$. Thus we have $t' = t_z$, or $y = y'$. (Q.E.D.)

REMARK: The above proof is illustrated in Figures 2.37 and 2.38.

Definition: $g(z) \equiv \{p : p \in P \text{ and } p \cdot z = 0\}$, where $z \in$ boundary Y.

Lemma 2.E.5:   *The set $g(z)$ is convex and $g(z)$ is an upper semicontinuous function of z.*

PROOF: Convexity follows from the convexity of P and the linearity of the inner product of z. (Check this for yourself; it is a simple exercise using the definition of a convex set.)

To prove the upper semicontinuity of $g(z)$, consider a sequence $\{z^q\} \in$ boundary Y such that $z^q \to z$. Then form a sequence $p^q \in g(z^q)$. We have to show that if $p^q \to p$, then $p \in g(z)$. For this, simply observe:

(i)   Since P is closed, $p \in P$.
(ii) By the continuity of inner product, $p \cdot z = 0$
      ($\because p^q \cdot z^q = 0$ implies $p \cdot z = 0$). Hence, $p \in g(z)$.   (Q.E.D.)

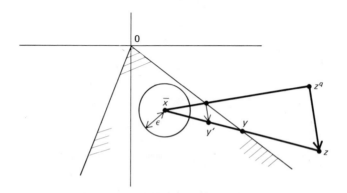

Figure 2.37.   An Illustration of y' and $B_\epsilon(\bar{x})$.

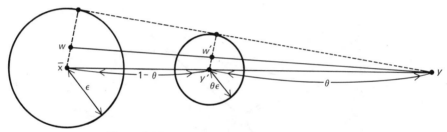

Figure 2.38.   An Illustration of $B_\epsilon(\bar{x})$ and $B_{\theta\epsilon}(y')$.

Definition: $F \equiv g \circ h \circ f$ where $f \equiv \sum_{i=1}^{m} f_i$.

REMARK: The function F is illustrated by Figure 2.40.

Theorem 2.E.3: *Under assumptions (A-1) through (A-6), there is a competitive equilibrium.*

PROOF: If $f(p) \in$ interior Y, then by (A-6) no consumer is satiated. Then by Lemma 2.E.3 (ii), $p \cdot f(p) = 0$. This contradicts the fact that $p \in P$. Hence $f(p) \notin$ interior Y for $p \in P$.

By Lemma 2.E.3 (i), Lemma 2.E.4, and Lemma 2.E.5, F is upper semi-continuous. Also F maps $p \in P$ to a convex subset $F(p) \subset P$. Hence by Kakutani's fixed point theorem, there exists a $\hat{p} \in F(\hat{p})$. Consider $[\hat{x}_1, \hat{x}_2, \ldots, \hat{x}_m, \hat{y}, \hat{p}]$ where $\hat{x}_i = f_i(\hat{p})$, $i = 1, 2, \ldots, m$, and $\hat{y} \equiv h(f(\hat{p})) = \hat{t}\bar{x} + (1 - \hat{t})\hat{x}$, where $\hat{x} \equiv \sum_{i=1}^{m} \hat{x}_i$, $0 \leq \hat{t} < 1$. By the definition of $\hat{y}, \hat{p} \cdot \hat{y} = 0$. Also $\hat{p} \cdot y \leq 0$ for all $y \in Y$, since $\hat{p} \in Y^*$ from $\hat{p} \in P$. Hence the profit condition, (ii), of a competitive equilibrium is satisfied. By the definition of f_i, the demand condition (i) of a competitive equilibrium is satisfied.

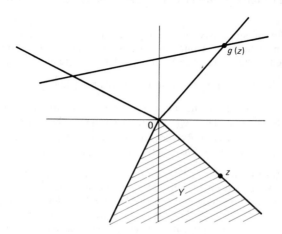

Figure 2.39.   An Illustration of $g(z)$.

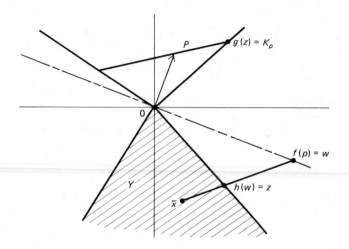

Figure 2.40.   An Illustration of $F(p)$.

Now we want to prove $\hat{t} = 0$, which implies condition (iii) of a competitive equilibrium. By the definition of $f_i(p)$, $\hat{p} \cdot \hat{x}_i \leq 0$ (the budget condition). Thus $\hat{p} \cdot \hat{x} \leq 0$. Moreover, $\hat{p} \cdot \hat{y} = 0$, but $\hat{p} \cdot \hat{y} = \hat{p} \cdot [\hat{t}\bar{x} + (1 - \hat{t})\hat{x}]$. Since $\hat{p} \cdot \bar{x} < 0$, and $\hat{p} \cdot \hat{x} \leq 0$ and $0 \leq \hat{t} < 1$, this implies $\hat{t} = 0$. Therefore $\hat{y} = \hat{x}$ and condition (iii) of competitive equilibrium is satisfied.   (Q.E.D.)

FOOTNOTES

1. Roughly the order is as follows: (a) (multiperson) two-commodity pure exchange economy; (b) (multiperson) multicommodity pure exchange economy; (c) introduction of production; (d) introduction of capital goods; and finally (e) introduction of money.

2. For the sake of simplicity, we leave out an explicit treatment of intermediate goods. The modification of our illustration with intermediate goods should be an easy exercise for the reader. See Walras [42] and Morishima [25].

3. See William Jaffé's "Translator's Notes" in Walras [42], pp. 549–553.

4. Assume that the functions with p and w as arguments—that is, v_i, x_j, a_{ij}—are homogeneous of degree zero. Then $x_i(p, w)$, for example, can be written as $x_i(1, p_2/p_1, \ldots, p_n/p_1, w_1/p_1, \ldots, w_m/p_1)$. By redefining symbols, we may write $(1, p_2/p_1, \ldots, w_m/p_1)$ as (p, w). This amounts to setting $p_1 = 1$.

5. We can easily show that Walras' Law holds if and only if the budget constraint of each consumer is satisfied as an equality. In general, a consumer can be satiated so that he may not spend all his income. Then the Walras law identity is replaced by an inequality such as $\sum p_j x_j \leq \sum w_i v_i$. Since the substance of Walras' Law is the individual's budget constraint, it in essence says that, whatever the market prices may be, the amount people wish to spend is equal to (or does not exceed) the amount

they desire to earn. It does not say that people spend all their income. The budget constraint is a constraint and *not* a result of any choice.

6. The problem may be stated as follows: Let $f_i(x_1, \ldots, x_n, z_1, \ldots z_m) = 0, i = 1, 2, \ldots,$ n, be the equilibrium system, where $x_1, \ldots, x_n$ are the "endogenous" variables and $z_1, \ldots, z_m$ are the "exogenous" variables. The problem is whether we can obtain $x_i = x_i(z_1, \ldots, z_m)$ such as to be consistent with the above set of equations. If we can, these x_i's define the **equilibrium values** of the endogenous variables and we call such $(x_1, \ldots, x_n)$ a **solution** of the above system. In the above, the number of equations is taken to be equal to the number of endogenous variables, for otherwise we cannot guarantee the existence of a solution even when the f_i's are all linear (affine). The well-known implicit function theorem guarantees the (local) existence of a unique solution in the neighborhood of a point (x°, z°), if certain assumptions are satisfied—especially that the Jacobian matrix $\left[\partial f_i / \partial x_j \right]$ evaluated at (x°, z°) is nonsingular. The assumptions of this theorem guarantee the global existence of a unique solution when the f_i's are all linear (affine). However, these assumptions are not sufficient for the global existence of a solution for the nonlinear case.

7. We note that Walras clearly realized the possibility of the nonexistence of equilibria for the two-commodity economy ([42], section 64, lesson 7).

8. In certain cases, the equality of the number of equations and variables is not even a necessary condition. An example is $x^2 + y^2 = 0$, in which the number of equations (=1) is different from the number of variables (=2), and yet there exists a unique real solution (that is, $x = 0$ and $y = 0$).

9. The above difficulty of the Walrasian system (that is, there is no guarantee that there exists a solution) was realized after Cassel's exposition [8] of the system. As a result of the simplicity and the popularity of Cassel's exposition, the system then became known as the **Walras-Cassel system**. For the reason that Cassel attracted Austrians, Hicks says, "As is known, there was a phase [in the 1920's] when Cassel's treatise was displacing those of the "historical" and "Austrian" schools in curricula of Central European countries: during such struggles its weakness would be carefully watched," ([15], p. 674). The difficulty discussed above was made clear in the seminar conducted by Karl Menger (a mathematician and the son of the famous economist Menger). For the summary of the discussions in Menger's seminar on the Cassel-Wald system, see Arrow and Debreu [3], pp. 287–289. Strictly speaking, the Casselian system is quite different from the Walrasian system. Cassel did not pay any attention to the behavior of each economic agent. He, in fact, proposed to reject altogether the procedure of deriving an individual's demand function from this hypothesized utility maximization behavior. Cassel *a priori* assumed the constancy of the a_{ij}'s and the v_i's.

10. In particular, condition (1) in the above is changed to $\sum_{j=1}^n a_{ij} x_j \leq v_i, i = 1, 2, \ldots, m$. The equality condition for this relation is a very stringent one, if we assume the a_{ij}'s and v_i's are all constants, as in the Casselian system. If, on the other hand, the a_{ij}'s and v_i's are functions of prices as in Walras, the equality assumption is not as strong as is generally believed. For then the equality *can* be achieved through changes in prices. The inequality of condition (1) allows the possibility of an excess supply of factors. If a factor is in excess supply, its price will be zero. In other words, the inequality allows the possibility of determining the division of factors into free and scarce (compare Zeuthen [43]).

11. Wald's work [39] was first presented at Karl Menger's seminar. His article [41] is the summary of the main results of [39] and [40]. These, together with the results from Menger's seminar, clearly designate this period as the dawn of modern eco-

nomics. Notably, von Neumann's first paper [26] on game theory was published in 1928, and his paper on the "von Neumann growth model" [27] was published in 1937. The latter paper clearly resembles modern activity analysis and also contains the basic idea of the duality theorems of linear programming.

12. Note that (8) presupposes that the functions (3) and (4) are globally invertible and that the supplies of productive factors (the v_i's) are completely inelastic with respect to all prices (p and w). Note also that the factor prices are left out in (8). In general, these assumptions are not guaranteed, and Wald's procedure of using (8) is illegitimate.

13. The procedure sketched here is the one prescribed by Kuhn [19]. DOSSO's procedure [13] is a little different from this, although the mathematical structure of the two procedures is essentially the same. Incidentally, there are some errors in DOSSO's proof of existence [13]. They are pointed out and corrected by K. Inada. See his "A Note on the Revision of the Proof of Dorfman, Samuelson, and Solow's Existence Theorem of General Equilibrium," *Economic Studies Quarterly*, XIII, February 1963.

14. If F is an upper semicontinuous function from a compact set X into itself, it can be shown easily that the image set $F(x)$, $x \in X$, is also compact. See, for example, Berge [6], section 1 of chapter VI (especially theorems 3 and 4 and the corollary of theorem 7). Note the distinction between his definition and our definition of upper semicontinuity. See our discussion in Chapter 2, Appendix to Section D.

15. See also C. B. Tompkins, "Sperner's Lemma and Some Extensions," chapter 15 in *Applied Combinatorial Mathematics*, ed. by E. F. Beckenbach, New York, Wiley, 1964, and E. Burger, *Introduction to the Theory of Games*, Englewood Cliffs, N.J., Prentice-Hall, 1963 (appendix).

16. Note that from the duality theorem, $\hat{p} \cdot \hat{x} = \hat{w} \cdot \hat{v}$ so that we have $\hat{w} \cdot (\hat{v} - A \cdot \hat{x}) = \hat{w} \cdot \hat{v} - (A' \cdot \hat{w}) \cdot \hat{x} = \hat{w} \cdot \hat{v} - \hat{p} \cdot \hat{x} = 0$, that is, condition (6) is satisfied. (See also Theorem 1.F.1.) Note also that $\hat{p} \cdot \hat{x} = \hat{w} \cdot \hat{v}$ implies that $(\hat{p}, \hat{x}, \hat{w})$ satisfies Walras' Law.

17. Suppose not. That is, suppose $(\hat{p}, \hat{x}, \hat{w})$ and (p^*, x^*, w^*) are two different equilibria. Since $\hat{x}$ maximizes $\hat{p} \cdot x$ for all $x \in X$, we have $\hat{p} \cdot \hat{x} \geq \hat{p} \cdot x$ for all $x \in X$ where $\hat{p} = f(\hat{x})$. In particular, $\hat{p} \cdot \hat{x} \geq \hat{p} \cdot x^*$. Similarly, $p^* \cdot x^* \geq p^* \cdot \hat{x}$ where $p^* = f(x^*)$, which implies that $\hat{p} \cdot \hat{x} < \hat{p} \cdot x^*$ from assumption (vi). This contradicts $\hat{p} \cdot \hat{x} \geq \hat{p} \cdot x^*$, which proves the uniqueness. The discussions of assumption (vi) will be postponed to the Appendix to Section E of this chapter and Chapter 3, Section E.

18. DOSSO [13] avoided the use of the inverse demand function.

19. In the issue of *Econometrica* before the one containing the article by Arrow and Debreu [3], McKenzie [20] showed the existence of a solution for Graham's model of world trade, which clearly resembles the model of Walrasian competitive markets. We may also note that this is probably the first article in economics to use Kakutani's fixed point theorem.

20. Sonnenschein [35] established the upper semicontinuity of $x_i(p)$ [hence also $x(p)$] without assuming the transitivity of the underlying individual preferences. The main result of [35], as the author puts it, is that "the transitivity of preferences can be replaced by the convexity of preferences in establishing the existence of demand functions." (p. 215).

21. Nikaido called the above relation with inequality the **Walras law in the general sense**, and the usual Walras law with equality the **Walras law in the narrow sense**. ([30], section 45; [31], p. 263)

22. A similar theorem was proved by Debreu [10] and it was also used in the proof of the existence of a competitive equilibrium. See also [11].

23. The use of Kakutani's fixed point theorem, which is an extension of Brouwer's fixed point theorem, is not a matter of mere technical convenience. Surprisingly enough,

it can be shown that the Gale-Nikaido lemma conversely implies Brouwer's fixed point theorem. See Uzawa [38] and Nikaido [31], pp. 268–269. This produces Uzawa's contention [38] that the existence of equilibria in the Walrasian system is in a sense equivalent to Brouwer's fixed point theorem. Nikaido then remarked ([31], p. 270): "The Walrasian general equilibrium theory [Walras, 1874] was published in the 1870's, while Brouwer's work on fixed points [Brouwer, 1909, 1910] appeared three decades later. It is therefore no wonder that Walras could not achieve a mathematical consolidation of the conjecture in the days before the advancement of topology; he should certainly not be criticized for his failure to achieve a mathematical solution, but should be admired for his mathematical imagination which let him formulate this well-posed conjecture."

24. For this purpose, the reader may also be interested in seeing Debreu [11], chapter 5, for example.

25. See (A-5) of the next subsection and footnote 31. This assumption implies that every consumer must be able to supply a positive amount of every unproduced commodity (such as labor). Arrow and Debreu [3] imposed a stronger assumption which requires that every consumer can supply a positive amount of every commodity. The relaxation of Arrow and Debreu's assumption is seen in McKenzie [21], [22]. In [22], McKenzie introduced the concept of "irreducibility." For a further discussion on the concept of irreducibility, see Moore [24]. See also Arrow [2], and J. T. Rader, "Pairwise Optimality and Noncompetitive Behavior," in *Papers in Quantitative Economics*, vol. 1, ed. by J. Quirk, and A. M. Zarley, Lawrence, Kansas, University of Kansas Press, 1968. In essence, the concept of **irreducibility** says that no matter how the consumers are partitioned into two groups, an increase in the initial assets held by the members of one group can be used to make possible an allocation which would improve the position of someone in the second group without damaging the position of anyone else there.

26. As Arrow [1] points out, the convexity of each consumer's preferences and of each producer's production set are "the empirically most vulnerable" assumptions. However, the nonconvexity of preferences would have no significant effect as long as each consumer is small enough compared to the economy. Recall our discussion on the core in the Appendix to Section C of this chapter. On the other hand, increasing returns to scale for each firm (which precludes the convexity of each firm's production set) over a sufficiently wide range may mean the appearance of large firms and the failure of the existence of a competitive equilibrium.

27. There is also a problem in the procedure of fixing the number of consumers in the economy, even if we assume that everybody can survive. But this seems to be much less serious than the problem that arises in fixing the number of firms. See Koopmans [17], pp. 64–65.

28. In particular we are concerned with his "special existence theorem," which provides the core of his proof for a more general case.

29. In proving the "existence of competitive equilibria," no assumptions on each producer's production set are required (only the assumptions on the aggregate production set of the total economy are required). This was first shown by Uzawa in 1956 (*Stanford Technical Paper* No. 40), later published as [37].

30. Note that the origin represents the point of the initial endowments, and the consumption set X_i represents the set of all possible trade (and consumption) for the ith consumer. In Figure 2.33, labor is assumed to be the only unproduced commodity. At point $\bar{x}$, a positive amount of the produced commodity, food, is received by consumer i. This restrictive assumption simplifies the proof in this subsection.

31. Since $\bar{x}_i \in$ interior Y, $p \cdot \bar{x}_i < 0$ for all $p \in P$. This means that the ith consumer is guaranteed a positive income above subsistence requirements for all $p \in P$. In this sense, (A-5) takes care of the subsistence problem.

REFERENCES

1. Arrow, K. J., "Economic Equilibrium," *International Encyclopedia of Social Sciences*, New York, Macmillan and Free Press, 1968.
2. ———, "The Firm in General Equilibrium," *Technical Report*, no.3, Harvard University, May 1969.
3. Arrow, K. J., and Debreu, G., "Existence of an Equilibrium for a Competitive Economy," *Econometrica*, 22, July 1954.
4. Arrow, K. J., and Hahn, F. H., *General Competitive Analysis*, San Francisco, Holden Day, 1971.
5. Aumann, R. J., "Existence of Competitive Equilibria in Markets with a Continuum of Traders," *Econometrica*, 34, January 1966.
6. Berge, C., *Topological Spaces*, New York, Macmillan, 1963 (French, 1959).
7. Brouwer, L. E. J., "Über Abbildung von Mannigfaltigkeiten," *Mathematischen Annalen*, 71, 1912.
8. Cassel, G., *Theory of Social Economy*, tr. by McCabe, London, T. Fisher Unwin, 1923.
9. Debreu, G., "A Social Equilibrium Existence Theorem," *Proceedings of the National Academy of Sciences of the U.S.A.*, 42, November 1952.
10. ———, "Market Equilibrium," *Proceedings of the National Academy of Sciences of the U.S.A.*, 42, November 1956.
11. ———, *Theory of Value*, New York, Wiley, 1959.
12. ———, "New Concepts and Techniques for Equilibrium Analysis," *International Economic Review*, 3, September, 1962.
13. Dorfman, R., Samuelson, P. A., and Solow, R. M., *Linear Programming and Economic Analysis*, New York, McGraw-Hill, 1958, esp. chap. 13.
14. Gale, D., "The Law of Supply and Demand," *Mathematics Scandinavica*, 3, 1955.
15. Hicks, J. R., "Linear Theory", *Economic Journal*, LXX, December 1960, reprinted in *Surveys of Economic Theory*, Vol. III, prepared for the American Economic Association and the Royal Economic Society, London, Macmillan, 1967.
16. Kakutani, S., "A Generalization of Brouwer's Fixed Point Theorem," *Duke Mathematical Journal*, 8, 1941.
17. Koopmans, T. C., *Three Essays on the State of Economic Science*, New York, McGraw-Hill, 1957.
18. Koopmans, T. C., and Bausch, A., "Selected Topics Involving Mathematical Reasoning," *SIAM Review*, 1, July 1959.
19. Kuhn, H. W., "On a Theorem of Wald," in *Linear Inequalities and Related Systems*, ed. by H. W. Kuhn, and A. W. Tucker, Princeton, N.J., Princeton University Press, 1956.
20. McKenzie, L. W., "On Equilibrium in Graham's Model of World Trade and Other Competitive Systems," *Econometrica*, 22, April 1954.
21. ———, "Competitive Equilibrium with Dependent Consumer Preferences," *in Proceedings of the Second Symposium in Linear Programming*, ed. by H. A. Antosiewicz, Washington, D.C., National Bureau of Standards, 1955.
22. ———, "On the Existence of General Equilibrium for a Competitive Market," *Econometrica*, 27, January 1959.

23.   ———, "On the Existence of General Equilibrium for a Competitive Market: Some Corrections," *Econometrica*, 29, April 1961.

24.   Moore, J. C., "On Pareto Optima and Competitive Equilibria, Part II. The Existence of Equilibria and Optima," *Krannert Institute Paper*, no. 269, April 1970.

25.   Morishima, M., "A Reconsideration of the Walras-Cassel-Leontief Model of General Equilibrium," in *Mathematical Methods in the Social Sciences, 1959*, ed. by Arrow, Karlin, and Suppes, Stanford, Calif., Stanford University Press, 1960.

26.   von Neumann, J., "Zur Theorie der Gesellschaftsspiele," *Mathematischen Annalen*, 100, 1928.

27.   ———, "Über ein Ökonomisches Gleichungssystem und eine Verallgemeinerund des Fixpunktsatzes," *Ergebnisse eines Mathematischen Kolloquims*, 1935–1936 (in English, "A Model of General Economic Equilibrium," *Review of Economic Studies*, VIII, 1945–1946).

28.   Nikaido, H., "On the Classical Multilateral Exchange Problem," *Metroeconomica*, 8, August 1956.

29.   ———, "A Supplementary Note to 'On the Classical Multilateral Exchange Problem,'" *Metroeconomica*, 9, December 1957.

30.   ———, *Introduction to Sets and Mappings in Modern Economics*, tr. by K. Sato, Amsterdam, North-Holland, 1970 (Japanese original, Tokyo, 1960).

31.   ———, *Convex Structures and Economic Theory*, New York, Academic Press, 1968.

32.   Quirk, J., and Saposnik, R., *Introduction to General Equilibrium Theory and Welfare Economics*, New York, McGraw-Hill, 1968.

33.   Scarf, H., "On the Computation of Equilibrium Prices," in *Ten Economic Studies in the Tradition of Irving Fisher*, New York, Wiley, 1967.

34.   Schlesinger, K., "Über die Produktiongleichungen der Ökonomischen Wertlehre," *Ergebnisse eines Mathematischen Kolloquiums*, 6, 1933–1934.

35.   Sonnenschein, H. F., "Demand Theory without Transitive Preferences," in *Preferences, Utility, and Demand*, ed. by J. S. Chipman *et. al.*, New York, Harcourt Brace Jovanovich, 1971.

36.   Starr, R. M., "Quasi-Equilibria in Markets with Non-Convex Preferences," *Econometrica*, 37, January 1969.

37.   Uzawa, H., "Aggregate Convexity and the Existence of Competitive Equilibrium," *Economic Studies Quarterly*, XII, January 1962.

38.   ———, "Walras' Existence Theorem and Brouwer's Fixed Point Theorem," *Economic Studies Quarterly*, XIII, March 1962.

39.   Wald, A., "Über die Eindeutige Positive Lösbarkeit der Neuen Produktionsgleichungen," *Ergebnisse eines Mathematischen Kolloquiums*, 6, 1933–1934.

40.   ———, "Über die Produktionsgleichungen der Ökonomischen Wertlehre," *Ergebnisse eines Mathematischen Kolloquiums*, 7, 1934–1935.

41.   ———, "Über Einige Gleichungssysteme der Mathematischen Ökonomie," *Zeitschrift für Nationalökonomie*, 7, 1936, (in English, "On Some Systems of Equations of Mathematical Economics," *Econometrica*, 19, October 1951).

42.   Walras, L., *Elements of Pure Economics* (1926 ed.), tr. by W. Jaffé, London, Allen & Unwin, 1954. (1st. ed., 1874).

43.   Zeuthen, F., "Das Prinzip der Knapphert, technische Kombination und ökonomische Qualität," *Zeitschrift für Nationalökonomie*, 4, 1933.

Appendix to Section E: On the Uniqueness of Competitive Equilibrium

The existence of a competitive equilibrium does not necessarily guarantee its uniqueness. This has been known to economists since Walras and Marshall. In fact, the conditions needed to ensure uniqueness are somewhat different from those needed to ensure existence. The purpose of this Appendix is to review briefly the uniqueness problem.

Let there be $n + 1$ commodities in the economy and assume that the 0th commodity can be chosen as the *numéraire*.[1] Let $f_i(p)$ be the excess demand function for the ith commodity, $i = 1, 2, \ldots, n$, where $p = (p_1, p_2, \ldots, p_n) \in \Omega^n$ (the nonnegative orthant of R^n) denotes the price vector. It is assumed that the f_i's are single-valued, continuous, and bounded from below. Define "equilibrium" as follows.

Definition: If the following conditions are satisfied, $\hat{p} \in \Omega^n$ is said to be an **equilibrium price vector**.

(1) $$f_i(\hat{p}) \leq 0, i = 0, 1, 2, \ldots, n$$

and

(2) $$\hat{p}_i f_i(\hat{p}) = 0, i = 0, 1, 2, \ldots, n \text{ (where } p_0 = 1)$$

Using Walras's Law, (1) and (2) can be equivalently rewritten (in vector notations) as[2]

(3) $$f(\hat{p}) \leq 0 \quad \text{and} \quad \hat{p} \cdot f(\hat{p}) = 0, \text{ where } f(\hat{p}) = [f_1(\hat{p}), \ldots, f_n(\hat{p})]$$

We assume that there *exists* an equilibrium price vector $\hat{p}$.

Needless to say, the value of p under which (1) and (2) hold may not be unique. International trade theorists, for example, have often encountered the possibility of multiple equilibria in connection with their simple two-commodity trade models. This is the situation when two offer curves intersect more than once. Our question here is: Under what conditions can we guarantee uniqueness? In Section E, we remarked that Wald [10] proved uniqueness assuming the following condition:

(R)   We have either $p \cdot x < p \cdot x'$ or $p' \cdot x' < p' \cdot x$, where $x = f(p)$ and $x' = f(p')$.

Then the following theorem is almost trivial to prove.

Theorem 2.E.4 (Wald):[3]   *Suppose (R) holds; then the equilibrium is unique.*

PROOF: Suppose there exist two equilibrium price vectors $\hat{p} \geq 0$ and $p^* \geq 0$ such that $\hat{p} \neq p^*$. Write $\hat{x} = f(\hat{p})$ and $x^* = f(p^*)$. By (R), we have either $\hat{p} \cdot \hat{x} < \hat{p} \cdot x^*$ or $p^* \cdot x^* < p^* \cdot \hat{x}$. But since $\hat{p}$ and p^* are equilibrium price vectors, it must be that $\hat{p} \cdot \hat{x} = 0$ and $p^* \cdot x^* = 0$, so we have either $\hat{p} \cdot x^* > 0$ or $p^* \cdot \hat{x} > 0$. But $\hat{p} \cdot x^* > 0$ is impossible for $x^* \leq 0$ ($\because p^*$ is an equilibrium price vector). Hence $p^* \cdot \hat{x} > 0$, which is also impossible, since $\hat{x} \leq 0$ ($\because \hat{p}$ is an equilibrium price vector).   (Q.E.D.)

REMARK: If x is interpreted as an excess demand vector for *all* the commodities of an *individual consumer*, then (R) refers to Samuelson's well-known weak axiom of revealed preference.[4] However, as remarked before, the plausibility of the weak revealed preference axiom for the entire economy is to be questioned.[5]

As a matter of fact, the most appropriate uniqueness theorem has not been fully explored. However, important mathematical theorems have recently been made available by Gale and Nikaido [3] and others in connection with their studies on the factor price equalization theorem,[6] and this line of thought turns out to be useful in the study of the uniqueness problem (Nikaido [7], p. 338).

To consider this, let $f(p)$ be a differentiable function from P into R^n where P is a "region" in R^n (that is, an open connected subset of R^n). For the time being (that is, as long as we are concerned with mathematical theorems), we do not adhere to the economic interpretation of $f(p)$ (such as "excess demand" vector). Let $F(p) = [f_{ij}]$ be the Jacobian matrix of $f(p)$, that is, $f_{ij} \equiv \partial f_i(p)/\partial p_j$.

Definition: An $n \times n$ matrix $A = [a_{ij}]$ is said to be **Hicksian** if it has all the principal minors of odd order negative and those of even order positive. In other words,

$$(4) \quad a_{ii} < 0, \qquad \begin{vmatrix} a_{ii} & a_{ij} \\ a_{ji} & a_{jj} \end{vmatrix} > 0, \qquad \begin{vmatrix} a_{ii} & a_{ij} & a_{ik} \\ a_{ji} & a_{jj} & a_{jk} \\ a_{ki} & a_{kj} & a_{kk} \end{vmatrix} < 0, \qquad \dots,$$

where $i, j, k, \dots, = 1, 2, \dots, n$.

Then the following proposition is available from Gale-Nikaido [3] and Nikaido [7].

Lemma 2.E.6:   *Assume the region P of R^n is rectangular and suppose the Jacobian matrix $F(p)$ is Hicksian for all $p \in P$. Then*

(i) *The mapping $f(p)$ is one-to-one for all $p \in P$.*
(ii) *The inequalities*
$$(5) \quad (p_i - a_i) [f_i(p) - f_i(a)] \geq 0, \quad i = 1, 2, \dots, n \text{ have only the trivial solution}$$
$p = a$.

With the help of this lemma, the following uniqueness theorem is easy to prove.

Theorem 2.E.5 (Nikaido):   *Let $f(p)$ be an excess demand vector as considered above, where f is differentiable and defined on a rectangular region P of Ω^n. Then the equilibrium price vector is unique if the Jacobian matrix $F(p)$ is Hicksian.*

PROOF: Suppose $\hat{p}$ and p^* are two equilibrium price vectors. In the inequalities (5), let $a = \hat{p}$ and $p = p^*$. Then the LHS of (5) can be rewritten as

$$(6) \qquad (p_i^* - \hat{p}_i)\left[f_i(p^*) - f_i(\hat{p})\right] = -\hat{p}_i f_i(p^*) - p_i^* f_i(\hat{p}) \geqq 0$$

by definition of equilibrium. Hence by (ii) of Lemma 2.E.6, $p^* = \hat{p}$.

$$\text{(Q.E.D.)}$$

REMARK: Suppose that the equilibrium relation is expressed in the Walras-Cassel equality form

$$(7) \qquad\qquad f_i(\hat{p}) = 0, \, i = 1, 2, \ldots, n$$

and suppose that such a $\hat{p}$ with $\hat{p} \geqq 0$ exists. Then (i) of Lemma 2.E.6 provides the uniqueness of $\hat{p}$ immediately.

Unless some economic justifications are found for the condition that $F(p)$ is Hicksian, Theorem 2.E.5 remains essentially a mathematical theorem. Here there is still much to be explored. The reader may find his own uniqueness theorems by exploring further economic interpretations of Theorem 2.E.5.

To illustrate such a line of thought, let us quote the following result in the literature, from which we shall prove one uniqueness theorem.

Lemma 2.E.7:   *Let $A = [a_{ij}]$ be an $n \times n$ matrix with $a_{ij} \geqq 0$ for all $i \neq j$. Then A is Hicksian if and only if*

(8) *There exists an $x \geqq 0$ such that $A \cdot x < 0$.*

PROOF: See Chapter 4, Section C.

To make use of this theorem, we assume

(G) $f_{ij} \geqq 0$ for all p and for all $i \neq j$.

That $f_{ij} > 0$ means that an increase (resp. decrease) in the price of the jth commodity will increase (resp. decrease) the excess demand for the ith commodity. Condition (G) is known to be the (**weak**) **gross substitutability** condition and plays an important role in the stability theorem of competitive equilibrium (see Chapter 3).

Next write

$$(9) \qquad\qquad f_i(p) = \tilde{f}_i(p, p_0), \, i = 1, 2, \ldots, n$$

and

$$(10) \qquad\qquad f_0(p) = \tilde{f}_0(p, p_0)$$

where $p_0 = 1$ and $f_0(p)$ signifies the excess demand function of the 0th commodity (*numéraire*). Observe that $\partial f_i / \partial p_j = \partial \tilde{f}_i / \partial p_j$ for all $i, j = 1, 2, \ldots, n$. As remarked before, the existence of a *numéraire* presupposes that $\tilde{f}_i(p, 1), i = 0, 1, 2, \ldots, n,$[7]

are homogeneous of degree zero with respect to all the arguments. Hence using Euler's equation we obtain

(11) $\sum_{j=1}^{n} \tilde{f}_{ij} p_j = -\tilde{f}_{i0},$ for all p, $i = 1, 2, \ldots, n,$

where $\tilde{f}_{ij} \equiv \partial \tilde{f}_i(p)/\partial p_j$, $i = 1, 2, \ldots, n, j = 0, 1, 2, \ldots, n$. Assume

(12) $\tilde{f}_{i0} > 0$ for all p, $i = 1, 2, \ldots, n^8$

The economic interpretation of (12) should be obvious. Clearly equations (11) and (12) imply that condition (8) is satisfied for the $n \times n$ Jacobian matrix $F(p)$ for all p. Hence, as a simple corollary of Theorem 2.E.5, we immediately obtain the following theorem.

Theorem 2.E.6:[9]   *Assume (G) and (12). Then the equilibrium is unique.*

PROOF: By Lemma 2.E.7, $F(p)$ is Hicksian for all p. Hence by Theorem 2.E.5, the equilibrium is unique.   (Q.E.D.)

This result has been known to economists since Wald [10]. Moreover, it can be proved quite simply without using the knowledge of Theorem 2.E.5 and Lemma 2.E.7. For such a proof, see Lemma 3.E.2. Lemma 3.E.3 provides the relation between condition (R) and gross substitutability. The difficulty of Theorem 2.E.6 is that the economic plausibility of gross substitutability is very questionable.

FOOTNOTES

1. As remarked before, the existence of a *numéraire* presupposes that the price of such a commodity is positive at least in equilibrium and that the excess demand for each commodity is homogeneous of degree zero with respect to *all* prices including that of the *numéraire* commodity.

2. By Walras' Law, we mean here that $\sum_{i=0}^{n} p_i f_i(p) = 0$ for all p. It is easy to see that, under this law, (1) and (2) hold if and only if (3) holds.

3. To prove this theorem, there is no need to assume the existence of a *numéraire*, as long as condition (R) is stated in a form which includes the *numéraire*. Then we can assert the uniqueness of the price vector (including the *numéraire* commodity) up to scalar multiples.

4. It may be worthwhile to recall Samuelson's **weak axiom of revealed preference.** Interpret x and x' as the consumption vectors of a particular *individual*. Let x and x' respectively, be chosen under p and p'. If x' is affordable at p, that is, $p \cdot x' \leq p \cdot x$, then x is revealed to be preferred to x', for he could have bought x'. If this is the case, x' cannot be revealed to be preferred to x; that is, $p' \cdot x \leq p' \cdot x'$ is impossible. Therefore $p \cdot \Delta x \leq 0$ (where $\Delta x \equiv x' - x$) implies $p' \cdot \Delta x < 0$, which is the weak axiom. By this axiom, we have $p' \cdot \Delta x < 0$ or $p \cdot \Delta x > 0$ (for a particular individual). See P. A. Samuelson, *Foundations of Economic Analysis*, Cambridge, Mass., Harvard University Press, 1947, chapter 5.

5. In other words, the statement that the weak axiom holds in the aggregate is not a

consequence of rational behavior but is an additional assumption. Hence, unless some behavioral background is discussed for such a statement, Theorem 2.E.4 is essentially a mathematical theorem. It can be shown that sufficiently small income effects could ensure such a statement.

6. See, for example, Inada [4], Nikaido [7], and Uekawa [8].

7. Besides, the price of the *numéraire* commodity must be positive, at least in equilibrium.

8. Note that conditions (G) (with strict inequalities) and (12) are inconsistent with homogeneity unless $p > 0$. To see this, suppose $p_i = 0$ for some $i = 1, 2, \ldots, n$. Then $\tilde{f}_i(\alpha p, \alpha) > \tilde{f}_i(p, 1)$ in view of (G) and (12), which contradicts the homogeneity condition (see Chapter 3, Section G). In other words, under such conditions, none of the commodities are free.

9. As in Theorem 2.E.5, $f(p)$ is an excess demand vector (deleting the *numéraire* commodity), which is differentiable and defined on a rectangular region P in Ω^n.

REFERENCES

1. Arrow, K. J., "Economic Equilibrium," *International Encyclopedia of Social Sciences*, New York, Macmillan and Free Press, 1968.

2. Arrow, K. J., Block, H. D., and Hurwicz, L., "On the Stability of the Competitive Equilibrium, II," *Econometrica*, 27, January 1959.

3. Gale, D., and Nikaido, H., "The Jacobian Matrix and Global Univalence of Mappings," *Mathematische Annalen*, 159, 1965.

4. Inada, K., "The Production Coefficient Matrix and the Stolper-Samuelson Condition," *Econometrica*, 39, March 1971.

5. McKenzie, L. W., "Matrices with Dominant Diagonals and Economic Theory," *Mathematical Methods in the Social Sciences, 1959*, ed. by Arrow, Karlin, and Suppes, Stanford, Calif., Stanford University Press, 1960.

6. Morishima, M., "A Generalization of the Gross Substitute System," *Review of Economic Studies*, XXXVII, April 1970.

7. Nikaido, H., *Convex Structure and Economic Theory*, New York, Academic Press, 1968.

8. Uekawa, Y., "On the Generalization of the Stolper-Samuelson Theorem," *Econometrica*, 39, March 1971.

9. Wald, A., "Über die Eindeutige Positive Lösbarkeit der Neuen Producktionsgleichungen," *Ergebnisse eines Mathematischen Kolloquiums*, 6, 1933–1934.

10. ———, "Über einigen Gleichungssysteme der Mathematischen Ökonomie," *Zeitschrift für Nationalökonomie*, 7, 1936 (in English, "On Some Systems of Equations of Mathematical Economics," *Econometrica*, 19, October 1951).

Section F

PROGRAMMING, PARETO OPTIMUM, AND THE EXISTENCE OF COMPETITIVE EQUILIBRIA[1]

In Chapter 1, we described the recent developments in the theory of non-linear programming. In this chapter, we have described one of the most important developments of economic theory, that is, the theory of competitive markets. The purpose of this section is to relate these two developments. Specifically, we will prove the optimality and the existence of competitive equilibria, as an application of the theory of nonlinear programming. The reader will see that the two developments, the theory of nonlinear programming and the theory of competitive equilibria, are thus closely related to each other in their structures. We may even say that the model of competitive equilibria is a programming model with economic content attached to it. And in a sense, the theory of nonlinear programming is a mathematical reformulation of the theory of competitive equilibria. Thus this section is intended to give a unified treatment of the problem of existence, welfare economics, and the theory of nonlinear programming. Moreover, as a result of this recognition, our treatment of the theory of competitive equilibria becomes very simple and straightforward, while retaining the generality of the model of the competitive market fairly well. Such simplicity will encourage further research.

We should mention one important predecessor in such an attempt. Negishi, in his ingenious paper [12], proved the existence of competitive equilibria by using the theory of nonlinear programming.[2] His formulation is based on the quasi-saddle-point characterization of the constrained maximum problem. Hence he assumed, among other things, the existence of the right-hand and left-hand derivatives of each producer's production function (his F_k). Moreover, the use of the quasi-saddle-point characterization complicated his formulation and the proof of the existence a great deal. Here we entirely avoid the use of each producer's production function—hence we do not impose any conditions on such functions as F_k (conditions such as concavity and the existence of the right-hand and left-hand derivatives of each F_k, as imposed by Negishi [12]).[3] Our treatment and proof will be much simpler than that of Negishi, yet our model of competitive equilibrium will be more general than Negishi's. The reader will note that the simplicity and generality of the present section is achieved by using the simple saddle-point characterization (rather than the quasi-saddle-point characterization) of optimality. In Negishi's paper, the characterization of competitive equilibrium as a Pareto optimum is not attempted, but we will attempt it here. The reader may note that the proof of the Pareto optimality characterization and the proof of existence parallel each other very closely. In Theorem 2.F.1, we prove that every Pareto optimum can be realized by competitive pricing; in Theorem 2.F.2, we prove the existence of competitive equilibria; and in Theorem 2.F.3 we show that such a competitive equilibrium will realize a Pareto optimum.

Let x_i be an n-vector of consumption by consumer i $(i = 1, 2, \ldots, m)$ and $\bar{x}_i$ be the initial resources held by the ith consumer, and let y_j be an n-vector of production by producer j $(j = 1, 2, \ldots, k)$. Let

$$ x \equiv \sum_{i=1}^{m} x_i, \quad \bar{x} \equiv \sum_{i=1}^{m} \bar{x}_i, \quad \text{and } y \equiv \sum_{i=1}^{k} y_j $$

where all externalities are assumed away.

Denote by X_i the consumption set of i and by Y_j the production set of j. We denote by X the aggregate consumption set and by Y the aggregate production set. We assume that the preferences of consumer i are represented by a continuous real-valued function $u_i(x_i)$.[4] Given price p, the profit of producer j can be written as $p \cdot y_j$. Pareto optimality and competitive equilibrium are defined (in the usual manner) as follows:

Definition (feasibility):   An array of consumption vectors $\{x_i\}$ is said to be **feasible** if there exists an array of production vectors $\{y_j\}$ such that $y + \bar{x} - x \geq 0$ with $x_i \in X_i$ for all i and $y_j \in Y_j$ for all j.

Definition (Pareto optimality):   A feasible $\{\hat{x}_i\}$ is said to be **Pareto optimal** if there does not exist a feasible $\{x_i'\}$ such that $u_i(x_i') \geq u_i(\hat{x}_i)$ for all $i = 1, 2, \ldots, m$ with strict inequality for at least one i.

Definition (competitive equilibrium):   An array of vectors $[\hat{p}, \{\hat{x}_i\}, \{\hat{y}_j\}]$ with $\hat{p} \geq 0$, $\hat{x}_i \in X_i$ for all i, and $\hat{y}_j \in Y_j$ for all j, is a **competitive equilibrium**, if the following hold:

   (i) $u_i(\hat{x}_i) \geq u_i(x_i)$ for all $x_i \in X_i$ with $\hat{p} \cdot x_i \leq \hat{p} \cdot \hat{x}_i$, $i = 1, 2, \ldots, m$.
   (ii) $\hat{p} \cdot \hat{y}_j \geq \hat{p} \cdot y_j$ for all $y_j \in Y_j$, $j = 1, 2, \ldots, k$.
   (iii) $\hat{x} \leq \hat{y} + \bar{x}$ and $\hat{p} \cdot (\hat{y} + \bar{x} - \hat{x}) = 0$.

Definition (satiation):   The ith consumer is **satiated at** x_i' if $u_i(x_i') \geq u_i(x_i)$ for all $x_i \in X_i$.

We assume the following:

(A-1)   There exist $x' \in X$, $y' \in Y$ such that $y' + \bar{x} - x' > 0$.[5]
(A-2)   The set Y is convex.[6]
(A-3)   The function $u_i(x_i)$ is continuous and concave for all $i = 1, 2, \ldots, m$.[7]
(A-4)   **(cheaper point)**   Given a point $\hat{x}_i$, if a price vector $\hat{p}$ prevails, there exists an $x_i' \in X_i$ such that $\hat{p} \cdot \hat{x}_i > \hat{p} \cdot x_i'$ for all i.

Notice also that our definition of feasibility tacitly assumes free disposability.

Theorem 2.F.1   *Under (A-1), (A-2), and (A-3), if $[\{\hat{x}_i\}, \hat{y}]$ is a Pareto optimum, then there exists a $\hat{p} \geq 0$ and $\{\hat{y}_j\}$ such that $[\hat{p}, \{\hat{x}_i\}, \{\hat{y}_j\}]$ is a competitive equilibrium, provided that (A-4) holds at this $\hat{p}$.*

PROOF: Let u be a vector function of which the ith component is $u_i(x_i)$. Since $[\{\hat{x}_i\}, \hat{y}]$ is a Pareto optimum, it is a solution of the following vector maximum problem:[8] Choose $\{x_i\}$ and y so as to maximize u subject to $x \leq y + \bar{x}$, and $x_i \in X_i$, $i = 1, \ldots, m$, and $y \in Y$. Hence, in view of (A-1), (A-2), and (A-3), there exists an $(\alpha, \hat{p})$ such that the following (1) and (2) hold:

(1) $$\alpha \cdot u + \hat{p} \cdot (y + \bar{x} - x) \leq \alpha \cdot \hat{u} + \hat{p} \cdot (\hat{y} + \bar{x} - \hat{x})$$

for all $x_i \in X_i$, $i = 1, 2, \ldots, m$, and $y \in Y$, where $\alpha \geq 0$, $\hat{p} \geq 0$, and $\alpha \neq 0$,[9] and $\hat{u} \equiv [u_1(\hat{x}_1), u_2(\hat{x}_2), \ldots, u_m(\hat{x}_m)]$;

(2) $$\hat{p} \cdot (\hat{y} + \bar{x} - \hat{x}) = 0, \qquad \hat{y} + \bar{x} - \hat{x} \geq 0$$

Condition (iii) of competitive equilibrium follows immediately from (2). Since y and $\hat{y}$ are in Y, we can find $y_j \in Y_j$ and $\hat{y}_j \in Y_j$, $j = 1, 2, \ldots, k$, such that $y = \sum_{j=1}^{k} y_j$ and $\hat{y} = \sum_{j=1}^{k} \hat{y}_j$. Put $x_i = \hat{x}_i$ for all i and $y_j = \hat{y}_j$ for all j except for $j = j_0$ in (1). Then $\hat{p} \cdot \hat{y}_{j_0} \geq \hat{p} \cdot y_{j_0}$ for all $y_{j_0} \in Y_j$. Since the choice of j_0 is arbitrary, this establishes condition (ii) of competitive equilibrium. Put $y = \hat{y}$ and $x_i = \hat{x}_i$ for all i except for $i = i_0$. Then we have

$$\alpha_{i_0} u_{i_0}(\hat{x}_{i_0}) - \alpha_{i_0} u_{i_0}(x_{i_0}) \geq \hat{p} \cdot \hat{x}_{i_0} - \hat{p} \cdot x_{i_0} \qquad \text{for all } x_{i_0} \in X_{i_0}$$

If $\alpha_{i_0} > 0$, then condition (i) of competitive equilibrium is satisfied for i_0. If $\alpha_{i_0} = 0$, then $\hat{p} \cdot x_{i_0} \geq \hat{p} \cdot \hat{x}_{i_0}$ for all $x_{i_0} \in X_{i_0}$.[10] This contradicts the cheaper point assumption, (A-4), so that $\alpha_{i_0} > 0$. Since the choice of i_0 is arbitrary, this establishes condition (i) of competitive equilibrium.

(Q.E.D.)

Corollary: *If there exists at least one consumer (say, i_0) who is not satiated at $\hat{x}_{i_0}$, then $\hat{p} \neq 0$.*

PROOF: From the proof of the theorem, we know

$$\alpha_i u_i(\hat{x}_i) - \alpha_i u_i(x_i) \geq \hat{p} \cdot \hat{x}_i - \hat{p} \cdot x_i \quad \text{for all } x_i \in X_i, \, \alpha_i > 0, \, i = 1, 2, \ldots, m$$

Now suppose $\hat{p} = 0$. Then $u_{i_0}(\hat{x}_{i_0}) \geq u_{i_0}(x_{i_0})$ for all $x_{i_0} \in X_{i_0}$. This contradicts the fact that i_0 is not satiated at x_{i_0}.
(Q.E.D.)

REMARK: Note that the cheaper point assumption plays a crucial role in establishing that each consumer indeed maximizes his satisfaction subject to his budget constraint. Without (A-4), we cannot say this, as was shown by

Arrow [1], although each consumer still minimizes his expenditure subject to a given satisfaction. See Section C of this chapter.

REMARK: That $\alpha_{i_0} = 0$ means that individual i_0 is completely "disregarded" by the society at a given Pareto optimal state $[\{\hat{x}_i\}, \hat{y}]$. If $\alpha_{i_0} = 0$, he gets the minimum possible income at this price vector p. As noted before, (A-4) avoids this possibility. As is well known, the society can be at a Pareto optimum when every member of the society except one is "disregarded" by the society. The importance of the cheaper point assumption became well known since Arrow's famous example [1]; however, its role in precluding such a case (that is, $\alpha_i = 0$) is not well recognized in the literature.

REMARK: Let $z = (x_1, \ldots, x_m, y)$ and define the set Z by $Z \equiv \{z: x \leq y + \bar{x}, y \in Y, x_i \in X_i, i = 1, 2, \ldots, m\}$. The sets X_i's and Y may not be compact, but we may assume that Z is compact without much difficulty.[11] Since the constraint set of the maximization problem in the above proof is Z, the compactness of Z (together with the continuity of the u_i's) guarantees the existence of a Pareto optimum as a result of the Weierstrass theorem.[12]

REMARK: Note that the competitive equilibrium in the above definition can be achieved by allocating the aggregate income of the society $\hat{p} \cdot (\hat{y} + \bar{x})$ to each consumer by the amount of $\hat{p} \cdot \hat{x}_i$, $i = 1, 2, \ldots, m$ [note that $\hat{p} \cdot \hat{x} = \hat{p} \cdot (\hat{y} + \bar{x})$ from (2), so all the income of the society is completely absorbed by each member of the society]. In other words, without such a reallocation of income, a given Pareto optimum can*not*, in general, be supported by competitive pricing.

To prove the "existence" of competitive equilibria, we have to show the existence of a price vector which would support the conditions of the competitive equilibrium without such a reallocation of income as discussed in the previous remark. Hence we have to rephrase condition (i) in the previous definition of competitive equilibrium. To do this, first note that the income of consumer i, denoted by M_i, when a price vector $\hat{p}$ prevails and the output vector for the jth producer is $\hat{y}_j$, can be written as

$$(3) \qquad M_i(\hat{p}, \hat{y}) \equiv \hat{p} \cdot \bar{x}_i + \max \left\{0, \sum_{j=1}^{k} \theta_{ji} \hat{p} \cdot \hat{y}_j\right\}$$

where θ_{ji} is the share of profits from j to i, $\sum_{i=1}^{m} \theta_{ji} = 1$, $i = 1, 2, \ldots, m$. Then condition (i) in the definition of competitive equilibrium is restated as

(i') $\qquad u_i(\hat{x}_i) \geq u_i(x_i)$ for all $x_i \in X_i$ with $\hat{p} \cdot x_i \leq M_i$, $i = 1, 2, \ldots, m$

To prove the existence, we impose the following additional assumptions.[13]

(A-5) The set Z is compact, where $Z \equiv \{(x_1, \ldots, x_m, y): x \leq y + \bar{x}, y \in Y, x_i \in X_i, i = 1, 2, \ldots, m\}$.

(A-6) **(Nonsatiation)** For every consumption x_i in X_i with $[\{x_i\}, y] \in Z$, there is a consumption in X_i preferred to x_i, $i = 1, 2, \ldots, m$.

(A-7) **(Survival)** There is an x_i^0 in X_i such that $x_i^0 < \bar{x}_i$ for all $i = 1, 2, \ldots, m$.

(A-8) **(The possibility of inaction)** $0 \in Y_j, j = 1, 2, \ldots, k$.

Theorem 2.F.2   *Under (A-1), (A-2), (A-3), (A-5), (A-6), (A-7), and (A-8), there exists a competitive equilibrium with a nonzero price vector.*

PROOF: Let $\alpha \in A$ where $A \equiv \{\alpha \in R^m: \sum_{i=1}^m \alpha_i = 1, \alpha_i \geq 0 \text{ for all } i\}$. Let $U \equiv \sum_{i=1}^m \alpha_i u_i(x_i)$ and consider the following problem:[14]

Maximize: U
$$x_i \in X_i, y \in Y$$

Subject to: $y + \bar{x} - x \geq 0$, $x_i \in X_i$, $i = 1, 2, \ldots, m$, and $y \in Y$

Hence, from the Kuhn-Tucker theorem,[15] there exists a $p' \geq 0$ such that the following (4) and (5) hold:

(4) $$U + p' \cdot (y + \bar{x} - x) \leq U' + p' \cdot (y' + \bar{x} - x')$$

for all $x_i \in X_i$, $i = 1, 2, \ldots, m$, $y \in Y$, where x_i' and y' are the optimal vectors for the above problem, and $U' \equiv \sum_{i=1}^m \alpha_i u_i(x_i')$:

(5) $$p' \cdot (y' + \bar{x} - x') = 0, \text{ and } y' + \bar{x} - x' \geq 0$$

In a manner similar to the proof of Theorem 2.F.1, we can immediately show that the following (6), (7), and (8) hold:

(6) $$p' \cdot y_j' \geq p' \cdot y_j \qquad \text{for all } y_j \in Y_j, j = 1, 2, \ldots, k$$

where the y_j' are obtained from y' as $y' = \sum_{j=1}^k y_j'$, $y_j' \in Y_j$, $j = 1, 2, \ldots, k$;

(7) $u_i(x_i') \geq u_i(x_i)$ for all $x_i \in X_i$ with $p' \cdot x_i \leq p' \cdot x_i'$, if $\alpha_i > 0$

(8) $p' \cdot x_i \geq p' \cdot x_i'$ for all $x_i \in X_i$, if $\alpha_i = 0$

Since there is no satiation consumption in Z as a result of assumption (A-6), (7) implies $p' \neq 0$. Hence we may normalize the price vector p' as follows:

(9) $$p_s'' \equiv \frac{p_s'}{\sum_{s=1}^n p_s'}, \qquad s = 1, 2, \ldots, n$$

Relations (4), (5), (7), and (8) all hold with p'' replaced for p'.

The rest of the proof is analogous to Negishi [12]. It is simply recorded here to keep this section sufficiently self-contained.

Since the set Z is bounded by (A-5), there exists a number M such that

$$\sum_{i=1}^m |M_i(p, y) - p \cdot x_i| < M \text{ for all } (x_1, \ldots, x_m, y) \in Z, \text{ and for all } p$$

Now define

$$\mu_i \equiv \max \ \{0, \ \alpha_i + (M_i(p, y) - p \cdot x_i)/M\}, \qquad i = 1, 2, \ldots, m$$

where p is a point in the $(n - 1)$-dimensional unit simplex.[16] Define α_i' by

$$\alpha_i' \equiv \frac{\mu_i}{\sum\limits_{i=1}^{m} \mu_i}$$

Note that α' is a point of the $(n - 1)$-dimensional unit simplex. Following Negishi [12], we construct the following mappings:[17]

(a) $\qquad\qquad\qquad\qquad \alpha \to [\{x_i'\}, y', p']$

(b) $\qquad\qquad\qquad [\{x_i'\}, y', p'] \to [\alpha', \{x_i'\}, y', p'']$

The point-to-set mapping (a) is the mapping from α to the saddle point of $U + p \cdot (y + \bar{x} - x)$. Its image is nonempty from (A-3) and (A-5) (see footnote 14), and the mapping is upper semicontinuous with compact and convex images.[18] The mapping (b) is a point-to-point mapping and is continuous.

Let $(x_1, \ldots, x_m, y)$ be an arbitrary point in Z. Let p be an arbitrary point in the $(n - 1)$ unit simplex. Combining (a) and (b), the mapping $[\alpha, \{x_i\}, y, p] \to [\alpha', \{x_i'\}, y', p'']$ is an upper semicontinuous mapping[19] from a convex compact set into itself whose image is nonempty and convex. Hence, from Kakutani's fixed point theorem,[20] there exists a fixed point $[\hat{\alpha}, \{\hat{x}_i\}, \hat{y}, \hat{p}]$. Since conditions (ii) and (iii) of competitive equilibrium are met by the construction of the mapping, it suffices to show that condition (i') of competitive equilibrium (C. E.) is satisfied. Note that (A-8) and condition (ii) of C. E. imply $\hat{p} \cdot \hat{y}_j \geqq 0$ for all j. Hence $M_i(\hat{p}, \hat{y}) = \hat{p} \cdot \bar{x}_i + \sum_{j=1}^{k} \theta_{ji} \hat{p} \cdot \hat{y}_j$. Note also that the $(M_i(\hat{p}, \hat{y}) - \hat{p} \cdot \hat{x}_i)$, $i = 1, 2, \ldots, m$, must be of equal sign or zero by the construction of the mapping. Hence, from (5), we have[21]

(10) $\qquad\qquad\qquad\qquad M_i(\hat{p}, \hat{y}) = \hat{p} \cdot \hat{x}_i$

Since there exist $x_i^0 < \bar{x}_i$ by (A-7), $\hat{\alpha}_i > 0$ for all $i = 1, 2, \ldots, m$, for otherwise it contradicts relation (8).[22] Hence, combining (7) and (10), we obtain condition (i') of competitive equilibrium.   (Q.E.D.)

REMARK: If we do not assume free disposability, then we cannot have a nonnegative price vector in Theorems 2.F.1 and 2.F.2. The prices of "undesired" commodities can be negative. To analyze such a case, we must alter the statement of the definition of feasibility. In other words, $[y + \bar{x} - x \geqq 0]$ should be replaced by $[y + \bar{x} - x = 0]$. Then our problem becomes the programming problem with an *equality* constraint. Although we can carry out our analysis analogously to that above, we can no longer use the saddle-point characterization of maximality. We have to rely upon the quasi-saddle-point characterization, for the Slater condition is no longer applicable and the Kuhn-Tucker constraint qualification or the classical rank condition would now be relevant. This forces us to introduce the undesirable assumption, that is, differentiability of the utility functions. The proper route should be in extending the theory of the saddle-point characterization which takes proper account of the equality constraint.

Theorem 2.F.3:   *Let* $[\{\hat{x}_i\}, \{\hat{y}_j\}, \hat{p}]$ *be a competitive equilibrium in Theorem 2.F.2; then* $[\{\hat{x}_i\}, \{\hat{y}_j\}]$ *is a Pareto optimum.*

PROOF: First note that $[\{\hat{x}_i\}, \{\hat{y}_j\}]$ maximizes $\sum_{i=1}^{m} \alpha_i u_i(x_i)$ (where $\alpha_i > 0$ for all i), subject to feasibility. Suppose $[\{\hat{x}_i\}, \{\hat{y}_j\}]$ is *not* a Pareto optimum. Then by the definition of Pareto optimum, there exist $\tilde{x}_i \in X_i, i = 1, 2, \ldots, m$, $\tilde{y}_j \in Y_j, j = 1, 2, \ldots, k$, such that $u_i(\tilde{x}_i) \geqq u_i(\hat{x}_i)$ for all i with strict inequality holding for at least one i, and $\tilde{x} \leqq \tilde{y} + \bar{x}$. In other words, there exists a feasible $[\{\tilde{x}_i\}, \{\tilde{y}_j\}]$ such that $\sum_{i=1}^{m} \hat{\alpha}_i u_i(\tilde{x}_i) > \sum_{i=1}^{m} \hat{\alpha}_i u_i(\hat{x}_i)$, contradicting the maximality of $[\{\hat{x}_i\}, \{\hat{y}_j\}]$.   (Q.E.D.)

FOOTNOTES

1. This section is a revised version of Takayama and El-Hodiri [15]; their work was developed from the discussions between Takayama and El-Hodiri during the summer of 1966, and the actual writing was done by Takayama. I am indebted to Takashi Negishi for comments.

2. One of the important by-products of such an approach is that we can avoid the concepts of demand correspondence and supply correspondence altogether.

3. Moreover, in Negishi's paper, X_i is nonnegative and contains the origin for all i. This means that *every* consumer has the *same* minimum subsistence consumption point, the origin, regardless of his physiological need.

4. For conditions which guarantee the existence of a continuous real-valued utility function, see Rader [12]. The reader may wish to note that one of his theorems (theorem 3) does not require the transitivity axiom of the preference ordering.

5. Note that if $y + \bar{x} - x < 0$ for all $x \in X$ and $y \in Y$, then the society cannot guarantee the survival of every one of its members.

6. Note that only the aggregate production set is assumed to be convex. Every production set does not have to be convex.

7. From the consideration below, we may also surmise that the theorems of nonlinear programming that we used can be extended to the case in which the maximand function is explicitly quasi-concave rather than concave. This conjecture is due to the fact that only explicit quasi-concavity is usually required in establishing the corresponding theorems of this section (see Theorem 2.C.2 and Theorem 2.E.3). Finally, we may note that the concavity implies the continuity in the interior of the domain (here X_i), but not necessarily at the boundary. This is important, for X_i may be a closed set.

8. We are using the following theorem. *Theorem*: Let Z be a convex subset in R^l and $f(z)$ be a vector function of which the ith component is $f_i(z)$. Let $f_i(z)$, $i = 1, 2, \ldots, m$, and $g_j(z), j = 1, 2, \ldots, n$, be concave functions on Z. Suppose also that there exists a $\bar{z} \in Z$ such that $g_j(\bar{z}) > 0, j = 1, 2, \ldots, n$ (Slater's condition). Then if $\hat{z}$ achieves a vector maximum of $f(z)$ subject to $g_j(z) \geqq 0, j = 1, 2, \ldots, n$, then there exist $\alpha \geqq 0, p \geqq 0$ ($\alpha \neq 0$) such that $(\hat{z}, \hat{p})$ is a saddle point of

$\alpha \cdot f(z) + p \cdot g(z)$. See Theorem 1.E.4. Also see Karlin [7], pp. 216–218, and Kuhn and Tucker [8], pp. 487–489. Note that the convexity of Y and X_i as well as the concavity of u_i is required in applying this theorem. Note also that assumption (A-1) provides Slater's condition, which implies Karlin's condition as stated in [7], p. 201. See also Section B of Chapter 1.

9. Here α_i can be interpreted as the "weight" attached by the society to the ith individual.

10. Note that this unfortunate consumer is still minimizing his expenditure.

11. To ensure the compactness of Z, assume, for example, that the X_i's are closed and bounded from below, Y is closed, and that "no-land-of-Cockaigne" holds for each Y_j. For the discussion of such a "compactification," see Arrow and Debreu [2], pp. 276–277, and p. 279; Debreu [5], pp. 76–78, pp. 84–86; and Nikaido [13], section 40.

12. The Weierstrass theorem asserts that a continuous (real-valued) function achieves its maximum (and a minimum) on a compact set, and this theorem can easily be extended to the case of a vector maximum.

13. These assumptions are analogous to those of Debreu [5], chapter 5. Assumptions (A-5) and (A-7) may sound too strong, and some readers may wish to generalize in the direction achieved by McKenzie [9]. It should be noted, however, that our set of assumptions used to prove existence (Theorem 2.F.2), is more general than that of Negishi [12]. We do not assume the existence of the right-hand and left-hand derivatives of each F_k. As we noted before, we, in fact, completely avoided the use of the individual production function F_k. Hence we do not assume that each F_k is concave. Note that the concavity of each F_k implies the *convexity* of *each* producer's production set. We only assume the convexity of the aggregate production set. Slater's condition for each F_k does not have to be assumed. Our assumption (A-1) is concerned with the aggregate sets. Note also that the assumption of Slater's condition for each F_k also implies that the production set for each producer must have a common interior point with the consumption set of *every* consumer (recall that the origin is the starvation point for each consumer in Negishi [12]).

14. In view of (A-3) and (A-5), the solution of the above maximization problem always exists because of the Weierstrass theorem.

15. We are using the following version of the Kuhn-Tucker theorem. *Theorem*: Let Z be a convex set in R^n, and $f(z)$, $g_j(z)$, $j = 1, 2, \ldots, m$, be concave functions on Z. Suppose also there exists a $\bar{z} \in Z$ such that $g_j(\bar{z}) > 0$ for all j (Slater's condition). Under these conditions, if $\hat{z}$ maximizes $f(z)$ subject to $g_j(z) \geq 0, j = 1, 2, \ldots, m$, then there exists a $\hat{p} \geq 0$ such that $(\hat{z}, \hat{p})$ is a saddle point of $[f(z) + p \cdot g(z)]$. A beautiful proof when $Z = R^n$ is provided by Uzawa [16]. The above slightly generalized version is provided by Karlin [7], pp. 201–203 (note that Slater's condition implies Karlin's condition), and Nikaido [13], section 37. See our discussion in Chapter 1, Section B (especially the corollary of Theorem 1.B.3).

16. Note that $\sum_{i=1}^m \mu_i > 0$, since $\sum_{i=1}^m \alpha_i = 1$ and $\sum_{i=1}^m [(M_i(p, y) - p \cdot x_i)/M] < 1$.

17. Note that the range of the mapping (a) is compact. This is due to the fact that the set Z is compact and the part of the range in which p' lives can be considered as a compact subset—say, $\bar{P}$—of the nonnegative orthant Ω^n of R^n; p' is bounded and it is obviously nonnegative. Without loss of generality, we may also assume that $\bar{P}$ is convex.

18. The image is convex because U is concave, the constraint set Z is convex (Theorem 1.C.5), and $\bar{P}$ is convex. Also recall here that the Cartesian product of convex sets is always convex. Since the graph of this mapping is a closed set, it is a closed

mapping (see Berge [3], p. 111). Furthermore, it is an upper semicontinuous (u.s.c.) mapping, since its range is compact as a result of our observation in the previous footnote. The importance of this is pointed out by Moore [11] (especially p. 133 and his footnotes 10 and 12 on p. 139), who corrected the impreciseness on this point in Negishi [12]. In general, a closed mapping is u.s.c. if the range space is compact (see Berge [3], p. 112, corollary of theorem 7). The image of the mapping (a) is compact, for the image of any u.s.c. mapping is always compact.

19. In general, the composite mapping of two u.s.c. mappings is also u.s.c. (see Berge [3], p. 113). For a generalization of this, see Moore [11].

20. Kakutani's fixed point theorem states the following: Let Z be a nonempty convex and compact subset of R^n. If F is an upper semicontinuous mapping from Z to Z such that for all $z \in Z$, the set $F(z)$ is nonempty and convex, then there exists a $\hat{z}$ (called a "fixed point") such that $\hat{z} \in F(\hat{z})$. Recall Section E of this chapter.

21. Note that $\hat{p} \cdot (\hat{y} + \bar{x}) = \sum_{i=1}^{m} M_i(\hat{p}, \hat{y})$. Hence $\sum_{i=1}^{m} [M_i(\hat{p}, \hat{y}) - \hat{p} \cdot \hat{x}_i] = \hat{p} \cdot (\hat{y} + \bar{x} - \hat{x})$, which is zero from (5). Since the $[M_i(\hat{p}, \hat{y}) - \hat{x}_i]$'s are all of equal sign or zero, this proves (10).

22. Since $\hat{p} \geq 0$, $x_i^0 < \bar{x}_i$ implies $\hat{p} \cdot x_i^0 < \hat{p} \cdot \bar{x}_i$. But $\hat{p} \cdot \bar{x}_i \leq M_i(\hat{p}, \hat{y}) = \hat{p} \cdot \hat{x}_i$, so that we have $\hat{p} \cdot x_i^0 < \hat{p} \cdot \hat{x}_i$. Now suppose the contrary, that is, $\alpha_i = 0$ for some i. Then (8) says that $\hat{p} \cdot x_i \geq \hat{p} \cdot \hat{x}_i$ for all $x_i \in X_i$; hence, in particular, $\hat{p} \cdot x_i^0 \geq \hat{p} \cdot \hat{x}_i$, which is a contradiction.

REFERENCES

1. Arrow, K. J., "An Extension of the Basic Theorems of Classical Welfare Economics," *Proceedings of the Second Berkeley Symposium on Mathematical Statistics and Probability*, ed. by J. Neyman, Berkeley, Calif., University of California Press, 1951.

2. Arrow, K. J., and Debreu, G., "Existence of an Equilibrium for a Competitive Economy," *Econometrica*, 22, July 1954.

3. Berge, C., *Topological Spaces*, tr. by Patterson, New York, Macmillan, 1963 (French original, 1959).

4. Debreu, G., "The Coefficient of Resource Utilization," *Econometrica*, 19, July 1951.

5. ———, *Theory of Value*, New York, Wiley, 1959.

6. Fenchel, W., *Convex Cones, Sets and Functions*, Princeton, 1953 (offset).

7. Karlin, S., *Mathematical Methods and Theory in Games, Programming, and Economics*, Vol. I, 1st ed., Reading, Mass., Addison-Wesley, 1959.

8. Kuhn, H. W., and Tucker, A. W., "Nonlinear Programming," *Proceedings of the Second Berkeley Symposium on Mathematical Statistics and Probability*, ed. by J. Neyman, Berkeley, Calif., University of California Press, 1951.

9. McKenzie, L. W., "On the Existence of General Equilibrium for a Competitive Market," *Econometrica*, 27, January 1959.

10. Moore, J. C., "Some Extensions of the Kuhn-Tucker Results in Concave Programming," *Papers in Quantitative Economics*, ed. by J. P. Quirk and A. M. Zarley, Lawrence, Kansas, University of Kansas Press, 1968.

11. ———, "A Note on Point-Set Mappings," *Papers in Quantitative Economics*, Vol. I,

ed. by J. P. Quirk and A. M. Zarley, Lawrence, Kansas, University of Kansas Press, 1968.

12. Negishi, T., "Welfare Economics and the Existence of an Equilibrium for a Competitive Economy," *Metroeconomica*, 12, Agosto–Dicembre 1960.

13. Nikaido, H., *Introduction to Sets and Mappings in Modern Economics*, tr. by K. Sato, Amsterdam, North-Holland, 1970 (Japanese original, Tokyo, 1960).

14. Rader, T., "Existence of a Utility Function to Represent Preferences," *Review of Economic Studies*, 30, October 1963.

15. Takayama, A., and El-Hodiri, M., "Programming, Pareto Optimum, and the Existence of Competitive Equilibria," *Metroeconomica*, XX, Gennaio–Aprile 1968.

16. Uzawa, H., "The Kuhn-Tucker Theorem in Concave Programming," in *Studies in Linear and Non-linear Programming*, ed. by Arrow, Hurwicz, and Uzawa, Stanford, Calif., Stanford University Press, 1958.

3

THE STABILITY OF COMPETITIVE EQUILIBRIUM

Consider an isolated (competitive) market for one commodity (say, A). Suppose that the demand for A, denoted by $D(p)$, is a function of its price p, and suppose also that the supply of A, denoted by $S(p)$, is also a function of its price. An equilibrium price, $\hat{p}$, is a price such that $D(\hat{p}) = S(\hat{p})$. Whether or not there exists such a $\hat{p}$ is the problem of the "existence" of an equilibrium. This existence of an equilibrium is guaranteed if the demand curve and the supply curve cross. If they cross at many points, then there are many equilibria. Suppose that the price of A, p, deviates from a certain equilibrium price—say, $\hat{p}$. The question now is what happens to the time path of p. In particular, we want to know if p will converge to the original $\hat{p}$. This is the question of "stability." To solve this "stability problem," we impose one basic assumption: an excess demand for A will raise its price, p, and an excess supply of A will lower its price. Mathematically, $dp/dt \gtreqless 0$ according to whether $D(p) - S(p) \gtreqless 0$. Here dp/dt denotes the time derivative of p. In order to facilitate our understanding of the problem, let us assume that there *exists* a *unique* equilibrium price $\hat{p}$ such that $D(\hat{p}) = S(\hat{p})$. When the question is posed in this manner, the answer is almost obvious from a diagrammatical analysis. The left-hand diagram in Figure 3.1 illustrates the case of a stable equilibrium and the right-hand diagram illustrates the case of an unstable equilibrium. The reader should easily be able to check the direction in which p moves when p is off the equilibrium price $\hat{p}$.

To consider a more general problem, let us now suppose that a certain economy is described by n equations which describe the "equilibrium relations" of the economy. Let $x = (x_1, x_2, \ldots, x_n)$ be the variables which should be determined from this system of n equations. Let the equilibrium relations of the economy be described by $f_i(x) = 0$, $i = 1, 2, \ldots, n$ [or $f(x) = 0$]. The value of x which satisfies the above system (assuming that there exists such an x) is called an **equilibrium value** of x, and we denote it by $\hat{x}$. The stability question is the problem

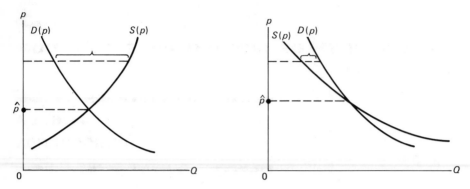

Figure 3.1.   Stability of an Isolated Market.

of what happens to the time path of x when it deviates from $\hat{x}$. In particular, we want to consider whether x will converge to $\hat{x}$. An example of such an equilibrium system is the system of a competitive market, where f_i denotes the excess demand for the ith commodity and x_i denotes the price of the ith commodity. Another example of an equilibrium system is the classical or the Keynesian macro equilibrium system, which typically consists of the equilibrium relations that describe the goods market, the money market, and the labor market.

Let us suppose that the initial value of x is given by x^0. Assume that x^0 is *not* an equilibrium value, that is, $f(x^0) \neq 0$. Let us suppose that this generates a certain adjustment process, from which the time path of x, denoted by $x(t)$, is described by the following system of equations.

$$F_i[x(t), t] = 0, \qquad i = 1, 2, \ldots, n$$

with $x(0) = x^0$; or $F[x(t), t] = 0$ with $x(0) = x^0$. Typically this system of equations is generated by a system of differential (difference) equations that describe the adjustment processes. The stability analysis is concerned with the solution of the above system or the question of whether $x(t)$ converges to an equilibrium value $\hat{x}$. Most typically, the system of differential equations which generates the above dynamic system may be written as follows:

$$\frac{dx_i(t)}{dt} = h_i[f(x(t))]$$

Or, more simply,

$$\frac{dx_i(t)}{dt} = h_i[f_i(x(t))]$$

In the case of a competitive equilibrium, this says that the movement of the ith price, $x_i(t)$, is a function of the excess demand for the ith commodity f_i (or excess demand for all the commodities f). When the problem is written in differential equation form, one suspects that the theory of stability developed for differential equations might be of some value. This was indeed the case in the development of the theory of the stability of a competitive equilibrium. In Section B, we survey the basic material on differential equations. This discussion will also be useful in later chapters.

Before concluding this introductory section, one important discussion is necessary on the distinction between the "Walrasian stability" and the "Marshallian stability."[1] In the introductory exposition of the stability problem of a competitive equilibrium above, we considered the basic postulate in the form of

$$\dot{p}_i(t) = h_i[f_i(p(t))], \qquad i = 1, 2, \ldots, n$$

where p_i is the price of the ith commodity and $p(t)$ is an n-vector in which the ith element is $p_i(t)$ and $\dot{p}_i(t) \equiv dp_i(t)/dt$. Also, $f_i(p(t))$ is the excess demand function for the ith commodity and h_i is any (fixed) monotone increasing differentiable real-valued function. For the case of an isolated market for one commodity, we write this equation as

$$\dot{p} = h[D(p(t)) - S(p(t))]$$

where h refers to some fixed monotone increasing differentiable real-valued function. Or, more simply,

$$\dot{p} = k[D(p(t)) - S(p(t))]$$

where $k > 0$ can be interpreted as the "speed of adjustment" of the market.

There are two important premises in the above formulation. One is that neither demanders nor suppliers can affect the price that prevails in the market, but rather they take it as given. This is the premise of a competitive market. The second premise is that the price is the only adjusting parameter of the market. At each instant of time, demanders and suppliers, respectively, adjust the quantities that they wish to demand and supply, based only on the information of the price given to them. This adjustment is assumed to be instantaneous. Then the price moves as described in the differential equation above. As price moves, the quantity of excess demand will vary and stability of the market is achieved when the price moves in such a way that the excess demand vanishes.

In contrast to such a price adjustment process, the quantity adjustment type mechanism is often considered. In Figure 3.2, suppose q^1 is the given quantity of the commodity. We denote by $D(q^1)$ and $S(q^1)$, respectively, the price that buyers are willing to pay and the price that sellers are charging for a given quantity q^1. The dynamic output adjustment equation for the above market can be written as

$$\dot{q} = \check{k}[D(q) - S(q)]$$

where $\check{k} > 0$ is the speed of adjustment of the market. This reflects the fact that if $D(q) > S(q)$, for example, the *suppliers* can profitably increase the quantity supplied. If the time path of the solution of the above differential equation con-

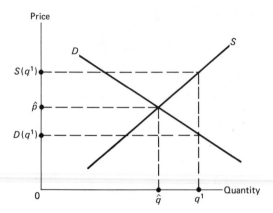

Figure 3.2. An Illustration of Output Adjustment.

verges to the equilibrium quantity $\hat{q}$ as t extends without limit, then the equilibrium is said to be "stable." Such a stability is often called the **Marshallian stability**, while the stability in the price adjusting market as discussed before is often called the **Walrasian stability**.

These two stability definitions apparently do not coincide. The market can be Walrasian stable (resp. unstable) but Marshallian unstable (resp. stable). In the literature, this is often illustrated by diagrams such as those shown in Figure 3.3. The diagrams should be self-explanatory.

However, comparison of the two concepts as shown in these diagrams contains a very serious confusion. In essence, these two concepts are in completely different dimensions and should *not* be compared in the same figure.

One source of this confusion is probably attributable to Hicks' remark ([1], p. 62) on the distinction between these concepts. He states that the Marshal-

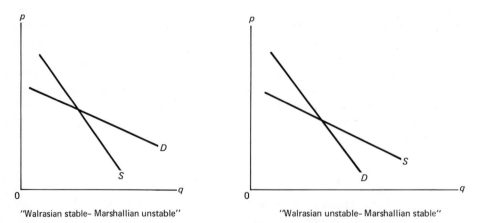

"Walrasian stable– Marshallian unstable"   "Walrasian unstable– Marshallian stable"

Figure 3.3. Two Concepts of Stability.

lian stability concept is more appropriate to conditions of monopoly than to those of perfect competition.

As Newman ([3], pp. 106–108) has pointed out, the common confusion about the Walrasian vs. the Marshallian stability lies in the failure to distinguish clearly the theory of exchange from the theory of production. The Marshallian stability conditions are explicitly designed for the theory of production, whereas the Walrasian price adjustment is more suited for the theory of exchange. Hence these two concepts cannot be compared in the same dimension. Thus the description of an equilibrium as Walrasian stable but Marshallian unstable is rather meaningless. It contains a "serious substantive error of muddling up exchange with production" (Newman [3], p. 107). As Newman has pointed out, this confusion is found frequently in the literature.

The next question is: What is the essential distinction between the problem of exchange and the problem of production? One answer is essentially the time involved in the two problems. Exchange can be considered as the "temporary" problem, whereas production is the "short-run" problem.[2] This is based on the recognition that producers take a significant period of time before attaining their optimum positions, whereas the consumer's adjustment can be much faster. Take, for example, an isolated market for one commodity—say, apples. When apples are harvested in the fall, the quantity that each producer can supply to the market may be considered to be fixed; hence, the total quantity of apples supplied to the market is fixed. The market thus characterized is that of exchange rather than that of production. The Walrasian adjustment process is one excellent way to explain the mechanism of reaching an equilibrium price. Once an equilibrium price is determined, the producers determine the next year's output based on the price of apples this year. Here the output-adjusting Marshallian mechanism is probably most relevant. Note that in this example the quantity of apples is fixed in the Walrasian adjustment process, whereas the price of apples is fixed in the Marshallian adjustment process. In this example the behavior of the market is very similar to that described in the Cobweb model.[3] In general, this does not have to be the case. For example, the market supply of a commodity can still be a function of price, even if the total amount is fixed (until the production of the next period is finished).

In any case, what the above example illustrates is that the Walrasian price adjustment process is more appropriate for the "temporary" period in which production is not completed, whereas the Marshallian adjustment is better suited to the "short-run" period in which the adjustment of output is explicitly considered. It is important to note that the Marshallian output adjustment process is, contrary to Hicks' remark, perfectly relevant for a competitive market. Producers in the above-described apple market are competitive in the sense that they take the market price of apples as given. The usual discussion that the Marshallian process is more appropriate for monopoly is thus wrong.

One typical and brilliant diagrammatical analysis of the Marshallian mechanism is found in Marshall's paper "The Pure Theory of Foreign Trade" (privately printed in 1879; the revision is reprinted in his *Money, Trade and Commerce*, London, Macmillan, 1923, appendix J). The curves drawn there became known later as "offer curves." The intersection of the two offer curves determines the equilibrium outputs of the two commodities involved. It is assumed that the consumers adjust to their optimum positions instantaneously and the Walrasian adjustment process is completed instantaneously (the stability in the Walrasian process is implicitly assumed). The adjustment from an off-equilibrium point to the equilibrium point described in the above article is purely that of output adjustment.[4]

We may remark that *both* Marshall and Walras clearly realized that there are these two types of adjustments and they both used them in the proper context.[5] Hence it may be rather misleading to call the stability in the price adjustment process the "Walrasian stability" and the stability in the output adjustment process the "Marshallian stability." But since this practice is already much too common, we will not change it. A difference between these two approaches is probably that Marshall emphasized the "short-run" output adjustment mechanism and utilized a diagrammatical technique for this adjustment, whereas Walras emphasized the "temporary" price adjustment mechanism and utilized a diagrammatical technique for this adjustment in his theory of two-person exchange.[6] Moreover, Walras [5], in his theory of production, treated the output adjustment process as the one that occurs *simultaneously* with the price adjustment process.[7]

The question still remains whether the Walrasian price adjustment process is *only* relevant to the theory of exchange. I believe it is not. As long as both demand and supply are functions of prices, the prices must be the final adjustment parameter. After the "temporary" and the "short-run" adjustments are completed, we should find an equilibrium position in which $D(p) = S(p)$. Hence, if we wish to abstract such "temporary" processes and "short-run" processes, we may simply assume that both demand and production adjust instantaneously to price and then consider the time path as described by $\dot{p} = k[D(p) - S(p)]$, and so on. In other words, we can still consider the price adjustment as the one that describes the mechanism for the final equilibrium (see Walras' theory of production [5]).[8]

In the later revival of the stability theory, starting from Hicks [1] and Samuelson [4], the Walrasian type of price adjustment has been the main issue and little attention has been paid to the output adjustment. This is rather unfortunate, but as long as the price is the sole independent variable in a competitive market, it may be natural to emphasize the price adjustment process (either as a theory of temporary equilibrium in exchange or as a theory of short-run equilibrium when all adjustments including output are completed).

In any case, this chapter is dedicated to exploring this recent development in the price-adjusting theory. We will examine both the mathematical technique and the conceptual difficulties in this recent development of the theory. The mathematical exploration serves as a beautiful example of the application of the theory of differential equations to economics.

A short summary of this chapter is now in order. After the exposition on the elements of the theory of differential equations in Section B, we start our discussion on the stability of competitive equilibria with a historical survey of the topic in Section C. In Section D, we give a proof of the global stability of a three-commodity market. This section is also useful as an illustration of the phase diagram technique which has recently turned out to be very useful in many other branches of economics. In Section E, we sketch the proof of the global stability of a competitive economy given by Arrow, Block, and Hurwicz, and in Section F, we make some important remarks on the stability analysis of a competitive market. In Section G, we discuss some basic problems involved in the dynamic adjustment equations, in particular the *tâtonnement* and the *non-tâtonnement* processes. We end the chapter with a short survey of Liapunov's "second method," which recently turned out to be useful in the stability analysis of a competitive equilibrium (Section H).

FOOTNOTES

1. I am indebted to Takashi Negishi for the subsequent remark. Clearly, mistakes, if there are any, are my own.
2. This approach is due to Marshall [2]. The terms such as "temporary" and "short run" are also his. Marshall's "long run" is, as is well known, concerned with the adjustment process which involves the adjustment of the capital stocks.
3. Such an intertemporal model which contains more than one (production) period is really *outside* the scope of the ordinary "stability" analysis, which is concerned with the adjustment process within the one-period model. The analysis of a multiperiod model usually belongs to the theory of growth, business cycles, and so forth.
4. For an excellent attempt to reconsider Marshall's study from this viewpoint, see A. Amano, "Stability Conditions in the Pure Theory of International Trade: A Rehabilitation of the Marshallian Approach," *Quarterly Journal of Economics*, LXXXII, May 1968.
5. For another study (besides Newman [3]) on the Marshallian vs. Walrasian stability conditions, see D. G. Davis, "A Note on Marshall versus Walrasian Stability Conditions," *Canadian Journal of Economics and Political Science*, 29, November 1963.
6. Marshall did not utilize diagrams for the price adjustment process. Walras did not utilize diagrams for his output (-price) adjustment process.
7. For the case of a single-commodity isolated market, an example of such a simultaneous adjustment process may be formulated as follows: $\dot{p} = k_1[D(p) - q]$ and $\dot{q} = k_2[p - S(q)]$, that is, the system of simultaneous differential equations. For further studies based on the view that the adjustment processes are simultaneous, see, for example, M. Morishima, "A Reconsideration of the Walras-Cassel-Leontief Model of General Equilibrium," in *Mathematical Methods in the Social Sciences, 1959*, ed. by K. J. Arrow, S. Karlin, and P. Suppes, Stanford, Calif., Stanford University Press, 1960, and E. Malinvaud, "Decentralized Procedures for Planning," in *Activity Analysis in the Theory of Growth and Planning*, ed. by E. Malinvaud and M. O. L. Bacharch, London, Macmillan, 1967.
8. Such a view may be represented by some of the above approaches to *simultaneous* adjustment of prices and outputs. Another view is that all the adjustments boil down to price adjustments after all. For example, Jones obtained the stability

condition interpreting the adjustment mechanism in the international trade equilibrium à la Marshall (that is, the intersection of the two countries' offer curves) as the one with the price-adjusting type. See R. W. Jones, "Stability Conditions in International Trade: A General Equilibrium Analysis," *International Economic Review*, 2, May 1961.

REFERENCES

1.   Hicks, J. R. *Value and Capital*, 2nd ed., Oxford, Clarendon Press, 1946.
2.   Marshall, A., *The Principles of Economics*, 8th ed., London, Macmillan, 1920.
3.   Newman, P., *The Theory of Exchange*, Englewood Cliffs, N.J., Prentice-Hall, 1965.
4.   Samuelson, P. A., *Foundations of Economic Analysis*, Cambridge, Mass., Harvard University Press, 1947.
5.   Walras, L., *Elements of Pure Economics*, 1926 ed., tr. by W. Jaffé, London, George Allen & Unwin, 1954.

Section B

ELEMENTS OF THE THEORY OF DIFFERENTIAL EQUATIONS

Before we pursue a discussion of the stability of a competitive equilibrium, let us review some basic material from the theory of differential equations. Not only has this technique been very useful in science and engineering, but it has also proved itself useful in economics. This is especially true in problems of dynamics, that is, problems that have "time" as an essential element, such as those found in the theory of the stability of an economic (micro or macro) equilibrium as well as in business cycle theory and growth theory. Hence this discussion is important for several branches of economics.

First let us consider a very simple example of an "(ordinary) differential equation":

$$\dot{x}(t) = ax(t), a \neq 0, \text{ where } \dot{x}(t) \equiv \frac{dx(t)}{dt}$$

Here $x(t)$ is a real-valued differentiable function defined on the real line, and a is some real number which is constant. The two most basic features of the above equation that one should note are the following:

(i)   The above equation holds for all values of t in the domain (here the entire real line).

(ii)   The function $x(t)$ is not *a priori* specified, that is, it is an "unknown" function.[1]

To "solve" a given differential equation(s) is to specify the unknown function(s) so that the given differential equation(s) is reduced to an identity(ies). For example, $x(t) = ce^{at}$, where c is some constant, will reduce the above differential equation to an identity. In other words, we have now "found" the unknown function, which turns out to be $x(t) = ce^{at}$; hence it is a "solution" of the above differential equation. The reader may immediately note that c can be any real number, as long as it is fixed. Hence there are infinitely many solutions. However, if we specify one more condition in the above equation such that $x(t^0) = x^0$, then this is no longer the case, for the above solution $x(t) = ce^{at}$ must satisfy this "boundary condition" (or "initial condition"). The constant c must take some fixed value, $c = x^0 e^{-at^0}$, so that the solution is now written as $x(t) = x^0 e^{a(t-t^0)}$. It is easy to check that this solution is unique up to the boundary condition; that is, if there exists another solution $\tilde{x}(t)$ such that $\tilde{x}(t^0) = x^0$, then $\tilde{x}(t) = x(t) = x^0 e^{a(t-t^0)}$. Often t^0 is taken to be 0. Then $c = x^0$ so that $x(t) = x^0 e^{at}$ is a (unique) solution. When an unspecified constant(s), such as c in the above example, is specified by a boundary condition(s), the solution thus obtained is often called a (*particular*) *solution*. The solution with an unspecified constant(s) is often called a *general solution*. The differential equation in the above example contains only the first derivative of the unknown function, and it is called a **first-order differential equation**. When the highest order of the derivative of the unknown function is n, it is called an **nth-order differential equation**. To obtain a particular solution of an nth-order equation, n boundary conditions are usually required. It is also possible that we have more than one unknown function. For example, there can be $x_1(t)$, $x_2(t)$, ..., $x_n(t)$ [or in vector notation, $x(t)$], that is, n unknown functions. For the first-order system of n simultaneous differential equations, n boundary conditions are usually required to obtain a particular solution of $x(t)$.

In passing, we should note one fundamental fact in the above example $\dot{x}(t) = ax(t)$. We observed that $x(t) = ce^{at}$ is a general solution and a particular solution is unique up to a boundary condition such as $x(t^0) = x^0$. In other words, in this example there *exists* a solution, and a particular solution is unique up to the boundary condition. This may not necessarily be the case when we are given a general form of a differential equation(s). However, without the existence (and uniqueness) of a solution, the study of differential equations will be meaningless or, at most, uninteresting. Hence the first fundamental theorem in the theory of differential equations is the one which gives the conditions under which a solution exists. This is stated later as the Cauchy-Peano theorem. We are now ready to begin a more formal discussion of differential equations.

Definition: Let f_i, $i = 1, 2, \ldots, n$, be real-valued functions defined on $X \otimes T$ where $X \subset R^n$ and $T \equiv (T^0, T^1) \subset R$. The system of equations

$$\dot{x}_i(t) = f_i[x_1(t), x_2(t), \ldots, x_n(t), t], \, i = 1, 2, \ldots, n$$

where $\dot{x}_i(t) \equiv dx_i(t)/dt$, or, in vector notation,

$$\dot{x}(t) = f[x(t), t]$$

is called a **system of n first-order differential equations**. An R^n-valued function $\phi(t)$ defined on a subinterval of T, (t^1, t^2), is called a **solution** of the system if

(i)   The function $\phi(t)$ is continuous on (t^1, t^2).

(ii) $\phi(t) \in X$ for all t in (t^1, t^2).

(iii) $\dot{\phi}(t) = f[\phi(t), t]$ for all t in (t^1, t^2), except possibly for the elements of some countable subset of (t^1, t^2).

Let $\dot{x}(t) = f[x(t), t]$ be a system of n first-order differential equations, which is defined as above. Let (x^0, t^0) be a point in $X \otimes T$ such that $x(t^0) = x^0$. We call (x^0, t^0) the **initial condition** if $\phi(t^0) = x^0$. We denote the solution which satisfies the initial condition by $\phi(t; x^0, t^0)$ or, if there is no danger of confusion, simply by $x(t; x^0, t^0)$, or $x(t; x^0)$, or even $x(t)$. The notation $x(t)$ is clearly sloppy, but it is often used in the engineering literature.

REMARK: The system of differential equations

$$\dot{x}(t) = f[x(t), t]$$

is sometimes contrasted with the following special case:

$$\dot{x}(t) = f[x(t)]$$

In the latter case, t does *not* explicitly appear on the right side of the equations. The former system is called a **nonautonomous system** and the latter is called an **autonomous system**.

REMARK: Let Φ be a continuous real-valued function defined on an open subset of R^{n+2}. Then the equation $\Phi[x(t), \dot{x}(t), \ldots, x^{(n)}(t), t] = 0$, where $x^{(n)}(t) \equiv d^n x(t)/dt^n$, is called an **$n$th-order differential equation**. In particular, if this is written in the form

$$x^{(n)}(t) = \tilde{\Phi}[x(t), \dot{x}(t), \ldots, x^{(n-1)}(t), t]$$

the change of variables, $y_1(t) = x(t)$, $y_2(t) = \dot{x}(t)$, $\ldots$, $y_n(t) = x^{(n-1)}(t)$, allows the equations to be rewritten in the following form, which is a system of n first-order differential equations:

$$\dot{y}_i = y_{i+1}, i = 1, 2, \ldots, n - 1$$
$$\dot{y}_n = \Phi[y_1(t), y_2(t), \ldots, y_n(t), t]$$

Hence it is sufficient to consider the theory of a system of n *first-order differential equations* (although it may not always be convenient).

Definition: Suppose that a system $\dot{x}(t) = f[x(t), t]$ can be written in the form

$$\dot{x}(t) = A(t) \cdot x(t) + u(t)$$

or equivalently

$$\dot{x}_i(t) = \sum_{j=1}^{n} a_{ij}(t) \, x_j(t) + u_i(t), \, i = 1, 2, \ldots, n$$

where $A(t) = [a_{ij}(t)]$; then the system is called **linear**. If $a_{ij}(t) = $ a constant for all t and for all i and j, then it is called a linear system of **constant coefficients**. The function $u(t)$ is called the **forcing function** *or* **control function** of the system, and if $u(t) \equiv 0$, the linear system is said to be **homogeneous**. Unless otherwise specified, we will be concerned primarily with the nonlinear system $\dot{x} = f[x(t), t]$.

The fundamental theorem in the theory of differential equations, as mentioned before, is the Cauchy-Peano theorem, which asserts the existence and uniqueness of the solution. For the purposes of later chapters (especially Chapter 8), we will state this theorem for a system which has a form slightly different from the one described above. We consider the form

$$\dot{x}(t) = f[x(t), u(t), t]$$

where $u(t)$ is a known (or *a priori* given) function (sometimes called a **control function**). It is an m vector-valued function of t [or $u(t) \in R^m$]. We may neglect this function for the purposes of this chapter. We now state the theorem.

Theorem 3.B.1 (Cauchy-Peano):   *Let $\dot{x}(t) = f[x(t), u(t), t]$ be a system of n first-order differential equations, where f is an R^n-valued function on $X \otimes R^m \otimes T$ [X is an open connected subset of R^n and $T = (T^1, T^2) \subset R$]. Suppose that the following conditions hold.*

(A-1)   *The function f is continuous on $X \otimes R^m \otimes T$.*
(A-2)   *The partial derivative $\partial f_i / \partial x_j$ exists and is continuous on $X \otimes R^m \otimes T$ for all i and $j = 1, 2, \ldots, n$.*
(A-3)   *The function $u(t)$ is "piecewise" continuous on T, that is, continuous on T except possibly for a countable number of points in T.*
(A-4)   *$(x^0, t^0) \in X \otimes T$.*

Then *there exists a function $\phi(t)$ from some interval (t^1, t^2) containing t^0 into R^n such that*[2]

   (i)   *The function $\phi(t)$ is continuous on (t^1, t^2) and $\phi(t^0) \in X$.*

   (ii) *$\phi(t^0) = x^0$.*

   (iii) *$\dot{\phi}(t) = f[\phi(t), u(t), t]$ (that is, $\phi(t)$ is a solution of the system).*

   (iv) *If $\psi(t)$ satisfies (i), (ii), and (iii) above on an interval (s^1, s^2), then $\phi(t) = \psi(t)$ on $(t^1, t^2) \cap (s^1, s^2)$ (that is, the solution which satisfies the initial condition is unique).*[3]

REMARKS:

    (i)   For the proof of this theorem, see Coddington and Levinson [5], chapter 1, or any standard textbook on differential equations.

    (ii) Note that no assumptions are made about the existence and continuity of the partial derivatives $\partial f_i/\partial u_k$.

    (iii) The theorem gives a *local* result, for it establishes the existence of a solution on an interval (t^1, t^2), which can be very small.

    (iv) In the statement of the theorem, R^m can be replaced by any subset of R^m which contains the closure of the range of $u(t)$.

    (v) Assumption (A-2) can be weakened; that is, it can be replaced by the following condition, called the **Lipschitz condition**.[4]

(A-2′)   There exists a constant $k > 0$ such that

$$\| f(x^1, u, t) - f(x^2, u, t) \| < k \| x^1 - x^2 \|$$

for all x^1, $x^2 \in X$ and $t \in T$, where $\| \ \|$ denotes the Euclidian norm.

REMARK: Since the Cauchy-Peano theorem gives only a local result, and since we are primarily concerned with global results in this chapter [that is, the process of $t \to \infty$ presupposes the existence of a unique solution on (t^0, ∞)], this theorem is only a guide for the existence of a solution. The global existence theorem has not been fully established as yet.[5] Henceforth we will often adopt a simple assumption such as the following: "We assume that there exists a unique solution to the system determined by the initial point (x^0, t^0)." This, however, does not diminish the importance of the Cauchy-Peano theorem.

REMARK: In the linear system $\dot{x}(t) = A(t) \cdot x(t) + u(t)$, assumptions (A-1) and (A-2) are clearly satisfied. Let $u(t)$ be continuous and let (x^0, t^0) be a point in $X \otimes T$. Then we can show that the unique solution which satisfies the initial condition exists and is such that (t^1, t^2) in the above theorem may be replaced by the whole domain of t, that is, T. In other words, for the linear case, the existence theorem gives a *global* result.

We will now discuss the stability of a system of n first-order differential equations, $\dot{x}(t) = f[x(t), t]$, as defined above.

Definition: A point $\hat{x} \in X$ in the above system of differential equations is called an **equilibrium point (state)** if $f(\hat{x}, t) = 0$ for all t. In the autonomous system, $\hat{x}$ is called an **equilibrium point** if $f(\hat{x}) = 0$.

We are concerned with the behavior of the solution, $\phi(t; x^0, t^0)$, which satisfies the boundary condition, $\phi(t^0; x^0, t^0) = x^0$ or, in short, $\phi(x^0, t^0) = x^0$. In particular, we are concerned with whether $\phi(t; x^0, t^0) \to \hat{x}$ as $t \to \infty$. There are two important concepts in this connection; one is concerned with the behavior of ϕ when x^0 is "sufficiently" close to $\hat{x}$, and the other is concerned with the behavior of ϕ when x^0 is an arbitrary point in the x-plane. The former is the one required for "local stability" and the latter is the one required for "global stability."

We should also note that the solution path $\phi(t; x^0, t^0)$ depends on t^0 as well as on x^0. Here we are concerned with the behavior of ϕ, regardless of the value of t^0; thus, for example, we can pick an arbitrary value of t^0, such as $t^0 = 0$. Hence our definition of stability is now stated in a form which is independent of the value of t^0.

Definition: An equilibrium state $\hat{x}$ is called **globally stable**, if $\phi(t; x^0, t^0) \rightarrow \hat{x}$ as $t \rightarrow \infty$ regardless of the value of (x^0, t^0). Or, more precisely, for any $\epsilon > 0$, there exists a $\bar{t}$ such that $\| \phi(t; x^0, t^0) - \hat{x} \| \leq \epsilon$ for all $t \geq t^0 + \bar{t}$, where $\| x^0 \| \leq \delta$ and $\delta > 0$ can be arbitrarily large. (Note that $\bar{t}$ in the above definition depends on ϵ but not on x^0 and t^0.)

Definition: An equilibrium state $\hat{x}$ is called **locally stable** if there exists a closed ball $B_\delta(\hat{x})$ about $\hat{x}$ with radius $\delta > 0$ such that $x^0 \in B_\delta(\hat{x})$ implies $\phi(t; x^0, t^0) \rightarrow \hat{x}$ as $t \rightarrow \infty$. More precisely, for any $\epsilon > 0$ there exists a $\delta(\epsilon)$ (that is, δ depends on ϵ) and a $\bar{t}(\epsilon, x^0)$ (that is, $\bar{t}$ depends on ϵ and x^0) such that $\| x^0 - \hat{x} \| \leq \delta$ implies $\| \phi(t; x^0, t^0) - \hat{x} \| \leq \epsilon$ for all $t \geq t^0 + \bar{t}$. (Note that in the above definition, $\bar{t}$ does not depend on t^0 although it depends on ϵ and x^0.)

> *REMARK*: In the above definitions of global and local stability, $\bar{t}$ may depend on t^0 and x^0, and δ may depend on t^0 as well as on ϵ. In order to discuss this, a more complete exposition of the stability concepts is necessary. We postpone this task to Section H of this chapter where, among other things, we will discuss how the above concepts are related to the concepts called *"uniform* global stability" and *"uniform* local stability." Since such a discussion will be confined solely to Section H, the reader need not worry about it here.

> *REMARK*: An equilibrium state may *not* be unique. In other words, there may exist many values of x such that $f(x, t) = 0$ for all t. The above definition of global stability is much too strong in this case, for it requires that the solution $\phi(t; x^0, t^0)$ go to a particular equilibrium state regardless of the initial point x^0. When there are multiple equilibria (each of which may or may not be isolated from the others), and if the solution $\phi(t; x^0, t^0)$ converges to some equilibrium point, then we may say that the **system is globally stable**. If every limit point of $\phi(t; x^0, t^0)$, as $t \rightarrow \infty$, is an equilibrium,[6] then the system is said to be **quasi-stable**. This concept was studied by Uzawa [8]. If the system is globally stable, then it is quasi-stable. The converse does not necessarily hold. However, if all the equilibrium points are distinct from each

other, then the quasi-stability of the system implies the global stability of the system.[7]

The following simple example may be useful to clarify some of the above concepts.

EXAMPLE: $\dot{x}(t) = -2x(t)$, $t \in R$, $x \in R$, and $x(t^0) = x^0$

Clearly $\hat{x} \equiv 0$ (for all t) is an "equilibrium state" of this equation. It is easy to see that this solution is unique. The solution of this differential equation is obtained as

$$\phi(t; x^0, t^0) = x^0 e^{-2(t-t^0)}$$

Clearly, $\phi(t; x^0, t^0) \to 0 \ (=\hat{x})$ as $t \to \infty$ *regardless* of the initial value, (x^0, t^0). In other words, the equilibrium point of the above differential equation is unique and globally stable. In general, given $\dot{x}(t) = a x(t), t \in R$, $x \in R$, and $x(t^0) = x^0$, $\hat{x} = 0$ is a unique equilibrium state. It can easily be seen that $\hat{x} = 0$ is globally stable if and only if $a < 0$.

A diagrammatical device is often useful to ascertain the stability property of an equilibrium state when the dimension of $x(t)$ is small (say, 1 or 2). To illustrate this, consider the following example:

EXAMPLE: $\dot{x}(t) = -\frac{1}{5}x^3(t)$, $t \in R$, $x \in R$, $x(t^0) = x^0$

Clearly, $\hat{x} = 0$ (for all t) is an equilibrium state. The above differential equation is illustrated in Figure 3.4. From the diagram it is clear that if $x > 0$, $\dot{x} < 0$ so that $x(t)$ decreases as t increases, and that if $x < 0$, $\dot{x} > 0$ so that $x(t)$ increases as t increases. Hence in either case $x(t) \to 0$ as $t \to \infty$, regardless of the initial position of x [or more precisely, regardless of the initial value, (x^0, t^0)]. It is also easy to see from the diagram that $\hat{x} = 0$ is a unique equilibrium state. The diagrammatical proof of a slightly more complicated case will be illustrated in Section D in connection with the

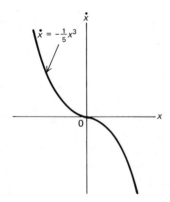

Figure 3.4.   An Illustration of Simple Proof of Stability.

proof of global stability of a competitive equilibrium for the three-commodity case. Such a diagrammatical technique is in general referred to as the **phase diagram technique**. Note that in this technique no explicit solution of the differential equation is sought.

Suppose that we now have the following homogeneous linear system with constant coefficients:

$$\dot{x}(t) = A \cdot x(t), \text{ where } A = [a_{ij}] \text{ is an } n \times n \text{ matrix}$$

Clearly $\hat{x} = 0$ is an equilibrium state and it is unique if A is nonsingular. From the remark on the Cauchy-Peano existence theorem, we know that there exists a unique solution. In fact, an explicit solution to the above system can easily be obtained. We state it as a theorem.

Theorem 3.B.2:   *Let* $\dot{x}(t) = A \cdot x(t)$ *be a given system of differential equations with* $x(0) = x^0$. *Then*

$$\phi(t; x^0) = e^{At} \cdot x^0$$

where[8]

$$e^{At} \equiv \sum_{k=0}^{\infty} A^k \frac{t^k}{k!}$$

(so that e^{At} *is an* $n \times n$ *matrix).*

REMARK: For an excellent but simple discussion of the explicit solution of the linear system, see, for example, Athans and Falb [1], pp. 125–149.

Suppose A has n *distinct real* eigenvalues,[9] $\lambda_1, \lambda_2, \ldots, \lambda_n$; then we know from the elementary theory of linear algebra that there exists a nonsingular $n \times n$ matrix P such that $P A P^{-1}$ is a diagonal matrix where the diagonal elements are $\lambda_1, \lambda_2, \ldots, \lambda_n$. Using this property we can easily rewrite the solution of the above linear system as follows.

Corollary: *If A, in the above system, has n distinct eigenvalues* $\lambda_1, \lambda_2, \ldots, \lambda_n$, *then the solution can be written as*

$$\phi(t; x^0) = P e^{\Lambda t} P^{-1} \cdot x^0$$

where P is an $n \times n$ *nonsingular matrix and*[10]

$$e^{\Lambda t} \equiv \begin{bmatrix} e^{\lambda_1 t} & 0 & 0 & \cdots & 0 \\ 0 & e^{\lambda_2 t} & 0 & \cdots & 0 \\ \cdots & \cdots & \cdots & \cdots & \cdots \\ 0 & 0 & \cdots & \cdots & e^{\lambda_n t} \end{bmatrix}$$

Hence in this case we can see that the stability property depends crucially on the eigenvalues, the λ_i's. In particular, if the λ_i's are all negative, then clearly $e^{\Lambda t} \to 0$ as $t \to \infty$. Hence the system is globally stable. In general, we have the following theorem, which holds even when the eigenvalues are not all distinct.

Theorem 3.B.3:   *Let $\dot{x}(t) = A \cdot x(t)$ be a given system of differential equations. The equilibrium point $\hat{x} = 0$ is globally stable if and only if the real part of any eigenvalue of A is negative.*

PROOF: See, for example, Bellman [2], [3], Coddington and Levinson [5], Birkoff and Rota [4], and Gantmacher [6].

REMARK: If a system is given in the form $\dot{x}(t) = A \cdot [x(t) - \hat{x}]$, then, clearly, $x(t) = \hat{x}$ is an equilibrium state and it is unique if A is nonsingular. Carrying out the change of variable $y(t) \equiv x(t) - \hat{x}$, we find that $\hat{y} = 0$ is the unique equilibrium state for $\dot{y}(t) = A \cdot y(t)$, and the above theorem can be applied immediately.

REMARK: If A is negative definite, then from the elementary theory of linear algebra, we know that all its eigenvalues are negative; hence the system is stable.

Given an arbitrary $n \times n$ matrix, we now wish to know whether all the eigenvalues of A have negative real parts. There is a famous theorem for this.

Theorem 3.B.4 (Routh-Hurwitz):   *A necessary and sufficient condition that all the roots of the equation*

$$a_0 \lambda^n + a_1 \lambda^{n-1} + \cdots + a_n = 0$$

with real coefficients have negative real parts is that the following conditions hold:

$$a_1 > 0, \quad \begin{vmatrix} a_1 & a_0 \\ a_3 & a_2 \end{vmatrix} > 0, \quad \begin{vmatrix} a_1 & a_0 & 0 \\ a_3 & a_2 & a_1 \\ a_5 & a_4 & a_3 \end{vmatrix} > 0, \cdots, \quad \begin{vmatrix} a_1 & a_0 & 0 & 0 & \cdots & \cdots \\ a_3 & a_2 & a_1 & a_0 & \cdots & \cdots \\ a_5 & a_4 & a_3 & a_2 & \cdots & \cdots \\ \cdots & \cdots & \cdots & \cdots & \cdots & \cdots \\ \cdots & \cdots & \cdots & \cdots & \cdots & \cdots \\ 0 & 0 & 0 & 0 & \cdots & a_n \end{vmatrix} > 0$$

Here a_0 is taken to be positive (if $a_0 < 0$, then multiply the equations by -1).

PROOF: See Gantmacher [6], chapter XV.

REMARK: The above condition is known as the **Routh-Hurwitz condition**. Its power lies in the fact that it provides a *necessary and sufficient* condition for stability. However, in actual application, its power is quite weak because of the computations required when n is large. In fact, when $n \geq 4$, the computation usually becomes too tedious.

Let us return to the (autonomous) nonlinear differential equation

$$\dot{x}(t) = f[x(t)]$$

to obtain the local property of the solution path. The standard procedure is to take a Taylor expansion of f about an equilibrium value $\hat{x}$, a point in which $f(\hat{x}) = 0$ (if there exists such a value), and then to disregard the second and higher order terms. Thus we obtain the linear differential equation

$$\dot{x}(t) = A \cdot [x(t) - \hat{x}]$$

where $A \equiv [a_{ij}]$ and $a_{ij} \equiv \partial f_i / \partial x_j$ (evaluated at $x = \hat{x}$) [in other words, $A \equiv f'(\hat{x})$, the Jacobian matrix of f at $\hat{x}$]. We call the linear system obtained in this manner the **linear approximation system**. It is clear that if an equilibrium point in the linear approximation system is (globally) stable, then it is locally stable in the original system. We should note, however, that the converse is *not* necessarily true. In other words, it is possible that an equilibrium point is locally or globally stable in the original system and is not stable in its linear approximation system. This is due to the fact that higher order terms may act favorably for stability. Consider the following example.

> **EXAMPLE:** $\dot{x}(t) = ax(t) - x(t)^3$. Clearly $\hat{x} = 0$ is an equilibrium point. If $a = 0$, $\hat{x} = 0$ is a globally stable equilibrium point. Its linear approximation system is $\dot{x}(t) = 0$ (when $a = 0$). Hence $\hat{x} = 0$ is *not* stable—the solution starting from an initial point x^0 always stays at x^0. In order to stress this fact, we call $\hat{x}$, an equilibrium point which is stable in the linear approximation system, **linear approximation stable**.[11] This point is often confused in the literature which applies Samuelson's "correspondence principle" to the comparative statics problem. Although the Routh-Hurwitz condition provides a necessary and sufficient condition for the stability of the linear approximation system, it does *not* necessarily provide a necessary condition for the (local) stability of the original (nonlinear) system owing to the reason discussed above. Hence the Routh-Hurwitz condition for the linear approximation system cannot, in general, be utilized in obtaining comparative statics results.

FOOTNOTES

1. Observe also that the unknown function here, $x(t)$, contains only one independent variable, t. This is the defining characteristic of an **ordinary** differential equation. If the unknown function contains more than one independent variable, then we have a "partial differential equation." Here we are solely concerned with ordinary differential equations.

2. Note that the interval (t^1, t^2) on which the solution $\phi(t)$ is defined is a subset of T. In other words, $\phi(t)$ may not be defined on the entire interval T. For example, consider $\dot{x} = x^2$, $x \in R$. Clearly $\phi(t) = -1/t$ is a solution which passes through $\phi(1) = -1$. However, $\phi(t)$ is not defined at $t = 0$. The existence theorem here asserts only the existence of $\phi(t)$ in a neighborhood of t^0, that is, (t^1, t^2).

3. When some of the assumptions of the theorem are violated, the solution which satisfies the initial condition, even if it exists, may not be unique. For example, consider $\dot{x} = \sqrt{x}$ if $x \geq 0$, and $\dot{x} = 0$ if $x < 0$, with $x \in R$ and $\phi(0) = 0$. Clearly $[\phi(t) = 0$ for all $t, -\infty < t < \infty]$ is a solution which satisfies $\phi(0) = 0$. However, $[\phi(t) = t^2/4$, if $t \geq 0$, and $\phi(t) = 0$, if $t \leq 0]$ is also a solution which satisfies $\phi(0) = 0$. Here (A-2) is violated at $x = 0$. Given the initial point (t^0, x^0), the problem of finding the solution $\phi(t)$, defined on (t^1, t^2), of a given system of differential equations which satisfies $\phi(t^0) = x^0$, is called the **initial value problem**.

4. It can be shown that if $f_i(x, t)$ has continuous partial derivatives, it satisfies the Lipschitz condition. But $f(x) = \sqrt{x}$ (where $x \in R$, $x \geq 0$) does not satisfy even the Lipschitz condition at $x = 0$. To see this, observe that $|\sqrt{x} - \sqrt{y}| = |x - y|/(\sqrt{x} + \sqrt{y})$ where $x \neq 0$ and $y \neq 0$. When x and y approach 0, $1/(\sqrt{x} + \sqrt{y})$ will increase indefinitely. In general, the Lipschitz condition [or (A-2)] is crucial to guarantee the uniqueness of the solution which satisfies $\phi(t^0) = x^0$. If f is not Lipschitzian [hence (A-2) is violated] but if all the other assumptions of Theorem 3.B.1 are satisfied, then all the conclusions of Theorem 3.B.1 follow except (iv); that is, the existence of $\phi(t)$ is guaranteed but not its uniqueness. Here the continuity of f is the crucial assumption for existence.

5. However, in specific cases, global existence (and uniqueness) can be ascertained. The procedure is as follows. Suppose that the solution $\phi(t)$ exists. Suppose f is bounded as well as continuous in $X \otimes T$. Then we can show that $\phi(t^1 + 0)$ [that is, $\lim \phi(t)$ as $t \rightarrow t^1$ with $t \geq t^1$] and $\phi(t^2 - 0)$ [that is, $\lim \phi(t)$ as $t \rightarrow t^2$ with $t \leq t^2$] both exist. Suppose $\phi(t^1 + 0)$ and $\phi(t^2 - 0)$ are in X; then the solution exists in neighborhoods of $(t^1 + 0)$ and $(t^2 - 0)$ by Theorem 3.B.1. In this way the solution can be "continued" or extended to an interval which is larger than (t^1, t^2) and, therefore, we can prove the existence (and the uniqueness) of solutions for the interval $(0, \infty)$ under certain assumptions. For the discussion of the "continuation" of solutions, the reader is referred to any standard textbook on differential equations.

6. In other words, if for some sequence t_q, $q = 1, 2, \ldots$, such that $t_q \rightarrow \infty$, $\lim \phi(t_q, x^0, t^0)$ as $q \rightarrow \infty$ exists, then $\lim \phi(t_q, x^0, t^0)$ as $q \rightarrow \infty$ is an equilibrium. As Uzawa ([8], p. 619) has shown, the concept of quasi-equilibrium in essence means that the "distance" between the set of equilibrium points and $\phi(t, x^0, t^0)$ converges to zero as $t \rightarrow \infty$.

7. In other words, whether or not equilibrium points are isolated is crucial. As an example of a system that is quasi-stable but not (globally) stable, consider the case in which $\phi(t, x^0, t^0)$ spirals toward the unit circle as t increases but approaches no single point on the unit circle, while the set of equilibrium points is the unit circle. See Section H of this chapter.

8. Let z be a scalar (real or complex). Then the exponential function e^z can be defined by $e^z \equiv \sum_{k=0}^{\infty} z^k/k!$; hence the definition of e^{At} below conforms with this definition. When z is a real number, then the above definition of e^z can be obtained as a consequence of the usual definition of e^z by using the Taylor expansion theorem.

9. Readers who are not familiar with the concept of eigenvalues are referred to the beginning of Section B, Chapter 4 (or any standard textbooks on matrix algebra).

10. Notice that the definition of $e^{\Lambda t}$ conforms with the above definition of e^{At}.
11. In the above example, $\dot{x} = -x^3$ (with $a = 0$), $\hat{x} = 0$ is *not* linear approximation stable.

REFERENCES

1. Athans, M., and Falb, P. L., *Optimal Control*, New York, McGraw-Hill, 1966, esp. chap. 3.
2. Bellman, R., *Stability Theory of Differential Equations*, New York, McGraw-Hill, 1953.
3. ———, *Introduction to Matrix Analysis*, New York, McGraw-Hill, 1960.
4. Birkoff, G., and Rota, C. C., *Ordinary Differential Equations*, Boston, Ginn & Co., 1962.
5. Coddington, E. A., and Levinson, N., *Theory of Ordinary Differential Equations*, New York, McGraw-Hill, 1955.
6. Gantmacher, F. R., *The Theory of Matrices*, Vol. II, New York, Chelsea Publishing Co., 1959 (tr. from Russian).
7. Samuelson, P. A., *Foundations of Economic Analysis*, Cambridge, Mass., Harvard University Press, 1947.
8. Uzawa, H., "The Stability of Dynamic Processes," *Econometrica*, 29, October 1961.

Section C

THE STABILITY OF COMPETITIVE EQUILIBRIUM— THE HISTORICAL BACKGROUND

We assume here that a competitive equilibrium is described by the following system of equations:

$$f_i(p_1, p_2, \ldots, p_n) = 0, \, i = 1, 2, \ldots, n \, [\text{or} f(p) = 0]$$

where p_i denotes the price of the ith commodity and f_i denotes the excess demand for the ith commodity,[1] and we consider its stability. The fundamental assumption in the stability analysis of a competitive market is that an excess demand for the ith commodity raises the price of the ith commodity and that an excess supply of the ith commodity lowers the price of the ith commodity. One may question this traditionally accepted assumption of the competitive market, but here we will proceed on the basis of this assumption. Note that if the market for a certain commodity is isolated from all the other markets, the stability analysis is not too difficult and its solution has already been indicated in Section A. The complications arise when we have repercussions among a number of markets.

The first satisfactory treatment of the stability of a competitive equilibrium was done by Léon Walras [18]. He solved this problem fairly completely for the two-commodity exchange economy. Hicks [7] extended the scope of the analysis to a multicommodity economy. For the multimarket case, we suspect naturally that repercussions among the various markets will complicate the analysis a great deal. In order to deal with this problem, following Hicks, we distinguish two concepts of "stability." An equilibrium in the market for the jth commodity (henceforth the jth market) is said to be **imperfectly stable** if the markets for all the other commodities are held in equilibrium (with possible adjustment of the prices of these goods) and there is stability in the jth market. Let $\hat{p}$ be an **equilibrium price vector** [that is, $f(\hat{p}) = 0$] (which is assumed to exist), and suppose that the price vector p deviates from this $\hat{p}$. In order to avoid complicating the discussion, let us assume that p lies in a certain small neighborhood of $\hat{p}$ (by this convention we would like to avoid for the time being the problem of multiple equilibria and local vs. global stability). Then the equilibrium in the jth market is said to be **imperfectly stable** if

   (i) $f_i(p) = 0$ for all $i \neq j$,

and

   (ii) $p_j > \hat{p}_j$ implies $f_j(p) < 0$ and $p_j < \hat{p}_j$ implies $f_j(p) > 0$.

The equilibrium in the jth market is said to have **perfect stability** if the above imperfect stability holds regardless of the number of the other markets adjusted to equilibrium, or more specifically, whether or not other prices are fixed or adjusted so as to maintain equilibrium in the relevant market [that is, for $i \neq j$, either $f_i(p) = 0$ or $p_i = $ constant]. If the equilibrium in every market in the economy is imperfectly stable (say, at $\hat{p}$), then Hicks states that the equilibrium of the *system* is **imperfectly stable**. If the equilibrium in every market in the economy is perfectly stable, then Hicks states that the equilibrium of the *system* is **perfectly stable**.

The Hicksian method of stability analysis is essentially that of comparative statics. By differentiating the equilibrium system $f(p) = 0$ at a certain equilibrium—say, $\hat{p}$—with respect to p_j and applying the definitions of perfect stability and imperfect stability (then repeating this for all $j = 1, 2, \ldots, n$), Hicks obtained the following condition for perfect stability for the equilibrium of the system:

$$a_{ii} < 0, \quad \begin{vmatrix} a_{ii} & a_{ij} \\ a_{ji} & a_{jj} \end{vmatrix} > 0, \quad \begin{vmatrix} a_{ii} & a_{ij} & a_{ik} \\ a_{ji} & a_{jj} & a_{jk} \\ a_{ki} & a_{kj} & a_{kk} \end{vmatrix} < 0, \ldots$$

for all $i, j, k, \ldots$, of the index set $\{1, 2, \ldots, n\}$. (See Quirk and Saposnik [16], pp. 153–160, as well as Hicks [7].) Here $a_{ij} \equiv \partial f_i / \partial p_j$, evaluated at $\hat{p}$, $i, j = 1, 2, \ldots, n$. It is to be noted that the Walrasian condition for the stability of the two-commodity economy corresponds to the first of the above conditions (that is, $a_{ii} < 0$). When an $n \times n$ matrix $A = [a_{ij}]$ satisfies the above condition, A is said to be **Hicksian**. The Hicksian condition for the imperfect stability was obtained as $\Delta_{ii}/\Delta < 0$, where Δ denotes the determinant of A and Δ_{ii} denotes the co-factor of A at a_{ii}.

The above Hicksian concepts of perfect and imperfect stability (in addition to the assumption of timeless and instantaneous adjustment) clearly have an air of artificiality about them and thus require some further examination. A careful scrutiny of these concepts will reveal that they may in fact have little to do with the stability problem that we are considering. Instead of checking these points, Samuelson [17] proposed a fresh approach to the problem. First, he writes the fundamental assumption of stability analysis as the following system of differential equations:

$$\frac{dp_i(t)}{dt} = k_i f_i [p_1(t), p_2(t), \ldots, p_n(t)], i = 1, 2, \ldots, n$$

Here k_i denotes the **speed of adjustment** of the ith market.[2] The fundamental assumption of stability analysis specifies that k_i is strictly positive. Then stability analysis is reduced to the problem of examining the dynamic system generated by the above system of differential equations. This amounts to examining the stability property of the above system of differential equations. Alternatively, one may also formulate the fundamental assumption of stability analysis in terms of the following system of difference equations:

$$p_i(t+1) - p_i(t) = k_i f_i [p(t)], i = 1, 2, \ldots, n$$

where $k_i > 0$ is the speed of adjustment of the ith market.

Whichever approach one takes, we say that an equilibrium (or, more specifically, an equilibrium price vector $\hat{p}$) is "stable" if the time path of the solution of the dynamic system, starting from an initial point p^0, converges to $\hat{p}$. When this is the case, Samuelson calls the equilibrium **truly dynamically stable**. We can distinguish here between local stability and global stability. Samuelson was mainly concerned with local stability. We may note that either one of the above dynamic systems describes the behavior of the price vector when it is not an equilibrium point. We can thus carry out the stability analysis by examining the stability property of either of the above dynamic systems. Partly because the theory of differential equations is more developed than the theory of difference equations, the later development occurs mostly through the differential equation approach.

This (dynamic) approach by Samuelson is conceptually much more transparent than Hicks's approach in the sense that it properly handles the general equilibrium nature of the stability analysis (that is, the repercussions among various markets). It also has the advantage that it makes clear the dynamic character of the adjustment process toward an equilibrium.

Samuelson then takes a linear approximation of the above system [that is, he takes only the linear terms of the Taylor expansion of $f_i(p)$ about an equilibrium price vector $\hat{p}$]. Noting that $f_i(\hat{p}) = 0$ from the definition of an equilibrium, we easily obtain

$$\frac{dp_i(t)}{dt} = \sum_{j=1}^{n} k_i a_{ij} [p_j(t) - \hat{p}_j], \ i = 1, 2, \ldots, n$$

where $a_{ij} \equiv \partial f_i / \partial p_j$ evaluated at $p = \hat{p}$; or, in vector notation

$$\frac{dp(t)}{dt} = K \cdot A \cdot [p(t) - \hat{p}]$$

where $A = [a_{ij}]$, and K is a diagonal matrix whose diagonal elements are k_i and whose nondiagonal elements are all zero. Then the stability analysis of a competitive market is reduced to the stability analysis of the above system of linear differential equations. We now recall the discussion of Section B, that is, a necessary and sufficient condition for stability is that all the eigenvalues of A have negative real parts. In order to establish this property for matrix A, we refer to the Routh-Hurwitz condition (Theorem 3.B.4).[3] We recall that stability in the above linear approximation system (that is, "linear approximation stability") implies local stability in the original system and that the converse of this statement is not necessarily true. In other words, an equilibrium point can be locally stable in the original system but it may not be stable in the linear approximation system. We note that as long as we deal with the stability of the linear approximation system, we can also use the theory of linear differential equations.

Samuelson then considers the relation between the Hicksian stability (the conditions of which were discussed above) and the true dynamic stability (in the linear approximation system). He concludes that (1) for the two-commodity case, the two conditions are equivalent, (2) for the three-commodity case, the Hicks condition for perfect stability (that is, that matrix A be Hicksian) is sufficient for true dynamic stability, and (3) for the n-commodity case ($n > 3$), the Hicks condition for perfect stability is neither necessary nor sufficient for true dynamic stability. This relation between Hicks' condition for perfect stability and dynamic stability is explained in more detail in the literature (for example, Samuelson [17], Lange [8], Metzler [10], and Morishima [11]), with the following results.

(i)   If A is symmetric (that is, $a_{ij} = a_{ji}$) and if $k_i = 1$ for all i, the Hicksian condition is equivalent to the dynamic condition (Samuelson and Lange). This can be seen easily by noting that if A is symmetric and Hicksian, then it is negative definite, which implies that the real parts of the eigenvalues of A are always negative.

(ii) If A is **quasi-negative definite** [that is, $(A + A')/2$ is negative definite where A' is the transpose of A], and if $k_i = 1$ for all i, then Hicks' condition is equivalent to the dynamic condition (Samuelson).

(iii) If the dynamic process is stable *regardless of* the values of the speeds of adjustment, then Hicks' condition must be satisfied (Metzler).

(iv) If A has all its nondiagonal elements positive ($a_{ij} > 0$, $i \neq j$), Hicks' condition is equivalent to the dynamic condition (Metzler).

In order to understand the meaning of statement (iv), let us consider the model of pure exchange. Let x_i denote the total demand for the ith commodity in the economy and $\bar{x}_i$ the total holdings of the ith commodity in the economy. We note that x_i is the sum of each consumer's demand for the ith commodity. Thus if x_{ik} denotes the demand for the ith commodity by the kth consumer and if there are m consumers in the economy,

$$x_i \equiv \sum_{k=1}^{m} x_{ik}$$

The excess demand function $f_i(p)$ may then be written as

$$f_i(p) \equiv x_i(p) - \bar{x}_i, \quad i = 1, 2, \dots, n$$

Then

$$a_{ij} \equiv \frac{\partial f_i}{\partial p_j} = \frac{\partial x_i}{\partial p_j} = \sum_{k=1}^{m} \frac{\partial x_{ik}}{\partial p_j}$$

(evaluated at $\hat{p}$). Hence $a_{ij} > 0$ if $\partial x_{ik}/\partial p_j > 0$ for all $k = 1, 2, \dots, m$. This means that for each consumer the demand for the ith commodity rises when the price of the jth commodity rises. There should be no confusion between this concept of substitutability and ordinary (net) substitutability. The latter is concerned with the (positive) effect of a change in the price of commodity j on the demand for commodity i *when real income is properly compensated*. Such a qualification of income compensation is absent in "gross substitutability." That is, when $\partial x_{ik}/\partial p_j > 0$ holds (for all p), we say that commodity i is a **gross substitute** of j for Mr. k with respect to the change in the price of j ($i \neq j$). Hence $a_{ij} > 0$ for all i and j ($i \neq j$) is guaranteed if all the commodities are gross substitutes for each other for every consumer in this pure exchange economy. We call this case, $a_{ij} > 0$ for all i and j ($i \neq j$), the **gross substitute** case.

This gross substitute case attracted the attention of many economists, and in 1958 (that is, about ten years after the publication of Samuelson's *Foundations* [17]), Hahn [6], Negishi [12], and Arrow and Hurwicz [2] independently proved that if $a_{ij} > 0$, $i \neq j$, then the equilibrium point is stable in the linear approximation system; hence it is locally stable in the original system. Note that in statement (iv) above, Hicks' condition for perfect stability is stated as a necessary and sufficient condition for dynamic stability. What Arrow and Hurwicz, Negishi, and Hahn proved is that Hicks' condition can be totally dispensed with in the gross substitute case. The novelty of their proof is that they take full advantage of the implications of the economic assumptions underlying the competitive model, such as Walras' Law, and the zero homogeneity of the individual's demand function. In 1959 Arrow, Block, and Hurwicz [1] finally proved that the original system is *globally* stable if all commodities are gross substitutes for each other and put an end to one of the major periods in the history of the stability of competitive markets. We may simply list some other major points considered after Samuelson [17].[4]

(i) The nonnegativity of the price vector has been explicitly considered (Nikaido and Uzawa [15]).

(ii) Expectation has been introduced into the model (Enthoven and Arrow [5] for the extrapolative expectation and Arrow and Nerlove [4] for adaptive expectation).

(iii) Non-*tâtonnement* processes have been introduced and examined.[5]

(iv) Some attempts to relax the gross substitutability assumption have been made. In the course of such attempts, important examples for unstable equilibrium have been discovered by Scarf (see Section F), which in turn cast dark shadows on the scope of the stability of competitive markets and the method of finding an equilibrium by such an adjustment mechanism of the markets.[6]

Finally, two remarks are in order. In the course of the proof, it was noticed that the speed of adjustment, k_i, is immaterial for the stability property. Arrow and Hurwicz [2] and Arrow, Block, and Hurwicz [1] noted that by choosing the units of measurement properly, we can choose $k_i = 1$ for all i and for all t.[7] If this is the case, our basic dynamic adjustment system is simplified as

$$\frac{dp_i(t)}{dt} = f_i[p_1(t), p_2(t), \ldots, p_n(t)], \ i = 1, 2, \ldots, n$$

or

$$\frac{dp(t)}{dt} = f[p(t)]$$

The second remark is concerned with the equilibrium state. In the system $f(p) = 0$, which defines an equilibrium state, we note that one commodity can be taken as the *numéraire* (for example, $p_0 = 1$). If every individual's budget relation holds with equality (that is, if everybody spends all his "income"—as a result of nonsatiation and the like), then we have the relation known as **Walras' Law**. That is, the price-weighted sum of *all* the excess demands is identically equal to zero. This relation is supposed to hold whether the economy is in equilibrium or not. When one of the prices is taken to be the *numéraire* and one of the equations in the system is dropped because of Walras' Law, we say that the system is a **normalized system**; otherwise it is a **nonnormalized system**. That one commodity can be chosen as *numéraire* depends on the homogeneity assumption.[8] For the nonnormalized system, none of the commodities is designated as *numéraire*, although the homogeneity of the excess demand functions is usually assumed to be still binding on the system. The Hicksian discussion on stability is based on the normalized system, while dynamic stability can be (and has been) discussed under either the normalized or the nonnormalized system. Interestingly enough, the proof of the dynamic stability of the normalized system is in general different from that of the nonnormalized system, and the stability relation between the two systems has not been studied thoroughly.

FOOTNOTES

1. Let there be $n + 1$ commodities. Assuming homogeneity, choose one commodity (say the 0-th commodity) as the *numéraire*. By Walras' Law one equation can be dropped and the above system of n equations describes the equilibrium. Recall our discussion in Section E of Chapter 2.

2. In a dynamic form, this means that the price of the ith commodity rises if its demand exceeds its supply and falls in the opposite case, the so-called "law of supply and demand."

3. As long as we are talking about linear approximation stability, the difference equation approach is as good as the differential equation approach. For the analysis of the stability of a nonlinear system, the differential equation approach is often more convenient. The condition which corresponds to the Routh-Hurwitz condition in this case is known as the **Schur-Cohn condition**. See Samuelson [17], for example.

4. For an excellent survey article on the stability problem of competitive equilibrium, see Negishi [13]. See also Quirk and Saposnik [16], especially chapter 5.

5. For the survey of this discussion, see Negishi [13] and Section G of this chapter.

6. In addition to these attempts, which deepened our understanding of the stability theory of competitive markets, important mathematical techniques were made known to economists and added to the list of standard tools of economic analysis. For example, the mathematical theory of the Leontief's input-output analysis was found to be relevant to stability analysis, resulting in the inclusion of the theory of "dominant diagonal matrices" in our box of standard tools (see Chapter 4). Also the importance of the Liapunov "second method" in economic analysis was recognized and added to our standard tools.

7. As Parry Lewis pointed out, this convention of setting $k_i = 1$ for all i "by a suitable choice of units of commodities" implies that these commodities have to be measured in peculiar units. Although this does not seem to affect the analysis by Arrow and Hurwicz [2] and Arrow, Block, and Hurwicz [1] with gross substitutability, serious confusions may occur unless these units of measurement and dimensions are kept carefully in mind. See J. P. Lewis, "Dimensions in Economic Theory," *Manchester School of Economic and Social Studies*, 31, September 1963. Moreover, we may also note that while the equilibrium may become stable for one set of speeds of adjustment, it may remain unstable for another set of speeds of adjustment. To illustrate this point, consider the case in which each market is stable when the repercussions from the other markets are ignored, but the equilibrium of the system as a whole is unstable for one set of speeds of adjustment; then, by making speeds of adjustment large enough in a sufficiently large number of markets, we may actually obtain the stability of the equilibrium of the system as a whole.

8. If there are n (instead of $n + 1$) commodities in the economy, $dp_i/dt = f_i(p_1, p_2, \ldots, p_n)$, $i = 1, 2, \ldots, n$, describes the adjustment mechanism of the *non*normalized system. Here none of the commodities is taken to be a *numéraire*.

REFERENCES

1. Arrow, K. J., Block, H. D., and Hurwicz, L., "On the Stability of the Competitive Equilibrium, II," *Econometrica*, 27, January 1959.

2. Arrow, K. J., and Hurwicz, L., "On the Stability of the Competitive Equilibrium, I," *Econometrica*, 26, October 1958.

3. ——, and ——, "Decentralization and Computation in Resource Allocation," in *Essays in Economics and Econometrics*, ed. by Phouts, Chapel Hill, N. C., University of North Carolina Press, 1960.

4. Arrow, K. J., and Nerlove, M., "A Note on Expectation and Stability," *Econometrica*, 26, April 1958.

5. Enthoven, A. C., and Arrow, K. J., "A Theorem on Expectations and the Stability of Equilibrium," *Econometrica*, 24, July 1956.

6. Hahn, F. H., "Gross Substitutes and the Dynamic Stability of General Equilibrium," *Econometrica*, 26, January 1958.

7. Hicks, J. R., *Value and Capital*, 2nd ed., Oxford, Clarendon Press, 1946.

8. Lange, O., *Price Flexibility and Employment*, Bloomington, Ind., Principia Press, 1944.

9. McKenzie, L. W., "Stability of Equilibrium and the Value of Positive Excess Demand," *Econometrica*, 28, July 1960.

10. Metzler, L., "Stability of Multiple Markets: The Hicks Conditions," *Econometrica*, 13, October 1945.

11. Morishima, M., "Notes on the Theory of Stability of Multiple Exchange," *Review of Economic Studies*, XXIV, 1957.

12. Negishi, T., "A Note on the Stability of an Economy Where All Goods Are Gross Substitutes," *Econometrica*, 26, July 1958.

13. ——, "The Stability of a Competitive Economy: A Survey Article," *Econometrica*, 30, October 1962.

14. ——, *The Theory of Price and Resource Allocation*, Tokyo, Toyokeizai Shimpo-sha, 1965 (in Japanese).

15. Nikaido, H., and Uzawa, H., "Stability and Nonnegativity in Walrasian Tâtonnement Process," *International Economic Review*, 1, January 1960.

16. Quirk, J., and Saposnik, R., *Introduction to General Equilibrium Theory and Welfare Economics*, New York, McGraw-Hill, 1968.

17. Samuelson, P. A., *Foundations of Economic Analysis*, Cambridge, Mass., Harvard University Press, 1947.

18. Walras, L., *Elements of Pure Economics*, 4th ed., tr. by Jaffé, London, George Allen & Unwin, 1954.

For a more complete bibliography on this topic, see Negishi [13].

A PROOF OF GLOBAL STABILITY FOR THE THREE-COMMODITY CASE (WITH GROSS SUBSTITUTABILITY)— AN ILLUSTRATION OF THE PHASE DIAGRAM TECHNIQUE

Here we consider a model of a competitive economy in which there are only three commodities. We prove the global stability of the system using a diagrammatical technique called the **phase diagram technique**. Since this technique has many applications in other branches of economics, such as macro-economics and growth theory, the reader will benefit by becoming familiar with its use. This technique was first introduced to economics by Marshall [3] and adapted by Hicks [2] to the stability analysis of a competitive market. But its first rigorous use with complete recognition of the assumptions made in its formulation was by Arrow and Hurwicz [1] in proving the global stability of the three-commodity economy. Our exposition is based chiefly on this paper. The discussion here will illustrate the use of the phase diagram technique as well as a proof of global stability, especially its use of economic assumptions involved in the system.

Let $f_i(p)$, where $p = (p_1, p_2, p_3)$, denote the excess demand function of the ith commodity. Consider the model of a competitive equilibrium described by

$$f_i(\hat{p}_1, \hat{p}_2, \hat{p}_3) = 0, \quad i = 1, 2, 3$$

or, in short, $f_i(\hat{p}) = 0$, $i = 1, 2, 3$. We assume

(A-1) (Gross substitutability) $f_{ij}(p) > 0$ for all values of p, $i \neq j$, $i, j = 1, 2, 3$.[1]
(A-2) (Homogeneity) $f_i(p)$, $i = 1, 2, 3$, are positively homogenous of degree 0 [that is, $f_i(\alpha p) = f_i(p)$ for all $\alpha > 0$, $\alpha \in R$].
(A-3) (Walras' Law) $\sum_{i=1}^{3} p_i f_i(p) = 0$ for all p.
(A-4) $p_i > 0$, $i = 1, 2, 3$.
(A-5) There exists at least one $\hat{p}$ such that $f_i(\hat{p}) = 0$ for all i.[2]

In view of (A-2), we henceforth normalize the price vector p such that $p_3 = 1$ always.[3]
Our dynamic adjustment process is described by

$$\dot{p}_i = k_i f_i(p_1, p_2, p_3), k_i > 0, i = 1, 2$$

Note that $f_1 = 0$ and $f_2 = 0$ imply $f_3 = 0$ from Walras' Law (that is, if the first two markets are brought into equilibrium, the third market is automatically brought into equilibrium). Hence it suffices to consider the adjustment process of the first two markets for the stability analysis.

Our problem is to find out whether or not the solution of the above system of differential equations, $p(t; p^0, 0)$, or simply $p(t; p^0)$, converges to the equilibrium price vector $\hat{p}$, where $\hat{p}$ is defined by $f_i(\hat{p}) = 0$, $i = 1, 2, 3$. The phase diagram technique is a device which shows the time path of $p(t; p^0)$ *without* explicitly solving the differential equations. The technique (for the present case) is essentially based on the fact that each $[\dot{p}_i = 0]$ curve or $[f_i(p) = 0]$ curve ($i = 1, 2,$) [that is, the locus of (p_1, p_2) such that $\dot{p}_i = k_i f_i(p) = 0$] divides the entire $(p_1\text{-}p_2)$-plane into two regions: the region in which $\dot{p}_i > 0$ and the region in which $\dot{p}_i < 0$, where $i = 1, 2$. Recall in this connection that $p_3 = 1$ always. Hence we can omit any consideration of p_3 or $\dot{p}_3$. This enables us to consider the problem in the two-dimensional plane.

First we ascertain the shape of the $[f_i(p) = 0]$ curves ($i = 1, 2$). We assert that they are both upward sloping and that they intersect only once [hence an equilibrium point, that is, a point in which $f_i(\hat{p}) = 0$ for all i, if it exists, is *unique*]. Moreover, we can assert that the $[f_2(p) = 0]$ curve intersects the $[f_1(p) = 0]$ curve "from the left." By checking the signs of $\dot{p}_1$ and $\dot{p}_2$ in the four regions defined by these two curves, we will be able to ascertain the global stability of $\hat{p}$. We now pursue this process in detail.

First observe that the following "Euler's equation" holds owing to the homogeneity assumption (A-2):

$$\sum_{j=1}^{3} f_{ij} p_j = 0 \qquad \text{for all } p, i = 1, 2, 3$$

Then in view of (A-1) and (A-4), we obtain

$$f_{ii} < 0 \qquad \text{for all } p, i = 1, 2, 3$$

Consider the values of p_1 and p_2 for which $f_1 = 0$. In the $(p_1\text{-}p_2)$-plane this defines a curve. We want to obtain the slope of this curve, that is, dp_2/dp_1. This can be obtained simply by differentiating $f_1 = 0$. That is, $f_{11}\, dp_1 + f_{12}\, dp_2 = 0 \,(\because p_3 = 1$ or $dp_3 = 0)$. Thus $dp_2/dp_1 = -f_{11}/f_{12}$, which is positive from the fact that $f_{ii} < 0$ for all i and from (A-1). Similarly, we obtain the slope of the curve defined by $f_2 = 0$ on the $(p_1\text{-}p_2)$-plane by differentiating $f_2 = 0$, that is, $f_{21}\, dp_1 + f_{22}\, dp_2 = 0$. Hence $dp_2/dp_1 = -f_{21}/f_{22}$, which again is positive. Thus we have established that both the $[f_1(p) = 0]$ curve and the $[f_2(p) = 0]$ curve are upward sloping.

Next we ascertain the signs of $\dot{p}_i$ in the region defined by these two curves. Since $f_{12} > 0$ for all p by (A-1), to the left (resp. right) of the $[f_1(p) = 0]$ curve, $f_1(p) > 0$ or $\dot{p}_1 > 0$ (resp. $f_1(p) < 0$ or $\dot{p}_1 < 0$). Since $f_{21} > 0$ for all p by (A-1), to the left (resp. right) of the $[f_2(p) = 0]$ curve, $f_2(p) < 0$ or $\dot{p}_2 < 0$ (resp. $f_2(p) > 0$ or $\dot{p}_2 > 0$). In establishing the above facts, we can use $f_{11} < 0$ and $f_{22} < 0$ instead of $f_{12} > 0$ and $f_{21} > 0$, respectively.

By (A-5), there exists at least one equilibrium point. Thus the two curves, the $[f_1(p) = 0]$ curve and the $[f_2(p) = 0]$ curve, intersect at least once. Now we assert that such an intersection happens only once. In other words, we assert that the equilibrium price vector $\hat{p}$ is unique. To show this, suppose the contrary, that is, suppose that there exists another equilibrium point $p^* > 0$, $f(p^*) = 0$ and $p^* \neq \hat{p}$, where $p_3^* = \hat{p}_3 = 1$. Then the $[f_1(p) = 0]$ curve and the $[f_2(p) = 0]$ curve intersect at least twice, that is, at points p^* and $\hat{p}$. Then at one of these two points— say, at p^*—the $[f_1(p) = 0]$ curve must intersect the $[f_2(p) = 0]$ curve from the left. This is illustrated in Figure 3.5.

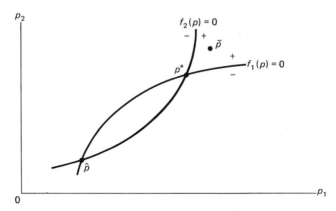

Figure 3.5.   The Proof of the Uniqueness of an Equilibrium.

Now consider a point $\tilde{p}$ in the diagram; $\tilde{p}$ is chosen such that $\tilde{p}_1 > p_1^*$ and $\tilde{p}_2 > p_2^*$. (Note that $\tilde{p}_3 = p_3^* = \hat{p}_3 = 1$). Then $f_1(\tilde{p}) > 0$ and $f_2(\tilde{p}) > 0$. Totally differentiate $f_3(p)$, and obtain

$$df_3 = f_{31} dp_1 + f_{32} dp_2 \quad (\because dp_3 = 0 \text{ for } p_3 = 1 \text{ always})$$

Compare the two points p^* and $\tilde{p}$. Since $f_3(p^*) = 0$, the above equation implies $f_3(\tilde{p}) > 0$ ($\because f_{31} > 0$, $f_{32} > 0$, $dp_1 > 0$, $dp_2 > 0$, so that $df_3 > 0$), so that $f_i(\tilde{p}) > 0$ for all $i = 1, 2, 3$. This contradicts Walras' Law, or (A-3), in view of (A-4). Hence we establish the uniqueness of an equilibrium point and that p^* cannot be an equilibrium point; that is, the $[f_2(p) = 0]$ curve intersects the $[f_1(p) = 0]$ curve from the left only (and the intersection point is $\hat{p}$).[4]

We now obtain the **phase diagram** illustrated in Figure 3.6, from which the global stability of $\hat{p}$ can easily be seen.[5] In the diagram the time paths of the price vector (p_1, p_2) corresponding to the two possible initial points (p_0 and p^0) are illustrated. For example, consider point p_0 in Figure 3.6. At p_0, $f_1 > 0$ and $f_2 < 0$ so that $\dot{p}_1 > 0$ and $\dot{p}_2 < 0$. In other words, p_1 increases whereas p_2 decreases over time. The price path of $[p_1(t), p_2(t)]$ eventually hits the $[f_1 = 0]$ curve—say, at point A where f_2 is still negative. At point A, then, $\dot{p}_1 = 0$ and $\dot{p}_2 < 0$, so that the price path enters the region in which $f_1 < 0$ and $f_2 < 0$, where both p_1 and p_2 decrease over time. Notice that the price path may hit the $[f_2 = 0]$ curve afterward— say, at point B. But at point B, $\dot{p}_1 < 0$. Hence the price path will "bounce back" to the region in which $f_1 < 0$ and $f_2 < 0$, approaching the equilibrium point.

The essence of the phase diagram proof of stability here, under gross sub-

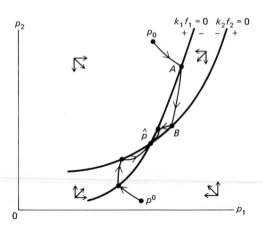

Figure 3.6.   An Illustration of the Phase Diagram.

stitutability, is that, regardless of the initial value of the price vector, the price path $[p_1(t), p_2(t)]$ is "trapped" inside the region in which $\dot{p}_1 < 0$ and $\dot{p}_2 < 0$ with $p_1 > \hat{p}_1$ and $p_2 > \hat{p}_2$, *or* inside the region in which $\dot{p}_1 > 0$ and $\dot{p}_2 > 0$ with $p_1 < \hat{p}_1$ and $p_2 < \hat{p}_2$.

FOOTNOTES

1. As before, f_{ij} denotes $\partial f_i / \partial p_j$.

2. We will observe that under the present set of assumptions, especially (A-2), the equilibrium $\hat{p}$ is unique. The proof of the existence of equilibrium is fairly simple under the present set of assumptions, (A-1) to (A-4), especially with gross substitutability. For such a proof, see H. Nikaido, "Generalized Gross Substitutability and Extremization," *Advances in Game Theory*, ed. by M. Presher, L. S. Shapley, and A. W. Tucker, Princeton, N.J., Princeton University Press, 1964. For a generalization of Nikaido's result which relaxes the assumption of the continuous differentiability of the excess demand functions, see K. Kuga, "Weak Gross Substitutability and the Existence of Competitive Equilibrium," *Econometrica*, 33, July 1965.

3. The normalization thus amounts to adding another equation $p_3 = 1$ to the system. Assumption (A-2) implies that if $\hat{p}$ is an equilibrium price vector, then $\alpha \hat{p}$ is also an equilibrium price vector for any $\alpha > 0$. By the normalization with $p_3 = 1$, this is no longer possible.

4. Using similar logic, we can prove easily that the $[f_1(p) = 0]$ curve will not overlap with the $[f_2(p) = 0]$ curve for any "interval." To see this, suppose that the two curves overlap over the interval between the two points p^* and $\tilde{p}$ in Figure 3.5. Then we have $f_i(p^*) = f_i(\tilde{p}) = 0$, $i = 1, 2$, so that $f_3(p^*) = f_3(\tilde{p}) = 0$. But using $df_3 = f_{31}dp_1 + f_{32}dp_2$ and $f_3(p^*) = 0$, we also obtain $f_3(\tilde{p}) > 0$. This contradicts $f_3(\tilde{p}) = 0$.

5. In general, let $\dot{x}(t) = f[x(t)]$, where $\dot{x}_i(t) = f_i[x(t)]$, be a given system of differential equations. The solution $x(t)$ of this differential equation defines a curve on the $(x_1$-$x_2)$-plane for a given initial point x_0, where t is taken to be the parameter. With the existence and the uniqueness of a (continuous) solution, such a curve is uniquely

drawn for each given x_0 and is continuous. Such a curve is called the **(solution) path** or **orbit**, and the (x_1, x_2)-plane on which the solution path is drawn is called the **phase space**. Since there can be many possible initial points, we can draw a family of the solution paths, each path corresponding to each initial point. The **phase diagram technique** is concerned with the technique of studying the behavior of the solution paths on the phase space, without actually solving the given system of differential equations.

REFERENCES

1. Arrow, K. J., and Hurwicz, L., "On the Stability of the Competitive Equilibrium, I," *Econometrica*, 26, October 1958.
2. Hicks, J. R., *Value and Capital*, 2nd ed., Oxford, Clarendon Press, 1946.
3. Marshall, A., *Money, Credit and Commerce*, London, Macmillan, 1923, appendix J (this appendix was originally published in 1879 as "The Pure Theory of Foreign Trade").

Section E

A PROOF OF GLOBAL STABILITY WITH GROSS SUBSTITUTABILITY— THE *n*-COMMODITY CASE

In this section we study the proof of the global stability of a competitive equilibrium due to Arrow, Block, and Hurwicz [1].[1] For this exposition, I benefited from an excellent survey article on the stability problem by Negishi [3] and a critical scrutiny of [1] by Hotaka [2]. We consider the following non-normalized system of an *n*-commodity pure exchange economy:[2]

$$(1) \quad \frac{dp_i(t)}{dt} = f_i[p_1(t), p_2(t), \ldots, p_n(t)] \equiv x_i[p_1(t), p_2(t), \ldots, p_n(t)] - \bar{x}_i$$

$$i = 1, 2, \ldots, n$$

where the functions f_i are defined on the interior of the nonnegative orthant of R^n and are assumed to be continuously differentiable. Here we adopt the Arrow-Hurwicz convention of setting all the speeds of adjustment equal to one by choosing units of measurement for each commodity properly. Denote the price vector $(p_1, p_2, \ldots, p_n)$ by p. It should be understood that p is a function of time, t; that is, $p = p(t)$. The price vector $p(t)$, which is the solution of the above system of equations, obviously depends on the initial condition, $p(0)$. We denote the value of $p(0)$ by p^0 and assume that it is positive. We also assume that, for any given initial price p^0, there exists a unique solution

$p(t, p^0), t \in [0, \infty)$ for the above dynamic system, there exists a positive equilibrium price vector $\hat{p}$ [that is, $f_i(\hat{p}) = 0, i = 1, 2, \ldots, n$], and the demand functions are single-valued and continuously differentiable. Finally, we assume that the following relations hold:

(A-1) (**Walras' Law**) $\sum_{i=1}^{n} p_i f_i(p) = 0$.
(A-2) (**Homogeneity**) $x_i(p) = x_i(\alpha p), i = 1, 2, \ldots, n$, for any positive number α.
(A-3) (**Gross substitutability**) $\partial x_i(p)/\partial p_j > 0$, for all $p, i \neq j, i, j = 1, 2, \ldots, n$.[3]

REMARK: All the above relations are assumed to hold for any $t \geq 0$ and $p(t) > 0$.[4] Thus we may rewrite Walras' Law as

$$\sum_{i=1}^{n} p_i(t) f_i[p(t)] = 0$$

The homogeneity assumption, (A-2), implies that $f_i(p)$ is homogeneous of degree zero. By Euler's equation,

$$\sum_{j=1}^{n} f_{ij} p_j = 0, i = 1, 2, \cdots, n$$

where $f_{ij} \equiv \partial f_i/\partial p_j$. In view of (A-3), $f_{ij} > 0, i \neq j, i, j = 1, 2, \ldots, n$.

Lemma 3.E.1:   *Assume Walras' Law; then we have*

$$\| p(t) \| = \| p(0) \| \textit{ for all } t \geq 0, \textit{ where } \| p(t) \|^2 \equiv \sum_{i=1}^{n} p_i^2(t)$$

PROOF: Differentiate $\| p(t) \|^2$ with respect to t. Then

$$\frac{d}{dt} \left[\sum_{i=1}^{n} p_i(t)^2 \right] = 2 \sum_{i=1}^{n} p_i(t) \dot{p}_i = 2 \sum_{i=1}^{n} p_i(t) f_i[p(t)] = 0 \; (\because \text{Walras' Law})$$

Hence $\| p(t) \| = \text{constant} = \| p(0) \|$.   (Q.E.D.)

Lemma 3.E.2:   *The homogeneity and the gross substitutability assumptions, that is, (A-2) and (A-3), imply that the equilibrium price vector is unique up to a positive scalar multiple.*

REMARK: This lemma states that any equilibrium price vector may be expressed in the form $\alpha \hat{p}$ where α is some positive number. Geometrically, this means that there is a *unique* "equilibrium *ray*" $\{\alpha \hat{p}: \alpha > 0\}$.

PROOF: Suppose not. In other words, let $\hat{p}$ and p^* be two equilibrium price vectors such that $p^* \neq \alpha \hat{p}$ for any positive α. Let $\hat{p}_1/p_1^* \equiv \min_i \{\hat{p}_1/p_1^*, \hat{p}_2/p_2^*, \ldots, \hat{p}_i/p_i^*, \ldots, \hat{p}_n/p_n^*\}$ and write $\mu \equiv \hat{p}_i/p_i^*$. By definition, $\mu \leq \hat{p}_i/p_i^*$ for all i, or $\hat{p}_i \geq \mu p_i^*$ for all i. Since $p^* \neq \alpha \hat{p}$ for any positive α, $\hat{p}_i > \mu p_i^*$ for some $i \neq I$. Write $\tilde{p}_i \equiv \mu p_i^*$. Then $\hat{p}_i \geq \tilde{p}_i$ for all i with strict inequality for some $i \neq I$. From the gross substitutability assumption, this implies $x_I(\hat{p}) > x_I(\check{p})$, and from the homogeneity assumption $f_i(p^*) = 0$ implies $f_i(\check{p}) = 0$. Thus we have $\bar{x}_I = x_I(\hat{p}) > x_I(\check{p}) = \bar{x}_I$. This is a contradiction. (Q.E.D.)

REMARK: A slight error by Arrow, Block, and Hurwicz [1] in this connection was pointed out by Hotaka [2].

REMARK: Note that Walras' Law is not used in the proof of Lemma 3.E.2.

REMARK: From Lemma 3.E.1, we know that $p(t)$ moves only along the sphere with radius $\| p(0) \|$. Hence Lemma 3.E.2 implies that if $p(t) \to \hat{p}$ (an equilibrium price vector), then $\hat{p}$ is unique, where $\hat{p}$ is confined to such a sphere.

Lemma 3.E.3: *Let $\hat{p}$ be an equilibrium price vector. Under the assumptions of Walras' Law, homogeneity, and gross substitutability, we have*

$$\sum_{i=1}^{n} \hat{p}_i f_i(p) > 0 \quad \text{for all } p > 0 \text{ such that } p \neq \alpha\hat{p} \text{ for any } \alpha > 0$$

PROOF: We illustrate the proof for the two-commodity case diagrammatically in Figure 3.7 and refer to Arrow, Block, and Hurwicz [1] and its revision by Hotaka [2] for the proof of the general case. This exposition for the two-commodity case is due to Negishi [3].

The point $\bar{x}$ in Figure 3.7 represents the total stock of the two commodities, that is, the vector $\bar{x} = (\bar{x}_1, \bar{x}_2)$. Let $\hat{p}$ be an equilibrium price vector; then $x_1(\hat{p}) = \bar{x}_1$ and $x_2(\hat{p}) = \bar{x}_2$. Let p be a price vector such that $p \neq \alpha\hat{p}$ for any positive number α. By Lemma 3.E.2, p is not an equilibrium price vector. As a result of Walras' Law, $\sum_{i=1}^{2} p_i x_i(p) = \sum_{i=1}^{2} p_i \bar{x}_i$. Hence a point $[x_1(p), x_2(p)]$ is on the line AB which passes through the point $\bar{x}$ and

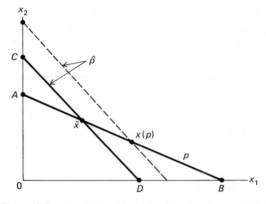

Figure 3.7. An Illustration of the Proof of Lemma 3.E.3.

whose slope is given by p. Let CD be the line which passes through the point $\bar{x}$ and whose slope is given by $\hat{p}$. We assume that $\hat{p}_1/\hat{p}_2 > p_1/p_2$ (under the assumption $\hat{p}_1/\hat{p}_2 < p_1/p_2$, the lemma can be proved analogously). In other words, we assume that the line CD is steeper than the line AB. This assumption means that $\hat{p}_1/p_1 > \hat{p}_2/p_2$. Write $\mu \equiv \hat{p}_2/p_2$. Then $\hat{p}_1 > \mu p_1$ and $\hat{p}_2 = \mu p_2$. Hence the gross substitutability assumption implies that $x_2(\hat{p}) > x_2(\mu p)$. But Walras' Law implies that $\mu p_1 x_1(\hat{p}) + \mu p_2 x_2(\hat{p}) = \mu p_1 \bar{x}_1 + \mu p_2 \bar{x}_2 = \mu p_1 x_1(\mu p) + \mu p_2 x_2(\mu p)$, so that we must have $x_1(\hat{p}) < x_1(\mu p)$. Using the homogeneity assumption, we get $x_1(p) = x_1(\mu p) > x_1(\hat{p}) = \bar{x}_1$, and $x_2(p) = x_2(\mu p) < x_2(\hat{p}) = \bar{x}_2$. Hence point $x(p) = [x_1(p), x_2(p)]$ must lie to the right of the point $\bar{x}$ in Figure 3.7. Now draw a line parallel to CD passing through the point $x(p)$. We see at once that $\hat{p} \cdot x(p) > \hat{p} \cdot \bar{x}$. Hence $\hat{p} \cdot f(p) > 0$ where $f(p) = [f_1(p), f_2(p)]$. 　　　　　　　　　　　　　　　　　　　　　(Q.E.D.)

REMARK:　This lemma states that in any disequilibrium situation, the sum of the excess demands weighted by the *equilibrium* prices is always positive. We recall that Samuelson's **weak axiom of revealed preference** states that $p \cdot \Delta x \leq 0$ implies $p' \cdot \Delta x < 0$, where $\Delta x \equiv x(p') - x(p)$. That this axiom holds for an individual is a consequence of rational behavior.[5] However, the statement that this axiom holds for the entire economy (that is, for the market demand as a whole) is *not* a consequence of rational behavior but is an additional assumption as we remarked in the Appendix to Section E, Chapter 2. In any case, suppose that this axiom holds *for the entire economy*. Walras' Law implies that $p \cdot x(p) = p \cdot \bar{x} = p \cdot x(\hat{p})$, where $\hat{p}$ is an equilibrium price vector, so that we have $p \cdot \Delta x = 0$ where $\Delta x \equiv x(\hat{p}) - x(p)$. Hence from the weak axiom of the revealed preference for the entire economy, we have $\hat{p} \cdot \Delta x < 0$. This means that $\hat{p} \cdot [x(\hat{p}) - x(p)] < 0$, or $\hat{p} \cdot [\bar{x} - x(p)] < 0$, which is nothing but the statement of the lemma. Hence Lemma 3.E.3 is also implied from the weak axiom of revealed preference for the entire economy.

REMARK:　We may recall that if the weak axiom holds in the aggregate (that is, the conclusion of Lemma 3.E.3), then the equilibrium is unique up to a positive scalar multiple.[6] To prove this, suppose not. That is, suppose there exists a $p^* \neq \alpha \hat{p}$ for any α, yet $f_i(p^*) = 0$ for all i. But by the assumption, we have $\sum_{i=1}^{n} \hat{p}_i f_i(p^*) > 0$, which is a contradiction. Note that gross substitutability is *not* needed in this proof. See the appendix to Section E, Chapter 2.

REMARK:　The uniqueness is nice,[7] but it is a rather restrictive phenomenon.[8] Note that the uniqueness here is a consequence of such restrictive assumptions as gross substitutability or the weak axiom in the aggregate.

Theorem 3.E.1 (Arrow-Block-Hurwicz):　*Let $\hat{p}$ be an equilibrium price vector. Under the assumptions of Walras' Law, homogeneity, and gross substitutability, the system described in equation (1) is globally stable.*

PROOF: We consider the Euclidian distance between $p(t)$ and $\hat{p}$ and show that this distance converges to zero as $t \to \infty$. Let $D(t) \equiv \| p(t) - \hat{p} \|^2 = \sum_{i=1}^{n} [p_i(t) - \hat{p}_i]^2$. From Lemma 3.E.1, $\| p(t) \| = \| p(0) \|$. Normalize $\hat{p}$ such that $\| \hat{p} \| = \| p(0) \|$. Differentiate $D(t)$ with respect to t. That is,

$$\frac{dD(t)}{dt} = \frac{d}{dt} \left[\sum_{i=1}^{n} \{p_i(t) - \hat{p}_i\}^2 \right] = 2 \sum_{i=1}^{n} \{p_i(t) - \hat{p}_i\} \frac{dp_i}{dt}$$

$$= 2 \sum_{i=1}^{n} \{p_i(t) - \hat{p}_i\} f_i(p) = 2 \left\{ \sum_{i=1}^{n} p_i(t) f_i(p) - \sum_{i=1}^{n} \hat{p}_i f_i(p) \right\}$$

$$= -2 \sum_{i=1}^{n} \hat{p}_i f_i(p) \quad (\because \text{Walras' Law}).$$

Hence $dD(t)/dt < 0$, by Lemma 3.E.3, as long as $p \neq \alpha \hat{p}$ for any $\alpha > 0$. If $p = \alpha \hat{p}$, then $dD(t)/dt = 0$ [since $f_i(\alpha \hat{p}) = 0$ for all i], and we are done; so we assume that $p \neq \alpha \hat{p}$. $dD(t)/dt < 0$ implies that the convergence of $p(t)$ to the equilibrium point, $\hat{p}$, is monotone. This monotone movement of $p(t)$ toward $\hat{p}$ does not preclude the possibility of $p(t)$ never reaching $\hat{p}$. In other words, $D(t)$ may be bounded away from 0. Suppose it is, that is, $p(t)$ is bounded away from $\hat{p}$. Let $P \equiv \{p: \| p \| = \| p(0) \|\}$. Then there exists an open ball $B_\epsilon(\hat{p})$ about $\hat{p}$ with radius $\epsilon > 0$ such that $p(t) \in \bar{P} \equiv P \setminus B_\epsilon(\hat{p})$, for all t. Since $\bar{P}$ is compact and dD/dt is continuous in p, dD/dt achieves its maximum in $\bar{P}$ (Weierstrass' theorem). Since $dD/dt < 0$ in $\bar{P}$, this implies that there exists a $\delta > 0$ such that $dD/dt \leq -\delta < 0$. Integrating both sides of the above inequality from 0 to t, we obtain $D(t) - D(0) \leq -\delta t$, or $D(t) \leq D(0) - \delta t$. Hence for t larege enough, $D(t) < 0$. This contradicts the condition that the norm is always nonnegative.   (Q.E.D.)

REMARK: In view of the above proof and the remark on uniqueness immediately following Lemma 3.E.3, the gross substitutability assumption is replaced by the assumption that the weak axiom holds in the aggregate.

REMARK: Arrow, Block, and Hurwicz also showed the proof in terms of the maximum norm, $D_m \equiv \max_i \{(p_i(t) - \hat{p}_i)/\hat{p}_i\}$ (instead of the Euclidian norm used above), under a weaker set of conditions. However, the proof is more difficult, and monotonicity of convergence in the maximum norm does not necessarily imply monotonicity of convergence in the Euclidian norm.

FOOTNOTES

1. It is possible to produce simpler proofs than the ones given by Arrow, Block, and Hurwicz [1]. However, our attempt here to sketch one of the proofs in [1] will be useful in enhancing our understanding of the stability problem. The facts that we pick up along the way in the present round-about manner of proof are of some economic interest in themselves.

2. Arrow, Block, and Hurwicz [1] also proved the stability of the normalized system.

3. The gross substitutability assumption can be stated without using derivatives (that is, without assuming differentiability) as follows: For any $j = 1, 2, \ldots, n$, we have $p_i = p_i'$ for all $i \neq j$ and $p_j < p_j'$, implying that $f_i(p) < f_i(p')$ for all $i \neq j$, where $p = (p_1, \ldots, p_n)$ and $p' = (p_1', \ldots, p_n')$. This is called **gross substitutability in the finite incremental form**.

4. It can be easily shown that the gross substitutability and homogeneity assumptions are inconsistent with each other if $p_i = 0$ for any i (Section F-c, of this chapter and Hotaka [2]). Therefore, under these two assumptions, the f_i's have no meaning if $p(t)$ is a boundary point of the nonnegative orthant of R^n. This obviously implies that if $\hat{p}$ is an equilibrium price vector [that is, $f_i(\hat{p}) = 0$, $i = 1, 2, \ldots, n$], then $\hat{p} > 0$. An error by Arrow, Block, and Hurwicz [1] in this connection was pointed out and corrected by Hotaka ([2], pp. 305–306), who also showed that these two assumptions *and* Walras' Law imply that if $p_i \to 0$ for some i (the other prices being fixed), then $f_i(p) \to \infty$.

5. A brief recollection of the weak axiom may be useful. Interpret x and x' as the consumption vectors of a particular *individual*. Let x and x', respectively, be chosen by him when p and p' prevail. Assume the uniqueness of the choice. If x' is affordable at p—that is, $p \cdot x' \leq p \cdot x$—then x is revealed to be preferred to x', for he could have consumed x'. If this is the case, x' cannot be revealed to be preferred to x; that is, it is impossible to have $p' \cdot x \leq p' \cdot x'$, with x' chosen under p'. In other words, $p \cdot \Delta x \leq 0$ implies $p' \cdot \Delta x < 0$. See P. A. Samuelson, *Foundations of Economic Analysis*, Cambridge, Mass., Harvard University Press, 1947, chapter 5.

6. We may recall that in the proof of the existence of a competitive equilibrium, Wald proved the uniqueness of equilibrium by assuming that the weak axiom holds in the aggregate.

7. When we have multiple equilibria, the property that $p(t, p^0)$ always converges to a particular equilibrium point regardless of p^0 is rather restrictive. Thus "uniqueness" is a nice property, especially when we are interested in global stability. However, multiple equilibria are not necessarily destructive in stability analysis. Recall Uzawa's concept of "quasi-stability" which we remarked upon in Section B. See also Section H.

8. It may suffice to recall the possibility of multiple intersections of the offer curves in the Mill-Marshall diagram in the theory of international trade.

REFERENCES

1. Arrow, K. J., Block, H. D., and Hurwicz, L., "On the Stability of the Competitive Equilibrium, II," *Econometrica*, 26, January 1959.

2. Hotaka, R., "Some Basic Problems on Excess Demand Functions," *Econometrica*, 39, March 1971.

3. Negishi, T., "The Stability of a Competitive Economy: A Survey Article," *Econometrica*, 30, October 1962.

Section F

SOME REMARKS

a.   AN EXAMPLE OF GROSS SUBSTITUTABILITY

From the previous analysis, it is clear that the gross substitutability assumption plays an important role in stability analysis. An interesting question, then, is: What sort of utility function will give rise to a demand function which exhibits the gross substitutability property? Arrow and Hurwicz [2] have presented such an example.[1] Suppose that Mr. i's preference ordering can be represented by the following real-valued (utility) function:[2]

$$(1) \qquad u_i(x_{i1}, x_{i2}, \ldots, x_{in}) = \sum_{j=1}^{n} \alpha_{ij} \log x_{ij}$$

where $\sum_{j=1}^{n} \alpha_{ij} = 1$, $\alpha_{ij} > 0$ for all i, j, and x_{ij} ($j = 1, 2, \ldots, n$) is the amount of the jth commodity consumed by Mr. i. We will show that the above utility function yields a demand function for Mr. i which exhibits the gross substitutability property. For notational simplicity, we will omit the subscripts i. In other words, we will represent Mr. i's preference ordering as

$$(2) \qquad u(x_1, x_2, \ldots, x_n) = \sum_{j=1}^{n} \alpha_j \log x_j, \ \sum_{j=1}^{n} \alpha_j = 1, \text{ and } \alpha_j > 0 \quad \text{for all } j$$

Now suppose that Mr. i maximizes his utility over his budget constraint and note that he consumes a positive amount of every commodity (that is, an interior solution is achieved for this constrained maximum problem).[3] Then the first-order condition (see Chapter 1, Section F) can be written in the following form:

$$(3) \qquad \frac{\partial u}{\partial x_j} = \lambda p_j, \quad j = 1, 2, \ldots, n$$

where λ is the Lagrangian multiplier for this problem. Since the above utility function is a concave function, this condition is also sufficient for the global maximum of the solution. From (2), $\partial u/\partial x_j$ can immediately be obtained as

$$(4) \qquad \frac{\partial u}{\partial x_j} = \frac{\alpha_j}{x_j}$$

Therefore, from (3) and (4), we have

$$(5) \qquad \frac{\alpha_j}{x_j} = \lambda p_j, \quad \text{or } \alpha_j = \lambda p_j x_j, \quad j = 1, 2, \ldots, n$$

Note that this implies $\lambda > 0$. This, in turn, implies that all the income is spent. In other words, if we denote Mr. i's income by M, then $M = \sum_{j=1}^{n} p_j x_j$. Now we sum equation (5) over j and obtain

$$1 = \sum_{j=1}^{n} \alpha_j = \sum_{j=1}^{n} \lambda p_j x_j = \lambda M$$

or

(6) $$M = \frac{1}{\lambda}$$

Suppose that all his income is obtained by selling his resources in the markets. Denote his initial holding of the jth resources by $\bar{x}_j$ (where we again omit the subscript i for notational simplicity). Then

(7) $$M \equiv \sum_{j=1}^{n} p_j \bar{x}_j$$

Using (5), (6), and (7), we then obtain

$$x_j = \alpha_j \frac{1}{\lambda p_j} = \alpha_j \frac{M}{p_j} = \alpha_j \frac{\sum_{j=1}^{n} p_j \bar{x}_j}{p_j}$$

Therefore

(8) $$\frac{\partial x_j}{\partial p_k} = \alpha_j \frac{\bar{x}_k}{p_j}, \quad k \neq j$$

Hence under the assumptions $p_j > 0$ and $\bar{x}_k > 0$ for all j and $k = 1, 2, \ldots, n$, all commodities are gross substitutes for Mr. i. Thus if everybody in the economy has the utility function specified by (2) (with the assumptions used above), the market demand function also exhibits the "gross substitutability" property.[4]

    To obtain the gross substitutability for the market demand function, we note (resuming the subscript i for Mr. i):

$$\sum_{i=1}^{m} x_{ij} = \frac{\alpha_j}{p_j} \sum_{i=1}^{m} \sum_{j=1}^{n} p_j \bar{x}_{ij}$$

Hence

$$\frac{\partial}{\partial p_k} \sum_{i=1}^{m} x_{ij} = \frac{\alpha_j}{p_j} \sum_{i=1}^{m} \bar{x}_{ik}, \quad k \neq j$$

which is positive if $p_j > 0$ and $\sum_{i=1}^{m} \bar{x}_{ik} > 0$.

b.   SCARF'S COUNTEREXAMPLE

In Section E, we established the global stability of a competitive equilibrium under the assumptions of Walras' Law, homogeneity, and gross substitutability. It is natural to ask how far we can relax these assumptions. In particular, we would like to know the extent to which gross substitutability can be relaxed. It was conjectured that gross substitutability could be replaced by a more plausible assumption on the utility function, such as quasi-concavity (that is, convex to the origin indifference curves). Scarf [18] has constructed examples that cast doubt on all such conjectures. His examples are useful in understanding the basic problem involved in the stability question. Here we explain one of them.

Consider a pure exchange economy consisting of three consumers and three commodities. Let x_{ij} be the consumption of commodity j ($j = 1, 2, 3$) by Mr. i ($i = 1, 2, 3$). Suppose that Mr. i's utility function, u_i, can be written in the following form.

$$u_1(x_{11}, x_{12}, x_{13}) = \min \{x_{11}, x_{12}\}$$

$$u_2(x_{21}, x_{22}, x_{23}) = \min \{x_{22}, x_{23}\}$$

$$u_3(x_{31}, x_{32}, x_{33}) = \min \{x_{31}, x_{33}\}$$

In other words, each individual desires only two commodities and wants them only in the fixed ratio (one to one). It can easily be seen (by analogy to the case of fixed production coefficients) that such a utility function gives rise to an L-shaped indifference curve (which is clearly convex to the origin!). Let $\bar{x}_{ij}$ be the initial holding of commodity j by Mr. i. Let us suppose that

$$\bar{x}_{ii} = 1, \text{ and } \bar{x}_{ij} = 0, \quad i \neq j$$

In other words, Mr. i ($i = 1, 2, 3$) only has one unit of commodity i and none of the other commodities. Scarf's indifference curve and the budget line are illustrated in Figure 3.8.

Note that, in view of the specifications of the utility functions, the income consumption path of each individual in Figure 3.8 is the 45-degree line, so that $x_{11} = x_{12}$, $x_{22} = x_{23}$, and $x_{31} = x_{33}$. Consider the change in the price indicated by the arrow in the diagram (a decrease in the price of commodity 2). It is clearly illustrated by the diagram that there is only an "income effect"; there is no "substitution effect." Hence for such indifference curves, the entire price change is absorbed into the income effect.

The excess demand for commodity 1 can be written as

(9)
$$\begin{aligned} x_1 - \bar{x}_1 &= (x_{11} + x_{21} + x_{31}) - (\bar{x}_{11} + \bar{x}_{21} + \bar{x}_{31}) \\ &= (x_{11} + x_{31}) - \bar{x}_{11} = (x_{11} - \bar{x}_{11}) + x_{31} \end{aligned}$$

The budget equation for Mr. 1 can be written as $p_1 x_{11} + p_2 x_{12} = p_1 \bar{x}_{11}$. But by our convention, $x_{11} = x_{12}$ and $\bar{x}_{11} = 1$. Hence $x_{11} = p_1/(p_1 + p_2)$ so that $x_{11} - \bar{x}_{11} =$

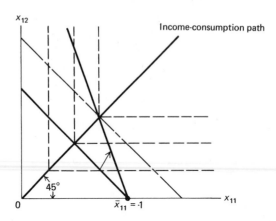

Figure 3.8.   Scarf's Counterexample (the Case of Mr. 1).

$-p_2/(p_1 + p_2)$. Similarly, x_{31} can be obtained from Mr. 3's budget equation, $p_1 x_{31} + p_3 x_{33} = p_3 \bar{x}_{33}$; that is, $x_{31} = p_3/(p_3 + p_1)$. Therefore, from (9), we obtain

(10-a)
$$x_1 - \bar{x}_1 = -\frac{p_2}{p_1 + p_2} + \frac{p_3}{p_3 + p_1}$$

Similarly we obtain

(10-b)
$$x_2 - \bar{x}_2 = -\frac{p_3}{p_2 + p_3} + \frac{p_1}{p_1 + p_2}$$

(10-c)
$$x_3 - \bar{x}_3 = -\frac{p_1}{p_3 + p_1} + \frac{p_2}{p_2 + p_3}$$

From equations (10-a, -b, -c), it is clear that there exists a unique "equilibrium price ray" $\hat{p}_1 = \hat{p}_2 = \hat{p}_3$.

We can write the dynamic adjustment equation as

(11)
$$\dot{p}_i(t) = x_i(t) - \bar{x}_i, \, i = 1, 2, 3$$

Now we want to show that $\| p(t) \| = $ constant for all t. To show this, we differentiate $\| p(t) \|$ with respect to t. In other words

$$\frac{d}{dt} \left[\sum_{i=1}^{3} p_i^2(t) \right] = 2 \sum_{i=1}^{3} p_i(t) \, \dot{p}_i = 2 \sum_{i=1}^{3} p_i(x_i - \bar{x}_i) = 0$$

Hence we conclude that $\| p(t) \|^2 = \sum_{i=1}^{3} p_i^2(t) = $ constant.[5]

Next we want to show that $\Pi_{i=1}^{3} p_i(t) = $ constant. To do so, differentiate this as follows:

$$\frac{d}{dt}\left[\prod_{i=1}^{3}p_i(t)\right] = \dot{p}_1p_2p_3 + \dot{p}_2p_3p_1 + \dot{p}_3p_1p_2$$

$$= (x_1 - \bar{x}_1)p_2p_3 + (x_2 - \bar{x}_2)p_3p_1 + (x_3 - \bar{x}_3)p_1p_2 = 0$$

The last equality is obtained by using equations (10-a, -b, -c).

Now we can show that the dynamic process (11) is not globally stable. First choose the initial prices $p_i(0)$, $i = 1$, 2, 3, such that $\sum_{i=1}^{3}p_i^2(0) = 3$ and $\prod_{i=1}^{3}p_i(0) \neq 1$. Then $\sum_{i=1}^{3}p_i^2(t) = 3$ and $\prod_{i=1}^{3}p_i(t) \neq 1$ for all t. Since $\sum_{i=1}^{3}p_i^2(t) = 3$, the only possible equilibrium prices are $\hat{p}_1 = \hat{p}_2 = \hat{p}_3 = 1$. Hence the solution of the above system of differential equations, (11), denoted by $p_i(t; p_i(0), 0)$, cannot converge to the equilibrium price $\hat{p}_i$ where $\hat{p}_1 = \hat{p}_2 = \hat{p}_3 = 1$.

We may observe the following facts in the above example.

(i)   There is no substitution effect.
(ii) The indifference curve is not strictly convex to the origin.
(iii) The indifference curve has a kink and hence is not differentiable.

These conditions are somewhat peculiar when compared with the ordinary Hicks-Slutsky model of consumer's behavior. Scarf [18] and Gale [5] also considered cases of instability in which the substitution effect is present (however, this effect is "smaller" than the income effect—Giffen's case). It is certainly difficult to say precisely under what conditions the instability arises. However, Scarf's examples indicate that instability may occur in a wide variety of cases.

c.   CONSISTENCY OF VARIOUS ASSUMPTIONS[6]

We have observed that a certain set of assumptions is necessary to prove the stability of a competitive equilibrium. A natural question now is whether the assumptions, by which we can guarantee the stability, are consistent with each other. It would also be nice to know some of the implications of these assumptions, other than the stability of a competitive equilibrium, given that they are consistent with each other. Following are some important observations on the *gross substitutability and homogeneity assumptions.*

These two assumptions can be inconsistent *unless* $p_i > 0$ for all *i*. For example, if we suppose $p_i \geq 0$ for all *i* with equality for some *i*, then we can get a contradiction. To see this, note that zero degree homogeneity (by definition) means $x_i(p) = x_i(\alpha p)$, $i = 1, 2, \ldots, n$, for any positive real number α, where x_i is the demand for the *i*th commodity. Now suppose that $p_{i_0} = 0$ for some i_0. Then the gross substitutability assumption implies $x_{i_0}(\alpha p) > x_{i_0}(p)$ for $\alpha > 1$. This contradicts the homogeneity condition.

However, if $p_i > 0$ for *all* i, then the three assumptions—gross substitutability, homogeneity, and Walras' Law—are consistent. Consider the following example of an excess demand function:[7]

$$f_i(p) = \frac{\sum_k a_{ki} p_k}{p_i}$$

where the a_{ki}'s are arbitrary constants such that $a_{ki} > 0$ for $k \neq i$ and $\sum_i a_{ki} = 0$. Since $\partial f_i / \partial p_k = a_{ki}/p_i > 0$ for $k \neq i$, the gross substitutability assumption is satisfied. Second, note that

$$\sum_i p_i f_i = \sum_i \frac{p_i}{p_i} \sum_k a_{ki} p_k = \sum_{i,k} a_{ki} p_k = \sum_k p_k \sum_i a_{ki} = 0$$

Hence Walras' Law is satisfied. Finally, note that $f_i(\alpha p) = (\sum_k a_{ki} \alpha p_k)/(\alpha p_i) = (\sum_k a_{ki} p_k)/p_i = f_i(p)$. Hence the homogeneity condition is satisfied.

d. NONNEGATIVE PRICES

The problem of the stability of a competitive equilibrium, as we have seen, is concerned with the following system of differential equations:

$$\dot{p}_i(t) = f_i[p_1(t), p_2(t), \ldots, p_n(t)], \; i = 1, 2, \ldots, n$$

If the f_i's are defined on an open connected set X, the Cauchy-Peano theorem guarantees the existence of a solution in a neighborhood of $t = 0$. But the Cauchy-Peano theorem does not guarantee the existence of a solution for the entire region $[0, \infty)$, with which stability analysis is concerned. A natural question is: Can we guarantee the existence of a solution for the entire region of t, $[0, \infty)$, by guaranteeing the existence of solutions in the local regions $[0, \epsilon_1]$, $[\epsilon_1, \epsilon_2]$, $[\epsilon_2, \epsilon_3]$, ..., and so forth? Suppose we can make these "continuations" by some suitable method.[8] We may find that we can not go further than in some region $[\epsilon_j, \epsilon_{j+1}]$, for when t is in the region $[\epsilon_j, \epsilon_{j+1}]$, the solution vector $p[t; p(0)]$, may lie outside the region X on which the f_i's are defined. Then the above differential equation system would not have solutions for the entire region $[0, \infty)$. In stability analysis, X is often taken as the positive or nonnegative orthant of R^n, or else $X = R^n$ with the explicit constraint $p \geq 0$. Hence the question here is one of negative prices. In other words, when t reaches the region $[\epsilon_j, \epsilon_{j+1}]$, the solution of $p_i[t; p(0)]$ may become negative for some i. Then p is outside the region X or violates the restriction $p \geq 0$ so that it becomes meaningless to discuss the question of whether or not $p[t, p(0)]$ converges to an equilibrium price vector $\hat{p}$ as t goes to ∞.

This nonnegativity condition for the price vector is often neglected in the literature. Explicit consideration is given to this problem in two masterpieces, [1] and [8]. Here we illustrate the problem by using some other studies.

One way to avoid the above difficulty is to modify the above system of differential equations such that, for each i,

$$\frac{dp_i(t)}{dt} = \begin{cases} 0, \text{ if } p_i(t) = 0 \text{ and } f_i[p_1(t), \ldots, p_n(t)] < 0 \\ f_i[p_1(t), \ldots, p_n(t)], \quad \text{for all other cases} \end{cases}$$

This approach is adopted by Arrow, Hurwicz, and Uzawa [3], Morishima [9], and Kose [7]. The advantage of this method is that we do not have to modify the stability analysis of the previous sections very much, if we assume the existence of a solution for the above modified system. The question now is whether we can guarantee the existence of a solution for this modified system. The ordinary Cauchy-Peano existence theorem is not applicable here because the right-hand side of this system may not be a continuous function of p. To see this, consider a sequence $\{p^q\}$ in X such that $p^q \rightarrow \bar{p}$ with $\bar{p} = 0$. Assume $f_i(\bar{p}) < 0$. Then the RHS of the above differential equation converges to 0, and not to $f_i(\bar{p})$, as $p^q \rightarrow \bar{p}$. Hence we indeed have a discontinuity. Unless a new existence theorem is proved for the above modified system, we are not being quite honest if we proceed with the stability analysis.

Nikaido and Uzawa [15] proposed the following alternative system:

(NU) $$\frac{dp_i(t)}{dt} = \max\{f_i[p_1(t), \ldots, p_n(t)], -p_i\}, i = 1, 2, \ldots, n$$

The right-hand side is a continuous function of p if f_i is continuous; hence the problem of discontinuity disappears. Using the continuity and the homogeneity of f_i, Nikaido and Uzawa proved a global existence theorem for the above system (by first showing that the continuity and the homogeneity imply the boundedness of the above system). The (NU) system states that when p_i happens to hit the "wall" of $p_i = 0$, then the RHS of (NU) is either 0 or positive. Hence the nonnegativity condition will be satisfied for the entire process. Moreover, the "switching" from $dp_i/dt = f_i$ to $dp_i/dt = -p_i$ is carried out continuously. In other words, when the sequence of prices, p^q, converges to $\bar{p}$ where one of the components (say, $\bar{p}_i$) of $\bar{p}$ is zero, $f_i(p^q)$ may become negative (it can be positive, but then there will be no such "switching"). But dp_i/dt would already have become $-\bar{p}_i = 0$. When $f_i(p^q) < -p_i$, the dynamic process is switched from $dp_i/dt = f_i$ to $dp_i/dt = -p_i$ continuously.

Another dynamic process for the adjustment of a competitive market was proposed by Nikaido [12]. The essential idea of this procedure was to utilize the Brown-von Neumann differential equation which had been developed in the study of the two-person zero-sum games. The Brown-von Neumann equation for the present case can be written as

$$\frac{dp_i(t)}{dt} = F_i[p_1(t), p_2(t), \ldots, p_n(t)] - G[p_1(t), \ldots, p_n(t)] p_i(t) \quad (i = 1, 2, \ldots, n)$$

$$F_i[p_1(t), p_2(t), \ldots, p_n(t)] \equiv \max\{f_i[p_1(t), \ldots, p_n(t)], 0\} \quad (i = 1, 2, \ldots, n)$$

$$G[p_1(t), p_2(t), \ldots, p_n(t)] \equiv \sum_{i=1}^{n} F_i[p_1(t), \ldots, p_n(t)]$$

In ending, we may note one criticism of the above three devices for avoiding the problem of negative prices. The process of "switching," whether continuous or discontinuous, is quite mechanical or artificial and little economic meaning can be given to it. If we understand the dynamic adjustment equation as simply "a rule of the game," as mentioned before, we may not have to question this. The switching rule is then a part of the rule. Since the dynamic adjustment equation involves an extremely difficult problem (which we discuss in the next section), we do not discuss this issue any further.

FOOTNOTES

1. We should not, however, emphasize gross substitutability too much. Hicks [6] considered "strongly asymmetrical income effects and extreme complementary" as causes of instability. Unfortunately, we do not have any important stability theorem that applies when the gross substitutability assumption is relaxed, although we do have some results for instability when this assumption is relaxed (cf. Scarf [18] and Gale [5]). See subsection b of this section. Recent studies by Morishima [10] and Ohyama [16] seem to offer interesting attempts when gross substitutability is absent. Unfortunately, [10] seems to contain a serious error.

2. Note that this is a logarithmic transformation (which is a monotone transformation) of a Cobb-Douglas type utility function $u_i = \Pi_{j=1}^{n} x_{ij}^{\alpha ij}$, $\sum_j \alpha_{ij} = 1$. Recall that a preference ordering is invariant under a monotone (increasing) transformation of the utility function.

3. This is due to our specification of the utility function, (2). For if consumption of one of the commodities becomes zero, then the consumer's utility becomes $-\infty$. As long as he has a positive income, this (zero utility) is certainly not optimal for him.

4. Recently Eisenberg [4] has shown that if each individual's utility function is of the Cobb-Douglas type (or more generally homogeneous), then the individual utility functions are "aggregated" to form a social welfare function, which is of the Cobb-Douglas (or homogeneous) type. Here the "social welfare function" is not used to describe the welfare level of the society, but rather it is used to describe the behavior of the society.

5. This result was proved in Lemma 3.E.1. The proof is recorded here to keep our exposition sufficiently self-contained.

6. For the expositions of this and the following subsections, I am indebted to Nikaido [13].

7. As we observed in subsection a, such an excess demand function can be obtained from the Cobb-Douglas type of utility function.

8. For "continuation" of the solution, recall our remark in Section B. For an explicit proof of the possibility of continuation under the present framework, see Nikaido ([14], pp. 338–339).

REFERENCES

1. Arrow, K. J., Block, H. D., and Hurwicz, L., "On the Stability of the Competitive Equilibrium, II," *Econometrica*, 27, January 1959.

2. Arrow, K. J., and Hurwicz, L., "On the Stability of the Competitive Equilibrium, I," *Econometrica*, 26, October 1958.

3. Arrow, K. J., Hurwicz, L., and Uzawa, H., eds., *Studies in Linear and Nonlinear Programming*, Stanford, Calif., Stanford University Press, 1958.

4. Eisenberg, E., "Aggregation of Utility Functions," *Management Science*, 7, July 1961.

5. Gale, D., "A Note on Global Instability of Competitive Equilibrium," *Naval Research Logistics Quarterly*, 10, March 1963.

6. Hicks, J. R., *Value and Capital*, 2nd ed., Oxford, Clarendon Press, 1946.

7. Kose, T., "Solutions of Saddle-Value Problems by Differential Equation," *Econometrica*, 24, January 1956.

8. McKenzie, L. W., "Stability of Equilibrium and the Value of Positive Excess Demand," *Econometrica*, 28, July 1960.

9. Morishima, M., "A Reconsideration of the Walras-Cassel-Leontief Model of General Equilibrium," in *Mathematical Methods in Social Sciences*, ed. by Arrow *et. al.*, Stanford, Calif., Stanford University Press, 1960.

10. ———, "A Generalization of the Gross Substitute System," *Review of Economic Studies*, XXXVII, April 1970.

11. Negishi, T., "The Stability of a Competitive Economy: A Survey Article," *Econometrica*, 30, October 1962.

12. Nikaido, H., "Stability of Equilibrium by the Brown-von Neumann Differential Equation," *Econometrica*, 27, October 1959.

13. ———, "The Tâtonnement Process and the Nonnegativity Condition," in *New Economic Analysis*, ed. by M. Morishima *et al.*, Tokyo, Sobunsha, 1960 (in Japanese).

14. ———, *Convex Structures and Economic Theory*, New York, Academic Press, 1968.

15. Nikaido, H. and Uzawa, H., "Stability and Nonnegativity in a Walrasian Tâtonnement Process," *International Economic Review*, 1, January 1960.

16. Ohyama, M., "On the Stability of Generalized Metzlerian Systems," *Review of Economic Studies*, XXXIX, April 1972.

17. Quirk, J., and Saposnik, R., *Introduction to General Equilibrium Theory and Welfare Economics*, New York, McGraw-Hill, 1968.

18. Scarf, H., "Some Examples of Global Instability of the Competitive Equilibrium," *International Economic Review*, 1, September 1960.

Section G

THE *TÂTONNEMENT* AND THE NON-*TÂTONNEMENT* PROCESSES

The following system of differential equations has been an essential part of the analysis of the dynamic adjustment process:

$$\frac{dp_i(t)}{dt} = f_i[p_1(t), p_2(t), \ldots, p_n(t)], i = 1, 2, \ldots, n$$

We pointed out in Section C (and in Section A) that this system reflects a fundamental assumption of stability analysis—that a positive excess demand for commodity i raises the price of i and a negative excess demand (that is, an excess supply) for commodity i lowers the price of i. The above system of differential equations is a straightforward mathematical formulation of this assumption.

This assumption, although it seems quite plausible, is beset with two serious difficulties: (1) its behavioral background, and (2) the unrealistic nature of the "*tâtonnement* process," of which the above system of differential equations is a mathematical formulation.

a. THE BEHAVIORAL BACKGROUND AND THE *TÂTONNEMENT* PROCESS

The first difficulty is that it is not clear whose behavior is described by the above system of differential equations. If it describes the behavior of each "market," it is not at all clear what type of economic agent is behind each market and what type of behavior leads to the above adjustment process. Walras [15] gave one ingenious answer. He assumed that all the traders gather in one place and that there exists a "market manager." The market manager quotes a price for the commodity (say, i). Then each trader writes the amount of that commodity that he wishes to buy or sell on a piece of paper (called a **ticket**). If there is an excess demand for i, the market manager raises the price of i, and if there is an excess supply of i, he lowers the price of i. Each time he quotes a new price, the "tickets" are again collected. This process continues until the excess demand becomes zero (that is, until an equilibrium price is called). Until then, no actual transaction takes place. This process is called the **tâtonnement process**. Two varieties of the *tâtonnement* process are discussed in the literature. The first assumes that this adjustment process is carried out simultaneously for all markets. The second assumes that this process is carried out in one market after another. In other words, first the adjustment process is carried out in the first market; after an equilibrium price is called in the first market, the adjustment process takes place in the second market, and so on. In each process, only one price is adjusted. For example, when the adjustment process is carried out in the ith market, only the price of commodity i is adjusted so as to bring the ith market into equilibrium. This process continues until the last market is in equilibrium; but by that time, the markets considered earlier are, generally, in disequilibrium again. Thus another "round" of adjustment is carried out from the first to the nth market. This cycle continues until *all* the markets are in equilibrium. The two varieties of *tâtonnement* process may be called the **simultaneous** *tâtonnement* **process** and the **successive** *tâtonnement* **process**, respectively. The dynamic process, $\dot{p} = f[p(t)]$, is a simultaneous process and the original *tâtonnement* process considered by Walras is a successive process. In any case, the crux of the *tâtonnement* process lies in the exchange of tickets with no actual trade being carried out until all the markets are in equilibrium,[1] and the crux of the stability analysis is to see whether such a *tâtonnement* process can bring all the markets into equilibrium. If so, we say that the *tâtonnement* process is a **stable process**. This is the problem that we have considered so far in this chapter.

Under the *tâtonnement* process, it is clear whose behavioral rule is described by $\dot{p}(t) = f[p(t)]$. This is the behavioral rule of the "market manager."[2] However, the question has not been completely answered yet, because we do not know why the market manager has to obey this behavioral rule. No straightforward explanation such as the profit maximization of producers or the utility maximization of consumers is given for this behavioral rule. Thus the stability analysis may be considered as an analysis which shows whether the *tâtonnement* process converges to an equilibrium *when* the market manager is instructed to behave according to $\dot{p} = f[p(t)]$. Since it is not clear who should establish this rule or why the market manager should behave according to this rule, we may consider this to be the "rule of the game." Thus we get only a partial answer to the question of the stability of the behavior which is described by this dynamic equation.

Some readers may not like the interpretation of the dynamic process $\dot{p} = f[p(t)]$ in terms of *tâtonnement* process, for it appears quite unrealistic to think of all traders being assembled in one place at one time to carry out the *tâtonnement* process as described. Thus we may come back to the original question: Whose behavior is described by this dynamic adjustment process? We end this inquiry into the behavioral background of the dynamic adjustment equation with the following acute observation by Koopmans ([5], p. 179):[3]

> If, for instance, the net rate of increase in price is assumed to be proportional to the excess of demand over supply, whose behavior is thereby expressed? And is the alternative hypothesis, that the rate of increase in supply is proportional to the excess of demand price over supply price any more plausible, or any better traceable to behavior motivations?

b. THE *TÂTONNEMENT* AND THE NON-*TÂTONNEMENT* PROCESSES

In the above description, we pointed out that no transactions are carried out in the *tâtonnement* process until all the markets reach equilibrium. The following passage from Takayama ([13], p. 142) summarizes the problems involved when we allow intermediate purchases and actual transactions in the adjustment process:

> If we admit actual purchases in the process towards equilibrium, the excess demand function is necessarily affected. This is because of the difference between the trader's purchasing power evaluated at the current price and the current holding of goods (before trade is carried out), *and* that evaluated at the changed price and the changed holding of goods (after trade has taken place), when Walras's law is effective and we do not assume "recontracting" in the tatonnement. Then the excess demand function is clearly changed and the eventual equilibrium will depend on the time path of "tâtonnement".

In terms of our equations, we defined $\hat{p}$, an equilibrium price vector, to be the one such that $f(\hat{p}) = 0$, and we then described the dynamic process by $dp(t)/dt =$

$f[p(t)]$. In other words, we used the same function f to denote the equilibrium relation and the dynamic process. If we allow intermediate purchases and actual transactions in the process, then this excess demand function f will change from time to time as the traders' income or purchasing power varies.[4] Hence the price vector which prevails when the market is finally cleared depends on the time path of the process and will, therefore, not generally be the same for any two processes. Thus the process does not describe at all how the economy actually reaches an equilibrium price vector $\hat{p}$, the very problem with which Walras was concerned.[5]

Here we may note that the stability analysis of the *tâtonnement* process, however unrealistic it may look, is one of fundamental importance in economics. Some of the reasons for this are as follows:

(i) It is a genuine model which describes how the economy can reach an equilibrium. As long as we describe our economy in terms of equilibrium relations such as $f(\hat{p}) = 0$, it is important to see how we can actually reach an equilibrium. Moreover, our economy may be constantly in disequilibrium as a result of changes in consumers' tastes, production technology, and the availability of resources in the economy. That is, the equilibrium relation may be constantly changing. Hence when the equilibrium relation $f(p) = 0$ moves to a new relation $\tilde{f}(p) = 0$, the price vector $\hat{p}$ with $f(\hat{p}) = 0$ does not necessarily sustain an equilibrium under the new relation. Hence if the economic model described by equilibrium relations is to be meaningful, it must contain a model of the adjustment mechanism, by which the equilibrium if disturbed could be restored.[6] [In the above example, if $\tilde{f}(p^*) = 0$ for a unique p^*, the mechanism which brings $\hat{p}$ to p^* should be established.] The *tâtonnement* process, if it is a stable process, offers such a model. We may also note that the dynamic stability analysis which has been described in this chapter *can* be relevant for a model which is more realistic and does not necessarily involve the *tâtonnement* process. The author once offered such a model [13]. Even if we grant that the *tâtonnement* process is unrealistic, this does not negate the importance of the dynamic stability analysis described in this chapter. Moreover, there exist adjustment processes in the real economy which resemble the *tâtonnement* process—for example, the stock market, the fish market, the corn market, and so on.

(ii) In Chapter 2, Section C, we showed that a competitive equilibrium is a Pareto optimal state. Moreover, a competitive equilibrium has a unique feature: a decentralized decision-making process. Even apart from the problem of individual incentives and the like, the decentralized process seems to have a clear advantage over a centralized decision-making process. It does not involve the almost impossible task (and accompanying costs) of collecting all the relevant data on each consumer's tastes, each firm's production set, the resource availability, and so on, so that the "center" may treat these data in such a way as to obtain a decision. Hence the model of a competitive equilibrium, whether it is realistic or not, offers an excellent prototype for the optimal organization of a society and can be used as a realistic means of achieving a social optimum (even by a socialist state). Thus when the model of a competitive equilibrium is viewed as a realistic device for achieving a Pareto optimum, we certainly should know how we can actually reach this "equilibrium" state. The *tâtonnement* process, if it is stable, offers exactly such a process.[7] See Arrow and Hurwicz [2], for example.[8]

Now let us return to the unrealistic elements of the *tâtonnement* process. How can all the traders in the economy gather in one place and exchange tickets? How can actual trade (and production) be prohibited until an equilibrium price has been achieved? Despite the fact that we can offer an example from a real economy which is based on the stability analysis described in this chapter but does not contain the above difficulties, it is certainly very important to consider models which explicitly avoid the unrealistic elements mentioned above. Such models have been developed recently and are known as non-*tâtonnement* processes. The only models of non-*tâtonnement* processes developed so far are pure exchange models. In such models, the dynamic adjustment equation $dp(t)/dt = f[p(t)]$ $(\equiv \sum x_i[p(t)] - \sum \bar{x}_i)$ is replaced by

$$\frac{dp_j(t)}{dt} = \sum_{i=1}^{m} x_{ij}[p(t), \bar{x}_1(t), \bar{x}_2(t), \ldots, \bar{x}_m(t)] - \sum_{i=1}^{m} \bar{x}_{ij}(t), j = 1, 2, \ldots, n$$

and

$$\frac{d\bar{x}_{ij}(t)}{dt} = F_{ij}[p(t), \bar{x}_1(t), \ldots, \bar{x}_m(t)], i = 1, 2, \ldots, m; j = 1, 2, \ldots, n$$

Here x_{ij} denotes Mr. i's demand for commodity j, $\bar{x}_{ij}(t)$ denotes Mr. i's holding of the commodity j at time $t(i = 1, 2, \ldots, m)$, and $\bar{x}_i(t)$ is a vector denoting $[\bar{x}_{i1}(t), \ldots, \bar{x}_{in}(t)]$. The functions F_{ij} denote the transaction rules that individuals follow to change their stock of commodities $\bar{x}_{ij}$. Thus $\sum_{i=1}^{m} \bar{x}_i(t)$ denotes the vector of all the commodities available in the economy at time t. In the case of pure exchange, $\sum_{i=1}^{m} \bar{x}_i(t)$ is clearly a constant for all t (which implies $\sum_{i=1}^{m} dF_{ij}/dt = 0$ for all j). It should be clear that $\bar{x}_{ij}(t)$ moves over time and this represents the essence of the non-*tâtonnement* process which allows intermediate purchases. In the non-*tâtonnement* process the resource allocation $\bar{x}(t) = [\bar{x}_1(t), \bar{x}_2(t), \ldots, \bar{x}_m(t)]$ as well as the price vector $[p_1(t), \ldots, p_n(t)]$ are the adjustment parameters of the system. We call $[p^*, \bar{x}^*]$ an **equilibrium state** of the non-*tâtonnement* process if

$$\sum_{i=1}^{m} x_{ij}[p^*, \bar{x}^*] = \sum_{i=1}^{m} \bar{x}_{ij} \left(= \sum_{i=1}^{m} \bar{x}_{ij}(0) \right), j = 1, 2, \ldots, n$$

We can define "stability" in terms of

$$[p(t), \bar{x}(t)] \rightarrow [p^*, \bar{x}^*] \text{ as } t \rightarrow \infty$$

Three kinds of non-*tâtonnement* processes are well known in the literature, all of which are confined to the model of the pure exchange economy:[9]

(i)   A **barter process** (Negishi [8]). In a barter exchange economy, to get something one must offer something else of equal value. Hence such an exchange does not alter the total value of the commodities held by each individual. That is,

$$\sum_{j=1}^{n} p_j \left(\frac{d\bar{x}_{ij}}{dt} \right) = \sum_{j=1}^{n} p_j F_{ij} = 0 \quad \text{for all } t, i = 1, 2, \ldots, m$$

Negishi [8] showed that the barter process is stable under the gross substitutability assumption.

However, one may ask whether or not we can avoid the use of the gross substitutability assumption in the adjustment of the non-*tâtonnement* process. This may be done by specifying the rule of exchange in the above barter process in more detail. In fact, the Edgeworth process and the Hahn-Negishi process are examples of such a process.

(ii) **Edgeworth process** (Uzawa [14], Hahn [3], Morishima [7]). This process is based on the assumption that each individual participates in the exchange as long as it increases his satisfaction. Hence in the Edgeworth exchange process, it is supposed that the utility of the stock of commodities held by each individual increases over time as a result of the exchange transactions (the process is named after Edgeworth who first described it in his paper originally written in 1891 and published in his *Papers Relating to Political Economy*, Vol. II, London, Macmillan, 1925). When the process reaches a Pareto optimal point, it cannot move any further by definition; hence it is an equilibrium point. Let u_i be Mr. i's utility function and consider the following constrained maximum problem:[10]

$$\text{Maximize:} \quad \sum_{i=1}^{m} \alpha_i u_i(x_i)$$

$$\text{Subject to:} \quad \sum_{i=1}^{m} x_{ij} = \sum_{i=1}^{m} \bar{x}_{ij}$$

$$\sum_{j=1}^{n} p_j x_{ij} = \sum_{j=1}^{n} p_j \bar{x}_{ij}, \text{ and}$$

$$u_i(x_i) \geq u_i(\bar{x}_i)$$

where $x_i = (x_{i1}, x_{i2}, \ldots, x_{in})$. Let $\hat{x} = (\hat{x}_1, \hat{x}_2, \ldots, \hat{x}_m)$ be a solution to this constrained maximum problem. Obviously for each t we have a different $\bar{x}_{ij}(t)$ and hence a different $\hat{x}$. The Edgeworth process moves in the direction of a solution of such a constrained maximum problem; that is,

$$\frac{d\bar{x}_{ij}}{dt} = \hat{x}_{ij}(t) - \bar{x}_{ij}(t), i = 1, \ldots, m; j = 1, 2, \ldots, n$$

Uzawa [14] claims that he has shown that the Edgeworth process is stable.[11]

(iii) **Hahn-Negishi process** ([4]). This is based on the assumption that if there is an excess supply of a certain commodity, then all the buyers of this commodity can achieve their desires, and that if there is an excess demand for a certain commodity, then all the sellers of this commodity can achieve their desires. The following relations illustrate this process:

(1) (Disequilibrium)   If $x_{ij}(t) - \bar{x}_{ij}(t) \neq 0$, then sign $\left[x_{ij}(t) - \bar{x}_{ij}(t) \right] = $ sign $\left[\sum_{i=1}^{m} x_{ij}(t) - \sum_{i=1}^{m} \bar{x}_{ij}(t) \right]$, for all $i = 1, 2, \ldots, m; j = 1, 2, \ldots, n$.

(2) (Equilibrium)   If $\sum_{i=1}^{m} x_{ij}(t) - \sum_{i=1}^{m} \bar{x}_{ij}(t) = 0$, then $x_{ij}(t) - \bar{x}_{ij}(t) = 0$, for all $i = 1, 2, \ldots, m$.

Statement (1) means that if there is an excess demand for j (that is, $\sum_i x_{ij} - \sum_i \bar{x}_{ij} > 0$), then all the sellers can sell (hence $x_{ij} - \bar{x}_{ij} = 0$ if Mr. i is a seller) and not all the buyers can buy (hence $x_{ij} - \bar{x}_{ij} \geq 0$ if Mr. i is a buyer). On the other hand, if $\sum_i x_{ij} - \sum_i \bar{x}_{ij} < 0$, then all the buyers can buy (hence $x_{ij} - \bar{x}_{ij} = 0$ if Mr. i is a buyer) but not all the sellers can sell (hence $x_{ij} - \bar{x}_{ij} \leq 0$ if Mr. i is a seller). Using properties (1) and (2), Hahn and Negishi [4] proved the stability of this process without using the gross substitutability assumption.

FOOTNOTES

1. Walras apparently was not fully aware of the significance of such a "false trading" (or "recontracting") for he introduced such a concept in his theory of *production* but there is no evidence that he considered it seriously in his theory of *exchange* (see Patinkin, [12] esp. Note B). Newman argues that Walras' *tâtonnement* was not meant to be a device to deal with false trading, but that "the device was meant to cope with—the problem of convergence of the 'excess demand' mechanism in *multiple market* situations." (See P. Newman, *The Theory of Exchange*, Englewood Cliffs, N. J., Prentice-Hall, 1965, p. 102.) Incidentally, for a modern mathematical treatment of the Walrasian successive *tâtonnement* process in the theory of pure exchange, see H. Uzawa, "Walras' Tâtonnement in the Theory of Exchange," *Review of Economic Studies*, XXVII, June 1960.

2. Negishi ([11], p. 135) has proposed that the "market manager" in the *tâtonnement* process may be regarded as the "incarnation of the competitive forces in the market." Although this is an interesting observation, it has an objectionable flavor of metaphysics, as was the case with the "invisible hand." Moreover, in most markets, it is not easy to think of such a "competitive force."

3. See also Arrow [1] and Takayama [13], for similar comments.

4. Or we may consider that f depends on the allocation of commodities among the traders (in the theory of pure exchange). Given a price vector p and an initial resource vector $\bar{x}_i = [\bar{x}_{i1}, \ldots, \bar{x}_{in}]$, trader i chooses his demand vector $x_i = (x_{i1}, \ldots, x_{in})$, so that we may write $x_i = x_i(p, \bar{x}_i)$. The market excess demand vector is defined as $\sum x_i - \sum \bar{x}_i$, which can, therefore, be written as $f(p, \bar{x}_1, \ldots, \bar{x}_m)$, assuming m traders in the economy. Now if actual transactions are allowed in the process, the $\bar{x}_i$'s (as well as p) change from time to time so that $dp(t)/dt = f[p(t), \bar{x}_1(t), \ldots, \bar{x}_m(t)]$. Here f does not change over time. See the latter part of this section.

5. Hahn [3] pointed out a rather artificial case in which intermediate transactions are allowed which have no effect on the distribution of welfare between individuals. This is the case in which no stocks of commodities exist but where there is a continuous flow of perishable commodities.

6. This is the point emphasized by Samuelson when he proposed the "correspondence

principle." Its application to macro-economics was emphasized by Patinkin [12].
But we cannot see the relevance of the *tâtonnement* process to macro-economics, for
we cannot quite visualize all people involved in a "macro-economy" gathered in one
place to exchange tickets.

7. Notice that the *tâtonnement* process offers a method of computing an equilibrium
   price vector without actually specifying the function f. In the process, $dp_i(t)/dt = k_i f_i[p(t)]$ [or $p_i(t + 1) = p_i(t) + k_i f_i[p(t)]$], for example, $f_i[p(t)]$, $i = 1, 2, \ldots, n$,
   can be easily computed by adding or subtracting the numbers recorded on the
   "tickets," so that the market manager does not have to know the functions f_i at
   all in computing the new price vector. If the process is stable, the price vector
   eventually comes close to the equilibrium vector.

8. There is a recent interest in the topic of "optimal" organization of society and possible adjustment processes toward an "optimal" state by economists such as L.
   Hurwicz, S. Reiter, J. Marschak, T. Marschak, R. Radner, and A. Camacho. The
   classical article on this topic is L., Hurwicz, "Optimality and Informational Efficiency
   in Resource Allocation Processes," in *Mathematical Methods in the Social Sciences*,
   ed. by K. J. Arrow, S. Karlin, and P. Suppes, Stanford Calif., Stanford University
   Press, 1960.

9. The proofs of stability for these processes can best be done by utilizing the Liapunov
   "second method" or its modified form. For a sketch of the proof, see Negishi [10].
   An exposition of the Liapunov second method will be given in the next section of
   this chapter.

10. Here the α_i's are assumed to be positive constants.

11. A minor flaw in [14] was pointed out by R. W. Ruppert and R. R. Russel in their
    "A Note on Uzawa's Barter Process," *International Economic Review*, 13, June 1972.

REFERENCES

1. Arrow, K. J., "Towards a Theory of Price Adjustment", in *The Allocations of Resources*, ed. by M. Abramovitz, Stanford, Calif., Stanford University Press, 1959.

2. Arrow, K. J., and Hurwicz, L., "Decentralization and Computation in Resource
   Allocation," in *Essays in Economics and Econometrics*, ed. by R. Phouts, Chapel Hill,
   N.C., University of North Carolina Press, 1960.

3. Hahn, F. H., "On the Stability of a Pure Exchange Equilibrium," *International
   Economic Review*, 3, May 1962.

4. Hahn, F. H., and Negishi, T., "A Theorem on Non-tâtonnement Stability," *Econometrica*, 30, July 1962.

5. Koopmans, T. C., *Three Essays on the State of Economic Science*, New York,
   McGraw-Hill, 1957.

6. Morishima, M., *Dynamic Economic Theory* (Dogakuteki Keizai Riron), Tokyo,
   Kobundo, 1950 (in Japanese).

7. ———, "The Stability of Exchange Equilibrium: An Alternative Approach," *International Economic Review*, 3, May 1962.

8. Negishi, T., "On the Formation of Prices," *International Economic Review*, 2, January
   1961.

9. ———, "On the Successive Barter Process," *Economic Studies Quarterly*, XII, January
   1962.

10.   ———, "Stability of a Competitive Economy: A Survey Article," *Econometrica*, 30, October 1962.

11.   ———,*Theories of Price and Resource Allocation* (Kakaku to Haibun no Riron), Tokyo, Toyo Keizai Shimpo-sha, 1965 (in Japanese)

12.   Patinkin, D., *Money, Interest and Prices*, 2nd ed., New York, Harper and Row, 1965.

13.   Takayama, A., "Stability in the Balance of Payments, A Multi-Country Approach," *The Journal of Economic Behavior*, 1, October 1961.

14.   Uzawa, H., "On the Stability of Edgeworth's Barter Process," *International Economic Review*, 3, May 1962.

15.   Walras, L., *Elements of Pure Economics*, tr. by Jaffé, London, George Allen & Unwin, 1954.

Section H

LIAPUNOV'S SECOND METHOD

In connection with the proof of the global stability of an equilibrium, people found that Liapunov's second method might be useful. The distance function adopted in the above proof of global stability by Arrow, Block, and Hurwicz may be considered a Liapunov function (of his "second method"). The first explicit use of this method was probably by McKenzie [7], who, in turn, acknowledges the idea to Arrow. The history of Liapunov's method, consisting of the "first method" and the "second method," goes back to 1892, but it was practically unknown until its French translation appeared in 1907 [1]. Since the 1930s, major developments in the theory of the stability of differential equations have occurred in the U.S.S.R. **Liapunov's first method** is to find explicit power series solutions, convergent near the origin, and then to deduce the stability from the behavior of the series, for large t. **Liapunov's second method**, on the other hand, makes no attempt to find explicit solutions. This allows a far greater range of applications for the second method than for the first. However, the second method cannot provide any *explicit* information on the actual behavior of the solutions.

Consider the following systems of differential equations:

(A) $$\frac{dx_i}{dt} = f_i(x_1, x_2, \ldots, x_n), i = 1, 2, \ldots, n$$

or

$$\frac{dx}{dt} = f(x), \text{ where } f: X \to R^n, X \subset R^n$$

(NA) $$\frac{dx_i}{dt} = f_i(x_1, x_2, \ldots, x_n; t), i = 1, 2, \ldots, n$$

or

$$\frac{dx}{dt} = f(x, t), \text{ where } f: X \otimes (-\infty, \infty) \rightarrow R^n, X \subset R^n$$

In both systems, f is assumed to be continuous.

As discussed in Section B, the system (A) is called the **autonomous system** and the system (NA) is called the **nonautonomous system**. Let $\hat{x}$ be an equilibrium point of the (A) system, that is, $f(\hat{x}) = 0$ [or $f(\hat{x}; t) = 0$ for all t, for (NA)]. We may choose $\hat{x} = 0$ if we wish. This is not really much of a restriction, for by defining $y \equiv x - \hat{x}$, we get a new system $dy/dt = f(y)$ [or $dy/dt = f(y; t)$] whose equilibrium point is the origin, that is, $\hat{y} = 0$. We assume that $\hat{x}$ is an *isolated* equilibrium point in the sense that there is no other equilibrium point in some open ball about $\hat{x}$. We assume that the initial point $x(t^0)$ (where t^0 is the "initial" time) lies inside this open ball. If the equilibrium is unique, we take this open ball to be the whole space in which both systems, (A) and (NA), are defined. We are concerned with the global stability of the solution of the above systems $x(t; x^0, t^0)$, which start from an initial point $x(t^0) \equiv x^0$.

We now define various concepts of stability. We assume that there exists a unique solution determined by the initial point and that it is continuous with respect to the initial point. We write the solution vector starting from (x^0, t^0) as $x(t; x^0, t^0)$.

Definition (S₁):   An equilibrium state $\hat{x}$ of a dynamic system is called **Liapunov stable** if for any real number $\epsilon > 0$ and any t^0 there exists a positive real number δ such that

$$\| x^0 - \hat{x} \| \leq \delta \text{ implies } \| x(t; x^0, t^0) - \hat{x} \| \leq \epsilon$$

for all $t \geq t^0$ where $\delta = \delta(\epsilon, t^0)$ (that is, δ is dependent on ϵ and t^0).[1]

> *REMARK:*   This concept is a local concept; that is, it refers to behavior near $\hat{x}$, since δ can be very small. Moreover, this does not say that $x(t; x^0, t^0)$ converges to $\hat{x}$. The concept of Liapunov stability is illustrated in Figure 3.9.[2]

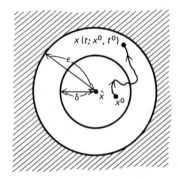

Figure 3.9.   An Illustration of Liapunov Stability.

In essence it says that if x^0 is sufficiently close to $\hat{x}$, then $x(t; x^0, t^0)$ remains bounded for all t.

Definition (S_2): An equilibrium state $\hat{x}$ of a dynamic system is called (**asymptotically**) **locally stable** if[3]

   (i)   It is Liapunov stable, *and*

  (ii) Every motion starting sufficiently close to $\hat{x}$ converges to $\hat{x}$ as $t \to \infty$. In other words, for any $\mu > 0$ there exists an $r = r(t^0) > 0$ and $T = T(\mu, x^0, t^0)$ such that $\| x^0 - \hat{x} \| \leq r(t^0)$ implies $\| x(t; x^0, t^0) - \hat{x} \| \leq \mu$, for all $t \geq t^0 + T$, where r and T are some real numbers dependent on t^0 and (μ, x^0, t^0), respectively.

REMARK: This again is a local concept, for $r(t^0)$ can be very small. A somewhat puzzling thing in the definition is that (S_1) (Liapunov stability) has to be mentioned even though we have (ii); that is, (ii) in the above definition alone does not necessarily imply (i). Kalman and Bertram ([3], pp. 375–376) gave the following example.

EXAMPLE: Consider the second-order system in polar coordinates

$$x = (r, \theta), 0 \leq r < \infty, 0 \leq \theta < 2\pi$$
$$\dot{r} = [\dot{g}(\theta, t)/g(\theta, t)] r$$

$$\dot{\theta} = 0$$

where $g(\theta, t) = \sin^2\theta/[\sin^4\theta + (1 - t \sin^2\theta)^2] + 1/(1 + t^2)$. Here (ii) of ($S_2$) is satisfied but (i) of (S_2) [that is, (S_1)] is not satisfied. However, if all motions are continuous in x^0, then we can show that if every motion sufficiently close to $\hat{x}$ converges *uniformly* to $\hat{x}$, then (S_1) holds (see [3], p. 376).

Definition (S_3): An equilibrium state $\hat{x}$ of a dynamic system is called (**asymptotically**) **globally stable**[4] if

   (i)   It is Liapunov stable, *and*

  (ii) Every motion converges to $\hat{x}$ *as* $t \to \infty$.

REMARK: If a system is autonomous [that is, $\dot{x} = f(x)$], then we can show that δ, r, and T in the preceding definitions do not depend on t^0. Hence (1) if $\hat{x}$ is Liapunov stable, it is uniformly Liapunov stable; and (2) if $\hat{x}$ is asymptotically locally stable, it is *uniformly* asymptotically locally stable. Moreover, we can show that if $\hat{x}$ is asymptotically globally stable it is uniformly asymptotically globally stable, the latter being defined as follows:

Definition (S_4): An equilibrium state $\hat{x}$ of a dynamic system is called **uniformly** (**asymptotically**) **globally stable** if

(i) It is *uniformly* Liapunov stable in the sense that δ in the definition of (S_1) does not depend on t^0, *and*

(ii) Every motion converges to $\hat{x}$ as $t \to \infty$ uniformly in t^0 and $\| x^0 \| \leq r$ where r is fixed and can be arbitrarily large. [That is, given *any* $r > 0$ and $\mu > 0$, there is some $T(\mu, r)$ such that $\| x^0 - \hat{x} \| \leq r$ implies $\| x(t; x^0, t^0) - \hat{x} \| \leq \mu$ for all $t \geq t^0 + T$.]

Definition (S_5):   An equilibrium state $\hat{x}$ of a dynamic system is called **(asymptotically) strongly uniformly globally stable**[5] if

(i) It is uniformly (**asymptotically**) globally stable, *and*

(ii) It is **uniformly bounded** in the sense that, for any given $r > 0$, there is some $B = B(r)$ such that $\| x^0 - \hat{x} \| \leq r$ implies $\| x(t^0; x^0, t^0) - \hat{x} \| \leq B$.

REMARK: The above concepts may be illustrated by Figure 3.10, where the arrow reads "implies" and "+ (autonomous)" reads "if the system is autonomous."

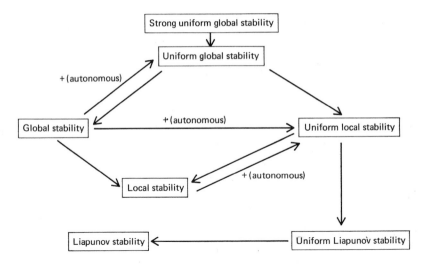

Figure 3.10.   Relations among Various Concepts of Stability.

We are now ready to state some of the major results obtained by Liapunov and his followers.

Theorem 3.H.1:   *Consider the autonomous system* (A) [*that is,* $\dot{x} = f(x)$] *with* $f(0) = 0$. *Suppose that there exists a real-valued continuously differentiable function* $V(x)$ *on X such that*

(i) $V(x) > 0$ for all $x \neq 0$, $V(0) = 0$,[6]
(ii) $dV[x(t; x^0, t^0)]/dt < 0$ for all $x(t; x^0, t^0) \neq 0$,[7]
(iii) $V(x) \to \infty$ with $\| x \| \to \infty$.

Then *the equilibrium state* $\hat{x} = 0$ *is uniformly globally stable, so that* $x(t; x^0, t^0) \to$ 0 *(for any* t^0 *and* x^0*), as* $t \to \infty$.

REMARK: The function $V(x)$ is called a **Liapunov function** of system (A).

EXAMPLE: Consider $\dot{x} = -x^3$, $x \in R$. Define the Liapunov function for this system by $V(x) \equiv x^2$. Conditions (i) and (iii) above are obviously satisfied. To show (ii), observe that $\dot{V} = -2x^4$.

The above theorem provides sufficient conditions for "complete" stability in the sense that the uniform global stability holds for the entire region X (which can be R^n). The next theorem provides sufficient conditions for the uniform global stability of a certain subregion of X.

Theorem 3.H.2:   *Consider* (A) *with* $f(0) = 0$ *and suppose that there exists a real-valued continuously differentiable function* $V(x)$ *on* X *and a region* $D \equiv \{x \in X: V(x) < k\}$ *which is nonempty and bounded such that*

(i) $V(x) > 0$ for all $x \neq 0$, $x \in D$, and $V(0) = 0$, and
(ii) $dV[x(t; x^0, t^0)]/dt < 0$ for all $x(t; x^0, t^0) \neq 0$, $x(t; x^0, t^0) \in D$.

Then $\hat{x} = 0$ *is Liapunov stable and* $x(t; x^0, t^0)$, *the solution of* (A), *converges to* $\hat{x} = 0$ *as* $t \to \infty$ *for any* t^0, *if* $x^0 \in D$.

REMARK: The function $V(x)$ in the above theorem is again called the **Liapunov function** of the system (A). Again, condition (ii) implies that the origin is the unique equilibrium point.

EXAMPLE: Consider the **van del Pol equation**, $\ddot{x} - \epsilon(x^2 - 1)\dot{x} + x = 0$ where $\epsilon > 0$,[8] or its equivalent form,[9] $\dot{x} = y + \epsilon(x^3/3 - x)$, $\dot{y} = -x$. Define the Liapunov function for this by $V(x, y) \equiv (x^2 + y^2)/2$. Then $\dot{V} = \epsilon x^2(x^2/3 - 1)$ along the solution path, so that $\dot{V} \leq 0$ if $x^2 \leq 3$. Define the region D by $D \equiv \{(x, y) \in R^2 : x^2 + y^2 < 3\}$. Then we have $\dot{V}(x, y) \leq 0$, as well as $V(x, y) \geq 0$, for all (x, y) in D [note that $V(x, y) = 0$ only when $(x, y) = (0, 0)$; that is, condition (i) of Theorem 3.H.2 is satisfied]. Now observe that $\dot{V}(x, y) = 0$ along the solution path only when $x = 0$, that is, only when (x, y) is on the y-axis. But if $x^0 = 0$ and $y^0 \neq 0$, then $\dot{V} < 0$ for any $t > t^0$, for $\dot{x} = y$ on the y-axis. This proves condition (ii) of Theorem 3.H.2. Therefore $x(t; x^0, y^0, t^0) \to 0$ and $y(t; x^0, y^0, t^0) \to 0$ as $t \to \infty$, provided that $(x^0, y^0) \in D$.

We now state the asymptotic stability theorem for the nonautonomous system.

Theorem 3.H.3:   *Consider the nonautonomous system (NA)*, $\dot{x} = f(x, t)$ *with* $f(0; t) = 0$ *for all t. Suppose that there exists a real-valued continuously differentiable function* $V(x, t)$ *on* $X \otimes (-\infty, \infty)$ *such that* $V(0, t) = 0$, *and*

   (i)   *There exist continuous nondecreasing real-valued functions* α *and* β *such that* $\alpha(0) = 0$ *and* $\beta(0) = 0$ *and* $0 < \alpha(\|x\|) \leq V(x, t) \leq \beta(\|x\|)$ *for all t and all* $x \neq 0$,

   (ii)   *There exists a continuous real-valued function* γ *such that* $\gamma(0) = 0$ *and* $dV[x(t; x^0, t^0), t]/dt \leq -\gamma(\|x\|) < 0$ *for all t and all* $x \neq 0$,[10]

   (iii) $\alpha(\|x\|) \rightarrow \infty$ *with* $\|x\| \rightarrow \infty$.

Then *the equilibrium state* $\hat{x} = 0$ *is strongly uniformly globally stable so that* $x(t; x^0, t^0) \rightarrow \hat{x} = 0$ *for any* x^0 *and* t^0 *when* $t \rightarrow \infty$. *The function* $V(x, t)$ *is called a* **Liapunov function** *of the system (NA)*.

   REMARK: For the proof of the above theorems, see Kalman and Bertram [3]; LaSalle and Lefshetz [4], chapter 2; and Yoshizawa [10], chapter 5.

   REMARK: If $V(x, t)$ in Theorem 3.H.3 is positive definite and if $dV[x(t; x^0, t^0), t]/dt \leq 0$ (instead of < 0), then we can merely say that $\hat{x} = 0$ is Liapunov stable.

   REMARK: Conditions (i), (ii), and (iii) of Theorem 3.H.3 can be restated as follows: There exist continuous positive definite functions $a(x)$, $b(x)$, and $c(x)$ such that

   (i) $a(x) \leq V(x, t) \leq b(x)$ for all t and all $x \neq 0$,

   (ii) $dV[x(t; x^0, t^0), t]/dt \leq -c(x)$, for all t and all $x \neq 0$, where $\|x\| < \infty$, *and*

   (iii) $a(x) \rightarrow \infty$ as $\|x\| \rightarrow \infty$.

   REMARK: The converse of Theorem 3.H.3 is also, in a sense, true. In particular, we can show the following: Let f in (NA) be Lipschitzian[11] and suppose that $f(0, t) = 0$ for all t. If $\hat{x} = 0$ is strongly uniformly globally stable, then there exists a real-valued function $V(x, t)$, infinitely differentiable in x and t, which satisfies the hypothesis of Theorem 3.H.3.[12]

   Functions α and β in (i) and (ii) of Theorem 3.H.3 are illustrated by Figure 3.11.

   As a result of the above theorems, the proof of the stability of a certain dynamic system can be obtained by finding a Liapunov function for the system. Many stability theorems in the literature are obtained as special cases of the above dynamic systems (A) and (NA). (For example, see Kalman and Bertram [3].)

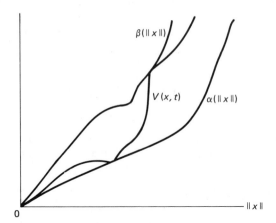

Figure 3.11.   An Illustration of α and β in Theorem 3.H.3.

An important stability condition for the linear case $[f(x) = A \cdot x$ where A is an $n \times n$ matrix with constant components$]$, that is, the Routh-Hurwitz condition, can be obtained from Theorem 3.H.1. (See, for example, Kalman and Bertram [3], pp. 381–382.) In mechanics or thermodynamics, a natural candidate for a Liapunov function is the amount of total energy[13] or, with the sign reversed, total entropy. The proof of the stability of a competitive equilibrium can be handled by finding a Liapunov function. Let $\dot{p} = f(p)$, where $p = (p_1, p_2, \ldots, p_n)$ denotes a price vector. This is clearly an autonomous system. The distance function $D(t)$ [or $D_m(t)$] introduced in the proof by Arrow, Block, and Hurwicz can be considered a Liapunov function, although they made no explicit use of Theorem 3.H.1. McKenzie [7] constructed the following Liapunov function for the above system:

$$V(t) = \sum_{i=1}^{n} p_i |f_i(p)|$$

that is, $V(t)$ is the sum of the absolute values of the excess demands multiplied by their prices. Clearly $V(t) > 0$, whenever $p \neq \hat{p}$ ($\hat{p} \equiv$ an equilibrium price vector), and $V = 0$ when $p = \hat{p}$. Hence, if we can show that $\dot{V} < 0$, the proof of the stability is almost complete. For a short sketch of the proof that $\dot{V} < 0$, we refer the reader to Negishi ([8], pp. 656–657). See also Chapter 4, Section D.

In the Liapunov method discussed above, it is assumed that the equilibrium point is either isolated or unique. However, it is often important to consider cases in which there are more than one equilibrium point which are not isolated. As we remarked in Section B, Uzawa [9] reconsidered Liapunov's second method to allow for such a case. Let $f: X \to R^n$ be continuous and consider a system of differential equations $\dot{x}(t) = f[x(t)]$. Let x^0 be the initial value of x at $t = 0$. Assume that, for any value of $x^0 \in X$, this system of differential equations has a unique solution $x(t, x^0)$ for all $t \geq 0$, which is continuous at x^0. Let E be the set of all equilibrium vectors, that is, $E \equiv \{\hat{x}: \hat{x} \in X \text{ and } f(\hat{x}) = 0\}$. Since $f(x)$ is continuous, E is closed in X.

Definition: The process $\dot{x} = f[x(t)]$ is called **quasi-stable** if its solution $x(t; x^0)$ satisfies the following conditions:

(i) Every limit point of $x(t, x^0)$, as t tends to infinity, is an equilibrium. That is, if for some sequence t^q, $q = 1, 2, \ldots$, such that $t^q \to \infty$, $\lim x(t^q, x^0)$, as $q \to \infty$, exists, then $\lim_{q \to \infty} x(t^q, x^0)$ is an equilibrium.

(ii) It is uniformly bounded; that is, for any given $r > 0$, there is some number $B = B(r)$ such that $\| x^0 - \hat{x} \| \leq r$ implies $\| x(t; x^0, t^0) - \hat{x} \| \leq B$.

REMARK: Uzawa [9] has shown that if the set X is closed, quasi-stability is equivalent to

(i') $\lim\limits_{t \to \infty} V[x(t; x^0)] = 0$,   where $V(x) \equiv \inf\limits_{\hat{x} \in E} |x - \hat{x}|, x \in X$

The function $V(x)$ signifies the distance between point x and the equilibrium set E. This function V will play the role of the Liapunov function.

REMARK: If the equilibrium points are isolated from each other, then condition (i') means nothing but the asymptotic convergence of $x(t, x^0)$ to some equilibrium point. The concept of quasi-stability, however, allows the case in which the equilibrium points are not isolated and the solution $x(t, x^0)$ does not necessarily converge to a particular point in the equilibrium set (see Section B of this chapter).

Uzawa then proved the following theorem and showed its application.

Theorem 3.H.4:   *Suppose that the solution $x(t; x^0, t^0)$ of $\dot{x} = f[x(t)]$ is contained in a compact set X, and*

(U)   *There exists a continuous function $V(x)$ defined on X such that $V[x(t, x^0)]$ is a strictly decreasing function with respect to t unless $x(t, x^0)$ is an equilibrium.*

Then *the process $\dot{x} = f[x(t)]$ is quasi-stable.*

REMARK: Uzawa called the function $V(x)$ above a **modified Liapunov function**. Unlike Liapunov's V, it is not assumed to be differentiable and positive definite.

As an illustration of such a theorem applied to stability analysis, consider the nonnormalized adjustment process of a competitive equilibrium:[14]

$$\frac{dp_i}{dt} = f_i[p(t)], i = 1, 2, \ldots, n$$

where we have

(i) (Homogeneity) $f_i(p) = f_i(\alpha p)$ for all $\alpha > 0$, and for all $p, i = 1, 2, \ldots, n$.
(ii) (Gross substitutability) $\partial f_i / \partial p_j > 0$ for all $i \neq j$ and for all p.

Assume that an equilibrium price vector exists, and denote it by $\hat{p}$. Assume further that the above system of differential equations has a unique solution $p(t; p^0)$ for all $t \geq 0$, which is continuous in p^0, where $p^0 > 0$.
  Following Uzawa [9], define the functions $V(p)$ and $v(p)$ by

$$V(p) \equiv \max \left\{\frac{p_1(t)}{\hat{p}_1}, \frac{p_2(t)}{\hat{p}_2}, \ldots, \frac{p_n(t)}{\hat{p}_n}\right\}$$

and

$$v(p) \equiv \min \left\{\frac{p_1(t)}{\hat{p}_1}, \frac{p_2(t)}{\hat{p}_2}, \ldots, \frac{p_n(t)}{\hat{p}_n}\right\}$$

The functions $V(p)$ and $v(p)$ are "proxies" for the distance between $p(t)$ and $\hat{p}$. These functions would play the role of the (modified) Liapunov function.[15]
  Without loss of generality, we may assume that $p_1(t)/\hat{p}_1 \geq p_i(t)/\hat{p}_i$ for all i. That is, $V(p) = p_1(t)/\hat{p}_1$, for some time interval, say, τ. To simplify the exposition, assume further that $V(p)$ and $v(p)$ are differentiable in t.[16] We, hence, observe that

$$\frac{dV(p)}{dt} = \frac{1}{\hat{p}_1}\frac{dp_1(t)}{dt} = \frac{1}{\hat{p}_1}[x_1(p) - \bar{x}_1]$$

$$= \frac{1}{\hat{p}_1}[x_1(\frac{\hat{p}_1}{p_1}p_1, \frac{\hat{p}_1}{p_1}p_2, \ldots, \frac{\hat{p}_1}{p_1}p_n) - \bar{x}_1] \qquad (\because \text{homogeneity})$$

Since $\hat{p}_1/p_1 \leq \hat{p}_i/p_i$ for all i with strict inequality for at least one i,[17] we have

$$x_1(\frac{\hat{p}_1}{p_1}p_1, \ldots, \frac{\hat{p}_1}{p_1}p_n) < x_1(\hat{p}_1, \ldots, \hat{p}_n) = \bar{x}_1$$

due to gross substitutability. Hence $dV/dt < 0$ for the time interval τ if $p(t; p^0)$ is not an equilibrium vector. A similar argument holds for any time interval so that $dV/dt < 0$ for all t, if $p(t; p^0)$ is not an equilibrium vector. Similarly, we can show that $dv/dt > 0$ for all t, if $p(t; p^0)$ is not an equilibrium vector. Hence the solution $p(t; p^0)$ is contained in a compact set $\{p : v(p^0) \leq p_i/\hat{p}_i \leq V(p^0), i = 1, 2, \ldots, n\}$ of positive vectors.[18] Hence by applying Theorem 3.H.4, every limit point of $p(t)$ as t tends to infinity is an equilibrium point. Hence there exists a sequence t^q such that $t^q \to \infty$ $(q \to \infty)$ and

$$\lim_{t^q \to \infty} \frac{p_i(t^q)}{\hat{p}_i} = 1, \, i = 1, 2, \ldots, n$$

Hence both $V[p(t^q; p^0)]$ and $v[p(t^q; p^0)]$ go to unity as $q \to \infty$. But

$$v[p(t; p^0)] \leq \frac{p_i(t; p^0)}{\hat{p}_i} \leq V[p(t; p^0)]$$

for all t and $i = 1, 2, \ldots, n$, and $V[p(t; p^0)]$ and $v[p(t; p^0)]$ are both bounded and monotonic. Therefore $\lim_{t \to \infty} p_i(t)/\hat{p}_i$ always exists and equals 1, for $i = 1, 2, \ldots, n$. This proves the uniqueness and global stability of the equilibrium price vector $\hat{p}$.

FOOTNOTES

1. We may show that if there is Liapunov stability for some initial time t^0, then there is Liapunov stability for any other initial time t^1, provided that all motions are continuous in the initial state.

2. In the above definition of Liapunov stability, if δ can be chosen independently of t^0, then $\hat{x}$ is said to be **uniformly Liapunov stable**. If $\hat{x}$ is not Liapunov stable, $\hat{x}$ is called **unstable**. An example of a *uniformly* Liapunov stable equilibrium is $\hat{x} = 0$ in $\dot{x} = 0, x \in R$.

3. As an example, consider $\dot{x} = -x/(t + 1), x \in R$. The solution can be written as $x(t; x^0, t^0) = x^0(t^0 + 1)/(t + 1)$. Then $\hat{x} = 0$ is asymptotically locally stable, since (1) $\|x(t; x^0, t^0)\| \leq \|x^0\|$ whenever $t \geq t^0$ (Liapunov stable) *and* (2) $x(t; x^0, t^0) \to 0$ as $t \to \infty$. If condition (i) in the definition is replaced by *uniform* Liapunov stability (that is, δ does not depend on t^0) *and* if r and T do not depend on t^0 in condition (ii), then $\hat{x}$ is said to be **uniformly (asymptotically) locally stable**. As an example, consider $\dot{x} = -x, x \in R$ and $\hat{x} = 0$. The point $\hat{x} = 0$ in the above example, $\dot{x} = -x/(t + 1), x \in R$, is *not uniformly* locally stable. See Yoshizawa [10], p. 96.

4. The phrase "globally stable" can be replaced by "stable in the large." Similarly, "locally stable" can be replaced by "stable in the small." The word "asymptotically" is often dropped in economics literature (although this is not usually the case in mathematics literature).

5. Often $\hat{x}$ is simply called **(asymptotically) uniformly globally stable**; that is, the word "strongly" is omitted. In this case no special name is given to the stability property of $\hat{x}$ under (S4).

6. That is, $V(x)$ is "positive definite." In general, any real-valued continuous function $V(x, t)$, defined on $X \otimes (-\infty, \infty)$ where $X \subset R^n$, is said to be **positive definite** in region $D \subset X$, if there exists a continuous real-valued function $W(x)$ defined on D such that $V(x, t) \geq W(x)$ for all t where $W(x) > 0$ if $x \neq 0$ and $W(0) = 0$.

7. That is, $\dot{V} < 0$ along the solution path $x(t; x^0, t^0)$. We may define such a $\dot{V}(x)$ by $\dot{V}(x) \equiv V_x(x) \cdot f(x)$, noting $\dot{x} = f(x)$, where V_x is the gradient vector of V. Clearly $\dot{V}(0) = 0$ since $f(0) = 0$. Note that condition (ii) implies that the origin is the unique equilibrium point, since if $\hat{x} \neq 0$ is an equilibrium point [that is, $f(\hat{x}) = 0$], then $\dot{V}(\hat{x}) = V_x(\hat{x})f(\hat{x}) = 0$, contradicting condition (ii).

8. The sign of ϵ is crucial. If $\epsilon < 0$, it is known that the only equilibrium point is the origin and it is unstable. Moreover, there is a unique "limit cycle" which surrounds

the origin. In economic theory such a differential equation (with $\epsilon < 0$) is associated with the so called "Kalecki-Kaldor model" of business cycles. The limit cycle is supposed to constitute the "business cycles." The name 'van del Pol' is due to his article, "Relaxation-Oscillations," *Philosophical Magazine*, series 7, vol. 2, November 1962.

9. This form is known as the "Liénard form." The present example is discussed in Yoshizawa [10].
10. Note that $dV[x(t, x^0, t^0), t]/dt \equiv V_x \cdot f[x(t, x^0, t^0), t] + \partial V/\partial t$.
11. That is, $\| f(x, t) - f(y, t) \| \leq k \| x - y \|$ where k is a positive constant.
12. This theorem is due to Massera. See J. L. Massera, "Contributions to Stability Theory." *Annals of Mathematics*, 64, 1956.
13. The following remark by Kalman and Bertram ([3], p. 371) is quite instructive.

   The principal idea of the second method is contained in the following physical reasoning: If the rate of change $dE(x)/dt$ of the energy $E(x)$ of an isolated physical system is negative for every possible state x, except for a single equilibrium state x_e, then the energy will continually decrease until it finally assumes its minimum value $E(x_e)$. In other words, a dissipative system perturbed from its equilibrium state will always return to it.

14. This illustration is from Uzawa [9], pp. 623–624.
15. The use of such proxies rather than the distance itself together with Theorem 3.H.4 simplify Uzawa's proof of global stability considerably.
16. In general, V and v are not necessarily differentiable in t, although they are continuous in t. However, the nondifferentiable case can be analyzed analogously. See Uzawa [9], pp. 623–624. Note that Theorem 3.H.4 requires only the continuity (and not the differentiability) of the modified Liapunov function.
17. For, otherwise, $p(t)$ is an equilibrium.
18. This proves $p(t; p^0) > 0$ for all $t \geq 0$, as long as $p^0 > 0$.

REFERENCES

1. Antosiewicz, H., "A Survey of Liapunov's Second Method," in *Contribution to Nonlinear Oscillations IV*, Princeton, N.J., Princeton University Press, 1958.
2. Hahn, W., *Theory and Application of Liapunov's Direct Method*, Englewood Cliffs, N.J., Prentice-Hall, 1963 (German original, 1959).
3. Kalman, R. E., and Bertram, J. E., "Control System Analysis and Design Via the 'Second Method' of Liapunov, I: Continuous-Time System," *Journal of Basic Engineering*, June 1960.
4. LaSalle, J., and Lefshetz, S., *Stability by Liapunov's Direct Method*, New York, Academic Press, 1961.
5. Liapunov, A. M., "Problem géneral de la stabilité du mouvement," *Annales de la Faculté de Sciences de l'Université de Toulouse* (2), 9, 1907, pp. 203–247 (in French). Reprinted in *Annals of Mathematical Study* No. 17, Princeton, N.J., Princeton University Press, 1949.
6. ———, *Stability of Motion*, New York, Academic Press, 1966.
7. McKenzie, L. W., "Stability of Equilibrium and the Value of Positive Excess Demand," *Econometrica*, 28, 1960.

8. Negishi, T., "The Stability of a Competitive Economy: A Survey Article," *Econometrica*, 30, October 1962.

9. Uzawa, H., "The Stability of Dynamic Processes," *Econometrica*, 29, October 1961.

10. Yoshizawa, T., *Introduction to Differential Equations*, Tokyo, Asakura-Shoten, 1967 (in Japanese).

11. Zubov, V. I., *Methods of A. M. Liapunov and their Application*, Netherlands, Noordhoff Gronigen, 1964.

4

FROBENIUS THEOREMS, DOMINANT DIAGONAL MATRICES, AND APPLICATIONS

In a general equilibrium model of an economy (such as the one we discussed in Chapter 2), there are usually two types of economic agents (consumers and producers) and various commodities. Each commodity is either reproducible or nonreproducible. The nonreproducible commodities are called "primary factors." In this section we call the reproducible commodities "goods." Each good is used for the production of other goods and/or consumption. In other words, it is demanded by producers and/or consumers, the two types of economic agents. When a general equilibrium model such as the Walras-Cassel model was popularized in the 1920s and 1930s, Wassily Leontief conceived of doing the empirical groundwork for it and actually attempted to do so using the U.S. economy as an example [8]. Thus we note that his path-breaking book has the subtitle "An Empirical Application of Equilibrium Analysis."

Let a_{ij} be the amount of the ith good used to produce one unit of the jth good $(i, j = 1, 2, \ldots, n)$. Let x_j be the amount of the jth good produced, and let c_i be the amount of the ith good used for (final) consumption purposes. Then the demand = supply equilibrium relation for each good is written as

(1) $$\sum_{j=1}^{n} a_{ij}x_j + c_i = x_i, i = 1, 2, \ldots, n$$

or, in vector notation,

(1') $$A \cdot x + c = x, \text{ where } A = \left[a_{ij}\right]$$

Here it is assumed that there is only one productive process which produces each good so that a_{ij} is constant for all i and j. (This assumption was adopted by Cassel and copied by Leontief.) The matrix A is called the **input-output matrix**. It was actually empirically estimated by Leontief [8]. To illustrate the use of the above relation, rewrite it as

(2) $$x = (I - A)^{-1} \cdot c$$

Here the matrix $(I - A)$ is assumed to be nonsingular. Now if we can predict the final consumption demand c, then x can be immediately computed from the above formula. Thus we can predict the output of each industry. This device was successfully used by Leontief for a post-World War II forecast and has become very popular since then. The input-output matrix (A) has been empirically estimated for many countries and its size has been considerably expanded in several of the countries. Many applications have been discovered for this type of study, and it is now called "input-output analysis." See, for example, Chenery and Clark [1] and Fukuchi [4]. It is considered an important tool for the analysis of economic decisions by governments.

Let us return to the basic relation of the input-output analysis, $(I - A) \cdot x = c$. Although this looks like a very simple relation, it conceals many difficult questions. At the outset we can immediately raise the following questions.

  (i) (**The existence problem**) For any given $c \geq 0$, can we guarantee that there exists an $\hat{x} \geq 0$ such that $(I - A) \cdot \hat{x} = c$? If so, is such an $\hat{x}$ unique?
  (ii) (**The nonsingularity problem**) Is the matrix $(I - A)$ nonsingular? If so, is $(I - A)^{-1} \geq 0$?

Clearly these two questions are very closely related. In fact, we can prove that (i) is answered affirmatively if and only if (ii) is answered in the affirmative. However, whether these questions can be answered in the affirmative is not at all obvious; $(I - A) \cdot x = c$ involves n equations and n unknowns for a given c, but this certainly does not guarantee the existence of x or its nonnegativity.

The study of the existence problem produced the following interesting conditions as necessary and sufficient for (i) to be answered in the affirmative.

(3) (**H-S**) $b_{11} > 0,$ $\begin{vmatrix} b_{11} & b_{12} \\ b_{21} & b_{22} \end{vmatrix} > 0,$ $\dots,$ $\begin{vmatrix} b_{11} & b_{12} & \cdots & b_{1n} \\ b_{21} & b_{22} & \cdots & b_{2n} \\ \cdots & \cdots & \cdots & \cdots \\ b_{n1} & b_{n2} & \cdots & b_{nn} \end{vmatrix} > 0$

where b_{ij} is the i-j element of matrix $B \equiv (I - A)$. In other words, for any $c \geq 0$, there exists a unique $\hat{x} \geq 0$ such that $A \cdot \hat{x} + c = \hat{x}$ if and only if all the successive principal minors of $(I - A)$ are positive. The condition (H-S) is now known as the **Hawkins-Simon condition**.

In order to obtain an intuitive understanding of this condition and the Leontief system, let us consider a simple two-industry (say, steel and coal) input-output model. In this case, the Hawkins-Simon condition is expressed as

(4) $1 - a_{11} > 0$ and $\begin{vmatrix} 1 - a_{11} & -a_{12} \\ -a_{21} & 1 - a_{22} \end{vmatrix} > 0$

Note that the second of the above conditions may also be written as

(5) $$(1 - a_{11})(1 - a_{22}) > a_{12}a_{21}$$

This coupled with $1 - a_{11} > 0$ in (4) implies $1 - a_{22} > 0$.

The conditions that $1 - a_{11} > 0$ and $1 - a_{22} > 0$ obviously mean that each industry produces positive net output of its own good. To ease the understanding of (5), suppose, for example, that $a_{22} = 0$, which means that the second industry (say, coal) requires none of its own input (that is, coal). Then equation (5) states that $1 > a_{11} + a_{12}a_{21}$, where a_{11} is the amount of steel required to produce a ton of steel directly and $a_{12}a_{21}$ represents the amount of steel required to make coal to make a ton of steel. That is, $(a_{11} + a_{12}a_{21})$, the total requirement of steel to produce a ton of steel as direct and indirect input, must be less than the amount of output (that is, a ton of steel). In other words, an intuitive meaning of condition (5) is that the unit production of any good must use less than one unit of itself as direct and indirect input. When the number of industries is more than two, there are additional strings of determinants than those indicated by (4), but the interpretation would always be that all subgroups of industries should be "self-sustaining," directly and indirectly.

The nature of the Leontief system and the Hawkins-Simon condition can be made more specific with the aid of a diagram. For this purpose, we first define two vectors α_1 and α_2 by

(6) $$\alpha_1 \equiv \begin{bmatrix} 1 - a_{11} \\ - a_{21} \end{bmatrix}, \quad \alpha_2 \equiv \begin{bmatrix} - a_{12} \\ 1 - a_{22} \end{bmatrix}$$

Clearly, α_1 and α_2 signify the input-output combination involved in a one-unit operation (that is, one unit of gross output) of the first and the second industry, respectively. In Figure 4.1, points A and B, respectively, denote α_1 and α_2. Point C denotes the final consumption vector c, and $(I - A)\cdot x = c$ can be written as $\alpha_1 x_1 + \alpha_2 x_2 = c$. Points $\bar{A}$ and $\bar{B}$, respectively, denote the vectors $\alpha_1 x_1$ and $\alpha_2 x_2$, and point C is obtained by the parallelogram law of vector addition from the two points $\bar{A}$ and $\bar{B}$.

Notice that in Figure 4.1 the positive angle between the OA and OB rays (that is, the angle θ) is less than 180°. As long as this condition holds, for *any* point in the nonnegative orthant of the $(c_1\text{-}c_2)$-plane except the origin, such as point C, we can find an $x_1 \geq 0$ and an $x_2 \geq 0$ (not vanishing simultaneously) such that $\alpha_1 x_1$ and $\alpha_2 x_2$ (such as points $\bar{A}$ and $\bar{B}$) add up to c. It is easy to see that if the slope of the OA ray is equal to or greater than the slope of the OB ray (that is, the angle θ is equal to or greater than 180°), then there does not exist a point in the nonnegative orthant of the $(c_1\text{-}c_2)$-plane (except the origin) such that $x_1 \geq 0$ and $x_2 \geq 0$ and $\alpha_1 x_1 + \alpha_2 x_2 = c$. Hence with the assumption of $1 - a_{11} > 0$ and $1 - a_{22} > 0$ tacitly made in the construction of Figure 4.1, a necessary and sufficient condition for an $x \geq 0$ to exist to satisfy $(I - A)\cdot x = c$ for any $c \geq 0$

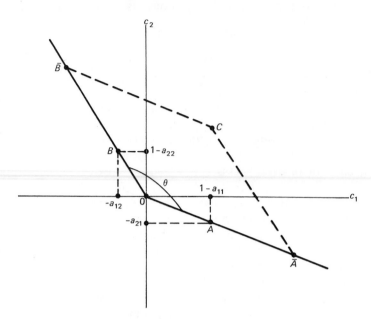

Figure 4.1. An Illustration of the Hawkins-Simon Condition.

is, for the two-industry case, that the slope of the OA ray be flatter than the slope of the OB ray. In other words,

(7)
$$\frac{a_{21}}{1 - a_{11}} < \frac{1 - a_{22}}{a_{12}}$$

which is nothing but condition (5) in the Hawkins-Simon condition.

Let c be a final demand vector. In order to obtain this bundle of goods, we need the "first-round" input requirements of the goods, namely, $A \cdot c$. But to obtain the bundle $A \cdot c$, we need the "second-round" input requirements of the goods, that is, $A \cdot (A \cdot c) = A^2 \cdot c$. Then on the third round, and so on, *ad infinitum*. Therefore the total requirements of the goods would be

(8)
$$c + A \cdot c + A^2 \cdot c + A^3 \cdot c + \cdots$$

Now the question arises whether this infinite series converges and is in fact equal to the bundle of goods produced in the economy, x. That is, the following problem is posed.

THE CONVERGENCE PROBLEM: Does the above series converge? If so, can we assert that

(9)
$$\sum_{k=0}^{\infty} A^k \cdot c = (I - A)^{-1} \cdot c$$

It turns out that this problem can be answered in the affirmative if and only if the existence problem or the nonsingularity problem is answered in the affirmative, or if and only if the Hawkins-Simon condition holds.

Empirically, the input-output matrix A is typically estimated for a particular year. Suppose that for that year we have $c > 0$ and $x \geq 0$. In other words, we have

(10)　　　　For a given particular $c > 0$, there exists an $x \geq 0$ such that
$$(I - A) \cdot x = c$$

Clearly if the answer to the existence problem is affirmative, (10) holds. What about the converse? We will prove later that the converse also holds. Then condition (10) becomes a necessary and sufficient condition for an affirmative answer to the existence problem, the nonsingularity problem, and the convergence problem, and it is also necessary and sufficient for the Hawkins-Simon condition (see Section C).

Obviously condition (10) can be restated as follows:

(11)　　　　There exists an $x \geq 0$ such that $(I - A) \cdot x > 0$

It will be shown later (see Section D) that condition (11) is equivalent to the following:

(12)　　　　There exists a $p \geq 0$ such that $(I - A)' \cdot p > 0$

where $(I - A)'$ is the transpose of $(I - A)$ and p may be interpreted as a "price" vector. The amount of "value-added" (per unit output) by the jth industry, v_j, can be defined as

(13)　　　　$$v_j \equiv p_j - \sum_{i=1}^{n} p_i a_{ij}, \ j = 1, 2, \ldots, n$$

Hence condition (12) can be interpreted as implying the existence of a price vector $p \geq 0$ such that the v_j computed by use of this p is positive for all j. Obviously the v_j's go to other factors of production such as labor.

Consider the following sums of the coefficients (a_{ij}'s) of the input-output matrix:

(14-a)　　　　$$r_i \quad \sum_{j=1}^{n} a_{ij}, \ i = 1, 2, \ldots, n$$

(14-b)　　　　$$s_j \equiv \sum_{i=1}^{n} a_{ij}, \ j = 1, 2, \ldots, n$$

where r_i and s_j signify the ith row sum and the jth column sum, respectively. Let $\bar{r} \equiv \max r_i$ for $i = 1, 2, \ldots, n$ and $\bar{s} \equiv \max s_j$ for $j = 1, 2, \ldots, n$. In the course of the study of the input-output matrix, it has become clear that *either* of the following two conditions, (15-a) and (15-b), is sufficient to answer the existence problem, the nonsingularity problem, and the convergence problem:

(15-a) $\bar{r} < 1$

(15-b) $\bar{s} < 1$

The conditions (15-a) and (15-b) are known as the (**Brauer-**) **Solow conditions** (see Section C). Condition (15-a) should not be surprising to the reader, for it simply asserts a special case of condition (11). That is, condition (15-a) asserts that condition (11) is realized by an x whose elements are all equal to one. Similarly, condition (15-b) asserts a special case of condition (12) [choose p in (12) with elements all equal to one]. In other words, condition (15-b) states that if we choose the unit of measurement of each good properly so that the price of each good is equal to one, then the valued-added (per unit output) of each good is positive.

In the course of these studies it was realized that the input-output matrix, A, has a special property, that is, all of its elements are nonnegative. By imposing this special nonnegativity restriction on the matrix, it was conjectured that we should be able to obtain stronger results than those listed in the usual textbooks on matrix algebra. Looking back into journals of mathematics, economists found that such matrices had been discussed at the beginning of the century by the German mathematicians Perron and Frobenius. Hence the theorem, now called the "(Perron-) Frobenius theorem," suddenly attracted a great deal of attention from economists.[1] A number of papers (by Metzler, Debreu-Herstein, Solow, Chipman, Morishima, Goodwin, and so on) have been published on the properties of A (the nonnegative matrix). (See Section C.) By using the properties of such an A, the nature of the $(I - A)$ matrix was made precise and clear (See Section D). All of these studies are treated in a unified fashion by McKenzie [9] and Nikaido [13]. The unifying concept here is taken from condition (11) or condition (12). McKenzie [9] thus discovered the relevance of the concept of "dominant diagonal matrices" in this context (see Sections C and D).

In retrospect, many of the results thus discovered with a great deal of effort by economists were already known, especially among Russian mathematicians. For this reason Karlin writes ([7], p. 289),

> Since 1908 there have been innumerable extensions and applications of the Frobenius results. . . . An impressive collection of these extensions is found in Gantmacher and Krein, which in addition develops much of the finer structure of the theory of positive matrices. . . . Unfortunately, economists continue to rediscover many of these theorems and to assign them thoroughly inaccurate priorities.

This comment may be rather harsh. We may add that the studies by Nikaido [13] and McKenzie [9], mentioned above, provide us with an interesting unifying view, which is certainly new in the literature. More importantly, we cannot overstress the fact that the structure of these mathematical theorems has been straightened out and their nature made intuitively clear to economists (as indicated above) through the Leontief input-output system.[2]

An interesting by-product of the study of the input-output matrix is the

study of the stability of a competitive market. The discussion of linear approximation stability is essentially concerned with the stability of the equilibrium of a
differential equation system of the form $\dot{p} = A \cdot p$. In connection with the stability
of this system, Metzler [10] (see also chapter 3, Section C) found that if $A = [a_{ij}]$
is such that $a_{ij} > 0$, $i \neq j$, then Hicks' stability condition is equivalent to the
stability of the equilibrium of the above differential equation. Recall that
Hicks' condition is that the successive principal minors of A alternate in sign.
This condition is obviously equivalent to saying that all the successive principal
minors of $(-A)$ are positive—in other words, A satisfies the Hawkins-Simon
condition!

Hence the study of the stability of a competitive market and input-output
analysis developed in parallel, and the unified theory as presented by McKenzie or
Nikaido has applications in both fields.

Clearly the economic applications of the theory of such matrices are not
confined to these two fields. For example, Metzler [11], Chipman [2], and Goodwin [6] in the 1950s considered an application to the multisectoral income
propagation of the Keynesian type model. Later, economists found applications
to the dynamic Leontief theory, the substitution theorem, the turnpike theorem,
and so forth. The purpose of this chapter is to study the properties of such matrices
in a systematic fashion and to show some of the applications. The theory
developed in this chapter is an extremely useful technique in economics and the
reader may find many unknown applications for it.[3] Some of the important
applications are explained in Section D.

A brief summary of this chapter is now in order. The most useful results
of this chapter are summarized in the beginning of Section D. Section D then
develops important applications of these results to various topics of economic
theory (such as the input-output analysis, the stability of competitive equilibrium,
and comparative statics). Section D thus illustrates the use of the basic results
of this chapter, enabling and motivating the reader to investigate further applications of the results.

Sections B and C do the major groundwork for Section D. Section B high-
lights well-known "(Perron-) Frobenius theorems" on matrices whose entries are
all nonnegative. Important concepts such as "indecomposable matrix" and
"primitive matrix" are explained in this connection. Section C discusses matrices
with "dominant diagonals," which play a key role in the type of problems discussed in Section A. The Frobenius theorems are crucial in obtaining some of
the important results in Section C.

The reader may find that Sections B and C, especially some of the proofs
of the theorems in these sections, are rather tedious to read. In the first reading
of these sections, it may therefore be advisable for the reader to skip reading
these proofs altogether. In fact, to understand Section D, the reader can even
skip reading the statements of these theorems (especially those in Section C).
Only familiarity with some of the basic concepts is really required for the reading
of Section D.[4]

FOOTNOTES

1. Morishima ([12], p. 1) claims that Frobenius' theorems were rediscovered independently by him, R. Goodwin, and T. Yasui.
2. For an excellent exposition of the input-output theory, see Dorfman, Samuelson, and Solow (DOSSO) [3], for example.
3. In these applications, the matrices whose off-diagonal elements are all nonnegative (such as the gross substitution matrix) or are all nonpositive (such as the Leontief input-output matrix) turn out to yield very sharp results. To honor the name of a pioneer of such a matrix, the matrix is often called the **Metzler matrix**.
4. The reader, if he so wishes, can therefore go directly to Section D, occasionally referring to previous sections for the concepts used. After reading Section D, he may then be more motivated to read the statements and proofs of the theorems in Sections B and C.

REFERENCES

1. Chenery, H. B., and Clark, P. G., *Interindustry Economics*, New York, Wiley, 1959.
2. Chipman, J. S., *The Theory of Inter-Sectoral Money Flows and Income Formation*, Baltimore, Md., Johns Hopkins University Press, 1951.
3. Dorfman, R., Samuelson, P. A., and Solow, R. M., *Linear Programming and Economic Analysis*, New York, McGraw-Hill, 1958.
4. Fukuchi, T., *Introduction to Linear Economics*, Tokyo, Toyo Keizai Shimpo-sha, 1963 (in Japanese).
5. Gantmacher, F. R., *The Theory of Matrices*, Vol. II, New York, Chelsea Publishing Co., 1959 (tr. from Russian).
6. Goodwin, R. M., "Does the Matrix Multiplier Oscillate?" *Economic Journal*, LX, December 1950.
7. Karlin, S., *Mathematical Methods and Theory in Games, Programming and Economics*, Vol. I, Reading, Mass., Addison-Wesley, 1959.
8. Leontief, W. W., *The Structure of American Economy, 1919–1939*, 2nd ed., New York, Oxford University Press, 1951.
9. McKenzie, L. W., "Matrices with Dominant Diagonals and Economic Theory," in *Mathematical Methods in the Social Sciences, 1959*, ed. by Arrow, Karlin, and Suppes, Stanford, Calif., Stanford University Press, 1960.
10. Metzler, L. A., "Stability of Multiple Markets: The Hicks Conditions," *Econometrica*, 13, October 1945.
11. ——, "A Multiple Region Theory of Income and Trade," *Econometrica*, 18, October 1950.
12. Morishima, M., *Interindustry Relations and Economic Fluctuations* (Sangyo-renkan to Keizai Hendo), Tokyo, Yuhikaku, 1955 (in Japanese).
13. Nikaido, H., *Introduction to Sets and Mappings in Modern Economics*, tr. by K. Sato, Amsterdam, North-Holland, 1970 (the Japanese original, Tokyo, 1960).
14. ——, *Convex Structures and Economic Theory*, New York, Academic Press, 1968.

FROBENIUS THEOREMS

We begin this section by recalling some of the basic concepts of linear algebra which are important in this chapter. Let A be an $m \times n$ matrix. Here we assume that all the elements of $A = [a_{ij}]$ are real numbers. Note that A is a linear function from R^n into R^m, in the sense that, for any x and y in R^n, we have $A \cdot (x \pm y) = A \cdot x \pm A \cdot y$ and $A \cdot (\alpha x) = \alpha A \cdot x$ for any real number α. On the other hand, any linear function from R^n into R^m can be written in matrix form. Clearly, A is a continuous function for any subset X of R^n into R^m. Hence if X is compact in R^n, $f(X)$ is compact in R^m. From now on we will confine ourselves to a square matrix, that is, let A be an $(n \times n)$ square matrix. Thus A is a linear continuous function from R^n into itself. If we have $A \cdot x = \lambda x$, $x \neq 0$, where x is an n-vector and λ is a scalar (real or complex), then we call λ an **eigenvalue** or **characteristic root** of A. The vector x is called the **eigenvector** (or **characteristic vector**) associated with λ. If we write the above equation in the form

(1) $$(\lambda I - A) \cdot x = 0$$

we can immediately see that if λ is an eigenvalue, then equation (1) has a solution $x \neq 0$, so that we have

(2) $$\phi(\lambda) = |\lambda I - A| = 0$$

That is, $(\lambda I - A)$ must be singular [here $|\lambda I - A|$ denotes the determinant of $(\lambda I - A)$]. Conversely, if λ is a solution of (2), then (1) has nonzero solution x. Hence (1) and (2) are really equivalent. Equation (2) is called the **characteristic equation** or **eigen equation** (of A). Clearly we may write (2) as

$$\phi(\lambda) = \lambda^n + a_1 \lambda^{n-1} + \cdots + a_{n-1} \lambda + a_n = 0$$

where the a_i's are functions of the a_{ij}'s. By a fundamental theorem of algebra, the above polynomial has n (not necessarily distinct) roots. Each root is not necessarily a real number. Hence an eigenvector is not necessarily a real vector.

EXAMPLES:

(a) $A = \begin{bmatrix} 1 & 1 \\ 1 & 1 \end{bmatrix}$, $\phi(\lambda) = \begin{vmatrix} \lambda - 1 & -1 \\ -1 & \lambda - 1 \end{vmatrix}$

$$= \lambda^2 - 2\lambda = \lambda(\lambda - 2) = 0 \qquad \therefore \lambda = 0 \text{ and } 2$$

(b) $A = \begin{bmatrix} 1 & 0 \\ 0 & 1 \end{bmatrix}$, $\phi(\lambda) = \begin{vmatrix} \lambda - 1 & 0 \\ 0 & \lambda - 1 \end{vmatrix} = (\lambda - 1)^2 = 0$

$$\therefore \lambda = 1 \text{ (double root)}$$

(c) $A = \begin{bmatrix} 0 & 1 \\ -1 & 0 \end{bmatrix}$, $\phi(\lambda) = \begin{vmatrix} \lambda & -1 \\ 1 & \lambda \end{vmatrix} = \lambda^2 + 1 = 0$

$\therefore \lambda = \pm i$ (complex roots)

When λ is a simple root of the characteristic equation, λ is called the **simple eigenvalue** (or **simple root**) of A.

We will now restrict ourselves to an $n \times n$ matrix whose *elements are all nonnegative*. First recall our conventions with regard to vector and matrix notation. Here x is a vector whose ith element is x_i, and A is a matrix whose i-j element is a_{ij}.

NOTATIONS:
(a) $x \geq 0$ if $x_i \geq 0$ for all i
   $x \geq 0$ if $x_i \geq 0$ for all i and $x_i > 0$ for some i (that is, $x \neq 0$)
   $x > 0$ if $x_i > 0$ for all i
(b) $A \geq 0$ if $a_{ij} \geq 0$ for all i and j
   $A \geq 0$ if $a_{ij} \geq 0$ for all i and j and $a_{ij} > 0$ for some i and j
   $A > 0$ if $a_{ij} > 0$ for all i and j

Although we are concerned here exclusively with an $(n \times n)$ square matrix A, the matrix A in the above notation does not have to be square. If $A \geq 0$, we call A a **nonnegative matrix**, and if $A > 0$, we call A a **(strictly) positive matrix** ($A \geq 0$ is often called a **semipositive matrix**). One may consider A as an input-output matrix so that a_{ij} denotes the amount of ith input needed to produce a unit of the jth output.

Definition: A **permutation** is a one-to-one function from the set $\{1, 2, 3, \ldots, n\}$ onto itself. We denote it by

$$\begin{pmatrix} i_1 i_2 \cdots i_n \\ j_1 j_2 \cdots j_n \end{pmatrix}$$

or

$$\sigma(i_k) = j_k, \quad k = 1, 2, \ldots, n$$

EXAMPLE: $\begin{pmatrix} 1 & 2 & 3 \\ 2 & 3 & 1 \end{pmatrix}$ is a permutation of $1 \to 2$, $2 \to 3$, and $3 \to 1$ [that is, $\sigma(1) = 2$, $\sigma(2) = 3$, and $\sigma(3) = 1$].

A **permutation matrix**, usually denoted by P, is the one which is obtained by permuting the columns (or rows) of the identity matrix. Or, more formally, it is defined as follows.

Definition: An $n \times n$ matrix $P = [p_{ij}]$ is called a **permutation matrix** if $p_{\sigma(j)j} = 1$,

$j = 1, 2, \ldots, n$ [resp. $p_{i\sigma(i)} = 1$, $i = 1, 2, \ldots, n$], and if $p_{ij} = 0$ for all $i \neq \sigma(j)$ [resp. $p_{ij} = 0$ for all $j \neq \sigma(i)$].

REMARK: The identity matrix itself is a permutation matrix. Every permutation matrix can be obtained by interchanging (two) columns (or rows) of the identity matrix a finite number of times.

EXAMPLE:

$$P = \begin{bmatrix} 0 & 0 & 1 \\ 1 & 0 & 0 \\ 0 & 1 & 0 \end{bmatrix}$$

is obtained by interchanging the columns as follows:

$$
\begin{matrix}
1 \; 2 \; 3 & 3 \; 2 \; 1 & 2 \; 3 \; 1
\end{matrix}
$$

$$
I = \begin{bmatrix} 1 & 0 & 0 \\ 0 & 1 & 0 \\ 0 & 0 & 1 \end{bmatrix} \rightarrow \begin{bmatrix} 0 & 0 & 1 \\ 0 & 1 & 0 \\ 1 & 0 & 0 \end{bmatrix} \rightarrow \begin{bmatrix} 0 & 0 & 1 \\ 1 & 0 & 0 \\ 0 & 1 & 0 \end{bmatrix}
$$

If σ is some permutation $\begin{pmatrix} 1 & 2 \ldots n \\ \alpha_1 \alpha_2 \ldots \alpha_n \end{pmatrix}$, we denote by P_σ the permutation matrix obtained by permuting the *columns* of the identity matrix I by σ. In the above example, σ was $\begin{pmatrix} 1 & 2 & 3 \\ 2 & 3 & 1 \end{pmatrix}$.[1] Similarly, the transpose P'_σ of P_σ can be obtained by permuting the *rows* of the identity matrix by σ. For example,

$$P'_\sigma = \begin{bmatrix} 0 & 1 & 0 \\ 0 & 0 & 1 \\ 1 & 0 & 0 \end{bmatrix}$$

is obtained by permuting the *rows* of the (3×3) identity matrix by the above σ. It can also be obtained by interchanging the rows as follows:

$$
I = \begin{bmatrix} 1 & 0 & 0 \\ 0 & 1 & 0 \\ 0 & 0 & 1 \end{bmatrix} \begin{matrix} 1 \\ 2 \\ 3 \end{matrix} \rightarrow \begin{bmatrix} 0 & 0 & 1 \\ 0 & 1 & 0 \\ 1 & 0 & 0 \end{bmatrix} \begin{matrix} 3 \\ 2 \\ 1 \end{matrix} \rightarrow \begin{bmatrix} 0 & 1 & 0 \\ 0 & 0 & 1 \\ 1 & 0 & 0 \end{bmatrix} \begin{matrix} 2 \\ 3 \\ 1 \end{matrix}
$$

It can be shown easily that $P'_\sigma = P_\sigma{}^{-1}$. Note that $P_\sigma{}^{-1} \cdot A \cdot P_\sigma$ (or $P'_\sigma \cdot A \cdot P_\sigma$) is the matrix obtained by permuting the rows *and* the columns by σ.

EXAMPLE:

$$\sigma = \begin{pmatrix} 1 & 2 & 3 \\ 2 & 3 & 1 \end{pmatrix}, A = \begin{bmatrix} a_{11} & a_{12} & a_{13} \\ a_{21} & a_{22} & a_{23} \\ a_{31} & a_{32} & a_{33} \end{bmatrix}$$

$$P_\sigma{}^{-1} \cdot A \cdot P_\sigma = \begin{bmatrix} a_{22} & a_{23} & a_{21} \\ a_{32} & a_{33} & a_{31} \\ a_{12} & a_{13} & a_{11} \end{bmatrix}$$

REMARK: If A is an input-output matrix, then $P_\sigma{}^{-1} \cdot A \cdot P_\sigma$ amounts to renaming (or renumbering) the industries in the economy by the permutation σ. If $\sigma = \begin{pmatrix} 1 & 2 & 3 \\ 2 & 3 & 1 \end{pmatrix}$, then the industries are renamed as follows: $1 \to 3, 2 \to 1$, and $3 \to 2$. Since the numbering or the naming of the industries should not alter what is going on in the economy, we may sometimes wish to perform $P_\sigma{}^{-1} \cdot A \cdot P_\sigma$ by choosing σ properly.

We are now ready to introduce the first important concept.

Definition: An $n \times n$ matrix A is called **decomposable** if there exists a permutation matrix P such that

$$P^{-1} \cdot A \cdot P = \begin{bmatrix} A_{11} & A_{12} \\ 0 & A_{22} \end{bmatrix}$$

where A_{11} and A_{22} are *square* submatrices.[2] If this is impossible, A is called **indecomposable**.

REMARK: This definition can be restated as follows: A is called "decomposable" if (1) there exists a partition $\{J, K\}$ of $N = \{1, 2, \ldots, n\}$, such that $N = J \cup K$ and $J \cap K = \emptyset$ with $J \neq \emptyset$ and $K \neq \emptyset$, and (2) $a_{ij} = 0$ for $i \in K$ and $j \in J$. That is,

$$\begin{array}{cc} & \begin{array}{cc} J & K \end{array} \\ \begin{array}{c} J \\ K \end{array} & \begin{bmatrix} A_{11} & A_{12} \\ 0 & A_{22} \end{bmatrix} \end{array}$$

REMARK: If A is the input-output matrix, we can interpret the decomposable matrix as follows: The whole economy is partitioned into two groups of industries, the J-group and the K-group. Any industry that belongs to the J-group does not require any inputs from the industries in the K-group. If A can be transformed by a permutation matrix P such that $P^{-1} \cdot A \cdot P = \begin{bmatrix} A_{11} & 0 \\ 0 & A_{22} \end{bmatrix}$, then A is called **completely decomposable**. In this case, not only do the industries in the J-group not require any inputs from the K-group industries, but also the K-group industries do not require any inputs from the J-group industries as well.

EXAMPLE:

$$A = \begin{bmatrix} 1 & 0 & 1 \\ 1 & 1 & 1 \\ 1 & 0 & 1 \end{bmatrix}$$

is decomposable by P_σ where $\sigma = \begin{pmatrix} 1 & 2 & 3 \\ 2 & 3 & 1 \end{pmatrix}$. That is,

$$P_\sigma^{-1} \cdot A \cdot P_\sigma = \begin{bmatrix} 1 & 1 & 1 \\ 0 & 1 & 1 \\ 0 & 1 & 1 \end{bmatrix}$$

In the above example, the decomposability is really obvious without performing P_σ. Another obvious case of decomposability is one in which all the elements in some row (or column) are zero. However, there are many cases in which this is not obvious. The following examples are given by Nikaido ([8], pp. 83–85).

(i) $A_1 = \begin{bmatrix} 0 & 1 & 0 \\ 0 & 0 & 1 \\ 1 & 0 & 0 \end{bmatrix}$ is indecomposable

(ii) $A_2 = \begin{bmatrix} 0 & 0 & 1 & 2 \\ 0 & 0 & 2 & 1 \\ 3 & 1 & 0 & 0 \\ 2 & 4 & 0 & 0 \end{bmatrix}$ is indecomposable

REMARK: The reader may wish to prove that A_1 and A_2 in the above examples are indeed indecomposable.

We now prove the following lemma.

Lemma 4.B.1: *Let A be a nonnegative indecomposable $n \times n$ matrix. Then $[I + A]^{n-1} > 0$, where I is the identity matrix.*

PROOF: It suffices to show that for every $x \geq 0$, $[I + A]^{n-1} \cdot x > 0$, for then by choosing

$$x = (\overbrace{0, 0, \ldots, 0, 1}^{i}, 0, \ldots, 0)$$

we have $[I + A]^{n-1} > 0$. To show that $[I + A]^{n-1} \cdot x > 0$ for any $x \geq 0$, it, in turn, suffices to show that the vector $y = [I + A] \cdot x$ always has fewer zero coordinates than x does. Suppose the contrary. Note that $y = x + A \cdot x$ and $A \cdot x \geq 0$, so that for each positive coordinate of x, there corresponds a positive coordinate of y. Thus x cannot have more positive coordinates than y. Hence x has the same zero coordinates as y. Without loss of generality, we may suppose that x and y have the form

$$x = \begin{bmatrix} u \\ 0 \end{bmatrix}, y = \begin{bmatrix} v \\ 0 \end{bmatrix}; \quad u > 0, v > 0$$

where u and v are of the same dimension. Let

$$A = \begin{bmatrix} A_{11} & A_{12} \\ A_{21} & A_{22} \end{bmatrix}$$

where A_{11} and A_{22} are square submatrices. Then $x + A \cdot x = y$ means that

$A_{21} \cdot u = 0$. Since $u > 0$, $A_{21} = 0$. This contradicts the indecomposability of A.   (Q.E.D.)

We now state and prove the important theorems called the **Frobenius theorems**.

Theorem 4.B.1 (Frobenius' theorem I):   *Let A be a nonnegative indecomposable $n \times n$ matrix. Then*

(i)   *A has an eigenvalue $\hat{\lambda} > 0$ such that*

(ii)   *An eigenvector $\hat{x} > 0$ can be associated with $\hat{\lambda}$.*

(iii) *The eigenvector $\hat{x}$ is unique up to a scalar multiple; that is, if $\hat{y}$ is an eigenvector associated with $\hat{\lambda}$, then $\hat{y} = \theta \hat{x}$ for some positive scalar θ.*

(iv)   *If $A \cdot x = \mu x$ for some $\mu \geq 0$ and $x \geq 0$, then $\mu = \hat{\lambda}$.*

(v)   *If ω is any eigenvalue of A, then $|\omega| \leq \hat{\lambda}$.*

(vi)   *The eigenvalue $\hat{\lambda}$ increases when any element of A increases; that is, if $A_1 \geq A_2 \geq 0$ and A_1 and A_2 are indecomposable,[3] then $\hat{\lambda}_{A_1} > \hat{\lambda}_{A_2}$, where $\hat{\lambda}_{A_1}$ and $\hat{\lambda}_{A_2}$, respectively, denote the $\hat{\lambda}$ associated with A_1 and A_2.*

(vii) *The eigenvalue $\hat{\lambda}$ is a simple root.*

Definition: The root $\hat{\lambda}$ in the above theorem is called the **Frobenius root of A**; it is denoted by $\hat{\lambda}_A$ or simply $\hat{\lambda}$.

PROOF OF THEOREM 4.B.1 (WIELANDT [12]):   Given $x \in R^n$, with $x \geq 0$, define $\lambda_x \equiv \max \{\lambda: A \cdot x \geq \lambda x, \lambda \in R\}$. Let $(A \cdot x)_i = \sum_{j=1}^{n} a_{ij} x_j$ and define $\lambda_i(x)$ by

$$\lambda_i(x) = \begin{cases} \dfrac{(A \cdot x)_i}{x_i} & \text{if } x_i > 0 \\ \infty & \text{if } x_i = 0 \text{ and } (A \cdot x)_i \neq 0 \\ \text{undefined} & \text{if } x_i = 0 \text{ and } (A \cdot x)_i = 0 \end{cases}$$

Observe that λ_x can also be written as

$$\lambda_x = \min_i \lambda_i(x)$$

The concept of λ_x is illustrated in Figure 4.2.

We are interested in establishing the existence of an $\hat{x} \geq 0$ which maximizes the value of λ_x over $x \geq 0$, for it turns out later that such a maximum value of λ_x will give the Frobenius root of A, with which the eigenvector $\hat{x}$ is associated. First note that $\lambda_x = \lambda_{\alpha x} \equiv \max \{\lambda: A \cdot (\alpha x) \geq \lambda(\alpha x), \lambda \in R\}$, where α is any positive number. Hence for the maximization of λ_x over $x \geq 0$, it suffices to restrict x to the following portion of the unit sphere, denoted by S:

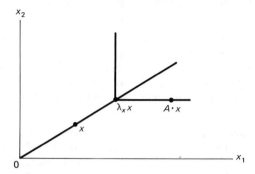

Figure 4.2.   An Illustration of λ_x.

$$S \equiv \{x \in R^n: \sum_{i=1}^{n} x_i^2 = 1, x \geq 0\}$$

If the function λ_x were continuous on S, then the existence of an $\hat{x}$ in S which maximizes λ_x is guaranteed by Weierstrass' theorem. However, λ_x can have discontinuities at the boundary points of S at which one of the coordinates vanishes, although it is continuous for all $x > 0$.

An ingenious way to avoid this difficulty of possible discontinuities of λ_x on S is used by Wielandt ([12], p. 644).[4] Define the set $\bar{S}$, in place of S, by

$$\bar{S} = \{y : y = (I + A)^{n-1} \cdot x, x \in S\}$$

Clearly $\bar{S}$ is compact, since S is compact (Theorem 0.A.17). Moreover, by Lemma 4.B.1, $\bar{S}$ consists solely of positive vectors. Multiply both sides of the inequality $A \cdot x \geq \lambda_x x$ by $(I + A)^{n-1} > 0$, and obtain $A \cdot y \geq \lambda_x y$, where $y \equiv (I + A)^{n-1} \cdot x$. Hence by the definition of λ_y, $\lambda_y \geq \lambda_x$. Hence, instead of considering the maximization of λ_x over S, it suffices to consider the maximization of λ_y over $\bar{S}$. Since $y \in \bar{S}$ implies $y > 0$, λ_y is continuous on $\bar{S}$ and achieves its maximum in $\bar{S}$, say, at $z > 0$, $z \in \bar{S}$.

Write $\hat{\lambda} \equiv \lambda_z$. Denote by $\hat{x}$ every vector for which $\hat{\lambda} = \lambda_{\hat{x}}$. Clearly $\hat{x} \geq 0$. We will prove that $\hat{\lambda}$ is a Frobenius root and $\hat{x}$ is its eigenvector. In other words, we will prove each statement of Frobenius' theorem I.

(i-a) $\hat{\lambda} > 0$. Let $u \equiv (1, 1, \ldots, 1) \in R^n$. Then $\lambda_u = \min_{1 \leq i \leq n} \sum_{j=1}^{n} a_{ij}$. Since no rows of an indecomposable matrix can consist only of zeros, $\lambda_u > 0$. Since $\hat{\lambda} \geq \lambda_u$, $\hat{\lambda} > 0$.

(i-b) *$\hat{\lambda}$ is an eigenvalue of A and $\hat{x}$ is its eigenvector, that is,* $A \cdot \hat{x} = \hat{\lambda}\hat{x}$. Suppose that $A \cdot \hat{x} \neq \hat{\lambda}\hat{x}$. By the definition of $\hat{\lambda}$, $A \cdot \hat{x} \geq \hat{\lambda}\hat{x}$, so that $A \cdot \hat{x} - \hat{\lambda}\hat{x} \geq 0$. Multiply both sides of this inequality by $(I + A)^{n-1} > 0$ (recall Lemma 4.B.1), and let $z \equiv (I + A)^{n-1} \cdot \hat{x}$. Then $(I + A)^{n-1} \cdot (A \cdot \hat{x} - \hat{\lambda}\hat{x}) > 0$, or $A \cdot z - \hat{\lambda}z > 0$. This contradicts the definition of $\hat{\lambda}$, for it implies that $A \cdot z - (\hat{\lambda} + \epsilon)z > 0$ for any sufficiently small $\epsilon > 0$, that is, $\lambda_z \geq (\hat{\lambda} + \epsilon) > \hat{\lambda}$. Hence $A \cdot \hat{x} = \hat{\lambda}\hat{x}$.

(ii) $\hat{x} > 0$. Let $z \equiv (I + A)^{n-1} \cdot \hat{x}$. Then by Lemma 4.B.1, $z > 0$. But $(I + A)^{n-1} \cdot \hat{x} = (1 + \hat{\lambda})^{n-1}\hat{x}$. Hence $0 < z = (1 + \hat{\lambda})^{n-1}\hat{x}$ so that $\hat{x} > 0$.

(iii) $\hat{x}$ *is unique up to a scalar multiple.* Let $\hat{y}$ be another eigenvector associated with $\hat{\lambda}$. Let $\theta \equiv \min_{1 \leq i \leq n} \hat{y}_i/\hat{x}_i$, and let $y \equiv \hat{y} - \theta\hat{x}$. Then $A \cdot y = A \cdot (\hat{y} - \theta\hat{x}) = \hat{\lambda}\hat{y} - \theta\hat{\lambda}\hat{x} = \hat{\lambda}y$. By definition of θ, $y \not> 0$. Suppose $y \neq 0$. Then $A \cdot y = \hat{\lambda}y$ means y is also an eigenvector associated with $\hat{\lambda}$. Hence using a proof similar to that of (ii), $y > 0$. This contradicts the condition that $y \not> 0$. Hence $y = 0$ or $\hat{y} = \theta\hat{x}$.

(iv) $A \cdot x = \mu x$ *and* $x \geq 0$ *imply that* $\mu = \hat{\lambda}$. Clearly A' is indecomposable if and only if A is indecomposable, where A' is the transpose of A. Denote the $\hat{\lambda}$ for A by $\hat{\lambda}_A$ and the $\hat{\lambda}$ for A' by $\hat{\lambda}_{A'}$; then we can easily show that $\hat{\lambda}_A = \hat{\lambda}_{A'}$. Hence there exists a $y > 0$ such that $A' \cdot y = \hat{\lambda}_{A'} \cdot y$. By assumption, $A \cdot x = \mu x$, $x \geq 0$. Consider the inner product $\mu\langle x, y\rangle = \langle \mu x, y\rangle = \langle A \cdot x, y\rangle = \langle x, A' \cdot y\rangle = \langle x, \lambda_{A'} y\rangle = \lambda_A\langle x, y\rangle$. Hence $(\lambda_A - \mu)\langle x, y\rangle = 0$. But $x \geq 0$, $y > 0$ imply that $\langle x, y\rangle > 0$, so that $\lambda_A - \mu = 0$.

(v) $|\omega| \leq \hat{\lambda}$. Let ω be an eigenvalue of A, so that $A \cdot x = \omega x$ for some $x \neq 0$. Taking the absolute values of both sides and using the triangular inequality, we obtain

$$A \cdot x^+ \geq |\omega| x^+$$

where x^+ is obtained by replacing all the elements of x by their absolute values. Hence $|\omega| \leq \lambda_x^+ \leq \hat{\lambda}$, where $\lambda_x^+ \equiv \max \{\lambda: A \cdot x^+ \geq \lambda x^+, \lambda \in R\}$.

(vi) $A_1 \geq A_2 \geq 0 \implies \hat{\lambda}_{A_1} > \hat{\lambda}_{A_2}$, *if* A_1 *and* A_2 *are indecomposable.*[5] Let $C \equiv \frac{1}{2}(A_1 + A_2)$; then C is also indecomposable. Consider the $\hat{\lambda}$ for C and denote it by $\hat{\lambda}_C$. Let $z > 0$ be its eigenvector [the existence of $\hat{\lambda}_C$ and $z > 0$ are guaranteed by (i) and (ii) above and the indecomposability of C]. Clearly $\hat{\lambda}_C z = C \cdot z \leq A_1 \cdot z$, since $A_1 \geq C$. Let $y > 0$ be an eigenvector associated with $\hat{\lambda}_{A_1'}$. Consider the inner product $\hat{\lambda}_C\langle y, z\rangle = \langle y, \hat{\lambda}_C z\rangle = \langle y, C \cdot z\rangle < \langle y, A_1 \cdot z\rangle = \langle A_1' \cdot y, z\rangle = \langle \hat{\lambda}_{A_1'} \cdot y, z\rangle = \hat{\lambda}_{A'}\langle y, z\rangle$. Hence $(\hat{\lambda}_{A'} - \hat{\lambda}_C)\langle y, z\rangle > 0$. But $y > 0$ and $z > 0$ imply that $\langle y, z\rangle > 0$, so that $(\hat{\lambda}_{A_1} - \hat{\lambda}_C) > 0$. Hence $\hat{\lambda}_{A_1} = \hat{\lambda}_{A_1'} > \hat{\lambda}_C$. Similarly, we can show that $\hat{\lambda}_C > \hat{\lambda}_{A_2}$ (in view of $C \geq A_2$), so that $\hat{\lambda}_{A_1} > \hat{\lambda}_{A_2}$.

(vii) $\hat{\lambda}$ *is a simple root.* (Proof omitted; see Gantmacher [4], p. 57, or Debreu and Herstein [1], p. 599.)   (Q.E.D.)

REMARK: The essential part of the above proof is (i). Note that (i) follows from Weierstrass' theorem, an elementary property of compact sets. An alternative proof using sequential compactness is provided by Nikaido [7]. Debreu and Herstein [1] gave a very simple and elegant proof by using Brouwer's fixed point theorem. It should be stressed, however, that we do not need such a powerful theorem to prove Frobenius' theorem I. Debreu and Herstein's proof of (i) goes roughly as follows:

(a) $x \geq 0$ *implies* $A \cdot x \geq 0$. If $A \cdot x = 0$, then A would have a column of zeros and would not be indecomposable.

(b) A *has an eigenvalue* $\hat{\lambda} > 0$. Let $\tilde{S} \equiv \{x \in R^n: x \geq 0, \sum_{i=1}^n x_i = 1\}$ be the

$(n-1)$ unit simplex. For each $x \in \check{S}$, we define $T(x) \equiv [1/\lambda(x)]\ A \cdot x$ where $\lambda(x) > 0$ is so determined that $T(x) \in \check{S}$ [by (a), such a $\lambda(x)$ exists for every $x \in \check{S}$]. The mapping $T(x)$ is illustrated in Figure 4.3. Clearly $T(x)$ is a continuous function from $\check{S}$ (which is compact and convex) into itself. Hence by Brouwer's fixed point theorem there exists an $\hat{x}$ in $\check{S}$ such that $\hat{x} = T(\hat{x}) = [1/\lambda(\hat{x})]\ A \cdot \hat{x}$. Finally, let $\hat{\lambda} \equiv \lambda(\hat{x})$.

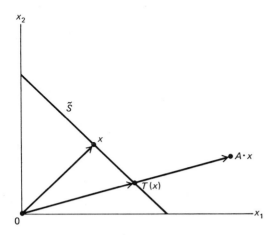

Figure 4.3.   An Illustration of $T(x)$.

Frobenius' theorem I is concerned with *indecomposable* nonnegative matrices. A similar theorem for arbitrary (hence possibly decomposable) non-negative matrices can be obtained by observing that every nonnegative matrix $A \geq 0$ can be represented as the limit of a sequence of positive matrices $A_q > 0$ (which are obviously indecomposable), that is

$$A = \lim_{q \to \infty} A_q \quad (A_q > 0, q = 1, 2, \ldots)^{[6]}$$

Theorem 4.B.2 (Frobenius' theorem II): *Let A be a nonnegative $n \times n$ matrix. Then*

(i)   *The matrix A has an eigenvalue $\hat{\lambda} \geq 0$ such that*

(ii) *With $\hat{\lambda}$ we can associate an eigenvector $\hat{x} \geq 0$.*

(iii) *If $A \cdot x \geq \mu x$ for some real number μ and $x \geq 0$, then $\hat{\lambda} \geq \mu$.*

(iv) *If ω is any eigenvalue of A, then $\hat{\lambda} \geq |\omega|$.*

(v)   *If $A_1 \geq A_2 \geq 0$, then $\hat{\lambda}_{A_1} \geq \hat{\lambda}_{A_2}$.*

PROOF: The proof is omitted.[7] See Gantmacher [4], pp. 66–68, or Debreu and Herstein [1], p. 600.

REMARK: In the above theorem, $\hat{\lambda}$ is again called the **Frobenius root of A** and $\hat{\lambda}_{A_1}$ denotes the Frobenius root of A_1. Owing to the lack of indecomposability we miss certain properties which hold for the indecomposable case (Frobenius' theorem I). In particular, note that if A is *not* indecomposable, then

(i)   The root $\hat{\lambda}$ can be zero.[8]

(ii) Some (not all) elements of $\hat{x}$ can be zero.

(iii) Both $\hat{x}$ and $\hat{y}$ with $\hat{y} \neq \theta\hat{x}$ for any $\theta \in R$ can be eigenvectors associated with $\hat{\lambda}$.

(iv) The root $\hat{\lambda}$ is not necessarily a simple root.

REMARK: Let $\hat{\lambda}(A)$ be the Frobenius root of $A \geq 0$ (decomposable or indecomposable). Then we can easily show that

(i) $\hat{\lambda}(A) = \hat{\lambda}(A')$ where A' is the transpose of A.

(ii) $\hat{\lambda}(\alpha A) = \alpha\hat{\lambda}(A)$ where α is any nonnegative real number.

(iii) $\hat{\lambda}(A^m) = \hat{\lambda}(A)^m$ where m is any positive integer.

The proofs of these propositions are left to the interested reader.

In the above discussion we observed that when a matrix does not have the indecomposability property, it also does not have all of the nice properties that we obtained in Theorem 4.B.1. Now we will impose an additional restriction on indecomposable nonnegative matrices to see whether we can obtain nicer properties for such matrices.

Definition: An $n \times n$ indecomposable matrix A is called **imprimitive** (or **cyclic**) if there exists a permutation matrix P such that

$$P^{-1} \cdot A \cdot P = \begin{bmatrix} 0 & A_{12} & 0 & 0 & \cdots & 0 \\ 0 & 0 & A_{23} & 0 & \cdots & 0 \\ 0 & 0 & 0 & A_{34} & \cdots & 0 \\ \cdots & \cdots & \cdots & \cdots & \cdots & \cdots \\ \cdots & \cdots & \cdots & \cdots & \cdots & \cdots \\ 0 & 0 & 0 & 0 & \cdots & A_{m-1,n} \\ A_{m1} & 0 & 0 & 0 & \cdots & 0 \end{bmatrix}$$

Here the 0's in the diagonal are square matrices, but the $A_{i,i+1} \geq 0$ are not necessarily square. If such a permutation does not exist, A is called **primitive** (or **acyclic**).

REMARK: This definition can also be stated as follows. An $n \times n$ indecomposable matrix $A = [a_{ij}]$ is called **imprimitive** (otherwise **primitive**) if

(i)   There exists a partition $\{J_1, J_2, \ldots, J_m\}$ of $N \equiv \{1, 2, \ldots, n\}$ such that $N = J_1 \cup J_2 \cup \ldots \cup J_m$, $J_i \cap J_j = \emptyset$ $(i \neq j)$, $J_i \neq \emptyset$, $i = 1, 2, \ldots, m$, and

(ii) $a_{ij} = 0 (i \notin J_{i-1}, j \in J_i)$, and $\sum_{i \in J_{i-1}} a_{ij} > 0 (j \in J_i)$, $i = 1, 2, \ldots, m$.

Here we regard J_0 as J_m. We note that this partition is not necessarily unique.

REMARK: Hence if A is imprimitive, it means that any industry which belongs to the J_i-group industries does use the outputs of the J_{i-1}-group industries but does not use the outputs of any other group of industries as inputs.

EXAMPLE: Nikaido ([7], section 21) gave the following example:

$$A = \begin{bmatrix} 0 & 0 & 0 & 0 & 0 & 1 \\ 0 & 0 & 0 & 0 & 5 & 0 \\ 0 & 0 & 0 & 3 & 0 & 0 \\ 0 & 4 & 0 & 0 & 0 & 0 \\ 6 & 0 & 0 & 0 & 0 & 0 \\ 0 & 0 & 2 & 0 & 0 & 0 \end{bmatrix} \text{ can be shown to be imprimitive}$$

1. Let $\sigma_1 = \begin{pmatrix} 1 & 2 & 3 & 4 & 5 & 6 \\ 1 & 4 & 2 & 6 & 3 & 5 \end{pmatrix}$; then by the permutation matrix P_{σ_1}, we have

$$P_{\sigma_1}^{-1} \cdot A \cdot P_{\sigma_1} = \begin{bmatrix} 0 & 0 & \boxed{\begin{matrix}0 & 1\end{matrix}} & 0 & 0 \\ 0 & 0 & \boxed{\begin{matrix}4 & 0\end{matrix}} & 0 & 0 \\ 0 & 0 & 0 & 0 & \boxed{\begin{matrix}0 & 5\end{matrix}} \\ 0 & 0 & 0 & 0 & \boxed{\begin{matrix}2 & 0\end{matrix}} \\ \boxed{\begin{matrix}0 & 3\end{matrix}} & 0 & 0 & 0 & 0 \\ \boxed{\begin{matrix}6 & 0\end{matrix}} & 0 & 0 & 0 & 0 \end{bmatrix}$$

Here the partition is $J_1 = \{1, 4\}$, $J_2 = \{2, 6\}$, $J_3 = \{3, 5\}$.

2. Also let $\sigma_2 = \begin{pmatrix} 1 & 2 & 3 & 4 & 5 & 6 \\ 1 & 6 & 3 & 4 & 2 & 5 \end{pmatrix}$; then

$$P_{\sigma_2}^{-1} \cdot A \cdot P_{\sigma_2} = \begin{bmatrix} 0 & \boxed{1} & 0 & 0 & 0 & 0 \\ 0 & 0 & \boxed{2} & 0 & 0 & 0 \\ 0 & 0 & 0 & \boxed{3} & 0 & 0 \\ 0 & 0 & 0 & 0 & \boxed{4} & 0 \\ 0 & 0 & 0 & 0 & 0 & \boxed{5} \\ \boxed{6} & 0 & 0 & 0 & 0 & 0 \end{bmatrix}$$

Here the partition is $J_1 = \{1\}$, $J_2 = \{6\}$, $J_3 = \{3\}$, $J_4 = \{4\}$, $J_5 = \{2\}$, and $J_6 = \{5\}$.

This example also shows that the partition which reveals the imprimitiveness is not necessarily unique. The relationships between the above concepts may be illustrated as follows:

$$\begin{cases} \text{decomposable} \\ \text{indecomposable} \begin{cases} \text{primitive (acyclic)} \\ \text{imprimitive (cyclic)} \end{cases} \end{cases}$$

We will now state the most important theorem on primitive (indecomposable) matrices.

Theorem 4.B.3: *A nonnegative indecomposable square matrix A is primitive if and only if its Frobenius root is* unique; *that is, there are no other eigenvalues of A whose absolute values are equal or greater than this.*

    PROOF: The proof is omitted. See Nikaido [7], section 21, and [9], section 8.3, for example.

    REMARK: From this theorem, we may define the "primitive matrix" in terms of its *unique* Frobenius root (see Gantmacher [4], p. 80, for example). In fact, if we define the primitive matrix in terms of the unique Frobenius root and define the acyclic matrix as above, then the above theorem can be restated as follows: A nonnegative indecomposable square matrix is acyclic if and only if it is primitive (see Solow [11], p. 40, for example).

    REMARK: Frobenius' theorem I asserts that if A is nonnegative and indecomposable, then its Frobenius root $\hat{\lambda}$ is a simple root and $\hat{\lambda} \geq |\omega|$ for any other eigenvalues ω of A. In other words, there can be an eigenvalue whose absolute value is as large as $\hat{\lambda}$. The above theorem asserts that if A is primitive, then there is no such root.

The following theorem is a rather easy corollary of Theorem 4.B.3.

Theorem 4.B.4: *A nonnegative indecomposable square matrix A is primitive if and only if some power of A is positive; that is, $A^m > 0$ for some positive integer $m \geq 1$.*

    PROOF: The proof is omitted. See Gantmacher [4], pp. 80–81, for example.

The following theorem, which is due to Frobenius, gives a sufficient condition for A to be primitive.

Theorem 4.B.5: *A nonnegative indecomposable square matrix A is primitive if it has at least one diagonal element which is positive.*

    PROOF: The proof is obvious from the definition of primitive matrices.

FOOTNOTES

1. Note that the second, third, and first columns of I now become the first, second, and third columns of P_σ. If A is any 3×3 matrix whose jth column is a_j—that is, $A = [a_1, a_2, a_3]$ —then $A \cdot P_\sigma = [a_2, a_3, a_1]$, under the above permutation.
2. It immediately follows from the definition that A is decomposable if and only if the transpose of A is decomposable.
3. In fact, it is not necessary to assume the indecomposability of both A_1 and A_2. It suffices to assume that only A_1 is indecomposable.

4. The "modified" compactness argument used by D. Glycopantis to prove the existence of the von Neumann path can be used as an alternative method to avoid this difficulty. See his "The Closed Linear Model of Production: A Note," *Review of Economic Studies*, XXXVII, April 1970. See also Section A of Chapter 6.

5. As remarked before, it suffices to assume that only A_1 is indecomposable. The proof is analogous to the one below. Note that the matrix C is still indecomposable as long as A_1 is indecomposable. If A_2 is decomposable, $\hat{\lambda}_C > \hat{\lambda}_{A_2}$ should be modified to $\hat{\lambda}_C \geqq \hat{\lambda}_{A_2}$, and to assert this we need the first two statements of Frobenius' theorem II. The proofs of these two statements do not presuppose the present statement (vi) of Frobenius' theorem I.

6. The proof based on this observation is given by Gantmacher [4]. Alternatively, observe that decomposable matrices can be written (by suitable permutation of rows and columns) in a form which has indecomposable submatrices on the principal diagonal. Then, using Frobenius' theorem I, we can obtain the theorem for the decomposable case. Such a proof is given by Debreu and Herstein [1].

7. The proof of statements (i) and (ii) can be sketched as follows. Let $A_q \rightarrow A$ as $q \rightarrow \infty$, where $A_q > 0$, and $x_q > 0$ is the eigenvector associated with λ_q. Let x_q be chosen such that x_q is in the unit sphere S. Since S is compact, the sequence $\{x_q\}$ has a convergent subsequence $\{x_{q_h}\}$ whose limit $\hat{x}$ is in S. Since $A_{q_h} \cdot x_{q_h} = \lambda_{q_h} x_{q_h}$ in this subsequence with $x_{q_h} > 0$ and $\lambda_{q_h} > 0$, we have $A \cdot \hat{x} = \hat{\lambda} \hat{x}$ where $\hat{x} \geq 0$ and $\hat{\lambda} \geq 0$ in the limit.

8. An obvious example is $A = 0$. It can be shown that a necessary and sufficient condition for $\hat{\lambda} = 0$ is that $A^m = 0$ for some positive integer m. In economic applications, such a case turns out to be rather uninteresting.

REFERENCES

1. Debreu, G., and Herstein, I. N., "Nonnegative Square Matrices," *Econometrica*, 21, October 1953.

2. Frobenius, G., "Über Matrizen aus Positiven Elementen," *Sitzungsberichte der Königlichen Preussichen Akademie der Wissenschaftan*, 1908, pp. 471–76, 1909, pp. 514–518.

3. ———, "Über Matrizen aus Nicht Negativen Elementen," *Sitzungberichte der Königlichen Preussichen Akademie der Wissenschaften*, 1912, pp. 456–477.

4. Gantmacher, F. R., *The Theory of Matrices*, Vol. II, New York, Chelsea Publishing Co., 1959 (tr. from Russian).

5. McKenzie, L. W., "Matrices with Dominant Diagonals and Economic Theory," in *Mathematical Methods in the Social Sciences, 1959*, ed. by Arrow, Karlin, and Suppes, Stanford, Calif., Stanford University Press, 1960.

6. Morishima, M., "The Mathematical Theory of the Leontief System," in his *Inter-Industry Relations and Economic Fluctuations*, Tokyo, Yuhikaku, 1955 (in Japanese).

7. Nikaido, H., *Introduction to Sets and Mappings in Modern Economics*, tr. by K. Sato, Amsterdam, North-Holland, 1970 (the Japanese original, Tokyo, 1960).

8. ———, *Linear Mathematics for Economics*, Tokyo, Baifukan, 1961 (in Japanese).

9. ———, *Convex Structures and Economic Theory*, New York, Academic Press, 1968.

10. Perron, O., "Zur Theorie der Matrizen," *Mathematischen Annalen*, 64, July 1907, pp. 248–263.

11. Solow, R. M., "On the Structure of Linear Models," *Econometrica*, 20, January 1952.

12. Wielandt, H., "Unzerlegbare, Nicht Negative Matrizen," *Mathematische Zeitschrift*, LII, März 1950, pp. 642–648.

Section C

DOMINANT DIAGONAL MATRICES

Consider the following relation which appears in the Leontief input-output analysis:

$$[I - A] \cdot x = c$$

Here $A \geq 0$ is the input-output matrix, x is the output vector, and c is the final demand vector. We may call $[I - A]$ the **Leontief matrix**. We begin this section by reminding the reader of some of our discussions in Section A.

Suppose we estimate the input-output table A for a particular year from the statistical data for this year. Suppose that $c > 0$ and also that $x > 0$. In other words, we have the following property for $[I - A]$.

(i) For some $c > 0$, there exists an $x > 0$ such that $[I - A] \cdot x = c.$[1]

Suppose now that we want to use this input-output table A to predict x for future years. This can be done if we can predict the final demand vector, c, for these years and if we can assume that A is "fairly" constant. This is a more or less usual procedure for the application of the input-output table A. However, there remains one obvious question: How can we guarantee the nonnegativity of the x-vector which corresponds to some future $c \geq 0$? In other words, we want to be able to make the following assertion.

(ii) For any $c \geq 0$, there exists an $x \geq 0$ such that $[I - A] \cdot x = c.$

In the course of studying this question, the condition that all the successive principal minors of $[I - A]$ be positive has been shown to be important. This condition is called the Hawkins-Simon condition, as pointed out in Section A.

Another question has arisen in connection with the problem of "dynamizing" the Leontief input-output relation. It is now known that the crucial condition here is that the absolute values (modulus) of A's eigenvalues are all less than one. It is also known that this condition is closely related to conditions (i) and (ii) above, that is, the Hawkins-Simon condition. In the course of those studies, the Frobenius theorems were rediscovered and have since played an important role in developments in this area. We now know that condition (i) is crucial in the study of the matrix $[I - A]$; for then the concept of the "dominant diagonal matrix" can be used by economists. The relationship of these properties of the matrix $[I - A]$ or of "dominant diagonal matrices" to other studies in economics, such as the theory of stability of a competitive market, has also been realized. McKenzie's article [11] brilliantly summarizes the whole of this unifying structure. Nikaido's work [16], which was published at about the same time, is partly devoted to displaying this unifying structure as well. The purpose of this section is to clarify the mathematical structure of these problems. Hence it is natural that our exposition rely heavily on McKenzie [11] and Nikaido [16]. We begin with the definition of a dominant diagonal matrix.

Definition: An n × n matrix $A = [a_{ij}]$ is said to have a **dominant diagonal** if there exist positive numbers $d_1, d_2, \ldots, d_n$ such that.

$$d_j|a_{jj}| > \sum_{i \neq j} d_i|a_{ij}|, \quad \text{for } j = 1, 2, \ldots, n$$

The phrase "a dominant diagonal" will be abbreviated "d.d."[2]

REMARK: As the defining property, we could have chosen

$$d_i|a_{ii}| > \sum_{j \neq i} d_j|a_{ij}|, \quad \text{for } i = 1, 2, \ldots, n$$

which would define **row dominance** as compared with **column dominance**. The choice of column dominance here is mainly for the convenience of the present exposition.

REMARK: The usual definition in the literature is that A is said to have a **dominant diagonal** if $|a_{jj}| > \sum_{i \neq j}|a_{ij}|$, for all j, which is due to Hadamard. If D is the diagonal matrix whose diagonal elements d_{ii} are the d_i's in column dominance, then $D \cdot A$ has a dominant diagonal in the Hadamard sense. The following theorem by McKenzie [11] is a slight extension of the theorem due to Hadamard in terms of the new definition. This theorem is a fundamental theorem for dominant diagonal matrices.

Theorem 4.C.1 (Hadamard, McKenzie):   *If an n × n matrix A has d.d., A is nonsingular.*

PROOF: Suppose A is singular. Then there exists an $x \neq 0$ such that $B' \cdot x = 0$ where $B = D \cdot A$ and D is a diagonal matrix with $d_{ii} > 0$ $(i = 1, 2, \ldots, n)$. (Here D is chosen so that A has d.d. with respect to D, that is, $|b_{jj}| > \sum_{i \neq j}|b_{ij}|$ for all $j = 1, 2, \ldots, n$.) Therefore, $x_j b_{jj} + \sum_{i \neq j} x_i b_{ij} = 0, j = 1, 2, \ldots, n$. Or $|x_j| |b_{jj}| = |\sum_{i \neq j} x_i b_{ij}| \leq \sum_{i \neq j}|x_i| |b_{ij}|, j = 1, 2, \ldots, n$. Let J be the index set such that $|x_j| \geq |x_i|$ for all $i = 1, 2, \ldots, n$, when $j \in J$. Then we have $|x_j|\,|b_{jj}| \leq \sum_{i\neq j}|x_i|\,|b_{ij}| \leq \sum_{i\neq j}|x_j|\,|b_{ij}|$ for $j \in J$. Or $|b_{jj}| \leq \sum_{i\neq j}|b_{ij}|$, $j \in J$. This contradicts the assumption that A has d.d. so that $|b_{jj}| > \sum_{i\neq j}|b_{ij}|$ for all j.   (Q.E.D.)

Theorem 4.C.2:   *If an $n \times n$ matrix A has d.d. that is positive, all its eigenvalues have positive real parts.*

PROOF (McKENZIE):   Consider $[\rho I - A]$. Suppose that ρ has a nonpositive real part; then $|\rho - a_{ii}| \geq |a_{ii}|$, $i = 1, 2, \ldots, n$. (Here the absolute value symbols mean modulus if complex values are being considered.) Hence $[\rho I - A]$ has d.d. and is nonsingular by the previous theorem. Hence ρ cannot be an eigenvalue of A ($\because$ if ρ is an eigenvalue of A, det $[\rho I - A] = 0$).
                    (Q.E.D.)

REMARK: Similarly, we can show that if A has d.d. that is negative, all its eigenvalues have negative real parts.

The next theorem is clearly important in the Leontief input-output theory. It characterizes condition (ii) in terms of the matrix with d.d.

Theorem 4.C.3:   *Let $B = [b_{ij}]$ be an $n \times n$ matrix with $b_{ii} > 0$ for all i and $b_{ij} \leq 0$ for $i \neq j$. Then there exists a unique $x \geq 0$ such that $B \cdot x = c$ for every $c \geq 0$ if and only if B has d.d.*

PROOF: We first prove sufficiency. Suppose that there exist $d_i > 0$, $i = 1, 2, \ldots, n$, with which B has d.d. By Theorem 4.C.1, B is nonsingular. Hence a unique solution x exists. To show $x \geq 0$, suppose that $x_j < 0$ for $j \in J \neq \emptyset$ and $x_j \geq 0$ for $j \notin J$, where J is a set of indices. Consider $\sum_{j \notin J} b_{ij}x_j + \sum_{j \in J} b_{ij}x_j = c_i \geq 0$ for $i \in J$. Multiplying by d_i and summing, we obtain

$$(*) \qquad \sum_{i \in J}\sum_{j \notin J} d_i b_{ij} x_j + \sum_{i \in J}\sum_{j \in J} d_i b_{ij} x_j = \sum_{i \in J} d_i c_i \geq 0$$

Clearly the first term on the left is nonpositive since $x_j \geq 0$ for $j \notin J$ and $b_{ij} \leq 0$ for $i \neq j$. By assumption of d.d., $\sum_{i \in J, i \neq j} d_i|b_{ij}| < d_j|b_{jj}|$ for all j, hence for $j \in J$. Since $b_{jj} > 0$, this implies that $\sum_{i \in J, i \neq j} d_i b_{ij} + d_j b_{jj} = \sum_{i \in J} d_i b_{ij} > 0$ for $j \in J$. Hence $\sum_{i \in J}\sum_{j \in J} d_i b_{ij} x_j < 0$; that is, the second term on the left-hand side of $(*)$ is negative. Thus the left-hand side of $(*)$ is negative, which is a contradiction.
    Now we prove necessity. Consider $B \cdot x = c$. By assumption, for any $c \geq 0$, there exists a unique $x \geq 0$. In particular, let $c > 0$. Then $x > 0$, since $b_{ii} > 0$ for all i and $b_{ij} \leq 0$, $i \neq j$. Hence B' has d.d. realized by this x. Then by the above, $B' \cdot p = \pi$ has a unique solution $p \geq 0$ for any $\pi \geq 0$. In particular, let $\pi > 0$; then $p > 0$, since $b_{ii} > 0$ for all i and $b_{ij} \leq 0$, $i \neq j$. In other words, B has d.d. with respect to this p.   (Q.E.D.)

The following theorem follows immediately from Theorem 4.C.3.

Theorem 4.C.4:   *Let $B = [b_{ij}]$ be an $n \times n$ matrix such that $b_{ij} \leq 0$ for $i \neq j$; then the following conditions are equivalent.*

   (I)   *There exists an $x \geq 0$ such that $B \cdot x > 0$.*
   (II) *For any $c \geq 0$, there exists an $x \geq 0$ such that $B \cdot x = c$.*
   (III) *The matrix B is nonsingular and $B^{-1} \geq 0$.*

   PROOF: We prove $(I) \Rightarrow (III) \Rightarrow (II) \Rightarrow (I)$.

   (i) $[(I) \Rightarrow (III)]$: Since $b_{ij} \leq 0$, $i \neq j$, $B \cdot x > 0$ implies that $b_{ii}x_i > -\sum_{j \neq i} b_{ij}x_j$ for all i so that $b_{ii} > 0$ for all i and $x > 0$. Hence B has d.d. with respect to this x. Therefore B is nonsingular by Theorem 4.C.1, and, by the previous theorem, for any $c \geq 0$, $B^{-1} \cdot c \geq 0$. Let

$$c_i \equiv (0, 0, \ldots, \overset{i}{1}, \ldots, 0)$$

Then $B^{-1} \cdot c \geq 0$, $i = 1, 2, \ldots, n$, which implies $B^{-1} \geq 0$.
   (ii) $[(III) \Rightarrow (II)]$: The proof follows trivially.
   (iii) $[(II) \Rightarrow (I)]$: The proof follows trivially.   (Q.E.D.)

REMARK: From the proof it is obvious that if B satisfies (I), then B has d.d. that is positive.

REMARK: Let B be the Leontief matrix $[I - A]$. Then conditions (I) and (II) are obviously restatements of our conditions (i) and (ii), respectively. Hence we now know that condition (i) is equivalent to condition (ii).

REMARK: Condition (I) can be restated as follows:

   (I) For some $c > 0$, $B \cdot x = c$ has a solution $x \geq 0$.

Nikaido [16] called (I) the **weak solvability condition** and (II) the **strong solvability condition**.

Theorem 4.C.5 (Hawkins-Simon):   *Let $B = [b_{ij}]$ be an $n \times n$ matrix with $b_{ij} \leq 0$, $i \neq j$; then the following two conditions are equivalent.*

   (I)   *There exists an $x \geq 0$ such that $B \cdot x > 0$.*
   (IV) $[$*or* **(H-S)**$]$ *All the successive principal minors of B are positive, that is,*

$$b_{11} > 0, \quad \begin{vmatrix} b_{11} & b_{12} \\ b_{21} & b_{22} \end{vmatrix} > 0, \ldots, \quad \begin{vmatrix} b_{11} & b_{12} & \cdots & b_{1n} \\ b_{21} & b_{22} & \cdots & b_{2n} \\ \cdots & \cdots & \cdots & \cdots \\ b_{n1} & b_{n2} & \cdots & b_{nn} \end{vmatrix} > 0$$

In other words,

$$\det B_k > 0, \ k = 1, 2, \ldots, n, \text{ where } B_k \equiv \begin{bmatrix} b_{11} & \cdots & b_{1k} \\ b_{21} & \cdots & b_{2k} \\ \cdots & \cdots & \cdots \\ b_{k1} & \cdots & b_{kk} \end{bmatrix}$$

REMARK: We call condition (H-S) the **Hawkins-Simon condition.**

PROOF $[(I) \Rightarrow (H\text{-}S)]$:   Condition (I) means there exist $x_j \geq 0$ such that $\sum_{j=1}^{n} b_{ij} x_j > 0$, $i = 1, 2, \ldots, n$. Since $b_{ij} \leq 0$, $i \neq j$, this implies $b_{ii} > 0$ for all i and that there exists $x_j \geq 0$ such that $\sum_{j=1}^{k} b_{ij} x_j > 0$ $(i = 1, 2, \ldots, n)$, for $k = 1$, $2, \ldots, n$, and $k = i$. In other words, condition (I) holds for all B_k, $k = 1, 2$, $\ldots, n$. Hence by Theorem 4.C.4, B_k is nonsingular. Now suppose that b_{ij} $(i \neq j)$ shrinks to zero. In this process condition (I) is clearly preserved so that the nonsingularity of B_k is also preserved. In other words, in this process of shrinking the b_{ij}'s $(i \neq j)$, $\det B_k$ will never be zero so that $\det B_k$ keeps the same sign. But in the limit of $b_{ij} = 0$ $(i \neq j)$, $\det B_k > 0$ since $b_{ii} > 0$ for all i. Hence $\det B_k$ must also be positive $(k = 1, 2, \ldots, n)$ for the original b_{ij} $(i \neq j)$. $[(H\text{-}S) \Rightarrow (I)]$: It suffices to show that (H-S)$\Rightarrow$(II). We prove this by mathematical induction. For $n = 1$, $b_{11} x_1 = c_1$. Condition (H-S) implies that $b_{11} > 0$. Hence for any $c_1 \geq 0$, there exists an $x_1 \geq 0$ such that $b_{11} x_1 = c_1$ (obviously $x_1 = c_1/b_{11}$). Suppose that (II) holds for $n - 1$, and we want to prove that it holds for n. Consider $\sum_{j=1}^{n} b_{ij} x_j = c_i$, $i = 1, 2, \ldots, n$ (or $B \cdot x = c$). We want to show that, for any $c = (c_1, c_2, \ldots, c_n) \geq 0$, there exists an $x = (x_1, x_2, \ldots, x_n) \geq 0$ such that $\sum_{j=1}^{n} b_{ij} x_j = c_i$, $i = 1, 2, \ldots, n$. Noting that $b_{11} > 0$ (hence $\neq 0$), we obtain $\sum_{j=1}^{n} b_{ij} x_j - [\sum_{j=1}^{n} b_{1j} x_j] b_{i1}/b_{11} = c_i - c_1 b_{i1}/b_{11}$ for $i = 2, 3, \ldots, n$. Define $b'_{ij} \equiv b_{ij} - b_{1j} b_{i1}/b_{11}$ and $c'_i \equiv c_i - c_1 b_{i1}/b_{11}$, $i = 2, 3, \ldots, n$, $j = 1, 2, \ldots, n$. Then we obtain $\sum_{j=2}^{n} b'_{ij} x_j = c'_i$, $i = 2, 3, \ldots, n$, and $b'_{11} = c'_1 = 0$. Note that

$$\begin{vmatrix} b_{11} & b_{12} & \cdots & b_{1k} \\ b_{21} & b_{22} & \cdots & b_{2k} \\ \cdots & \cdots & \cdots & \cdots \\ b_{k1} & b_{k2} & \cdots & b_{kk} \end{vmatrix} = \begin{vmatrix} b_{11} & b'_{12} & \cdots & b'_{1k} \\ 0 & b'_{22} & \cdots & b'_{2k} \\ \cdots & \cdots & \cdots & \cdots \\ 0 & b'_{k2} & \cdots & b'_{kk} \end{vmatrix} = b_{11} \begin{vmatrix} b'_{22} & \cdots & b'_{2k} \\ \cdots & \cdots & \cdots \\ \cdots & \cdots & \cdots \\ b'_{k2} & \cdots & b'_{kk} \end{vmatrix}$$

Since $\det B_k > 0$, $k = 1, 2, \ldots, n$ [by (H-S)], we obtain

$$\begin{vmatrix} b'_{22} & \cdots & b'_{2k} \\ \cdots & \cdots & \cdots \\ \cdots & \cdots & \cdots \\ b'_{k2} & \cdots & b'_{kk} \end{vmatrix} > 0, \ k = 2, 3, \ldots, n$$

That is, the (H-S) condition holds for the $(n - 1) \times (n - 1)$ matrix $[b'_{ij}]$. Then by the induction hypothesis, $\sum_{j=2}^{n} b'_{ij} x_j = c'_j$ has a nonnegative solution $(x_2, \ldots, x_n)$ for any nonnegative $(c'_2, \ldots, c'_n)$. Let $c = (c_1, c_2, \ldots, c_n) \geq 0$ be an arbitrary vector. Compute c'_i, $i = 2, 3, \ldots, n$, from $c'_i = c_i - c_1 b_{i1}/b_{11}$; $c'_i \geq 0$ since $b_{i1} \leq 0$, $i \neq 1$, and $b_{11} > 0$. Then obtain $x_2, x_3, \ldots, x_n \geq 0$ and obtain x_1 from $x_1 = [c_1 - \sum_{j=2}^{n} b_{1j}x_j]/b_{11}$. Since $b_{1j} \leq 0, 1 \neq j$, and $b_{11} > 0$, x_1 is also nonnegative. Hence $B \cdot x = c$ has a solution $x \geq 0$ for any $c \geq 0$. Thus (II) holds for n.   (Q.E.D.)

REMARK: The proof of $[(\text{H-S}) \Rightarrow (\text{I})]$ is due to Nikaido [16], section 3, and [17], p. 92.

REMARK: Combining Theorem 4.C.4 and Theorem 4.C.5, we can say that conditions (I), (II), (III), and (IV) are all equivalent.

Corollary: *Let* $B = [b_{ij}]$ *be an* $n \times n$ *matrix with* $b_{ij} \leq 0, i \neq j$. *Then* (*H-S*) *implies that all the principal minors of* B *are positive,*[3] *that is,*

$$(\textbf{h-s}), \quad b_{ii} \; > \; 0, \quad \begin{vmatrix} b_{ii} & b_{ij} \\ b_{ji} & b_{jj} \end{vmatrix} \; > \; 0, \quad \begin{vmatrix} b_{ii} & b_{ij} & b_{ik} \\ b_{ji} & b_{jj} & b_{jk} \\ b_{ki} & b_{kj} & b_{kk} \end{vmatrix} \; > \; 0, \cdots$$

PROOF: By Theorem 4.C.5, (H-S) implies that condition (I) holds. That is, for some $c > 0$ there exists an $x \geq 0$ such that $B \cdot x = c$. Then renumber the coordinates of x and c and renumber the b_{ij}'s correspondingly. Clearly, (I) holds throughout this process. Hence by Theorem 4.C.5 (H-S) holds for the new system. Since the renumbering can be any permutation of $\{1, 2, \ldots, n\}$, condition (h-s) holds.   (Q.E.D.)

REMARK: This (h-s) is the so-called "Hawkins-Simon condition." Gantmacher called the above corollary the **Kotelyanskii theorem** ([5], pp. 71–73).[4]

Theorem 4.C.6:   *Suppose* B *is written as* $B = [\rho I - A]$ *where* $A = [a_{ij}]$ *is an* $n \times n$ *nonnegative matrix (that is,* $A \geq 0$*) and* ρ *is a positive real number.*[5] *Then any one of the conditions* (*I*), (*II*), (*III*), *and* (*IV*) *is equivalent to the following condition:*[6]

$$\text{The series } \frac{1}{\rho} \sum_{k=0}^{\infty} \left(\frac{A}{\rho} \right)^k \text{ is convergent.}$$

PROOF (NIKAIDO)[7]:   We prove the above equivalence by showing the equivalence of the above condition and (III). First we show that (III) implies the above condition with the sum of the series being $[\rho I - A]^{-1}$. Let $T_m \equiv [\sum_{k=0}^{m}(A/\rho)^k]/\rho$. Then

$$(1) \qquad T_m \cdot [\rho I - A] = [\rho I - A] \cdot T_m = I - \frac{A^{m+1}}{\rho^{m+1}}$$

This implies that $[\rho I - A] \cdot T_m \leq I$. Hence $T_m \leq [\rho I - A]^{-1}$ in view of (III), so that the sequence $\{T_m\}$ is bounded from above. But $T_0 \leq T_1 \leq T_2 \leq \ldots$, since $\rho > 0$. Hence T_∞ is convergent. Write $T_\infty \equiv T$. Since $A^{m+1}/$

$\rho^{m+1} = \rho T_{m+1} - \rho T_m \to 0$ as $m \to \infty$, from (1) we obtain $(\rho I - A) \cdot T = I$, or $T = [\rho I - A]^{-1}$. Conversely, if T_∞ is convergent, then (1) converges to $T \cdot [\rho I - A] = [\rho I - A] \cdot T = I$, since $A^{m+1}/\rho^{m+1} \to 0$, as above. That is, $[\rho I - A]$ is invertible and $[\rho I - A]^{-1} = T$. Since $T_m \geq 0$, $T \geq 0$ so that $[\rho I - A]^{-1} \geq 0$.
(Q.E.D.)

We now come to using the Frobenius theorem. Let $A = [a_{ij}]$ be an $n \times n$ nonnegative matrix, and consider $B = [\rho I - A]$ where ρ is some real number. Clearly $b_{ij} \leq 0$, $i \neq j$. We prove the following theorem.

Theorem 4.C.7:   *Let $B \equiv \rho I - A$, where $A = [a_{ij}] \geq 0$ and $\rho \in R$; then the following conditions are all equivalent.*[8]

(I′)   *There exists an $x \geq 0$ such that $B \cdot x > 0$.*
(V′)   *The real parts of all the eigenvalues of B are positive.*
(VI′)   *We have $\rho > \hat{\lambda}_A$, where $\hat{\lambda}_A$ is the Frobenius root of A.*

PROOF: Let ω be an eigenvalue of A; then by definition $0 = \det[\omega I - A] = \det[-\omega I + A] = \det[(\rho - \omega)I - (\rho I - A)]$. Hence any eigenvalue of B can be written in the form $(\rho - \omega)$. We now prove this theorem in the following order: (I′) $\Rightarrow$ (V′) $\Rightarrow$ (VI′) $\Rightarrow$ (I′).
[(I′) $\Rightarrow$ (V′)]: Condition (I′) implies that B has d.d. Hence (V′) follows by Theorem 4.C.2.
[(V′) $\Rightarrow$ (VI′)]: By (V′), we have $\text{Re}(\rho - \omega) > 0$, where ω is any eigenvalue of A and $\text{Re}(\rho - \omega)$ denotes the real part of $(\rho - \omega)$. By Frobenius' theorem II, A has a maximal nonnegative eigenvalue $\hat{\lambda}_A$. Since $\hat{\lambda}_A$ is a real root, $\rho - \hat{\lambda}_A = \text{Re}(\rho - \hat{\lambda}_A) > 0$. Hence $\rho > \hat{\lambda}_A$.
[(VI′) $\Rightarrow$ (I′)]: By Frobenius' theorem II, condition (iii), if $A \cdot x \geq \rho x$ for some $x \geq 0$ and for some real number ρ, then we have $\hat{\lambda}_A \geq \rho$. Hence if $\hat{\lambda}_A < \rho$, then for any $x \geq 0$ we have $A \cdot x < \rho x$, or $[\rho I - A] \cdot x > 0$, which in turn implies that (I′) holds.
(Q.E.D.)

REMARK: In view of Theorems 4.C.4 and 4.C.5 these conditions are also equivalent to (II), (III), and (IV) for this $B = [\rho I - A]$.

We now come back to our original matrix $B = [b_{ij}]$ with $b_{ij} \leq 0$, $i \neq j$. We want to write B in the form of $[\rho I - A]$, for some $A \geq 0$. To do this, let ρ be a positive number which is big enough so that $[\rho I - B] \geq 0$. Write $A \equiv \rho I - B$. Then we can write $B = \rho I - A$, where $A \geq 0$. Hence, using Theorem 4.C.7, we at once obtain the following theorem.

Theorem 4.C.8:   *Conditions (I), (II), (III), and (IV) are all equivalent to the following condition.*

(V)   *The real parts of all the eigenvalues of B are positive.*

PROOF: By Theorem 4.C.7, condition (V) is equivalent to the condition

$\rho > \hat{\lambda}_A$ where $\hat{\lambda}_A$ is the Frobenius root of A. This, in turn, is equivalent to condition (I).   (Q.E.D.)

Corollary (Metzler):   *Let A be an $n \times n$ nonnegative matrix and $\hat{\lambda}_A$ be its Frobenius root. Then a necessary and sufficient condition for $\hat{\lambda}_A < 1$ is that all the principal minors of $[I - A]$ are positive.*

PROOF: This is a result of (VI') $\Leftrightarrow$ (IV') [or (H-S)].   (Q.E.D.)

When we considered $[\rho I - A]$, we simply assumed $A \geq 0$. If, in addition, A is indecomposable, we can get a stronger result. But first we prove the following lemma.

Lemma: *Let $A = [a_{ij}]$ be an $n \times n$ nonnegative matrix. Suppose $A \cdot x \leq \mu x$ for some $\mu \in R$ and $x \geq 0$. Then if A is indecomposable, $x > 0$.[9]*

PROOF: Suppose $x \not> 0$. Then we may write $x = \begin{bmatrix} x' \\ 0 \end{bmatrix}$, where $x' > 0$. Write

$A \equiv \begin{bmatrix} A_{11} & A_{12} \\ A_{21} & A_{22} \end{bmatrix}$ accordingly. Then $A \cdot x \leq \mu x$ implies $A_{21} \cdot x' \leq \mu 0 = 0$.

Hence $A_{21} = 0$. This contradicts the indecomposability of A.   (Q.E.D.)

Theorem 4.C.9:   *Let $A = [a_{ij}]$ be an $n \times n$ nonnegative indecomposable matrix and let ρ be a real number. Consider $B \equiv \rho I - A$. Then the following conditions are equivalent.*

(I')   *There exists an $x \geq 0$ such that $B \cdot x > 0$.*
(VII')   *There exists an $x \geq 0$ such that $B \cdot x \geq 0$.*
(VIII')   *The matrix B is nonsingular and $B^{-1} > 0$.*

REMARK: Condition (VII') is a strengthening of (I'), and (VIII') is a strengthening of (III'), where condition (III') means (III) holds when B can be written as $B = \rho I - A$, $A \geq 0$.

PROOF: [(VII') $\Leftrightarrow$ (I')]: Condition (I') $\Rightarrow$ (VII') follows trivially. Hence it suffices to show that (VII') $\Rightarrow$ (I'). By assumption, there exists an $x \geq 0$ such that $B \cdot x \geq 0$. Clearly $x \neq 0$. Hence $x \geq 0$. Let A' be the transpose of A and let $\hat{\lambda}_{A'}$ be its Frobenius root with associated eigenvector y. Since A is indecomposable, so is A'. Thus by Frobenius' theorem I, $y > 0$. We have $A' \cdot y = \hat{\lambda}_{A'} y$. Write $B \cdot x \equiv c$, where $c \geq 0$. Then $\rho x = A \cdot x + c \geq A \cdot x$. Consider the inner product of y and ρx: $\rho \langle y, x \rangle = \langle y, \rho x \rangle > \langle y, A \cdot x \rangle = \langle A' \cdot y, x \rangle = \langle \hat{\lambda}_{A'} y, x \rangle = \hat{\lambda}_{A'} \langle y, x \rangle$. Since $\langle y, x \rangle > 0$, we have $\rho > \hat{\lambda}_{A'}$. Since the Frobenius root of A (denoted by $\hat{\lambda}_A$) is equal to $\hat{\lambda}_{A'}$, we have $\rho > \hat{\lambda}_A$. Since (VI') $\Leftrightarrow$ (I') by Theorem 4.C.7, (I') follows.

$[(VIII') \Leftrightarrow (I')]$: It suffices to show that $(VIII') \Leftrightarrow (III')$ since $(III') \Leftrightarrow$ (I') by Theorem 4.C.4. Since $(VIII') \Rightarrow (III')$ follows trivially, it remains to show that $(III') \Rightarrow (VIII')$.

$[(III') \Rightarrow (VIII')]$: Let $c \geq 0$ be an arbitrary semipositive vector. By assumption, $B^{-1} \geq 0$. Hence $x \equiv B^{-1} \cdot c \geq 0$. We will show that $x > 0$. Note that $B \cdot x = c$ implies $\rho x = A \cdot x + c \geq A \cdot x$, so that $x \geq 0$. Hence by the previous lemma, $x > 0$. Choose

$$c = (0, 0, \ldots, \overbrace{0, 1, 0}^{i}, \ldots, 0)$$

Then $B^{-1} \cdot c > 0$ means that the ith column of B^{-1} is strictly positive. Let $i = 1, 2, \ldots, n$. Thus $B^{-1} > 0$.   (Q.E.D.)

Theorem 4.C.10 (Brauer [1], Solow [19]):   *Let* $A = [a_{ij}]$ *be an* $n \times n$ *nonnegative indecomposable matrix. Let* $r_i \equiv \sum_{j=1}^{n} a_{ij}, i = 1, 2, \ldots, n$ *(row sum). If* $\rho \geq r_i$ *for all* i *with strict inequality for some* i, *then* $\rho > \hat{\lambda}_A$, *where* $\hat{\lambda}_A$ *is the Frobenius root of* A.

PROOF: Let $c_i \equiv \rho - r_i$ and $B \equiv \rho I - A$. Then $B \cdot x = c$ has a solution $x = (1, 1, \ldots, 1)$. Hence condition (VII') holds, so that condition (VI') follows; that is, $\rho > \hat{\lambda}_A$.   (Q.E.D.)

REMARK: If we let $s_j \equiv \sum_{i=1}^{n} a_{ij}, j = 1, 2, \ldots, n$ (column sum), we can show analogously that if $\rho \geq s_j$ for all j with strict inequality for some j, then $\rho > \hat{\lambda}_A$.

REMARK: If $B = [I - A]$, this condition gives a sufficient condition for $\hat{\lambda}_A < 1$.

REMARK: If $r_i < \rho$ for all i (or $s_j < \rho$ for all j), then condition (I') immediately follows so that $\hat{\lambda}_A < \rho$. No indecomposability assumption is necessary. In fact, this condition provides a trivial (but very useful) sufficient condition for conditions (I'), (II'), and so on, to hold.

REMARK: The following proposition is a slight generalization of Brauer-Solow's result.

Theorem 4.C.11: (Fisher [4], Takayama [20]):   *Let* $A = [a_{ij}]$ *be an* $n \times n$ *nonnegative matrix (not necessarily indecomposable) and let* $\hat{\lambda}_A$ *be its Frobenius root. Let* $s_j \equiv \sum_{i=1}^{n} a_{ij}, j = 1, 2, \ldots, n$ *(column sum) and let* $\bar{s} \equiv \max_j s_j$ *and* $\underline{s} \equiv \min_j s_j$; *then we have* $\underline{s} \leq \hat{\lambda}_A \leq \bar{s}$, *and if, in particular,* $s_j = 1$ *for all* j, *then* $\hat{\lambda}_A = 1$. *A similar proposition can be obtained with respect to the row sums of* A.

PROOF: Let $\hat{x} = (\hat{x}_1, \ldots, \hat{x}_n) \geq 0$ be the eigenvector associated with $\hat{\lambda}_A$. By definition, we have $\hat{\lambda}_A \hat{x} = A \cdot \hat{x}$, that is, $\hat{\lambda}_A \hat{x}_i = \sum_{j=1}^{n} a_{ij} \hat{x}_j, i = 1, 2, \ldots, n$. Summing over i, we obtain

$$\hat{\lambda}_A \sum_{i=1}^{n} \hat{x}_i = \sum_{i=1}^{n} \sum_{j=1}^{n} a_{ij}\hat{x}_j = \sum_{j=1}^{n} \hat{x}_j \left(\sum_{i=1}^{n} a_{ij} \right) = \sum_{j=1}^{n} \hat{x}_j s_j$$

Hence

$$\hat{\lambda}_A = \frac{\sum_{j=1}^{n} \hat{x}_j s_j}{\sum_{i=1}^{n} \hat{x}_i}$$

(that is, $\hat{\lambda}_A$ is a nonnegative weighted average of the column sums, the s_j's). The statement of the theorem follows immediately from this relation.

(Q.E.D.)

REMARK: Takayama [20] proved the theorem for the case when $s_j = 1$ for all j. Fisher's result [4] as recorded above is more general, but his method of proof is identical with that of Takayama [20]. Hence in essence it is only a slight generalization.

Finally we may point out the interesting discussion on the "choice of units" by Fisher [3]. Consider the Leontief system $A \cdot x + c = x$. Suppose the jth element of x and c (that is, the jth good) is to be measured in new units. Then the jth row of A must be multiplied by, and the jth column divided by, the same appropriate conversion factor. In other words, the shift of units will convert the original matrix A to

$$A^* \equiv D \cdot A \cdot D^{-1}$$

where D is an $n \times n$ diagonal matrix with positive diagonal elements. Write $x^* \equiv D \cdot x$ and $c^* \equiv D \cdot c$; then the original system can be rewritten with new units as $A^* \cdot x^* + c^* = x^*$. Then we can show easily that if A is indecomposable, there exists a set of units in which all column (row) sums of A^* are equal to its Frobenius root. To prove this, first note that A and A^* have the same Frobenius root (say, $\hat{\lambda}_A$) and that if $\hat{x} > 0$ is the eigenvector of A associated with $\hat{\lambda}_A$, then $D \cdot \hat{x}$ is the eigenvector of A^* associated with $\hat{\lambda}_A$. Then set $d_i = 1/\hat{x}_i$, $i = 1, 2, \ldots, n$, where d_i is the ith diagonal element of D. Then the above proposition follows immediately from $A^* \cdot (D \cdot \hat{x}) = \hat{\lambda}_A (D \cdot \hat{x})$.

With this observation, we can immediately obtain the following corollary of Theorem 4.C.10 (see Fisher [3], p. 446, for a decomposable case).

Corollary: *Let A be indecomposable. Then a necessary and sufficient condition for $1 > \hat{\lambda}_A$ is that there exist a set of units in which all column (row) sums are at most unity, and one such sum is less than unity.*

In this connection, we may also recall the definition of dominant diagonal matrices. By this definition, the Leontief matrix $[I - A]$, where $A \geq 0$, has dominant diagonals if there exist $d_j > 0$ such that $d_j(1 - a_{jj}) > \sum_{i \neq j} d_i a_{ij}, j = 1, 2, \ldots, n$; that is, $1 > \sum_{i=1}^{n} (d_i/d_j) a_{ij}, j = 1, 2, \ldots, n$. In other words, $[I - A]$ has dominant diagonals if and only if the column sums are less than unity with an appropriate shift of units. In the definition of dominant diagonals, we noted that McKenzie extended the usual definition. We can now see easily that the dominant diagonals in McKenzie's extended sense are equivalent to the existence of a set of units in which the matrix in question has dominant diagonals in the usual sense (see Fisher [3], p. 448).

FOOTNOTES

1. Note that this condition is equivalent to the following condition: For some $c > 0$, there exists an $x \geq 0$ such that $[I - A] \cdot x = c$. That is, $x > 0$ can be replaced by a weaker statement $x \geq 0$. To see this, write $[I - A] \cdot x = c > 0$ as $x_i - \sum_{j=1}^{n} a_{ij} x_j = c_i > 0$ for all i, and observe that this requires $x_i > 0$ for all i anyway.

2. Define $M = [m_{ij}]$ from $A = [a_{ij}]$ as follows: $m_{ij} = -|a_{ij}|, i \neq j$ and $m_{ii} = |a_{ii}|$. Then it is easy to see that A has a dominant diagonal if and only if there exists a $d > 0$ such that $M' \cdot d > 0$, where M' is the transpose of M. Clearly this condition is closely related to the above condition (i) for the Leontief matrix.

3. Therefore the condition (H-S) is equivalent to the condition (h-s).

4. Hawkins and Simon [7] obtained (h-s) and Nicholas Georgescu-Roegen obtained (H-S) in his "Some Properties of a Generalized Leontief Model," in *Activity Analysis of Production and Allocation*, ed. by T. C. Koopmans, New York, Wiley, 1951 (theorem 7), reprinted with revision and "A Postcript (1964)" in his *Analytical Economics*, Cambridge, Mass., Harvard University Press, 1966.

5. If (IV) [that is, (H-S)] holds, then $\rho > 0$ is automatically implied if $a_{11} > 0$, for (H-S), among other things, requires $\rho - a_{11} > 0$.

6. In the proof it will be shown that if the series is convergent it is equal to $[\rho I - A]^{-1}$.

7. See Nikaido [17], p. 97, and [16], section 19.

8. Note that the prime in (I′), (V′), and (VI′) indicates that B has the specific form $[\rho I - A]$, where $A \geq 0$ is a given nonnegative square matrix.

9. In view of this lemma, we can immediately assert that if $A \cdot x \leq \mu x$ for some μ and $x \geq 0, x \not> 0$, then A is decomposable. In fact, we can also show the converse of this statement, that is, if A is decomposable, then $A \cdot x \leq \mu x$ for some μ and $x \geq 0$, $x \not> 0$. The proof of this follows easily from the definition of decomposability.

REFERENCES

1. Brauer, A., "Limits for the Characteristic Roots of a Matrix," *Duke Mathematical Journal*, 13, September 1946.

2. Debreu, G., and Herstein, I. N., "Nonnegative Square Matrices," *Econometrica*, 21, October 1953.

3. Fisher, F. M., "Choice of Units, Column Sums, and Stability in Linear Dynamic Systems with Nonnegative Square Matrices," *Econometrica*, 33, April 1965.

4. ———, "An Alternate Proof and Extension of Solow's Theorem on Nonnegative Square Matrices," *Econometrica*, 30, April 1962.

5. Gantmacher, F. R., *The Theory of Matrices*, Vol. II, New York, Chelsea Publishing Co., 1959 (tr. from Russian).

6. Hawkins, D., "Some Conditions of Macro-economic Stability," *Econometrica*, 16, October 1948.

7. Hawkins, D., and Simon, H. A., "Note: Some Conditions of Macro-economic Stability," *Econometrica*, 17, July–October 1949.

8. Herstein, I. N., "Comments on Solow's 'Structure of Linear Models,'" *Econometrica*, 20, October 1952.

9. Karlin, S., *Mathematical Methods and Theory in Games, Programming and Economics*, Vol. 1, Reading, Mass., Addison-Wesley, 1959.

10. McKenzie, L. W., "An Elementary Analysis of the Leontief System," *Econometrica*, 25, July 1957.

11. ——, "Matrices with Dominant Diagonals and Economic Theory," in *Mathematical Methods in Social Sciences, 1959*, ed. by Arrow, Karlin, and Suppes, Stanford, Calif., Stanford University Press, 1960.

12. Metzler, L. A., "Stability of Multiple Markets: The Hicks Conditions," *Econometrica*, 13, October 1945.

13. ——, "A Multiple Region Theory of Income and Trade," *Econometrica*, 18, October 1950.

14. Morgenstern, O., ed., *Economic Activity Analysis*, New York, Wiley, 1954, esp. articles by Wong, Y. K., and Woodbury, M. A.

15. Mosak, S. L., *General Equilibrium Theory in International Trade*, Bloomington, Ind., Principia Press, 1944.

16. Nikaido, H., *Introduction to Sets and Mappings in Modern Economics*, tr. by K. Sato, Amsterdam, North-Holland, 1970 (the Japanese original, Tokyo, 1960).

17. ——, *Convex Structures and Economic Theory*, New York, Academic Press, 1968.

18. Price, G. G., "Bounds for Determinates with Dominant Principal Diagonals," *Proceedings of the American Mathematical Society*, 2, 1951.

19. Solow, R. M., "On the Structure of Linear Models," *Econometrica*, 20, January 1952.

20. Takayama, A., "Stability in the Balance of Payments: A Multi-Country Approach," *Journal of Economic Behavior*, 1, October, 1961 (the paper presented at the Washington meeting of the Econometric Society, 1959, resumé, *Econometrica*, 28, July 1960).

Section D
SOME APPLICATIONS

a. SUMMARY OF RESULTS

We begin this section by summarizing some of the results obtained in the previous section. In order to make it easy to refer to these results, we will present them as theorems.

Theorem 4.D.1:   *Let $B = [b_{ij}]$ be an $n \times n$ matrix with $b_{ij} \leq 0$ for $i \neq j$. Then the following five conditions are mutually equivalent.*

(I)   *There exists an $x \geq 0$ such that $B \cdot x > 0$ (that is, for some $c > 0$, there exists an $x \geq 0$ such that $B \cdot x = c$).*[1]
(II)   *For any $c \geq 0$, there exists an $x \geq 0$ such that $B \cdot x = c$.*
(III)   *The matrix B is nonsingular and $B^{-1} \geq 0$.*
(IV) [*or* **(H-S)**]   *All the successive principal minors of B are positive. In other words,*

$$b_{11} > 0, \quad \begin{vmatrix} b_{11} & b_{12} \\ b_{21} & b_{22} \end{vmatrix} > 0, \cdots, \quad \begin{vmatrix} b_{11} & b_{12} \cdots b_{1n} \\ b_{21} & b_{22} \cdots b_{2n} \\ \cdots\cdots\cdots\cdots \\ b_{n1} & b_{n2} \cdots b_{nn} \end{vmatrix} > 0$$

(V)   *The real parts of all the eigenvalues of B are positive.*

PROOF: The proof is obvious from Theorem 4.C.8.

The matrix B is often written in the form $B \equiv [\rho I - A]$, where $A \geq 0$. Clearly Theorem 4.D.1 is applicable to this B. In fact, we can say even more in this case as is done in our next theorem.

Theorem 4.D.2:   *Let $A = [a_{ij}]$ be an $n \times n$ nonnegative matrix. Let $B \equiv [\rho I - A]$, where ρ is a real number and I is the identity matrix. Then the following six conditions are mutually equivalent.*

(I′)   *There exists an $x \geq 0$ such that $B \cdot x > 0$.*
(II′)   *For any $c \geq 0$, there exists an $x \geq 0$ such that $B \cdot x = c$.*
(III′)   *The matrix B is nonsingular and $B^{-1} \geq 0$.*
(IV′) [**(H-S)**]   *All the successive principal minors of B are positive.*
(V′)   *The real parts of all the eigenvalues of B are positive.*
(VI′)   *We have $\rho > \hat{\lambda}_A$ where $\hat{\lambda}_A$ is the Frobenius root of A.*

If, in addition, A is indecomposable, then any of the above conditions is equivalent to either of the following conditions:

(VII′)   *There exists an $x \geq 0$ such that $B \cdot x \geq 0$.*
(VIII′)   *The matrix B is nonsingular and $B^{-1} > 0$.*

PROOF: The proof is obvious from Theorems 4.C.7, 4.C.8, and 4.C.9.

REMARK: From Theorem 4.C.6, the first six conditions [(I′)–(VI′)] are equivalent to the following condition, if $\rho > 0$.

(IX′)   The series $\dfrac{1}{\rho} \sum_{k=0}^{\infty} \left(\dfrac{A}{\rho}\right)^k$ is convergent.

REMARK: As it was remarked in Theorem 4.C.6, if the series

$$\frac{1}{\rho}\sum_{k=0}^{\infty}\left(\frac{A}{\rho}\right)^{k}$$

is convergent, it is equal to $[\rho I - A]^{-1}$.

In the above theorems we are concerned with B such that $b_{ij} \leq 0$ for $i \neq j$, that is, such that all its off-diagonal elements are nonpositive. Suppose, on the contrary, that all the off-diagonal elements are nonnegative. We know that such a matrix appears in the stability analysis of a competitive market as the gross substitution matrix; hence we may suspect that if we know the properties of such a matrix, it will have many applications in economics. But the properties of such a matrix can immediately be obtained from the above theorems. Let $\tilde{B}$ be a (square) matrix whose off-diagonal elements are all nonnegative, and let $B \equiv -\tilde{B}$. Then clearly all the off-diagonal elements of B are nonpositive. Thus Theorem 4.D.1 can be applied and we obtain the following theorem.

Theorem 4.D.3:   *Let $\tilde{B}$ be an $n \times n$·matrix whose off-diagonal elements are all nonnegative. Then the following conditions are mutually equivalent*:

(I″)   *There exists an $x \geq 0$ such that $\tilde{B} \cdot x < 0$.[2]*
(II″)   *For any $c \leq 0$, there exists an $x \geq 0$ such that $\tilde{B} \cdot x = c$.*
(III″) *The matrix $\tilde{B}$ is nonsingular and $\tilde{B}^{-1} \leq 0$.*
(IV″)   *The successive principal minors of $\tilde{B}$ alternate in sign; that is, if $\tilde{B}_k$ is the successive principal minor of $\tilde{B}$ of order k, then $(-1)^k \tilde{B}_k > 0, k = 1, 2, \ldots, n$. In other words, $\tilde{B}$ is* **Hicksian**.
(V″)   *The real parts of all the eigenvalues of $\tilde{B}$ are negative.*
        If $\tilde{B}$ is written in the form $\tilde{B} = [A - \rho I]$ where $A \geq 0$ and ρ is a real number, then any of the above conditions is equivalent to the following:
(VI″)   *We have $\rho > \hat{\lambda}_A$, where $\hat{\lambda}_A$ is the Frobenius root of A.*
        If, in addition, A is indecomposable, then any of the above six conditions is equivalent to either of the following conditions:
(VII″) *There exists an $x \geq 0$ such that $\tilde{B} \cdot x \leq 0$.*
(VIII″) *The matrix $\tilde{B}$ is nonsingular and $\tilde{B}^{-1} < 0$.*

Finally we prove the following theorem, which will be useful and important in several economic applications.

Theorem 4.D.4:   *Let B be an $n \times n$ matrix such that $b_{ij} \leq 0$ for $i \neq j$. Then the following four conditions are mutually equivalent.*

(I)   *There exists an $x \geq 0$ such that $B \cdot x > 0$.*
(Ĭ)   *There exists a $p \geq 0$ such that $B' \cdot p > 0$ where B' is the transpose of B.*
(I*) *There exists an $x > 0$ such that $B \cdot x > 0$.*
(Ĭ*) *There exists a $p > 0$ such that $B' \cdot p > 0$.*

PROOF: From Theorem 4.D.1, condition (I) holds if and only if $B^{-1} \geq 0$ [condition (III)]. But by a well-known relation in elementary linear algebra, $(B^{-1})' = (B')^{-1}$. Thus $B^{-1} \geq 0$ is true if and only if $(B')^{-1} \geq 0$. Then applying Theorem 4.D.1 again, this is true if and only if there exists a $p \geq 0$ such that $B' \cdot p > 0$. Hence (I) and (Ǐ) are equivalent.

To show the equivalence of (I) and (I*), we recall that if there exists an $x \geq 0$ such that $B \cdot x > 0$, x must be strictly positive since $b_{ii} > 0$.[3] Conversely, if there exists an $x > 0$ such that $B \cdot x > 0$, then condition (I) clearly follows. Similarly, (I*) holds if and only if there exists a $p > 0$ such that $B' \cdot p > 0$. Combining this with the first part of the theorem, we obtain the second part of the theorem.   (Q.E.D.)

REMARK: In the first part of the proof of Theorem 4.D.4, we use the relation (I) $\Leftrightarrow$ (III). By noting that the eigenvalues of a matrix are the same as the eigenvalues of its transpose, we can prove the same statement using the relation (I) $\Leftrightarrow$ (V).

REMARK: The equivalence (I*) $\Leftrightarrow$ (Ǐ*) in Theorem 4.D.4 implies that B' has a dominant diagonal *if and only if* B has a dominant diagonal.[4]

REMARK: We also note that Theorem 4.D.4 can be proved directly from Theorem 4.C.3. To do this, simply note that $B \cdot x > 0$ for some $x > 0$ means that B' has a dominant diagonal. Hence, from Theorem 4.C.3, $B' \cdot p = \pi > 0$ has a solution $p > 0$. The converse holds similarly.

b.   INPUT-OUTPUT ANALYSIS

Let A be an input-output matrix so that a_{ij} denotes the amount of the ith good necessary to produce one unit of the jth good. Obviously $A \geq 0$. Let c and x be the final demand vector and the output vector, respectively. The basic relation of (static) input-output analysis is written as

$$[I - A] \cdot x = c$$

First, let A be computed for a particular year and let x and c be obtained for the year as well. Clearly $c > 0$ and $x > 0$, and all the off-diagonal elements of $[I - A]$ are nonpositive. Hence condition (I) of Theorem 4.D.1 is satisfied for $[I - A]$. Suppose that this technology matrix A is expected to be fairly constant for some years. Then by predicting the final demand vector c_f for some future year, we can easily compute the output vector for that particular year as $x_f = [I - A]^{-1} \cdot c_f$. In order to apply the above theorems, we consider the following two questions mentioned before.

(i)   For any $c_f \geq 0$, does there exist an $x_f \geq 0$ such that $[I - A] \cdot x_f = c_f$?
(ii)   Is $[I - A]$ nonsingular? If so, is $[I - A]^{-1} \geq 0$?

By use of Theorem 4.D.1, we can immediately answer both these questions in the affirmative. Questions (i) and (ii) are nothing but conditions (II) and (III) of

Theorem 4.D.1, respectively. By Theorem 4.D.2, we must also have $1 > \hat{\lambda}_A$ where $\hat{\lambda}_A$ is the Frobenius root of A. Conversely, if $1 > \hat{\lambda}_A$, we can answer questions (i) and (ii) in the affirmative. Thus $1 > \hat{\lambda}_A$ offers a characterization of this problem in terms of the matrix A.

Suppose that some elements of the final demand vector c (for the year in which A is estimated) are zero. In other words, $c \geq 0$ (instead of $c > 0$). This is possible if certain goods are used only as intermediate goods. Can we again answer questions (i) and (ii) above in the affirmative? The questions can be answered "yes" by referring to Theorem 4.D.2. In other words, if A is indecomposable, we can say that, for any $c_f \geq 0$, there exists an $x_f \geq 0$ such that $[I - A] \cdot x_f = c_f$ and that $[I - A]$ is nonsingular with $[I - A]^{-1} > 0$.

Suppose that there exists an $x > 0$ such that $[I - A] \cdot x = c$ for some c. Then from Theorem 4.D.4, this is true if and only if there exists a $p > 0$ such that $[I - A]' \cdot p > 0$. In order to understand the economic significance of this statement, let us suppose that this productive system is realized in a competitive equilibrium. Then we may suppose that a set of prices $p_i > 0$, $i = 1, 2, \ldots, n$, will be established for the n goods. Then $\sum_{i=1}^{n} p_i a_{ij}$ constitutes the payment by the jth industry for the goods used to produce one unit of the jth good (that is, "raw material cost"). Since each industry presumably uses some primary factors (such as labor) for the production, we must have

$$p_j > \sum_{i=1}^{n} p_i a_{ij}, \text{ if } x_j > 0 \, (j = 1, 2, \ldots, n)$$

or

$$[I - A]' \cdot p > 0 \text{ if } x > 0, \text{ where } [I - A]' \text{ is the transpose of } [I - A]$$

Conversely, suppose that $[I - A]' \cdot p > 0$ for some p. Then by paying an amount equal to $[I - A]' \cdot p$, for the primary factors, we can achieve positive output $x > 0$ under this competitive equilibrium. This illustrates a use of Theorem 4.D.4 in input-output analysis.

Above we observed that $[I - A]' \cdot p$ represents the payments for the primary factors. In fact, it represents the vector of the value added per unit of output in each industry. Suppose there is only one kind of primary factor, "labor," and let us denote the amount of labor necessary to produce one unit of the jth good by l_j. Assume l_j is constant for all $j = 1, 2, \ldots, n$. Cases in which there are more than one primary factor can be analyzed analogously and hence are omitted from the subsequent discussion. Let us suppose the competitive condition holds so that wages in each industry are equalized. Denote this wage by w. The cost of production per unit output of the jth good is $v_j \equiv [\sum_{i=1}^{n} p_i a_{ij} + w l_j]$. The "profit" per unit output of the jth good is simply $[p_j - v_j]$. Let $\pi_j \equiv [p_j - v_j]/v_j$. Then π_j is the rate of profit per unit of "working capital" in the jth industry. So far π_j can be different from industry to industry. Under the competitive condition π_j will be equalized for all industries. [In the long run, π_j will be zero, as noted by Walras. Here we are also considering the intermediate step (that is, $\pi > 0$) to this "Walrasian long run".] Then write $\pi \equiv \pi_1 = \pi_2 = \cdots = \pi_n$. Let l denote the n-vector whose jth component is l_j. Then from the definition of π_j and the condition on the π_j's, we obtain

$$[I - A]' \cdot p - wl = \pi [A' \cdot p + wl]$$

or

$$p = (1 + \pi) [A' \cdot p + wl]$$

Assume $\pi \geq 0$; then $1 + \pi \neq 0$. Hence $[\rho I - A'] \cdot p = wl$ where $\rho \equiv 1/(1 + \pi)$. From Theorem 4.D.2, a necessary and sufficient condition that there exists a $p \geq 0$ such that this relation holds for any $wl \geq 0$ is simply $\rho > \hat{\lambda}_A$ where $\hat{\lambda}_A$ is the Frobenius root of A (hence also of A'). This means

$$\frac{1}{1+\pi} > \hat{\lambda}_A$$

Under this condition, $[\rho I - A']$ is nonsingular and $[\rho I - A']^{-1} \geq 0$ as a result of condition (III″) of Theorem 4.D.2. Then p is explicitly obtained as

$$p = [\rho I - A']^{-1} \cdot wl \qquad \text{for a given } w$$

c.   THE EXPENDITURE LAG INPUT-OUTPUT ANALYSIS

In an earlier study of input-output analysis, Solow [21] considered the following system of difference equations:

$$x(t) = A \cdot x(t - 1) + c$$

where $A = [a_{ij}]$ is an $(n \times n)$ matrix and $x_j(t)$ is the output vector in period t. This system may be justified by the assumption that the demand for the ith good by the jth industry in period t [that is, $x_{ij}(t)$] is proportional to this industry's sales (= output) in period $t - 1$ [that is, $x_j(t - 1)$]. Here a_{ij} is simply defined by $a_{ij} \equiv x_{ij}(t)/x_j(t - 1)$. It should be noted that the meaning of a_{ij} here is slightly different from that of the input-output (production) coefficient in the ordinary sense as discussed above. Here A denotes the expenditure relations in this model.[5]

Consider the stationary state in which $x(t) = x(t - 1) = x^*$ for all t. Then we have $x^* = A \cdot x^* + c$, or $[I - A] \cdot x^* = c$. Two questions immediately arise.

(i)   Does $x(t) \to x^*$, as $t \to \infty$?
(ii) Is $[I - A]$ nonsingular and is $[I - A]^{-1} \geq 0$?

The first question is the problem of stability and the second question is the problem of the existence of a nonnegative solution. From Theorem 4.D.1, we know immediately that $[I - A]$ is nonsingular and $[I - A]^{-1} \geq 0$ if and only if $1 > \hat{\lambda}_A$ where $\hat{\lambda}_A$ is the Frobenius root of A.

In order to understand the stability question, let us carry out the following successive substitutions:

$$x(1) = A \cdot x(0) + c$$
$$x(2) = A \cdot x(1) + c = A^2 \cdot x(0) + (I + A) \cdot c$$
$$x(3) = A \cdot x(2) + c = A^3 \cdot x(0) + (I + A + A^2) \cdot c$$
$$\cdots \cdots \cdots \cdots \cdots \cdots \cdots \cdots$$
$$x(t) = A \cdot x(t - 1) + c = A^t \cdot x(0) + (I + A + \cdots + A^{t-1}) \cdot c$$

Then from the remark following Theorem 4.D.2, we can say that $A^t \to 0$ as $t \to \infty$ if and only if $1 > \hat{\lambda}_A$, and that $\sum_{t=0}^{\infty} A^t \cdot c$ is convergent and equal to $[I - A]^{-1} \cdot c$ ($\equiv x^*$). Therefore $x(t) \to [I - A]^{-1} \cdot c$ as $t \to \infty$ if and only if $1 > \hat{\lambda}_A$. Hence we see that the stability question and the problem of the existence of a nonnegative solution are really equivalent.

d. MULTICOUNTRY INCOME FLOWS

Another application of our theorems is in the stability problem of the (naive) Keynesian multiplier model with a multisector specification (see Chipman [3], Metzler [8] and [9], and Morishima [11], for example). The "multisector" model can be a "multi-industry" model or a "multicountry" model. Here we will illustrate this application in terms of a multicountry model of income flows. Let there be n countries in the world and let $U_{ij}(t)$ be country j's demand for country i's goods for consumption purposes in period t. Let $V_{ij}(t)$ be country j's demand for country i's goods for investment purposes in period t. Let $Y_j(t)$ be the national income of country j in period t. We assume the following expenditure lag model.

$$U_{ij}(t) = \alpha_{ij} Y_j(t - 1) + u_{ij}, \qquad i, j = 1, 2, \ldots, n$$
$$V_{ij}(t) = \beta_{ij} Y_j(t - 1) + v_{ij}, \qquad i, j = 1, 2, \ldots, n$$

where α_{ij}, u_{ij}, β_{ij}, v_{ij} are all constants. We then assume the following equilibrium relations.

$$Y_i(t) = \sum_{j=1}^{n} U_{ij}(t) + \sum_{j=1}^{n} V_{ij}(t), \qquad i = 1, 2, \ldots, n$$

Write $\alpha_{ij} + \beta_{ij} \equiv a_{ij}$ and $\sum_{j=1}^{n} (u_{ij} + v_{ij}) \equiv c_i$. Then the above relations can be combined and written as

$$Y_i(t) = \sum_{j=1}^{n} a_{ij} Y_j(t - 1) + c_i, \qquad i = 1, 2, \ldots, n$$

or in matrix-vector notation,

$$Y(t) = A \cdot Y(t - 1) + c, \text{ where } A = [a_{ij}]$$

This is exactly the same equation as that for the Leontief expenditure lag type model discussed above. As we observed there, the following three conditions are all equivalent.

(i) $Y(t) \to [I - A]^{-1} \cdot c$ as $t \to \infty$.

(ii) $[I - A]$ is nonsingular and $[I - A]^{-1} \geq 0$.

(iii) $1 > \hat{\lambda}_A$ where $\hat{\lambda}_A$ is the Frobenius root of A.

More complicated models are discussed by Morishima [11] and others.

e.   A SIMPLE DYNAMIC LEONTIEF MODEL

Above we considered a dynamic model of input-output analysis based on an expenditure lag. We noted there that A is no longer a technological input-output matrix unless a certain restrictive assumption is made. Another way to dynamize the static Leontief model is to introduce a production lag (instead of an expenditure lag). Then A, in the new dynamized model, represents the technological matrix. We will discuss a simple version of such a model. Let us suppose that the production of each good takes one period. Production periods will vary from good to good in an actual economy, but by defining **one period** as the largest common divisor of the production periods of all the goods, we may suppose that the production period for every good is equal to one (see, Chapter 6, Section A). Let $x_i(t)$ be the output of the ith good in the tth period. At the beginning of the tth period [that is, at the end of the $(t - 1)$th period], the amount of the ith good available is $x_i(t - 1)$. This is used for production in the tth period. Hence we have, for $t = 1, 2, \ldots,$

$$x_i(t - 1) = \sum_{j=1}^{n} a_{ij} x_j(t) + c_i(t), \text{ or } x(t - 1) = A \cdot x(t) + c(t)$$

Here a_{ij} is the input-output coefficient in the ordinary sense. We now ask whether there exists a balanced growth solution to the above system, starting from an arbitrary $c(0)$, where **balanced growth** means, for $t = 1, 2, \ldots,$

$$x_i(t) = \alpha \, x_i(t - 1), \text{ and } c_i(t) = \alpha \, c_i(t - 1), \, i = 1, 2, \ldots, n$$

Here α is a positive constant (called the **growth factor**), and $\alpha > 1$ means "growth" and $\alpha < 1$ means "decay" of the economy. Write $\alpha \equiv 1 + \gamma$; then γ is called the **growth rate**. Substitute the above balanced growth relation into the original system of difference equations to obtain, for $t = 0, 1, 2, \ldots,$

$$[\rho I - A] \cdot x(t) = c(t) \text{ where } \rho \equiv \frac{1}{\alpha}$$

When $t = 0$, $[\rho I - A] \cdot x(0) = c(0)$. And $x(t) = \alpha^t x(0)$ and $c(t) = \alpha^t c(0)$ along this balanced growth path. A necessary and sufficient condition for the existence of a solution $x(0) \geq 0$ for any $c(0) \geq 0$ is given by Theorem 4.D.2 as $\rho > \hat{\lambda}_A$ (or $1/\alpha > \hat{\lambda}_A$), where $\hat{\lambda}_A$ is the Frobenius root of A [(II') $\Leftrightarrow$ (VI')]. Hence $\rho > \hat{\lambda}_A$

gives a necessary condition for the existence of a balanced growth solution starting from an arbitrary initial $c(0) \geq 0$. Conversely, if $\rho > \hat{\lambda}_A$, we can also obtain the above balanced growth solution. Hence a necessary and sufficient condition for the existence of a balanced growth path with growth factor α is $1/\alpha > \hat{\lambda}_A$. Note that if $c(0) = 0$ and $1/\alpha > \hat{\lambda}_A$, then $c(t) = 0$ and $x(t) = 0$ for all t. In order to achieve $x(t) > 0$ for all t, we need the indecomposability of A. Suppose that for some $c(0) \geq 0$ there exists an $x(0) \geq 0$ such that $[\rho I - A] \cdot x(0) = c(0)$. Then condition (VII') of Theorem 4.D.2 is satisfied, provided that A is *indecomposable*. Then from condition (VIII'), $[\rho I - A]$ is nonsingular and $[\rho I - A]^{-1} > 0$. Hence $x(0) > 0$ with $c(0) \geq 0$, so that $x(t) = \alpha^t x(0) > 0$ for all t. In these considerations it is important to realize that the initial output vector cannot be arbitrary; it must be equal to $[\rho I - A]^{-1} \cdot c(0)$.

Now suppose that the households form an industry with labor as its output. Labor is now considered a good rather than a primary factor, and thus $c(t) = 0$ for all t. Then balanced growth with a positive growth factor in the above dynamic system is possible if and only if there exists a $\rho > 0$ such that $[\rho I - A] \cdot x(0) = 0$. If A is indecomposable, then we know that there exists a unique $\hat{\lambda}_A > 0$ and an $x(0) > 0$, such that $A \cdot x(0) = \hat{\lambda}_A x(0)$. Then set $\hat{\lambda}_A = \rho$. In other words, if A is indecomposable, there exists a unique balanced growth path whose growth factor is equal to $1/\hat{\lambda}_A$ where $\hat{\lambda}_A$ is the Frobenius root of A. Note that we cannot choose the initial $x(0)$ arbitrarily.

The basic weakness in the above dynamic analysis is that there is no consideration of the stock of goods. A proper treatment of this will give rise to the so-called "dynamic Leontief model," which we discuss in Chapter 6. There we show that there exists a balanced growth path, corresponding to the Frobenius root, and we will discuss the conditions for the "convergence" to this path starting from an *arbitrary* given initial *stock* of goods.

f.   STABILITY OF COMPETITIVE EQUILIBRIUM

Let $f_i(p)$, $i = 0, 1, \ldots, n$, be the excess demand function for the ith good in a competitive trading system. As in Chapter 3, we consider the following system of dynamic adjustment equations:

$$\frac{dp_i(t)}{dt} = f_i[p(t)], i = 0, 1, \ldots, n$$

where $p(t) = [p_0(t), p_1(t), \ldots, p_n(t)]$. Let $\hat{p}$ be an isolated equilibrium price so that (i) $f_i(\hat{p}) = 0$, $i = 0, 1, \ldots, n$, and (ii) $\hat{p}$ is unique in a certain open ball about $\hat{p}$. Assume $\hat{p} > 0$. Assume also that the f_i's are differentiable, and expand the above relation about $\hat{p}$ according to Taylor's expansion. Then taking only the first-order term of the Taylor series, we obtain

$$\frac{dp_i(t)}{dt} = \sum_{j=0}^{n} a_{ij}[p_j(t) - \hat{p}_j], i = 0, 1, \ldots, n$$

where $a_{ij} \equiv \partial f_i / \partial p_j$ evaluated at $p = \hat{p}$.

The question is whether or not $p_j(t) \to \hat{p}_j$ as $t \to \infty$ for all j. Since the above system is linear, a global solution $p(t)$ always exists for all $t \geq 0$. Assume the solution $p(t)$ remains positive for all $t \geq 0$. But owing to the linear approximation procedure, the stability of the above system does not establish global stability, although it does establish local stability. Write

$$q_i(t) \equiv p_i(t) - \hat{p}_i, \, i = 0, 1, \ldots, n$$

Then the above system can be rewritten as

$$\frac{dq_i(t)}{dt} = \sum_{j=0}^{n} a_{ij} q_j(t), \, i = 0, 1, \ldots, n$$

We impose the following two assumptions:

(A-1) (Walras' Law) $\sum_{i=0}^{n} f_i(p) p_i = 0$ (for all p).

(A-2) (Homogeneity) $f_i(p)$ is positively homogeneous of degree zero (for all p), $i = 0, 1, \ldots, n$.

In view of Walras' Law, if $f_i(p) = 0$, $i = 1, 2, \ldots, n$, then $f_0(p) = 0$. By homogeneity, we may set one of the prices—say, p_0—equal to unity (*numéraire*). Therefore, the equilibrium is described by

$$f_i(\hat{p}) = 0, \, i = 1, 2, \ldots, n$$

and the linear system of dynamic adjustment is written as

$$\frac{dp_i(t)}{dt} = \sum_{j=0}^{n} a_{ij} [p_j(t) - \hat{p}_j], \, i = 1, 2, \ldots, n$$

or

$$\frac{dq_i(t)}{dt} = \sum_{j=1}^{n} a_{ij} q_j(t)$$

since $p_0(t) = \hat{p}_0 = 1$ for all t. In matrix notation, we may rewrite this as

$$\frac{dq(t)}{dt} = A \cdot q(t)$$

where $q(t) = [q_1(t), \ldots, q_n(t)]$ and $A = [a_{ij}]$, $i, j = 1, 2, \ldots, n$. Our problem is to ascertain whether $q(t) \to 0$ as $t \to \infty$ in the above system of differential equations. Needless to say, $p(t) \to \hat{p}$ if and only if $q(t) \to 0$. From the elementary theory of differential equations (see Chapter 3, Section B), it is known that $q(t) \to 0$ as $t \to \infty$ *if and only if* the real parts of all the eigenvalues of A are negative. Hence the question is reduced to finding the condition that will guarantee that the real parts of all the eigenvalues of A are negative. If A is symmetric, then negative definiteness gives this condition; this result is given by Samuelson (see

Chapter 3, Section C). However, the symmetry of A is hard to justify. Metzler observed that if $a_{ij} > 0$ $(i \neq j)$, then this condition on the eigenvalues is equivalent to Hicks' condition (that is, A is "Hicksian"). In 1958, Arrow and Hurwicz [1], Hahn [4], and Negishi [15] independently proved that if $a_{ij} > 0, i \neq j$ (**gross substitutability**), then this condition on the eigenvalues follows. In other words, linear approximation stability is implied by the strong gross substitutability condition. The essential idea was to utilize such economic laws as Walras' Law and the homogeneity of the excess demand functions.

Instead of gross substitutability, we impose a slightly weaker condition.

(A-3) $a_{ij} \geqq 0$ for all $i \neq j$, where $a_{ij} \equiv \partial f_i / \partial p_j$ evaluated at $\hat{p}$ $(i, j = 0, 1, \ldots, n)$.

This assumption is known as the **weak gross substitutability** assumption.

We are now ready to prove the (linear approximation) stability of the normalized system.

Theorem 4.D.5:   *Under (A-3), the normalized system $\dot{q}(t) = A \cdot q(t)$ is stable, that is, $q(t) \rightarrow 0$ as $t \rightarrow \infty$, provided that either one of the following conditions holds.*[6]

(i)   *Assumption (A-1) and $a_{0j} > 0, j = 1, 2, \ldots, n$.*
(ii)   *Assumption (A-2) and $a_{i0} > 0, i = 1, 2, \ldots, n$.*

PROOF:

(i)   First use (A-1) (that is, Walras' Law) and $a_{0j} > 0$ for $j \neq 0$. From (A-1) we have $\sum_{i=0}^{n} \hat{p}_i a_{ij} = a_{0j} < 0$ for all j. Hence condition (I″) of Theorem 4.D.3 is satisfied for A' where A' is the transpose of A, which implies (I″) also holds for A from Theorem 4.D.4. Hence condition (V″) of Theorem 4.D.3 holds, which in turn implies the stability.

(ii)   Now use (A-2) (that is, homogeneity) and $a_{i0} > 0$, for $i \neq 0$. The homogeneity implies $\sum_{j=0}^{n} a_{ij} \hat{p}_j = 0$ (Euler's equation). Or $\sum_{j=0}^{n} a_{ij} \hat{p}_j = -a_{i0} < 0$, for all i. Hence condition (I″) of Theorem 4.D.3 is satisfied for A', which implies that condition (V″) also holds for A. This again establishes stability.   (Q.E.D.)

REMARK: The above proofs are not exactly the same as those of Negishi and Hahn. This is understandable, for, at the time of their proofs, the structure of Theorem 4.D.3 was not well recognized. However, our proofs are essentially based on their ideas. Note also that we only required $a_{ij} \geqq 0$ $(i \neq j)$[7] (called the **weak gross substitute case**) instead of $a_{ij} > 0$ $(i \neq j)$.

REMARK: As remarked above, Metzler [9] proved that under gross substitutability, the condition for dynamic stability (that is, the eigenvalues with negative real parts) is equivalent to the Hicksian condition (that is, the alternating sign of the successive principal minors). In other words, Metzler proved part of Theorem 4.D.3 by establishing the equivalence between conditions (V") and (IV"). The Hahn-Negishi theorem indicated the connection between conditions (V") and (I") of Theorem 4.D.3.

We now prove the global stability of the nonnormalized differential equation system, $\dot{p} = f(p)$. For the other systems (normalized system or difference equation system), the reader can attempt a similar proof. The essential idea is to use Liapunov's second method. (For Liapunov's second method for a difference equation system, see Kalman and Bertram [5].) We will use our theorems to show $\dot{V} < 0$ (or $\Delta V < 0$ for the difference equation system), where V is Liapunov's function (as described in Chapter 3, Section H).

Theorem 4.D.6: *Let $p(t; p^0)$ be the solution price vector for the system $\dot{p}(t) = f[p(t)]$, with the initial condition $p(0) = p^0$. Assume Walras' Law (A-1), homogeneity (A-2), and*

(A-3') $f_{ij}(p)$ ($\equiv \partial f_i(p)/\partial p_j) \geqq 0$ *for all $i \neq j$ ($i, j = 0, 1, \ldots, n$) and for all p.*

Then $p(t; p^0) \to \hat{p}$ as $t \to \infty$ where $f(\hat{p}) = 0$, regardless of the initial point p^0.

REMARK: Clearly, (A-3') is a stronger assumption than (A-3). In the above theorem, it is tacitly assumed that the equilibrium price vector $\hat{p}$ is unique up to a positive scalar multiple, which is certainly the case if (A-3') is strengthened to the following: $f_{ij}(p) > 0$ for all $i \neq j$ and for all p (see Lemma 3.E.2.) The following proof is, in essence, due to McKenzie [6].

PROOF: We use Liapunov's second method. Define $V[f(p)] \equiv \frac{1}{2}\sum_{i \in J}f_i^2(p)$, where $f(p) = [f_0(p), \ldots, f_n(p)]$ and $J \equiv \{i: f_i(p) > 0\}$. In other words, J is the set of indices for goods whose excess demands are positive. Obviously the set J changes as prices move from time to time. We shall show that V is a Liapunov function. First note that $V(f) > 0$ if $f \neq 0$, so that $V(f) = 0$ if and only if $f = 0$.[8] By Lemma 3.E.1, $\| p(t) \| = \| p(0) \|$ for all t, so that we can confine our attention to such a path of $p(t)$. This in particular implies that the equilibrium price vector $\hat{p}$ is unique in which $\| \hat{p} \| = \| p(0) \|$. Also $V(f) > 0$ for all $p(t) \neq \hat{p}$. We now show that $\dot{V}(f) < 0$ for all $p(t) \neq \hat{p}$. Consider

$$\frac{dV[p(t)]}{dt} = \sum_{i \in J}\sum_{j=0}^{n}f_i f_{ij}\dot{p}_j = \sum_{i \in J}\sum_{j=0}^{n}f_i f_{ij}f_j = \sum_{i \in J}\sum_{j \in J}f_i f_{ij}f_j + \sum_{i \in J}\sum_{j \notin J}f_i f_{ij}f_j$$

where $f_{ij} \equiv f_{ij}(p) \equiv \partial f_i(p)/\partial p_j$ (that is, evaluated at p rather than $\hat{p}$). From (A-3') ($f_{ij} \geqq 0$, $i \neq j$) and $f_j \leqq 0$ for $j \notin J$, we have $\sum_{i \in J}\sum_{j \notin J}f_i f_{ij}f_j \leqq 0$. We now show that $\sum_{i \in J}\sum_{j \in J}f_i f_{ij}f_j < 0$. From the definition of J, $f_i > 0$ for $i \in J$. By Walras' Law, $\sum_{i=0}^{n}p_i f_{ij} = -f_j, j = 0, 1, \ldots, n$. Hence $\sum_{i \in J}p_i f_{ij} \leqq -f_j < 0$, for $j \in J$. Therefore $F'_j \cdot p_J < 0$, where F'_j is the transpose of $F_J = [f_{ij}], i, j \in J$; p_J is the vector $[p_j]$ where j is taken from J. Also by homogeneity, $\sum_{j \in J}f_{ij}p_j + \sum_{j \notin J}f_{ij}p_j = 0$ for all i, so that $\sum_{j \in J}f_{ij}p_j \leqq 0$ for $i \in J$, or $F_J \cdot p_J \leqq 0$.

Consider $F_J^* \equiv (F_J + F'_J)$. Then $F_J^* \cdot p_J < 0$, so that condition (I'') of Theorem 4.D.3 is satisfied for F_J^*. Hence the real parts of all the eigenvalues of F_J^* are negative as a result of condition (V''). Since F_J^* is symmetric, the eigenvalues of F_J^* are all real,[9] so that they are all negative. Hence F_J^* is negative definite,[10] that is, $x \cdot F_J^* \cdot x < 0$ for all $x \neq 0$. Since $x \cdot F_J^* \cdot x = 2x \cdot F_J \cdot x$, this implies $x \cdot F_J \cdot x < 0$ for all $x \neq 0$. Hence $p_J \cdot F_J \cdot p_J < 0$. From Walras' Law, f_J and f are zero together, where $f \equiv (f_0, \ldots, f_n)$. Hence we have established $\dot{V}[f(p)] < 0$ for $f \neq 0$. Hence $f \to 0$ as $t \to \infty$.   (Q.E.D.)

REMARK: The proof for the normalized system is similar. Or, alternatively, use $\hat{p} \cdot f(p) > 0$ (Lemma 3.E.3); that is, define $V \equiv \sum (p_i - \hat{p}_i)^2$ so that $\dot{V} = 2(p - \hat{p}) \cdot \dot{p} = 2(p - \hat{p}) \cdot f(p) < 0$ for all $p \neq \hat{p}$ by Lemma 3.E.3 and (A-1). Here we normalize p by $\sum p_i(t) = 1$ for all t.

g.   COMPARATIVE STATICS

Suppose that a certain economic system is described by

$$f_i(x_1, x_2, \ldots, x_n) = 0, \ i = 1, 2, \ldots, n$$

or simply

$$f(x) = 0$$

Such a system can describe the set of certain equilibrium relations or the set of certain optimization conditions. An example of the former interpretation is that f_i and x_i are respectively taken as the excess demand for and the price of the ith commodity. The value of x (say, $\hat{x}$) which satisfies the above relations $f(x) = 0$ is called the **equilibrium value** of x. Clearly the equilibrium value of x is not necessarily unique.

In order to consider a shift of the above system, rewrite the system as

$$f_i(x_1, \ldots, x_n; \alpha, \beta, \ldots) = 0, \ i = 1, 2, \ldots, n$$

or simply $f(x; \alpha, \beta, \ldots) = 0$, where all the second partial derivatives of f_i ($i = 1, 2, \ldots, n$) with respect to $x_1, x_2, \ldots, x_n$ and $\alpha, \beta, \ldots$ are assumed to exist and be continuous in the domain. Here $\alpha, \beta, \ldots$ are the **shift parameters** or **exogenous variables**. The equilibrium value of x clearly depends on the values of $\alpha, \beta, \ldots$. The concept of an equilibrium value of x is meaningful only after the values of $\alpha, \beta, \ldots$ are specified—say, as $\hat{\alpha}, \hat{\beta}, \ldots$. If the f_i's are "well-behaved," then we can write such dependence relations as

$$x_i = x_i(\alpha, \beta, \ldots), \ i = 1, 2, \ldots, n$$

or simply $x = x(\alpha, \beta, \ldots)$, where the function x is continuously differentiable in some region S about $(\hat{\alpha}, \hat{\beta}, \ldots)$, *and*

$$f[x(\alpha, \beta, \ldots); \alpha, \beta, \ldots] = 0, \quad \text{for all } (\alpha, \beta, \ldots) \text{ in the region } S$$

Obviously the f_i's are not so "well-behaved" in general, so that an explicit functional relation such as $x = x(\alpha, \beta, \ldots)$ may not be obtained, either locally or globally. A set of mathematical conditions guaranteeing the "local" possibility is known as the **implicit function theorem**.[11] In this case S is some neighborhood of $(\hat{\alpha}, \hat{\beta}, \ldots)$, which can be very small.

   Comparative statics is concerned with the effect of a change in one or more of the shift parameters $\alpha, \beta, \ldots$ on the equilibrium value of x. The comparative statics analysis can be local or global, depending on whether the region S is large [for example, so that it covers all possible values of $(\alpha, \beta, \ldots)$] or S is confined to a certain (small) neighborhood of $(\hat{\alpha}, \hat{\beta}, \ldots)$. The local analysis in connection with the classical optimization theory was discussed in the Appendix to Section F, Chapter 1.[12]

   Partially differentiate the system $f[x(\alpha, \beta, \ldots); \alpha, \beta, \ldots] = 0$ with respect to one of the shift parameters—say, α (while keeping the other parameters, β, $\gamma, \ldots$, constant)—we obtain

$$\sum_{j=1}^{n} f_{ij} \frac{\partial x_j}{\partial \alpha} + b_i = 0, i = 1, 2, \ldots, n, \quad \text{for all } (\alpha, \beta, \ldots) \text{ in } S$$

where $f_{ij} \equiv \partial f_i / \partial x_j$ and $b_i \equiv \partial f_i / \partial \alpha$ with $x = x(\alpha, \beta, \ldots)$. In matrix form, we may rewrite this as

$$F \cdot x_\alpha + b = 0$$

where $F = [f_{ij}]$, $b = [b_i]$, and x_α is the n-vector whose jth element is $\partial x_j / \partial \alpha$. Assuming that F is nonsingular, we can rewrite the above equation as

$$x_\alpha = -F^{-1} \cdot b, \quad \text{for all } (\alpha, \beta, \ldots) \text{ in } S \text{ where } x = x(\alpha, \beta, \ldots)$$

which is called the **fundamental equation of comparative statics**.[13] The solution x_α indicates the effect of a change in α on the equilibrium value of x in the region S.

   The use of the theorems of this section in comparative statics is clear. They can be applied when all the off-diagonal elements of F have a definite sign. If $f_{ij} \leq 0$ for all $i \neq j$, then we can use Theorem 4.D.1, and if $f_{ij} \geq 0$ for all $i \neq j$, then we can use Theorem 4.D.3.

   For example, suppose that f_i and x_i, respectively, denote the excess demand for and the price of the ith commodity. Let α represent the taste of the consumers. Let there be $(n + 1)$ commodities $(i = 0, 1, \ldots, n)$. Assume homogeneity and let commodity 0 be the *numéraire* $(x_0 = 1)$. Assume that the equilibrium of the market can be described by n equations: $f_i[x(\alpha, \beta, \ldots); \alpha, \beta, \ldots] = 0, i = 1, 2, \ldots, n$, for $(\alpha, \beta, \ldots)$ in the region S. From homogeneity, we have

$$\sum_{j=0}^{n} f_{ij} x_j = 0, i = 0, 1, 2, \ldots, n, \quad \text{for all } (x; \alpha, \beta, \ldots)$$

Assume now that $f_{ij} > 0$ for all $i \neq j(0, 1, \ldots, n)$ and for all x (gross substitutability). Then we obtain

$$\sum_{j=1}^{n} f_{ij} x_j < 0, \qquad \text{for all } i \text{ and for all } (x; \alpha, \beta, \ldots)$$

Therefore the $n \times n$ matrix $F = [f_{ij}]$ satisfies condition (I'') of Theorem 4.D.3. We are now ready to consider the so-called **Hicksian laws of comparative statics**. As an illustration, we show that a shift in demand from the *numéraire* to commodity k raises the price of k and the prices of all other commodities. For this purpose, set $b_k \equiv \partial f_k / \partial \alpha = 1$ and $b_i \equiv \partial f_i / \partial \alpha = 0$ for all $i \neq k$ $(i, k = 1, 2, \ldots, n)$. Since F is indecomposable and condition (I'') of Theorem 4.D.3 holds, condition (VII') also holds so that F is nonsingular and $F^{-1} < 0$. Hence $x_\alpha = - F^{-1} \cdot b$ implies $x_\alpha > 0$; that is, the price of all the commodities (except that of the *numéraire*) must rise.[14]

We now turn to another illustration, the theory of the firm. Consider a firm that produces a single product y using n inputs, $x_1, x_2, \ldots, x_n$, with the production function $\Phi(x)$. Let p be the price of the product and w the factor price vector, which are all taken as positive constants given to the firm. Assume that the firm maximizes its profit $py - w \cdot x$ subject to $\Phi(x) \geq y$ and $x \geq 0$. Assume further that

(i) $\partial \Phi / \partial x_i > 0, i = 1, 2, \ldots, n$ for all $x > 0$.
(ii) There exists an $\bar{x} \geq 0$ and a $\bar{y} \geq 0$ such that $\Phi(\bar{x}) > \bar{y}$ (Slater's condition).
(iii) The Hessian matrix of Φ is negative definite for all x.

Condition (iii) implies that Φ is a strictly concave function. Under these assumptions, the following set of conditions together with $\Phi(\hat{x}) = \hat{y}$ gives a necessary and sufficient characterization of a unique global maximum:

$$f_i\left(\hat{x}, \frac{w}{p}\right) \equiv \frac{\partial \Phi(\hat{x})}{\partial x_i} - \frac{w_i}{p} = 0, i = 1, 2, \ldots, n$$

where we assume that the optimal values, $\hat{x}$ and $\hat{y}$, are strictly positive.[15]

First consider the effect of the minimum wage regulation (MWR) on employment. Suppose that a *local* government imposes a minimum wage rate $\bar{w}_n$ which is above w_n. Assume that this does not disturb the market in such a way as to change p and $w_1, \ldots, w_{n-1}$. Thus $p, w_1, w_2, \ldots, w_{n-1}, \bar{w}_n$ are taken as (positive) constants to the firm. This is again a problem of comparative statics.[16] Assume that there exists a continuously differentiable function $x = x(w/p)$ such that $f_i[x(w/p), w/p] = 0, i = 1, 2, \ldots, n$, for all w/p in some region S of w/p. Then the partial differentiation of f_i with respect to w_n yields

$$\sum_{j=1}^{n} f_{ij} \frac{\partial x_j}{\partial w_n} + b_i = 0, i = 1, 2, \ldots, n, \qquad \text{for all } w/p \text{ in } S$$

where we now define the f_{ij}'s and the b_i's by $f_{ij} \equiv \partial f_i / \partial x_j = (\partial^2 \Phi / \partial x_i \partial x_j) \equiv \Phi_{ij}$ and

$b_i \equiv \partial(-w_i/p)/\partial w_n$, respectively. Note that $b_i = 0$ for all $i \neq n$ and that $b_n = -1/p$. Since the Hessian matrix of Φ is negative definite, the Hessian matrix of Φ is Hicksian (see Chapter 1, Section E). Assume further[17]

(iv) $f_{ij} > 0$ for all $i \neq j$, for all x.

Then noting that condition (IV') of Theorem 4.D.3 is satisfied and that $F = [f_{ij}]$ is indecomposable, we can conclude that condition (VII'') is also satisfied. In other words, F is nonsingular and $F^{-1} < 0$ for all x. Therefore we obtain

$$\frac{\partial x_j}{\partial w_n} < 0, j = 1, 2, \ldots, n, \quad \text{for all } w/p \text{ in } S \text{ where } x = x(w/p)$$

In other words, a local MWR always decreases the employment of labor and all other factors, provided that the above assumptions are satisfied.[18]

In order to explore the above line of thinking further, let us suppose that the price of the kth factor changes, where k is not restricted to n. Then the partial differentiation of the system $\Phi_i[x(w/p)] - w_i/p = 0$ (where $\Phi_i \equiv \partial\Phi/\partial x_i$), $i = 1, 2, \ldots, n$, with respect to w_k, again yields

$$\sum_{j=1}^{n} f_{ij} \frac{\partial x_j}{\partial w_k} + b_i = 0, k = 1, 2, \ldots, n, \quad \text{for all } \frac{w}{p} \text{ in } S$$

where $b_i = 0$ if $i \neq k$, $b_k = -1/p$, and $f_{ij} = \Phi_{ij}$. It is often assumed in general equilibrium theory that commodities are gross substitutes. Our question now is whether we can extend the list of these commodities to factors. In particular, we want to examine whether $\partial x_j/\partial w_k > 0$ for all $j \neq k$, that is, whether an increase in the kth factor price will increase the demand for the jth factor when $j \neq k$. Consider again the "normal" case in which $f_{ij} > 0$, for all $i \neq j$, and for all x. Then we can apply Theorem 4.D.3 again. Observing that the negative definiteness of the Hessian matrix Φ implies condition (IV') of Theorem 4.D.3 and that $F = [f_{ij}]$ is indecomposable, we can conclude that condition (VIII') is satisfied. In other words, F is nonsingular and $F^{-1} < 0$ for all x. Hence we conclude[19]

$$\frac{\partial x_j}{\partial w_k} < 0 \quad \text{for all } j \neq k, j, k = 1, 2, \ldots, n, \quad \text{for all } \frac{w}{p} \text{ in } S \text{ where } x = x\left(\frac{w}{p}\right)$$

In other words, "normally" factors are not gross substitutes but rather "gross complements." This is the conclusion obtained by Rader [19].[20] The economic interpretation of this result can be found in [19], p. 40.

FOOTNOTES

1. Since $b_{ij} \leq 0$ for all $i \neq j$, $B \cdot x > 0$ with $x \geq 0$ implies $x > 0$. This was also noted in the proof [step (i)] of Theorem 4.C.4. Hence condition (I) says that B' (that is, the transpose of B) has d.d.

2. This means that like (I'), $\tilde{B}$ has d.d.

3. The same argument is used in the proof [step (i)] of Theorem 4.C.4.

4. We can also conclude that an arbitrary matrix—say, A (that is, the one whose off-diagonal elements do not necessarily have a definite sign)—has a dominant diagonal if and only if its transpose A' has a dominant diagonal. To see this, recall that (by the definition of a dominant diagonal) $A = [a_{ij}]$ has d.d. if and only if the matrix $M = [m_{ij}]$, where $m_{ij} \equiv -|a_{ij}|$, $i \neq j$, $m_{ii} = |a_{ii}|$, has d.d. Note that M is a B matrix in Theorem 4.D.4.

5. It is, however, possible to interpret A as the technology matrix, if we assume that sales expectations are made on the basis of simple extrapolation of all industries; that is, the sales of the last period $x(t-1)$ are expected to continue as sales of this period so that $A \cdot x(t-1) + c$ signifies the expected demands for the goods in period t. The advantage of this interpretation is that we can interpret A as the technology matrix.

6. In proving local stability, it suffices to assume that (A-1) or (A-2) holds *at* the equilibrium $\hat{p}$. The theorem is often referred to as the *Hahn-Negishi theorem*. Hahn used (A-1) and Negishi used (A-2).

7. Strictly speaking, we also required that $a_{0j} > 0$ or $a_{i0} > 0$, $i, j = 1, 2, \ldots, n$, where the 0th commodity is the *numéraire*. This also implies that the choice of the *numéraire* is important.

8. Obviously, $f = 0$ implies $V(f) = 0$.

9. It is well known and easy to show that all the eigenvalues of any symmetric matrix are real.

10. It is well known in matrix theory that a symmetric matrix is negative definite if and only if its eigenvalues are all negative (for the proof, see any textbook on matrix theory).

11. As remarked earlier in Chapter 1, the (local) implicit function theorem roughly states the following. Let $f_i(\hat{x}; \hat{\alpha}, \hat{\beta}, \ldots) = 0$ for some $\hat{x}$ and for some $(\hat{\alpha}, \hat{\beta}, \ldots)$. Assume that $\det[a_{ij}] \neq 0$, where $a_{ij} = \partial f_i / \partial x_j$, evaluated at $(\hat{x}, \hat{\alpha}, \hat{\beta}, \ldots)$. Then there exists a neighborhood N of $(\hat{\alpha}, \hat{\beta}, \ldots)$ and a unique continuously differentiable function g such that $g(\hat{\alpha}, \hat{\beta}, \ldots) = \hat{x}$ and $f[g(\alpha, \beta, \ldots); \alpha, \beta, \ldots] = 0$ for all $(\alpha, \beta, \ldots)$ in N. See W. H. Fleming, *Functions of Several Variables*, Reading, Mass., Addison-Wesley, 1965, and most textbooks on advanced calculus.

12. The use of comparative statics, as remarked in the above, is not confined to optimization theory; that is, the above system, $f(x, \alpha, \ldots) = 0$ is not necessarily made up of first-order conditions.

13. See Samuelson [20], which also contains an excellent exposition of comparative statics (especially chapters 2 and 3). Also see the Appendix to Section F, Chapter 1.

14. For the other Hicksian laws of comparative statics, see Mundell [14]. See also Morishima [13], pp. 3–14.

15. Recall Section F of Chapter 1 (especially subsection c).

16. There seems to be a widespread misunderstanding among labor economists with regard to the comparative statics nature of the problem. For example, in their study of the MWR of New York City, M. Benewitz, and R. E. Weintraub wrote, "Economic theorists assert, as a logical deduction from the diminishing returns, that elasticity of the demand for labor is negative. This means that a rise in the wage rate will lead to a decline in employment." See their "Employment Effects of a Local Minimum Wage," *Industrial and Labor Relations Review*, 17, January 1964, p. 283. The error seems to be in confusion between shifts of a curve and movements along a curve; the employment of other factors as well as labor adjust to a new level of the wage rate, which causes a shift of the marginal productivity curve of labor.

Also recall the famous controversy between Lester and Machlup in the *American Economic Review* (in the 1940s) with regard to the validity of the marginal productivity theory. See also J. M. Peterson, "Employment Effects of Minimum Wages, 1938–50," *Journal of Political Economy*, LXV, October 1957, as well as our footnote 18.

17. This means that an increase in the employment of the *j*th factor will increase the marginal (physical) productivity of the *i*th factor, if $i \neq j$. This means that factors are used in conjunction with each other rather than as substitutes. This so-called "Wicksell's Law" is termed the **normal** case by Rader [19]. The case in which this assumption is slightly weakened to $f_{ij} \geq 0$ for all $i \neq j$ can be analyzed in a method similar to the subsequent analysis. Also note that the crucial condition for the **global** invertibility of Φ [that is, the existence of the unique inverse Φ^{-1}, for all $(w_1/p, \ldots, w_n/p)$] in the Gale-Nikaido theorem is satisfied if the Hessian matrix of Φ is Hicksian. See Nikaido [18], section 20, and our Chapter 2, Appendix to Section E.

18. If some of the assumptions are violated (which is quite plausible), it is possible that a local MWR may increase the employment of labor. Such an analysis is carried out by Takayama [22]. For example, suppose the demand function of the product is $p(y) = y^{-0.4}$ (a complete monopoly) and the production function is $y = LK$. Then we can show that the profit-maximizing value of (L, K) is unique and that the imposition of MWR increases the employment of labor L. If $p = ay^{-1/\eta}$ and $y = bL^{\alpha}K^{\beta}$, where $\eta > 1, \alpha, \beta > 0$, and $a, b > 0$, then a necessary and sufficient condition that the imposition of MWR increase the employment of labor is computed as $[1 - \varepsilon(\alpha + \beta)]/(\varepsilon\alpha - 1) > 0$ where $\epsilon \equiv 1 - 1/\eta$. Hence the empirical findings that the imposition of MWR does not necessarily decrease the amount of labor employment do not constitute a sufficient reason to refute the marginal productivity theory.

19. If $f_{ij} \geq 0$, $i \neq j$, condition (VI″) of Theorem 4.D.3 is equivalent to (III″) instead of (VIII″). In other words, F is nonsingular and $F^{-1} \leq 0$, which slightly weakens the conclusion to $\partial x_j/\partial w_k \leq 0$, for all $j \neq k$.

20. A similar conclusion was obtained by M. Morishima in "A Note on a Point in Value and Capital," *Review of Economic Studies*, XXI, 1953–1954 (which is cited in Rader [19]). See also D. V. T. Bear, "Inferior Inputs and the Theory of the Firm," *Journal of Political Economy*, LXXIII, June 1965. Note that the above analysis of MWR (Takayama [22]) essentially establishes the same result.

REFERENCES

1. Arrow, K. J., and Hurwicz, L., "On the Stability of the Competitive Equilibrium, I," *Econometrica*, 26, October 1958.

2. Bellman, R., *Introduction to Matrix Analysis*, New York, McGraw-Hill, 1960.

3. Chipman, J. S., *The Theory of Inter-Sectoral Money Flows and Income Formation*, Baltomore, Md., Johns Hopkins University Press, 1951.

4. Hahn, F. H., "Gross Substitutes and the Dynamic Stability of General Equilibrium," *Econometrica*, 26, January 1958.

5. Kalman, R. E., and Bertram, J. E. "Control System Analysis and Design Via the "Second Method" of Lyapunov, II, Discrete-Time Systems," *Journal of Basic Engineering*, June 1960.

6. McKenzie, L. W., "Matrices with Dominant Diagonals and Economic Theory," in

Mathematical Methods in the Social Sciences, 1959, ed. by Arrow, Karlin, and Suppes, Stanford, Calif., Stanford University Press, 1960.

7. ———, "An Elementary Analysis of the Leontief System," *Econometrica*, 25, July 1959.

8. Metzler, L. A., "Underemployment Equilibrium in International Trade," *Econometrica*, April 1942.

9. ———, "Stability of Multiple Markets: The Hicks Conditions," *Econometrica*, 13, October 1945.

10. ———, "A Multiple Region Theory of Income and Trade," *Econometrica*, 18, October 1950.

11. Morishima, M., "The International Inter-relatedness of Economic Fluctuations," in his *Inter-Industry Relations and Economic Fluctuations*, Tokyo, Yuhikaku, 1955 (in Japanese).

12. ———, *Introduction to the Inter-Industry Analysis*, Tokyo, Sobun-sha, 1956 (in Japanese).

13. ———, *Equilibrium, Stability and Growth*, Oxford, Oxford University Press, 1964.

14. Mundell, R. A., "The Homogeneity Postulate and the Law of Comparative Statics," *Econometrica*, 33, April 1965.

15. Negishi, T., "A Note on the Stability of an Economy Where All Goods Are Gross Substitutes," *Econometrica*, 26, July 1958.

16. Nikaido, H., *Introduction to Sets and Mappings in Modern Economics*, tr. by K. Sato, Amsterdam, North-Holland, 1970 (the Japanese original, Tokyo, 1960).

17. ———, *Linear Mathematics for Economics*, Tokyo, Baifukan, 1961 (in Japanese).

18. ———, *Convex Structures and Economic Theory*, Academic Press, N.Y., 1968.

19. Rader, T., "Normally, Factor Inputs Are Never Gross Substitutes," *Journal of Political Economy*, 76, January/February 1968.

20. Samuelson, P. A., *Foundations of Economic Analysis*, Cambridge, Mass., Harvard University Press, 1947.

21. Solow, R. M., "On the Structure of Linear Models," *Econometrica*, 20, January 1952.

22. Takayama, A., "Minimum Wage and Unemployment," Purdue University, March 1967 (unpublished manuscript).

5

THE CALCULUS OF VARIATIONS AND THE OPTIMAL GROWTH OF AN AGGREGATE ECONOMY

ELEMENTS OF THE CALCULUS OF VARIATIONS AND ITS APPLICATIONS

a. STATEMENT OF THE PROBLEM

Consider the following (Riemann) integral:

$$J \equiv \int_a^b f[t, x(t), x'(t)]\, dt, \text{ where } x'(t) \equiv \frac{dx}{dt}$$

and a and b are some constants. The function $x(t)$ can either be real-valued or R^n-valued. Clearly the value of this integral depends on the function $x(t)$. By changing the function $x(t)$, we can get different values of J. Suppose we are given a certain class of functions X (for example, the set of all differentiable functions defined on the closed interval $[a, b]$). Then we can consider the problem of choosing a function $x(t)$ from the class of functions X such as to maximize the integral J, subject to the conditions $x(a) = \alpha$ and $x(b) = \beta$. This is the type of problem that the calculus of variations is concerned with.

The simplest problem in the calculus of variations is probably the problem of finding the curve which joins two fixed points on the plane with the minimum distance. Given the two points A and B in Figure 5.1, a curve joining A and B can be represented by $x(t)$ with $x(a) = \alpha$ and $x(b) = \beta$.

Given an "arc" (or "path") $x(t)$, the distance along each infinitesimal segment of $x(t)$ is $ds = \sqrt{(dt)^2 + (dx)^2} = \sqrt{1 + x'(t)^2}\, dt$. Hence the distance between A and B along this arc can simply be computed as

$$J_D \equiv \int_a^b \sqrt{1 + x'(t)^2}\, dt, \text{ where } x'(t) \equiv \frac{dx}{dt}$$

The problem then is one of finding a function ("arc") $x(t)$ from the set of differentiable functions[1] to minimize the above integral J_D subject to $x(a) = \alpha$ and $x(b) = \beta$. This problem is called the **minimum distance problem**.

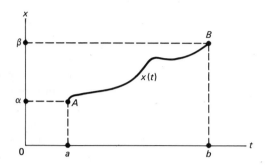

Figure 5.1.   The Minimum Distance Problem.

The answer to the above problem is obviously the straight line joining A and B. This answer can readily be obtained without applying any of the theorems in the calculus of variations. However, we can use this problem to illustrate the nature of the technique of the calculus of variations.

The first major development in the calculus of variations came as a result of a little more difficult problem first discussed by Galileo in 1630 and then by John Bernouilli in 1696. The problem was solved by John Bernouilli himself and by James Bernouilli, Newton, and L'Hospital. The problem (later called the **brachistochrone problem**) was as follows: Let O and A be two fixed points in a vertical plane and consider a particle with mass sliding from O to A under the force of gravity along a certain curve connecting O and A on this vertical plane. The problem is to find a curve such that the particle moves from O to A in the least amount of time. The problem is illustrated in Figure 5.2. Here O is taken as the origin of the coordinates.

Using elementary mechanics, we can prove that the problem can be reduced to one of minimizing the following integral:[2]

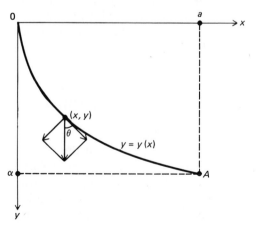

Figure 5.2   The Brachistochrone Problem.

$$J_B = \int_0^a \sqrt{\frac{1 + y'(x)^2}{2gy}}\, dx$$

Here $y(x)$ [with $y(0) = 0$ and $y(a) = \alpha$] denotes the curve joining O and A, and g denotes the gravitational constant.

Later it was discovered that the calculus of variations provided a unified view of many problems in physics. For example, in optics it is known that light travels in such a way that it traverses the distance between two given points in the least possible time (**Fermat's principle**). In classical mechanics, W. Hamilton discovered that the motion of a system of n particles (in the x-y-z-plane) can be explained by the minimization of the following integral:

$$\int_{t^0}^{t^1} (T - U)\,dt, \qquad \text{where } t \text{ denotes time}$$

Here $T \equiv T[x_1(t),\ y_1(t),\ z_1(t),\ \ldots,\ x_n(t),\ y_n(t),\ z_n(t)]$ and $U \equiv U[x_1(t), \ldots, z_n(t)]$, respectively, denote the kinetic and the potential energy of the system at time t. (This principle is called **Hamilton's principle**.) Similar theorems hold in the field of electricity and magnetism and in Einstein's theory of relativity.

We may note that in the 1920s and 1930s, specialists in the calculus of variations, men such as Roos and Evans, were greatly interested in economics. For a complete bibliography of their works, the reader is referred to Evans [3], p. 166. Unfortunately, there was hardly any response from economists at the time, except that some of their results were incorporated by R. G. D. Allen ([1], chapter XX) in 1938. A simple problem discussed by them which is summarized in Allen [1] is the problem of dynamic monopoly.

Consider a complete monopolist who produces and sells a single good X. Suppose that his cost function is given by $C(x)$, where x denotes the amount of output of X. Suppose that the price of X at time t is given by $p(t)$. Assume that the function $p(t)$ is differentiable and let $\dot{p}(t) \equiv dp(t)/dt$. Let us suppose the demand function of X is given by $D = D[p(t), \dot{p}(t)]$ where $\dot{p}$ represents a "speculative" element. The monopolist's profit per unit of time is obviously $Dp(t) - C(x)$ where $x = D$. Suppose that he wants to find the optimal pricing policy $p(t)$ so as to maximize his profit over a period of time, say, $[0, T]$. In other words, he wants to find the function $p(t)$ which will maximize the following integral subject to the boundary conditions $p(0) = p^0$ and $p(T) = \bar{p}$

$$\int_0^T [Dp(t) - C(x)]\,dt = \int_0^T \{D[p(t), \dot{p}(t)]\,p(t) - C[D(p(t), \dot{p}(t))]\}\,dt$$

where $x = D$ and $\dot{p} \equiv dp/dt$. This is again a variational problem.

During the period of this interest in economics by specialists in the calculus of variations, Frank Ramsey [5] considered the problem of maximizing social welfare over time. Ramsey's problem is again a problem in the calculus of variations. This problem, once forgotten, has recently attracted enormous attention and was solved, to a certain extent, by Koopmans and Cass. We take up this problem in Section D as another illustration of the application of the calculus of variations to economics.

b.   EULER'S EQUATION

We now obtain the first-order necessary condition for the maximization (or minimization) problems discussed above. The emphasis will be on the exposition and the intuitive understanding of the derivation. Hence some sacrifice of mathematical rigor is inevitable. Moreover, we will consider only the simplest problem. We go to a more general analysis in the next section.

Let X be the set of all real-valued (and single-valued) continuously differentiable functions defined on the closed interval $[a, b]$ (**admissible functions**). We want to find a function $x(t)$ in X which maximizes (or minimizes) the following integral:

(1)
$$J[x] \equiv \int_a^b f[t, x(t), x'(t)] \, dt$$

where $x'(t) \equiv dx/dt$, subject to $x(a) = \alpha$ and $x(b) = \beta$. We assume that f possesses continuous first and second partial derivatives with respect to all its arguments.

Assume that there exists a function $\hat{x}(t)$ in X which maximizes (or minimizes) J.[3] Consider an arbitrary differentiable function (called the **displacement**) $h(t) \in X$ such that $h(a) = 0$ and $h(b) = 0$. Let ϵ be a real number and define $x_\epsilon(t) \in X$ by

(2)
$$x_\epsilon(t) \equiv \hat{x}(t) + \epsilon h(t)$$

By assumption, $J[x_\epsilon]$ attains its maximum (or minimum) when $\epsilon = 0$. Regarding $J[x_\epsilon]$ as a function of ϵ and assuming an interior maximum (or minimum), this means

(3)
$$\frac{\partial}{\partial \epsilon} J[x_\epsilon] = 0$$

where the partial derivative $\partial J[x_\epsilon]/\partial \epsilon$ is evaluated at $\epsilon = 0$. But we have

(4)
$$\frac{\partial}{\partial \epsilon} J[x_\epsilon]\Big|_{\epsilon=0} = \left[\frac{\partial}{\partial \epsilon} \int_a^b f[t, \hat{x} + \epsilon h, \hat{x}' + \epsilon h'] \, dt \right]_{\epsilon=0}$$

$$= \int_a^b \hat{f}_x h \, dt + \int_a^b \hat{f}_{x'} h' \, dt$$

where $\hat{f}_x$ and $\hat{f}_{x'}$ denote the partial derivatives of f, respectively, with respect to its second and third argument evaluated at $\epsilon = 0$.

Integration by parts yields

(5)
$$\int_a^b \left[\hat{f}_{x'} h' \right] dt = \hat{f}_{x'} h \Big|_a^b - \int_a^b \left[\frac{d\hat{f}_{x'}}{dt} h \right] dt$$

$$= - \int_a^b \left[\frac{d\hat{f}_{x'}}{dt} h \right] dt \qquad [\because h(a) = h(b) = 0]$$

provided we tacitly assume that $d\hat{f}_{x'}/dt$ exists. Therefore, we obtain from (3), (4), and (5)

(6)
$$\frac{\partial}{\partial\epsilon} J[x_\epsilon]_{|\epsilon=0} = \int_a^b \left[\hat{f}_x - \frac{d}{dt}\hat{f}_{x'}\right] h(t)dt = 0$$

This is true for any $h(t) \in X$ with $h(a) = h(b) = 0$. To be able to conclude from (6) that $\hat{f}_x - d\hat{f}_{x'}/dt = 0$, we prove the following lemma, which is often called the **fundamental lemma of the calculus of variations**.

Lemma: *Let $F(t)$ be a given continuous function on $[a, b]$. Let X_0 be the set of all continuous functions on $[a, b]$ such that $h(t) \in X_0$ implies $h(a) = h(b) = 0$. Suppose that $\int_a^b F(t) h(t) dt = 0$ for all $h(t) \in X_0$. Then $F(t)$ is identically equal to zero for all $t \in [a, b]$.*

    PROOF: Suppose $F(\bar{t}) \neq 0$ at some point $\bar{t}$ in $[a, b]$, say, $F(\bar{t}) > 0$. Then, from the continuity of $F(t)$, $F(t) > 0$ in some interval $[c, d]$ where $c < d$, $\bar{t} \in [c, d]$, and $[c, d] \subset [a, b]$. Choose $h(t) \in X_0$ such that $h(t) > 0$ for $t \in (c, d)$ and $h(t) = 0$ for $t \notin (c, d)$. Then $\int_a^b F(t) h(t)dt > 0$, which is a contradiction.   (Q.E.D.)

Using this lemma and noting the continuity of $\hat{f}_{x'}$, we obtain from (6) that

(7)
$$\hat{f}_x - \frac{d}{dt}\hat{f}_{x'} = 0, \text{with } \hat{x}(a) = \alpha, \hat{x}(b) = \beta$$

This equation is called **Euler's equation (condition)** and gives a *necessary condition* (the first-order condition) for the maximum (or the minimum) of the integral J.[4]

    REMARK: Since $\hat{f}_{x'} = \hat{f}_{x'}[t, \hat{x}(t), \hat{x}'(t)], \hat{f}_x - d\hat{f}_{x'}/dt = 0$ means

$$\hat{f}_x - \frac{\partial \hat{f}_{x'}}{\partial t} - \frac{\partial \hat{f}_{x'}}{\partial \hat{x}}\hat{x}' - \frac{\partial \hat{f}_{x'}}{\partial \hat{x}'}\hat{x}'' = 0$$

This is a second-order ordinary differential equation where the unknown function is $\hat{x}(t)$. The two boundary conditions are given by $\hat{x}(a) = \alpha$ and $\hat{x}(b) = \beta$.

    REMARK: The above remark also reveals that if $\hat{f}_{x'}$ is a differentiable function with respect to its arguments (that is, $d\hat{f}_{x'}$ exists), then $d\hat{f}_{x'}/dt$ exists; $d\hat{f}_{x'}/dt$ exists if and only if $\hat{x}''$ exists [that is, $\hat{x}(t)$ is twice differentiable]. The twice differentiability of $\hat{x}(t)$ is a rather strong assumption, for $\hat{x}(t)$ is an unknown function and, in defining the objective integral $J \equiv \int_a^b f[t, x(t), x'(t)] dt$, only the differentiability of $x(t)$ is required. For this reason, Euler's equation is often expressed in the following form:

(8)
$$\hat{f}_{x'} = \int_a^t \hat{f}_x d\tau + \text{const}$$

This equation can be obtained formally by integrating Euler's equation. When $d\hat{f}_{x'}/dt$ does not exist, this procedure of integrating Euler's equation is illegitimate since Euler's equation itself is illegitimate. However, the above equation can be directly obtained from (3) and (4) and the integration by parts of the *first* term of the RHS of (4). Thus Euler's equation (7) implies (8). But (8) does not necessarily imply (7). However, if $\partial \hat{f}_{x'}/\partial \hat{x}'$ (denoted by $\hat{f}_{x'x'}$) exists and is nonzero everywhere in the domain of f, then it can be shown that (8) always implies (7). It is interesting to observe that $\hat{x}(t)$ then has a higher order of differentiability than the admissible functions. When the condition $\hat{f}_{x'x'} \neq 0$ is satisfied, we call the above problem **regular**.

REMARK: In the above discussion we assumed that the function inside the integral J has the form $f[t, x(t), x'(t)]$. In certain cases it may lack certain arguments, and useful formulae can be obtained for such special cases. Consider, for example, the case where f lacks t so that it has the form $f[x(t), x'(t)]$. First note that

$$\frac{df}{dt} = f_x x' + f_{x'} x''$$

But for the optimal path $\hat{x}(t)$, Euler's condition is satisfied so that $\hat{f}_x = d\hat{f}_{x'}/dt$. Hence we have [along the optimal arc $\hat{x}(t)$]:

$$\frac{d\hat{f}}{dt} = \left[\frac{d}{dt}\hat{f}_{x'}\right]\hat{x}' + \hat{f}_{x'}\hat{x}'' = \frac{d}{dt}\left[\hat{f}_{x'}\hat{x}'\right]$$

where $\hat{f} \equiv f[\hat{x}(t), \hat{x}'(t)]$ and $\hat{f}_{x'} \equiv \partial \hat{f}/\partial x'$. Therefore, we obtain the following condition in place of Euler's condition:

(9) $$\hat{f} = \hat{f}_{x'}\hat{x}' + c$$

where c is some constant.

c.   SOLUTIONS OF ILLUSTRATIVE PROBLEMS

In subsection a we discussed the nature of the variational problem by giving some examples of actual problems, and in subsection b we obtained the first-order condition equation for a simple case. Here we solve the problems presented in subsection a by using Euler's equation. Since we have not discussed sufficiency conditions, our discussion here will naturally be confined to the necessary condition and the path which satisfies Euler's necessary condition. We will not discuss whether there exists a path which satisfies Euler's equation. In the application of Euler's equations (7) or (9), we omit the ^ for notational simplicity.

1. THE MINIMUM DISTANCE PROBLEM

We are to find an $x(t) \in X$ such as to

$$\text{Minimize: } J_D \equiv \int_a^b \sqrt{1 + (x')^2} \, dt$$

$$\text{Subject to: } x(a) = \alpha \text{ and } x(b) = \beta$$

Write $\sqrt{1 + (x')^2} \equiv f_D$; then Euler's condition is written as

$$\frac{\partial f_D}{\partial x} = \frac{d}{dt}\left[\frac{\partial f_D}{\partial x'}\right]$$

Since f_D contains no x, $\partial f_D / \partial x = 0$. Hence

$$\frac{\partial f_D}{\partial x'} = \frac{x'}{\sqrt{1 + (x')^2}} = \text{const.}$$

In other words, $x'(t) = \gamma$ (constant). Hence $x(t) = \gamma t + \sigma$. Since $x(a) = \alpha$, and $x(b) = \beta$, we obtain $x(t) = [(\alpha - \beta)/(a - b)]t + (a\beta - \alpha b)/(a - b)$. This is the equation which denotes the desired straight line.

2. THE BRACHISTOCHRONE PROBLEM

Here we are to find a $y(x)$ such as to

$$\text{Minimize: } J_B \equiv \int_0^a \sqrt{\frac{1 + (y')^2}{2gy}} \, dx$$

$$\text{Subject to: } y(0) = 0 \text{ and } y(a) = \alpha$$

Write $f_B \equiv \sqrt{[1 + (y')^2]/(2gy)}$. Since f_B does not explicitly contain x, we use formula (9).

In other words,

$$f_B = \left(\frac{\partial f_B}{\partial y'}\right)y' + c, \qquad \text{where } c \text{ is some constant}$$

or

$$\sqrt{\frac{1 + (y')^2}{2gy}} = \frac{(y')^2}{\sqrt{2gy[1 + (y')^2]}} + c$$

We find, on multiplying, squaring, and collecting terms, that

$$y = \frac{k}{1 + (y')^2} \qquad \text{where } k \equiv \frac{1}{2gc^2}$$

We proceed with the following parametric representation of y':

$$y' = \tan \omega$$

Hence

$$y = \frac{k}{1 + (y')^2} = \frac{k}{1 + \tan^2\omega} = k \cos^2\omega$$

Thus $y' = -2k \cos \omega \sin \omega \, d\omega/dx = \tan \omega$, so that $d\omega/dx = -1/(2k \cos^2\omega)$. Thus $dx = -2k \cos^2\omega \, d\omega = -k(1 + \cos 2\omega)d\omega$. Hence integration yields

$$x = -k(\omega + \tfrac{1}{2}\sin 2\omega) + (\text{constant})$$

Write $2\omega = \pi - \theta$ and note that $\sin (\pi - \theta) = \sin \theta$. Then we may write

$$x = k_1(\theta - \sin \theta) + k_2$$

where k_1 and k_2 are some constants. Obviously $k_1 = k/2$. Also y can be obtained as follows:

$$y = k \cos^2\omega = \frac{k}{2}(1 + \cos 2\omega) = \frac{k}{2}[1 + \cos (\pi - \theta)]$$

$$= \frac{k}{2}[1 - \cos \theta] = k_1 [1 - \cos \theta]$$

In other words, we have obtained the parametric representation of the solution as

$$x = k_1 (\theta - \sin \theta) + k_2$$

$$y = k_1(1 - \cos \theta)$$

These equations define a family of "cycloids" with cusps on the x-axis. A unique curve is determined by the boundary conditions

$$y(0) = 0 \quad \text{and} \quad y(a) = \alpha$$

3. A PROBLEM OF DYNAMIC MONOPOLY

We are to find the function $p(t)$ which minimizes

$$J_M \equiv \int_0^T \left\{ D[p(t), \dot{p}(t)] \, p(t) - C \left[D[p(t), \dot{p}(t)] \right] \right\} \, dt$$

subject to $p(0) = p^0$ and $p(T) = \bar{p}$ (where, we may recall, $x = D$). Denote the inside of the above integral by f_M; that is, $J_M \equiv \int_0^T f_M dt$. Since f_M does not contain t explicitly, we can use formula (9) in place of Euler's equation, that is,

$$f_M = \frac{\partial f_M}{\partial \dot{p}} \dot{p} + \delta, \text{ where } \delta \text{ is some constant}$$

Thus $pD - C = [pD_{\dot{p}} - C'D_{\dot{p}}] \dot{p} + \delta$, where $D_{\dot{p}} \equiv \partial D/\partial \dot{p}$ and $C' \equiv dC/dx$. Clearly, C' signifies the marginal cost function. The above equation is a first-order differential equation, the solution of which involves two arbitrary constants that can be determined by the boundary conditions $p(0) = p^0$ and $p(T) = \bar{p}$. The following special case illustrates the problem. Let

$$D[p, \dot{p}] = ap + b\dot{p} + c, \qquad a < 0$$

$$C(x) = \alpha x^2 + \beta x + \gamma$$

where a, b, c, α, β, and γ are all constants. The solution for this particular problem can be obtained as follows (see Allen [1], pp. 535–536, for example, or try it yourself):

$$p(t) = \tilde{p} + Ae^{\lambda t} + Be^{-\lambda t}$$

where $\tilde{p}$ and λ are defined by

$$\tilde{p} \equiv \frac{c - (2\alpha c + \beta)\, a}{2a\,(a\alpha - 1)} \qquad \text{and} \qquad \lambda \equiv \frac{1}{b}\sqrt{\frac{a(\alpha a - 1)}{\alpha}}$$

The constants A and B are determined from the boundary conditions $p(0) = p^0$ and $p(T) = \bar{p}$.

FOOTNOTES

1. The analysis can be extended to the case of continuous functions (instead of differentiable functions).

2. Let m be the mass of the particle. The gravitational force F is given by $F = mg$, where g is the gravitational constant. The force F is decomposed into its normal and tangential components. The former plays no part in the motion. Let ds be the tangential distance along the curve at point (x, y). Since $\cos \theta = dy/ds$ (note $ds^2 = dx^2 + dy^2$), the tangential component of F at (x, y) is equal to $F \cos \theta = mg\, dy/ds$. Hence the acceleration along ds is equal to $g\, dy/ds$. That is, $dv/dt = g\, dy/ds$ where $v \equiv ds/dt$ (velocity along ds). Thus we obtain $v\, dv = g\, dy$. Integrating this and using the initial condition $y = 0$, $v = 0$, we have $v = \sqrt{2gy}$. Therefore $dt = ds/v = \sqrt{1 + y'^2}\; dx/\sqrt{2gy}$. Hence for the required duration, we obtain the expression $J(y) = \int_0^a \sqrt{(1 + y'^2)/2gy}\; dx$.

3. The existence of an optimal function $\hat{x}(t)$ is not at all obvious in many problems and the proof of the existence should be supplied separately. But such a proof will exceed the scope of the present section. We may also note that $\hat{x}(t)$, even if it exists, may not be unique.

4. Solve equation (7) regarding $\hat{x}$ as an unknown function of t. The solution $\hat{x}(t)$ of (7) will provide the equation that the optimal path must satisfy. It is important to realize, however, that this $\hat{x}(t)$ does not necessarily maximize (or minimize) the objective integral J, since equation (7), in general, only provides a necessary condition and *not* a sufficient condition for the optimum. In Section B, we prove that *under certain concavity conditions* equation (7) also provides a sufficient condition for the optimum.

REFERENCES

1. Allen, R. G. D., *Mathematical Analysis for Economists*, London, Macmillan, 1938, esp. chap. XX.

2. Bliss, G. C., *Lectures on the Calculus of Variations*, Chicago, Ill., University of Chicago Press, 1946.

3. Evans, G. C., *Mathematical Introduction to Economics*, New York, McGraw-Hill, 1930.

4. Gelfand, I. M., and Fomin, C. V., *Calculus of Variations*, Englewood Cliffs, N. J., Prentice-Hall, 1963 (tr. from Russian).

5. Ramsey, F. P., "A Mathematical Theory of Saving," *Economic Journal*, XXXVIII, December 1928.

6. Shilov, G. Y., *Mathematical Analysis*, Oxford, Pergamon Press, 1965 (tr. from Russian).

7. Tomiyama, K., *The Logic of Modern Physics*, Tokyo, Iwanami, 1956 (in Japanese).

Section B

SPACES OF FUNCTIONS AND THE CALCULUS OF VARIATIONS[1]

a. INTRODUCTION

In the last section, we considered the problem of finding a function $x(t)$ from the set $X_{[a,b]}$ of differentiable real-valued functions defined on the closed interval $[a, b]$ such as to maximize the following integral:

$$J[x] \equiv \int_a^b f[t, x(t), x'(t)] \, dt$$

The alert reader may already have noticed the resemblance of the above problem to the ordinary nonlinear programming problem that we discussed in Chapter 1. The set $X_{[a,b]}$ of continuously differentiable real-valued functions on $[a, b]$ is a linear space. The function $J[x]$ is a real-valued function defined on $X_{[a,b]}$. The problem is to find an $\hat{x} \in X_{[a,b]}$ which maximizes $J[x]$. As a matter of fact, this analogy is the same even if we take $x(t)$ as a continuously differentiable function of $[a, b]$ into R^n, that is, $x(t) = [x_1(t), x_2(t), \ldots, x_n(t)]$, and $X_{[a,b]}$ is the collection of such vector-valued continuously differentiable functions on $[a, b]$. The function $x'(t)$ in $J[x]$ is simply defined by $x'(t) \equiv [x_1'(t), \ldots, x_n'(t)]$, where $x_i'(t) \equiv dx_i(t)/dt$. What then is the difference between the above problem and the ordinary nonlinear programming problem? The crucial difference is simply that the linear space $X_{[a,b]}$ is no longer finite dimensional. In the exposition of ordinary nonlinear programming, the choice set is typically a finite dimensional Euclidian space, and theorems are developed under this basic assumption. But there is no guarantee that the theorems that hold for a finite dimensional Euclidian space remain valid for an infinite dimensional linear space.

However, it is interesting to note that many theorems in the theory of nonlinear programming for the finite dimensional Euclidian space can be re-proved without too much difficulty (sometimes almost word for word) for infinite dimensional linear spaces. There may be some unexpected difficulties in this task, but if we accomplish it, we obtain a general theory of nonlinear programming which covers both the finite dimensional and infinite dimensional cases. In particular, such a theory will include the classical calculus of variations problem as a special case. We may note that this corresponds to a trend in modern mathematics to review the classical results of analysis for spaces of functions (or function spaces); this field of study is known as **functional analysis**.

Extensive work along this line has been done by Hurwicz in his seventy-page article, "Programming in Linear Spaces" [5]. Textbooks on the calculus of variations have been written from the viewpoint of function spaces (see Gelfand and Fomin [3] and Shilov [10]; for the exposition of this section we are indebted to them). We note that our Chapter 1 was written in the same spirit as was the Hurwicz article. Although we confined our attention to the finite dimensional case, we remarked in several places that the definitions and theorems could be extended to the infinite dimensional case. This was done, for example, in the definitions of derivatives and in the proof of the Kuhn-Tucker main theorem (Theorem 1.D.3).

In this section we shall explicitly state our problem as a "nonlinear programming" problem for the infinite dimensional case and proceed with our analysis. Euler's condition will be rigorously and more systematically obtained under this procedure. However, we will not follow this procedure through to its completion. In other words, we will not be concerned here with developing all the results of the classical calculus of variations from the viewpoint of nonlinear programming in infinite dimensional vector spaces. One reason is that this attempt has not been completed yet. In the meantime, a new development suddenly attracted a great deal of attention from mathematicians. This development became a matter of vital interest to American mathematicians after the publication (and translation) of the book by Pontryagin and his students [8]. This was followed by the work of Hestenes [4] and his students, in which all the major results of the classical calculus of variations have been obtained and extended by this new approach. The most important extension is probably the incorporation of inequality constraints in a natural way. Active research and development in this field (known as **optimal control theory**), which we will summarize in Chapter 8, is being carried out vigorously. This new approach resembles Hurwicz's approach [5] in the sense that it recognizes the problem as a choice problem in infinite dimensional space, but it is different in the sense that it does not come out as a natural extension of the ordinary linear and nonlinear programming theory. An interesting novelty in viewing and formulating variational problems is seen in the Pontryagin-Hestenes approach. A natural question now is whether we can develop the ordinary nonlinear programming theory for the finite dimensional case from this new formulation. The answer should be yes, but how? This task has been partly accomplished recently by Canon, Cullum, and Polak [2]. However, we will not go into this problem here. Furthermore, in this section we restrict ourselves to the simplest problem, that is, the problem in which there are no constraints and the "end points" such as a and b are fixed.

b.   SPACES OF FUNCTIONS AND OPTIMIZATION

We begin our discussion by reminding the reader of some basic definitions (see Chapter 0, Section A, and Chapter 1, Section C).

Definition: A set X of elements x, y, z, ... of any kind is called a **linear space** (or **vector space**) over the real field if X is closed under "addition" (denoted by $+$) and multiplication by real numbers such as α, β, and so on, and if the following axioms (for any x, y, $z \in X$ and for any α, $\beta \in R$) are satisfied:

(L-1) $x + y = y + z$.
(L-2) $(x + y) + z = x + (y + z)$.
(L-3) $\exists$ an element "0" ("zero") such that $x + 0 = x$ for any $x \in X$.
(L-4)   For each $x \in X$, there exists an element "$-x$" such that $x + (-x) = 0$.
(L-5) $\alpha(\beta x) = (\alpha\beta) x$.
(L-6) $\alpha(x + y) = \alpha x + \alpha y$.
(L-7) $(\alpha + \beta) x = \alpha x + \beta x$.

Definition: A linear space X is said to be **normed** if to each element $x \in X$ there corresponds a *nonnegative* number $\| x \|$ (called the **norm** of x) such that (1) $\| x \| = 0$ if and only if $x = 0$; (2) $\| x + y \| \leq \| x \| + \| y \|$ for any x, $y \in X$; and (3) $\| \alpha x \| = |\alpha| \| x \|$ for any $\alpha \in R$.

Definition: Let X be a linear space. Any function from X into R is called a **functional** on X. A functional J on X is called a **linear functional** on X if (1) $J[\alpha x] = \alpha J[x]$ for any $x \in X$ and $\alpha \in R$, and (2) $J[x + y] = J[x] + J[y]$ for any x, $y \in X$.

Definition: Let X be a normed linear space. A functional J is said to be **continuous at x^0** if, for any $\epsilon > 0$, there exists a $\delta > 0$ such that $\| x - x^0 \| < \delta$ implies $|J[x] - J[x^0]| < \epsilon$. When J is continuous at every point of X, J is called **continuous in X**.

    REMARK: It can be shown fairly easily that

      (i)   A linear functional on X is continuous in X if it is continuous at one point $x^0 \in X$.

      (ii)   A linear functional is continuous if and only if it is bounded (that is, there exists a μ such that $|J[x]| \leq \mu \| x \|$ for all $x \in X$). For the proofs of the above statements, see Kolmogorov and Fomin [7], pp. 77–78, for example (or the reader may try it himself).

EXAMPLE: Let $C_{[a,b]}$ be the set of all (bounded) continuous real-valued functions $x(t)$ defined on a closed interval $[a, b]$. Then $C_{[a,b]}$ is a linear space.[2] $\| x \| \equiv \sup_{a \le t \le b} |x(t)|$ is a norm.[3] Note that there can be many kinds of norms. $J[x] \equiv \int_a^b x(t)dt$ (Riemann integral) is a continuous linear functional on $C_{[a,b]} \cdot J[x] \equiv \int_a^b \alpha(t)x(t)dt$, where $\alpha(t)$ is a given function in $C_{[a,b]}$, is also a continuous linear functional.

REMARK: The normed linear space will be considered as a metric space with the metric naturally induced by the norm.

Definition: Let X be a normed linear space. A functional J on X is said to be **differentiable at** x^0 where $x^0 \in X$, if there exists a continuous linear functional ϕ on X such that $\Delta J[x^0; h] \equiv J[x^0 + h] - J[x^0] = \phi[h] + o(\| h \|)$, where $o(\| h \|)$ is an infinitesimal of higher order than h(Landau's o), that is,

$$\lim_{h \to 0} \frac{o(\| h \|)}{\| h \|} = 0$$

The functional J is said to be **differentiable in** X, if it is differentiable at each x in X.

We may recall that when X is finite (say, n) dimensional, $\phi[h]$ can be written as $\phi \cdot h$ where ϕ is an n-vector. Note that $\phi[h]$ denotes the *value* of the linear functional ϕ at h. The linear functional ϕ is called the **first derivative of** J and is denoted by J' or $J'[x^0]$; $\phi[h]$ is called the **first differential** (or the **first variation**) of J and is denoted by $dJ[x^0; h]$ or $dJ[h]$.[4]

REMARK: Needless to say, for a fixed x^0, $\phi[h]$ depends only on h. However, if x^0 changes, $\phi[h]$ also changes.[5] Hence $\phi[h]$ may be written as $\phi[x^0; h]$. It can be shown that, given x^0, the differential $\phi[h]$ of a differentiable function is unique, which makes the above definition meaningful.

REMARK: A linear functional J is obviously always differentiable since, by definition,

$$J[x + h] - J[x] = J[h]$$

REMARK: From the above definition, we can say that a linear functional is differentiable if its increment $\Delta J[x]$ is split into the two parts: a linear functional of h and an infinitesimal of higher order of h, that is, $o(\| h \|)$.

Definition: A functional $J[x]$ on a normed linear space X is said to be **twice differentiable at** x^0 where $x^0 \in X$, if there exists a linear functional ϕ and a quadratic functional Q such that

$$\Delta J[x^0; h] = J[x^0 + h] - J[x^0] = \phi[h] + Q[h, h] + o(\| h \|^2)$$

Here $o(\| h \|^2)$ is the infinitesimal of higher order than $\| h \|^2$, that is, $\lim_{h \to 0}$ $o(\| h \|^2)/\| h \|^2 = 0$. $Q[h, h]$ is called the **second differential** (or **second varia-tion**) of J at x^0 and is denoted by $d^2 J[x^0; h]$ or $d^2 J[h]$. When J is twice differentiable for all $x \in X$, J is said to be **twice differentiable in** X.

> REMARK: We may recall the definition of the quadratic functional (Chapter 1, Section E,). A real-valued function $Q(x, x)$ on a linear space X is called a **quadratic functional** on X if it is a bilinear functional.

> REMARK: Since a quadratic functional on R^n can be written as a quadratic form, $Q[h, h]$ in the above definition can be written as $Q[h, h] = \frac{1}{2} h \cdot A \cdot h$, where $A \equiv [a_{ij}]$ is an $n \times n$ matrix, $h \in R^n$, that is, $h \equiv (h_1, h_2, \ldots, h_n)$, and $a_{ij} = \partial^2 J/\partial x_i \partial x_j$ evaluated at $x = x^0$. If the a_{ij}'s are bounded in the neighborhood of x^0 (that is, if there exists a μ such that $|a_{ij}| \leq \mu$ for all i and j), then $h \cdot A \cdot h \leq \sum_{i,j} \mu h_i h_j \leq \mu n^2 \| h \|^2$, where we may define $\| h \|$ by

(a)
$$\| h \| \equiv \left[\sum_{i=1}^n h_i^2 \right]^{\frac{1}{2}}$$

or

(b)
$$\| h \| = \max_{1 \leq i \leq n} \{ |h_i| \}$$

We now turn to the problem of maximization (or minimization) in an infinite dimensional space. The reader will readily recognize that our discussions here are strictly analogous to the ones in the *unconstrained* maximization (or minimization) problem for a finite dimensional case (see Chapter 1, Section C).

Definition: Let $J[x]$ be a functional (not necessarily linear) defined over a normed linear space X.

(i) The functional $J[x]$ is said to achieve its **local maximum** (resp. **local minimum**) at $\hat{x} \in X$, if there exists an open ball $B_\epsilon(\hat{x})$ about $\hat{x}$ with radius ϵ such that $B_\epsilon(\hat{x}) \subset X$ and $J[\hat{x}] \geq J[x]$ (resp. $J[\hat{x}] \leq J[x]$) for all $x \in B_\epsilon(\hat{x})$. If $J[\hat{x}] > J[x]$ (resp. $J[\hat{x}] < J[x]$) for all $x \in B_\epsilon(\hat{x})$ whenever $x \neq \hat{x}$, we say that J achieves its **unique local maximum** (resp. **unique local minimum**) at $\hat{x}$.

(ii) We say that J achieves its **global maximum** (resp. **global minimum**) at $\hat{x} \in X$ if $J[\hat{x}] \geq J[x]$ (resp. $J[\hat{x}] \leq J[x]$) for all $x \in X$. If $J[\hat{x}] > J[x]$ (resp. $J[\hat{x}] < J[x]$) whenever $x \neq \hat{x}$, then we say that J achieves its **unique global maximum** (resp. **unique global minimum**) at $\hat{x}$.

> REMARK: When $J[x]$ has either a local maximum or a local minimum at $\hat{x}$, it is said to have a **local extremum** at $\hat{x}$, and similarly for **unique local extremum**, **global extremum**, and **unique global extremum**.

> REMARK: It should be clear that if $\hat{x}$ furnishes a global maximum (resp.

global minimum) of $J[x]$, it also furnishes a local maximum (resp. local minimum) of $J[x]$, but not vice versa. In other words, local maximality is necessary for global maximality but is not sufficient.

Theorem 5.B.1:   *Let $J[x]$ be a differentiable functional defined over a normed linear space X. A necessary condition for $J[x]$ to have a local (or global) extremum at $\hat{x} \in X$ is that its differential vanishes at $x = \hat{x}$; that is, $dJ[\hat{x}; h] = 0$ for all h.*

PROOF: From the definition of a differential, $\Delta J[\hat{x}; h] \equiv J[\hat{x} + h] - J[\hat{x}]$ $= dJ[\hat{x}; h] + \delta \| h \|$ where $\delta \equiv o(\| h \|)/\| h \|$. By the definition of $o(\| h \|)$, $\delta \rightarrow 0$ as $h \rightarrow 0$. Hence $\Delta J[\hat{x}; h]$ and $dJ[\hat{x}; h]$ have the same sign [that is, $\Delta J[\hat{x}; h] \geq 0$ (or ≤ 0) depending on whether $dJ[\hat{x}; h] \geq 0$ (or ≤ 0) for sufficiently small h]. Now suppose that $dJ[\hat{x}; h^0] \neq 0$ for some admissible h^0. Since dJ is a linear functional in h, $dJ[\hat{x}; -\theta h^0] = -\theta \, dJ[\hat{x}; h^0] \neq 0$ for any real $\theta \neq 0$. Let $\theta > 0$ be small enough. Then $\Delta J[\hat{x}; h]$ can be neither always ≥ 0 nor ≤ 0, for arbitrary small h (or small θ). This contradicts the assumption that $J[x]$ has a (local) extremum at $\hat{x}$ [that is, $(J[\hat{x}] - J[x])$ has a definite sign in some neighborhood of $\hat{x}$].   (Q.E.D.)

REMARK: When $X = R^n$, we used the "chain rule" (Theorem 1.C.2) for the proof of the above theorem (Theorem 1.C.6). By noting that the chain rule also holds in an infinite dimensional (normed linear) space, we may prove Theorem 5.B.1. in the way we proved the finite dimensional case (Theorem 1.C.6). Let X, Y, and Z be normed linear spaces. Let f be a function from X into Y and g be a function from $f(X) \subset Y$ into Z. Let f be differentiable at x^0 and g be differentiable at $f(x^0)$. The chain rule for this case simply states that for $h \equiv g \circ f$, $h'(x^0) = g'[f(x^0)] \circ f'(x^0)$. The proof of Theorem 5.B.1 then goes as follows: Let $h \in X$ be such that $\| h \| = 1$. Consider $\Phi(\theta) \equiv J[\hat{x} + \theta h]$ where $\theta \in R$. Then $\Phi(\theta)$ is a function from R into itself. By assumption, $\Phi(\theta)$ has a local extremum at $\theta = 0$; hence by elementary calculus, $\Phi'(0) = 0$. By the chain rule, $\Phi'(0) = J'[\hat{x}] \cdot h$. Thus $J'[\hat{x}] = 0$ or $dJ[\hat{x}] = 0$.

REMARK: It may have to be recalled that X does not have to be a *finite* dimensional linear space. For example, $x(t)$ may be in $C_{[a,b]}$ with a certain norm. Then the fact that $J[x]$ has a local maximum at $\hat{x}$ means that $J[\hat{x}] - J[x] \geq 0$ for some neighborhood of the curve $\hat{x}(t)$, where the "neighborhood" is defined in terms of the metric induced by the norm of $C_{[a,b]}$.

Theorem 5.B.2:   *Let $J[x]$ be a twice differentiable functional defined on a normed linear space X. A necessary condition for $J[x]$ to have a local (or global) minimum at $x = \hat{x}$ is that*

$$d^2J[\hat{x}; h] \geq 0 \qquad \text{for all } h$$

PROOF: By definition, we have

$$\Delta J[\hat{x}; h] \equiv J[\hat{x} + h] - J[\hat{x}] = dJ[\hat{x}; h] + d^2J[\hat{x}; h] + o(\| h \|^2)$$

By Theorem 5.B.1, $dJ[\hat{x}; h] = 0$. Hence $\Delta J[\hat{x}; h]$ and $d^2J[\hat{x}; h]$ have the same sign for sufficiently small $\| h \|$. Suppose $d^2J[\hat{x}; h^0] < 0$ for some h^0. Then from the bilinearity of the quadratic functional $d^2J[\hat{x}; h]$, we have

$$d^2J[\hat{x}; \theta h^0] = \theta^2 d^2J[\hat{x}; h^0] < 0 \quad \text{for any } \theta \neq 0$$

Hence $\Delta J[\hat{x}; h]$ can be made negative for an arbitrarily small $\| h \|$, which contradicts the assumption that $J[x]$ has a local minimum at $x = \hat{x}$.

(Q.E.D.)

REMARK: Similarly, we can easily prove that $d^2J[\hat{x}; h] \leq 0$ is a necessary condition for $\hat{x}$ to furnish a local maximum for $J[x]$. We call $d^2J[\hat{x}; h] \geq 0$ (or ≤ 0 for maximum) the **second-order necessary condition** for a local minimum (or maximum). For the finite dimensional case, recall Theorem 1.E.15.

Definition: A quadratic functional $Q[x]$ defined on a normed linear space X is called **strongly positive definite** if there exists a constant $\theta > 0$ such that

$$Q[x] \geq \theta \| x \|^2 \quad \text{for all } x \in X$$

Theorem 5.B.3:   *A sufficient condition for a functional $J[x]$ to have a unique local minimum at $x = \hat{x}$, given that the first differential at $\hat{x}$ vanishes (that is, $dJ[\hat{x}; h] = 0$), is that its second differential at $\hat{x}$, $d^2J[\hat{x}; h]$, be strongly positive definite.*

PROOF: Since $dJ[\hat{x}; h] = 0$, we have $\Delta J[\hat{x}; h] = d^2J[\hat{x}; h] + \epsilon \| h \|^2$, where $\epsilon \equiv o(\| h \|^2)/\| h \|^2$ (that is, $\epsilon \to 0$ as $h \to 0$). By assumption, there exists a $\theta > 0$ such that $d^2J[\hat{x}; h] \geq \theta \| h \|^2$ for all h. Hence we obtain

$$\Delta J[\hat{x}; h] = d^2J[\hat{x}; h] + \epsilon \| h \|^2 \geq (\theta + \epsilon) \| h \|^2$$

For ϵ small enough (that is, $\| h \|$ small enough) with $h \neq 0$, we have $\theta + \epsilon > 0$. Hence $\Delta J[\hat{x}; h] > 0$.

(Q.E.D.)

REMARK: In a finite dimensional space, the strong positive definiteness of a quadratic form is equivalent to its positive definiteness. In the general case (not necessarily finite dimensional), strong positive definiteness can be stronger than positive definiteness. Hence in the above sufficiency condition, the strong positive definiteness of $d^2J[\hat{x}; h]$ cannot be replaced by the positive definiteness (that is, $d^2J[\hat{x}; h] > 0$ for all h). The following example is given by Shilov ([10], pp. 90–91): $J[x] \equiv \int_0^1 x^2(t)[t - x(t)] dt$, where $x(t)$ is continuously differentiable on $[0, 1]$. Let $\hat{x}(t) \equiv 0$. Then $dJ[\hat{x}; h] = dJ[0; h] = 0$. Moreover $d^2J[\hat{x}; h] = d^2J[0; h] = \int_0^1 th^2(t)\,dt$, which is positive for every $h(t) \neq 0$. But we can easily pick a function $x(t)$ such that $J[x; h] < 0$; that is, $J(x)$ does not achieve a minimum at $\hat{x}(t) \equiv 0$.

REMARK: Theorem 5.B.3 is formulated in terms of minimum. For the maximum problem, we can say $\hat{x}$ furnishes a unique local maximum of $J[x]$, if $dJ[\hat{x}; h] = 0$ *and* if there exists a $\theta > 0$ such that $d^2J[\hat{x}; h] \leq -\theta \| h \|$ for all h.

c.   EULER'S CONDITION AND A SUFFICIENCY THEOREM

Let $x(t) = [x_1(t), \ldots, x_n(t)]$ and $x'(t) = [x_1'(t), \ldots, x_n'(t)]$ where $x_i(t)$, $i = 1, 2, \ldots, n$, are real-valued continuously differentiable functions defined on the closed interval $[a, b]$, and $x_i'(t) \equiv dx_i(t)/dt, i = 1, 2, \ldots, n$. Let us denote this by $x_i(t) \in D_{[a,b]}$ or $x(t) \in D^n_{[a,b]}$. Now consider the following specific form of $J[x]$.

$$J[x] \equiv \int_a^b f[t, x(t), x'(t)]\,dt$$

Here f is defined in an open subset of R^{2n+1} which includes the space of $[t, x(t), x'(t)]$ which is defined for $a \leq t \leq b$. The function f is assumed to possess continuous first and second partial derivatives with respect to t, x, and x'. With this explicit form of $J[x]$, we realize at once that the general problem of minimization (or maximization) of $J[x]$ turns out to be that of the *calculus of variations*.

Let us now consider a "displacement" of $x(t)$ by $h(t)$, where $h(t) \in D^n_{[a,b]}$ with $h_i(a) = h_i(b) = 0, i = 1, 2, \ldots, n$.

$$\Delta J[x; h] \equiv J[x + h] - J[x]$$
$$= \int_a^b \{ f[t, x(t) + h(t), x'(t) + h'(t)] - f[t, x(t), x'(t)] \}\,dt$$

For notational simplicity, write the $2n$-vectors as $(x, x') \equiv y$ and $(h, h') \equiv k$. Clearly $(x + h, x' + h') = y + k$. From the differentiability of f with respect to y, we have, for each fixed t,

$$f[t, x + h, x' + h'] - f[t, x, x'] = f[t, y + k] - f[t, y]$$
$$= f_y \cdot k + o(\| k \|)$$

where $f_y \equiv (\partial f/\partial x_1, \ldots, \partial f/\partial x_n')$. Here the norm $\| k \|$ is defined as

$$\| k \| \equiv \max_{a \leq t \leq b} \{ |h_1(t)|, \ldots, |h_n(t)|, |h_1'(t)|, \ldots, |h_n'(t)| \}$$

Alternatively, we can carry out a similar analysis with the following norm:

$$\| k \| \equiv \max_{a \leq t \leq b} \left[\sum_{i=1}^n h_i^2(t) + \sum_{i=1}^n (h_i'(t))^2 \right]^{\frac{1}{2}}$$

Note that $o(\| k \|)$ depends on t and y as well as on k, so that we may write $o(\| k \|) = r(t, y, k)$. Assume that the second partial derivatives of the function $f(t, y)$ with respect to y are bounded by N (in absolute value), so that we have[6]

$$|o(\| k \|)| \leq \tfrac{1}{2}N(2n)^2 \| k \|^2$$

Hence we obtain

$$\Delta J[x; h] = \int_a^b (f_y \cdot k)\, dt + \int_a^b o(\| k \|)\, dt$$

$$\leq \int_a^b (f_y \cdot k)\, dt + 2Nn^2 \int_a^b \mu^2\, dt \qquad \text{for } \| k \| \leq \mu$$

In other words,

$$\Delta J[x; h] \leq \int_a^b (f_y \cdot k)\, dt + 2N\, n^2(b - a)\, \mu^2 \qquad \text{for } \| k \| \leq \mu$$

Thus we see that the increment of the functional $J[x]$ is split into a principal linear part (linear with respect to k) and an infinitesimal of higher order. For the latter, note that $\lim_{\mu \to 0} [2N\, n^2(b - a)\, \mu^2]/\mu = 0$. Hence $J[x]$ is differentiable and its differential has the form

$$dJ[x; h] \equiv \int_a^b (f_y \cdot y)\, dt \equiv \int_a^b \left[\frac{\partial f}{\partial x_1} h_1 + \cdots + \frac{\partial f}{\partial x_n} h_n + \frac{\partial f}{\partial x'_1} h'_1 + \cdots + \frac{\partial f}{\partial x'_n} h'_n \right] dt$$

In other words, if f, defined on an Euclidian space, is differentiable with respect to x and x', and if the *second* partial derivatives of f with respect to x and x' are bounded, then the functional J is differentiable and its first differential is written as above.

From Theorem 5.B.1, a necessary condition for J to have an extremum is that its first differential vanish. Hence for the above J, we ought to have, for the optimal arc $x(t)$,

$$dJ = \int_a^b \left[\sum_{i=1}^n \frac{\partial f}{\partial x_i} h_i + \sum_{i=1}^n \frac{\partial f}{\partial x'_i} h'_i \right] dt = 0$$

To obtain the Euler condition, we assume that $x(t)$ is twice differentiable and then perform integration by parts for the terms which involve h'_i in the above equation.

$$\int_a^b \sum_{i=1}^n \frac{\partial f}{\partial x'_i} h'_i\, dt = \sum_{i=1}^n \frac{\partial f}{\partial x'_i} h_i \Big|_a^b - \int_a^b \sum_{i=1}^n \left[\frac{d}{dt} f_{x'_i} \right] h_i\, dt$$

where $f_{x'_i} \equiv \partial f/\partial x'_i$. The first term on the right of the above equation is zero since $h_i(a) = h_i(b) = 0$. Hence we have

$$dJ = \int_a^b \left[\sum_{i=1}^n f_{x_i} h_i - \left(\sum_{i=1}^n \frac{d}{dt} f_{x_i'} \right) h_i \right] dt$$

$$= \int_a^b \left\{ \sum_{i=1}^n \left[f_{x_i} - \left(\frac{d}{dt} f_{x_i'} \right) \right] h_i \right\} dt = 0$$

for all $h_i(t)$, $i = 1, 2, \ldots, n$, where $f_{x_i} \equiv \partial f / \partial x_i$ and $f_{x_i'} \equiv \partial f / \partial x_i'$. Since all the increments $h_i(t)$ are independent and arbitrary, we obtain, by setting all except one to zero, that

$$\int_a^b \left\{ \left[f_{x_i} - \frac{d}{dt} (f_{x_i'}) \right] h_i \right\} dt = 0, \quad \text{for all } h_i(t)$$

Hence from the fundamental lemma of the calculus of variations (Section A), we must have (noting the continuity of $df_{x_i'} / dt$ which is due to the continuous differentiability of $f_{x_i'}$)

(E) $$f_{x_i} - \frac{d}{dt} (f_{x_i'}) = 0, \, i = 1, 2, \ldots, n$$

This is a (necessary) condition that the optimal arc must satisfy and it is called **Euler's condition** for the *n*-variable case.

REMARK: When $x(t)$ is *not* twice differentiable, then we cannot get (E) as we discussed in Section A. We instead obtain

$$\int_a^t f_{x_i} dt = f_{x_i'} + c, \, i = 1, 2, \ldots, n, \text{ where } c \text{ is some constant}$$

We may obtain the expression for the second differential d^2J for

$$J[x] \equiv \int_a^b f[t, x(t), x'(t)] \, dt$$

by assuming that all the second partial derivatives of f exist and are continuous, and by using Taylor's expansion. For example, if $x(t)$ is real-valued (instead of R^n-valued), then

$$d^2J = \frac{1}{2} \int_a^b \left[f_{xx} h^2 + 2 f_{xx'} hh' + f_{x'x'} h'^2 \right] dt$$

A similar expression can be obtained readily when x is R^n-valued. Then using Theorems 5.B.2 and 5.B.3, we can obtain expressions of the second-order necessary conditions and sufficient conditions. These conditions are known by the names of Legendre, Weierstrass, Jacobi, and so on. The simplest is the Legendre condition for necessity (of a minimum), which states

$$f_{x'x'} \geq 0$$

when x is real-valued. For a maximum, it is

$$f_{x'x'} \leq 0$$

Since discussions of these conditions are tedious, we omit them entirely. We will, however, prove the following remarkable sufficiency theorem, which has its counterpart for the finite dimensional case (see Theorem 1.C.7).

Theorem 5.B.4: *Let $f[t, x(t), x'(t)]$ be differentiable with respect to $x(t)$ and $x'(t)$, where $x(t)$ is an R^n-valued twice differentiable function on the closed interval $[a, b]$ with $x(a) = \alpha$ and $x(b) = \beta$. Suppose that f is a concave function in $x(t)$ and $x'(t)$. Then a necessary and sufficient condition that $\hat{x}(t)$ maximizes the integral*

$$J[x] \equiv \int_a^b f[t, x(t), x'(t)]\, dt$$

is that it satisfies the Euler condition

$$\frac{\partial f}{\partial x} = \frac{d}{dt}\left[\frac{\partial f}{\partial x'}\right], \text{ with } x(a) = \alpha \text{ and } x(b) = \beta$$

PROOF: The necessity is obvious, so we prove the sufficiency. Let $\hat{x}(t)$ and $\hat{x}'(t)$ satisfy the above Euler equation. Denote $f[t, \hat{x}(t), \hat{x}'(t)]$ by $\hat{f}$, and let $\partial \hat{f}/\partial \hat{x} \equiv \hat{f}_x$, $\partial \hat{f}/\partial \hat{x}' \equiv \hat{f}_{x'}$. Then, we can write the following string of an inequality and equalities:

$$J[x] - J[\hat{x}] = \int_a^b (f - \hat{f})dt \leq \int_a^b [(x - \hat{x})\cdot \hat{f}_x + (x' - \hat{x}')\cdot \hat{f}_{x'}]\, dt$$

$$(\because \text{concavity})$$

$$= \int_a^b (x - \hat{x})\cdot (\hat{f}_x - \frac{d}{dt}\hat{f}_{x'})dt + (x - \hat{x})\cdot \hat{f}_{x'}\Big|_a^b$$

$$[\because \text{ The integration by parts yield} \int_a^b (x' - \hat{x}')\cdot \hat{f}_{x'}dt = (x - \hat{x})\cdot \hat{f}_{x'}\Big|_a^b$$

$$- \int_a^b (x - \hat{x})\frac{d}{dt}(\hat{f}_{x'})dt]$$

$$= (x - \hat{x})\cdot \hat{f}_{x'}\Big|_a^b [\because \text{ Euler's equation}]$$

$$= 0 \ [\because \text{ fixed end points, that is, } x(a) = \hat{x}(a) = \alpha \text{ and } x(b) = \hat{x}(b) = \beta]$$

$$(\text{Q.E.D.})$$

REMARK: It can easily be seen from the above proof that if f is *strictly* concave in x and x', then $\hat{x}(t)$ provides a *unique* global maximum. Note also that if f is convex (resp. *strictly* convex in x and x'), then $\hat{x}(t)$ provides a global minimum (resp. *unique* global minimum).

REMARK: Any integral evaluated at a single point is obviously zero. Also, any integral evaluated on a set of countably many points is zero. Therefore, if two (integrable) functions $u(t)$ and $v(t)$ differ only for countably many points in $[a, b]$, then the values of the integrals of these functions from a to b will be the same. Hence the "uniqueness" of an optimal solution in the above only means uniqueness except for countably many points.

REMARK: As we noted in Section A, the above theorem does *not* say that there does exist such an $\hat{x}(t)$. It is possible that there is no solution for the differential equation, that is, Euler's equation. The existence of $\hat{x}(t)$ is simply assumed in the above theorem.

REMARK: This theorem was obtained by the author and presented as a lecture at the University of Minnesota in the spring of 1966. See Takayama [11]. It is now a special case of Mangasarian's theorem in optimal control theory (see Theorem 8.C.5).

FOOTNOTES

1. For the first reading, this section can safely be skipped, except for Theorem 5.B.4. The major purpose of this section (except for Theorem 5.B.4) is to clarify the basic underlying mathematical structure of the calculus of variations problem (rather than to provide theorems useful for practical applications), which then will be useful for further theoretical studies on this topic. Theorem 5.B.4 can be read independently of the rest of this section, and it provides a useful result in applications. That is, under "concave cases" the Euler condition is sufficient (as well as necessary) for a global maximum.

2. Define addition and scalar multiplication pointwise; that is, for any $x(t)$ and $y(t) \in C_{[a,b]}$, define $(x + y)(t) \equiv x(t) + y(t)$ and $(\alpha x)(t) \equiv \alpha x(t)$. The zero element is $x(t) \equiv 0$ for all t and $(-x)(t) \equiv -x(t)$.

3. With this norm, $C_{[a,b]}$ is a Banach space. We may recall that the **Banach space** is defined as a normed linear space which is "complete" as a metric space induced by the norm. A metric space is called **complete** if every Cauchy sequence is convergent. In general, C_X, the set of all bounded continuous real-valued functions on a topological space X, is a Banach space with the norm $\| x \| \equiv \sup |x(t)|$. Convergence of a sequence $\{x^q\}$ with respect to this norm is a "uniform convergence." The sequence $\{x^q\}$ is said to **converge to x_0 uniformly** if for any $\epsilon > 0$ there exists a $\bar{q}$ such that $q \geq \bar{q}$ implies $|x^q(t) - x_0(t)| < \epsilon$. It is crucial that $\bar{q}$ does not depend on t. If $\bar{q}$ depends on t, then we have a **pointwise convergence**. That the space C_X is complete amounts to the fact that $x^q \to x_0$ (uniformly) and $x^q \in C_X$ for each q implies $x_0 \in C_X$. The norm in the above, $\|x\| \equiv \sup |x(t)|$, is often called the **uniform norm**.

4. Clearly the definitions of differentiability and differentials depend on the choice of the norm. However, as remarked earlier (Chapter 1, Section C), the choice of the norm really does not matter in *finite* dimensional spaces; that is, if J is differentiable at x^0 in one norm, then J is differentiable at x^0 in any other norm and the differentials at x^0 under any norm are the same.

5. If ϕ is continuous at x^0 with respect to x, J is said to be **continuously differentiable at** x^0. If J is continuously differentiable at each x in X, J is said to be **continuously differentiable in** X.

6. If the second partial derivatives of f in y (denoted by f_{yy}) exist, then we have, by the well-known Taylor theorem, $r(t, y, k) = \frac{1}{2}\Sigma_{i,j}f_{yy}(t, y + \theta k)k_i k_j$, for some θ, $0 < \theta < 1$. For the Taylor theorem, see any standard textbook on advanced calculus.

REFERENCES

1. Bliss, G. A., *Lectures on the Calculus of Variations*, Chicago, Ill., University of Chicago Press, 1946.

2. Canon, M., Cullum, C., and Polak, E., "Constrained Maximization Problem in Finite-Dimensional Spaces," *Journal of SIAM Control*, Vol. 4, no. 3, 1966.

3. Gelfand, I. M., and Fomin, S. V., *Calculus of Variations*, Englewood Cliffs, N.J., Prentice-Hall, 1963 (tr. from Russian).

4. Hestenes, M. R., *Calculus of Variations and Optimal Control Theory*, New York, Wiley, 1966.

5. Hurwicz, L., "Programming in Linear Spaces," in *Studies in Linear and Nonlinear Programming*, ed. by Arrow, Hurwicz, and Uzawa, Stanford, Calif., Stanford University Press, 1958.

6. ———, "Programming Involving Infinitely Many Variables and Constraints," in *Activity Analysis in the Theory of Growth and Planning*, ed. by Malinvaud and Bacharach, London, Macmillan, 1967.

7. Kolmogorov, A. N., and Fomin, S. V., *Elements of the Theory of Functions and Functional Analysis*, Vol. I, Rochester, N.Y., Grayrock, 1957 [tr. from 1st (1954) Russian ed.].

8. Pontryagin, L. S., Boltyanskii, V. G., Gamkrelidze, R. V., and Mishchenko, E. R., *The Mathematical Theory of Optimal Processes*, New York, Interscience, 1962 [tr. from Russian (1961) ed.].

9. Ritter, K., "Duality for Nonlinear Programming in a Banach Space," *SIAM Journal of Applied Mathematics*, vol. 15, no. 2, March 1967.

10. Shilov, G. Y., *Mathematical Analysis*, Oxford, Pergamon Press, 1965, esp. chap. III (tr. from Russian).

11. Takayama, A., "On the Structure of the Optimal Growth Problem," *Krannert Institute Paper*, No. 178, Purdue University, June 1967.

Section C

A DIGRESSION: THE NEO-CLASSICAL AGGREGATE GROWTH MODEL

In the next section we treat the problem of optimal growth of an aggregative economy. We will argue that we can consider the problem as a straightforward application of the calculus of variations. However, before we turn to this problem, a short summary of the discussion on the aggregate growth model is probably useful and hence we digress here from our main topic to do the summary work. Although this section will serve as an introduction to modern growth theory, it has nothing to do with the calculus of variations, so that those readers who are familiar with this much of growth theory may, without too much difficulty, skip this section.[1]

Let us suppose that the economy can be characterized by one sector, which produces "national product," Y. Let us suppose that this is produced by two factors, labor (L) and capital (K), with the following production function

$$(1) \qquad Y_t = F(L_t, K_t)$$

where t denotes time. Denoting consumption by X_t and investment by I_t, equilibrium in the output market (output $Y_t =$ the demand for the output) is described by

$$(2) \qquad Y_t = X_t + I_t$$

Assuming that the amount of depreciation of capital at each instant of time is a constant proportion (μ) of the existing stock of capital,[2] the amount of gross investment must be equal to $\dot{K}_t + \mu K_t$, where $\dot{K}_t \equiv dK_t/dt$. That is,

$$(3) \qquad \dot{K}_t + \mu K_t = I_t$$

Assume that labor grows at a constant rate n, so that we have

$$(4) \qquad L_t = L_0 e^{nt}$$

where L_0 is the amount of labor available at $t = 0$. So far, there are four equations above but there are five variables, L_t, K_t, Y_t, I_t, X_t, excluding time t. Hence by adding one more equation we can "close" the model; that is, if these five equations are somewhat "nice," we should be able to solve for these five variables with respect to t. The fifth equation which can be used to close the model is the equation which describes the consumption behavior. A common behavioral assumption here is that the amount of consumption is a constant fraction of net income.

(5) $$X_t = (1 - s)(Y_t - \mu K_t)$$

Here s is a constant, a fraction between 0 and 1, called the **average propensity to save** and $(1 - s)$ is called the **average propensity to consume**. The usual justification for this is the famous empirical observation due to Simon Kuznets for U.S. data.[3] The saving behavior implied by (5) is called the **proportional saving behavior**.

The above model is quite well known in the literature, but the following two important remarks are sometimes forgotten.

(i) In equation (1), L_t denotes the amount of labor input and in equation (4), L_t denotes the total amount of labor available in the economy. Hence the fact that the same notation L_t is used in those two equations means that full employment of labor is assumed. Similarly, K_t in equation (1) denotes the amount of capital input and K_t in equation (3) is the amount of the total stock of capital available in the economy. Hence the fact that the same notation K_t is used in these two equations means that full employment of capital is assumed. It is true that the economy can deviate from such a full employment state from time to time. But if we are interested in the long-run behavior of the economy, we might as well consider such unemployment states as "short-run" phenomena and abstract our model from them (at least as a first approximation).

(ii) Equation (1) describes the equilibrium relation in the output market. Nothing is mentioned about how this equilibrium can be achieved. Typically, such an equilibrium can be achieved through flexibility of certain price variables such as the price of output (vis-à-vis money) and/or the rate of interest. A full consideration of this mechanism involves the consideration of other markets such as the money market. The above model is abstracted from this consideration. This abstraction parallels the previous assumption of full employment where the mechanism of how full employment of labor and capital can be achieved is not considered. In the model, the full employment equilibrium in the output market is maintained through adjustments in investment I_t. That is, investment is assumed to be completely "passive"; the amount of I_t is automatically adjusted to the level just equal to the amount of saving.

In order to analyze the properties of the model, we have to make some preliminary comments about the production function. Following a standard convention, we assume that F is defined on the nonnegative orthant of R^2 and that it exhibits constant returns to scale with diminishing returns with respect to each factor. That F exhibits constant returns to scale means $F(\alpha L_t, \alpha K_t) = \alpha F(L_t, K_t)$ for any positive real number α. That F exhibits diminishing returns with respect to each factor can be described as (assuming that F is twice differentiable) $\partial^2 F/\partial L_t^2 < 0$ and $\partial^2 F/\partial K_t^2 < 0$ for all values of L_t and K_t in the domain. This means that MPP_L, the marginal physical product of labor ($\partial F/\partial L_t$), decreases as L_t increases and that MPP_K, the marginal physical product of capital ($\partial F/\partial K_t$), decreases as K_t increases. The well-known example of such a production function is the Cobb-Douglas function, $F(L_t, K_t) = L_t^{1-\alpha} K_t^\alpha, 0 < \alpha < 1$.

From the assumption of constant returns to scale on F, for $L_t > 0$ we can rewrite equation (1) as

$$Y_t = L_t F(1, \frac{K_t}{L_t}) = L_t f(k_t), \text{ where } k_t \equiv \frac{K_t}{L_t} \text{ and } f(k_t) \equiv F(1, \frac{K_t}{L_t})$$

In other words,

(6) $$y_t = f(k_t), \text{ where } y_t \equiv \frac{Y_t}{L_t}$$

Henceforth we will assume $L > 0$ always (that is, labor is indispensable for production). The function f is a real-valued differentiable function defined on the half real line $[0, \infty)$.

We can prove the following two lemmas, both of which are important in aggregate growth theory, fairly easily: (for the sake of notational simplicity, we omit the subscript t in these two lemmas.)

Lemma 5.C.1: $MPP_L = f(k) - k f'(k), \text{ and } MPP_K = f'(k)$.

PROOF: $MPP_L \equiv \partial F/\partial L = \partial [Lf(k)]/\partial L = f(k) + Lf'(k)(-K/L^2) = f(k) - kf'(k)$. $MPP_K \equiv \partial F/\partial K = \partial [Lf(k)]/\partial K = Lf'(k)(1/L) = f'(k)$.

(Q.E.D.)

Lemma 5.C.2:   Let $L > 0$, $K > 0$. Then $\partial^2 F/\partial L^2 < 0$ for all $L > 0$, $K > 0$ if and only if $f''(k) < 0$ for all $k > 0$, and $\partial^2 F/\partial K^2 < 0$ for all $L > 0$, $K > 0$ if and only if $f''(k) <$ for all $k > 0$.

PROOF: We use Lemma 5.C.1.

$$\frac{\partial^2 F}{\partial L^2} = \frac{\partial}{\partial L} [f(k) - kf'(k)] = f'(k)\left(\frac{-K}{L^2}\right) - \left(\frac{-K}{L^2}\right)f'(k) - kf''(k)\left(\frac{-K}{L^2}\right)$$

$$= k^2 f''(k)\frac{1}{L}$$

From this the first statement of the lemma follows immediately. Also

$$\frac{\partial^2 F}{\partial K^2} - \frac{\partial}{\partial K}[f'(k)] = f''(k)\frac{1}{L}$$

From this the second statement of the lemma follows immediately.

(Q.E.D.)

A corollary of Lemma 5.C.1 is that if $f'(k) > 0$ for all $k \geq 0$, then the marginal physical product of capital is always positive. Respectively, $f'(0)$ and $f''(0)$ denote the right-hand derivative of f and f' at 0. The production function with constant

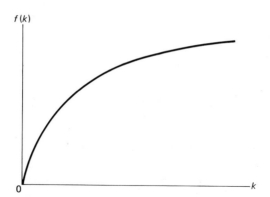

Figure 5.3.   An Illustration of Production Function.

returns to scale and diminishing returns with respect to each factor is illustrated in Figure 5.3. The reader should note that both (i) $f'(k) > 0$ for all $k \geq 0$ and (ii) $f''(k) < 0$ for all $k \geq 0$ are satisfied in the diagram. Note also that $f(0) = 0$, that is, that capital is indispensable for production, is assumed in the diagram.

The next task is to simplify the above set of equations. From equations (1), (2), and (3), we can immediately obtain

$$F(L_t, K_t) = X_t + (\dot{K}_t + \mu K_t)$$

Dividing both sides of the equation by $L_t(> 0)$ and writing $x_t \equiv X_t/L_t$, we obtain

(7)
$$f(k_t) = x_t + \frac{\dot{K}_t}{L_t} + \mu k_t$$

But

$$\dot{k}_t = \frac{\dot{K}_t}{L_t} - \frac{\dot{L}_t}{L_t} k_t$$

Since equation (4) implies $\dot{L}_t/L_t = n$, we obtain

$$\frac{\dot{K}_t}{L_t} = \dot{k}_t + n k_t$$

Combining this equation with (7), we obtain

(8)
$$\dot{k}_t = f(k_t) - \lambda k_t - x_t, \text{ where } \lambda \equiv n + \mu$$

This is the **fundamental equation** of the (neo-classical) aggregate growth model.

Definition: The time path (k_t, x_t) is called a **(neo-classical aggregate) feasible (growth) path**, if it satisfies equation (8) and $k_t \geq 0$, $x_t \geq 0$. If *in addition* it satisfies the prescribed initial conditions k_0 and x_0, then it is called the **attainable path** with respect to k_0 and x_0.

> REMARK: It should be clear that any path $(L_t, K_t, Y_t, X_t, I_t)$ which satisfies equations (1), (2), (3), and (4) can be completely described by the path (k_t, x_t) which satisfies equation (8). This is because (8) is obtained from (1), (2), (3), and (4), and from any path (k_t, x_t) which satisfies equation (8) we can obtain a path $(L_t, K_t, Y_t, X_t, I_t)$ which satisfies equations (1), (2), (3), and (4).

Clearly there are many attainable paths starting from the same point (k_0, x_0). This is due to the fact that there are two "unknowns" in equation (8). We can close the model by specifying the behavior of consumption. Robert Solow [15], following Harrod and Domar, adopted the consumption behavior as described in equation (5). By dividing both sides of (5) by L_t and referring to (6), we obtain

$$(9) \qquad x_t = (1 - s) \left[f(k_t) - \mu k_t \right]$$

Hence combining (9) and (8), we have

$$(10) \qquad \dot{k}_t = sf(k_t) - \lambda^* k_t, \qquad \text{where } \lambda^* \equiv n + s\mu$$

We now impose the following assumptions

(A-1) $f'(k) > 0$ and $f''(k) < 0$ for all $k \geq 0$.
(A-2) $f(0) = 0$.
(A-3) $f'(0)$ is "sufficiently" large or, more specifically, $f'(0) > \lambda^*/s$.
(A-4) $f'(\infty)$ is "sufficiently" small or, more specifically, $f'(\infty) < \lambda^*/s$.
(A-5) $0 < s \leq 1$.

Assumptions (A-3) and (A-4) are often written in a stronger form as

(A-3') $f'(0) = \infty$.
(A-4') $f'(\infty) = 0$.

We are now ready to state and prove the theorem due to Solow [15].[4]

Theorem 5.C.1 (Solow):   *Under assumptions (A-1) to (A-5), there exists a feasible path (k_s, x_s), which is unique, where k_s and x_s are some positive constants, such that any attainable growth path with the proportional saving behavior converges monotonically to it (that is, $k_t \to k_s$ and $x_t \to x_s$ monotonically) as $t \to \infty$, regardless of the initial value of $k_0 > 0$, where k_s and x_s are determined by $sf(k_s) = \lambda^* k_s$ and $x_s \equiv (1 - s)\left[f(k_s) - \mu k_s \right]$.*

> PROOF: Under assumptions (A-1) to (A-5), we can have the situation as illustrated in Figure 5.4. It is important to note that assumptions (A-1) to (A-5) guarantee the unique intersection of the λ^*k-line (from below) with the $sf(k)$-curve at a positive value of k, k_s, as illustrated in Figure 5.4, which

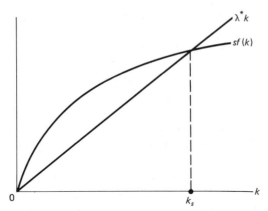

Figure 5.4.　An Illustration of the Proof of Solow's Theorem.

proves the existence and the uniqueness of the path (k_s, x_s) with $k_s > 0$ and $x_s > 0$. The rest of the proof is also easy. As is clear from Figure 5.4, $k_t \gtreqless k_s$ according to whether $sf(k_t) \lesseqgtr \lambda^* k_t$. But equation (10) states that $\dot{k}_t \lesseqgtr 0$ according to whether $sf(k_t) \lesseqgtr \lambda^* k_t$. Hence $\dot{k}_t \lesseqgtr 0$ according to whether $k_t \gtreqless k_s$. In other words, if $k_t > k_s$, then $\dot{k}_t < 0$ so that k_t decreases over time. If $k_t < k_s$, then $\dot{k} > 0$ so that k_t increases over time. And if $k_t = k_s$, then $\dot{k}_t = 0$ so that k_t stays at k_s.　　　　　　　　　　　　　　　　　　　　　　　　(Q.E.D.)

REMARK:　Starting from k_0, what will be the amount of time required to reach a certain prescribed value k^*? To find this, note

$$t(k^*) \equiv \int_{k0}^{k^*} \frac{dt}{dk}\, dk = \int_{k0}^{k^*} \frac{1}{\dot{k}}\, dk = \int_{k0}^{k^*} \frac{1}{sf(k) - \lambda^* k}\, dk$$

Recall that

$$sf(k) - \lambda^* k \begin{cases} > 0 \text{ if } k < k_s \\ < 0 \text{ if } k > k_s \end{cases}$$

Theorem 5.C.1 establishes that k approaches k_s monotonically. Hence $t(k^*)$ is meaningful only when k^* is such that $k_0 \le k^* \le k_s$ or $k_s \le k^* \le k_0$.[5] Let $k_0 \ne k_s$. The question is: What is the amount of time necessary to reach k_s when $k_s \ne k_0$? This can be resolved by considering the two cases $k_0 < k_s$ and $k_0 > k_s$. In either of these two cases it is elementary to see that

$$\lim_{k^* \to k_s} t(k^*) = \infty$$

since $sf(k^*) \to \lambda^* k^*$ as $k^* \to k_s$. In other words, it takes an infinite amount of time to reach the path (k_s, x_s).[6]

REMARK: As was seen in the proof, (A-1) to (A-5) are used to guarantee the existence and the uniqueness of a positive k_s, that is, the existence and uniqueness of a path (k_s, x_s) with $k_s > 0$ and $x_s > 0$. The reader can easily think of many alternative sets of assumptions which guarantee the existence and the uniqueness of a positive k_s.[7] This path (k_s, x_s) may be referred to as **Solow's path**. Note that in Solow's path, labor, L_t, and capital, K_t, grow at the same rate n (because $K_t/L_t = $ constant k_s), and Y_t and X_t also grow at this rate n [because $f(k_s)$ and $(1 - s)f(k_s)$ are constant]. Investment I_t also grows at this rate because of equation (2). Hence the above theorem establishes that the path of $(L_t, K_t, Y_t, X_t, I_t)$ approaches a "balanced growth" path in which these variables all grow at the same rate as time extends without limit, regardless of the initial value of these variables. This global stability theorem was not quite established in Solow's original paper [15]. A further scrutiny and proof of this theorem with an explicit recognition of key assumptions is due to Okamoto and Inada [10].

REMARK: If $F(L, K) = L^{1-\alpha}K^\alpha$, $0 < \alpha < 1$ (the Cobb-Douglas case), for example, then $f(k) = k^\alpha$. Solow's path requires that $sf(k_s) = \lambda^* k_s$, or $k_s = (s/\lambda^*)^{1/(1-\alpha)}$

REMARK: Solow's path may be illustrated as a ray from the origin with its slope equal to k_s, as illustrated in Figure 5.5. Note, however, that k_t approaching k_s as $t \to \infty$ does not guarantee that the (L_t, K_t) configuration in the L-K-plane asymptotically converges to the k_s-ray (as illustrated by the dotted line in Figure 5.5). In fact, such an asymptotic convergence is impossible for the present model, as is shown by Deardorf [3]. Let δ_t be the vertical distance of the (L_t, K_t) path from the k_s-ray; that is, $\delta_t \equiv (k_s - k_t)L_t$. Deardorf argues that $\delta_t \to 0$ is impossible and that $\delta_t \to \infty$ is more plausible.

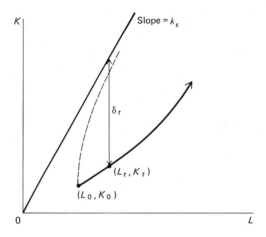

Figure 5.5. An Illustration of Solow's Theorem.

One basic premise in Solow's theorem is that consumption is a constant proportion of income. This is a rather awkward assumption, for it means that the overall (average) propensity to save is constant regardless of income distribution between the two factors. Empirical evidence may not mean too much in this connection, for it is an interplay of various other factors such as technological progress, international trade, and factor movements. An alternative assumption on consumption behavior is the one adopted by the classical economists, that is, the assumption that the workers save nothing and the capitalists save a certain constant fraction of their gross income. We call this the **classical saving behavior**. The capitalists' income can be described by $(MPP_k)K$, which, from Lemma 5.C.1, is equal to $f'(k)K$. Letting $\bar{s}$ be the capitalists' average propensity to save, where $0 < \bar{s} < 1$, the following equation now replaces equation (5).

(11) $$\bar{s}f'(k_t)K_t = Y_t - X_t$$

Note that X consists of consumption by capitalists and by workers, so that

(12) $$X_t = (1 - \bar{s})f'(k_t)K_t + [f(k_t) - k_t f'(k_t)]L_t$$

We can check easily that the X_t thus obtained satisfies (11) with $Y_t = L_t f(k_t)$. By dividing both sides of (11) by L_t, we obtain

$$\bar{s}f'(k_t)k_t = f(k_t) - x_t$$

Combining this equation with the fundamental equation (8), we obtain (assuming $k_t > 0$)

(13) $$\frac{\dot{k}_t}{k_t} = \bar{s}f'(k_t) - \lambda, \quad \text{where } \lambda = n + \mu$$

Under (A-1), (A-3'), and (A-4'), we can draw Figure 5.6, from which we can immediately assert the existence and the uniqueness of k_c such that $\bar{s}f'(k_c) = \lambda$

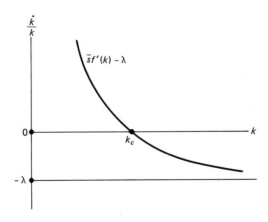

Figure 5.6.   An Illustration of Equation (13).

and $k_c > 0$. Moreover, the time path of k_t is quite apparent from Figure 5.6. Thus we can easily determine $\dot{k}_t \gtreqless 0$ according to whether $k_t \lesseqgtr k_c$. As k_t approaches k_c, x_t approaches x_c, where x_c can easily be obtained from (12), that is,

$$x_c = (1 - \bar{s})f'(k_c)k_c + [f(k_c) - k_c f'(k_c)]$$

or

(14) $$x_c = f(k_c) - \bar{s}f'(k_c)k_c$$

Hence we have established the following theorem.

Theorem 5.C.2: *Under assumptions (A-1), (A-3'), and (A-4') with the classical saving behavior, there exists a unique feasible path (k_c, x_c) with $k_c > 0$ and $x_c > 0$, such that any attainable path (k_t, x_t) approaches it monotonically as $t \to \infty$ regardless of the initial value of k_0, where k_c and x_c are respectively determined by $\bar{s}f'(k_c) = \lambda$ and equation (14).*

> REMARK: We may call (k_c, x_c) the **classical path**. Theorem 5.C.2 establishes global stability for the classical path, which is again a balanced growth path of $(L_t, K_t, Y_t, X_t, I_t)$. It can also be shown that the time required to reach the classical path is infinity. Hence, like Solow's theorem, the above theorem establishes "asymptotic" stability for the classical path. Note that the above method of proof can also be used to prove Solow's theorem. For this, simply divide (10) by k_t and observe that we obtain an equation similar to (13). Such a proof is used in Okamoto and Inada [10].

The above two theorems lead us to focus our attention on balanced growth paths.

Definition: A neo-classical feasible path (k_t, x_t) is called a **golden age path**[8] if k_t and x_t are both constant over time.

> REMARK: In other words, the set of all the golden age paths is the set of all the balanced growth paths of $(L_t, K_t, Y_t, X_t, I_t)$ which satisfy equations (1) to (4).

Since k_t and x_t are constant in the golden age paths, we write them simply as k and x, respectively. Note that $\dot{k} = 0$ in the golden age paths. Hence from equation (8), we obtain

(15) $$x = f(k) - \lambda k$$

Then under assumptions (A-1), (A-2), (A-3'), and (A-4'), the locus of the (k, x)'s which satisfy equation (15) can be illustrated by Figure 5.7. It is clear from Figure 5.7 that there exists a unique positive value of k which maximizes x globally subject

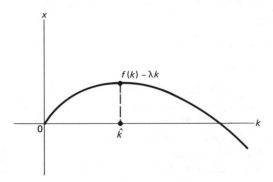

Figure 5.7.   An Illustration of Equation (15).

to (15). We denote it by $\hat{k}$. Formally we obtain this by maximizing $[f(k) - \lambda k]$ with respect to k. The first-order condition can be obtained as

$$\frac{d}{dk}[f(k) - \lambda k] = 0$$

or

(16) $$f'(k) = \lambda$$

There exists, in view of (A-1), only one value of k which satisfies (16), and $\hat{k}$ is this value. Note that (A-1) guarantees the strict concavity of f and hence of $[f(k) - \lambda k]$. Thus (16) gives a necessary and sufficient condition for the unique global maximum (Theorem 1.C.7). Even without such a remark this may be obvious from Figure 5.7. We now define a very important concept.

Definition: A golden age path which maximizes per capita consumption x at every instant of time is called the **golden rule path**.[9]

In view of this definition, the above consideration has really established the theorem which can be stated as follows.

Theorem 5.C.3:   *Under assumptions (A-1), (A-2), (A-3'), and (A-4'), there exists a unique golden rule path, $(\hat{k}, \hat{x})$, where $\hat{k}$ and $\hat{x}$ are respectively defined by $f'(\hat{k}) = \lambda$ and $\hat{x} \equiv f(\hat{k}) - \lambda \hat{k}$.*

REMARK: Thus in the golden rule path the marginal productivity of capital $f'(\hat{k})$ is equal to the rate of population growth (n) plus the rate of depreciation (μ). The above theorem was established by quite a number of different economists. See Phelps [11], Robinson [14], Swan [17], von Weizsäcker [20], Allais [1], and Desrousseaux [4].

REMARK: It is easy to see that (A-3′) in the theorem can be relaxed to
(**A-3″**) $f'(0) > \lambda$.

Also assumption (A-4′) can be relaxed to
(**A-4″**) $f'(\infty) < \lambda$.

REMARK: It is important to recall that the golden rule path is that path which maximizes per capita consumption in the set of all the golden age paths (that is, balanced growth paths). It disregards the historically given value of k_0 (or L_0 and K_0). In other words, there is no guarantee that the historically given value of k_0 is actually on the golden rule path. This seriously undermines the usefulness of this concept. However, as we shall see in the next section, we can assert that, under a certain situation, an "optimal" path which starts from an arbitrary given k_0 converges to the golden rule path as time extends without limit. From this theorem, the concept of the golden rule path becomes important.

FOOTNOTES

1. A complete survey of macro growth theory is not attempted here. For such an attempt, see, for example, Hahn and Matthews [7].
2. This implies, of course, that Y is *gross* national product and I is *gross* investment. If instead we take Y as net national product, then we can put $\mu = 0$. Then I is taken as net investment. This convention is adopted by Solow [15] and others.
3. The theoretical justification for this from a "long-run" standpoint by Deusenberry is well known. See J. Deusenberry, *Income, Saving and the Theory of Consumer Behavior*, Cambridge, Mass., Harvard University Press, 1949.
4. As remarked in footnote 2, Solow has no explicit consideration of depreciation. A similar model and a similar theorem were also obtained by Swan [16], although he assumed that the production function is of the Cobb-Douglas form. Tobin [19] obtained a similar but more general model that incorporates money. But he did not obtain the stability theorem like Theorem 5.C.1.
5. In other words, we preclude such cases as $k^* < k_0 < k_s$ and $k_s < k_0 < k^*$.
6. It may be of some interest to investigate what is the time required for the actual path to come "close enough" to the path (k_s, x_s). This clearly depends on such parameters as s, n, μ, and k_0. There was a debate between R. Sato and K. Sato on this point. See, for example, K. Sato, "On the Adjustment Time in Neo-Classical Growth Models," *Review of Economic Studies*, XXXIII, July 1966.
7. For example, we can have the case in which the $f(k)$-curve is mound-shaped, that is, $f'(k) < 0$ for sufficiently large k (capital satiation). The essential point here is that the $sf(k)$-curve intersects the $\lambda^* k$-line from the "left" with only one point of intersection. If the rate of population growth n (hence λ^*) is not constant but depends on per capita income, and thus is a function of k, we can have multiple equilibria with a mixture of stable and unstable ones. This has been studied by such economists as R. R. Nelson, H. Leibenstein, J. Buttrick, and J. Niehans. This is used as a rationale for the "big-push" thesis. However, we may question why $n (= \dot{L}/L)$ rather than L is a function of y.

8. The name is used to emphasize its mythological character. See J. Robinson, *The Accumulation of Capital*, 2nd. ed., London, Macmillan, 1965, p. 99.

9. For the Cobb-Douglas case, that is, $f(k) = k^{\alpha}, 0 < \alpha < 1$, the value of k in the golden rule path is easily obtained as $\hat{k} = (\alpha/\lambda)^{1/(1-\alpha)}$. Note that, for this case, $\hat{k} \gtreqless k_s$ according to whether $\alpha \gtreqless s$, if $\lambda = \lambda^*$.

REFERENCES

1. Allais, M., "The Influence of the Capital-Output Ratio on Real National Income," *Econometrica*, 30, October 1962.

2. Champernowne, D. G., "Some Implications of Golden Age Conditions When Savings Equal Profits," *Review of Economic Studies*, XXIX, June 1962.

3. Deardorf, A. V., "Growth Path in the Solow Neoclassical Growth Model," *Quarterly Journal of Economics*, LXXXIV, February 1970.

4. Desrousseaux, J., "Expansion table et taux d'interet optimal," *Annales de Mines*, November 1961.

5. Domar, E. D., *Essays in the Theory of Growth*, London, Oxford University Press, 1957.

6. Haavelmo, T., *A Study in the Theory of Investment*, Chicago, Ill., University of Chicago Press, 1960.

7. Hahn, F. H., and Matthews, R. C. O., "The Theory of Economic Growth: A Survey," *Economic Journal*, LXXIV, December 1964.

8. Harrod, R. F., "Second Essay in Dynamic Theory," *Economic Journal*, LXX, June 1960.

9. Meade, J. E., *A Neo-classical Theory of Economic Growth*, London, George Allen and Unwin, 2nd. ed., 1962 (1st. ed. 1961).

10. Okamoto, T., and Inada, K., "A Note on the Theory of Economic Growth," *Quarterly Journal of Economics*, LXXVI, August 1962.

11. Phelps, E. S., "The Golden Rule of Accumulation: A Fable for Growthmen," *American Economic Review*, LI, September 1961.

12. ———, "Second Essay on the Golden Rule of Accumulation," *American Economic Review*, LV, September 1965.

13. ———, *Golden Rules of Economic Growth*, New York, W.W. Norton, 1966.

14. Robinson, J., "A Neo-Classical Theorem," *Review of Economic Studies*, XXIX, June 1962.

15. Solow, R. M., "A Contribution to the Theory of Economic Growth," *Quarterly Journal of Economics*, LXX, February 1956.

16. Swan, T. W., "Economic Growth and Capital Accumulation," *Economic Record*, XXXII, November 1956.

17. ———, "Growth Models of Golden Ages and Production Functions," in *Economic Development with Special Reference to East Asia, Proceedings of International Economic Conference*, ed. by Barrill, London, Macmillan, 1963.

18. Takayama, A., "Per Capita Consumption and Growth: A Further Analysis," *Western Economic Journal*, V, March 1967.

19. Tobin, J., "A Dynamic Aggregative Model," *Journal of Political Economy*, LXIII, April 1955.

20. von Weizsäcker, C. C., *Wachstum, Zins und Optimale Investitionsquote*, Basel, Kyklos-Verlag, 1962.

Section D

THE STRUCTURE OF THE OPTIMAL GROWTH PROBLEM FOR AN AGGREGATE ECONOMY[1]

a. INTRODUCTION

In the previous section we discussed an aggregate model of economic growth. The model we considered can be described by the following three equations:

$$(1) \qquad Y_t = F(L_t, K_t)$$

$$(2) \qquad \dot{K}_t + \mu K_t = Y_t - X_t$$

$$(3) \qquad \frac{\dot{L}_t}{L_t} = n$$

This economy produces a single output, Y, using two inputs, labor (L) and capital (K); X denotes the amount of consumption. The rate of depreciation is denoted by μ and the subscript t denotes time. In the previous section we observed that, by adding the equation which describes the consumption (or saving) behavior *and* by specifying the initial capital and labor (or the capital:labor ratio k_0 if F is homogenous of degree one), we can "close" the model and thus completely describe the time path of each variable.

In this section we ask a different question. Instead of specifying the consumption behavior, we ask: What is the necessary amount of consumption at each instant time in order to maximize a certain target while satisfying the above three equations (the **feasibility condition**) *and* the prescribed boundary conditions? Clearly such a target must be based on the satisfaction that one can obtain from the stream of consumption. The question thus posed casts a genuine question of choice. If we consume more at present, then we have less saving so that the amount of capital stock in the future will be less compared with the case in which we save more (that is, consume less) at present. This, in turn, implies that we have less output and less consumption (unless we eat up the capital accumulated) in the future compared with the case in which we save more at present. Hence, although we can get more satisfaction at present as we consume more now, we will have less satisfaction in the future. The question is: What is the optimal amount of present consumption? In this verbal presentation of the problem, we implicitly assumed that our time consists of only two periods, present and future. In general, there are more than two periods. But this does not create too much difficulty.

Supposing that we can choose the time path of consumption on a time continuum, we may ask what the optimal time path of consumption is. Let $x_t \equiv X_t/L_t$ be per capita consumption of the economy. One obvious target function which the economy may wish to choose is

(4)
$$I \equiv \int_0^T x_t \, dt$$

where T is the planning horizon. Here the society wishes to maximize the total sum of per capita consumption over time, satisfying the feasibility condition, equations (1) to (3), and the boundary condition (say, k_0 and k_T). In Figure 5.8 we illustrate two types of consumption streams. The α-curve denotes the "thrifty type" of economy, that is, one which chooses less consumption at present or in the immediate future, while the β-curve denotes the "nonthrifty type." The problem here is to compare the area under the α-curve up to the T-line with the area under the β-curve up to the T-line. If the former, for example, has a larger area than the latter, we say that the former is "better" than the latter under the target prescribed in equation (4). Clearly curves such as α and β are not drawn arbitrarily; they must satisfy the "feasibility" prescribed by equations (1), (2), and (3). The optimal program we choose under the prescribed target equation (4) is the one which gives the largest area under the curve up to the T-line.

As alert readers may have already realized, such an optimal program depends on the length of the planning horizon T. If the planning horizon T is longer, the thrifty type of program may eventually be "better" than the nonthrifty type, as it pays off at a later time. However, if T is short enough, the thrifty type of program will not be optimal. Then a question arises as to what should be the length of this planning horizon. Should it be 5 years, 10 years, or longer? This is a rather

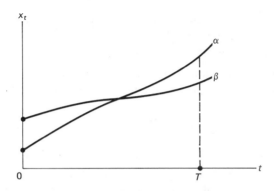

Figure 5.8.   An Illustration of Optimal Consumption Problem.

difficult problem. However, there is one serious objection to a *finite T*, however large *T* may be. What happens after time *T*? If we allow the accumulated capital to be used up, then the optimal program must be such that there is no capital stock left after time *T*. Thus the people in the economy will starve to death after time *T*. Even if we do not allow ourselves to eat up the accumulated capital, one essential difficulty remains: the arbitrariness of the cut-off point. When we decide the size of *T*, we automatically decide to ignore the time after *T*, and such a *T* is arbitrarily chosen for there is no *a priori* criterion by which to choose the size of *T*. The general consensus among economists about this point seems to be to choose *T* = ∞ in order to avoid such an arbitrary cut-off point.

There are, however, some difficulties in the infinite horizon formulation as well. First, as astronomers tell us, our world may cease to exist after some few billions of years (which is still finite!). Second, there is always the problem of uncertainty. In particular, how do we know that our technology (that is, the production function) will be the same for the next hundred or thousand years (which is, incidentally, much shorter than "some few billion years").

One answer is that the optimal program may not be particularly sensitive to what we do a hundred years later but depends more crucially on what we do in the neighborhood of the present. As Koopmans [22] discovered, all the "eligible" paths in his formulation closely approach some fixed balanced growth path; hence they all look the same for a large time horizon. In other words, the infinite horizon formulation, contrary to some people's expectation, may really describe the immediate future more than it does the infinite future. In this connection, the following analogy due to Gale ([14], p. 2) may be useful.

> One is guiding a ship on a long journey by keeping it lined up with a point on the horizon even though one knows that long before that point is reached the weather will change (but in an unpredictable way) and it will be necessary to pick up a new course with a new reference point, again on the horizon rather than just a short distance ahead.

Another justification simply admits that the infinite horizon formulation is more convenient and revealing. On this point, Arrow ([1], p. 92) writes

> As elsewhere in mathematical approximation to the real world, it is frequently more convenient and more revealing to proceed to the limit to make a mathematical infinity in the model correspond to the vast futurity of the real world.

So much for the discussion of the size of *T*. The next question is to find a more sensible target function than the one described in equation (4). One answer is

$$(5) \qquad\qquad J_T \equiv \int_0^T u(x_t)e^{-\rho t}dt$$

where *u* is a utility function associated with the "representative" individual in the society and ρ is the time discount factor. Clearly the target described in (4) is a special case of the one described in (5), where $u(x_t) = x_t$ and $\rho \equiv 0$. In elementary economics, we usually argue that a utility function of the form $u(x_t) = x_t$ is rather unrealistic. Instead, we say that the "marginal utility" is decreasing with an increasing amount of consumption. We now impose such an assumption. In other words, throughout this section, we assume that u is defined on $[0, \infty)$, is twice differentiable, and

(A-1) $\qquad\qquad\qquad u'(x_t) > 0$ and $u''(x_t) < 0 \qquad$ for all $x_t \geqq 0$

Under this assumption, $u(x_t)$ is a strictly monotone and strictly concave function. [Here $u'(0)$ and $u''(0)$, respectively, refer to the right-hand derivative of u and u' at $x = 0$.]

The question of discounting the future (that is, $\rho > 0$) is not an easy one. Frank Ramsey, who first studied the optimal saving problem systematically, argued that ρ should be equal to zero, for it is "unethical" to discount the utility of our descendants compared to the utility of ourselves. The welfare of different generations should be equally weighted. However, Koopmans [21] and Koopmans, Diamond, and Williamson [25] have discovered that a utility function of all consumption paths, which at the same time exhibits time neutrality and satisfies other reasonable postulates on utility functions, does not exist. Since this question has not been settled yet, we will not discuss it further. For the time being, we assume that ρ is constant and nonnegative.

For the infinite horizon formulation, equation (5) is rewritten as

(6) $$J \equiv \int_0^\infty u(x_t) e^{-\rho t} dt$$

Thus our problem is now to find the time path of x_t which maximizes J subject to the feasibility conditions (1), (2), and (3) with the prescribed value of the initial capital-labor ratio k_0 (assuming constant returns to scale) and the nonnegativity of each variable.

The question thus formulated, however, casts another problem immediately. That is, how can we guarantee that J converges? If, for some feasible paths with a prescribed k_0, the integral J does not converge (say, goes to ∞), the above formulation becomes meaningless.[2] This question of convergence is especially acute when $\rho = 0$. Ramsey [35] solved this question beautifully by constructing some reference path, say, $\hat{u}$, and converting the problem to one of maximizing

(7) $$J_R \equiv \int_0^\infty [u(x_t) - \hat{u}] \, dt$$

Note that both J and J_R are bounded from below for the optimal path under the monotonicity of the utility function u, assuming that the economy is "productive" in the sense that it allows a strictly positive path of consumption starting from a given k_0. When $\rho > 0$, the easiest way to guarantee the convergence of J is simply to assume that the function u is bounded from above (that is, satiation). (See also footnotes 12 and 16.)

So much for the discussion of the formulation of the problem. We now proceed to the solution of the problem thus formulated. This question of the optimal saving problem was first formulated and solved to a certain extent by Ramsey in 1928 [35]. Then the problem was almost forgotten for some time probably as a result of the Great Depression and the war. Then in the 1950s there was a revival of the problem with enthusiasm and it was solved by Koopmans [22] and Cass [6] in the early 1960s.[3] Cass formulated the problem in terms of Pontryagin's maximum principle, reflecting the fashion during the time the paper was written. (We shall take up such a formulation in Chapter 8.) As we will see in this section, we really do not need this new technique, the full understanding of which requires a considerable mathematical maturity. Instead, we will use only the knowledge of the elementary theory of the calculus of variations that we discussed in Section A. Koopmans' paper [22], although masterly and very penetrating, is long, consisting of sixty-three printed pages, and his proofs are sometimes difficult. This difficulty is partly the result of his thorough and important examination of the "eligibility" conditions for the "feasible path."

We can simplify the treatment considerably if we realize the fact that the whole problem is a straightforward application of the elementary part of the classical calculus of variations. We will see that the "phase diagram" will be very useful and vital in our analysis. There is one basic difference between his and our approach. Koopmans first eliminates the ineligible paths, then chooses the optimal (eligible) path from the set of eligible (attainable) paths, whereas we first eliminate the paths which do not satisfy the Euler condition as "nonoptimal," and then choose the eligible (optimal) path from the set of the attainable paths that satisfy Euler's condition. In the process of obtaining the set of attainable paths that satisfy Euler's condition, we use the elementary theory of the calculus of variations.

To solve our problem, we first have to simplify the constraint equations (1), (2), and (3). This procedure of simplification has already been discussed in the previous section, assuming that F exhibits constant returns to scale. In short, for $L_t > 0$, equations (1), (2), and (3) are reduced to

$$(8) \qquad \dot{k}_t = f(k_t) - \lambda k_t - x_t$$

where $k_t \equiv K_t/L_t$ (*capital:labor ratio*), $x_t \equiv X_t/L_t$, $f(k_t) \equiv F(L_t, K_t)/L_t$. We call the path (k_t, x_t) the **feasible path** if it satisfies (8). If, in addition, it satisfies the arbitrarily prescribed initial value k_0 and the terminal value k_T, we call it the **attainable path**. When $T \to \infty$, k_T will not be specified. The problem, then, is the following:[4]

$$\text{Maximize: } J_T \equiv \int_0^T u(x_t)e^{-\rho t}dt$$

Subject to: $\dot{k}_t = f(k_t) - \lambda k_t - x_t$, and $k_t \geq 0$, $x_t \geq 0$ for all t

with the prescribed values of $k_0 > 0$ and $k_T \geq 0$.

We first observe that x_t in the target function can be expressed in terms of k_t and $\dot{k}_t$ in view of the constraint equation (8). In other words, the problem may be reformulated as follows:

$$\text{Maximize:} \int_0^T u[f(k_t) - \lambda k_t - \dot{k}_t]e^{-\rho t}\,dt$$

$$\text{Subject to:} \ k_t \geq 0, \ x_t \geq 0 \text{ for all } t$$

with the prescribed values of $k_0 > 0$ and $k_t \geq 0$.

The nonnegativity constraints $k_t \geq 0$, $x_t \geq 0$, do not cause any trouble here. For, as we will see later, the **solution path** obtained by neglecting the nonnegativity condition is in fact in the nonnegative orthant.

Neglecting the nonnegativity condition, we can immediately apply the Euler condition to choose x_t so as to maximize the integral J_T from the set of attainable paths. In other words, our problem is now converted to the calculus of variations problem without the constraint. Thus letting

(9) $$\Phi(t, k_t, \dot{k}_t) \equiv u[f(k_t) - \lambda k_t - \dot{k}_t]e^{-\rho t}$$

we can write Euler's condition as follows:

(10) $$\frac{\partial \Phi}{\partial k_t} = \frac{d}{dt}\left[\frac{\partial \Phi}{\partial \dot{k}_t}\right]$$

where the partial derivatives are evaluated at the optimal path $\hat{k}_t$. For notational simplicity we henceforth omit ($\char`\^$), which denotes the optimal path. Equation (10) gives a necessary condition for k_t to be an optimal path. By utilizing (9), (10) can be computed as

(11) $$\dot{x}_t = \frac{-u'}{u''}[f'(k_t) - (\lambda + \rho)]$$

This is a necessary condition for an optimum. It is also sufficient for a unique optimum, as we proved in Section B (Theorem 5.B.4), if Φ is strictly concave in k_t and $\dot{k}_t$ (as long as T is finite).

Thus we have obtained two equations, (8) and (11). The former describes the feasibility condition and the latter describes the optimality condition. The path (k_t, x_t) which satisfies both equations is called the **feasible Euler path**. By prescribing the values of two boundary conditions k_0 and k_T, we can obtain the solution path of the problem as described.

We now ask the question: What happens to the path (k_t, x_t) which satisfies both feasibility (8) and optimality (11) with the initial condition k_0, when the planning horizon T is sufficiently large (where k_T is no longer fixed)? As we argue later, there can be three such possible types of paths, depending on the initial condition. We argue that two of these three paths create some difficulties for a sufficiently large T. Hence we call the paths in these two classes **noneligible**. The path in the third class does not create such a difficulty and it is called an **eligible**

path. We show that the eligible path which satisfies both feasibility (8) and Euler's condition (11) is such that it monotonically approaches the "modified golden rule path" (whose concept is to be defined later) regardless of the initial k_0 as T increases. It can be shown that the integral J (for $\rho > 0$) or J_R (for $\rho = 0$) converges along such a path. The eligible Euler feasible path thus obtained will be better than any other feasible path starting from the same initial point k_0 for any sufficiently large T. This criterion of choosing the **optimal path** corresponds to the one proposed by von Weizsäcker [52] as the "overtaking criterion."

Finally, one remark about the feasibility condition (8), in particular the shape of $f(k_t)$, should be mentioned. In the neo-classical model as described in the previous section, we supposed a strictly concave shape of f, that is, $f'(k_t) > 0$ and $f''(k_t) < 0$ for all k_t. However, there is one other type of production function that is quite common in the literature of economic growth and development. This production function has the assumption of a constant capital:output ratio[5]. In this case, $F(L_t, K_t)$ has the form

(12) $$Y_t = \frac{1}{\sigma} K_t$$

where σ is a positive constant denoting the capital:output ratio. Notice that labor, L_t, is not explicitly involved in this production function. By dividing both sides by L_t we obtain

(13) $$y_t = \frac{1}{\sigma} k_t, \text{ where } y_t \equiv \frac{Y_t}{L_t}$$

In other words, by identifying $f(k_t)$ with $(1/\sigma)k_t$, we can consider the present case as a special case of the production function considered above.[6] We can use the same conditions (8) and (11), with $f(k_t)$ now identified as $f(k_t) = (1/\sigma)k_t$. Equation (8) can now be rewritten as

(14) $$\dot{k}_t = \frac{1}{\sigma}[1 - \sigma\lambda]k_t - x_t$$

b. THE CASE OF A CONSTANT CAPITAL:OUTPUT RATIO

During the revival period of the optimal growth problem in the 1950s and early 1960s, there were important discussions by Tinbergen [47], [48], Chakravarty [9], Goodwin [15], and others, before we reached the culmination by Koopmans [22] and Cass [6]. They considered the case in which there exists a constant capital:output ratio with a special form of the utility function and a finite planning horizon. Such a case clearly constitutes the simplest possible case in the problem formulated in subsection a. We now will attempt to critically survey the literature during this period, especially [48], [9], and [15]. We will show that the model with a constant capital:output ratio yields a difficulty when the planning horizon is infinite. That is, the optimal path in this case does not exist at all in many cases. Chakravarty [9] considered a finite horizon problem as did Goodwin [15]. There, in terms of numerical examples, he made the very interesting conjecture that the optimal attainable path is "insensitive" with respect to the terminal capital stock k_T and also that it is insensitive with respect to the planning horizon T. We will show that these conjectures are true under a general framework, which will shed some light on a later controversy between Chakravarty and Maneschi.[7] We note that our sensitivity analysis deals with a simple case of Brock's elegant analysis [5]. We point out that, in the Chakravarty-Goodwin case, the optimal program for a sufficiently large T approximates the program in which consumption is kept at the subsistence level forever. The discussion of this subsection will be useful to increase the reader's understanding of the problem involved in the constant capital:output ratio case and of the basic technique employed in the analysis, as well as some of the basic difficulties involved in the optimal growth problem of an aggregate economy.

With these preliminary remarks we now proceed with our analysis. First rewrite the Euler equation, (11), for the case of a fixed capital:output ratio, that is,

$$(15) \qquad \dot{x}_t = -\frac{u'}{u''}\left[\frac{1}{\sigma} - (\lambda + \rho)\right]$$

Since $f(k_t) - \lambda k_t - \dot{k}_t [= (1/\sigma - \lambda)k_t - \dot{k}_t]$ is a linear function in k_t and $\dot{k}_t$ (hence concave) and u is a strictly concave function, the Euler condition, (15), is sufficient for a global optimum as well as necessary (assuming that T is finite). The optimal feasible path is the one which satisfies equations (14) and (15) simultaneously with $k_t \geq 0$ and $x_t \geq 0$. We may replace the condition $x_t \geq 0$ by $x_t \geq \bar{x}$, where $\bar{x}$ is the subsistence level of consumption. We may note that Chakravarty assumes $\bar{x} = 0$.

In the formulation of the problem by Tinbergen, Goodwin, and Chakravarty, the depreciation of capital is not explicit. In our formulation, this amounts to putting $\mu = 0$. Also these three people assumed that there is no time discount for the future consumption so that $\rho = 0$. Tinbergen and Chakravarty in the main assumed that there is no population growth in the economy so that $n = 0$ (thus $\lambda = 0$). Goodwin gives a numerical example of the problem in which he assumes $n = 0.01$ and $\sigma = 4$ (see [15], pp. 773–774). Hence all the treatments of Tinbergen, Chakravarty, and Goodwin can be considered as special cases of the following assumption:

(A-2) $\qquad\qquad\qquad 1 - \sigma(\lambda + \rho) > 0$

The case in which $1 - \sigma(\lambda + \rho) < 0$ can be discussed *mutatis mutandis* so that the analysis for this case can be omitted from our discussion. We may note that if $1 - \sigma(\lambda + \rho) < 0$, then the path constrained by equation (15) requires the economy continuously to reduce per capita consumption (that is, $\dot{x}_t < 0$), since $u' > 0$ and $u'' < 0$ by (A-1). This is an uninteresting case. We may note that (A-2) implies $1 - \sigma\lambda > 0$. If $1 - \sigma\lambda \leq 0$, then, from equation (14), any feasible path (with x_t some positive constant) must undergo a decrease in capital stock and the economy must disappear for a sufficiently large T in order to keep some positive level of consumption. Otherwise, the amount of per capita consumption must become zero and everyone in the society will eventually starve to death. Therefore, the case $(1 - \sigma\lambda \leq 0)$ is uninteresting. Note that (A-2), among others, implies that ρ cannot be too large, and in fact, if we accept $\rho = 0$, (A-2) can easily be accepted as a realistic assumption.

The studies by Tinbergen, Goodwin, and Chakravarty all assume the following specific form of the utility function,[8] which obviously satisfies (A-1), for $x_t > \bar{x}$:

(16) $$u'(x_t) = (x_t - \bar{x})^{-v}, \qquad v > 0$$

or

(17) $\quad u(x_t) = \log(x_t - \bar{x})$ if $v = 1$, and $u(x_t) = \dfrac{1}{1-v}(x_t - \bar{x})^{1-v}$ if $0 < v \neq 1$

Here u is defined for $x_t > \bar{x}$ if $v = 1$ and for $x_t \geq \bar{x}$ for $0 < v < 1$. In (16) and (17), $\bar{x}$ is the subsistence level of consumption. If we suppose $u(x) > 0$ for some value of $x > \bar{x}$, then v cannot be greater than 1. Goodwin assumes that $v = 1$. Tinbergen quotes the figures from Frisch's study of 1931 which, for example, says $v = 0.6$ for American workers ([48], p. 482). The specification of the utility function as above may cause strong opposition from the view point of the cardinality of utility. However, since one of the purposes of this section is to survey the past studies, we want to keep the explicit form of the utility function as defined above.

With the above specification of the utility function, the Euler equation (15) can be rewritten as

(18) $\quad \dot{x}_t = \alpha(x_t - \bar{x})$, where $\alpha \equiv \dfrac{1}{\sigma v}\left[1 - \sigma(\lambda + \rho)\right] > 0$ from (A-2)

The solution of this differential equation can immediately be obtained as

(19) $$x_t = \bar{x} + Ae^t$$

where $\alpha > 0$ from (A-2), and A is a constant determined by the boundary conditions. Equation (14) can now be rewritten as

(20) $\quad \dot{k}_t - \beta k_t = -(\bar{x} + Ae^{\alpha t})$, where $\beta \equiv \dfrac{1}{\sigma}(1 - \sigma\lambda) > 0$ from (A-2)

This is a simple linear differential equation, and its solution can be obtained as

(21) $$k_t = \frac{\bar{x}}{\beta} + (B - At)e^{\beta t}, \text{ if } \alpha = \beta$$

(22) $$k_t = \frac{\bar{x}}{\beta} + \frac{A}{\beta - \alpha}e^{\alpha t} + Be^{\beta t}, \text{ if } \alpha \neq \beta$$

The two constants A and B are to be determined by the boundary conditions. One of them is obviously the initial value of k. We can consider several candidates for the other. Goodwin chooses the terminal growth rate $\dot{Y}_T/Y_T$. Since the capital: output ratio is constant and the rate of labor growth is constant, this amounts to choosing $\dot{k}_T/k_T$.[9] Chakravarty chooses the terminal stock of capital k_T as the other boundary condition. In either case, the specification of the two boundary conditions determines the values of A and B, and hence specifies completely the optimal attainable path of (k_t, x_t). We may note that Goodwin assumes $v = 1$ and $\rho = 0$ so that $\alpha = \beta$, whereas Tinbergen and Chakravarty consider the case in which $v < 1$ and $\rho = 0$ so that $\alpha \neq \beta$. In other words, Goodwin considers a special case of the time path (k_t, x_t) described by equations (20) and (21), while Tinbergen and Chakravarty considered a special case of the path of (k_t, x_t) described by (20) and (22).

To pursue the analysis further, let us assume $\bar{x} = 0$. This amounts to choosing the origin properly and does not constitute a loss of generality. (One may, if he so desires, redefine x_t, k_t by $x_t - \bar{x}$ and $k_t - \bar{x}/\beta$, respectively.) Then (19), (21), and (22) can be rewritten respectively as

(23) $x_t = Ae^{\alpha t}$, regardless of the relative size of α and β

(24) $k_t = (B - At)e^{\beta t}$, when $\alpha = \beta$

(25) $k_t = \dfrac{A}{\beta - \alpha} e^{\alpha t} + Be^{\beta t}$, when $\alpha \neq \beta$

Write the two boundary conditions as

(26) $k_0 = a$ and $k_T = b$, where we assume $a > 0$ and $b \geq 0$

Note that if $a = 0$, then $k_t = 0$ and $x_t = 0$ for all t. We may disregard this uninteresting case. Using (26), we can obtain expressions for A and B as follows:

CASE I: $\alpha = \beta$

(27) $A = \dfrac{a - be^{-\beta T}}{T}$

(28) $B = a$

CASE II: $\alpha \neq \beta$

(29) $A = (\alpha - \beta)\dfrac{ae^{\beta T} - b}{e^{\alpha T} - e^{\beta T}}$

(30) $B = a + \dfrac{A}{\alpha - \beta}$

We may rewrite (29) as follows:

(31) $A = (\alpha - \beta)\dfrac{a - be^{-\beta T}}{e^{(\alpha-\beta)T} - 1}$

We now examine the nonnegativity condition, that is, $k_t \geq 0$, $x_t \geq 0$ for all t. Clearly whether this condition is satisfied or not depends on the magnitudes of

A and B. So far as equations (27) to (30) are concerned, A and B can be either negative or positive depending on the size of T and the relative sizes of a and b. For example, if T is sufficiently small and b is sufficiently large relative to a, then we may have $a < be^{-\beta T}$, so that $A < 0$ in (27). A necessary and sufficient condition for $x_t \geq 0$ for all t is, in view of (23), that $A \geq 0$ regardless of the relative size of α and β. $A \geq 0$ holds [in view of (27) and (29)] if and only if

$$(32) \qquad ae^{\beta T} \geq b, \text{ regardless of the relative size of } \alpha \text{ and } \beta$$

We assume that this condition holds, for otherwise $x_t < 0$ (for all t).

In order to consider the condition in which $k_t \geq 0$ for all t, we obtain the expressions for k_t using (24), (25), (27), (28), (29), and (30):

$$(33) \qquad k_t = ae^{\beta t}\frac{(T-t)}{T} + \frac{bt}{T}, \qquad \text{when } \alpha = \beta$$

$$(34) \qquad k_t = ae^{\beta t} - (ae^{\beta t} - b)\frac{e^{\alpha t} - e^{\beta t}}{e^{\alpha T} - e^{\beta T}}, \qquad \text{when } \alpha \neq \beta$$

which can be rewritten as

$$(35) \quad k_t = \frac{1}{e^{\alpha T} - e^{\beta T}}\left[ae^{\beta t}\{(e^{\alpha T} - e^{\beta T}) - (e^{\alpha t} - e^{\beta t})\} + b(e^{\alpha t} - e^{\beta t})\right] \text{ (when } \alpha \neq \beta)$$

In view of (33), $k_t \geq 0$ for all t, when $\alpha = \beta$. Also in view of (35), $k_t \geq 0$ for all t, when $\alpha \neq \beta$. In fact, $k_t > 0$ for all t, $0 \leq t < T$, regardless of the relative size of α and β as long as $\alpha > 0$.

In order to investigate what happens when T is large enough, take the limit as $T \to \infty$ in (27), (28), (29), and (30). We then obtain:

$$(36) \qquad\qquad A = 0, B = a, \text{ when } \alpha = \beta$$

$$(37) \qquad\qquad A = 0, B = a, \text{ when } \alpha > \beta$$

$$(38) \qquad\qquad A = (\beta - \alpha)a, B = 0, \text{ when } \alpha < \beta$$

Hence in view of (23), (24), and (25), we obtain:

$$(39) \qquad\qquad x_t = 0, \qquad \text{for all } t, \text{ when } \alpha \geq \beta$$

$$(40) \qquad\qquad x_t = (\beta - \alpha)ae^{\alpha t}, \qquad \text{for all } t, \text{ when } \alpha < \beta$$

$$(41) \qquad\qquad k_t = ae^{\beta t}, \qquad \text{for all } t, \text{ when } \alpha \geq \beta$$

$$(42) \qquad\qquad k_t = ae^{\alpha t}, \qquad \text{for all } t, \text{ when } \alpha < \beta$$

Note that when $\alpha < \beta$, we obtain, in view of (40) and (42), the following relation:

$$(43) \qquad\qquad x_t = (\beta - \alpha)k_t, \quad \text{for all } t$$

In other words, x_t and k_t grow at the same rate α and the ratio between them is constant (that is, $\beta - \alpha$). For $\alpha \geq \beta$, we do not have such a solution.

Define the **limit path** as the path which is specified by (39) and (41) [or (40) and (42)]. What can we infer from the limit path? One important implication is that such a path gives an approximation of the optimal path when the planning horizon is large enough.

Can we infer anything about the infinite horizon problem? First note that we cannot specify the terminal stock b for the infinite horizon problem. It is certainly meaningless to talk about the capital:labor ratio for the infinite future, that is, the date which we can never reach! Therefore, strictly speaking, the solution of the infinite horizon problem is *not* the limit of the finite horizon problem. The problem is altered with regard to the specification of the terminal stock b.

The reader may then wonder whether we can replace the boundary condition $k_T = b$ by a condition such as $\lim_{T\to\infty} k_T = b$. Then the terminal condition is specified. But we can immediately see that the limit path then does not give a solution of the infinite horizon problem, by simply observing $k_t \to \infty$ as $t \to \infty$ in the limit path. In other words, if we adopt the limit path approach for the infinite horizon problem, the terminal condition should not be specified.

Furthermore, the limit path is *not*, in general, a solution of the infinite horizon problem anyway, even if the terminal condition is unspecified. This is easy to see by assuming $\alpha \geq \beta$ and recalling (39). In other words, if $\alpha \geq \beta$, $x_t = 0$ for all t in the limit path; that is, consumption must be kept at the subsistence level forever. Clearly the path in which $x_t = 0$ for all t cannot be an "optimal" path. In fact, it gives the worst possible path if $\beta > 0$, since it is possible for the economy to sustain itself at more than the subsistence level. To see this, it suffices to choose x_t such that $0 < x_t \leq \beta a$ and examine (14). Clearly such a path is attainable and k_t is non-decreasing in t. Such a path is certainly better than the path in which the economy is kept at the subsistence level for all t.

What then can we infer from this? The appropriate conclusion is that the solution of the infinite horizon problem does *not* exist if $\alpha \geq \beta$. Actually a simple procedure, which does not involve the tedious process of obtaining the limit path, will also reveal this. First note that the solution must satisfy the feasibility condition (14), and the Euler condition, (18) or (23).[10] Any path which satisfies these two conditions is called the feasible Euler path. The feasible Euler path is not necessarily a **solution path** (an **optimal path**), that is, the solution of the optimization problem. We then have to proceed to screen the solution path out of the set of all feasible Euler paths. The test used in this screening process is called the **eligibility test**. Note that if $x_0 = 0$, then $x_t = 0$ for all t by Euler's condition (23). Since the society can sustain itself at more than the subsistence level, the path in which $x_t = 0$ for all t is not "eligible" for the solution path. Recall (24) and (25). Then if $x_0 > 0$ and $\alpha \geq \beta$, k_t eventually becomes negative for a sufficiently large t [$\because A > 0$ from (23) and $x_0 > 0$]. In other words, if $\alpha \geq \beta$, none of the feasible Euler paths is "eligible" for the solution path; that is, the solution path for the infinite horizon problem does not exist.

Since the above conclusion crucially hinges on whether $\alpha \geq \beta$ or $\alpha < \beta$, let us obtain the condition under which $\alpha < \beta$. This can easily be obtained from the definitions of α and β in (18) and (20), and we can conclude that the necessary and sufficient condition for $\alpha < \beta$ is

$$(44) \qquad\qquad v(1 - \sigma\lambda) > 1 - \sigma(\lambda + \rho)$$

Hence, in particular, when $\rho = 0$ (no future discount), the necessary and sufficient condition for $\alpha < \beta$ is simplified to

$$(45) \qquad\qquad v > 1$$

As we remarked earlier, if we assume $u(x) > 0$ for some $x > 0$, v cannot be greater than one. Hence, in this case, $\alpha \geq \beta$ must hold as long as $\rho = 0$. Note that if $\rho > 0$, then $v \leq 1$ is necessary for $\alpha \geq \beta$, and that $v > 1$ is sufficient for $\alpha < \beta$ [in view of (44)]. Goodwin's case ($v = 1, \lambda > 0, \rho = 0$) and Chakravarty's model ($v \leq 1, \lambda > 0, \rho = 0$), as well as the above-mentioned Tinbergen case ($\lambda = \rho = 0$, $v < 1$), all yield the case in which $\alpha \geq \beta$. An interesting example of $\alpha < \beta$ may be the case in which $\lambda = 0, \rho > 0$, and $v \geq 1$.

Tinbergen considered the infinite horizon problem with the above specification (which amounts to $\alpha > \beta$) and contended that his article is "an unsuccessful attempt to find a simple solution to the problem of optimum savings" ([48], p. 481). Both Goodwin and Chakravarty considered the finite horizon problem; hence there is no such "unsuccessful" story.

For the finite horizon problem, the limit path represents an approximation to the case in which T is sufficiently large. The only question that remains is how the economy can tolerate spending most of its time near the subsistence level. The present contention of the author is that this is not a small criticism, although such a judgment may be a matter of taste.

Confining ourselves to the finite horizon problem, there is a way to avoid the above-mentioned problem of the "arbitrary cut-off point." This is the "sensitivity analysis" explored by Brock [5]. Postponing its full discussion to the Appendix, we now *illustrate* this analysis for the present problem. Assuming that T is finite, this analysis examines questions such as the effect of a change in the terminal stock $k_T = b$ and a change in the terminal date T on the optimal consumption program. Then we find out that the *optimal consumption program is "insensitive," at least for a certain initial period, with respect to these changes, if T is large enough.* As remarked before, Chakravarty [9] conjectured such insensitivities by constructing certain numerical examples. These problems were then solved under a general framework with both linear and nonlinear production functions by Brock [5]. Our consideration here offers a simple case of Brock's result. Also note that Brock dealt with a discrete time model while ours is a continuous time model.

We first consider the effect of a change in the terminal stock requirement k_T, assuming T is fixed. Write the optimal path for $k_T = b_1$ as (k_t^1, x_t^1) and the optimal path for $k_T = b_2$ as (k_t^2, x_t^2). Similarly, we write the values of

A and B for $k_T = b_1$ as A_1 and B_1 and those for $k_T = b_2$ as A_2 and B_2. Then using (23) to (25) and (34), we can compute the following, where we assume $b_1 > b_2$:

CASE I: $\alpha = \beta$

(46) $x_t^1 - x_t^2 = e^{\alpha t}(A_1 - A_2) = e^{\alpha t}(b_2 - b_1)\dfrac{e^{-\beta T}}{T} < 0$ (which implies $x_t^1 < x_t^2$)

(47) $k_t^1 - k_t^2 = te^{\alpha t}(A_2 - A_1) = te^{\alpha t}(b_1 - b_2)\dfrac{e^{-\beta T}}{T} > 0$ (which implies $k_t^1 > k_t^2$)

CASE II: $\alpha \neq \beta$

(48) $x_t^1 - x_t^2 = e^{\alpha t}(A_1 - A_2)$

$$= (b_2 - b_1)e^{\alpha t}\frac{\alpha - \beta}{e^{\alpha T} - e^{\beta T}} < 0 \text{ (which implies } x_t^1 < x_t^2)$$

(49) $k_t^1 - k_t^2 = \dfrac{e^{\alpha t} - e^{\beta t}}{e^{\alpha T} - e^{\beta T}}(b_1 - b_2) > 0$ (which implies $k_t^1 > k_t^2$)

Hence on the optimal path, an increase in the terminal stock requirement k_T implies a decrease in x_t for *each* t and an increase in k_t for *each* t. Moreover, when $\alpha = \beta$, the distance between x_t^1 and x_t^2 can be made arbitrarily small for each t by choosing T sufficiently large and t sufficiently small; also the distance between k_t^1 and k_t^2 can be made arbitrarily small for each t by choosing a sufficiently large T, provided that t is sufficiently small. In other words, the optimal path is "insensitive" to a change in the terminal stock k_T for a certain initial period when T is sufficiently large, provided that $\alpha = \beta$. The degree of this insensitivity (that is, the choice of T and t) can be precisely computed from (46) and (47).

In order to see whether a similar conclusion can be obtained for $\alpha \neq \beta$, we rewrite (48) and (49), respectively, as follows.

(50) $x_t^1 - x_t^2 = e^{\alpha t}\dfrac{(b_2 - b_1)(\alpha - \beta)}{e^{\beta T}(e^{(\alpha - \beta)T} - 1)} = e^{\alpha t}\dfrac{(b_2 - b_1)(\beta - \alpha)}{e^{\alpha T}(e^{(\beta - \alpha)T} - 1)}$

(51) $k_t^1 - k_t^2 = (b_1 - b_2)\dfrac{e^{\alpha t} - e^{\beta t}}{e^{\beta T}(e^{(\alpha - \beta)T} - 1)} = (b_1 - b_2)\dfrac{e^{\beta t} - e^{\alpha t}}{e^{\alpha T}(e^{(\beta - \alpha)T} - 1)}$

Hence the distance between x_t^1 and x_t^2 can again be made arbitrarily small for each t by choosing T large enough (relative to t), when $\alpha \neq \beta$. Also the distance between k_t^1 and k_t^2 can again be made arbitrarily small for each t by choosing T large enough (relative to t), when $\alpha \neq \beta$. The choice of T with a given distance between x_t^1 and x_t^2 (resp. k_t^1 and k_t^2) and with a given value of t can be computed precisely from (50) [resp. (51)].

Next we consider the effect of a change in the planning horizon T on the optimal path. Write the optimal path for the T-period problem as (k_t^T, x_t^T) and the optimal path for the T'-period problem as $(k_t^{T'}, x_t^{T'})$. Assume $T' > T$. Using (23) to (25) and (34), compute the following:

CASE I: $\alpha = \beta$

$$(52) \qquad x_t^{T'} - x_t^T = e^{\alpha t}\delta_T, \text{ where } \delta_T \equiv a\left(\frac{1}{T'} - \frac{1}{T}\right) - b\left(\frac{e^{-\beta T}}{T'} - \frac{e^{-\beta T'}}{T}\right)$$

$$(53) \qquad\qquad\qquad k_t^{T'} - k_t^T = -te^{\alpha t}\delta_T$$

CASE II: $\alpha \neq \beta$

$$(54) \qquad x_t^{T'} - x_t^T = e^{\alpha t}(\alpha - \beta)\Delta_T, \text{ where } \Delta_T \equiv \frac{a - be^{-\beta T'}}{e^{(\alpha-\beta)T'} - 1} - \frac{a - be^{-\beta T}}{e^{(\alpha-\beta)T} - 1}$$

$$(55) \qquad\qquad\qquad k_t^{T'} - k_t^T = -(e^{\alpha t} - e^{\beta t})\Delta_T$$

Note that δ_T and Δ_T can be made arbitrarily close to zero by choosing T sufficiently large (regardless of the relative size of α and β). Hence, for each fixed t, both the distance between x_t^T and $x_t^{T'}$ and the distance between k_t^T and $k_t^{T'}$ can be made arbitrarily close to zero, by choosing T sufficiently large (relative to t), regardless of the relative size of α and β.

Note also that if $b = 0$, then $\delta_T < 0$ so that $x_t^{T'} < x_t^T$ and $k_t^{T'} > k_t^T$ when $\alpha = \beta$. Also $b = 0$ implies that $\Delta_T \lessgtr 0$ according to whether $\alpha \gtrless \beta$. Hence $x_t^{T'} < x_t^T$ and $k_t^{T'} > k_t^T$, when $\alpha \neq \beta$. In other words, the monotonicities of x_t^T and k_t^T with respect to T can be achieved whenever we have $b = 0$. Note that a necessary and sufficient condition for such monotonicities can be computed from (52) to (55) for the case in which $b > 0$.[11] Also note that we have established the insensitivity of the optimal path with respect to T without regard to any such monotonicities.

Hence we obtained the conclusion that the optimal path is insensitive both to a change in the planning horizon T and to a change in the terminal stock k_T for a certain initial period. I believe that this is a precise formalization of Chakravarty's conjecture, where he confined himself to numerical examples.

In the above we noted the following features of the constant capital:output ratio model when $\alpha \gtreqless \beta$.

(i) The solution of the infinite horizon problem does not exist.
(ii) Although the sensitivity results hold for the finite horizon problem, the solution for a sufficiently large T approximates the program in which consumption is kept at the subsistence level for a long period of time.

These observations lead us to suspect the plausibility of the constant capital: output ratio model. In the next subsection we take up a nonlinear specification of the production function, that is, the case in which the assumption of a constant capital:output ratio does not hold. We then show that under a certain set of plausible assumptions, the solution of the infinite horizon problem always converges to a balanced growth path ("modified golden rule path"). In the Appendix to Section D, we show that the sensitivity results hold in general, including such a nonlinear case.

Here we should also recall the problem of the inequality between the natural rate of growth and the warranted rate of growth in the Harrod-Domar model. In other words, we have to ask ourselves the question whether we can really describe the "optimal" path without any significant consideration of the growth of labor. Will not such a path be bounded by the ceiling of the growth with "full employment of labor"? Will not such a path cause continuously increasing unemployment of labor? Will not the productivity of capital $(1/\sigma)$ be decreased with the increase in the capital:labor ratio? There are no clear answers to these questions as long as we retain the assumption of a constant capital:labor ratio.

c. NONLINEAR PRODUCTION FUNCTION WITH INFINITE TIME HORIZON

In this subsection we consider the case in which there is substitution between labor and capital in the production function. In other words, we are dealing with equation (8), where f is some nonlinear function of k. We consider the problem in which the time horizon is infinite. This is the problem that was posed and answered by Koopmans [22] and Cass [6]. We will see that with a nonlinear specification of the production function, the difficulty that arose in the previous section will not arise here. The assumptions that we impose on the function f are as follows:

(A-3) $f'(k) > 0$ and $f''(k) < 0$ for all $k \geqq 0$.
(A-4) $f'(0) = \infty, f'(\infty) = 0$, and $f(0) = 0$.

Here $f'(0)$ and $f''(0)$, respectively, are the right-hand derivatives of f and f' at 0. Note that $f'(k) > 0$ for all k means that the marginal physical product of capital is always positive and $f''(k) < 0$ means that the marginal physical product of capital (labor) is a decreasing function with respect to capital (labor); $f(0) = 0$ means that capital is indispensable for production. These assumptions are also introduced in the previous section. Under (A-3) and (A-4), we can draw the following familiar diagram. Note that (A-3) and (A-4) guarantee the existence of a unique solution for $f(k) = \lambda k$. We denote the value of k which satisfies this equation by $\bar{k}$. Note also that the first assumption of (A-4) is strategic in avoiding the uninteresting possibility of $f(k) - \lambda k < 0$ for all k (such a possibility would mean that the economy must eventually disappear, *regardless* of the optimality condition), in order to keep the consumption positive $(x > 0)$. It can also be seen from Figure 5.9 that if $k_0 > \bar{k}, \dot{k} < 0$, regardless of the optimality condition, in order to keep the consumption positive.[12] It is, in any case, very important

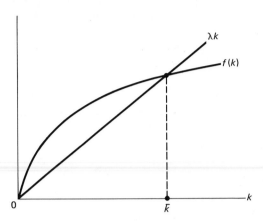

Figure 5.9.   An Illustration of Production Function.

to see that the "nonlinear" specification of f creates an essential difference from the "linear" specification of f where the capital:output ratio is assumed to be constant. In the subsequent analysis, we shall show that, under the nonlinear specification of f (also of F), there exists a unique optimal attainable path for the infinite horizon problem, which approaches the modified golden rule path. The "modified golden rule path" will be defined later. (It is equal to the golden rule path when the discount factor ρ is equal to zero.)

To obtain this result, we need one more specification on the utility function in addition to (A-1):

(A-5) $\lim u(x) \to -\infty$ as $x \to 0$ with $x \geq 0$.

This assumption is due to Koopmans [22]. He explains that "this means a strong incentive to avoid periods of very low consumption as much as is feasible" (p. 241). If $x_t = 0$ for any (small) time interval, then by (A-5) the objective integral diverges to $-\infty$. That is, (A-5) in essence guarantees an interior solution.

We are now ready to proceed with our analysis. As discussed in subsection a, we first solve the problem with a finite horizon, and then examine the optimal feasible path when T extends without limit. Thus our first task is to maximize the integral J_T [equation (5)] subject to feasibility. This is a straightforward calculus of variations problem, of which the Euler condition is already obtained [equation (11)]. Now note that since f is strictly concave in k from (A-3) and u is a strictly concave function from (A-5), Φ is a strictly concave function in k and $\dot{k}$. Hence the Euler condition as given in (11) is sufficient (as well as necessary) for a unique global maximum (Theorem 5.B.4). Ignoring the possibility of a corner solution (which may arise due to the nonnegativity condition $k_t \geq 0$, $x_t \geq 0$), the feasible Euler path is the one that satisfies equations (11) and (8) simultaneously. Hence the time path of k_t and x_t can be analyzed simply in terms of the following phase diagram, where we now confine our attention to the nonnegative orthant of the $(x - k)$-plane in view of the nonnegativity constraint.

In Figure 5.10, $\hat{k}(\rho)$ is defined as the value of k which satisfies the following equation:

(56) $$f'(k) = \lambda + \rho$$

From (A-3) and (A-4), $\hat{k}(\rho)$ lies between 0 and $\bar{k}$. Also, $\hat{x}(\rho)$ in Figure 5.10 is defined by the following equation:

(57) $$\hat{x}(\rho) \equiv f(\hat{k}(\rho)) - \lambda\hat{k}(\rho)$$

In Figure 5.10, the vertical line starting from $\hat{k}(\rho)$ represents the set of (k, x) combinations which satisfy equation (11), so that $\dot{x} = 0$ along this line, $\dot{x} > 0$ to the left of this line, and $\dot{x} < 0$ to the right of this line [which follows from (A-3)]. The mound-shaped curve in Figure 5.10 represents the set of (k, x) combinations which satisfy $x = f(k) - \lambda k$, so that $\dot{k} = 0$ along this curve, $\dot{k} < 0$ above the curve, and $\dot{k} > 0$ below the curve. Hence we can obtain the arrows in Figure 5.10 and trace various paths of (k_t, x_t) on the diagram. Therefore, given the initial k_0 and another boundary condition—say, k_T—we can completely describe the shape of the time path of (k_t, x_t) on Figure 5.10. It may be interesting to observe that all the optimal paths of (k_t, x_t) arch toward the path of $[\hat{k}(\rho), \hat{x}(\rho)]$ when T is sufficiently large.[13] This phenomenon is the basis of the theorem which Samuelson called the "consumption turnpike theorem" [36].

Let us now turn to the problem with an infinite time horizon. We are now concerned with the problem of maximizing J as defined in (6) subject to feasibility. The problem can simply be analyzed by tracing the feasible Euler paths as

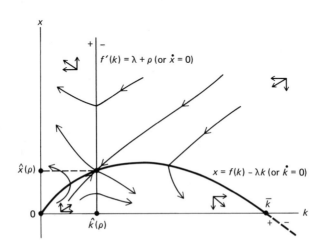

Figure 5.10. Phase Diagram for the Nonlinear Case.

462 CALCULUS OF VARIATIONS AND OPTIMAL GROWTH OF AN AGGREGATE ECONOMY

described in the above diagram. From the diagram it is clear that there are three kinds of feasible Euler paths, (k_t, x_t), namely,

(**Type A**) $k_t > \hat{k}(\rho)$ for all $t > \bar{t}$ (for some $\bar{t} > 0$).

(**Type B**) $k_t \rightarrow \hat{k}(\rho)$ and $x_t \rightarrow \hat{x}(\rho)$ as $t \rightarrow \infty$.

(**Type C**) $k_t < \hat{k}(\rho)$, for all $t > \bar{t}$ (for some $\bar{t} > 0$).

Along the type A path, $x_t < \hat{x}(\rho)$ as well as $k_t > \hat{k}(\rho)$ from some time on (say after $t = t_0$). Then we can always improve on a given type A path by consuming the capital stock (disinvesting) in some interval beginning at t_0 until k_t diminishes to $\hat{k}(\rho)$, while we raise x_t to $\hat{x}(\rho)$. After this, we maintain $\hat{x}(\rho)$ and $\hat{k}(\rho)$, and we obtain a path superior to a given type A path. In other words, the type A path cannot be optimal. Along the type C path, $\dot{k}_t < 0$ for all $t > \bar{t}$ so that k_t is decreasing over time, yet x_t is nondecreasing over time as can be seen from the above phase diagram. Hence k_t eventually goes to some negative value for a sufficiently long passage of time.[14] This violates our assumption of $k_t \geqq 0$ for all $t \geqq 0$. Hence both the type A and type C paths are not eligible for the infinite horizon problem. Note that when we consider the problem of $t \rightarrow \infty$ (hence also $T \rightarrow \infty$), we do not pre-specify the value of k_T.

What about the type B path? If ρ is positive, then the integral J defined in (6) along the type B path is clearly convergent, so that we obtain a unique eligible path which is feasible and satisfies Euler's condition, for any positive initial k_0.[15] The path approaches monotonically to $[\hat{k}(\rho), \hat{x}(\rho)]$ as time extends without limit.[16] If ρ is zero, then the integral J defined in (6) along the type B path is not convergent. However, the problem of divergence in this case can be avoided if we redefine the target function as follows:

$$(7) \qquad J_R \equiv \int_0^\infty [u(x_t) - u(\hat{x})] dt \qquad \text{where } \hat{x} \equiv \hat{x}(0)$$

Along the type B path, we can show that the integral J_R is convergent; hence the feasible Euler path of type B is eligible for the infinite horizon problem under this new target function J_R.[17] This Ramseyian device is also used by Koopmans [22]. We now obtain the following theorem.

Theorem 5.D.1 (Ramsey-Koopmans-Cass): *Under assumptions (A-1), (A-3), (A-4), and (A-5), we have*

    (i) $\rho > 0$: *Given an arbitrary initial value of k, an optimal feasible and eligible path is unique and it converges to the path* $[\hat{k}(\rho), \hat{x}(\rho)]$ *monotonically. The optimality is defined in the sense of maximizing the integral J, and this integral is convergent for this optimal path.*

    (ii) $\rho = 0$: *Given an arbitrary initial value of k, an optimal feasible and eligible path is unique, and it converges to the path* $[\hat{k}(0), \hat{x}(0)]$ *monotonically. The optimality*

*is defined in the sense of maximizing the integral J_R, and this integral is convergent
for this optimal path.*

REMARK: If $k_0 = \hat{k}(\rho)$, then the optimal feasible path is simply the path of
$[\hat{k}(\rho), \hat{x}(\rho)]$ for all $t \geq 0$. The target is the integral J when $\rho > 0$ and J_R when
$\rho = 0$.

REMARK: The path of $[\hat{k}(\rho), \hat{x}(\rho)]$ is the familiar "golden rule path" à la
Phelps, Robinson, and so on, when $\rho = 0$. We can, in general, call the path of
$[\hat{k}(\rho), \hat{x}(\rho)]$ with $\rho \geq 0$ the **modified golden rule path**.

The importance of the above theorem may be emphasized. It gives a
completely new significance to the golden rule path. As discussed in Section C,
the concept of the golden rule path can be severely criticized on the grounds
that it neglects the historically given stocks of capital and labor, and that its
choice set is restricted to the golden age paths. This means that even if the
historically given value of the capital:labor ratio happens to be on the golden
rule path, it only maximizes per capita consumption in the choice set which is
limited to the set of the golden age paths. Theorem 5.D.1 gives an answer to
both of these criticisms. In other words, it says that the path which maximizes the
"Ramsey sum" of utility over the infinite horizon (that is, J_R) converges to the
golden rule path regardless of the initial value of k_0, as long as it satisfies the
eligibility conditions. Here the choice set is not limited to the golden age paths,
so that k_t can fluctuate over time (in fact, along this optimal attainable eligible
path, k_t approaches $\hat{k}(\rho)$ monotonically—hence, in general, it is not constant). If
we have a positive discount factor ($\rho > 0$), the theorem says that the optimal

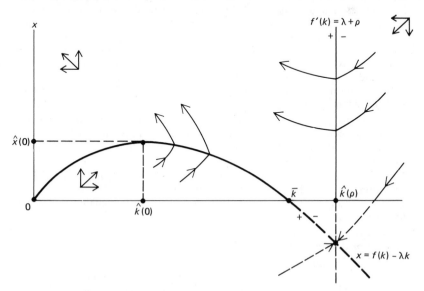

Figure 5.11.   An illustration of the Case with a Negative Discount Factor.

attainable eligible path converges monotonically to the "modified golden rule path."

Koopmans [22] observed that the above theorem is, in general, no longer true when the time discount factor ρ is negative. The wicked character of the optimal feasible path when $\rho < 0$ may be illustrated by the phase diagram of Figure 5.11. In this case, there exists no feasible Euler path which is eligible for the infinite horizon problem. Note also that if $\hat{k}(\rho)$ takes the value between $\hat{k}(0)$ and $\bar{k}$, then, using a similar phase diagram, a proposition analogous to the previous theorem should follow even if $\rho < 0$, since the intersection of the $\dot{k} = 0$ curve and the $\dot{x} = 0$ line occurs for a positive value of k (and x).

FOOTNOTES

1. This section was first presented by the author as a lecture at the University of Minnesota in the spring of 1966. See Takayama [46]. For a recent survey of the same problem, see Koopmans [24], for example. In the first reading of this section, the reader may skip reading subsection b.

2. This point is discussed by Chakravarty [8].

3. There exists an extensive literature on this topic including recent textbook expositions. The earlier contributions on this problem in addition to [35], [22], and [6], include: Tinbergen [47] and [48], Goodwin [15], Black [4], Chakravarty [8] and [9], Dasgupta [12], Horvat [18] and [19], Leontief [27], Meade [31], Samuelson [36], Sen [38] and [39], Stone [45] and von Weizsäcker [52]. (Discussion on "investment criteria" in the 1950s by Sen, Eckstein, and others, especially in the *Quarterly Journal of Economics*, also belongs to this category of problem.) An extension to the multisector model has been attempted since the pioneering work by Samuelson and Solow [37]. More recent turnpike theorems obviously belong to this category. We take up this topic later (Chapter 7, Section A). See also a further extension of this multisector growth model by Gale [14]. We also discuss this later (Chapter 7, Section B). The extension to the two-sector optimization model is attempted by Kurz [26], Srinivasan [43], Stoleru [44], Johansen [20], Uzawa [50] and [51], Atsumi [3], and so on. See also J. Z. Drabicki and A. Takayama, "On the Optimal Growth of the Two Sector Economy," *Krannert Institute Paper*, No. 383, January 1973.

4. We implicitly assume that the economy can "eat up" the existing stock of capital: that is, the economy can increase the amount of consumption by reducing the existing stock of capital. Cass [6], and Arrow and Kurz [2] considered the optimal growth problem by explicitly banning this possibility.

5. It is often referred to in connection with the "Harrod-Domar model." This representation of a production function implicitly assumes that labor is not scarce. Harrod's and Domar's original models are more sophisticated than the one with such an assumption.

6. This also implies either that Y is defined as "net" (rather than gross) national product *or* that the capital good is assumed to last forever.

7. See [11], [29], and [30].

8. Note that $v = -(x_t - \bar{x})u''/u'$, which signifies the **elasticity of marginal utility**. The crux of such a specification of the utility function is the constancy of this elasticity.

9. Goodwin's framework is a little more complicated. He asks the question of "transforming an economy characterized by the Old, low productivity technique into one consisting entirely of the New, high productivity technique." And T is determined as the year of the completion of this transformation. However, so far as the mathematical structure is concerned, his model is essentially the same as that of Tinbergen and Chakravarty. Hence we treat these models together.

10. For the infinite horizon problem, the objective integral is the J of (6) when $\rho > 0$ and it is the J_R of (7) when $\rho = 0$. Both J and J_R yield the same Euler's equation.

11. Such a condition would be a much sharper result than Brock's result (Theorem 3 in [5]). However, this sharpness is obtained at quite a high price, that is, the specification of the production function as a constant capital:output ratio.

12. Hence, if $k_0 > \bar{k}$, $k_t < k_0$ for all $t > 0$, so that $f(k_t) \leq f(k_0)$ for all $t \geq 0$ for any attainable path. Therefore x_t, hence also $u(x_t)$, is bounded from above for all t if x_t is to come only from the current output. That is, $x_t \leq f(k_0)$ for all $t \geq 0$. Also if $k_0 \leq \bar{k}$, we can show that, for any attainable path, $k_t \leq \bar{k}$ for all $t \geq 0$ (by setting $x_t = 0$ for all t, **the path of pure accumulation**). Hence again, x_t and $u(x_t)$ are bounded from above for all $t \geq 0$. Therefore, $u(x_t)$ is bounded from above regardless of whether $k_0 > \bar{k}$ or $k_0 \leq \bar{k}$, so that the convergence of the integral J is guaranteed for any attainable path whose value of J does not diverge to $-\infty$, provided that $\rho > 0$. In other words, we can solve the convergence problem discussed earlier without setting an upper bound on u, if x_t is to come only from the current output. For the other case, that is, when the capital can be "eaten up," the proof of convergence is slightly more complicated; yet it can be handled analogously as above by noting that x_t cannot go up for an indefinite period of time.

13. See Samuelson [36], p. 490. A linear approximation of our system will yield a catenary solution. We may note that our formulation completely avoids such a linear approximation.

14. From (11) and (A-4), $x_t \to \infty$ as $k_t \to 0$ along the type C path. Hence from (8) there exists a constant $\delta > 0$ such that $\dot{k}_t < -\delta$ from some time on ($\because f$ is bounded from above for all k). This shows that k_t will eventually become negative. On the other hand, if the capital cannot be "eaten up," then x_t is bounded by the current output, that is $x_t \leq f(k_t)$. In figure 5.10, the reader can easily draw the picture of this bound (called the *boundary curve*). Then along the type C path, x_t will hit the boundary curve, where $\dot{k}_t = -\lambda k_t$, and x_t and k_t will approach the origin along the boundary curve. In this case k_t will never become negative and the above eligibility test fails.

15. In the theory of differential equations, the point $[\hat{k}(\rho), \hat{x}(\rho)]$ is a saddle point, and the type B path is its stable branches. This can be confirmed by linearizing the dynamic equations (8) and (11) around $[\hat{k}(\rho), \hat{x}(\rho)]$, and showing that the eigenvalues of the coefficient matrix are real and of opposite signs. See any standard textbooks on differential equations.

16. Therefore, we have shown that the feasible Euler path which is eligible must be the type B path. The converse remains to be shown: that is whether the feasible Euler path which satisfies the end-point conditions k_0 and $\hat{k}(\rho)$ is indeed optimal compared to any attainable path starting from k_0. But this can be done easily by using a method analogous to the proof of Theorem 5.B.4 together with the end-point conditions k_0 and $\hat{k}(\rho)$. The improper integrals which appear in the above proof are bounded from above in view of footnote 12. Since any attainable path with $x_t = 0$ for a certain interval of time cannot be optimal in view of (A-5), we can delete such paths from our consideration. Hence the improper integrals which appear in the proof are bounded from below also, and thus they are well-defined. Note also

that the uniqueness of the optimal path is provided for by the strict concavity of the function u.

17. Our Euler condition (11), under this target function, can be transformed as $u'(x_t)\dot{k}_t = u(\hat{x}) - u(x_t)$. This is the Keynes-Ramsey rule which says that "the net increase in capital per worker multiplied by the marginal utility of consumption per worker at any time equals the excess of the maximum sustainable utility level over the current utility level." See Koopmans [22], p. 243, and also pp. 272–273. As we will show in the next section, his equation (28) corresponds to our equation (11). As Koopmans has shown, the time necessary to reach the golden rule path is infinity.

REFERENCES

1. Arrow, K. J., "Applications of Control Theory to Economic Growth," in *Mathematics of the Decision Sciences*, Pt. 2, ed. by G. B. Dantzig and A. F. Veinott, Providence, R. I., American Mathematical Society, 1968.

2. Arrow, K. J., and Kurz, M., "Optimal Growth with Irreversible Investment in a Ramsey Model," *Econometrica*, 38, March 1970.

3. Atsumi, H., "Neoclassical Growth and the Efficient Program of Capital Accumulation," *Review of Economic Studies*, XXXII, April 1965.

4. Black, J., "Optimum Savings Reconsidered, or Ramsey Without Tears," *Economic Journal*, LXXII, June 1962.

5. Brock, W. A., "Sensitivity of Optimal Growth Paths with Respect to a Change in Target Stocks," *Zeitschrift für Nationalökonomie*, Supp. 1, 1971 (originally presented at the Purdue Meeting of the Kansas-Missouri Seminar on Quantitative Economics, October 1969).

6. Cass, D., "Optimum Growth in an Aggregate Model of Capital Accumulation," *Review of Economic Studies*, XXXII, July 1965.

7. ———, "Optimum Growth in an Aggregative Model of Capital Accumulation: A Turnpike Theorem," *Econometrica*, 34, October 1966.

8. Chakravarty, S., "The Existence of an Optimum Savings Program," *Econometrica*, 30, January 1962.

9. ———, "Optimal Savings with Finite Horizon," *International Economic Review*, 3, September 1962.

10. ———, "Optimal Investment and Technical Progress," *Review of Economic Studies*, XXXI, June 1964.

11. ———, "Optimal Savings with Finite Horizon: A Reply," *International Economic Review*, 7, January 1966.

12. Dasgupta, A., "A Note on Optimum Savings," *Econometrica*, 32, July 1964.

13. Farrell, M. J., and Hahn, F. H., ed., *Infinite Programmes in Economics*, Edinburgh, Oliver & Boyd, 1967 (*Review of Economic Studies*, January 1967 issue).

14. Gale, D., "On Optimal Development in a Multi-Sector Economy," *Review of Economic Studies*, XXXIV, January 1967.

15. Goodwin, R. M., "The Optimal Growth Path for an Underdeveloped Economy," *Economic Journal*, LXXI, December 1961.

16. Harrod, R. F., "Second Essay in Dynamic Theory," *Economic Journal*, LXX, June 1960.

17. Hicks, J. R., *Capital and Growth*, Oxford, Clarendon Press, 1965.

18. Horvat, B., "The Optimum Rate of Saving: A Note," *Economic Journal*, LXVII, March 1958.

19. ———, "The Optimum Rate of Investment," *Economic Journal*, LXVIII, December 1958.

20. Johansen, L., "Saving and Growth in Long-Term Programming Models," in *Econometric Analysis for National Economic Planning*, ed. by Hart, P. E., Mills, G., and Whitaker, J. K., London, Butterworth, 1964.

21. Koopmans, T. C., "Stationary Ordinal Utility and Impatience," *Econometrica*, 28, April 1960.

22. ———, "On the Concept of Optimal Economic Growth," in *The Econometric Approach to Development Planning*, Pontificiae Academiae Scientiarvm Scriptvm Varia, Amsterdam, North-Holland, 1965 (also "Discussion," pp. 289–300).

23. ———, "On Flexibility of Future Preferences," in *Human Judgement and Optimality*, ed. by Bryan and Shelly, New York, Wiley, 1966.

24. ———, "Objectives, Constraints and Outcomes in Optimal Growth Models," *Econometrica*, 35, January 1967.

25. Koopmans, T. C., Diamond, R. A., and Williamson, R. E., "Stationary Utility and Time Perspective," *Econometrica*, 32, January-April 1964.

26. Kurz, M., "Optimal Paths of Capital Accumulation under Minimum Time Objective," *Econometrica*, 33, January 1965.

27. Leontief, W., "Theoretical Note on Time Preference, Productivity of Capital, Stagnation, and Economic Growth," *American Economic Review*, XLVIII, March 1958.

28. ———, "Time Preference and Economic Growth: A Reply," *American Economic Review*, XLIX, December 1959.

29. Maneschi, A., "Optimal Savings with Finite Planning Horizon: A Note," *International Economic Review*, 7, January 1966.

30. ———, "Optimal Savings with Finite Planning Horizon: A Rejoinder," *International Economic Review*, 7, January 1966.

31. Meade, J. E., *Trade and Welfare: Mathematical Supplement*, London, Oxford University Press, 1955.

32. Mirrlees, J., "Optimal Growth When Technology is Changing," *Review of Economic Studies*, XXXIV, January 1967.

33. Phelps, E., "The Ramsey Problem and the Golden Rule of Accumulation," in Phelps, *Golden Rules of Economic Growth*, New York, W. W. Norton, 1966.

34. Pontryagin, L. S., Boltyanskii, V. G., Gamkrelidze, R. V., and Mishchenko, E. R., *The Mathematical Theory of Optimal Processes*, New York, Interscience, 1962, (tr. by Trirogoff and Neustadt from Russian).

35. Ramsey, F. P., "A Mathematical Theory of Saving," *Economic Journal*, XXXVIII, December 1928.

36. Samuelson, P. A., "A Catenary Turnpike Involving Consumption and the Golden Rule," *American Economic Review*, LV, June 1965.

37. Samuelson, P. A., and Solow, R. M., "A Complete Capital Model Involving Heterogeneous Capital Goods," *Quarterly Journal of Economics*, LXX, November 1956.

38. Sen, A. K., "A Note on Tinbergen on the Optimum Rate on Saving," *Economic Journal*, LXVII, December 1957.

39. ———, "On Optimising the Rate of Saving," *Economic Journal*, LXXI, September 1961.

40. Shell, K., "Applications of Pontryagin's Maximum Principle to Economics," in *Mathematical Systems, Theory and Economics*, ed. by H. W. Kuhn and G. P. Szegö, Berlin, Springer-Verlag, 1969.

41. Solow, R. M., "A Contribution to the Theory of Economic Growth," *Quarterly Journal of Economics*, LXX, February 1956.

42. Srinivasan, T. N., "Investment Criteria and Choice of Techniques of Production," *Yale Economic Essays*, 2, Spring 1962.

43. ———, "Optimal Savings in a Two-Sector Model of Growth," *Econometrica*, 32, July 1964.

44. Stoleru, L. G., "An Optimal Policy for Economic Growth," *Econometrica*, 33, April 1965.

45. Stone, R., "Misery and Bliss: A Comparison of the Effect of Certain Forms of Savings Behaviour on the Standard of Living of a Growing Community," *Economia Internazionale*, VIII, Febraio 1955.

46. Takayama, A., "On the Structure of the Optimal Growth Problem," *Krannert Institute Paper*, Purdue University, No. 178, June 1967.

47. Tinbergen, J., "The Optimum Rate of Saving," *Economic Journal*, LXVI, December 1956.

48. ———, "Optimum Savings and Utility Maximization over Time," *Econometrica*, 28, April 1960.

49. Tobin, J., "Economic Policy as an Objective of Government Policy," *American Economic Review*, LIV, May 1964.

50. Uzawa, H., "Optimal Growth in a Two-Sector Model of Capital Accumulation," *Review of Economic Studies*, XXXI, January 1964.

51. ———, "Optimal Technical Change in an Aggregative Model of Economic Growth," *International Economic Review*, 5, January 1965.

52. von Weizsäcker, C. C., "Existence of Optimal Programs of Accumulation for an Infinite Time Horizon," *Review of Economic Studies*, XXXII, April 1965.

53. Westfield, F. M., "Time-Preference and Economic Growth: Comment," *American Economic Review*, XLIX, December 1959.

54. Yaari, M. E., "On the Existence of an Optimal Plan in Continuous-time Allocation Process," *Econometrica*, 32, October 1964.

Appendix to Section D: A Discrete Time Model of One-Sector Optimal Growth and Sensitivity Analysis

a.   INTRODUCTION

In Section D, we have assumed that time t is a continuum or, more specifically, that it is represented by real numbers. The purpose of this section is to construct a one-sector optimal growth model when time t is not a continuum but

discrete, that is, when it is represented by integers. Such an analysis in economics is known as "period analysis" and it is used in many fields of economics other than growth theory, such as the stability theory of competitive markets, business cycle theory, macro theory, and so on. In period analysis, difference equations rather than differential equations often become the main tool of analysis. In many cases, differential equations are known to be the better tool for use by theoreticians, because there are many more readily available theorems in the (mathematical) theory of differential equations than in the theory of difference equations. However, in some cases, difference equations are an equally good or even better tool of analysis. In fact, the present topic of optimal growth may provide such an example. In any case, this topic enables us to compare the two optimization techniques, nonlinear programming and the calculus of variations. In many cases, topics which can be analyzed by the calculus of variations can also be analyzed by the usual nonlinear programming technique. We will use period analysis in multisector growth models (Chapters 6 and 7). In Chapter 6, Section B, the use of the difference equation technique is illustrated, and in Chapter 7, Section B, the use of the nonlinear programming technique is illustrated. The present analysis may serve as a bridge to these later models. We may also note that these later models can be formulated in terms of differential equations and/or the calculus of variations. The rationale for the use of period analysis does not particularly lie in the tools of analysis that one employs. An important merit of period analysis is that this mode of analysis is often very useful in making explicit the crucial roles of "periods" in certain economic occurrences. For example, it is often noted that consumption may depend on income of the previous "period." As is well known, the recognition of this phenomenon is an important starting point of modern business cycle theory. In this case, one "period" is defined as the length of time in which a consumer's reaction is delayed. Similarly, we can consider many cases in which "periods" may play important roles in economic analysis, such as the "gestation period" of investment, the "duration period" of fixed capital, and the adjustment lag of the labor market compared with other markets (say, the money market).

It should be noted that the point made in the previous paragraph has no direct relevance to the fact that the time element in human economic activities is often discrete in the sense that many offices open only during daytime, some markets open only once a week, and so on. It is certainly possible to define "period" by one day or one week depending upon such "realistic" considerations. But unless there are certain crucial economic meanings attached to such calendar periods, one can often use differential equations (instead of difference equations) by supposing that a day, week, or year shrinks to a point of time, and still obtain meaningful results.[1]

The analysis of this Appendix does not provide an example of a case in which the definition of a period is of crucial significance to the conclusion. The analysis turns out to be merely a discrete analogue of the continuous time analysis of Section D. We obtain results essentially similar to those obtained there. We should, however, stress that one unit of a "period" is not arbitrarily defined. It is explicitly defined as a unit of a production period. Such an explicit recognition of the meaning of a "period" is very important, once one has decided to carry out his analysis in terms of period analysis. In the literature, such a consideration is often missing, so that there are several different period analyses for presumably the same problem, each obtaining a different conclusion.

In this Appendix, we obtain most of the results of the one-sector optimal growth model in Section D, such as the optimality condition and the convergence of the optimal attainable path to the modified golden rule path. However, our emphasis here is on the following:

(i)   A rigorous formulation of the discrete time model for the present topic.
(ii) The illustration of the use of nonlinear programming for the present topic.
(iii) The obtaining of some important additional results—in particular, the existence and uniqueness of the optimal attainable path and Brock's theorem on sensitivities [2].

The existence theorem is not a particularly easy topic when we use the calculus of variations and differential equations. However, when we use nonlinear programming, the simple Weierstrass theorem is often sufficient for this purpose. We have already illustrated sensitivity analysis in Section D for the case of a constant capital:output ratio. We will now record general results with the proofs.

b.   MODEL

We define the notations L_t, K_t, X_t, I_t, and so on, as we have done in the two previous sections, except that t now refers to period t. The labor supply equation is now written as

(1) $L_t = (1 + n)^t L_0,$ or $\dfrac{L_{t+1}}{L_t} = (1 + n)$, where $n \geqq 0$

We write the basic equilibrium relation in the output market as follows:

(2) $X_{t+1} + I_{t+1} = F(L_t, K_t)$

The basic assumption involved here is that the unit period is chosen to be the "production period." That is, it is assumed that production is not instantaneous but takes a certain period of time, and that period is chosen to be a one unit time period. It is assumed that the stock of capital does not depreciate within the period but depreciates *suddenly* at the end of each period at the rate μ, $0 < \mu < 1$ (when the production of each period is completed). Hence we can write the production function as $F(L_t, K_t)$; that is, the value K_t is unchanged during the entire tth period, and at the end of the tth period, the capital stock inherited from the previous period suddenly declines from K_t to $(K_t - \mu K_t)$.

However, at the beginning of the $(t + 1)$th period, a part of the output produced during the tth period is now available for increasing the capital stock. It is assumed that if I_{t+1} is the amount to be invested in the $(t + 1)$th period, then the entire amount of I_{t+1} is invested *at the beginning* of the $(t + 1)$th period. Hence K_{t+1}, the stock of capital available for production in the $(t + 1)$th period, is written as

$$K_{t+1} = (K_t - \mu K_t) + I_{t+1}$$

or

$$I_{t+1} = K_{t+1} - (K_t - \mu K_t)$$

Combining this with (2), we obtain

(3) $$X_{t+1} + [K_{t+1} - (K_t - \mu K_t)] = F(L_t, K_t)$$

or

$$X_{t+1} + (K_{t+1} - K_t) = F(L_t, K_t) - \mu K_t$$

Consumption, unlike investment, does not have to take place all at once at the beginning of the period. That is, the amount X_{t+1} is consumed during the entire $(t + 1)$th period

In the literature, there does not seem to be a consensus on the form of the basic output equilibrium relation such as (3), when time is discrete. For example, Samuelson ([7], p. 273) writes the corresponding equation as

(4) $$X_t + (K_{t+1} - K_t) = F(L_t, K_t) - \mu K_t$$

Notice that X_{t+1} in (3) is replaced by X_t in (4). One interpretation is that production takes place instantaneously, unlike our assumption concerning production. We proceed with our analysis using (3).[2]

Assume again that F is homogeneous of degree one, and write

(5) $$F(L_t, K_t) = L_t f(k_t), \text{ where } k_t \equiv \frac{K_t}{L_t}$$

Dividing (3) by L_{t+1} and using (1) and (5), we obtain

(6) $$x_{t+1} + k_{t+1} - \frac{k_t - \mu k_t}{1 + n} = \frac{f(k_t)}{1 + n}$$

where $$x_{t+1} \equiv \frac{X_{t+1}}{L_{t+1}} \quad \text{and} \quad k_{t+1} \equiv \frac{K_{t+1}}{L_{t+1}}$$

We can rewrite (6) as

(7) $$x_{t+1} + k_{t+1} = g(k_t)$$

where

(8) $$g(k_t) \equiv \frac{1}{1 + n} [f(k_t) + (k_t - \mu k_t)]$$

We impose the following assumptions on f.

(A-1) $f(0) = 0, 0 < f'(k_t) < \infty$ and $f''(k_t) \leq 0$ for all $k_t < \infty$.

For the meaning of these assumptions, the reader is referred to Section C. Note that $f''(k_t) = 0$ (for all k_t) corresponds to the case in which the capital:output ratio is a constant. Note also that (A-1) implies the following:

(A-1') $g(0) = 0, 0 < g'(k_t) < \infty$ and $g''(k_t) \leq 0$ for all $k_t < \infty$

This, among other things, implies that the function g is concave.

We assume that the economy is endowed with the stock of a good whose per capita amount is equal to a. We also assume that the economy is required to bequeath a stock of that good to the amount of b per capita at the end of the Tth period. Thus we have the following conditions:

(9)
$$x_0 + k_0 = a$$

and

(10)
$$k_T = b$$

If $a = 0$, then $k_0 = 0$ as well as $x_0 = 0$, which in turn implies that $k_t = 0$, and $x_t = 0$ for all t in view of $g(0) = 0$ and (7).[3] In order to avoid this uninteresting case, we assume $a > 0$ and that

(A-2) (a) There exists a unique $\bar{k}, 0 < \bar{k} < \infty$, such that $g(\bar{k}) - \bar{k} = 0$, or
 (b) $g'' = 0$ for all $k_t \geq 0$ (and $\bar{k} = \infty$).

In terms of f, this can be expressed as[4]

(A-2') (a) There exists a unique $\bar{k}, 0 < \bar{k} < \infty$, such that $f(\bar{k}) = \lambda \bar{k}$, where $\lambda \equiv \mu + n$, or
 (b) $f'' = 0$ for all $k_t \geq 0$ (and $\bar{k} = \infty$).[5]

Recall that an assumption similar to part (a) of (A-2') was imposed in the Cass-Koopmans model which we discussed in Section D.

Now consider the problem of finding a path such that $k_t = k > 0$ and $x_t = x > 0$, for all $t = 0, 1, \ldots, T$ (k, x are constants). That is, we ask whether there exists a *nonzero balanced* growth path.[6] This problem is reduced to one of finding $k > 0, x > 0$, such that

(11)
$$k + x = a \text{ and } x = g(k) - k$$

It is clear from Figure 5.12 that such a path exists uniquely, if $a < \bar{k}$. We call such a path **the balanced growth (or the golden age) path with respect to** a, and we denote it by $\{k^*(a), x^*(a)\}$. Note that $\bar{k} > k^*(a) > 0$ and $x^*(a) > 0$. We henceforth assume

(A-3) (a) $a < \bar{k}$, when $g'' < 0$ for all $k_t \geq 0$, or
 (b) $g(k_t) - k_t > 0$ for all $k_t > 0$, when $g'' = 0$ for all $k_t \geq 0$.

It is important to note that this consideration implies that the economy is capable of growing with strictly positive values of X_t and K_t (or x_t and k_t),

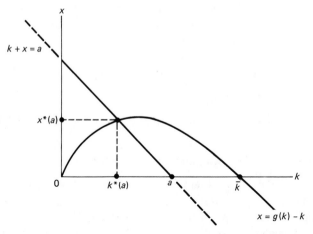

Figure 5.12.   The Existence of the Balanced Growth Path.

as long as the initial condition satisfies (A-3), for we can then choose $x_t = x^*(a)$ and $k_t = k^*(a)$. On the other hand, we may consider **the path of pure accumulation** or the **path of subsistence** with respect to a, which is defined by

(12) $k_0 = a,$ $k_{t+1} = g(k_t), t = 0, 1, \ldots, T - 1,$ $x_t = 0, t = 0, 1, \ldots, T$

The path of pure accumulation is illustrated in Figure 5.13.

When $a > \bar{k}$ and $f'' < 0$ [so that (A-3) is violated], then k_t monotonically *declines* to $\bar{k}$ in the path defined by (12), as t increases. This is an uninteresting case and may be considered as another justification of (A-3).[7]

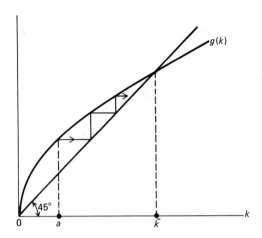

Figure 5.13.   The Path of Pure Accumulation.

C. THE OPTIMAL ATTAINABLE PATHS

Consider now the following T-period optimization problem:

$$\text{Maximize: } U \equiv \sum_{t=0}^{T} u(x_t)(1 + \rho)^{-t}$$
$$(k_t, x_t)$$

Subject to: $x_t + k_t = g(k_{t-1}), t = 1, 2, \ldots, T, x_0 + k_0 = a, k_T = b$

and $x_t \geq 0, k_t \geq 0, t = 0, 1, \ldots, T$

Here $\rho \geq 0$ is the discount rate and u is the utility function with the following assumption:

(A-4) $u(0) = -\infty, u'(x_t) > 0,$ and $u''(x_t) < 0$ for all x_t.

The solution to the above problem is called an **optimal (attainable) path** starting from a and ending at b. We denote this by $[\hat{k}_t(a, b; T), \hat{x}_t(a, b; T)]$, or, unless confusion might result, simply by $(\hat{k}_t, \hat{x}_t)$ or $[\hat{k}_t(b), \hat{x}_t(b)]$.

On the other hand, the path $(k_t, x_t), t = 0, 1, \ldots, T$, which satisfies the above constraints

(13) $x_t + k_t = g(k_{t-1}), t = 1, 2, \ldots, T$

(14) $x_0 + k_0 = a, k_T = b$

is called an **attainable path** starting from a and ending at b. When only (13) is imposed and (14) is disregarded, it is called a **feasible path**. Clearly the optimal attainable path is the path which maximizes U among the set of all attainable paths. Note that the set of attainable paths can be empty, so that there may not exist a solution for the above maximization problem. For example, b may be so large that the economy cannot attain it within the prescribed T periods, even if $x_t = 0$ for all t (the path of pure accumulation). We may denote the set of all the attainable paths by $A(a, b; T)$. For the infinite horizon problem $(T \to \infty)$, this set is denoted by $A(a, \infty)$, or simply $A(a)$, where we do not impose the constraint such as $\lim_{T \to \infty} k_T = b$.

We assume that the set of attainable paths is nonempty, for otherwise it is meaningless to consider the problem. It can be shown that the **attainable set** $A(a, b; T)$ is compact in the $(2T + 2)$ dimensional Euclidian space. To show this, let $(k_t{}^q, x_t{}^q), q = 1, 2, \ldots,$ be a sequence such that

(15) $x_t{}^q + k_t{}^q = g(k_{t-1}^q), t = 1, 2, \ldots, T$

(16) $x_0{}^q + k_0{}^q = a, k_T{}^q = b$

and

(17) $k_t{}^q \to k_t^*$ and $x_t{}^q \to x_t^*$

Then we have $x_t^* + k_t^* = g(k_{t-1}^*), x_0^* + k_0^* = a,$ and $k_T^* = b,$ since g is continuous.[8] That is, the set $A(a, b; T)$ is a closed set. Since it is obviously bounded, it is compact.[9] Thus, the attainable set $A(a, b; T)$ is nonempty and compact. Hence, in view of the Weierstrass theorem (Theorem 0.A.18) and the continuity of u, there always exists a solution for the above nonlinear programming problem. That is, the existence of an optimal attainable path is demonstrated.[10]

Next we consider the nonnegativity of the optimal attainable path. In fact, we can show, under a certain assumption, that $\hat{k}_t > 0, \hat{x}_t > 0$, for all $t = 0, 1, \ldots, T$ (except possibly for $k_T = b$, which can be zero), where $(\hat{k}_t, \hat{x}_t)$ denotes an optimal attainable path. To consider this problem, first suppose that $b = k^*(a)$. Then it is clear that the path (k_t, x_t), in which $k_t = k^*(a) > 0, x_t = x^*(a) > 0, t = 0, 1, \ldots, T$, is an attainable path. Then in view of the assumptions that $u(0) = -\infty$ and $f(0) = 0$,[11] we have

(18) $\hat{k}_t > 0, \hat{x}_t > 0$, for all $t = 0, 1, \ldots, T$ (except possibly for k_T)

That is, we have an "interior solution" for the above maximization problem. Now suppose that $b < k^*(a)$. Then we can similarly conclude that we have an interior solution [that is, (18) holds] since the path (k_t, x_t) in which $k_t = k^*(a), x_t = x^*(a)$, $t = 0, 1, \ldots, T - 1$, and $k_T = b, x_T = g[k^*(a)] - b = a - b$, is an attainable path and $k_t > 0, x_t > 0$, for all t along this path. Henceforth we impose the following assumption:

(A-5) $b \leq k^*(a)$.

Note that if $b = 0$, then this condition is always satisfied. We leave it to the interested readers to work out the implications of the case in which (A-5) is not satisfied.

We now assert the uniqueness of an optimal path. Although we should be able to assert this by way of the Lagrangian of the above maximization problem and using assumptions such as $u'' < 0$ in (A-4) and $g' > 0$ in (A-1'), here we will prove uniqueness directly from the problem because that method has applications to some other problems; in particular, we will use it for the multisector case (Chapter 7, Section B). First, for the sake of notational simplicity, write $x \equiv (x_0, x_1, \ldots, x_T)$ and $k \equiv (k_0, k_1, \ldots, k_T)$, so that $U(x) \equiv \sum_{t=0}^{T} u(x_t)(1 + \rho)^{-t}$.

We first assert that the strict concavity of u(that is, $u'' < 0$) implies that the optimal consumption path $\hat{x}$ is unique. To show this, suppose that $(\hat{k}, \hat{x})$ and (k', x') are two optimal attainable paths with $\hat{x} \neq x'$. That is, $U(\hat{x}) = U(x')$ and $a - \hat{x}_0 - \hat{k}_0 = 0, g(\hat{k}_{t-1}) - \hat{x}_t - \hat{k}_t = 0, t = 1, 2, \ldots, T, \hat{k}_T - b = 0, a - x_0' - k_0' = 0$, $g(k_{t-1}') - x_t' - k_t' = 0, t = 1, 2, \ldots, T, k_T' - b = 0$. Define a new path $(\check{k}_t, \check{x}_t)$ by

(19) $$\check{x}_t = \tfrac{1}{2}(\hat{x}_t + x_t'), t = 0, 1, \ldots, T - 1$$

(20) $$\check{k}_0 = a - \check{x}_0, \check{k}_t = g(\check{k}_{t-1}) - \check{x}_t, t = 1, 2, \ldots, T$$

(21) $$\check{x}_T = g(\check{k}_{T-1}) - b$$

Then $(\check{k}_t, \check{x}_t)$ is an attainable path. Note that $\check{k}_0 = \tfrac{1}{2}(\hat{k}_0 + k_0')$. Hence, from the concavity of g, we obtain

(22) $\tilde{x}_1 + \check{k}_1 = g(\check{k}_0) \geq \frac{1}{2}g(\hat{k}_0) + \frac{1}{2}g(k'_0) = \frac{1}{2}(\hat{x}_1 + \hat{k}_1) + \frac{1}{2}(x'_1 + k'_1)$

$$= \tilde{x}_1 + \frac{1}{2}(\hat{k}_1 + k'_1)$$

Here the equality holds if $\hat{k}_0 = k'_0$. Hence we obtain $\check{k}_1 \geq \frac{1}{2}(\hat{k}_1 + k'_1)$, with equality holding when $\hat{k}_0 = k'_0$. This in turn implies

(23) $\tilde{x}_2 + \check{k}_2 = g(\check{k}_1) \geq g(\frac{1}{2}\hat{k}_1 + \frac{1}{2}k'_1) \geq \frac{1}{2}g(\hat{k}_1) + \frac{1}{2}g(k'_1)$

$$= \frac{1}{2}(\hat{x}_2 + \hat{k}_2) + \frac{1}{2}(x'_2 + k'_2) = \tilde{x}_2 + \frac{1}{2}(\hat{k}_2 + k'_2)$$

Hence we obtain $\check{k}_2 \geq \frac{1}{2}(\hat{k}_2 + k'_2)$. Here the equality holds if $\hat{k}_0 = k'_0$ and $\hat{k}_1 = k'_1$. Repeating the above argument, we obtain

(24) $\tilde{x}_T + b = g(\check{k}_{T-1}) \geq g(\frac{1}{2}\hat{k}_{T-1} + \frac{1}{2}k'_{T-1}) \geq \frac{1}{2}g(\hat{k}_{T-1}) + \frac{1}{2}g(k'_{T-1})$

$$= \frac{1}{2}(\hat{x}_T + b) + \frac{1}{2}(\hat{x}'_T + b) = \frac{1}{2}(\hat{x}_T + x_T) + b$$

Here the equality holds when $\hat{k}_t = k'_t$ for all $t = 0, 1, \ldots, T$. Therefore $\tilde{x}_T \geq \frac{1}{2}(\hat{x}_T + x'_T)$ with equality holding when $\hat{k}_t = k'_t$ for all $t = 0, 1, 2, \ldots, T$. Then in view of the monotonicity and the strict concavity of u, we obtain

(25) $$U(\tilde{x}) \geq U(\frac{1}{2}\hat{x} + \frac{1}{2}x') > \frac{1}{2}U(\hat{x}) + \frac{1}{2}U(x') = U(\hat{x})$$

which is a contradiction. Note that the above consideration does not preclude the possibility that $\hat{k} \neq k'$. We now show that this is impossible. Suppose that $(\hat{x}, \hat{k})$ and $(\hat{x}, k')$ are two optimal attainable paths. Then observe from the attainability that

(26) $$g(\hat{k}_{t-1}) - \hat{k}_t = g(k'_{t-1}) - k'_t, \, t = 1, 2, \ldots, T$$

Since $\hat{k}_T = k'_T = b$, so $\hat{k}_{T-1} = k'_{T-1}$ as a result of the monotonicity of g.[12] Then using the relation (26) successively, we obtain $\hat{k}_t = k'_t$, $t = 0, 1, 2, \ldots, T$, which in turn is consistent with $a - \hat{k}_0 = a - k'_0$. Thus we obtain $\hat{k} = k'$. Note that in the above proof the crucial assumption is $g' > 0$ and not $g'' < 0$. That is, the strict concavity of g (or $g'' < 0$) is not crucial.

Having demonstrated the existence and the uniqueness of the optimal attainable path, we now proceed to the characterization of such a path. To ease the notation, we define the following h-functions within the constraints of the above maximization problem:

(27) $$h_0(k_0, x_0) \equiv a - x_0 - k_0$$

(28) $$h_t(k_{t-1}, k_t, x_t) \equiv g(k_{t-1}) - x_t - k_t, \, t = 1, 2, \ldots, T$$

Note that k_T may be replaced by b, so that it can be dropped from the list of the control variables.[13] In order to obtain the first-order characterization of the above maximization problem, we next examine the rank constraint qualification.[14] For this purpose, define the $(T + 1) \times (2T + 1)$ matrix H as

(29)
$$H \equiv \begin{bmatrix} \dfrac{\partial h_0}{\partial k_0} & \dfrac{\partial h_0}{\partial k_1} & \cdots & \dfrac{\partial h_0}{\partial k_{T-1}} & \dfrac{\partial h_0}{\partial x_0} & \cdots & \dfrac{\partial h_0}{\partial x_T} \\[2ex] \dfrac{\partial h_1}{\partial k_0} & \dfrac{\partial h_1}{\partial k_1} & \cdots & \dfrac{\partial h_1}{\partial k_{T-1}} & \dfrac{\partial h_1}{\partial x_0} & \cdots & \dfrac{\partial h_1}{\partial x_T} \\[2ex] \cdots & \cdots & \cdots & \cdots & \cdots & \cdots & \cdots \\[1ex] \cdots & \cdots & \cdots & \cdots & \cdots & \cdots & \cdots \\[2ex] \dfrac{\partial h_T}{\partial k_0} & \dfrac{\partial h_T}{\partial k_1} & \cdots & \dfrac{\partial h_T}{\partial k_{T-1}} & \dfrac{\partial h_T}{\partial x_0} & \cdots & \dfrac{\partial h_T}{\partial x_T} \end{bmatrix}$$

Since the number of effective constraints for the above problem is $(T + 1)$, the rank constraint qualification of this problem states that the rank of matrix H should ·be equal to $(T + 1)$. It is easy to see that this condition is in general satisfied by actually computing H in view of (27) and (28) (and evaluating the matrix along the optimal attainable path).

We now define the Lagrangian function L of the above problem as

(30)
$$L \equiv \sum_{t=0}^{T} u(x_t)(1 + p)^{-t} + \sum_{t=0}^{T} p_t h_t$$

where $p_0, p_1, \ldots, p_T$ are the Lagrangian multipliers. Since the constraint qualification is satisfied, the following first-order condition gives a set of necessary conditions for an optimum (recall Chapter 1, Section D):

(31)
$$\frac{\partial \hat{L}}{\partial k_t} = -p_t + p_{t+1} g'(\hat{k}_t) = 0, \, t = 0, 1, \ldots, T - 1$$

(32)
$$\frac{\partial \hat{L}}{\partial x_t} = u'(\hat{x}_t)(1 + p)^{-t} - p_t = 0, \, t = 0, 1, 2, \ldots, T$$

Note that we do not have the inequalities $\partial \hat{L}/\partial k_t \leq 0$, and $\partial \hat{L}/\partial x_t \leq 0$, for we ruled out the corner solution (that is, $\hat{k}_t = 0$, $\hat{x}_t = 0$, for some t) by (A-5) and the assumptions $u(0) = -\infty$, $f(0) = 0$. Note that we have $p_t > 0$ for all $t = 0$, 1, 2, $\ldots$, T in view of (32) and the assumption $u'(x_t) > 0$ for all x_t. There are $(2T + 1)$ conditions in (31) and (32). These together with the $(T + 1)$ constraints (that is, $h_t = 0$, $t = 0, 1, \ldots, T$) determine the optimal value of the $(2T + 1) + (T + 1)$ variables (that is, k_t, $t = 0, 1, \ldots, T - 1$; x_t, p_t, $t = 0, 1, \ldots, T$).

It is easy to show that (31) and (32) together with the constraints (13) and (14) also give a set of sufficiency conditions for a (global) optimum in view of the concavity of u and g. Since the optimal attainable path is unique, these conditions give a set of necessary and sufficient conditions for a unique global optimum. We now turn to a study of these conditions. First we note that conditions (31) and (32) can be rewritten as

(33)
$$u'(\hat{x}_t) = u'(\hat{x}_{t+1}) \frac{g'(\hat{k}_t)}{1 + p}, \, t = 0, 1, \ldots, T - 1$$

There are T conditions in (33), which, together with the $(T + 2)$ conditions in (13) and (14), completely determine the value of the $(2T + 2)$ variables $\hat{k}_t$, $\hat{x}_t$, $t = 0$, $1, \ldots, T$.

The economic meaning of (33) is easy to see. By reducing consumption by one unit of the good, the loss of utility is $u'(\hat{x}_t)$ for the tth period. By investing this one unit, there is a gain in "net" output[15] by the amount of $g'(k_t)$. This, in turn, gives an increase in utility by the amount of $u'(\hat{x}_{t+1}) g'(\hat{k}_t)/(1 + p)$. Hence the equality (33) gives nothing but the competitive intertemporal arbitrage condition. It is easy to rewrite (33) in the following equivalent form:

(33′)
$$u'(\hat{x}_{t+1}) - u'(\hat{x}_t) = -\frac{u'(\hat{x}_{t+1})}{1 + p}\left[g'(\hat{k}_t) - (1 + p)\right]$$

It should be clear that this corresponds to the Euler equation obtained in Section D of this chapter.

We summarize some of the results obtained obove.

Theorem 5.D.2:   *Under assumptions (A-1), (A-2), (A-3), (A-4), and (A-5), we have the following:*

(i)   *The balanced growth path $[k^*(a), x^*(a)]$ starting from $a > 0$ exists, is unique, and $k^*(a) > 0$, $x^*(a) > 0$.*

(ii)   *The optimal attainable path $(\hat{k}_t, \hat{x}_t)$ starting from $a > 0$ and ending at $k_T = b \geq 0$ exists, is unique, and $\hat{k}_t > 0$, $\hat{x}_t > 0$ for all $t = 0, 1, 2, \ldots, T$, with the possible exception that $k_T = b = 0$.*

(iii)   *A necessary and sufficient condition for the path to be optimal and attainable is given by (33), (13), and (14).*

We now define the concept of competitiveness.

Definition: The attainable path $(\hat{k}_t, \hat{x}_t)$ starting from a and ending at b is called **competitive** if there exist nonnegative numbers ("prices") p_t such that

(34)
$$u(\hat{x}_t)(1 + p)^{-t} - p_t\hat{x}_t \geq u(x_t)(1 + p)^{-t} - p_t x_t$$
$$\text{for all } x_t \geq 0, t = 0, 1, \ldots, T$$

and

(35)
$$p_t g(\hat{k}_{t-1}) - p_{t-1}\hat{k}_{t-1} \geq p_t g(k_{t-1}) - p_{t-1}k_{t-1}$$
$$\text{for all } k_{t-1} \geq 0, t = 1, \ldots, T$$

REMARK: Relation (34) in the definition of competitiveness implies the well-known condition that consumers maximize utility subject to the budget constraint; that is,

(36) $u(\hat{x}_t) \geq u(x_t)$ for all $x_t \geq 0$ such that $p_t x_t \leq p_t \hat{x}_t$, $t = 0, 1, \ldots, T$

Condition (35) corresponds to the well-known profit maximization condition for the producers.

We now prove the following important corollary of Theorem 5.D.2, which is proved by Gale [4] in the multisector context.

Corollary: *An attainable path is competitive if and only if it is optimal.*

PROOF: In view of (iii) of Theorem 5.D.2, an attainable path is optimal if and only if there exist p_t, $t = 0, 1, \ldots, T$, all ≥ 0, such that

$$(37) \quad \sum_{t=0}^{T} u(\hat{x}_t)(1 + \rho)^{-t} + p_0(a - \hat{x}_0 - \hat{k}_0) + \sum_{t=1}^{T} p_t[g(\hat{k}_{t-1}) - \hat{x}_t - \hat{k}_t]$$

$$\geq \sum_{t=0}^{T} u(x_t)(1 + \rho)^{-t} + p_0(a - x_0 - k_0) + \sum_{t=1}^{T} p_t[g(k_{t-1}) - x_t - k_t]$$

for all $k_t, x_t \geq 0$, $t = 0, 1, \ldots, T$. Set $x_t = \hat{x}_t$ for all $t = 0, 1, \ldots, T$, except for $t = t_0$. Then we obtain (34), the first condition of competitiveness, since the choice of t_0 is arbitrary. Next set $k_t = \hat{k}_t$ for all $t = 1, \ldots, T$, except for $t = t_0$, and $x_t = \hat{x}_t$ for all $t = 0, 1, \ldots, T$. Since the choice of t_0 is arbitrary, we establish (35), the second condition of competitiveness. In other words, we established that optimality implies competitiveness.

To show the converse, first note the following simple identity:

$$(38) \qquad p_0 a - p_T b = p_0 a - p_T b, \text{ where } k_T = \hat{k}_T = b$$

Then summing both sides of (34), (35), and (38), we obtain (37), which establishes the converse.   (Q.E.D.)

We now turn to the problem in which t becomes "very large," which is obviously meaningful when T is large enough. Define $\hat{k}(\rho)$ and $\hat{x}(\rho)$ by

$$(39) \qquad\qquad g'[\hat{k}(\rho)] = 1 + \rho$$

and

$$(40) \qquad\qquad \hat{x}(\rho) = g[\hat{k}(\rho)] - \hat{k}(\rho)$$

Here we assume $g''(k) < 0$ for all k and impose assumption (A-2), part (a). Then $[\hat{k}(\rho), \hat{x}(\rho)]$ defines the modified golden rule path for the present discrete time model. Note that $0 < \hat{k}(\rho) < \bar{k}$. Recall now the two basic equations of the present model, that is, (7) for feasibility and (33') for optimality. Then, in view of $g''(k_t) < 0$ for all k_t and $u''(x_t) < 0$ for all x_t, we can easily conclude from (33') that

$$(41) \qquad\qquad \hat{x}_{t+1} - \hat{x}_t \gtreqless 0 \text{ according to whether } \hat{k}_t \lesseqgtr \hat{k}(\rho)$$

We rewrite condition (7) as

(7')
$$k_{t+1} - k_t = g(k_t) - k_t - x_{t+1}$$

Hence we can easily conclude that

(42) $\hat{k}_{t+1} - \hat{k}_t \gtreqless 0$ according to whether $g(\hat{k}_t) - \hat{k}_t - \hat{x}_{t+1} \gtreqless 0$

We can now draw a phase diagram similar to the one used in Section D. Applying our argument of the "eligibility condition," we can obtain the same conclusion we obtained in Section D, which we list as another corollary of Theorem 5.D.2.

Corollary (Ramsey-Koopmans-Cass): *As* $t \to \infty$ *(and* $T \to \infty$*),* $\hat{x}_t \to \hat{x}(\rho)$ *and* $\hat{k}_t \to \hat{k}(\rho)$*, regardless of the initial stock a.*

d.   SENSITIVITY ANALYSIS: BROCK'S THEOREM[16]

Finally we turn to the sensitivity analysis. Following Brock [2], we consider the "sensitivity" of the optimal attainable path with respect to the final stock b and with respect to the planning horizon. Here we can allow the case in which $g''(k_t) = 0$ for all k_t. Moreover, the subsequent analysis can allow for "autonomous" changes in u and g; that is, $u(x_t)$ can be replaced by $u(x_t, t)$ and $g(k_t)$ can be written as $g(k_t, t)$. The second argument t in these functions signifies the autonomous shifts of these functions. For example, $u(x_t, t)$ can involve the case in which there is a change in the discount rate as well as taste over time, and $g(k_t, t)$ can mean technological progress. We may then rewrite our feasibility condition (7) accordingly as

(7") $x_{t+1} + k_{t+1} = g(k_t, t), t = 0, 1, \ldots, T - 1$

It can be shown fairly easily, by repeating our earlier argument, that the optimality condition (33) can be rewritten accordingly as

(33")
$$u'(\hat{x}_t, t) = u'(\hat{x}_{t+1}, t) \frac{g'(k_t, t)}{1 + \rho}$$

where prime (') obviously means the partial derivative with respect to the first argument of the relevant functions. In fact, we can omit the discount factor $(1 + \rho)^{-t}$ from the target function U and simply rewrite $U \equiv \sum_{t=0}^{T} u(x_t, t)$, for the second argument t of u takes care of such a time discount. We may then omit $(1 + \rho)$ from (33").

Denote the T-period optimal attainable path starting from a and ending at b_1 and b_2, respectively, by $[\hat{k}_t(b_1), \hat{x}_t(b_1)]$ and $[\hat{k}_t(b_2), \hat{x}_t(b_2)]$, and let $b_1 > b_2$. First assume $\hat{k}_0(b_1) \leq \hat{k}_0(b_2)$, and we obtain a contradiction. $\hat{k}_0(b_1) \leq \hat{k}_0(b_2)$ implies

(43)
$$\hat{x}_0(b_1) \geq \hat{x}_0(b_2)$$

because $\hat{x}_0(b_1) + \hat{k}_0(b_1) = a = \hat{x}_0(b_2) + \hat{k}_0(b_2)$. This in turn implies that $u'[\hat{x}_0(b_1), t] \leq u'[\hat{x}_0(b_2), t]$. Write

(44)
$$P_t(b_1) \equiv u'[\hat{x}_t(b_1), t], P_t(b_2) \equiv u'[\hat{x}_t(b_2), t]$$
$$g'_t(b_1) \equiv g'[\hat{k}_t(b_1), t], g'_t(b_2) \equiv g'[\hat{k}_t(b_2), t]$$

to save space. Then we have

(45-a)
$$P_0(b_1) \leq P_0(b_2)$$

(45-b)
$$g'_0(b_1) \geq g'_0(b_2)$$

(45-c)
$$g_0(b_1) \leq g_0(b_2)$$

Hence, from (33″) and (45-b),

(46)
$$\frac{P_0(b_1)}{P_1(b_1)} = \frac{g'_0(b_1)}{1+\rho} \geq \frac{g'_0(b_2)}{1+\rho} = \frac{P_0(b_2)}{P_1(b_2)}$$

Therefore, from (46) and (45-a),

(47)
$$\frac{P_1(b_1)}{P_1(b_2)} \leq \frac{P_0(b_1)}{P_0(b_2)} \leq 1$$

Hence $P_1(b_1) \leq P_1(b_2)$, which means $\hat{x}_1(b_1) \geq \hat{x}_1(b_2)$. Then, together with (45-c) *and* feasibility, (13),

(48) $\hat{k}_1(b_1) - \hat{k}_1(b_2) = [g_0(b_1) - \hat{x}_1(b_1)] - [g_0(b_2) - \hat{x}_1(b_2)]$

$$= [g_0(b_1) - g_0(b_2)] - [\hat{x}_1(b_1) - \hat{x}_1(b_2)] \leq 0$$

Repeating the above argument, we obtain

(49) $\hat{k}_t(b_1) \leq \hat{k}_t(b_2)$ for all $t = 1, 2, \ldots, T$

which contradicts $\hat{k}_T(b_1) = b_1 > b_2 = \hat{k}_T(b_2)$. Therefore we have

(50) $k_0(b_1) > k_0(b_2)$

Repeating the above argument, we obtain

(51) $\hat{k}_t(b_1) > \hat{k}_t(b_2)$ for all $t = 0, 1, \ldots, T$, and
     $\hat{x}_t(b_1) < \hat{x}_t(b_2)$ for all $t = 1, 2, \ldots, T$

That is, an increase in the final stock requirement increases $\hat{k}_t$ and decreases $\hat{x}_t$ for *each* t in the optimal attainable path.

Next we consider the effect of changing the planning horizon T. We denote the optimal attainable path starting from a and ending at b for the T-period problem by $[\hat{k}_t^T(b), \hat{x}_t^T(b)]$. Hence, for example, $\hat{k}_T^{T+1}(0)$ denotes the (per capita) stock of capital in period T in the $(T + 1)$-period optimal attainable path starting from a and ending at $k_{T+1} = 0$.

We now compare two optimal attainable paths, both starting from a and ending at 0 with the only difference being the planning horizon, T for one and $(T + 1)$ for the other. Then $\hat{k}_{T+1}{}^{T+1}(0) = \hat{k}_T{}^T(0) = 0$, but $\hat{k}_T{}^{T+1}(0) > 0$; for if $\hat{k}_T{}^{T+1}(0) = 0$, then $\hat{x}_{T+1}{}^{T+1}(0) = 0$, which implies $u[\hat{x}_{T+1}{}^{T+1}, T + 1] = -\infty$. Next observe that

$$(52) \qquad \hat{k}_t{}^{T+1}(0) = \hat{k}_t{}^T\left(\hat{k}_T{}^{T+1}(0)\right), t = 0, 1, \ldots, T$$

for otherwise one can always increase the value of U for the $(T + 1)$-period program with $(\hat{k}_{T+1}{}^{T+1} = 0)$ by following the path $\hat{k}_t{}^T(\hat{k}_T{}^{T+1}(0))$, $t = 0, \ldots, T$ (that is, up to the Tth period). Since $\hat{k}_T{}^{T+1}(0) > 0$, (52) implies

$$(53) \qquad 0 = \hat{k}_T{}^T(0) < \hat{k}_T{}^T\left(\hat{k}_T{}^{T+1}(0)\right)$$

Hence, in view of (51) and (53), we obtain

$$(54) \qquad \hat{k}_t{}^T(0) < \hat{k}_t{}^{T+1}(0) \qquad \text{for each } t = 0, 1, \ldots, T$$

and

$$\hat{x}_t{}^T(0) > \hat{x}_t{}^{T+1}(0) \qquad \text{for each } t = 0, 1, \ldots, T$$

Repeating the argument, we have for each t,

$$(55) \qquad \hat{k}_t{}^T(0) < \hat{k}_t{}^{T+1}(0) < \hat{k}_t{}^{T+2}(0) < \cdots$$

and

$$\hat{x}_t{}^T(0) > \hat{x}_t{}^{T+1}(0) > \hat{x}_t{}^{T+2}(0) > \cdots$$

In other words, an increase in the planning horizon with zero terminal stocks always increases the optimal (per capita) stock for each t and decreases the optimal (per capita) consumption for each t.
Next note that

$$(56) \qquad \hat{k}_t{}^T(0) \leq \bar{k}_t \qquad \text{for all } t = 0, 1, \ldots, T; T = 1, 2, \ldots$$

where $\bar{k}_t$ denotes k_t in the path of pure accumulation. Hence, for each t, $\hat{k}_t{}^T(0)$ is a monotone increasing sequence with respect to T, which is bounded from above. Hence $\lim_{T \to \infty} \hat{k}_t{}^T(0)$ exists. Denote this by $\hat{k}_t$. Also $\hat{x}_t{}^T(0)$ is a monotone decreasing sequence with respect to T, which is bounded from below by zero. Hence $\lim_{T \to \infty} \hat{x}_t{}^T(0)$ exists. Denote this by $\hat{x}_t$. The path $(\hat{k}_t, \hat{x}_t)$ is attainable in view of the continuity of g.

This convergence is the essential result in the sensitivity analysis with respect to T, for it asserts that the distance between $\hat{k}_t{}^T(0)$ and $\hat{k}_t{}^{T'}(0)$ and the distance between $\hat{x}_t{}^T(0)$ and $\hat{x}_t{}^{T'}(0)$ can be made arbitrarily small, at least for certain initial periods when T and T' are sufficiently large. Also note that $(\hat{k}_t, \hat{x}_t)$ corresponds to the path obtained by Koopmans and Cass for the infinite horizon problem (which also implies that $\hat{k}_t$ does not converge to 0 when $t \to \infty$).

We summarize the above results as follows:

Theorem 5.D.3 (Brock):   *Under (A-1) and (A-4), we have (51) and (55), and the optimal attainable path for the T-period problem with no terminal stock requirements,* $[\hat{k}_t^T(0), \hat{x}_t^T(0)]$, *converges (for each t) to a limit path* $(\hat{k}_t, \hat{x}_t)$ *as* $T \to \infty$.

Can we assert that $[\hat{k}_t^T(b), \hat{x}_t^T(b)]$ also converges to $(\hat{k}_t, \hat{x}_t)$ when $b > 0$, as $T \to \infty$? Brock [2] proved the following corollary (his theorem 3), which asserts, in essence, that if b is below a certain value, then such a convergence holds.

Corollary: *If* $b < \varliminf_{t \to \infty} \hat{k}_t$, *then* $\lim_{T \to \infty} \hat{k}_t^T(b)$ *exists and equals* $\hat{k}_t$.

REMARK: Before we prove this corollary, we may have to explain the mathematical concept $\varliminf$ (or lim inf). Let $\{x^q\}$ be a sequence of real numbers and let X be the set of real numbers x (including ∞ and $-\infty$) such that $x^{q_s} \to x$ for some subsequence $\{x^{q_s}\}$ of $\{x^q\}$. Then $\varliminf$ (or lim inf) and $\varlimsup$ (or lim sup) are defined as[17]

$$\text{(57)} \qquad\qquad \varlimsup_{q \to \infty} x^q \equiv \text{lub of } X$$

and

$$\text{(58)} \qquad\qquad \varliminf_{q \to \infty} x^q \equiv \text{glb of } X$$

Write $\varliminf_{q \to \infty} x^q \equiv \hat{x}$. Then we can show easily that $\hat{x} \in X$, and that if $\alpha < \hat{x}$ then there exists an integer N such that $q \geq N$ implies $x^q > \alpha$. (That is, for a given $\epsilon > 0$, there exists an N such that $q \geq N$ implies $x^q > \hat{x} - \epsilon$.) Similar results hold for lim sup. We now turn to the proof of the above corollary.

PROOF: By assumption, $b < \varliminf_{t \to \infty} \hat{k}_t$. Hence there exists a T_0 such that

$$\text{(59)} \qquad\qquad \hat{k}_t > b, \text{ for } t \geq T_0$$

For $T \geq T_0$, choose N, which depends on T, such that

$$\text{(60)} \qquad\qquad \hat{k}_T^T(b) \equiv b < \hat{k}_T^N(0)$$

which is possible since $\hat{k}_t^N(0)$ unconditionally converges to $\hat{k}_t$ by (55) and $\hat{k}_t > b$ by (59). Then by (51) we have

$$\text{(61)} \qquad\qquad \hat{k}_t^T(b) < \hat{k}_t^N(0), \ t = 0, 1, \dots, T$$

Therefore, using (51) again, we obtain

$$\text{(62)} \qquad\qquad \hat{k}_t^T(0) \leq \hat{k}_t^T(b) < \hat{k}_t^N(0), \ t = 0, 1, \dots, T$$

with equality when $b = 0$. Observe that $\hat{k}_t^T(0) \to \hat{k}_t$ as $T \to \infty$ and $\hat{k}_t^N(0) \to \hat{k}_t$ as $N \to \infty$. Since $N \to \infty$ as $T \to \infty$, (62) implies that $\hat{k}_t^T(b) \to \hat{k}_t$ (for each t) as $T \to \infty$.

(Q.E.D.)

REMARK: This corollary shows that as long as b is below the bound $\lim_{t \to \infty} \hat{k}_t$, the optimal attainable path is insensitive to changes in the terminal stock b, for certain initial periods. In other words, as long as b_1 and b_2 are below the bound, the distance between $\hat{k}_t^T(b_1)$ and $\hat{k}_t^T(b_2)$ can be made arbitrarily small for certain initial periods by choosing T sufficiently large.

FOOTNOTES

1. This does not preclude the importance of period analysis in the empirical contexts. For example, in empirical econometric research one is often forced to use period analysis since the time series data are tabulated at discrete time intervals (for example, GNP). In optimization models, one may be able to change the policy (or control) variables only at discrete time intervals as a result of practical considerations. Then such a time interval may define the period.

2. We should note that our specification of the model is *not* the only way to produce equation (3). Our point here is simply that we should make the specification explicit to avoid possible misunderstanding.

3. We here adopt the convention that zero is the subsistence level of consumption. Hence $x_t = 0$ for all t means that the economy is at the subsistence level all the time.

4. In the literature, the following alternative assumptions are used in place of (A-2'), part (a): $f'(0) = \infty$ and $f'(\infty) = 0$. See Sections C and D. Clearly this implies the present assumption, (A-2'), part (a).

5. This is the case of a constant capital:output ratio. Obviously for such a case, (A-2), part (a), cannot be imposed.

6. If $k_{t_0} = 0$ for some t_0, then $f(0) = 0$ implies $x_t = 0$, $k_t = 0$ for all $t > t_0$. This is an uninteresting case of "balanced growth."

7. See Koopmans [6], p. 237, for example. When $a = \bar{k}$, then $k_t = \bar{k}$ and $x_t = 0$ for all t except possibly for $t = T$ and $T - 1$. This is again a trivial and uninteresting case.

8. Recall the definition of continuous functions and note that the linear (affine) functions are continuous everywhere in the domain. The function g is continuous because it is differentiable.

9. Each of $k_t, x_t, t = 0, 1, 2, \ldots, T$, is bounded from below by 0; $k_t, t = 0, 1, 2, \ldots, T$, are bounded from above by the path of pure accumulation; $x_t, t = 0, 1, 2, \ldots, T$, are bounded from above by $g'(k_t) < \infty$ for all $k_t < \infty$ *and* equation (7). Let $\bar{x}_t, \bar{k}_t, t = 0, 1, 2, \ldots, T$, be these upper bounds and consider rectangles S_t in R^2 defined by $S_t = \{(x_t, k_t): 0 \le k_t \le \bar{k}_t, 0 \le x_t \le \bar{x}_t\}, t = 0, 1, \ldots, T$. Clearly the S_t's are compact; hence in view of Tychonoff's theorem $\otimes_{t=0}^T S_t$ is also compact in R^{2T+2} with respect to the product topology (Theorem 0.A.15). As a closed subset of the compact set, $A(a, b; T)$ is compact.

10. Consider $S_t, t = 0, 1, 2, \ldots,$ *ad inf.* Define $S \equiv \otimes_{t=0}^\infty S_t$. Then S is again compact as a result of the Tychonoff theorem. Hence $A(a)$ with $T \to \infty$ is compact as a closed subset of S. Hence, using the Weierstrass theorem again, we can assert the existence of an optimal attainable program for the *infinite* horizon problem ($T = \infty$), as long as $U(x_0, x_1, \ldots) \equiv \sum_{t=0}^\infty u(x_t)(1 + \rho)^{-t}$ remains continuous and bounded. This argu-

ment is used to prove existence by Beale and Koopmans [1]. A different proof of existence for a more general model which involves factor-augumenting technological progress is provided by Brock and Gale [3]. They also showed the possible non-existence of an optimal attainable path in such an economy (if the discount rate ρ is below a certain critical value). See also Gale and Sutherland [5].

11. If, in (k_t, x_t), $x_t = 0$ for some t, then this path becomes "infinitely worse" than $(k^*(a), x^*(a))$, because $u(0) = -\infty$. If $k_t = 0$ for some t, then $f(0) = 0$ implies that $x_{t+1} = k_{t+1} = \cdots = x_T = k_T = 0$.

12. That is, $g'(k_t) > 0$ for all $k_t \geq 0$.

13. It is certainly possible to take into account the constraint $k_T = b$ explicitly. We can also modify this constraint to $k_T \geq b$. However, as long as $u' > 0$ everywhere (that is, nonsatiation), $k_T \geq b$ will produce the same solution to the above maximization problem as in the case in which $k_T = b$. The reader should be able to carry out the analysis when the constraint $k_T = b$ or $k_T \geq b$ is explicitly taken into account.

14. We can certainly use other constraint qualifications. However, as long as every function in the constraints is differentiable, we might as well use the classical rank condition, for it is convenient to deal with the equality constraints (see Chapter 1, Section D, in particular, Theorem, I.D.6.).

15. "Net" means net or depreciation (μ) *and* population growth (n). Recall (8).

16. We are heavily indebted to Brock [2] for the argument here. Our effort is simply expository.

17. "lim inf" and "lim sup" are the abbreviations of limit inferior and limit superior, respectively. Needless to say, lub stands for the least upper bound (supremum), and glb stands for the greatest lower bound (infimum).

REFERENCES

1. Beale, R., and Koopmans, T. C., "Maximizing Stationary Utility in a Constant Technology," *SIAM Journal of Applied Mathematics*, 17, September 1969.

2. Brock, W. A., "Sensitivity of Optimal Growth Paths with Respect to a Change in Target Stocks," *Zeitschrift für Nationalökonomie*, Supp. 1, 1971 (originally presented at the Purdue Meeting of the Kansas-Missouri Seminar on Quantitative Economics, October 1969).

3. Brock, W. A., and Gale, D., "Optimal Growth under Factor Augmenting Progress," *Journal of Economic Theory*, vol. 1, October 1969.

4. Gale, D., "On Optimal Development in a Multisector Economy," *Review of Economic Studies*, XXXIV, January 1967.

5. Gale, D., and Sutherland, W. R., "Analysis of a One Good Model of Economic Development," in *Mathematics of the Decision Sciences*, Part 2, ed. by G. B. Dantzig and A. F. Veinott, Providence, R. I., American Mathematical Society, 1968.

6. Koopmans, T. C., "On the Concept of Optimal Economic Growth," in *The Econometric Approach to Development Planning*, Pontificiae Academiae Scientarum Varia, Amsterdam, North-Holland, 1965.

7. Samuelson, P. A., "A Turnpike Refutation of the Golden Rule in a Welfare-Maximizing Many Year Plan," in *Essays on the Theory of Optimal Economic Growth*, ed. by K. Shell, Cambridge, Mass., M.I.T. Press, 1967.

6

MULTISECTOR MODELS OF ECONOMIC GROWTH

a. INTRODUCTION

If we had to name the most important immediate forerunner of modern mathematical economics, we would not hesitate to choose John von Neumann for his model of economic growth presented in his 1937 paper [22]. Not only did this paper provide the first explicit nonaggregate model in capital and growth theory, but also it presented (1) the first explicit activity analysis model of production and (2) the first abstract model of a competitive economy (together with Wald's model in his papers published in 1935 and 1936), which lead to the models of the 1950s (see Chapter 2, Section E). In addition to the modern character of the model, the problems that von Neumann dealt with are also modern. In particular, he was concerned with the path that gives the maximal rate of growth and the price implication of such a path. In the first part of this section, we present the model as formulated now so as to convey its modern character. In subsection b, we prove his major results in an elementary fashion.

Because of the innovative character of the paper, many papers have been written on the von Neumann models, but we restrict ourselves to his growth model as such and exclude its impact on other developments such as activity analysis and the theory of competitive markets.

A major effort has been devoted to simplifying the proof of von Neumann's major theorem in the original paper. To prove his theorem von Neumann used Brouwer's fixed point theorem. Later, Loomis [15], Georgescu-Roegen [5], Gale [3], and Karlin [11] all provided elementary proofs. The proof of the existence of the balanced growth path with the maximal growth rate can be separated from the proof of the price implication of such a path. The essence of the proof of the existence is simply to utilize the compactness of the relevant set of production. Our proof in subsection b also follows this line. In this connection, we may note a formal similarity to the theory of nonnegative matrices in which the existence of the Frobenius root can be proved by utilizing the compactness of a certain set, although it can also be proved by using Brouwer's fixed point theorem (see Chapter 4). For the proof of the price implication of the maximal rate balanced growth path, Georgescu-Roegen, Gale, and Karlin made direct use of the separation theorem of convex sets. We use, instead, the fundamental theorem of concave functions (Chapter 1, Section B). It is true that this theorem is derived from the separation theorem, but the use of this fundamental theorem will avoid many steps in the proof (which is hence much simpler) compared with those necessary in the proof which uses the separation theorem directly.

Another major effort devoted to the von Neumann model is in the direction of the generalization of the model and its results. Essentially there are three weaknesses in the original paper:

(i)   There is no discussion of the irreducibility of the model, and there is no proof that the value of output at each time period is positive.

(ii) The growth paths that von Neumann considered were restricted to the "balanced growth paths," that is, paths in which all commodities grow at the same rate.

(iii) There is no explicit treatment of consumption.

The major contributions to eliminating the first weakness were made by Kemeny, Morgenstern, and Thompson [12], Thompson [21], and Gale [3]. The major breakthrough concerning the second point came in the form of the turnpike theorem by DOSSO [2] and later followers such as Radner and McKenzie. The turnpike theorem will be discussed in the next chapter. The introduction of consumption was attempted by Morishima [18]. We discuss these three weaknesses here under subsection c.

Consider an economy that transforms the stock of n commodities x, an n-vector, into the stock of n commodities y, an n-vector, in one time period. This time period can be considered as a unit "production period." This transformation can be represented by (x, y), a point in R^{2n}. Here x is an "input" vector and y is an "output" vector. There are certainly many input-output combinations that are possible in the economy. The set of such input-output combinations, that is, the collection of these (x, y)'s which are technically possible in the economy, is called the **technology set** or the **production set** of the economy and is denoted by T. Clearly, elements of x or y can be zero. The concept of T is essentially the same as the concept of a production set in activity analysis (see Chapter 0, Section C). A point of caution is that x and y here are explicitly vectors of the *stocks* of commodities rather than the *flows* of commodities.

At first glance, the concept of a production process, especially the concept of a production *period*, may seem absurd. There are two apparent difficulties. One is the problem of the simultaneous inputs and outputs, and the other is the problem of differences in production periods. Let us view these two difficulties separately. The first difficulty is the assumption that in the beginning of each period all the commodities are *simultaneously* fed into the process and at the end of the period all the commodities are *simultaneously* produced. In reality, such a simultaneous input or output rarely occurs. More commonly, various commodities are fed into the process at different points in time and various commodities are produced from time to time. However, such "successive" inputs and outputs can be handled simply as follows. Consider a production process in which inputs go into the production process at time t_0 and t_1 and outputs come out at time t_2 and t_3. Then we can "decompose" such a production process into three "steps." In other words, the commodities that are fed in at time t_0 produce certain "intermediate commodities," and at t_1, new inputs, together with these intermediate commodities, are fed in. At time t_2 certain commodities are produced as final outputs together with the higher order intermediate goods. At time t_3 only the final outputs are produced. Hence, including these intermediate commodities in the classification of commodities, in each of the production periods (t_0, t_1), (t_1, t_2), (t_2, t_3), all the commodities are simultaneously fed in at the beginning of the period and produced at the end of the period. We only consider such "decomposed" processes.

The second apparent difficulty in the concept of a production period lies in the difference in the actual time period from process to process. This can simply be handled as follows. Suppose there are only three processes z_1, z_2, and z_3 such that z_1 takes 30 days, z_2 takes 60 days, and z_3 takes 45 days. Take the greatest common divisor of these three periods $\{30, 60, 45\}$—that is, 15—and define this 15 days as a unit period of production. Then z_1 is decomposed into two steps. In other words, at the end of the first period (that is, at the end of 15 days), the process produces certain "intermediate" (or unfinished) commodities, and during the second period of production these intermediate commodities are all transformed into the final commodities of the process z_1. Thus, at the end of the second period (that is, at the end of 30 days), this process z_1 is completed.

Hence, by choosing the unit of period properly and by properly including the "intermediate" commodities in the list of commodities, we can avoid the two difficulties and can proceed meaningfully to our analysis. Time in this economy elapses with the succession of such production periods, and each production process is in the technology set T. We assume that this set T is constant over time. This implies, among other things, that there is no technological progress in the economy.

In the original von Neumann presentation of the model, a concrete explanation about the input-output vector (x, y) is given. Let a_{ij} be the amount of the ith commodity needed as an input in a one-unit operation of the jth process (or "activity"). Let b_{ij} be the amount of the ith commodity produced in a one-unit operation of the jth process. Let there be n commodities and m processes in the economy. Let $A = [a_{ij}]$ and $B = [b_{ij}]$ be $n \times m$ matrices whose entries are non-negative real numbers and possibly zero for some elements. Let a^j be an n-vector whose ith element is a_{ij} and let b^j be an n-vector whose ith element is b_{ij}. Some of the a_{ij}'s and the b_{ij}'s can be zero. One unit operation of the jth process transforms

a^j to b^j. Let $z(t)$ be an m-vector whose jth element, $z_j(t)$, signifies the level of operation of the jth process in period t; $z_j(t) \geq 0$ for all j and t. The vector $z(t)$ is called the **activity level vector** (or **process level vector**) in period t. That $x(t)$ (often denoted also as x_t) is an input vector in period t means that $x(t)$ can be written as

$$x(t) = \sum_{j=1}^{m} a^j z_j(t)$$

for some $z_j(t) \geq 0$ $(j = 1, 2, \ldots, m)$. Similarly, that $y(t)$ (or y_t) is an output vector in period t means that it can be written as

$$y(t) = \sum_{j=1}^{m} b^j z_j(t)$$

for some $z_j(t) \geq 0$ $(j = 1, 2, \ldots, m)$. The assumption that the technology set T is constant implies that these a_{ij}'s and b_{ij}'s are constant over time for some $z_j(t) \geq 0$ $(j = 1, 2, \ldots, m)$. Allow "free disposability"; that is, if the process (x, y) is in the technology set, then there is a nonnegative m-vector z such that

$$x \geq A \cdot z \quad \text{and} \quad 0 \leq y \leq B \cdot z$$

Hence, the von Neumann technology set T_N can be written as

$$T_N \equiv \{(x, y): x \geq A \cdot z, 0 \leq y \leq B \cdot z, \text{for some } z \geq 0\}$$

That T_N is constant over time can be expressed by saying that A and B are constant over time. Note that the set T_N is a convex polyhedral cone with its vertex at the origin.

The following assumptions are then imposed by von Neumann.

(A$_N$-1) $a_{ij} \geq 0, b_{ij} \geq 0$ for all i and j.
(A$_N$-2) $A + B > 0$, that is, $a_{ij} + b_{ij} > 0$ for all i and j.

The second assumption is rather unrealistic, for even if (A$_N$-2) holds, $a_{ij} = 0$ implies $b_{ij} > 0$, and $b_{ij} = 0$ implies $a_{ij} > 0$, which means that *every* commodity is either used as an input or produced as an output in *every* production process. It is quite possible that certain commodities may not be involved in some processes either as inputs or as outputs. About this point, Morishima remarked that "in the process of producing sewing machines, a banana is neither produced as a by-product, nor is it used as a raw material" ([19], p. 20).

Kemeny, Morgenstern, and Thompson [12] modified the above assumptions as follows:

(A-i) $a_{ij} \geq 0$ and $b_{ij} \geq 0$ for all i and j.
(A-ii) For any j, there exists at least one i such that $a_{ij} > 0$.
(A-iii) For any i, there exists at least one j such that $b_{ij} > 0$.

Assumption (A-ii) means that every process uses some commodity as an input, which implies "the impossibility of the land of Cockaigne." Assumption (A-iii) means that every commodity is producible by some process. Assumptions (A-ii) and (A-iii) modify (A_N-2) in a significant way.

Karlin [11], in his formulation of the von Neumann model, did not use the von Neumann specification of the technology set in terms of the matrices A and B. Hence he did not adopt the above specification of assumptions in terms of the a_{ij}'s and the b_{ij}'s. Rather, he abstracted the essential nature of the von Neumann technology by supposing that the technology set T of the economy is specified by the following four assumptions.

(A-1) T is a closed convex cone in Ω^{2n}, the nonnegative orthant of R^{2n}.

(A-2) (Free disposability) $(x, y) \in T$, $x' \geqq x$, and $0 \leqq y' \leqq y$ imply $(x', y') \in T$.

(A-3) (The impossibility of the land of Cockaigne) $(0, y) \in T$ implies $y = 0$.

(A-4) (The "productiveness") For any i, there exists an $(x, y) \in T$ such that $y_i > 0$ (that is, every commodity is producible).

> REMARK: As remarked in the exposition of activity analysis (Chapter 0, Section C), "T is a convex cone" implies additivity, proportionality (that is, complete divisibility and constant returns to scale), and the possibility of inaction.

> REMARK: In view of (A-1), (A-4) is equivalent to the following:

> **(A-4')**   There exists an $(x, y) \in T$ such that $y > 0$.

It is easy to see that the von Neumann technology set T_N with (A-i) to (A-iii) is a special case of the technology set T with (A-1) to (A-4). To see this, note that (A-i) together with the definition of T_N imply (A-1) and (A-2); (A-ii) implies (A-3); and (A-iii) implies (A-4).

The economy transforms the stock of commodities at the beginning of period $x(t)$ to the stock of commodities $y(t)$ by spending one time period, such that $(x(t), y(t)) \in T$, where T satisfies (A-1) to (A-4). Thus the movement of the economy can be depicted schematically by Figure 6.1.

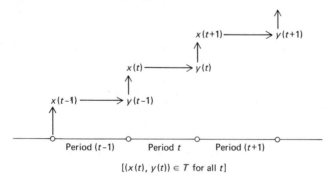

[$(x(t), y(t)) \in T$ for all t]

Figure 6.1.   Economic Growth in the von Neumann Economy.

Von Neumann restricted his consideration to the set of **balanced growth paths**, that is, the paths of $(x(t), y(t))$ such that $(x(t), y(t)) \in T$ and $y(t) = \alpha x(t)$ for some $\alpha > 0$. He allows $\alpha < 1$ so that the economy may decay rather than grow. The question then is whether there *exists* a balanced growth path that has the maximal rate of growth and whether such a path can be supported under a certain economic system. The first question to consider is the problem of maximizing α over the set of balanced growth paths, and the second is the problem of the economic interpretation (in particular, the price implication) of the balanced growth path which gives the maximal rate. The reader may realize that this question is analogous to either of the following two problems in modern economic literature:

(i) *Activity analysis*: the existence of an efficient point in a production set and the assertion that every efficient point can be realized as a profit maximization point (Theorem 0.C.3).

(ii) *Welfare economics*: the existence of a Pareto optimal point and the assertion that every Pareto optimal point can be supported by competitive pricing (Theorem 1.C.2).

b. MAJOR THEOREMS

We now proceed to the investigation of the two major problems stated above: (1) the existence of the balanced growth path with a maximal rate, and (2) the price implication of such a path.

Definition: Define a real-valued function $\alpha(x, y)$ on T as

$$\alpha(x, y) \equiv \max_{\alpha \in R} \{\alpha : y \geq \alpha x\}, \text{ where } (x, y) \neq 0$$

The value of $\alpha(x, y)$ is called the **rate of expansion** of the process (x, y) in T.

REMARK: For $(0, 0)$, $\alpha(x, y)$ cannot be defined. Note also that, owing to (A-3), $(0, y) \notin T$ if $y \geq 0$. Hence $\alpha(x, y)$ is not defined on such points under (A-3). Thus $\alpha(x, y)$ is not defined for $(0, 0)$ and $(0, y)$ with $y \geq 0$. Since $x \geq 0$ and $y \geq 0$, this means that $\alpha(x, y)$ is defined only when $x \geq 0$. This implies that $\alpha(x, y) \geq 0$. The concept of "rate of expansion" is illustrated in Figure 6.2. As an example of $\alpha(x, y) = 0$, consider $x = (0, 1)$ and $y = (2, 0)$. Note that $\alpha(x, y)$ may be less than 1; hence the process can produce "decay" rather than "expansion." Writing $x = (x_1, x_2, \ldots, x_n)$ and $y = (y_1, y_2, \ldots, y_n)$, we can also write the above definition of the expansion rate as follows. Let $\alpha_i(x, y)$, $i = 1, 2, \ldots, n$, be defined as

$$\alpha_i(x, y) \equiv \begin{cases} \dfrac{y_i}{x_i} & \text{if } x_i > 0 \\ \infty & \text{if } x_i = 0 \text{ and } y_i > 0 \\ \text{undefined if } x_i = 0 \text{ and } y_i = 0 \end{cases}$$

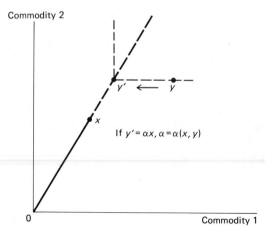

Commodity 2

If $y' = \alpha x$, $\alpha = \alpha(x, y)$

0

Commodity 1

Figure 6.2.   An Illustration of the Rate of Expansion.

Then

$$\alpha(x, y) = \min_i \alpha_i(x, y) \qquad \text{for } x \geq 0$$

As is clear from Figure 6.2, the concept of the rate of expansion is that of a "balanced growth path," that is, a ray from the origin. Given (x, y), if y is not on the ray from the origin passing through x, y is brought into such a ray as illustrated in Figure 6.2 ($y \to y'$).

Since $\alpha(x, y)$ is a function of (x, y), the value of $\alpha(x, y)$, the expansion rate, varies from process to process. The following theorem asserts that there exists a process $(\hat{x}, \hat{y})$ in T which gives the maximum rate of expansion. The essential argument for this existence theorem is the standard compactness argument if we assume that $\alpha(x, y)$ is continuous.

Theorem 6.A.1:   *Under the assumptions (A-1) to (A-4), there exists an $(\hat{x}, \hat{y}) \in T$ such that $\hat{y} = \hat{\alpha}\hat{x}$, where $\hat{\alpha} \equiv \alpha(\hat{x}, \hat{y})$, and $\hat{\alpha} \geq \alpha(x, y)$ for all $(x, y) \in T$ with $x \geq 0$. Also we have $0 < \hat{\alpha} < \infty$.*

PROOF: Let $\overline{T}$ be the intersection of T with the unit sphere (with the center at the origin) in R^{2n}. Since T is closed, $\overline{T}$ is also closed, which in turn implies that $\overline{T}$ is compact. Suppose $\alpha(x, y)$ is continuous for all points of T (or $\overline{T}$). Then $\alpha(x, y)$ achieves a maximum on $\overline{T}$ by Weierstrass' theorem (Theorem 0.A.18). However, as Glycopantis [6] pointed out, $\alpha(x, y)$ can be discontinuous (for such an example, see [6], p. 296). This, in essence, is due to the fact that the domains of the functions $\alpha_i(x, y)$ are not identical. To avoid this difficulty, define the subset T_i of T as

$$T_i \equiv \{(x, y) \in T : \alpha(x, y) = \alpha_i(x, y)\}$$

Clearly, $T \setminus \{0\} = \cup_i T_i$. Let $\tilde{T}_i \equiv T_i \cup \{0\}$, and let (x^q, y^q) be a convergent sequence in $\tilde{T}_i$ with limit (x^0, y^0). Then, since $y_k^q/x_k^q \geq y_i^q/x_i^q$ for $(x^q, y^q) \neq 0$ implies that $y_k^0/x_k^0 \geq y_i^0/x_i^0$, we have $\alpha(x^0, y^0) = \alpha_i(x^0, y^0)$. That is, $(x^0, y^0) \in \tilde{T}_i$ so that the $\tilde{T}_i$'s are *closed* cones. Also the functions $\alpha_i(x, y)$ are continuous except when they are undefined. Let T_i^* be the intersection of $\tilde{T}_i$ with the unit sphere in R^{2n}. Then the T_i^*'s are compact. Hence, from Weierstrass' theorem, $\alpha_i(x, y)$ achieves its maximum b_i on T_i^*. Choose the maximum of the b_i's over i, which clearly exists. Thus we have shown that there exists an $(x^*, y^*) \in \bar{T}$ such that $\alpha(x^*, y^*) \geq \alpha(x, y)$ for all $(x, y) \in \bar{T}$ ($\because \cup_i T_i = T_i \setminus \{0\}$). Write $\hat{\alpha} \equiv \alpha(x^*, y^*)$. Since T is a cone, for any $(x, y) \in T$ with $x \geq 0$, there exists an $(\bar{x}, \bar{y})$ in $\bar{T}$ such that $(\lambda \bar{x}, \lambda \bar{y}) = (x, y)$ for some $\lambda > 0$, $\lambda \in R$ [note $(\bar{x}, \bar{y}) = (x, y)/\|(x, y)\|$]. However, by the definition of $\alpha(x, y)$, we have $\alpha(x, y) = \alpha(\lambda \bar{x}, \lambda \bar{y}) = \alpha(\bar{x}, \bar{y})$. Since $\alpha(x^*, y^*) \geq \alpha(x, y)$ for all $(x, y) \in \bar{T}$ with $x \geq 0$, we then obtain that $\alpha(x^*, y^*) \geq \alpha(x, y)$ for all $(x, y) \in T$ with $x \geq 0$. From the free disposability assumption (A-2), we can find an $(\hat{x}, \hat{y})$ in T such that $\alpha(\hat{x}, \hat{y}) = \alpha(x^*, y^*)$ and $\hat{y} = \hat{\alpha} \hat{x}$. Thus $\hat{\alpha} \equiv \alpha(\hat{x}, \hat{y}) \geq \alpha(x, y)$ for all $(x, y) \in T$ with $\hat{y} = \hat{\alpha} \hat{x}$. Finally, we show that $0 < \hat{\alpha} < \infty$. From (A-4) there exists an $(\tilde{x}, \tilde{y})$ in T such that $\tilde{y} > 0$. Since $\alpha(\tilde{x}, \tilde{y}) > 0$ and $\hat{\alpha} \geq \alpha(\tilde{x}, \tilde{y})$, $\hat{\alpha} > 0$. $\hat{\alpha} < \infty$ clearly follows from (A-3) and $\hat{y} = \hat{\alpha} \hat{x}$.   (Q.E.D.)

REMARK: In the above proof (which is in essence due to [6]), we observe that the possible discontinuities of the function $\alpha(x, y)$ make it necessary to complicate the "compactness" proof. Note that in the above proof the continuity of $\alpha(x, y)$ is neither established nor utilized. The proof relies on the continuity of $\alpha_i(x, y)$.

REMARK: We may recall that the "failure" of the "compactness" proof (as a result of the lack of continuity) also appeared in the proof of the Frobenius theorem (Theorem 4.B.1). The reader may, therefore, wish to consider Theorem 6.A.1 and the Frobenius theorem under a unified framework.

REMARK: For the case of $n = 1$, that is, a one commodity economy, the above proof can be illustrated by Figure 6.3.

REMARK: The definition of $\alpha(x, y)$ reduces the rate of expansion to the rate in the corresponding balanced growth path, as was illustrated in the definition of $\alpha(x, y)$. Hence Theorem 6.A.1 simply asserts that there exists a balanced growth path which maximizes the rate of expansion in the set of all the balanced growth paths in the economy. We call such a path the **von Neumann path**. It is important to notice that the von Neumann path is not necessarily unique. In the above illustrations, the von Neumann path was supposed to constitute a unique ray from the origin. But, as McKenzie [16] emphasized in connection with the turnpike theorem, this is not necessarily the case. The set of von Neumann paths, in general, constitutes a facet.

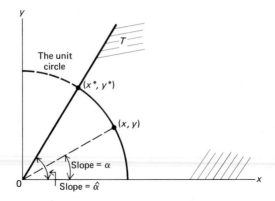

Figure 6.3.   An Illustration of the Proof of Theorem 6.A.1.

REMARK: Theorem 6.A.1 essentially asserts the existence of the following nonlinear programming problem and states some properties of its solution.

$$\text{Maximize: } \alpha$$
$$\underset{(x,\,y)}{}$$
$$\text{Subject to: } y - \alpha x \geqq 0 \text{ and } (x, y) \in T$$

Since α is a function of (x, y), neither the constraints nor the maximand function is linear. The solution of the above problem is denoted by $\hat{\alpha} \equiv \alpha(\hat{x}, \hat{y})$. If we introduce the von Neumann technology, $y = B \cdot z$ and $x = A \cdot z$, explicitly, then the above problem is written:

$$\text{Maximize: } \alpha$$
$$\underset{z}{}$$
$$\text{Subject to: } [B - \alpha A] \cdot z \geqq 0 \text{ and } z \geqq 0$$

As Gale noted ([4], p. 312), this problem yields the following problem, which appears strikingly analogous to the dual problem of linear programming.

$$\text{Minimize: } \beta$$
$$\underset{p}{}$$
$$\text{Subject to: } p \cdot [B - \beta A] \leqq 0 \text{ and } p \geqq 0$$

Then using exactly the same argument as in the proof of Theorem 6.A.1, we show that there exists a solution $\hat{\beta}$ for the above problem. In general, we cannot, however, show that $\hat{\beta} = \hat{\alpha}$, although it can be shown that $\hat{\beta} \leqq \hat{\alpha}$. The above "dual problem" can have various economic interpretations. If $p \cdot a^j > 0$, the ratio $p \cdot b^j / p \cdot a^j$ is meaningful and signifies return divided by cost, a kind of "profit ratio" of the jth activity. The inequality $p \cdot [B - \beta A] \leqq 0$ means $(p \cdot b^j)/(p \cdot a^j) \leqq \beta$ whenever $p \cdot a^j > 0$. In other words, β is the maximum profit rate. In a competitive economy with free entry, competition forces this to a minimum. A second interpretation of β is as an *interest factor*. Suppose each activity is financed by borrowing and suppose also that one dollar borrowed at the beginning of the period is paid back by β dollars. Then $p \cdot b^j - \beta p \cdot a^j$ is the profit of the jth activity and thus $p \cdot [B - \beta A] \leq 0$ indicates that no activity will make a profit, the well-known principle in a competitive economy.

Returning to the original model à la Karlin, we prove the following theorem, which gives the price implication of Theorem 6.A.1 and increases our understanding of the above "dual problem."

Theorem 6.A.2: *Under assumptions (A-1) to (A-4), there exists a $\hat{p}$ such that $\hat{p} \geq 0$ and $\hat{p} \cdot (y - \hat{\alpha}x) \leq 0$ for all $(x, y) \in T$.*

PROOF: By definition of $\hat{\alpha}$, there exists no (x, y) in T such that $y - \hat{\alpha}x > 0$ [∵ if there exists an $(x', y') \in T$ such that $y' - \hat{\alpha}x' > 0$, then there exists an $\epsilon > 0$ such that $y' - (\hat{\alpha} + \epsilon)x' > 0$, so that $\hat{\alpha}$ is not the maximum expansion ratio—contradiction]. Since T is convex and the function $f(x, y) \equiv y - \hat{\alpha}x$ is concave (in fact linear), we can apply the fundamental theorem of concave functions, that is, Theorem 1.B.2. From this theorem, there exists a $\hat{p} \geq 0$ such that $\hat{p} \cdot f(x, y) \leq 0$ for all $(x, y) \in T$.   (Q.E.D.)

REMARK: We can prove Theorem 6.A.2 directly from the separation theorem by considering two convex sets: $\{y - \hat{\alpha}x : (x, y) \in T, \| (x,y) \| \leq 1\}$ and the interior of Ω^n. For such a proof, see Karlin [11], pp. 339–340. We note, however, that Theorem 6.A.2 follows immediately once we recall the fundamental theorem (Theorem 1.B.2). The above proof illustrates the usefulness of the fundamental theorem.

REMARK: As we discussed above in connection with the "dual problem," $(\hat{p} \cdot y)/(\hat{p} \cdot x)$ is the "profit ratio" of process (x, y), whenever $\hat{p} \cdot x > 0$. Theorem 6.A.2 states that this does not exceed the maximum expansion rate. Note that this theorem also implies that $\hat{\beta} \leq \hat{\alpha}$. Gale ([4], p. 316) gave an example of $\hat{\beta} < \hat{\alpha}$.

The following theorem, originally due to von Neumann [22], is now an immediate corollary of Theorems 6.A.1 and 6.A.2.

Theorem 6.A.3 (von Neumann):   *Let A and B respectively be the input and the output matrices in the von Neumann technology. Then under assumptions (A-1) to (A-4) there exist $\hat{\alpha} > 0$, $\hat{z} \geq 0$, and $\hat{p} \geq 0$, where $\hat{\alpha} \in R$, $\hat{z} \in R^m$, and $\hat{p} \in R^n$, such that*

(i) $[B - \hat{\alpha}A] \cdot \hat{z} \geq 0$
(ii) $\hat{p} \cdot [B - \hat{\alpha}A] \leq 0$
(iii) $\hat{p} \cdot [B - \hat{\alpha}A] \cdot \hat{z} = 0$

PROOF: Let $(\hat{x}, \hat{y})$ be the process which gives rise to the maximum expansion rate $\hat{\alpha}$ in Theorem 6.A.1; then there exists a $\hat{z} \geq 0$ such that $\hat{y} = \hat{\alpha}\hat{x}, \hat{y} \leq B \cdot \hat{z}$, and $\hat{x} \geq A \cdot \hat{z}$. Hence $B \cdot \hat{z} \geq \hat{\alpha} A \cdot \hat{z}$, or (i) is shown, since $\hat{\alpha} > 0$ and $\hat{y} \geq 0$. $\hat{z} \geq 0$. To show (ii) of Theorem 6.A.3, recall Theorem 6.A.2. Then we have $\hat{p} \cdot [B - \hat{\alpha}A] \cdot z \leq 0$ with $\hat{p} \geq 0$ for all $z \geq 0$, so that $\hat{p} \cdot [B - \hat{\alpha}A] \leq 0$ with $\hat{p} \geq 0$. Thus (ii) is shown. To show (iii), note that (i) and $\hat{p} \geq 0$ imply $\hat{p} \cdot [B - \hat{\alpha}A] \cdot \hat{z} \geq 0$, so that $\hat{p} \cdot [B - \hat{\alpha}A] \cdot \hat{z} = 0$, in view of (ii).

(Q.E.D.)

REMARK: The relation (iii) of Theorem 6.A.3 states that if the jth activity yields negative profit, the corresponding activity level z^j is zero, and that if the ith commodity is expanding at a rate greater than $\hat{\alpha}$, being "oversupplied," its price $\hat{p}_i$ is zero.

In order to increase our understanding of Theorem 6.A.3, let us consider more closely the original von Neumann model [22] in terms of the matrix $[A, B]$. Let $z(t)$ and $p(t)$ denote the activity level vector in period t and the price vector in period t, respectively. Let $\beta(t)$ be the interest factor in period t. Then we have the following "equilibrium" relations.

(i) $A \cdot z(t + 1) \leq B \cdot z(t)$
(ii) $p(t + 1) \cdot [B \cdot z(t) - A \cdot z(t + 1)] = 0$
(iii) $\beta(t) p(t) \cdot A \geq p(t + 1) \cdot B$
(iv) $[\beta(t) p(t) \cdot A - p(t + 1) \cdot B] \cdot z(t) = 0$

The interpretation of the above four relations is as follows:

(i)   It is impossible to consume more of each commodity (in the production process) than is available.
(ii)   If a commodity is in excess supply, its price becomes zero.
(iii) The production process will make no positive profit and the maximum profit is zero.
(iv)   If a process yields negative profits, it will not be used.

Now assume balanced growth in the sense that

$$z(t + 1) = \alpha z(t), p(t + 1) = p(t) = p \text{ (constant)} \quad \text{for all } t$$

and

$$\beta(t) = \beta \text{(constant)} \quad \text{for all } t$$

Then writing $z(0) \equiv z$, we can rewrite the above four relations as:

(i') $[B - \alpha A] \cdot z \geq 0$
(ii') $p \cdot [B - \alpha A] \cdot z = 0$
(iii') $p \cdot [B - \beta A] \leq 0$
(iv') $p \cdot [B - \beta A] \cdot z = 0$

We may call the quadruplet $[\hat{z}, \hat{p}, \hat{\alpha}, \hat{\beta}]$ which satisfies the above four relations the **von Neumann quadruplet**. Theorem 6.A.3 asserts the existence of such a quadruplet with $\hat{\alpha} = \hat{\beta} > 0$ and $\hat{z} \geq 0$, $\hat{p} \geq 0$. It is important to note that in this interpretation of the model, $\hat{\alpha}$ is *not* defined as the maximum expansion factor. An interpretation in terms of the dual maximization and minimization problems that Gale conceived is not intended here. Strictly speaking, $\hat{\beta}$ here is not interpreted as the solution of Gale's minimization problem. The model (i') to (iv') *describes* the workings of a closed economy as interpreted above with the fundamental assumption of balanced growth. That is, the interpretation here is that of a descriptive model and not that of a planning model. However, it should also be noted that Theorem 6.A.3 provides a "planning" interpretation. In other words, $\hat{\alpha}$ in the von Neumann quadruplet *can* be interpreted as the maximum expansion factor. This means that if the economy is organized as described by (i') to (iv') with the attached interpretations, it will maximize the expansion factor α. This result is analogous to a result in the theory of competitive equilibrium, namely, that every competitive equilibrium realizes a Pareto optimum.

c.   TWO REMARKS

Irreducibility

In Theorem 6.A.3, we proved the existence of $[\hat{\alpha}, \hat{p}, \hat{z}]$ with $\hat{\alpha} > 0, \hat{p} \geq 0$, and $\hat{z} \geq 0$, such that

$$[B - \hat{\alpha}A] \cdot \hat{z} \geq 0, \hat{p} \cdot [B - \hat{\alpha}A] \leq 0, \text{ and } \hat{p} \cdot [B - \hat{\alpha}A] \cdot \hat{z} = 0$$

We may call this triplet $[\hat{\alpha}, \hat{p}, \hat{z}]$ the **von Neumann equilibrium** of the $[A, B]$ economy. However, in the conclusion of Theorem 6.A.3, or the definition of the von Neumann equilibrium, the possibility that $\hat{p} \cdot B \cdot \hat{z} = 0$ is *not* precluded. The condition $\hat{p} \cdot B \cdot \hat{z} = 0$ means (intuitively) that the total value of all commodities produced in the von Neumann equilibrium is zero. This is rather annoying. Gale [3] apparently realized this and considered the "regular" von Neumann model, where the "regularity" is defined in terms of $B \cdot \hat{z} > 0$. Clearly $B \cdot \hat{z} > 0$, together with $\hat{p} \geq 0$, implies $\hat{p} \cdot B \cdot \hat{z} > 0$. Thompson [21] and Kemeny, Morgenstern, and Thompson [12] also realized this and explicitly introduced the condition $\hat{p} \cdot B \cdot \hat{z} > 0$ into the definition of the von Neumann equilibrium.

A natural question now is: What then is the condition which would guarantee that $\hat{p} \cdot B \cdot \hat{z} > 0$? Gale [3] and [4] introduced "irreducibility," the concept which is analogous to the indecomposability of the Frobenius theorem. It turns out that this concept of "irreducibility" plays an important role in the above question.

Definition: The set of indices I, a subset of $N \equiv \{1, 2, \ldots, n\}$, is called an **independent subset** if it is possible to produce commodity $i \in I$, without consuming any commodity $i \in I'$, where $I' \equiv N \setminus I$. That is, I is independent if there exists J, a subset of $M \equiv \{1, 2, \ldots, m\}$, such that $a_{ij} = 0$ for $i \in I'$ and $j \in J$, and $b_{ij} > 0$

for all $i \in I$ and for some $j \in J$. The input-output matrix $[A, B]$ is said to be **irreducible** if $I' = \emptyset$.

REMARK: Hence, if the model is reducible, there is a certain permutation of rows and columns of A (that is, renumbering of indices) such that A is decomposed as

$$
\begin{array}{cc}
 & J \quad\quad J' \\
\begin{array}{c} I \\ \\ I' \end{array} &
\left[
\begin{array}{c:c}
A_{11} & A_{12} \\
\hdashline
0 & A_{22}
\end{array}
\right]
\end{array}
$$

Theorem 6.A.4:   *Let A and B, respectively, be the input and the output matrices in the von Neumann technology. Suppose there exist $\hat{\alpha} > 0$, $\hat{z} \geq 0$, $\hat{p} \geq 0$, $\hat{\alpha} \in R$, $\hat{z} \in R^m$, and $\hat{p} \in R^n$ such that (i), (ii), and (iii) of Theorem 6.A.3 hold. Then if the input-output matrix $[A, B]$ is irreducible, we have $\hat{p} \cdot B \cdot \hat{z} > 0$.*

PROOF: Renumber j and partition $\hat{z}$ such that $\hat{z} = (\hat{z}^0, \hat{z}^1)$, where $\hat{z}^0 > 0$ and $\hat{z}^1 = 0$. Let J be the set of indices where $\hat{z}^0 > 0$ (so that $J' \equiv M \backslash J$ is the set of indices where $\hat{z}^1 = 0$). Let b_i be the m-vector whose jth element is b_{ij}. Let I be the set of indices i such that $b_i \cdot \hat{z} > 0$ (so that $I' \equiv N \setminus I$ is the set of indices i where $b_i \cdot \hat{z} = 0$). Renumbering i and j, A and B respectively can be partitioned as

$$
\begin{array}{cc}
 & J \quad\; J' \\
\begin{array}{c} I \\ \\ I' \end{array} &
\left[
\begin{array}{c:c}
A_{11} & A_{12} \\
\hdashline
A_{21} & A_{22}
\end{array}
\right]
\end{array}
\quad \text{and} \quad
\begin{array}{cc}
 & J \quad\; J' \\
\begin{array}{c} I \\ \\ I' \end{array} &
\left[
\begin{array}{c:c}
B_{11} & B_{12} \\
\hdashline
B_{21} & B_{22}
\end{array}
\right]
\end{array}
$$

By assumption of the theorem, $B \cdot \hat{z} \geq \hat{\alpha} A \cdot \hat{z}$, which, in turn, means $B_{11} \cdot \hat{z}^0 \geq \hat{\alpha} A_{11} \cdot \hat{z}^0$ and $B_{21} \cdot \hat{z}^0 \geq \hat{\alpha} A_{21} \cdot \hat{z}^0$ ($\because \hat{z}^1 = 0$). But $B_{21} \cdot \hat{z}^0 = 0$ by definition of I and J ($\because 0 = B_{21} \cdot \hat{z}^0 + B_{22} \cdot \hat{z}^1 = B_{21} \cdot \hat{z}^0$). Hence $\hat{\alpha} A_{21} \cdot \hat{z}^0 \leq 0$, or $A_{21} \cdot \hat{z}^0 \leq 0$ since $\hat{\alpha} > 0$. But $A_{21} \cdot \hat{z}^0 \geq 0$, since $A_{21} \geq 0$ and $\hat{z}^0 > 0$, so that we must have $A_{21} \cdot \hat{z}^0 = 0$. This, in view of $A_{21} \geq 0$ and $\hat{z}^0 > 0$, implies that $A_{21} = 0$. That is, $a_{ij} = 0$ for $i \in I', j \in J$. Since $[A, B]$ is irreducible by assumption, the set I' must be empty. That is, $I = N$, so that $b_i \cdot \hat{z} > 0$ for all $i = 1, 2, \ldots, n$. Hence $B \cdot \hat{z} > 0$, which implies $\hat{p} \cdot B \cdot \hat{z} > 0$.

(Q.E.D.)

REMARK: The above proof is based on Gale [4], p. 315.

REMARK: If we have assumptions (A-i) through (A-iii), then we can prove the above theorem without irreducibility. See Kemeny, Morgenstern, and Thompson [12]. For alternative proofs, see Howe [10], p. 638, or Nikaido [20], p. 146.

The von Neumann Model with Consumption (Morishima)

One basic criticism of the von Neumann model is that it has no explicit treatment of consumption. It is assumed that "consumption of goods takes place only through the processes of production which include necessities of life consumed by workers" ([22], p. 2). Explicit introduction of consumption and labor into the model is attempted by Morishima [18] and was reconsidered by Haga and Otsuki [7] in terms of the duality theorem of linear programming. Our purpose here is to sketch this Morishima model and understand the way in which consumption is explicitly treated in the model.

The starting point of Morishima's model is the following model, originally due to Kemeny, Morgenstern, and Thompson [12].

$$
(1) \qquad A \cdot z(t + 1) \leq B \cdot z(t)
$$

$$
(2) \qquad \beta(t) \, p(t) \cdot A \geq p(t + 1) \cdot B
$$

$$
(3) \qquad p(t + 1) \cdot A \cdot z(t + 1) = p(t + 1) \cdot B \cdot z(t)
$$

$$
(4) \qquad \beta(t) \, p(t) \cdot A \cdot z(t) = p(t + 1) \cdot B \cdot z(t)
$$

$$
(5) \qquad p(t + 1) \cdot B \cdot z(t) > 0
$$

As we remarked earlier, the addition of (5) is novel in Kemeny, Morgenstern, and Thompson [12] and in Thompson [21]. The point of departure is the explicit introduction of labor into the model. Let L be the m-vector whose jth element is l_j, where l_j is the amount of labor necessary for the one unit operation of the jth production process. L is assumed to be constant for all t. Assume that there is only one kind of homogeneous labor in the economy and that the wage rate of this labor in period t is equal to $w(t)$. Assume also that labor is indispensable for every production process, that is, $l_j > 0$ for all j. The cost of production in period t is no longer equal to $p(t) \cdot A$ but, instead, equals $[p(t) \cdot A + w(t)L]$, assuming that wages are paid at the beginning of the production period. Hence the above relations (2) and (4) may be rewritten as

$$
(2') \qquad \beta(t) [p(t) \cdot A + w(t)L] \geq p(t + 1) \cdot B
$$

$$
(4') \qquad \beta(t) [p(t) \cdot A + w(t)L] \cdot z(t) = p(t + 1) \cdot B \cdot z(t)
$$

If, on the other hand, the wage is paid at the end of the production period, then $\beta(t) [p(t) \cdot A + w(t)L]$ in (2') and (4') should be modified accordingly. Morishima called the former "Marx-von Neumann" and the latter "Walras-von Neumann." Since the Walras-von Neumann model can be considered analogously to the Marx-von Neumann model, we will stick to the above Marx-von Neumann equations (2') and (4'). Let $E(t)$ be the total "profit" (or "capitalists' income") in period t. That is, we define $E(t)$ by

$$
(6) \qquad E(t) \equiv [p(t) \cdot B - p(t - 1) \cdot A - w(t - 1)L] \cdot z(t - 1)
$$

Then, in view of (4'), we have

(7) $E(t) = [\beta(t-1) - 1] [p(t-1) \cdot A + w(t-1)L] \cdot z(t-1)$

Let $d_i(t)$ be the capitalists' consumption of commodity i in period t, and let $d(t)$ be the n-vector whose ith element is $d_i(t)$. Let c be the average propensity to consume of the capitalists, so that we have

(8) $cE(t) = p(t) \cdot d(t)$

where c is assumed to be a positive constant for all t as long as $E(t) \geq 0$. We suppose that $E(t) < 0$ implies $d(t) = 0$, so that $c = 0$ whenever $E(t) < 0$. Let $e(t)$ be the workers' consumption vector in period t. Assuming that the workers consume all their wage income, we have

(9) $W(t) = p(t) \cdot e(t)$

where $W(t) \equiv w(t)L \cdot z(t)$.
        Equations (1) and (3) are now modified (in view of the above considerations) as

(1') $B \cdot z(t-1) \geq A \cdot z(t) + e(t) + d(t)$

(3') $p(t) \cdot B \cdot z(t-1) = p(t) \cdot A \cdot z(t) + W(t) + cE(t)$

Morishima [18] supposed the functional relations $d_i(t) = \check{d}_i[p(t), E(t)]$ and $e_i(t) = \check{e}_i[p(t), W(t)]$, which are assumed to be homogeneous of degree 0 with respect to their respective arguments. It is further assumed that the Engel elasticity of consumption is unity so that $\check{d}$ and $\check{e}$ can be written explicitly in the following form:

(10) $d(t) = \dfrac{E(t)}{\sum_{i=1}^{n} p_i(t)} f[q(t)]$ and $e(t) = \dfrac{W(t)}{\sum_{i=1}^{n} p_i(t)} g[q(t)]$

where $q(t) \equiv p(t)/(\sum_{i=1}^{n} p_i(t))$, f and g are n-vectors, and $\sum_{i=1}^{n} p_i(t) > 0$ for all t is assumed. Note that $E(t) < 0$ implies $f = 0$ by assumption. Defining $\mu(t)$ by $\mu(t) \equiv w(t)/(\sum_{i=1}^{n} p_i(t))$, $e(t)$ can be further rewritten as $e(t) = \mu(t)g[q(t)]L \cdot z(t)$. Here μ may be interpreted as the "real wage rate."
        Morishima [18] retains the fundamental balanced growth assumption à la von Neumann so that

(11) $z(t) = \alpha z(t-1), p(t) = \text{constant} = p$
                    $w(t) = \text{constant} = w, \beta(t) = \text{constant} = \beta$

Also the unit of measurement of the commodities is chosen properly so that $\sum_{i=1}^{n} p_i = 1$. Note that this convention implies $p = q$ and $\mu = w$. Then, using (7) and (10), the model consisting of (1'), (2'), (3'), (4'), and (5) can be rewritten as

(12) $B \cdot z \geq \alpha [A \cdot z + wg(p)L \cdot z] + (\beta - 1) [p \cdot A + wL] \cdot z \cdot f(p)$

(13) $\beta [p \cdot A + wL] \geq p \cdot B$

(14) $$p \cdot B \cdot z = [\alpha + (\beta - 1)c] \ (p \cdot A \cdot z + wL \cdot z)$$

(15) $$\beta [p \cdot A + wL] \cdot z = p \cdot B \cdot z$$

(16) $$p \cdot B \cdot z > 0$$

Here p, z, α, β, and w are all constants. The value $[p^*, z^*, \alpha^*, \beta^*, w^*]$ which satisfies (12) to (16) is the von Neumann equilibrium à la Morishima. Morishima ([18], pp. 356–359) showed the existence of $[p^*, z^*, \alpha^*, \beta^*]$ such that $p^* \geq 0$ and $z^* \geq 0$, *with a given value of w* > 0, which satisfies (12) to (16) [with some additional results, such as $\beta^* - 1 > 0$ implies that $\alpha^* - 1 = s(\beta^* - 1)$, were $s \equiv (1 - c)$, and so on]. The basic assumptions used for the proof are (i) $a_{ij} \geq 0$, $b_{ij} \geq 0$ for all i and j, and (ii) for every i, there exists at least one j such that $b_{ij} > 0$. Compare these with the three assumptions (A-i) to (A-iii) introduced by Kemeny, Morgenstern, and Thompson [12], and note that the assumption that for each j there exists at least one i such that $a_{ij} > 0$ is dropped. The assumption $l_j > 0$ for all j replaces this assumption, for this itself implies "no land of Cockaigne."

One should note that this model is not complete. There is no mechanism to determine w. One way to close the model is to introduce a labor supply equation and equilibrium in the labor market (= full employment) through fluctuations in w. Another way is simply to assume the existence of (Marxian) underemployment so that w is constant at the subsistence level.

It should also be noted that there is no mechanism in the model that determines (absolute) money prices. To determine money prices, we have to introduce an equation which describes the money market.

Finally, we should recall one fundamental assumption involved in the Morishima model, that is, the balanced growth assumption in the sense of (11). Nothing is said about what happens if the historically given stocks of commodities are not on such balanced growth paths and how a particular balanced growth path $[p^*, z^*, \alpha^*, \beta^*, w^*]$ is chosen. On this point, Morishima inherits the basic difficulty of von Neumann.

REFERENCES

1. Champernowne, D. G., "A Note on J. v. Neumann's Article on 'A Model of Economic Equilibrium'," *Review of Economic Studies*, XIII, 1945–1946.
2. Dorfman, R., Samuelson, P. A., and Solow, R. M., *Linear Programming and Economic Analysis*, New York, McGraw-Hill, 1958.
3. Gale, D., "The Closed Linear Model of Production," in *Linear Inequalities and Related Systems*, ed. by H. W. Kuhn and A. W. Tucker, Princeton, N.J., Princeton University Press, 1956.
4. ———, *The Theory of Linear Economic Models*, New York, McGraw-Hill, 1960.
5. Georgescu-Roegen, N., "The Aggregate Linear Production Function and Its Applications to von Neumann's Economic Model," in *Activity Analysis of Production and Allocation*, ed. by T. C. Koopmans, New York, Wiley, 1951.

6. Glycopantis, D., "The Closed Linear Model of Production: a Note," *Review of Economic Studies*, XXXVII, April 1970.

7. Haga, H., and Otsuki, M., "On a Generalized von Neumann Model," *International Economic Review*, 6, January 1965.

8. Hahn, F. H., and Matthews, R. C. O., "The Theory of Economic Growth: A Survey," *Economic Journal*, LXXIV, December 1964.

9. Hicks, J. R., *Capital and Growth*, Oxford, Clarendon Press, 1965.

10. Howe, C. W., "An Alternative Proof of the Existence of General Equilibrium in a von Neumann Model," *Econometrica*, 28, July 1960.

11. Karlin, S., *Mathematical Methods and Theory in Games, Programming and Economics*, Vol. 1, Reading, Mass., Addison-Wesley, 1959.

12. Kemeny, J. G., Morgenstern, O., and Thompson, G. L., "A Generalization of the von Neumann Model of an Expanding Economy," *Econometrica*, 24, April 1956.

13. Koopmans, T. C., "Analysis of Production as an Efficient Combination of Activities," in *Activity Analysis of Production and Allocation*, ed. by T. C. Koopmans, New York, Wiley, 1951.

14. ———, "Economic Growth at a Maximal Rate," *Quarterly Journal of Economics*, LXXVII, August 1964.

15. Loomis, L. H., "On a Theorem of von Neumann," *Proceedings of National Academy of Science*, 32, 1946.

16. McKenzie, L. W., "Turnpike Theorems for a Generalized Leontief Model," *Econometrica*, 31, January–April 1963.

17. ———, "Maximal Paths in the von Neumann Model," in *Activity Analysis in the Theory of Growth and Planning*, ed. by E. Malinvaud and M. O. L. Bacharach, London, Macmillan, 1967.

18. Morishima, M., "Economic Expansion and the Interest Rate in Generalized von Neumann Models," *Econometrica*, 28, April 1960 (also chap. V of his *Equilibrium, Stability and Growth, A Multi-Sectoral Analysis*, Oxford, Clarendon Press, 1964).

19. ———, "A Multi-Sectoral Analysis of Balanced Growth," in *New Economic Analysis*, ed. by M. Morishima, M. Shinohara, and T. Uchida, Tokyo, Sobunsha, 1960 (in Japanese).

20. Nikaido, H., *Convex Structures and Economic Theory*, New York, Academic Press, 1968.

21. Thompson, G. L., "On the Solution of a Game-theoretic Problem," in *Linear Inequalities and Related Systems*, ed. by H. W. Kuhn and A. W. Tucker, Princeton, N.J., Princeton University Press, 1956.

22. von Neumann, J., "Über ein ökonomisches Gleichungs-System und eine Verallgemeinerung des Brouwerschen Fixpunktsatzes," in *Ergebnisse eines Mathmatischen Kolloquiums*, ed. by K. Menger, no. 8, 1937 (tr. as "A Model of General Equilibrium," *Review of Economic Studies*, XIII, no. 1, 1945–1946).

23. Winter, S. G., "Some Properties of the Closed Linear Model of Production," *International Economic Review*, 6, May 1965.

THE DYNAMIC LEONTIEF MODEL

a. INTRODUCTION

The dynamic Leontief model is a natural extension of the static input-output Leontief model to a dynamic case. As in the static case, the general equilibrium interaction among various industries in an economy is explicitly taken into account. Like the static model, the dynamic model is also used extensively for empirical purposes to ascertain the industrial structure of particular economies for forecasting, planning, and so on.

Theoretically speaking, the dynamic Leontief model can be considered a special case of the von Neumann model, in which there is only one production process available for the production of each good (the "fixed coefficient assumption") and no joint output is allowed except that capital goods may be considered as joint outputs in the sense that they are transferred from one period to the next.

The essential idea in dynamizing the static Leontief model seems to have come from the Harrod-Domar model. Hence the assumption of fixed capital coefficients is essential in the model.

The fixed coefficients assumption or the strict linearity of the model, although a useful assumption for empirical purposes, causes serious theoretical difficulties in the dynamic Leontief model because of its rigidity. The most notable of such difficulties is known as **causal indeterminacy**. That is, unless the initial output vector and stock vector are on a certain ray from the origin, it may so happen that the output and the stock of at least one good may become negative for sufficiently large t. Thus, waking up on a bright Monday morning, one may find that the dynamic Leontief economy, which had started with a positive initial stock of commodities, has realized a negative stock of some commodity!

There have been various attempts to rescue the dynamic Leontief model from this difficulty. One useful concept in this connection turns out to be that of "relative stability," developed by Solow and Samuelson [39]. That is, if the coefficient matrices A and B satisfy certain conditions, then there exists a balanced growth path in which all outputs (or stocks) grow at the same rate such that the ratio between the output (or stock) of the balanced growth path and the actual output (or stock) for each good converges to a certain *positive* constant, as time extends without limit, *regardless* of the initial configuration of outputs and stocks. (Incidentally, the definitions of coefficient matrices A and B will be given at the beginning of subsection b. Here we simply proceed with our discussion without worrying about the definitions of A and B.)

It turns out that the study of this question is concerned with a system of first-order, linear, homogenous difference equations of the form

$$x(t + 1) = M \cdot x(t)$$

where M is an $n \times n$ constant matrix and $x(t)$ [and $x(t + 1)$] is an n-vector. In the (closed) dynamic Leontief model, it turns out that M is written as $M = I + B^{-1}(I - A)$.

A necessary and sufficient condition for the relative stability of the above system was discovered by Tsukui [42]. It states that the above system is relatively stable if and only if there exists a positive integer m such that $M^m > 0$. Observe that by iteration the above system of difference equations yields

$$x(t) = M^t \cdot x(0)$$

Thus Tsukui's theorem means that, for a sufficiently large t (say, m), the output of every good becomes positive regardless of the initial point, $x(0) \geq 0$.

This is an interesting result even from a purely mathematical viewpoint, for a system of difference equations such as $x(t + 1) = M \cdot x(t)$ can appear in many fields of economics other than the dynamic Leontief system. Hence it has many potential applications.

Coming back to the dynamic Leontief system, suppose now that the coefficient matrices A and B are such that we do not have relative stability. Then we are back to the problem of causal indeterminacy. In general, there is nothing which would guarantee the relative stability of the system. The answer to this question of causal indeterminacy under these general circumstances can be sought from two directions. One is to convert the (deterministic) dynamic Leontief model into a planning model, in which case the problem of causal indeterminacy can be avoided trivially by explicitly introducing the nonnegativity of the output and the stock vectors (for all t) in the constraints. The nontrivial part of this conversion procedure is to change the equalities in the Leontief system into inequalities. The procedure of converting the deterministic Leontief model to a planning model, thus avoiding the problem of causal indeterminacy, was developed by Solow [38]. Since the coefficient matrices A and B are fixed so that the system is linear, he obtained a linear programming model. Then considering the dual problem of this linear programming model and interpreting the dual variables as "price" variables, Solow obtained a remarkable result: the price implication of the output system of the dynamic Leontief model.

Preserving linearity in the sense of linear homogeneity of the production processes, we can still avoid the problem of causal indeterminacy by explicitly introducing some sort of "nonlinearity" into the system. In particular, we may point out the following three kinds of "nonlinearity" to avoid causal indeterminacy.

(i) Allow factor substitution in the production processes. In this case, the a_{ij}'s and b_{ij}'s in the matrices A and B are no longer fixed but are functions of prices. Moreover, labor can be introduced in this substitution mechanism.

(ii) Allow demand (of consumer) substitution. In the usual dynamic Leontief model, the final demand vector $c(t)$ is exogenously given; but we may allow it to depend on prices.

(iii) Introduce a "floor" and "ceiling," just as Hicks [13] introduced them into Samuelson's business cycle model. As Goodwin [8] observed, this essentially amounts to introducing nonlinearity into the system.

It is easy to see that causal indeterminacy could be avoided by (i) and/or (ii). If the stock of a certain good decumulates in a certain period(s) (too close to zero), then the scarcity of this good would, in general, cause an increase in its marginal productivity and/or an increase in its marginal utility. This would increase the demand for the good, thus increasing its price. This, in turn, would cause an increase in its supply, which would avoid the stock of the good decumulating to zero.

That labor can be introduced in the mechanism of producer's substitution in (i) has another important implication in the sense that it will avoid another major difficulty in the dynamic Leontief model with fixed coefficients. We now discuss this difficulty. Under full employment of capital, the output vector $x(t)$ may follow the law of motion described by a system of difference equations such as $x(t + 1) = M \cdot x(t) + d(t)$ [where $d(t)$ is exogeneously given owing to final demand] in the open Leontief model in which labor is explicitly introduced. As long as there is a fixed relation between the labor input and the output of each good, the movement of $x(t)$ will uniquely determine the labor requirement in the economy. Let it be $L(t)$. Suppose this $L(t)$ does not correspond to the actual supply of labor. There is no mechanism in the usual dynamic Leontief system to eliminate the gap between $L(t)$ and the supply of labor. For example, suppose the supply of labor is given exogenously by population and the like, and grows proportionately such that $L(t) = L_0(1 + n)^t$. Suppose also that the output determined by $x(t + 1) = M \cdot x(t) + d(t)$ is given by $x(0)(1 + \mu)^t +$ (constant). Then we have ever-expanding unemployment of labor if $n > \mu$. If, on the other hand, $n < \mu$, then the output system such as $x(t + 1) = M \cdot x(t) + d(t)$ is meaningless, for such a growth of output is impossible due to the labor constraint. This difficulty can be avoided by introducing labor in the mechanism of producer's substitution. In other words, if labor grows faster than is required, then the price of labor will go down and encourage the use of labor in the production vis-à-vis other factors. This, in turn, will increase the labor requirement. In other words, the labor coefficients—the amounts of labor necessary to produce one unit of each good—are not fixed constants but functions of prices.

Morishima [26] introduced nonlinearity of type (i). However, he was apparently misled by his desire to obtain the substitution theorem for the dynamic Leontief system. He was concerned with reducing nonlinearity to linearity by arguing that only one set of values of the a_{ij}'s and b_{ij}'s will be chosen regardless of the value of final demand, rather than with the problem of causal indeterminacy *per se*.

In spite of his difficulty in establishing the substitution theorem for the dynamic case, his attempt to build the dynamic Leontief model with an explicit recognition of producer's substitution and to prove the existence and the uniqueness of the equilibrium values of the variables is very important. Besides, his model has an interesting feature in that his treatment of prices and Solow's assumption on prices represent two polar assumptions in the treatment of prices in the dynamic Leontief model.

After all, the problem of finding a proper price system for the dynamic Leontief model is not an easy one. In fact, Solow writes ([38], p. 30),

> The price-valuation side of the dynamic Leontief system has been pretty thoroughly neglected. So far as I know, a complete history of the literature on this subject can be given in a paragraph.

This is because of the obvious reason that in the Leontief model there is no explicit discussion of consumer's and producer's substitution in which prices can play a vital role. As remarked above, consumer's substitution is neglected because of the exogenous treatment of final demand, and producer's substitution is neglected because of the fixed coefficient assumption. However, it is not correct to say that there is no price formation in the dynamic Leontief system. We can still follow the logical implication of the model as it stands by supposing that each commodity is evaluated by certain prices in a systematic manner and asking what the implications of such an evaluation are. In the literature, two examples of the price system under the competitive framework are well known: Solow's system and Morishima's system.

In subsection b, we sketch the output system of the usual dynamic Leontief system. There we take up topics such as relative stability and causal indeterminacy. This subsection will also be useful to introduce and illustrate an important technique of economics, that is, difference equations. However, the complete discussion of this technique is not attempted. The reader, if he wishes to do so, should be able to easily convert the discussion of the present section in terms of differential equations.

In subsection c, we sketch the price system of the dynamic Leontief model based on Solow [38]. It should be understood that a competitive intertemporal arbitrage relation under the assumption of perfect foresight is crucial in this price system.

In subsection d, we take up Solow's conversion of the deterministic Leontief model to a planning model and discuss the price implications based on such a model, and finally, in subsection e, we deal with the Morishima model.

In the course of reading this section, it is hoped that the reader will become aware of the difficulties inherent in the linear system with fixed coefficients. Although such a system may be very useful for empirical purposes, it is, after all, a linear approximation of a nonlinear system. The difficulty posed by causal indeterminacy seems to be that of stretching properties that may hold only locally (that is, in the neighborhood in which the linear approximation is a good approximation) to a global domain which is inevitable as $t \to \infty$.

b. THE OUTPUT SYSTEM

Let $x(t)$ be an n-vector whose ith element is $x_i(t)$, the output of the ith good in period t. Let $A = [a_{ij}]$ be an $n \times n$ matrix, where a_{ij} denotes the current input of the ith good used per unit of the jth good. Let $B = [b_{ij}]$ be an $n \times n$ matrix, where b_{ij} denotes the quantity of the ith good invested in the jth industry in order to increase the output of that industry by one unit. Let $\bar{c}_i(t)$ be the final demand (such as consumption demand) of the ith good in period t. Then the total demand for the ith good in period t is

$$(1) \qquad \sum_{j=1}^{n} a_{ij}x_j(t) + \sum_{j=1}^{n} b_{ij}[x_j(t+1) - x_j(t)] + \bar{c}_i(t)$$

The second term of this expression can be understood by supposing that the production of each good requires a stock of goods (such as "capital") as well as current inputs (such as "raw materials"). In other words, suppose that, in the production of one unit of the jth good, b_{ij} units of the stock of the jth good are necessary as a capital good. Let $K_{ij}(t)$ be the amount of the stock of the ith good required as capital in the jth industry in period t. Then we have

$$(2) \qquad b_{ij}x_j(t) = K_{ij}(t)$$

Let $K_i(t)$ be the total stock of the ith good required as a capital good in the economy in period t, that is, $K_i(t) \equiv \sum_{j=1}^{n} K_{ij}(t)$. Then we have [in view of (2)]

$$(3) \qquad K_i(t) = \sum_{j=1}^{n} b_{ij}x_j(t)$$

Assume that capital is **freely transferable** from one industry to another, and assume also the **full employment of capital** so that $K_i(t)$ in (3) also denotes the *supply* of the ith capital as well as its demand ($i = 1, 2, \ldots, n$). Then

$$(4) \qquad I_i(t) = \Delta K_i(t) \equiv K_i(t+1) - K_i(t) = \sum_{j=1}^{n} b_{ij}[x_j(t+1) - x_j(t)]$$

where $I_i(t)$ is the amount of the ith good demanded (and supplied) for "investment" purposes.[1] Expression (1) may be interpreted as (demand as a current input) + (investment demand) + (final demand) for the ith good.

Since $x_i(t)$ denotes the output of the ith good in period t, the basic supply $=$ demand equilibrium relation for the ith good can now be written as

$$(5) \qquad x_i(t) = \sum_{j=1}^{n} a_{ij}x_j(t) + \sum_{j=1}^{n} b_{ij}[x_j(t+1) - x_j(t)] + \bar{c}_i(t)$$

or in matrix form,

$$(6) \qquad x(t) = A \cdot x(t) + B \cdot [x(t+1) - x(t)] + \bar{c}(t)$$

where $\bar{c}(t)$ is an n-vector whose ith element is $\bar{c}_i(t)$. We may also rewrite (6) as

(6′) $x(t) = A \cdot x(t) + \Delta K(t) + \bar{c}(t)$ and $K(t) = B \cdot x(t)$

where $\Delta K(t) \equiv K(t + 1) - K(t)$. Here free transferability and full employment of capital are assumed. Equation (5) or (6) [or (6′)] denotes the **basic output equation of the dynamic Leontief system**. The matrix A is called the **current input coefficient matrix** and matrix B is called the **capital coefficient matrix**. The purpose of this subsection is to study the behavior of $x(t)$ over time, as described by equation (6).

It is assumed that

(A-1) $a_{ij} \geq 0$ and $b_{ij} \geq 0$ for all $i, j = 1, 2, \ldots, n$, and the a_{ij}'s and the b_{ij}'s are all constant over time.

The constancy of the a_{ij}'s and b_{ij}'s signifies that there is no technological progress. As remarked earlier, the above system of the dynamic Leontief model can be considered a special case of the von Neumann growth model in which there is only one production process in each industry ("fixed coefficients") and joint output is allowed only in the sense that each production process uses stocks of goods which are transferred from one period to the next.[2]

In order to facilitate further analysis, we impose the following assumption:[3]

(A-2) The matrix B is nonsingular.

Thus we can rewrite (6) as

(7) $x(t + 1) = [I + B^{-1} (I - A)] \cdot x(t) - B^{-1}\bar{c}(t)$

where I is the n-dimensional identity matrix.

In order to sharpen our analysis, let us restrict our attention to the **closed (dynamic) Leontief system**. In other words, we set $\bar{c}(t) = 0$ for all t. Then (7) can be rewritten as

(8) $x(t + 1) = [I + B^{-1}(I - A)] \cdot x(t)$

or, in short,

(8′) $x(t + 1) = M \cdot x(t),$ where $M \equiv [I + B^{-1}(I - A)]$

This is a system of n first-order, linear, homogenous difference equations with constant coefficients. Suppose that λ_i is an eigenvalue of M; then it is known that the following is a particular solution:

(9) $\check{x}(t) = \lambda_i{}^t x^i$

where x^i is an eigenvector associated with λ_i. That this is a solution of (8) can be checked easily by substituting this into (8) and noticing that (8) is reduced to an identity. If all the eigenvalues of M are distinct, then the n particular solutions in the form of (9) $(i = 1, 2, \ldots, n)$ are linearly independent, and the general solution of (8) can be written as

(10) $\hat{x}(t) = h_1\lambda_1{}^t x^1 + \cdots + h_n\lambda_n{}^t x^n$

where $h_1, h_2, \ldots, h_n$ are determined by the n initial (boundary) conditions. The fact that this is a solution of (8) can be checked easily by noticing that (10) reduces (8) to an identity.

In general, the λ_i's are complex numbers and the x^i's can contain negative elements, so that a solution (9) may not have any economic meaning. Suppose, however, that one of the eigenvalues—say, λ_1—is a positive (real) number and that an eigenvector associated with it—say, x^1—is a positive vector (that is, $x^1 > 0$); then a solution

$$(11) \qquad\qquad x^*(t) = \lambda_1^t x^1$$

does make economic sense, because this tells us that if the initial output vector, $x(0)$, of the economy is x^1 (or its positive constant multiple, say, $h_1 x^1$), then the economy is capable of "balanced growth" (at the rate of λ_1) for $\lambda_1 > 1$ or "balanced decay" for $0 < \lambda_1 < 1$. We simply call the path such as (11) a **balanced growth path** or a **balanced growth solution**. This is an interesting conclusion, for if the initial output vector $x(0)$ is x^1 or its (positive) constant multiple, then, in the economy in which (8) holds, the output of every good grows (or decays) at the same rate λ_1.

A natural question that follows from this consideration is: What are the conditions which would guarantee the existence of a positive eigenvalue λ_1 and a positive eigenvector x^1 associated with it? An immediate thought about this is to consider the case where M is a nonnegative matrix. For if M is a nonnegative indecomposable matrix, then owing to the Frobenius theorem (Theorem 4.B.1), there exists a positive eigenvalue (called the Frobenius root) and a positive eigenvector associated with it. That is, simply by taking the Frobenius root as λ_1 and the associated eigenvector as x^1, we have a balanced growth solution, (11).

However, there is one basic difficulty, namely, the question of how we can guarantee that $M \equiv [I + B^{-1}(I - A)]$ is a nonnegative matrix. In general, M will not be nonnegative. To see this, consider the following example by DOSSO ([4], p. 297):

EXAMPLE 1:

Let
$$A = \begin{bmatrix} \frac{1}{3} & \frac{1}{3} \\ \frac{1}{3} & \frac{1}{3} \end{bmatrix}, \qquad B = \begin{bmatrix} 1 & 0 \\ 0 & 1 \end{bmatrix}$$

Then
$$M \equiv [I + B^{-1}(I - A)] = \begin{bmatrix} \frac{5}{3} & -\frac{1}{3} \\ -\frac{1}{3} & \frac{5}{3} \end{bmatrix}$$

However, the fact that M is not a nonnegative matrix may not preclude the possibility that the system of difference equations, (8), contains a balanced growth solution. Hence, we want to find a set of plausible assumptions under which there exists a balanced growth solution of (8). To do this, first assume that the matrix $[I - A]$ has a dominant diagonal, that is,

(A-3)   There exists an $x \geq 0$, $x \in R^n$ such that $(I - A) \cdot x > 0$.

Then, using Theorem 4.D.2, we can conclude that $(I - A)$ is nonsingular and $(I - A)^{-1} \geq 0$. Since $B \geq 0$ by (A-1), $(I - A)^{-1}B$ is also nonnegative. If, in addition, A is indecomposable, $(I - A)^{-1} > 0$ so that $(I - A)^{-1}B > 0$ in view of the nonsingularity of B.[4] But A may not be indecomposable; hence we simply assume that

(A-4) $(I - A)^{-1}B$ is indecomposable.

Then, owing to the Frobenius theorem (Theorem 4.B.1), there exists a maximal eigenvalue $v > 0$ with which a positive eigenvector $\bar{x} > 0$ is associated.[5] In other words,

$$(12) \qquad (I - A)^{-1}B \cdot \bar{x} = v\bar{x}, \text{where } v > 0 \text{ and } \bar{x} > 0$$

Then $\rho \equiv 1/v$ is an eigenvalue of $B^{-1}(I - A)$ and its associated eigenvector is $\bar{x}$, since $B^{-1}(I - A) \cdot \bar{x} = (1/v)\bar{x}$ by (12). Therefore,

$$(13) \qquad (1 + \rho)\bar{x} = [I + B^{-1}(I - A)] \cdot \bar{x} = M \cdot \bar{x}$$

Since $1 + \rho > 0$ and $\bar{x} > 0$, we discover the desired result, namely, a positive eigenvalue of M and a positive eigenvector associated with it. Thus setting $\lambda \equiv 1 + \rho$ and $x^1 \equiv \bar{x}$, the economy is capable of balanced growth in the form of (11), even if M is not nonnegative. That is,

$$(14) \qquad x^*(t) = (1 + \rho)^t \bar{x}$$

We are now interested in the long-run character of the movement of $\hat{x}(t)$, the solution of (8), when it starts from an *arbitrary* given initial vector $x(0)$ instead of a particular one such as $\bar{x}$(or x^1). For this purpose, the following concept turns out to be important.

Definition (relative stability):   Let $x(t + 1) = M \cdot x(t)$ be a system of difference equations where M is an $n \times n$ constant matrix. Suppose that $x^*(t) = \lambda^t \bar{x} > 0$ is a particular solution of this system of difference equations. Let $\hat{x}(t)$ be a solution of this system starting from an arbitrary initial vector $\hat{x}(0) \geq 0$. Then the balanced growth solution $x^*(t)$ is said to be **relatively stable** if

$$(15) \qquad \lim_{t \to \infty} \frac{\hat{x}_i(t)}{x_i^*(t)} = \sigma \qquad \text{exists such that } \infty > \sigma > 0 \text{ and } \sigma \text{ is independent}$$

of i, where i stands for the ith component

REMARK: The concept of relative stability is really independent of whether the motion of $x(t)$ is described by a system of linear difference equations such as (8). Essentially, if $\hat{x}(t)$ behaves according to a certain law of motion (which can be anything) starting from the initial value $\hat{x}(0)$, and if there exists a reference path $x^*(t)$ [for example, $x^*(t) = \lambda^t \bar{x}$], which is positive for all t, then the definition such as the one described by (15) holds.

REMARK: One of the crucial features of the concept of relative stability is that $\hat{x}(t)$ can start from any arbitrary initial point. That is, regardless of the initial value $\hat{x}(0)$, relation (15) holds if $x^*(t)$ is relatively stable. Suppose $\hat{x}(t)$ and $\hat{x}^0(t)$ are two solutions starting from $\hat{x}(0)$ and $\hat{x}^0(0)$, respectively, such that $\hat{x}(t) > 0$ for all t. Then noting that $\hat{x}_i^0(t)/\hat{x}_i(t) = [\hat{x}_i^0(t)/x_i^*(t)]/[\hat{x}_i(t)/x_i^*(t)]$, we can conclude that if there exists a balanced growth path $x^*(t) > 0$ which is relatively stable, then $\lim_{t \to \infty} [\hat{x}_i^0(t)/\hat{x}_i(t)]$ also converges to a constant which is independent of i.

In Figure 6.4, we illustrate the concept of relative stability in such a way that $\hat{x}(t)$ asymptotically approaches the balanced growth path $x^*(t)$. Contrary to a common misunderstanding, this asymptotic convergence is *not* necessary in the concept of relative stability. In other words, that $x^*(t)$ is relatively stable does *not* necessarily imply that $\hat{x}(t) \to x^*(t)$ as $t \to \infty$. An example of such a case is given by Nikaido ([32], section 22) as follows:

EXAMPLE 2:   Let $M = \begin{bmatrix} 3 & 1 \\ 1 & 3 \end{bmatrix}$. Then the eigenvalues of M are 4 and 2 and the general solution can be written as

$$(16) \qquad \hat{x}(t) = h_1 4^t \begin{bmatrix} 1 \\ 1 \end{bmatrix} + h_2 2^t \begin{bmatrix} 1 \\ -1 \end{bmatrix}$$

where $\begin{bmatrix} 1 \\ 1 \end{bmatrix}$ and $\begin{bmatrix} 1 \\ -1 \end{bmatrix}$ are the eigenvectors associated with 4 and 2, respectively. Clearly,

$$(17) \qquad x_i^*(t) = 4^t, \; i = 1, 2$$

is a balanced growth path of the economy. If the initial output vector is such that $x_1(0) = 2$ and $x_2(0) = 0$, then the path of the output of each good, determined by

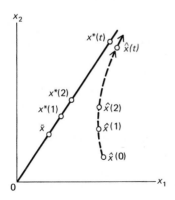

Figure 6.4.   An Illustration of Relative Stability.

(16), is

(18) $$\hat{x}_1(t) = 4^t + 2^t \quad \text{and} \quad \hat{x}_2(t) = 4^t - 2^t$$

Hence $\hat{x}_1(t)/x_1^*(t)$ and $\hat{x}_2(t)/x_2^*(t)$ both approach 1 as $t \to \infty$; that is, $x^*(t)$ is relatively stable. But the Euclidian distance between $\hat{x}(t)$ and $x^*(t)$ in period t is given by

(19) $$\| \hat{x}(t) - x^*(t) \| \equiv \sqrt{[\hat{x}_1(t) - x_1^*(t)]^2 + [\hat{x}_2(t) - x_2^*(t)]^2}$$

$$= \sqrt{2}\, 2^t,$$

which goes to ∞ as $t \to \infty$.

An important application of the concept of relative stability was given by Solow and Samuelson [39] in their 1953 article, in which they considered the following system of n first-order nonlinear difference equations:

(20) $$x_i(t + 1) = H_i[x_1(t), x_2(t), \ldots, x_n(t)], i = 1, 2, \ldots, n$$

or simply

$$x(t + 1) = H[x(t)]$$

Here the H_i, $i = 1, 2, \ldots, n$, are assumed to be real-valued, continuously differentiable,[6] linear homogeneous functions defined on the nonnegative orthant of R^n. The H_i's are in general nonlinear functions. Hence the system of linear difference equations such as (8), or $x(t + 1) = M \cdot x(t)$ where M is an $n \times n$ matrix, is an example of the above system.

Solow and Samuelson [39] imposed the following assumption on the functions H_i.

(SS)   The partial derivatives of H_i are *all positive* for all $x(t)$, $i = 1, 2, \ldots, n$.

Under this assumption they proved that the system of difference equations, (20), has a unique balanced growth solution that is relatively stable. This theorem is known as the **Solow-Samuelson theorem**.

The assumption (SS) is very strong. Considering (20) as a dynamic system of output growth in which H_i describes the production relation[7] (as in Solow and Samuelson [39]), this assumption means not only that every good is useful in the production of every other good, but also that if we have only one good, then we can produce *all* the other goods. Our model (8)—that is, $x(t + 1) = M \cdot x(t)$—does not, in general, satisfy this assumption for it requires that *all* the elements of M be positive.

Attempts to simplify the proof and to generalize the basic result of the Solow-Samuelson theorem have been made by Suits [40], Muth [30], Morishima [27] and [28], and Nikaido [33].[8] Since the Frobenius theorem plays an important role in the linear system, such as (8) (as explained above), it can easily be conjectured that the Frobenius theorem can be extended to a nonlinear case and can be applied to the Solow-Samuelson model, (20). Morishima [28] and Nikaido [33] substantiated such a conjecture.

Here we will not go into the exposition of the above attempts at the generalization of the Solow-Samuelson theorem and the nonlinear extension of the Frobenius theorem.[9] Instead we will come back to the original closed Leontief system (8), $x(t + 1) = M \cdot x(t)$. As we remarked before, we cannot establish the relative stability of a balanced growth solution for this system by directly applying the original Solow-Samuelson theorem, since M can contain zero and negative elements. However, Tsukui [42] proved that relative stability can be established if there exists a positive integer m such that $M^m > 0$. We prove below the essence of his result, which we call **Tsukui's lemma**. Clearly the application of this lemma is not confined to the dynamic Leontief problem *per se*.[10]

Tsukui's Lemma: *Let $M \equiv [I + F]$ be an $n \times n$ matrix, where F is nonsingular and $F^{-1} > 0$.[11] Then there exists a positive integer m such that $M^m > 0$ if and only if there exists an eigenvalue λ_1 of M such that $\lambda_1 > |\lambda_i|$ where the λ_i, $i = 2, 3, \ldots,$ n, are the other eigenvalues of M.*

PROOF: Let λ_i, μ_i, and $v_i (i = 1, 2, \ldots, n)$ be the eigenvalues for the matrices $(I + F), (I + F)^m$, and F^{-1}, respectively. Let x^i, y^i, z^i be the corresponding eigenvectors so that

(21) $(I + F) \cdot x^i = \lambda_i x^i, (I + F)^m \cdot y^i = \mu_i y^i, (F^{-1}) \cdot z^i = v_i z^i$

Note that $(I + F)^2 \cdot x^i = (I + F) \cdot (\lambda_i x^i) = \lambda_i^2 x^i$. Similarly, we have

(22) $(I + F)^m \cdot x^i = \lambda_i^m x^i$

Also note that $(F^{-1}) \cdot z^i = v_i z^i$ implies $(1/v_i) z^i = F \cdot z^i$, which in turn implies $(I + F) \cdot z^i = (1 + 1/v_i) z^i$. Hence we have

(23) $\lambda_i^m = \mu_i, 1 + \dfrac{1}{v_i} = \lambda_i$, and $x^i = y^i = z^i, i = 1, 2, \ldots, n$

We are now ready to prove the statement of the theorem.

(Necessity) Suppose $M^m > 0$ or $(I + F)^m > 0$, for some integer $m > 0$. Then M^m is indecomposable and primitive; hence there exists a positive eigenvalue μ_1 (Frobenius' root) such that $\mu_1 > |\mu_i|, i = 2, \ldots, n$, and an eigenvector $y^1 > 0$ associated with μ_1. This implies that $\lambda_1 > |\lambda_i|, i = 2, \ldots, n$, and $x^1 > 0$, for $\lambda_1^m = \mu_1$ and $x^1 = y^1$ by (23), which is the desired result.

(Sufficiency) Let v_1 be the Frobenius root of $F^{-1} > 0$, so that $F^{-1} \cdot x^1 = v_1 x^1$. Then $v_1 > 0$ and $x^1 > 0$. Moreover, $\lambda_1 = 1 + 1/v_1 > 0$. Since the transpose of a matrix has the same set of eigenvalues as the original matrix, we have $v_1 u^1 = u^1 \cdot (F^{-1})$, so that $(1/v_1) u^1 = u^1 \cdot F$. Moreover, $u^1 > 0$, since

$F^{-1} > 0.$[12] Then note the following relations:

(24) $\lambda_i(u^1 \cdot x^i) = u^1 \cdot (\lambda_i \cdot x^i) = u^1 \cdot (I + F) \cdot x^i$

$$= [u^1(1 + \frac{1}{v_1})] \cdot x^i = (1 + \frac{1}{v_1})(u^1 \cdot x^i)$$

Since $\lambda_1 = 1 + 1/v_1$ and also $\lambda_1 > |\lambda_i|$ for all $i = 2, \ldots, n$, by assumption,[13] this implies

(25) $u^1 \cdot x^i = 0, i = 2, \ldots, n$

Let e^i be the n-dimensional column vector whose ith component is 1 and all other components are zero, and consider the system of difference equations $x(t + 1) = M \cdot x(t)$.

Then, assuming that all the eigenvalues of M are distinct,[14] the general solution of this system of difference equations is [as discussed in connection with (10)]

$$\hat{x}(t) = h_1 \lambda_1{}^t x^1 + \cdots + h_n \lambda_n{}^t x^n$$

where the $h_i, i = 1, 2, \ldots, n$, are determined by the initial conditions. Hence a path starting from e^i must satisfy

(26) $\hat{x}(0) = e^i = h_1 x^1 + \cdots + h_n x^n$

so that

(27) $M^t \cdot e^i = h_1 \lambda_1{}^t x^1 + \cdots + h_n \lambda_n{}^t x^n$

since the λ_i's are the eigenvalues of M and the x^i's are the eigenvectors of M associated with the λ_i's, $i = 1, 2, \ldots, n$. Also (26) implies

(28) $u^1 \cdot e^i = \sum_{i=1}^{n} h_i(u^1 \cdot x^i) = h_1 u^1 \cdot x^1$

in view of (25). Since $x^1 > 0$ and $u^1 > 0$, we have

(29) $h_1 = \frac{u^1 \cdot e^i}{u^1 \cdot x^1} > 0$

Since $\lambda_1 > |\lambda_i|, i = 2, 3, \ldots, n$, and $\lambda_1 > 0$, $x^1 > 0$ by assumption, (27) implies that there exist (finite) positive integers $k_i, i = 1, 2, \ldots, n$, such that

(30) $M^t \cdot e^i > 0$ for $t \geq k_i$

Let m_i be the smallest of such k_i's and let $m \equiv \max \{m_1, m_2, \ldots, m_i, \ldots, m_n\}$. Then $M^m \cdot e^i > 0$ for all $i = 1, 2, \ldots, n$, so that

(31) $M^m > 0$

as desired.   (Q.E.D.)

We are now ready to consider the relative stability property of a balanced
growth solution of the system of difference equations $x(t + 1) = M \cdot x(t)$, where
$M \equiv (I + F)$. Consider the following particular solution, which is a (meaningful)
balanced growth solution if $\lambda^1 > 0$ and $x^1 > 0$:

(32) $x^*(t) = \lambda_1{}^t x^1$

Hence, assuming that all the eigenvalues of M are distinct,[15] the solution $x^*(t)$
is relatively stable (by definition) if and only if

(33) $\dfrac{\hat{x}_j(t)}{x_j^*(t)} = \dfrac{\sum_{i=1}^{n} h_i \lambda_i{}^t x_j^i}{\lambda_1{}^t x_j^1} \to \sigma > 0$ as $t \to \infty, j = 1, 2, \ldots, n$

where x_j^i is the jth element of x^i, $i = 1, 2, \ldots, n$, and $\hat{x}(t)$ is the general solution
written in the form of (10), whose jth element is $\hat{x}_j(t)$. It is clear then that the
balanced growth path $x^*(t)$ is relatively stable if and only if $\lambda_1 > |\lambda_i|, i = 2, \ldots, n$,
with $h_1 > 0$. Hence, in view of the previous lemma, we can conclude the following.

Theorem 6.B.1: *Suppose there exists a positive integer m such that $M^m > 0$ with
with $F^{-1} > 0$; then the balanced growth solution $x^*(t)$ as defined in (32) is relatively
stable, where $\lambda_1{}^m$ is the Frobenius root of M^m. Conversely, if the solution $x^*(t)$ is
relatively stable and $F^{-1} > 0$, then there exists a positive integer m such that
$M^m > 0$.[16]*

> REMARK: Nikaido ([32], section 22) proved the first half of this theorem
> for the case $m = 1$ (that is, $M > 0$), which is a special case of the Solow-
> Samuelson theorem.

> REMARK: The matrix M is not necessarily a nonnegative matrix in the
> above theorem. However, if M is a nonnegative matrix, then λ_1 becomes
> the Frobenius root of M. Moreover, if M is nonnegative and indecomposable
> (but not necessarily $M > 0$), then from Theorem 4.B.4 there exists a positive
> integer m such that $M^m > 0$ if and only if M is *primitive*. Hence we obtain the
> following corollary.

Corollary: *Let M be a nonnegative indecomposable matrix. Then if M is primitive, the balanced growth solution $x^*(t)$ as defined in (32) is relatively stable.
Conversely, if the solution $x^*(t)$ is relatively stable and if $F^{-1} > 0$, then M is
primitive.*

> REMARK: The result of the first part of this corollary is also obtained in
> Nikaido [32], pp. 110–113.

Above, we remarked that the balanced growth path $x^*(t)$ defined by (32) is relatively stable if and only if $\lambda_1 > |\lambda_i|$, $i = 2, \ldots, n$. However, the examination of (33) also reveals that the path $x^*(t)$ is relatively unstable if

(34) $$\lambda_1 < |\lambda_i|, \quad i = 2, \ldots, n$$

Now suppose that $M^{-m} > 0$ for some positive integer m where M^{-m} is defined by $(M^m)^{-1}$. Write the Frobenius root of M^{-m} as ρ_1 and observe that $\rho_1 > |\rho_i|$, $i = 2, \ldots, n$, and $1/\rho_i = \mu_i = \lambda_i^m$, $i = 1, 2, \ldots, n$, which in turn implies condition (34). On the other hand, if $M = I + F$, where $F^{-1} > 0$, and if (34) holds, we can prove that there exists a positive integer m such that $M^{-m} > 0$. The proof is analogous to the sufficiency proof of Tsukui's lemma. Therefore, we obtain the following direct opposite to Tsukui's lemma, which is also due to Tsukui [44].

Theorem 6.B.2 (relative instability theorem): *Let $M \equiv [I + F]$ be an $n \times n$ matrix, where F is nonsingular and $F^{-1} > 0$. Then there exists a positive integer m such that $M^{-m} > 0$ if and only if there exists an eigenvalue λ_1 of M such that $\lambda_1 < |\lambda_i|$ where λ_i, $i = 2, 3, \ldots, n$, are the other eigenvalues of M.*

> *REMARK:* Recent empirical studies on the dynamic Leontief system such as Tsukui [44] indicate that the condition $M^{-m} > 0$ for some m is more common in practice than $M^m > 0$ for some m. If this is the case, the output system is relatively unstable.[17]

In the dynamic Leontief system where $M \equiv I + B^{-1}(I - A)$, we may impose conditions on A and B such as $A \geq 0$, $B \geq 0$, B is nonsingular, $(I - A)$ is nonsingular with $(I - A)^{-1} > 0$, and $0 \leq a_{ij} < 1$ for all i and j. However, these conditions are not sufficient to guarantee that $M^m > 0$ for some positive integer m. In other words, even setting aside its empirical validity, the condition $M^m > 0$ for some m is not necessarily satisfied theoretically. To see this, recall Example 1 above (which is due to DOSSO [4]). As we noted, we have

$$M \equiv I + B^{-1}(I - A) = \begin{bmatrix} \dfrac{5}{3} & -\dfrac{1}{3} \\ -\dfrac{1}{3} & \dfrac{5}{3} \end{bmatrix}$$

The eigenvalues of M can be computed easily as 2 and $\frac{4}{3}$ with the corresponding eigenvectors $\begin{bmatrix} 1 \\ -1 \end{bmatrix}$ and $\begin{bmatrix} 1 \\ 1 \end{bmatrix}$ (or their constant multiples). Hence, the general solution of (8), $x(t + 1) = M \cdot x(t)$, can be written as

(35) $$\hat{x}_1(t) = h_1 2^t + h_2\left(\frac{4}{3}\right)^t, \quad \hat{x}_2(t) = -h_1 2^t + h_2\left(\frac{4}{3}\right)^t$$

where h_1 and h_2 are to be determined by the boundary conditions, say, $\hat{x}_1(0) =$

$h_1 + h_2$ and $\hat{x}_2(0) = -h_1 + h_2$. If $\hat{x}_1(0)$ and $\hat{x}_2(0)$ are such that $h_1 = 0$, then the economy is on a balanced growth path $x_i^*(t) = h_2(\frac{4}{3})^t$, $i = 1, 2$. On the other hand, if $\hat{x}_1(0)$ and $\hat{x}_2(0)$ are such that $h_1 \neq 0$, then one of the outputs eventually becomes negative. For example, if $h_1 > 0$, then $\hat{x}_2(t) < 0$ for all $t > \bar{t}$ for some $\bar{t}$. Note that the balanced growth solution $h_1 2^t$ is impossible for any $h_1 > 0$ under the assumption that $x(0) \geq 0$, that is, $x_i(0) \geq 0$, $i = 1, 2$, with strict inequality for at least one i.[18] In other words, we have shown for the present dynamic Leontief system that one of the outputs eventually becomes negative except when the boundary conditions are such that the economy is actually on its only balanced growth path $x_i^*(t) = h_2(\frac{4}{3})^t$, $i = 1, 2$. We may note that if $\hat{x}_i(t)$ becomes negative for $t > \bar{t}$, then $K_i(t)$, the stock of this ith good, also becomes negative for $t > \bar{t}$ in view of (3). Clearly, negative output and a negative stock of goods do not make any economic sense in the present discussion. Such a possibility in a dynamic Leontief system is called "causal indeterminacy."[19]

Definition: If the relative configuration of the initial outputs (or the initial stock of goods) does not coincide with that of any possible balanced growth path of the economy, then the growth path *may* ultimately reach a situation at which the output (and the stock) of at least one good becomes negative. If this happens, then we say that we have **causal indeterminacy**.

Clearly this possibility of causal indeterminacy seriously undermines the dynamic Leontief model. Note also that if the economy possesses a balanced growth path which is relatively stable, then there is no causal indeterminacy in such an economy. This is, as mentioned earlier, another point of crucial importance in the concept of relative stability.

c.   THE PRICE SYSTEM[20]

Assume that our economy is equipped with "money" which can be produced at no cost and which functions as a medium of exchange as well as a unit of account by which the price of each good is measured. Let $p(t)$ be the price vector in period t, whose ith element $p_i(t)$ denotes the price of the ith good in period t. We assume that the production of all goods takes exactly one period and that prices are constant throughout each period. It is assumed that no individual can affect the price of any good that prevails in the market (the "competitiveness" assumption).

Consider a bundle of goods denoted by the vector $b_j = (b_{1j}, b_{2j}, \ldots, b_{nj})$. This bundle of goods gives the necessary configuration of capital equipment for the production of one unit of the jth good. The value of this bundle is equal to $v_j \equiv p(t) \cdot b_j = \sum_{i=1}^{n} p_i(t) b_{ij}$. Consider an individual who has money in the amount of v_j at the beginning of period t. Suppose he can either lend this (say to a "bank") at the rate of interest $r(t)$ or invest it in the production of the jth good.

We assume that no individual can affect the interest rate which prevails in the economy and that $r(t)$ is the rate which prevails in the economy throughout period t. By lending at this rate in period t, he can obtain

(36) $$\left[1 + r(t)\right] v_j(t)$$

at the beginning of the $(t + 1)$th period.

Suppose that, instead of lending his money, he invests it in the production of the jth good. Then he can buy the configuration of capital equipment which is necessary for the production of the jth good in the amount of exactly one unit with his money v_j. Assume for the sake of simplicity that (homogeneous) labor is the only primary factor. Let a_{0j} be the amount of labor necessary to produce one unit of the jth good. Let $p_0(t)$ be the price of labor ("wages") in period t and assume that wages and the material cost are paid at the end of the period (that is, at the beginning of the following period). Then the wage cost and the material cost for the production of one unit of the jth good in period t are given, respectively, by

$$p_0(t + 1)a_{0j} \quad \text{and} \quad \sum_{i=1}^{n} p_i(t + 1)a_{ij} = p(t + 1) \cdot a_j$$

where $a_j = \left[a_{1j}, a_{2j}, \ldots, a_{nj}\right]$. The current profit for period t per unit production of the jth good is thus given by

$$\pi_j(t) \equiv p_j(t + 1) - p_0(t + 1)a_{0j} - p(t + 1) \cdot a_j$$

Since the configuration of capital equipment b_j will be worth $p(t + 1) \cdot b_j$ at the beginning of period $(t + 1)$, the total value of his assets at the beginning of period $(t + 1)$ is given by

(37) $$\pi_j(t) + p(t + 1) \cdot b_j$$

Assuming the competitive arbitrage condition, it should be immaterial in equilibrium whether one lends the v_j or invests it in the production of the jth good; the above expression, (37), must be equal to the one given by (36). In other words, we have

$$\pi_j(t) + p(t + 1) \cdot b_j = \left[1 + r(t)\right] v_j$$

or

(38) $$p_j(t + 1) - p_0(t + 1)a_{0j} - p(t + 1) \cdot a_j + p(t + 1) \cdot b_j = \left[1 + r(t)\right] p(t) \cdot b_j$$

Recalling that $v_j(t) \equiv p(t) \cdot b_j$, and rearranging terms after dividing both sides of (38) by $v_j(t)$, we obtain

(39) $$\frac{v_j(t + 1) - v_j(t)}{v_j(t)} + \frac{\pi_j(t)}{v_j(t)} = r(t)$$

This is the well-known equation of capital theory. We may consider $v_j(t)$ the price of a unit capacity to produce the jth good. A usual way of interpreting (39) is as follows: Suppose a person has one unit of money (say, a "dollar") with which he can buy the capacity for the jth good in the amount of $1/v_j(t)$.[21] One unit of this capacity is worth $v_j(t + 1)$ in period $(t + 1)$ so that $v_j(t + 1)/v_j(t)$ is the value of the capacity of the original $(1/v_j(t))$ units. Moreover, $(1/v_j(t))$ units of capacity yield current profits of $\pi_j(t)/v_j(t)$ in period t. On the other hand, one dollar, if it is loaned to a "bank," will be worth $[1 + r(t)]$ at the beginning of the $(t + 1)$th period. Thus, in equilibrium, we have

$$(40) \qquad \frac{v_j(t + 1)}{v_j(t)} + \frac{\pi_j(t)}{v_j(t)} = 1 + r(t)$$

which is obviously equivalent to (39).

Coming back to (38), this relation must hold for all $j = 1, 2, \ldots, n$. Hence, recalling that a_j is the jth row of A and b_j is the jth row of B, we obtain

$$(41) \qquad p(t + 1) \cdot [I - A + B] = [1 + r(t)] p(t) \cdot B + p_0(t + 1) a_0$$

where a_0 is an n-vector whose jth element is a_{0j}. This is the **basic price equation of the dynamic Leontief system**. This equation is the "dual" of the output equation (7), which we may rewrite as

$$(7') \qquad B \cdot x(t + 1) = [I - A + B] \cdot x(t) - \bar{c}(t)$$

In the above exposition of the derivation, for the sake of convenience, we introduced such concepts as "money" and "bank" (or lending possibility). But these are not essential concepts in the construction of the economy. "Money" is introduced to measure prices, the $p_j(t)$'s, and to facilitate transactions, and "bank" is introduced solely to facilitate the concept of the rate of interest. If there are neither "banks" nor any lending possibilities, then $r(t)$ is considered the **own rate of interest** in period t. Assuming that $p(t)$ and $p(t + 1)$ are given, we may then consider equation (39) as the *defining equation* of the own rate of interest, $r(t)$.

Assuming again that B is nonsingular [assumption (A-2)], we can rewrite (41) as

$$(42) \qquad p(t + 1) = [1 + r(t)] \, p(t) \cdot [I + (I - A)B^{-1}]^{-1} + W$$

where $W \equiv p_0(t + 1) a_0 \cdot [I - A + B]_\bullet^{-1}$. This equation corresponds to (7) for the output system. In obtaining (42), the nonsingularity of $[I + (I - A)B^{-1}]$ is implicitly assumed.

In the closed dynamic Leontief system in which labor is subsumed as one of the industries, the term W does not appear, so that (42) is simplified to

$$(43) \qquad p(t + 1) = [1 + r(t)] p(t) \cdot [I + (I - A)B^{-1}]^{-1}$$

This is again a system of n first-order, linear, homogeneous difference equations. We should note the one fundamental assumption in the above procedure of obtaining (43). That is, one has to know $p(t + 1)$ in period t. Clearly, $p(t + 1)$ is a future price in period t; thus this is the assumption of **perfect foresight**.[22]

We may also note that this system of equations, (43), is not self-contained. That is, there are $(n + 1)$ unknown time profiles (the prices of n goods and the interest rate), whereas (43) contains only n equations. If we specify $r(t)$, then we can solve this system of equations for $p_i(t)$, $i = 1, 2, \ldots, n$. An unspecified interest rate is appropriate in the present model, for there is no mechanism in the model which determines the interest rate. Alternatively, if we set one of the goods to be the *numéraire* (say $p_1(t) = 1$ for all t), then (43) determines $r(t)$ and $p_i(t)$, $i = 2, \ldots, n$. But then there is no mechanism in the model which determines the absolute prices. The banking system, demand for money, and the like, are not discussed. In his treatment of the dynamic Leontief price system, Solow proposed "to let the interest rate hang and treat it as an arbitrary function of time" ([38], p. 36). Then, soon after this statement, he assumed $r(t)$ constant for all t (p. 36). Jorgenson [15], in proving his dual stability theorem, assumed that $r(t) = 0$ for all t. Here let us also assume $r(t) = 0$ for all t, so that we now have

$$(44) \qquad\qquad p(t + 1) = p(t) \cdot N$$

where $N \equiv [I + (I - A)B^{-1}]^{-1}$. Let ξ_i, $i = 1, 2, \ldots, n$, be the eigenvalues of N with corresponding eigenvectors $\bar{p}_i$, $i = 1, 2, \ldots, n$, that is,

$$(45) \qquad\qquad \bar{p}_i \cdot N = \xi_i \bar{p}_i, \qquad i = 1, 2, \ldots, n$$

If all the eigenvalues of N are distinct, then the general solution of (44) can be written as

$$(46) \qquad\qquad \hat{p}(t) = g_1 \xi_1{}^t \bar{p}_1 + \cdots + g_n \xi_n{}^t \bar{p}_n$$

where the g_i, $i = 1, 2, \ldots, n$, are constants which are determined by the initial conditions. Hence again the behavior of $\hat{p}(t)$ over time depends on the eigenvalues of N, the ξ_i's.

In order to study the eigenvalues of N, let ζ_i, $i = 1, 2, \ldots, n$, be the eigenvalues of $(I - A)B^{-1}$ with corresponding eigenvectors $\bar{q}_i$, $i = 1, 2, \ldots, n$. That is,

$$(47) \qquad\qquad \bar{q}_i \cdot (I - A)B^{-1} = \zeta_i \bar{q}_i, \qquad i = 1, 2, \ldots, n$$

Then

$$(48) \qquad\qquad \bar{q}_i [I + (I - A)B^{-1}] = (1 + \zeta_i) \bar{q}_i, \quad i = 1, 2, \ldots, n$$

That is, the $(1 + \zeta_i)$'s are the eigenvalues of $[I + (I - A)B^{-1}]$. Then we have

$$(49) \qquad\qquad \bar{q}_i \cdot [I + (I - A)B^{-1}]^{-1} = \frac{\bar{q}_i}{1 + \zeta_i}, \qquad i = 1, 2, \ldots, n$$

Hence in view of (45), we obtain

(50) $$\xi_i = \frac{1}{1 + \zeta_i} \quad \text{and} \quad \bar{p}_i = \bar{q}_i, i = 1, 2, \ldots, n$$

Therefore, to study the eigenvalues of N, it suffices to study the eigenvalues of $(I - A)B^{-1}$. But the eigenvalues of $(I - A)B^{-1}$ are equal to the eigenvalues μ_i of $B^{-1}(I - A)$, $i = 1, 2, \ldots, n$. Hence we have $\zeta_i = \mu_i$, $i = 1, 2, \ldots, n$, so that we obtain

(51) $$\xi_i = \frac{1}{\lambda_i}, \qquad i = 1, 2, \ldots, n$$

since $\lambda_i = 1 + \mu_i$, $i = 1, 2, \ldots, n$.

The output system (8), $x(t + 1) = M \cdot x(t)$, has a balanced growth path which is relatively stable if and only if there exists a positive eigenvalue λ_1 of M such that $\lambda_1 > |\lambda_i|$, $i = 2, \ldots, n$, with $\bar{x}^1 > 0$, where $\bar{x}^1$ is the eigenvector associated with $\lambda_1 > 0$. The relevant balanced growth path which is relatively stable is $x^*(t) = \lambda_1^t \bar{x}^1$. But if $\lambda_1 > |\lambda_i|$, $i = 2, \ldots, n$, then we have, in view of (51),

(52) $$\xi_1 < |\xi_i|, \qquad i = 2, \ldots, n$$

The price equation which corresponds to the balanced growth path $x^*(t) = \lambda_1^t \bar{x}^1$ can be written as

$$p^*(t) = \xi_1^t \bar{p}_1$$

where $\xi_1 > 0$ and $\bar{p}_1 > 0$ as long as $\lambda_1 > 0$ and $\bar{x}^1 > 0$. Hence if $x^*(t)$ is relatively stable, then $p^*(t)$ is *not* relative stable, for the ratio $\hat{p}_i(t)/p_i^*(t)$, $i = 1, 2, \ldots, n$, does not, in general, converge to a constant as $t \to \infty$ in view of (46). Conversely, if there exists a $\xi_1 > 0$ and the corresponding eigenvector $\bar{p}_1 > 0$ such that $\xi_1 > |\xi_i|$, $i = 2, \ldots, n$, then we have $\lambda_1 < |\lambda_i|$, $i = 2, \ldots, n$. Hence the balanced growth path $x^*(t)$ is not relatively stable. We may call this result the **(Solow-Jorgenson) dual stability theorem** in view of Solow [38] and Jorgenson [15].[23]

Finally, let us examine whether it is possible for the price vector to be constant for all t. Coming back to (41), put $p(t + 1) = p(t) = \text{constant} \equiv p$, and $p_0(t) = \text{constant} \equiv p_0$. Then we obtain

(53) $$p = p \cdot A + rp \cdot B + p_0 \cdot a_0$$

In other words, if the initial price vectors $p(0)$ and $p_0(0)$ happen to be such that $p(0) = p$ and $p_0(0) = p_0$ and that p and p_0 satisfy (53), then all the prices are constant for all t. For the special case $r = 0$ and $p_0 = a_0 = 0$, that is, the case we are considering in connection with (44), we have $p = 0$, assuming $(I - A)$ is nonsingular. This can also be seen from (44) directly. This means that in the closed Leontief system with $r = 0$, the only constant price case is the case in which all the prices are zero. The constant price solution is the one that Morishima [26] is concerned with. A discussion of this is given in subsection e.

d.   INEQUALITIES AND OPTIMIZATION MODEL (SOLOW)

The phenomenon of causal indeterminacy brings up the following question: Under what conditions can we guarantee the existence of nonnegative output and stock vectors, $x(t)$ and $K(t)$, for all t, which satisfy a system of difference equations such as (8)? This question, in a sense, resembles the Walras-Wald problem of the existence of a competitive equilibrium as a solution of a system of simultaneous equations. We recall (Chapter 2, Section E, subsection a) that this problem is solved by allowing inequalities in the system. We may then naturally conjecture that the problem of causal indeterminacy can also be avoided by allowing inequalities in the system. This is precisely the route that Solow [38] investigated. Following Solow, we consider the following system [instead of (6')]:

$$(54) \qquad x(t) = A \cdot x(t) + \Delta K(t) + \bar{c}(t)$$

and

$$(55) \qquad K(t) \geq B \cdot x(t), \text{ with } x(t) \geq 0 \text{ and } K(t) \geq 0$$

Note that the important feature is that inequalities are introduced as $K(t) \geq B \cdot x(t)$. This, of course, means that we allow the possibility that output may fail to use up all of the available capacity; that is, excess capacity may exist.[24] The introduction of these inequalities relaxes the "tightness" of the original equality system such as (6') or (8). However, we can no longer define a unique output path $x(t)$ [and a stock path $K(t)$] as a solution of a given system of difference equations such as (8). The above relations (54) and (55) define only a "feasible" path of an output vector and a stock vector, $x(t)$ and $K(t)$. Clearly there can be many $x(t)$ and $K(t)$ which would satisfy the above relations (54) and (55), even if the initial conditions—say, $K(0)$—are uniquely given. In other words, (54) and (55) define only the *set* of feasible paths.

What then can we say about the output path and the stock path which would actually be chosen in the economy? The answer to this question should seem obvious to any economics student, that is, that "it depends on the demand conditions." But what demand conditions? The best way to understand this is probably to consider the above dynamic system in terms of a diagram. Write $d(t) \equiv A \cdot x(t) + \bar{c}(t)$, which determines the demand for goods (net of accumulation) in period t, once $x(t)$ is determined. At each t, $K(t)$ is given to the economy and the possible values of output are determined by $K(t) \geq B \cdot x(t)$, $x(t) \geq 0$. For $t = 0$ this is illustrated by the area inside (and including the boundary) $OEFG$ in Figure 6.5. Suppose that point P is chosen, which is an output vector in period 0, that is, $x(0)$. Then deducting $d(0) \equiv [d_1(0), d_2(0)]$, we obtain point Q, which, in terms of (54), defines the increase in the stock of goods in period 0, $\Delta K(0) = K(1) - K(0)$, from which $K(1)$, the stock vector in the next period, is determined.

It may be plausible to assume that $x(0)$ is chosen such that $x(0)$ is on the frontier (that is, the kinked line EFG), for any other point (that is, point inside) can be improved upon.[25] However, the choice of location of $x(0)$ on the EFG line is a

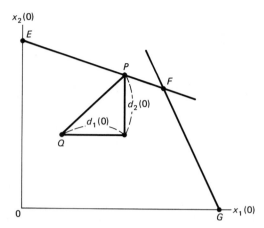

Figure 6.5.   Feasible Set.

matter of the demand conditions. In this connection, we should note that point Q and point P are related in a definite way, for vector $d(0)$ is uniquely specified once $x(0)$ is specified. Hence the choice of $x(0)$ is uniquely related to the choice of $\Delta K(0)$ if the equality (54) is to hold, so that $K(1)$ is determined in a definite way. In other words, the "demand condition" simultaneously determines the output vector of the current period [here $x(0)$] and the stock vector of the next period [here $K(1)$]. Once the stock vector of the next period is determined, we are ready to consider the next period by taking the stock vector of this period as a new initial condition.

Solow [38] then proposed to consider this demand condition as a solution of an optimization model. Suppose, for example, that the demand condition is not determined in a decentralized way as the sum of each individual's desires or tastes but is rather determined by the central planning authority in such a fashion as to optimize a certain target.

As such a target (following Solow), we choose a weighted sum of the terminal capital stocks, $\sum_{i=1}^{n} \alpha_i K_i(T)$, or $\alpha \cdot K(T)$, where $\alpha \geq 0$. Recalling our discussion in Chapter 1, Section E, we may regard this as the vector maximum problem of maximizing $K(T)$. In any case, given the value of α, our problem now is a simple linear programming problem of maximizing $\alpha \cdot K(T)$ subject to

$$(I - A) \cdot x(t) \geq \bar{c}(t) + \Delta K(t),\ t = 0, 1, 2, \ldots, T - 1$$

$$K(t) \geq B \cdot x(t),\ t = 0, 1, 2, \ldots, T - 1$$

and

$$x(t) \geq 0,\ K(t) \geq 0,\ t = 0, 1, 2, \ldots, T$$

Note that we now allow an excess supply of goods [that is, $x(t) \geq A \cdot x(t) + \Delta K(t) + \bar{c}(t)$] as well as excess capacity. The constraints $(I - A) \cdot x(t) \geq \bar{c}(t) + \Delta K(t)$ and $K(t) \geq B \cdot x(t)$ are written out as follows (here write $C \equiv I - A$):

$$
\begin{bmatrix}
I & 0 & 0 & \cdots & 0 & 0 & -C & 0 & 0 & \cdots & 0 \\
-I & I & 0 & \cdots & 0 & 0 & 0 & -C & 0 & \cdots & 0 \\
0 & -I & I & \cdots & 0 & 0 & 0 & 0 & -C & \cdots & 0 \\
\cdots & \cdots & \cdots & \cdots & \cdots & \cdots & \cdots & \cdots & \cdots & & \cdots \\
0 & 0 & 0 & \cdots & -I & I & 0 & 0 & 0 & \cdots & -C \\
0 & 0 & 0 & \cdots & 0 & 0 & B & 0 & 0 & \cdots & 0 \\
-I & 0 & 0 & \cdots & 0 & 0 & 0 & B & 0 & \cdots & 0 \\
0 & -I & 0 & \cdots & 0 & 0 & 0 & 0 & B & \cdots & 0 \\
\cdots & \cdots & \cdots & \cdots & \cdots & \cdots & \cdots & \cdots & \cdots & & \cdots \\
0 & 0 & 0 & \cdots & -I & 0 & 0 & 0 & 0 & \cdots & B
\end{bmatrix}
\begin{bmatrix}
K(1) \\ K(2) \\ K(3) \\ \vdots \\ K(T) \\ x(0) \\ x(1) \\ x(2) \\ \vdots \\ x(T-1)
\end{bmatrix}
\leqq
\begin{bmatrix}
K(0)-\bar{c}(0) \\ -c(1) \\ -c(2) \\ \vdots \\ -c(T-1) \\ K(0) \\ 0 \\ 0 \\ \vdots \\ 0
\end{bmatrix}
$$

Clearly the choice variables here are $K(t)$, $t = 1, 2, \ldots, T$, and $x(t)$, $t = 0, 1, 2, \ldots, T - 1$. Clearly, it is possible to generalize the above maximization problem by adding the primary resource constraints such as $a_0 \cdot x(t) \leqq L(t)$ where $L(t)$ is the exogenous supply of labor in period t. Since such an analysis would be analogous to the subsequent one, we shall leave it to the interested reader.

In order to consider the price implications of the above problem, Solow considered the dual of this linear programming problem, which can be easily obtained by constructing the dual constraints from the above original constraints. That is, the dual constraints are explicitly written out as follows:

$$
\begin{bmatrix}
I & -I & 0 & \cdots & 0 & 0 & -I & 0 & \cdots & 0 \\
0 & I & -I & \cdots & 0 & 0 & 0 & -I & \cdots & 0 \\
0 & 0 & I & \cdots & 0 & 0 & 0 & 0 & \cdots & 0 \\
\cdots & \cdots & \cdots & \cdots & \cdots & \cdots & \cdots & \cdots & \cdots & \cdots \\
0 & 0 & 0 & \cdots & -I & 0 & 0 & 0 & \cdots & -I \\
0 & 0 & 0 & \cdots & I & 0 & 0 & 0 & \cdots & 0 \\
-C' & 0 & 0 & \cdots & 0 & B' & 0 & 0 & \cdots & 0 \\
0 & -C' & 0 & \cdots & 0 & 0 & B' & 0 & \cdots & 0 \\
0 & 0 & -C' & \cdots & 0 & 0 & 0 & B' & \cdots & 0 \\
\cdots & \cdots & \cdots & \cdots & \cdots & \cdots & \cdots & \cdots & \cdots \\
0 & 0 & 0 & \cdots & -C' & 0 & 0 & 0 & \cdots & B'
\end{bmatrix}
\begin{bmatrix}
u(0) \\ u(1) \\ u(2) \\ \vdots \\ u(T-2) \\ u(T-1) \\ q(0) \\ q(1) \\ q(2) \\ \vdots \\ q(T-1)
\end{bmatrix}
\geqq
\begin{bmatrix}
0 \\ 0 \\ 0 \\ \vdots \\ 0 \\ \alpha \\ 0 \\ 0 \\ 0 \\ \vdots \\ 0
\end{bmatrix}
$$

Here $u(t)$, $t = 0, 1, \ldots, T - 1$, and $q(t)$, $t = 0, 1, \ldots, T - 1$, are the dual variables, and B' and C' are, respectively, the transposes of B and C. We thus obtain the following set of constraints for the dual problem:

(56) $$u(t) - u(t + 1) - q(t + 1) \geqq 0, \quad t = 0, 1, 2, \ldots, T - 2$$

(57) $$u(T - 1) \geqq \alpha$$

and

(58) $$-C' \cdot u(t) + B' \cdot q(t) \geqq 0, \quad t = 0, 1, 2, \ldots, T - 1$$

as well as the nonnegativity constraints, $u(t) \geq 0, q(t) \geq 0, t = 0, 1, \ldots, T - 1$. The objective of this dual problem is to minimize

$$u_0 \cdot \left[K(0) - \bar{c}(0) \right] - \sum_{t=1}^{T-1} u(t) \cdot \bar{c}(t) + q(0) \cdot K(0)$$

$$= - \sum_{t=0}^{T-1} u(t) \cdot \bar{c}(t) + \left[u(0) + q(0) \right] \cdot K(0)$$

Let $\hat{K}(t), t = 1, 2, \ldots, T$, and $\hat{x}(t), t = 0, 1, \ldots, T - 1$, be a solution of the original problem, and let $\hat{u}(t), t = 0, 1, 2, \ldots, T - 1$, and $\hat{q}_t, t = 0, 1, \ldots, T - 1$, be a solution of the dual problem. Then applying the LP duality theorem (see Theorem 1.F.1), we can easily conclude that

(59) $$\alpha \cdot \hat{K}(T) = \left[\hat{u}(0) + \hat{q}(0) \right] \cdot K(0) - \sum_{t=0}^{T-1} \hat{q}(t)\bar{c}(t)$$

(60) $\quad \hat{K}(t) > 0$ implies $\hat{u}(t) - \hat{u}(t + 1) - \hat{q}(t + 1) = 0, t = 0, 1, \ldots, T - 2$

(61) $$\hat{K}(T) > 0 \quad \text{implies} \quad \hat{u}(T - 1) = \alpha$$

(62) $\quad \hat{x}(t) > 0 \quad \text{implies} \quad - C' \cdot \hat{u}(t) + B' \cdot \hat{q}(t) = 0, t = 0, 1, 2, \ldots, T - 1$

(63) $\hat{u}(t) > 0 \quad \text{implies} \quad \hat{x}(t) = A \cdot \hat{x}(t) + \Delta \hat{K}(t) + \bar{c}(t), t = 0, 1, 2, \ldots, T - 1$

(64) $\quad \hat{q}(t) > 0 \quad \text{implies} \quad \hat{K}(t) = B \cdot \hat{x}(t), t = 0, 1, 2, \ldots, T - 1$

(65) $\quad \hat{K}_j(t) > \left[B \cdot \hat{x}(t) \right]_j \quad \text{implies} \quad \hat{q}_j(t) = 0, t = 1, 2, \ldots, T - 1$

Following Solow [38], we interpret $\hat{u}(t)$ as the vector of commodity prices in period t, discounted back to the present, and $\hat{q}(t)$ as the vector of stock rents discounted back to the present. In terms of the previous notations

(66) $$\hat{u}(t) = \frac{p(t)}{\Pi_{\tau=1}^t \left[1 + r(\tau) \right]}, \quad \hat{u}(0) = p(0) \quad \text{and} \quad \hat{u}(t) \geq 0$$

Let $R(t)$ denote the undiscounted vector of stock rents. Then

(67) $$\hat{q}(t) = \frac{R(t)}{\Pi_{\tau=1}^t \left[1 + r(\tau) \right]}, \quad \hat{q}(0) = R(0) \quad \text{and} \quad \hat{q}(t) \geq 0$$

Now assuming that all stocks are always positive, that is, $\hat{K}(t) > 0$ for all t, we obtain from (60)

(68) $$\left[1 + r(t) \right] p(t) = R(t + 1) + p(t + 1)$$

from which we can easily obtain

(69) $$\frac{p_j(t + 1) - p_j(t)}{p_j(t)} + \frac{R_j(t + 1)}{p_j(t)} = r(t), \text{ for all } t$$

which corresponds to our old intertemporal-arbitrage equilibrium condition (39). Note that $R_j(t + 1)$ corresponds to $\pi_j(t)$, which is the current profit (own rent) of period t from a spectrum of equipment which has a capacity of producing one unit of the jth good. On the other hand, $R_j(t)$ is the rent on a stock consisting of one unit of the jth good. Also from (61) we obtain [by assuming $\hat{K}(T) > 0$]

(70) $$\alpha = \frac{p(T - 1)}{\Pi_{\tau=1}^{T-1}[1 + r(\tau)]}$$

Using (66) and (67), the constraint $-C' \cdot u(t) + B' \cdot q(t) \geq 0$ can be written as

(71) $-C' \cdot p(t) + B' \cdot R(t) \geq 0,$ or $p(t) \leq A' \cdot p(t) + B' \cdot R(t)$

Suppose $\hat{K}(t) > 0$ for all t so that (60) holds; then we have

(72) $(B + C)' \cdot p(t + 1) \leq [1 + r(t)] B' \cdot p(t),$ for all t

If $\hat{x}(t) > 0$, then (71) holds with equality for all t in view of (62). Hence (72) holds with equality for all t, and we can easily rewrite it as the basic price equation (43) in the dynamic Leontief system. [If we had incorporated the labor constraint $a_0 \cdot x(t) \leq L(t)$ in the original maximization problem, we would obtain equation (42) instead.]

If some stock is not held for some period, that is, if $\hat{K}_j(t) = 0$ for some j and some t, then (69) does not necessarily hold with equality. In other words,

(73) $$\frac{p_j(t + 1) - p_j(t)}{p_j(t)} + \frac{R_j(t + 1)}{p_j(t)} \leq r(t)$$

The strict inequality here would induce a holder of the stock to get rid of it. We henceforth assume $\hat{K}_j(t) > 0$ for all j and for all t.

Suppose that $\alpha_j > 0$, that is, the terminal stock of the jth good is positively weighted. Then we can show that $u_j(t) > 0$ for all t. To see this, observe that, owing to (60), $\hat{u}_j(t) = 0$ implies $\hat{u}_j(t + 1) = 0$ and $\hat{q}_j(t + 1) = 0$, so that $\hat{u}_j(t + 2) = \hat{u}_j(t + 3) = \cdots = \hat{u}_j(T - 1) = 0$. But $\hat{u}_j(T - 1) = \alpha_j > 0$. Hence $\hat{u}_j(t) = 0$ is impossible for any t. Therefore, assuming $\alpha > 0$, we can conclude that $\hat{u}(t) > 0$ for all t. Hence, in view of (63), we obtain

(74) $\hat{x}(t) = A \cdot \hat{x}(t) + \Delta \hat{K}(t) + \bar{c}(t),$ for all t

In terms of Figure 6.5 this means that the output must always be chosen on the frontier, that is, the kinked line EFG, as we remarked earlier.

If the stock of the jth good has excess capacity in period t, then in view of (65), we have $\hat{q}_j(t) = 0$, so that $R_j(t) = 0$. Then, owing to (69),

(75) $p_j(t + 1) = [1 + r(t)] p_j(t)$

In other words, the nominal price of the jth good will increase simply at the compound rate of interest $r(t)$.

What does this all add up to? It may be worthwhile to recapitulate some of the results obtained above.

(i)   The problem of causal indeterminacy can be avoided simply by converting the equalities to inequalities, that is, by allowing excess capacity of capital together with the nonnegativity constraint.

(ii)   The dual variables $u(t)$ and $q(t)$ play the role of prices in the competitive mechanism. For example, the competitive intertemporal arbitrage equation (69) is obtained by interpreting the dual variables as prices.

(iii) The values of the dual variables can be computed explicitly by solving the dual linear programming problem.

(iv)   There are certain important relations between prices $[p(t)$ and $R(t)]$ and the real variables $[x(t)$ and $K(t)]$ implied by relations (59) to (65). Some of them are obtained as (69), (71), (72), (73), (74), and (75). The possibility of zero prices and of excess capacity is a novel feature in the present formulation.

(v)   The price equation (43) holds if $\hat{K}(t) > 0$ and $\hat{x}(t) > 0$ for all t.

Finally, we should stress that the above model à la Solow is a planning model and not a descriptive model of an economy. Although it can be interpreted as an "optimal path" generated by a "competitive" mechanism, it does not describe the mechanism nor the equilibrium of a competitive dynamic economy. This is in marked contrast to Morishima's model, which we describe in the next subsection. However, if we recall the treatment of a competitive (static) equilibrium in terms of linear programming (with the duality theorem) by Kuhn [18] and DOSSO [4] (see our Chapter 2, Section E, subsection a), we realize immediately that we can construct a model for a competitive dynamic economy utilizing the above planning model and prove various properties of the model such as existence, and so on. In other words, we may consider the above planning model as a part of a descriptive model.

There is another possible route of development in the above planning model, and that is dropping the assumption of fixed coefficients and allowing various production processes for the production of one or more goods, while still retaining the basic planning character of the model. A natural question which then arises is that of characterizations of the "optimal path." The turnpike theorems that we discuss in the next chapter (Section A) are concerned with this question, under the assumption that the planning horizon T is long enough. This route is further investigated by Gale, and others, with a more satisfactory treatment of consumption (Section B of Chapter 7).

e.   MORISHIMA'S MODEL OF THE DYNAMIC LEONTIEF SYSTEM

Another important model of the dynamic Leontief system is provided by Morishima [26] and [27]. The essential difference here from the usual dynamic

Leontief model is that the production coefficients such as the a_{ij}'s and b_{ij}'s are no longer assumed to be constant. That is, these coefficients can now vary depending on changes in the prices of goods (which are used as factors of production) as well as on changes in the wage rate.[26]

One of the important objectives of Morishima in the above-mentioned papers was to prove that the coefficients, the a_{ij}'s and b_{ij}'s, are, in fact, constant. Although these coefficients are allowed to vary, only fixed values are chosen in equilibrium so that the usual analysis of the dynamic Leontief system with fixed coefficients could be justified. This is an extension of the famous substitution theorem[27] of Samuelson from a static to a dynamic case.

Although we will argue that his dynamic substitution theorem holds only for very limited cases, his introduction of the possibility of factor substitution is a very important contribution. For example, as we remarked in subsection a, it could enable us to avoid the difficulty of causal indeterminacy which is inherent in the dynamic Leontief model with fixed coefficients. In other words, suppose that for certain period(s) of time, the stock of some good diminishes. Then, under the usual circumstances, such a decumulation would increase the marginal productivity of this good when it is used as a factor of production, which may, in turn, encourage the production of this good. Hence the decumulation of the stock of this good could be stopped, thus avoiding causal indeterminacy.[28]

We do not, however, attempt to prove this observation rigorously in this subsection. We leave this to the interested reader. Here, instead, we try to build a foundation for such an attempt by discussing Morishima's model critically.

This will enable the reader to understand how the model is to be constructed when factor substitution is allowed. In this connection we may also point out an interesting feature in Morishima's model, that is, he distinguishes capital goods from noncapital goods explicitly, so there are goods that are never used as capital goods (unlike the usual Leontief model in which the nonsingularity of the B matrix is assumed).

Second, Morishima's model represents a polar assumption with regard to the treatment of the price equation compared with our price equation (41) à la Solow [38]. In other words, as we will discuss later, whereas (41) represents the dynamic price equation with changing prices but perfect foresight, Morishima's price equation is based on the assumption that entrepreneurs always expect prices to remain constant.[29]

Substitution of goods as factors of production can be explicitly introduced by considering the production function for each good in the usual neo-classical way. In other words, omitting t for the sake of notational simplicity, we have

$$(76) \qquad x_j = f_j(x_{0j}, x_{1j}, \ldots, x_{nj}), \quad j = 1, 2, \ldots, m$$

$$(77) \qquad x_k = f_k(x_{0k}, x_{1k}, \ldots, x_{nk}), \quad k = m + 1, \ldots, n$$

where x_{ij} is the amount of the ith good used for the production of the jth (non-capital) good and x_{ik} is the amount of the ith good used for the production of the kth (capital) good. When $i = 0$, it refers to labor. It is assumed that (homogeneous) labor is the only primary factor of production. Assuming that these production functions (f_j's and f_k's) exhibit constant returns to scale (that is, linear homogeneity), and then dividing both sides of the above equations by x_j or x_k, we obtain

(78) $1 = f_i(a_{0i}, \ldots, a_{mi}, b_{m+1,i}, \ldots, b_{ni}), i = 1, 2, \ldots, n$

where a_{ji} and b_{ki} are now defined as $a_{ji} \equiv x_{ji}/x_j, j = 0, 1, \ldots, m$, and $b_{ki} \equiv x_{ki}/x_k$, $k = m + 1, \ldots, n, (i = 1, 2, \ldots, n)$.

Unlike the usual dynamic Leontief system, these a_{ji}'s and b_{ki}'s are not constant. They are assumed to depend on prices, thus reflecting the substitutability of these goods as factors of production. That is,

(79) $a_{ji} = a_{ji}(p_0, p_1, \ldots, p_n), j = 0, 1, \ldots, m; i = 1, 2, \ldots, n$

(80) $b_{ki} = b_{ki}(p_0, p_1, \ldots, p_n), k = m + 1, \ldots, n; i = 1, 2, \ldots, n$

It is assumed that $a_{ji} \geq 0$ and $b_{ki} \geq 0$ for all i, j, and k. The a_{ji}'s and b_{ki}'s may be chosen to minimize the cost of production subject to the production constraints (76) and (77) [or (78)].

The treatment of price equations in Morishima [26] is of the traditional Walrasian type and is different from Solow's. Let p_i ($i = 1, 2, \ldots, m$) be the price of the noncapital good i, p_k ($k = m + 1, \ldots, n$) be the price of capital service k, and p_0 be the wage rate. Let P_k be the price of new capital good k and let $\delta'_k P_k$ and $\delta''_k P_k$ be the depreciation charges and the insurance premium, respectively, to be deducted from the gross income p_k of one unit of capital good $k (k = m + 1, \ldots, n)$. Then the net price of capital service k is $p_k - (\delta'_k + \delta''_k)P_k$. Let r be the rate of interest. Following Walras [46], Morishima supposed that the net price of each capital service is equal to rP_k. That is, $p_k - (\delta'_k + \delta''_k)P_k = rP_k$, or[30]

(81) $P_k = \dfrac{p_k}{r + \delta_k}, \delta_k \equiv \delta'_k + \delta''_k, k = m + 1, \ldots, n$

Under a regime of perfect competition, owing to free entry and exit of firms, profit is zero for all industries. Thus we have, for each period,

(82) $p_i = \displaystyle\sum_{j=0}^{m} a_{ji} p_j + \sum_{k=m+1}^{n} b_{ki} p_k, i = 1, \ldots, m$

(83) $P_i = \displaystyle\sum_{j=0}^{m} a_{ji} p_j + \sum_{k=m+1}^{n} b_{ki} p_k, i = m + 1, \ldots, n$

Define the matrices A_1, B_1, A_2, B_2, by

$$A_1 \equiv \begin{bmatrix} a_{11} & a_{12} & \cdots & a_{1m} \\ a_{21} & a_{22} & \cdots & a_{2m} \\ \cdots & \cdots & \cdots & \cdots \\ \cdots & \cdots & \cdots & \cdots \\ a_{m1} & a_{m2} & \cdots & a_{mm} \end{bmatrix}, B_1 \equiv \begin{bmatrix} b_{m+1,1} & b_{m+1,2} & \cdots & b_{m+1,m} \\ b_{m+2,1} & b_{m+2,2} & \cdots & b_{m+2,m} \\ \cdots & \cdots & \cdots & \cdots \\ \cdots & \cdots & \cdots & \cdots \\ b_{n1} & b_{n2} & \cdots & b_{nm} \end{bmatrix}$$

$$A_2 \equiv \begin{bmatrix} a_{1,m+1} & a_{1,m+2} & \cdots & a_{1n} \\ a_{2,m+1} & a_{2,m+2} & \cdots & a_{2n} \\ \cdots & \cdots & \cdots & \cdots \\ \cdots & \cdots & \cdots & \cdots \\ a_{m,m+1} & a_{m,m+2} & \cdots & a_{mn} \end{bmatrix}, B_2 \equiv \begin{bmatrix} b_{m+1,m+1} & \cdots & \cdots & b_{m+1,n} \\ b_{m+2,m+1} & \cdots & \cdots & b_{m+2,n} \\ \cdots & \cdots & \cdots & \cdots \\ \cdots & \cdots & \cdots & \cdots \\ b_{n,m+1} & \cdots & \cdots & b_{nn} \end{bmatrix}$$

Then writing $p^1 = (p_1, p_2, \ldots, p_m)$, $p^2 = (p_{m+1}, \ldots, p_n)$, $P^2 = (P_{m+1}, \ldots, P_n)$, $l_1 = (a_{01}, \ldots, a_{0m})$, and $l_2 = (a_{0,m+1}, \ldots, a_{0n})$, we can rewrite (82) and (83) as

$$(84) \qquad\qquad p^1 = p^1 \cdot A_1 + p^2 \cdot B_1 + p_0 l_1$$

$$(85) \qquad\qquad P^2 = p^1 \cdot A_2 + p^2 \cdot B_2 + p_0 l_2$$

Let δ be an $(n - m) \times (n - m)$ diagonal matrix whose kth diagonal element is δ_{m+k} (where all the off-diagonal elements are zero). Then in view of (81), (85) can be rewritten as

$$(86) \qquad P^2 = [p^1 \cdot A_2 + p^2 \cdot B_2 + p_0 l_2] \cdot \delta + r[p^1 \cdot A_2 + p^2 \cdot B_2 + p_0 l_2]$$

Let $p \equiv (p_1, \ldots, p_n) = (p^1, p^2)$, and define $\overline{A}, \overline{B}$, and l by

$$(87) \qquad \overline{A} \equiv \begin{bmatrix} A_1 & A_2 \cdot \delta \\ B_1 & B_2 \cdot \delta \end{bmatrix}, \qquad \overline{B} \equiv \begin{bmatrix} 0_1 & A_2 \\ 0_2 & B_2 \end{bmatrix}, \qquad l \equiv \begin{bmatrix} l_1 \\ l_2 \cdot (rI + \delta) \end{bmatrix}$$

where 0_1 and 0_2 are, respectively, $m \times m$ and $(n - m) \times m$ matrices whose elements are all zero. Then $\overline{A}$ and $\overline{B}$ are both $n \times n$ matrices, and l is an n-vector. With these notations we can now rewrite (84) and (86) as

$$(88) \qquad\qquad p = p \cdot \overline{A} + rp \cdot \overline{B} + p_0 l$$

These matrices $\overline{A}$ and $\overline{B}$ correspond to A and B in the usual dynamic Leontief model. As a result of the convention that there are goods which cannot be used as capital goods, matrix $\overline{B}$ contains columns whose elements are all zero.

We can easily compare the above price equation of Morishima with the Solow equation (41) by recalling that (41) is reduced to (53) when all prices are constant, which corresponds to the above Morishima equation (88). This makes us suspect that Morishima's equation is a special case of the Solow type equation, (41), that is, the case in which all the prices are constant. Reexamination of equation (81) may strengthen this conviction, for this equation is true only when prices are constant, so there are no capital gains or losses by holding a stock of goods.

However, to say that Morishima's equation is a special case of Solow's equation may be a bit too strong. The best stand with regard to this comparison can be found in Solow's own writing, where he states ([38], p. 32):

> Morishima's model and mine can be reconciled by recognizing that they represent polar assumptions about price expectations. I assume that entrepreneurs have perfect foresight and (correctly) expect prices to change, and I ask what price movements are then logically consistent. Morishima assumes that entrepreneurs always expect prices to remain constant although in fact they do change from time to time in order to clear markets, and he asks what set of constant prices (and interest rate) can actually be made to endure. It's a toss-up which assumption does more violence to reality.

In other words, what Morishima [26] was concerned with is the possibility of enduring constant prices. Since he wished to prove the dynamic substitution theorem in which prices are uniquely chosen (thus constant), he must find the set of prices (and interest rate) that can be kept constant. Therefore, his way of treatment of the price equation is a natural consequence of his interest in proving his dynamic substitution theorem.[31]

We now count the number of equations and the number of unknowns. For this purpose, first note that the matrices $\overline{A}$ and $\overline{B}$ are completely specified once the price vector (p_0, p) is given. Hence we may write (88) as

$$(89) \qquad p = p \cdot \overline{A}(p_0, p) + rp \cdot \overline{B}(p_0, p) + p_0 l$$

which we may also write as

$$(89') \qquad \Phi(p_0, p, r) = 0$$

It is well known (and can be shown easily) that the a_{ji}'s and the b_{ki}'s are all homogeneous of degree zero in (p_0, p). Hence we have $\overline{A}(\alpha p_0, \alpha p) = \overline{A}(p_0, p)$ and $\overline{B}(\alpha p_0, \alpha p) = \overline{B}(p_0, p)$ for any positive number α. Hence (89) implies

$$(90) \qquad \alpha p = \alpha p \cdot \overline{A}(\alpha p_0, \alpha p) + r(\alpha p) \cdot \overline{B}(\alpha p_0, \alpha p) + \alpha p_0 l$$

for any $\alpha > 0$. In other words,

$$(91) \qquad \Phi(\alpha p_0, \alpha p, r) = 0$$

for any $\alpha > 0$. In view of the homogeneity of Φ in (p_0, p), we may impose the following price normalization equation:[32]

$$(92) \qquad \sum_{i=0}^{n} p_i = 1$$

Equations (89) and (92) combined provide us with $(n + 1)$ equations. There are $(n + 2)$ variables to be determined within the system, that is, $p_i, i = 0, 1, \ldots, n$, and r. Hence if we can preassign the value of either p_0 or r, the system is completely specified. This is schematically described by

(93-a) $$r \to (p_0, p)$$

(93-b) $$p_0 \to (p, r)$$

The values of (p_0, p) or (p, r) thus determined define the **equilibrium** values of the system. Note that the mechanism described in (93) does not determine the absolute (monetary) prices of the goods. This is because there are two degrees of freedom in (89) and one of them is controlled by (92). Alternatively, we may specify *both* r and p_0 exogenously where (92) is not binding; then the absolute prices of the goods can all be specified.

As we remarked in Chapter 1, Section E, subsection a, the procedure of counting the number of equations and the number of unknowns merely checks the consistency of the model and does neither prove the existence nor the uniqueness of the equilibrium values of the unknowns. The task of establishing the existence, uniqueness, and nonnegativity of the equilibrium values was attempted by Morishima [26]. The problem of existence is not a particularly difficult one. The continuity of the linear maps $\overline{A}(p_0, p)$ and $\overline{B}(p_0, p)$ immediately establishes the continuity of $\Phi(p_0, p, r)$. For the $r \to (p_0, p)$ determination, it then suffices to consider a continuous map Φ from a unit simplex $\{(p_0, p): \sum_{i=0}^{n} p_i = 1\}$ into itself and to apply the Brouwer fixed point theorem (Theorem 2.E.2). The existence of the equilibrium values for the $p_0 \to (p, r)$ specification can be proved analogously.[33] For an attempt to prove the uniqueness, the reader is referred to Morishima [26]. Unfortunately, Morishima [26] apparently forgot to prove the nonnegativity of the equilibrium values. Take the case of the $p_0 \to (p, r)$ specification, for example. Just looking at (89), it can immediately be seen that if p_0 is large enough, r may have to be negative to preserve the nonnegativity of the (p_0, p) vector by (92). Hence it is not surprising to find the brilliant example due to Georgescu-Roegen [5], in which the value of r is negative when the value of p_0 is preassigned. Such a defect can be remedied if we can set an upper bound on the value of p_0. Morishima and Murata [29] thus "remedied" this defect simply by assuming such a bound.[34]

That the value of (p_0, p) is uniquely determined for a given value of r, or that the value of (p, r) is uniquely determined for a given value of p_0, has a very important implication; it means that the a_{ji}'s and b_{ki}'s remain constant regardless of any change in the values of the final demand for goods, provided that these changes do not disturb the preassigned values of r and p_0. This means, under certain assumptions, that a perfectly competitive economy would choose to produce each good by *one* process. Hence (as remarked before) the above result, essentially obtained by Morishima [26], is considered an extension of Samuelson's famous substitution theorem for the static Leontief system to the case of intertemporal production (see, for example, Hahn and Matthews [9], p. 870).

Under what circumstances are the values of r and p_0 determined in such a way that they are undisturbed by changes in the final demand for goods? An obvious case is the "Keynesian situation" in which the money rate of interest r is fixed owing to the "liquidity trap" in the money market and/or the money wage rate is fixed owing to its rigidity in the labor market.[35] However, except for such rather extreme cases, we cannot, in general, establish that the values of r and p_0 are undisturbed by changes in the final demand for goods. This obviously undermines the use of Morishima's substitution theorem in the dynamic Leontief system described above, contrary to the belief by Morishima [26] and Hahn and Matthews [9].

To illustrate this point, consider the $p_0 \rightarrow (p, r)$ determination. In this case, the equilibrium value of (p, r) is uniquely determined as long as the value of p_0 is given. But if the value of p_0, that is, the wage rate, changes, the values of p and r also move, thus causing changes in the values of the a_{ji}'s and the b_{ki}'s. This is not the case for the substitution theorem of the static Leontief model.[36]

Theoretically speaking, the (absolute) values of p_0 and r are determined under a broader general equilibrium system which incorporates the markets ignored in the above consideration—that is, the markets for labor, money, bonds, and so on—with the introduction of the store of value as a function of money as well as of bonds. If we incorporate these markets into our analysis, it is more difficult, at least for this author, to accept Morishima's basic postulate of constant prices, for constant prices presuppose certain assumptions with regard to the supply of money and the like.[37] Suppose now that prices change over time. Then the basic equation (89) is no longer valid, for it lacks the term that signifies price changes which certainly affects the profit condition.[38] This factor, among others, may destroy the homogeneity of the function Φ, which in turn makes the price normalization equation (92) invalid.

In this connection, we may point out that within the profession an active interest has arisen recently in incorporating money (which, among other things, functions as a store of value) into a growth model (see Tobin [41] and the appendix to this section, for example).[39] Although such an analysis in the literature has so far been confined to the model in which there is only one commodity besides labor, it is certainly possible to extend it to a multicommodity model by using the dynamic Leontief system as discussed in this section.

Keeping this in mind, let us return to the constant price world to explore further implications of such a model. Consider (89) and normalize the price vector p by the wage rate p_0 instead of the price normalization represented by equation (92). Thus rewrite (89) as

(94) $$\bar{p} = \bar{p} \cdot A^*(\bar{p}) + r\bar{p} \cdot B^*(\bar{p}) + l$$

where $\bar{p} \equiv (\bar{p}_1, \ldots, \bar{p}_n)$, $\bar{p}_i \equiv p_i/p_0$, $i = 1, 2, \ldots, n$, $A^*(\bar{p}) \equiv \bar{A}(1, p/p_0)$, and $B^*(\bar{p}) \equiv \bar{B}(1, p/p_0)$. There are n equations in (94) with $(n + 1)$ variables, $\bar{p}$ and r. Suppose that the value of r is preassigned, and ask the question whether it is possible to have identical technology matrices A^* and B^* for two different values of r. If it is possible, we call such a phenomenon **reswitching of techniques**.[40] If the relation between r and $\bar{p}$ is one-to-one, then "reswitching" is obviously impossible.[41] Note that the relation between r and $\bar{p}$ may not be one-to-one, even if the functions $A^*(\bar{p})$ and $B^*(\bar{p})$ are continuous and one-to-one.

Actually we can also show that reswitching is impossible even in the absence of a one-to-one relation between r and $\bar{p}$,[42] if $\bar{p}$ is strictly positive for all relevant changes in r. To prove this, let r and r' be two interest rates, and suppose that reswitching is possible. In other words, suppose that we have the same matrices A^* and B^* for both r and r'. Since $A^*(\bar{p})$ and $B^*(\bar{p})$ are one-to-one, we have the same $\bar{p}$ for r and r'. Therefore

(95-a) $$\bar{p} = \bar{p} \cdot A^* + r\bar{p} \cdot B^* + l$$

and

(95-b) $$\bar{p} = \bar{p} \cdot A^* + r'\bar{p} \cdot B^* + l$$

Hence

(96) $$(r - r')\bar{p} \cdot B^* = 0$$

Since $\bar{p} > 0$ by assumption, we obtain $r = r'$ as long as at least one element of B^* is positive. This proves the impossibility of the reswitching of techniques.

Let us now turn to the determination of outputs in the above system. Let $x_j(t)$, $j = 1, 2, \ldots, m$, represent the output of noncapital good j and let $x_k(t)$, $k = m + 1, \ldots, n$, represent the output of capital good k. Then we have

(97) $$x_j(t) = \sum_{i=1}^{n} a_{ji} x_i(t) + \bar{c}_j(t), j = 1, 2, \ldots, m$$

where $\bar{c}_j(t)$, $j = 1, 2, \ldots, m$, represents the final demand for the ith noncapital good. Here, unlike the usual dynamic Leontief system, $\bar{c}_j$ as well as the a_{ji}'s are functions of the prices $(p_0, p_1, \ldots, p_n)$.

Let $y_k(t)$ be the existing quantity of capital in period t. Assuming that all the existing capital goods are all fully employed we have

(98) $$y_k(t) = \sum_{i=1}^{n} b_{ki} x_i(t), k = m + 1, \ldots, n$$

Since the obsolete and destroyed portions of capital goods are $\delta_k y_k(t)$, $k = m + 1, \ldots, n$, we obtain

(99) $$x_k(t) = \delta_k y_k(t) + [y_k(t + 1) - y_k(t)] + \bar{c}_k(t), k = m + 1, \ldots, n$$

where $\bar{c}_k(t)$ is the final demand for capital good k. Hence, in view of (98), we obtain

(100) $$x_k(t) = \sum_{i=1}^{n} a_{ki} x_i(t) + \sum_{i=1}^{n} b_{ki}[x_i(t + 1) - x_i(t)] + \bar{c}_k(t) k = m + 1, \ldots, n$$

where $a_{ki} \equiv \delta_k b_{ki}$, $i = 1, 2, \ldots, n$, and $k = m + 1, \ldots, n$. Defining the matrices $\check{A}$ and $\check{B}$ by

$$\text{(101)}\qquad \dot{A} \equiv \begin{bmatrix} A_1 & A_2 \\ \delta \cdot B_1 & \delta \cdot B_2 \end{bmatrix}, \quad \check{B} \equiv \begin{bmatrix} 0_1 & 0_3 \\ B_1 & B_2 \end{bmatrix}$$

where 0_1 and 0_3 are respectively $m \times m$ and $m \times (n - m)$ matrices whose elements are all zero, we can write (97) and (100) as

$$\text{(102)}\qquad x(t) = \dot{A} \cdot x(t) + \check{B} \cdot \left[x(t + 1) - x(t) \right] + \bar{c}(t)$$

which corresponds to our earlier output equation (6). Note that, unlike the case in the usual dynamic Leontief system, $\dot{A}$ and $\check{B}$, respectively, are different from $\bar{A}$ and $\bar{B}$, which appeared in the price equation. This is a result of the distinction between capital goods and noncapital goods and the introduction of the δ_k-factors. However, we should also note that the determination of the a_{ji}'s and b_{ki}'s (by relative prices) simultaneously determines $\bar{A}$, $\bar{B}$, $\dot{A}$, and $\check{B}$. Note that the addition of (102) to the system increases the number of equations by n, corresponding to the addition of the n variables $x_i(t)$, $i = 1, 2, \ldots, n$. Hence we still have essentially two degrees of freedom, as discussed earlier. In other words, we need to specify two variables—say, r and p_0—to specify completely the equilibrium values of all the variables. Specification of these variables requires the consideration of markets other than the goods market, in particular the money market and the labor market.

In the above model, as in the usual dynamic Leontief model, it is assumed that the final demand vector $\bar{c}(t)$ is given exogenously; that is, $\bar{c}(t)$ is given as an explicit function of t. This means, of course, that the usual treatment and the above treatment of the dynamic Leontief model completely assume away two important choices of consumers, namely, consumers' substitution among various goods owing to changes in prices and the choice between present and future consumption. Extensions of the dynamic Leontief model in these directions are again left to the interested reader. We may, however, point out that this will add more flexibility to the Leontief model, in the sense that it will help to avoid the difficulty posed by causal indeterminacy.

FOOTNOTES

1. Interpreting $\left[K_i(t + 1) - K_i(t) \right]$ as a **net** increase in the stock of the ith good, $I_i(t)$ is the **net** investment of the ith good. In other words, we abstract the depreciation of the stock of goods by properly interpreting the b_{ij}'s.
2. That is, the production process of the ith industry produces the stock of the ith good (for the next period) as a joint output.
3. In reality, many goods are never used as capital goods for the production of certain goods. On this ground, it is often argued that (A-2) is a serious weakness of the dynamic Leontief model. However, in the actual computation of B, items such as raw materials and inventories should be included. Then (A-2) is quite realistic, contrary to the widespread belief on this point. I am indebted to Jinkichi Tsukui for pointing this out to me.
4. Since $B \geq 0$ is nonsingular, every row and every column of B contain at least one positive element. Since $(I - A)^{-1} > 0$, this proves that $(I - A)^{-1}B > 0$.

5. That is, if ω is any other eigenvector of $(I - A)^{-1}B$, then $v \geqq |\omega|$. If A is indecomposable so that $(I - A)^{-1}B > 0$, then (A-4) is automatically satisfied. Moreover, $(I - A)^{-1}B$ for this case is primitive so that ρ is unique, or $v > |\omega|$ (recall Theorems 4.B.3 and 4.B.5).

6. The continuous differentiability of H_i (everywhere in the domain) means that H_i possesses continuous partial derivatives (everywhere in the domain), for all $i = 1, 2, \ldots, n$.

7. The function H_i is not necessarily the production function of the ith good. Given the quantities of various goods in period t, $x(t)$, the quantity of the ith good in period $t + 1$, $x_i(t + 1)$, is given by H_i. Therefore, H_i can be a complex mixture of many production processes in the economy. Hence this Solow-Samuelson model is sometimes called the **sausage machine model** (see Hahn and Matthews [9], p. 872). Note that joint output is allowed in the model, for H_i does not necessarily imply a particular production process (for the production of the ith good). The quantity represented by $x_i(t)$ can be either a "stock" or "flow" of the ith good, although in Solow and Samuelson [39] it is taken as the "flow" ("output") of the ith good.

8. Hahn and Matthews' work [9] contains a simple exposition of the Solow-Samuelson theorem for the two-good case (pp. 872–873).

9. There is an excellent exposition in Nikaido ([33], pp. 149–161) of the generalization of the Solow-Samuelson theorem and the nonlinear extension of the Frobenius theorem. The assumptions of the differentiability of the H_i's and of the positivity of the partial derivatives of the H_i's in the Solow-Samuelson theorem are replaced by the continuity and the "monotonicity" of the H_i's (see theorem 10.7 of [33], pp. 160–161, especially).

10. Tsukui [43] and McKenzie [23], for example, applied this result to the proofs of their turnpike theorems.

11. Define F by $F \equiv M - I$. The dynamic Leontief system (8) is a special case of this in which $F \equiv B^{-1}(I - A)$ or $M \equiv I + B^{-1}(I - A)$. Note that $F^{-1} > 0$ does not necessarily imply $M > 0$. Also note (from the subsequent proof) that $F^{-1} > 0$ is required only in the sufficiency part of the theorem. Furthermore, the assumption of $F^{-1} > 0$ can be weakened so that F^{-1} is nonnegative, indecomposable, and primitive.

12. The eigenvector u^1 is that associated with the Frobenius root v_1 for the transpose of F^{-1}.

13. Since v_1 is the Frobenius root of F^{-1}, $v_1 > |v_i| (i = 2, \ldots, n)$. Moreover, $1 + 1/v_1 > |1 + 1/v_i| (i = 2, \ldots, n)$ since $\lambda_1 > |\lambda_i| (i = 2, \ldots, n)$ by assumption. However, $v_1 > |v_i| (i = 2, \ldots, n)$ and $1 + 1/v_1 > |1 + 1/v_i| (i = 2, \ldots, n)$ are not inconsistent with each other. For some readers, an inconsistency may appear to occur, if, for example, more than one eigenvalue of F^{-1} is positive. But this is not true. The assumption of $\lambda_1 > |\lambda_i| (i = 2, \ldots, n)$ precisely rules out such a possibility.

14. That the eigenvalues of M are all distinct is not essential in the subsequent arguments. The reader can easily extend our analysis to the case in which there are multiple roots. For such a case, the general solution is written as $\hat{x}(t) = \sum_{i=1}^{n} h_i(t)\lambda_i{}^t$, where $h_i(t)$ is now a polynomial in t, the order of which is less than the multiplicity of λ_i, and where these λ_i's are distinct. (See any introductory treatment on difference equations.)

15. That the eigenvalues of M are all distinct is not essential in the subsequent arguments and theorems. It essentially amounts to rewriting $\sum_{i=1}^{n} h_i \lambda_i{}^t x_j{}^i$ as $\sum_{i=1}^{n} h_{ij}(t)\lambda_i{}^t$ where $h_{ij}(t)$ is now a polynomial in t, the order of which is less than the multiplicity of λ_i, and where these λ_i's are distinct.

16. This follows from the sufficiency part of the proof of the previous lemma. The root

$\lambda_1{}^m$ is the Frobenius root of $M^m > 0$, since $\lambda_1{}^m > |\lambda_i{}^m|$, $i = 2, \ldots, n [\because \lambda_1 > |\lambda_i|,$ $i = 2, \ldots, n]$. Note that the assumption $F^{-1} > 0$ can be weakened so that F^{-1} is nonnegative, indecomposable, and primitive. Incidentally, the x^1 in (32) is a positive vector as is clear from the proof of Tsukui's lemma.

17. When the output system (6) is replaced by $x(t) = A \cdot x(t) + B \cdot [x(t) - x(t - 1)] + \bar{c}(t)$, where the coefficients in B now can be interpreted similarly to the coefficients in the usual acceleration principle, then relative stability is considered to be empirically more plausible. I owe this observation to Jinkichi Tsukui. In this system, investment is assumed to be "passive," that is, it takes place only to supplement the excess demand for capacity in the preceding period.

18. It suffices to show that we cannot have $h_2 = 0$. To show this, suppose the contrary, or $h_2 = 0$. Then $x_1(0) = -x_2(0)(=h_1)$, which contradicts $x(0) \geq 0$.

19. Our Example 1, as an illustration of causal indeterminacy, is due to DOSSO [4].

20. The formulation of the price system here is due to Solow [38]. See also DOSSO [4] and Samuelson [35].

21. Assume perfect divisibility of the capital good.

22. Because (43) is obtained by comparing only two periods, the assumption is also known as that of "*myopic* perfect foresight."

23. Observing this, Jorgenson proved Solow's conjecture that in the closed Leontief model, if the output system is relatively stable, then the price system is relatively unstable and vice versa, provided that $n \geq 2$. A similar result is obtained by Uzawa [45], M. Fukuoka, and H. Niida.

24. In other words, unlike the notation in subsection b, $K(t)$ denotes only the supply of capital and does not denote the demand for capital, whereas $\Delta K(t)$ denotes the demand for an increase in the supply of capital.

25. Mathematically speaking, this means that although inequality may be allowed in (54) [that is, $x(t) \geq A \cdot x(t) + \Delta K(t) + \bar{c}(t)$], only the equality case is chosen. Such a choice can be justified if for each good there exists an individual who is not satiated with the good.

26. One difference between [26] and [27] is that in [26] such a neo-classical "smooth" substitution with a continuum of activities is assumed, whereas in [27] a "discrete" substitution with a finite number of activities is assumed. Although the latter resembles "reality" more closely, there is little theoretical difference between the two approaches. Hence we mostly adhere to the simpler neo-classical· case [26].

27. Since the "substitution theorem" asserts that the input coefficients are in fact fixed, it is often (perhaps more properly) called the **nonsubstitution theorem**.

28. If we allow such a price flexibility and factor substitution, then all the factors (here labor and the stocks of goods = capital) are fully employed. Hence Morishima's model is in sharp contrast to Solow's excess capacity model [38] described in subsection d. It resembles more closely Solow's neo-classical revision [37] of the Harrod-Domar model. Morishima's model also contrasts sharply with Jorgenson's descriptive excess capacity model [16] which converts Solow's optimization model [38] to a descriptive model, allowing excess capacities but sticking to the fixed coefficients of production (as in Solow [38]). Jorgenson's model [16] thus also aims to remove the difficulty of causal indeterminacy and the dual stability theorem, but has unfortunately attracted severe criticism by McManus [25].

29. In other words, Morishima assumed static expectations. As we will discuss later, he then asked: What set of constant prices can actually be made to endure so that such an expectation is realized for each t (which also, in fact, implies perfect fore-

sight)? Such a state of constant prices is sustained, except for knife edge cases, only on a balanced growth or decay path [often termed the **steady state (growth) path**]. These two polar assumptions with regard to prices and expectation—that is, perfect foresight with changing prices and static foresight with constant prices—are quite common in growth theory literature. Both these assumptions are clearly unrealistic. This rather unfortunate state of the theory is, among other things, due to the fact that we do not have any elaborate theory with regard to future expectation and uncertainty. See also the Appendix to this section.

30. As in Walras [46], part V, (81) is crucial in Morishima in establishing the consistency of the system with capital accumulation or decumulation under constant prices (that is, a balanced growth or decay path). Note that (81) also signifies that the returns to various capital goods are equal, or $[p_k - (\delta'_k + \delta''_k)P_k]/P_k$ is the same for all k (and equal to r). This means that capital goods are freely transferable among industries. In the absence of price changes, r is equal to the interest rate (or the own rate of interest in the moneyless economy).

31. As we remarked earlier, the state of constant prices is sustained, except for knife edge cases, only in a state of balanced growth or decay. It is not clear how the economy reaches such a steady state starting from a historically given initial point. This question, in spite of its great importance, was not investigated by Morishima, thus undermining the significance of his work.

32. Choose $\alpha \equiv 1/\sum_{i=0}^{n} p_i$ and let $\tilde{p}_i \equiv \alpha p_i$, $i = 0, 1, \ldots, n$. Then clearly $\sum_{i=0}^{n} \tilde{p}_i = 1$. The imposition of (92) amounts to writing p_i for each such $\tilde{p}_i$ and dropping the homogeneity from (89) or (89′).

33. There is a slight complication that we must take care of in the proof. That is, it is easy to see from (89) that if r is large enough, it may not be possible to have a positive p_0; hence it may be impossible to find a "fixed point" in the simplex.

34. However, it is not quite clear from Morishima and Murata [29] what is the mechanism that sets the upper bound of the wage rate p_0.

35. Morishima [26] pointed out another situation, the "Ricardo-Marx" case, in which the "real" wage rate is fixed as a result of the "reserve army" of labor and so on ([26], p. 69). Here the "real" wage rate means the "money" wage rate p_0 deflated by a certain price index (see [26], p. 66).

36. Unlike in Morishima [26], it seems more natural to emphasize the $r \to (p_0, p)$ determination as a dynamic substitution theorem. In this case, as long as r is given, the a_{ji}'s and the b_{ki}'s are fixed regardless of p *and* p_0. Since r reflects intertemporal choice (hence it is abstracted away from the static theory), the static substitution theorem may be considered as a special case (that is, $r = 0$) of the $r \to (p_0, p)$ determination.

37. With the introduction of money, which functions as a store of value, the state of balanced growth or decay of the real goods sector does not necessarily imply constant absolute prices, although relative prices may be constant. This seems to be an obvious point, but it is often forgotten in growth theory literature.

38. It will not be too difficult to modify (89) if we assume perfect foresight. The real task, of course, is to modify (89) under a suitable assumption with regard to expectations concerning future prices.

39. For a recent survey of such a theory, see, for example, Burmeister and Dobell [1], chapter 6.

40. The reswitching of techniques has the following important implication: If it occurs, then it is impossible to say that a lower interest rate implies (in steady-state equili-

brium) a more mechanized technology. Owing to the significance of this statement, the problem of the reswitching of techniques has excited a part of the profession. See, for example, the symposium on "Paradoxes in Capital Theory," *Quarterly Journal of Economics*, LXXX, November 1966, which argues that reswitching is possible under an activity analysis type technology. See also Burmeister and Dobell [1], especially sections 8.6 and 9.2.

41. Although reswitching is possible in an activity analysis type model, it is not possible under the smooth neo-classical technology (see theorem 5 of [1], p. 279). For a recent discussion of this problem, see D. A. Starrett, "Switching and Reswitching in a General Production Model," *Quarterly Journal of Economics*, LXXXIII, November 1969.

42. In the "smooth" neo-classical technology (as in Morishima [26]), it may be natural to assume that $A^*(\bar{p})$ and $B^*(\bar{p})$ are continuous and single-valued (and even one-to-one). However, in the activity analysis type "discrete" technology, such an assumption would be absurd.

REFERENCES

1. Burmeister, E., and Dobell, A. R., *Mathematical Theories of Economic Growth*, London, Macmillan, 1970.

2. Chakravarty, S., *Capital and Development Planning*, Cambridge, Mass., M.I.T. Press, 1969.

3. Domar, E. D., *Essays in the Theory of Growth*, New York, Oxford University Press, 1957.

4. Dorfman, R., Samuelson, P. A., and Solow, R. M., *Linear Programming and Economic Analysis*, New York, McGraw-Hill, 1958.

5. Georgescu-Roegen, N., "Book Review: Morishima, M., *Equilibrium, Stability and Growth—A Multi-Sectoral Analysis*," *American Economic Review*, LV, March 1965.

6. ———, *Analytical Economics*, Cambridge, Mass., Harvard University Press, 1966.

7. Goodwin, R., "A Non-linear Theory of the Cycle," *Review of Economics and Statistics*, XXXII, November 1950.

8. ———, "The Non-linear Accelerator and the Persistence of Business Cycles," *Econometrica*, 19, January 1951.

9. Hahn, F. H., and Matthews, R. C. O., "The Theory of Economic Growth: A Survey," *Economic Journal*, LXXIV, December 1964.

10. Harrod, R. F., "An Essay in Dynamic Theory," *Economic Journal*, XLIX, March 1939.

11. ———, *Towards a Dynamic Economics*, London, Macmillan, 1948.

12. ———, "Domar and Dynamic Economics," *Economic Journal*, LXIX, September 1959.

13. Hicks, J. R., *A Contribution to the Theory of the Trade Cycle*, Oxford, Clarendon Press, 1950.

14. Jorgenson, D. W., "On Stability in the Sense of Harrod," *Economica*, XXVII, August 1960.

15. ———, "A Dual Stability Theorem," *Econometrica*, 28, October 1960.
16. ———, "Stability of Dynamic Input-Output System," *Review of Economic Studies*, XXVIII, February 1961.
17. ———, "The Structure of Multi-sector Dynamic Models," *International Economic Review*, 2, September 1961.
18. Kuhn, H. W., "On a Theorem of Wald," in *Linear Inequalities and Related Systems*, ed. by H. W. Kuhn and A. W. Tucker, Princeton, N.J., Princeton University Press, 1956.
19. Leontief, W. W., *The Structure of American Economy, 1919–39*, 2nd ed., New York, Oxford University Press, 1951.
20. ———, "Structural Change," in *Studies in the Structure of the American Economy*, by W. W. Leontief *et al.*, New York, Oxford University Press, 1953.
21. ———, "Dynamic Analysis," in *Studies in the Structure of the American Economy*, by W. W. Leontief *et al.*, New York, Oxford University Press, 1953.
22. ———, *Input-Output Economics*, New York, Oxford University Press, 1966.
23. McKenzie, L. W., "Turnpike Theorems for a Generalized Leontief Model," *Econometrica*, 31, January–April 1963.
24. McManus, M., "Self-Contradiction in Leontief's Dynamic Model," *Yorkshire Bulletin*, 9, May 1957.
25. ———, "Notes on Jorgenson's Model," *Review of Economic Studies*, XXX, June 1963.
26. Morishima, M., "A Dynamic Leontief System with Neo-Classical Production Function," chap. III in his *Equilibrium, Stability and Growth: A Multi-Sectoral Analysis*, Oxford, Clarendon Press, 1965 (a revision of his paper in *Econometrica*, 26, July 1958.)
27. ———, "An Alternative Dynamic System with a Spectrum of Technique," chap. IV in his *Equilibrium, Stability and Growth: A Multi-Sectoral Analysis*, Oxford, Clarendon Press, 1965 (a revision of his paper in *Econometrica*, 27, October 1959).
28. ———, "Generalization of the Frobenius-Wielandt Theorems for Non-negative Square Matrices," *Journal of London Mathematical Society*, 36, 1961 (also in his *Equilibrium, Stability and Growth*, appendix).
29. Morishima, M., and Murata, Y., "An Input-Output System Involving Nontransferable Goods," *Econometrica*, 36, January 1968.
30. Muth, J. F., "A Note on Balanced Growth," *Econometrica*, 22, October 1954.
31. Neisser, H., "Balanced Growth under Constant Returns to Scale," *Econometrica*, 22, October 1954.
32. Nikaido, H., *Introduction to Sets and Mappings in Modern Economics*, tr. by K. Sato, Amsterdam, North-Holland, 1970 (the Japanese original, Tokyo, 1960).
33. ———, *Convex Structures and Economic Theory*, New York, Academic Press, 1968.
34. Samuelson, P. A., "Abstract of a Model Concerning Substitutability in Open Leontief Models," in *Activity Analysis of Production and Allocation*, ed. by T. C. Koopmans, New York, Wiley, 1951.
35. ———, "Market Mechanisms and Maximization," in *The Collected Scientific Papers of Paul A. Samuelson*, Vol. 1, Cambridge, Mass., M.I.T. Press, 1966.

36. Sargan, J. D., "The Instability of the Leontief Dynamic Model," *Econometrica*, 26, July 1958.

37. Solow, R. M., "A Contribution to the Theory of Economic Growth," *Quarterly Journal of Economics*, LXX, February 1956.

38. ———, "Competitive Valuation in a Dynamic Input-Output System," *Econometrica*, 27, January 1959.

39. Solow, R. M., and Samuelson, P. A., "Balanced Growth under Constant Returns to Scale," *Econometrica*, 21, July 1953.

40. Suits, D. B., "Dynamic Growth Under Diminishing Returns to Scale," *Econometrica*, 22, October 1954.

41. Tobin, J., "Money and Growth," *Econometrica*, 33, December 1965.

42. Tsukui, J., "On a Theorem of Relative Stability," *International Economic Review*, 2, May 1961.

43. ———, "Efficient and Balanced Growth Paths in Dynamic Input-Output System— A Turn-Pike Theorem," *Economic Studies Quarterly*, XIII, September 1962 (in Japanese).

44. ———, "Application of a Turn-Pike Theorem to Planning for Efficient Accumulation: An Example for Japan," *Econometrica*, 36, January 1968.

45. Uzawa, H., "Causal Indeterminacy of the Leontief Dynamic Input-Output System," *Economic Studies Quarterly*, XII, September 1961.

46. Walras, L., *Elements of Pure Economics*, tr. by W. Jaffé, Homewood, Ill., Richard D. Irwin, 1954.

Appendix to Section B: Some Problems in the Dynamic Leontief Model— The One-Industry Illustration[1]

The purpose of this Appendix is to illustrate some of the difficulties inherent in the dynamic Leontief model by taking a simple one-industry model as an example. Clearly, by using such an example, we ignore some important aspects of the model, such as the interrelatedness among the industries. Moreover, we cannot discuss such an important concept as a "balanced growth path" in the one-industry illustration, and hence we ignore one important difficulty in the dynamic Leontief model: that of causal indeterminacy.

However, the simplicity of the one-industry model will serve to make some important features of the model stand out as well as clearly illustrate some weaknesses of the model. In this Appendix, we point out these weaknesses and try to show their repercussions on other markets such as the labor market and the money market, which are often neglected in the dynamic Leontief model.

We should, however, note that the purpose of this Appendix is not to build a complete model of the one-industry economy. It is rather to point out some of the important difficulties in the usual dynamic Leontief model using a simpler model. The task of constructing a more general dynamic Leontief model by taking account of these criticisms is left to the interested reader.

In order to maintain connection with our discussion of the one-industry growth model in Chapter 5, we use the notation adopted there. In other words, Y_t = output, X_t = consumption, K_t = capital stock, L_t = labor, and I_t = investment. Since we adopt the difference equation formulation here, the subscript t now refers to period t (instead of time t). The basic equation in the dynamic Leontief model is the equilibrium relation in the goods market, stating that supply is equal to demand. In the one-industry model, Y_t is considered to be the final output and the use of this good for intermediate purposes (such as "raw material") is netted out. That is, Y_t is the output after we deduct a portion of the output used for intermediate purposes. Thus matrix A in the (dynamic) Leontief model is not explicit in the model. In any case, we obtain the well-known identity that the total demand for Y_t consists of investment and consumption. Hence the *equilibrium* relation in the goods market is, as it is well known,

$$(1) \qquad\qquad Y_t = I_t + X_t$$

As in the usual Harrod-Domar model, I_t is derived from the "acceleration principle" in the sense that

$$(2) \qquad\qquad \sigma I_t = Y_{t+1} - Y_t$$

where σ is assumed to be a positive constant and is called the **relation** or **accelerator coefficient**. This equation *can* be derived from the following consideration. Let K_t be the stock of capital goods available in period t. Assuming away depreciation and obsolescence, or taking Y_t net of these, we have

$$(3) \qquad\qquad K_{t+1} - K_t \equiv \Delta K_t = I_t$$

That is, an investment in period t becomes a capacity increase in period $t + 1$. Suppose now that the production function for the output can be written as

$$(4) \qquad\qquad Y_t = \sigma K_t$$

where $\sigma > 0$ is a constant. Note that K_t here means the amount of capital employed in period t. That the same notation K_t is used for the supply of capital in period t implies that we are assuming the *full employment of capital*. Thus (2) can be obtained easily from (3) and (4).

Equations (1) and (2) can be rewritten as

$$(5) \qquad\qquad Y_t = \frac{1}{\sigma}[Y_{t+1} - Y_t] + X_t$$

which corresponds to (6) in Section B. Here $1/\sigma$ corresponds to the B matrix, and there is nothing which corresponds to the A matrix.

It is certainly possible to specify consumption, such as

$$(6) \qquad\qquad X_t = (1 - s)Y_t + \bar{c}$$

where s denotes the marginal propensity to save (which is assumed to be constant and $0 < s \leq 1$), and $\bar{c} \geq 0$ is a constant. In the Harrod-Domar model, the specification of the behavior of consumption as above is made explicit. Moreover, it is usually assumed that $\bar{c} = 0$. The closed Leontief model in which consumption is included corresponds to a special case of the above, that is, the case in which $X_t = 0$ for all t, or $s = 1$ and $\bar{c} = 0$ for all t. The open Leontief model with a fixed bundle of final consumption corresponds to a special case of the above, that is, the case in which $X_t =$ constant, or $s = 1$ and $X_t = \bar{c} > 0$. However, it is also to be noted that, in the general open Leontief model, X_t may not be constant over t but rather is given exogenously as an explicit function of time t. In any case, as long as X_t is given either in the induced form such as (6) or in an exogenous manner as a function of t, we can solve for Y_t explicitly as a function of t.

We may consider the present model to consist of four equations, (1), (3), (4), and (6), and four variables (Y_t, K_t, X_t, I_t) to be determined in the system. If X_t is given exogenously, then equation (6) drops out from this list and the variable X_t is also dropped accordingly. In the latter case, we simply obtain Y_t from (5), and in the former case, we obtain the following equation by combining (5) and (6):

$$
(7) \qquad Y_{t+1} = (1 + s\sigma) Y_t - \bar{c}\sigma
$$

From this, Y_t is obtained explicitly as a function of time. Then K_t is obtained from (4), I_t is obtained from either (2) or (3), and X_t is obtained from (5).

The solution of equation (7) is easily found to be

$$
(8) \qquad Y_t = (1 + s\sigma)^t (Y_0 - Y^*) + Y^*
$$

where $Y^* = \bar{c}/s$ and Y_0 is the initial output. Clearly, as long as $Y_0 > Y^*$, the economy is capable of growth. In the usual Harrod-Domar model, $\bar{c}$ is assumed to be zero (thus $Y^* = 0$) so that $Y_0 > Y^*$ will always hold, and the economy grows at a constant rate, $s\sigma$, that is,

$$
(9) \qquad Y_t = Y_0(1 + s\sigma)^t
$$

When $s = 1$, the growth rate is equal to σ, which corresponds to the balanced growth path in the closed dynamic Leontief model, and $1/\sigma$ corresponds to the eigenvalue of the B matrix.

Although it is not emphasized in the literature, the above model gets into trouble when $\bar{c} > 0$ and $Y_0 < Y^*$, for then Y_t becomes negative for sufficiently large t.

Most of the discussions of the dynamic Leontief model, including ours, avoid this problem by considering the closed Leontief model. In the one-sector version, this amounts to assuming $\bar{c} = 0$ (as well as $s = 1$) or $X_t \equiv 0$ for all t. As remarked earlier, there is no difficulty of causal indeterminacy in the present model, for there is only one sector in the economy [whose growth is described by (9) regardless of the initial point Y_0].

We are now ready to describe another difficulty inherent in the fixed coefficient model. Let l be the amount of labor necessary to produce one unit of output. Suppose this is a fixed constant. In order to avoid the above difficulty, assume $Y_0 > Y^*$ so that Y_t *grows* over time according to (8). As Y_t grows over time, the labor requirement, denoted by L_t, also grows according to lY_t, or

$$(10) \qquad L_t = \left[(1 + s\sigma)^t (Y_0 - Y^*) + Y^*\right]l$$

Clearly, the actual supply of labor may not grow at the same rate, and there is no mechanism in the economy to equilibrate the supply and the requirement of labor. To illustrate this point, assume $\bar{c} = 0$ or $Y^* = 0$ following the usual Harrod-Domar convention, so that (10) is rewritten as

$$(11) \qquad L_t = Y_0(1 + s\sigma)^t l$$

Suppose the supply of labor, $\bar{L}_t$, grows at a constant rate n, so that

$$(12) \qquad \bar{L}_t = L_0(1 + n)^t$$

If $n > s\sigma$, then there is an ever-increasing unemployment of labor, and it is hard to conceive of any society which can tolerate this. If $n < s\sigma$, on the other hand, then the output growth described by (9) is impossible. The output can grow only as much as labor grows, namely at the rate n. This, in turn, implies an ever-increasing unemployment of capital, for the full employment of capital requires the increase of output at the rate $s\sigma$ ($> n$ by assumption). Here the fixity of the capital coefficient σ is crucial for this dilemma. It is certainly hard to conceive that such an ever-increasing unemployment of capital is possible and that there is any continuing investment (or capital construction) as required by (1) in such an economy.

Let us now turn to the price implication of the above system. Let p_t be the price of the good (which is also the capital good) in period t. Suppose one has $p_t K_t$ dollars; then he can buy K_t units of capital in period t, which are worth $p_{t+1} K_t$ dollars in period $(t + 1)$ (where depreciation and obsolescence are assumed away). By employing L_t units of labor, he can produce Y_t units of the good, which are worth $p_{t+1} Y_t$ in period $(t + 1)$. Let w_t be the wage rate in period t. Then the current profit, in period t, can be computed as $\left[p_{t+1} Y_t - w_t L_t\right]$, so that the current profit per unit dollar (denoted by π_t) is

$$\pi_t \equiv \frac{p_{t+1} Y_t - w_t L_t}{p_t K_t}$$

or

$$(13) \qquad \pi_t = \frac{\sigma}{p_t}\left[p_{t+1} - w_t l\right]$$

where $\sigma \equiv Y_t/K_t$ and $l \equiv L_t/Y_t$. Here we assume (as in Section B, subsection c) that the wage is paid at the end of each production period.

We can now write the intertemporal arbitrage equation (with perfect foresight)[2] as

(14)
$$p_{t+1}K_t + [p_{t+1}Y_t - w_tL_t] = (1 + r_t)(p_tK_t)$$

which can be rewritten as

(14')
$$\frac{p_{t+1}}{p_t} + \frac{\sigma}{p_t}[p_{t+1} - w_tl] = 1 + r_t$$

where r_t is the interest rate in period t. This is also written as

(15)
$$\frac{p_{t+1} - p_t}{p_t} + \frac{\sigma}{p_t}[p_{t+1} - w_tl] = r_t$$

Equation (14) or (15) corresponds to equation (39) in Section B.

Following Morishima [16], we now ask whether constant prices are possible in (15). That is, setting $r_t = r$, $w_t = w$, and $p_t = p^*$, we obtain from (15)

(16)
$$p^* = r\frac{p^*}{\sigma} + wl$$

which corresponds to Morishima's price equation (88) in Section B, where $1/\sigma$ corresponds to Morishima's B matrix. From (16), p^* can be obtained as

(17)
$$p^* = \frac{\sigma wl}{\sigma - r}$$

which is meaningful only when $\sigma > r$.

Following Solow [23], let us *not* assume that the price p_t is constant, but assume that both r_t and w_t are constant so that $r_t = r$ and $w_t = w$. Then solving the above difference equation (14') or (15), we can easily obtain

(18)
$$p_t = (p_0 - p^*)\left(\frac{1 + r}{1 + \sigma}\right)^t + p^*$$

where p^* is defined in (17).

In the knife edge case ($\sigma = r$), $p_t = p_0$ for all t. For all practical purposes, σ is likely to be larger than r. If this is the case, then regardless of the initial value p_0, p_t converges to p^* as $t \to \infty$.[3] If we assume $r = 0$ as in Solow [23] and Jorgenson [14], this assumption of $\sigma > r$ obviously holds. As a matter of fact, if $\sigma < r$, then something very strange will happen in the system, namely, $p_t \to \infty$ as $t \to \infty$ with $p_0 > p^*$.

I hope that the above discussion has made clear the type of assumptions buried in Morishima [16], Solow [23], and Jorgenson [14]. Their conclusions depend crucially on these conditions. In general, neither r_t nor w_t is constant, and r_t is not necessarily equal to 0. The assumption of $\sigma > r$ is not explicit in the usual discussions of the price system of the dynamic Leontief system. The assumption of $r = 0$ is not crucial in proving the convergence of p_t to p^* as $t \to \infty$. It can be relaxed to $\sigma > r$.

Morishima introduced factor substitution into the model so that coefficients such as l and σ are no longer fixed constants. The factor substitution in the present model amounts to incorporating the following production function

$$(19) \qquad\qquad Y_t = F(L_t, K_t)$$

which was introduced by Solow [23] and others in connection with the one-sector model (recall Chapter 5, Section C). Assuming the linear homogeneity of F and dividing both sides of (19) by Y_t, we obtain

$$(20) \qquad 1 = F(l_t, \frac{1}{\sigma_t}), \text{ where } l_t \equiv \frac{L_t}{Y_t} \text{ and } \sigma_t \equiv \frac{Y_t}{K_t}$$

which corresponds to our equation (78) in Section B. Notice that subscript t is now attached to l and σ. If we follow Morishima in [16], these coefficients l_t and σ_t are now chosen to minimize the unit cost $[w_t l_t + \check{p}_t/\sigma_t]$ subject to (20),[4] where $\check{p}_t$ is the price of the capital service of the good. Then we may write the optimal values of l_t and σ_t as

$$(21) \qquad\qquad l_t = l(\check{p}_t, w_t)$$

$$(22) \qquad\qquad \sigma_t = \sigma(\check{p}_t, w_t)$$

which correspond to (79) and (80) in Section B. Let $p_t = \text{constant} \equiv p^*$, $w_t = \text{constant} \equiv w$, and $r_t = \text{constant} \equiv r$. Then we obtain (16), and moreover there is a unique relation between p^* and $\check{p}^*$ such as[5]

$$(23) \qquad\qquad p^* = \frac{\check{p}^*}{r}$$

which corresponds to Morishima's (81) in Section B. The price equation (16) can be rewritten [in view of (23)] as

$$(24) \qquad\qquad \check{p}_t = \check{p}^* = \frac{r\check{p}^*}{\sigma_t} + rwl_t \qquad \text{for all } t$$

which corresponds to Morishima's price equation (88) in Section B. Equations (21), (22), (23), and (24) determine the values of $\check{p}^*$, p^*, l_t, and σ_t with a given set of r and w, which is the essence of the dynamic substitution theorem of Morishima, which we discussed in subsection e.

The analysis above is incomplete in the sense that there are still two degrees of freedom—say, r and w—in the model. The model will become self-contained after we explicitly introduce the money market and the labor market. It is to this task that we now turn.

We take up the money market first. Let M_t be the supply of money exogenously controlled by the monetary authority and let M be the demand function for money. We suppose that equilibrium in the money market is written as[6]

$$(25) \qquad M_t = M(r_t, p_t Y_t, A_t), \text{ where } A_t = M_t + p_t K_t$$

The demand function M is taken to be homogeneous of degree one with respect to $p_t Y_t$ and A_t, for otherwise it would not be independent of the monetary units which are used to measure $p_t Y_t$ and A_t. Thus (25) can be rewritten as

(26)
$$\frac{M_t}{p_t} = M\left(r_t, Y_t, \frac{A_t}{p_t}\right)$$

We assume labor is employed up to the point where the marginal productivity of labor is equal to the real wage rate.[7] Then we have

(27)
$$\frac{w_t}{p_t} = \frac{\partial}{\partial L_t} F(L_t, K_t)$$

Assuming that the production function F is homogeneous of degree one, so that we can write $F(L_t, K_t) = L_t f(k_t)$ where $k_t \equiv K_t/L_t$ and $f(k_t) \equiv F(1, k_t)$, we have

(28)
$$\frac{w_t}{p_t} = f(k_t) - k_t f'(k_t)$$

where $f'(k_t) = df(k_t)/dk_t$. We assume that the supply of labor is given exogenously and that it grows at a constant rate n. Since, in this Appendix, L_t denotes the demand for labor, the following equation now signifies the equilibrium relation in the labor market:

(29)
$$L_t = L_0(1 + n)^t$$

We may suppose that the equilibrium in the labor market is achieved through fluctuation in the real wage rate w_t/p_t. The earlier difficulty of ever-increasing unemployment of labor can then be avoided. In fact, the full employment of labor, namely, (29), can be guaranteed by assuming the flexibility of the real wage rate. In other words, unemployment of labor lowers w_t/p_t, which, in view of (28), increases the employment of labor with a given K_t. The reverse will happen with an excess demand for labor.[8]

Our model now consists of equations (1), (3), (6), (14), (19), (26), (28), and (29). If consumption X_t is not to be specified, then equation (6) is to be dropped.

If depreciation is explicitly introduced into the model, then (3) can be modified to

(3')
$$I_t = (K_{t+1} - K_t) + \delta K_t$$

where δ is the rate of depreciation and I_t now denotes gross investment instead of net investment. Corresponding to this, Y_t now denotes gross output instead of net output. As a result of the explicit introduction of depreciation, (14') should be modified to[9]

(14'')
$$\frac{p_{t+1}}{p_t}(1 - \delta) + \frac{\sigma_t}{p_t}[p_{t+1} - w_t l_t] = 1 + r_t$$

where $\sigma_t \equiv Y_t/K_t$ and $l_t \equiv L_t/Y_t$.

Note that equations (1), (3'), and (19) are summarized as

(30) $$F(L_t, K_t) = (K_{t+1} - K_t) + \delta K_t + X_t$$

This together with (14''), (19), (26), (28), and (29) will determine the time paths of $L_t, K_t, Y_t, p_t, w_t,$ and r_t once the consumption specification, such as (6), is made.

It is certainly possible to describe this model in terms of differential equations, which can be written as

(31) $$F(L_t, K_t) = \dot{K}_t + \mu K_t + X_t$$

where μ is the *instantaneous* rate of depreciation,[10]

(32) $$\dot{p}_t + p_t[(1 - \mu) + \sigma_t] = (1 + r_t)p_t + \sigma_t w_t l_t$$

where $\sigma_t \equiv Y_t/K_t$ and $l_t \equiv L_t/Y_t$,

(33) $$\frac{M_t}{p_t} = M\left[r_t, F(L_t, K_t), \frac{A_t}{p_t}\right]$$

and

(34) $$L_t = L_0 e^{nt}$$

where n now denotes the *instantaneous* rate of labor growth. Assuming the linear homogeneity of F, we can obtain the following equation from (31) and (34):

(35) $$\dot{k}_t = f(k_t) - \lambda k_t - x_t$$

where $k_t \equiv K_t/L_t$, $x_t \equiv X_t/L_t$, $\lambda \equiv n + \mu$, and $f(k_t) \equiv F(1, k_t)$. Since M is homogeneous of degree one in p_t, Y_t and A_t, we have[11]

(36) $$\frac{m_t}{p_t} = M\left[r_t, f(k_t), k_t + \frac{m_t}{p_t}\right]$$

where $m_t \equiv M_t/L_t$. We may also rewrite (32) as[12]

(37) $$\frac{\dot{p}_t}{p_t}k_t + [(1 - \mu)k_t + f(k_t)] = (1 + r_t)k_t + \frac{w_t}{p_t}$$

Equations (35), (36), (37), and (28) determine the time path of $[k_t, p_t, r_t, w_t]$, once the behavior of per capita consumption x_t is specified and the per capita money supply m_t is determined. The model can be complicated further (and generalized) by introducing government expenditures and taxes explicitly. This complication can be handled by reformulating the equilibrium relation of the goods market (1) and by formulating explicitly the relation among government expenditures, taxes, and the money supply. We leave this to the interested reader.

Note that equations (37) and (28) can be combined to yield[13]

(38) $$r_t = [f'(k_t) - \mu] + \Phi_t$$

where $\Phi_t \equiv \dot{p}_t/p_t$, the rate of inflation or deflation. Equation (38) implies that there is inflation ($\Phi_t > 0$) or deflation ($\Phi_t < 0$) at time t, depending on whether the **money interest rate** r_t exceeds or falls short of the "net" marginal productivity of capital, $[f'(k_t) - \mu]$, at time t. Price stability ($\Phi_t = 0$) is achieved if and only if $r_t = f'(k_t) - \mu$.

Per capita consumption x_t depends on the choice between present consumption and future consumption (present savings) for each individual and on the income distribution among people (say, between the capitalists and the workers). Hence x_t would, in general, depend on variables such as r_t, p_t, w_t, and so on. There is one simple specification of x_t which ignores all such considerations, namely, the proportional savings behavior, $X_t = (1 - s)[Y_t - \mu K_t]$. Or

(39) $$x_t = (1 - s)[f(k_t) - \mu k_t]$$

where $0 < s \leq 1$ is assumed to be constant.[14]

If we adopt this specification of x_t, then (35) is simplified to

(40) $$\dot{k}_t = sf(k_t) - (n + s\mu)k_t$$

so that the time path of k_t becomes independent of the other part of the model. This is the case Solow was concerned with in his 1956 paper [22]. As we proved in Chapter 5, Section C, we can show that, under somewhat plausible assumptions, k_t monotonically approaches a constant value k_s (called Solow's path) as $t \to \infty$,[15] where k_s is defined by

(41) $$sf(k_s) = (n + s\mu)k_s$$

This occurs regardless of the specification of the other part of the model. For example, the capital:labor ratio k_t as specified by (40) and the per capita output y_t move independently of the money supply.

Following Tobin's path-breaking works ([27] and [28]), there has arisen a rather heated discussion on "money and growth." In view of the above consideration, it is not surprising to observe that the main feature of these "money and growth" models often lies in their departure from the consumption specification such as (39). More sophisticated behavioral relations on consumption than (39) can be imposed by recognizing that "income" arises also from a change in the real value of cash balances as well as from production. Assuming that money consists only of "outside money," Tobin [28] and others imposed

(42) $$X_t = (1 - s)\left[F(L_t, K_t) - \mu K_t + \frac{d}{dt}\left(\frac{M_t}{p_t}\right)\right]$$

where M_t denotes outside money (government noninterest-bearing debt). The introduction of a term such as $d(M_t/p_t)/dt$, which signifies capital gains or losses, constitutes the major path through which money affects the working of the economy (in the "money and growth" literature). Following Shell, Sidrauski, and Stiglitz [20], we may call $[F(L_t, K_t) - \mu K_t + d(M_t/p_t)/dt]$ the **real purchasing**

power or the **purchasing power in terms of the real good**. If we recognize that the price of money in terms of the real good is $1/p_t$ and if we denote it by p_{mt}, then $d(M_t/p_t)/dt = \dot{p}_{mt}M_t + p_{mt}\dot{M}_t$, where $p_{mt} \equiv 1/p_t$. Also denote the "net output" by Q_t; that is, $Q_t \equiv F(L_t, K_t) - \mu K_t$. Then (42) may also be written as[16]

$$(43) \qquad X_t = (1 - s)[Q_t + \dot{p}_{mt}M_t + p_{mt}\dot{M}_t]$$

Alternatively, we may assume that the money value of consumption is a constant function of the money value of income. Then instead of (42) or (43), we have

$$(44) \qquad p_t X_t = (1 - s)[p_t Q_t + \dot{M}_t + \dot{p}_t K_t]$$

The two specifications (43) and (44) are fundamentally different. As is well known, (44) involves money illusion (see Burmeister and Dobell [1], pp. 166–167). We proceed by using (43) or (42).

Write the per capita real cash balances as $z_t \equiv m_t/p_t$. Also write the rate of change in the money supply as $\theta_t \equiv \dot{M}_t/M_t$. Then, dividing both sides of (42) by L_t, we obtain[17]

$$(45) \qquad x_t = (1 - s)[f(k_t) - \mu k_t + z_t(\theta_t - \Phi_t)]$$

Combining this with (35), we obtain

$$(46) \qquad \dot{k}_t = sf(k_t) - (n + s\mu)k_t - (1 - s)z_t(\theta_t - \Phi_t)$$

Rewrite (36) as

$$(47) \qquad z_t = M[r_t, f(k_t), k_t + z_t]$$

Assume that $\partial M/\partial r_t < 0$, $\partial M/\partial f > 0$, and $1 > \partial M/\partial(k_t + z_t) > 0$.[18] Then we can show that (47) may be rewritten as

$$(48) \qquad r_t = g(k_t, z_t)$$

where $\partial g/\partial k_t > 0$ and $\partial g/\partial z_t < 0$.[19] Equations (46) and (48), respectively, signify equilibrium in the goods market and the money market. Combining (48) with the intertemporal arbitrage equation (38) we obtain

$$(49) \qquad \Phi_t = -[f'(k_t) - \mu - g(k_t, z_t)]$$

Using (49), we can rewrite (46) as

$$(50) \quad \dot{k}_t = sf(k_t) - (n + s\mu)k_t - (1 - s)z_t[\theta_t - \{f'(k_t) - \mu - g(k_t, z_t)\}]$$

Next, noting that[20]

$$(51) \qquad \dot{z}_t = (\theta_t - n - \Phi_t)z_t$$

we obtain from (49)

$$(52) \qquad \frac{\dot{z}_t}{z_t} = \Psi(k_t, z_t; \theta_t)$$

where

(53) $$\Psi(k_t, z_t; \theta_t) \equiv \theta_t - n + [f'(k_t) - \mu - g(k_t, z_t)]$$

Equations (50) and (52) then define the equilibrium path of (k_t, z_t) for a pre-assigned value of θ_t. Once the path of (k_t, z_t) is determined, the rate of price change Φ_t is determined by (49). The dynamic behavior of (k_t, z_t) can be studied by constructing a phase diagram in the (k_t, z_t)-plane using (50) and (52). The construction of the phase diagram also reveals the condition for the existence and uniqueness of the steady state path in which $\dot{z}_t = 0$ and $\dot{k}_t = 0$. This task is left to the interested reader. Such an analysis can be seen, for example, in Burmeister and Dobell ([1], Chapter 6). In this connection, note that (46) and (51) imply

(54) $$\dot{k}_t = sf(k_t) - (n + s\mu)k_t - (1 - s)(\dot{z}_t + nz_t)$$

Hence, if the steady state path $(\bar{k}, \bar{z})$ is ever achieved, then

(55) $$sf(\bar{k}) = (n + s\mu)\bar{k} + (1 - s)n\bar{z}$$

Therefore, assuming that $f'(k_t) > 0$ for all k_t and $\bar{k} > 0$, (55) implies

(56) $$\bar{k} < k_s$$

where k_s is the value of k in Solow's steady state path defined by (41). Equation (56) implies that per capita output under the present steady state path is lower than that under Solow's steady state path, that is, $f(\bar{k}) < f(k_s)$. Note that these conclusions are independent of the rate of change in the money supply, θ_t.[21] It is, however, to be stressed that the convergence to the steady state path under the present model does not necessarily hold (unlike in Solow's theorem in [22]).[22] Hence the value of any statement with regard to the steady state path under the present model is not very great.

   Above we assumed that the rate of change of the money supply θ_t is exogenously given. Alternatively, we may suppose that the monetary authority manipulates θ_t so as to maintain price stability (that is, $\Phi_t = 0$ for all t).[23] Imposing $\Phi_t = 0$, we obtain from (46), (51), and (49)

(57) $$\dot{k}_t = sf(k_t) - (n + s\mu)k_t - (1 - s)z_t\theta_t$$

(58) $$\dot{z}_t = z_t(\theta_t - n)$$

(59) $$f'(k_t) = g(k_t, z_t) + \mu$$

Note that (59) implies

(60) $$\frac{dz_t}{dk_t} = \frac{f'' - g_k}{g_z}$$

where $g_k \equiv \partial g/\partial k_t$ and $g_z \equiv \partial g/\partial z_t$. Hence, assuming that $g_k > 0, g_z < 0$, and $f'' < 0$, we obtain $dz_t/dk_t > 0$.[24] Therefore, we may write

(61) $$z_t = \zeta(k_t), \text{ where } \zeta' \equiv \frac{d\zeta}{dk_t} > 0$$

In order to facilitate our study of the above system, it is necessary to explore the meaning of (47) further. We noted that (47) can be written as (48). Now note that (47) can also be written as

(62) $$z_t = h(k_t, r_t)$$

where $\partial h/\partial k_t > 0$ and $\partial h/\partial r_t < 0$, assuming again $\partial M/\partial r_t < 0$, $\partial M/\partial y_t > 0$, and $1 > \partial M/\partial(k_t + z_t) > 0$.[25] Assume that for a sufficiently large value $\bar{r} = \bar{r}(k)$, the demand for money is zero. Then we have

(63) $$0 = h(k, \bar{r}(k))$$

Assume further that the function $\bar{r}(k)$ satisfies

(64) $$0 < \bar{r}(k) < \infty, \bar{r}'(k) > 0, \text{ and } \lim_{k \to \infty} \bar{r}(k) \equiv R > 0$$

The fact that $\bar{r}(k) > 0$ means that the transaction demand for money is positive. The shape of $\bar{r}(k)$ is illustrated in Figure 6.6.

Assuming that $f''(k) < 0$, $f'(0) = \infty$, and $f'(\infty) = 0$, the shape of $[f'(k) - \mu]$ is also illustrated in Figure 6.6. As is clear from the diagram, under the above assumptions, there exists a unique value of $\check{k} > 0$ which satisfies

(65) $$f'(\check{k}) = \bar{r}(\check{k}) + \mu$$

Now return to (61) or

(61') $$z_t = \zeta(k_t) = h[k_t, f'(k_t) - \mu]$$

Obviously $\bar{r}(k_t) \geq f'(k_t) - \mu$ by the definition of $\bar{r}(k_t)$, so that k_t cannot be less than $\check{k}$, as is clear from Figure 6.6. The shape of $\zeta(k_t)$ is illustrated in Figure 6.7.[26]

We are now ready to study the system consisting of (57), (58), and (59) [or (61')]. Note that (57) and (58) yield an equation which is the same as (54), and note that (61') implies that $\dot{z}_t = \zeta' \dot{k}_t$. Then we obtain

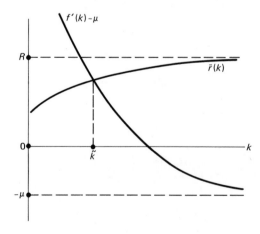

Figure 6.6. $\bar{r}(k)$ and $\check{k}$.

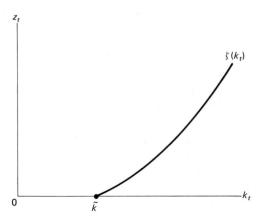

Figure 6.7.   An Illustration of $\zeta(k_t)$.

(66) $$\left[1 + (1 - s)\zeta'\right]\dot{k}_t = sf(k_t) - (n + s\mu)k_t - (1 - s)n\zeta(k_t)$$

The dynamic behavior of k_t can now be deduced easily from Figure 6.8.

It is clear from Figure 6.8 that there exists a unique k^* with $0 < k^* < k_s$ which is defined by

(67) $$sf(k^*) = (n + s\mu)k^* + (1 - s)n\zeta(k^*)$$

Moreover, from (66) we can immediately conclude that k_t converges to k^* monotonically as $t \to \infty$, regardless of the initial value of k_0. In other words, k^* is globally stable. If k_t converges to k^* monotonically, then from (61′) we can also conclude that z_t converges monotonically to z^*, where $z^* \equiv \zeta(k^*)$. Note that at (k^*, z^*), $\dot{k}_t = \dot{z}_t = 0$, so that (58) implies $\theta_t = n$; that is, the money supply is increasing at the rate of population growth. Moreover, if $k_t < k^*$, then $z_t < z^*$, and z_t is monotonically increasing, so that (58) implies $\theta_t > n$. On the other hand, if $k_t > k^*$, then we can similarly conclude that $\theta_t < n$. The precise formula for θ_t can be computed from (57), (58), and (59). Some of the above conclusions may be summarized as follows:

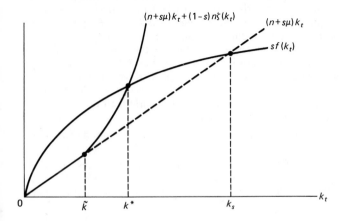

Figure 6.8..   Dynamics of k_t.

Proposition: *Under the above specification and the assumptions of the model, if the monetary authority manipulates the money supply so as to maintain price stability, then there exists a unique steady state path (k^*, z^*), where $0 < k^* < k_s$, which is globally stable. Along the stipulated price stability path of the money supply, $\theta_t \gtreqless n$ according to whether $k_t \lesseqgtr k^*$.*

The relation between money and growth in connection with the one-industry model has recently attracted the attention of many economists since Tobin's fundamental paper [28]. We have simply traced and developed some thoughts along these lines. Since active research is still being done on this topic, we do not go any further.[27] The above analysis is an exercise under the rather limited conditions of perfect foresight, full employment, and no fiscal elements.[28] The reader may wish to extend our analysis by realizing these limitations. However, the purpose of this Appendix is fulfilled if the reader realizes some of the inherent difficulties in the dynamic Leontief model.

FOOTNOTES

1. The major result on money and growth in this appendix is taken from Takayama [26].
2. Note that intertemporal arbitrage is concerned only with two periods (t and $t + 1$). Hence this perfect foresight assumption is often called **myopic perfect foresight**, as mentioned before.
3. Recall that $p^* > 0$ only when $\sigma > r$.
4. This is clearly myopic, and can be justified under Morishima's assumption of a stationary state. When we divert ourselves from the steady state (or balanced growth) assumption, it is desirable to reconsider this decision rule. Here we simply assume that such a "long-range" decision rule is reduced to the present myopic rule.
5. Note that in (23), depreciation and obsolescence are assumed away.
6. Here A_t signifies the money value of assets. An alternative formulation with regard to monetary equilibrium is $M_t = M(r_t, p_t K_t, A_t)$. See Tobin [28], for example. Following Tobin [28], we may assume that there are only two kinds of assets, (outside) money, and the stock of capital, which certainly justifies the definition of A_t in (25). However, (25) can incorporate private (nongovernmental) bonds, and signify a part of the portfolio equilibrium of the three types of assets, M, K, and, private bonds. The introduction of interest-yielding government bonds will complicate the formulation, although the essence of the conclusions in this Appendix will still remain. On the other hand, if there are no bonds, equation (15) [and also (14″) and (32), which will appear later as a modified version of (15)] becomes the *defining* equation of the own rate of interest (or the money rate of return on the physical capital) and does not show the intertemporal arbitrage relation. In this case, (25) describes the portfolio equation of M and K alone.
7. The behavioral rule of cost minimization (for each period) is the major background for this result.
8. Assume, for example, that w_t adjusts the labor market. Then an excess demand (resp. supply) of labor will increase (resp. lower) w_t with a given p_t, thus increasing (resp. lowering) w_t/p_t. It is usually assumed that p_t adjusts the goods market. This

adjustment mechanism takes place within the framework of the Hicksian week. Here it is assumed that such an equilibrium is achieved in order to focus attention on the equilibrium path. Under the Keynesian framework, w_t has downward rigidity; that is, an excess supply of labor will not reduce w_t.

9. With $p_t K_t$ dollars, one can buy K_t units of capital in period t, which are worth $p_{t+1}(K_t - \delta K_t)$ dollars in period $t + 1$. The current profit in t is $p_{t+1} Y_t - w_t L_t$. Hence we have the intertemporal arbitrage equation $p_{t+1}(K_t - \delta K_t) + (p_{t+1} Y_t - w_t L_t) = (1 + r_t) p_t K_t$. From this, we can deduce (14″).

10. Equation (32) corresponds to (14″). Note that (32) cannot be obtained by simply setting $\Phi_{t+1} = p_t + \dot{p}_t$ in (32). To obtain (32), first observe the following intertemporal arbitrage equation under perfect foresight for the continuous time case,

$$p_t = \int_t^\infty \rho_\tau e^{-\mu(\tau - t)} e^{-\int_t^\tau r_\alpha \, d\alpha} \, d\tau$$

where $\rho_\tau \equiv p_\tau \sigma_\tau - w_\tau \sigma_\tau l_\tau$, and we assume that the integral converges. The term inside the integral gives the present value of the quasi-rent for time τ. Totally differentiating the above equation with respect to t, we obtain $\dot{p}_t = -[p_t \sigma_t - w_t \sigma_t l_t] + \mu p_t + r_t p_t$, from which we obtain (32). In this derivation of (32), no assumption is made with regard to the myopic nature of intertemporal arbitrage. It is assumed that r_τ is known for all future time (τ). However, (32) can also be obtained by assuming the myopic nature of intertemporal arbitrage (that is, the arbitrage is concerned only with the current time and the next instant of time).

11. Suppose that we have the alternative formulation $M_t = M[r_t, p_t K_t, A_t]$. Then under a suitable set of assumptions we can conclude that $M_t / (p_t K_t)$ is a function of r_t alone and that it is a decreasing function.

12. Equation (37) is obtained from (32), which assumes perfect foresight in the intertemporal arbitrage relation. In general, $(\dot{p}_t / p_t)$ should be replaced by $E(\dot{p}_t / p_t)$, which denotes the expected rate of price change at t. However, if $(\dot{p}_t / p_t) \neq E(\dot{p}_t / p_t)$, that is, if expectations turn out to be incorrect, then some sort of learning device to correct such a mistake is necessary. One device which is used in the literature to cope with this problem is the simple "adaptive expectations" postulate of the form $\dot{\pi}_t = \epsilon(\dot{p}_t / p_t - \pi_t)$, where π_t denotes $E(\dot{p}_t / p_t)$ and $\epsilon \geq 0$ signifies the speed of adjustment in expectations. It says that the rate of adjustment in the current expected rate of price change is linearly dependent on the error made in predicting the *current* rate of change. No doubt this device can be useful. The reader can, if he is interested, modify our analysis accordingly using this device. However, the fundamental question with regard to the background of this device from the viewpoint of rational behavior is still unclear.

13. Equation (38) says that the money rate of interest (r_t) is equal to the net marginal productivity of capital $[f'(k_t) - \mu]$ plus the rate of inflation (or deflation) Φ_t.

14. In (39), it is assumed that consumption is a constant fraction of *net* national product. Alternatively, we may assume that consumption is a constant fraction of *gross* national product. Then (39) is simply written as

(39′) $x_t = (1 - s)f(k_t)$

15. This conclusion will be unaltered even if (39) is replaced by (39′). In that case, the definition of k_s needs to be modified to the one specified by

(41′) $sf(k_s) = \lambda k_s$

16. Consider the possibility that real output is very low, or to dramatize the story,

consider the case in which $F(L_t, K_t) = 0$. The consumption specification (42) or (43) then says that usual bounds on s such as $0 < s < 1$ are absurd. If $d(M_t/p_t)/dt < 0$, $X_t < 0$, which is absurd. If, on the other hand, $d(M_t/p_t)/dt$ is positive and large enough, $X_t > 0$. Assuming that one does not "eat up" the capital that is already invested, this is again absurd, for this then implies that one can live by paper money alone. Hence we may naturally impose the *constraint* such as $0 \leq X_t \leq F(L_t, K_t)$.

17. Actually, several other alternative specifications are possible. See, for example, Levhari and Patinkin [15] and Stein [25]. Note also that if $E(\dot{p}_t/p_t) \neq \dot{p}_t/p_t$, then capital gains or losses due to miscalculation should also be introduced in defining the purchasing power. This point seems to be ignored in the literature.

18. It is easy to see that $\partial M/\partial r_t < 0$ and $\partial M/\partial f > 0$ from the usual Keynesian hypothesis on liquidity preference; $\partial M/\partial (k_t + z_t) > 0$ or $\partial M/\partial A_t > 0$ says that money is not an inferior good; and $1 > \partial M/\partial (k_t + z_t)$ says that an extra dollar of wealth will not all be held in the form of money.

19. The proof of this statement is left to the reader.

20. Equation (51) is obtained from $z_t \equiv m_t/p_t$. Equation (51) implies that in the steady state path in which $\dot{z}_t = 0$, $\Phi_t = \theta_t - n$; that is, the rate of price change is equal to the rate of change of the money supply minus the rate of population increase.

21. However, the actual values of $\bar{k}$ and $\bar{z}$, in general, depend on θ_t. This is often called the **nonneutrality of money**. The conclusion that "money matters" is rather obvious in view of the change of the consumption specification from (39) to (45).

22. In various money and growth models, it has been established that the steady state path under the present specifications is not globally (nor locally) stable. See, for example, Burmeister and Dobell [1] and Nagatani [18].

23. To me, this is a much more acceptable hypothesis than the usual one in the money and growth literature which assumes that the monetary authority keeps the rate of money change (θ_t) constant *forever*, regardless of the state of the economy.

24. In other words, if price stability is maintained, then k_t and z_t move together. Needless to say, (59) signifies that if price stability is maintained, then the marginal physical productivity of capital is equal to the rate of depreciation plus the rate of interest.

25. The proof is again left to the reader.

26. Such an illustration of $\zeta(k_t)$ is also seen in Burmeister and Dobell ([1], p. 169).

27. For a recent survey of the discussion on "money and growth," the reader is referred to Stein [25] and Burmeister and Dobell [1].

28. Another major limitation is that we are concerned only with the equilibrium path in which temporary (or momentary) equilibrium in all markets is achieved (instantaneously). For pioneering studies in which "disequilibrium" is allowed in this context, see, for example, Rose [19], Stein [24], and Tsiang [30]. In essence, they assume the price of the good changes if and only if there is disequilibrium in the goods market. Writing I_t and S_t, respectively, for planned investment and planned saving at t, they (somewhat arbitrarily) imposed that $\dot{K}_t = \eta I_t + (1 - \eta)S_t$, where η is a constant with $0 \leq \eta \leq 1$.

REFERENCES

1. Burmeister, E., and Dobell, A. R., *Mathematical Theories of Economic Growth*, New York, Macmillan, 1970.

2. Domar, E. D., "Capital Expansion, Rate of Growth and Employment," *Econometrica*, 14, April 1946.

3. ———, "Expansion and Employment," *American Economic Review*, XXXVII, March 1947.

4. ———, *Essays in the Theory of Growth*, New York, Oxford University Press, 1957.

5. Dorfman, R., Samuelson, P. A., and Solow, R. M., *Linear Programming and Economic Analysis*, New York, McGraw-Hill, 1958.

6. Georgescu-Roegen, N., "Book Review: Morishima, M., *Equilibrium, Stability and Growth: A Multi-Sectoral Analysis*," *American Economic Review*, LV, March 1965.

7. Hahn, F. H., "On Money and Growth," *Journal of Money, Credit and Banking*, 1, May 1969.

8. Hahn, F. H., and Matthews, R. C. O., "The Theory of Economic Growth: A Survey," *Economic Journal*, LXXIV, December 1964.

9. Harrod, R. F., "An Essay in Dynamic Theory," *Economic Journal*, XLIX, March 1939.

10. ———, *Towards a Dynamic Economics*, London, Macmillan, 1948.

11. ———, "Domar and Dynamic Economics," *Economic Journal*, LXIX, September 1959.

12. Hicks, J. R., *A Contribution to the Theory of the Trade Cycle*, Oxford, Clarendon Press, 1950.

13. Johnson, H. G., "The Neoclassical One-Sector Growth Model: A Geometrical Exposition and Extension to a Monetary Economy," *Economica*, XXXIII, August 1966.

14. Jorgenson, D., "A Dual Stability Theorem," *Econometrica*, XXVIII, October 1960.

15. Levhari, D., and Patinkin, D., "The Role of Money in a Simple Growth Model," *American Economic Review*, LVIII, September 1968.

16. Morishima, M., "A Dynamic Leontief System with Neo-Classical Production Function," chap. III in his *Equilibrium, Stability and Growth: A Multi-Sectoral Analysis*, Oxford, Clarendon Press, 1965 (a revision of his paper in *Econometrica*, 26, July 1958).

17. Morishima, M., and Murata, Y., "An Input-Output System Involving Nontransferable Goods," *Econometrica*, 36, January 1968.

18. Nagatani, K., "Professor Tobin on Money and Economic Growth," *Econometrica*, 38, January 1970.

19. Rose, H., "Real and Monetary Factors in the Business Cycle," *Journal of Money, Credit and Banking*, 1, May 1969.

20. Shell, K., Sidrauski, M., and Stiglitz, J. E., "Capital Gains, Income and Saving," *Review of Economic Studies*, XXXVI, January 1969.

21. Sidrauski, M., "Inflation and Economic Growth," *Journal of Political Economy*, LXXXIV, October 1966.

22. Solow, R. M., "A Contribution to the Theory of Economic Growth," *Quarterly Journal of Economics*, LXX, February 1956.

23. ———, "Competitive Valuation in a Dynamic Input-Output System," *Econometrica*, 27, January 1959.

24. Stein, J. L., "Neoclassical and Keynes-Wicksell Monetary Growth Models," *Journal of Money, Credit and Banking*, 1, May 1969.

25. ———, "Monetary Growth Theory in Perspective," *American Economic Review*, LX, March 1970.

26. Takayama, A., "A Note on Money and Growth," *Krannert Institute Paper* No. 305, Purdue University, March 1971.

27. Tobin, J., "A Dynamic Aggregative Model," *Journal of Political Economy*, LXIII, April 1955.

28. ———, "Money and Growth," *Econometrica*, 33, December 1965.

29. ———, "The Neutrality of Money in Growth Models: A Comment," *Economica*, XXXIV, February 1967.

30. Tsiang, S. C., "A Critical Note on the Optimum Supply of Money," *Journal of Money, Credit and Banking*, 1, May 1969.

7

MULTISECTOR OPTIMAL GROWTH MODELS

TURNPIKE THEOREMS

---

a. INTRODUCTION

Consider a trip from a suburb of Chicago to a suburb of New York City. There are many routes that one could take. The fastest way is probably not the route that is the shortest, that is, the route that is approximately a straight line between the two suburbs. The fastest route is probably to get to the "turnpike" as quickly as possible and travel on it until reaching an exit that leads to the destination. This is true even if the "turnpike" appears to be a very roundabout route compared to a straight line between the starting point and the terminal point.

In the problem of economic growth, one may wonder whether or not there is a path of growth that resembles a "turnpike," that is, a growth path on which an economy should spend most of its time. This problem was considered by Dorfman, Samuelson, and Solow (DOSSO) [2] with respect to the von Neumann type of growth model. They conjectured that there is such a path and that it is none other than the von Neumann growth path, that is, the path which maximizes the growth rate among the set of balanced growth paths. This conjecture was first proved rigorously by Morishima [22] and Radner [25] for the n-commodity case. Since then, there have been many extensions and variations of the basic theorem. For example, we list the following important papers: McKenzie [17], [18], [19], and [20], Nikaido [23], Inada [10], Tsukui [28], [29], and [30], Drandakis [3], Winter [35], and expository articles by Koopmans [14] and Hahn-Matthews [7] for simpler cases. Because of the variations in these numerous papers, the theorem is often referred to in the plural form as **turnpike theorems**.

Let us now describe the essence of these turnpike theorems more specifically. The basic model is the von Neumann (or at least a von Neumann type) economy with n-commodities. The vector of historically given initial stocks of the commodities is given arbitrarily. It is supposed that the economy wishes to maximize the vector of the *final stocks* of commodities or the utility function which is defined with regard to only the final stocks of commodities as its arguments. Then, in terms of this optimality criterion, the "best" way for the economy to achieve its goal is to spend "most" of its time "sufficiently close" to the von Neumann growth path, regardless of the initial point, provided that the planning horizon (that is, the terminal time) is sufficiently far away. In almost all versions of the turnpike theorems, it is not advocated that the optimal path actually be on the von Neumann path most of the time; it is only required that it spend most of the time "sufficiently close" to the von Neumann path. Hence the above Chicago–New York analogy is not quite accurate.

The above statement of the essence of the turnpike theorems may be illustrated by a simple diagram (see Figure 7.1). The turnpike theorems essentially require that the "optimal" path *arch toward* the von Neumann path; it is in this sense that the von Neumann path plays the role of the "turnpike." It is important to note that in the statement above, optimality is defined with respect to the final state only and that, unlike the analogy of the Chicago–New York trip, the terminal point is not given whereas the time to reach the terminal state is specified. It is possible to conjecture that the "turnpike property" of arching toward a certain path holds for other types of models. Optimality may depend on the interim states as well as on the final state, or the final state may be given and optimality may be defined to minimize the time in reaching the final state.

The significance of the turnpike theorems for the von Neumann model and the von Neumann theorem should now be clear. As we remarked in Chapter 6, Section A, it saves the von Neumann theorem from its two basic criticisms: the von Neumann path ignores the historically given stocks of commodities and consideration is restricted to balanced growth paths. The situation is analogous to the Ramsey-Koopmans-Cass theorem for the one-sector economy concerning the golden age path (recall Chapter 5, Section D).

Aside from the number of commodities, there is, however, one important

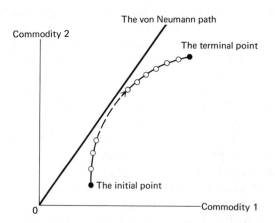

Figure 7.1.   An Illustration of a Turnpike Theorem.

difference between the turnpike theorems and the Ramsey-Koopmans-Cass theorem. In the latter, consumption is explicit in the model and the optimality depends on the interim states as well as on the terminal state. The extension of the turnpike theorems in this direction was first achieved by Atsumi [1] for a two-commodity economy and then by Gale [6] and McKenzie [21] for an *n*-commodity economy. Such an extension will be discussed in the next section of this chapter.[1]

The purpose of this section is *not* to survey all the literature on the turnpike theorems.[2] There is too much for such a limited space. In this section, we are mainly concerned with giving an expository account of the turnpike theorem due to Radner [25]. Radner's turnpike theorem has been criticized and extended by many writers, but the elegance of the paper and the excellence of the method of proof are generally agreed upon. In fact, his basic method of proof may also be found in several papers which have extended his result (including the papers which deal with consumption explicitly). See, for example, McKenzie [20].

In subsection b, we develop the basic model for the Radner turnpike theorem. In subsection c, we digress from the turnpike theorem and develop a "profit maximizing characterization" of the optimal feasible path, which is not discussed by Radner but is very important since this characterization is implied by a competitive market. Here the theorem is strictly analogous to the one in activity analysis and the price implication of the Pareto optimum in the theory of competitive markets. In subsection d, we proceed to the proof of the Radner turnpike theorem. In the proof of this theorem, the lemma due to Radner is essential.

b.   THE BASIC MODEL AND OPTIMALITY

Consider an economy which produces *n* commodities. Let (x_t, y_t) denote the production process in period *t* where x_t and y_t, respectively, denote an input vector and an output vector. Let *T* be the set of such processes which are technologically feasible in the economy. For the meaning of the production "period," the reader is reminded of our discussion in Chapter 6, Section A. We assume:

(A-1)   The set *T* is a closed cone in the nonnegative orthant of the $2n$-dimensional real space, R^{2n}.

(A-2)   (No land of Cockaigne) $(0, y) \in T$ implies $y = 0$.

The model described above is the von Neumann type "closed" model of production, in which there is no explicit treatment of consumption.

Definition (feasibility):   Given *N*, the span of the programming periods, and given the vector of initial commodity stocks, $\bar{x}_0$, a sequence $\{x_t\}$, $t = 0, 1, \ldots, N$, is called a **feasible path** with respect to $\bar{x}_0$, if $(x_t, x_{t+1}) \in T$, $t = 1, \ldots, N - 1$, and $x_0 = \bar{x}_0$.

Definition (von Neumann path):   A triplet $(\hat{x}, p, \lambda)$, where $\hat{x}$ and p are nonzero elements in the nonnegative orthant of R^n and $\lambda \in R$ with $\lambda > 0$, is called a **von Neumann triplet** or a **von Neumann equilibrium**, if

(i) $(\hat{x}, \lambda\hat{x}) \in T$

(ii) $p \cdot (y - \lambda x) \leq 0$ for all $(x, y) \in T$

We call the process $(\hat{x}, \lambda\hat{x})$ a **von Neumann process**. The ray from the origin through $\hat{x}$ is called the **von Neumann ray** (with respect to $\hat{x}$) or the **von Neumann (growth) path** (with respect to $\hat{x}$). This ray is denoted by the set $\{x: x \in R^n, x = \alpha\hat{x}, \alpha \geq 0, \alpha \in R\}$. In the above triplet, p is called the **(von Neumann) price**, and λ is called the **(von Neumann) interest factor** [or sometimes the **(von Neumann) growth factor**]. An evaluation of process $(x, y) \in T$ by $p \cdot (y - \lambda x)$, where p is the von Neumann price and λ is the von Neumann interest factor, is called the **von Neumann value** (or the **von Neumann profit**) of the process (x, y).

> *REMARK*:   Set $y = \lambda\hat{x}$ and $x = \hat{x}$ in condition (ii) of the definition of the von Neumann triplet. Then we have $p \cdot (y - \lambda x) = p \cdot (\lambda\hat{x} - \lambda\hat{x}) = 0$. In other words, the von Neumann value of the von Nuemann process $(\hat{x}, \lambda\hat{x})$ is zero.

> We now assume:

(A-3)   There exists a von Neumann triplet.

> *REMARK*:   In Chapter 6, Section A, we proved the "von Neumann theorem" which asserts the existence of a von Neumann triplet under (A-1), (A-2), and the following:

> **(Convexity)** T is convex.
> **(Free disposability)** $(x, y) \in T$, $x' \geq x$ and $0 \leq y' \leq y$ imply $(x', y') \in T$.
> **(Productiveness)**   There exists an $(x, y) \in T$ such that $y > 0$.

Radner imposed the following assumption which qualifies the von Neumann triplet:

(A-4)   Let $(\hat{x}, p, \lambda)$ be a von Neumann triplet. Then $p \cdot (y - \lambda x) < 0$ for all (x, y)'s in T that are not *proportional* to $(\hat{x}, \lambda\hat{x})$, that is, those (x, y)'s in T which are not on the von Neumann ray *with respect to $\hat{x}$.*

> *REMARK*:   It is important to note that (A-4) guarantees the uniqueness of a von Neumann ray. Radner remarked that (A-4) can be obtained from the following assumption:

> **(A-4′)**   The set T has a nonempty interior and is a **strictly convex cone**, in the sense that $z, z' \in T$, with z' not proportional to z, implies $\theta z + (1 - \theta)z'$ is in the interior of T for any θ where $0 < \theta < 1$.

> That (A-4′) implies (A-4) can be proved as follows. Suppose (A-4) does not hold, so that there exists an $(x', y') \in T$, which is not proportional to

$(\hat{x}, \lambda\hat{x})$, but $p \cdot (y' - \lambda x') = 0$. Let $(x, y) \equiv \frac{1}{2}(\hat{x}, \lambda\hat{x}) + \frac{1}{2}(x', y')$. Then $p \cdot (y - \lambda x) = 0$. But (x, y) is in the interior of T from (A-4'). Hence for sufficiently small a and b, $(x + a, y + b) \in T$ and $p \cdot (b - \lambda a) > 0$. The last inequality implies that $p \cdot [(y + b) - \lambda(x + a)] > 0$, which contradicts that $(\hat{x}, p, \lambda)$ is a von Neumann triplet [see condition (ii) of the definition of the von Neumann triplet].

REMARK: Assumption (A-4') is very restrictive for it precludes the case in which T is a convex polyhedral cone. Morishima [22] assumed that T is a convex polyhedral cone but imposed a quite restrictive assumption which in fact implies the *uniqueness* of the von Neumann ray.

The economy has preferences among the feasible sequences $\{x_t\}_0^N$. It is assumed that these preferences depend only upon the terminal state x_N and that the preference is represented by a real-valued function $u(x)$ defined on the non-negative orthant of R^n. Following Radner [25], we impose the following assumptions on u:

(A-5) The function $u(x)$ is nonnegative and continuous and there exists an $\bar{x} \geq 0$, $\bar{x} \in R^n$, such that $u(\bar{x}) > 0$.
(A-6) The function $u(x)$ is homogeneous of degree one.

An obvious example is $u(x) = p^* \cdot x$, where p^* is a nonzero n-vector whose elements are all nonnegative. The vector p^* can be interpreted as the price or the weight vector associated with the terminal commodity vector. Another example of $u(x)$ is the "Cobb-Douglas" utility function

$$u(x) = \prod_{i=1}^{n} x_i \alpha_i, \; \alpha_i > 0, \; \sum_{i=1}^{n} \alpha_i = 1$$

We are now ready to define the optimal feasible path.

Definition (optimality): A feasible path $\{x_t\}$, $t = 0, 1, 2, \ldots, N$, starting from $\bar{x}_0$, is said to be **optimal** if it maximizes $u(x_N)$ among the set of all the feasible paths starting from $\bar{x}_0$.

c. FREE DISPOSABILITY AND THE CONDITIONS FOR OPTIMALITY
If we allow free disposability, the optimal feasible path can then be considered as a solution of the following nonlinear programming problem:

PROBLEM I:

Maximize: $u(y_N)$
$\{(x_t, y_t)\}_0^N$
Subject to:
$x_t \leq y_{t-1}$, $t = 1, 2, \ldots, N$
$x_0 \leq \bar{x}_0$
and $(x_t, y_t) \in T$, $t = 0, 1, \ldots, N$

Here the inequalities presuppose free disposability. With free disposability, a **feasible path** (starting from $\bar{x}_0$) is now defined as a sequence $\{(x_t, y_t)\}$, $t = 0$, $1, \ldots, N$, such that $x_t \leqq y_{t-1}$, $t = 1, 2, \ldots, N$, $x_0 \leqq \bar{x}_0$ and $(x_t, y_t) \in T$ for all t.

Now consider the following vector maximum problem:

PROBLEM II:

$$\text{Maximize: } y_N$$
$$\{(x_t, y_t)\}_0^N$$

Subject to:
$$x_t \leqq y_{t-1}, t = 1, 2, \ldots, N$$
$$x_0 \leqq \bar{x}_0$$
$$\text{and } (x_t, y_t) \in T, t = 0, 1, \ldots, N$$

Here the inequalities again presuppose free disposability. Suppose, for example, u is concave and "Slater's condition" holds [that is, there exists an $(\bar{x}, \bar{y}) \in T$ such that $\bar{x} < x_0$ and $\bar{x} < \bar{y}$]; then the solution to Problem II may be regarded as a solution to Problem I with the following particular utility function:

$$u(y_N) = p^* \cdot y_N, p^* \geqq 0, p^* \neq 0$$

(Recall Theorem 1.E.4.) Clearly this utility function, as remarked before, satisfies assumptions (A-5) and (A-6). Since it may be rather artificial to conceive of a utility function for the economy in which the consumers are not explicit, the formulation of optimality in terms of Problem II may be better than that in terms of Problem I. In this subsection, we use the formulation in terms of Problem II.

> *REMARK:* In the above, we assumed free disposability and used the inequality constraints. This was done to utilize the ready-made theorems developed in Chapter 1, and hence to relate the present discussion to that chapter. In general, the free disposability assumption is not essential, and the results in the present subsection follow in the main without such an assumption by using the equality constraints.

Here we may digress from Radner's discussion of the turnpike theorem and characterize the optimal feasible path (à la Problem II). In other words, by applying a theorem on vector maximum (especially Theorem 1.E.4), we can assert the following:

Theorem 7.A.1:   *Suppose $\{(\hat{x}_t, \hat{y}_t)\}$, $t = 0, 1, \ldots, N$, is a solution to Problem II and suppose that there exists an $(\bar{x}, \bar{y}) \in T$ such that $\bar{x} < \bar{x}_0$ and $\bar{x} < \bar{y}$. Then there exist $p^* \geqq 0$, $p^* \neq 0$, and $p_t \geqq 0$, $t = 0, 1, \ldots, N$, such that*

$$p_{t+1} \cdot \hat{y}_t - p_t \cdot \hat{x}_t \geqq p_{t+1} \cdot y_t - p_t \cdot x_t, t = 0, 1, \ldots, N - 1$$

for all $(x_t, y_t) \in T$, $t = 0, 1, \ldots, N - 1$,

$$p^* \cdot \hat{y}_N - p_N \cdot \hat{x}_N \geqq p^* \cdot y_N - p_N \cdot x_N$$

for all $(x_N, y_N) \in T$, and

$$p_t \cdot (\hat{y}_{t-1} - \hat{x}_t) = 0, \ t = 1, \ldots, N$$

$$p_0 \cdot (\bar{x}_0 - \hat{x}_0) = 0$$

REMARK: By interpreting the p_t's as prices, the above inequalities signify that profit in each period is maximized. A similar theorem is proved by McKenzie [19] using the separation theorem. The result corresponds to that of Malinvaud [15] and Koopmans [13].

PROOF: Note that the saddle-point condition implies the above *equalities* and

$$p^* \cdot \hat{y}_N + \sum_{t=1}^{N} p_t \cdot (\hat{y}_{t-1} - \hat{x}_t) + p_0 \cdot (\bar{x}_0 - \hat{x}_0)$$

$$\geq p^* \cdot y_N + \sum_{t=1}^{N} p_t \cdot (y_{t-1} - x_t) + p_0 \cdot (\bar{x}_0 - x_0)$$

for all (x_t, y_t)'s in T. Then rewrite this inequality as

$$(p^* \cdot \hat{y}_N - p_N \cdot \hat{x}_N) + \sum_{t=0}^{N-1} (p_{t+1} \cdot \hat{y}_t - p_t \cdot \hat{x}_t) + p_0 \cdot \bar{x}_0$$

$$\geq (p^* \cdot y_N - p_N \cdot x_N) + \sum_{t=0}^{N-1} (p_{t+1} \cdot y_t - p_t \cdot x_t) + p_0 \cdot \bar{x}_0$$

Then set $(x_t, y_t) = (\hat{x}_t, \hat{y}_t)$ for all t except $\bar{t}$. Noting that the choice of $\bar{t}$ is arbitrary, we obtain the conclusion of the theorem.   (Q.E.D.)

REMARK: If the relations in the conclusion of the theorem hold with $p^* > 0$ and if $\{(\hat{x}_t, \hat{y}_t)\}$ is feasible, then $\{(\hat{x}_t, \hat{y}_t)\}$ is optimal. In other words, the converse of the above theorem also holds if $p^* > 0$. This is easy to see by recalling Theorem 1.E.5.

REMARK: If $\bar{x}_0$ is *on* the von Neumann ray with respect to $(\hat{x}, p, \lambda)$, where $\hat{x} \geq 0$, $p > 0$, and $\lambda > 0$, then we can show that the von Neumann path $\{(\hat{x}, \lambda \hat{x})\}$ starting from $\bar{x}_0 \geq 0$ satisfies the conditions (that is, conclusions) of the previous theorem, and hence is optimal because of the previous remark.[3] To see this, first note that $\bar{x}_0 = \alpha \hat{x}$ for some $\alpha > 0$, since $\bar{x}_0$ is on the von Neumann ray. Without loss of generality, we may choose $\hat{x}$ so that $\bar{x}_0 = \hat{x}$. Now set

$$\hat{x}_t \equiv \lambda^t \hat{x}, \quad \hat{y}_t \equiv \lambda^{t+1} \hat{x}, \quad p_t \equiv \lambda^{-t} p, \quad t = 0, 1, 2, \ldots, N$$

(λ is interpreted as the growth factor or the interest factor.) Then observe that

$$p_{t+1} \cdot \hat{y}_t - p_t \cdot \hat{x}_t = (\lambda^{-(t+1)} p) \cdot (\lambda^{t+1} \hat{x}) - (\lambda^{-t} p) \cdot (\lambda^t \hat{x}) = 0, \quad \text{for all } t$$

On the other hand, in view of condition (ii) of the definition of the von

Neumann equilibrium,

$$p \cdot (y_t - \lambda x_t) \leq 0, \qquad \text{for all } (x_t, y_t) \in T$$

That is,

$$p_{t+1} \cdot y_t - p_t \cdot x_t \leq 0, \qquad \text{for all } (x_t, y_t) \in T$$

Hence we obtain

$$p_{t+1} \cdot \hat{y}_t - p_t \cdot \hat{x}_t \geq p_{t+1} \cdot y_t - p_t \cdot x_t, \quad \text{for all } (x_t, y_t) \in T, t = 0, 1, \ldots, N$$

where we set $p^* = p_{N+1}$. It is elementary to see that the other conditions set in Theorem 7.A.1 also hold.

REMARK: The above theorem is, in essence, concerned with the saddle-point characterization of the optimal feasible program. Let us now consider the quasi-saddle-point characterization. To do this, first write the production set T as

$$T \equiv \{(x, y): F(x, y) \geq 0, (x, y) \in \Omega^{2n}\}$$

where the production function F is assumed to be continuously differentiable and concave. Consider Problem II and assume again that the Slater condition holds for this problem [that is, there exists an $(\bar{x}, \bar{y}) \in \Omega^{2n}$ such that $\bar{x} < \bar{x}_0, \bar{x} < \bar{y}$, and $F(\bar{x}, \bar{y}) > 0$]. The Lagrangian of this problem can be written as

$$p^* \cdot y_N + \sum_{t=1}^{N} p_t \cdot (y_{t-1} - x_t) + p_0 \cdot (\bar{x}_0 - x_0) + \sum_{t=0}^{N} q_t F(x_t, y_t)$$

Let $(\hat{x}_t, \hat{y}_t)$, $t = 0, 1, 2, \ldots, N$, be the solution for Problem II. Write the ith element of $\hat{x}_t, \hat{y}_t, p_t$, and p^* as $\hat{x}_t^i, \hat{y}_t^i, p_t^i$, and p_i^*, respectively. Then, assuming an interior solution for all t (that is, $\hat{x}_t > 0$ and $\hat{y}_t > 0$ for all t) and $p^* > 0$, the following quasi-saddle-point conditions are necessary and sufficient for an optimum:

$$-p_t^i + q_t \frac{\partial F(\hat{x}_t, \hat{y}_t)}{\partial x_t^i} = 0, \, i = 1, 2, \ldots, n; \, t = 0, 1, \ldots, N$$

$$p_{t+1} + q_t \frac{\partial F(\hat{x}_t, \hat{y}_t)}{\partial y_t^i} = 0, \, i = 1, 2, \ldots, n; \, t = 0, 1, \ldots, N-1$$

$$p_i^* + q_N \frac{\partial F(\hat{x}_N, \hat{y}_N)}{\partial y_N^i} = 0, \, i = 1, 2, \ldots, n$$

$$\hat{y}_{t-1} - \hat{x}_t \geq 0, \, p_t \cdot (\hat{y}_{t-1} - \hat{x}_t) = 0, \, t = 1, 2, \ldots, N$$

$$\bar{x}_0 - \hat{x}_0 \geq 0, \, p_0 \cdot (\bar{x}_0 - \hat{x}_0) = 0$$

$$F(\hat{x}_t, \hat{y}_t) \geq 0, \, q_t F(\hat{x}_t, \hat{y}_t) = 0, \, t = 0, 1, 2, \ldots, N$$

$$p^* > 0, \, p_t \geq 0, \, q_t \geq 0, \, t = 0, 1, 2, \ldots, N$$

Here $\partial F(\hat{x}_t, \hat{y}_t)/\partial y_t{}^i$ and $\partial F(\hat{x}_t, \hat{y}_t)/\partial x_t{}^i$ denote that these partial derivatives are evaluated at $(\hat{x}_t, \hat{y}_t)$. Assume $p_t > 0$ and $q_t > 0$ for all t. Then we have $\hat{y}_{t-1} = \hat{x}_t,\ t = 1, 2, \ldots, N,\ \hat{x}_0 = \overline{x}_0$, and $F(\hat{x}_t, \hat{y}_t) = 0,\ t = 0, 1, 2, \ldots, N$. Moreover, the first two sets of conditions yield

$$\frac{\partial F(\hat{x}_{t-1}, \hat{y}_{t-1})/\partial y_{t-1}{}^i}{\partial F(\hat{x}_{t-1}, \hat{y}_{t-1})/\partial y_{t-1}{}^j} = \frac{\partial F(x_t, y_t)/\partial x_t{}^i}{\partial F(\hat{x}_t, \hat{y}_t)/\partial x_t{}^j}, t = 1, \ldots, N, \text{ and } i, j = 1, \ldots, n$$

This is the famous intertemporal efficiency condition obtained by DOSSO [2]. In other words, this corresponds to the following remark by them ([2], p. 312):

> A necessary condition for intertemporal efficiency is the following: the MRS between any two goods regarded as outputs of the previous period must equal their MRS as inputs for the next period.

This condition is illustrated in Figure 7.2 for the two-commodity case. The location of the production isoquant for producing y_t obviously depends on the location of y_t. In Figure 7.2, the above (tangency) condition determines the location of $\hat{y}_t$.

In the vector maximum problem (that is, Problem II), $\hat{y}_N$ (and hence the path leading to $\hat{y}_N$) are not, in general, unique. The value of p^* depends on $\hat{y}_N$. However, in Problem I, $\hat{y}_N$ is unique if the utility function u is strictly quasi-concave. Then p^* is unique, and the path $(\hat{x}_t, \hat{y}_t)$ that leads to $\hat{y}_N$ can be unique (as can be seen from Figure 7.2).

d.   THE RADNER TURNPIKE THEOREM

We now proceed to Radner's turnpike theorem returning to the model developed in subsection b. His turnpike theorem states that any optimal feasible path, *regardless of the initial commodity vector* $\overline{x}_0$, spends most of the time sufficiently "close" to the von Neumann ray. To define "closeness," we have to define "distance."

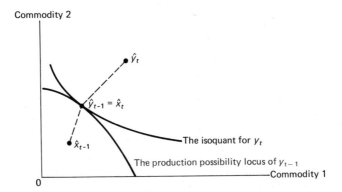

Figure 7.2.   An Illustration of the Intertemporal Optimality Condition.

Definition: The **(Radner) distance** between two vectors z' and z'' is defined as

$$d(z', z'') \equiv \left\| \frac{z'}{\|z'\|} - \frac{z''}{\|z''\|} \right\|$$

where $\|z\|$ refers to the Euclidian norm, that is, $\|z\| \equiv (z \cdot z)^{\frac{1}{2}}$.

REMARK: In this definition, it is not essential that $\|z\|$ be the Euclidian norm. It can be replaced by other norms such as $\|z\| \equiv \sum_{i=1}^{n} |z_i|$. The essential point is that the distance between two vectors be measured in a "normalized way." The above concept of distance may be illustrated in Figure 7.3.

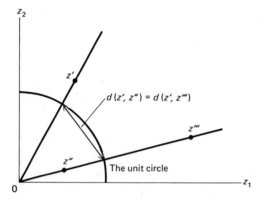

Figure 7.3. An Illustration of Distance.

In proving the main theorem, Radner first proved the following lemma, which is crucial to the proof of his main theorem. It is often referred to as **Radner's lemma.** Here we do *not* assume free disposability.

Radner's Lemma: *Suppose that (A-1), (A-2), (A-3), and (A-4) hold, and let $(\hat{x}, p, \lambda)$ be a von Neuman triplet. Then for any $\epsilon > 0$, there exists a $\delta, 0 < \delta < \lambda$, such that $(x, y) \in T$ and $d(x, \hat{x}) \geq \epsilon$ imply $p \cdot y \leq (\lambda - \delta)(p \cdot x)$.*

REMARK: If $(x, y) \in T$ is on a von Neumann ray, then $p \cdot y = \lambda(p \cdot x)$; that is, the value of the output is λ times the value of the input. Radner's lemma asserts that whenever the distance from the process $(x, y) \in T$ to a given von Neumann ray [or, equivalently, to $(\hat{x}, \lambda\hat{x})$] exceeds some number ϵ, then the value of the output falls short of λ times the value of the input for such a process (x, y), by some proportion δ, as long as $p \cdot x > 0$. In other words, there is a certain "value loss" associated with such a process. It is easy to see that the lemma is crucial in establishing the turnpike theorem. Suppose, for example, that a feasible program $\{x_t\}$, $t = 0, 1, \ldots, N$, deviates from a given von Neumann path in many periods. Then the sum of the values lost may be excessive. If we could link the "value loss" to the optimality criterion, we would be able to obtain a turnpike theorem. Note that the uniqueness of the von Neumann ray appears to be essential, for if the von Neumann ray were not unique, a process not on a certain von Neumann ray might be on another von Neumann ray, thus causing no "value loss." The possibility of multiple von Neumann rays, which is assumed away both in Radner [25] and Morishima [22], is fully explored by McKenzie ([17] and [20]). It is argued that the collection of von Neumann rays constitutes a facet of T and that the turnpike theorem is then concerned with the conditions under which the optimal feasible path arches toward this facet (which can be n-dimensional). Radner's theorem is concerned with a special case in which this facet is one-dimensional. However, the proof for such a general case is analogous to that for the present case, and, in fact, McKenzie's method is essentially similar to Radner's method. Here, for the sake of simplicity, we assume the uniqueness of the von Neumann ray by way of (A-4).

We now turn to the proof of Radner's lemma.

PROOF:

(i) Since $p \cdot (y - \lambda x) \leq 0$ for all $(x, y) \in T$, $p \cdot x = 0$ implies $p \cdot y = 0$ whenever $(x, y) \in T$. Thus the conclusion of the lemma follows trivially when $p \cdot x = 0$. We may, henceforth, assume $p \cdot x \neq 0$, or $p \cdot x > 0$. Note that $p \cdot x \neq 0$ also precludes the case in which $x = 0$. Hence we take $x \neq 0$. [Note that the assertion of the lemma (with $p \cdot x > 0$) is that $(p \cdot y)/(p \cdot x) - \lambda < -\delta < 0$, that is, $[(p \cdot y)/(p \cdot x) - \lambda]$ is bounded away from 0.]

(ii) Define the set T_1 by

$$T_1 \equiv \{y: (x, y) \in T \text{ and } \| x \| = 1\}$$

We claim T_1 is bounded; otherwise there exists a sequence (x^s, y^s) such that $\| x^s \| = 1$ and $\| y^s \| \to \infty$ as $s \to \infty$. Since $x^s \neq 0$, we may choose y^s so that $y^s \neq 0$. Consider a sequence $(x^s/\| y^s \|, y^s/\| y^s \|)$ ($\because$ since $y^s \neq 0$, $\| y^s \| > 0$, so that the division by $\| y^s \|$ is possible). This is clearly a bounded sequence; hence it contains a convergent subsequence. Let $(\bar{x}, \bar{y})$ be its limit. Since $(x^s/\| y^s \|, y^s/\| y^s \|) \in T$ ($\because T$ is a cone) and since T is a closed set by (A-1), $(\bar{x}, \bar{y}) \in T$. Since $\| y^s \| \to \infty, \bar{x} = 0$. But $\| (y^s/\| y^s \|) \| = 1$ for all s so that $\| \bar{y} \| = 1$, or $\bar{y} \neq 0$. In other words, $(0, \bar{y}) \in T$ with $\bar{y} \neq 0$. This contradicts (A-2). Thus T_1 is bounded.

(iii) Now suppose that there is an $\epsilon > 0$ and a sequence $\{(x^q, y^q)\}$, $q = 1$, 2, ..., with $(x^q, y^q) \in T$ for all q for which $x^q \neq 0$ and $d(x^q, \hat{x}) \geq \epsilon > 0$ but for which $[(p \cdot y^q)/(p \cdot x^q) - \lambda] \to 0$ as $q \to \infty$. We will show that this will lead to a contradiction by using the fact just established that T_1 is bounded. Consider a sequence $\{(\check{x}^q, \check{y}^q)\}$ defined by $\check{x}^q \equiv x^q/\| x^q \|$ and $\check{y}^q \equiv y^q/\| x^q \|$ (the division by $\| x^q \|$ is possible as $x^q \neq 0$). Since T is a cone by (A-1), $(\check{x}^q, \check{y}^q) \in T$ for all $q = 1, 2, \ldots$. Moreover, $(\check{x}^q, \check{y}^q) \in T_1$ for all q. Hence $\{(\check{x}^q, \check{y}^q)\}$ is a bounded sequence. Therefore it contains a convergent subsequence. Let $(\check{x}, \check{y})$ be the limit of this subsequence. Because T is closed by (A-1), $(\check{x}, \check{y}) \in T$. Since $\| \check{x}^q \| = 1$ for all q,

$\| \tilde{x} \| = 1$, or $\tilde{x} \neq 0$. Since $(p \cdot y^q)/(p \cdot x^q) = (p \cdot \tilde{y}^q)/(p \cdot \tilde{x}^q)$ and $(p \cdot y^q)/(p \cdot x^q) \to \lambda$ as $q \to \infty$ by assumption, we have $(p \cdot \tilde{y})/(p \cdot \tilde{x}) = \lambda$ by the continuity of the inner product. Therefore $p \cdot \tilde{y} = \lambda(p \cdot \tilde{x})$. But $d(\tilde{x}^q, \hat{x}) = d(x^q, \hat{x}) \geq \epsilon > 0$ by assumption, for all $q = 1, 2, \ldots$, so that $d(\tilde{x}, \hat{x}) \geq \epsilon > 0$, which, in turn, implies $(\tilde{x}, \hat{y})$ cannot be proportional to $(\hat{x}, \lambda\hat{x})$; hence $p \cdot \tilde{y} < \lambda(p \cdot \tilde{x})$, from (A-4). This contradicts the above equality $p \cdot \tilde{y} = \lambda(p \cdot \tilde{x})$. Hence $(p \cdot y^q)/(p \cdot x^q)$ cannot approach λ. Note that $(p \cdot y^q)/(p \cdot x^q) - \lambda < 0$ for any $(x^q, y^q) \in T$ that is not proportional to $(\hat{x}, \lambda\hat{x})$ (with $p \cdot x^q > 0$). This does not preclude the possibility that $[(p \cdot y^q)/(p \cdot x^q) - \lambda]$ approaches 0. But we have just denied this possibility. This proves that $[(p \cdot y)/(p \cdot x) - \lambda]$ is bounded away from zero whenever $(x, y) \in T$ and $d(x, \hat{x}) \geq \epsilon > 0$. The fact that $\delta \leq \lambda$ is obvious, for otherwise $p \cdot y < 0$, which is a contradiction.   (Q.E.D.)

The next step of Radner's proof of his turnpike theorem is to construct a reference path which coincides with the von Neumann ray except for the initial state, and then to show that this reference path is better than any feasible path that departs too far and for too long from the von Neumann ray (hence such a path cannot be optimal). Note that this reference path itself may not be optimal. Before we proceed to the statement and the proof of the Radner turnpike theorem, we introduce the following additional assumptions:

(A-7)   An initial commodity vector $\bar{x}_0$ is given such that there exists a real number $k > 0$ such that $(\bar{x}_0, k\hat{x}) \in T$.
(A-8)   There exists a real number $a > 0$ such that $u(x) \leq a(p \cdot x)$ for all commodity vectors x.
(A-9) $u(\hat{x}) > 0$.

REMARK: Assumption (A-8) is satisfied if, for example, all the coordinates of p are positive. Assumption (A-7) is satisfied if, for example, there is free disposability and x_0 provides positive amounts of all those commodities. This assumption enables the economy to reach the von Neumann ray one period after the initial time, starting from an arbitrary initial point $\bar{x}_0$. Assumption (A-7) can be slightly weakened as follows: An initial vector $\bar{x}_0$ is given such that there exists a feasible sequence $\{x_t\}$, $t = 0, 1, \ldots, N_0(N_0 \geq 1)$, starting from the given value of $\bar{x}_0$ at $t = 0$, such that $x_{N0} = k\hat{x}$ for some $k > 0$. In other words, the economy can reach the von Neumann ray within a finite number of periods. Assumption (A-9) can be weakened as follows (as pointed out by Radner [25]): For some integer $N_1 \geq 0$ and some commodity vector y for which $u(y) > 0$, there is a feasible sequence from $\hat{x}$ to y in N_1 periods.

Theorem 7.A.2 (Radner's turnpike theorem):   *Let $(\hat{x}, p, \lambda)$ be a von Neumann triplet. Suppose that assumptions (A-1) to (A-9) hold. Let $\{\hat{x}_t\}$, $t = 0, 1, 2, \ldots, N$, be an optimal feasible path with respect to $\bar{x}_0$. Then, for any $\epsilon > 0$, there is a number $\bar{N}$ such that the number of periods in which $d(x_t, \hat{x}) \geq \epsilon$ cannot exceed $\bar{N}$.*

PROOF: First we define a **reference path** $\{\tilde{x}_t\}$, $t = 0, 1, 2, \ldots, N$, as a feasible path such that

$$\tilde{x}_0 = \bar{x}_0, \; \tilde{x}_1 = k\hat{x}$$

and

$$\tilde{x}_t = k\lambda^{t-1}\hat{x}, \; t = 1, 2, \ldots, N$$

The existence of a $k > 0$ is guaranteed by (A-7). Let $\{x_t\}$, $t = 0, 1, \ldots, N$, be an arbitrary feasible path which starts from a given initial point $\bar{x}_0$. Consider any $\epsilon > 0$. Then for any t for which $d(x_t, \hat{x}) \geq \epsilon$, there exists a $\delta > 0$ such that

$$p \cdot x_{t+1} \leq (\lambda - \delta)p \cdot x_t$$

by Radner's lemma. Also

$$p \cdot x_{t+1} \leq \lambda p \cdot x_t$$

for any $(x_t, x_{t+1}) \in T$. Suppose that $d(x_t, \hat{x}) \geq \epsilon$ for N' periods. Then we have

$$p \cdot x_N \leq (\lambda - \delta)^{N'}\lambda^{N-N'}(p \cdot \bar{x}_0)$$

Then, by (A-8), there exists an $a > 0$ such that

$$u(x_N) \leq a(p \cdot x_N) \leq a(\lambda - \delta)^{N'}\lambda^{N-N'}(p \cdot \bar{x}_0)$$

On the other hand, by the homogeneity of u, (A-6),

$$u(\tilde{x}_N) = k\lambda^{N-1}u(\hat{x})$$

Hence, in view of (A-9), we have

$$\frac{u(x_N)}{u(\tilde{x}_N)} \leq b\left(\frac{\lambda - \delta}{\lambda}\right)^{N'}, \text{ where } b \equiv \frac{a\lambda p \cdot \bar{x}_0}{ku(\hat{x})}$$

Hence for $\{x_t\}$ to be an optimal feasible path with respect to $\bar{x}_0$, it is necessary that

$$b\left(\frac{\lambda - \delta}{\lambda}\right)^{N'} \geq 1$$

or

$$\log b + N' \log \frac{\lambda - \delta}{\lambda} \geq 0$$

Here it is essential to note that $\delta < \lambda$; for, otherwise, $\log\left[(\lambda - \delta)/\lambda\right]$ makes no sense. The above inequality can be rewritten as

$$N' \leq \frac{\log b}{\log\left(\dfrac{\lambda}{\lambda - \delta}\right)}$$

Define $\bar{N}$ by

$$\bar{N} \equiv \max \left\{ 1, \frac{\log b}{\log\left(\frac{\lambda}{\lambda - \delta}\right)} \right\}$$

(Q.E.D.)

REMARK: The number $\bar{N}$ gives the maximum number of periods that any optimal feasible path can remain at a distance exceeding ϵ from the von Neumann ray. It is crucial to observe that $\bar{N}$ is independent of the planning period N. Hence if N is sufficiently large, N becomes sufficiently larger than $\bar{N}$ and any optimal feasible path starting from an arbitrary initial point spends "most" of its time within the ϵ-distance from the von Neumann ray. Note also that Radner's theorem (just as several other versions of the turnpike theorems) does not advocate that any optimal feasible path must be on the von Neumann ray most of the time. It requires only that it must be sufficiently close to the von Neumann ray most of the time.

One of the difficulties in Radner's turnpike theorem is that it does not preclude the possibility that an optimal feasible path may run out of the neighboring ϵ-cone of the von Neumann ray around the halfway point of the entire programming period. In other words, the optimal feasible path may enter and leave the neighboring ϵ-cone several times. In this sense, Radner's theorem is sometimes referred to as a **hop-skip-jumping turnpike theorem** or a **weak turnpike theorem**. This possibility can, with certain additional assumptions, be ruled out. Such a theorem is often referred to as a **strong turnpike theorem**. In terms of the Radner type model, such a theorem is proved by Nikaido [23] and Inada [10].[4] Nikaido [23] imposed the following assumptions in addition to the assumptions of Radner's theorem.

(N-1) For any $x \geq 0$ there is some y such that $(x, y) \in T$, where y can be 0.
(N-2) $\hat{x} > 0$.
(N-3) The function $u(x)$ is such that $x > x' \geq 0$ implies $u(x) > u(x')$.

Assumption (N-1) is related to but weaker than the usual free disposability assumption, which says that $(x, y) \in T$, $x' \geq x$, and $y' \leq y$ imply $(x', y') \in T$. Assumption (N-3) is satisfied if, for example, $u(x) = p^* \cdot x$ with $p^* > 0$.

Under these additional assumptions, Nikaido's strong turnpike theorem ([23], p. 154) asserts the following:

For any $\epsilon > 0$, there is a number N_1 such that, for any N and for any optimal feasible program, $\{\hat{x}_t\}$, $t = 0, 1, \ldots, N$, starting from an arbitrarily given x_0, we have

$$d(\hat{x}_t, \hat{x}) < \epsilon \qquad for \ N_1 \leq t \leq N - N_1$$

FOOTNOTES

1. The extension of the turnpike theorems to the model in which consumption is allowed may be referred to as the **neo-turnpike theorems**.

2. For an excellent attempt to survey various turnpike theorems, see Turnovsky [32], for example.

3. Obviously this is not necessarily true, if the prescribed initial stock $\bar{x}_0$ is not on the von Neumann ray. On the other hand, we can conclude that any balanced growth path other than the von Neumann path is not optimal even if the initial stock $\bar{x}_0$ is on such a path. This is owing to the observation made in the previous remark that the converse of the above theorem also holds.

4. In this connection, we should point out Tsukui's contribution [28]. In a Leontief type model with alternative techniques, he proved a strong turnpike theorem as well as other results. The result of this paper overlaps with those in McKenzie [17], Drandakis [3], and Tsukui [29]. As in [29], Tsukui in [28], also proved a "dual theorem" which shows the turnpike behavior of the shadow prices of the efficient path about the von Neumann price ray. Strikingly enough, his [28] was apparently completed in February 1961 (as a Ph.D. thesis at the Hitotsubashi University), and it appears to be independent even of pioneering works by Morishima [22] and Radner [25]. Tsukui's contribution in [28] seems to be unduly ignored. In this connection, the truly pioneering nature of the Japanese edition (published in 1957) of Furuya and Inada [4] in the turnpike literature should be emphasized. Incidentally, Nikaido [23] was apparently written under the stimulus of Tsukui [28] (see [23], p. 151).

REFERENCES

1. Atsumi, H., "Neoclassical Growth and the Efficient Program of Capital Accumulation," *Review of Economic Studies*, XXXII, April 1965.

2. Dorfman, R. A., Samuelson, P. A., and Solow, R. M., *Linear Programming and Economic Analysis*, New York, McGraw-Hill, 1958, chap. 12.

3. Drandakis, E. M., "On Efficient Accumulation Paths in the Closed Production Model," *Econometrica*, 34, April 1966.

4. Furuya, H., and Inada, K., "Balanced Growth and Intertemporal Efficiency in Capital Accumulation," *International Economic Review*, 3, January 1962.

5. Gale, D., "The Closed Linear Model of Production," in *Linear Inequalities and Related Systems*, ed. by H. W. Kuhn, and A. W. Tucker, Princeton, N.J., Princeton University Press, 1956.

6. ———, "On Optimal Development in a Multi-Sector Economy," *Review of Economic Studies*, XXXIV, January 1967.

7. Hahn, F. H., and Matthews, R. C. O., "The Theory of Economic Growth: A Survey," *Economic Journal*, LXXIV, December 1964.

8. Hicks, J. R., "The Story of Mare's Nest," *Review of Economic Studies*, XXVIII, February 1961.

9. ———, *Capital and Growth*, Oxford, Clarendon Press, 1965.

10. Inada, K., "Some Structural Characteristics of Turnpike Theorems," *Review of Economic Studies*, XXXI, January 1964.

11. Karlin, S., *Mathematical Methods and Theory in Games, Programming and Economics*, Vol. 1, Reading, Mass., Addison-Wesley, 1959.

12. Kemeny, J. G., Morgenstern, O., and Thompson, G. L., "A Generalization of the von Neumann Model of an Expanding Economy," *Econometrica*, 24, April 1956.

13. Koopmans, T. C., "Analysis of Production as an Efficient Combination of Activities," in *Activity Analysis of Production and Allocation*, ed. by T. C. Koopmans, Cowles Foundation Monograph, No. 13, New York, Wiley, 1951, chap. 3.

14. ———, "Economic Growth at a Maximal Rate," *Quarterly Journal of Economics*, LXXVIII, August 1964.

15. Malinvaud, E., "Capital Accumulation and Efficient Allocation of Resources," *Econometrica*, 21, April 1953.

16. ———, "Efficient Capital Accumulation: A Corrigendum," *Econometrica*, 30, July 1962.

17. McKenzie, L. W., "Turnpike Theorems for a Generalized Leontief Model," *Econometrica*, 31, January–April 1963.

18. ———, "The Dorfman-Samuelson-Solow Turnpike Theorem," *International Economic Review*, 4, January 1963.

19. ———, "The Turnpike Theorem of Morishima," *Review of Economic Studies*, XXX, October 1963.

20. ———, "Maximal Paths in the von Neumann Model," in *Activity Analysis in the Theory of Growth and Planning*, ed. by E. Malinvaud and M. O. L. Bacharach, London, Macmillan, 1967.

21. ———, "Accumulation Programs of Maximum Utility and the von Neumann Facet," in *Value, Capital and Growth, Papers in Honour of Sir John Hicks*, ed. by J. N. Wolfe, Edinburgh, Edinburgh University Press, 1968.

22. Morishima, M., "Proof of a Turnpike Theorem: The 'No Joint Production' Case," *Review of Economic Studies*, XXVIII, February 1961.

23. Nikaido, H., "Persistence of Continual Growth Near the von Neumann Ray," *Econometrica*, 32, January 1964.

24. Radner, R., *Notes on the Theory of Economic Planning*, Athens, Greece, Center of Economic Research, 1963.

25. ———, "Paths of Economic Growth that are Optimal with Regard Only to Final States: A Turnpike Theorem," *Review of Economic Studies*, XXVIII, February 1961.

26. Samuelson, P. A., "Efficient Paths of Capital Accumulation in Terms of the Calculus of Variations," in *Mathematical Methods in the Social Sciences, 1959*, ed. by Arrow, Karlin, and Suppes, Stanford, Calif., Stanford University Press, 1960.

27. Thompson, G. L., "On the Solution of a Game Theoretic Problem," in *Linear Inequalities and Related Systems*, ed. by H. W. Kuhn and A. W. Tucker, Princeton, N.J., Princeton University Press, 1956.

28. Tsukui, J., "Efficient and Balanced Growth Paths in a Dynamic Input-Output System—A Turnpike Theorem," *Economic Studies Quarterly*, XIII, 1, 1962 (in Japanese).

29. ———, "Turnpike Theorem in a Generalized Dynamic Input-Output System," *Econometrica*, 34, April 1966.

30. ———, "The Consumption and the Output Turnpike Theorems in a von Neumann Type of Model—A Finite Term Problem," *Review of Economic Studies*, XXXIV, January 1967.

31. ———, "Application of a Turnpike Theorem to Planning for Efficient Accumulation: An Example of Japan," *Econometrica*, 36, January 1968.

32. Turnovsky, S. J., "Turnpike Theorems and Efficient Economic Growth," Chapter 10 of *Mathematical Theories of Economic Growth*, by E. Burmeister and A. R. Dobell, New York, Macmillan, 1970.

33. von Neumann, J., "A Model of General Economic Equilibrium," *Review of Economic Studies*, XII, 1, 1945–46 (originally published in German, 1937).

34. Winter, S. G., "Some Properties of the Closed Linear Model of Production," *International Economic Review*, 6, May 1965.

35. ———, "The Norm of a Closed Technology and the Straight-Down-the-Turnpike Theorem," *Review of Economic Studies*, XXXIV, January 1967.

Section B

MULTISECTOR OPTIMAL GROWTH WITH CONSUMPTION

a. INTRODUCTION

In spite of all the excitement in the profession, the turnpike theory, at least in its earlier versions, has one major weakness: It assumes that the utility function is a function of the terminal stock of commodities only. This means that the economy's concern about the intermediate periods is restricted only to their effect on the terminal stock of commodities. The utility function in the (earlier) turnpike theory is defined only on the terminal stock of commodities and not on the stock of commodities in any intermediate period. As Koopmans remarked, "the purpose of economic activity is by implication assumed to be the fastest growth rather than the enjoyment of life by all generations" ([9], p. 357).

Ramsey, Koopmans, and Cass have overcome these shortcomings of the turnpike theory for a one-commodity economy. We have already discussed their problem in Chapter 5, Section D. For a multisector model Gale [6], then McKenzie [13], have made major progress and have provided an almost complete solution of the problem. In their treatment of the problem, the utility function depends on every intermediate state as well as on the terminal state. If s_t represents the state of period t relevant to satisfaction, Gale's utility function is represented as $\sum_{t=1}^{N} u(s_t)$ for an N-period program, or as $\sum_{t=1}^{\infty} u(s_t)$ for an infinite horizon program. Gale and McKenzie are concerned primarily with the optimal program when the time horizon is infinite. In this sense, they are addressing the same question for the multisector optimal growth problem that Ramsey, Koopmans, Cass, and so on, addressed for the one-sector optimal growth problem. Gale shows the existence of an optimal path by actually constructing such a path, which at the same time exhibits the basic characteristics of the optimal path. In arriving at this major result, Gale utilizes Radner's procedure in proving his turnpike theorem; hence a concept analogous to the von Neumann ray becomes essential in his procedure. For this purpose, he defines the concept of an "optimal stationary program"; then the "loss" associated with paths which deviate from this "optimal stationary program" plays a crucial role in establishing his major theorem. He confesses, "it may well be true that there is a more direct way of obtaining our existence theorem," but "the facts we pick up along the way are of economic interest in themselves describing properties of an 'optimal path'" ([6], p. 1).

Although in showing the existence and in characterizing the optimal path we essentially follow Gale's procedure, our presentation is more expository. In addition, it differs from Gale's presentation in the following respects:

(i) Gale assumed that the utility function is defined on the input-output process adopted at each period. If (x_t, y_t) denotes such a process, then $s_t = (x_t, y_t)$, and $\sum u(x_t, y_t)$ represents his utility series. Here (x_t, y_t) includes consumption activities such as eating cakes as well as production activities such as producing cakes. Although he claims that this is "the conceptually correct way" ([6], p. 6), and although he may be right in his defense, this has the weakness of obscuring the distinction between the production activity and the consumption activity, with minor implications such as obscuring the role of consumers' satiation. Certainly an activity of consuming cakes is essentially different from an activity of producing cakes and in economics it is often very important to make this distinction clear. It would be difficult to rewrite the entire theory of competitive markets (such as described in Chapter 2) by adopting Gale's procedure. Hence in this section we assume that the utility function is defined on consumption vectors instead of on input-output vectors. Such a procedure is certainly the case for the one-sector optimal growth theory à la Ramsey, Koopmans, and Cass.

(ii) In the discussion of the "optimal stationary program," Gale [7] utilized his new results in the theory of nonlinear programming and developed the Kuhn-Tucker theorem. We show that we can do the same job by utilizing the ordinary concave programming theory (Chapter 1, Section B) without any new result.

(iii) Brock [3] worries about Gale's assumption of strict concavity of the utility function. His worry is mainly due to the fact that it does not include the "von Neumann" economy. Although he followed Gale in defining a utility function on input-output vectors, Brock simplified Gale's procedure on one important point which we call "Brock's lemma." For a discussion of his other important contribution on the "weakly maximal program," the reader is referred to his paper [3].

A rough preview of this section is now in order. First, we may note that we agree with Gale about the importance of appreciating various "sceneries" in connection with the present problem. In subsection b, we formulate the basic model of this section. Then in subsection c, we discuss the finite horizon problem. There we show that every "competitive" program is "optimal" and that every "optimal" program is "competitive" (Theorems 7.B.1 and 7.B.2). (As pointed out by Malinvaud [11], similar theorems for the infinite horizon case would not hold without an important modification, that is, "cost minimization.") In subsection d, we switch to the finite horizon problem. First, we introduce the concept of "optimal stationary program" (**O.S.P.**). Theorem 7.B.3 asserts its existence and Theorem 7.B.4 asserts the price implications of the optimal stationary program. In the corollaries of Theorem 7.B.4, we discuss (i) the consumers' nonsatiation conditions which guarantee semipositiveness and strict positiveness of the price vector associated with the O.S.P, and (ii) the conditions which guarantee the uniqueness of the O.S.P. In subsection e, we compare an arbitrary "attainable" program (for the infinite horizon problem) with the O.S.P. In Theorem 7.B.5, we assert that no attainable program is "infinitely better" than the O.S.P. In Theorem 7.B.6, we characterize the attainable paths which are not "infinitely worse" than the O.S.P. (called the "eligible programs"). Theorem 7.B.7 establishes the existence of an eligible attainable program, and in Theorem 7.B.8, we assert that every eligible attainable program converges to the O.S.P. if the O.S.P. is unique. In subsection f, we turn to the optimal program for the infinite horizon problem and by Theorem 7.B.9, prove the crucial result of this section, the existence of the optimal attainable program. Before we prove Theorem 7.B.9, we introduce Brock's lemma, which is crucial to this theorem.

b.   THE MODEL

Consider an economy with n commodities. Let (x_t, y_t) denote the production process in period t where x_t and y_t, respectively, denote the (stock) input vector and the (stock) output vector. Let T be the set of such processes which are technologically feasible in the economy. Thus T is the **technology set** (or the **production set**) of the economy. Let c_t denote a consumption vector of the economy and let C be the set of all possible consumption vectors (not necessarily technologically feasible) in the economy. We assume that:

(A-1)   (i) The set T is a nonempty, compact, and convex subset of R^{2n}, and
    (ii) C is a nonempty, compact, and convex subset of R^n.

The set T is bounded because of some sort of resource limitation, which we clarify in an example later in this subsection, and C is bounded from below for the obvious reason of subsistence, and so on. We may assume that C is bounded from above owing to the physiological limitation of personal consumption, for if C is not bounded from above and if the economy can "grow" indefinitely as time extends without limit, then the above assumption would not hold. However, the justification for the upper bound of C may not be acceptable to some readers. One way to avoid this question is to introduce consumers' satiation, which imposes a practical upper bound on consumption; for example, recall Ramsey's "bliss" in [16]. Another way is to suppose an upper bound on capital accumulation resulting from capital satiation. The latter may be more acceptable. (See, for example, McKenzie [13].) If there is an upper bound on capital accumulation, then this, together with the lower bound on the consumption set, will practically make the relevant "attainable" set bounded, which makes the relevant consumption set bounded. In this connection, we may remind the reader of the procedure in the theory of competitive equilibria, in which the attainable set is "compactified." (See Debreu [4], pp. 76–78.)

In any case, we proceed with our analysis under the assumption that both T and C are bounded. Since both T and C are compact, $T \otimes C$ is also compact. That $T \otimes C$ is nonempty and convex follows from the fact that a product of nonempty convex sets is nonempty and convex. Hence (A-1) implies that $T \otimes C$ is nonempty, compact, and convex. Let r_0 denote the vector of the stock of commodities made available at the beginning of period 0. It is called the **initial resource vector**. Let Z be the set of all possible initial resource vectors. We assume that Z is a nonempty bounded subset of R^n.

We assume that the welfare of the society in period t can be represented by the utility function $u(c_t)$ such that:

(A-2)   The utility function $u(c_t)$ is continuous and concave on C.

Consider a sequence $\{(x_t, y_t, c_t)\}$, $t = 0, 1, 2, \ldots, N$, such that

(a) $(x_t, y_t) \in T,$ $t = 0, 1, 2, \ldots, N$
(b) $c_t \in C,$ $t = 0, 1, 2, \ldots, N$
(c) $x_0 + c_0 \leq r_0,$ $r_0 \in Z$
(d) $x_t + c_t \leq y_{t-1},$ $t = 1, 2, \ldots, N$

We call such a sequence $\{(x_t, y_t, c_t)\}$ an **N-period attainable program starting from** r_0. The set of all the N-period attainable programs starting from r_0 is denoted by $A_N(r_0)$. When $N \to \infty$, we can analogously define the **infinite horizon attainable program starting from** r_0. The movement of our economy, that is, a sequence $\{(x_t, y_t, c_t)\}$ where $(x_t, y_t) \in T$ and $c_t \in C$, is described by Figure 7.4

We now discuss an important example of the economy described above.

EXAMPLE: We consider an economy in which n "commodities" and one type of "labor" are involved. The essential characteristics of this "labor" are that it is indispensable for any production process and that it grows at a constant rate μ. Let a_{ij} be the amount of the ith commodity input per unit operation of the jth process and let b_{ij} be the amount of the ith commodity output per unit operation of the jth process. Here the unit operation of each process is measured by one unit input of "labor." We assume that $a_{ij} \geq 0$ and $b_{ij} \geq 0$ for all i and j. Let A and B be $n \times m$ matrices such that $A = [a_{ij}]$ and $B = [b_{ij}]$. The technology set may be defined as $\{(A \cdot v, B \cdot v): v \geq 0,$ $v \in R^m\}$, which is a convex polyhedral cone; hence it is closed but *not* bounded. Let L_t be the total labor available in period t. By assumption,

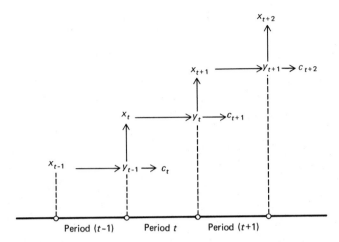

Figure 7.4.   An Illustration of the Movement of the Economy.

$L_t = (1 + \mu)L_{t-1}$. Assume $L_t > 0$ for all t. Let $\tilde{c}_t$ be the aggregate consumption vector of the economy. Assume that the consumption set is the entire nonnegative orthant of R^n. Let $R_0 \geqq 0$ be the initial resources. Then we have

PROGRAM α

$$A \cdot v_0 + \tilde{c}_0 \leqq R_0$$

$$A \cdot v_t + \tilde{c}_t \leqq B \cdot v_{t-1}, \qquad t = 1, 2, \ldots, N$$

$$0 \leqq \sigma \cdot v_t \ \leqq L_t, v_t \geqq 0 \text{ and } \tilde{c}_t \geqq 0, \qquad t = 0, 1, \ldots, N$$

where $\sigma \equiv (1, 1, \ldots, 1) \in R^m$

Divide both sides of these inequalities by L_t and set $c_t \equiv \tilde{c}_t/L_t, z_t \equiv v_t/L_t$, and $r_0 \equiv R_0/L_0$. Then we obtain

$$A \cdot z_0 + c_0 \leqq r_0$$

$$A \cdot z_t + c_t \leqq \frac{B \cdot z_{t-1}}{1 + \mu}, \qquad t = 1, 2, \ldots, N$$

$$0 \leqq \sigma \cdot z_t \ \leqq 1, z_t \geqq 0 \text{ and } c_t \geqq 0, \qquad t = 0, 1, \ldots, N$$

Write $x_t \equiv A \cdot z_t$ and $y_{t-1} = B \cdot z_{t-1}/(1 + \mu)$. Let $T \equiv \{(x_t, y_t): x_t = A \cdot z_t, y_t = B \cdot z_t/(1 + \mu), 0 \leqq \sigma \cdot z_t \leqq 1\}$. Clearly, T is nonempty, compact, and convex. We can now construct an attainable program.

PROGRAM β

$$(x_t, y_t) \in T, c_t \in \Omega^n$$

$$x_t + c_t \leqq y_{t-1}, \qquad t = 1, 2, \ldots, N$$

$$x_0 + c_0 \leqq r_0$$

Clearly program α and program β are equivalent in the sense that there exists a one-to-one correspondence by the rule defined above. Hence the set of utility sequences $u(\tilde{c}_t / L_t)$ in program α and the set of utility sequences $u(c_t)$ in program β are identical. Therefore, it suffices to consider only program β.

C.   FINITE HORIZON: OPTIMALITY AND COMPETITIVENESS
We now consider the following maximization problem for the finite-period problem:

$$\text{Maximize: } \sum_{\{(x_t, y_t, c_t)\}}^{N} \sum_{t=0}^{N} u(c_t)$$

$$\text{Subject to: } \{(x_t, y_t, c_t)\} \in A_N(r_0)$$

A solution $\{(\hat{x}_t, \hat{y}_t, \hat{c}_t)\}$ of the above problem is called an **optimal (attainable) program** with respect to $A_N(r_0)$. Note that a solution to the above problem may not exist. First of all, $A_N(r_0)$ may be empty. Moreover, even if $A_N(r_0)$ is not empty, the solution still may not exist. We now state the following assumptions:

(A-3)   The set $A_N(r_0)$ is nonempty and compact.
(A-4)   **(Productiveness)** Given r_0, there exist $(\bar{x}_t, \bar{y}_t) \in T, t = 0, 1, \ldots, N$, and $\bar{c}_t \in C$ such that $\bar{x}_t + \bar{c}_t < \bar{y}_{t-1}, t = 1, 2, \ldots, N$, and $\bar{x}_0 + \bar{c}_0 < r_0$.

Although the nonemptiness of T and C in (A-1) can be considered as preliminary to (A-3), it is not sufficient. For example, if r_0 is too small, then there exists no $c \in C$ and $(x, y) \in T$ such that $x + c \leqq r_0$. Assumption (A-4) implies that the economy is capable of expansion starting from r_0. Note the strict inequality in $\bar{x}_t + \bar{c}_t < \bar{y}_{t-1}$.

We can now assert that if (A-3) holds and if u is continuous by (A-2), then there exists an optimal program for $A_N(r_0)$ as a result of the Weierstrass theorem (Theorem 0.A.18). If u is *strictly* concave, we can show that the sequence $\{\hat{c}_t\}$ is unique. However, this does not imply that there exists a *unique* $(\hat{x}_t, \hat{y}_t) \in T$ corresponding to this unique $\hat{c}_t$. In other words, there can be many $(x_t, y_t) \in T$ such that $\{(x_t, y_t, \hat{c}_t)\} \in A_N(r_0)$ is optimal.

The problem thus stated very much resembles some problems which appear in the theory of competitive markets (for example, the Pareto optimum problem), and therefore we can obtain analogous results. The basic methodology is again nonlinear programming. We first define the following concept.

Definition (competitiveness): An N-period program $\{(\hat{x}_t, \hat{y}_t, \hat{c}_t)\}$ starting from r_0 with $(\hat{x}_t, \hat{y}_t) \in T$ and $\hat{c}_t \in C$ is called **competitive** if there exists a sequence of n-vectors $p_t \geq 0$, $t = 0, 1, 2, \ldots, N, N+1$ (called "price" vectors), such that

(i) $u(\hat{c}_t) - u(c_t) \geq p_t \cdot (\hat{c}_t - c_t)$ for all $c_t \in C, t = 0, 1, 2, \ldots, N$

(ii) $p_{t+1} \cdot \hat{y}_t - p_t \cdot \hat{x}_t \geq p_{t+1} \cdot y_t - p_t \cdot x_t$ for all $(x_t, y_t) \in T, t = 0, 1, \ldots, N$

(iii) $\{(\hat{x}_t, \hat{y}_t, \hat{c}_t)\} \in A_N(r_0), p_0 \cdot (r_0 - \hat{c}_0 - \hat{x}_0) = 0, p_t \cdot (\hat{y}_{t-1} - \hat{c}_t - \hat{x}_t) = 0$
$$t = 1, 2, \ldots, N \quad \text{and} \quad p_{N+1} = 0$$

REMARK: We define **competitiveness** for an infinite horizon program in a strictly analogous fashion.

REMARK: Condition (ii) is the condition for profit maximization and condition (iii) says that a competitive program must be attainable and that if a commodity is in excess supply for each period, its price becomes zero. Note that condition (i) implies that $u(\hat{c}_t) \geq u(c_t)$ for all $c_t \in C$ with $p_t \cdot \hat{c}_t \geq p_t \cdot c_t$, $t = 0, 1, 2, \ldots, N$, that is, utility is maximized subject to the budget condition. Note also that our definition is analogous to that of competitive equilibrium (Chapter 1, Section F).

REMARK: Strictly speaking, the supposition of an aggregate utility function is a very uncomfortable assumption. Instead, we may consider a society which consists of "consumers" who are immortal (immortal consumers can be justified by conceiving of each consumer as a family unit) and then define the utility function for each consumer. Many of the theorems and definitions in this section would then follow with suitable changes (for example, maximization of a real-valued function u is converted to vector maximization of a vector-valued function). We leave this task to interested readers. We should note, however, that there is a clear simplification in the exposition as a result of the supposition of an aggregate utility function, which also has the advantage of giving stronger results. Gale [6], for example, adopted this supposition of an aggregate utility function.

Our first theorem is analogous to the theorem that every competitive equilibrium is a Pareto optimum.

Theorem 7.B.1: *If a program $\{(\hat{x}_t, \hat{y}_t, \hat{c}_t)\} \in A_N(r_0)$ is competitive, then it is optimal.*

PROOF: Let $\{(x_t, y_t, c_t)\}$ be any other program in $A_N(r_0)$. By conditions (i) and (iii) of competitiveness, we have

(1)
$$u(\hat{c}_0) - u(c_0) \geq p_0 \cdot (\hat{c}_0 - c_0)$$
$$= p_0 \cdot (r_0 - \hat{x}_0) - p_0 \cdot (r_0 - x_0) = p_0 \cdot x_0 - p_0 \cdot \hat{x}_0$$

(2) $u(\hat{c}_t) - u(c_t) \geq p_t \cdot (\hat{c}_t - c_t) \geq p_t \cdot (\hat{y}_{t-1} - \hat{x}_t) - p_t \cdot (y_{t-1} - x_t)$
$$1 \leq t \leq N$$

(3) $$0 = p_{N+1} \cdot \hat{y}_N - p_{N+1} \cdot y_N$$

Summing from 0 to N and rearranging terms,

(4) $\sum\limits_{t=0}^{N} u(\hat{c}_t) - \sum\limits_{t=0}^{N} u(c_t) \geq \sum\limits_{t=0}^{N} \left[(p_{t+1} \cdot \hat{y}_t - p_t \cdot \hat{x}_t) - (p_{t+1} \cdot y_t - p_t \cdot x_t) \right]$

Then in view of condition (ii) of competitiveness, the RHS of the above inequality is nonnegative, which implies

$$\sum_{t=0}^{N} u(\hat{c}_t) \geq \sum_{t=0}^{N} u(c_t)$$

(Q.E.D.)

Next we prove the converse of the above theorem, which is analogous to the theorem in the theory of competitive markets that every Pareto optimum point can be achieved as a competitive equilibrium point.

Theorem 7.B.2: *Under (A-2) and (A-4), if $\{(\hat{x}_t, \hat{y}_t, \hat{c}_t)\}$ is an optimal program with respect to $A_N(r_0)$, then it is competitive.*

PROOF: By the hypothesis of the theorem, $\{(\hat{x}_t, \hat{y}_t, \hat{c}_t)\}$ maximizes

$$\sum_{t=0}^{N} u(c_t)$$

subject to $r_0 \geq x_0 + c_0, y_{t-1} \geq x_t + c_t, t = 1, 2, \ldots, N$
and $(x_t, y_t) \in T, c_t \in C, t = 0, 1, 2, \ldots, N$

Since u is concave and since Slater's condition is satisfied from (A-4), we can apply the Kuhn-Tucker-Uzawa theorem of concave programming (Theorem 1.B.3 and its corollary). In other words, there exist $p_t \geq 0, t = 0, 1, 2, \ldots, N$, such that

(5) $\sum\limits_{t=0}^{N} u(\hat{c}_t) + p_0 \cdot (r_0 - \hat{x}_0 - \hat{c}_0) + \sum\limits_{t=1}^{N} p_t \cdot (\hat{y}_{t-1} - \hat{x}_t - \hat{c}_t)$

$\geq \sum\limits_{t=0}^{N} u(c_t) + p_0 \cdot (r_0 - x_0 - c_0) + \sum\limits_{t=1}^{N} p_t \cdot (y_{t-1} - x_t - c_t)$

for all $c_t \in C, (x_t, y_t) \in T, t = 0, 1, 2, \ldots, N$

and

(6) $$p_0 \cdot (r_0 - \hat{x}_0 - \hat{c}_0) + \sum_{t=1}^{N} p_t \cdot (\hat{y}_{t-1} - \hat{x}_t - \hat{c}_t) = 0$$

We set $p_{N+1} = 0$. Since $r_0 - \hat{x}_0 - \hat{c}_0 \geq 0$ and $\hat{y}_{t-1} - \hat{x}_t - \hat{c}_t \geq 0, t = 1, 2, \ldots, N$, owing to $\{(\hat{x}_t, \hat{y}_t, \hat{c}_t)\} \in A_N(r_0)$, condition (iii) of competitiveness follows from (6) and $p_{N+1} = 0$. Condition (5) can be rewritten as follows:

(7)
$$\sum_{t=0}^{N} u(\hat{c}_t) - p_0 \cdot (\hat{x}_0 + \hat{c}_0) + \sum_{t=1}^{N} p_t \cdot (\hat{y}_{t-1} - \hat{x}_t - \hat{c}_t)$$

$$\geq \sum_{t=0}^{N} u(c_t) - p_0 \cdot (x_0 + c_0) + \sum_{t=1}^{N} p_t \cdot (y_{t-1} - x_t - c_t)$$

for all $(x_t, y_t) \in T$ and $c_t \in C$, $t = 0, 1, 2, \ldots, N$

In particular, put $x_t = \hat{x}_t$, $y_t = \hat{y}_t$ for all $t = 0, 1, 2, \ldots, N$, and $c_t = \hat{c}_t$ for all $t = 0, 1, 2, \ldots, N$, except for t_0. Then we obtain

(8)
$$u(\hat{c}_{t_0}) - p_{t_0} \cdot \hat{c}_{t_0} \geq u(c_{t_0}) - p_{t_0} \cdot c_{t_0} \qquad \text{for all } c_{t_0} \in C$$

Since the choice of t_0 is arbitrary, this establishes condition (i) of competitiveness. Next put $c_t = \hat{c}_t$ in relation (7) for all $t = 0, 1, \ldots, N$, and $x_N = \hat{x}_N$. Then we obtain

$$\sum_{t=0}^{N-1} p_{t+1} \cdot (\hat{y}_t - y_t) \geq \sum_{t=0}^{N-1} p_t \cdot (\hat{x}_t - x_t)$$

for all $(x_t, y_t) \in T$, $t = 0, 1, \ldots, N - 1$. Now set $x_t = \hat{x}_t$ and $y_t = \hat{y}_t$ for all $t = 0, 1, \ldots, N - 1$, except for t_0; then we obtain

(9)
$$p_{t_0+1} \cdot (\hat{y}_{t_0} - y_{t_0}) \geq p_{t_0} \cdot (\hat{x}_{t_0} - x_{t_0}) \qquad \text{for all } (x_{t_0}, y_{t_0}) \in T$$

Note that the choice of t_0 is arbitrary, so that (9) holds for any $t_0 = 0, 1, \ldots, N - 1$. Next put $c_t = \hat{c}_t$, $x_t = \hat{x}_t$, and $y_t = \hat{y}_t$ (for $t = 0, 1, \ldots, N - 1$) in relation (7), and obtain

$$-p_N \cdot \hat{x}_N \geq -p_N \cdot x_N$$

or

$$p_{N+1} \cdot \hat{y}_N - p_N \cdot \hat{x}_N \geq p_{N+1} \cdot y_N - p_N \cdot x_N$$

since $p_{N+1} = 0$. Thus we have established condition (ii) of competitiveness.
(Q.E.D.)

d. OPTIMAL STATIONARY PROGRAM

From now on we consider only *infinite* horizon programs, so we use such words as "program" and "attainable program" without explicitly stating "infinite horizon," unless it is desirable to make it explicit. A sequence $\{(x_t, y_t, c_t)\}$ is a **feasible program** if $(x_t, y_t) \in T$, $c_t \in C$, and $x_t + c_t \leq y_{t-1}$, $t = 1, 2, \ldots$. If in addition $x_0 + c_0 \leq r_0$, then it is an **attainable program** starting from r_0. The set of all the feasible programs will be denoted by A. The set of all the attainable programs starting from r_0 will be denoted by $A(r_0)$. The crucial difference between A and $A(r_0)$ is whether the initial condition $(x_0 + c_0 \leq r_0)$ is specified. In A, the historically given initial vector r_0 is ignored. In other words, $A(r_0) \equiv \{\{(x_t, y_t, c_t)\} \in A: x_0 + c_0 \leq r_0\}$. *We henceforth assume that the set $A(r_0)$ (and also A) is nonempty.*

We first consider a program $\{(x, y, c)\}$ in A such that each of the x, y, and c is constant over time. Such a program, if it exists, is called a **stationary program** or a **golden age program**. The concept is analogous to that of the "golden age path" for the one-sector optimal program (Chapter 5, Section C) or the balanced growth path (Chapter 6, Section A). Next consider the program which maximizes $u(c)$ among the set of stationary programs. Such a concept is analogous to that of the golden rule path or the von Neumann path.

Definition: A constant sequence $\{(\hat{x}, \hat{y}, \hat{c})\} \in A$ is called an **optimal stationary program** (O.S.P.) or a **golden rule path** if it is a solution to the following nonlinear programming problem:

$$\underset{(x,\, y,\, c)}{\text{Maximize: } u(c)}$$

$$\text{Subject to: } x + c \leq y$$
$$(x, y) \in T \text{ and } c \in C$$

where x, y, and c are constant over time. Note that in the concept of O.S.P., the initial condition r_0 is disregarded.

To consider the above problem we make the following assumption:

(A-5)   There exist $(\bar{x}, \bar{y}) \in T$ and $\bar{c} \in C$ such that $\bar{x} + \bar{c} < \bar{y}$.

One distinction between (A-4) and (A-5) must be made clear; in (A-5), the historically given initial resource vector is ignored. Under (A-1) and (A-5), the set $\{(x, y, c): (x, y, c) \in T \otimes C, x + c \leq y\}$ is nonempty and compact. Then the continuity of u in (A-2) insures the existence of a solution to the above nonlinear programming problem (that is, the existence of an O.S.P.). Hence we assert the following theorem.

Theorem 7.B.3:   *Under (A-1), (A-2), and (A-5), there exists an O.S.P.*

REMARK: In establishing this theorem the strict inequality $(<)$ in (A-5) can be weakened to the weak inequality $(\leq)$.

We now prove the following important theorem which is in Gale $[6]$.

Theorem 7.B.4:   *If $\{(\hat{x}, \hat{y}, \hat{c})\}$ is an O.S.P. and if (A-2) and (A-5) are satisfied, then there exists a $p \geq 0, p \in R^n$, such that*

(10) $$u(c) + p \cdot (y - x - c) \leq u(\hat{c}) + p \cdot (\hat{y} - \hat{x} - \hat{c})$$
$$\textit{for all } (x, y) \in T \textit{ and } c \in C$$

and

(11) $$p \cdot (\hat{y} - \hat{x} - \hat{c}) = 0, \qquad \hat{y} - \hat{x} - \hat{c} \geq 0$$

PROOF: By definition of O.S.P., the theorem can be obtained by applying the theorem for the saddle-point characterization in concave programming (see the corollary of Theorem 1.B.3). The "productiveness assumption," (A-5), provides Slater's condition.   (Q.E.D.)

REMARK: The converse of the above theorem holds and its proof is easy (see Theorem 1.B.4).

REMARK: We call the p obtained in Theorem 7.B.4 the **price vector associated with O.S.P.** It corresponds to the von Neumann price vector.

REMARK: The above inequality holds, *a fortiori*, for all $(x, y) \in T$ and $c \in C$ such that $x + c \leq r_0$ for a given $r_0 \in Z$ [provided that such an (x, y, c) exists].

If $\hat{c}$ in the above theorem is not a satiation consumption [that is, if there exists a $c' \in C$ such that $u(c') > u(\hat{c})$], then we can also assert that $p \neq 0$. To see this, suppose $p = 0$ in the inequality (10); then $u(\hat{c}) \geq u(c)$ for all $c \in C$, which contradicts $\hat{c}$ being a nonsatiation consumption. Suppose we strengthen this assumption of nonsatiation such that, for $\hat{c}$, there exists a $_i\hat{c}' \equiv (\hat{c}_1, \hat{c}_2, \ldots, c'_i, \ldots, \hat{c}_n) \in C$ such that $u(_i\hat{c}') > u(\hat{c})$, for *all* $i = 1, 2, \ldots, n$. This means that the consumption vector for $\hat{c}$ can be improved by changing the amount of consumption of *any* commodity. In other words, at $\hat{c}$, the consumption of no commodity reaches a satiation point. We call this assumption the **strong nonsatiation assumption,** and we call the former assumption ["there exists a $c' \in C$ such that $u(c') > u(\hat{c})$"] the **weak nonsatiation assumption.** If this strong nonsatiation assumption holds, then we can assert that p is strictly positive. To see this, suppose the contrary, so that $p_{i_0} = 0$ for some i_0 in $\{1, 2, \ldots, n\}$. Let $c_i = \hat{c}_i$, $x_i = \hat{x}_i$, and $y_i = \hat{y}_i$ for all $i = 1, 2, \ldots, n$, except for $i = i_0$ in inequality (10). Then we have $u(\hat{c}) \geq u(_{i_0}\hat{c})$ for all $_{i_0}\hat{c} \in C$ where $_{i_0}\hat{c} \equiv (\hat{c}_1, \hat{c}_2, \ldots, \hat{c}_{i_0}, \ldots, \hat{c}_n)$. This contradicts the strong nonsatiation assumption. We may summarize this as a corollary of Theorem 7.B.4.

Corollary 1:   *In Theorem 7.B.4,*

(i)   *If the weak nonsatiation assumption holds, then $p \geq 0$.*
(ii)   *If the strong nonsatiation assumption holds, then $p > 0$.*

It should be clear that the O.S.P. is not necessarily unique. If $u(c)$ is a strictly concave function of c, then we can assert that $\hat{c}$ is unique. But this does not guarantee that the associated input-output vector $(\hat{x}, \hat{y})$ is unique, unless T has some special feature. Here we point out one such feature, that is, the strict convexity of the set T.

Definition: The set T is said to be **strictly convex** if $(x, y) \in T$, $(x', y') \in T$, and $(x, y) \neq (x', y')$ imply that there exists an $(\check{x}, \check{y}) \in T$ such that, for some θ, $0 < \theta < 1$,

$$\check{x} \leqq \theta x + (1 - \theta)x'$$

and

$$\check{y} > \theta y + (1 - \theta)y'$$

Corollary 2:   *Suppose that u is strictly concave and that both T and C are convex. Let $(\hat{x}, \hat{y}, \hat{c})$ be an O.S.P. Then*

(i) *$\hat{c}$ is unique.*

(ii) *If, in addition, the assumptions of Theorem 7.B.4 hold with $p \neq 0$ and if T is strictly convex, then the $(\hat{x}, \hat{y})$ associated with $\hat{c}$ is also unique. Thus $(\hat{x}, \hat{y}, \hat{c})$ is a unique O.S.P.*

PROOF:

(i) We first assert that the strict concavity of u implies the uniqueness of $\hat{c}$. To prove this, suppose that $(\hat{x}, \hat{y}, \hat{c})$ and (x', y', c') are two O.S.P.'s such that $\hat{c} \neq c'$. Note that $u(\hat{c}) = u(c')$ by the definition of O.S.P. Let $\tilde{c} \equiv \frac{1}{2}(\hat{c} + c')$, $\tilde{x} \equiv \frac{1}{2}(\hat{x} + x')$, and $\tilde{y} \equiv \frac{1}{2}(\hat{y} + y')$. Clearly $\tilde{x} + \tilde{c} \leqq \tilde{y}$. Also $(\tilde{x}, \tilde{y}) \in T$ and $\tilde{c} \in C$ resulting from the convexity of T and C. Hence the constraints for the defining programming problem are all satisfied for $(\tilde{x}, \tilde{y}, \tilde{c})$. But owing to the strict concavity we have

$$u(\tilde{c}) > \frac{1}{2}[u(\hat{c}) + u(c')] = u(\hat{c})$$

which is a contradiction.

(ii) Next we show that the input-output vector $(\hat{x}, \hat{y})$ associated with $\hat{c}$ is unique under the strict convexity of T. To show this, suppose the contrary so that both $(\hat{x}, \hat{y}) \in T$ and $(x', y') \in T$ are associated with $\hat{c}$, where $(\hat{x}, \hat{y}) \neq (x', y')$. In other words, both $(\hat{x}, \hat{y}, \hat{c})$ and $(x', y', \hat{c})$ are solutions of the defining programming problem of O.S.P. Since the assumptions of Theorem 7.B.4 hold, the necessary and sufficient condition for O.S.P.— that is, the relations (10) and (11)—holds. In view of (11) and the assumption that both $(\hat{x}, \hat{y}, \hat{c})$ and $(x', y', \hat{c})$ are O.S.P.'s, we have

$$0 = p \cdot (\hat{y} - \hat{x} - \hat{c}) = p \cdot (y' - x' - \hat{c})$$

or

$$p \cdot (\hat{y} - \hat{x}) = p \cdot (y' - x') = p \cdot \hat{c}$$

But because of the strict convexity of T, $(\hat{x}, \hat{y}) \in T$, $(x', y') \in T$, and $(\hat{x}, \hat{y}) \neq (x', y')$ imply that there exists an $(x^*, y^*) \in T$ such that, for some $\theta, 0 < \theta < 1$,

$$x^* \leqq \theta \hat{x} + (1 - \theta)x'$$

$$y^* > \theta \hat{y} + (1 - \theta)y'$$

Hence, using $p \neq 0$, we obtain

$$p \cdot (y^* - x^*) > \theta p \cdot (\hat{y} - \hat{x}) + (1 - \theta)p \cdot (y' - x') = p \cdot \hat{c}$$

or

$$p \cdot (y^* - x^* - \hat{c}) > 0$$

Set $x = x^*$, $y = y^*$, and $c = \hat{c}$ in relation (10), and note (11). Then we obtain

$$p \cdot (y^* - x^* - \hat{c}) \leq 0$$

which is a contradiction. (Q.E.D.)

REMARK: As we remarked in subsection a, Gale [6] and Brock [3] assumed that u is a function of (x, y) rather than of c and suppressed c from their entire analysis. Hence in Gale [6], his assumption of the strict concavity of u implies the uniqueness of his O.S.P., $(\hat{x}, \hat{y})$, without any assumption such as the strict convexity of T. However, as Brock pointed out, the strict concavity of $u(x, y)$ precludes the von Neumann type model from the analysis. Brock therefore assumed the concavity of $u(x, y)$ instead of its strict concavity to allow for the von Neumann model. To obtain some of his major theorems, he also assumed that the O.S.P. is unique. We may wish to obtain the conditions, other than the strict convexity of T and the strict concavity of u, which would imply the uniqueness of the O.S.P. We leave this to the interested reader.

REMARK: The uniqueness of the optimal attainable program $\{(\hat{x}_t, \hat{y}_t, \hat{c}_t)\}$ for the finite horizon problem can be established in a manner similar to that in the above Corollary 2.

e. O.S.P. AND ELIGIBILITY
The relations (10) and (11) of Theorem 7.B.4 imply

(12) $u(\hat{c}) - u(c) \geq 0$ for all $(x, y) \in T$ and $c \in C$ such that $p \cdot (y - x - c) \geq 0$

Consider any attainable program $\{(x_t, y_t, c_t)\}$ with $y_{t-1} - x_t - c_t \geq 0$ starting from an arbitrary r_0 in Z, and consider a particular O.S.P. Relation (12) means that there can be no utility gains along such a path compared with the O.S.P. if we ignore the initial condition of the program. This observation will be central in establishing the following.

(i)   The utility sequence of any attainable program cannot be infinitely better than that of the O.S.P. (Theorem 7.B.5).

(ii) An attainable program can be "infinitely worse" than the O.S.P. by deviating from it sufficiently. The characterization of such a path is given by Theorem 7.B.6.

(iii) Any attainable program that is not "infinitely worse" must converge to the O.S.P. asymptotically (Theorem 7.B.8), if the O.S.P. is unique.

The situation is very much analogous to the procedure used by Radner, who utilizes the "value loss" associated with any path deviating from the von

Neumann ray in establishing his turnpike theorem (see Section A of this chapter). Following Gale [6], we now establish the above statements one by one. First we prove the following.

Theorem 7.B.5:   *Suppose that $\{(\hat{x}, \hat{y}, \hat{c})\}$ is an O.S.P. and that (A-1), (A-2), and (A-5) hold. Then, for any N and for any attainable program $\{(x_t, y_t, c_t)\}$ starting from any given $r_0 \in Z$, there exists an M such that*

(13)
$$\sum_{t=0}^{N} (u_t - \hat{u}) \le M, \text{ where } u_t \equiv u(c_t) \text{ and } \hat{u} \equiv u(\hat{c})$$

PROOF: Using (A-2) and (A-5), we apply Theorem 7.B.4. Then there exists a $p \ge 0$ such that

(14) $u(c) + p \cdot (y - x - c) \le u(\hat{c})$ for all $(x, y) \in T$ and $c \in C$

or

(15) $u(c_t) - \hat{u} \le p \cdot (x_t + c_t - y_t)$ for all $(x_t, y_t) \in T$ and $c_t \in C$

$$t = 0, 1, 2, \ldots, N$$

Now suppose $\{(x_t, y_t, c_t)\} \in A$ so that $x_t + c_t \le y_{t-1}, t = 1, 2, \ldots, N$. Then summing both sides of the above inequality (15) over t, we obtain the following relation for $\{(x_t, y_t, c_t)\} \in A_N(r_0)$:

(16)
$$\sum_{t=0}^{N} (u_t - \hat{u}) \le \sum_{t=0}^{N} p \cdot (x_t + c_t - y_t)$$

$$= p \cdot (x_0 + c_0) + \sum_{t=1}^{N} p \cdot (x_t + c_t - y_{t-1}) - p \cdot y_N$$

$$\le p \cdot (x_0 + c_0 - y_N) \le p \cdot r_0 - p \cdot y_N$$

The last two inequalities hold because $x_t + c_t \le y_{t-1}$ and $x_0 + c_0 \le r_0$ with $p \ge 0$. Since T and Z are bounded, there exists a real number M, independent of N, such that

(17)
$$p \cdot r_0 - p \cdot y_N \le M$$

Hence

$$\sum_{t=0}^{N} (u_t - \hat{u}) \le M \qquad \text{(Q.E.D.)}$$

REMARK: Following the above convention, we henceforth write $u_t \equiv u(c_t)$ and $\hat{u} \equiv u(\hat{c})$.

REMARK: As remarked before, the above theorem establishes that there is no attainable program which is infinitely better than the O.S.P.,

$\{(\hat{x}, \hat{y}, \hat{c})\}$. However, there is nothing discussed so far that precludes the possibility that there exists an attainable program which is infinitely worse than the O.S.P. To consider this problem, we introduce the concept of "eligibility."

Definition: An infinite horizon attainable program $\{(x_t, y_t, c_t)\}$, starting from an arbitrary given $r_0 \in Z$, is called **eligible** if its associated utility series is bounded from below; that is, there exists a real number E such that

$$(18) \qquad \sum_{t=0}^{N} (u_t - \hat{u}) \geq E \qquad \text{for any } N$$

Theorem 7.B.6:   *If an attainable program* $\{(x_t, y_t, c_t)\}$ *starting from any given* $r_0 \in Z$ *is not eligible, and if (A-1), (A-2), and (A-5) hold, then*

$$(19) \qquad \sum_{t=0}^{N} (u_t - \hat{u}) \to -\infty \qquad as \qquad N \to \infty$$

PROOF: Since $\{(x_t, y_t, c_t)\}$ is not eligible for any E, there exists an $\bar{N}$ dependent on E such that

$$(20) \qquad \sum_{t=0}^{\bar{N}} (u_t - \hat{u}) < E$$

Also, in view of relation (15), we have

$$(21) \qquad \sum_{t=\bar{N}+1}^{N} (u_t - \hat{u}) \leqq \sum_{t=\bar{N}+1}^{N} p \cdot (x_t + c_t - y_t)$$

$$= p \cdot (x_{\bar{N}+1} + c_{\bar{N}+1} - y_{\bar{N}}) + \sum_{t=\bar{N}+2}^{N} p \cdot (x_t + c_t - y_{t-1})$$

Since $x_t + c_t - y_{t-1} \leqq 0$ for all t for $\{(x_t, y_t, c_t)\} \in A(r_0)$, this implies

$$(22) \qquad \sum_{t=\bar{N}+1}^{N} (u_t - \hat{u}) \leqq p \cdot (x_{\bar{N}+1} + c_{\bar{N}+1} - y_{\bar{N}}) < B$$

where B is a bound independent of $\bar{N}$ and N, and B is obtained by the compactness of T and C. Hence combining (20) and (22), we obtain

$$(23) \qquad \sum_{t=0}^{N} (u_t - \hat{u}) < E + B \qquad \text{for } N > \bar{N}$$

It follows that

$$(24) \qquad \sum_{t=0}^{N} (u_t - \hat{u}) \to -\infty \qquad as \qquad N \to \infty$$

since E can be any (absolutely large) negative number.   (Q.E.D.)

REMARK: Thus every attainable program is noneligible if and only if its associated utility series diverges to $-\infty$ as $N \to \infty$. In other words, every attainable program is either eligible or its associated utility series diverges to $-\infty$ as $N \to \infty$.

The next theorem in order is the one which asserts the asymptotic convergence of every eligible attainable program to the O.S.P. (if it is unique). However, here we need to make an important digression. We establish that there exists an eligible attainable program; otherwise any discussion on the eligible attainable program would be vacuous. The existence of an eligible attainable program is not really obvious. For example, it may so happen that even an attainable program (not necessarily eligible) starting from a given r_0 may not exist. This is the case when the initial resource vector r_0 is so small that there does not exist any $c_0 \in C$ such that $x_0 + c_0 \leq r_0$ for any x_0. This difficulty may be handled by assumption (A-6) below. However this does not establish the existence of a program that is *eligible*. To do this we impose assumption (A-7) below.

(A-6) There exist an $(x, y) \in T$ and a $c \in C$ such that $x + c \leq y$ and $x + c \leq r_0$.
(A-7) The function u has a "bounded steepness" at $\hat{c}$. (The concept of "bounded steepness" was introduced by Gale [6], and it is defined as follows.)

Definition: The function $u(c)$ is said to have a **bounded steepness** at $\hat{c} \in C$ if there exists a positive number σ, dependent on $\hat{c}$, such that

$$(25) \qquad |u(c) - u(\hat{c})| \leq \sigma \| c - \hat{c} \|, \text{ for all } c \in C$$
$$\text{where } \| c - \hat{c} \| \text{ may be any convenient norm on } R^n$$

Assumption (A-6) is a slight modification of (A-5). Here the additional restriction $x + c \leq r_0$ is imposed. Note that if $x + c > r_0$, then this "productive" process (x, y) does not have any meaning for the economy starting from r_0. Assumption (A-6) is regarded as a restriction on the initial resource vector r_0, given a certain productive technology. Assumption (A-7) corresponds to the well-known Lipschitz condition in which the relation in (25) holds for any c *and* $\hat{c}$ in C.

We now state and prove a theorem for the existence of an eligible attainable program.

Theorem 7.B.7: *Suppose that an O.S.P., $(\hat{x}, \hat{y}, \hat{c})$, exists. Then under (A-1), (A-6), and (A-7), there exists an eligible attainable path starting from an arbitrary given r_0 in Z.*

PROOF: By (A-6), there exist an $(x, y) \in T$ and a $c \in C$ such that $x + c \leq y$ and $x + c \leq r_0$. Define $x_1, y_1,$ and c_1 as

$$(26) \qquad x_1 \equiv (1 - \lambda)\hat{x} + \lambda x, \text{ where } 0 \leq \lambda < 1$$

$$(27) \qquad y_1 \equiv (1 - \lambda)\hat{y} + \lambda y$$

$$(28) \qquad c_1 \equiv (1 - \lambda)\hat{c} + \lambda c$$

Note that $x_1 + c_1 = (1 - \lambda)(\hat{x} + \hat{c}) + \lambda(x + c) \leqq (1 - \lambda)(\hat{x} + \hat{c}) + \lambda y$; hence $x_1 + c_1 \leqq y$, for, otherwise, we obtain $x_1 + c_1 > (1 - \lambda)(\hat{x} + \hat{c}) + \lambda y$ by choosing λ close enough to one. The convexity of T implies $(x_1, y_1) \in T$ and the convexity of C implies $c_1 \in C$.

We now define the sequence $\{x_t, y_t, c_t)\}$, $t = 1, 2, \ldots$, by the rule

$$(29) \qquad x_t \equiv (1 - \lambda^t)\hat{x} + \lambda^t x = \hat{x} + \lambda^t(x - \hat{x})$$

$$(30) \qquad y_t \equiv (1 - \lambda^t)\hat{y} + \lambda^t y = \hat{y} + \lambda^t(y - \hat{y})$$

and

$$(31) \qquad c_t \equiv (1 - \lambda^t)\hat{c} + \lambda^t c = \hat{c} + \lambda^t(c - \hat{c})$$

Next we note that

$$(32) \qquad x_t = (1 - \lambda)\hat{x} + \lambda x_{t-1}$$

because

$$(1 - \lambda)\hat{x} + \lambda x_{t-1} = (1 - \lambda)\hat{x} + \lambda[(1 - \lambda^{t-1})\hat{x} + \lambda^{t-1}x]$$
$$= (1 - \lambda^t)\hat{x} + \lambda^t x = x_t$$

Similarly, we have

$$(33) \qquad y_t = (1 - \lambda)\hat{y} + \lambda y_{t-1}$$

and

$$(34) \qquad c_t = (1 - \lambda)\hat{c} + \lambda c_{t-1}$$

We now show that $x_t + c_t \leqq y_{t-1}$ and $(x_t, y_t) \in T$ for all $t = 1, 2, \ldots$. First note that this is true for $t = 1$ by putting $y_0 \equiv y$. Next, by mathematical induction on t,

$$(35) \; x_{t+1} + c_{t+1} = (1 - \lambda)\hat{x} + \lambda x_t + (1 - \lambda)\hat{c} + \lambda c_t$$
$$= (1 - \lambda)(\hat{x} + \hat{c}) + \lambda(x_t + c_t) \leqq (1 - \lambda)\hat{y} + \lambda y_{t-1} = y_t$$

using $x_t + c_t \leqq y_{t-1}$. Also $(x_t, y_t) \in T$ means $(x_{t+1}, y_{t+1}) \in T$, owing to the convexity of T. That $c_t \in C$ for all $t = 1, 2, \ldots$, can also be shown easily by mathematical induction. First recall $c_1 \in C$. Then the convexity of C with $\hat{c} \in C$ and $c_t \in C$ implies $c_{t+1} \in C$ in view of (34). Let $x_0 \equiv x$ and $c_0 \equiv c$. Then $x_0 + c_0 \leqq r_0$. Hence $\{(x_t, y_t, c_t)\}$, $t = 0, 1, 2, \ldots$, constitutes an attainable program.

To show that the program is eligible, note that u has a bounded steepness by (A-7). In other words, there exists a $\sigma > 0$ such that

$$(36) \qquad |u(c_t) - u(\hat{c})| = |u[\hat{c} + \lambda^t(c - \hat{c})] - u(\hat{c})|$$

$$\leqq \sigma\lambda^t \|c - \hat{c}\|, \; t = 0, 1, 2, \ldots$$

Summing this inequality over t and recalling $0 \leq \lambda < 1$, we obtain

$$(37) \qquad \sum_{t=0}^{\infty} |u_t - \hat{u}| \leq \frac{\sigma}{1 - \lambda} \| c - \hat{c} \| \qquad \text{(Q.E.D.)}$$

We will now prove that every eligible attainable program starting from any $r_0 \in Z$ converges to the O.S.P. Here we have to recall that the O.S.P. is not necessarily unique. If this is the case, convergence to the O.S.P. has little meaning. One way to avoid this problem is simply to assume the uniqueness of the O.S.P. As remarked before, the strict concavity of u and the strict convexity of T will imply the uniqueness of the O.S.P. The interested reader may attempt to find other conditions which would guarantee the uniqueness of the O.S.P. Another way to handle the situation is to consider the set of all the O.S.P.'s with the recognition that the O.S.P. is not necessarily unique. Then the convergence to a unique O.S.P. will be replaced by convergence to such a set. This procedure will be analogous to the one that McKenzie [12] used to establish a turnpike theorem in terms of the "von Neumann facet" instead of the unique von Neumann ray. For such a study, see McKenzie [13]. With this remark, we now prove the following theorem.

Theorem 7.B.8: *Suppose that (A-2) and (A-5) hold and that $(\hat{x}, \hat{y}, \hat{c})$ is the unique O.S.P. with strict convexity of T and strict concavity of u. Then if an attainable program $\{(x_t, y_t, c_t)\}$ starting from r_0 is eligible, then $\{(x_t, y_t, c_t)\}$ converges to $(\hat{x}, \hat{y}, \hat{c})$ as $t \to \infty$, regardless of the value of r_0 in Z.*

PROOF: By the hypothesis of the present theorem, Theorem 7.B.4 holds, so that relation (15) also follows. (See the proof of Theorem 7.B.5.) Rewriting relation (15), we obtain

$$(38) \qquad u_t - \hat{u} = p \cdot (x_t + c_t - y_t) - \beta_t, \quad t = 0, 1, 2, \ldots$$

for all $(x_t, y_t) \in T$ and $c_t \in C$, where $u_t \equiv u(c_t)$, $\hat{u} \equiv u(\hat{c})$, and $\beta_t \geq 0$ for all t. Summing this, we obtain

$$(39) \qquad \sum_{t=0}^{N} (u_t - \hat{u}) = \sum_{t=0}^{N} p \cdot (x_t + c_t - y_t) - \sum_{t=0}^{N} \beta_t$$

$$= p \cdot (x_0 + c_0 - y_N) + \sum_{t=1}^{N} p \cdot (x_t + c_t - y_{t-1}) - \sum_{t=0}^{N} \beta_t, \qquad \text{for all } N$$

Since $x_t + c_t \leq y_{t-1}$ for all $t = 1, 2, \ldots$, and $x_0 + c_0 \leq r_0$ for $\{(x_t, y_t, c_t)\} \in A(r_0)$, we have

$$(40) \qquad \sum_{t=0}^{N} (u_t - \hat{u}) \leq p \cdot (r_0 - y_N) - \sum_{t=0}^{N} \beta_t, \quad N = 0, 1, \ldots$$

Because T and Z are bounded, there exists an M such that $p \cdot (r_0 - y_N) \leq M$.

But the eligibility of $\{(x_t, y_t, c_t)\}$ implies that there exists an E such that $E \leq \sum_{t=0}^{N}(u_t - \hat{u})$. Hence we have

$$E \leq \sum_{t=0}^{N}(u_t - \hat{u}) \leq M - \sum_{t=0}^{N}\beta_t$$

or

(41)
$$\sum_{t=0}^{N}\beta_t \leq M - E, \, N = 0, 1, \ldots$$

Since $\left\{\sum_{t=0}^{N}\beta_t\right\}$, $N = 0, 1, 2, \ldots$, is a monotone nondecreasing sequence with an upper bound because of (41), $\beta_t \to 0$ as $t \to \infty$.

Since u is strictly concave, T is strictly convex, and Slater's condition holds by (A-5), the O.S.P. $(\hat{x}, \hat{y}, \hat{c})$ is a unique choice of $(\hat{x}, \hat{y}) \in T$ and $\hat{c} \in C$ which maximizes the function

(42)
$$\Phi(x, y, c) \equiv u(c) + p \cdot (y - x - c)$$

where $(x, y, c) \in T \otimes C$, and $\Phi(\hat{x}, \hat{y}, \hat{c}) = u(\hat{c})$. But from (38)

$$\Phi(x_t, y_t, c_t) = u(\hat{c}) - \beta_t$$

and since $\beta_t \to 0$ as $t \to \infty$, it follows that

$$\Phi(x_t, y_t, c_t) \to \Phi(\hat{x}, \hat{y}, \hat{c}) \qquad \text{as} \qquad t \to \infty$$

Hence from the strict concavity of u, the strict convexity of T, and the continuity of u, we have

$$(x_t, y_t) \to (\hat{x}, \hat{y}) \text{ and } c_t \to \hat{c} \qquad \text{as} \qquad t \to \infty \qquad \text{(Q.E.D.)}$$

REMARK: For the case in which $(\hat{x}, \hat{y}, \hat{c})$ may *not* be a unique O.S.P., see Brock ([3], his lemma 4).

Corollary: *Suppose that the assumptions of the previous theorem hold. Then $\sum_{t=0}^{\infty}(u_t - \hat{u})$ converges to a finite value.*

PROOF: Let $\{(x_t, y_t, c_t)\}$ be an eligible attainable program. Then $(x_t, y_t, c_t) \to (\hat{x}, \hat{y}, \hat{c})$ as $t \to \infty$. From (39) and eligibility, we obtain

(43)
$$\sum_{t=1}^{N} p \cdot (x_t + c_t - y_{t-1}) = \sum_{t=0}^{N}(u_t - \hat{u}) + p \cdot (y_N - x_0 - c_0) + \sum_{t=0}^{N}\beta_t$$

$$\geq E + p \cdot (y_N - r_0) + \sum_{t=0}^{N}\beta_t, \qquad \text{for all } N$$

Here a real number E which is independent of N exists owing to the eligibility of the program. Since $\sum_{t=0}^{\infty}\beta_t$ is convergent (from the proof of Theorem

7.B.8) and $y_N \to \hat{y}$ as $N \to \infty$, the series $\sum_{t=1}^{\infty} p \cdot (x_t + c_t - y_{t-1})$ is bounded from below by $\tilde{E} - p \cdot r_0$ where $\tilde{E} \equiv E + p \cdot \hat{y} + \sum_{t=0}^{\infty} \beta_t$, a fixed number. (Since Z is bounded, $p \cdot r_0$ is also bounded.) Since $p \geqq 0$ and $(x_t + c_t - y_{t-1}) \leqq 0$ for $\{(x_t, y_t, c_t)\} \in A(r_0)$, and $\sum_{t=1}^{\infty} p \cdot (x_t + c_t - y_{t-1})$ is bounded from below, this series $\sum_{t=1}^{\infty} p \cdot (x_t + c_t - y_{t-1})$ is monotone nonincreasing and converges to a finite value. Therefore, in view of equation (39) and recalling again that $y_N \to \hat{y}$ as $N \to \infty$, $\sum_{t=0}^{N}(u_t - \hat{u})$ converges to a fixed value.

(Q.E.D.)

f.   OPTIMAL PROGRAM FOR AN INFINITE HORIZON PROBLEM

Now we turn to the question of the (infinite horizon) "optimal program." Clearly such a program must be an attainable program. In other words, the optimality must be defined in the set of (infinite horizon) attainable programs (starting from the same initial point). It is tempting to define the optimal program as an attainable program $\{(x_t, y_t, c_t)\}$ which maximizes

$$(44) \qquad \sum_{t=0}^{\infty} u(c_t)$$

or

$$(45) \qquad \sum_{t=0}^{\infty} \frac{u(c_t)}{(1 + \rho)^t}, \qquad \text{where } \rho \geqq 0 \text{ is a discount factor}$$

Following Ramsey [16] and Gale [6], we assume that the discount factor is zero. But we cannot simply adopt the target function such as (44), for such a target may diverge to infinity in many attainable programs. To avoid such a situation for infinite horizon programs, we define optimality as follows.

Definition: An attainable program $\{(\hat{x}_t, \hat{y}_t, \hat{c}_t)\}$ starting from the initial resource vector r_0 is said to be **optimal** if there exists an $\overline{N}$ such that, for any attainable program $\{(x_t, y_t, c_t)\}$ starting from the same r_0,

$$(46) \qquad \sum_{t=0}^{N} [u(\hat{c}_t) - u(c_t)] \geqq 0 \qquad \text{for all } N \geqq \overline{N}$$

REMARK: In the literature relation (46) is often referred to as defining the program $\{(\hat{x}_t, \hat{y}_t, \hat{c}_t)\}$ that **overtakes** the program $\{(x_t, y_t, c_t)\}$. Hence the above definition says that $\{(\hat{x}_t, \hat{y}_t, \hat{c}_t)\}$ is optimal if it overtakes all the attainable programs starting from the same r_0. This concept, which ingeniously avoids the problem of divergence to infinity for infinite horizon programs, is due to von Weizsäcker [20] and Atsumi [2].

REMARK: It is possible to define and consider weaker concepts of optimality than the one defined above. For such a treatment, see Brock [3].

The question that we wish to ask now is whether there exists an optimal attainable program and, if so, what the characteristics of such a program are. Gale answered both questions simultaneously by constructing such a program. This is probably the most important although the most tedious part of his paper [6]. Brock in a recent paper [3] has simplified this tedious procedure. In this simplification, the following lemma, which we call Brock's lemma, plays a central role.

Brock's Lemma: *Suppose that (A-1), (A-2), and (A-5) hold. Let $\{(x_t, y_t, c_t)\}$ be an attainable program starting from an arbitrary given $r_0 \in Z$. Assume that an eligible attainable program exists starting from r_0. Let $(\hat{x}, \hat{y}, \hat{c})$ be an O.S.P. with an associated price vector p. Then there exists a nonnegative sequence $\{\delta_t\}_{t=0}^{N}$ associated with $\{(x_t, y_t, c_t)\}$ such that*

(47)
$$\sum_{t=0}^{N} (u_t - \hat{u}) = p \cdot (r_0 - y_N) - \sum_{t=0}^{N} \delta_t, \quad for \ N = 0, 1, 2, \ldots$$

where $u_t \equiv u(c_t)$ and $\hat{u} \equiv u(\hat{c})$

Moreover, there exists an attainable program $\{(\hat{x}_t, \hat{y}_t, \hat{c}_t)\}$ starting from r_0 such that its associated series $\sum_{t=0}^{\infty} \delta_t$ is minimal in the class of attainable programs starting from a given r_0.

PROOF:

(i)   Recall equation (38) and set

(48)
$$\delta_t \equiv -p \cdot (x_t + c_t - y_{t-1}) + \beta_t, \ t = 1, 2, \ldots$$

and

$$\delta_0 \equiv -p \cdot (x_0 + c_0 - r_0) + \beta_0$$

Then we obtain

$$\sum_{t=0}^{N} (u_t - \hat{u}) = p \cdot (r_0 - y_N) - \sum_{t=0}^{N} \delta_t, \ N = 0, 1, \ldots$$

Since $x_t + c_t \leqq y_{t-1}$, for all $t = 1, 2, \ldots$, and $x_0 + c_0 \leqq r_0$, for any attainable $\{(x_t, y_t, c_t)\}$, we have $\delta_t \geqq 0$ for all $t = 0, 1, 2, \ldots$. This proves the first statement of the lemma.

(ii)   Consider an attainable program $\{(x_t, y_t, c_t)\}$ starting from an arbitrary given r_0 which is eligible. Then for any $N = 0, 1, 2, \ldots$, there exist E and $\overline{B}$ such that

(49)
$$E \leqq \sum_{t=0}^{N} (u_t - \hat{u}) = p \cdot (r_0 - y_N) - \sum_{t=0}^{N} \delta_t \leqq \overline{B} - \sum_{t=0}^{N} \delta_t$$

where the existence of a bound $\overline{B}$, independent of N and $r_0 \in Z$, can be asserted owing to the boundedness of T and Z. Therefore we have

$$(50) \qquad \sum_{t=0}^{N} \delta_t \leq \overline{B} - E, \quad N = 1, 2, \ldots .$$

Hence $\sum_{t=0}^{\infty} \delta_t < \infty$ (that is, bounded from above), for any eligible and attainable $\{(x_t, y_t, c_t)\}$ starting from $r_0 \in Z$.

(iii) Given any $\{(x_t, y_t, c_t)\}$ starting from a given r_0, we can obtain the associated sequence of $\delta_t \geq 0$, $t = 0, 1, 2, \ldots$, defined in (48). Let α be defined by

$$(51) \qquad \alpha \equiv \inf \left\{ \sum_{t=0}^{\infty} \delta_t : \{\delta_t\} \text{ is associated with an attainable } \{(x_t, y_t, c_t)\} \right.$$
$$\left. \text{starting from } r_0 \right\}$$

Here the infimum is taken over the set of all attainable $\{(x_t, y_t, c_t)\}$ starting from a given r_0. Since an eligible program exists by assumption, $\alpha < \infty$ [see step (ii) of the proof]. Starting from r_0, there may not exist any attainable program such that its associated series is equal to α. Our task now is to show that there does exist such a program. That is, we wish to find an attainable program $\{(\hat{x}_t, \hat{y}_t, \hat{c}_t)\}$ starting from r_0 such that its associated sequence $\{\hat{\delta}_t\}$ is such that

$$(52) \qquad \alpha = \sum_{t=0}^{\infty} \hat{\delta}_t$$

In other words, we wish to find a program $\{(\hat{x}_y, \hat{y}_t, \hat{c}_t)\}$ such that its associated series $\sum_{t=0}^{\infty} \hat{\delta}_t$ is minimal in the class of programs starting from a given r_0.

(iv) By the definition of α, there exists an attainable program $\{x_t^N, y_t^N, c_t^N\}$ starting from r_0 with its associated series $\sum_{t=0}^{\infty} \delta_t^N$ such that

$$(53) \qquad \sum_{t=0}^{\infty} \delta_t^N \leq \alpha + \frac{1}{N+1}, \quad N = 0, 1, 2, \ldots$$

Now for a given t, consider (x_t^N, y_t^N, c_t^N) as a sequence over N, where $N = 0, 1, 2, \ldots$. Then owing to the compactness of $T \otimes C$, it contains a convergent subsequence whose limit is in $T \otimes C$. That is, there exists an $\{N'\} \subset \{N\}$ such that

$$(54) \qquad (x_t^{N'}, y_t^{N'}, c_t^{N'}) \rightarrow (\hat{x}_t, \hat{y}_t, \hat{c}_t) \qquad \text{as } N' \rightarrow \infty$$

where $(\hat{x}_t, \hat{y}_t) \in T$ and $\hat{c}_t \in C$. Note that $x_t^{N'} + c_t^{N'} \leq y_{t-1}^{N'}$ for all t, so that we have $\hat{x}_t + \hat{c}_t \leq \hat{y}_t$. Hence $\{(\hat{x}_t, \hat{y}_t, \hat{c}_t)\} \in A(r_0)$. Owing to the compactness of $T \otimes C$, the boundedness of Z, and the continuity of u, the sequence $\{\delta_t^{N'}\}$ (sequence with respect to N') is bounded for each t [recall equations (38) and (48)]. Hence for each t there exists a convergent subsequence of $\{\delta_t^{N'}\}$; that is, there exists a subsequence $\{M\} \subset \{N'\}$ such that, for each $t = 0, 1, 2, \ldots$,

$$(55) \qquad \delta_t^M \rightarrow \hat{\delta}_t \qquad \text{as } M \rightarrow \infty$$

It is clear from the continuity of u and the definition of δ_t that $\{\delta_t\}$ corresponds to the program $\{(\hat{x}_t, \hat{y}_t, \hat{c}_t)\}$ [recall equations (38) and (48)]. Hence

$$(56) \qquad\qquad \sum_{t=0}^{\infty} \hat{\delta}_t \geq \alpha$$

by the definition of α.

Write $\beta \equiv \sum_{t=0}^{\infty} \hat{\delta}_t$. Suppose $\beta > \alpha$. Then choose r_1 and r_2 such that

$$(57) \qquad\qquad \beta > r_2 > r_1 > \alpha$$

Choose N_0 large enough so that

$$(58) \qquad\qquad \sum_{t=0}^{N_0} \hat{\delta}_t \geq r_2$$

Next choose M_0, $M_0 \in \{M\}$, so that $M \geq M_0$ implies

$$(59) \qquad\qquad \sum_{t=0}^{N_0} \delta_t{}^M \geq r_1$$

which is possible because $\delta_t{}^M \to \hat{\delta}_t$ as $M \to \infty$. But in view of (53), we also have

$$(60) \qquad\qquad \alpha + \frac{1}{M+1} \geq \sum_{t=0}^{\infty} \delta_t{}^M \geq \sum_{t=0}^{N_0} \delta_t{}^M$$

Then in view of (59), we have

$$(61) \qquad\qquad \alpha + \frac{1}{M+1} \geq r_1$$

This is a contradiction, for $\alpha < r_1$ implies that we can choose M large enough so that $\alpha + 1/(M+1) < r_1$.   (Q.E.D.)

REMARK: The program $\{(\hat{x}_t, \hat{y}_t, \hat{c}_t)\}$, obtained in the above lemma, is called the **program with minimal associated series** $(\sum_{t=0}^{\infty} \hat{\delta}_t)$. It is easy to see that this program is an eligible program.

Theorem 7.B.9:   *Suppose that (A-1), (A-2), and (A-5) hold, that an eligible attainable program exists starting from r_0, and that the O.S.P. is unique. Then there exists an attainable program $\{(\hat{x}_t, \hat{y}_t, \hat{c}_t)\}$ starting from r_0 such that, for any attainable program $\{(x_t, y_t, c_t)\}$ starting from the same r_0, there exists an $\bar{N}$ such that*

$$(62) \qquad\qquad \sum_{t=0}^{N} [u(\hat{c}_t) - u(c_t)] \geq 0 \quad \text{for all } N \geq \bar{N}$$

PROOF: Let $\{(\hat{x}_t, \hat{y}_t, \hat{c}_t)\}$ be the program with minimal associated series $\sum_{t=0}^{\infty} \hat{\delta}_t$, which is obtained in the previous lemma. We claim that this is the optimal program that is desired in Theorem 7.B.9. As remarked before, this program is an eligible attainable program. In view of Theorem 7.B.6, we need only compare eligible attainable programs.

From (47) of Brock's lemma, we obtain

$$(63) \quad \sum_{t=0}^{N} \left[u(\hat{c}_t) - u(c_t) \right] = p \cdot \left[r_0 - r_0 + (y_N - \hat{y}_N) \right] + \sum_{t=0}^{N} \delta_t - \sum_{t=0}^{N} \hat{\delta}_t$$

Also as a result of the eligibility of the two programs and the uniqueness of the O.S.P., $y_N \to \hat{y}$ and $\hat{y}_N \to \hat{y}$ as $N \to \infty$. By definition, $\sum_{t=0}^{\infty} \hat{\delta}_t$ is the minimal series so that $\sum_{t=0}^{\infty} \delta_t \geq \sum_{t=0}^{\infty} \hat{\delta}_t$. Hence the conclusion of the theorem follows from (63).   (Q.E.D.)

REFERENCES

1. Arrow, K. J., Hurwicz, L., and Uzawa, H., "Constraint Qualification in Maximization Problems," *Naval Research Logistics Quarterly*, 8, June 1961.

2. Atsumi, H., "Neoclassical Growth and the Efficient Program of Capital Accumulation," *Review of Economic Studies*, XXXII, April 1965.

3. Brock, W. A., "On Existence of Weakly Maximal Programmes in a Multi-Sector Economy," *Review of Economic Studies*, XXXVII, April 1970.

4. Debreu, G., *Theory of Value*, Cowles Foundation Monograph, No. 17, New York, Wiley, 1959.

5. Drandakis, E. M., "On Efficient Accumulation Paths in the Closed Production Model," *Econometrica*, 34, April 1966.

6. Gale, D., "On Optimal Development in a Multi-Sector Economy," *Review of Economic Studies*, XXXIV, January 1967 (also "Correction," *Review of Economic Studies*, XXXVIII, July 1971).

7. ———, "A Geometric Duality Theorem with Economic Applications," *Review of Economic Studies*, XXXIV, January 1967.

8. Koopmans, T. C., "Analysis of Production as an Efficient Combination of Activities," in *Activity Analysis of Production and Allocation*, ed. by T. C. Koopmans, Cowles Foundation Monograph, No. 13, New York, Wiley, 1951, chap. 3..

9. ———, "Economic Growth at a Maximal Rate," *Quarterly Journal of Economics*, LXXVIII, August 1964.

10. ———, "On the Concept of Optimal Economic Growth," in *The Econometric Approach to Development Planning*, Pontificiae Academiae Scientiarvm Scriptvm Varia, Amsterdam, North-Holland, 1965.

11. Malinvaud, E., "Capital Accumulation and Efficient Allocation of Resources," *Econometrica*, 21, April 1953 (also "A Corrigendum," *Econometrica*, 30, July 1962).

12. McKenzie, L. W., "Turnpike Theorems for a Generalized Leontief Model," *Econometrica*, 31, January–April 1963.

13. ———, "Accumulation Programs of Maximum Utility and the von Neumann Facet," in *Value, Capital and Growth, Papers in Honour of Sir John Hicks*, ed. by J. N. Wolfe, Edinburgh, Edinburgh University Press, 1968.

14. Nikaido, H., *Convex Structures and Economic Theory*, New York, Academic Press, 1968.

15. Radner, R., "Paths of Economic Growth that Are Optimal with Regard Only to Final States: A Turnpike Theorem," *Review of Economic Studies*, XXVIII, February 1961.

16. Ramsey, F. P., "A Mathematical Theory of Saving," *Economic Journal*, XXXVIII, December 1928.

17. Tsukui, J., "Turnpike Theorem in a Generalized Dynamic Input-Output System," *Econometrica*, 34, April 1966.

18. ———, "The Consumption and the Output Turnpike Theorems in a von Neumann Type of Model—A Finite Term Problem," *Review of Economic Studies*, XXXIV, January 1967.

19. Uzawa, H., "The Kuhn-Tucker Theorem in Concave Programming," in *Studies in Linear and Non-Linear Programming*, ed. by K. J. Arrow, L. Hurwicz, and H. Uzawa, Stanford, Calif., Stanford University Press, 1958.

20. von Weizsäcker, C. C., "Existence of Optimal Programs of Accumulation for an Infinite Time Horizon," *Review of Economic Studies*, XXXII, April 1965.

8

DEVELOPMENTS OF OPTIMAL CONTROL THEORY AND ITS APPLICATIONS

Section A

PONTRYAGIN'S MAXIMUM PRINCIPLE

a. OPTIMAL CONTROL: A SIMPLE PROBLEM AND THE MAXIMUM PRINCIPLE

Consider the problem of shooting a guided missile to intercept an airplane. The location of the missile at time $\bar{t}$ can be described by a three-dimensional vector-valued function $x(\bar{t})$. The problem is to obtain the "optimal" trajectory $x(t)$ so that it maximizes or minimizes a certain objective. For example, the objective may be to minimize the time for the missile to reach the airplane. Clearly $x(t)$ can be "controlled" by a number of variables. Thus we may consider that the trajectory of the missile $x(t)$ is controlled by the fuel consumption of the missile at time t and the angle between the direction of thrust and the "flat" of the earth at time t.[1] These variables are, in general, denoted by an r-dimensional vector-valued function $u(t)$. The function $x(t)$ is, in general, an n-dimensional vector-valued function, and hence the problem is, in general, to obtain the trajectory $x(t)$ by choosing a function $u(t)$ so as to maximize or minimize a certain objective. This problem is an **optimal control problem** and the theory for such a problem is called **optimal control theory**. Examples of optimal control are vast and one can find many such examples in everyday life. Some problems are very complex and some are quite trivial (in the sense that the solution can be found easily). For example, a trivial problem is to minimize the time required to fill a bathtub with water by controlling the amount of water running from a faucet at each instant of time. We can find many such problems in economics.[2] The problem of optimal growth as discussed in Chapter 5, Section D, is an example. In that problem, we were concerned with finding the time path of per capita consumption so as to maximize the discounted sum (or the integral) of the utilities obtained from future consumptions. Corresponding to the optimal time path of per capita consumption, we obtained the trajectory of the capital:labor ratio.

Not only has the (modern) optimal control theory revolutionized the

600

traditional control theory in various fields of engineering, but also it has attracted attention throughout our society. It can be considered a mathematical theory with applications extending to all of human activity. Mathematically, optimal control theory is closely related to the calculus of variations, as can be suggested by the problem of optimal growth. In fact, optimal control theory provides a link to the vast literature on the calculus of variations.[3] And, by contrast to the classical calculus of variations, optimal control theory incorporates general constraints imposed on the problem in a direct and natural way.[4] The work by the famous Russian mathematician L. S. Pontryagin and his associates [11] is chiefly responsible for this new approach.[5] Although pioneering works were done by F. A. Valentine in 1937, E. J. McShane in 1939 and 1940, and M. R. Hestenes in 1949, this new approach has attracted a huge audience of mathematicians, engineers, economists, and so on, only after the publication (of the English translation) of Pontryagin *et al.* [11]. Especially since the publication of this work, the literature in the field of optimal control theory has been increasing very rapidly,[6] and already includes a number of good textbooks (for example, [2], [8], and [9]).

The basic result of Pontryagin *et al.* [11] is called *Pontryagin's maximum principle*, which is concerned with the necessary conditions for optimality.[7] This condition is analogous to the maximization of the Lagrangian in the classical theory of nonlinear programming. Further results by Hestenes [5] and others extended this condition to incorporate various kinds of constraints.

The purpose of this chapter is to give an expository account of this theory and to illustrate it with some applications in economics. Since a rigorous exposition of optimal control theory requires a book, and since there are several such books available, our exposition here is rather intuitive.

Consider a system of n first-order differential equations

$$(1) \qquad \dot{x}_i(t) = f_i[x(t), u(t), t], \, i = 1, 2, \ldots, n$$

where $x(t) \equiv [x_1(t), x_2(t), \ldots, x_n(t)]$ and $u(t) \equiv [u_1(t), u_2(t), \ldots, u_r(t)]$. Here the f_i's, x_i's, and u_k's are all real-valued functions. The boundary conditions for (1) are given by

$$(2) \qquad x_i(t_0) = x_i^0, \, i = 1, 2, \ldots, n$$

If we specify the $u_k(t)$'s—say, $u(t) = \hat{u}(t)$—then, assuming the uniqueness and the existence of a solution, we can completely and uniquely specify the solution path $x(t; x^0, t^0)$ of the above differential equations. The Cauchy-Peano theorem discussed in Chapter 3, Section B, is a theorem on the (local) existence and the uniqueness of a solution.

In optimal control theory, we do not specify $u(t)$ *a priori*, but rather we choose $u(t)$ from a set of functions—say, U—in order to maximize (or minimize) a certain target. In this sense, the vector-valued function $u(t)$ is called a **control**. The variables $u_k(t)$, $k = 1, 2, \ldots, r$, are called the **control variables**. The range of the

$u(t)$'s in U is denoted by $\overline{U}$. The region $\overline{U}$ is called the **control region** and U is called the **set of admissible controls**. When $u(t) \in U$, $u(t)$ is called an **admissible control (function)**. In this section, we assume that the control region $\overline{U}$ is independent of $x(t)$ and t. The case in which $\overline{U}$ is restricted by a constraint such as $g(x, u, t) \geq 0$ will be discussed in Section C. Throughout this chapter, we assume that U is restricted to the set where $u(t)$ is "piecewise continuous." By **piecewise continuous** we mean that a function is continuous except possibly at a finite number of points.[8] It is important to note that discontinuities are allowed for the control functions (recall footnote 7). Notice that the control region $\overline{U}$ can be a closed set. In other words, $\overline{U}$ can incorporate a constraint such as

$$0 \leq u(t) \leq 1 \quad \text{for all } t$$

Such a bound may appear if, for example, $u(t)$ is the propensity to save at time t.

The f_i's are assumed to be continuous in each x_i, u_k, and t, and possess continuous partial derivatives with respect to each x_i and t. The range of $x(t)$ is denoted by X, which is assumed to be an open connected subset of R^n. The boundary point (x^0, t_0) must be such that $x^0 \in X$ and $t_0 \in (t_1, t_2)$. It is required that $x(t)$ be continuous and have piecewise continuous derivatives.

We now set the target as follows (where T is a fixed constant):

(3) $$S \equiv \sum_{i=1}^{n} c_i x_i(T), \text{ where } T \in (t_1, t_2)$$

and consider the problem of choosing $u(t) \in U$ so as to

Maximize: S

Subject to: $\dot{x}_i(t) = f_i[x(t), u(t), t]$, and $x_i(0) = x_i^0$, $i = 1, 2, \ldots, n$

Once such a control function denoted by $\hat{u}(t)$ is found, we should be able to find the corresponding function $\hat{x}(t)$ as a solution of the system of differential equations (1). The variables $x_i(t)$, $i = 1, 2, \ldots, n$, which are assumed to be continuous in t, are called the **state variables**. It is important to note that the derivative of each state variable is in the constraints, but no derivatives of the control functions are involved in either the target function or the constraints. This is sometimes used to distinguish the state variables from the control variables. Although t often refers to *time* t, in practical applications, this does not have to be the case, of course. See, for example, El-Hodiri [4], pp. 122–126. However, following the usual convention, we nickname t as "time" t.

We now state the most basic theorem in this chapter, which is concerned with the above problem.

Theorem 8.A.1: *Under the above specifications of the problem, in order that $\hat{u}(t)$ be a solution of the above problem with the corresponding state variable $\hat{x}(t)$, it is necessary that there exist a nonzero, continuous vector-valued function $p(t) \equiv [p_1(t), p_2(t), \ldots, p_n(t)]$ such that*[9]

(i) $p(t)$ *together with* $\hat{u}(t)$ *and* $\hat{x}(t)$ *solve the following* **Hamiltonian system:**

(4) $$\dot{x}_i = \frac{\partial \hat{H}}{\partial p_i}, \; \dot{p}_i = \left[-\frac{\partial \hat{H}}{\partial x_i}, i = 1, 2, \ldots, n \right]$$

where H is defined by

(5) $$H\left[x(t), u(t), t, p(t)\right] \equiv \sum_{i=1}^{n} p_i(t) f_i\left[x(t), u(t), t\right]$$

(*which is called the* **Hamiltonian**)*, and* $\hat{H} \equiv H\left[\hat{x}(t), \hat{u}(t), t, p(t)\right]$

(ii) $H\left[\hat{x}(t), \hat{u}(t), t, p(t)\right] \geq H\left[\hat{x}(t), u(t), t, p(t)\right]$ *for all* $u(t) \in U$, *that is, H is maximized with respect to* $u(t)$

(iii) $p_i(T) = c_i, i = 1, 2, \ldots, n$

REMARK: To avoid any misunderstanding, one notational remark is in order. For example, the sentence, $\dot{p}_i = -\partial \hat{H}/\partial x_i$, where $\hat{H} \equiv \left[\hat{x}(t), \hat{u}(t), t, p(t)\right]$, should be taken to mean that $\dot{p}_i = -\partial H/\partial x_i$, where the partial derivative $\partial H/\partial x_i$ is evaluated at $\left[\hat{x}(t), \hat{u}(t), t, p(t)\right]$. That is, $\partial \hat{H}/\partial x_i$ is not the derivative of $\hat{H}$ with respect to x_i (which is clearly meaningless).

REMARK: In view of the fact that H is to be maximized [condition (ii)], this theorem is called the **maximum principle**, by Pontryagin *et al*. [11]. Thus the above theorem is known as **Pontryagin's maximum principle**. Theorem 8.A.1 gives the necessary conditions for $\hat{u}(t)$ to be optimal. It was later shown by Mangasarian [10] and others that these conditions are also sufficient (for a global optimum) if the f_i's are concave in x and u. We discuss Magasarian's theorem in Section C. Note that the above necessary conditions do not guarantee the existence of an optimal control $\hat{u}(t)$; they are only the conditions that are implied by optimality, assuming the existence of an optimal control $\hat{u}(t)$. As remarked above, the local existence of $\hat{x}(t)$ which satisfies the system of differential equations (1), conditional upon the existence of $\hat{u}(t)$, is guaranteed by the assumption that the f_i's are continuously differentiable in the x_i's and t (the Cauchy-Peano theorem). An alert reader may have realized the similarity between the above problem and the ordinary nonlinear programming problem. The p_i's correspond to the Lagrangian multipliers, and H corresponds to the Lagrangian. The maximization of the Lagrangian is now converted to the maximization of the Hamiltonian. Pontryagin *et al.* called the $p_i(t)$'s the **auxiliary variables**. They are also called the **multipliers** or the **costate variables**.

REMARK: It is important to note that in the above formulation of the problem, T is *a priori* fixed and $x(T)$ is *not a priori* specified. We determine $\hat{x}(t)$ from the differential equation $\dot{x} = f\left[x(t), u(t), t\right]$, once $\hat{u}(t)$ is specified, and we obtain $\hat{x}(T)$ from $\hat{x}(t)$. The third condition in the theorem, $p_i(T) = c_i, i = 1, 2, \ldots, n$, is called the **transversality condition** and its role is to provide the additional conditions required due to the fact that $x(T)$ is not *a priori* specified. For a good and relatively elementary discussion of the transversality condition, see Pontryagin *et al.* [11], especially chapter 1, section 2.

REMARK: Each $\dot{x}_i = \partial\hat{H}/\partial p_i$, $i = 1, 2, \ldots, n$, is reduced to the constraint equation (1), that is, $\dot{x}_i = f_i[\hat{x}(t), \hat{u}(t), t]$, $i = 1, 2, \ldots, n$. The equations $\dot{p}_i = -\partial\hat{H}/\partial x_i$, $i = 1, 2, \ldots, n$, are rewritten as

$$\dot{p}_i = -\sum_{j=1}^{n} p_j \frac{\partial\hat{f}_j}{\partial x_i}, \quad i = 1, 2, \ldots, n$$

where $\hat{f}_j$ denotes $f_j[\hat{x}(t), \hat{u}(t), t]$. In other words, Theorem 8.A.1 produces $2n$ first-order differential equations with $2n$ boundary conditions $x_i(t_0) = x^0$ and $p_i(T) = c_i$, $i = 1, 2, \ldots, n$; hence the actual solution of the above problem is reduced to solving a system of differential equations. Clearly this system is unsolvable unless the function $u(t)$ is specified. The choice of $u(t)$ depends upon condition (ii) (that is, the maximization of H). The triplet $[\hat{x}(t), \hat{u}(t), p(t)]$ thus found in Theorem 8.A.1 is called the **optimal triplet** or the **solution triplet**. The pair $[\hat{x}(t), \hat{u}(t)]$ is called the **optimal pair** or the **solution pair**.

REMARK: Note that the target function as described in (3) is more general than it appears, as it includes the following target function:

(6)
$$I \equiv \int_0^T f_0[x(t), u(t), t]\,dt$$

To see this, define $x_0(t)$ by $\dot{x}_0 = f_0[x(t), u(t), t]$ with $x_0(0) = 0$. Then $I = x_0(T)$, which is clearly a special case of (3). Hence the problem of maximizing I subject to (1) and (2) can be converted to the problem of simply maximizing $x_0(T)$ subject to (1), (2), and $\dot{x}_0 = f_0[x(t), u(t), t]$ and $x_0(0) = 0$. We can then immediately apply Theorem 8.A.1.

REMARK: In the above formulation of the problem, we defined the target function by $S \equiv \sum_{i=1}^{n} c_i x_i(T)$. We noted in the above remark that an integral target in the form of

$$I \equiv \int_0^T f_0[x(t), u(t), t]\,dt$$

can be converted into the form of S. The converse is also true. In other words, the target in the form of S can be converted to the above integral form. To see this, note that

$$S \equiv \sum_{i=1}^{n} c_i x_i(T) = \int_0^T \sum_{i=1}^{n} c_i \dot{x}_i(t)\,dt + \sum_{i=1}^{n} c_i x_i(0)$$

Hence if the $x_i(0)$'s are fixed, the maximization of S is equivalent to the maximization of the integral

$$J \equiv \int_0^T \sum_{i=1}^n c_i \dot{x}_i(t) dt$$

Hence the maximization of S subject to $x_i(0) = x_i^0$, $\dot{x}_i = f_i[x(t), u(t), t]$, $i = 1, 2, \ldots, n$, is reformulated as follows:

Maximize: $\displaystyle\max_{u(t)} \int_0^T f_0[x(t), u(t), t] dt$

Subject to: $\dot{x}_i = f_i[x(t), u(t), t]$ and $x_i(0) = x_i^0$, $i = 1, 2, \ldots, n$

where $f_0[x(t), u(t), t] \equiv \displaystyle\sum_{i=1}^n c_i f_i[x(t), u(t), t]$

REMARK: If $\hat{u}$ is in the interior of the control region $\bar{U}$ and if each f_i is continuously differentiable in u (so that H is continuously differentiable in u), then condition (ii) implies

$$\frac{\partial \hat{H}}{\partial u_k} = 0, \, k = 1, 2, \ldots, r$$

and $\hat{u}$ is in the interior of $\bar{U}$ if $\bar{U}$ is an open set. Note that $\partial \hat{H}/\partial u_k = 0$ for all k means that the maximization of $\hat{H}$ usually implies r independent conditions. Conversely, if H is a concave function in the u_k's, then the equations $\partial \hat{H}/\partial u_k = 0$ for all k imply condition (ii). It is important to note, however, that the power of condition (ii) is specifically that $\bar{U}$ is not restricted to being an open set; in fact, $\bar{U}$ can be a closed set. For example, if $u_k(t)$ is restricted by $0 \leq u_k(t) \leq 1$ for all k, then $\bar{U}$ is the closed interval which is a closed set. Since $u_k(t)$ can be any piecewise continuous function, $\hat{u}_k(t)$ may be such that, for each k,

$$\hat{u}_k(t) = 0 \quad \text{for } t_0 \leq t < \bar{t}$$
$$\hat{u}_k(t) = 1 \quad \text{for } \bar{t} \leq t \leq t_1$$

Such a solution, as remarked before, is called the **bang-bang solution**[10] and is obtained very often in practical applications. For example, consider the problem of filling a bathtub with water from a faucet in a minimal amount of time. The amount of water that can be run from the faucet at each instant of time is the control. Let the unit of the volume of water be chosen such that the maximum rate at which water can be run into the tub is equal to one. Thus the control $u(t)$ is restricted by $0 \leq u(t) \leq 1$. The solution of this bathtub problem is obviously $u(t) = 1$, for $0 \leq t < T$, and $u(t) = 0$, for $t = T$, where T is the point of time at which the tub is full. That is, we obtain a kind of bang-bang solution. Note also that in this problem T is not specified *a priori*, unlike in the problem stated for Theorem 8.A.1. We consider such a case later.

REMARK: If we define M by

(7) $$M[\hat{x}(t), t, p(t)] \equiv \sup_{u(t) \in U} H[\hat{x}(t), u(t), t, p(t)]$$

then condition (ii) of Theorem 8.A.1 can be rewritten as

$$H[\hat{x}(t), \hat{u}(t), t, p(t)] = M[\hat{x}(t), t, p(t)]$$

REMARK: Those readers who are familiar with the calculus of variations problem with differential equation constraints should be able to see that Theorem 8.A.1 may be reduced to a well-known result in the calculus of variations when $\hat{u}(t)$ is in the interior of $\overline{U}$. To see this, note that the problem is reduced to one of maximizing

$$\int_0^T \sum_{i=1}^n c_i \dot{x}_i(t) dt \quad \text{subject to (1) and (2)}$$

since the constant term $-\sum_{i=1}^n c_i x_i(0)$ will not affect the solution $[\hat{x}(t), \hat{u}(t)]$. Then form the "Lagrangian," $\Phi \equiv \sum_{i=1}^n c_i \dot{x}_i + \sum_{i=1}^n p_i(\dot{x}_i - f_i)$. Viewing this as a calculus of variations problem, we can write Euler's conditions here as

$$\frac{d}{dt}\frac{\partial \Phi}{\partial \dot{x}_i} = \frac{\partial \Phi}{\partial x_i} \quad \text{and} \quad \frac{d}{dt}\frac{\partial \Phi}{\partial \dot{u}_k} = \frac{\partial \Phi}{\partial u_k}, \quad \text{for all the } i\text{'s and } k\text{'s}$$

The first condition gives $\dot{p}_i = -\partial \hat{H}/\partial x_i$ [condition (i) of Theorem 8.A.1] and the second condition gives condition (ii) of Theorem 8.A.1 if $\hat{u}(t)$ is in the interior of $\overline{U}$.

b.   THE PROOF OF A SIMPLE CASE

We now give a proof of Theorem 8.A.1. Since the proof of Theorem 8.A.1 in general is quite complicated and takes a great deal of space, we give the proof for a special case only. In particular, we consider the case in which the functions f_i, $i = 1, 2, \ldots, n$, take the following special form:

(8) $$f_i[x(t), u(t), t] \equiv \sum_{j=1}^n a_{ij}(t)x_j(t) + \phi_j[u(t), t], i = 1, 2, \ldots, n$$

In other words, the f_i's are linear in the state variables, and the control variables are separable from the state variables. Because of this, the proof is greatly simplified and will enhance the reader's understanding of Theorem 8.A.1. The proof for this simple case is based on Kopp [7]. The reader who is interested in more general cases is referred to Leitmann [9], chapter 1, as well as to other works on the topic, such as Hestenes [5].

In order to present the proof, we now repeat the problem with which Theorem 8.A.1 is concerned.

PROBLEM:

Maximize: $S \equiv \sum_{i=1}^{n} c_i x_i(T)$, where T is fixed

$\underset{u(t)}{}$

Subject to:

(9) $\dot{x}_i = f_i[x(t), u(t), t], i = 1, 2, \ldots, n$

(10) $x_i(0) = x_i{}^0$ (fixed), $i = 1, 2, \ldots, n$

and

(11) $u(t) \in U$

where $x(t) \equiv [x_1(t), \ldots, x_n(t)]$ and $u(t) \equiv [u_1(t), \ldots, u_r(t)]$.

First we define the "auxiliary variables" $p_i(t)$, $i = 1, 2, \ldots, n$, by

(12) $\dot{p}_i(t) = -\sum_{j=1}^{n} p_j(t) \dfrac{\partial \hat{f}_j}{\partial x_i}$, $p_i(T) = c_i$, $i = 1, 2, \ldots, n$

Here $\partial \hat{f}_j / \partial x_i$ denotes $\partial f_j / \partial x_i$ evaluated at $[\hat{x}(t), \hat{u}(t), t]$. Define the function H by

(13) $H[x(t), u(t), t, p(t)] \equiv \sum_{i=1}^{n} p_i(t) f_i[x(t), u(t), t]$

where $p(t) \equiv [p_1(t), \ldots, p_n(t)]$; it is clear from the definition of the $p_i(t)$'s that

(14) $\dot{p}_i(t) = -\dfrac{\partial \hat{H}}{\partial x_i}$, where $\hat{H} \equiv H[\hat{x}(t), \hat{u}(t), p(t)]$

We assume that an optimal control vector $\hat{u}(t)$ has been found and let $\hat{x}(t)$ be the corresponding state vector. We are concerned with the characterization of this solution pair $[\hat{x}(t), \hat{u}(t)]$. Consider now a variation $\Delta u(t)$ from the optimal control vector $\hat{u}(t)$ such that $\hat{u}(t) + \Delta u(t) \in U$, and let $\Delta x(t)$ be the resulting total variation from the optimal state vector $\hat{x}(t)$. Then from (9), we have

(15) $\sum_{i=1}^{n} p_i \Delta \dot{x}_i = \sum_{i=1}^{n} p_i[f_i(\hat{x} + \Delta x, \hat{u} + \Delta u, t) - f_i(\hat{x}, \hat{u}, t)]$

Hence we obtain

(16) $\displaystyle\int_0^T \sum_{i=1}^{n} p_i \Delta \dot{x}_i dt = \int_0^T \sum_{i=1}^{n} p_i[f_i(\hat{x} + \Delta x, \hat{u} + \Delta u, t) - f_i(\hat{x}, \hat{u}, t)] dt$

Integration by parts of the LHS of the above equation yields

(17) $\displaystyle\int_0^T \sum_{i=1}^{n} p_i \Delta \dot{x}_i dt = \sum_{i=1}^{n} p_i \Delta x_i \Big|_0^T - \int_0^T \sum_{i=1}^{n} \dot{p}_i \Delta x_i dt$

Then, rewriting the second term of the RHS of (17) by utilizing (12), and using (16) and (17), we obtain

(18)
$$\sum_{i=1}^{n} p_i \Delta x_i \bigg|_0^T = - \int_0^T \sum_{i=1}^{n} \sum_{j=1}^{n} p_i(t) \frac{\partial \hat{f}_i}{\partial x_j} \Delta x_j dt$$

$$+ \int_0^T \sum_{i=1}^{n} p_i \left[f_i(\hat{x} + \Delta x, \hat{u} + \Delta u, t) - f_i(\hat{x}, \hat{u}, t) \right] dt$$

Since the initial state vector $x(0)$ is assumed to be fixed, $\Delta x(0) = 0$. Note that in (12), $p_i(T)$ is chosen such that $p_i(T) = c_i$. Hence we have

(19)
$$\sum_{i=1}^{n} p_i \Delta x_i \bigg|_0^T = \sum_{i=1}^{n} c_i \Delta x_i(T) \equiv \Delta S$$

where ΔS is the total variation of the payoff function S.

To consider the RHS of (18), expand f_i in a Taylor series about $(\hat{x}, \hat{u} + \Delta u, t)$ and obtain

(20)
$$f_i(\hat{x} + \Delta x, \hat{u} + \Delta u, t) - f_i(\hat{x}, \hat{u}, t) = f_i(\hat{x}, \hat{u} + \Delta u, t) - f_i(\hat{x}, \hat{u}, t)$$

$$+ \sum_{j=1}^{n} \frac{\partial f_i(\hat{x}, \hat{u} + \Delta u, t)}{\partial x_j} \Delta x_j + \frac{1}{2} \sum_{j=1}^{n} \sum_{k=1}^{n} \frac{\partial^2 f_i(\hat{x} + \xi \Delta x, \hat{u} + \Delta u, t)}{\partial x_j \partial x_k} \Delta x_j \Delta x_k$$

where $0 \le \xi \le 1$. Here it is assumed that the first and second continuous partial derivatives of f exist. From (18), (19), and (20), we obtain

(21)
$$\Delta S = \int_0^T \sum_{i=1}^{n} p_i \left[f_i(\hat{x}, \hat{u} + \Delta u, t) - f_i(\hat{x}, \hat{u}, t) \right] dt$$

$$+ \int_0^T \sum_{i=1}^{n} \sum_{j=1}^{n} p_i \left\{ \frac{\partial}{\partial x_j} \left[f_i(\hat{x}, \hat{u} + \Delta u, t) - f_i(\hat{x}, \hat{u}, t) \right] \right\} \Delta x_j dt$$

$$+ \frac{1}{2} \int_0^T \sum_{i=1}^{n} \sum_{j=1}^{n} \sum_{k=1}^{n} p_i \frac{\partial^2 f_i(\hat{x} + \xi \Delta x, \hat{u} + \Delta u, t)}{\partial x_j \partial x_k} \Delta x_j \Delta x_k dt$$

Now recall our special form of the f_i's, that is, equation (8). Then, owing to (8), the last two members of the RHS of (21) vanish and ΔS becomes

(22)
$$\Delta S = \int_0^T \left[H(\hat{x}, \hat{u} + \Delta u, t) - H(x, u, t) \right] dt$$

A sufficient condition for a maximum of the payoff function S at $(\hat{x}, \hat{u}, t)$ is clearly $\Delta S < 0$, and a sufficient condition for $\Delta S < 0$, in turn, is obtained from (22) as

(23)
$$H(\hat{x}, \hat{u} + \Delta u, t) - H(\hat{x}, \hat{u}, t) < 0$$

for all $0 \le t \le T$.

To obtain a *necessary condition* for a maximum of S, a special condition on the control vector is chosen, that is,

$$\text{(24)} \qquad \Delta u = (0, \ldots, 0, \Delta u_i, 0, \ldots, 0)$$

and $\Delta u_i = 0$ except in the interval (t_1, t_2), where $t_1 < t_2$. Now suppose we have

$$\text{(25)} \qquad H(\hat{x}, \hat{u} + \Delta u, t) - H(\hat{x}, \hat{u}, t) > 0$$

for some interval between 0 and T. If the interval (t_1, t_2) is chosen to include the interval over which relation (25) is satisfied, then $\Delta S > 0$. A similar argument may be presented for all the control variables. But $\Delta S > 0$ contradicts the fact that S achieves a maximum at $(\hat{x}, \hat{u}, t)$. Hence by denying (25), we obtain the following necessary condition

$$\text{(26)} \qquad H(\hat{x}, \hat{u} + \Delta u, t) - H(\hat{x}, \hat{u}, t) \leq 0$$

In other words, the maximum of S at $(\hat{x}, \hat{u}, t)$ implies that H is maximized at $(\hat{x}, \hat{u}, t)$ with respect to the control vector u. Thus condition (ii) of Theorem 8.A.1 is proved. Conditions (i) and (iii) are obvious from our choice of the p_i's in equation (12). Thus the proof is complete.

c. VARIOUS CASES

As already remarked, the above theorem is concerned with the case in which the time horizon (T) is fixed and the end-point $x(T)$ is *not a priori* fixed (it is determined from the solution of the problem). However, in many circumstances this may not be the case. For example, if the target of the problem is to minimize the time (T) to reach a certain target, then T is not *a priori* specified but it is rather obtained as a solution of the problem. Such a problem is called the **time optimal problem**. In general, we can formulate various problems depending, first, on whether or not some (or all) coordinates of the state vector $x(T)$ are *a priori* fixed and, second, on whether or not the "final time" (T) is fixed.

A few examples are now in order. In the problem of minimizing the time to fill a bathtub, the final state $x(T) = 100$ (%) is *a priori* fixed, but the final time T is not specified; it is determined as a solution of the problem. In the problem of shooting a missile to intercept an airplane in a minimum amount of time, both the final time T and the final state $x(T)$ are unspecified. They are determined as a part of the solution. In the optimal growth problem of maximizing the discounted sum (integral) of utilities over time $[0, T]$ with fixed initial and terminal capital:labor ratios, k_0 and k_T, both the final time T and the final state $k(T)$ are *a priori* fixed.

We now turn to a general consideration of such problems. First we discuss the case in which m coordinates of the terminal value of the state vector, $x(T)$, are *a priori* fixed, where $m < n$ or $m = n$. Next we consider the case in which the final time T is not *a priori* fixed.

(i) **The Right-Hand End-Point $x(T)$ Partially Specified:** In other words

(27) $$x_i(T) = x_i^T, i = 1, 2, \ldots, m \text{ (fixed)}, m \leq n$$

and no conditions are specified for $x_i(T)$, $i = m + 1, \ldots, n$. In this case we rewrite the transversality condition of Theorem 8.A.1 as follows:

(28) $$p_i(T) = c_i + \lambda_i, i = 1, 2, \ldots, m$$

(29) $$p_i(T) = c_i, i = m + 1, \ldots, n$$

Here the λ_i's are unknown variables that are constant over time. Note that in (27) we have m new equations, which corresponds to m new variables, the λ_i's. The rest of Theorem 8.A.1 holds as it is. Clearly, Theorem 8.A.1 with condition (iii) revised as above is a generalization of the original Theorem 8.A.1. Note that the original theorem is concerned with the case in which $m = 0$ [that is, none of the $x_i(T)$'s are *a priori* specified]. A further generalization of the theorem is obtained if, instead of specification (27), we have the following functional specification on the right-hand end-point $x(T)$:

(30) $$F_j[x(T)] = 0, j = 1, 2, \ldots, m$$

where the F_j's are real-valued differentiable functions. Clearly (27) is a special case of (30) in which $F_j[x(T)] = x_j(T) - x_j^T, j = 1, 2, \ldots, m$. In this case, the transversality conditions (28) and (29) are rewritten as

(31) $$p_i(T) = c_i + \sum_{j=1}^m \lambda_j \frac{\partial F_j}{\partial x_i(T)}, i = 1, 2, \ldots, n$$

where the λ_j's are unspecified variables which are constant over t.[11] It should be clear that (31) is a generalization of (28) and (29) in the sense that (28) and (29) are obtained from (31) (not vice versa). Thus by replacing the transversality condition (iii) by (31), we obtain a further generalization of Theorem 8.A.1.

(ii) **Final Time Open:** We now turn to the consideration of the case in which the "terminal time" T is not *a priori* specified. Since T is not specified, we have one additional degree of freedom in the system. Hence one additional equation is required, which is written as follows:

(32) $$\sum_{i=1}^n p_i(T)\dot{x}_i(T) = 0$$

In view of the constraint equations $\dot{x}_i = f_i[x(t), u(t), t]$, $i = 1, 2, \ldots, n$, equation (32) can be rewritten as

(33) $$H[\hat{x}(T), \hat{u}(T), T, p(T)] \equiv \sum_{i=1}^n p_i(T)f_i[\hat{x}(T), \hat{u}(T), T] = 0$$

Here $[\hat{x}(T), \hat{u}(T), p(T)]$ denotes the solution triplet at T. In terms of $M[\hat{x}(T), T, p(T)]$ as defined in (7), (33) can be rewritten as

(34) $$M[\hat{x}(T), T, p(T)] = 0$$

In the case of an autonomous system in which the f_i's do not explicitly depend on t (that is, $f_i[x(t), u(t)]$), (33) or (34) can be rewritten as

(35) $M[\hat{x}(t), p(t)] = H[\hat{x}(t), \hat{u}(t), p(t)] = 0$ for *all* t

To see this, first note

$$\frac{d}{dt} M[\hat{x}(t), p(t)] = \sum_{i=1}^{n} \frac{\partial \hat{H}}{\partial x_i} \dot{\hat{x}}_i + \sum_{i=1}^{n} \frac{\partial \hat{H}}{\partial p_i} \dot{p}_i$$

Hence, in view of condition (i) of Theorem 8.A.1, we have $dM[\hat{x}(t), p(t)]/dt = 0$, or $M[\hat{x}(t), p(t)]$ = constant for all t. Thus (34) implies (35).

We are now ready to summarize the modifications considered in (i) and (ii).

FIXED VS. VARIABLE END POINTS [MODIFICATION OF TRANSVERSALITY CONDITION (iii)]:

$$x_i(T) = x_i^T, \ i = 1, \ 2, \ \ldots, \ m(m \leq n) \left.\right] \left[\begin{array}{l} p_i(T) = c_i + \lambda_i, \ i = 1, \ 2, \ \ldots, \ m \\ \end{array}\right.$$
$$x_i(T) = \text{unspecified}, \ i = m + 1, \ \ldots, \ n \left.\right] \left[\begin{array}{l} p_i(T) = c_i, \ i = m + 1, \ \ldots, \ n \end{array}\right.$$

"FINAL TIME" OPEN:

autonomous $H[\hat{x}(t), \ \hat{u}(t), \ p(t)] = 0,$ for all t

nonautonomous $H[\hat{x}(T), \ \hat{u}(T), \ T, \ p(T)] = 0$

FIXED "FINAL TIME":   The two conditions given above for the case of open final time are not required for the case of fixed final time.

Theorem 8.A.1 with the above modifications in (i) and (ii) may be called the **generalized Theorem 8.A.1**. However, for the sake of simplicity, we will henceforth refer to this simply as **Theorem 8.A.1**. With these modifications, we are ready to derive the results for various interesting cases as corollaries of Theorem 8.A.1. Not only will these corollaries give us some readily available results, they will also enhance the reader's understanding of Theorem 8.A.1. In fact, the reader will observe that all the theorems listed in chapter 1 of Pontryagin *et al.* [11] are really special cases of this theorem.

(α)   **FIXED-TIME WITH FIXED-END POINTS PROBLEM:**   We consider the following problem in which the final time T is fixed (with fixed end-points):

Maximize: $\displaystyle\int_0^T f_0[x(t), u(t), t]\, dt$
$\quad{}_{u(t)}$

Subject to: $\dot{x}_i = f_i[x(t), u(t), t], \ i = 1, 2, \ldots, n$
and $x_i(0) = x_i^0, \ x_i(T) = x_i^T, \ i = 1, 2, \ldots, n$

Here T is fixed and both the initial and terminal end points, x_i^0 and x_i^T, are also fixed. To consider this problem, define $x_0(t)$ by $\dot{x}_0 = f_0[x(t), u(t), t]$, $x_0(0) = 0$. Then, as we noted earlier, the problem is converted to one of maximizing $x_0(T)$ subject to $\dot{x}_i = f_i[x(t), u(t), t], \ i = 0, 1, 2, \ldots, n$, and $x_0(0) = 0$,

$x_i(0) = x_i^0$, $x_i(T) = x_i^T$, $i = 1, 2, \ldots, n$. Applying Theorem 8.A.1, we obtain the following theorem.

Theorem 8.A.2 (Pontryagin *et al.* **[11], pp. 67–68):** *In the above problem, in order that $[\hat{x}(t), \hat{u}(t)]$ be optimal, it is necessary that there exist a nonzero $(n + 1)$-vector-valued continuous function $p(t) \equiv [p_0(t), p_1(t), \ldots, p_n(t)]$, which has piecewise continuous derivatives, such that*

(i)   *$\hat{x}_0(t)$, $\hat{x}(t)$, $\hat{u}(t)$, and $p(t)$ solve the following Hamiltonian system:*

$$\dot{x}_i = \frac{\partial \hat{H}}{\partial p_i}, \quad \dot{p}_i = -\frac{\partial \hat{H}}{\partial x_i}, i = 0, 1, 2, \ldots, n$$

where

$$H[x(t), u(t), t, p(t)] \equiv \sum_{i=0}^{n} p_i(t) f_i[x(t), u(t), t]$$

and

$$\hat{H} \equiv H[\hat{x}(t), \hat{u}(t), t, p(t)]$$

(ii)   *$H[\hat{x}(t), \hat{u}(t), t, p(t)] \geq H[\hat{x}(t), u(t), t, p(t)]$, for all $u(t) \in U$*
(iii)   *$p_0(t) = $ constant ≥ 0, for all t, $0 \leq t \leq T$*

REMARK: Because of the fixed time assumption, conditions such as $\hat{H} = 0$ do not appear in the above theorem. Note that $\dot{p}_0 = -\partial \hat{H}/\partial x_0 = 0$; hence $p_0(t) = $ constant for all t. The $p_i(T)$, $i = 1, 2, \ldots, n$, are left unspecified because the $x_i(T) = x_i^T$, $i = 1, 2, \ldots, n$, are fixed. Note that $p_0(T) = 1$ cannot be concluded in general, since the solution pair $[\hat{x}(t), \hat{u}(t)]$ with $\hat{x}_i(0) = x_i^0$ and $\hat{x}_i(T) = x_i^T$, $i = 1, 2, \ldots, n$, will imply the specification of $f_0[\hat{x}(t), \hat{u}(t), t]$, and hence its integral, $x_0(T)$. The proof of $p_0(T) \geq 0$ [which, in view of $p_0(t) = $ constant for all t, implies the nonnegativity in condition (iii)] requires a further consideration and it is omitted here. We may note, however, that if we can show that $p_0(T) \neq 0$ [so that $p_0(T) > 0$], then we can take $p_0(T) = 1$.[12] The condition which guarantees $p_0(T) \neq 0$ is analogous to the "normality condition" in nonlinear programming, which is discussed in Chapter 1 (especially Sections B and D).

REMARK: In the ordinary nonlinear programming problem of maximizing a real-valued function $f(u)$ subject to $g_j(u) \geq 0, j = 1, 2, \ldots, m, u \in U \subset R^n$, we can obtain the following theorem (Fritz John's theorem; recall also Theorem 1.B.3).
       If $\hat{u}$ is a solution of the above problem, then there exist multipliers p_0, $p_1, \ldots, p_m$ (all constants), not vanishing simultaneously, such that

$$p_0 f(\hat{u}) + \sum_{j=1}^{m} p_j g_j(\hat{u}) \geq p_0 f(u) + \sum_{j=1}^{m} p_j g_j(u), \text{ for all } u \in U$$

and

$$\sum_{j=1}^{m} p_j g_j(\hat{u}) = 0$$

Clearly condition (ii) of Theorem 8.A.2 corresponds to the first condition in the above theorem for the optimization of the ordinary nonlinear programming problem. As we remarked in Chapter 1, the condition which guarantees $p_0 > 0$ (rather than $p_0 \geq 0$) is called the **normality condition**.

(β) FINAL TIME OPEN WITH FIXED END POINT (NONAUTONOMOUS CASE): Consider the following problem.

$$\text{Maximize:}\ \underset{u(t)}{\int_0^T} f_0[x(t), u(t), t]\, dt$$

Subject to: $\dot{x}_i = f_i[x(t), u(t), t], i = 1, 2, \ldots, n$
and $\quad x_i(0) = x_i{}^0, x_i(T) = x_i{}^T, i = 1, 2, \ldots, n$

Here both the initial and terminal end points, the $x_i(0)$'s and $x_i(T)$'s, are fixed, but final time T is *not a priori* specified. To consider this problem, define $x_0(t)$ by $\dot{x}_0 = f_0[x(t), u(t), t]$ and $x_0(0) = 0$ and utilize the generalized Theorem 8.A.1 for the case of fixed end points with final time open.

Theorem 8.A.3 (Pontryagin *et al.* **[11], pp. 60–61):** *In the above problem, in order that $[\hat{x}(t), \hat{u}(t)]$ be optimal, it is necessary that there exist a nonzero $(n + 1)$-vector-valued continuous function $p(t) \equiv [p_0(t), p_1(t), \ldots, p_n(t)]$, which has piecewise continuous derivatives, such that*

(i) *$\hat{x}_0(t)$, $\hat{x}(t)$, $\hat{u}(t)$, and $p(t)$ solve the following Hamiltonian system:*

$$\dot{x}_i = \frac{\partial \hat{H}}{\partial p_i}, \dot{p}_i = -\frac{\partial \hat{H}}{\partial x_i}, i = 0, 1, 2, \ldots, n$$

where

$$H[x(t), u(t), t, p(t)] \equiv \sum_{i=0}^{n} p_i(t) f_i[x(t), u(t), t]$$

and

$$\hat{H} \equiv H[\hat{x}(t), \hat{u}(t), t, p(t)]$$

(ii) $H[\hat{x}(t), \hat{u}(t), t, p(t)] \geq H[\hat{x}(t), u(t), t, p(t)]$, *for all $u(t) \in U$*

(iii) $H[\hat{x}(T), \hat{u}(T), T, p(T)] = 0$

(iv) $p_0(t) = \text{constant} \geq 0 \quad$ *for all $t, 0 \leq t \leq T$*

REMARK: Condition (iii) of the above theorem is necessary because the final time is open (for a nonautonomous case). The fact that $p_0(t) = \text{constant}$

for all t follows from $\dot{p}_0 = -\partial \hat{H}/\partial x_0 = 0$. The $p_i(T)$, $i = 1, 2, \ldots, n$, are left unspecified because the $x_i(T)$, $i = 1, 2, \ldots, n$, are specified. Note that $p_0 = 0$ is possible in the above theorem.

(γ) TIME OPTIMAL PROBLEM (NONAUTONOMOUS CASE): Consider the following problem.

> Minimize: T
> $u(t)$
>
> Subject to: $\dot{x}_i = f_i[x(t), u(t), t]$, $i = 1, 2, \ldots, n$
> and $\quad x_i(0) = x_i^0$, $x_i(T) = x_i^T$, $i = 1, 2, \ldots, n$

Here both the $x_i(0)$'s and the $x_i(T)$'s are fixed but T is open. The problem is called the **time optimal problem**, for it is concerned with minimizing the time for the transfer from a fixed point x_i^0 to another fixed point x_i^T satisfying the differential equation $\dot{x}_i = f_i[x(t), u(t), t]$, $i = 1, 2, \ldots, n$. Clearly this is a special case of the above problem (β) with $f_0[x(t), u(t), t] = -1$ for all t. Hence defining the Hamiltonian $\tilde{H}$ by

$$\tilde{H}[x(t), u(t), t, p(t)] \equiv -p_0(t) + \sum_{i=1}^{n} p_i(t)f_i[x(t), u(t), t]$$

we can apply Theorem 8.A.3 and obtain the following theorem (here we define $H[x(t), u(t), t, p(t)] \equiv \sum_{i=1}^{n} p_i(t)f_i[x(t), u(t), t]$ and note that $\tilde{H} = -p_0 + H$).

Theorem 8.A.4 (Pontryagin *et al.* **[11], p. 65):** *In the above problem, in order that* $[\hat{x}(t), \hat{u}(t)]$ *be optimal, it is necessary that there exist a nonzero n-vector-valued continuous function* $p(t) \equiv [p_1(t), p_2(t), \ldots, p_n(t)]$, *which has piecewise continuous derivatives, such that*

(i) $\hat{x}(t)$, $\hat{u}(t)$ *and* $p(t)$ *solve the following Hamiltonian system:*

$$\dot{x}_i = \frac{\partial \hat{H}}{\partial p_i}, \quad \dot{p}_i = -\frac{\partial \hat{H}}{\partial x_i}, i = 1, 2, \ldots, n$$

where

$$\hat{H} \equiv H[\hat{x}(t), \hat{u}(t), t, p(t)] \equiv \sum_{i=1}^{n} p_i(t)f_i[\hat{x}(t), \hat{u}(t), t]$$

(ii) $H[\hat{x}(t), \hat{u}(t), p(t)] \geq H[\hat{x}(t), u(t), p(t)]$ *for all* $u(t) \in U$

(iii) $H[\hat{x}(T), \hat{u}(T), T, p(T)] \geq 0$

REMARK: The above condition (iii) follows from $p_0(T) \geq 0$ and

$$\tilde{H}[\hat{x}(T), \hat{u}(T), T, p(T)] \equiv -p_0(T) + H[\hat{x}(T), \hat{u}(T), T, p(T)] = 0$$

(δ)   **FINAL TIME OPEN WITH FIXED END POINTS (AUTONOMOUS CASE):**
Consider the following problem.

(a)   Maximize: $\int_0^T f_0[x(t), u(t)]\, dt$
                $u(t)$

             Subject to: $\dot{x}_i = f_i[x(t), u(t)]$, $i = 1, 2, \ldots, n$
             and $x_i(0) = x_i^0$, $x_i(T) = x_i^T$, $i = 1, 2, \ldots, n$

Here T is not specified. This is a special case (autonomous case) of the problem considered for Theorem 8.A.3. Here, owing to the autonomous character of the problem, condition (iii) of Theorem 8.A.3 is modified as

(36) $H[\hat{x}(t), \hat{u}(t), p(t)] = 0$ for all $t, 0 \leq t \leq T$

The rest of Theorem 8.A.3 holds as is.

Next consider the following time optimal problem for the autonomous case.

(b)   Minimize: T
                $u(t)$

             Subject to: $\dot{x}_i = f_i[x(t), u(t)]$, $i = 1, 2, \ldots, n$
             and $x_i(0) = x_i^0$, $x_i(T) = x_i^T$, $i = 1, 2, \ldots, n$

This is a special case (autonomous case) of the problem considered for Theorem 8.A.4. Here, owing to the autonomous character of the problem, condition (iii) of Theorem 8.A.4 is modified to the following condition:

(37) $H[\hat{x}(t), \hat{u}(t), p(t)] \geq 0$ and constant for all $t, 0 \leq t \leq T$

Thus we obtain the following theorem.

Theorem 8.A.5 (Pontryagin *et al.* **[11], p. 19 and pp. 20–21):** *The necessary conditions for $[\hat{x}(t), \hat{u}(t)]$ to be a solution of problem (δ-a) are obtained by replacing condition (iii) of Theorem 8.A.3 by condition (36). (The other conditions of Theorem 8.A.3 hold as they are.) The necessary conditions for $[\hat{x}(t), \hat{u}(t)]$ to be a solution of problem (δ-b) are the same as those in Theorem 8.A.4, except that condition (iii) of the theorem is replaced by condition (37).*

(ε)   **FIXED-TIME WITH VARIABLE RIGHT-HAND END POINTS PROBLEM:**
Now consider the following problem:

             Maximize: $\int_0^T f_0[x(t), u(t), t]\, dt$
                $u(t)$

             Subject to: $\dot{x}_i = f_i[x(t), u(t), t]$, $i = 1, 2, \ldots, n$
             and $x_i(0) = x_i^0$, $i = 1, 2, \ldots, n$

Here T is fixed but the $x_i(T)$, $i = 1, 2, \ldots, n$, are *not* fixed. Again defining $x_0(t)$ by $\dot{x}_0 = f_0[x(t), u(t), t]$, $x_0(0) = 0$, we can convert the above problem to one of maximizing $x_0(T)$. Thus applying Theorem 8.A.1, we obtain the following theorem.

Theorem 8.A.6 (Pontryagin *et al.* **[11], p. 69):** *In the above problem, in order that* $[\hat{x}(t), \hat{u}(t)]$ *be optimal it is necessary that there exist a nonzero* $(n + 1)$-*vector-valued continuous function* $p(t) \equiv [p_0(t), p_1(t), \ldots, p_n(t)]$, *which has piecewise continuous derivatives, such that*

(i) $\hat{x}_0(t)$, $\hat{x}(t)$, $\hat{u}(t)$, *and* $p(t)$ *solve the following Hamiltonian system:*

$$\dot{x}_i = \frac{\partial \hat{H}}{\partial p_i}, \dot{p}_i = -\frac{\partial \hat{H}}{\partial x_i}, i = 0, 1, 2, \ldots, n$$

where

$$H[x(t), u(t), t, p(t)] \equiv \sum_{i=0}^{n} p_i(t) f_i[x(t), u(t), t]$$

and

$$\hat{H} \equiv H[\hat{x}(t), \hat{u}(t), t, p(t)]$$

(ii) $H[\hat{x}(t), \hat{u}(t), t, p(t)] \geqq H[\hat{x}(t), u(t), t, p(t)]$, *for all* $u(t) \in U$

(iii) $p(T) = (1, 0, \ldots, 0)$ [*that is,* $p_0(T) = 1$ *and* $p_i(T) = 0$, $i = 1, 2, \ldots, n$]

(iv) $p_0(t) = 1$ *for all* t

REMARK: Owing to the transversality condition for the variable end points, $p_i(T) = 0$ for all $i = 1, 2, \ldots, n$. Since $p(T) \equiv [p_0(T), p_1(T), \ldots, p_n(T)]$ is a nonzero vector, this implies $p_0(T) \neq 0$, or $p_0(T) > 0$. Thus without loss of generality we may take $p_0(T)=1$. Hence we obtained condition (iii), especially $p_0(T) = 1$, *without* mentioning anything about the normality condition.

REMARK: Note that condition (i) of the above theorem implies $\dot{p}_0 = -\partial \hat{H}/\partial x_0 = 0$, so that $p_0(t) = $ constant for all t. Hence $p_0(t) = 1$ for all t in view of condition (iii); that is, condition (iv) follows. Thus we may write H as $H = f_0 + \sum_{i=1}^{n} p_i f_i$.

REMARK: It may be of some interest to obtain Theorem 8.A.1 as a special case of Theorem 8.A.6. To do this, recall the remark for Theorem 8.A.1 which noted that the problem of maximizing $S \equiv \sum_{i=1}^{n} c_i x_i(T)$ subject to $\dot{x}_i = f_i[x(t), u(t), t]$, $x_i(0) = x_i^0$, $i = 1, 2, \ldots, n$, can be converted to the following problem:

Maximize: $\displaystyle\int_0^T f_0[x(t), u(t), t]\,dt$
$\scriptstyle u(t)$

Subject to: $\dot{x}_i = f_i[x(t), u(t), t], i = 1, 2, \ldots, n$

and $x_i(0) = x_i^0, i = 1, 2, \ldots, n$

where $\displaystyle f_0[x(t), u(t), t] \equiv \sum_{i=1}^{n} c_i f_i[x(t), u(t), t]$

Then apply Theorem 8.A.6. The Hamiltonian H is defined by $H \equiv p_0 f_0 + \sum_{i=1}^{n} p_i f_i$, which, in view of the definition of f_0, can also be written as $H = \sum_{i=1}^{n} q_i f_i$, where $q_i(t) \equiv c_i p_0(t) + p_i(t), i = 1, 2, \ldots, n$. Conditions (i) and (ii) of Theorem 8.A.1 follow immediately from conditions (i) and (ii) of Theorem 8.A.6. Condition (iii) of Theorem 8.A.1 follows from condition (iii) of Theorem 8.A.6 by noting that $p_0(T) = 1$ and $p_i(T) = 0, i = 1, 2, \ldots, n$, imply $q_i(T) = c_i, i = 1, 2, \ldots, n$.

d.   AN ILLUSTRATIVE PROBLEM: THE OPTIMAL GROWTH PROBLEM

Consider the optimal growth problem discussed in Section D of Chapter 5. Suppose that we are to choose $x(t)$, the time path of per capita consumption, such as to

Maximize: $\displaystyle\int_0^T u[x(t)]e^{-\rho t}\,dt$

Subject to: $\dot{k}(t) = f[k(t)] - \lambda k(t) - x(t)$

with $k(0) = k_0 > 0, k(T) = k_T > 0, k(t) \geq 0, x(t) \geq 0$

The notations used here are the same as those used in Chapter 5, Section D: $\rho \geq 0$ is the discount factor, $k(t)$ is the capital:labor ratio at time t, λ is the rate of population growth plus the rate of capital depreciation, f is the per capita production function, and u is the utility function. We adopt assumptions similar to the ones used in subsection c of Chapter 5, Section D. In particular, we assume the following:

(A-1) $u'(x) > 0$ and $u''(x) < 0$ for all $x \geq 0$.
(A-2) $f(k) < \infty, f'(k) > 0$, and $f''(k) < 0$ for all $k \geq 0$.
(A-3) $f(0) = 0, f'(0) = \infty$, and $f'(\infty) = 0$.

One may notice that this problem is a special case of the general optimal control problem. Here $x(t)$ is the control variable and $k(t)$ is the state variable. The control region for this problem is the entire nonnegative region, which is a closed set. Here we assume that the final time T is fixed and the final state $k(T)$ is fixed. Hence Theorem 8.A.2 is relevant to this problem. The Hamiltonian H is defined by

(38) $H[k(t), x(t), t, p(t)] \equiv u[x(t)]e^{-\rho t} + p(t)[f[k(t)] - \lambda k(t) - x(t)]$

Strictly speaking, H should be

(39)
$$p_0 u [x(t)] e^{-\rho t} + p(t) [f[k(t)] - \lambda k(t) - x(t)]$$

Then condition (ii) of Theorem 8.A.2 implies

(40)
$$p_0 u [x(t)] e^{-\rho t} + p(t) \Big[f[\hat{k}(t)] - \lambda \hat{k}(t) - x(t) \Big]$$
$$\leq p_0 u [\hat{x}(t)] e^{-\rho t} + p(t) \Big[f[\hat{k}(t)] - \lambda \hat{k}(t) - \hat{x}(t) \Big]$$
$$\text{for all } x(t) \geq 0, 0 \leq t \leq T$$

Now if $p_0 = 0$ [note that $p_0(t) = $ constant and ≥ 0 from condition (iii) of Theorem 8.A.2], then

(41)
$$p(t)x(t) \geq p(t)\hat{x}(t) \qquad \text{for all } x(t) \geq 0, 0 \leq t \leq T$$

Since p_0 and $p(t)$ cannot vanish simultaneously, we obtain $p(t) \neq 0$ for all t. If $p(t) < 0$, then (41) implies that $\hat{x}(t) \geq x(t)$ for all $x(t) \geq 0$; thus $\hat{x}(t)$ is unbounded. This is impossible since $\hat{x}(t)$ must be bounded from above because of the feasibility condition $\dot{k}(t) = f[k(t)] - \lambda k(t) - x(t)$. (Recall footnote 12 of Chapter 5, Section D.) Hence $p(t) > 0$ for all t. Set $x(t) = 0$ in (41) and obtain

(42)
$$0 \geq p(t)\hat{x}(t) \qquad \text{for all } t, 0 \leq t \leq T$$

Since $p(t) > 0$ for all t, this implies that $\hat{x}(t) = 0$ for all t. If we impose Koopmans' assumption

(43)
$$\lim_{\substack{x \to 0 \\ x > 0}} u(x) = -\infty$$

then $\hat{x}(t) = 0$ (for all t) cannot be optimal. However, even without (43), we can guarantee that $\hat{x}(t) = 0$ (for all t) is not optimal. To see this, notice that the productivity conditions imposed by (A-2) and (A-3) permit the existence of $\bar{x}(t) > 0$ for all t, which is technically feasible in the economy. Since $u'(x) > 0$ for all x, the path with $\bar{x}(t)$ is better than the path with $\hat{x}(t)$; that is, $\hat{x}(t) = 0$ for all t cannot be optimal. Hence (42) is a contradiction so that (41) is also a contradiction. This then implies that $p_0 = 0$ is a contradiction. Therefore we obtain $p_0 > 0$. We can now choose p_0 to be unity without loss of generality since all the necessary conditions for optimality in the various theorems (such as Theorem 8.A.2) stated so far in this section will not be affected by this choice. This then justifies our definition of the Hamiltonian in (38). The above rather lengthy consideration, which justifies $p_0 = 1$, is usually ignored in the literature.

Furthermore, note that with $p_0 = 1$, (40) may be rewritten as

(44)
$$u[\hat{x}(t)] e^{-\rho t} - u[x(t)] e^{-\rho t} \geq p(t)\hat{x}(t) - p(t)x(t)$$
$$\text{for all } x(t) \geq 0, 0 \leq t \leq T$$

If we assume (43), then (44) implies

(45) $$\hat{x}(t) > 0 \quad \text{for all } t, 0 \leq t \leq T$$

so that we have an interior solution (that is, the optimal control is in the interior of the control region). Later we will see that (45) can also be justified under an alternative assumption such as (63).

The Hamiltonian system for the present problem is written as

(46) $$\dot{k}(t) = f[\hat{k}(t)] - \lambda\hat{k}(t) - \hat{x}(t) \left(= \frac{\partial\hat{H}}{\partial p}\right)$$

and

(47) $$\dot{p}(t) = -p(t)\left[f'[\hat{k}(t)] - \lambda\right]\left(= -\frac{\partial\hat{H}}{\partial k}\right)$$

where ($\wedge$) over $\partial H/\partial p$ and $\partial H/\partial k$ signifies that these partial derivatives are evaluated at $[\hat{k}(t), \hat{x}(t)]$. Assuming an interior solution (that is, $\hat{x}(t) > 0$ for all t), condition (ii) of Theorem 8.A.2 can be rewritten as[13]

(48) $$\frac{\partial\hat{H}}{\partial x} = 0$$

Equation (48) can be spelled out as

(49) $$p(t) = u'[\hat{x}(t)]e^{-\rho t}$$

Since $u'(x) > 0$ for all x, this implies that $p(t) > 0$ for all t. From (49) we obtain

(50) $$\hat{x}(t) = -\frac{\hat{u}'}{\hat{u}''}\left[f'[\hat{k}(t)] - (\lambda + \rho)\right]$$

where $\hat{u}' \equiv u'[\hat{x}(t)]$ and $\hat{u}'' \equiv u''[\hat{x}(t)]$. This is exactly the same equation which is obtained as the Euler equation in the calculus of variations formulation of this optimal growth problem, discussed in Section D of Chapter 5. Hence combining this with the feasibility equation, we can obtain exactly the same phase diagram obtained there (if we assume $u' > 0$ for all x). The extension to the infinite horizon problem can be carried out by examining the "eligibility conditions" as we did there, and thus we can omit this from the present discussion.

Here we may note another important implication of the maximum principle. The maximality of the Hamiltonian H implies the following inequality [set $p_0 = 1$ in (40)]:

(51) $$u[\hat{x}(t)]e^{-\rho t} + p(t)\left[f[\hat{k}(t)] - \lambda\hat{k}(t) - \hat{x}(t)\right]$$
$$\geq u[x(t)]e^{-\rho t} + p(t)\left[f[\hat{k}(t)] - \lambda\hat{k}(t) - x(t)\right]$$
$$\text{for all } x(t) \geq 0$$

This can be rewritten as

(52)
$$e^{-\rho t}\left[u[\hat{x}(t)] - u[x(t)] \right] \geq p(t)\left[\hat{x}(t) - x(t) \right]$$
$$\text{for all } x(t) \geq 0, 0 \leq t \leq T$$

as already observed in (44). From (52) we obtain

(53)
$$u[\hat{x}(t)] - u[x(t)] \geq 0$$
$$\text{for all } x(t) \geq 0, 0 \leq t \leq T, \text{ with } p(t)\left[\hat{x}(t) - x(t) \right] \geq 0$$

In other words, the satisfaction from consumption is maximized along the optimal path for *each* instant of time subject to the budget constraint. From (52) we also obtain

(54)
$$p(t)\left[x(t) - \hat{x}(t) \right] \geq 0$$
$$\text{for all } x(t) \geq 0, 0 \leq t \leq T, \text{ with } u[x(t)] - u[\hat{x}(t)] \geq 0$$

In other words, the consumption expenditure [at "implicit prices" $p(t)$] reaches its minimum along the optimal path at *each* instant of time in the set of paths with utility equal to or exceeding that of the optimal path $[\hat{k}(t), \hat{x}(t)]$. Relations (52), (53), and (54) and their interpretations are the generalizations of Koopmans' proposition F([6], pp. 245–246), for our propositions are concerned with each instant of time. Note also that (49) and (52) yield

(55)
$$u[\hat{x}(t)] - u[x(t)] \geq u'[\hat{x}(t)]\left[\hat{x}(t) - x(t) \right]$$
$$\text{for all } x(t) \geq 0, 0 \leq t \leq T$$

In other words, at *any* instant of time, the excess of $\hat{x}(t)$ over $x(t)$ multiplied by the marginal utility of the optimal consumption at t cannot exceed the excess of utility at $\hat{x}(t)$ over that at $x(t)$.

In fact, the above formulation (51) in terms of the maximum principle and the subsequent implications discussed above should hold even if we replace $u[x(t)]e^{-\rho t}$ and $f[k(t)]$ by more general functions $u[x(t), t]$ and $f[k(t), t]$, where u and f are continuously differentiable in t [as well as in $x(t)$ and $k(t)$]. The function $u[x(t), t]$ allows the possibility of a nonconstant discount, and $f[k(t), t]$ allows the possibility of technological progress. We may rewrite relations (52), (53), and (54) in terms of these new functions u and f as follows:

(52′)
$$u[\hat{x}(t), t] - u[x(t), t] \geq p(t)\left[\hat{x}(t) - x(t) \right]$$
$$\text{for all } x(t) \geq 0, 0 \leq t \leq T$$

(53′)
$$u[\hat{x}(t), t] - u[x(t), t] \geq 0$$
$$\text{for all } x(t) \geq 0, 0 \leq t \leq T, \text{ with } p(t)\left[\hat{x}(t) - x(t) \right] \geq 0$$

(54′)
$$p(t)\left[x(t) - \hat{x}(t) \right] \geq 0$$
$$\text{for all } x(t) \geq 0, 0 \leq t \leq T, \text{ with } u[x(t), t] - u[\hat{x}(t), t] \geq 0$$

The interpretations of these relations follow analogously.

In the above interpretations, it is clear that Pontryagin's "auxiliary variable" $p(t)$ plays the role of the "implicit (or shadow) price." Hence the Pontryagin maximum principle which, among other things, asserts that the maximization of a certain function or integral implies the existence of an auxiliary variable $p(t)$, has, in turn, a very important implication in economics. The situation is strictly analogous to the one in the theory of nonlinear programming in which the maximization implies the existence of the Lagrangian multipliers that play the role of "prices." Koopmans [6] defines the price of output by "the present value of the marginal (instantaneous) utility of consumption at time t." This corresponds precisely to our relation (49), obtained from the maximum principle (note that Koopmans used neither the maximum principle nor the calculus of variations). Define $\check{p}(t)$ by

$$(56) \qquad \check{p}(t) \equiv p(t) \left[f'[\hat{k}(t)] - \lambda \right]$$

That is, $\check{p}(t)$ is the (present) value of the "net" marginal productivity of capital at time t. Using this relation, the optimality equation (47) can be rewritten in the following simple form:

$$(57) \qquad \check{p}(t) + \dot{p}(t) = 0$$

This relation is the same as the one obtained by Koopmans [6] (his proposition I).

Now suppose that we *alter* the above problem such that the terminal endpoint of the state variable, $k(T)$, is *not a priori* specified (with time T still fixed); then we apply Theorem 8.A.6, a theorem for the variable end-points problem. With this modification, the above analysis holds as it is[14] except for two crucial points: (1) We do not have to prove that $p_0 > 0$ (since $p_0 = 1$ for all t), and (2) we have the following transversality condition:

$$(58) \qquad p(T) = 0$$

In view of (49), (58) is rewritten as

$$(59) \qquad u'[x(T)]e^{-\rho T} = 0$$

where we assume that $\rho > 0$. Notice that (59) implies that $u'(x) = 0$ for some x if T is finite. In other words, as long as T is finite, (A-1) looks like it should be modified so as to allow satiation in consumption.

However, as Arrow ([1], p. 88) has shown, we can (and should) modify (58) and hence (59) by recognizing the fact that the terminal state is constrained by the condition $k(T) \geq 0$. In other words, (58) and (59) should, respectively, be rewritten as follows. (For the derivation, see Arrow [1], or Section C of this chapter.)

$$(58') \qquad p(T) \geq 0 \quad \text{and} \quad p(T)k(T) = 0$$

$$(59') \qquad u'[x(T)] e^{-\rho T} \geq 0 \quad \text{and} \quad u'[x(T)]k(T)e^{-\rho T} = 0$$

Hence, if we have $u'(x) > 0$ for all x (no satiation) so that $p(T) > 0$, we must have $k(T) = 0$. This condition then replaces (58). Thus $k(0) = k_0$ and $k(T) = 0$ specify the two boundary conditions for (46) and (47).

To analyze the present problem, we will consider a phase diagram which is different from the one used in Chapter 5, Section D. For this purpose, first note that (A-1) [especially $u''(x) < 0$ for all x] and (49) imply

(60)
$$\hat{x}(t) = g[q(t)]$$

where

(61)
$$q(t) \equiv p(t)e^{\rho t} = u'(\hat{x}_t), \quad g \equiv (u')^{-1}, g' < 0 \quad \text{for all } q$$

In view of (60), (46) can be rewritten as

(62)
$$\dot{k}(t) = f[\hat{k}(t)] - \lambda\hat{k}(t) - g[q(t)]$$

The relation between q and $\hat{x}$ is illustrated in Figure 8.1.

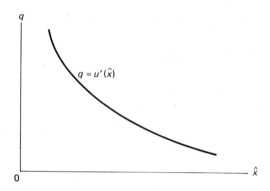

Figure 8.1. The Relationship between q and $\hat{x}$.

Note that if we impose the following assumption à la Cass [3],

(63)
$$\lim_{\substack{x \to 0 \\ x > 0}} u'[x] = \infty$$

we can again assert that the solution is an interior solution, that is, $\hat{x}(t) > 0$ for all t.[15]

Now recalling the definition of $q(t)$ in (61), we rewrite equation (47) as

(64)
$$\dot{q} = -q(t)[f'[\hat{k}(t)] - (\lambda + \rho)]$$

Hence we obtain the phase diagram from equations (62) and (64) as in Figure 8.2.

The transversality condition (58') means that $q(T) \geq 0$ and $q(T)k(T) = 0$. Suppose that satiation is not allowed so that $u'(x) > 0$ for all x. Then $q(T)$ cannot be zero. Hence, as remarked earlier, the transversality condition is replaced by $k(T) = 0$. This means that it is always better to "eat up" the capital to increase con-

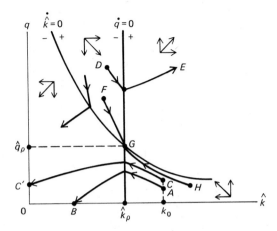

Figure 8.2.   An Alternative Phase Diagram for the Optimal Growth Problem.

sumption for some period of time and leave nothing after the planning horizon. This reflects the fact that $k(T)$ is not *a priori* specified by $k(T) = k_T$. The optimal attainable path would in general be unique up to the boundary conditions $k(0) = k_0$ and $k(T) = 0$. It is illustrated by a curve such as the CC' path in Figure 8.2. A curve such as the AB path cannot be optimal, because at point B we have $q = 0$ so that $u' = 0$, which violates the nonsatiation assumption. Note that a path such as the DE path in Figure 8.2 cannot be optimal whether or not satiation in consumption is allowed, because the transversality condition (58') cannot be satisfied in any way.

What happens for the infinite horizon problem ($T = \infty$)? As long as we do not specify the terminal stock $k(T)$ when $T \to \infty$, the problem is identical with the usual optimal growth problem, that is, the one discussed in Section D of Chapter 5, except in one important aspect. How should the transversality condition be modified for the infinite horizon problem? Note that when $T \to \infty$ the problem of satiation discussed above does not arise, since $p(T) = 0$ when $T \to \infty$ as long as $u'(x)$ is bounded (by the bound on the movement of x). In other words, the condition in the form of either (58) or (58') is satisfied as $T \to \infty$. The real question here is whether such a condition indeed constitutes a condition for optimality. In other words, the question we have to ask is: What is a transversality condition at infinity?

Mathematically speaking, the "transversality conditions" refer to the conditions which require that the state variables be in a particular target set at the terminal point (see, for example, Pontryagin *et al* [11], p. 49). For the finite horizon problem, the values of the state variables would have a definite meaning; but the meaning of the limit of these values when $T \to \infty$ is ambiguous, for the limit may not exist for all attainable paths.[16] Hence the phrase "transversality conditions" is rather meaningless for the infinite horizon problem. Although for the infinite horizon case the condition $[p(T) \to 0$ as $T \to \infty]$ may appear to be a natural extension of the transversality condition $[p(T) = 0$ for finite $T]$, counterexamples have been discovered where this is not true.[17] In general, appropriate conditions for the infinite horizon problem, which replace the transversality conditions for the finite horizon problem, are not known. However, for the present problem of optimal growth, Arrow [1] pointed out that the following condition happens to be necessary for optimality, as long as $\rho > 0$:[18]

(65) $$\lim_{T \to \infty} p(T) \geqq 0 \quad \text{and} \quad \lim_{T \to \infty} p(T)k(T) = 0$$

In other words, the simple extension of the finite horizon transversality condition (58') holds in this particular case.

Clearly any path in which $x(t)$ approaches a finite value as $t \to \infty$ will satisfy condition (65) so long as $\rho > 0$. It can be shown easily that of the paths illustrated in Figure 8.2, only the FG path and the HG path satisfy condition (65) [note that $k(t) \to \hat{k}_\rho$ implies $\hat{x}(t) \to \hat{x}_\rho$ from (46)]. Hence assuming the existence of a unique optimal attainable path, we have FG as the optimal attainable path if $k_0 < \hat{k}_\rho$ and we have HG as the optimal attainable path if $k_0 > k_\rho$. Here $[\hat{k}_\rho, \hat{x}_\rho]$ is the modified golden rule path discussed in Chapter 5, Section D.[19]

In the above analysis, we assumed that $\rho > 0$ (positive discount factor). Suppose now that $\rho = 0$. Then the condition such as $\lim_{T \to \infty} u'[x(T)]k(T) = 0$ which would correspond to (65) does not hold in general. That is, condition (65) is false when $\rho = 0$. As Koopmans ([6], proposition C and lemma 3) has shown, the following condition is necessary for the present problem, with $\rho = 0$:

(66) $$\lim_{T \to \infty} u'[x(T)] = u'(\hat{x}_\rho) \quad \text{and} \quad \lim_{T \to \infty} k(T) = \hat{k}_\rho$$

or

(67) $$\lim_{T \to \infty} p(T) = u'(\hat{x}_\rho) \quad \text{and} \quad \lim_{T \to \infty} p(T)k(T) = u'(\hat{x}_\rho)\hat{k}_\rho \ (\neq 0)$$

Thus in the case where $\rho = 0$, condition (65) is replaced by condition (66) or (67).

Condition (66) reconfirms our conclusion that the only optimal attainable path is the one which converges to the golden rule path. Needless to say, the maximand integral for the case of $\rho = 0$ should be changed to

$$\int_0^\infty \left\{ u[x(t)] - u[\hat{x}_\rho] \right\} dt$$

in order to handle the problem of the convergence of the maximand integral (see Chapter 5, Section D).

Note that condition (67) is a counterexample to the conjecture that the transversality condition for the finite horizon problem is simply extended to the infinite horizon problem by setting $T \to \infty$. Such a conjecture would be false in general regardless of whether there is a restriction on the final state (such as $k(T) \geqq 0$).

When there are no restrictions on the final state, the transversality condition required in Theorem 8.A.6 is $p_i(T) = 0$, $i = 1, 2, \ldots, n$. However, the condition that $p_i(T) = 0$, $i = 1, 2, \ldots, n$, as $T \to \infty$ may fail to hold for the infinite horizon problem. A counterexample, which is due to H. Halkin, is reported by Arrow and Kurz.[20] In view of the importance of the problem, we reproduce Halkin's counterexample here.

Consider a control problem which maximizes

$$\int_0^\infty \left[1 - y(t)\right] v(t) dt$$

subject to $\dot{y}(t) = \left[1 - y(t)\right] v(t)$, $-1 \leq v(t) \leq 1$, and $y(0) = 0$, where $y(t) \in R$ denotes the state variable and $v(t) \in R$ denotes the control variable. Observe that

$$\int_0^\infty \left[1 - y(t)\right] v(t) dt = \int_0^\infty \dot{y}(t) dt = \lim_{t \to \infty} y(t)$$

But by direct integration, $y(t) = 1 - e^{-V(t)}$ where $V(t) \equiv \int_0^t v(\tau) d\tau$. Hence $y(t) < 1$ for all t. Hence any choice of v, $-1 \leq v \leq 1$, for which $\lim_{t \to \infty} V(t) = \infty$ is optimal. For example, $v(t) = v_0$ (constant), where $0 < v_0 < 1$, is optimal. The Hamiltonian for this problem is

$$H \equiv \left[1 + p(t)\right]\left[1 - y(t)\right] v(t)$$

where $p(t)$ is the auxiliary variable. Since $v(t) = v_0$ is a solution, it maximizes H. Since v_0 is in the interior of $\left[-1, 1\right]$, the control region, the maximality of H with respect to v in turn implies that $\partial H / \partial v = \left[1 + p(t)\right]\left[1 - y(t)\right] = 0$. Hence $p(t) = -1$ for all t, since $y(t) < 1$ for all t. Owing to the continuity of $p(t)$, $\lim_{t \to \infty} p(t) = -1$ and *not* 0.

FOOTNOTES

1. The above problem of shooting a guided missile is a favorite example in the literature of optimal control theory. An expository account of the solution of this problem can be found, for example, in Leitmann [9], section 8, chapter 2, and in Saaty and Bram [12].
2. See, for example, K. Shell ed., *Essays on the Theory of Optimal Economic Growth*, Cambridge, Mass., M.I.T. Press, 1967, as well as Arrow [1], El-Hodiri [4], and Shell [13]. See also G. Hadley and M. C. Kemp, *Variational Methods in Economics*, Amsterdam, North-Holland, 1971.
3 The development of the classical calculus of variations reached its culmination in the 1930s, especially at the University of Chicago.
4. The major results in optimal control theory and the relation between the calculus of variations and optimal control theory are discussed in Hestenes [5] in a systematic and unified way. The major content of this work was published in 1965 in the *Journal of SIAM Control*.
5. It received the Lenin Prize in 1962.

6. See, for example, the *Journal of SIAM Control.*

7. In [11], Pontryagin *et al.* emphasized that the range space of the control function can be a closed set (hence a "corner solution" can be discussed in a satisfactory way). In addition to this, they allowed the "control function" $u(t)$ to be "piecewise continuous," and thus they obtained a satisfactory treatment of the "bang-bang" solution (the solution which jumps from one corner to another). The term "piecewise continuity" will be defined shortly.

8. Here the discontinuity is limited to the **first kind**; that is, the left-hand and the right-hand limits are finite ($\lim_{t\to a, t<a} u(t)$ and $\lim_{t\to a, t>a} u(t)$ are both finite), although they are not equal. Note that the definition of piecewise continuity does not exclude the possibility of a function which is continuous over the entire interval.

9. The functions $p(t)$ as well as $x(t)$ are required to have piecewise continuous derivatives (as well as to be continuous) on the interval (t_1, t_2). [The possible discontinuities of $\dot{p}(t)$ and $\dot{x}(t)$ occur at the points of discontinuity of $u(t)$.] Since $p(t)$ is continuous for all t in the closed finite interval, it must be bounded in the same interval. The function $\hat{u}(t)$ is called the **optimal control**, and $\hat{x}(t)$ is called the **optimal trajectory**.

10. It is important to note that the bang-bang solution assumes that the jump in the control is "costless" or "inertialess."

11. An intuitive way to understand (31) is to convert the problem of maximizing $S \equiv \sum c_i x_i(T)$ subject to $F_j[x(T)] = 0$, $j = 1, 2, \ldots, m$, to one of maximizing $\tilde{S} \equiv S + \sum \lambda_j F_j$ and set $\partial \tilde{S}/\partial x_i(T) = p_i(T)$. See Kopp [7], pp. 260–261.

12. If $p_0(T) = 1$, then $p_0(t) = 1$ for all t. Thus the Hamiltonian can be written as $H = f_0 + \sum_{i=1}^{n} p_i f_i$. It is, however, important to note that there is a distinct possibility that $p_0(t) = 0$ for all t. Note also that $p_0(T) = 0$ implies $p_0(t) = 0$ for all t since $p_0(t) = $ constant for all t.

13. Notice that if we *assume* an interior solution in the first place, the proof of normality (that is, the proof of $p_0 > 0$) can be greatly simplified. To see this, note that (48), in view of (39), means $p_0 u' e^{-\rho T} = p(t)$ in the presence of p_0. Hence if $p_0 = 0$, we have $p(t) = 0$ for all t. This contradicts that p_0 and $p(t)$ do not vanish simultaneously for any t. Since $p_0 \geq 0$ by (iii) of Theorem 8.A.2, this proves $p_0 > 0$. Notice that in the text we first proved $p_0 > 0$ *without* using the interior solution assumption, and then *derived* an interior solution in (45).

14. Hence all the relations such as (52), (53), (54), and (55) also hold.

15. This is due to the fact that Pontryagin's auxiliary variable $p(t)$ is continuous and hence bounded for all $0 \leq t \leq T$ [hence for the present problem $q(t)$ is bounded]. More rigorously, when we do *not* assume the interior solution and allow the possibility of a corner solution (that is, the possibility of $\hat{x} = 0$), then equation (48) should be replaced by $\partial \hat{H}/\partial x \leq 0$ with equality if $\hat{x}(t) > 0$. Thus, instead of (49), we will have $p(t) \geq u'[\hat{x}(t)] e^{-\rho t}$. If $p(t)$ is bounded and if (63) holds, then $\hat{x}(t)$ cannot be zero so that $\hat{x}(t) > 0$ for all t.

16. Denote the state vector by $x(t)$ as we did earlier in this section. The transversality conditions require that $x(T)$ be in a certain set, where T is the terminal value of t. The problem is that the limit of $x(T)$ for $T \to \infty$ may not exist for all feasible paths $x(t)$.

17. Counterexamples will be provided later in this section.

18. For a discussion that such a condition is necessary under a more general context, and also for a useful discussion of the transversality condition, see W. A. Brock, "What *Is* a Transversality Condition at Infinity?" University of Rochester, 1969 (unpublished).

19. That is, $\hat{k}_\rho$ and $\hat{x}_\rho$ are respectively defined by $f'(\hat{k}_\rho) = \lambda + \rho$ and $\hat{x}_\rho \equiv f(\hat{k}_\rho) - \lambda \hat{k}_\rho$.

20. See, K. J. Arrow and M. Kurz, *Public Investment, the Rate of Return, and Optimal Fiscal Policy,* Baltimore, Md., Johns Hopkins Press, 1970, p. 46. See also Shell [13].

REFERENCES

1. Arrow, K. J., "Applications of Control Theory to Economic Growth," in *Mathematics of the Decision Sciences*, Part 2, ed. by G. B. Dantzig and A. F. Veinott, Providence, R.I., American Mathematical Society, 1968.

2. Athans, M., and Falb, P. L., *Optimal Control*, New York, McGraw-Hill, 1966.

3. Cass, D., "Optimum Growth in an Aggregative Model of Capital Accumulation," *Review of Economic Studies*, XXXII, July 1965.

4. El-Hodiri, M. A., *Constrained Extrema: Introduction to the Differentiable Case with Economic Applications*, Berlin, Springer-Verlag, 1971.

5. Hestenes, M. R., *Calculus of Variations and Optimal Control Theory*, New York, Wiley, 1966.

6. Koopmans, T. C., "On the Concept of Optimal Economic Growth," in *The Econometric Approach to Development Planning*, Pontificiae Academiae Scientiarvm Scriptvm Varia, Amsterdam, North-Holland, 1965.

7. Kopp, R. E., "Pontryagin Maximum Principle," in *Optimization Techniques*, ed. by G. Leitmann, New York, Academic Press, 1962.

8. Lee, E. B., and Markus, L., *Foundations of Optimal Control Theory*, New York, Wiley, 1967.

9. Leitmann, G., *An Introduction to Optimal Control*, New York, McGraw-Hill, 1966.

10. Mangasarian, O. L., "Sufficient Conditions for the Optimal Control of Nonlinear Systems," *Journal of SIAM Control*, vol. 4, February 1966.

11. Pontryagin, L. S., Boltyanskii, V. G., Gamkrelidze, R. V., and Mishchenko, E. F., *The Mathematical Theory of Optimal Processes*, New York, Interscience, 1962 (tr. by K. N. Trirogoff from Russian original). (A translation by D. E. Brown was published by Macmillan, 1964.)

12. Saaty, T. L., and Bram, J., *Nonlinear Mathematics*, New York, McGraw-Hill, 1964, esp. chap. 5.

13. Shell, K., "Applications of Pontryagin's Maximum Principle to Economics," in *Mathematical Systems, Theory and Economics*, ed. by H. W. Kuhn and G. P. Szegö, Berlin, Springer-Verlag, 1969.

14. Takayama, A., "On the Structure of the Optimal Growth Problem," *Krannert Institute Paper*, No. 178, Purdue University, June 1967.

Section B

SOME APPLICATIONS

a.   REGIONAL ALLOCATION OF INVESTMENT[1]

Consider an economy consisting of two regions (1 and 2),[2] each producing one and the same output, *Y* (called the "national product"). The output of each region is an increasing function of the capital input; hence an increase in the capital stock of each region will result in an increase in the output of that region. The increase in the stock of capital in a region is due to an increase in the investment in that region. Assume that the total investment funds are pooled in a central agency and allocated to the two regions. Then the increase in the investment in a region depends on the allocation of the total investment funds. Assume that total investment funds come from the total savings of the people in the economy. The question is: What is the "optimal" allocation of the total investment funds?

This was the question posed and analyzed by Rahman [10] in his Ph.D. dissertation at Harvard. His analysis, which was in terms of dynamic programming, was reformulated by Intriligator [6] in terms of Pontryagin's maximum principle. Although the reformulation is ingenious, Intriligator's conclusions do not coincide with Rahman's result. This is because of errors involved in Intriligator's analysis. Rahman, in his rebuttal [11], commented on this but failed to come up with a complete and precise analysis. The latter was provided by Takayama ([14] and [15]).

The model presented in the Rahman-Intriligator studies is a very simple one. A linear target is maximized subject to linear differential equations with constant coefficients. Because of its simplicity, this model is very useful as an illustration of Pontryagin's maximum principle. The reader, if he wishes, can always construct a more general model and analyze it in a similar manner.

Assume that the output of each region $Y_i(i = 1, 2)$ is produced with a fixed capital:output ratio so that we have

$$Y_i = b_i K_i, \quad i = 1, 2$$

where K_i denotes the stock of capital in region i and $1/b_i > 0$ denotes the capital: output ratio in the ith region. The variables such as Y_i and K_i are all functions of time t so that we may write $Y_i(t)$ and $K_i(t)$. However, for the sake of notational simplicity, we omit the notation for time except where it might cause confusion to do so. Since the investment funds for the two regions come from the saving done in the whole economy, we have

(1) $$\dot{K}_1 + \dot{K}_2 = s_1 Y_1 + s_2 Y_2$$

where the dot refers to the total derivative with respect to t; that is, $\dot{K}_1 \equiv dK_1/dt$, and so on. Here we assume that the propensity to save s_i of each region is constant for all t and that $0 < s_i < 1$. Defining g_i by

$$g_i \equiv b_i s_i, \quad i = 1, 2$$

we can rewrite (1) as follows:

(2) $$\dot{K}_1 + \dot{K}_2 = g_1 K_1 + g_2 K_2$$

Let $\beta = \beta(t)$ be the proportion of investment allocated to region 1. This β may be called the **allocation parameter**. Clearly $(1 - \beta)$ is the proportion of investment allocated to region 2. Then we have the following set of equations:

(3-a) $$\dot{K}_1 = \beta(g_1 K_1 + g_2 K_2)$$

(3-b) $$\dot{K}_2 = (1 - \beta)(g_1 K_1 + g_2 K_2)$$

with arbitrarily given initial capital stocks $K_1(t_0) = K_1{}^0 > 0$ and $K_2(t_0) = K_2{}^0 > 0$. It is obvious that

(4) $$0 \leq \beta \leq 1$$

The problem facing the economic planner is to choose $\beta(t)$ so as to maximize some objective function. The objective considered by Rahman is to maximize income at some given future terminal time T. In other words, his problem is to[3]

Maximize: $Y_1(T) + Y_2(T) \ [= b_1 K_1(T) + b_2 K_2(T)]$
Subject to: conditions (3) and (4)

Following the maximum principle, especially Theorem 8.A.1, we first define the Hamiltonian as follows:

(5) $$H \equiv p_1 \beta(g_1 K_1 + g_2 K_2) + (1 - \beta)p_2(g_1 K_1 + g_2 K_2)$$

where p_i's are "auxiliary variables" and satisfy the following transversality conditions [see (iii) of Theorem 8.A.1]:

(6) $$p_1(T) = b_1, \ p_2(T) = b_2$$

The Hamiltonian system consists of (3) and the following equations:

(7) $$\dot{p}_i = -\frac{\partial \hat{H}}{\partial K_i}, \quad i = 1, 2$$

Henceforth we omit ($\hat{\ }$), which denotes the optimality, for the sake of notational simplicity.

According to the maximum principle we choose the control variables so as to maximize H.[4] Noting that $H = [\beta(p_1 - p_2) + p_2](g_1 K_1 + g_2 K_2)$, we obtain[5]

(8) $$\beta = 1 \text{ if } p_1 > p_2 \quad \text{and} \quad \beta = 0 \text{ if } p_1 < p_2$$

Equations (7) and (6) can be rewritten as

(7') $$\dot{p}_1 = - [\beta(p_1 - p_2) + p_2] g_1, \quad p_1(T) = b_1$$
$$\dot{p}_2 = - [\beta(p_1 - p_2) + p_2] g_2, \quad p_2(T) = b_2$$

Hence, observing that $\dot{p}_1/\dot{p}_2 = g_1/g_2$ from the above, we obtain[6]

(9) $$p_1(t) = \frac{g_1}{g_2}p_2(t) + \frac{b_1 b_2}{g_2}(s_2 - s_1), \ p_1(T) = b_1, \ p_2(T) = b_2$$

or

(9') $$p_1(t) - p_2(t) = \frac{g_1 - g_2}{g_2}p_2(t) + \frac{b_1 b_2}{g_2}(s_2 - s_1)$$

If $g_1 > g_2$ and $s_2 > s_1$ (also for $g_1 = g_2$ and $s_2 > s_1$, or $g_1 > g_2$ and $s_2 = s_1$), then $p_1 > p_2$ always. Hence, $\beta = 1$. In particular if the saving rates in both regions are the same, we should obviously invest all the funds in that region where productivity of capital, b, is higher. Similarly, if the productivities are the same ($b_1 = b_2$), we should invest all the funds in the region where the saving rate is higher.[7] In this case, therefore, there is no switch for our control variable β. Since this is rather obvious, one may wonder why Intriligator was misled to conclude that there is always a "switch" at the terminal date.

In order to understand the more difficult case $g_1 > g_2$, $s_1 > s_2$,[8] we draw a diagram for equation (9), as in Figure 8.3. Although in Figure 8.3, p_2^* is to the right of b_2, in fact, it may be on either side of b_2. The value of p_2^* is obtained by setting $p_1 = p_2$ in (9):

$$(10) \qquad p_2^* = \frac{s_1 - s_2}{g_1 - g_2} b_1 b_2 \qquad \text{(which is positive by assumption)}$$

We can easily show that:

$$(11) \qquad p_2^* \gtreqqless b_2 \text{ according to whether } b_2 \gtreqqless b_1$$

CASE i: $b_2 > b_1$

This is the case depicted in Figure 8.3. Let t^* be the point of time at which $p_2(t)$ takes the value of p_2^*, and let t_0 be the initial point of time. Since both p_1 and p_2 are monotone decreasing functions of time t from equation (7'), the point t^* is unique and we can consider case i as composed of two subcases.

(i-a) $t_0 < t^*$

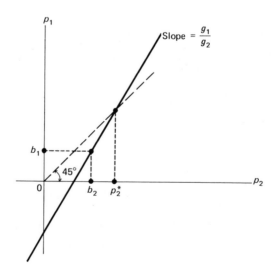

Figure 8.3.   Rahman's Objective with $b_2 > b_1$.

There is a *switch* such that

$$\beta = 1 \quad \text{for } t_0 \leq t < t^*$$

$$\beta = 0 \quad \text{for } t^* \leq t \leq T$$

In other words, this is a case of "bang-bang" control.

(i-b) $t_0 > t^*$

In this case there is no switch and $\beta = 0$ all the time.

In order to find the value of t^*, we solve the following differential equation:

$$\dot{p}_2 = - \left[\beta (p_1 - p_2) + p_2 \right] g_2 \quad \text{where } \beta = 0 \text{ and } p_2(T) = b_2$$

and we obtain

(12) $$p_2(t) = b_2 e^{g_2(T-t)}$$

Equating $p_2(t)$ to p_2^*, the value of which is given in (10), we obtain the exact expression for the switching time t^* as follows:

(13) $$t^* = T - \frac{1}{g_2} \log\left(\frac{s_1 - s_2}{g_1 - g_2} b_1 \right)$$

CASE ii: $b_2 < b_1$

This case is illustrated in Figure 8.4. From the diagram it is clear that $p_1 > p_2$ always so that $\beta = 1$ always. In fact, this should be obvious. Region 1 has a higher propensity to save and a higher productivity.

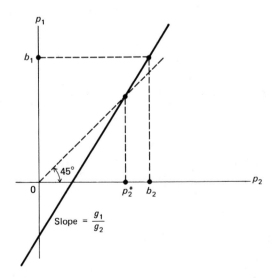

Figure 8.4.   Rahman's Objective with $b_1 > b_2$.

As an alternative objective for the planner, Intriligator proposed to maximize per capita consumption over the planning period. Since consumption, X, is given by $X = (1 - s_1)b_1K_1 + (1 - s_2)b_2K_2$, his target function can be written as

$$\int_0^T \frac{X}{N} dt$$

where N is the population of the economy.[9] Assuming that population grows exponentially at a constant rate n so that[10] $N = e^{nt}$ and letting ρ be the time discount rate for the future consumption, we may rewrite our target function as follows:

$$\int_0^T e^{-\lambda t}\left[(1 - s_1)b_1K_1 + (1 - s_2)b_2K_2\right] dt$$

where

$$\lambda \equiv \rho + n$$

and ρ is assumed to be nonnegative (that is, $\rho \geq 0$). Our problem now is to choose $\beta(t)$ so as to maximize the above target subject to conditions (3) and (4).

To apply Theorem 8.A.6, we first define the Hamiltonian as

$$H \equiv e^{-\lambda t}(b_1K_1 + b_2K_2) + \left[\beta(p_1 - p_2) + p_2 - e^{-\lambda t}\right](g_1K_1 + g_2K_2)$$

and the Hamiltonian system consists of (3) and the following equations:

$$(15) \qquad \dot{p}_i = -\frac{\partial \tilde{H}}{\partial K_i} = -e^{-\lambda t}b_i - \left[\beta(p_1 - p_2) + p_2 - e^{-\lambda t}\right]g_i, \quad i = 1, 2$$

with $p_1(T) = p_2(T) = 0$.[11] The value of β which maximizes $\tilde{H}$ is again

$$(16) \qquad \beta(t) = 1 \text{ if } p_1(t) > p_2(t) \text{ and } \beta(t) = 0 \text{ if } p_1(t) < p_2(t)$$

From (15), we can easily obtain the following expression:

$$(17) \qquad p_1(t) - p_2(t) = \frac{g_1 - g_2}{g_2}p_2(t) + \frac{b_1}{\lambda s_2}(e^{-\lambda t} - e^{-\lambda T})(s_2 - s_1)$$

Hence if $g_1 > g_2$ and $s_1 < s_2$[12] (instead of $s_1 > s_2$), then $p_1(t) - p_2(t) > 0$ for all $t < T$, and the optimal policy is to invest the entire fund in the first region. However, if $s_1 > s_2$ (together with $g_1 > g_2$ and $\lambda \neq 0$), then we cannot arrive at any immediate conclusion about the optimal policy. This forces us to reconsider the problem under Intriligator's target function from a completely fresh viewpoint.

To do this, we obtain from (15) the following equation:

$$(18) \qquad \dot{p}_1 - \dot{p}_2 = -\left[\beta(p_1 - p_2) + p_2\right](g_1 - g_2) + \left[(1 - s_2)b_2 - (1 - s_1)b_1\right]e^{-\lambda t}$$

If $\sigma \equiv (1 - s_2)b_2 - (1 - s_1)b_1$ is negative,[13] then $\dot{p}_1 - \dot{p}_2 < 0$ for optimal values of β, provided that $g_1 \geq g_2$.[14] If $g_1 > g_2$ and $s_1 < s_2$, then $b_1 > b_2$, which is required in order that $\sigma < 0$. Note, however, that σ can be negative even if we have $g_1 > g_2$ and $s_1 > s_2$. Since $p_1(T) = p_2(T) = 0$, $\dot{p}_1(t) - \dot{p}_2(t) < 0$ for all $t < T$ implies $p_1(t) - p_2(t) > 0$ for all $t < T$. Hence the optimal value of β is equal to one. In other words, if $g_1 \geq g_2$ and $\sigma < 0$, we have $\beta = 1$. The same conclusion holds when $g_1 > g_2$ and $\sigma \leq 0$.

However, when $\sigma > 0$, $\dot{p}_1 - \dot{p}_2$ is *not* necessarily negative. In the subsequent analysis, we assume $\sigma > 0$. First we define $q_i(t) \equiv p_i(t)e^{\lambda t}$, $i = 1, 2$. It should be clear that, for all $t \leq T$, $q_1(t) \gtreqless q_2(t)$ according to whether $p_1(t) \gtreqless p_2(t)$. We also note that $q_i(t) \gtreqless 0$ according to whether $p_i(t) \gtreqless 0$ for each t, $i = 1, 2$. From this we can conclude that $q_1(T) = q_2(T) = 0$ and that $q_i(t) > 0$, $i = 1, 2$, for all $t < T$. With this definition of $q_i(t)$, we immediately have the following equations:

(19) $$\dot{p}_i = (\dot{q}_i - \lambda q_i)e^{-\lambda t}, \; i = 1, 2$$

We can also show that $\dot{q}_i(t) < 0$, $i = 1, 2$, for all $t < T$ for $\beta = 1$ or 0, if we assume that $g_i > \lambda$, $i = 1, 2$.[15] Using the definitions of the $q_i(t)$ and (19), we now consider (18) for the two cases $\beta = 0$ and $\beta = 1$.

CASE i: $q_1 < q_2$ (that is, $\beta = 0$)

In this case equation (18) can be rewritten as[16]

(20) $$\dot{q}_1 - \dot{q}_2 = -\left[-\lambda \frac{q_1 - q_2}{g_1 - g_2} + q_2 \right](g_1 - g_2) + \sigma$$

Hence $\dot{q}_1 - \dot{q}_2 = 0$ if and only if the values of (q_1, q_2) satisfy the following equation:

(21) $$-\lambda q_1 + (g_1 - g_2 + \lambda)q_2 = \sigma$$

The locus of (q_1, q_2) values which satisfy (21) is clearly a straight line in the $(q_1 \text{-} q_2)$-plane and divides the entire plane into two parts, that is, the region where $\dot{q}_1 - \dot{q}_2 > 0$ and the region where $\dot{q}_1 - \dot{q}_2 < 0$. We should also recall that we are concerned only with the region where $q_1 < q_2$ with $q_i \geq 0$, $i = 1, 2$. This implies that we are concerned only with the nonnegative region below the 45° line in the $(q_1 \text{-} q_2)$-plane where $\dot{q}_1 - \dot{q}_2 > 0$.[17] We call the region which satisfies these requirements the "relevant region." The relevant region for the present case ($q_1 < q_2$) is illustrated by the shaded triangle in Figure 8.5.

CASE ii: $q_1 > q_2$ (that is, $\beta = 1$)
In this case, (18) can be rewritten as

(22) $$\dot{q}_1 - \dot{q}_2 = -\left[-\lambda \frac{q_1 - q_2}{g_1 - g_2} + q_1 \right](g_1 - g_2) + \sigma$$

Hence $\dot{q}_1 - \dot{q}_2 = 0$ if and only if the values of (q_1, q_2) satisfy the following equation:

(23) $$(g_1 - g_2 - \lambda)q_1 + \lambda q_2 = \sigma$$

The locus of (q_1, q_2) pairs which satisfy (23) is clearly a straight line in the

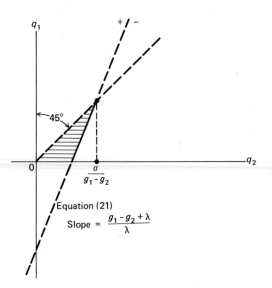

Figure 8.5. Case a: $q_1 < q_2$ with $g_1 - g_2 + \lambda > 0$.

$(q_1\text{-}q_2)$-plane and divides the entire plane into two parts, that is, the region where $\dot{q}_1 - \dot{q}_2 > 0$ and the region where $\dot{q}_1 - \dot{q}_2 < 0$. We should recall that we are concerned with the case in which $q_1 > q_2$; hence the "relevant region" in the present case is the region above the 45° line in the $(q_1\text{-}q_2)$-plane where $\dot{q}_1 - \dot{q}_2 < 0$.[18] We are again concerned with the nonnegative values of q_1 and q_2. The sign of the slope of the straight line which satisfies (23) will differ according to whether $g_1 - g_2 - \lambda > 0$ or < 0.[19] We illustrate the relevant region for the case $q_1 > q_2$ with $g_1 - g_2 - \lambda > 0$ by the shaded triangle in Figure 8.6.

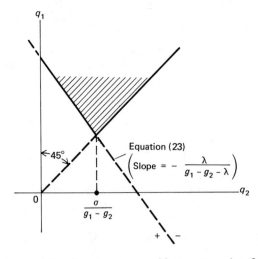

Figure 8.6. Case b: $q_1 > q_2$ with $g_1 - g_2 - \lambda > 0$.

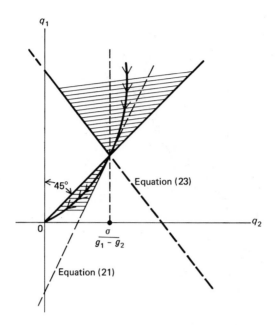

Figure 8.7.   Intriligator's Objective with $g_1 - g_2 - \lambda > 0$.

In Figure 8.7, we combine Figures 8.5 and 8.6, and we obtain the path of (q_1, q_2), which is illustrated by an arrowed line. In Figure 8.8, we illustrate the case in which $g_1 - g_2 - \lambda < 0$, when $q_1 > q_2$. The optimal path of (q_1, q_2) is again indicated by an arrowed line. Note that in both cases—that is, $g_1 - g_2 - \lambda > 0$ and $g_1 - g_2 - \lambda < 0$—there is a possibility of a switch of the optimal policy from $\beta = 1$ to $\beta = 0$. For example, in the case of $g_1 - g_2 - \lambda > 0$, the optimal value of β is equal to one until $q_1(t^*) = q_2(t^*) = \sigma/(g_1 - g_2)$, and then it switches to zero until the terminal point of time T. The same holds for the case of $g_1 - g_2 - \lambda < 0$.

Finally, let us obtain the switching time t^*. This can be done by noting that $q_1(t^*) = q_2(t^*) = \sigma/(g_1 - g_2)$. The explicit expression for $q_1(t)$ with $\beta = 1$ is written as[20]

$$(24) \qquad q_1(t) = \left[\frac{(1 - s_1)b_1}{g_1 - \lambda} \right] \left[e^{(g_1 - \lambda)(T - t)} - 1 \right]$$

Define A as

$$(25) \qquad A \equiv \frac{(g_1 - \lambda)\sigma}{(1 - s_1)b_1(g_1 - g_2)}$$

Then the switching time t^* is obtained as

$$(26) \qquad t^* = T - \frac{1}{g_1 - \lambda} \log (A + 1)$$

If $g_1 > \lambda$, then $A > 0$. Hence if T is sufficiently large so that the RHS of (26) is

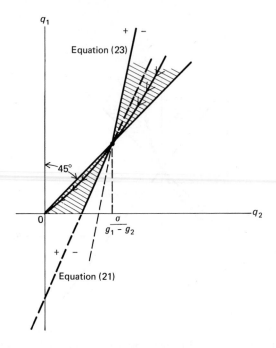

Figure 8.8. Intriligator's Objective with $g_1 - g_2 - \lambda < 0$.

positive, there is a switch of the optimal policy at $t = t^*$. If T is not big enough, there is no switch and the optimal policy will always be $\beta = 0$. If $g_1 < \lambda$, then $A < 0$; hence as long as the difference between g_1 and λ is not too large,[21] $\log(A + 1) < 0$, and there is again a possibility of a switch of the optimal policy at $t = t^*$ provided T is sufficiently large so that the RHS of (26) is positive.

This finishes our analysis under Intriligator's target function. We summarize the results as follows:

(i) $g_1 > g_2$, $s_1 < s_2$ (or $g_1 = g_2$, $s_1 < s_2$; $g_1 > g_2$, $s_1 = s_2$; or $g_1 > g_2$, $\lambda = 0$): $\beta = 1$ always.

(ii) $g_1 > g_2$, $\sigma \leqq 0$: $\beta = 1$ always.[22]

(iii) $g_1 = g_2$, $\sigma > 0$: $\beta = 0$ always.[23]

(iv) $g_1 > g_2$, $\sigma > 0$: possibility of a switch from $\beta = 1$ to $\beta = 0$.

Our results now can be summarized in the following table.[24]

	$s_1 > s_2$		$s_1 < s_2 (b_1 > b_2)$
Rahman's objective function	$b_1 < b_2$ switch	$b_1 > b_2$ $\beta = 1$	$\beta = 1$
Intriligator's objective function	$\sigma > 0$ switch	$\sigma \leqq 0$ $\beta = 1$	$\beta = 1$

We may now discuss whether the model is really plausible or not. The first question is whether we can assume that the b_i's are kept constant, since the b_i's may decline, owing to the law of diminishing returns, as capital accumulates. One reason the b_i's may be kept from declining is that labor is freely available so that the capital:labor ratio is kept constant. However, this is impossible in a full-employment economy unless the total labor supply increases at the same rate as capital. Even in an economy with an "unlimited" supply of labor, it is not easy to conceive of a mechanism which would determine the total employment of labor and the allocation of this labor to different regions such that the capital:labor ratio would remain constant in each region.

Apart from this, a more important question is the implication of our optimal policy which says that the planner should invest all the funds in one region only (say, region 1). If the income is growing in region 1 while the income in region 2 is stagnant, there may be a migration of labor from region 2 to region 1. It is not quite clear whether there should be a mechanism to stop this and whether we should consider the effect of this migration on productivity and the propensity to save of each region. In short, the question we ought to face is whether we can keep labor implicit in our model.

> *ADDENDUM*:   Here we record the explicit expressions for $p_i(t)$ and $\dot{p}_i(t)$, $i = 1, 2$, as functions of time, corresponding to the optimal values of β under Intriligator's objective function. They can be obtained by putting $\beta = 1$ or 0 in equation (15) and solving the linear differential equations thus obtained subject to the boundary conditions $p_1(T) = p_2(T) = 0$.[25]

CASE i: $\beta = 1$

(27)
$$p_1(t) = e^{-\lambda t} \left[\frac{(1 - s_1)b_1}{g_1 - \lambda} \right] \left[e^{(g_1 - \lambda)(T - t)} - 1 \right]$$

(28)
$$\dot{p}_1(t) = e^{-\lambda t} \left[\frac{(1 - s_1)b_1}{g_1 - \lambda} \right] \left[\lambda - g_1 e^{(g_1 - \lambda)(T - t)} \right]$$

(29)
$$\dot{p}_2(t) = -e^{-\lambda t} \left[(1 - s_2)b_2 + \frac{(1 - s_1)b_1}{g_1 - \lambda} g_2 \left[e^{(g_1 - \lambda)(T - t)} - 1 \right] \right]$$

To obtain the expression for $p_2(t)$, we rewrite (17) as

(17′)
$$p_2(t) = \frac{g_2}{g_1} \left[p_1(t) + \frac{b_2}{\lambda s_1} (s_1 - s_2) \left[1 - e^{-\lambda(T - t)} \right] e^{-\lambda t} \right]$$

Then substituting (27) into this, we immediately obtain the expression for $p_2(t)$. Note that $e^{(g_1 - \lambda)(T - t)} \gtrless 1$ according to whether $g_1 \gtrless \lambda$, for all $t < T$. Therefore from (27), (28), and (29) we obtain $p_1(t) > 0$, $\dot{p}_1(t) < 0$ and $\dot{p}_2(t) < 0$, for all $t < T$. Since $p_2(T) = 0$, we also have $p_2(t) > 0$ for all $t < T$. Using (19), (27), and (28), we can easily show that $\dot{q}_1(t) < 0$ for all $t < T$. If $g_1 > \lambda$, we can also show that $\dot{q}_2(t) < 0$ for all $t < T$.[26]

CASE ii: $\beta = 0$

(30)
$$p_2(t) = e^{-\lambda t} \left[\frac{(1 - s_2)b_2}{g_2 - \lambda} \right] \left[e^{(g_2 - \lambda)(T - t)} - 1 \right]$$

(31)
$$\dot{p}_1(t) = -e^{-\lambda t} \left[(1 - s_1)b_1 + \frac{(1 - s_2)b_2}{g_2 - \lambda} g_1 \left[e^{(g_2 - \lambda)(T - t)} - 1 \right] \right]$$

(32)
$$\dot{p}_2 = e^{-\lambda t} \left[\frac{(1 - s_2)b_2}{g_2 - \lambda} \right] \left[\lambda - g_2 e^{(g_2 - \lambda)(T - t)} \right]$$

The expression for $p_1(t)$ can be obtained by substituting (30) into (17'). Using an argument analogous to the one above, we can show that $p_i(t) > 0$ and $\dot{p}_i(t) < 0$, $i = 1, 2$, for all $t < T$. Using (19), (30), and (32), we can show that $\dot{q}_2(t) < 0$ for all $t < T$. Also if $g_2 > \lambda$, we can show that $\dot{q}_1(t) < 0$ for all $t < T$.

b.   OPTIMAL GROWTH WITH A LINEAR OBJECTIVE FUNCTION[27]

Here again we take up the optimal growth problem. The only change we make here is that the objective integral is now defined as

(33)
$$J \equiv \int_0^\infty x_t e^{-\rho t} dt, \text{ where } \rho > 0$$

The constraints, which are exactly the same as before, are

(34)
$$\dot{k}_t = f(k_t) - \lambda k_t - x_t, \text{ and } x_t \geq 0, \ k_t \geq 0$$

The notations are also the same as before: x_t, per capita consumption; k_t, capital:labor ratio; ρ, discount factor; λ, rate of population growth (n) + rate of depreciation (μ); and $f(k_t)$, per capita production function. The subscript t refers to time t. Once again it is assumed that $\lambda > 0$.

This change in the objective function implies a special form of the utility function, that is, $u(x_t) = x_t$, so that the marginal utility is constant (and is equal to 1). The objective (33), the discounted sum of the per capita consumption stream, is in fact quite common in the literature. From the mathematical viewpoint, the crucial change is that the function inside the objective integral is now a linear function with respect to the control variable.

Let s_t be the propensity to save at time t, that is,

(35)
$$s_t \equiv \frac{Y_t - X_t}{Y_t} = \frac{f(k_t) - x_t}{f(k_t)}$$

so that $x_t = (1 - s_t) f(k_t)$. We rewrite the objective integral (33) and the constraint (34) as follows:[28]

(36)
$$J \equiv \int_0^\infty (1 - s_t) f(k_t) e^{-\rho t} dt$$

(37) $$\dot{k}_t = s_t f(k_t) - \lambda k_t, \; s_t \leqq 1, \; k_t \geqq 0$$

In order to emphasize the corner solution, we further assume that $s_t \geqq 0$. Thus s_t is assumed to be bounded in the unit closed interval

(38) $$0 \leqq s_t \leqq 1$$

The fact that $s_t \geqq 0$ means that consumption does not exceed current income; that is, gross investment I_t is nonnegative. This signifies that we do not allow capital to be "eaten up" (except for depreciation), which means that once the output is invested as capital stock it is not used for the purpose of consumption. The assumption of $I_t \geqq 0$ is often called the **irreversibility of investment** (see Arrow [1], for example).

Note three (mathematical) features in the present formulation of the optimal growth problem: (1) the objective function is linear in the control (s_t); (2) the RHS of the differential equation constraint (37) is again linear in s_t; and (3) the control is in the closed region prescribed by (38). Under these features, it will be observed that we obtain a "corner solution" as a usual case. Since it is typically supposed in the classical calculus of variations that the control region is an open set, the corner solution requires special consideration. However, the Pontryagin maximum principle, in which the control region can be a closed set, is well suited for the analysis of this problem. Moreover, the solution of the above problem is such that there is a jump in the optimal control from a corner solution to an interior solution. Hence the assumption of the piecewise continuity of the control function is useful.

The problem is to choose the time path of s_t so as to maximize J defined in (36) subject to (37) and (38) with a given k_0. The solution path is called the **optimal attainable path** (with respect to k_0). For this problem s_t is the control variable and k_t is the state variable. We consider this problem as the one with open terminal end point and apply Theorem 8.A.6. The Hamiltonian for this problem is

(39) $$H[k_t, s_t, t, p_t] \equiv e^{-\rho t}(1 - s_t)f(k_t) + p_t[s_t f(k_t) - \lambda k_t]$$

Omitting (^), which indicates optimality, for the sake of notational simplicity, we write the three necessary conditions from Theorem 8.A.6.[29]

(i) The variables k_t, s_t, p_t solve the Hamiltonian system which consists of (37) and the following equation:

(40) $$\dot{p}_t = -\left[e^{-\rho t}(1 - s_t)f'(k_t) + p_t[s_t f'(k_t) - \lambda]\right]$$

(ii) The Hamiltonian H is maximized with respect to s_t.
(iii) The right-hand end-point condition: $\lim_{t \to \infty} p_t = 0$.

In order to simplify the problem, define q_t by

(41) $$q_t \equiv p_t e^{\rho t} \qquad t < \infty$$

Then $e^{-pt}\dot{q}_t - pe^{-pt}q_t = \dot{p}_t$ so that (40) can be rewritten as

(42) $$\dot{q}_t = (\lambda + p)q_t - \pi_t f'(k_t)$$

where π_t is defined as

(43) $$\pi_t \equiv (1 - s_t) + s_t q_t = 1 + (q_t - 1)s_t$$

In terms of q_t, condition (iii) can be rewritten as

(44) $$\lim_{t\to\infty} q_t e^{-pt} = 0$$

Note also that H can be rewritten in terms of q_t and π_t as follows:

(45) $$H = e^{-pt}[\pi_t f(k_t) - \lambda k_t q_t]$$

Hence condition (ii), the maximization of H with respect to s_t, is realized if and only if π_t is maximized with respect to s_t. Thus

(46) $$s_t = 0 \text{ if } q_t < 1 \quad \text{and} \quad s_t = 1 \text{ if } q_t > 1$$

Note also that

(47) $$\pi_t = 1 \text{ if } s_t = 0 \quad \text{and} \quad \pi_t = q_t \text{ if } s_t = 1$$

In other words, the choice of s_t depends on whether q_t is greater or less than 1, and corresponding to this choice of s_t, π_t is specified in (47). Using such a choice of s_t and the specification of π_t [which in turn is a result of condition (ii)], we investigate the Hamiltonian system [condition (i)]. Therefore we consider our problem by distinguishing the two cases ($q_t > 1$ and $q_t < 1$).

CASE i: $q_t > 1$

In this case $s_t = 1$ and $\pi_t = q_t$ in view of (46) and (47) so that (37) and (42) can be rewritten, respectively, as

(48) $$\dot{k}_t = f(k_t) - \lambda k_t$$

(49) $$\dot{q}_t = -[f'(k_t) - (\lambda + p)]q_t$$

The phase diagram for these two differential equations is depicted in Figure 8.9 [assuming, as before, that $f'(k) > 0, f''(k) < 0$ for all $k \geq 0, f'(0) = \infty$, and $f'(\infty) = 0$].

Here $\bar{k}$ and k^* are respectively defined by the following equations:

(50) $$f(\bar{k}) = \lambda\bar{k}$$

(51) $$f'(k^*) = \lambda + p$$

Note that k^* is the capital:labor ratio in the modified golden rule path, the concept of which was already discussed in Chapter 5, Section D.

Hence, in Figure 8.9, if the initial capital:labor ratio, k_0, is less than k^*, then there exists a path (k_t, q_t) which starts from $[k_0, q(k_0)]$ and reaches the state $(k^*, 1)$. It can be easily shown that such a path reaches the state $(k^*, 1)$ within a finite amount of time—say, T—and along this path q_t is always greater than 1. Assuming that $k_0 < k^*$, we define another path

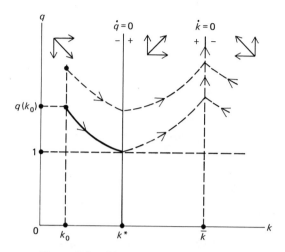

Figure 8.9. Phase Diagram When $q_t > 1$.

(k_t', q_t'), which is the same as the above path for the period $0 \leq t \leq T$ but is $(k^*, 1)$ for $t > T$.

We may now examine whether the path $(k^*, 1)$ satisfies the system of differential equations (37) and (42). To do this, first note that $q_t = 1$ implies $\pi_t = 1$, and for the path $(k^*, 1)$, $\dot{k}_t = 0$ and $\dot{q}_t = 0$. Therefore, (37) and (42) are reduced to

$$(52) \qquad\qquad 0 = s_t f(k^*) - \lambda k^*$$

$$(53) \qquad\qquad 0 = (\lambda + \rho) - f'(k^*)$$

Equation (53) is obviously satisfied by the definition of k^* [see (51)]. Equation (52) is satisfied if and only if s_t takes the value

$$(54) \qquad\qquad s_t = s^* \equiv \frac{\lambda k^*}{f(k^*)} \quad \text{for all } t$$

Note that $s^* > 0$, and that $k^* < \bar{k}$ implies $s^* < 1$. Hence we have $0 < s^* < 1$, which satisfies (38). Thus $(k^*, 1)$ satisfies both (37) and (42).

Hence the path (k_t', q_t') defined above satisfies all three conditions of the maximum principle for this problem, including condition (iii) [or (44)]. It can be easily shown that along this path (k_t', q_t'), the integral J defined by (36) also converges.

CASE ii: $q_t < 1$

In this case $s_t = 0$ and $\pi_t = 1$ in view of (46) and (47), so that (37) and (42) can be rewritten respectively as

$$(55) \qquad\qquad \dot{k}_t = -\lambda k_t$$

$$(56) \qquad\qquad \dot{q}_t = (\lambda + \rho)q_t - f'(k_t)$$

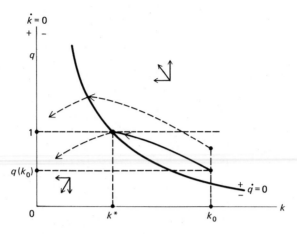

Figure 8.10.   Phase Diagram When $q_t < 1$.

The phase diagram for these two differential equations is depicted in Figure 8.10.

If $k_0 > k^*$, there exists a path (k_t, q_t), starting from $[k_0, q(k_0)]$, such that it reaches the state $(k^*, 1)$. This is also illustrated by an alternative phase diagram, Figure 8.11, which again can be obtained from (55) and (56). It can be shown that it reaches $(k^*, 1)$ within a finite amount of time—say, $\overline{T}$.

Assuming $k_0 > k^*$, we therefore define the path, denoted by (k_t'', q_t''), as the above path for the period $0 \le t \le \overline{T}$ and $(k^*, 1)$ for $t > \overline{T}$. Clearly (k_t'', q_t'') satisfies all three conditions of the maximum principle for the present problem, including condition (44). Also, along this path, the integral J defined by (36) converges.

We may summarize the above discussion in the following theorem.

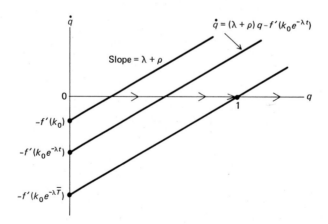

Figure 8.11.   An Alternative Phase Diagram When $q_t < 1$.

Theorem 8.B.1:   *For the above model, given an arbitrary initial value of k, there is a unique optimal attainable path which is characterized as follows:*

    (i) $k_0 < k^*$: $s_t = 1$, *and after k_t reaches k^*, $k_t = k^*$ for all such t; that is, the path (k_t^I, q_t^I).*

    (ii) $k_0 > k^*$: $s_t = 0$, *and after k_t reaches k^*, $k_t = k^*$ for all such t; that is, the path (k_t^{II}, q_t^{II}).*

    (iii) $k_0 = k^*$: $k_t = k^*$ for all t and $s_t = s^* = \lambda k^*/f(k^*)$.

In other words, the optimal attainable path is the one that reaches the modified golden rule path (k^*, x^*) [where $x^* \equiv (1 - s^*)f(k^*)$] with a maximum speed and stays thereafter on it. This optimal attainable path is illustrated in Figure 8.12.

    Thus the solution path is such that if $k_0 < k^*$, the economy maximizes savings from current income until time T and after time T maintains a constant saving ratio s^*; if $k_0 > k^*$, the economy minimizes saving from current income until time $\overline{T}$ and after time $\overline{T}$ maintains a constant saving ratio s^*. As is clear from the above diagrams, the optimal saving ratio is a kind of bang-bang control or, more precisely, "bang-off" (or "bang-coast") control.

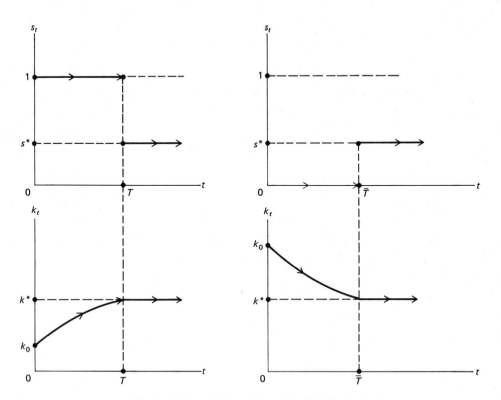

Figure 8.12.   An Illustration of the Solution Path.

FOOTNOTES

1. This subsection is taken from Takayama ([14] and [15]), which were originally developed in his lectures at the University of Minnesota in the spring of 1966.

2. Our analysis can be modified to a two-sector economy (for example, agriculture and industry). It can also be extended to an n-region or n-sector economy without too much difficulty. An attempt for the two-sector economy is made by Bruno [3].

3. We can also consider the objective function in the form of $c_1 Y_1(T) + c_2 Y_2(T)$ where c_i is some weight attached to the income of each region by the planner. The analysis, in this case, will be analogous to the one which we develop below. It is also possible to consider different propensities to save of each factor (labor, capital, and so on). The analysis will be similar as long as we assume fixed coefficients of production. For such variations, see, for example, Dorfman [5].

4. The maximum principle, as it is presented and proved by Pontryagin *et al.* [9], gives necessary conditions for the optimum. Since the right-hand sides of equations (3-a) and (3-b) are linear (hence concave) functions of β, K_1 and K_2, the maximum principle is also sufficient for the optimum. See Mangasarian [8] and Section C of this chapter.

5. We can interpret p_i as the "shadow price" of investment in the ith region. Condition (8) can be interpreted simply as investing the entire fund in the region where the "shadow price" of investment is higher.

6. From (7'), it should be clear that $p_1(t) > 0$ and $p_2(t) > 0$, for $0 \le t \le T$, for the optimal values of β (0 or 1).

7. If $g_1 = g_2$ and $s_1 = s_2$, the two regions would look exactly the same to the planner, so that the choice between the two would be indifferent.

8. Since the name of the region is arbitrary, this exhausts all the possible cases.

9. We can certainly extend our analysis to the case in which the target function is more generally defined as $\int_0^T (X/N)e^{-\rho t}dt + a_1 K_1(T) + a_2 K_2(T)$ where ρ is a time discount factor for future consumption and a_i is a weight attached by the planner for the capital stock in the ith region at time T.

10. We choose the units of population properly so that the initial amount of pupulation is equal to one.

11. We can show that $p_1(t)$ and $p_2(t)$ are positive, $0 \le t < T$, if $\beta = 1$ or 0.

12. Or: (i) $g_1 = g_2$, $s_1 < s_2$; (ii) $g_1 > g_2$, $s_1 = s_2$; (iii) $g_1 > g_2$, $\lambda = 0$.

13. If $g_1 > g_2$ and $s_1 > s_2$, then $[(1 - s_2)b_2 - (1 - s_1)b_1]$ is not necessarily negative.

14. This is because we can show that $p_1(t) > 0$ and $p_2(t) > 0$, for all $t < T$, if $\beta = 1$ or 0, and that the optimal value of β is either 0 or 1. In the Addendum to this subsection, we show our proof for $p_1(t)$, $p_2(t) > 0$, for all $t < T$, if $\beta = 1$ or 0. In the argument that follows, we assume that $g_1 > g_2$. If $g_1 = g_2$ and $\sigma > 0$, then $\dot{p}_1 - \dot{p}_2 > 0$ so that $p_1 - p_2 < 0$ for all $t < T$. In other words, the optimal policy is to invest the entire fund in the second region ($\beta = 0$). When $g_1 = g_2$ and $\sigma < 0$, $\beta = 1$ always. But this case is already covered by case i of footnote 12.

15. See the Addendum to this subsection.

16. We may recall that $g_1 > g_2$ by assumption.

17. This is due to the fact that $\dot{q}_1 - \dot{q}_2 > 0$ implies $q_1 - q_2 < 0$ for all $t < T$ since $q_1(T) = q_2(T) = 0$. If $\dot{q}_1 - \dot{q}_2 < 0$, then $q_1 > q_2$, which is a case that should be excluded from the assumption of the present case ($q_1 < q_2$). We also note that $q_i \ge 0$, $i = 1, 2$, for all $t \le T$. Hence we are concerned with the nonnegative orthant of the (q_1-q_2)-plane.

18. Again this is due to the fact that $\dot{q}_1 - \dot{q}_2 < 0$ implies $q_1 - q_2 > 0$ for all $t < T$ since $q_1(T) = q_2(T) = 0$.

19. If we approximate the discount factor ρ by the current market rate of interest, the g_i's may become much larger than $\lambda(\equiv n + \rho)$, where n is the rate of population growth. Note also that if this is the case, both $q_i(t)$, $i = 1, 2$, decrease over time for all $t < T$.

20. See the Addendum to this subsection, especially (27), and recall that $p_1(t) \equiv q_1(t)e^{-\lambda t}$.

21. If the difference between g_1 and λ is too big, then $(A + 1)$ is negative and (26) makes no sense. We may avoid such a possibility altogether by assuming that $g_1 > \lambda$.

22. In this case, $b_1 > b_2$. Needless to say, $b_1 > b_2$ and $g_1 > g_2$ do not necessarily imply $\sigma \leqq 0$.

23. In this case, $b_1 < b_2$.

24. Here we assume that $g_1 > g_2$.

25. Some of the computational procedure can be simplified by transforming the $p_i(t)$ to $q_i(t)$ and noting (19).

26. Use (19), (29), (17'), and (27).

27. This part is also from my lectures at the University of Minnesota given in the spring of 1966. This is a simplification of Uzawa's model [16], which involves the two sectors, material output and knowledge. This simplification illuminates the significance of a linear objective more dramatically.

28. The condition that $x_t \geqq 0$ or, equivalently, $s_t \leqq 1$, implicitly assumes that the starvation level of consumption is zero. If we want to explicitly consider a positive level of consumption as the starvation level, then we alter this condition to $x_t \geqq \bar{x} > 0$ or, equivalently, $s_t \leqq \bar{s} < 1$, where $\bar{x}$ is the starvation level of consumption and $\bar{s}$ is the corresponding propensity to save. However, this change will not alter the subsequent analysis in any essential way as we simply assume $\bar{x} = 0$.

29. Using a proof similar to the one used in Mangasarian's theorem [8], or in Theorem 8.C.5, we can show that these conditions are also sufficient for optimality. Note also that condition (iii) below needs a proof, for Theorem 8.A.6 is concerned only with the finite horizon problem.

REFERENCES

1. Arrow, K. J., "Optimal Capital Policy with Irreversible Investment," in *Value, Capital, and Growth, Papers in Honour of Sir John Hicks*, ed. by J. N. Wolfe, Edinburgh, Edinburgh University Press, 1968.

2. ———, "Applications of Control Theory to Economic Growth," in *Mathematics of the Decision Sciences*, Part 2, ed. by G. B. Dantzig and A. F. Veinott, Providence, R. I., American Mathematical Society, 1968.

3. Bruno, M., "Optimal Accumulation in Discrete Capital Models," in *Essays on the Theory of Optimal Economic Growth*, ed. by K. Shell, Cambridge, Mass., M. I. T. Press, 1967.

4. Cass, D., "Optimum Growth in an Aggregative Model of Capital Accumulation," *Review of Economic Studies*, XXXII, July 1965.

5. Dorfman, R., "Regional Allocation of Investment: Comment," *Quarterly Journal of Economics*, LXXII, February 1963.

6. Intriligator, M. S., "Regional Allocation of Investment: Comment," *Quarterly Journal of Economics*, LXXIII, November 1964.

7. Koopmans, T. C., "On the Concept of Optimal Economic Growth," in *The Econometric Approach to Development Planning*, Pontificiae Academiae Scientiarvm Scriptvm Varia, Amsterdam, North-Holland, 1965 (also "Discussion" on pp. 289–300).

8. Mangasarian, O. L., "Sufficient Conditions for the Optimal Control of Nonlinear Systems," *Journal of SIAM Control*, vol. 4, February 1966.

9. Pontryagin, L. S., *et al.*, *The Mathematical Theory of Optimal Processes*, tr. by Trirogoff, New York, Interscience, 1962.

10. Rahman, M. A., "Regional Allocation of Investment," *Quarterly Journal of Economics*, LXXII, February 1963.

11. ———, "Regional Allocation of Investment: Continuous Version," *Quarterly Journal of Economics*, LXXV, February 1966.

12. Takayama, A., "On the Structure of the Optimal Growth Problem," *Krannert Institute Paper*, No. 178, Purdue University, June 1967.

13. ———, "Per Capita Consumption and Growth: A Further Analysis," *Western Economic Journal*, V, March 1967.

14. ———, "Regional Allocation of Investment: A Further Analysis," *Quarterly Journal of Economics*, LXXXI, May 1967.

15. ———, "Regional Allocation of Investment: Corrigendum," *Quarterly Journal of Economics*, LXXXII, August, 1968 (also *Krannert Institute Paper*, No. 186, Purdue University, August 1967).

16. Uzawa, H., "Optimal Technical Change in an Aggregative Model of Economic Growth," *International Economic Review*, 5, January 1965.

Section C

FURTHER DEVELOPMENTS IN OPTIMAL CONTROL THEORY

a. CONSTRAINT: $g[x(t), u(t), t] \geqq 0$

In many applications of optimal control theory it is necessary to consider explicitly constraints of the following form:

$$(1) \qquad g_j[x(t), u(t), t] \geqq 0, j = 1, 2, \ldots, m$$

or, in vector notation,

$$(2) \qquad g[x(t), u(t), t] \geqq 0$$

We refer to constraints of the form (1) or (2) as the "*g*-**constraints**." In the g-constraints, it is important to note that the control function $u(t)$ explicitly enters the g-function. Throughout this section, our g-function contains $u(t)$.[1]

With the above constraints, we consider the following control problem.

PROBLEM I:

$$\text{Maximize:} \quad I \equiv \int_0^T f_0[x(t), u(t), t]\, dt$$
$$\scriptstyle u(t) \in U$$

$$\text{Subject to:} \quad \dot{x}_i = f_i[x(t), u(t), t], i = 1, 2, \ldots, n$$
$$g_j[x(t), u(t), t] \geq 0, j = 1, 2, \ldots, m$$
$$x_i(0) = x_i^0, i = 1, 2, \ldots, n$$

Here f_0, the f_i's, and the g_j's are assumed to be continuously differentiable in (x, u, t)-space. The functions $x_i(t)$, $i = 1, 2, \ldots, n$, $0 \leq t \leq T$, are continuous, and the $u_i(t)$, $i = 1, 2, \ldots, r$, are piecewise continuous. In this problem the final time T is fixed and the terminal end points, the $x_i(T)$'s, are not specified.

Here we shall not attempt a full exposition of the maximum principle with the g-constraints (1). Instead, following Arrow [1], we simply give below a heuristic explanation of the main result for Problem I.

First we consider the above problem *without* the constraints (1); the problem is then reduced to the one discussed for Theorem 8.A.6. Hence we obtain the necessary conditions described in that theorem. The essential part of Theorem 8.A.6 is the maximization of H with respect to u. That is, for each t,

$$(3) \qquad H[\hat{x}(t), \hat{u}(t), t, p(t)] \geq H[\hat{x}(t), u(t), t, p(t)] \qquad \text{for all } u(t) \in U$$

where

$$(4) \qquad H[x(t), u(t), t, p(t)] \equiv f_0 + \sum_{i=1}^m p_i f_i$$

Now we add constraints (1) to the problem and consider the maximization of H as a constrained maximum problem, that is, the problem of maximizing H subject to the constraints (1). Thus (3) may now be replaced by

$$(5) \qquad \hat{u}(t) \text{ maximizes } H[\hat{x}(t), u(t), t, p(t)] \text{ (for each } t)$$

$$\text{subject to } g_j[\hat{x}(t), u(t), t] \geq 0, j = 1, 2, \ldots, m, \text{ and } u(t) \in U$$

Let us now define the **Lagrangian** L (or the **generalized Hamiltonian**) by

$$(6) \qquad L[x(t), u(t), t, p(t), q(t)] \equiv H[x(t), u(t), t, p(t)]$$

$$+ \sum_{j=1}^m q_j(t) g_j[x(t), u(t), t]$$

where H is defined by (4), and the $q_j(t)$'s are the "multipliers" associated with the g-constraints. Then, in view of our discussions in Chapter 1, the maximization of L implies the following conditions for each t, provided the "constraint qualification"[2] holds:[3]

(7) $\dfrac{\partial \hat{L}}{\partial u_i} = 0, i = 1, 2, \ldots, r$, where $\hat{L} \equiv L[\hat{x}(t), \hat{u}(t), t, p(t), q(t)]$

(8) $q(t) \cdot g[\hat{x}(t), \hat{u}(t), t] = 0$ and $q(t) \geq 0$, where $q(t) \equiv [q_1(t), \ldots, q_m(t)]$

or

$$q_j(t)g_j[\hat{x}(t), \hat{u}(t), t] = 0 \text{ and } q_j(t) \geq 0 \quad \text{for each } j = 1, 2, \ldots, m$$

$$(\because g_j[\hat{x}(t), \hat{u}(t), t] \geq 0 \text{ for all } j)$$

The constraint qualification was discussed in detail in Chapter 1. Here we simply remind the reader of some conditions of the Arrow-Hurwicz-Uzawa theorem [2] (Theorem 1.D.4).

Lemma: *Any one of the following conditions provides the constraint qualification*:

(i) *The functions $g_j[x, u, t]$, $j = 1, 2, \ldots, m$, are all convex functions in u.*

(ii) *The functions $g_j[x, u, t]$, $j = 1, 2, \ldots, m$, are all linear functions in u.*

(iii) *The functions $g_j[x, u, t]$, $j = 1, 2, \ldots, m$, are all concave functions in u and there exists a $\bar{u} \in \bar{U}$ such that $g_j[\hat{x}, \bar{u}, t] > 0$, for all j.*

(iv) *The functions $g_j[x, u, t]$, $j = 1, 2, \ldots, m$, satisfy the rank condition for each t; that is, the rank of $[\partial g_j / \partial u_i]_E$ [evaluated at $(\hat{x}, \hat{u})$ where E denotes that j is taken from the effective constraints] must be equal to the number of effective constraints in $g_j(\hat{x}, \hat{u}, t) \geq 0, j = 1, 2, \ldots, m$.[4]*

We can now state the necessary conditions for Problem I.

Theorem 8.C.1:   *Assuming that the constraint qualification holds, in order that $\hat{u}(t)$ be a solution of Problem I with the corresponding state variable $\hat{x}(t)$, it is necessary that there exist vector-valued functions $p(t) \equiv [p_1(t), p_2(t), \ldots, p_n(t)]$ and $q(t) \equiv [q_1(t), q_2(t), \ldots, q_m(t)]$[5], where the $p_i(t)$'s are continuous and have piecewise continuous derivatives and the $q_j(t)$'s are piecewise continuous and continuous at all points of continuity of $\hat{u}(t)$, such that*

(i) *The function $p(t)$ together with $\hat{u}(t)$ and $\hat{x}(t)$ solve the following **Hamiltonian system**:*

(9) $\dot{x}_i = \dfrac{\partial \hat{L}}{\partial p_i}$ and $\dot{p}_i = -\dfrac{\partial L}{\partial x_i}, i = 1, 2, \ldots, n,$

for each interval on which $\hat{u}(t)$ is continuous

(ii) $H[\hat{x}(t), \hat{u}(t), t, p(t)] \geq H[\hat{x}(t), u(t), t, p(t)]$

for all $u(t) \in U$ such that $g_j[\hat{x}(t), u(t), t] \geq 0, j = 1, 2, \ldots, m$.

(iii) $\dfrac{\partial \hat{L}}{\partial u_i} = 0, i = 1, 2, \ldots, m,$ and

(10) $\qquad q_j(t)g_j\big[\hat{x}(t), \hat{u}(t), t\big] = 0, \quad q_j(t) \geq 0, \quad j = 1, 2, \ldots, m$

(iv) $\dfrac{d}{dt}\hat{L} = \dfrac{\partial}{\partial t}\hat{L}$ [6]

(v) $p_i(T) = 0, i = 1, 2, \ldots, n$

REMARK: If L is a concave function in u, then condition (iii) implies condition (ii).[7] The function L is concave in u if, for example, f_0, the f_i's, and the g_j's are all concave in u and the p_i's are all nonnegative.

REMARK: A typical situation in economics is that the control $u(t)$ is constrained by the nonnegativity condition, that is,

(11) $\qquad\qquad\qquad u_i(t) \geq 0, i = 1, 2, \ldots, r$

We can treat this as a special case of the g-constraints in which $g_0[x(t), u(t), t] \equiv u(t) \geq 0$. Then the L-function can be written as

(12) $\qquad\qquad L \equiv H + q(t)\cdot g + \mu(t)\cdot u(t)$

where

$$H\big[x(t), u(t), t, p(t)\big] \equiv f_0\big[x(t), u(t), t\big] + \sum_{i=1}^{n} p_i(t)f_i\big[x(t), u(t), t\big]$$

and

$$q(t) \equiv \big[q_1(t), \ldots, q_m(t)\big], g \equiv \big[g_1, \ldots, g_m\big], g_j \equiv g_j\big[x(t), u(t), t\big]$$
$$j = 1, 2, \ldots, m, \mu(t) \equiv \big[\mu_1(t), \ldots, u_r(t)\big]$$

Then condition (iii) [with (10)] of the above theorem implies[8]

(13) $\qquad \dfrac{\partial \hat{L}_+}{\partial u_i} \leq 0 \quad$ and $\quad \dfrac{\partial \hat{L}_+}{\partial u_i}\hat{u}_i = 0, i = 1, 2, \ldots, r$

where

$$\hat{H} \equiv H\big[\hat{x}(t), \hat{u}(t), t, p(t)\big] \quad \text{and} \quad \hat{L}_+ \equiv \hat{H} + \sum_{j=1}^{m} q_j(t)g_j\big[\hat{x}(t), \hat{u}(t), t\big]$$

Conversely, if (13) holds, then we can easily find multipliers $\mu_i(t) \geq 0$, $i = 1, 2, \ldots, n$, so that condition (iii) of the above theorem is satisfied. An alert reader may have realized that this procedure and condition (13) are analogous to those discussed in connection with the nonnegative quasi-saddle-point condition in Chapter 1, Section D.

REMARK: It should also be realized that Pontryagin's maximum principle as discussed in Section A can be considered as a special case of Theorem

8.C.1, in which $g_j[x(t), u(t), t] \geq 0$ takes the form $g_j[u(t)] \geq 0, j = 1, 2, \ldots, m$, or the constraint region $\bar{U}$ is restricted by the g-constraint.

In many problems of economics, it may be desirable to impose the following condition explicitly:[9]

(14) $$x_i(T) \geq 0, \ i = 1, 2, \ldots, n$$

To do so, we first alter the objective functional of Problem I as follows:

(15) $$J \equiv \int_0^T f_0[x(t), u(t), t] \, dt + \sum_{i=1}^n c_i x_i(T)$$

where T is fixed, $x(T)$ is not specified, and the c_i, $i = 1, 2, \ldots, n$, are some fixed constants. The transversality condition for Problem I with this change in the objective is

(16) $$p_i(T) = c_i, \ i = 1, 2, \ldots, n$$

instead of condition (v) of the above theorem. Now suppose that each c_i is chosen such that it is a sufficiently large positive number if $x_i(T) < 0$ and is zero if $x_i(T) \geq 0$. This choice of the c_i's amounts to putting a prohibitively high penalty for negative $x_i(T)$'s so that in the optimal program, negative $x_i(T)$'s are avoided. Thus we can guarantee $x_i(T) \geq 0$ for all i. In view of this choice of the c_i's, the transversality condition (16) should be rewritten as [10]

(17) $$p_i(T) \geq 0 \quad \text{and} \quad p_i(T)\hat{x}_i(T) = 0, \ i = 1, 2, \ldots, n$$

Hence we obtain the following corollary of Theorem 8.C.1.

Corollary: *Assuming that the constraint qualification is satisfied, in order that $[\hat{x}(t), \hat{u}(t)]$ be a solution pair of Problem I, with the additional constraint $x_i(T) \geq 0$, $i = 1, 2, \ldots, n$, it is necessary that there exist continuous (and bounded) vector-valued functions $p(t)$ and $q(t)$ such that conditions (i), (ii), (iii), and (iv) of the previous theorem hold and condition (17) holds instead of condition (v).*

REMARK: If the objective functional for Theorem 8.C.1 is replaced by the one with an infinite horizon,

(18) $$I_\infty \equiv \int_0^\infty f_0[x(t), u(t), t] \, dt$$

then assuming that an optimal policy exists, all the conclusions of the above corollary except condition (17) and all the conclusions of Theorem 8.C.1 except condition (v) hold. As remarked at the end of Section A, the appropriate conditions which replace the transversality conditions (17) or (v) (of Theorem 8.C.1) for the infinite horizon problem are not yet known in a general form. So far it is necessary to prove such conditions for each case.

In other words, conditions such as

$$\lim_{t \to \infty} p(t) \geq 0 \quad \text{and} \quad \lim_{t \to \infty} p(t)\hat{x}(t) = 0 \left[\text{or} \lim_{t \to \infty} p(t) = 0\right]$$

are, in general, *false*. Halkin's example, which we discussed at the end of Section A, and (Koopmans') condition (66) of Section A constitute counter-examples.

b. HESTENES' THEOREM

In an important paper [5] and later in a book [6] that discusses the relation between the classical calculus of variations and optimal control theory, Hestenes presented a general formulation of the necessary conditions for optimality in optimal control theory and the proofs of his major theorems. The formulation is general enough to cover constraints of the type $g[x(t), u(t), t] \geq 0$, equality constraints, integral constraints with both inequalities and equalities, as well as ordinary differential equation constraints of the Pontryagin type. The formulation also introduces the "control parameter."

An example of the integral constraint problem follows.

PROBLEM II:

$$\text{Maximize:} \quad \int_0^T f_0[x(t), u(t), t] \, dt$$
$$u(t) \in U$$

$$\text{Subject to:} \quad \dot{x}_i = f_i[x(t), u(t), t], \, i = 1, 2, \ldots, n$$
$$x_i(0) = x_i^0, \, and$$

$$(19) \quad J_k[x, u] \equiv \int_0^T h_k[x(t), u(t), t] \, dt \geq 0, \, k = 1, 2, \ldots, l$$

Here T is fixed and the $x_i(T)$'s are unspecified. The integral constraint in the above problem is stated in the form of an inequality.[11]

Let $[\hat{x}(t), \hat{u}(t)]$ be a solution pair of the above problem. Assuming all functions, f_0, the f_i's, and the h_k's, are continuously differentiable with respect to their arguments, we have the following theorem describing the necessary conditions of optimality.

Theorem 8.C.2: *Suppose $[\hat{x}(t), \hat{u}(t)]$ is a solution of the above problem. Assume that the constraint qualification holds. Then there exist multipliers p_0, $p_i(t)$, $i = 1$, 2, \ldots, n, λ_k, $k = 1, 2, \ldots, l$, not vanishing simultaneously on $0 \leq t \leq T$, and a function H,*

$$(20) \quad H[x(t), u(t), t, p(t)] \equiv p_0 f_0[x(t), u(t), t]$$

$$+ \sum_{i=1}^{n} p_i f_i[x(t), u(t), t] + \sum_{k=1}^{l} \lambda_k h_k[x(t), u(t), t]$$

such that the following relations hold:

(i-a) *The multipliers p_0, λ_k, $k = 1, 2, \ldots, l$, are constants and $\lambda_k \geq 0, k = 1, 2, \ldots, l$, with $\lambda_k J_k[\hat{x}, \hat{u}] = 0$.*

(i-b) *The multipliers $p_i(t)$, $i = 1, 2, \ldots, n$, are continuous and have piecewise continuous derivatives.*

(ii) *The functions $\hat{x}(t)$, $\hat{u}(t)$, $p(t)$ satisfy the equations*

$$(21) \qquad \dot{x}_i = \frac{\partial H}{\partial p_i}, \quad \dot{p}_i = -\frac{\partial H}{\partial x_i}, \qquad i = 1, 2, \ldots, n$$

Moreover, we have

$$(22) \qquad \frac{d}{dt}\hat{H} = \frac{\partial}{\partial t}\hat{H}, \text{ on each interval in which } \hat{u}(t) \text{ is continuous}$$

(iii) *The relation*

$$(23) \quad H[\hat{x}(t), \hat{u}(t), t, p(t)] \geq H[\hat{x}(t), u(t), t, p(t)], \qquad \text{for all } u(t) \in U$$

holds.

(iv) *The transversality condition*

$$(24) \qquad p_i(T) = 0, i = 1, 2, \ldots, n$$

holds.

REMARK: If the terminal end points, the $x_i(T)$'s, are fixed such that $x_i(T) = x_i^T$, $i = 1, 2, \ldots, n'$, where $n' \leq n$, then the above transversality condition (iv) is replaced by

$$(25\text{-}a) \qquad x_i(T) = x_i^T, i = 1, 2, \ldots, n'$$

and

$$(25\text{-}b) \qquad p_i(T) = 0, i = n' + 1, n' + 2, \ldots, n$$

EXAMPLE: Consider a consumer who wishes to maximize the sum of his satisfaction from consumption over his lifetime. Assume, for the sake of simplicity, that he knows that his life span is T, and that he also knows the time path of the price vector p_t, of his consumption bundle c_t, and his income y_t, over his entire life span. Let r be the market rate of interest which is assumed to be a positive constant. Assume that this consumer is "competitive" (that is, "small" enough relative to the economy) so that his choice of c_t for any t will not affect the p_t and r that prevail in the market. Let M be his total (discounted) income; that is, $M \equiv \int_0^T e^{-rt} y_t \, dt$. Let a differentiable real-valued function $u(c_t)$ represent his satisfaction from the consumption vector c_t. Let C be his consumption set. His problem is to choose the time path of consumption c_t from C such as to maximize his satisfaction over time subject to his budget constraint. That is,

Maximize: $\displaystyle\int_0^T e^{-\rho t} u(c_t) dt$
$\quad c_t$

Subject to: $\displaystyle\int_0^T p_t \cdot c_t e^{-rt} dt \leqq M \quad \left[\text{or } \int_0^T \left(\frac{M}{T} - p_t \cdot c_t e^{-rt}\right) dt \geqq 0\right]$
and $\quad c_t \in C$

where it is assumed that the consumer is not interested in leaving any bequest to his children.[12] Here ρ is the discount factor, which is assumed to be constant over time, and $\rho \geqq 0$; $\rho > 0$ indicates a preference for present consumption. In this problem, c_t is the control variable and there is no state variable. In order to apply Theorem 8.C.2, we define a function

$$(26) \qquad H[c_t] \equiv p_0 e^{-\rho t} u(c_t) + \lambda \left[\frac{M}{T} - p_t \cdot c_t e^{-rt}\right]$$

where λ is the multiplier corresponding to the integral budget constraint. Then in view of the above theorem, we obtain the following necessary conditions for $\hat{c}_t$ to be a solution:

$$(27) \qquad p_0 e^{-\rho t} u(\hat{c}_t) + \lambda \left(\frac{M}{T} - p_t \cdot \hat{c}_t e^{-rt}\right) \geqq p_0 e^{-\rho t} u(c_t) + \lambda \left(\frac{M}{T} - p_t \cdot c_t e^{-rt}\right)$$

for all $c_t \in C$, where $\lambda \geqq 0$, and

$$(28) \qquad \lambda \left[M - \int_0^T p_t \cdot \hat{c}_t e^{-rt} dt\right] = 0$$

If $p_0 = 0$, then $\lambda > 0$ (the multipliers do not vanish simultaneously). Then (27) is reduced to $p_t \cdot \hat{c}_t \leqq p_t \cdot c_t$ for all $c_t \in C$. Assuming that there exist $\bar{c}_t \in C$ such that $p_t \cdot \bar{c}_t < p_t \cdot \hat{c}_t$ (the "cheaper point assumption"), this cannot happen so that $p_0 > 0$. We can then choose $p_0 = 1$. Thus rewrite (27) as follows:

$$(27') \quad e^{-\rho t} u(\hat{c}_t) + \lambda \left(\frac{M}{T} - p_t \cdot \hat{c}_t e^{-rt}\right) \geqq e^{-\rho t} u(c_t) + \lambda \left(\frac{M}{T} - p_t \cdot c_t e^{-rt}\right)$$

for all $c_t \in C$, where $\lambda \geqq 0$. If there exist $\tilde{c}_t \in C$ such that $u(\tilde{c}_t) > u(\hat{c}_t)$ for all t ("nonsatiation"), then $\lambda > 0$. For if $\lambda = 0$, then we obtain $u(\hat{c}_t) \geqq u(c_t)$ for all $c_t \in C$ from condition (27'), which contradicts the above nonsatiation assumption. If $\lambda > 0$, then (28) implies

$$(28') \qquad M = \int_0^T p_t \cdot \hat{c}_t e^{-rt} dt$$

In other words, all of his income is spent over his lifetime. This is certainly a natural consequence under the nonsatiation assumption.

Now rewrite (27′) as

(29) $e^{-\rho t}[u(\hat{c}_t) - u(c_t)] \geq \lambda[p_t \cdot \hat{c}_t - p_t \cdot c_t] e^{-rt}$ for all $c_t \in C$

Thus, for $\lambda > 0$,

(30) $u(\hat{c}_t) \geq u(c_t)$ for all $c_t \in C$ such that $p_t \cdot \hat{c}_t \geq p_t \cdot c_t$

and

(31) $p_t \cdot \hat{c}_t \leq p_t \cdot c_t$ for all $c_t \in C$ such that $u(c_t) \geq u(\hat{c}_t)$

Condition (30) says that this consumer maximizes his satisfaction at *each* instant of time over those consumptions whose values do not exceed the value of the optimal consumption $\hat{c}_t$. Condition (31) says that, for the optimal consumption bundle, his consumption expenditure is minimized at *each* instant of time over those consumption bundles which would give him satisfaction that is higher than or equal to the satisfaction obtained from $\hat{c}_t$.

The control variable $u(t)$ is a function of time t. In many cases it may so happen that we can choose a variable that does not depend on t. Such a variable is called a **control parameter**. Let $b \equiv [b_1, b_2, \ldots, b_a]$ be an α-dimensional vector which denotes the control parameter. Let $B \subset R^\alpha$ be the set to which b is restricted. Consider the following problem.

PROBLEM III:[13]

Maximize: $\psi(b) + \int_0^T f_0[x(t), u(t), t] dt$
$\qquad \scriptstyle u(t) \in U, b \in B$

Subject to: $\dot{x}_i = f_i[x(t), u(t), t], i = 1, 2, \ldots, n$

$\qquad g_j[x(t), u(t), t] \geq 0, j = 1, 2, \ldots, m$

$\qquad x_i(0) = x_i^0 \text{ (fixed)}, x_i(T) = x_i^T(b), i = 1, 2, \ldots, n$

$\qquad T = T(b)$

The problem we considered before, the one with final time open and variable terminal end points, can be considered as a special case of the above problem in which $b = T$. The time optimal problem can also be considered as a special case when $T = b$, $\psi(b) \equiv 0$, $f_0 \equiv -1$, or with $b = T$, $\psi(b) = -b$, $f_0 \equiv 0$. The problem with the fixed terminal end points is reduced to the case in which $x_i^T(b) = x_i^T$ (= constant), $i = 1, 2, \ldots, n$. In economics, the problem of investing a large fixed capital may be a once-and-for-all choice (which may be the case in the peak-load problem). Then such an investment can be considered as a control parameter (see the next section).

Suppose there exists a solution $[\hat{u}(t), \hat{b}]$ of the above problem with the corresponding state variable $\hat{x}(t)$; then we have the following theorem, which gives a set of necessary conditions for an optimum.

Theorem 8.C.3: *Suppose $[\hat{x}(t), \hat{u}(t), \hat{b}]$ is a solution of the above problem and the constraint qualification holds. Then there exist multipliers p_0, $p_i(t)$, $i = 1, 2, \ldots, n$, $q_j(t)$, $j = 1, 2, \ldots, m$, not vanishing simultaneously on $0 \leq t \leq T$, and a function L,*

$$(32) \quad L[x(t), u(t), t, p(t), q(t)] \equiv H[x(t), u(t), t, p(t)] + \sum_{j=1}^{m} q_j(t)\, g_j[x(t), u(t), t]$$

where

$$(33) \qquad H[x(t), u(t), t, p(t)] \equiv p_0 f_0[x(t), u(t), t] + \sum_{i=1}^{n} p_i f_i[x(t), u(t), t]$$

such that the following relations hold:

(i-a) *The multiplier p_0 is a nonnegative constant[14] and the multipliers $p_i(t)$, $i = 1, 2, \ldots, n$, are continuous and have piecewise continuous derivatives.*

(i-b) *The multipliers $q_j(t)$, $j = 1, 2, \ldots, m$, are piecewise continuous and are continuous at each point of continuity of $\hat{u}(t)$. Moreover, for each j,*

$$(34) \qquad\qquad q_j(t) \geq 0, \quad \text{and} \quad q_j(t) g_j[\hat{x}(t), \hat{u}(t), t] = 0$$

This may be written as $q \geq 0$ and $q \cdot \hat{g} = 0$, where

$$q \equiv [q_1, q_2, \ldots, q_m], \hat{g} \equiv [\hat{g}_1, \hat{g}_2, \ldots, \hat{g}_m]$$

$$\hat{g}_j \equiv g_j[\hat{x}(t), \hat{u}(t), t], j = 1, 2, \ldots, m$$

(ii) *The functions $\hat{x}(t)$, $\hat{u}(t)$, $p_i(t)$, $i = 1, 2, \ldots, n$, $q_j(t)$, $j = 1, 2, \ldots, m$, satisfy the Hamiltonian system*

$$(35) \qquad\qquad \dot{x}_i = \frac{\partial L}{\partial p_i}, \quad \dot{p}_i = -\frac{\partial L}{\partial x_i}, \quad i = 1, 2, \ldots, n$$

for the interval on which $\hat{u}(t)$ is continuous and

$$(36) \qquad\qquad \frac{\partial \hat{L}}{\partial u_i} = 0, \quad i = 1, 2, \ldots, r$$

where

$$\hat{L} \equiv L[\hat{x}(t), \hat{u}(t), t, p(t), q(t)]$$

Moreover, we have

$$(37) \qquad\qquad \frac{d}{dt}\hat{L} = \frac{\partial}{\partial t}\hat{L}$$

on each interval of continuity of $\hat{u}(t)$ and the function $\hat{L}$ is continuous on $0 \leq t \leq T$.

(iii) $\qquad H[\hat{x}(t), \hat{u}(t), t, p(t)] \geq H[\hat{x}(t), u(t), t, p(t)]$
$\qquad\qquad$ *for all $u(t) \in U$ such that $g_j[\hat{x}(t), u(t), t] \geq 0, j = 1, 2, \ldots, m$*

(iv) *(transversality condition)*

$$(38) \qquad\qquad -p_0 \frac{\partial \psi}{\partial b_j} - \hat{L}^T \frac{\partial T}{\partial b_j} + \sum_{i=1}^{n} p_i(T) \frac{\partial x_i^T}{\partial b_j} = 0$$

where

$$\hat{L}^T \equiv L[\hat{x}(T), \hat{u}(T), T, p(T), q(T)]$$

REMARK: The last condition, (iv), summarizes (or generalizes) the simple transversality conditions discussed in Section A. In particular,

(a) T is fixed and $b_i \equiv x_i^T$: $p_i(T) = 0, i = 1, 2, \ldots, n$.

(b) T is unspecified and the x_i^T's are fixed: Set $b = T$ and obtain

$$L[\hat{x}(T), \hat{u}(T), T, p(T), q(T)] = 0$$

REMARK: It can be shown that (37) is a consequence of (34) and (35).

REMARK: Note that if T is fixed and $b_i \equiv x_i^T$, $i = 1, 2, \ldots, n$, then Problem III is reduced to Problem I; hence Theorem 8.C.3 is reduced to Theorem 8.C.1. In this case, $p_0 > 0$ so that we can choose $p_0 = 1$. To carry out a proof of this, note the transversality condition $p_i(T) = 0, i = 1, 2, \ldots, n$, and suppose, for example, that the rank constraint qualification holds at $t = T$ so that the rank of the matrix $[\partial \hat{g}_j / \partial u_i]$ for $j \in E$ (where E is the set of indices for the effective constraints at $t = T$) is equal to the number of the effective constraints (for $t = T$). Now suppose that p_0 is not positive so that $p_0 = 0$. Since $p_i(T) = 0$ for all i, we obtain, for $t = T$, $\hat{L} = q(T) \cdot g[\hat{x}(T), \hat{u}(T), T] = 0$. Hence condition (36) implies that $\partial \hat{L} / \partial u_k = \sum_{j=1}^{m} q_j(T) \hat{g}_{jk}^T = 0$, $k = 1, 2, \ldots, r$, where $\hat{g}_{jk}^T \equiv \partial g_j / \partial u_k$ evaluated at $[\hat{x}(T), \hat{u}(T), T]$. Let q_E be the vector whose jth element is $q_j(T), j \in E$. Note that $q_j(T) = 0$ for $j \notin E$ from relation (34). Let G_E be the matrix whose (j,k)th element is $\hat{g}_{jk}^T$, $j \in E$, of the above relation; then we obtain $q_E \cdot G_E = 0$. But the rank constraint qualification means that the rank of G_E is equal to the dimension of q_E so that $q_E = 0$; hence $q_j(T) = 0$ for all j. Therefore we have $p_0 = 0$, $p_i(T) = 0, i = 1, 2, \ldots, n, q_j(T) = 0, j = 1, 2, \ldots, m$, which contradicts the condition that the multipliers do not vanish simultaneously; hence, $p_0 > 0$. If we assume the Slater type condition [condition (iii) of the lemma] instead of the rank condition, the proof is simpler. To see this, suppose that there exists a $\bar{u}(T) \in \bar{U}$ such that $g_j[\hat{x}(T), \bar{u}(T), T] > 0$ for all j. Then condition (34) implies $q_j(T) = 0$ for all j. Thus again the multipliers vanish simultaneously for $t = T$ under the assumption $p_0 = 0$.

We are now ready to proceed to a more general theorem which is due to Hestenes [5]. Again let $x(t), t_0 \leq t \leq t_1$, be a state variable, which is a continuous n-vector-valued function, let $u(t), t_0 \leq t \leq t_1$, be a control variable which is a piecewise continuous r-vector-valued function, and let b be a control parameter which is an α-dimensional vector. Here t_0 and t_1 are not necessarily fixed but are functions of the control parameter b. It may be convenient to refer to the arc of an $(n + r + \alpha)$-dimensional vector $[x(t), u(t), b], t_0 \leq t \leq t_1$, by a single letter z, that is,

$$(39) \qquad z: [x(t), u(t), b], t_0 \leq t \leq t_1$$

The general problem to be considered here is that of maximizing a function

$$(40) \qquad I_0[z] \equiv \psi_0(b) + \int_{t_0}^{t_1} f_0[x(t), u(t), b, t] dt$$

in a class of arcs

$$z: [x(t), u(t), b], t_0 \leq t \leq t_1$$

satisfying the following conditions

$$(41) \qquad \dot{x} = f_i[x(t), u(t), b, t], i = 1, 2, \ldots, n$$

$$(42) \qquad g_j[x(t), u(t), b, t] \geq 0, j = 1, 2, \ldots, m'$$

$$(43) \qquad g_j[x(t), u(t), b, t] = 0, j = m' + 1, m' + 2, \ldots, m$$

$$(44) \qquad I_k(z) \geq 0, k = 1, 2, \ldots, l'$$

$$(45) \qquad I_k(z) = 0, k = l' + 1, l' + 2, \ldots, l$$

where I_k is defined as

$$(46) \qquad I_k \equiv \psi_k(b) + \int_{t_0}^{t_1} h_k[x(t), u(t), b, t] dt, k = 1, 2, \ldots, l$$

and

$$(47) \qquad t_0 = t_0(b), t_1 = t_1(b)$$

$$(48) \qquad x_i(t_0) = x_i^0(b), x_i(t_1) = x_i^1(b), i = 1, 2, \ldots, n$$

The problem thus formulated is called the **optimal control problem of Bolza-Hestenes**. The name Bolza is introduced because a similar calculus of variations problem was discussed by O. Bolza. This problem may also be referred to as the **problem of Hestenes**. The solution of the above problem is denoted by

$$\hat{z}: [\hat{x}(t), \hat{u}(t), \hat{b}], t_0 \leq t \leq t_1$$

We assume

(A-1) All functions, ψ_0, f_0, f_i's, g_j's, ψ_k's, h_k's, t_0, t_1, x_i^0's, and x_i^1's, are continuously differentiable on a set X of points in the (x, u, b, t)-space.

Let X_0 be a set of all elements (x, u, b, t) in X satisfying $g_j[x, u, b, t] \geq 0$, $j = 1, 2, \ldots, m'$, $g_j(x, u, b, t) = 0, j = m' + 1, \ldots, m$. This set X_0 is called the **set of admissible elements**. We assume further that

(A-2) The matrix

$$(49) \qquad \left(\frac{\partial g}{\partial u}, \delta_{ij} g_j \right)$$

has rank m at each element $[\hat{x}(t), \hat{u}(t), \hat{b}, t]$ in X_0, where δ_{ij} is "Kronecker's delta" defined by $\delta_{ij} = 1$ if $i = j$ and $\delta_{ij} = 0$ if $i \neq j$, and $\partial g / \partial u$ is the Jacobian matrix of g with respect to u evaluated at $[\hat{x}(t), \hat{u}(t), \hat{b}, t]$.

The matrix (49) can be written out as

$$(50) \quad \begin{bmatrix} \dfrac{\partial g_1}{\partial u_1} & \dfrac{\partial g_1}{\partial u_2} & \cdots & \dfrac{\partial g_1}{\partial u_r} & g_1 & 0 & 0 & \cdots & 0 \\[2mm] \dfrac{\partial g_2}{\partial u_1} & \dfrac{\partial g_2}{\partial u_2} & \cdots & \dfrac{\partial g_2}{\partial u_r} & 0 & g_2 & 0 & \cdots & 0 \\[2mm] \cdots & \cdots & \cdots & \cdots & \cdots & \cdots & \cdots & \cdots & \cdots \\[2mm] \dfrac{\partial g_m}{\partial u_1} & \dfrac{\partial g_m}{\partial u_2} & \cdots & \dfrac{\partial g_m}{\partial u_r} & 0 & 0 & 0 & \cdots & g_m \end{bmatrix}$$

In other words, this is an $m \times (m + r)$ matrix. The rank of a rectangular matrix is defined as the number of linearly independent rows, which is equal to the number of linearly independent columns. The above matrix has rank m if and only if the matrix

$$(51) \quad \left(\frac{\partial g_E}{\partial u} \right)$$

has rank s, where E is the set of indices in which the g_j's are **effective**, that is,

$$(52) \quad E \equiv \{ j : g_j[\hat{x}, \hat{u}, \hat{b}, t] = 0 \}$$

and s is the number of these effective constraints. In other words, (A-2) says that the rank of $(\partial g_E / \partial u)$ is equal to the number of the effective constraints. If all the g_j-constraints are inequality constraints (so that $m' = m$), then (A-2) amounts to the rank constraint qualification discussed in subsection a [see condition (iv) of the lemma and Arrow-Hurwicz-Uzawa [2]].

Theorem 8.C.4 (Hestenes):   *Suppose that the arc*

$$\hat{z}: [\hat{x}(t), \hat{u}(t), \hat{b}], \quad t_0 \leq t \leq t_1$$

is a solution of the above problem and suppose that (A-1) and (A-2) hold. Then there exist multipliers

$$p_0, p_i(t), q_j(t), \lambda_k, \quad i = 1, 2, \ldots, n; j = 1, 2, \ldots, m; k = 1, 2, \ldots, l$$

not vanishing simultaneously on $t_0 \leq t \leq t_1$ and functions L and Ψ where

$$(53) \quad L[x(t), u(t), b, t, p(t)] \equiv H[x(t), u(t), b, t, p(t)] + \sum_{j=1}^{m} q_j(t) g_j[x(t), u(t), b, t]$$

with H defined as

(54)
$$H[x(t), u(t), b, t, p(t)] \equiv p_0 f_0[x(t), u(t), b, t]$$

$$+ \sum_{i=1}^{n} p_i f_i[x(t), u(t), b, t] + \sum_{k=1}^{l} \lambda_k h_k[x(t), u(t), b, t]$$

and

(55)
$$\Psi(b) \equiv p_0 \psi_0(b) + \sum_{k=1}^{l} \lambda_k \psi_k(b)$$

such that the following relations hold:

(i-a) *The multipliers p_0, λ_k, $k = 1, 2, \ldots, l$, are constants, and $\lambda_k \geq 0$, $k = 1, 2, \ldots, l'$, with*

(56)
$$\lambda_k I_k[\hat{x}(t), \hat{u}, \hat{b}] = 0, \quad k = 1, 2, \ldots, l$$

(i-b) *The multipliers $p_i(t)$, $i = 1, 2, \ldots, n$, are continuous and have piecewise continuous derivatives.*

(i-c) *The multipliers $q_j(t)$, $j = 1, 2, \ldots, m$, are piecewise continuous and are continuous at each point of continuity of $\hat{u}(t)$. Moreover, for each j, $1 \leq j \leq m'$, we have*

(57)
$$q_j(t) \geq 0, \quad q_j(t) g_j[\hat{x}(t), \hat{u}(t), \hat{b}, t] = 0$$

The last equation may be rewritten as

(58)
$$q \cdot \hat{g} = 0$$

where
$$q \equiv [q_1, q_2, \ldots, q_m] \text{ and } \hat{g} \equiv [\hat{g}_1, \hat{g}_2, \ldots, \hat{g}_m]$$
$$\hat{g}_j \equiv g_j[\hat{x}(t), \hat{u}(t), \hat{b}, t], j = 1, 2, \ldots, m$$

(ii) *The functions $\hat{x}(t)$, $\hat{u}(t)$, $p_i(t)$, $i = 1, 2, \ldots, n$, $q_j(t)$, $j = 1, 2, \ldots, m$, satisfy the* **Euler-Lagrange-Hamiltonian** *equations*

(59)
$$\dot{x}_i = \frac{\partial L}{\partial p_i}, \quad \dot{p}_i = -\frac{\partial L}{\partial x_i}, \quad i = 1, 2, \ldots, n$$

(60)
$$\frac{\partial \hat{L}}{\partial u_i} = 0, \quad i = 1, 2, \ldots, r$$

where $\hat{L} \equiv L[\hat{x}(t), \hat{u}(t), \hat{b}, t, p(t), q(t)]$. Moreover, we have

(61)
$$\frac{d}{dt}\hat{L} = \frac{\partial}{\partial t}\hat{L}$$

on each interval of continuity of $\hat{u}(t)$ and the function $\hat{L}$ is continuous on $t_0 \leq t \leq t_1$.

(iii) *The following formula holds:*

(62)
$$H[\hat{x}(t), \hat{u}(t), \hat{b}, t, p(t)] \geq H[\hat{x}(t), u(t), \hat{b}, t, p(t)]$$

for all $[\hat{x}(t), u(t), \hat{b}, t]$ in X_0. Or equivalently,

$$H[\hat{x}(t), u(t), \hat{b}, t, p(t)]$$

is maximized with respect to u subject to $[\hat{x}(t), u(t), \hat{b}, t] \in X$ *and* $g_j[\hat{x}(t),$
$u(t), b, t] \geq 0, j = 1, 2, \ldots, m', g_j[\hat{x}(t), u(t), b, t] = 0, j = m' + 1, \ldots, m.$

(iv) *The* **transversality condition**

$$(63) \quad -\frac{\partial \psi}{\partial b_j} + \left[-\hat{L}^s \frac{\partial t_s}{\partial b_j} + \sum_{i=1}^{n} p_i(t_s) \frac{\partial x_i^s}{\partial b_j} \right]\Bigg|_{s=0}^{s=1} = \int_{t_0}^{t_1} \frac{\partial \hat{L}}{\partial b_j} dt, j = 1, 2, \ldots, \alpha$$

holds, where

$$\hat{L}^s \equiv L[\hat{x}(t_s), \hat{u}(t_s), \hat{b}, t_s, p(t_s), q(t_s)], s = 0, 1$$

REMARK: If f_0, the f_i's, g_j's, and h_k's do not contain b explicitly (so that
L does not contain b explicitly), then the right-hand side of the transversality
condition is identically equal to zero. If, in addition, t_0 is fixed and does
not depend on t and the x_i^0's are fixed, the transversality condition is further
simplified to

$$(64) \quad -\frac{\partial \psi}{\partial b_j} + \left[-\hat{L}^1 \frac{\partial t_1}{\partial b_j} + \sum_{i=1}^{n} p_i(t_1) \frac{\partial x_i^1}{\partial b_j} \right] = 0, j = 1, 2, \ldots, \alpha$$

Writing $t^1 = T$ and $x_i^1 = x_i^T$, we can obtain the transversality condition (38)
discussed in Theorem 8.C.3.

C. A SUFFICIENCY THEOREM

All the theorems we have discussed so far have been concerned with the
necessary conditions for optimality. A naturally important question is: Under
what conditions are these conditions also sufficient for optimality? In the case of
ordinary nonlinear programming and the calculus of variations, several important
sufficiency theorems exist; however, in each case there exists a simple but powerful
sufficiency theorem which implies optimality when the relevant functions are
concave. Here we prove such a theorem, which is a generalization of a theorem
due to Mangasarian [9].

We consider a problem in which $x(t)$ is the state variable and $u(t)$ is the
control variable. The function $x(t)$ is an n-dimensional vector-valued continuous
function and $u(t)$ is an r-dimensional vector-valued piecewise continuous function. The problem is as follows:

Maximize: $\quad I[x, u] \equiv \psi_0[x(0), x(T)] + \int_0^T f_0[x(t), u(t), t] dt$

Subject to:

$$(65) \quad \dot{x}_i = f_i[x(t), u(t), t], i = 1, 2, \ldots, n$$

$$(66) \quad g_j[x(t), u(t), t] \geq 0, j = 1, 2, \ldots, m$$

$$(67) \quad \psi_k[x(0)] + \int_0^T h_k[x(t), u(t), t] dt \geq 0, \quad k = 1, 2, \ldots, l'$$

(68) $\psi_k[x(T)] + \int_0^T h_k[x(t), u(t), t]\, dt \geq 0, \qquad k = l' + 1, \ldots, l$

Note that in Mangasarian [9], there are no integral constraints. In this problem both the initial and the terminal time (that is, 0 and T) are assumed to be fixed. Regarding the vector $[x(0), x(T)]$ as a control parameter b, we can apply the Hestenes theorem. Thus, under suitable assumptions, we have the following set of necessary conditions in order that $[\hat{x}(t), \hat{u}(t)]$ be optimal:

(i)   There exist multipliers p_0, $p(t) \equiv [p_1(t), \ldots, p_n(t)]$, $q(t) \equiv [q_1(t), \ldots, q_m(t)]$, and $\lambda \equiv [\lambda_1, \ldots, \lambda_l]$, such that

(i-a) p_0 and λ are constants and $\lambda \geq 0$, with

(69) $\lambda \cdot [\hat{\phi} + \int_0^T \hat{h}\, dt] = 0$, where $\hat{\phi} \equiv [\hat{\phi}_1, \ldots, \hat{\phi}_l]$

$\hat{\phi}_k \equiv \psi_k[\hat{x}(0)], k = 1, 2, \ldots, l', \hat{\phi}_k \equiv \psi_k[\hat{x}(T)], k = l' + 1, \ldots, l$

$\hat{h} \equiv [\hat{h}_1, \hat{h}_2, \ldots, \hat{h}_l]$, and $\hat{h}_k \equiv h_k[\hat{x}(t), \hat{u}(t), t], k = 1, 2, \ldots, l$

(i-b) $p_i(t)$, $i = 1, 2, \ldots, n$, are continuous and have piecewise continuous derivatives.

(i-c) $q_j(t)$, $j = 1, 2, \ldots, m$, are piecewise continuous and are continuous at each point of continuity of $\hat{u}(t)$ and $q_j(t) \geq 0$ for all j with

(70) $q \cdot \hat{g} = 0$, where $\hat{g} \equiv [\hat{g}_1, \cdots, \hat{g}_m]$, $\hat{g}_j \equiv g_j[\hat{x}(t), \hat{u}(t), t]$, $j = 1, 2, \ldots, m$

(ii) The functions $\hat{x}(t)$, $\hat{u}(t)$, $p(t)$, and $q(t)$ satisfy the following differential equations:

(71) $\dot{x}_i = \dfrac{\partial L}{\partial p_i}, \qquad \dot{p}_i = -\dfrac{\partial L}{\partial x_i}, \qquad i = 1, 2, \ldots, n$

(72) $\dfrac{\partial \hat{L}}{\partial u_i} = 0, \qquad i = 1, 2, \ldots, r$

where $\hat{L}$ is defined by

(73) $\hat{L} \equiv L[\hat{x}(t), \hat{u}(t), t, p(t), q(t)]$

and

(74) $L[x(t), u(t), t, p(t), q(t)] \equiv p_0 f_0[x(t), u(t), t]$

$+ \sum_{i=1}^{n} p_i(t) f_i[x(t), u(t), t] + \sum_{j=1}^{m} q_j(t) g_j[x(t), u(t), t]$

$+ \sum_{k=1}^{l} \lambda_k h_k[x(t), u(t), t]$

(iii) The following transversality conditions hold:

(75)
$$\frac{\partial \hat{\Psi}}{\partial x_i(0)} + p_i(0) = 0, \, i = 1, 2, \ldots, n$$

(76)
$$\frac{\partial \hat{\Psi}}{\partial x_i(T)} - p_i(T) = 0, \, i = 1, 2, \ldots, n$$

where

(77) $\hat{\Psi} \equiv \psi_0[\hat{x}(0), \hat{x}(T)] + \lambda \cdot \hat{\phi}$, where $\hat{\phi} \equiv [\hat{\phi}_1, \ldots, \hat{\phi}_{l'}, \ldots, \hat{\phi}_l]$

Denote the gradient vector of f_0 with respect to x, evaluated at $[\hat{x}, \hat{u}]$, by $\hat{f}_{0x}$. Define $\hat{f}_{0u}$ similarly. Define the Jacobian matrix of $f \equiv [f_1, f_2, \ldots, f_n]$ (where $f_i \equiv f_i[x(t), u(t), t]$) with respect to x, evaluated at $(\hat{x}, \hat{u})$, by $\hat{f}_x$. Similarly, define $\hat{f}_u, \hat{g}_x, \hat{g}_u$. Denote the Jacobian matrix of h with respect to x (resp. u), evaluated at $(\hat{x}, \hat{u})$, by $\hat{h}_x$ (resp. $\hat{h}_u$). Also denote the Jacobian matrix of ϕ with respect to $x(0)$ [resp. $x(T)$], evaluated at $[\hat{x}(0), \hat{x}(T)]$, by $\hat{\phi}_{x(0)}$ [resp. $\hat{\phi}_{x(T)}$]. Define $\hat{\psi}_{0x(0)}$ and $\hat{\psi}_{0x(T)}$ similarly. Then conditions (71) and (72) can be rewritten respectively as

(78) $\dot{x} = f, \quad \dot{p} = - [p_0 \hat{f}_{0x} + p \cdot \hat{f}_x + q \cdot \hat{g}_x + \lambda \cdot \hat{h}_x]$

(79) $\hat{f}_{0u} + p \cdot \hat{f}_u + q \cdot \hat{g}_u + \lambda \cdot \hat{h}_u = 0$

Conditions (75) and (76) can be rewritten respectively as

(80) $\hat{\psi}_{0x(0)} + \lambda \cdot \hat{\phi}_{x(0)} + p(0) = 0$

(81) $\hat{\psi}_{0x(T)} + \lambda \cdot \hat{\phi}_{x(T)} - p(T) = 0$

We now impose the following assumptions (here when we say that a vector-valued function is concave, we mean that every component is concave):

(A-3)   The functions $f_0[x, u, t], f[x, u, t], g[x, u, t]$, and $h[x, u, t]$ are all concave and differentiable in (x, u) for $t \in [0, T]$.

(A-4)   The functions $\psi_0[x(0), x(T)]$ and $\psi[x(0), x(T)]$ are concave and differentiable in $x(0)$ and $x(T)$.

Now we can state our theorem.

Theorem 8.C.5: *For the above problem, if (A-3) and (A-4) hold, then all the necessary conditions (i), (ii), and (iii), stated above, are also sufficient for $[\hat{x}(t), \hat{u}(t)]$ to be a global optimum solution of the problem, provided that $p_0 = 1$ and the following additional condition holds:*

(82) $p(t) \geq 0 \quad$ *for all t*

If the concavity in (A-3) and (A-4) is replaced by strict concavity, then the optimality is "unique."

PROOF: Let $x(t)$ and $u(t)$ satisfy the constraints (65) to (68). The proof is carried out by writing a string of equalities and inequalities. For simplicity, we denote $f_0[\hat{x}(t), \hat{u}(t), t]$ by f_0 and we deal similarly with f, g, u, w, and ψ.

$$I[\hat{x}, \hat{u}] - I[x, u] = \int_0^T (\hat{f}_0 - f_0)dt + (\hat{\psi}_0 - \psi_0)$$

(a)
$$\geqq \int_0^T \left[(\hat{x} - x)\cdot\hat{f}_{0x} + (\hat{u} - u)\cdot\hat{f}_{0u}\right] dt + \left[\hat{x}(0) - x(0)\right] \cdot \hat{\psi}_{0x(0)}$$
$$+ \left[\hat{x}(T) - x(T)\right] \cdot \hat{\psi}_{0x(T)}$$

(b)
$$= \int_0^T \left[-(\hat{x} - x)\cdot (p\cdot\hat{f}_x + q\cdot\hat{g}_x + \lambda\cdot\hat{h}_x + \dot{p}) - (\hat{u} - u)\cdot(p\cdot\hat{f}_u + q\cdot\hat{g}_u + \lambda\cdot\hat{h}_u)\right] dt - \left[\hat{x}(0) - x(0)\right] \cdot \left[p(0) + \lambda\cdot\hat{\psi}_{x(0)}\right]$$
$$+ \left[\hat{x}(T) - x(T)\right] \cdot \left[p(T) - \lambda\cdot\hat{\psi}_{x(T)}\right]$$

(c)
$$= \int_0^T \left[-(\hat{x} - x)\cdot (p\cdot\hat{f}_x + q\cdot\hat{g}_x + \lambda\cdot\hat{h}_x) + p\cdot(\hat{f} - f)\right.$$
$$\left. -(\hat{u} - u)\cdot(p\cdot\hat{f}_u + q\cdot\hat{g}_u + \lambda\cdot\hat{h}_u)\right] dt - \left[\hat{x}(0) - x(0)\right] \cdot (\lambda\cdot\hat{\psi}_{x(0)})$$
$$- \left[\hat{x}(T) - x(T)\right] \cdot (\lambda\cdot\hat{\psi}_{x(T)})$$

(d)
$$\geqq \int_0^T \left[p\cdot(f - \hat{f}) + q\cdot(g - \hat{g}) + \lambda\cdot(h - \hat{h}) + p\cdot(\hat{f} - f)\right] dt$$
$$- \left[\hat{x}(0) - x(0)\right] \cdot (\lambda\cdot\hat{\psi}_{x(0)}) - \left[\hat{x}(T) - x(T)\right] \cdot (\lambda\cdot\hat{\psi}_{x(T)})$$

(e)
$$\geqq \int_0^T \lambda\cdot(h - \hat{h})dt - \left[\hat{x}(0) - x(0)\right] \cdot (\lambda\cdot\hat{\psi}_{x(0)})$$
$$- \left[\hat{x}(T) - x(T)\right] \cdot (\lambda\cdot\hat{\psi}_{x(T)})$$

(f)
$$\geqq \int_0^T \lambda\cdot(h - \hat{h})dt + \lambda\cdot(\psi - \hat{\psi})$$

(g)
$$\equiv \int_0^T \lambda\cdot h dt + \lambda\cdot\psi$$

(h)
$$\geqq 0$$

Following are the reasons the above relations hold:

Inequality (a) by the differentiability and the concavity of f_0 and ψ_0.[15]
Equation (b) by (78), (79), (80), and (81).
Equation (c) by integration by parts, (65), and the continuity of $x(t)$, $\hat{x}(t)$ and $p(t)$.

Inequality (d) by the differentiability and concavity of f, g, and h, $q(t) \geqq 0$, and (82) [note that this is the only step in the proof where (82) is used].

Inequality (e) by (70), $q(t) \geqq 0$, and (66).

Inequality (f) by the concavity and differentiability of ψ, and by $\lambda \geqq 0$.

Equation (g) by (69).

Inequality (h) by $\lambda \geqq 0$, (67), and (68).

If the concavity of f_0, ψ_0, f, g, h, and ψ is replaced by strict quasi-concavity, then the inequalities in steps (a), (d), and (f) are replaced by strict inequality for $[x, u] \neq [\hat{x}, \hat{u}]$.   (Q.E.D.)

REMARK: The above proof is essentially the same as that in Mangasarian [9]. The idea of the proof is clearly due to Kuhn and Tucker [7].

REMARK: The assumption represented by condition (82) and the concavity of f can be replaced by the weaker condition that $p \cdot f$ is concave in (x, u). Note also that if $f_i(x, u, t)$ is linear in (x, u), then (82) is *not* needed for this i. [Recall step (d).]

REMARK: Any integral evaluated at a single point is obviously zero. Also, any integral evaluated on a set of countably many points is zero. Hence, for any (integrable) function $y(t)$ and $y'(t)$, $\int_0^T y(t)dt = \int_0^T y'(t)dt$ if $y(t)$ and $y'(t)$ are different only for countably many points in $[0, T]$, that is, if they are identical "almost everywhere." Therefore the "uniqueness" of an optimal solution in the optimal control problem only means the uniqueness almost everywhere. Recall that we made the same remark in connection with Theorem 5.B.4.

Suppose that the initial point is fixed as

$$x(0) = x^0$$

Then this condition replaces transversality condition (75). Similarly, if the right-hand end-point is fixed as $x(T) = x^T$, then this replaces transversality condition (76). With this remark, we can easily prove the following corollary.

Corollary:

(i)   *If $x(0) = x^0$ [or $x(T) = x^T$], and if $h_k \equiv 0$ for all k, then Theorem 8.C.5 holds with (69), (75) [or (76)], and $\lambda \geqq 0$, and the vector λ, all deleted.*

(ii) *If $x(0) = x^0$ and $x(T) = x^T$, and if $h_k \equiv 0$ for all k, then Theorem 8.C.5 holds with (69), (75), (76), and $\lambda \geqq 0$, and the vector λ, all deleted.*

This completes our discussion on the theory of optimal control. Theorem 8.C.4 provides us with a set of necessary conditions for a quite general class of problems, and Theorem 8.C.5 guarantees the sufficiency of these necessary conditions for an important class of problems. However, there are still two important topics that we have left out. One is the problem of bounded state variables, which we mentioned already.[16] And the other is the problem of the *existence* of an optimal control. Those interested in this topic of existence are referred to L. Cesari, "Existence Theorems for Optimal Solutions in Pontryagin and Lagrange Problems," *Journal of SIAM Control*, vol. 3, no. 3, 1966 (and perhaps his two articles in *Transactions of American Mathematical Society*, 124, September 1966).[17]

FOOTNOTES

1. When the g-function lacks the $u(t)$ (the case of **bounded state variables**), the optimal control problems become quite difficult and tedious, and are beyond the scope of our exposition. The interested readers are referred to Hestenes ([6], chapter 8) and Russak [10], for example. See also footnote 16.

2. The constraint qualification is the qualification imposed on the constraint to guarantee "normality." In other words, if the constraint qualification does not hold, then L must be written as $L \equiv q_0 H + \sum_{j=1}^{m} q_j g_j$, where q_0 can be zero. The constraint qualification in this context can be interpreted as the qualification imposed on the constraint to guarantee $q_0 > 0$. (Note that if $q_0 > 0$, we can choose $q_0 = 1$, for we can always redefine the multipliers q_j by q_j/q_0. Recall our discussion on the normality condition in Chapter 1.)

3. More precisely, the notation $\partial \hat{L}/\partial u_i$ means $\partial L/\partial u_i$ evaluated at $[\hat{x}(t), \hat{u}(t), t, p(t), q(t)]$ for each t. In the subsequent discussion, we use the notation $\partial \hat{L}/\partial x_i$, $\partial \hat{L}/\partial p_i$ in the same sense.

4. That constraint $g_j[x, u, t] \geq 0$ is effective means $g_j[\hat{x}, \hat{u}, t] = 0$. In the subsequent discussion we refer to condition (iv) as the **rank constraint qualification**.

5. The p_i's and the q_j's are often called **multipliers**. It is important to note that in the definition of the functions L and H, the multiplier corresponding to f_0 (that is, p_0) is set equal to one. This is due to the fact that the present problem corresponds to the one considered in Theorem 8.A.6. In other words, this is the case with variable right-hand end-points. As should be clear from our discussion in Section A, if the right-hand end-points are fixed, then in general we do not obtain $p_0 = 1$. In this case, H should be defined as $H \equiv p_0 f_0[x(t), u(t), t] + \sum_{i=1}^{n} p_i f_i[x(t), u(t), t]$ with $p_0 \geq 0$ (constant) and the definition of L should be modified accordingly.

6. More precisely, $\hat{L}$ is continuous along $[\hat{x}(t), \hat{u}(t), t]$ and has a piecewise continuous derivative given by $\partial \hat{L}/\partial t$ on each interval on which $\hat{u}(t)$ is continuous. From conditions (i) and (iii), we obtain $d\hat{L}/dt = (\partial \hat{L}/\partial x) \cdot \dot{x} + (\partial \hat{L}/\partial u) \cdot \dot{u} + (\partial \hat{L}/\partial t) + (\partial \hat{L}/\partial p) \cdot \dot{p} + (\partial \hat{L}/\partial q) \cdot \dot{q} = (\partial \hat{L}/\partial t) + (\partial \hat{L}/\partial q) \cdot \dot{q} = (\partial \hat{L}/\partial t) + \hat{g} \cdot \dot{q}$, where $\hat{g} \equiv g[\hat{x}(t), \hat{u}(t), t]$. If $\hat{g}_j = 0$, then $\hat{g}_j \cdot \dot{q}_j = 0$. On the other hand, if $\hat{g}_j > 0$ on some interval, then $q_j \cdot \hat{g}_j = 0$ [condition (iii)] means $q_j(t) = 0$ (= constant) for this interval so that $\dot{q}_j = 0$ for this interval. Thus we have $\hat{g}_j \cdot \dot{q}_j = 0$ for this interval. In other words, we have $\hat{g}_j \cdot \dot{q}_j = 0$ for all j so that $d\hat{L}/dt = \partial \hat{L}/\partial t$.

7. Clearly, if L is not concave in u, then condition (iii) does not necessarily imply condition (ii). It is important to note that condition (ii) always implies condition (iii) provided that the constraint qualification holds.

8. From condition (iii), $\partial \hat{L}/\partial u_i = 0$ and $\mu_i(t) \geq 0$, $\mu_i(t)\hat{u}_i(t) = 0$, $i = 1, 2, \ldots, r$. But

$\partial \hat{L}/\partial u_i = \partial \hat{L}_+ /\partial u_i + \mu_i(t)$. From this condition (13) follows.

9. Clearly such a condition is unnecessary if we consider the fixed terminal end points problem [that is, the $x_i(T)$'s are all fixed].

10. There is a slight inaccuracy in the above argument to show (17): that is, the c_i's are to be *a priori* fixed, and should not be chosen after the signs of the $x_i(T)$'s are determined. For a more accurate argument, see Arrow [1]. There is still another kind of inaccuracy. Since $p(T) = 0$ is not necessarily true anymore, strictly speaking, H should now be redefined as $H = p_0 f_0 + \sum_{i=1}^n p_i f_i [x(t), u(t), t]$ where $p_0 \geqq 0$ (and L should be redefined accordingly). (See the proof of Theorem 8.A.6.) However, following Arrow [1], we implicitly assume here the normality $p_0 > 0$, so that we can take $p_0 = 1$. Actually, in many problems with the constraint $x(T) \geqq 0$ we can find a solution by ignoring this constraint and then observe that this constraint is satisfied by $\hat{x}(T) > 0$. In such a case, we may solve the problem by *replacing* condition (17) by the usual condition $p(T) = 0$. [If $\hat{x}(T) > 0$ in (17), we have $p(T) = 0$.]

11. The integral constraint, especially with equality, is often called the **isoperimetric constraint**, gaining this name from a famous **isoperimetric problem** in the calculus of variations which is concerned with finding the curve enclosing the greatest area among all closed curves of a given length. "Isoperimetric" means "with the same perimeter." Such a constraint is expressed in the integral form.

12. This integral constraint contains the assumption that the consumer can borrow or lend any amount at the fixed rate of interest r. An alternative assumption is that there is a bound (say, zero) on the amount that he can borrow. For further discussions of the problem of the lifetime allocation of consumption, see, for example, M. E. Yaari, "On the Consumer's Lifetime Allocation Process," *International Economic Review*, 5, September 1964, and K. Avio, "Age-Dependent Utility in the Lifetime Allocation Problem," *Krannert Institute Paper*, No. 260, Purdue University, November 1969. Recall that the same example was used in Section A of Chapter 1.

13. We can formulate this problem in such a way that the f_i's, g_j's, and h_k's all contain the control parameter b explicitly as well as $x(t)$, $u(t)$, and t. However, without loss of generality, we can also assume that b does not appear in the f_i's, g_j's, and h_k's, since it can be eliminated by introducing the new state variables $x_{n+i}(t)$ subject to the conditions $\dot{x}_{n+i} = 0$ and $x_{n+i}(t_0) = x_{n+i}(t_1) = b_i$, $i = 1, 2, \ldots, \alpha$.

14. It is important to note the possibility of $p_0 = 0$.

15. Recall Theorem 1.C.3.

16. It is not difficult to illustrate the basic method involved in such a problem by a simple example. Suppose that we have the well-known constraint in economics, $x(t) \geqq 0$, in addition to the usual f-, g- and h- constraints discussed in this section. If $x_i(t) > 0$, then the constraint is ineffective and can be disregarded. If $x_i(t) = 0$, then we must have $\dot{x}_i(t) \geqq 0$ to satisfy the constraint. Since $\dot{x}_i = f_i(x, u, t)$, this amounts to adding an additional constraint $f_i(x, u, t) \geqq 0$. Let $v_i(t)$ be the multiplier corresponding to this constraint, and define the Lagrangian by $L \equiv H + q \cdot g + v \cdot f$, where $H \equiv p_0 f_0 + p \cdot f + \lambda \cdot h$, $f \equiv (f_1, \ldots, f_n)$ and $v \equiv (v_1, \ldots, v_n)$. Then it is easy to see that the necessary conditions for optimality consist of the usual conditions described in Theorem 8.C.4 *and* $v(t) \geqq 0$, $v(t) \cdot f[\hat{x}(t), \hat{u}(t), t] = 0$ and $v(t) \cdot \hat{x}(t) = 0$. Needless to say, if $\hat{x}(t) > 0$ then $v(t) = 0$ and the problem is reduced to the one without the constraint $x(t) \geqq 0$.

17. See also the following works: A. F. Filipov, "On Certain Questions in the Theory of Optimal Control," *Journal of SIAM Control*, vol. 1, no. 1, 1962; R. A. Gambill, "Generalized Curves and the Existence of Optimal Controls," *Journal of SIAM Control*, vol. 1, no. 3, 1963; and E. B. Lee and L. Markus, *Foundations of Optimal Control Theory*, New York, Wiley, 1967.

REFERENCES

1. Arrow, K. J., "Applications of Control Theory to Economic Growth," in *Mathematics of the Decision Sciences*, Part 2, ed. by G. B. Dantzig and A. F. Veinott, Providence, R.I., American Mathematical Society, 1968.
2. Arrow, K. J., Hurwicz, L., and Uzawa, H., "Constraint Qualifications in Nonlinear Programming," *Naval Research Logistics Quarterly*, vol. 8, January 1961.
3. Berkovitz, L. D., "Variational Methods in Problems of Control and Programming," *Journal of Mathematical Analysis and Applications*, 3, August 1961.
4. Guinn, T., "Weakened Hypotheses for the Variational Problem Considered by Hestenes," *Journal of SIAM Control*, vol. 3, no. 3, 1965.
5. Hestenes, M. R., "On Variational Theory and Optimal Control Theory," *Journal of SIAM Control*, vol. 3, no. 1, 1965.
6. ———, *Calculus of Variations and Optimal Control Theory*, New York, Wiley, 1966.
7. Kuhn, H. W., and Tucker, A. W., "Non-linear Programming," *Proceedings of the Second Berkeley Symposium on Mathematical Statistics and Probability*, ed. by J. Neymann, Berkeley, Calif., University of California Press, 1951.
8. Lee, E. B., "A Sufficient Condition in the Theory of Optimal Control," *Journal of SIAM Control*, vol. 1, no. 3, 1963.
9. Mangasarian, O. L., "Sufficient Conditions for the Optimal Control of Nonlinear Systems," *Journal of SIAM Control*, 4, February 1966.
10. Russak, B., "On Problems with Bounded State Variables," *Journal of Optimization Theory and Applications*, 5, February 1970.

Section D

TWO ILLUSTRATIONS: THE CONSTRAINT $g\left[x(t),\ u(t),\ t\right] \geq 0$ AND THE USE OF THE CONTROL PARAMETER

In this section we illustrate the theorems developed in Section C by considering two problems which will enhance the reader's understanding of these theorems. In particular, we discuss the optimal growth problem and the peak-load problem. The peak-load problem is also useful as an illustration of the use of the control parameter.

a. OPTIMAL GROWTH ONCE AGAIN[1]

We again consider the problem of optimal growth because familiarity with this subject will help the reader to understand the theory developed in Section C. Here we discuss optimal growth problems with explicit consideration given to the inequality g- constraint. The notations of the problem are the following: N_t, labor force; K_t, capital stock; I_t, gross investment; X_t, consumption; n, rate of population growth; μ, rate of capital depreciation; ρ, discount factor; F, production function; u, utility function; subscript t, time t. (Refer to Chapter 5, Section C.) Then our problem can be written as follows:

$$\text{Maximize:} \quad \int_0^\infty u\left[\frac{X_t}{N_t}\right] e^{-\rho t} dt, \quad \rho > 0$$
$$\small{(X_t, I_t)}$$

Subject to:

(1) $$F(N_t, K_t) - X_t - I_t \geqq 0$$

(2) $$\dot{K}_t + \mu K_t = I_t$$

(3) $$N_t = N_0 e^{nt}$$

(4) $$K_t \geqq 0$$

(5) $$X_t \geqq 0$$

It is important to note the explicit introduction of the inequality constraint (1). This inequality means that the goods can be in excess supply. Previously we stated (1) in the form of an equality, signifying demand = supply equilibrium in the goods market. By thus stating (1) in the form of an equality, we could solve (1) with respect to I_t so that we obtained $\dot{K}_t + \mu K_t = F(N_t, K_t) - X_t$ from (1) and (2). Hence we were able to eliminate I_t from the system. Now (1) is stated in the form of an inequality and, therefore, elimination of I_t from the system is impossible. Note that I_t (as well as X_t) is now considered as a control variable. Assuming the linear homogeneity of F so that $F(N_t, K_t) = N_t f(k_t)$, where $k_t \equiv K_t/L_t$ and $f(k_t) \equiv F(1, k_t)$, we can rewrite the above problem as follows:

$$\text{Maximize:} \quad J \equiv \int_0^\infty u(x_t) e^{-\rho t} dt, \quad \rho > 0$$
$$\small{x_t, i_t}$$

Subject to:

(6) $$f(k_t) - x_t - i_t \geqq 0$$

(7) $$\dot{k}_t = i_t - \lambda k_t, \quad \text{where } \lambda \equiv n + \mu$$

(8) $$k_t \geqq 0, \quad k_0 \text{ is given}$$

(9) $$x_t \geqq 0$$

where $x_t \equiv X_t/N_t$ and $i_t \equiv I_t/N_t$. Equation (7) is obtained from (2) and (3). We retain the assumptions made before for this problem: $f'(k) > 0, f''(k) < 0$ for all k, $f'(0) = \infty, f'(\infty) = 0, f(0) = 0$, and $u''(x) < 0$ for all x. Thus f is strictly concave in k, and u is strictly concave in x. Viewing this problem as an optimal control problem, x_t and i_t are the control variables and k_t is the state variable. Here k_∞ is not fixed. We first proceed with our analysis *without* explicit consideration of the state variable constraint (8). Introducing the multipliers p_t, r_t, and v_t, we define the function L as follows:

$$(10) \qquad L \equiv L[k_t, x_t, i_t, t, p_t, r_t, v_t]$$

$$\equiv u(x_t)e^{-\rho t} + p_t(i_t - \lambda k_t) + r_t[f(k_t) - x_t - i_t] + v_t x_t$$

Note that the rank constraint qualification is trivially satisfied, for we can observe[2]

$$\left| \begin{array}{cc} \dfrac{\partial}{\partial x}[f(k) - x - i] & \dfrac{\partial}{\partial i}[f(k) - x - i] \\[2ex] \dfrac{\partial x}{\partial x} & \dfrac{\partial x}{\partial i} \end{array} \right| = \left| \begin{array}{cc} -1 & -1 \\ 1 & 0 \end{array} \right| = 1 \neq 0$$

Then, in view of Theorem 8.C.1, the solution $[\hat{k}_t, \hat{x}_t, \hat{i}_t]$ of the above problem must satisfy the following conditions:[3]

(i)   The variables $\hat{k}_t$, $\hat{x}_t$, $\hat{i}_t$, p_t, r_t, and v_t must satisfy the Euler-Lagrange-Hamiltonian equations

$$(11) \qquad \dot{\hat{k}}_t = \frac{\partial \hat{L}}{\partial p_t}, \qquad \dot{p}_t = -\frac{\partial \hat{L}}{\partial k_t}$$

$$(12) \qquad \frac{\partial \hat{L}}{\partial x_t} = 0 \quad \text{and} \quad \frac{\partial \hat{L}}{\partial i_t} = 0, \quad \text{where } \hat{L} \equiv L[\hat{k}_t, \hat{x}_t, \hat{i}_t, t, p_t, r_t, v_t]$$

(ii)   The relations

$$(13) \qquad r_t \geq 0, \qquad r_t[f(\hat{k}_t) - \hat{x}_t - \hat{i}_t] = 0$$

and

$$(14) \qquad v_t \geq 0, \qquad v_t \hat{x}_t = 0$$

hold.

(iii) $$H[\hat{k}_t, \hat{x}_t, \hat{i}_t, p_t] \geq H[\hat{k}_t, x_t, i_t, p_t]$$

for all $[\hat{k}_t, x_t, i_t]$ which satisfy $f(\hat{k}_t) - x_t - i_t \geq 0$ and $x_t \geq 0$, where

$$(15) \qquad H[k_t, x_t, i_t, p_t] \equiv u(x_t)e^{-\rho t} + p_t(i_t - \lambda k_t)$$

(iv) The right-hand end-point condition

$$(16) \qquad \lim_{t \to \infty} p_t \geq 0 \quad \text{and} \quad \lim_{t \to \infty} p_t \hat{k}_t = 0$$

must hold. (See Arrow [1], pp. 92–93, and recall our discussion at the end of Section A.)

Condition (11) can be written as equation (7) for the optimal path and

(17)
$$\dot{p}_t = \lambda p_t - r_t f'(\hat{k}_t)$$

Also (12) can be written as

(18)
$$u'(\hat{x}_t)e^{-\rho t} - r_t + v_t = 0$$

and

(19)
$$p_t - r_t = 0$$

Clearly condition (iii) implies relations (12), (13), and (14) under the assumption that the constraint qualification holds. Moreover, the converse [that is, (12), (13), and (14) imply condition (iii)] also holds, because L is (strictly) concave in $\hat{x}_t$ and $\hat{i}_t$ in view of the (strict) concavity of u. Note also that (19), in view of $r_t \geqq 0$, implies

(20)
$$p_t \geqq 0$$

Moreover, (19) and (17) imply

(21)
$$\dot{p}_t = -p_t[f'(\hat{k}_t) - \lambda]$$

Define a new variable q_t by

(22)
$$q_t \equiv p_t e^{\rho t} \qquad \text{for } t < \infty$$

Then $\dot{q}_t e^{-\rho t} - \rho e^{-\rho t} q_t = \dot{p}_t$ so that (21) can be rewritten as

(23)
$$\dot{q}_t = -q_t[f'(\hat{k}_t) - (\lambda + \rho)]$$

In view of (14) and (19), (18) can be rewritten as

(24)
$$u'(\hat{x}_t)e^{-\rho t} \leqq p_t$$

or

(24′)
$$u'(\hat{x}_t) \leqq q_t \qquad \text{for } t < \infty$$

Then assuming $u'(x_t) > 0$ (nonsatiation) for all $x_t \geqq 0$, or at least for the optimal per capita consumption path $\hat{x}_t$, (24) [or (24′)] implies

(25)
$$p_t > 0$$

or

(25′)
$$q_t > 0 \qquad \text{for } t < \infty$$

Then (13) combined with (19) implies

(26)
$$f(\hat{k}_t) - \hat{x}_t - \hat{i}_t = 0$$

In other words, constraint (6) holds with equality. It is important to note that the equality constraint is obtained as a result of the explicit recognition of the nonsatiation assumption.

Combining (26) with (11), we now obtain

(27) $$\dot{k}_t = f(\hat{k}_t) - \lambda \hat{k}_t - \hat{x}_t$$

If we further assume $\lim_{x \to 0, x > 0} u'(x) = \infty$ [or $\lim_{x \to 0, x > 0} u(x) = -\infty$], then from (24) [or condition (iii)] and the boundedness of the multiplier p_t, we must have

(28) $$\hat{x}_t > 0 \qquad \text{for the solution path}$$

Therefore, in view of (14), we must have $v_t = 0$ so that we obtain the following equation from (18) and (19):

(29) $$u'(\hat{x}_t)e^{-\rho t} = p_t$$

or

(29') $$u'(\hat{x}_t) = q_t$$

Combining (23), (27), and (29'), we can draw the phase diagram on either the $(x-k)$-plane or the $(q-k)$-plane. The rest of the analysis is the same as that carried out in Section A. Recall that the nonnegativity of the state variable—that is, condition (8)—is satisfied along the optimal path which converges to the modified golden rule path. And along this path, the right-hand end-point condition (16) is satisfied, and the integral J converges.

In the above analysis, it is not assumed that $i_t \geq 0$. In other words, i_t or I_t can be negative. This means $\dot{K}_t + \mu K_t$ can be negative. If $\dot{K}_t < 0$, then the economy may "eat up" the capital accumulated in the past. We may suppose that this is impossible. In other words, we introduce the assumption of the **irreversibility of investment**, that is, $I_t \geq 0$ (or $i_t \geq 0$). This means that investment once made in physical form cannot be converted into consumer goods; hence the economy cannot "eat up" the capital accumulated in the past. Such a problem is discussed by Arrow [2] and Arrow and Kurz [3], but we omit it here.

b. TWO PEAK-LOAD PROBLEMS[4]

Consider a monopoly which produces a single *nonstorable* good Y_t (say, electricity). The output of Y_t depends on the initial investment of fixed capital K and the vector of inputs of the variable factors L_t. We assume that there is a constant relation between L_t and Y_t; that is, $L_t = aY_t$, where a is the vector of variable inputs required per unit of output. We assume that a is constant over t and Y_t. The subscript t refers to time, and hence it also signifies that the relevant variable is a function of time. We also assume that as Y_t increases, the degree of utilization of the fixed capital increases. Let bY_t denote the degree of such a utilization. Then there is a capacity limit given by the relation $bY_t \leqq K$. We assume that b is a positive constant. It is important to note that the suffix t is not attached to K; that is, K is not a function of time. The demand function for the output of the firm is given by $D(p_t, t)$, where p_t is the price of the output at time t. Thus if p_t is constant for all t (say, $p_t = \overline{p}$), we can draw the time path of demand for the output as illustrated in Figure 8.13.

Suppose that the firm is required to produce an output that will meet the peak demand. If the firm builds a capacity which will meet the peak demand, then there will be an excess capacity during the nonpeak periods, for the output is nonstorable by the assumption of the peak-load problem. Such a loss of excess capacity can be reduced if the firm sets a higher price for a peak period, thus "flattening" the demand curve. One version of the peak-load problem is that of choosing the amount of initial investment K and the time path of price so as to minimize such a "loss."

Let w be the price vector of L and T be the planning horizon of the firm.[5] For the sake of simplicity, we assume that the capital lasts for the period T with the same efficiency and w is constant over time and over the relevant range of output.[6] We also assume that the initial purchase of capital stock costs the firm r dollars per unit of capital at each t.[7] Assume that r is a positive number.

There are at least two types of targets that the firm might wish to achieve. In one case, the firm wishes to maximize total social welfare over time. This may be the case when the firm is owned by a public authority, for example. In the other case, the firm wishes to maximize the total profit over time. This may be the case when the firm is privately owned. The solution may be different in each of the two cases; then the problem of optimal public regulation occurs.

First we consider the case in which the firm wishes to maximize social welfare over time. This formulation of the peak-load problem seems to be more common in the literature (see, for example, Williamson [11] and Steiner [8]). The definition of "social welfare" or at least its maximization will cause well-known difficulties. We assume that the "optimum conditions" of production and exchange are satisfied elsewhere in the economy in order to avoid the "second best" digression. We also assume that the social welfare at each instant of time

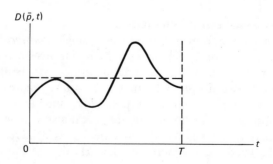

Figure 8.13.   An Illustration of the Peak-Load Problem.

is measured by (total revenue) plus (consumer's surplus) minus (social cost). That is,

$$(30) \qquad\qquad W_t = TR_t + S_t - TC_t$$

where W_t = social welfare, TR_t = total revenue, S_t = consumers' surplus, and TC_t = total social cost, each at time t.

The demand function may be expressed as $Y_t = D(p_t, t)$. However, assuming $D_p < 0$ for all p_t and t, we can globally invert the function D, and we may write the demand function as[8]

$$(31) \qquad\qquad p_t = P(Y_t, t), \qquad \text{where } P_Y \equiv \frac{\partial P}{\partial Y_t} < 0$$

Notice that the firm can select either the price policy of choosing the time path of p_t or the output policy of choosing the time path of Y_t. However, in view of the demand relation $Y_t = D(p_t, t)$ or $p_t = P(Y_t, t)$, the choice of one policy automatically implies the choice of the other policy. In other words, it does not make any difference whether we suppose the firm adopts the price policy or the output policy. Thus if the firm adopts the price policy, it has a uniquely implied output policy determined by $Y_t = D(p_t, t)$. Here we suppose that the firm adopts the output policy (that is, the policy of choosing the time path of Y_t). The price policy is then implied by $p_t = P(Y_t, t)$. The demand function is illustrated in the traditional manner in Figure 8.14. Note that as t changes (say, from t_1 to t_2), the demand curve shifts.

The total revenue plus consumers' surplus at time t, when Y_t is chosen, is given by

$$(32) \qquad\qquad TR_t + S_t = \int_0^{Y_t} P(y_t, t)\,dy_t$$

We denote (32) as follows:

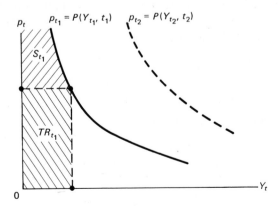

Figure 8.14.   Welfare and Demand Curves in the Peak-Load Problem.

$$(33) \qquad F(Y_t, t) \equiv \int_0^{Y_t} P(y_t, t)dy_t$$

Assume again that w, r, a, and b are all constant over time and over the relevant range of output. Then total social cost at time t, that is, TC_t, is given by

$$(34) \qquad TC_t \equiv (w \cdot a)Y_t + rK$$

Thus total social benefit over the period of time $[0, T]$ is given by

$$(35) \quad W \equiv \int_0^T W_t dt \equiv \int_0^T (TR_t + S_t - TC_t)dt \equiv \int_0^T [F(Y_t, t) - (w \cdot a)Y_t - rK] dt$$

The analysis with a positive future discount (that is, $W \equiv \int_0^T W_t e^{-\sigma t}dt, \sigma > 0$, where σ is social discount rate) is analogous to the subsequent analysis; hence it is left as an exercise to the interested reader.

We are now ready to formulate the present version of the peak-load problem.

PROBLEM I:

$$\text{Maximize:} \underset{Y_t, K}{\quad} W \equiv \int_0^T [F(Y_t, t) - (w \cdot a)Y_t - rK] dt$$

Subject to:

$$(36) \qquad K \geq bY_t$$

and

$$(37) \qquad Y_t \geq 0$$

Viewing this as an optimal control problem, Y_t is the control variable and K is the control parameter. There is *no* state variable in this problem. We assume, for the sake of simplicity, that K is perfectly divisible. In order to apply Hestenes' theorem, we define the following function L:

$$(38) \qquad \begin{aligned} L &\equiv L[Y_t, K, q_t, \mu_t] \\ &\equiv \psi_0[F(Y_t, t) - (w \cdot a)Y_t - rK] + q_t[K - bY_t] + \mu_t Y_t \end{aligned}$$

Here ψ_0, q_t and μ_t are the multipliers. Using Hestenes' theorem, we now have the following necessary conditions for $\hat{Y}_t$ and $\hat{K}$ to be optimal:

(i) $\psi_0 \geq 0$ (constant), $q_t \geq 0$, $\mu_t \geq 0$, for all t, and ψ_0, q_t, and μ_t do not vanish simultaneously. Moreover, $\mu_t \hat{Y}_t = 0$, for all t.

(ii) $\dfrac{\partial \hat{L}}{\partial Y_t} = 0$, where $\hat{L} \equiv L[\hat{Y}_t, \hat{K}, q_t, \mu_t]$, for all t; that is,

(39) $\psi_0\{\hat{F}_Y - (w \cdot a)\} - bq_t \leq 0$ and $[\psi_0\{\hat{F}_Y - (w \cdot a)\} - bq_t] \hat{Y}_t = 0$, for all t where $\hat{F}_Y \equiv \partial F(\hat{Y}_t, t)/\partial Y_t$.

(iii) The following relations hold:

(40) $$q_t(\hat{K} - b\hat{Y}_t) = 0 \text{ and } \hat{K} \geq b\hat{Y}_t, \text{ for all } t$$

(iv) The following relation also holds:

(41) $$\psi_0[F(\hat{Y}_t, t) - (w \cdot a)\hat{Y}_t - r\hat{K}] \geq \psi_0[F(Y_t, t) - (w \cdot a)Y_t - r\hat{K}]$$

for all t, and for all Y_t such that $\hat{K} \geq bY_t$ and $Y_t \geq 0$.

(v) The following transversality condition holds:

(42) $$\int_0^T (-\psi_0 r + q_t)dt = 0$$

Noting that $\hat{F}_Y \equiv P(\hat{Y}_t, t)$ in view of (33), and assuming an interior solution for $\hat{Y}_t$ (that is, $\hat{Y}_t > 0$ for all t) so that $\mu_t = 0$ for all t, we can rewrite the relation (39) as follows:[9]

(43) $$\psi_0[P(\hat{Y}_t, t) - (w \cdot a)] = bq_t, \quad \text{for all } t$$

Or writing $\hat{p}_t \equiv P(\hat{Y}_t, t)$, we have

(44) $$\psi_0(\hat{p}_t - w \cdot a) = bq_t, \quad \text{for all } t$$

The rank constraint qualification for this problem is trivially satisfied, for we can observe

(45) $$\frac{\partial (K - bY_t)}{\partial Y_t} = -b \neq 0, \quad \text{for all } t$$

Next we show $\psi_0 > 0$ so that we can take $\psi_0 = 1$. To see this, simply note the relation (44). If $\psi_0 = 0$, then (44) implies $q_t = 0$. Since we assumed $\hat{Y}_t > 0$ (the interior solution) (so that $\mu_t = 0$), this means that all the multipliers (ψ_0, q_t, and μ_t) vanish simultaneously. This contradicts condition (i) in the above. Hence the relations (44), (41), and (42) can now be rewritten as follows:

(46) $P(\hat{Y}_t, t) - w \cdot a = bq_t$, for all t, or $q_t = [P(\hat{Y}_t, t) - w \cdot a]/b$, for all t

(47) $F(\hat{Y}_t, t) - (w \cdot a)\hat{Y}_t - r\hat{K} \geq F(Y_t, t) - (w \cdot a)Y_t - r\hat{K}$, for all t

or

(48) $$F(\hat{Y}_t, t) - (w \cdot a)\hat{Y}_t \geq F(Y_t, t) - (w \cdot a)Y_t, \quad \text{for all } t$$

and for all Y_t such that $\hat{K} \geq bY_t$, $Y_t \geq 0$. Also,

(49) $$\int_0^T (q_t - r)dt = 0, \text{ or } rT = \int_0^T q_t dt$$

Relation (47) means that W_t is maximized subject to the constraints at each instant of time.

Conditions (46), (47), (49), and (40) constitute necessary conditions for $(\hat{Y}_t, \hat{K})$ to be optimal. Assuming $\partial^2 F/\partial Y_t^2 = \partial P/\partial Y_t < 0$, W_t is a concave function in Y_t and K, so that condition (47) is implied from condition (46). Therefore, in view of Mangasarian's theorem (Theorem 8.C.5), conditions (40), (46), and (49) constitute a set of necessary and sufficient conditions for an optimum. In other words, conditions (40), (46), and (49) completely describe the solution of the problem, $\hat{Y}_t, \hat{q}_t, \hat{K}, t \in [0, T]$. Notice that if $q_t > 0$ for all t, then $\hat{K} = b\hat{Y}_t, t \in [0, T]$ replaces (40). In general, q_t can be zero for some t, although $q_t > 0$ holds over a certain period of time in view of (49).

If the firm has an existing stock of capital $\overline{K}$, then $\hat{K}$ is written as $\hat{K} = \overline{K} + \hat{K}_a$, where K_a is the additional capital requirement. If $\hat{K} \geq \overline{K}$, then our analysis above follows word for word, except that it should be reinterpreted accordingly. If $\hat{K} < \overline{K}$, a slight modification of the analysis would be necessary, and r would presumably be zero. If $r = 0$, (49) implies $q_t = 0$ for "almost all" t (that is, for all t except for a countable number of isolated points in $[0, T]$), so that we have $P(\hat{Y}_t, t) = w \cdot a$ for almost all t. We proceed with our analysis for $\hat{K} \geq \overline{K}$.

From (46) and (49) we obtain

$$(50) \qquad \int_0^T P(\hat{Y}_t, t)dt = T[w \cdot a + br]$$

Let A be a subset of $[0, T]$ in which $\hat{Y}_t = \hat{Y}$, where $\hat{Y} = \hat{K}/b$. That is, A is the set of "top-peak" periods (the periods in which full capacity output is achieved). Since $q_t = 0$ for $t \notin A$ in view of (40), we have

$$(51) \qquad \hat{p}_t \equiv P(\hat{Y}_t, t) = w \cdot a \qquad \text{for } t \notin A$$

from (46). Therefore $\hat{p}_t$ is constant for all $t \notin A$.

The essence of the solution described above is that optimal outputs are equal and prices are unequal for $t \in A$, while optimal outputs are unequal and prices are equal for $t \notin A$.

Using (46) and (49), we may rewrite (50) in the following form:

$$(52) \qquad \int_A [P(\hat{Y}_t, t) - w \cdot a] = \int_A bq_t = brT$$

where $\int_A$ denotes the integration in t over the range of A.

The profit of the firm at time t is written as $\pi_t \equiv (p_t - w \cdot a)Y_t - rK$. Then under the above prescribed optimal policy, the total profit over the whole period is computed as

$$
\begin{aligned}
(53) \qquad \int_0^T &[(\hat{p}_t - w \cdot a)\hat{Y}_t - r\hat{K}] \, dt \\
&= \int_A bq_t\hat{Y}_t - \int_0^T (r\hat{K})dt \\
&= \int_A q_t\hat{K} - rT\hat{K} = 0
\end{aligned}
$$

In other words, the profit over the whole planning horizon should be zero.

Now suppose that the demand function P is such that $q_t > 0$ for all t so that $A = [0, T]$ (that is, full capacity output always occurs). Then $\hat{Y}_t = \hat{K}/b = $ constant $(\equiv \hat{Y})$ for all t, so that the value of $\hat{Y}$ is determined by (50) as follows:

$$(54) \qquad \int_0^T P(\hat{Y}, t)dt = T\left[w\cdot a + br\right]$$

The value of $\hat{K}$ can then be determined as $\hat{K} = b\hat{Y}$.

For the sake of illustration, suppose further that

$$(55\text{-a}) \qquad P(Y_t, t) = P_1(Y_t) \qquad \text{for } t \in T_1 \subset [0, T]$$

$$(55\text{-b}) \qquad P(Y_t, t) = P_2(Y_t) \qquad \text{for } t \in T_2 \subset [0, T]$$

where $T_1 \cap T_2 = \emptyset$ and $T_1 \cup T_2 = [0, T]$. We may call T_1 "day" and T_2 "night." Let the length of periods in T_1 and T_2 be τ_1 and τ_2, respectively. Then (54) can be rewritten as

$$(56) \qquad \tau_1 P_1(\hat{Y}) + \tau_2 P_2(\hat{Y}) = T\left[w\cdot a + br\right]$$

where $\tau_1 + \tau_2 \equiv T$. The solution $\hat{Y}$ indicated in (56) can be illustrated by Figure 8.15, which corresponds to Steiner's solution for the "shifting-peak" case ([8], p. 588), as generalized by Williamson [11].

In general, we have periods in which full capacity is not achieved. An extreme case is the case in which

$$(57\text{-a}) \qquad P(Y_t, t) = P_3(Y_t) \qquad \text{for } t \in A$$

$$(57\text{-b}) \qquad P(Y_t, t) = P_4(Y_t) \qquad \text{for } t \notin A$$

That is, the demand curve is fixed as long as $t \in A$ or $t \notin A$. Let α be the sum of

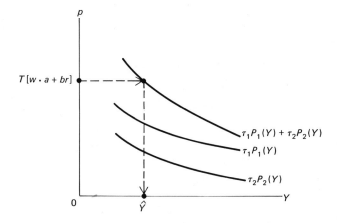

Figure 8.15.   An Illustration of the Solution When Full Capacity Is Achieved Always.

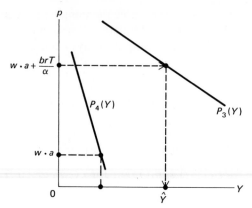

Figure 8.16. An Illustration of the Solution When Full Capacity Is Not Necessarily Achieved.

the lengths of the periods in A. Noting that (52) implies

$$(58) \qquad \alpha P_3(\hat{Y}) = \alpha(w \cdot a) + br T$$

for this case, we can illustrate the solution in Figure 8.16, which corresponds to Steiner's solution for the "firm-peak" case ([8], p. 588), as generalized by Williamson [11].

It may be of some interest to consider the case in which there is no shift in the demand function, in other words, where $P_t = P(Y_t)$. Then we may suppose that $[0, T] = A$ (that is, the full capacity output is achieved always), so that $\hat{Y}_t = \hat{Y}$ (constant) for all t. Hence in view of (46), we obtain $q_t =$ constant. Then from (49) we have

$$(59) \qquad q_t = r \qquad \text{for all } t$$

Therefore, from (46), we have

$$(60) \qquad \hat{p}_t = w \cdot a + rb$$

We define the **long-run marginal cost**, MC_t, by

$$(61) \qquad MC_t \equiv \frac{\partial}{\partial Y_t} \left[(w \cdot a) Y_t + rK \right]$$

Evaluating MC_t along the optimal path $\hat{Y}$ and $\hat{K} \, (= b\hat{Y})$, we obtain

$$(62) \qquad MC_t = w \cdot a + rb = \hat{p}_t \qquad \text{for all } t$$

which corresponds to the conventional rule of marginal cost pricing.

We now suppose that the firm wishes to maximize profit over time. Let π_t be the profit for time t. Then we have

$$(63) \qquad \begin{aligned} \pi_t &\equiv p_t Y_t - w \cdot L_t - rK \\ &= (p_t - w \cdot a) Y_t - rK \\ &= (p_t - w \cdot a) D(p_t, t) - rK \end{aligned}$$

Note that once p_t is set, the firm knows the demand for output by $D(p_t, t)$ and hence produces an amount $Y_t = D(p_t, t)$.

The firm is supposed to maximize

(64)
$$\pi \equiv \int_0^T \pi_t e^{-\rho t} dt$$

where $\rho \geq 0$ denotes the discount rate for the firm. We assume $\rho = 0$ for the sake of simplicity. The analysis in which $\rho > 0$ is analogous to the subsequent analysis; hence it is left as an exercise for the interested reader. We are now ready to state our problem.

PROBLEM II:

$$\underset{p_t, K}{\text{Maximize:}} \int_0^T \left[(p_t - w \cdot a) D(p_t, t) - rK \right] dt$$

Subject to:

(65)
$$K - bD(p_t, t) \geq 0$$

and

(66)
$$p_t \geq 0$$

Viewing this as an optimal control problem, K is the control parameter and p_t is the control variable. There is no state variable. We again assume, for the sake of simplicity, that capital K is perfectly divisible.

Then, in view of the optimal control theorem, we first define the function L by

(67)
$$L[p_t, K, q_t, \mu_t] \equiv \psi_0 [(p_t - w \cdot a) D(p_t, t) - rK]$$
$$+ q_t [K - bD(p_t, t)] + \mu_t p_t$$

Here ψ_0, q_t, and μ_t are multipliers. Although the same notation is used for these multipliers (as well as L) as in the previous problem, their values can, of course, be different from the corresponding ones in the previous problem. The same notation is used purely for the sake of notational simplicity. Using Hestenes' theorem, we now have the following necessary conditions for p_t^* and K^* to be optimal:

(i)   The multipliers ψ_0, q_t, and μ_t do not vanish simultaneously and $\psi_0 \geq 0$ (constant), $q_t \geq 0$, $\mu_t \geq 0$, for all t. Moreover, $\mu_t p_t^* = 0$, for all t.

(ii) $\dfrac{\partial L^*}{\partial p_t} = 0$, where $L^* \equiv L(p_t^*, K^*, q_t, \mu_t)$, for all t, that is,

$$(68) \qquad \phi_0\{D^* + (p_t^* - w \cdot a)D_p^*\} - q_t b D_p^* \leqq 0$$

$$\text{and } [\phi_0\{D^* + (p_t^* - w \cdot a)D_p^*\} - q_t b D_p^*] \, p_t^* = 0 \quad \text{for all } t$$

where $D^* \equiv D(p_t^*, t)$ and $D_p^* \equiv \partial D(p_t^*, t)/\partial p_t$. Assuming the interior solution for p_t^*, that is, $p_t^* > 0$, for all t (so that $\mu_t = 0$ for all t), this relation holds with equality. Thus we have[10]

$$(69) \qquad \phi_0[D^* + (p_t^* - w \cdot a)D_p^*] - q_t b D_p^* = 0, \qquad \text{for all } t$$

(iii) The following relation holds:

$$(70) \qquad q_t(K^* - bD^*) = 0, \qquad \text{for all } t$$

(iv) The following relation also holds:

$$(71) \quad \phi_0[(p_t^* - w \cdot a)D(p_t^*, t) - rK^*] \geqq \phi_0[(p_t - w \cdot a)D(p_t, t) - rK^*]$$

for all t and for all p_t such that $K^* \geqq bD(p_t, t)$ and $p_t \geqq 0$.

(v) The following transversality condition holds:

$$(72) \qquad \int_0^T (-\phi_0 \, r + q_t)dt = 0$$

We may assume that

$$(73) \qquad \frac{\partial}{\partial p_t}[K - p_t D(p_t^*, t)] \neq 0, \qquad \text{for all } t$$

In other words, we may assume that the rank constraint qualification is satisfied because

$$(74) \qquad D_p^* \neq 0, \text{ or } D_p^* < 0$$

from the assumption on the demand function. This implies $\phi_0 > 0$. To see this, suppose $\phi_0 = 0$. Then the relation (69) with condition (74) implies $q_t = 0$. Since $\mu_t = 0$ from $p_t^* > 0$, all the multipliers vanish, contradicting condition (i) above. Thus $\phi_0 > 0$, so that we may choose $\phi_0 = 1$. Conditions (69), (71), and (72) are now simplified as follows:[11]

$$(75) \qquad D^* = -(p_t^* - w \cdot a - q_t b)D_p^*, \qquad \text{for all } t$$

$$(76) \qquad (p_t^* - w \cdot a)D(p_t^*, t) \geqq (p_t - w \cdot a)D(p_t, t)$$

for all t and for all p_t such that $K^* \geqq bD(p_t, t)$ and $p_t \geqq 0$.

$$(77) \qquad \int_0^T (q_t - r)dt = 0, \quad \text{or} \quad rT = \int_0^T q_t dt$$

Note that relation (76) means that the "current profit" (that is, profit except for capital cost) as well as the total profit are to be maximized at each instant of time.

Conditions (75), (76), (77), and (70) constitute necessary conditions for an optimum for the present problem. Moreover, if we assume $D_{pp} \equiv \partial^2 D/\partial p_t^2 \leq 0$ for all p, then our π_t (hence π also) is a concave function so that these conditions are also sufficient for an optimum (again in view of Mangasarian's theorem or Theorem 8.C.5).

We now proceed to further characterizations of the above solution. First, we define the elasticity of demand by

$$(78) \qquad \eta_t \equiv \eta(p_t, t) \equiv \frac{-p_t D_p}{D} > 0, \text{ with } D_p < 0$$

Then we can rewrite (75) as

$$(79) \qquad (\eta_t^* - 1)p_t^* = \eta_t^*(w \cdot a + q_t b), \quad \text{for all } t$$

where $\eta_t^* \equiv \eta(p_t^*, t)$. Since $(w \cdot a + q_t b) > 0$, (79) requires that

$$(80) \qquad \eta_t^* > 1, \quad \text{for all } t$$

Define ϵ_t^* by $\epsilon_t^* \equiv \eta_t^*/(\eta_t^* - 1)$. Then

$$(81) \qquad \epsilon_t^* > 1 \quad \text{for all } t$$

Also (79) can be rewritten as[12]

$$(82) \qquad p_t^* = \epsilon_t^*(w \cdot a + q_t b), \quad \text{for all } t$$

Therefore

$$(83) \qquad \int_0^T p_t^* dt = \int_0^T \epsilon_t^*(w \cdot a + q_t b) dt$$

Note that (81) and (82) imply

$$(84) \qquad p_t^* - w \cdot a > p_t^* - \epsilon_t^*(w \cdot a) = \epsilon_t^* q_t b \geq 0, \quad \text{for all } t$$

In other words, current profits ($p_t^* - w \cdot a$) are always positive, whereas they are zero for "non-top-peaks" (that is, $t \notin A$) for the welfare maximizing monopoly.

Next let B be the subset of $[0, T]$ such that $bD(p_t^*, t) = K^*$. In other words, B is the set of "top peaks." Clearly, B can be different from A. For $t \notin B$, we have $bD(p_t^*, t) < K^*$. Hence $q_t = 0$ for $t \notin B$. Thus, in view of (82), we obtain

$$(85) \qquad p_t^* = \epsilon_t^*(w \cdot a), \quad t \notin B$$

Since $\epsilon_t^* > 1$, the optimal price p_t^* exceeds the operational cost $w \cdot a$ for $t \notin B$. Note also that ϵ_t^*, in general, changes from time to time. Hence p_t^* is not necessarily constant for $t \notin B$, while in the welfare maximization problem p_t^* is constant (and equal to $w \cdot a$) during the non-top-peaks (that is, $t \notin A$).

Using (84), (81), and (77) successively, total profit over the entire period can be shown to be positive. In other words

$$(86) \qquad \pi^* \equiv \int_0^T \left[(p_t^* - w \cdot a)D^* - rK^* \right] dt$$

$$> \int_0^T \left[(\epsilon_t^* q_t b)D^* - rK^* \right] dt$$

$$> \int_0^T \left[q_t b D^* - rK^* \right] dt$$

$$= \int_B q_t b D^* - rK^* T = 0$$

where $\int_B$ denotes the integration in t over the range of B. Recall that, in the case of a welfare maximizing monopoly, total profit is zero.

Now for the sake of illustration, assume that η_t^* is constant over t. An example of a demand function that yields a constant η_t^* is

$$(87) \qquad D(p_t, t) = \delta(t)p_t^{-\eta^*}$$

where $\eta^* > 1$ is some constant and $\delta(t)$ signifies the time shift of the demand function (it is easy to check that η^* satisfies the definition of the elasticity of demand). If η_t^* is constant, ϵ_t^* is also constant so we denote it by ϵ^*. For this case total profit is computed by using (82) and (77) as

$$(88) \qquad \pi^* \equiv \int_0^T \left[(p_t^* - w \cdot a)D^* - rK^* \right] dt$$

$$= \int_0^T \left[\{(\epsilon^* - 1)w \cdot a + q_t b\}D^* - rK^* \right] dt$$

$$= T(\epsilon^* - 1)w \cdot a$$

That is, total profit is larger when ϵ^* (or the degree of monopoly $1/\eta^*$) is larger.

When ϵ_t^* is constant, (83) can be rewritten as

$$(89) \qquad \int_0^T p_t^* \, dt = \epsilon^*(w \cdot a + br)T$$

Suppose further that the demand conditions are such that $q_t > 0$ for all t. Then $Y^* = D(p_t^*, t)$ for all t, where $Y^* \equiv K^*/b$. Using this relation, we obtain

$$(90) \qquad p_t^* = P(Y^*, t), \qquad \text{for all } t$$

For the sake of illustration, suppose also that relation (55) holds for the function P. Then (89) and (90) yield

$$(91) \qquad \tau_1 P_1(Y^*) + \tau_2 P_2(Y^*) = \epsilon^* T(w \cdot a + br)$$

The diagrammatical illustration of (91) is strictly analogous to that of (56).

Since $\epsilon^* > 1$, $Y^* < \hat{Y}$, so that $K^* < \hat{K}$. That is, capacity for the profit maximizing monopoly tends to be less than the socially optimum amount. It is easy to prove that this conclusion also holds even if ϵ_t^* changes over time.

If, on the other hand, the demand conditions are those specified by (57), then (82) and (77) imply

$$(92) \qquad \beta P_3(Y^*) = \beta \epsilon^*(w \cdot a) + brT$$

where β is the size of B. The illustration of the solution Y^* is strictly analogous to that of (58). Again, $\epsilon^* > 1$ implies that $Y^* < \hat{Y}$ and $K^* < \hat{K}$, *provided that* $\alpha = \beta$.

FOOTNOTES

1. This subsection relies heavily on Arrow [1].
2. The examination of the constraint qualification is often neglected in the practical application of optimal control theory. This is a bad practice.
3. Note that p_0 in the definition of the L-function, the multiplier attached to the maximand function (inside the integral), which appears in Hestenes' theorem, is set equal to one. To prove this, modify (18) and (29) with p_0. Then using (19) and the fact that the multipliers do not vanish simultaneously, we obtain a contradiction by supposing $p_0 = 0$. Notice also that the rank constraint qualification is satisfied for this problem. Incidentally, condition (16) may be replaced by a more usual condition $\lim_{t \to \infty} p_t = 0$ without changing the argument and the conclusions in essence.
4. This subsection is probably the first application of optimal control theory to the peak-load problem. The problem can also be solved by using the ordinary nonlinear programming technique. See Takayama [9].
5. The choice of T is a difficult problem indeed. We omit the discussion of the choice of a finite T. We may note that all the arguments in the literature assume that time is discrete, and usually assume that there are only two periods to facilitate a diagrammatical analysis. For an example of n-period analysis, see Steiner [8]. We may also note that there is no literature so far that treats the problem with a continuum of time.
6. That w is constant with respect to Y means that the firm is small in the (variable) factor markets. That w is constant with respect to t is an assumption purely for the sake of simplicity. This is the assumption adopted in the literature.
7. Consider, for example, that the firm borrows money to purchase the initial capital stock K, and assume that this borrowing amounts to repaying r dollars per unit of capital K at each instant of time for the period $[0, T]$.
8. We will assume that $p_t > 0$ implies $Y_t = D(p_t, t) > 0$ for all t.
9. In view of the assumption made in footnote 8 and $F_Y < 0$, $\hat{Y}_t > 0$ implies $\hat{p}_t \equiv F_Y(\hat{Y}_t, t) > 0$.
10. In view of the assumption made in footnote 8, $p_t^* > 0$ implies $D^* \equiv D(p_t^*, t) > 0$.
11. Equation (75) can be rewritten as $p_t^* + D^*/D_p^* = w \cdot a + q_t b$. But $D^* = Y_t^*$ and $1/D_p^* = \partial P(Y_t^*, t)/\partial Y_t \equiv P_{\hat{Y}}^*$. Hence the LHS of this equation is $p_t^* + P_{\hat{Y}}^* Y_t^* = \partial(p_t^* Y^*)/\partial Y_t$, which signifies the marginal revenue. The RHS of the equation, $w \cdot a + q_t b$, will signify the "marginal cost." Therefore equation (75) may be interpreted as the familiar rule, $MR_t = MC_t$.

12. Note that $\epsilon_t^* = 1/(1 - 1/\eta_t^*)$, and that $1/\eta_t^*$ is the well-known **degree of monopoly** à la Lerner. Notice that ϵ_t is greater, the greater the degree of monopoly. From footnote 11, $(w \cdot a + q_t b)$ is equal to the marginal revenue. Hence (82) signifies the usual rule that the difference between the price and the marginal revenue increases as the degree of monopoly increases.

REFERENCES

1. Arrow, K. J., "Applications of Control Theory to Economic Growth," in *Mathematics of the Decision Sciences*, Part 2, ed. by G. B. Dantzig and A. F. Veinott, Providence, R. I., American Mathematical Society, 1968.

2. ———, "Optimal Capital Policy with Irreversible Investment," in *Value, Capital, and Growth, Papers in Honour of Sir John Hicks*, ed. by J. N. Wolfe, Edinburgh, Edinburgh University Press, 1968.

3. Arrow, K. J., and Kurz, M., "Optimal Growth with Irreversible Investment in a Ramsey Model," *Econometrica*, 38, March 1970.

4. Buchanan, J. M., "Peak Loads and Efficient Pricing: Comment," *Quarterly Journal of Economics*, LXXX, August 1966.

5. Hirschleifer, J., "Peak Loads and Efficient Pricing: Comment," *Quarterly Journal of Economics*, LXXII, August 1958.

6. Houthakker, H. S., "Electricity Tariffs in Theory and Practice," *Economic Journal*, LXI, March 1951.

7. ———, "Peak Loads and Efficient Pricing: Further Comment," *Quarterly Journal of Economics*, LXXII, August 1958.

8. Steiner, P. O., "Peak Loads and Efficient Pricing," *Quarterly Journal of Economics*, LXXI, November 1957.

9. Takayama, A., "On the Peak-Load Problem," *Krannert Institute Paper*, No. 251, Purdue University, June 1969.

10. Turvey, R., "Peak-Load Pricing," *Journal of Policitical Economy*, 76, January–February 1968.

11. Williamson, O. E., "Peak-Load Pricing and Optimal Capacity," *American Economic Review*, LVI, September 1966.

Section E

THE NEO-CLASSICAL THEORY OF INVESTMENT AND ADJUSTMENT COSTS— AN APPLICATION OF OPTIMAL CONTROL THEORY[1]

a.   INTRODUCTION

The essence of the present treatment of the theory of investment is the behavioral assumption that a firm maximizes the present value of net cash flows subject to constraints such as a production function and a capital accumulation equation. Hence it is a part of dynamic decision theory. Since the firm determines both the demand for factors such as labor as well as the demand for investment, the name "theory of investment" seems slightly inappropriate. Rather it should be termed the dynamic theory of the firm.

Whatever we call it, there seems to be quite a bit of confusion in the theory of investment. The purpose of this section is partly expository in the sense that we attempt to correct these confusions and partly illustrative in the sense that we present various theories in a unified and generalized fashion.

First there is the argument (Haavelmo [20] and Lerner [43], for example) which says that there is no investment demand schedule for an individual firm. Assuming that the firm is competitive and small enough and that all prices are constant, the firm can and would adjust instantaneously to the desired stock of capital, which is constant. In this case, investment is always equal to the amount of depreciation and there is no investment function as such. Thus Haavelmo, for example, concludes the following ([20], p. 216):

> What we should reject is the naive reasoning that there is a 'demand schedule'
> for investment which would be derived from a classical scheme of producer's
> behavior in maximizing profit.

The capital is adjusted to the desired level instantaneously at the initial time and it will be kept constant over the whole planning horizon ([20], p. 163).

Jorgenson, being apparently distressed by this, argued that "it is possible to derive a demand function for investment based on purely neoclassical considerations" ([27], p. 133). The secret of Jorgenson's innovative procedure of obtaining the investment demand schedule is to change prices, notably the price of capital goods, over time ([27], p. 149). The amount of investment then changes over time depending on the time path of the prices.

However, as Tobin ([61], p. 157) noticed, nothing basic is changed. If all prices are assumed (or expected by the firm) to be constant, then the amount of investment is also constant over time in Jorgenson's model. In other words, the

basic characteristic of the Haavelmo-Lerner treatment, the instantaneous adjustment to the desired capital stock, is unchanged in Jorgenson's treatment.

The instantaneous adjustment to the desired stock of capital, in essence,
implies that the volume of investment I_t is unbounded. In other words, if we write

$$I_{min} \leqq I_t \leqq I_{max}$$

this assumption of unbounded investment means $I_{min} = -\infty$ and $I_{max} = \infty$. The
assumption of $I_{max} = \infty$ is often justified under the assumption of a competitive
firm. I believe that this justification is quite confusing. Even though I_{max} may
be very large for each firm, it should still be finite.

A more serious difficulty, however, is in the assumption of $I_{min} = -\infty$.
This is a silly assumption at the macro-economic level. But even at the microeconomic level, it is difficult to accept this assumption because it means that
the firm is able to sell the capital good already installed in any amount at the price
of a newly produced capital good. This is obviously unrealistic. Here it may suffice
to quote Arrow ([7], p. 2):

> From a realistic point of view, there will be many situations in which the sale
> of capital goods cannot be accomplished at the same price as their purchase.
> There are installation costs, which are added to the purchase price but cannot
> be recovered on sale; indeed, there may on the contrary be additional costs
> of detatching and moving machinery. Again sufficiently specialized machinery
> and plants have little value to others. So resale prices may be substantially
> below replacement costs.

Arrow, however, goes to the other extreme by assuming that resale of capital
goods is impossible, or by assuming $I_{min} = 0$; that is, the imposition of the constraint $I_t \geqq 0$ for all t.

Mathematically speaking, both Haavelmo [20] and Jorgenson [27] utilized
the classical calculus of variations and thus implicitly ignored the constraint
$I_{min} \leqq I_t \leqq I_{max}$. A more plausible mathematical technique is optimal control
theory. Not only can this constraint be incorporated into the analysis in a satisfactory manner by using the optimal control technique, but also this technique
enables us to realize the "bang-bang" nature of the solution and to understand
why instantaneous adjustment is optimal to the firm if I_{max} is sufficiently large
and if I_{min} is sufficiently small. These are not clear in the rather naive applications
of the calculus of variations as seen in Haavelmo [20] and Jorgenson [27]
(also [25], [28], and so on).

In subsection b, we formulate the problem explicitly as an optimal control
problem, and we conclude the following for the nonconstant returns to scale case:

1. The investment policy for the firm is to reach the "long-run" desired stock
   of capital (K^*) as soon as possible (that is, $\hat{I}_t = I_{max}$ if $K_0 < K^*$, and $\hat{I}_t = I_{min}$
   if $K_0 > K^*$), and after reaching K^* to remain at K^*.
2. The "long-run" desired stock of capital, K^*, is determined by the usual marginal
   productivity principle.

3. The above conclusions imply that the investment demand changes once over time when the capital stock reaches K^* (except for the case in which $K_0 = K^*$).

4. The (Lerner-Haavelmo-Jorgenson) conclusion of instantaneous adjustment *cannot* occur for the continuous time model (see, for example, [20] and [27]), regardless of the sizes of I_{max} and I_{min}, as long as they are finite. This is simply because the integral over a point of time—say, at $t = 0$—is zero. For the discrete time model, instantaneous adjustments can occur (see, for example, Takayama [59]).

5. However, if the sizes of I_{max} and $|I_{min}|$ are large enough, then the time required to reach K^* can be made very small; that is, an "almost" instantaneous adjustment occurs.

These conclusions may appear to be intuitively obvious. However, this does not negate the importance of deriving these results rigorously in mathematical terms.[2] In particular, at the end of subsection b we also observe that the above conclusions will be altered greatly if the production function exhibits constant returns to scale.

Another confusion in connection with the neo-classical investment theory is that the Keynesian theory of the marginal efficiency of capital is irrelevant to the neo-classical theory and hence is dismissed (see, for example, Jorgenson [27]). In subsection b, we observe that the Keynesian rule of the marginal efficiency of capital is, in essence, the same as the neo-classical marginal productivity rule.

As remarked earlier, the crucial feature of the Lerner-Haavelmo-Jorgenson theory of investment is instantaneous and frictionless adjustment to the desired stock of capital. Commenting on Jorgenson [27], Tobin remarked ([61], p. 158):

> Jorgenson's investment demand schedule cannot serve the analytical purposes for which such a schedule is desired, and one must look elsewhere for a determinate theory of investment. At the level of a single firm, this may be derived from frictional or adjustment costs.

We then have an increasing literature on the investment function which introduces adjustment costs explicitly (by economists such as Eisner and Strotz, Treadway, Lucas, Gould, and Uzawa).

In subsection c, we discuss the theory of investment with adjustment costs. In a typical treatment of this topic in the literature (see Eisner and Strotz [14], Lucas [45], and Gould [18], for example), it is assumed that the adjustment cost function is strictly convex and quadratic, and it is concluded that the optimal investment (as well as the optimal capital stock) is uniquely determined and *constant* over time and that the capital stock monotonically approaches the "long-run" desired level as time extends without limit. Note that, in obtaining this result, it is assumed in the literature that the adjustment cost function is quadratic. In subsection c, we will observe that such an assumption is not essential.

Moreover in obtaining the above result, it is usually assumed that the production function exhibits constant returns to scale. Although the constant returns to scale assumption might be convenient for macro-economic analysis in dealing with the exhaustion of the product problem, such an assumption might not hold for an individual firm. In subsection c, we also discuss the case of nonconstant returns to scale. We then conclude that the optimal investment is no longer constant over time, but rather monotonically approaches a certain limit as time extends without limit. In other words, we will observe that the constant returns to scale assumption is crucial in obtaining the conclusion in which the optimal investment is constant over time.

Subsection d contains three remarks. The first remark is concerned with the "response function." If the optimal investment demand is determinate and constant (say, I) as in the case of adjustment costs with a constant returns to scale production function, then we obtain an equation such as (see, for example, Gould [18]):

$$\dot{K}_t = \delta(\bar{K} - K_t)$$

where $\bar{K} \equiv \bar{I}/\delta$ and δ is the rate of depreciation. Viewing $\bar{K}$ as the "long-run" desired stock of capital, this equation seems to define the usual "response function" which is often seen in the empirical literature. Our first remark in subsection d is a critical note on such a claim.

The second remark in subsection d is a critical summary of Uzawa's treatment of adjustment costs, the "Penrose effect". The third remark is concerned with a possible extension of investment theory. Among other things, we point out that essentially the same results follow for the complete monopoly case.

b. THE CASE OF NO ADJUSTMENT COSTS

Consider a firm that wishes to maximize the sum of the present value of net cash flows W_t for all future time, W, where W is defined by

(1) $$W \equiv \int_0^\infty e^{-rt} W_t dt$$

where

(2) $$W_t \equiv p_t Q_t - w_t L_t - q_t I_t$$

Here we use the following notations: Q_t, output; L_t, labor input; I_t, investment; p_t, price of output; w_t, wage rate; q_t, price of capital goods; and r, discount rate.[3] There are three constraints in this maximization problem. The first is the production function, which we write as

(3) $$Q(L_t, K_t) - Q_t = 0$$

where K_t is the stock of capital. The second is the capital accumulation constraint, which, following the literature, we write as

(4) $$\dot{K}_t = I_t - \delta K_t$$

where δ denotes the rate of depreciation ($0 < \delta < 1$).

It is important to note that (4) contains a crucial assumption with regard to depreciation, that is, "depreciation by evaporation." Equation (4) together with $I_t \geq 0$ and $K_0 > 0$ imply that the capital good continues to exist forever.[4]

The third constraint is that the volume of investment is bounded, that is,

(5) $$I_{\min} \leq I_t \leq I_{\max} \quad \text{for all } t$$

A typical lower bound $I_{\min}$ is 0, or $I_t \geq 0$, which was introduced and called, as mentioned earlier, the "irreversibility of investment" in the literature by Arrow and so on. As we will see later, the constraint (5) is crucially significant in the present problem in which the "adjustment costs" are ignored.

It is supposed that the firm chooses the time stream of L_t and I_t (hence also K_t and Q_t) so as to maximize the present value of all future profits, W, subject to (3), (4), and (5), $L_t \geq 0$, $K_t \geq 0$ ($Q_t \geq 0$), and a given stock of initial capital K_0. Such a maximization problem is considered by Jorgenson [27] and others, except that the constraint (5) is often ignored.

Before embarking on solving the above maximization problem, the following remarks may be useful in revealing the assumptions which are often implicit in the literature.

REMARKS:

(i)   It is assumed that the firm takes the prices (p_t, w_t, q_t) which prevail at each t as given data. The output can be sold in any quantity at time t at the price p_t, and the firm's employment of labor L_t and investment I_t do not affect the prices w_t and q_t for each time t.

(ii) It is assumed that the firm knows all future prices p_t, w_t, and q_t for all $t \geq$ 0 with perfect certainty (perfect foresight). Alternatively, it is assumed that the firm has a certain *definite* expectation for these prices for all $t \geq$ 0.[5] When their expectation turns out to be incorrect in the future, they correct their program. If instead, these future prices are not expected with probability one but rather they are expected with a certain probability distribution, then the maximization problem should be altered. In other words, the procedure of first solving the problem with a definite expectation (that is, expectation with probability one) with regard to future prices and then of solving another problem when these prices turn out to be different from the originally expected value, does *not*, in general, give a truly optimal solution for the firm.

We now solve the above maximization problem. To sharpen our analysis and to highlight the problems involved, we consider a simple but important case in which p_t, w_t, and q_t are expected to be constants for all t. Therefore, we write p_t, w_t, and q_t as p, w, and q, respectively. The case in which these prices change over time is left to the interested reader.

First we substitute (2) and (3) into (1) and rewrite the firm's maximization problem as follows:

PROBLEM I: Choose the time path of L_t and I_t so as to

Maximize: $\int_0^\infty e^{-rt}\left[pQ(L_t, K_t) - wL_t - qI_t\right]dt$

Subject to: $\dot{K}_t = I_t - \delta K_t$

$I_{\min} \leqq I_t \leqq I_{\max}$

$L_t \geqq 0, K_t \geqq 0$

and a given value of K_0

We view this as an optimal control problem in which L_t and I_t are the control variables and K_t is the state variable. To solve this problem, define the Hamiltonian as[6]

(6) $H \equiv e^{-rt}\left[pQ(L_t, K_t) - wL_t - qI_t\right] + \mu_t\left[I_t - \delta K_t\right]$

The set of necessary conditions for an optimum is written as[7]

(7) $$\frac{d\hat{K}_t}{dt} = \frac{\partial \hat{H}}{\partial \mu_t}$$

(8) $$\dot{\mu}_t = -\frac{\partial \hat{H}}{\partial K_t}$$

(9) $e^{-rt}\left[pQ(\hat{L}_t, \hat{K}_t) - w\hat{L}_t - q\hat{I}_t\right] + \mu_t\left[\hat{I}_t - \delta\hat{K}_t\right]$

$\geqq e^{-rt}\left[pQ(L_t, \hat{K}_t) - wL_t - qI_t\right] + \mu_t\left[I_t - \delta\hat{K}_t\right]$

for all $L_t \geqq 0$ and I_t with $I_{\min} \leqq I_t \leqq I_{\max}$

(10) $$\lim_{t \to \infty} \mu_t = 0$$

As remarked in Sections A and C, condition (10) can be replaced by "Arrow's condition,"

(10′) $$\lim_{t \to \infty} \mu_t \geqq 0 \quad \text{and} \quad \lim_{t \to \infty} \mu_t \hat{K}_t = 0$$

by explicitly introducing the constraint $\lim_{t \to \infty} \hat{K}_t \geqq 0$. But the analysis and the conclusion would be the same as the present one. Condition (9) signifies the maximization of the Hamiltonian H with respect to the control variables L_t and I_t. Setting $L_t = \hat{L}_t$ for all t, condition (9) implies

(11) $(\mu_t - e^{-rt}q)\hat{I}_t \geqq (\mu_t - e^{-rt}q)I_t$ for all I_t with $I_{\min} \leqq I_t \leqq I_{\max}$

In other words,

(12-a) $\hat{I}_t = I_{\max}$ if $\mu_t > e^{-rt}q$

(12-b) $\hat{I}_t = I_{\min}$ if $\mu_t < e^{-rt}q$

(12-c) $\hat{I}_t \in [I_{\min}, I_{\max}]$ if $\mu_t = e^{-rt}q$

Now the significance of the constraint (5), $I_{\min} \leqq I_t \leqq I_{\max}$, should be apparent.

If there are no such bounds, $\hat{I}_t = \infty$ when $\mu_t > e^{-rt}q$ and $\hat{I}_t = -\infty$ when $\mu_t < e^{-rt}q$; both of these conditions do not make too much sense either economically or mathematically. The usual calculus of variations approach as seen in Jorgenson (for example, [25], [27], [28], and so on) is thus rather inappropriate for the present case. Note that the solution described in (12) arises from the fact that the terms inside the objective integral and the constraint function are both linear in I_t. This "bang-bang" characteristic described in (12) is ignored in the literature.

By setting $I_t = \hat{I}_t$ for all t in (9), we obtain[8]

(13) $$p\hat{Q}_L - w \leq 0 \quad \text{and} \quad (p\hat{Q}_L - w)\hat{L}_t = 0$$

where $\hat{Q}_L \equiv \partial Q/\partial L_t$ evaluated at $(\hat{L}_t, \hat{K}_t)$. Assuming $\hat{L}_t > 0$ for all t, we obtain

(14) $$\hat{Q}_L = \frac{w}{p}$$

which is the familiar marginal productivity rule with respect to labor.

Conditions (7), (8), and (10) are respectively rewritten as[9]

(15) $$\dot{\hat{K}}_t = \hat{I}_t - \delta\hat{K}_t$$

(16) $$\dot{\lambda}_t = (r + \delta)\lambda_t - p\hat{Q}_K$$

where

$$\lambda_t \equiv \mu_t e^{rt} \quad \text{and} \quad \hat{Q}_K \equiv \frac{\partial Q}{\partial K_t} \quad [\text{evaluated at } (\hat{L}_t, \hat{K}_t)]$$

and

(17) $$\lim_{t \to \infty} \lambda_t e^{-rt} = 0$$

In terms of λ_t, (12) is rewritten as

(18-a) $$\hat{I}_t = I_{\max} \qquad \text{if } \lambda_t > q$$

(18-b) $$\hat{I}_t = I_{\min} \qquad \text{if } \lambda_t < q$$

(18-c) $$\hat{I}_t \in [I_{\min}, I_{\max}] \qquad \text{if } \lambda_t = q$$

Therefore (15) is now rewritten as

(19-a) $$\dot{\hat{K}}_t = I_{\max} - \delta\hat{K}_t \qquad \text{if } \lambda_t > q$$

(19-b) $$\dot{\hat{K}}_t = I_{\min} - \delta\hat{K}_t \qquad \text{if } \lambda_t < q$$

(19-c) $$\dot{\hat{K}}_t = \hat{I}_t - \delta\hat{K}_t \qquad \text{if } \lambda_t = q, \text{ where } \hat{I}_t \in [I_{\min}, I_{\max}].$$

Note that if the function Q is concave, conditions (14), (16), (17), and (19) are sufficient as well as necessary for $(\hat{K}_t, \hat{L}_t, \hat{I}_t)$ to be optimal.[10]

Assume that (14) can be rewritten as[11]

(20) $$\hat{L}_t = L(\hat{K}_t, \frac{w}{p})$$

and write $pQ_K(\hat{L}_t, \hat{K}_t) = pQ_K\left[\hat{L}_t(\hat{K}_t, \frac{w}{p}), \hat{K}_t\right] \equiv \phi(\hat{K}_t)$; that is,

$$(21) \qquad \qquad \hat{Q}_K = \frac{\phi(\hat{K}_t)}{p}$$

where it is recalled that w/p is a constant.

Assume that $\phi' < 0$[12] for all $\hat{K}_t$ at each t. Then the phase diagram which describes the time path of $(\hat{K}_t, \lambda_t)$ can now be constructed from (16) and (19) as illustrated in Figure 8.17.

In Figure 8.17, it is assumed that $I_{\min} < 0$, and K^* is defined from

$$(22) \qquad \qquad q = \frac{\phi(K^*)}{r + \delta}$$

From Figure 8.17, it is clear that the only path that is eligible[13] is the one that approaches K^*, which is described by the heavy lines. Mathematically,[14]

$$(23\text{-a}) \qquad \qquad \dot{\hat{K}}_t = I_{\max} - \delta\hat{K}_t \qquad \text{if } K_0 < K^*$$

$$(23\text{-b}) \qquad \qquad \dot{\hat{K}}_t = I_{\min} - \delta\hat{K}_t \qquad \text{if } K_0 > K^*$$

$$(23\text{-c}) \qquad \qquad \hat{K}_t = K^* \qquad \text{if } K_0 = K^*$$

From (23-a), $\hat{K}_t$ is explicitly obtained for $K_0 < K^*$ as follows:

$$(23'\text{-a}) \qquad \qquad \hat{K}_t = K_0 e^{-\delta t} + \frac{I_{\max}}{\delta}(1 - e^{-\delta t})$$

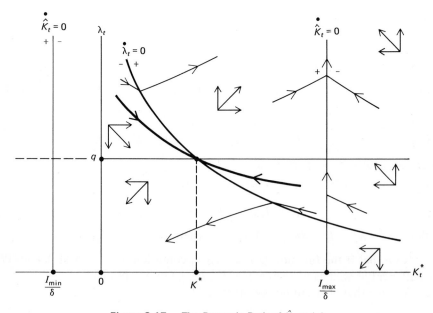

Figure 8.17.   The Dynamic Path of $\hat{K}_t$ and λ_t.

Therefore assuming $I_{\min} = 0$, we can describe the optimal path of investment as follows:

(24-a) $(K_0 < K^*)$

$$\hat{I}_t = I_{\max} \quad \text{for all } t, 0 \le t \le T^*$$
$$\hat{I}_t = \delta K^*(\equiv I^*) \quad \text{for all } t > T^*$$

(24-b) $(K_0 > K^*)$

$$\hat{I}_t = 0 \quad \text{for all } t, 0 \le t \le T^{**}$$
$$\hat{I}_t = I^*(\equiv \delta K^*) \quad \text{for all } t > T^{**}$$

(24-c) $(K_0 = K^*)$

$$\hat{I}_t = I^* (\equiv \delta K^*) \quad \text{for all } t \ge 0$$

Here T^* in (24-a) and T^{**} in (24-b) are computed respectively from

$$K^* = K_0 e^{-\delta T^*} + \frac{I_{\max}}{\delta}(1 - e^{-\delta T^*})$$

and

$$K^* = K_0 e^{-\delta T^{**}}$$

In other words,[15]

(25-a) $$T^* \equiv \frac{1}{\delta} \log \frac{I_{\max} - \delta K_0}{I_{\max} - \delta K^*} > 0$$

(25-b) $$T^{**} \equiv \frac{1}{\delta} \log \frac{K_0}{K^*} > 0$$

The optimal policy in (24) may be described as the one by which the firm reaches K^* as soon as possible, and after reaching K^*, remains there. It is illustrated in Figure 8.18.

We call K^* the **long-run desired stock of capital**. If $\hat{K}_t = \text{constant} = K^*$, then

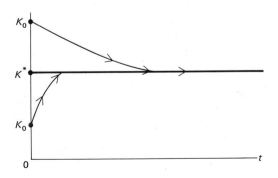

Figure 8.18. The Time Path of $\hat{K}_t$.

from (20), $\hat{L}_t = $ constant $\equiv L^*$. Recalling (14) and (22), the values of L^* and K^* are determined by

(26-a)
$$Q_L(L^*, K^*) = \frac{w}{p}$$

(26-b)
$$Q_K(L^*, K^*) = \frac{(r + \delta)q}{p}$$

Here $(r + \delta)q$ signifies the rent for capital; hence (26-a) and (26-b) are the famous marginal productivity rules. To see that $(r + \delta)q$ is the rent for capital, suppose that one unit of the capital good is rented with rent c. The physical quantity of one unit of capital good at time t will be decayed to $e^{-\delta t}$; hence the rental payment will be $ce^{-\delta t}$. Therefore, if the capital good is rented for an infinite future, the present value of rent over all future time will be

(27)
$$\int_0^\infty ce^{-\delta t}e^{-rt}dt = \int_0^\infty ce^{-(\delta + r)t}dt = \frac{c}{r + \delta}$$

The intertemporal arbitrage relation will equate this with the price of a unit of capital, so that[16]

(28)
$$q = \frac{c}{r + \delta} \quad \text{or} \quad c = (r + \delta)q$$

Relations (27) and (28) are also obtained by Jorgenson [27] (in a more complicated manner).

Suppose that the firm is in the long-run steady state (L^*, K^*). Then in view of (27) and (28), we immediately realize that (26-b) can be rewritten as

(29)
$$q = \int_0^\infty pQ_K^* e^{-(\delta + r)t}dt$$

where $Q_K^* \equiv \partial Q/\partial K_t$ evaluated at (L^*, K^*). This is the famous Keynesian rule of the marginal efficiency of capital which states that the demand for the stock of capital is determined by the equality between the unit price of capital and the present value of all future income from an additional unit of capital. Since equations (26-b) and (29) are equivalent, the Keynesian rule of the marginal efficiency of capital coincides with the neo-classical marginal productivity rule, if the firm is on the path (L^*, K^*). A similar observation with regard to the equivalence between the marginal efficiency rule and the marginal productivity rule can be made in terms of a discrete time model with depreciation by "sudden death" (see Takayama [59]). Therefore, we disagree with the following view which is taken by Jorgenson ([27], p. 152) as well as others: "Keynes' construction of the demand function for investment must be dismissed as inconsistent with the neoclassical theory of optimal capital accumulation."

Needless to say, Keynes does not explicitly impose some of the above assumptions. In other words, in Keynes, prices may change over time, the firm may not be a price taker, and the demand function that the firm (if monopolistic) faces may change in the future. Therefore Keynes obtained a rule which is much less explicit than (29); that is,

$$q = \int_0^\infty R_t e^{-(\delta + r)t} dt$$

where R_t is the "*expected* rate of return" on capital at time t, that is, R_t is the expected revenue minus the expected operating cost (not including the depreciation cost) per additional unit of capital.

It is important to observe that the values of L^* and K^* are equal to the ones determined by maximizing the "short-run" (or instantaneous) profit

$$pQ(L, K) - wL - cK$$

In other words, the "long-run" solution (L^*, K^*) for the dynamic optimization problem is reduced to the one for the static optimization problem. The myopic rule is optimal after all from the long-run viewpoint.

With constant prices, the effect of changes in parameters such as p, w, q, and r on L^* and K^* can easily be obtained from (26-a) and (26-b) by using the usual comparative statics procedure. For this purpose, assume, for example, that $Q_{LL}^* Q_{KK}^* - Q_{LK}^{*2} > 0$, $Q_{LL}^* < 0$, $Q_{KK}^* < 0$, and $Q_{LK}^* > 0$. Then it can be established, for example, that $\partial L^*/\partial r < 0$, $\partial K^*/\partial r < 0$, $\partial L^*/\partial w < 0$, and $\partial K^*/\partial w < 0$. Since $I^* \equiv \delta K^*$, we also obtain $\partial I^*/\partial r < 0$ and $\partial I^*/\partial w < 0$.

Assuming that the values of K^* and L^* are uniquely determined by (26-a) and (26-b), these values are constant as long as the prices (w, p, q, and r) are constant. In this case, I^* is also constant and equal to the amount of depreciation δK^*. In other words, the firm's investment is constant after it reaches K^*. Jorgenson [27] obtained results in which $\hat{I}_t$ changes over time. This is due to the fact that he allowed the price of capital q to vary over time, while he in the main assumed all other prices (p, w, and r) constant.[17] It is not quite clear why he allowed this asymmetry with regard to the expectation of future prices.

Finally, let us consider the case in which the production function $Q(L_t, K_t)$ is homogeneous of degree one (constant returns to scale). In this case, $Q_{LL} Q_{KK} - Q_{LK}^2 = 0$ for all (L_t, K_t), and the above analysis should be modified. Note that, in this constant returns to scale case, $Q_L(L_t, K_t)$ and $Q_K(L_t, K_t)$ are both homogeneous of degree zero. Then in view of (14), $\hat{K}_t/\hat{L}_t$ is constant ($\equiv \hat{k}$) for the fixed value of w/p, as long as $Q_{LL} < 0$ and $Q_{KK} < 0$ for all (L_t, K_t). Hence $\hat{Q}_K = \hat{Q}_K(1, \hat{k})$ is also constant.[18] Hence in view of (17), the λ_t which satisfies (16) is obtained as

(30) $$\lambda_t = \frac{p\hat{Q}_K}{r + \delta} = \text{constant} (\equiv \hat{\lambda})$$

provided that $\delta > 0$. Hence, assuming that $I_{\min} = 0$, the optimal investment is obtained as

(24'-a) $I_t = I_{\max}$ if $\hat{\lambda} > q$

(24'-b) $I_t = 0$ if $\hat{\lambda} < q$

For the knife edge case in which $\hat{\lambda} = q$, the optimal value of investment is in-determinate. The results (24'-a) and (24'-b) correspond to the ones obtained by Thompson and George [60] in a slightly more complicated situation [in partic-ular, they set $I_{\max}$ as a known function of time, say, $I_{\max} = M(t)$]. Since $\hat{\lambda}$ can be interpreted as the (shadow) demand price of capital and q is the (market) supply price of capital, the economic interpretation of (24'-a) and (24'-b) should be self-evident. Note also that we have (by definition of $\hat{\lambda}$)

$$\hat{Q}_K \gtreqless \frac{(r + \delta)q}{p} \text{ according to whether } \hat{\lambda} \gtreqless q$$

The marginal productivity rule with respect to capital as defined by (26-b) holds only for the "knife edge" case in which $\hat{\lambda} = q$. In Figure 8.19, we illustrate the case in which $\hat{\lambda} > q$ (with $0 < r + \delta < 1$).

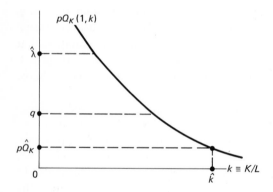

Figure 8.19.   An Illustration of $\hat{\lambda} > q$.

The time path of the optimal stock of capital is obtained from (15) and (24') as

(23'-a) $\hat{K}_t = K_0 e^{-\delta t} + \dfrac{I_{\max}}{\delta}(1 - e^{-\delta t})$ if $\hat{\lambda} > q$

(23'-b) $\hat{K}_t = K_0 e^{-\delta t}$ if $\hat{\lambda} < q$

Clearly,

$$\lim_{t \to \infty} \hat{K}_t = \frac{I_{\max}}{\delta} \quad \text{if } \hat{\lambda} > q$$

$$\lim_{t \to \infty} \hat{K}_t = 0 \quad \text{if } \hat{\lambda} < q$$

The time path of $\hat{K}_t$ for the constant returns to scale case is illustrated in Figure 8.20.

We have remarked that $\hat{\lambda} = q$ is the "knife edge" case. Although this may be

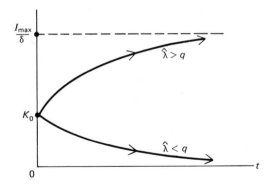

Figure 8.20.   The Time Path of $\hat{K}_t$ (the Constant Returns to Scale Case).

true for the behavior of an individual firm, the situation $\hat{\lambda} \neq q$ cannot continue forever, if every firm behaves under the rule described above and if every firm has
more or less the same production function (that is, the same technical efficiency).
For example, if $\hat{\lambda} > q$, the total demand for capital for the market as a whole
would exceed its supply and the price of the capital good (q) would sooner or
later rise to the point at which $\hat{\lambda} = q$. Notice that in the meantime, the demand
for labor would increase as $\hat{K}_t$ increases in order to keep $\hat{k}$ constant, which
might push up the real wage rate. Then the value of $\hat{k}$ would decrease to keep the
relation $\hat{Q}_L = w/p$, which in turn would increase $\hat{\lambda}$. In other words, the equilibrium
would be realized at an increased level of $\hat{\lambda}$. In any case, if $\hat{\lambda} = q$ is to be achieved
sooner or later, then $\hat{\lambda} = q$ is not really a knife edge case. Notice also that under
$\hat{\lambda} = q$, the marginal productivity rule with respect to capital, (26-b), is also
realized, although the volumes of optimal investment and capital stock become
indeterminate.

c.   THE CASE WITH ADJUSTMENT COSTS

Introduction

In the above analysis, it is assumed that the firm can obtain any amount of
investment I_t without affecting the investment price q_t. This is true for each t,
and it does not matter whether q_t is constant over time or not. This assumption
has recently been criticized on the basis of the "fixity" of capital. Fixity of capital
was considered to be the basis of Marshall's well-known distinction between
"short-run" and "long-run" analyses.

What then is the "fixity" of capital? Although there are a number of ways
to introduce this concept into the firm's maximization problem, here we consider
it as the cost per unit of gross investment *rising* with the investment rate. This
cost behavior can be rationalized, for example, (1) by postulating a monopsonistic
capital goods market, or (2) by introducing internal costs of investment which
are the sum of purchase costs (with either perfect or imperfect factor markets)
and installation costs. What then is the mathematical specification of such adjust-

ment costs of capital? Eisner and Strotz [14], Lucas [45], and Gould [18] suggested the following form to replace $q_t I_t$:

$$(31) \qquad\qquad C_t = C(I_t)$$

where $C(I_t) > 0$, $C'(I_t) > 0$, $C''(I_t) > 0$ for all $I_t > 0$, $C'(0) \geq 0$, and $C(0) = 0$.[19] The condition $C''(I_t) > 0$ means that adjustment costs will be greater, on the average, the greater the rate of investment.

On the other hand, Lucas [47], viewing the adjustment cost as the internal cost of the output foregone, introduced adjustment costs by altering the usual production function (3) to the following form:

$$(32) \qquad\qquad Q_t = Q(L_t, K_t, I_t)$$

where it is assumed that $\partial Q / \partial I_t < 0$ and $\partial^2 Q / \partial I_t^2 < 0$ for all $(L_t, K_t, I_t) > 0$.[20]

Clearly, the choice of the mathematical formulation may affect the conclusion. Such a choice would depend on empirical considerations and will vary between industries. Here we simply adopt the form presented in (31).

The firm's maximization problem is now slightly altered by this modification; q_t is no longer exogenous to the problem. In the definition of H in (6), we should replace $q_t I_t$ by $C(I_t)$. In other words, we rewrite the firm's problem as follows.

PROBLEM II: Choose the time path of L_t and I_t so as to

Maximize: $\displaystyle\int_0^\infty e^{-rt} \left[pQ(L_t, K_t) - wL_t - C(I_t) \right] dt$

Subject to: $\dot{K}_t = I_t - \delta K_t$

$I_{\min} \leq I_t \leq I_{\max}$

$L_t \geq 0,\ K_t \geq 0$

and a given value of K_0

Write the Hamiltonian H now as [21]

$$(6') \qquad H \equiv e^{-rt} \left[pQ(L_t, K_t) - wL_t - C(I_t) \right] + \mu_t \left[I_t - \delta K_t \right]$$

and define λ_t again by[22]

$$\lambda_t \equiv \mu_t e^{rt}$$

Denote again the optimal path by $(\hat{K}_t, \hat{L}_t, \hat{I}_t)$. Assuming that the function Q is concave and noting that C is (strictly) concave, the following conditions are sufficient as well as necessary for an optimum:

$$(33) \qquad\qquad \frac{d\hat{K}_t}{dt} = \hat{I}_t - \delta \hat{K}_t$$

$$(34) \qquad\qquad \dot{\lambda}_t = (r + \delta)\lambda_t - p\hat{Q}_K$$

where $\hat{Q}_K \equiv \partial Q / \partial K_t$ evaluated at $(\hat{L}_t, \hat{K}_t)$;

(35)
$$\hat{Q}_L = \frac{w}{p}$$

where $\hat{Q}_L \equiv \partial Q / \partial L_t$ evaluated at $(\hat{L}_t, \hat{K}_t)$;

(36)
$$\lambda_t = C'(\hat{I}_t)$$

and[23]

(37)
$$\lim_{t \to \infty} \lambda_t e^{-rt} = 0$$

In obtaining (35), it is assumed that $\hat{L}_t > 0$. In obtaining (36), it is assumed that $I_{min} < \hat{I}_t < I_{max}$. It is important to note that the introduction of adjustment costs by the function C enables us to assume the existence of an interior solution.[24] In other words, the "bang-bang" characteristic of the optimal investment in the previous section disappears with the introduction of adjustment costs.

Nonconstant Returns to Scale

In the literature with adjustment costs, it is usually assumed that the production function Q is homogeneous of degree one. However, unless we consider the investment problem on the macro-economic level and worry about the exhaustion of the product, there seems to be no need to assume constant returns to scale. Here we consider the nonconstant returns to scale case. Following the previous section, we specifically assume that $Q(L_t, K_t)$ satisfies the following condition:

(38) $Q_{LL} < 0, Q_{KK} < 0, Q_{LK} > 0,$ and $Q_{LL}Q_{KK} - Q_{LK}^2 > 0$

for the "relevant" neighborhood of the optimal path $(\hat{L}_t, \hat{K}_t)$.[25]

Then, as we did in the previous subsection, we can obtain $\hat{L}_t$ from (35) as

(39)
$$\hat{L}_t = L\left(\hat{K}_t, \frac{w}{p}\right)$$

and write

(40)
$$p\hat{Q}_K \equiv \phi(\hat{K}_t)$$

where $\phi' < 0$ for all $\hat{K}_t$ at each t.

Since $C''(I_t) > 0$ for all I_t, we may write, in view of (36),

(41)
$$\hat{I}_t = g(\lambda_t), \quad \text{for all } \lambda_t \geq C'(0)$$

where $g' > 0$ for all λ_t. Using (33), (34), (40), and (41), we can construct the phase diagram shown in Figure 8.21 to describe the dynamic path of λ_t and $\hat{K}_t$.

The equation for the $(\dot{\lambda}_t = 0)$-curve is

(42-a)
$$\lambda_t = \frac{\phi(\hat{K}_t)}{r + \delta} \left[= \frac{p\hat{Q}_K}{r + \delta} \right]$$

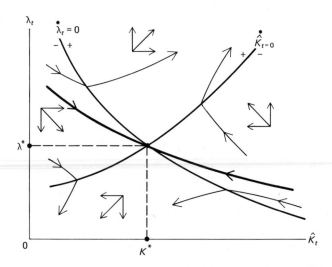

Figure 8.21. The Dynamic Path of $(\lambda_t, \hat{K}_t)$.

and the equation for the $(\dot{\hat{K}}_t = 0)$-curve is

$$(42\text{-b}) \qquad\qquad \hat{K}_t = \frac{g(\lambda_t)}{\delta}$$

The values of λ_t and $\hat{K}_t$ at the intersection of these two curves are denoted by λ^* and K^*, respectively, and are defined by the following equations:

$$(43\text{-a}) \qquad\qquad \lambda^* = \frac{\phi(K^*)}{r + \delta}$$

$$(43\text{-b}) \qquad\qquad K^* = \frac{g(\lambda^*)}{\delta}$$

In order to have $K^* > 0$, we require that

$$(44) \qquad\qquad \lambda^* > C'(0)$$

Moreover, from (43) we can easily see that

$$(45) \qquad\qquad \frac{\partial K^*}{\partial r} < 0, \frac{\partial \lambda^*}{\partial r} < 0, \frac{\partial K^*}{\partial p} > 0, \frac{\partial \lambda^*}{\partial p} > 0$$

Hence, writing $I^* \equiv g(\lambda^*)$, we obtain

$$(45') \qquad\qquad \frac{\partial K^*}{\partial r} < 0, \frac{\partial I^*}{\partial r} < 0, \frac{\partial K^*}{\partial p} > 0, \frac{\partial I^*}{\partial p} > 0$$

In other words, an increase in the interest rate (resp. the price of output) lowers (resp. increases) the "long-run" desired stock of capital (K^*) and investment (I^*).

There are three types of $(\hat{K}_t, \lambda_t)$-paths in Figure 8.21: (1) the path in which both $\hat{K}_t$ and λ_t decreases over time; (2) the path in which $\lambda_t \to \infty$; (3) the path in which $\hat{K}_t \to K^*$ as $t \to \infty$. Clearly only the third type of path is eligible.[26]

In the third path, $\hat{K}_t$ monotonically approaches K^*, as indicated in Figure 8.21. Notice that at K^*

$$(46) \qquad \hat{I}_t = I^* \equiv g(\lambda^*) = \delta K^*$$

as we can see from (43-b). In other words, the optimal investment at (K^*, λ^*) is just equal to the amount of depreciation. Now observe that

$$(47) \qquad \hat{I}_t - \delta \hat{K}_t = \hat{I}_t - I^* - (\delta \hat{K}_t - \delta K^*)$$
$$= [g(\lambda_t) - g(\lambda^*)] - \delta(\hat{K}_t - K^*)$$

In the third path, λ_t approaches λ^* as $\hat{K}_t$ approaches K^*. Therefore, from (47), $\hat{I}_t - \delta \hat{K}_t$ approaches zero as $\hat{K}_t$ approaches K^*. This implies that it takes an infinite amount of time to reach the steady state (K^*, λ^*). We thus conclude the following:

$$(48\text{-a}) \quad K_0 < K^*: \quad \frac{d\hat{K}_t}{dt} > 0, \frac{d\hat{I}_t}{dt} < 0 \quad \text{for all } t \geq 0, \quad \lim_{t \to \infty} \hat{K}_t = K^*, \lim_{t \to \infty} \hat{I}_t = I^*$$

$$(48\text{-b}) \quad K_0 > K^*: \quad \frac{d\hat{K}_t}{dt} < 0, \frac{d\hat{I}_t}{dt} > 0 \quad \text{for all } t \geq 0, \quad \lim_{t \to \infty} \hat{K}_t = K^*, \lim_{t \to \infty} \hat{I}_t = I^*$$

$$(48\text{-c}) \quad K_0 = K^*: \quad \hat{K}_t = K^* \text{ and } \hat{I}_t = I^* \quad \text{for all } t \geq 0$$

In Figure 8.22, we illustrate the time path of optimal investment $\hat{I}_t$.

Notice also that

$$(49) \qquad \frac{d\hat{K}_t}{dt} = \hat{I}_t - \delta \hat{K}_t = (\hat{I}_t - I^*) + \delta(K^* - \hat{K}_t)$$

Since $\hat{I}_t \neq I^*$ for all $t \geq 0$, we have

$$(50) \qquad \frac{d\hat{K}_t}{dt} \neq \delta(K^* - \hat{K}_t) \quad \text{for any } t$$

In other words, the usual response function which appears in the literature cannot hold for any t (see subsection d).

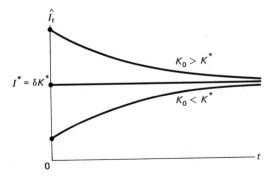

Figure 8.22.   The Time Path of $\hat{I}_t$.

Constant Returns to Scale

In this case, $Q_{LL}Q_{KK} - Q_{LK}{}^2 = 0$ for all (L_t, K_t) and $\phi' \equiv 0$. On the other hand, equation (35) uniquely determines the value of the capital:labor ratio $\hat{k}$ for each fixed w/p, as long as $Q_{LL} < 0$ and $Q_{KK} < 0$ for all (L_t, K_t). Therefore the value of $\hat{Q}_K$ becomes constant for all t.[27] Write $p\hat{Q}_K \equiv \hat{c}$. Then from (34) we have

$$(51) \qquad \dot{\lambda}_t = (r + \delta)\lambda_t - \hat{c}$$

This is a linear differential equation, and its solution is obtained as

$$(52) \qquad \lambda_t = \frac{\hat{c}}{r + \delta} + Ae^{(r+\delta)t}$$

where A is the integrating constant. In view of the right end-point condition (37), A must be zero. Hence

$$(53) \qquad \lambda_t = \frac{\hat{c}}{r + \delta} (\equiv \hat{\lambda})$$

which corresponds to (30). Then in view of (36) with $C'' > 0$, and hence in view of (41), we obtain

$$(54) \qquad \hat{I}_t = g\left[\frac{\hat{c}}{r + \delta}\right] \equiv \bar{I} \ (= \text{a positive constant})$$

for all t, where it is assumed that

$$(55) \qquad \frac{\hat{c}}{r + \delta} > C'(0)$$

Therefore we conclude that the optimal investment is constant and positive for all t. Notice that we obtained this result *without* assuming the quadratic approximation of the adjustment cost function which is the usual convention in the literature.[28]

Since the function g is monotone increasing, it is easy to conclude

$$(56) \qquad \frac{\partial \bar{I}}{\partial r} < 0, \frac{\partial \bar{I}}{\partial p} > 0, \frac{\partial \bar{I}}{\partial \delta} < 0$$

in view of (54).

The path of the optimal capital stock $\hat{K}_t$ is easily obtained from (33) as

$$(57) \qquad \frac{d\hat{K}_t}{dt} = \bar{I} - \delta\hat{K}_t$$

The solution of this linear differential equation is easily obtained as

$$(58) \qquad \hat{K}_t = \frac{\bar{I}(1 - e^{-\delta t})}{\delta} + K_0 e^{-\delta t}$$

Notice that $\hat{K}_t$ monotonically approaches $\bar{K}$ as $t \to \infty$ regardless of the values of

K_0, where $\bar{K}$ is defined by

(59)
$$\bar{K} \equiv \frac{\bar{I}}{\delta}$$

Notice also that

$$\frac{\bar{I}}{\delta}(1 - e^{-\delta t}) = \int_0^T \bar{I} e^{-\delta \tau}\, d\tau$$

Thus the first term on the RHS of (58) signifies the investment accumulated up to time t. The second term of the RHS of (58) is the initial capital stock left over at time t. The time path of $\hat{K}_t$ is illustrated in Figure 8.23. It takes an infinite amount of time to reach $\bar{K}$ if K_0 is different from $\bar{K}$.

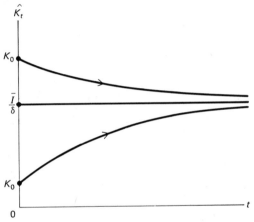

Figure 8.23.   The Time Path of $\hat{K}_t$.

In view of (56) and (58), we also obtain

(60)
$$\frac{\partial \hat{K}_t}{\partial r} < 0 \text{ and } \frac{\partial \hat{K}_t}{\partial p} > 0 \qquad \text{for all } t$$

Notice that the strict convexity of the function C (that is, $C'' > 0$) guarantees the uniqueness of the optimal investment as a result of (54), and thus guarantees the uniqueness of $\hat{K}_t$ from (58), which in turn implies the uniqueness of $\hat{L}_t$ since $\hat{K}_t/\hat{L}_t \equiv \hat{k} = $ constant. In other words, the strict convexity guarantees the uniqueness of the solution $(\hat{K}_t, \hat{L}_t, \bar{I})$ (almost everywhere), in spite of the fact that Q is homogeneous of degree one, and hence not *strictly* concave.

d. SOME REMARKS

The Response Function

In subsection b, we pointed out that the firm adjusts very quickly to its "long-run" desired stock of capital K^* if the adjustment is cost free and frictionless and if $I_{\max}$ is large enough or $I_{\min}$ is small enough. This more or less corresponds to the

Lerner-Haavelmo observation. If all the prices, p_t, w_t, q_t, and r, are constant, then the desired stock of capital K^*, whose value depends on the parameters p, w, q, and r, would be constant. In Jorgenson's study [27], these prices are not constant; hence the desired stock of capital is not constant, and is hence denoted by K_t^*.

Jorgenson and his associates then insisted that the actual stock of capital K_t is in general different from the desired level. In "reality," the firm cannot adjust its stock of capital to the desired level instantaneously and frictionlessly. Hence the investment demand at time t will be determined in such a way as to accommodate this adjustment.

Suppose that the response mechanism is represented in such a way that actual capital is a weighted average of all past levels of desired capital with geometrically declining weight. That is

(61)
$$K_t = \sum_{\tau=1}^{\infty} \alpha_\tau \hat{K}_{t-\tau}$$

where[29]

(62)
$$\sum_{\tau=1}^{\infty} \alpha_\tau = 1 \quad \text{and} \quad \alpha_\tau \geq 0, \tau = 1, 2, \ldots$$

In the continuous time model, such a *distributed lag* can be represented by

(63)
$$K_t = \int_0^{\infty} \alpha_\tau \hat{K}_{t-\tau} d\tau$$

where

(64)
$$\int_0^{\infty} \alpha_\tau d\tau = 1 \quad \text{and} \quad \alpha_\tau \geq 0 \quad \text{for all } \tau \geq 0$$

If the lag function α_t is a simple exponential lag

(65)
$$\alpha_t = \alpha e^{-\alpha t}, \alpha > 0$$

then it is well known that (63) can be rewritten as[30]

(66)
$$\dot{K}_t = \alpha(\hat{K}_t - K_t)$$

where α may be termed the **response parameter** or the **speed of adjustment**.

It is possible to select a lag function other than the above simple exponential lag, and the specification of the lag function would, in general, affect the results. For example, in their empirical studies of comparing alternative theories of investment, Jorgenson and Siebert ([29], p. 688) remarked the following:

> Misspecification of the lag distribution for a given theory of investment behavior may bias the results of our comparison. Accordingly, we choose the best lag distribution for each alternative specification of desired capital from among the class of general Pascal distributed lag functions.[31]

In a number of empirical studies of the investment function, Jorgenson and his associates have obtained good statistical fits for Jorgenson's "neo-classical" theory. (See, for example, [24], [25], and [29]–[37].)

However, there is a serious difficulty in the above procedure. In obtaining the desired stock of capital, it is assumed that the adjustment is instantaneous and frictionless. Hence the imposition of a response function such as (61) or (66) for empirical estimation is a serious inconsistency in theory (regardless of the specification of the lag function), for it implies that the adjustment to the desired stock of capital is neither instantaneous nor frictionless. If the adjustment is not instantaneous and involves some friction, then this should be incorporated in the maximization behavior of the firm. Thus, with regard to the treatment of the investment function by Jorgenson and his associates, Uzawa [65] comes to the following conclusion:

> It goes without saying that the investment function ... which is derived from logically completely inconsistent assumptions, cannot have any economic and empirical significance, no matter how good the statistical fit of that function may be. (Translation is mine.)

In other words, a response mechanism such as (61) or (66) affects the profits, and hence affects the desired stock of capital.

The introduction of adjustment costs by such authors as Treadway [62], Lucas [45] and [47], and Gould [18], as described in subsection c is, no doubt, based on serious skepticism about the above difficulty in the studies by Jorgenson and his associates.

However, the result they obtained is remarkable. As we can observe from our discussion in subsection c [especially from equations (57) and (59)], if the production function exhibits constant returns to scale with respect to labor and capital and if the adjustment cost function is strictly convex with respect to investment (I_t), then we obtain a result which states that $I_t = \overline{I}$ (constant) for all t and

(67)
$$\frac{d\hat{K}_t}{dt} = \delta(\overline{K} - \hat{K}_t)$$

where δ is the rate of depreciation. From (67) it is concluded that it is optimal for the firm to adjust in the way described by (66) where $\alpha = \delta$.

Now we should comment on this result. As remarked earlier, this result depends crucially on the assumption of constant returns to scale. As we showed in subsection c, we cannot obtain a nice response function such as (66) for the case of nonconstant returns to scale.

Secondly, one crucial assumption in the formulation by Gould, Treadway, Lucas, and so on, is that there is no lag between the investment decision and the realization of the decision. This is in sharp contrast to the usual rationalization of a time lag. For example, Jorgenson made the following (empirically) very sound remark ([25], p. 2):

> ... we divide the investment process into separate stages. The first stage of the process is a change in the demand for capital services. Subsequent to an alteration in demand for capital services, architectural and engineering plans must be drawn up, cost estimates prepared, funds appropriated and funds committed through the issuing of orders for equipment or the letting of contracts for construction. Actual investment expenditure is the final stage in the investment process. Only after a given investment project has passed through each of the intermediate stages can actual investment expenditure take place.

Clearly this seems to be the motivation of the empirical studies by Jorgenson and his associates. In the adjustment cost study as described in subsection c, such a time lag is ignored.

It is possible to argue, at least in a purely theoretical framework, that as long as all future prices are known to the firm and as long as the firm remains competitive (that is, a pure price taker), the firm would lay out the investment plans for all future time. Hence, except for the initial period, the time lag as described by Jorgenson does not matter. If, for example, there is a construction lag of θ, the order will be given out θ periods in advance.

Obviously this is unrealistic, as the firm usually neither knows all future prices, nor, as assumed in subsection c, expects constant prices. However, the basic criticism of the studies by Jorgenson and his associates still stands: If there is such a time lag, it ought to be incorporated into the optimization procedure of the firm.

The introduction of this time lag into the maximization problem with changing future prices together with the cost of adjustments is left to the interested reader. One problem remains: The response function, such as (66), is not likely to come out as a criterion function for the maximization anymore. The present study, as a critical summary of the existing theory, is only intended to serve as a framework for such a study in the future.

Uzawa on the "Penrose Effect"

Uzawa in a number of papers proposed to take a closer look at the actual behavior of firms, and in particular he argued that we should utilize the study by Penrose [54].[32]

He summarizes the **Penrose effect** as follows ([64], p. 4):

> The managerial and administrative abilities required by a firm in the process of growth are basically different from those which are needed in the mere management of the existing administrative structure of the firm. The nature of such a process may be conveniently summarized by a schedule relating the level of investment ... with the rate by which the stock of real capital available to the firm grows.

Uzawa postulates the following functional relation

(68)
$$\frac{I_t}{K_t} = \pi\left(\frac{\dot{K}_t}{K_t}\right)$$

where $\pi' > 0$ and $\pi'' > 0$; $\pi'' > 0$ signifies that the marginal effect of investment upon the growth process is diminishing.[33] The π-schedule depends on how the managerial and administrative resources are accumulated in the course of the growth of the firm. Notice that K_t in (68) is *not* the usual physical capital stock, but rather it incorporates the scarcity of managerial and administrative resources.

In essence, the Penrose effect seems to treat the managerial and administrative resources as another factor of production. It is assumed that such resources are directly related to the accumulated physical stock of capital. Moreover, instead of directly relating $\dot{K}_t$ to I_t, Uzawa's Penrose function relates $\dot{K}_t/K_t$ to I_t/K_t. These conventions enable him to avoid the problem of how to measure managerial and administrative resources,[34] to simplify mathematical deduction considerably, and thus to obtain some definite conclusions.

The Penrose function is illustrated in Figure 8.24 and it is called the **Penrose curve**.

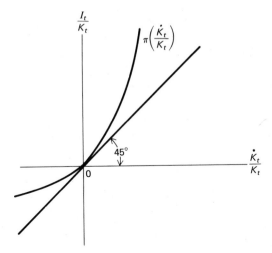

Figure 8.24. The Penrose Curve.

It is important to realize that the administrative and managerial resources which define the Penrose curve specify a kind of adjustment cost.[35] In other words, Uzawa's formulation of the investment function is in the same line of development as the investment theory which takes account of adjustment costs such as that of Treadway, Lucas, Gould, and so on; however, Uzawa's theory is perhaps more sophisticated than theirs.

Note also that by the specification of the Penrose function, the usual depreciation relation

(69) $$\dot{K}_t = I_t - \delta K_t$$

is already included. This relation may be considered as the case in which the Penrose curve takes a special form:

(69') $$\frac{I_t}{K_t} = \frac{\dot{K}_t}{K_t} + \delta$$

The problem of the firm is again to maximize the present value of all future profits subject to the constraints

$$Q(L_t, K_t) - Q_t = 0 \quad \text{and} \quad \frac{I_t}{K_t} = \pi\left(\frac{\dot{K}_t}{K_t}\right)$$

It is again assumed that all prices, p, w, q, and r, are kept constant.

Notice that the usual depreciation equation or equation (69') is replaced by equation (68), which denotes the Penrose effect. Equation (69) should be dismissed, for under the present circumstances it misses the essence of the Penrose effect, that is, the scarcity of managerial and administrative resources. On the other hand, if we assume that the physical capital is a single entity with units measurable in a normal way, then an equation such as (69) or variants thereof cannot be avoided. This then causes an inconsistency with the Penrose function. However, Uzawa's K_t is *not* the usual physical capital stock, as remarked above. Instead, it incorporates the scarcity of managerial and administrative resources. Moreover, Uzawa supposed that a spectrum of different capital goods is used. In order to avoid the difficulty involved in measuring the (real) unit of capital[36] and to incorporate the Penrose effect into his analysis, he invented an index to represent the unit. We omit such a discussion by simply referring the reader to his [66], pp. 637–639.[37]

We are now ready to state Uzawa's problem as an optimal control problem.

PROBLEM III: Choose L_t and Z_t so as to[38]

Maximize: $\displaystyle \int_0^\infty e^{-rt}\left[pQ(L_t, K_t) - wL_t - q\pi\left(\frac{Z_t}{K_t}\right)K_t\right]dt$

Subject to: $\dot{K}_t = Z_t$

$Z_{\min} \leqq Z_t \leqq Z_{\max}$

$K_t \geqq 0, L_t \geqq 0$

and a given value of K_0

Here K_t is the state variable and Z_t and L_t are the control variables. The introduction of a new control variable like Z_t is a standard practice in control theory.

We omit the discussion of the procedure of obtaining the solution to this problem, for it is already described in Uzawa ([64] and [66]), and the reader, if he so wishes, should easily be able to obtain it by himself.[39]

Assuming the linear homogeneity[40] of the function Q, Uzawa obtained the following results:

(70-a) $\hat{z}_t = $ constant $(\equiv \hat{z})$ for all t

(70-b) $\hat{k}_t = $ constant $(\equiv \hat{k})$ for all t

(70-c) $\lambda_t = $ constant $(\equiv \hat{\lambda})$ for all t

where $\hat{z}_t \equiv \hat{Z}_t / \hat{K}_t$ and $\hat{k}_t \equiv \hat{K}_t / \hat{L}_t$. The value of $\hat{k}$ is determined by $\hat{Q}_L = w/p$ as a result of the homogeneity assumption. The value of $\hat{z}$ is obtained as a solution of the problem of maximizing

(71) $$v \equiv \frac{\hat{c} - q\pi(z)}{r - z} \qquad \text{where } \hat{c} \equiv p\hat{Q}_K$$

with respect to z.[41]

Since $\hat{Z}_t / \hat{K}_t \equiv \hat{z}_t$ and $\hat{I}_t / \hat{K}_t = \pi(\hat{z}_t)$, the above solution implies

(72) $$\hat{K}_t = K_0 e^{\hat{z}t}$$

(73) $$\hat{I}_t = I_0 e^{\hat{z}t}$$

where $I_0 \equiv K_0 \pi(\hat{z})$, and

(74) $$\hat{L}_t = L_0 e^{\hat{z}t}$$

where $L_0 \equiv K_0 / \hat{k}$. In other words, once $\hat{z}$ is determined to be a positive constant, the firm's demand for labor and capital (and investment) grows exponentially. This solution is in sharp contrast to the solutions obtained in subsections b and c, in which there exist stationary values for optimal labor, capital, and investment. My concern with Uzawa's solution is simply that this can be in contradiction to the assumption that the firm is competitive and a pure price taker. If the firm keeps growing according to Uzawa's solution, then it may become large compared with the rest of the economy. Certainly the entire economy may be growing at the same time so that the relative position of the firms may be kept small enough to be competitive. But this is something which remains to be shown.

However, Uzawa's theory is apparently aiming at a theory of aggregate investment, which is clear from his various papers. Then the above inconsistency may not be of any serious consequence. One natural question at this point is whether or not the supply of labor grows exponentially at the rate z^* as its demand prescribes. This is obviously highly unlikely. Then there is a possible gap between demand for and supply of labor at the aggregate level, and the real wage rate will increase or decrease depending on whether there is an excess demand for or an excess supply of labor. The firm then changes the plan accordingly. A similar situation exists with respect to the supply of capital. The supply of capital is obviously funded from saving. Thus there is a possible gap between the demand for and supply of capital. Uzawa did realize these points. Assuming that the supply of labor grows at a constant rate and devising a theory of saving, he concluded that there is a steady state solution in the economy which is dynamically stable. It is assumed that the firm makes its decision on the assumption that the current interest rate and prices continue to remain the same for all future times. Clearly, the firm realizes its expectations are wrong in every case, for these prices and the interest rate change continuously over time. It is assumed that the firm never learns from past experience, which, to me, is highly dubious.

In this connection, the following confession by Uzawa with regard to the weakness of his theory seems to be pertinent ([66], pp. 651–652):

> However, the most serious limitation of the present analysis is the hypothesis that the aggregative behavior of each of two major sectors of the national economy may be explained in terms of the representative unit which behaves itself in a way similar to each individual unit. It might be less objectionable for a static or stationary analysis, but an economic model which is purportedly analyzing the mechanism of a growing economy would be deemed questionable if enough attention were not paid to the process of aggregation.

Needless to say, if the economy is in the stationary state, all the prices and the interest rate will presumably be constant; hence there should be no problem of aggregation nor should there be a problem of not learning from past experience. However, in Uzawa's investment theory, the firm wishes to expand exponentially without any limit; hence it cannot be a static theory. In other words, it seems that his theory also contains an inconsistency.

Some Extensions

As remarked earlier, the purpose of the present study is partly expository; hence several heroic assumptions are made to highlight some of the problems involved and to obtain the basic framework for analysis in investment theory. Although these assumptions are also seen in the literature, one may wish to weaken or modify some or all of them.

One assumption that may bother the reader is that of constant prices. If the economy is in a steady state or on a balanced growth path, then this assumption may be acceptable. However, if the economy is not in such a state, prices are not constant and may in fact be constantly changing. Hence a firm's investment program made under the assumption that the present prices are expected to continue forever is bound to be revised.

As is well known, this is a difficult problem in any theory which involves time explicitly, and actual trading occurs from time to time. A well-known assumption, alternative to the above static foresight assumption, is the one of perfect foresight. There it is assumed that the economic agent (in our case the firm) knows all future prices with perfect certainty. Under this assumption, the economic agent never makes a mistake with regard to future prices, and hence the agent does not have to revise his program because of past mistakes in forecasting nor does he have to learn from past mistakes. This perfect foresight assumption is thus useful in building a theoretically consistent model. But it is obviously an unrealistic assumption to make for a theory intended to explain the behavior of the firm. The firm does make mistakes with regard to the forecasting of future prices; hence it has to revise its program from time to time.

An obvious generalization here is to introduce an element of risk into forecasting and incorporate the firm's utility function with regard to risks into the analysis. Commenting on Jorgenson, Karl Borch has made the following remark ([24] p. 273):

> There are at least two generalizations which immediately suggest themselves as desirable: to replace the constant discount rate by a utility function which expresses a preference for the timing of payments and to introduce a probability distribution or a stochastic process to allow for the uncertainty associated with future payments.

But then he immediately admits (p. 273):[42]

> If it should be possible to construct a realistic theory of investment along these or other lines, it will be a very complex model, and it may contain so many parameters that it will be virtually impossible to test the theory against observations.

Another assumption that one may object to is that the firm is a pure price taker. Two interesting grounds for investigation are the behavior of an oligopolistic firm and that of a completely monopolistic firm. As is well known, the theory of the oligopolistic firm entails difficult problems. However, the theory of the complete monopoly, about which we can make a few remarks, is not difficult.

If the firm is a complete monopoly, it is no longer a price taker but rather a price setter. The firm has a demand function $Q_t = D(p_t)$ for its output (where $D' < 0$ for all p_t). Assuming that this can be rewritten in the inverse form $p_t = p(Q_t)$, the firm's revenue at time t may be expressed as $p(Q_t)Q_t$, which in turn can be expressed as a function of L_t and K_t. Therefore the firm's profit at time t, W_t, is written as[43]

(75-a) (with no adjustment costs) $\qquad W_t = G(L_t, K_t) - wL_t - qI_t$

(75-b) (with adjustment costs) $\qquad W_t = G(L_t, K_t) - wL_t - C(I_t)$

where

(76) $\qquad G(L_t, K_t) \equiv p(Q_t)Q_t \quad \text{with} \quad Q_t = Q(L_t, K_t)$

It can then be immediately seen that nothing basic is changed mathematically. The function $pQ(L_t, K_t)$ is replaced by $G(L_t, K_t)$. If we replace the concavity assumption of Q with that of G, our analysis in subsections b and c follows almost word for word. Notice that the choice of the path (L_t, K_t) implies the choice of the output path Q_t, which in turn implies the choice of the price by $p_t = p(Q_t)$.

In the case of no adjustment costs, the firm will adjust to the long-run optimal stock of capital and labor (K^* and L^*) very quickly as long as I_{max} is large enough or I_{min} is small enough. Both K^* and L^* are determined by the famous rule that marginal revenue equals marginal cost or, equivalently, that the marginal revenue product equals the factor price. In other words, L^* and K^* are determined by[44]

(77-a) $$G_L(L^*, K^*) = w$$

(77-b) $$G_K(L^*, K^*) = (r + \delta)q$$

where $G_L \equiv \partial G/\partial L$ and $G_K \equiv \partial G/\partial K$. Hence the optimal price p^* is given by

(78) $$p^* = p(Q^*), \text{ where } Q^* \equiv Q(L^*, K^*)$$

Note that the optimal price is constant over time.

The adjustment costs case can be analyzed analogously and is left to the interested reader. Here we only point out one difficult problem. The optimal capital stock, in this case, is in general not constant but changes over time. Here the optimal output price changes over time. For example, if it increases monotonically while the optimal path of labor employment is constant, then the optimal output increases over time, so that the optimal price decreases over time. The consumer eventually knows about this and may postpone present consumption of the good. In other words, the demand for output shifts over time. Or, more appropriately, the demand function in the form of $Q_t = D(p_t)$ or $p_t = p(Q_t)$ is inappropriate for the analysis; the demand for the output at each t depends on the time path of p_t. In other words, the firm's maximization problem must be based on such a demand function rather than on the simple one $Q_t = D(p_t)$.

FOOTNOTES

1. This note is a revised version of my lecture given at Purdue University, May 1971, which is recorded in A. Takayama, "The Neoclassical Theory of Investment and Adjustment Costs," *Krannert Institute Paper*, no. 349, Purdue University, April 1972.

2. A similar attempt is made by Arrow [7], for example, in the model in which labor is not explicitly introduced.

3. It is assumed that r is constant for all t. It can be interpreted as the current interest rate, if the firm can borrow or lend any amount at this rate r.

4. This assumption on depreciation contrasts, in the present analysis, to the so-called "depreciation by sudden death" assumption, which means that the capital goods last for a finite period of time with a constant efficiency and then "die" suddenly at the end of that period (that is, they are scrapped with zero value). The assumption of depreciation by evaporation ("radioactive" decay) is a very common assumption in the literature dealing with the continuous time model.

5. In the classical stationary state where everything is repeated over and over again, all prices are constant. Hence everybody expects all prices to remain constant and their expectations are always correct (perfect foresight). This makes the classical theory simple and elegant. But in a dynamic economy, the problem of future expectations causes very difficult problems.

6. Rigorously speaking, the Hamiltonian should be defined as

$$\check{H} \equiv v e^{-rt}\big[pQ(L_t, K_t) - wL_t - qI_t\big] + \mu_t\big[L_t - \delta K_t\big]$$

where v is a multiplier as well as μ_t, and v is constant for all t and nonnegative. But it is possible that $v = 0$. Under certain plausible assumptions we can prove $v > 0$, and thus we can set $v = 1$. Recall Theorem 8.A.6.

7. The optimal values of K_t, L_t, and I_t are denoted respectively by $\hat{K}_t$, $\hat{L}_t$, and $\hat{I}_t$. The circumflex ($\cdot$) in the partial derivatives $\partial \hat{H}/\partial \mu_t$ and $\partial \hat{H}/\partial K_t$ denotes that they are evaluated at $(\hat{K}_t, \hat{L}_t, \hat{I}_t)$.

8. In other words, we obtain

$$pQ(\hat{L}_t, \hat{K}_t) - w\hat{L}_t \geq pQ(L_t, \hat{K}_t) - wL_t$$

for all $L_t \geq 0$, which means the maximization of $pQ(L_t, \hat{K}_t) - wL_t$ with respect to L_t. This in turn implies (13). It is assumed that this maximum is achieved at a finite value of $\hat{L}_t$. Denote $Q(L_t, \hat{K}_t)$ by $\tilde{Q}(L_t)$ and assume $\tilde{Q}' > 0$. Assume also $\tilde{Q}'' < 0$ for all L_t and $\tilde{Q}(0) = 0$, $\tilde{Q}'(0) > w/p$, $\tilde{Q}'(\infty) = 0$. Then we can easily prove that a finite $\hat{L}_t$ exists and that $\hat{L}_t$ is unique and strictly positive. Moreover, (13) gives a sufficient (as well as necessary) condition for $\hat{L}_t$ to maximize $pQ(L_t, \hat{K}_t) - wL_t$.

9. From (8), we obtain $\dot{\mu}_t = \mu_t \delta - e^{-rt}pQ_K$. Then observing that $\dot{\lambda}_t = \dot{\mu}_t e^{rt} + r\lambda_t$, we obtain (16).

10. This is a result of Mangasarian's theorem. See his [49], or our Theorem 8.C.5.

11. Assume that the function $Q(L_t, K_t)$ satisfies the following conditions for some "relevant" neighborhood of the path $(\hat{L}_t, \hat{K}_t)$: $Q_{LL} < 0$, $Q_{KK} < 0$, $Q_{LL}Q_{KK} - Q_{LK}{}^2 > 0$ (which implies the strict concavity of Q in this neighborhood), and $Q_{LK} > 0$, where $Q_{LL} \equiv \partial^2 Q/\partial L^2$, $Q_{LK} \equiv \partial^2 Q/\partial L \partial K$, $Q_{KK} \equiv \partial^2 Q/\partial K^2$. The condition $Q_{LK} > 0$ is referred to as the "normal" case by Trout Rader (see Section D, Chapter 4). We cannot impose this condition for all $L_t \geq 0$ and $K_t \geq 0$, for then the strict concavity of Q for the entire domain, $L_t \geq 0$ and $K_t \geq 0$, together with $Q(0, 0) = 0$, imply diminishing returns to scale, which forces the scale of operation Q_t to zero under the competitive market (in the traditional sense of Viner [69]). In the literature, it is sometimes observed that the assumption of the strict concavity of Q is imposed together with $Q(0, 0) = 0$, hence causing a slight inconsistency. This inconsistency was pointed out by Proctor [56]. The "relevant" neighborhood of $(\hat{L}_t, \hat{K}_t)$ is slightly ambiguous phraseology, but the meaning should be clear from the usual Knightian cost function which appears in standard textbooks of intermediate price theory. A more precise specification of this is left to the interested reader.

12. We can obtain $\phi' = p[Q_{LL} Q_{KK} - Q_{LK}{}^2]/Q_{LL}$, which is negative under the assumptions made in the previous footnote.

13. There are in essence three types of paths: (1) $\hat{K}_t < 0$ within a finite t; (2) $\lambda_t \to \infty$ with $\dot{\lambda}_t = (r + \delta)\lambda_t - $ (constant); (3) $\hat{K}_t \to K^*$. Clearly the first type of path violates the restriction $\hat{K}_t \geq 0$, and the second type violates condition (17). Hence only the third type of path is eligible. In the above discussion of type (1) path, it is implicitly assumed that $I_{min} < 0$. When $I_{min} \geq 0$, the discussion should be modified.

14. Equation (23-a) may be rewritten as $\dot{K}_t = \delta(K_{max} - \hat{K}_t)$, where $K_{max} \equiv I_{max}/\delta$. This may be considered as the response equation for the period in which $K_0 < K^*$. A similar response equation can be obtained for the period in which $K_0 > K^*$ by replacing K_{max} by $K_{min} \equiv I_{min}/\delta$.

15. We assume that $I_{max} > \delta K^*$, that is, $I_{max} > I^*$. Note that $T^* > 0$ for any large I_{max} (except for $+ \infty$). In other words, the firm does *not* adjust instantaneously, although T^* can be very small, for I_{max} can be very large. In the limiting case of $I_{max} = +\infty$, we have $T^* = 0$.

16. If the capital good is rented for a finite period of time—say, T—then the intertemporal arbitrage relation is

$$q = \int_0^T ce^{-(\delta + r)t}\, dt + qe^{-(\delta + r)T}$$

This yields the same relation as before; that is, $c = (r + \delta)q$.

17. He seems to have failed to observe the adjustment mechanism required to reach the "long-run" state (for our case K^*), since he relied on a rather crude use of the calculus of variations instead of the optimal control technique. In other words, he considered only the case in which the desired stock of capital is equal to the "long-run" desired level.

18. We can also observe that $\phi' \equiv 0$. Note also that $Q_{LL} < 0$ if and only if $Q_{KK} < 0$ for the constant returns to scale case with $Q_{LK} \neq 0$.

19. As a specific form of $C(I_t)$, we may consider $q(I_t)I_t$, where $q(I_t) > 0$, $q'(I_t) > 0$, and $q''(I_t) > 0$ for all $I_t > 0$. It is easy to check that the conditions for the function C are satisfied by these specifications for the function q.

20. As a simple form of (32), we may consider $Q_t = Q(L_t, K_t) - C(I_t)$ with $C' > 0$, $C'' > 0$ and $C(0) = 0$. Such a specification is considered in Treadway ([62], p. 67, his equation (9)).

21. As noted in footnote 6, we should have the multiplier v attached to the term $e^{-rt}\left[pQ(L_t, K_t) - wL_t - C(I_t) \right]$. We again omit the discussion concerning the assumptions which lead to $v = 1$.

22. Clearly the values of μ_t and λ_t will in general be different from the ones in the previous section. However, for the sake of notational simplicity, we use the same notations for the multipliers.

23. Again it is possible to replace (37) by "Arrow's conditions," $\lim_{t \to \infty} \mu_t \geq 0$ and $\lim_{t \to \infty} \mu_t \hat{K}_t = 0$ (or equivalent conditions in terms of λ_t), and this will yield the same analysis and conclusions as the present one.

24. The problem is to find the assumptions to guarantee the existence of $\hat{I}_t$ which maximizes $\left[-e^{-rt}C(I_t) + \mu_t I_t \right]$ or, equivalently, $\left[\lambda_t I_t - C(I_t) \right]$ for each t such that $I_{\min} < \hat{I}_t < I_{\max}$. Assuming that $C'(I_t) > 0$ and $C''(I_t) > 0$ for all $I_t > 0$, $C(0) = 0$, and that $C'(0)$ is small enough, the existence of a unique $\hat{I}_t > 0$ can be proved easily if $\lambda_t > 0$. Here we also assume that $I_{\min} \leq 0$ and that $I_{\max}$ is sufficiently large. Note that (36) implies $\lambda_t > 0$.

25. Recall our discussion in footnote 11.

26. The first type of path violates the conditions $\hat{K}_t \geq 0$ and $\lambda_t > C'(0)$. Using (34), we can show that the second type of path violates condition (37).

27. We denote again the optimal path for the present case by $(\hat{K}_t, \hat{L}_t, \hat{I}_t)$; $\hat{Q}_K$ denotes $\partial Q/\partial K$ evaluated at $(\hat{L}_t, \hat{K}_t)$.

28. Gould and others assumed the quadratic approximation of the adjustment cost function, that is, $C(I_t) = aI_t + bI_t^2$ where $a > 0$ and $b > 0$. See, for example, [18] p. 48.

29. If $\hat{K}_{t-1} = \hat{K}_{t-2} = \cdots$ and if they are all equal to $\hat{K}_t$, then the RHS of (61) gives $(\alpha_1 + \alpha_2 + \cdots)\hat{K}_t$. On the other hand, in this case, the LHS of (61) should be equal to $\hat{K}_t$. Therefore $\alpha_1 + \alpha_2 + \cdots = 1$.

30. See, for example, Allen [4], pp. 88–89.

31. Solow has proposed the Pascal probability distribution for the lag function. Jorgenson [26] generalized this function. For a survey of distributed lags, see, for example, Griliches [17]. In connection with the above quotation from Jorgenson and Siebert [29], J. A. Swanson made the following remark to me: "J & S choose the 'best' lag in an inappropriate manner; viz., by choosing that lag structure which minimizes

sample residual variance. This procedure, developed by Theil, is appropriate only for non-stochastic regressors, but J & S have $I_{t-\tau}$ as regressors!" By "J & S," Swanson seems to have been referring to Jorgenson and Stephenson [32].

32. See, for example, Uzawa [64], [65], [66], [67], and [68].

33. A powerful outcome of the assumption $\pi'' > 0$ is that the uniqueness of the optimal path of capital accumulation K_t^* is obtained, even if the production function is homogeneous of degree one. See Uzawa [66], p. 642. In addition to the above restrictions on the function π, Uzawa ([64], p. 4; [66], p. 641) also imposed the following conditions: $\pi(0) = 0$ and $\pi'(0) = 1$. These conditions are assumed to hold for mathematical convenience and do not impair the generality of his argument.

34. The crucial feature of managerial and administrative resources is that they are not usually bought and sold in the market; hence the market prices of these resources usually do not exist. This then creates the problem of how to measure them.

35. In other words, Uzawa claims that the crucial feature of the "fixity of capital" is in the limitational character of administrative and managerial resources.

36. Notice that, in Problems I and II, there is really no problem of how to measure the units of capital, output, labor, and cost of adjustment. In the profit function, pQ_t, wL_t, qI_t, and $C(I_t)$ all enter in dollar terms. Notice also that as long as all prices are constant, the maximization of $\int_0^\infty e^{-rt} [pQ_t - wL_t - qI_t] \, dt$ will give the same result as that of the maximization of the present value of *real* profit $\int_0^\infty e^{-rt} [Q_t - wL_t/p - qI_t/p] \, dt$.

37. This does not deny the importance of such a treatment. In fact, this is one of the most important features of Uzawa's theory, reflecting clearly the influence of Joan Robinson.

38. Uzawa maximizes the present value of real profit $\int_0^\infty e^{-rt} [Q(L_t, K_t) - wL_t/p - \pi(Z_t/K_t)K_t] \, dt$, where his convention with regard to the measurement of units (mathematically) amounts to setting $p = q$.

39. Assuming the concavity of Q and an interior solution, the following conditions are necessary and sufficient for an optimum: $\dot{K}_t = \hat{Z}_t$; $\dot{\lambda}_t = r\lambda_t - [p\hat{Q}_K - q(\pi - \hat{\pi}'\hat{Z}_t/\hat{K}_t)]$; $\hat{Q}_L = w/p$; $\lambda_t = q\hat{\pi}'$; $\lim_{t\to\infty} e^{-rt}\lambda_t = 0$. Here the optimal path is again denoted by $(\hat{K}_t, \hat{L}_t, \hat{Z}_t)$. Also $\hat{\pi}'$ denotes $d\pi/dz_t$ evaluated at $\hat{z}_t$ where $z_t \equiv Z_t/K_t$. Similarly, $\hat{\pi} \equiv \pi(\hat{z}_t)$, $\hat{Q}_K \equiv Q_K(\hat{L}_t, \hat{K}_t)$ and $\hat{Q}_L \equiv Q_L(\hat{L}_t, \hat{K}_t)$.

40. The reader can easily analyze the case of nonconstant returns to scale. The analysis will be analogous to the one in subsection c. The results are different from Uzawa's.

41. The range of the variation of z is assumed to be restricted to $0 \leq z \leq r$ and $0 \leq q\pi(z) \leq \hat{c}$. It is shown then that $0 < \hat{z} < r$.

42. There is a more difficult problem involved. The firm may not be able to ascertain the probability distribution of its future prices or payments. Recall the famous Knightian distinction between risk and uncertainty.

43. It is assumed that there is no monopsony in the labor market. In the case of no adjustment costs, it is further assumed that there is no monopsony in the capital market.

44. Compare (77) with equations (26-a) and (26-b).

REFERENCES

1. Alchian, A. A., "The Rate of Interest, Fisher's Rate of Return Over Costs and Keynes' Internal Rate of Return," in *The Management of Corporate Capital*, ed. by E. Solomon, Glenco, Ill., Free Press, 1959.

2. ———, "The Basis of Some Recent Advances in the Theory of Management of the Firm," *Journal of Industrial Economics*, XIV, November 1965.

3. Allen, R. G. D., *Mathematical Economics*, 2nd ed., London, Macmillan, 1965.

4. ———, *Macro-Economic Theory*, London, Macmillan, 1969.

5. Arrow, K. J., "Optimal Capital Policy, the Cost of Capital and Myopic Decision Rules," *Annals of the Institute of Statistical Mathematics*, 16, 1964 (Tokyo).

6. ———, "Optimal Capital Adjustment," in *Studies in Applied Probability and Management Science*, ed. by K. J. Arrow, S. Karlin, and H. Scarf, Stanford, Calif., Stanford University Press, 1962.

7. ———, "Optimal Capital Policy with Irreversible Investment," in *Value, Capital and Growth, Papers in Honour of Sir John Hicks*, ed. by J. N. Wolfe, Edinburgh, Edinburgh University Press, 1968.

8. Arrow, K. J., Beckman, M. J., and Karlin, S., "The Optimal Expansion of the Capacity of a Firm," in *Studies in the Mathematical Theory of Inventory and Production*, ed. by K. J. Arrow, S. Karlin, and H. Scarf, Stanford, Calif., Stanford University Press, 1958.

9. Arrow, K. J., and Kurz, M., *Public Investment, the Rate of Return and Optimal Fiscal Policy*, Baltimore, Md., Johns Hopkins Press, 1970.

10. Bailey, M. J., "Formal Criteria for Investment Decisions," *Journal of Political Economy*, 67, October 1969.

11. ———, *National Income and the Price Level*, 2nd ed., New York, McGraw-Hill, 1971, Chap. 8.

12. Chenery, H. B., "Overcapacity and the Acceleration Principle," *Econometrica*, 20, January 1952.

13. Eisner, R., "A Distributed Lag Investment Function," *Econometrica*, 28, January 1960.

14. Eisner, R., and Strotz, R. H., "Determinants of Business Investment," in *Impacts of Monetary Policy*, by D. B. Suits *et al.*, Englewood Cliffs, N.J., Prentice-Hall, 1963.

15. Eisner, R., and Nadiri, M. I., "Investment Behavior and the Neo-Classical Theory," *Review of Economics and Statistics*, L, August 1968.

16. Fisher, I. N., *The Theory of Interest*, New York, Macmillan, 1930.

17. Griliches, Z., "Distributed Lags: A Survey," *Econometrica*, 35, January 1967.

18. Gould, J. P., "Adjustment Costs in the Theory of Investment of the Firm," *Review of Economic Studies*, XXXV, January 1968.

19. ———, "The Use of Endogenous Variables in Dynamic Models of Investment," *Quarterly Journal of Economics*, LXXXIII, November 1969.

20. Haavelmo, T., *A Study in the Theory of Investment*, Chicago, Ill., University of Chicago Press, 1961.

21. Hestenes, M. R., *Calculus of Variations and Optimal Control Theory*, New York, Wiley, 1966.

22. Hirshleifer, J., "On the Theory of Optimal Investment Decision," in the *Management of Corporate Capital*, ed. by E. Solomon, Glenco, Ill., Free Press, 1959.

23. ———, *Investment, Interest and Capital*, Englewood Cliffs, N.J., Prentice-Hall, 1970.

24. Jorgenson, D. W., "Capital Theory and Investment Behavior," *American Economic*

Review, LIII, May 1963. (Also "Discussion" by C. F. Christ, E. Mansfield, and K. Borch.)

25. ———, "Anticipations and Investment Behavior," in *Brookings Quarterly Econometric Model of the United States*, ed. by E. Kuh, G. Fromm, and L. R. Klein, Amsterdam, North-Holland, 1965.

26. ———, "Rational Distributed Lag Functions," *Econometrica*, 34, January 1966.

27. ———, "The Theory of Investment Behavior," in *Determinants of Investment Behavior*, ed. by R. Ferber, New York, NBER, 1967 (reprinted in *Macroeconomic Theory, Selected Readings*, ed. by H. R. Williams and J. D. Huffnagle, New York, Appleton-Century-Crofts, 1969).

28. ———, "The Demand for Capital Services", in *Economic Models, Estimations and Risk Programming: Essay in Honor of Gerhard Tintner*, ed. by K. A. Fox, J. K. Sengupta, and G. V. L. Narasimham, Berlin, Springer-Verlag, 1969.

29. Jorgenson, D. W., and Siebert, C. D., "A Comparison of Alternative Theories of Corporate Investment Behavior," *American Economic Review*, LXIII, September 1968.

30. ———, and ———, "Optimal Capital Accumulation and Corporate Investment Behavior," *Journal of Political Economy*, 76, November/December 1968.

31. Jorgenson, D. W., and Stephenson, J. A., "The Time Structure of Investment Behavior in U.S. Manufacturing, 1947–60," *Review of Economics and Statistics*, XLIX, February 1967.

32. ———, and ———, "Investment Behavior in U.S. Manufacturing, 1947–60" *Econometrica*, 35, April 1967.

33. ———, and ———, "Anticipations and Investment Behavior in U.S. Manufacturing, 1947–60," *Journal of American Statistical Association*, 64, March 1969.

34. ———, and ———, "Issues in the Development of the Neo-Classical Theory of Investment Behavior," *Review of Economics and Statistics*, LI, August 1969.

35. Jorgenson, D. W., Hunter, J., and Nadiri, M. I., "A Comparison of Alternative Economic Models of Quarterly Investment Behavior," *Econometrica*, 38, March 1970.

36. ———, ———, and ———, "The Predictive Performance of Econometric Models of Quarterly Investment Behavior," *Econometrica*, 38, March 1970.

37. Jorgenson, D. W., and Handel, S. S., "Investment Behavior in U.S. Regulated Industries," *Bell Journal of Economics and Management Science*, 2, Spring 1971.

38. Jorgenson, D. W., McCall, J. J., and Radner, R., *Optimal Replacement Policy*, Amsterdam, North-Holland, 1967.

39. Keynes, J. M., *General Theory of Employment, Interest and Money*, London, Macmillan, 1936.

40. Klein, L. R., "Studies in Investment Behavior," in *Conferences on Business Cycles*, New York, NBER, 1951.

41. Koyck, L. M., *Distributed Lags and Investment Analysis*, Amsterdam, North-Holland, 1954.

42. Kuh, E., "Theory and Institutions in the Study of Investment Behavior," *American Economic Review*, LIII, May 1963.

43. Lerner, A. P., *The Economics of Control; Principles of Welfare Economics*, New York, Macmillan, 1944.

44. ———, "On Some Recent Developments in Capital Theory," *American Economic Review*, LV, May 1965.

45. Lucas, R. E., "Optimal Investment Policy and the Flexible Accelerator," *International Economic Review*, 8, February 1967.

46. ———, "Tests of a Capital Theoretic Model of Technological Change," *Review of Economic Studies*, XXXIV, April 1967.

47. ———, "Adjustment Costs and the Theory of Supply," *Journal of Political Economy*, 75, August 1967.

48. Lutz, F., and Lutz, V., *The Theory of Investment of the Firm*, Princeton, N.J., Princeton University Press, 1951.

49. Mangasarian, O. L., "Sufficient Conditions for the Optimal Control of Nonlinear Systems," *Journal of SIAM Control*, 4, February 1966.

50. Masse, P. B. D., *Optimal Investment Decisions*, Englewood Cliffs, N.J., Prentice-Hall, 1962.

51. Nadiri, M. I., and Rosen, S., "Interrelated Factor Demand Functions," *American Economic Review*, LIX, September 1969.

52. Nerlove, M., *Distributed Lags and Demand Analysis*, USDA, Handbook No. 141, Washington, D. C., 1958.

53. Newlyn, W. T., *Theory of Money*, Oxford, Clarendon Press, 1962, esp. chap. 8.

54. Penrose, E. T., *The Theory of the Growth of the Firm*, Oxford, Blackwell, 1959.

55. Pontryagin, L. S., Boltyanskii, V. G., Gamkrelidze, R. V., and Mischchenko, E. F., *The Mathematical Theory of Optimal Processes*, tr. by K. N. Trirogoff, New York, Interscience, 1962.

56. Proctor, M. S., "Two Equivalence Theorems for Fisherian and Neoclassical Investment Criteria," Purdue University, 1971.

57. Ramsey, J. B., "The Marginal Efficiency of Capital, the Internal Rate of Return, and Net Present Value: An Analysis of Investment Criteria," *Journal of Political Economy*, 78, September/October 1970.

58. Samuelson, P. A., "Some Aspects of the Pure Theory of Capital," *Quarterly Journal of Economics*, LI, May 1937.

59. Takayama, A., "A Note on Marginal Efficiency of Capital and Marginal Productivity of Capital," Purdue University, February 1971.

60. Thompson, R. G., and George, M. D., "Optimal Operations and Investment of the Firm," *Management Science*, 15, September 1968.

61. Tobin, J., "Comment," in *Determinants of Investment Behavior*, ed. by R. Ferber, New York, NBER, 1967.

62. Treadway, A. B., "What is Output? Problems of Concept and Measurement," in *Production and Productivity in the Service Industries*, ed. by V. Fuchs, New York, Columbia University Press, 1969.

63. ———, "On the Rational Multivariate Flexible Accelerator," *Econometrica*, 39, September 1971.

64. Uzawa, H., "The Penrose Effect and Optimum Growth," *Economic Studies Quarterly*, XIX, March 1968.

65. ———, "A New Theory of the Investment Function," *Nihon Keizai Shimbun*, July 1969 (in Japanese).

66. ———, "Time Preference and the Penrose Effect in a Two Class Model of Economic Growth," *Journal of Political Economy*, 77, July/August 1969.

67. ———, "Towards a Keynesian Model of Monetary Growth," IEA Conference on the Theory of Economic Growth, 1970.

68. ———, "Diffusion of Inflationary Process in a Dynamic Model of International Trade," presented at the Far Eastern Meeting of the Econometric Society, June 1970.

69. Viner, J., "Cost Curves and Supply Curves," *Zeitschrift für Nationalökonomie*, 1931 [reprinted in *Readings in Price Theory*, ed. by G. J. Stigler, and K. E. Boulding, with "Supplementary Note (1950)," Chicago, Ill., Irwin, 1952].

70. Witte, J., "The Microfoundations of the Social Investment Function," *Journal of Political Economy*, 71, October 1963.

71. Wright, J. F., "Notes on the Marginal Efficiency of Capital," *Oxford Economic Papers*, n.s., 15, June 1963.

Name Index

Subject Index

Abelian group, 6
Accelerator coefficient, 542
Accumulation point, 21
Activity, 46
  level, 48, 489
Activity analysis, xix, 45–54, 140–142,
    486, 491
  two fundamental theorems of, 51–53
Acyclic matrix, 376, 377, 378
Addition, 5
Adjustment costs, 687, 688, 689, 697,
    698, 699, 711
  no, 688, 711, 715
  quadratic approximation of, 702, 714
Adjustment process
  output, 297, 299, 300, 301
  price, 297, 299, 300, 301
  simultaneous, 300, 301
  Walrasian, 299
Admissible control, 602
  set of, 602
Admissible function, 413, 602
Affine function, 15 (*see* Linear (affine)
    function)
Allocation, 207
  feasible, 207
Arithmetic mean theorem, 127
Arrow-Block-Hurwicz theorem, 328
Arrow-Enthoven theorem, 110, 133, 139,
    147
  relevant variable, 110, 150
  stated, 110–111

Arrow-Hurwicz-Uzawa (A-H-U) condi-
    tions, 94, [*see* Condition (A-H-U)]
Arrow-Hurwicz-Uzawa (A-H-U) theorem,
    93, 95, 96, 98, 102, 103, 105, 106,
    111, 131, 132, 139, 147, 150, 648
  further note, 102–108
  stated, 93–94
Associative law, 5
Asymptotically, 356
Autonomous system, 304, 306, 348, 349,
    350, 353, 610, 611, 615
  conditions for global stability,
    350–351
  conditions for quasi-stability, 354
  conditions for uniform global stability,
    351
  defined, 304
  equilibrium point (defined), 306
Auxiliary variables, 603, 621, 626, 629
Average cost, 167
Average propensity to consume, 433
Average propensity to save, 433
Axiom of extension, 1
Axiom of specification, 1

Balanced growth path, 398, 399, 438,
    440, 446, 459, 472, 478, 484, 486,
    487, 491, 492, 493, 500, 503, 509,
    515, 516, 521, 538, 543, 584
Banach space, 92, 101, 430
  defined, 101
Bang-bang control, 605, 626, 631, 643,

Total quasi-ordering, 177, 180, 235, 265
  defined, 177
Transformation, 3
Transversality condition, 603, 610, 611,
  616, 621, 622, 623, 624, 625, 626,
  629, 650, 652, 655, 656, 660, 662,
  664, 675, 680
  at infinity, 623–625, 626, 650–651
  stated in the most general form, 660
Triangular inequality, 8, 9
True dynamic stability, 315, 316
Truncated production cone, 50, 51
Tsukui's lemma, 513, 516, 537
  stated, 513
Turnpike property, 560
Turnpike theorem, xxi, 464, 527,
  559–575
  feasible path, 561, 564
  free disposability and optimality,
    563–567
  hop-skip-jumping, 572
  intertemporal efficiency condition, 567
  optimal path, 563
  strong, 572
  value loss in, 568, 569
  weak, 572
  Twice continuously differentiable func-
    tion, 79, 122, 123, 128, 152, 246
  defined, 79
Twice differentiable function, 120, 121,
  414, 423, 424, 427, 428, 429
Twice differentiable at a point, 120, 422
  defined, 120
Tychonoff's theorem, 29, 484
  stated, 29

Unconstrained maximum, 75, 82–85,
  123–124
Uncountable set, 32
Uniform convergence, 430
Uniform norm, 430
Uniformly bounded, 350, 354
Upper bound, 4
Upper contour set, 66, 178, 267
Upper inverse, 250, 255
Upper semicontinuous function,
  239–242, 250–254, 259, 261, 262,
  263, 276, 293
  defined, 240, 251
Upper semicontinuous at a point, 239,
  250
Util, 206

Utility function, 109, 150, 179–181,
  184, 188, 207, 229, 234, 264, 338
  aggregate, 146, 581
  defined, 179
  existence of, 180
  indirect, 162
Utility index, 179
Utility possibility set, 209

Value-added, 363, 395
van del Pol equation, 351
Vector(s), 6, 15
  linear combination of, 10
  nonnegative linear combination of, 17,
    111
Vector local maximum, 113
Vector maximum, 112–113, 115, 116,
  209, 289, 291, 564, 567
  defined, 112–113
  problem, 73, 112–117, 128, 141, 142,
    144
Vector space, 6, 420 (*see* Linear space)
Vector subspace, 6 (*see* Linear subspace)
von Neumann
  equilibrium, 497, 501, 562
  facet, 592
  growth factor, 562
  interest factor, 562
  path, 379, 493, 560, 562, 573, 584
  price, 562
  process, 562
  profit, 562
  quadruplet, 497
  triplet, 562, 568, 570
  value, 560
von Neumann (growth) model, xxi, 276,
  486–502, 508, 560
  dual problem, 494–495
  existence of maximum rate of expan-
    sion, 492
  existence of price vector, 495
  independent subset, 497
  interest factor, 495
  irreducibility, 497–498
  maximum profit rate, 494
  rate of expansion, 491, 493, 496
  regular, 497
  von Neumann theorem, 495–496, 560
von Neumann model with consumption
  Marx-von Neumann model, 499
  Morishima's treatment of, 499-501
  Walras-von Neumann model, 499